DAYS OUT
IN
BRITAIN & IRELAND 1995

BRITAIN'S MOST COMPREHENSIVE GUIDE TO HERITAGE AND LEISURE ATTRACTIONS

CAMELOT THEME PARK

HISTORIC HOUSES, CASTLES & GARDENS
MUSEUMS & GALLERIES
INDUSTRIAL HERITAGE & ANCIENT MONUMENTS
WILDLIFE PARKS & NATURE RESERVES
THEME PARKS & CHILDREN'S ATTRACTIONS

Produced by AA Publishing

Maps prepared by the Cartographic Department of The Automobile Association

Maps © The Automobile Association 1995

Directory generated by the AA Establishment Database, Information Research and Control, Hotel and Touring Services

Cover artwork by PPD, Basingstoke

Editorial contributions by Phil Bryant

Typeset by Avonset, Midsomer Norton, nr Bath

Colour origination by Daylight Colour Art Pte, Singapore

Printed and bound in Great Britain by St Ives plc

Head of Advertisement Sales: C J Heard 01256 20123 ext 21544
Advertisement production: Karen Weeks 01256 20123 ext 21545

The contents of this book are believed correct at the time of printing. Nevertheless, the Publishers cannot be held responsible for any errors or omissions or for changes in the details given in this guide or for the consequences of any reliance on the information provided in the same. Every effort has been made to ensure accuracy in this guide. However, things do change and we would welcome any information to help keep the book up to date.

Descriptions of places in this guide are based on information supplied in good faith by the establishments in advance of publication and correct to the best of their knowledge at that time. Details, particularly those relating to prices, opening hours and events, are always liable to change.

A CIP catalogue record for this book is available from the British Library

Published by AA Publishing, which is a trading name of Automobile Association Developments Limited whose registered office is Norfolk House, Priestley Road, Basingstoke, Hampshire RG24 9NY, Registered number 1878835.

ISBN 0 7495 0905 8

Cover photograph: Blickling Hall, Norfolk © Picture Colour Library Ltd

Cadbury World is the only attraction in Britain that is totally dedicated to the history, manufacture,  taste and sheer love of chocolate.

NOW MORE TO SEE

In fact, some 2 million people, including over 15,000 coach groups, have already followed the chocolate trail to discover for themselves the  fascinating history of the UK's favourite treat.

Thousands have been irresistibly tempted into our Chocolate Shop at the end of the trail, many of them to buy our exclusive Cadbury World Assortment (available nowhere else in the world) or to see what's on offer in Bargain Corner.

EVERYONE'S FAVOURITE CENTRE IS NOW EVEN TASTIER.

NOW EVEN MORE FUN FOR KIDS

 Today, there are even more reasons why Cadbury World is everyone's favourite centre.

NOW MORE TO DO

We've added exciting new features, like our very own 'Fantasy Factory' - a surefire hit with younger visitors, and many other features have been refurbished and improved.

So if you're looking for an excursion that's a racing certainty to pack them in, a trip to Cadbury World is sure to be everyone's favourite.

For bookings and further information on opening days times and admission prices telephone our group bookings line today on **0121-451 4159.**

THE CHOCOLATE EXPERIENCE

CADBURY WORLD, P.O. BOX 1958, LINDEN ROAD, BOURNVILLE, BIRMINGHAM B30 2LD.

1895-1995
The restoration period

The splendour of the British landscape is celebrated the world over. Our country homes and historic places attract admirers in their millions each year.

It's hard to imagine otherwise.

Yet, in 1895, our national assets - unique and irreplaceable - were under threat. And were it not for the labours of three visionary

Powis Castle.

Victorians, the Britain we know and love might be a very different place indeed.

Together they founded the National Trust to preserve places of historic interest and natural beauty for ever, for everyone.

One hundred years later, as Britain's leading conservation charity, we care for some 400 historic properties and gardens, 547 miles of breathtaking coastline and over half a million acres of magnificent countryside.

National treasures painstakingly restored, lovingly maintained, and preserved, for generations more to enjoy.

For a free Centenary Map Guide and information on any National Trust properties, events or for membership details telephone:

0181-464 1111.

Alternatively write to: The National Trust, Centenary Information Office, P.O. Box 39, Bromley, Kent BR1 1NH.

Elisabeth Vigee Lebrun, self-portrait 1791.

THE NATIONAL TRUST CENTENARY

PHOTOGRAPHY: N.T.P.L. - ANGELO HORNAK, IAN SHAW

CONTENTS

There are details of well over 2,000 fascinating places to visit in this guide which covers England, Scotland, Wales, the Channel Islands and the Isle of Man with – for 1995 – greatly extended coverage of Northern Ireland and the Irish Republic – so wherever you are, you should find just the place for your day out.

Looking at Our Past

Above A 'Victorian' lady stitches her tapestry at Morwellham Quay, Devon.

At the poet Wordsworth's house in Cockermouth, Cumbria, a 'cook' and a blazing fire show something of life below stairs.

Do you want to know what it feels like to be locked in a tiny prison cell? Or would you prefer to learn how to catch herring? Maybe something gentler appeals, like playing Victorian parlour games?

These are just some of the many things you can do in 'living' museums throughout the British Isles. Once, according to the dictionary, museums were just 'repositories for the collection, exhibition and study of objects of artistic, scientific and educational interest', but many of today's museums have come to life, offering 'hands-on' experiences involving touch, hearing, taste and even smell.

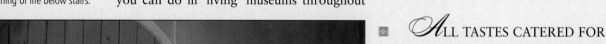

ALL TASTES CATERED FOR

There is hardly a corner of the United Kingdom or Ireland that cannot draw on its past or present in some way, to enthrall visitors of all ages. At West Stow (Suffolk), for example, there is a reconstruction of a real pagan Anglo-Saxon settlement; Poldark Mine and Heritage Complex (Cornwall) explains the history of Cornish tin-mining – an industry all but dead – and the modern distiller's skill can be viewed at Edradour Distillery (Tayside Region), even though production methods date back to 1825. A 'wee dram' is offered here before you leave – one of the more adult hands-on experiences!

Perhaps not everyone in the family relishes visiting a museum, but once you pass the turnstile, a living museum with its many attractions and activities seduces and charms, however esoteric the theme.

◯UT IN THE OPEN

A possible benefit of saying farewell to our industrial present – like coal-mining and ship-building – is that there is more industrial past to conserve. Many museums now make sure we will never lose sight of how life was before mechanisation or computer-aided manufacturing. What was it like working in a slate mine, Grandad? Did you really sit at the loom all day, Grandma? Did your father really harvest the wheat with just a scythe, Uncle Ted?

One of the first such places to be preserved and opened to the public was Abbeydale Industrial Hamlet, a 200-year-old agricultural steelworks near Sheffield, where several times a year you can see a wide variety of craftsmen at work. Devon's Morwellham Quay, once 'the greatest copper port in Queen Victoria's empire', leads you through its underground workings on a tramway, dresses you up in Victorian costume for a photograph and invites you to play games your great-grandparents played.

Gwent's 'Big Pit' closed as a working coal mine in 1980, but you can still don a safety helmet and cap lamp and descend the 300ft shaft to find out what generations of South Walian miners encountered every day. At Chatham's Historic Dockyard (Kent) you can live through more than 400 years of ship-

building history. There's a working ropery, sail and flag-makers craft workshops and 47 Scheduled Ancient Monuments in what was, until 1984, a functioning Royal dockyard.

Canals are also an integral feature of our industrial heritage. The Ellesmere Port Boat Museum (Cheshire) has more than 60 boats, restored warehouses and workshops, and puts on many special events during the year. There are events too at the National Waterways Museum in Gloucester, recently judged one of the top seven museums in Europe, and at the Canal Museum in Stoke Bruerne (Northants) you can take a boat trip through the mile-long Blisworth Tunnel.

Cardiff's once-notorious docklands are now home to the Welsh Industrial and Maritime Museum, offering working exhibits galore – a waterwheel, steam and gas engines, a steam turbine and a Rolls Royce jet engine are all on show. Children's activities are held in the locally-famous 'Q Shed' during school holidays and on the regular steam days there are evocative smells for aficionados.

A good sense of smell will also heighten your enjoyment if you go to Walsall's Leather Museum. Here you can see traditional leathergoods being made, and talk to leather-workers about their craft, in a town which still boasts more than 100 leather companies.

At Tralee in Co Kerry there is a realistic re-construction of an Irish medieval town – complete with sounds and smells!

Left Closed as a working mine in 1980, Big Pit coal mine at Blaenavon, Gwent, has a new lease of life as an exciting museum where visitors can go 300ft underground to experience the life of a miner.

A fully stocked co-operative shop is just one of the many features of the re-created town at Beamish Open Air Museum, Co Durham.

Right An unusual Fishermen's Museum at Hastings, East Sussex, shows something of the hard life of sailors in the past, be they fishermen or smugglers.

A TASTE OF ADVENTURE

Much further north, in Scotland's Grampian Region, the Buckie Drifter encourages you to experience life during the herring boom years of long ago. You can sign on as a crew member of a steam drifter and listen to the lively conversation of the women as they pack the catch in barrels. Grimsby's Fishing Heritage Centre offers other maritime delights. Here you can indulge all your senses in a series of recreated environments, travelling from the town's once-drab back streets to the cold and distant fishing grounds beyond the Arctic Circle – and home again.

Another aspect of life in a sea-faring nation was smuggling. For some reason we view the smugglers of the 18th century in a romantic light, but in acres of labyrinthine caverns and passages deep below Hastings (East Sussex), you can see how it really was. Life-size tableaux and push-button automated models dramatically depict the tough life of the south coast's long-dead contrabandists.

BACK TO BASICS

Life for most people, however, was less risky than for smugglers, and museums recreating how we once lived can be found throughout the British Isles. In Edinburgh, The People's Story museum, housed in the city's 16th-century tolbooth, contains a prison cell, a 1930s pub and a 1940s kitchen, all with authentic smells and sounds. At Cregneish on the Isle of Man, the furniture and everyday equipment of crofting communities is displayed in realistic settings.

Buildings of important historical or cultural interest, that were in the way of developments and would have been lost to the bulldozer forever, have been reconstructed in a number of open-air museums. From the early medieval barn to the 1947 prefab, there are plenty of examples of vernacular building types at museums like Weald and Downland (West Sussex) Beamish (Co. Durham), Chiltern Open Air Museum (Bucks), the Welsh Folk Museum (South Glamorgan), Ulster Folk and Transport (Co Down) and Bunratty Castle (Co Clare). Whole villages have been recreated, often with schools and shops. Many of the houses have been restored and furnished in their period style. In a number of places, like Wigan Pier (Greater Manchester), actors bring the inhabitants of the past alive or re-enact battles or even, as at Kentwell Hall (Suffolk), bring the whole place to life for a whole month with 200 people recreating every aspect of life in the 16th century.

On Poole Quay in Dorset, in a carefully restored late-medieval merchant's house called Scaplen's Court, you can observe domestic life through the ages. On certain days the Victorian kitchen comes alive, as the fire is lit in the cooking range and food is prepared, just as it used to be. But if you want to go further back in time, Bede's World (Tyne & Wear) prepares Anglo-Saxon feasts throughout the year, and a new museum and landscape are being developed to portray life in 7th and 8th-century Northumbria.

❧ TRAVEL THROUGH TIME ❧

High-tech equipment is behind the success of many museums, such as the Plymouth Dome, where you can also travel through time, exploring the sounds and smells of an Elizabethan street, dodging the 18th-century press gangs, strolling with film stars on an ocean liner and witnessing the city's devastation during the Blitz. High-resolution cameras enable you to zoom in on ships in Plymouth Sound, and computers help you to identify naval vessels on their way in and out of Devonport dockyard.

There are considerably older smells and sounds at Canterbury Tales (Kent), as you

The Weald and Downland Open Air Museum at Singleton, West Sussex, offers the chance to sit around the central fire in the Great Hall of a medieval manor house. The range of rescued buildings covers hundreds of years of history.

soon discover when you become one of Chaucer's happy band of pilgrims walking from Southwark to pay homage at the allegedly miracle-working tomb of St Thomas à Becket in Canterbury Cathedral. True to its name, Timespan (Highland Region), travels even further back, beginning its story with the Picts and the Vikings and ending with the North Sea oilfields. Everything is portrayed in a series of life-size sets with realistic sound effects and an audio-visual programme.

Experiences of a very different kind may be encountered in the Channel Islands. Guernsey and Jersey's Underground Hospitals were built by the occupying German forces during World War II and here, in the echoing corridors and chambers, you can attempt to re-live the hardships endured by the tunnellers, all prisoners of war. In North Yorkshire is yet another reminder of World War II. Eden Camp was built in 1942 for German and other prisoners of war but today it is the Modern History Theme Museum where the drama, hardships and humour of domestic life in the war years unfold.

☙ Ｄown on the Farm ❧

Farm life too, has undergone considerable change in recent years, and the Common Agricultural Policy ensures that the process continues. Reminders of less bureaucratic times can be found at places like Acton Scott (Shropshire), where the old rotation system is used to grow the crop types of around 1900. All the work is done by hand or horse power, and with old machines such as steam threshers. Eighteenth-century life among the horses can be experienced at Palace Stables Heritage Centre in Co Armagh, where audio-commentary, life-size models and spectacular murals bring it all to life.

Over at Gressenhall in Norfolk, the Rural Life Museum focuses on agriculture, rural crafts and village life, with working reconstructions. There are daily demonstrations of a 1920s farm in operation, with tireless Suffolk Punch horses and rare breeds of cattle, pigs and horned sheep.

And so we could go on. Small islands we may be, but our many and varied ancestors have unwittingly left us a rich legacy. We all share a curiosity about what their life was like, and it is thanks to living museums that we will not forget. ▨

ABOUT THIS BOOK

ntries in this guide are alphabetical under county and town. Towns or cities of outstanding interest have an entry giving a general description and mentioning features (such as cathedrals or streets) not necessarily included in this guide.

OPENING DATES quoted in the guide are inclusive - for instance, where you see Apr-Oct, that place will be open from the beginning of April to the end of October.

PRICES quoted are, as far as possible, those which are expected to be in force in 1995. However, some establishments have been unable to give us their projected prices and for those we have given 1994 prices prefixed by an asterisk. If no price is quoted, you should check with the establishment concerned before you visit. A number of the places which do not charge admission at all may ask for a voluntary donation.

TELEPHONE NUMBERS throughout the United Kingdom have changed from 16 April 1995 and all area codes starting with 0 now start 01. In Leeds, Sheffield, Nottingham, Leicester and Bristol the STD code has changed completely. We have given the new telephone numbers throughout the guide. The STD code is shown

SYMBOLS
In order to give you as much information as possible in the space available, we have used the following symbols in the guide:

	ENGLISH	FRANÇAIS	DEUTSCH	ITALIANO	ESPAÑOL
☎	Telephone number	Numéro de téléphone	Telefonnummer	Numero telefonico	Número telefónico
♿	Suitable for visitors in wheelchairs	Les invalidens fauteuils roulants pourrant y accéder	Für Rollstuhltahrer zugänglich	Accessibile agli handicappeti	Acondicionado para visitantes en silla de reudas
✳	Indicates 1994 price	Prix 1994	1994 Preise	Indica i prezzi del 1994	Indica los precios de 1994
Ⓟ	Parking at Establishment	Stationnement à l'établissement	Parken an Ort und Stelle	Parcheggio in loco	Aparcamiento en el establecimiento
☕	Refreshments	Rafraîchissements	Erfrischungen	Snack-bar	Refrescos
✗	Restaurant	Restaurant	Restaurant	Ristorante	Restaurante
🚫	No dogs	Chiens non permis	Hundeverbot	Cani non accettati	Se prohiben los perros
🚌	No coaches	Les groupes en cars pas admis	Keine Reisebusgesellschaften	Non si accettano comitive in pullman	Non se admiten los grupos de viajeros en autobús

ABBREVIATIONS In the same way, we have abbreviated certain pieces of information:

	ENGLISH	FRANÇAIS	DEUTSCH	ITALIANO	ESPAÑOL
AM	Ancient Monument	Monument ancien	Historiches Gebaude	Monumento storico	Monumento histórico
AM(Cadw)	Ancient Monument (Wales)	Monument ancien (Pays de Galles)	Historiches Gebaude (Walisland)	Monumento storico (Galles	Monumento histórico (Gales)
EH	English Heritage	English Heritage	English Heritage	English Heritage	English Heritage
NT	National Trust	National Trust	National Trust	National Trust	The National Trust
NTS	National Trust for Scotland	National Trust en Ecosse	National Trust in Schottland	National Trust per la Scozia	The National Trust de Escocia
BH	Bank Holidays	Jours fériés	Bankfeiertage	Festività nazionale	Días festivos (bancos y comercio)
PH	Public Holidays	Jours fériés	Feiertage	Festività nazionale	Días festivos
Etr	Easter	Pâques	Ostern	Pasqua	Semana Santa
ex	except	sauf	ausser	eccetto	excepto
IR£	Irish punts	Punts irlandais	Punts Irisch	Punts irlandesi	Punts irlandeses
Free	Admission free	Entrée gratuit	Freier eintritt	Ingresso gratuito	Entrada gratuita
£1	Admission £1	Entrée £1	Eintritt £1	Ingresso £1	Entrada £1
ch 50p	Children 50p	Enfants 50p	Kinder 50p	Bambini 50p	Niños 50p
ch 15 50p	Children under 15 50p	Enfents de moins de 15 ans 50p	Kinder unter 15 Jahren 50p	Bambini sotto i 15 anni 50p	Los niños de menores de 15 años 50p
P	Parking nearby	Stationnement tout près	Parken in der Nähe	Parcheggio nelle vicinanze	Aparcamiento cerca del
Pen	Senior Citizens	Retraites	Rentner	Pensionati	Jubilados
Party	Special or reduced rates for parties booked in advance	Tarifs spéciaux ou réduits pour groupes réservés d'advance	Sondertarife oder Ermässigungen für im voraus bestellte Gesellschaften	Tariffe speciali o ridotte per comitive che prenotano in anticipo	Tarifas especiales o reducidas para los grupos de viajeros que reserven de anternano
Party 30+	Special or reduced rates for parties of 30 or more booked in advance	Tarifs spéciaux ou réduits pour groupes de 30 ou plus réservés d'advance	Sondertarife oder Ermässigungen für im voraus bestellte Gesellschaften von wenigstens 30 Personen	Tariffe speciali o ridotte per comitive di 30 o più persone che prenotano in anticipo	Tarifas especiales o reducidas para grupos de 30 viajeros, o más, que reserven de anternano

in brackets, or with a dash, before the telephone number. An exchange name is only shown if it differs from the town in the heading, but you will only need to refer to the exchange name if you are in the area and need to use the local code.

If dialling Northern Ireland from England use the normal STD code, but for The Republic you need to prefix the number with 00 (this has changed from 01).

VISITORS WITH DISABILITIES should look for the wheelchair symbol showing where all or most of the establishment is accessible to wheelchair-bound visitors. We strongly recommend that you telephone in advance of your visit to check the exact details, particularly regarding access to toilet and refreshment facilities. **Guide dogs** are usually accepted where the establishments show the 'No Dogs' symbol – unless stated otherwise. For the **hard of hearing** induction loops are indicated.

PHOTOGRAPHY is restricted in some places and there are many where it is only allowed in specific areas. Visitors are advised to check with places of interest on the rules for taking photographs and the use of video cameras.

EACH COUNTRY IS COLOUR CODED FOR EASE OF IDENTIFICATION

KEY TO COLOUR CODING

ENGLAND

CHANNEL ISLANDS

SCOTLAND

SCOTTISH ISLANDS

WALES

NORTHERN IRELAND

REPUBLIC OF IRELAND

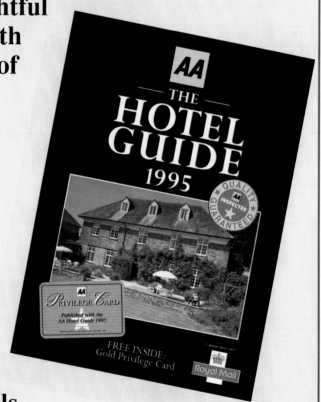

AVON

BATH

Bath owes its fame and beauty to its hot water springs. The Celts had a shrine to the water goddess Sulis here, but Bath's story really begins with the Romans. They called it Aquae Sulis, and enjoyed the pleasures of soaking in the warm water over four centuries. The extensive remains of their baths are at the heart of the city, near the handsome medieval Abbey church. Most of Bath today, however, dates from Georgian times, when the fashionable world came to 'take the waters' in a social round led by Beau Nash, and described - not always kindly - by writers such as Jane Austen. The city is still filled with elegant Georgian terraces and other buildings of mellow Bath stone, notably the celebrated Pulteney Bridge, Circus and Royal Crescent. Highlights among the many places to visit include No 1 Royal Crescent, the Roman Baths and the neighbouring Pump Room. Nearly every street is attractive, with stylish shops to add to the pleasure of wandering. Should the hilly streets prove exhausting, the Kennet and Avon Canal has boating and a towpath walk. The city also has a rich cultural life, and an arts festival each May.

American Museum
BATH
Claverton Manor (2.5m E off A36)
☎(01225) 460503
Claverton Manor is two miles south east of Bath, in a beautiful setting above the River Avon. The house was built in 1820 by Sir Jeffrey Wyatville, and is now a museum of American decorative arts. A series of rooms show American life from the 17th to 19th centuries, with special sections on American Indians and the Shakers, a distinctive collection of quilts, and miniature rooms. The gardens are also well worth seeing, and include an American arboretum and a replica of George Washington's garden at Mount Vernon. The Folk Art Gallery and the New Gallery are among the many exhibits in the grounds along with seasonal exhibitions. Winston Churchill made his first political speech here in 1897. Special events for 1995 include: American Civil War Camp Life (13-14 May), American Indian Weekend (10-11 June), American

Independence Day Displays (1-2 July), American Civil War Weekend (16-17 September).
Open 25 Mar-5 Nov, Tue-Sun 2-5. Gardens 1-6. BH Sun & Mon 11-5.
✱£5 (ch £2.50, pen £4.50). Grounds only £2 (ch £1). Disabled free.
🅿 ♨ ⅏ (ramps provided) toilets for disabled shop ⊛

Bath Industrial Heritage Centre
BATH
Camden Works, Julian Rd
☎(01225) 318348
The centre houses the Bowler collection, the entire stock-in-trade of a Victorian brass founder, general engineer and aerated water manufacturer, displayed so as to capture the atmosphere of the original premises. Also here is 'The Story of Bath Stone', with a replica of a mine face before mechanisation, and a Bath cabinet-maker's workshop, complete with tools and original drawings. A series of temporary exhibitions will include displays from the collection of travelling exhibitions, and there will be a series of lectures throughout the year.
Open all year, Etr-1 Nov, daily 10-5; Nov-Etr, wknds 10-5. (Closed 25-26 Dec).
✱£3 (ch, pen & students £2). Family ticket £7.50.
🅿 ♨ shop ⊛

Bath Postal Museum
BATH
8 Broad St
☎(01225) 460333
Ralph Allen, 18th-century postal reformer and Postmaster of Bath, developed and expanded the mail routes throughout the country. John Palmer, another Bath citizen later the same century, was instrumental in introducing the first nationwide mail coach service. In May 1840 the world's first postage stamps, the famous Penny Black, were sold and sent from the building now occupied by the Bath Postal Museum. The museum has displays on written communications throughout history, exhibitions and films, and of course stamps.
Open all year, Mon-Sat 11-5; Sun 2-5. Parties by appointment. (Closed Good Fri, 25-26 Dec & 1 Jan).
🅿 (200 yds) ♨ ⅏ toilets for disabled shop ⊛
Details not confirmed for 1995

The Book Museum
BATH
Manvers St
☎(01225) 466000
The Museum includes an exhibition of first and early editions of authors who lived in Bath, such as Jane Austen and Charles Dickens.
Open all year, Mon-Fri 9-1 & 2.15-5.30, Sat 9.30-1. (Closed 25 Dec & BH).

THE AMERICAN MUSEUM
Claverton Manor, Bath.
Telephone: (01225) 460503.

18 period furnished rooms from 17th/19th centuries showing domestic life during that period. Galleries of pewter, glass, maps, Folk Art and textiles (over 50 quilts on display). Seasonal exhibitions in the New Gallery. Many exhibits in beautiful gardens, American Arboretum.

OPEN – 25th March to 5th November
2 to 5 every day (except Monday).
Bank Holiday Weekends – Sun & Mon 11 to 5 p.m.

Gardens open 1 to 6 p.m.

Admission charge
Light lunches and teas with American cookies.

£2 (ch £1).
🅿 (NCP) shop ⊛ ⅏

British Folk Art Collection
BATH
Countess of Huntingdon Chapel, The Vineyard/Paragon
☎(01225) 446020
Formerly the Museum of English Native Art, the collection consists of a comprehensive selection of 18th and 19th-century paintings, depicting people, pursuits and incidents which are both revealing and entertaining. Also on show are shop signs, weather vanes and country furniture.
Open all year, Tue-Sat & BH Mon 10.30-5 also Sun Apr-Oct 2-5. (Closed Xmas period).

£2 (ch, pen, students & UB40's £1.50). shop ⊛

The Building of Bath Museum
BATH
Countess of Huntingdons Chapel, The Vineyards, The Paragon
☎(01225) 333895
This museum reveals the story behind Georgian Bath. Here visitors can discover how the buildings of the splendid city were built, decorated and lived in. Exhibits include full-size reconstructions, artefacts, tools and a series of spectacular models, including one of the entire city with push button illumination. This exhibition is the perfect introduction to Bath.
Open Mar-16 Dec, Tue-Sun & BH's 10.30-5.
£2.50 (ch & pen £1.50). Party 10+.
🅿 (500 mtrs) ⅏ shop ⊛

Holburne Museum & Craft Study Centre
BATH
Great Pulteney St
☎(01225) 466669
This elegant and historic building in a lovely garden setting, has 17th-and 18th-century collections of fine and decorative art, notably silver, porcelain, glass, maiolica, furniture and Old Masters, including Gainsborough. These are displayed together with work by 20th-century artists and crafts people, which embraces ceramics, woven and printed textiles, calligraphy and furniture. Ther is an annual programme of exhibitions, lectures, and events. Study facilities by appointment. Special events for 1995 include: A Nest of Nightingales - The Linley family and musical life in 18th-century Bath, plus related events and lectures (15 April-18 June).
Open mid Mar-mid Dec, Mon-Sat & BHs 11-5, Sun 2.30-6. (Closed Mon Etr & Nov).
✱£3.50 (ch £1.50, UB40 & student £2, other concessions £3). Family ticket £7.

Bath's famous Pump Rooms stand beside the city's medieval abbey. The Pump Rooms are built over the Roman temple built at source of the only hot spring in Britain.

➜

🅿 🛗 ♿ *(lift to all floors and ramps where necessary) toilets for disabled shop* ✗

Museum of Costume
BATH ▰▰▰▰▰

Assembly Rooms, Bennett St
☎ (01225) 461111
The Museum of Costume is one of the largest and most prestigious collections of fashionable dress for men, women and children covering the late 16th century to the present day. It is housed in Bath's famous 18th-century Assembly Rooms designed by John Wood the Younger in 1771. The special exhibition Up To Date: Fashion 1963-1993 will continue throughout 1995.
Open all year, Mon-Sat 10-5, Sun 11-5. (Closed 25 & 26 Dec).
✳ *£3.20 (ch £2). Prices under review*
P *(10 mins walk)* ♿ *toilets for disabled shop* ✗

No 1 Royal Crescent
BATH ▰▰▰▰▰

☎ (01225) 428126
Bath is very much a Georgian city, but most of its houses have naturally altered over the years to suit changing tastes and lifestyles. Built in 1768 by John Wood the Elder, No 1 Royal Crescent has been restored to look as it would have done some 200 years ago. Two floors are furnished as they might have been in the 18th century, with pictures, china and furniture of the period, and there is also an interesting kitchen. Note the first-floor windows, which are the original length: all the others in the Royal Crescent were lengthened downwards in the 19th century. The house was once the home of the Duke of York, famed for marching his 10,000 men up the hill and down again.
Open Mar-29 Oct, Tue-Sun 10.30-5; 31 Oct-10 Dec, Tue-Sun 10.30-4. Open BH Mon. (Closed Good Fri). Last admission 30 mins before closing.
✳ *£3.50 (ch, students & pen £2.50). Family ticket £8*
P *shop* ✗

Roman Baths & Pump Room
BATH ▰▰▰▰▰

Abbey Church Yard
☎ (01225) 461111 ext 2785
The descent to the Roman baths is a step back in time. The remains give a vivid impression of life nearly 2000 years ago. The baths, built next to Britain's only hot spring, served the sick and the pilgrims visiting the adjacent Temple of Sulis Minerva. The Spring was a sacred site lying within the courtyard of the Temple. Votive offerings and temple treasures discovered during the excavations of the Spring can be seen in the museum display.
Today, the Temple Courtyard is beneath the Pump Room. This building became a

popular meeting place in the 18th century when Bath became the leading resort for fashionable society. Inside the present Pump Room there is now a restaurant where morning coffee, lunches and teas can be taken to the accompaniment of music from the Pump Room Trio. The hot spa water can also be sampled.
Open all year, Apr-Jul & Sep, daily 9-6; Aug daily 9-6 & 8pm-10pm; Oct-Mar, Mon-Sat 9.30-5, Sun 10.30-5. Disabled visitors free admission to ground floor areas. Last admission 30 minutes before closing.
Admission fee payable.
✗ *licensed* ♿ *toilets for disabled shop* ✗

Royal Photographic Society
BATH ▰▰▰▰▰

The Octagon, Milsom St
☎ (01225) 462841
The Octagon was built in 1796 as a chapel, but is now the headquarters of the world's oldest photographic society. A huge collection of cameras, the first photograph, and other classics are displayed. Temporary exhibitions often include top contemporary work. A variety of workshops, seminars and talks will be held throughout the year.
Open all year, daily 9.30-5.30, last admission 4.45pm. (Closed 25-26 Dec).
P *(5 mins walk)* 🍴 ✗ *licensed* ♿ *(chair lift to all floors) toilets for disabled shop* ✗
Details not confirmed for 1995

Sally Lunn's Refreshment House & Museum
BATH ▰▰▰▰▰

4 North Pde Passage
☎ (01225) 461634
The history of this Tudor building can be traced back to Roman times. It is the oldest home in Bath, and became a popular meeting place in the 18th century. In the cellars, a fascinating museum reveals the findings of recent excavations. Here too is the original kitchen, with its faggot oven, Georgian cooking range and a collection of baking utensils. The traditional 'Sally Lunn' is still served in the restaurant: it is a bread like the French 'brioche', made with eggs and butter, popularly believed to have been named after its first maker, who came to Bath in 1680.
Open all year, museum - Mon-Fri 10-6, Sat 10-6, Sun 12-6; refreshment rooms: Mon 10-6, Tue-Sat 10am-10.30pm & Sun 12-10.30pm. (Closed 25-26 Dec & 1 Jan). 30p (ch, students & pen free).
P *(8 mins walk)* 🍴 ✗ *licensed (braille menu for the blind) shop* ✗ ♿

BRISTOL ▰▰▰▰▰
Bristol has been a crossroads of world exploration and trade since long before John Cabot left its quay for the

New World in 1496. It was the main port for exporting the wool that made the West Country wealthy and during the 18th century Bristol flourished on the slave trade. Many of her fine terraces and grand buildings were built on the enormous riches this created. Clifton, once a village on the steep cliffs above the docks is the most attractive part and is where the University is to be found. Brunel's famous suspension bridge was built to provide access from Clifton across the deep Avon Gorge. Nowadays Bristol is no longer a major trading port and many of the dock areas have been restored to provide leisure facilities.

Blaise Castle House Museum
BRISTOL ▰▰▰▰▰

Henbury Rd, Henbury (4m NW of city, off B4057)
☎ (0117) 9506789
The 'castle' is an 18th-century mansion built for a Quaker banker, and is now Bristol's Museum of Social History. It stands in extensive grounds which were planned by Humphry Repton. Nearby Blaise Hamlet is a picturesque little estate village designed by John Nash.
Open all year, daily 10-6.
P *(100 yds)* ♿ *shop* ✗
Details not confirmed for 1995

Bristol City Museum & Art Gallery
BRISTOL ▰▰▰▰▰

Queen's Rd
☎ (0117) 9223571
The museum has regional and international collections representing ancient history, natural sciences, and fine and applied arts. Displays include dinosaurs, Bristol ceramics, silver, Chinese and Japanese ceramics. Temporary exhibitions are held in the New Solaglass Gallery.
Open all year, daily 10-5.
P *(NCP 400 yds)* 🍴 ♿ *(lift) toilets for disabled shop* ✗
Details not confirmed for 1995

Bristol Industrial Museum
BRISTOL ▰▰▰▰▰

Prince's Wharf, Prince St
☎ (0117) 9251470
The museum is housed in a converted dockside transit shed. Motor and horse-drawn vehicles from the Bristol area are shown, with locally built aircraft and aero-engines. Railway exhibits include the industrial locomotive 'Henbury', steamed about once a month. There are also machines used in local industry, and displays on the history of the port.
Open all year, Tue-Sun 10-1 & 2-5. Open BH Mon.
🅿 *(charged)* ♿ *toilets for disabled shop* ✗
Details not confirmed for 1995

Bristol Zoo Gardens
BRISTOL ▰▰▰▰▰

Clifton (on A4176)
☎ (0117) 9738951
Set in beautiful gardens, the Zoo provides a haven for some of the world's most endangered wildlife. There are tigers, penguins, seals, an aquarium, reptile house, lake island for monkeys, an invertebrate house and much more. Other features include an adventure playground, zoolympics trail and activity centre. Special events held throughout the year include bird flying displays, classical and jazz concerts and theatre porductions. Many events are held during the school holidays.
Open all year, daily (ex 25 Dec) from 9am. Closing times approx 6pm (summer) 5pm (winter).
£5.50 (ch 3-13 £2.50, pen £4).
🅿 *(charged)* 🍴 ✗ *licensed* ♿ *toilets for disabled shop* ✗

Cabot Tower & Brandon Hill Nature Reserve
BRISTOL ▰▰▰▰▰

Brandon Hill, Great George St
☎ (0117) 9252748
The tower stands over 100ft high, giving superb views for photography, and was built in 1897-8 to commemorate Cabot's arrival in North America on 24 June 1497. It stands on Brandon Hill, a municipal park since 1924, and is surrounded by a rock garden and ornamental ponds. There is also a nature reserve which was created as one of the first urban reserves in Britain. It features ponds, a hay meadow, butterfly garden, mini forest and heathland plot.
Open all year. Tower normally 9.30-dusk; Nature Reserve & Park open all times; Nature Reserve HQ open weekdays, 11-3. Free.
P ♿ *shop*

Exploratory Hands-on-Science Centre
BRISTOL ▰▰▰▰▰

Bristol Old Station, Temple Meads
☎ (0117) 9252008 & 9225944 (info line)
As its name suggests, this is a museum which invites the visitor to try things out. Bubbles and bridges, lights and lasers, mechanics and mirrors - they are all here to discover and enjoy. Come to the Exploratory and find out for yourself! New attractions include a planetarium and a hands-on music and sound gallery with the world's largest acoustic guitar. Special events are held during major school holidays.
Open all year, daily 10-5 (Closed 21-26 Dec).
✳ *£4 (ch £2.50, ch under 5 free). Party 10+.*
P *(NCP 50 yds)* 🍴 ♿ *toilets for disabled shop* ✗

Georgian House
BRISTOL ▰▰▰▰▰

7 Great George St
☎ (0117) 9211362
A carefully preserved example of a late-18th-century merchant's town house, with many original features and furnished to illustrate life both above and below stairs.
Open all year, Tue-Sat, 10-1 & 2-5. Open BH Mon.
✗
Details not confirmed for 1995

Harveys Wine Museum
BRISTOL ▰▰▰▰▰

12 Denmark St
☎ (0117) 9275036
Founded in 1796 by a Bristol merchant, Harveys of Bristol is one of the oldest and most famous wine firms, and has been based here since the company started. The wine cellars date back to the 1220s and Bristol cream sherry was first blended in the cellars in the 1880s. Now the cellars house a collection devoted to wine including 18th-century drinking glasses, bottles, decanters, and corkscrews. There are guided tours with tutored tastings for groups (minimum 30). It is often possible for other visitors

Furnished throughout to show life in an 18th-century merchant's home, the exquisitely restored interior of Bristol's Georgian House shows the elegance of this wealthy trading city at its peak.

to join groups but please telephone in advance to check. Special events are planned throughout the year to mark the museum's 30th anniversary. Please telephone for details.
Open all year, Mon-Fri 10-1 and 2-5, Sat 10-5. Closed BH.
£2.50 (concessions £1.50). Family ticket £5.
P *(5 mins walk) (parking meters)* ✗ *licensed shop* ⚓

John Wesley's Chapel (The New Room)
BRISTOL
36 The Horsefair, Broadmead
☎ (0117) 9264740
This is the oldest Methodist chapel in the world. It was built in 1739 and extended in 1748, both times by John Wesley. Both chapel and living rooms above are preserved in their original form. John Wesley Day is 24 May.
Open all year, daily 10-4. (Closed Sun, Weds in winter & BH). Upstairs rooms closed 1-2pm.
✱*Donation requested. £2 for guided tour.*
P *(100yds)* ♿ *shop* ⚓

Maritime Heritage Centre
BRISTOL
Gas Ferry Rd
☎ (0117) 9260680
The centre explores 200 years of Bristol shipbuilding, with special reference to Charles Hill & Son, and their predecessor, James Hillhouse.
Open all year, daily 10-6, 5pm in winter; (Closed 24 & 25 Dec).
P *(charged)* ♿ *toilets for disabled* ⚓
Details not confirmed for 1995

Red Lodge
BRISTOL
Park Row
☎ (0117) 9211360
The house was built in 1590 and then altered in 1730. It has fine oak panelling and carved stone chimneypieces and is furnished in the style of both periods.

The garden has recently been laid out in Elizabethan style.
Open all year, Tue-Sat 10-1 & 2-5. Open BH Mon.
P *(NCP)* ⚓
Details not confirmed for 1995

SS Great Britain
BRISTOL
Great Western Dock, Gas Ferry Rd (off Cumberland Rd)
☎ (0117) 9260680
The SS *Great Britain* was built and launched in Bristol on 19 July 1843. She was the first ocean-going propeller-driven, iron ship in history. Designed by Isambard Kingdom Brunel, she had a varied active life for 43 years, both as a liner and a cargo vessel. Her first voyages were to America, then for some 25 years she carried thousands of emigrants to Australia: the voyages to Australia were interrupted twice when she became a troop ship for the Crimean War and the Indian Mutiny. Abandoned in the Falkland Islands in 1886, her wreck provided storage facilities in Port Stanley for 50 years. In 1970 what remained of her rusting carcass was towed back to Bristol and she is now being restored to her original 1843 appearance at the Great Western Dock in which she was built.
Open all year daily 10-6, 5pm in winter. (Closed 24 & 25 Dec).
£3.40 (ch & pen £2.30)
P *(charged)* ♿ *shop* ⚓

Clevedon Court
CLEVEDON
(off B3130)
☎ (01275) 872257
Clevedon Court is a remarkably complete manor house of around 1320. Additions have been made in each century, so it is now a pleasing variety of styles, with an 18th-century terraced garden. One owner, Sir Edmund Elton, was a celebrated potter, and there is a display of his work.
Open 2 Apr-28 Sep, Wed, Thu, Sun & BH Mon 2.30-5.30. Last admission 5pm.
£3.40 (ch £1.60, ch under 17 must be accompanied). Party 20+ by arrangement.
P ♿ ⚓
(NT)

Dyrham Park
DYRHAM
(8m N of Bath)
☎ (0117) 937 2501
Dyrham Park is a splendid William and Mary house, with interiors which have hardly altered since the late 17th century. It has contemporary Dutch-style furnishings, Dutch pictures and blue-and-white Delft ware. Around the house is an ancient park with fallow deer. Jazz Festival 30 June-1 July 1995.
Open - House & garden Apr-29 Oct, daily ex Thu & Fri 12-5.30. (Last admission 5pm or dusk). Park open all year, daily 12-5.30 or dusk if earlier. (Closed 25 Dec).
£4.80 (ch £2.40). Park only £1.60 (ch 80p).
P ♿ ✗ *toilets for disabled shop* ⚓ *(ex in dog walk area).*
(NT)

Radstock, Midsomer Norton & District Museum
RADSTOCK
Barton Meade House, Haydon (1m S on Haydon/Kilmersden rd)
☎ (01761) 437722
A local history museum, run by volunteers, housed in the 18th-century barn of a former dairy and cheese-making farm located in the old North Somerset coalfield. Features include a reconstructed coalface, miner's cottage, model railway, agricultural implements, a 1930's Co-op shop, a blacksmith's shop, mining photographs, chapel china and leisure bygones. There is also a Victorian schoolroom. Temporary exhibitions are held throughout the year.
Open Jan-Nov, Sat 10-4, Sun & BH's 2-5.
✱*£1.50 (concessions 50p)*
P ♿ *shop*

International Helicopter Museum
WESTON-SUPER-MARE
Weston Airport, Locking Moor Rd
☎ (01934) 635227
A unique collection of more than 50 helicopters and autogyros is on display. This is given a further dimension by exhibits of models, photographs and components to illustrate how the aircraft work. There is a ride simulator, and from March to September on the second Sunday in the month, 'Open Cockpit Days' are held when visitors can try out the pilot's seat of a real helicopter, and receive instructions from museum guides. Helicopters from this museum are also featured in the Weston Super Helidays (29-30 July), which take place on the seafront and include flying and static displays of up to 50 helicopters. New for 1995 are several new exhibits inlcuding the first Russian attack helicopter in a UK museum.
Open all year, Mar-Oct, daily 10-6 & Nov-Feb, 10-4.
£3 (ch under 5 free, 5-15 £2, pen £2.50). Family ticket £8. Party 15+.
P ♿ *toilets for disabled shop*

Woodspring Museum
WESTON-SUPER-MARE
Burlington St
☎ (01934) 621028
This museum, housed in the workshops of the Edwardian Gaslight Company, is set around a central courtyard with displays on the seaside holiday, an old chemist's shop, a dairy, and a lion fountain with Victorian pavement mosaics. Adjoining the museum is Clara's Cottage, a Westonian home of the 1900s with period kitchen, parlour, bedroom and back yard. One of the rooms has an additional display of Peggy Nisbet dolls. Other displays in the museum include a gallery of wildlife in the district, Mendip minerals, mining and local archaeology. There are also costume rooms, an exhibition of early bicycles and a display on the dentist in 1900. Changing exhibitions are held in the Temporary Exhibitions Gallery.
Open all year, Tue-Sun 10-5 & BH Mon. (Closed Xmas, New Year & Good Fri).
P *(400 yds)* ♿ *(induction loop) toilets for disabled shop* ⚓
Details not confirmed for 1995

'Ship-shape and Bristol fashion' refers to the days when Bristol was a great sea-faring port. Built in Bristol in 1843, *SS Great Britain* was part of that era.

BEDFORDSHIRE

Houghton House
AMPTHILL
(N off A418)
Now a ruin, the mansion was built for Mary Countess of Pembroke, the sister of Sir Philip Sidney. Inigo Jones is thought to have been involved in work on the house, which is said to be the 'House Beautiful' in Bunyan's 'Pilgrim's Progress'.
Open all reasonable times.
Free.
P &
(EH)

Bedford Museum
BEDFORD
Castle Ln
☎(01234) 353323
The museum is devoted to local history and natural history, with 19th-century room sets and displays of birds and mammals, agriculture, archaeology, fossils and minerals. There is a changing programme of children's activities, temporary exhibitions and special events.
Open all year, Tue-Sat 11-5, Sun 2-5. (Closed Mon ex BH Mon afternoon, Good Fri & Xmas).
Free.
P & (lift available on request) *toilets for disabled shop* ✿

Cecil Higgins Art Gallery & Museum
BEDFORD
Castle Close
☎(01234) 211222
The rooms in this award-winning recreated Victorian mansion are arranged in the manner of a house still lived in, to authenticate the atmosphere. The adjoining gallery has an outstanding collection of ceramics, glass and watercolours, and is set in gardens leading down to the river embankment. A regular programme of thematic exhibitions is taken from the gallery's own collection of watercolours, prints and drawings.
Open all year, Tue-Sat 11-5, Sun 2-5, BH Mon 2-5. (Closed Mon, Good Fri & 25-26 Dec).
Free.
P (50 yds) & *toilets for disabled shop* ✿

Moot Hall
ELSTOW
☎Bedford (01234) 228342 (office hrs)
The restored medieval timber-framed market hall has a collection of 17th-century furniture and items relating to the life and times of John Bunyan, who was born nearby. These include a fine collection of his works, notably *Pilgrim's Progress.*
Open Etr-30 Oct, Tue-Sat & BH's 2-5; Sun 2-5.30. (Closed Mon ex BH's).
P & *shop* ✿
Details not confirmed for 1995

Leighton Buzzard Railway
LEIGHTON BUZZARD
Pages Park Station, Billington Rd (0.75m SE on A4146)
☎(01525) 373888
The original light railway was built to carry sand in 1919, and after its redundancy in 1967 the railway society took over its three and a half mile length. It is now a 2ft gauge passenger-carrying line through varied scenery with over 50 locomotives, including 12 resident steam engines from West Africa, India, Spain and Britain. The line is now one of England's foremost narrow gauge preservation centres. A programme of industrial train displays and locomotive viewing will take place throughout the year. Special events planned for 1995 include: Easter Steam Weekend (14-17 April), VE Day event (8 May), Heritage Weekend (3-4 June), Wild West Day (2 July), Autumn steam-up (9-10 September).
Open, operating dates Suns, 2 Apr-15 Oct, Etr wknd & BH Mons. Also Weds 7 Jun-

LUTON HOO
THE WERNHER COLLECTION

The works of Carl Fabergé, the Russian Court jeweller which are on view at Luton Hoo, are part of the finest private Collection of works of art in Great Britain, which includes continental treasures rarely seen in English Country Houses.

There are many paintings, costume and other personal possessions of the Russian Imperial Family Romanov, complemented by the acquisition of memorabilia of Father Gibbes who was tutor to the Tsarevitch. All the Russian Collection has been redesigned and redisplayed in and around the beautiful Chapel — extensively restored to its original decorative splendour, and in 1991, consecrated into the Russian Orthodox Church and dedicated to the memory of Tsar Nicholas II and the Imperial Family.

Other treasures in the House are Old Master Paintings, magnificent Tapestries, English and French Porcelain, European Ceramics, Furniture, Byzantine and Medieval Ivories, Sculpture, Bronzes and Renaissance Jewellery.

OPEN 11 APRIL – 15 OCTOBER 1995
RESTAURANT OPENS AT 12 NOON
Gardens 12 noon-6.00pm House 1.30-5.45pm (Last admission to House 5.00pm)
N.B. House & gardens CLOSED MONDAYS
except BANK HOLIDAYS – open 10.30am.
The House & gardens will be open for pre-booked
private parties only on Tuesdays, Wednesdays &
Thursdays and for general viewing on Fridays, Saturdays & Sundays
Luton Hoo, Luton, Bedfordshire LU1 3TQ Tel: (01582) 22955

23 Aug, Thurs 3-24 Aug , Sats 3 Jun, 5-26 Aug & 9 Sep. Trains run to Stonehenge Works. Return journey lasts 1hr. Trains run between 11am-3.10pm (4.30 Sun & BH Mons). Xmas trains run Sat & Sun 2-24 Dec advanced booking advised.
Return ticket £4 (ch 2-15 £1, pen £3 & ch under 2 free). Party 10+.
P ♿ & (platform & train access for wheelchairs) *toilets for disabled shop*

Luton Hoo (The Wernher Collection)
LUTON
(entrance at Park Street gates)
☎(01582) 22955
Set in parkland landscaped by 'Capability' Brown is a magnificent country mansion originally designed by Robert Adam, and remodelled in 1903 for Sir Julius Wernher, a diamond magnate. Thoroughly equal to the splendid exterior is the fabulous Wernher Collection of art treasures, the finest private collection in Great Britain, which includes continental items rarely seen in English country houses. The famous Russian collection with works by Carl Fabergé, the Russian court jeweller, paintings, costume and other personal possessions of the Imperial Family, has been redesigned and redisplayed in and around the beautiful chapel, recently restored to its original decorative splendour, consecrated in 1991 into the Russian Orthodox Church and dedicated to the memory of Tsar Nicholas II and the Imperial family.
Other treasures in the house include Old Master paintings, magnificent tapestries, English and French porcelain, Byzantine and medieval ivories, sculpture, bronzes and Renaissance jewellery. Special events planned for 1995 include an interior design exhibition (October) and Christmas gift fair (November).
Open 11 Apr-15 Oct, Fri, Sat & Sun 1.30-5.(Closed Mon ex BH's). Tue-Thu pre-booked groups only.

✱Houses & Gardens £5.50 (ch £2.50, pen £5). Gardens only £2.50 (concessions £2.25).
P ♿ ✗ *licensed* & (ramp access to cafeteria) *toilets for disabled shop* ✿

Luton Museum & Art Gallery
LUTON
Wardown Park, Old Bedford Rd
☎(01582) 746722
A Victorian mansion standing in Wardown Park contains displays illustrating the natural and cultural history, archaeology and industries of the area. Follow the development of Luton's hat industry in the 19th and 20th centuries and admire the extensive hat and lace collections. Also on view are costumes, dolls, straw marquetry, decorative and fine arts, several Victorian settings and the Bedfordshire and Hertfordshire Regimental Collections. Extensive redisplay work is due to start early in 1995 so please telephone before making a special visit.
Open all year, Mon-Sat 10-5, Sun 1-5 (Closed Xmas & 1 Jan).
Free.
P ♿ & *toilets for disabled shop* ✿

The Shuttleworth Collection
OLD WARDEN
Old Warden Aerodrome (2m W from rdbt on A1, Biggleswade by-pass)
☎Northill (01767) 627288
Housed in seven hangars on a classic grass aerodrome, 30 working historic aeroplanes span the progress of aviation with exhibits ranging from a 1909 Bleriot to a 1941 Spitfire. A garage of roadworthy motor vehicles explores the eras of the 1898 Panhard Levassor to the Railton sports car of 1937.
Open all year, daily 10-4 (3pm Nov-Mar). Closed 10 days at Xmas, up to and including 1 Jan.
P ✗ *licensed* & (passageways between hangars are ramped) *toilets for disabled shop* ✿
Details not confirmed for 1995

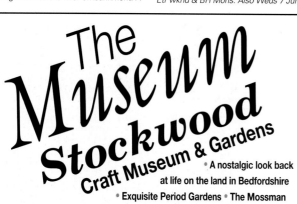

Wrest Park House & Gardens
SILSOE
☎ (01525) 860152
Notable 18th-century garden layout with formal canals and alterations by 'Capability' Brown. The early 18th-century Baroque banqueting house is by Thomas Archer and Bowling Green House by Betty Langley.
Open Apr-Sep, wknds & BH's 10-6.
🅿 ☕ ⌖
(EH)
Details not confirmed for 1995

Stagsden Bird Gardens
STAGSDEN
(5m W of Bedford, on A422)
☎ Bedford (01234) 822745
A breeding centre for many species of birds, including owls, cranes, pheasants, waterfowl and old breeds of poultry. There is also a fine collection of shrub roses.
Open all year, daily 11-6 or dusk. (Closed 25 Dec)
✤£2.50 (ch £1 & pen £2).
🅿 & shop ⌖

Whipsnade Wild Animal Park
WHIPSNADE
☎ (01582) 872171
The Park is set in 600 acres of beautiful parkland and is the home to almost 2500 animals. Wallabies, peacocks, mara and Chinese water deer roam freely among the woods, and many of the animals here are rare and endangered species in the wild. Whipsnade's conservation and breeding programmes for endangered species are known and respected worldwide. Things to see and do include unique free flying birds of the world demonstrations, World of Sealions, Elephants at Work, Discovery Centre, Woodland Bird Walk, Wolf Wood, Chimpanzee Island, Passage through Asia, Children's Farm, the Great Whipsnade Railway and Tiger Falls. Explore the park by foot, car or the free Trailbreaker Roadtrain. Events at Whipsnade include an Easter Egg Hunt, Steam Weekend, Teddy Festival and Christmas Wonderland.
Open all year, Mar-Oct, Mon-Sat 10-6, Sun & BH 10-7. Nov-Feb, 10-dusk. (Closed 25 Dec).
Nov-Feb: £3.50 (ch £2.75, pen £3, car £3). Mar-Oct: £7.25 (ch £5.50, pen £6, car £6). Prices under review.
🅿 (charged) ☕ ✕ licensed & (free entry for disabled cars) toilets for disabled shop ⌖

Woburn Abbey & Deer Park
WOBURN
☎ (01525) 290666
This palatial 18th-century mansion is the home of the Duke of Bedford. The house dates from 1744 but was remodelled in 1802 by Henry Holland. Originally a Cistercian abbey, the Dukes of Bedford have lived at Woburn since 1547. There is a valuable art collection in the house with paintings by Canaletto, Rembrandt, Van Dyck, Gainsborough and many others. There is also an extensive collection of 18th-century furniture, both French and English. Fourteen state apartments on view and the private apartments are shown when not in use by the family. The house stands in 3000 acres of parkland, famous for its collection of varieties of deer. Special events held during the year include craft fairs, a gardening festival, Jaguar car rally, antiques fair; please telephone for details.
Open, Abbey Sat & Sun only Jan-25 Mar, 11-4; 26 Mar-30 Oct daily 11-4. Deer Park Sat & Sun only Jan-25 Mar, 10.30-3.45; 26 Mar-30 Oct daily 10-4.45 (4.30 Sun).
✤Abbey & Deer Park £6.50 (ch over 12yrs £3, pen £5.50). Family ticket £12.50-£15.50. Deer Park only car & passengers £5. Motorcycles & passengers £2.
🅿 ☕ ✕ licensed & (wheelchairs accommodated by prior arrangement) toilets for disabled shop garden centre ⌖

There is an opportunity to take a dray ride after meeting the horses and learning their history at the Courage Shire Horse Centre.

Woburn Safari Park
WOBURN
Woburn Park (from M1, junc 13)
☎ (01525) 290407
Within the 3000 acres of parkland belonging to Woburn Abbey, is an area of over 300 acres set aside as a wild animal kingdom. A collection of many species of animal has made Woburn justifiably famous among Safari Parks. Woburn's own safari road passes through an African plains area stocked with eland, zebra, hippos and rhinos. Then through the well-keepered tiger and lion enclosures and on past bears and monkeys. The pets' corner, sea lion and parrot shows, and elephant displays, are all popular attractions. Special events are held on all Bank Holidays and during summer school holidays. The large new leisure complex also offers a boating lake and adventure playground.
Open Mar-Oct, daily 10-5. 2 Nov-Mar, wknds 11-3 weather permitting.
❄*£7.50 (ch & pen £5).*
🅿 ✗ *licensed & toilets for disabled shop* ⊘

BERKSHIRE

Basildon Park
BASILDON
☎ *Pangbourne (01734) 843040*
This lovely 18th-century house, built of golden Bath stone, fell into decay in the 20th century, but was rescued and beautifully restored by Lord and Lady Iliffe. The first feature to impress the visitor is the classical front with its splendid central portico and pavilions. Inside there are delicate plasterwork decorations on the walls and ceilings and an elegant staircase. The most impressive room is the Octagon drawing room, with its fine pictures and furniture, and three big windows overlooking the River Thames. The Shell Room and Bamboo Room are also notable for their decorations. There is a small formal garden, and a pretty terrace garden overlooks the grounds. National Trust centenary events will be held throughout

the season. Children's Day (4 June), Jazz concert (19 August), Gilbert and Sullivan Lantern Light Gala (20 August).
Open Apr-Oct, Wed-Sat 2-6; Sun & BH Mon noon-6. Last admission 5.30. (Closed Good Fri & Wed following BH). House & grounds £3.60, family ticket £9; Grounds only £1.50, family ticket £3.75.
🅿 🅿 & *toilets for disabled shop* ⊘ *(ex in grounds)*
(NT)

Beale Park
BASILDON
Lower Basildon (signposted from M4 junc 12)
☎ *Reading (01734) 845172*
Ornamental pheasants, peacocks, parrots, owls, cranes and wildfowl can be seen here in a pleasant riverside setting (a designated area of Outstanding Natural Beauty), together with Highland cattle and rare breeds of sheep, a pets' corner and a tropical house. There is a craft centre, and a children's playground with paddling pools and sandpits. There is also excellent fishing in season. The park has an information/education facility, and numerous events and exhibitions are held during the year.
River trips are another attraction, and a narrow gauge railway runs around the park every day. Amidst all this is the unusual focal point of the mausoleum, built by Mr Child Beale in memory of his parents, surrounded by a large and varied collection of statues, fountains and walks. Special events for 1995 include: craft fair/show (August), model ship/marine festivals (May and October), fireworks (November), car rallies and horse shows.
Open daily, Feb-Sep 10-6. Oct-Dec 10-5. Last admission 4pm. £4 (ch under 3 free, 3-16 £2.50, students £2 pen £3). Disabled £2 (disabled ch free). Unemployed half price for up to 2 adults plus 2 ch. Party.
🅿 🅿 & *(wheelchair available, parking) toilets for disabled shop* ⊘

Dorney Court
ETON
Dorney
☎ *Burnham (01628) 604638*

This enchanting brick and timber manor house (c1440) stands in a tranquil setting. It has tall Tudor chimneys and a splendid great hall and has been the home of the present family since 1510.
Open Etr wknd, then Sun & BH Mon in May; Jun-Sep, Sun-Tue 2-5.30 (last admission 5pm). £4 (ch 9 £2, pen & NT members £3.60).
🅿 🅿 *shop garden centre* ⊘

Courage Shire Horse Centre
MAIDENHEAD
Cherry Garden Ln, Maidenhead Thicket (off A4 .5m W of A4/A423/A423M jct)
☎ *Littlewick Green (01628) 824848*
Visitors are free to wander around and meet the horses, or take a free tour with an experienced guide who will introduce you to the horses and explain the care and history of the 'gentle giants' of the equestrian world. See the harness maker at work, and certain days will find the farrier or cooper in attendance. Dray rides are also available.
Open Mar-Oct, daily 10.30-5. Last admission 4pm (5pm Jul-Sep & Special Event Days) £2.80 (ch & pen £2). Party 10+.
🅿 🅿 & *(wheelchair available) toilets for disabled shop*

Newbury District Museum
NEWBURY
The Wharf
☎ *(01635) 30511*
The museum is situated in two picturesque and historic buildings in the centre of Newbury, the Cloth Hall built in 1627, and the Granary built in 1720. Apart from local history and archaeology, birds and fossils, the museum displays costume and other decorative art. Special features are the two Civil War battles of Newbury (1643 and 1644) and the history of ballooning.

Open all year, Apr-Sep Mon-Sat (ex Wed) 10-5, Sun & BH's 1-5; Oct-Mar Mon-Sat (ex Wed) 10-4. Open Wed during school holidays.
🅿 *(15yds) & shop* ⊘
Details not confirmed for 1995

Blake's Lock Museum
READING
Gasworks Rd
☎ *(01734) 590630*
Reading's museum of industrial heritage on the banks of the River Kennet houses a wealth of displays including a Victorian printer's workshop, bakery, barber's shop and a fully restored gypsy caravan. There are boat trips during the summer months. Special events during 1995 include: Reading Waterfest - a celebration of Reading's waterways (June), and an exhibition from spring, Reading at War: The Home Front.
Open all year, Tue-Fri 10-5, Sat, Sun & BH Mon 2-5. Parties by arrangement.
🅿 & *toilets for disabled shop* ⊘
Details not confirmed for 1995

Museum of English Rural Life
READING
University of Reading, Whiteknights Park (2m SE on A327)
☎ *(01734) 318660*
This museum houses a fascinating national collection of agricultural, domestic and crafts exhibits, including wagons, tools and a wide range of other equipment used in the English countryside over the last 150 years. Family groups will find the exhibitions especially attractive, and special facilities such as videos and teaching packs are available for school parties, on request. The museum also contains very extensive documentary and photographic archives, which can be studied by appointment.

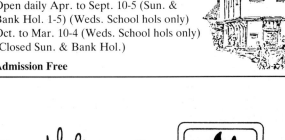

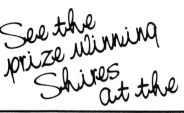

Open all year, Tue-Sat, 10-1 & 2-4.30. (Closed BH's & Xmas-New Year).
£1 (ch free & pen 75p).
🅿 & shop 🐾

The Museum of Reading
READING
The Town Hall, Blagrave St
☎ (01734) 399800
Discover the development of Reading through the ages from a Saxon settlement on the banks of the River Kennet to the commercial heart of today's Thames Valley. Experience the crowning of a medieval king, the sounds of singing in the Abbey, the smells of Victorian Reading - biscuits baking and beer brewing. Also on show is a full-size Victorian replica of the Bayeux Tapestry. Three new galleries are due to open mid 1995 - the Silchester Gallery with a permanent display from the Roman town of Silchester, a special exhibitions gallery with items from Reading's extensive art collection, and a resource gallery with a special fun area for the under 7s.
Open all year, Tue-Sat 10-5, Sun & BH 2-5.
Free.
🅿 🍽 ✗ licensed & toilets for disabled shop 🐾

Wellington Country Park & National Dairy Museum
RISELEY
(off B3349)
☎ Reading (01734) 326444
The country park consists of 600 acres of woodland and meadows, set around a lake in the countryside between Reading and Basingstoke. The National Dairy Museum in the grounds outlines the history of the dairy industry in Britain. There is also a Thames Valley Time Trail, which traces the development of earth and mineral resources in the area. Other attractions are the collections farm animals, a deer park and a miniature steam railway. Five nature trails are marked out, in addition to a fitness course and adventure playground. It is also possible to fish, sail, windsurf and row here. Special events for 1995 include: Easter Fun Days, Animal Day (8 May and 13 August), Teddy Bears' Picnic (mid June).
Open all year, Mar-Oct, daily 10-5.30 & winter wknds 10-dusk.
Prices under review.
🅿 🍽 & (fishing platform for disabled) toilets for disabled shop

WINDSOR
The town of Windsor owes its existence to the famous castle which has been a home of British monarchs for almost 900 years. The castle, on its outcrop above the River Thames, stands above the town like a stately galleon, dominating every aspect of life there. It is the largest inhabited castle in the world and through the ages has been much altered. Most of the present structure was due to work done by George IV and many of the buildings in the town are from this period. Windsor also flourished during the Victorian period and the town's station was built to celebrate Queen Victoria's Jubilee. The south and east of the town are bounded by 5000 acres of Windsor Great Park. Across the river is Eton, England's most famous school, founded by Henry VI in 1440 and educator of no less than 20 British Prime Ministers.

Crown Jewels of the World
WINDSOR
47-50 Peascod St
☎ (01753) 833773
This glittering exhibition displays the crown and court jewels of some 12 countries including Austria, Britain, France, Germany, Russia and Iran. Faithfully re-created by gem craftsmen and master jewellers the collection consists of over 150 crowns, tiaras, swords, sceptres,

royal and imperial jewels, and replicas of famous diamonds; most of the originals no longer exist. Lectures and film shows are planned for 1995.
Open 27 Mar-Oct, daily 11-5. Other times by arrangement.
£3.50 (ch £2, pen & student £2.50). Family ticket £10. Party.
🅿 (300yds) shop 🐾

Exhibition of The Queen's Presents & Royal Carriages
WINDSOR
Windsor Castle
☎ (01753) 831118
A regularly changing display of gifts given by foreign governments to The Queen.
Open all year, times vary with season.
❋£1.60 (ch 17 80p & pen £1.40). Prices under review.
🅿 (200 yds) & toilets for disabled 🐾

Frogmore House
WINDSOR
Home Park (entrance from B3021)
☎ (01753) 831118 (recorded info)
The long and distinguished history of Frogmore House dates back even further than the present building of 1618, being previously owned by Henry VIII. Subsequent residents have included Charles II's architect, Hugh May, who built the present house, a Duke of Northumberland, Queen Charlotte, Queen Victoria and Queen Mary. It has 19 rooms, and an original mural, discovered only six years ago during redecoration, can be seen on the stairway.
Open Aug-Sep.
Prices under review.
🅿 shop 🐾

Household Cavalry Museum
WINDSOR
Combermere Barracks, St Leonards Rd
☎ (01753) 868222 ext 5203
This is one of the finest military museums in Britain. There are comprehensive displays of the uniforms, weapons, horse furniture (tack, regalia, etc) and armour used by the Household Cavalry from 1600 to the present day.
Open all year Mon-Fri (ex BH) 9-12.30 & 2-4.30.
❋£2 (ch 50p & pen £1). Party.
& shop 🐾

St George's Chapel
WINDSOR
☎ (01753) 865538
The chapel is an impressive feature of Windsor Castle. Begun in 1475 by Edward IV, and completed in the reign of Henry VIII, it is a fine example of Perpendicular architecture which, with its large windows, gives a light and spacious effect. The magnificent fan vaulting on the ceiling, the chantries, the ironwork and intricate carving on the choir stalls, all add to this superb building. The choir stalls are dedicated to the Order of Knights of the Garter founded by Edward III. Each stall displays the arms of every knight who has sat there and above it are the banner and crested helm of the present holder.
Open weekdays 10-4, Sun 2-4. (Closed 26 & 27 Apr, 16-19 Jun, 24-25 Dec & occasionally at short notice).
Free entry to the Chapel is included in the price of entry to the precincts.
& shop 🐾

Savill Garden (Windsor Great Park)
WINDSOR
(via Wick Ln, Englefield Green, near Egham)
☎ (01753) 860222
The Savill Garden covers some 35 acres of woodland and includes hundreds of different varieties of plants. It is at its peak in spring but, with its range of shrubs such as magnolias and rhododendrons, rock plants, herbaceous borders and formal rose gardens, there is a wealth of colour and interest throughout the year. Special events for 1995 include a spring plant fair (13 May) and an autumn plant fair (26 August).
Open all year, daily 10-6 (10-4 Nov -Feb).·

The massive Round Tower of Windsor Castle looms over the River Thames and dominates the town.

(Closed 25-26 Dec).
£3.30 (ch 16 free, pen £2.80). Party 20+.
🅿 ✗ licensed & toilets for disabled shop garden centre 🐾

Valley Gardens (Windsor Great Park)
WINDSOR
(off A30)
☎ (01753) 860222
These gardens are near Virginia Water, a lake created in the 18th century. The gardens cover some 400 acres of woodland and are noted especially for their outstanding range of rhododendrons, camellias, magnolias and other trees and shrubs. It is worth visiting at any time of the year as there are plants for each season.
Open all year, daily sunrise-sunset.
Free to pedestrians.
🅿 (charged) & toilets for disabled ♿

Windsor Castle
WINDSOR
☎ (01753) 831118
The castle, which covers 13 acres is the official residence of HM The Queen and the largest inhabited castle in the world. It was begun as a wooden fort by William the Conqueror, but has been added to by almost every other monarch. Henry II erected the first stone building, including the famous Round Tower. Among the many alterations since then were those made in the 14th century by Edward III; the 17th century when the Castle began to be altered from a fortress to a palace; and the 19th century when Edward III enlarged the royal apartments and also founded the Order of Knights of the Garter, based at Windsor. Substantial rebuilding was done during the reign of Charles II and Sir Jeffrey Wyattville (1766-1840) was the architect for alterations made by George IV. The castle is in three parts - the Upper Ward which includes the State Apartments, the Middle Ward, with its Round Tower, and the Lower Ward where St George's Chapel is situated.
Queen Mary's Dolls House which is the exquisite dolls' house, designed for Queen Mary in the 1920s by Lutyens, is

also displayed at Windsor Castle. Every piece of furniture, decoration, tableware and equipment in the miniature house has been carried out in perfect detail on a scale of 1:12.
Open all year - but subject to closure at short notice. Telephone 01753 831118 for detailed information.
Prices under review. Single admission charge gives access to the Precincts, St George's Chapel, the State Apartments and The Gallery. Queen Mary's Dolls' House is also open to the public for a small additional charge.
🅿 (400yds) & (except The Gallery) toilets for disabled shop 🐾

BUCKINGHAMSHIRE

Buckinghamshire County Museum
AYLESBURY
St Mary's Square, Church St
☎ (01296) 88849
Old parish rooms next to the churchyard house displays on local history and temporary exhibitions while the main museum is closed for refurbishment.
Open all year, Mon-Sat 10-1.30 & 2-5. (Closed Good Fri, 25-26 Dec & 1 Jan & BH's).
🅿 (200 yds) & shop 🐾
Details not confirmed for 1995

Bekonscot Model Village
BEACONSFIELD
Warwick Rd (2.7m junc 2 M40, 4m junc 16 M25).
☎ (01494) 672919
Bekonscot is a miniature world where time has stood still for 66 years. A wonderland of make-believe with a model railway, airfield, castles, mine, a new elevated walkway, and a unique teaching aid showing rural England in the 1930s.
Open 12 Feb-30 Oct, daily 10-5.
£3 (ch £1.50, pen & students £2). Party 13+.
🅿 🍽 & (wheelchair loan) toilets for disabled shop 🐾
See advertisement on page 20

BEKONSCOT

The oldest model village in the world

Warwick Road, Beaconsfield, Bucks HP9 2PL (01494) 672919

A miniature world where time has stood still for 66 years.
Come and lose yourself in a wonderland of make-believe.
Picnic facilities – Playground – Refreshments – Souvenir Shop –
Elevated Walkway

Open: Daily mid February-end October — 10.00-5.00

| Adult £3.00 | Child £1.50 | Concessions £2 |

By road: Jnct 2 M40. **By train:** Marylebone/Beaconsfield

Chiltern Open Air Museum
CHALFONT ST GILES
Newland Park, Gorelands Ln (off B4442)
☎(01494) 871117 & 875542
The museum aims to preserve traditional Chilterns buildings by rebuilding them here. Among the buildings dismantled and brought to the site are a toll house, cart sheds, stables, granaries, a forge, barns, an Iron Age house, a pair of 18th-century cottages and a 1947 prefab. There is a nature trail through the 45 acres of parkland and there is also an adventure playground. Numerous events are held throughout the year including Transport Day (14 May), Woodworking Weekend (10-11 June), Family Days (27-28 August), and a Victorian Christmas Weekend (2-3 December).
Open Apr-29 Oct, Wed-Sun & BH 2-6. Also Tue in Aug.
£3 (ch 16 & over 60's £2.50, ch 5 free). Family ticket £10.
P 🍴 & *(Braille guide books & taped guides available, wheelchairs) toilets for disabled shop*

Milton's Cottage
CHALFONT ST GILES
Dean Way
☎(01494) 872313
This timber-framed, 16th-century cottage with its charming garden, is the only surviving home in which John Milton lived and worked. He completed *Paradise Lost* and started *Paradise Regained* here. First editions of these works are among the many rare books on display. Milton's parlour is due to open in 1995.
Open Mar-Oct, Wed-Sun 10-1 & 2-6. Also open Spring & Summer BH.
£2 (ch 15 60p). Party 20+.
P & *shop* ⌀

Chicheley Hall
CHICHELEY
(A422 between Newport Pagnell and Bedford)
☎North Crawley (01234) 391252
Built for Sir John Chester between 1719 and 1723, this is one of the finest and least-altered 18th-century houses in England, with wonderful Georgian craftsmanship in its brickwork, carving, joinery and plasterwork. It has a naval museum, English sea pictures and furniture, and an 18th-century dovecote.
Open Etr Sun then Apr-May & Aug, Sun & BH Mon 2.30-6. Last entry 5pm. Booked parties at most times.
£3 (ch £1.50). Parties 20+.
P 🍴 & *shop* ⌀

Cliveden
CLIVEDEN
☎Burnham (01628) 605069
The 375 acres of garden and woodland overlook the River Thames, and include a magnificent parterre, topiary, lawns with box hedges, and rose and water gardens. The palatial house, home of the Astors, is now a hotel, 3 rooms only of the house can be visited on certain afternoons.

Special events for 1995 include: Children's Day (4 June), Open Air Theatre Gala Performance (25 June), Open Air Theatre Festival (28 June-9 July).
Open Grounds Mar-Oct daily 11-6, Nov-Dec daily 11-4. House Apr-Oct, Thu & Sun 3-6 by timed ticket. (Last admission 5.30) Grounds: £4. House: £1 extra. Family ticket £10.
P ✕ *licensed & (powered vehicle available) toilets for disabled shop* ⌀ *(ex in woodland)*
(NT)

Wycombe Local History & Chair Museum
HIGH WYCOMBE
Castle Hill House, Priory Av
☎(01494) 421895
The museum is situated in an 18th-century house set in attractive and historic grounds. The displays explore the history of the Wycombe area focusing on a unique collection of country chairs. There are temporary exhibitions on different subjects which change every month, with activities for children and some special events at weekends.
Open all year, Mon-Fri 10-5; Sat 10-1 & 2-5; Sun (seasonal-please telephone for details).
Free.
P & *shop* ⌀

Hughenden Manor
HUGHENDEN
(1.5m N of High Wycombe, on W side of A4128)
☎High Wycombe (01494) 532580
Benjamin Disraeli, later Earl of Beaconsfield and twice Prime Minister, bought the house in 1847 and lived there until his death in 1881. It still has many of his books and other possessions. A Victorian Craft Fair is planned for 10-11 June 1995.
Open 5-27 Mar, Sat & Sun only 2-6. Apr-Oct, House & Gardens, Wed-Sat 2-6 & Sun & BH Mon 12-6 (5pm 4-30 Oct). Last admission 5.30. (Closed Good Fri).
❊*£3.60(ch £1.80). Family ticket £9.*
P & *(braille leaflet and taped guide) toilets for disabled shop* ⌀ *(ex in park & car park only)*
(NT)

Courthouse
LONG CRENDON
(2m N of Thame, via B4011)
Probably built as a wool store in the early 1400s, but also used as a manorial courthouse until the late 19th century, the timber-framed building stands out, even in a picturesque village of 16th-and 17th-century cottages. Although the windows and doors have been altered and the chimney stack is Tudor, the magnificent timber roof is original. Flower Festival 24-25 June 1995.
Open, Upper storey Apr-Sep, Wed 2-6, Sat, Sun & BH Mons 11-6.
£1
P *(street)* ⌀
(NT)

Claydon House
MIDDLE CLAYDON
(off A413, entrance by North drive only).
☎Steeple Claydon (01296) 730349 & 730693
The rather sober exterior of this 18th-century house gives no clue to the extravagances that lie inside, in the form of fantastic rococo carvings. Ceilings, cornices, walls and overmantels are adorned with delicately carved fruits, birds, beasts and flowers by Luke Lightfoot, and his Chinese room is particularly splendid. The second Earl of Verney commissioned Lightfoot to decorate the rooms and built many other additions to the house besides; but his ambition eventually bankrupted him and by 1783 he had to sell up. His successor proceeded to demolish two-thirds of the house. Florence Nightingale was a frequent visitor and relics of her Crimean experiences are displayed here. Special events for 1995 include concerts on 4 and 17 June.
Open Apr-Oct, Sat-Wed 1-5, BH Mon 1-5 or dusk if earlier. Last admission half hour before closing.
£3.60. Family ticket £9.
P 🍴 & *(Braille guide) toilets for disabled* ⌀ *(ex car park)*
(NT)

Pitstone Windmill
PITSTONE
(off B488)
Now restored and fully operative, this is one of England's oldest postmills, and still contains part of the original structure built in 1627.
Open May-Sep, Sun & BH Mon 2.30-6. (Last admission 5.30).
❊*£1*
P *(200yds)* ⌀
(NT)

Buckinghamshire Railway Centre
QUAINTON
Quainton Rd Station (off A41, signposted from A41 & A413)
☎(01296) 655720 & 655450 (info)
The Centre houses an interesting and varied collection of about 20 locomotives with 40 carriages and wagons from places as far afield as South Africa, Egypt and America. Many items date from the last century, while others were built as recently as the 1960s. Visitors can take a ride on full-size and miniature steam trains and stroll around the 20-acre site to see locomotives and rolling stock. Other memorabilia is displayed in a small museum. The Centre regularly runs steam locomotive driving courses for visitors including 2 hours on the footplate actually driving and firing a steam engine. Events planned for 1995 include: Thomas the Tank Engine weekends (1-2 July and 23-24 September), Vintage Car Rally (27-28 August), Santa Specials in December.
Open with engines in steam Apr-Oct, Sun & BH Mon; Jun-Aug, Wed; 11am-6pm. (last admission 5pm). Dec Sat & Sun Santa's Magical Steamings-advanced booking recommended. Also open for static viewing Sun Jan-Mar 11-4 & Sat Jan-Oct 11-4.
£4 (ch & pen £2.50). Family ticket £11. Static viewing £1.50 (ch & pen £1).
P 🍴 & *toilets for disabled shop*

Stowe House
STOWE
☎Buckingham (01280) 813650
Set within the National Trust's landscaped gardens, Stowe is one of the most majestic houses of the 18th century. Stowe owes its pre-eminence to the vision and wealth of two owners. Viscount Cobham called in the leading designers of the day to lay out the gardens and commissioned several leading architects - Vanbrugh, Gibbs, Kent and Leoni - to decorate them with garden temples. From 1750 to 1779 Earl Temple, his nephew and successor, continued to expand and embellish both gardens and house. The house has now become a major public school.
Open 25 Mar-11 Apr & 4 Jul-1 Sep. May occasionally be closed if booked for private functions. Please ring for confirmation.
£2 (ch £1).
P & *shop*

Stowe Landscape Gardens
STOWE
☎Buckingham (01280) 822850
One of the supreme creations of the Georgian era, the first formal layout was adorned with many buildings by Vanbrugh, Kent and Gibbs; in the 1730s Kent designed the Elysian Fields in a more naturalistic style, one of the earliest examples of the reaction against formality, leading to the evolution of the landscape garden; miraculously, this beautiful garden survives; its sheer scale must make it Britain's largest work of art. Special events for 1995 include: Children's Day (4 June), Music and Fireworks (15 July).
Open 25 Mar-16 Apr, daily; 17 Apr-2 Jul, Mon, Wed, Fri & Sun; 3 Jul-3 Sep daily; 4 Sep-29 Oct, Mon, Wed & Fri; 27 Dec-7 Jan, daily. 10-5 (or dusk if earlier). Last admission 1hr before closing. (Closed 24-26 Dec).
£3.80. Family ticket £9.50.

Cliveden's magnificent water garden overlooks the Thames, The gardens feature temples by Giacomo Leoni, formal walks and some fine examples of topiary.

STOWE LANDSCAPE GARDENS

The Cradle of English Landscape Gardening

Laid out between 1713 and 1775, thereafter unaltered.
One of the supreme creations of the Georgian Era.
580 acres adorned with 32 garden temples and monuments.
3 miles N.W. of Buckingham.

Grounds open:
1995: 25 Mar to 16 Apr daily; 17 Apr to 2 July Mon, Wed, Fri, Sun;
3 July to 3 Sep daily; 4 Sep to 20 Oct Mon, Wed, Fri, Sun;
27 Dec to 7 Jan daily.
10am-5pm or dusk if earlier.

MORNING COFFEE, LIGHT LUNCHES & TEA AVAILABLE

House open:
NOT N.T. (£2 extra) 25 Mar to 11 Apr; 4 July to 1 Sep; daily,
except Sat, 2-5pm.

For further details please telephone: 01280 822850

ADMISSION £3.80		REDUCTIONS FOR FAMILIES

P 🚻 ♿ *(unsuitable manual wheelchairs,powered batricars available) toilets for disabled shop*
(NT)

Waddesdon Manor
WADDESDON
(gates off A41)
☎ Aylesbury (01296) 651211 & 651282
In 1874 Baron Ferdinand de Rothschild acquired this Buckinghamshire hilltop which became the site for the Destailleur designed château, around which is set one of the finest late Victorian formal gardens and parks designed by Laine. The collection on the ground floor was reopened in 1994, after restoration, along with newly remodelled wine cellars. A magnificent suite of French 18th-century panelled rooms on the first floor are due to open in 1995. The elegant cast iron rococo-style aviary, built in 1889, contains mainly softbill birds and some parrots.
Open, Grounds & Aviary only Mar-22 Dec, Wed-Sun 12-5, Sat, Sun, Good Fri & BH Mon 12-6. House 6 Apr-15 Oct, Thu-Sat 1-6, Sun, BH Mon & Good Fri 11-6, also open Wed 1-6 in Jul & Aug. Last admission 5.
Grounds & Aviary £3 (ch 5 free, ch 5-17 £1.50). Family ticket £7.50. House - State Reception rooms £6 (ch 5 free, ch 5-17 £4.50). House - First Floor Exhibition rooms £6 (ch 5 free, ch 5-17 £4.50). Combined ticket £8 (ch 5-17 £6.50).
P ✗ *licensed* ♿ *toilets for disabled shop*
(NT)

West Wycombe Caves
WEST WYCOMBE
(on A40)
☎ High Wycombe (01494) 524411
The entrance to West Wycombe caves is halfway up the hill that dominates the village. On the summit stands the parish church and the mausoleum of the Dashwood family. The caves are not natural but were dug on the orders of Sir Francis Dashwood between 1748 and 1752. Sir Francis, the Chancellor of the Exchequer, was also the founder of the Hell Fire Club, whose members were reputed to have practised black magic. The caves, which extend to approximately one-third of a mile underground, are supposed to have been one of their venues. The entrance consists of a large forecourt with flint walls, from which a brick tunnel leads into the caves, where tableaux and curiosities are exhibited in various chambers, including the Great Hall of Statues.
Open all year, Mar-Oct, daily 11-6; Nov-Feb, Sat & Sun 1-5.
£2.50 (ch & pen £1.25). Party 20+.
P 🚻 ♿ *shop garden centre* ✿

West Wycombe Park
WEST WYCOMBE
☎ High Wycombe (01494) 524411
Set in 300 acres of beautiful parkland, the house was rebuilt in the Palladian style, between 1745 and 1771, for Sir Francis Dashwood. Inside there is a good collection of tapestries, furniture and paintings. Of particular note are the painted ceilings by Borgnis. The park was laid out in the 18th century and given an artificial lake and classical temples, some of which were designed by Nicholas Revett. The Temple of Venus has recently been reconstructed. The park was later rearranged by a follower of 'Capability' Brown. Special events for 1995 include: Fête Champêtre - The Battle of Trafalgar (7-9 July).
Open, House & grounds Jun-Aug, Sun-Thu 2-6. Grounds only Apr & May, Sun & Wed 2-6 & Etr, May Day & Spring BH Sun & Mon 2-6. Last admission 5.15. Entry by timed tickets on wkdays.
£4. Grounds only £2.50. Family ticket £10.
P ♿ ✿
(NT)

WADDESDON MANOR

Waddesdon, Nr. Aylesbury, Bucks, HP18 0JH
Tel: (01296) 651282   Fax: (01296) 651293

Waddesdon Manor was designed by the French architect G-H Destailleur in the 1870s for Baron Ferdinand de Rothschild from the Austrian branch of the family. The Renaissance style château was conceived as a showcase for the Baron's prodigious collection of works of art, which includes French royal furniture, Savonnerie carpets and Sèvres porcelain as well as important portraits by Gainsborough and Reynolds and works by Dutch and Flemish masters of the 17th century.

In 1986 far reaching programme of maintenance and conservation work was undertaken by the Rothschild family. The Collection on the ground floor was reopened last year and the newly remodelled Wine Cellars containing an exceptional 'library' of Rothschild vintages, were put on public view for the first time. This year the restoration will be complete with the inauguration of newly created rooms on the first floor. These include a magnificent suite of French 18th century panelled rooms, an exhibition of Sèvres porcelain, and the paintings of Leon Bakst showing the Rothschild family in the story of Sleeping Beauty. In addition, a number of works of art from Lord Rothschild's family are being put on loan. Restoration work in the Garden has included repairs to the fountains and garden sculpture, reinstatement of the 19th century Parterre and extensive replanting of shrubs and trees.

Location: On A41 between Aylesbury & Bicester.

Open: House 6 April to 15 October: Thurs to Sat 1-6; Sun, BH Mon & Good Fri: 11-6 also open Wed 1-6 in July & August.

Last admission 5. Grounds, Aviary, Shops, Licensed Restaurant: 1 March to 22 December: Wed to Sun & BH Mon 11-6. Private tours of the House by special arrangement.

Admission: Grounds, Aviary, Shops, Licensed Restaurant & Parking: £3, children £1.50. House - State Reception Rooms: £6, children over 5 only £4.50. First Floor Exhibition Rooms: £6, children over 5 only £4.50. Combined ticket £8, children over 5 £6.50. Additional charge to House on Sun, BH Mon & Good Fri: Adults & children £1. Guide dogs in grounds only.

The imposing marble-clad entrance hall of the FitzWilliam Museum in Cambridge. Built between 1827 and 1875, the museum houses one of Britain's most impressive art and antique collections.

Ascott
WING
(.50m E, on S side of A418)
☎*Aylesbury (01296) 688242*
The house, once the property of the de Rothschilds, was given to the National Trust in 1950. The bequest included a collection of French and Chippendale furniture, pictures by such notable painters as Hogarth, Gainsborough and Rubens. There is also a collection of paintings by Hobbema, Cuyp and other Dutch painters. The collection of Oriental porcelain has some outstanding pieces of K'ang Hsi and of the Ming and Sung dynasties.
Outside there are 260 acres of land of which 12 are gardens. There are many unusual trees, with thousands of naturalised bulbs, and also a formal garden.
Open, House & garden: 5 Apr-7 May & Sep, Tue-Sun 2-6. Garden only: 6 Apr & 18 May-31 Aug, every Wed & last Sun in each month 2-6. Last admission to house 5pm.
House & garden £5 (ch £2.50). Garden only £3
P ♿ *toilets for disabled*
(NT)

CAMBRIDGESHIRE

CAMBRIDGE
The heart of the ancient university city is the row of colleges which lines the River Cam and overlooks the Backs on the other side of the river. This area of lawns and trees was reclaimed from rough marshland by Richard Bently, Master of Trinity College from 1669 to 1734, and it makes a lovely place to walk. In medieval times, this would have been a very different scene: the Cam was a busy commercial river, and the town was a centre for trade. The university is considered to have begun in 1209, when a group of students arrived after fleeing from riots in Oxford. The colleges are open to the public on most days during daylight, though there are certain restrictions during term time. A good place to start is King's College Chapel, with its glorious fan vaulting. There is a permanent exhibition, 'Kings: The Building of a Chapel', which brings together the chapel's history, architecture, art, heraldry and music. From here, the colleges of Trinity, St John's, Clare and others can easily be reached on foot - or hire a bicycle to see the city in the authentic way.

Cambridge & County Folk Museum
CAMBRIDGE
2/3 Castle St
☎*(01223) 355159*
The timber-framed White Horse Inn is an appealing setting for the folk museum. It houses items covering the everyday life of the people of Cambridgeshire from 1650 to the present day. There are also temporary exhibitions. Special exhibitions and children's activity days take place throughout the year.
Open all year, Mar-Sep, Mon-Sat 10.30-5, Sun 2-5. Oct-Feb, Tue-Sat 10.30-5, Sun 2-5. (Closed Mon ex school hols & pre-booked school parties). Last admissions 30 mins before closing.
£1 (ch 5-16, disabled, students, UB40s & pen 50p)
P (300 yds) ♿ *(braille & tape guides) shop*

Fitzwilliam Museum
CAMBRIDGE
Trumpington St
☎*(01223) 332900*
The Fitzwilliam is one of the oldest museums in Britain, and is housed in an imposing building designed for the purpose in 1834. In the early days, it was only open to 'properly dressed' members of the public, and then only three days a week. The museum has particularly good English and Continental ceramics and English glass, with some outstanding Oriental work, and paintings by Titian, Veronese, Canaletto and many other famous names, including leading French Impressionists. There are Egyptian, Greek and Roman antiquities, and other treasures include medieval illuminated manuscripts, ivories, miniatures, carvings and armour. There are special exhibitions throughout the year. Regular guided tours for which a small charge is made are conducted on Sundays at 2.30pm. Other times by prior arrangment, telephone for details.
Open all year Tue-Sat 10-5, Sun 2.15-5 plus Etr Mon, Spring & Summer BH. (Closed Good Fri, May Day & 24 Dec-1 Jan).
Free.
P (400 yds) ♿ *(preferably pre-arranged) toilets for disabled shop*

Scott Polar Research Institute
CAMBRIDGE
Lensfield Rd
☎*(01223) 336540*
The institute is an international centre for polar studies, and has a museum with displays of Arctic and Antarctic expeditions, with special emphasis on those of Captain Scott. Other exhibits include Eskimo work and other arts of the polar regions. Also shown are displays on current scientific exploration. A special exhibition is shown every summer.
Open all year, Mon-Sat 2.30-4. (Closed some public & university hols).
Free.
♿ *shop*

University Botanic Garden
CAMBRIDGE
Cory Lodge, Bateman St (1.5m S)
☎*(01223) 336265*
The garden was founded in 1762, mainly for the study of medicinal plants, and was transferred to its present site in 1846. It now covers 40 acres and has interesting collections of trees and shrubs; botanical groups of herbaceous perennials; along with a lake, woodland and rock garden. The glasshouses contain sub-tropical and tropical plants. Features include a Winter Garden, Chronological Bed, Scented Garden and collection of native British plants. The Gardens hold nine National Collections including Geranium, Tulip and Alchemilla.
Open all year daily 10-6 (summer), 10-5 (autumn & spring), (10-4) winter. Glasshouses 10-12.30 & 2-4. Closed 25-26 Dec. Entry by Bateman St and Hills Rd gates on weekdays & by Bateman Street gate on weekends & BH.
£1.50 (ch 3-17 & pen £1). Between Nov & Feb charges made Sat, Sun & BH's only.
P ♿ *(scented garden for the visually impaired) toilets for disabled shop*

University Museum of Archaeology & Anthropology
CAMBRIDGE
Downing St
☎*(01223) 337733*
The museum covers man's development from the earliest times throughout the world, with anthropology displays and extensive sections on British archaeology and local archaeology in particular. A new exhibition 'Changing Traditions' opens in 1995.
Open all year Mon-Fri 2-4, Sat 10-12.30. (Closed 1 wk Etr, Aug BH & 24 Dec-2 Jan)
Free.
♿

Duxford Airfield
DUXFORD
(off junc 10 of M11 on A505)
☎*Cambridge (01223) 835000*
This former Battle of Britain fighter station has hangars dating from World War I. It is now home to most of the Imperial War Museum's collection of military aircraft, armoured fighting vehicles, midget submarines and other large exhibits. There are over 120 historic aircraft on the airfield, and also on display is the Duxford Aviation Society's collection of civil aircraft, including the prototype Concorde 01. Special themed exhibits include a US 8th Air Force Exhibition. Major flying displays are held in summer, and pleasure flights can be taken during summer weekends. Those with aircraft may apply to land them at the airfield; those without can try the popular flight simulator. There is an adventure playground. 1995 events include VE Day Anniversary event in May, Flying Legends Air Show in July, Duxford Air Show in September, and the Autumn Air Show in October.
Open all year, mid Mar-Oct daily 10-6; Nov-mid Mar daily 10-4. (Closed 24-26 Dec)
Admission prices under review.
P ♿ *(wheelchair available) toilets for disabled shop*

The Stained Glass Museum
ELY
The Cathedral
☎*(01353) 667735 ext 147*
The museum is situated in the cathedral and was established in 1972 to rescue and preserve fine stained glass, which might otherwise be lost and is the only one of its kind in the country. Models show how stained-glass windows are designed and made. There is an exhibition of approximately 80 panels dating from the 13th century to the present day, they are displayed at eye level in back-lit cases. A large panel, from the Royal Collection at Windsor, is on loan to the museum for twenty years and depicts George III from a portrait by Sir Joshua Reynolds executed by James Pearson in 1793. An audio tour lasts 25 minutes, and there are activities for children.
Open Mar-Oct, Mon-Fri 10.30-4, Sat & BH 10.30-4.30 & Sun 12-3. Also wknds throughout year & during school holidays.
£1.80 (ch & students & pen £1). Party 10+.
P 400yds shop

Hamerton Wildlife Centre
HAMERTON
☎*(01832) 293362*
A wildlife breeding centre, dedicated to the practical conservation of endangered species including otters, gibbons, marmosets, lemurs, wildcats, meerkats, Britain's only group of breeding sloths and many more. There is also a large and varied bird collection, with several species unique to Hamerton. Over 120 species in all. Other attractions include a children's play area, and undercover viewing of many mammals. Special events for 1995 include falconry demonstrations.
Open Summer daily 10.30-6; winter daily 10.30-4. (Closed Xmas)
**£3.50 (pen £3 & ch 5-14 £2). Family ticket available. Party 15+*
P ♿ *toilets for disabled shop*

Cromwell Museum
HUNTINGDON
Grammar School Walk
☎*(01480) 425830*

The museum is in a restored Norman building, which was first a hospital and then became a school in the 16th century. Oliver Cromwell (born in the town in 1599) was a pupil, so was Samuel Pepys (born 1640). It now houses some of Cromwell's possessions, family portraits and items relating to the Civil Wars and Commonwealth.
Open all year, Apr-Oct, Tue-Fri 11-1 & 2-5, Sat & Sun 11-1 & 2-4; Nov-Mar, Tue-Fri 1-4, Sat 11-1 & 2-4, Sun 2-4. (Closed BH's ex Good Fri)
Free.
P (200 yds) shop ⊗

Linton Zoological Gardens
LINTON
Hadstock Rd
☎*Cambridge (01223) 891308*
Conservation and education are the main concerns of this zoo which was established in 1972. The many species of animals and birds are housed in landscaped enclosures as like their natural habitats as possible. Especially interesting are the Sumatran tigers, giant Aldabra tortoises - the largest herd outside the tropics, a fine collection of owls, binturongs and the famous Toco toucans - the only young to be bred in Britain were born here. All around the enclosures are fine shrubberies and exotic trees. Special events for 1995 include: Meet the Boa Days, Owl Encounters and Fun with Fossils.
Open daily 10-6 or dusk (ex 25 Dec). Last admission 45 minutes before closing time.
✳*£3.75 (ch 2-13 £2.75, pen £3.50).*
P ⊠ ⟁ *toilets for disabled shop* ⊗

Anglesey Abbey
LODE
A medieval undercroft has survived from the priory founded here in 1135, but the house dates mainly from 1600. Thomas Hobson of 'Hobson's choice' was one of the owners. A later owner was Lord Fairhaven, who amassed the huge collection of pictures, including hundreds of views of Windsor Castle. He also laid out the beautiful Georgian-style gardens, which are set with urns and statues.
Open House: 29 Mar-15 Oct, Wed-Sun & BH Mon 1-5; Closed Good Fri. Garden: 29 Mar-9 Jul, Wed-Sun & BH Mon 11-5.30; 10 Jul-5 Sep, daily 11-5.30; 6 Sep-29 Oct, Wed-Sun 11-5.30. Lode Mill: 29 Mar-29 Oct, Wed-Sun & BH Mons 1.30-5.15.
£4.80 (ch £2.40). Sun & BH Mon £5.80. Garden only £3. Sun & BH Mon £3.50. Party 15+.
P ⊠ ✗ *licensed* ⟁ *(electric 2 seater vehicle, braille guide) toilets for disabled shop garden centre* ⊗
(NT)

City of Peterborough Museum & Art Gallery
PETERBOROUGH
Priestgate
☎*(01733) 343329*
Articles made by Napoleonic prisoners-of-

war at Norman Cross prison camp are on display here as well as exhibits of local geology, archaeology, social and natural history. Paintings are displayed along with a small collection of ceramics and glass, and there are regular temporary exhibitions.
Open all year, Tue-Sat 10-5; (Closed Good Fri & Xmas). Please telephone before weekend visits.
Free.
P (300yds) ⟁ *(main floors accessible) toilets for disabled shop* ⊗

Longthorpe Tower
PETERBOROUGH
☎*(01733) 268482*
Rare wall paintings of religious and educational subjects are on show in this 13th-to 14th-century fortified house, which formerly belonged to the the de Thorpe family.
Open Apr-Sep, daily 10-6 Jul-Aug weekends only.
£1. (ch 50p, students, pen & UB40 80p).
⊗
(EH)

Abbey Gatehouse
RAMSEY
Abbey School
The ruins of this 15th-century gatehouse, together with the 13th-century Lady Chapel, are all that remain of the abbey. Half of the gatehouse was taken away after the Dissolution. Built in ornate late-Gothic style, it has panelled buttresses, and friezes around both the doorway and the oriel window above it.
Open Apr-Oct, daily 10-5 (or dusk).
Free.
⊗
(NT)

Norris Museum ST IVES
The Broadway
☎*(01480) 465101*
The Norris Museum has a comprehensive collection of Huntingdonshire local history. Exhibits include fossils and archaeology. Also displayed is some fine work in bone and straw carried out by French prisoners at Norman Cross, and Huntingdonshire lace. Scenes by local artists are displayed in the new art gallery.
Open all year, May-Sep, Mon-Fri 10-1 & 2-5, Sat 10-12 & 2-5, Sun 2-5; Oct-Apr, Mon-Fri 10-1 & 2-4, Sat 10-12.
Free.
P (100 yds) ⟁ shop

Nene Valley Railway
WANSFORD
Wansford Station (A1 west of Peterborough)
☎*Stamford (01780) 782854*
A preserved steam railway with seven-and-a-half miles of track with locomotives and rolling stock from Europe and the UK. Passengers can enjoy a leisurely train ride along the River Nene. There is a museum, engine shed, model railway, cafe and souvenir shop. There are

Part of the Imperial War Museum, Duxford Airfield displays and restores a fascinating collection of planes from a 1916 BE2c fighter to a Concorde prototype.

facilities for the disabled at Wansford and a specially adapted carriage on each train. Special events are planned throughout 1995 to celebrate the 150th anniversary of the railway into Peterborough; the Nene Valley Railway occupies the eastern section of the line built in 1845.
Open all year on Sun; May-Aug, also Sat, Wed & some other weekdays; Sep-Oct, wkends only.
Admission under review.
P ⊠ ⟁ *(disabled access to trains) toilets for disabled shop*

Wimpole Hall
WIMPOLE
(junc of A14 and A603)
☎*Cambridge (01223) 207257*
Although Wimpole Hall is one of the grandest mansions in East Anglia, it is perhaps the 360 acres of parkland that make it unusual. The parkland was devised and planted by no less than four of the country's celebrated landscape designers, Charles Bridgeman, 'Capability' Brown, Sanderson Miller and Humphrey Repton. Under the pastures lie the remains of a medieval village with evidence of tracks and ridge-and-furrow farming. The house, which was given to the National Trust in 1976, dates back to 1640, but was altered into a large 18th-century mansion with a Georgian façade. The inside is the work of a number of important architects. Lord Harley's library and the gallery are the work of James Gibbs, and the Yellow Drawing Room was designed by Sir John Soane in about 1793. The chapel has a wonderful painted *trompe l'oeil* ceiling by Sir James Thornhill.
Open 25 Mar-5 Nov, Tue-Thu, Sat, Sun 1-5, BH Sun & Mon 11-5. Also open Fri 4-25 Aug. (Closed Good Fri).
£4.50 (ch £2.25). Party. Joint ticket with Home Farm £6 (ch £2.50).
P ✗ *licensed* ⟁ *(braille guide, battery operated vehicle) toilets for disabled shop* ⊗ *(ex park only)*
(NT)

Wimpole Home Farm
WIMPOLE
☎*Cambridge (01223) 207257*
When built in 1794, the Home Farm was one of the most advanced agricultural enterprises in the country. The group of thatched and timbered buildings was designed by Sir John Soane for the 3rd Earl of Hardwicke. The Great Barn, now restored, holds a display of farm machinery and implements of the kind used at Wimpole over the past two centuries. On the farm there is a wide selection of rare breeds of domestic animals, including the black-and-white Bagot goat which was rescued from extinction. In the stables,

there are once more the rare breed of Suffolk Punch horses. A special children's corner and a woodland play area are additional attractions.
Open 11 Mar-5 Nov; Tue-Thu & Sat-Sun, also Fri Jun-Aug & Mon 4-28 Aug. 10.30-5. (Open BH Mon & Fri ex closed Good Fri); Nov-4 Mar Sat & Sun 11-5.
£3.50 (ch £1.75). Party. Joint ticket with Hall & Farm £6 (ch £2.50).
P ⊠ ⟁ *(braille guide) toilets for disabled shop* ⊗
(NT)

Peckover House & Garden
WISBECH
North Bank
☎*(01945) 583463*
In a town with many elegant Georgian merchant's houses, Peckover House is one of the finest. It is named after a banker who purchased the house in 1777. His bank was part of the group which formed Barclays Bank in 1896. The house dates from 1722 and the interior has Rococo decoration in plaster and wood. The two-acre garden is a delightful and colourful example of Victorian planting, still with its 19th-century design. In the kitchen garden there are greenhouses with orange trees still bearing fruit after 250 years.
Open, House, garden & tearoom: Apr-Oct, Sun, Wed & BH Mon 2-5.30. Garden only: Apr-Oct, Sat, Mon & Tue 2-5.30.
✳*House & garden £2.40 (ch £1.20). Party 20+. Garden only £1.*
⊠ ⟁ ⊗
(NT)

Wisbech & Fenland Museum
WISBECH
Museum Square (on A17)
☎*(01945) 583817*
The museum contains a fine collection of ceramics and *objets d'art* and has a new gallery of geology. There are exhibits on the archaeology and natural history of Wisbech and the surrounding Fenland. Many items relate to Fenland life. Also of interest are the pictures; oils, water colours and photographs; the European and Oriental art; and exhibitions: Thomas Clarkson - Slavery and the Slave Trade, and History from Coins. Parish Registers, and a collection of over 14,000 books including early manuscripts, originally forming the library of the literary society, are in the town library. There is a programme of special exhibitions and evening lectures.
Open all year, Tue-Sat 10-5 (4pm Oct-Mar). Closed Xmas.
Free. (Museum libraries & archives available by appointment only).
P (100 yds) shop ⊗

Set in over 1300 acres pf country park, with 15 acres of formal and informal Victoria gardens, Lyme Park boasts an imposing Palladian front and courtyard.

CHESHIRE

Adlington Hall
ADLINGTON
(5m N of Macclesfield, 0.5m off A523)
☎ Prestbury (01625) 829206
This fine house is a lovely blend of Tudor timber-framing and 18th-century brick. Handel is said to have played the Bernard Smith organ in the Great Hall. The wilderness includes many interesting follies including a yew walk, lime avenue, temple to Diana and Chinese bridge. Special events for 1995 include craft fairs (7-8 May and 12-13 August).
Open Good Fri-Sep, Sun & BH 2-5.30.
Parties on weekdays by arrangement.
House & gardens £4 (ch £1.50). Party 25+
🅿 ⬛ & shop ⌘

Beeston Castle
BEESTON
(off A49)
☎ Bunbury (01829) 260464
This ruined stronghold dates back to around 1220 and was built by the Earl of Chester in an almost inaccessible position. Set on a steep hill, the ruins include the remains of the inner and outer wards, and give spectacular views of the surrounding countryside. An exhibition explains the history of the castle.
Open all year, Apr-Sep, daily 10-6; Oct, daily 10-4; Nov-Mar daily 10-4 or dusk if earlier. Closed 24-26 Dec & 1 Jan.
£2.20 (ch £1.10, pen, students & UB40 £1.70).
🅿 ⌘
(EH)

Capesthorne Hall
CAPESTHORNE
(On A34 between Congleton and Wilmslow)
☎ Chelford (01625) 861221 & 861779
Capesthorne has been the home of the Bromley-Davenport family and their ancestors, the Capesthornes and the Wards, since Domesday times. The present house, replacing an earlier timber-framed structure dates from 1719 and was designed by the Smiths of

Warwick. It was subsequently altered by Edward Blore in 1837 and after a disastrous fire in 1861 the whole of the centre portion was rebuilt by Anthony Salvin.
Capesthorne contains a great variety of sculptures, paintings and other contents including a collection of American Colonial furnishings. There are gardens, lakes, a nature trail and woodland walks.
Open Apr Suns; May & Aug-Sep Wed & Sun; Jun-Jul Tue-Thu & Sun. Park & Garden 12-6, Hall 2-4.
🅿 ⬛ ✗ licensed & toilets for disabled shop
Details not confirmed for 1995

CHESTER
Chester is one of Britain's most appealing cities. It is famed for its picturesque black and white buildings, but it is also a lively town that does not simply live on its past. The best way to start a visit is to walk around the medieval walls; there are small museums in some of the towers. The star attraction within the walls is the group of double-decker streets called the Rows, where stairs lead up to first-floor shops. The town is filled with timber-framed buildings, many of which are more Victorian than medieval, but are nonetheless attractive. There is also a Norman cathedral, extensively restored by Sir George Gilbert Scott. Roman Chester should not be forgotten. The city began as an important Roman military base, and the remains of a Roman amphitheatre lie outside the walls. To get a feel of Roman times, visit the Grosvenor Museum, which has evocative items such as memorial stones to Roman soldiers and their families.

Cheshire Military Museum
CHESTER
The Castle
☎ (01244) 327617
Exhibits from the history of the Cheshire Regiment, Cheshire Yeomanry, 5th Royal Inniskilling Dragoon Guards, and 3rd Carabiniers. VE Day exhibition May 1995.

Open all year, daily 9-5. (Closed Xmas & New Year).
50p (ch & pen 30p).

Chester Heritage Centre
CHESTER
St Michael's Church, Bridge St Row
☎ (01244) 321616
The centre aims to introduce visitors to the history of Chester's buildings and encourage then to explore the city. There are displays and an audio visual show with new features including exhibitions planned for 1995
Open Mon-Sat 11-5, Sun 2-5. Closed Good Fri, 24-26 Dec & 1 Jan. Telephone (0244) 321616 for further details.
Admission fee payable.
🅿 (440yds) shop ⌘

Chester Visitor Centre
CHESTER
Vicars Ln (opposite Roman Amphitheatre)
☎ (01244) 351609
Over 2000 years of Chester's history are illustrated by a video and a life-size reconstruction of a scene in the Chester Rows during Victorian times. There is a tourist information desk and guided tours depart regularly from the Centre. Working craft shops offer a large variety of gifts. Craft fairs take place on Bank Holiday weekends.
Open all year daily 9am-6pm.
Free.
🅿 ⬛ & shop

Chester Zoo
CHESTER
Upton-By-Chester (2m N of city centre off A41)
☎ (01244) 380280
This is one of Europe's finest zoological gardens, with 5500 animals in 110 acres of enclosures and landscaped gardens. The tropical house, aquarium, waterbus rides and overhead mono-rail system are added attractions.

Open all year, daily from 10-variable closing times. Last admission 3.30 Winter, 5.30 Summer. (Closed 25 Dec). £7 (ch 3-15 & pen £4.50). Party 15+
🅿 ⬛ ✗ licensed & (wheelchairs for hire) toilets for disabled shop ⌘

Grosvenor Museum
CHESTER
27 Grosvenor St
☎ (01244) 321616
This award-winning museum tells the story of the Roman army in Chester, and has a reconstructed Roman graveyard full of original tombstones. Other attractions include the Chester Race Cups which are part of a dazzling display of silver; period rooms which date from the 1680s to the 1920s; and the Natural History Gallery where visitors can learn of the past and present wildlife of Chester.
Open all year, Mon-Sat 10.30-5, Sun 2-5. (Closed Good Fri, 24-26 Dec & 1 Jan). Free, donations welcome. (under review)
🅿 (440yds) ⬛ & shop ⌘

Cholmondeley Castle Gardens
CHOLMONDELEY
(off A49/A41)
☎ (01829) 720383
The extensive pleasure gardens are dominated by a romantic Gothic Castle built in 1801 of local sandstone. The gardens are imaginatively laid out with fine trees and water gardens, and have been extensively replanted from the 1960s with rhododendrons, azaleas, cornus, acer and many other acid loving plants. There are also herbaceous borders, a rose and lavender garden, lovely lakeside and woodland walks, rare breeds of farm animals, inlcuding llamas, and an ancient private chapel. Special events are held throughout the year, please telephone for details.
Open May-1 Oct, Wed & Thu 12-5, Sun & BH 12-5.30. Apr Sun & BH Mon 12-5.30.
£2.60 (ch 75p, pen £1.80).

P ⚇ & (disabled car park near tearoom) toilets for disabled shop garden centre

Lyme Park
DISLEY
☎(01663) 762023
Surrounded by wild moorland, Lyme Park is an Elizabethan house at the core, but it was transformed in the 17th and 18th centuries. Notable features include the handsome Palladian front and courtyard, the elaborate Baroque ceiling of the grand staircase, and the intricate woodcarvings in the saloon, by Grinling Gibbons. Earlier Elizabethan decorative carving can be seen in the drawing room and the Long Gallery. The house's fine pictures and furnishings include Mortlake tapestries. The house is set amidst 15 acres of formal and informal Victorian gardens, and is surrounded by a 1377-acre country park. Other attractions include tearooms, an adventure playground, orienteering, and fishing. Details of events are available on request.
Open - Hall, Apr-Oct, 1.30-5. (Closed Thur & Fri).Telephone for details (01663) 766492. Park all year, Gardens Apr-Oct daily 11-5.
House & Garden £3; Garden only £1; Park £3 per car.
P ⚇ & (by arrangement) toilets for disabled shop ❀ (ex park on lead) (NT)

Boat Museum
ELLESMERE PORT
Dockyard Rd
☎0151-355 5017
The museum occupies a historic dock complex at the junction of the Shropshire Union and Manchester Ship Canals. These docks were one of the most important points for transferring goods between sea-going vessels and the smaller craft of the inland waterways. There are over 60 floating craft, ranging from a small weedcutter to a 300-ton coaster, many of which visitors can climb aboard and explore. Boat trips are also available. There are eight indoor exhibitions on canal life and local history which are housed in the restored warehouses of the dock, together with period worker's cottages, blacksmith's forge and working engines. The original restored steam engines can be seen 'in steam' on the first Sunday of each month. Many special events and craft courses take place throughout the year including: craft fair (March) traditional boat gathering (Easter), a festival of boats linking in wih Ellesmere Port's Bicentenary (July), Keels and Wheels - vintage and classic car show (July), model boats extravaganza (August Bank Holiday).
Open Summer daily 10-5. Winter daily (ex Thu & Fri) 11-4. (Closed 25 & 26 Dec). £4.70 (ch £3.20, pen & students £3.70). Family ticket £14.50.
P ⚇ & (resources pack for blind & deaf) toilets for disabled shop

Gawsworth Hall
GAWSWORTH
(2.5m S of Macclesfield on A536)
☎North Rode (01260) 223456
This fine Tudor black-and-white manor house was the birthplace of Mary Fitton, thought by some to be the 'Dark Lady' of Shakespeare's sonnets. Pictures and armour can be seen in the house, which also has a tilting ground - now thought to be a rare example of an Elizabethan pleasure garden. Special events for 1995 include craft fairs May and August Bank Holidays, and open-air theatre June-August.
Open 8 Apr-8 Oct, 2-5.30. £3.40 (ch £1.70). Party 20+.
P ⚇ & shop ❀

Jodrell Bank Science Centre & Arboretum
JODRELL BANK SCIENCE CENTRE & ARBORETUM
☎Lower Withington (01477) 571339
The Science Centre stands at the feet of one of the largest, fully-steerable radio telescopes in the world, the Lovell telescope, a landmark both in Cheshire and in the world of astronomy. There are exhibitions on space, astronomy and satellites. Interactive exhibits enable visitors to 'get to grips' with science. There are shows every half-hour in the Planetarium and outside, visitors may walk through 35 acres of tree-lined walkways in the Arboretum, beautiful in every season, and visit the Environmental Discovery Centre. Special events for 1995 include 200 Years of Computing (15 April-24 May) and various exhibitions and events celebrating trees in our culture.
Open daily 3rd weekend in Mar-last weekend in Oct, 10.30-5.30. Winter weekends & Xmas holidays (ex 25 Dec) 11-4.30.
✲£3.50 (ch £1.90, pen £2.50) includes Exhibition, Planetarium, Arboretum & Environmental Discovery Centre. Family ticket £10.50. Children under 5 not admitted to the Planetarium.
P ⚇ & toilets for disabled shop ❀

Tatton Park
KNUTSFORD
(3.5m from M6, junc 19, or M56 junc 7)
☎(01565) 654822
England's most complete historic estate, Tatton Park is one of the great playgrounds of the north-west, with gardens and a 1000-acre country park offering fishing, sailing and walking, as well as various events throughout the year. The centrepiece is the great Georgian mansion, whose gardens were first laid out by Humphry Repton, followed in the 19th century by Sir Joseph Paxton, who designed the Italian-style terraces in front of the house. Later, in the 20th century, Japanese gardeners created a Japanese garden with a Shinto temple beside one of the lakes, and also to be seen are an orangery and a fern house, as well as colourful expanses of flowers. The park is big enough to absorb its

visitors and still provide room for wildlife, and the mere is especially interesting for its wildfowl in winter. A variety of signposted walks includes an historic landscape trail. The house itself has sumptuous furnishings and pictures including two Canalettos. Also of interest are the kitchens and cellars. The Home Farm is stocked with animals and working as it was fifty years ago. Old Hall is the original medieval manor house and a guided tour transports you through five hundred years of Tatton history. An adventure playground is the newest feature. There is a regular programme of special events.
Open Apr-Sep, Park 10.30-6, Gardens, 10.30-5 Mansion, Farm & Old Hall, 12-4,(all ex Park closed Mon ex BH Mon); 1-24 Oct Mansion, Farm & Old Hall wknds only. 25 Oct-Mar, Park 11-5, Gardens 11-4. (Closed Mon & 24-25 Dec), Farm Sun only & Shop 11.30-4. (Last admission 1hr before closure).
All-in ticket £8 (ch 15 £5) Family £24; Mansion £2.50 (ch 15 £1.50) Family £7.50; Gardens £2.50 (ch 15 £1.50) Family £7.50; Old Hall £2.50 (ch 15 £1.50) Family £7.50; Farm & stables £2.50 (ch 15 £1.50) Family £7.50. Any two attractions £4 (ch 15 £2.50) Family £12.
P (charged) ⚇ ✗ licensed & (Old Hall & Farm not accessible) toilets for disabled shop garden centre ❀ (ex in Park & Gardens) (NT)

Hare Hill
MACCLESFIELD
(4m N off B5087)
☎(01625) 828981
The beautiful parkland at Hare Hill also features a pretty walled garden and pergola. A brilliant display of rhododendrons and azaleas can be seen in late spring.
Open 30 Mar-30 Oct Wed, Thu, Sat, Sun & BH Mons 10-5.30. Parties by written appointment with the Head Gardener.

Special openings (to see rhododendrons & azaleas) 13 May-3 Jun daily 10-5.30; (Closed Nov-Mar).
✲£2.50 (ch £1.25). £1.50 per car (refundable on entry to garden).
P (charged) & ❀ (NT)

Macclesfield Silk Museum
MACCLESFIELD
Heritage Centre, Roe St
☎(01625) 613210
The silk museum presents the story of silk in Macclesfield through a colourful audio-visual programme, exhibitions, textiles, garments, models and room settings. It is situated in the Heritage Centre, formerly a Sunday school for child labourers. A full programme of musical and artistic events is available throughout the year at the Heritage Centre.
Open all year, Mon-Sat 11-5, Sun & BH Mon 1-5. (Closed Good Fri, 24-26 Dec & 1 Jan)
Admission fee payable.
P ⚇ ✗ licensed & (ramps & chairlift) toilets for disabled shop ❀

Paradise Mill
MACCLESFIELD
Park Ln
☎(01625) 618228
An award-winning museum where knowledgeable guides, many of them former silk mill workers, illustrate the silk production process with the help of demonstrations from weavers. The museum was a working silk mill until 1981 when the last handloom weaver retired, and 26 handlooms have been fully restored in their original setting. Exhibitions and room settings give an impression of working conditions at the mill during the 1930s.
Open all year, BH Mon & Tue-Sun 1-5 (1-4 in winter). (Closed Good Fri, 24-26 Dec & 1 Jan).
Admission fee payable.
P (400 yds) & shop ❀

THE BOAT MUSEUM
Ellesmere Port
Visit Britain's Premier Canal Museum which is set within a historic dock complex and houses the world's largest floating collection of canal and river craft.

A working museum with eight indoor exhibitions telling the story of canals, workers' cottages, blacksmith's forge, stables, steam engines, boat trips, shop and chandlery, cafe, disabled facilities and free parking.

Situated 100 yards from Junction 9 of M53.

Open: 10-5 April – October (Daily)
11-4 November – March (Closed Thursday & Friday)
Admission Charge
Telephone: 0151-355 5017

West Park Museum
MACCLESFIELD
West Park, Prestbury Rd
☎(01625) 619831
A small but significant collection of Egyptian antiquities can be seen at this museum, together with a wide range of fine and decorative arts. The paintings on display are from the 19th and early 20th centuries and include the work of the bird artist, Charles Tunnicliffe. Items relating to local history are also shown. The museum was established in 1898 by the Brocklehurst family, and is on the edge of one of the earliest parks founded by voluntary subscriptions.
Open all year, Tue-Sun 2-5 (1-4 in winter). (Closed Mon ex BH, Good Fri, 25-26 Dec & 1 Jan).
Free.
P *(5mins)* & shop %

Stapeley Water Gardens
NANTWICH
London Rd, Stapeley (off junc 16 M6, 1m S of Nantwich on A51)
☎(01270) 623868 & 628628
Stapeley Water Gardens consists of four main areas. The Palms is a glass pavilion which is home to Koi carp, Giant Amazon water-lilies, sharks, piranhas, parrots and exotic flowers, whilst the two-acre Water Garden Centre houses, amongst other things, the National Collection of water-lilies. Dinky toys and fully-restored military vehicles are on display in the Yesteryear Museum. The site also has the home of a large angling centre.
Open Mon-Fri 9-6, wknds & BHs 10-6/7pm. (Winter 9-5, wknds & BHs 10-5). The Palms Tropical Oasis open from 10am, closing times as Garden Centre. The Palms Tropical Oasis £3.15 (ch £1.65, pen £2.25). The Yesteryear Museum £2.65 (ch £1.50, pen £1.95). Joint ticket £5.25 (ch £2.85, pen £3.85).
P 🍴 ✕ *licensed* & *(free wheelchair loan service) toilets for disabled shop garden centre* %

Liverpool University Botanic Gardens (Ness Gardens)
NESTON
Ness Gardens (off A540 near Ness-on-Wirral)
☎0151-336 2135 & 0151-336 7769
A place of learning and also a place of beauty containing fine trees and shrubs, rock terraces, water gardens, herbaceous borders and rose collections. Plants may be purchased in the gift shop. For children there is an exciting adventure playground. There is also a regular programme of lectures, courses and special events throughout the year for which tickets must be obtained in advance.
Open all year, Nov-Feb, daily 9.30-4; Mar-Oct, daily 9.30-dusk. Closed 25 Dec. £3.50 (ch 10 free, 10-18 & pen £2.50). Family ticket £8.
P 🍴 ✕ *licensed* & *(wheelchair route) toilets for disabled shop garden centre* %

Nether Alderley Mill
NETHER ALDERLEY
Congleton Rd (1.5m S of Alderley Edge on E side of A34)
☎*Wilmslow (01625) 523012*
This fascinating water-mill was originally built in the 15th century, and is a lot larger inside than its outward appearance would suggest. Inside there are tandem overshot water-wheels, original Elizabethan timber work, and Victorian machinery which has been restored to full working order after being derelict for 30 years. The original atmosphere of a working mill has been preserved as far as possible, and wheat is ground occasionally for demonstration purposes, water permitting.
Open Apr-May & Oct, Wed, Sun & BH Mon 1-4.30; Jun-Sep, Tue-Sun & BH Mon 1-5. Parties by arrangement.
P *shop* %
(NT)
Details not confirmed for 1995

Arley Hall & Gardens
NORTHWICH
Great Budworth (5m N)
☎(01565) 777353
Owned by the same family since medieval times, the present Arley Hall is a good example of the early Victorian Jacobean style and contains fine furniture, plasterwork, panelling and family portraits. There is also a private family chapel designed by Anthony Salvin. The gardens rank amongst the finest in the country and extend over 12 acres. Winner of the Christie's HHA 'Garden of the Year' award in 1987 they include a magnificent double herbaceous border, shrub rose collection, walled garden, unique clipped Ilex avenue, yew hedges, herb garden, scented garden and a woodland garden with rhododendrons, azaleas and exotic trees. Various events held throughout the year include, for 1995, performing arts firework and laser extravaganza (1 July), craft fair (8-9 July), Garden Design Show (29-30 July), flower show (August), antiques fair (13-15 October).
Open 8 Apr-1 Oct, Tue-Sun & BH 12-5. (Groups 11-9 & special arrangements during winter)
Gardens, Grounds & Chapel £2.80 (ch 6-16 £1.40); Family ticket £7. Hall £1.80 (ch 6-16 90p); Family ticket £4.50. Party 15+.
P 🍴 ✕ *licensed* & *(ramps) toilets for disabled shop garden centre*

Peckforton Castle
PECKFORTON
Stone House Ln (off A49 towards Taporley)
☎*Tattenhall (01829) 260930*
This 19th-century castle was described by Sir Gilbert Scott as 'the largest and most carefully and learnedly executed Gothic mansion of the present day ... not only a Castle in name but it is a real ... medieval fortress, capable of standing a siege from an Edwardian army'. The silhouette of this impressive castle can be seen for many miles across the Cheshire Plain with its castellated ramparts and round hexagonal towers. The Great Hall is stone vaulted with a minstrels' gallery and fine staircase around a central pentagonal well contributing to the Grade I listed status of Peckforton. Special events include family entertainment every Sunday and Bank Holidays, and medieval re-enactments.
Open 14 Apr-10 Sep, daily 10-6. £2.50 (concessions £1.50). Party 20+
P 🍴 & *toilets for disabled shop* %

Norton Priory
RUNCORN
Tudor Rd, Manor Park
☎(01928) 569895
Displays tell the fascinating story of the transformation of the medieval priory into a Tudor manor house and then into an elegant Georgian mansion amid fine gardens. Special events for 1995 include: May Day at the Priory (8 May), sculpture workshops (6-24 August), family fun and games (28 August), archaeological extravaganza (9 September).
Open all year, Apr-Oct, Mon-Fri 12-5; Sat, Sun & BHs 12-6; Nov-Mar daily 12-4. (Closed 24-26 Dec & 1 Jan). Walled Garden open Mar-Oct.
£2.50 (ch 5-16, students, UB40's & pen £1.30).
P 🍴 & *(wheelchairs available, Braille guide, audio tapes, parking) toilets for disabled shop garden centre* % *(ex woodland garden)*

Little Moreton Hall
SCHOLAR GREEN
(4m SW of Congleton on A34)
☎*Congleton (01260) 272018*
Perhaps one of the best examples of half-timbered architecture in England, Little Moreton Hall stands with moat and gatehouse in all its original and ornate glory. Although building began about 100 years earlier, by 1580 the house was much as it is today. Inside, the long gallery, the chapel and the great hall are its most splendid features and notable too are some of the pieces of oak furniture. Special events for 1995 include open-air theatre 'The Merchant of Venice' (13-15 and 20-22 July). Regular music and dance events are held at weekends.
Open Apr-Sep, Wed-Sun 12-5.30, BH Mon 11-5.30; Oct Sat & Sun 12-5.30. (Closed Good Fri).
£3.50 (ch £1) Family ticket £8. Parking £2, refundable on entry to Hall.
P *(charged)* ✕ *licensed* & *(wheelchair & electric vehicle available, Braille guide) toilets for disabled shop* %
(NT)

Quarry Bank Mill & Styal Country Park
STYAL
Quarry Bank Mill (off B5166, 1.5m N of Wilmslow)
☎*Wilmslow (01625) 527468*
Quarry Bank Mill is a Georgian cotton mill now restored as a working museum of the cotton industry and powered by a waterwheel. There are galleries illustrating all aspects of the textile process, spinning, weaving, dyeing etc and the role of the founders (the Gregs), pioneers of the factory system. Other attractions include the factory 'colony' nearby with its shop, cottages and chapels. The original 1790 apprentice house, which was the home of young pauper apprentices, is fully restored and open to visitors as a 'living exhibit'. The garden is laid out in Victorian 'utilitarian' style, growing fruits, vegetables and herbs using the same methods as 150 years ago. The museum is still developing, therefore displays and facilities will be changed from time to time. The mill is set in a lovely valley and there are pleasant walks through woodland or by the deep ravine of the River Bollin. Events planned for 1995 include: a Steam Weekend (17-18 June), Harvest Home (23-24 September), Archive Exhibition 1795-1995 (9 October - 19 November), Spooky Tours (28 October).
Mill open all year, Apr-Sep daily 11-6 (last admission 4.30); Oct-Mar Tue-Sun 11-5 (last admission 3.30). Apprentice House & Gardens, Tue-Fri, as Mill opening times during School Hols, Wed-Fri 2pm-Mill closing time during school term. Sat & Sun as for Mill. (Closed Mon all year ex BH Mon). Country Park open daily dawn-dusk.
❋*Mill and Apprentice House £4.50 (ch £3.20). Mill £3.50 (ch £2.50). Apprentice House & Garden £3 (ch £2.30). Styal Country Park £1.50 per car.*
P *(charged)* 🍴 ✕ *licensed* & *toilets for disabled shop* % *(ex in Park)*
(NT)

Catalyst
WIDNES
Mersey Rd
☎0151-420 1121
Catalyst is where the science and technology of the chemical industry comes alive. A feast of 'hands-on' exhibits explore the chemical industry, its heritage and and its effect on our lives. Fun for all the family. Voted North West Museum of the Year and North West Visitor Attraction of the Year 1992. A range of special events is planned throughout the year, including half term, Easter and summer holiday workshops, please telephone for details.
Open all year, Tue-Sun daily 10-5. (Closed Mon ex BH's, 24-26 Dec & 1 Jan). £3 (ch £2, concessions £2.50). Family ticket £8.25.
P 🍴 & *toilets for disabled shop* %

CLEVELAND

Gisborough Priory
GUISBOROUGH
☎(01287) 638301
The remains of the east end of the 14th-century church make a dramatic sight here. The priory was founded in the 12th century for Augustinian canons.
Open all year Good Fri-Oct, daily 10-5; Nov-Maundy Thu, Wed-Sun 10-4. Closed 24 Dec-1 Jan.
& %
(EH)

Hartlepool Art Gallery
HARTLEPOOL
Church Square
☎(01429) 266522 ext 2610
From August 1995, the building that was once the parish church of West Hartlepool becomes both an art gallery and museum with permanent displays of Japanese armour and ivories, oriental ceramics and statuary. Access to the church tower reveals displays on bellringing and church clocks, extensive panoramic views out to sea and across the North York moors. There is a full programme of temporary exhibitions.
Open all year, Tue-Sun 10-5 (closed Good Fri, Xmas & 1 Jan).
Free.
P 🍴 & *(remote controlled video unit) toilets for disabled shop* %

HMS Trincomalee Trust
HARTLEPOOL
Jackson Dock (follow brown heritage signs)
☎(01429) 223193
Situated at Jackson's Dock, the main attraction is *HMS Trincomalee* launched in 1817 and the oldest British warship afloat today and now undergoing restoration. Locally-built small craft can alo be seen. Visitor centre and shop.
Open all year, Mon-Fri 1.30-4.30, wknds & BH 10-4.30. (Closed Xmas & New Year).
❋£2.50 (concessions £1.50)
P & *shop* %

Museum of Hartlepool
HARTLEPOOL
Jackson Dock
☎(01429) 266522 ext 2610

Open from 29 April 1995, the museum has exhibits showing the history of Hartlepool including Roman and Anglo-Saxon times and medieval pirates. Step inside a 19th-century shipyard or board a 28ft local fishing vessel. There is also the *Winsfield Castle*, a paddlesteamer built in Hartlepool in 1934, which now houses touring exhibitions and the café. There are also a variety of small traditional sailing craft afloat in the dock. From 29 April 1995 for the following week there will be major events to celebrate the opening. 23-25 June 1995: Midsummer traditional North East sailing boat rally.
Open all year, Tue-Sun 10-5 (closed 25-26 Dec & 1 Jan).
Free.
🅿 🖲 & *toilets for disabled shop* ✇

Captain Cook Birthplace Museum
MIDDLESBROUGH
Stewart Park, Marton (3m S on A172 at Stewart Park, Marton)
☎ *(01642) 311211*
Opened to mark the 250th anniversary of the birth of the voyager in 1728, this museum illustrates the early life of James Cook and his discoveries with temporary exhibitions. Located in spacious and rolling parkland, the site also offers outside attractions for the visitor, including a conservatory of tropical plants, and assorted animals and fowl housed in small and accessible paddocks. There are Captain Cook Birthday Celebrations in October.
Open all year, summer Tue-Sun 10-5.30, winter 9-4. Last ticket 30 mins before closing. (Closed 25-26 Dec & 1 Jan).
✳£1.20 (ch & pen 60p). Family ticket £3.
🅿 🖲 & *(lift to all floors, car parking) toilets for disabled shop* ✇

Dorman Museum
MIDDLESBROUGH
Linthorpe Rd
☎ *(01642) 813781*
Middlesbrough has a rich industrial heritage and is now the administrative centre of Teesside. This museum illustrates its social and industrial growth, its natural history and geological features, by permanent exhibitions and a varied programme of temporary displays.
Open all year Tue-Sat 10-6. (Closed 25-26 Dec & 1 Jan).
Free.
🅿 & *toilets for disabled shop* ✇

Ormesby Hall
ORMESBY
☎ *Middlesbrough (01642) 324188*
An 18th-century mansion, Ormesby Hall has stables attributed to John Carr of York. Plasterwork, furniture and 18th-century pictures can be seen.
Open Apr-Oct, Wed, Thu, Sat, Sun & BH Mon & Good Fri 2-5.30. Last admission 5pm.
House & Gardens £2 (ch £1). Family ticket £4. Garden only £1 (50p).
🅿 🖲 & *toilets for disabled shop* ✇
(NT)

RNLI Zetland Museum
REDCAR
5 King St
☎ *(01642) 484402*
The museum portrays the lifeboat, maritime, fishing and local history of the area, including its main exhibit 'The Zetland' - the oldest lifeboat in the world dating from 1800. There is also a replica of a fisherman's cottage c1900 and almost 2000 other exhibits. The museum is housed in an early lifeboat station, now a listed building.
Open May-Sep, daily 11-4. Also Etr & Boxing Day. Other times by appointment.
Free.
🅿 *(charged)* & *shop*

Saltburn Smugglers
SALTBURN-BY-THE-SEA
(adjoining Ship Inn)
☎ *(01287) 625252*
The Saltburn Smugglers re-creates the 18th-century Ship Inn using a series of authentic room settings with sound and

lighting effects to tell the story of smuggling on the Cleveland coast. There is a tourist information centre and a souvenir shop.
Open all year, Etr-Sep, daily 10-6; Oct-Etr, wknds 10.30-4.
£1.50 (ch £1). Family ticket £4. Party.
🅿 *(200 mtrs) (charged in summer)* & *shop* ✇ *guide dogs*

Tom Leonard Mining Museum
SKINNINGROVE
Deepdale
☎ *Guisborough (01287) 642877*
The museum offers visitors an exciting and authentic underground experience on the site of the old Loftus mine, and a chance to see how the stone was drilled, charged with explosives and fired. Exhibits include a collection of original tools, lamps, safety equipment, old photographs and domestic objects, providing a glimpse of mining life both above and below ground.
Open Apr-Oct, daily 1-5 (last admission 3.45pm). Nov-Mar, schools & parties only. Parties by arrangement.
£2 (ch 75p).
🅿 & *shop* ✇

Preston Hall Museum
STOCKTON-ON-TEES
Yarm Rd (3m S on A135)
☎ *Eaglescliffe (01642) 781184*
The museum illustrates Victorian social history, with reconstructions of period rooms and a street with working craftsmen including blacksmith, cobbler, farrier and toymaker. The collections include costume, toys, arms and armour. The museum is set in a large park with an aviary, children's play area and nature trails. Special events for 1995 include: historic vehicle show (1-2 July), summer carnival (2-3 September).
Open all year, Etr-Sep, daily 10-5.30; Oct-Etr, daily 10-4.30. Last admission 30 mins before closing. (Closed Good Fri, 25-26 Dec & New Year).
Free.
🅿 *(charged)* 🖲 & *toilets for disabled shop* ✇

CORNWALL & ISLES OF SCILLY

Duke of Cornwall's Light Infantry Museum
BODMIN
The Keep, Victoria Barracks (on B3268)
☎ *(01208) 72810*
The museum was started at the Depot in 1925 and contains Armoury and Medals displays, a Uniforms room, and the Main Gallery with pictures and relics devoted to the major campaigns of the Regiment from 1702 to 1945.
Open all year Mon-Fri, 8-5 (ex BH).
£1 (ch 16 50p).
🅿 *shop*

Pencarrow
BODMIN
Washaway (3m N on unclass road off A389)
☎ *St Mabyn (01208) 841369*
This Georgian house is still a family home, and has a superb collection of pictures, furniture and porcelain. The 50 acres of formal and woodland gardens include a Victorian rockery, Italian and American gardens, a lake, an ice house and an ancient British encampment. There are over 600 different rhododendrons and an internationally acclaimed conifer collection. There is also a craft centre and a children's play area.
Open Etr-15 Oct, Mon-Thu & Sun, 1.30-5; BH Mon & Jun-10 Sep 11-5. (Last tour of the House 5pm)
🅿 🖲 & *toilets for disabled shop & plant shop* ✇ *(ex gardens)*
Details not confirmed for 1995

The inner keep and curtain wall of Pendennis Castle at Falmouth were built by Henry VIII to guard the entrance to the Carrick Roads.

Cotehele
CALSTOCK
St Dominick (2m E of St Dominick)
☎ *Liskeard (01579) 50434 & 51222*
The granite house dates from 1485 and was built for the Edgcumbe family. They moved south to Mount Edgcumbe in the 16th century, and have left Cotehele virtually untouched, apart from some building work in 1627. Inside there are tapestries, embroideries, furniture and armour; and outside there is a beautiful garden on different levels. It has a medieval dovecote. There is a restored manorial water mill in the valley below, and an outstation of the National Maritime Museum. The restored sailing barge 'Shamrock' can be seen from the quay.
Open Apr-Oct, House & Restaurant daily (ex Fri) 11-5.30; (11-5 in Oct). Garden & Mill Shop 11-5. Last admission 30 mins before closing. Nov-Mar garden only open daylight hours. Quay Gallery daily 12-5.30
House & Grounds £5. Grounds £2.50. Party.
🅿 ✗ *licensed* & *(braille guide) toilets for disabled shop* ✇
(NT)

North Cornwall Museum & Gallery
CAMELFORD
The Clease
☎ *(01840) 212954*
The museum is set in a building that was used for making coaches and wagons. There are sections on agriculture, slate and granite quarrying, and wheelwright's tools, and other displays include cobbling, dairy work and the domestic scene from lace bonnets to early vacuum cleaners. The gallery holds various exhibitions during the year. A small exhibition about Camelford and end of World War II is planned for 1995.
Open Apr-Sep, Mon-Sat 10-5.
£1.25 (ch 75p, pen & students £1).
🅿 *(50 yds)* & *shop* ✇

Chysauster Ancient Village
CHYSAUSTER ANCIENT VILLAGE
☎ *(01736) 61889*
Eight drystone masonry houses leading off a courtyard and incorporating a

characteristic Cornish underground chamber or 'fogou'. Adjoining the dwellings are byres. Inhabited between 1st and 3rd centuries AD.
Open all year, Apr-Sep, daily 10-6; Oct 10-4.
£1.50 (ch 80p, pen, students & UB40 £1.10).
✇
(EH)

Dobwalls Family Adventure Park
DOBWALLS
(0.5 N of A38)
☎ *Liskeard (01579) 20325 & 21129*
Dobwalls invites visitors to ride on its two-mile-long stretches of miniature American railroads. There are steam and diesel locos, and visitors can take the Rio Grande ride through the forests or the Union Pacific route over the prairies. Ten scaled-down locomotives include the Union Pacific Big Boy, and there are tunnels, embankments, lakes and canyons. Also at Dobwalls is Adventureland - eight action-packed areas filled with adventure play equipment including aerial cableways and three totally enclosed slides. There are also remote-controlled model boats and American-style trucks and trailers, a shooting gallery, Aquablasters and an Edwardian 'penny' amusement arcade.
Open Etr-Sep, daily 10-6 (last admission 4.30pm). Oct, Sat & Sun only & school half term (check as dates may differ). Prices under review.
🅿 🖲 & *(motorised & manual wheelchairs available) toilets for disabled shop*

Thorburn Museum & Gallery
DOBWALLS
(N of A38)
☎ *Liskeard (01579) 20325 & 21129*
'Mr Thorburn's Edwardian Countryside' is a unique combination of art and audio-visual display opened by HRH Prince Charles in 1986. A collection of major paintings by the wildlife artist Archibald Thorburn (1860-1935) is set in a reconstruction of the countryside, complete with sights, sounds and smells. The exhibition of watercolours and prints by wildlife and dog artist Steven Townsend will continue throughout 1995.
Open Etr-Sep, daily 10-6 (last admission

➤

A jagged granite stack called The Armed Knight forms the last outcrop of England at Land's End, pounded constantly by Atlantic rollers.

4.30pm). Oct, Sat & Sun only & school half term (check as dates may differ).
❋Prices under review.
P ♨ & (audio tour, braille, induction loop. Wheelchairs available) toilets for disabled shop

Cornwall Maritime Museum
FALMOUTH
2 Bells Court, Market St
☎(01326) 316745 & 212851
The Museum is situated in the building which one house the offices of the Packet Services. It gives a fascinating introduction to all aspects of the Cornwall Maritime Heritage, from sailors' superstitions through shipbuilding to smugglers in its new exhibition 'Cornwall and the Sea'. The history of the Falmouth Packet ships is covered in detail in a special gallery and there is a good collection of model ships of all types along with nautical artefacts in other galleries. During 1995 an exhibition, 'Art and the Sailor', will be held in conjunction with Falmouth Art Gallery.
Open all year, daily May-Sep 10-4; Oct-Apr, Mon-Sat 10-3.
£1 (ch 50p). Family ticket £2.50.
P (800yds) shop ⚘

Pendennis Castle
FALMOUTH
☎(01326) 316594
Pendennis was built to guard the waterways of the Carrick Roads, and was one of Henry VIII's many coastal forts. It is surrounded by later 16th-century fortifications, and now houses an exhibition of coastal defences of the Tudor period.
Open all year, Apr-Sep, daily 10-6; Oct daily, 10-4; Nov-Mar, daily 10-4. Closed 24-26 Dec & 1 Jan.
£2.20 (ch £1.10, concessions £1.70).
P & ⚘
(EH)

St Catherine's Castle
FOWEY
The ruined stronghold was one of the many castles built by Henry VIII to defend the coast. It was restored in 1855.
Open all year, any reasonable time.

Free.
(EH)

Godolphin House
GODOLPHIN CROSS
(situated between Townshend and Godolphin)
☎Penzance (01736) 762409
The former home of the Earls of Godolphin dates from the 15th century, but is most notable for the colonnades added in 1635. Inside is Wootton's painting Godolphin Arabian one of the three Arab stallion ancestors of all British bloodstock. The original stables house a small display of maps and interesting documents, and also old farm wagons. The Poldark Fayre will be held here during the second week of September 1995.
Open May & Jun, Thu 2-5, Tue & Thu 2-5; Jul-Sep, Aug, Tue 2-5, Thu 10-1 & 2-5.
Open BH Mons. Parties by arrangement at anytime throughout the year including Sun.
£3 (ch £1). Party 15+.
P ♨ & toilets for disabled shop (plants) ⚘

World in Miniature
GOONHAVERN
Bodmin Rd (on B3285)
☎Truro (01872) 572828
There are four major attractions for the price of one at this enchanting theme park. Visitors can stroll amongst the world's most famous landmarks such as the Taj Mahal and the Statue of Liberty, all in miniature scale, set in spectacular gardens. Then there is Tombstone, a wild-west town complete with saloon, bank, shops, livery stable and jail. The Adventure Dome is the original super cinema 180 direct from the USA where you experience the thrills and spills of two great films without leaving your seat. Finally, there are the gardens, twelve acres of beautifully landscaped grounds with over 70,000 plants and shrubs.
Open 27 Mar-30 Oct, daily 10-4 (5pm Jul-Aug).
£4 (ch 4-14 £1.75, pen £3.50). Family ticket £10.
P ♨ & toilets for disabled shop garden centre

Cornish Seal Sanctuary, Marine Animal Rescue Centre
GWEEK
☎Mawgan (01326) 221361
Here at the largest seal sanctuary in Europe an average of 30 sick and injured seals are rescued and cared for each year and then returned to the wild when fully recovered. With 10 pools, and a host of seals and sea lions, the highlight of a visit are the daily feeding times (six in summer and four in winter). Other attractions include the main exhibition with static and audio-visual displays, the hospital, safari bus rides, gift shop, cafe, seasonal barbecue, guided nature trail walks during the summer months, extensive picnic and play areas, an underwater viewing observatory, and children's quiz trail with scratch cards.
Open all year, daily 9-6. (4pm in winter). (Closed 25 Dec).
£4.50 (ch 4-14 £2.95, pen £3.50, students £3, disabled £2).
P ♨ & (wheelchair available) toilets for disabled shop

Flambards Village Theme Park
HELSTON
Culdrose Manor (0.5m S on A3083)
☎(01326) 573404
Three award-winning, all-weather attractions can be visited on one site here. Flambards Victorian Village is an evocative recreation of streets, shops and house interiors from the turn of the century, including a 'time capsule' chemist's shop. Britain in the Blitz is a life-size wartime street featuring shops, a pub and a living room with Morrison shelter; and Cornwall Aero Park covers the history of aviation from 'those magnificent men in their flying machines' to Concorde. Cornwall's Exploratorium, is a 'hands-on' science playground for the whole family. There are many rides from the gentle to the daring, including Flambards Family Log Flume, the

fabulous Cyclopter Monorail, Balloon Race, Space Mission, Superbob and Dragon Coaster. Other attractions include a maze, the Hall of Miscellany, a huge children's playground and picnic area. Various events due to take place in 1995 include the annual Easter Bonnet Parade, and exhibitions to mark the activities of the Special Operations Executive and the Secret Intelligence Service 1940-1943.
Open 12 Apr-29 Oct, daily 10-last admission 3.30pm. Park closes 5pm. Extended opening 23 Jul-1 Sep, Mon-Fri 10-3.30 Sat & Sun 10-5, last admission 4.30pm. Park closes 7pm.
Admission fee payable,
P ♨ & (wheelchairs available) toilets for disabled shop garden centre ⚘

Helston Folk Museum
HELSTON
Old Butter Market
☎(01326) 564027 & 572340
The Old Butter Market has been converted into a lively folk museum dealing with the town and the Lizard Peninsula.
Various exhibitions are held in summer.
Open all year, Mon, Tue & Thu-Sat 10.30-1 & 2-4.30, Wed 10.30-noon.
P (400 yds) & shop ⚘
Details not confirmed for 1995

Land's End
LAND'S END
☎Penzance (01736) 871501 & 871844
The most westerly point of mainland England draws countless visitors to its dramatic cliff scenery. On a clear day the Isles of Scilly, 28 miles away, can be seen together with the Wolf Rock Lighthouse and the Seven Stones Reef, where the Torrey Canyon met its end in 1967. The 200-acre site is the setting for wild coastal walks and amazing natural rock formations; and innovative exhibitions have been set up to trace the geology, wildlife and maritime history of the area. On the southernmost tip of the

peninsula are two small smugglers' coves linked by a tunnel which local miners carved through the headland. The Last Labyrinth, Man against the Sea and Spirit of Cornwall exhibitions can be seen along with an audio-visual show. Visitors can take a ride on the land train to the Land of Greeb with its animals, craftsmen and model village. Special events for 1995 include: Cornwall Vintage Vehicle Display (4 June), Steam Rally (17-18 June), Air Day (2 August).
Open all year, site & exhibitions 10-dusk. Times adjustable during winter. Closed 24-25 Dec.
❋£5.50 (pen £5). Under review.
🅿 (charged) 🍴 ✖ licensed ♿ (free admission for disabled & helper) toilets for disabled shop (some restricted areas)

Lanhydrock
LANHYDROCK
☎Bodmin (01208) 73320
Lanhydrock is approached along an avenue of beeches through a wooded park. It looks Tudor, but only the charming gatehouse, entrance porch and north wing date from the 16th century. The rest was rebuilt after a fire in 1881, and the house now gives a vivid picture of life in Victorian times. The 'below stairs' sections are particularly interesting and include a mighty kitchen, larders, dairy, bakehouse, cellars, and servants' quarters. Notable among the grander rooms is the long gallery, which has a moulded ceiling showing Old Testament scenes. The windows overlook the formal gardens with their clipped yews and bronze urns; the higher garden famed for its magnolias and rhododendrons, climbs the hillside behind the house.
Open Apr-Oct: House daily (ex Mon), but open BH Mon 11-5.30 (11-5 in Oct). Gardens daily. Last admission half hour before closing. Winter Gardens Nov-Mar during daylight hours.
❋House & Grounds £5.40. Grounds £2.50. Famil ticket £13.50. Party.
🅿 ✖ licensed ♿ (braille guide) toilets for disabled shop ⌖ (ex in Park)
(NT)

Lanreath Farm & Folk Museum
LANREATH
Churchtown
☎(01503) 220321
Implements and equipment from the farmhouse, dairy and farmyard are displayed, together with mill workings rescued from a derelict mill house. Demonstrations of local crafts are given on weekday afternoons from 2-4pm. Play phones, pets, and models to operate make it a fun place as well as educational.
Open Etr-May & Oct, daily 11-5; Jun-Sep, daily 10-6.
£2.25 (ch £1, under 5 free). Party.
🅿 ♿ shop

Launceston Castle
LAUNCESTON
☎(01566) 772365
Dominating this old market town is the ruin of the 12th-and 13th-century castle. It was stormed and changed hands four times during the Civil Wars, despite its impregnable appearance. The town that grew up outside the walls was the capital of Cornwall until 1838, when the assizes were moved to Bodmin.
Open all year, Apr-Sep, daily 10-6; Oct 10-4. Closed 24-26 Dec & 1 Jan.
£1.30 (ch 70p, students, pen & UB40 £1)
♿ (outer bailey only) ⌖
(EH)

Launceston Steam Railway
LAUNCESTON
Newport
☎(01566) 775665
The Launceston Steam Railway links the historic town of Launceston with the hamlet of New Mills. Travelling through the glorious countryside of the Kensey Valley, the trains are hauled by locomotives built in Victoria's reign. Tickets are valid for unlimited travel on

the day of issue so you can break your journey at various points along the track. At New Mills there are a range waymarked footpaths, a riverside picnic area and a water mill. Launceston Station houses railway workshops, a transport museum, gift shop and book shop. There will be two engines in steam and double-headed trains on Wednesdays in July and August.
Open Good Fri-21 Apr & Oct, Tue & Sun, then Jun-Sep, daily 10.30-4.30. (Closed Sat). Also Santa Weekends in Dec incl. 24 & 26 Dec.
❋£3.80 (ch £2.60, pen £3.30). Family ticket £12. Dogs 50p.
🅿 🍴 ♿ shop

Lawrence House
LAUNCESTON
9 Castle St
☎(01566) 773277 & 773047
The local history museum of this proud Cornish town is housed in one of several well-preserved red brick Georgian houses, and was once a rendezvous for French officer prisoners during the Napoleonic wars. The displays and artefacts all relate to the history and social history of Launceston.
Open Apr-early Oct, Mon-Fri 10.30-4.30. Other times by appointment. Closed BH's.
❋Free but donations requested.
(NT)

Monkey Sanctuary
LOOE
St Martins (4m E off B3253)
☎(01503) 262532
A protected breeding colony of rare Amazon woolly monkeys enjoy life here in the wooded grounds of Murrayton monkey sanctuary. Visitors can get close to the monkeys but are advised to bring children under four on dry days only. Talks are given morning and afternoon.
Open 2 wks Etr then May-Sep, Sun-Thu 10.30-5.
❋£3.50 (ch £1.70 & pen £2.50).
🅿 🍴 ♿ toilets for disabled shop ⌖

Trengwainton Garden
MADRON
Penzance
☎Penzance (01736) 63021
Rhododendrons and magnolias grow in profusion at Trengwainton, along with many plants that won't usually grow outdoors in Britain. The mild climate means that seed collected on expeditions to the Far East and southern hemisphere have flourished to produce a magnificent display in this 20th-century garden.
Open Mar-Oct, Wed-Sat also BH Mon & Good Fri 10.30-5.30. (Mar & Oct 11-5). Last admission 30 mins before closing.
£2.60.
🅿 ♿ (braille guide) toilets for disabled
(NT)

St Michael's Mount
MARAZION
(.5m S of A394)
☎(01736) 710507
Rising like a fairytale castle from the sea, St Michael's Mount can be reached on foot by a causeway at low tide, or by ferry at high tide in the summer only. It has been a church, priory, fortress and a private home in its time, and is still the home of Lord St Levan, whose ancestor St John Aubyn acquired it in 1660. The house is a medieval castle to which a magnificent east wing was added in the 1870s. There are splendid plaster reliefs of hunting scenes, Chippendale furniture in the elegant Blue Drawing Room, and collections of armour and pictures.
Open Apr-end Oct, Mon-Fri 10.30-5.30. Last admission 4.45. Mar-May special educational visits by prior arrangement, Tue only.
❋£3.50 Family ticket £9. Party.
🅿 🍴 ✖ licensed shop (Apr-Oct) ⌖
(NT)

'The Jungle' of palm ferns and bamboo forms part of the Lost Gardens of Heligan which lay untouched for 70 years.

Glendurgan
MAWNAN SMITH
☎Bodmin (01208) 74281
This delightful garden, set in a valley above the River Helford, was started by Alfred Fox in 1820. The informal landscape contains beautiful trees and shrubs from all over the world, including the Japanese loquat, Mexican cypress and tree ferns from New Zealand. There is also a walled garden, a maze and a Giant's Stride which is popular with children. *Open Mar-Oct, Tue-Sat & BH Mon 10.30-5.30 (last admission 4.30). (Closed Good Fri).*
£2.80.
🅿 🍴 ♿ (braille guide) toilets for disabled ⌖
(NT)

Folk Museum
MEVAGISSEY
East Quay
☎(01726) 843568
The museum is housed in an 18th-century boat builder's shed. It stands at the far end of the north quay in this old fishing village, famous in its day for pilchards and smuggling. Displays include fishing gear, china clay industry implements, a cider press, domestic items, pictures and models.
Open Etr wk 11-6; Etr-May 2-4; Jun-Sep 11-6.
30p (ch & pen 10p).
P (on quay,200yds) ♿ ⌖

World of Model Railways
MEVAGISSEY
Meadow St
☎(01726) 842457
Over 2000 British, Continental and American models are on display in this museum, which also features an impressively realistic layout for the models to run through, with urban and rural areas, a 'working' fairground, an Alpine ski resort with cable cars, and a Cornish china clay pit, all reproduced in miniature. The model shop is an added attraction.
Open 2 wks Etr, then Spring BH-1 Oct 11-5. Probably open Oct 1-4 (October half term 11-5).

❋£2.45 (ch & pen £1.90)
P (200 yds) ♿ shop

Animal World
NEWQUAY
Trenance Park
☎(01637) 873342
Education and conservation are the key issues at this exciting Zoological Centre. Apart from attractions such as the Monkey enclosures, penguin pool, tropical house and lion house all of which have been designed for maximum 'creature comfort' the park also boasts a Maze, an Oriental Garden, an activity Play Park, a Tarzan Trail Assault Course, and a tortoise enclosure which houses the tortoises that the Zoo is given each year. There are regular feeding times with talks, and animal encounter sessions.
Open Etr-Oct, daily 9.30-6; Nov-Etr 10-4.
£4 (ch £2.50, pen £3 & disabled £2)
🅿 (charged) 🍴 ♿ shop ⌖

Dairy Land Farm World
NEWQUAY
Summercourt (on A3058)
☎Mitchell (01872) 510246
Dairy Land Farm World was the first farm diversification of its kind in the UK. Here, visitors can watch while the cows are milked to music on a spectacular merry-go-round milking machine. The life of a Victorian farmer and his neighbours is explored in the Heritage Centre, and a Farm Nature Trail demonstrates farming and nature in harmony with informative displays along pleasant peaceful walks. Children will have fun getting to know the farm animals in the safety of the Farm Park. They will also enjoy the playground, assault course and indoor play areas.
Open daily, late Mar-Oct 10.30-5.30. Xmas opening telephone for details.
❋£4.50 (ch £3.30, pen £4.20). Party.
🅿 🍴 ✖ licensed ♿ (wheelchairs for loan; disabled viewing gallery - milking) toilets for disabled shop ⌖

The Lost Gardens of Heligan
PENTEWAN
(signposted from A390 & B3273)
☎Mevagissey (01726) 844157 & 843566
Covering an area of 57 acres, this is the largest garden reclamation project in ➤

Britain. Four walled gardens are being restored to their former glory including the re-planting of Victorian varieties of fruit and vegetables. A feature of the garden is 'The Jungle' - a collection of palms, tree ferns and bamboo. The visitor will find plenty to see here including a New Zealand and an Italian garden, a grotto, wishing well and rockeries. Various events are held throughout the year including walks, horticultural events, theatre workshops and educational courses.
Open all year, daily 10-4.30 (Closed 25 Dec).
£2.80 (ch £1.60, pen £2.40)
P ♨ & *toilets for disabled shop garden centre*

The Maritime Museum
PENZANCE
19 Chapel St (opposite the Admiral Benbow)
☎(01736) 68890 & 63324 (winter/after hours)
Treasures recovered from wrecks by the diving teams of Roland Morris are on display here, including gold and silver from the first treasure found in British waters. A man-o'-war display shows an full-scale section of a 1730 warship, including the gun-decks. Ship models, sailor's crafts, guns, instruments, shipwrights' tools and figureheads can also be seen.
Open Apr-Oct, daily 10-5
£1.50 (ch 5 75p). Family ticket £4
P (150 yds) shop

Cornish Engines
POOL
East Pool
☎Redruth (01209) 216657
Impressive relics of the tin mining industry, these great beam engines were used for pumping water from 2000ft below and for lifting men and ore from the workings below ground.
Open Apr-Oct, daily 11-5.30 (Oct 11-5). Last admission 30 mins before closing.
£2.
P *shop* ♨
(NT)

Probus Gardens
PROBUS
(on A390 between St Austell & Truro)
☎St Austell (01726) 882597
Permanent displays show many aspects of garden layout, plant selection and the effects of climate. Propagation of plants and trees is shown and there are exhibitions of fruit, herbs, vegetables and cultural trials. The emphasis here is on choosing the right foliage and flowers to suit individual requirements and environment. There is an historical plant collection, geological displays and an outdoor exhibition of sculpture. Special

events are advertised in the local press.
Open all year, 2 Apr-2 Oct, daily 10-5; 3 Oct-Mar, Mon-Fri 10-4.30. Adviser on duty Tue 2-5.
£2.40 (ch free).
P ♨ & *shop garden centre* ♨

Trewithen
PROBUS
Grampound Rd (on A390)
☎St Austell (01726) 882763 & 882418
The Hawkins family has lived in this charming, intimate country house since it was built in 1720. The internationally renowned landscaped garden covers some 30 acres and grows camellias, magnolias and rhododendrons as well as many rare trees and shrubs seldom seen elsewhere. The nurseries are open all year.
Open, House Apr-Jul & Aug BH, Mon & Tue 2-4. Gardens open Mar-Sep, Mon-Sat 10-4.30, also Sun in Apr & May.
✱*House £3 (ch £1.50); Gardens £2.50 (ch £1.50)*
P ♨ & *toilets for disabled garden centre*

Restormel Castle
RESTORMEL
☎(01208) 872687
With a commanding view over the Fowey Valley, Restormel is the best-preserved castle of its period in this area. Much of what survives dates from the 13th century, including a notable round keep; the castle was abandoned in the 16th century.
Open all year, Apr-Sep, daily 10-6; Oct 10-4. Closed 24-26 Dec & 1 Jan.
£1.30 (ch 70p, concessions £1).
P & ♨
(EH)

St Agnes Leisure Park
ST AGNES
(S on B3277)
☎(01872) 552793
The leisure park is set in several acres of mature landscaped gardens. Attractions include Cornwall in Miniature, the Lost World of the Dinosaurs, a Super X Simulator, an animated circus, the haunted house and fairyland. The park is illuminated after dark.
Open 2 Apr-15 Jul & 8 Sep-29 Oct, daily 10-6 (last entry 4pm); 16 Jul-7 Sep, daily 10am-10pm (last entry 9pm).
Admission fee payable.
P ♨ & *toilets for disabled shop*

Charlestown Shipwreck & Heritage Centre
ST AUSTELL
Quay Rd, Charlestown (1.25m SE A3061)
☎(01726) 69897 & 812345
Charlestown is a small and unspoilt village with a unique sea-lock china-clay port. It was purpose built in the 18th century by Charles Rashleigh. The

Shipwreck and Heritage Centre houses the largest display of shipwreck artefacts in the UK, along with a series of lifesize tableaux and photographs depicting village life, an audio-visual describing the local heritage, a Scarborough Lifeboat and a lifeboat display. An important 'History of Diving' display is a recent addition to the Centre.
Open Mar-Oct, daily 10-5 (later in high season). Last admission 1 hour before closing. Bookings taken out of season. Admission fee payable.
P *(charged)* ♨ ✗ *licensed* & *(ramps) toilets for disabled shop* ♨

Wheal Martyn China Clay Heritage Centre
ST AUSTELL
Carthew (2m N on B3274)
☎(01726) 850362
The Wheal Martyn Museum tells the story of Cornwall's most important present-day industry: china clay production. The open-air site includes a complete 19th-century clayworks, restored for this purpose. There are huge granite-walled settling tanks, working water-wheels and a wooden slurry pump. Other exhibits include a 220ft pan kiln, horse-drawn wagons and two steam locomotives used in the industry, and a restored 1914 Peerless lorry.
The story of china clay in Cornwall over two centuries is shown using indoor displays. There is also a short slide and sound programme, and a working pottery.
Outside again there are nature trails, a children's adventure trail and the spectacular viewing area of a modern china-clay pit.
Open Apr-Oct, 10-6 (last admission 5pm).
£3.90 (ch £1.95, pen £3.20)
P ♨ & *shop*

ST IVES
(Park your car at Lelant Station and take advantage of the park and ride service. The fee includes parking and journeys on the train between Lelant and St Ives during the day).

Barbara Hepworth Museum & Sculpture Garden
ST IVES
Barnoon Hill
☎Penzance (01736) 796226
Turner visited St Ives in 1811. Then, after the railway was established in 1880, the town became a popular haunt for artists; what was once a busy fishing port took on a distinctly Bohemian atmosphere as the net-lofts and fish-cellars were converted into studios. The house and garden that Dame Barbara Hepworth called home from 1949 until her death in

1975 is now a museum displaying 47 sculptures and drawings covering the period 1928-74, photographs, documents and other memorablia. Visitors can also visit her workshops, which house a selection of tools and some unfinished carvings. Administered jointly with the Tate Gallery St Ives.
Open all year, Apr-Oct, Mon-Sat 11-7, Sun & BHs 11-5; Nov-Mar, Tue-Sun 11-5. (Closed 24-26 Dec).
Admission included with Tate Gallery, St Ives. £2.50 (concessions £1.50)
P *(880 yds)* & *shop* ♨

Tate Gallery St Ives
ST IVES
Porthmeor Beach
☎(01736) 796226
This new gallery presents displays based on the Tate Gallery's collections of modern art related to Cornwall covering the years c1925-75.
Open all year, Apr-Oct, Mon-Sat 11-7 (9 Tue & Thu); Sun & BHs 11-5; Nov-Mar, Tue-Sun 11-5, (Closed 24-25 Dec).
£2.50 (includes one child under 11), concessions £1.50. Family ticket £10/£5(2 adults & 2 children; valid for 2 weeks. Party 10+
P ♨ ✗ *licensed* & *toilets for disabled shop* ♨

St Mawes Castle
ST MAWES
☎(01326) 270526
The castle at St Mawes was built by Henry VIII in the 1540s, roughly the same time as Pendennis Castle in Falmouth. Together they were to guard the mouth of the Fal estuary; their present state of excellent preservation is largely due to their comparatively trouble-free history. Smaller but built in the same 'clover leaf' design as Pendennis, St Mawes particularly is renowned as a fine example of military architecture. The dungeons, barrack rooms and cannon lined walls provide great interest for both adults and children.
Open all year Apr-Sep, daily 10-6; Oct 10-4; Nov-Mar, Wed-Sun 10-4. Closed 24-26 Dec & 1 Jan.
£1.50 (ch 80p, concessions £1.10)
P & ♨
(EH)

Carn Euny Ancient Village
SANCREED
(1m SW)
Four courtyard houses and a number of round houses dating from the 1st century BC can be seen at Carn Euny. There is also a 66ft long 'fogou': a subterranean passage leading to a circular chamber and used as a hiding place by the ancient inhabitants of this site.
Open any reasonable time.
Free.
P
(EH)

Old Post Office
TINTAGEL
☎(01804) 770024
A small, 14th-century manor house, with an ancient roof of thick uneven slates, it served as a receiving office for letters from 1844 to 1892, hence its name.
Open Apr-Oct, daily 11-5.30, (Oct 11-5). Last admission 30 mins before closing.
✱*£2.*
P *(opposite)* & *(braille guide) shop*
(NT)

Tintagel Castle
TINTAGEL
☎Camelford (01840) 770328
The romantic castle ruins have been divided by the erosion of the sea and make a dramatic sight. The castle was built by Reginald, Earl of Cornwall, in about 1145, and most of the remaining ruins date from the 13th century. They became famous in the 19th century as the site of King Arthur's birthplace and castle; and in fact there is some evidence of a stronghold here in the 5th-8th centuries which covers Arthur's time. There are also the remains of a Celtic

Overlooking the River Fowey and surrounded by a 60ft wide moat, Restormel Castle is one of the oldest, most romantic ruins in Cornwall.

monastery, founded on the peninsula about AD500 and abandoned by 1086. A small site exhibition covers the history of the site.
Open all year, Apr-Sep, daily 10-6; Oct 10-4; Nov-Mar, Tue-Sun 10-4. Closed 24-26 Dec & 1 Jan.
£2.20 (ch £1.10, concessions £1.70).
shop ⌘
(EH)

Antony House
TORPOINT
(2m NW, off A374)
☎ *Plymouth (01752) 812191*
A fine, largely unaltered mansion, built in brick and Pentewan stone for Sir William Carew between 1711 and 1721. The stable block and outhouses remain from an earlier 17th-century building. Most of the rooms in the house are panelled and contain contemporary furniture and family portraits.
The grounds, which overlook the River Lynher, were redesigned by Humphry Repton. They include an 18th-century dovecote and, near the river estuary, the Bath Pond House, with plunge bath and a panelled changing room (may be seen only after previous written application to the administrator).
Open Apr-Oct, Tue-Thu & BH Mons (also Sun Jun-Aug), 1.30-5.30. Last admission 4.45.
❋*£3.60. Party. Woodland Garden (not NT) £1. Combined Gardens only £2.50.*
🅿 *(braille guide) shop ⌘*
(NT)

Cornish Shire Horse Centre
TREDINNICK
Trelow Farm (off A39)
☎ *Rumford (01841) 540276*
This 120-acre farm specialises in Shire Horses, and visitors can see mares with foals. There are two horse shows a day which take place under cover and are fully seated, and cart rides are also available. The work of the blacksmith is also on display and there is a museum of carriages, a video room and the largest display of show harnesses in the country. The unique owl sanctuary enable owls to fly freely in a twilight atmosphere. There is a children's world of adventure playground, and small animals and special rare breeds can be seen.
Open Good Fri-Oct daily 10-5. (Closed Sat in Oct)
🅿 💺 ✗ *licensed & toilets for disabled shop*
Details not confirmed for 1995

Trelissick Garden
TRELISSICK GARDEN
☎ *Truro (01872) 862090 & 865808*
A beautiful woodland park of some 370 acres overlooking the Fal estuary. The park was mainly laid out between 1844 and 1913 but the gardens were designed later, between 1937 and 1955. The grounds have been immaculately kept and offer spectacular views from walks through beech trees and oaks.
The location of the garden, near the sea and sheltered by woodland, has allowed many unusual and exotic plants to be grown. There are sub-tropical plants, some from such distant places as Chile and Tasmania. The gardens are particularly noted for their camellias, magnolias and hydrangeas, of which there are over 100 kinds. There is also a large walled garden with fig trees and climbers, and a shrub garden. Plants are available in the garden shop. There is also an Art and Craft Gallery by the House Farm Courtyard.
Open Mar-Oct, Mon-Sat 10.30-5.30, Sun 12.30-5.30, Restaurant 12-5.30 (closes at 5 in Mar & Oct). Woodland walks open Nov-Feb. Last admission 30 mins before closing.
❋*£3.40. Family ticket £8.50.*
🅿 *(charged) ✗ licensed & (Braille guide) toilets for disabled shop ⌘ (ex in woodland walk & park)*
(NT)

Trerice
TRERICE
☎ *Newquay (01637) 875404*
Built in 1571 for Sir John Arundell, the picturesque Elizabethan house has unusual curved and scrolled gables, which may have been influenced by Sir John's stay in the Netherlands. The hall has an imposing window of 576 panes of glass, and throughout the house are fine plasterwork ceilings. A museum of lawnmowers is housed in the barn. The garden includes an orchard of Cornish fruit trees.
Open Apr-Oct, Wed-Mon 11-5.30, (Oct 11-5). Last admission 30 mins before closing.
House £3.60. Party.
🅿 ✗ *licensed & (braille guide) toilets for disabled shop ⌘*
(NT)

Royal Cornwall Museum
TRURO
River St (follow A390 towards town centre)
☎ *(01872) 72205*
The museum has interesting and well-laid out displays on the history of the county, and it also has a world-famous collection of minerals. There are paintings and drawings, including a number of Old Masters, and some excellent exhibits of pottery, pewter, Japanese ivories, lacquerwork and toys. An extension houses two temporary exhibition galleries and a cafe. Other galleries house displays of mining and minerals, archaeology, Cornish history, and Egyptian artefacts; a natural history gallery is planned for 1995.
Open all year, Mon-Sat 10-5. Library closes 1-2. (Closed BHs).
£1.50 (unaccompanied ch 50p, pen & students £1)
🅿 *(200 yds) 💺 ✗ & (lift) toilets for disabled shop ⌘*

Poldark Mine and Heritage Complex
WENDRON
(on B3297)
☎ *Helston (01326) 573173*
This Cornish tin mine has three levels open to the public; an 18th-century village, museums and a cinema showing a film on the history of Cornish mining. On the surface there are restaurants, shops, gardens and children's amusements. The area around the mine has been laid to lawn and shows the West Country's largest collection of antiquities, including a 40ft beam engine.
Open Etr-Oct, daily 10-5.30 (last admission 4).
Admission fee payable.
🅿 💺 ✗ *licensed & shop (ex grounds)*

Wayside Museum
ZENNOR
(4m W of St Ives, on B3306)
☎ *Penzance (01736) 796945*
This is the oldest private museum in Cornwall, founded in 1935, and covers every aspect of life in Zennor and District from 3000BC to the 1930s. Over 5000 items are displayed in eleven workshops and rooms covering wheelwrights, blacksmiths, agriculture, fishing, wrecks, mining, domestic and archaeological artefacts. A photographic exhibition entitled People of Past Zennor tells the story of the village and its people. The Miller's Cottage has a kitchen, parlour, mill and three working waterwheels. The delightful gardens are bounded on one side by a river. The majority of displays are under cover.
Open Etr-Oct, daily 10-6 & fine evenings during high season.
£1.85 (ch £1.25, pen £1.50). Party 10+.
🅿 💺 *shop ⌘*

CUMBRIA

South Tynedale Railway
ALSTON
The Railway Station, Hexham Rd (0.25m N, on A686)
☎ *(01434) 381696*
Running along the beautiful South Tyne valley, this narrow-gauge railway follows the route of the former Alston to Haltwhistle branch. At present the line runs between Alston and Gilderdale, but an extension of the lines to Kirkhaugh in Northumberland is expected to open in 1995. Special events for 1995 include: Teddy Bear Day (31 May), Transport Extravaganza Weekend (1-2 July), Friends of Thomas Weekend (21-22 October), Santa Specials in December.
Open 1,2,8,9, 14-23 & 29-30 Apr daily; May, wknds & BHs; Jun-Oct, Tue-Thu & wknds (daily Jul & Aug); Dec, Santa & Mince Pie Specials. Please enquire for times of trains.
❋*£2-£2.60 (ch £1-£1.30). Party 10+.*
Prices under review.
🅿 💺 & *(railway carriage for wheelchairs-pre-booking required) toilets for disabled shop*

Appleby Castle Conservation Centre
APPLEBY-IN-WESTMORLAND
(on A66, castle is top of the main street)
☎ *Appleby (017683) 51402*
The grounds of this beautifully preserved Castle provide a natural setting for a Farm Park featuring rare breeds of British farm animals and also a large collection of ornamental waterfowl and unusual birds. The fine Norman Keep and the Great Hall of the house are open to the public. Clifford family portraits and part of the Nanking Cargo are on display in the Hall. The view from the top of the ancient Keep is spectacular and well worth a visit. An added attraction is the introduction of a Nursery Garden in the old walled kitchen garden. The buildings

in the Old Stable Courtyard, provide a home for the National School of Falconry, encorporating a display on the history of this ancient sport. The magnificent birds of prey are on display to visitors of the Castle grounds when they are not being used for tuition in the school. A varied programme of events is planned throughout the season, please telephone for further information.
Open 8 Apr-Sep, daily 10-5 (last admission); Oct, daily 10-4.
£3.50 (ch £1.50, under 5 free & pen £2). Family ticket £9 (2 adults+2 children). Party 20+.
🅿 💺 ✗ & *(assistance available) toilets for disabled shop garden centre*

Furness Abbey
BARROW-IN-FURNESS
(1.5m NE on unclass road)
☎ *(01229) 823420*
Built in 1147, Furness Abbey is impressive even as a ruin. The extensive remains of the church and other buildings are a reminder that this was a very wealthy Cistercian establishment, and the setting is the beautiful 'Glen of Deadly Nightshade' near Barrow.
Open all year, Apr-Sep, daily 10-6; Oct 10-4; Nov-Mar, daily 10-4. Closed 24-26 Dec & 1 Jan.
£2.20 (ch £1.10, concessions £1.70). Admission price includes a free Personal Stereo Guided Tour.
🅿 & ⌘
(EH)

Lanercost Priory
BRAMPTON
(2.5m NE)
☎ *(016977) 3030*
The priory was founded in around 1166 by William de Vaux, for Augustinian canons. The nave of the church has survived and is still used, and makes a strange contrast with the ruined priory buildings around.
Open Apr-Sep, daily 10-6.
£1 (ch 50p, concessions 80p).
🅿 & ⌘
(EH)

Furness Abbey, now an awe-inspiring ruin in a quiet Cumbrian valley, was once Britain's second most rich and powerful Cistercian monastery.

Brough Castle
BROUGH
(on A66)
☎ 0191-261 1585
Standing on the site of the Roman Verterae, the castle was built in the 12th and 13th centuries to replace a stronghold destroyed by the Scots. The later castle also fell into ruin, but was restored in the 17th century by Lady Ann Clifford. The keep and curtain walls can be seen.
Open any reasonable time.
✍
(EH)

Brougham Castle
BROUGHAM
(off A66)
☎ (01768) 62488
12th-to 14th-century castle, repaired in late 17th-century.
Open Apr-Sep, daily 10-6; Oct 10-4.
£1.30 (ch 70p, pen, student & UB40 £1)
(EH)

Border Regiment & King's Own Royal Border Regiment Museum
CARLISLE
Queen Mary's Tower, The Castle
☎ (01228) 32774
Three hundred years of the regiment's history are illustrated with trophies, weaponry, models, silver and pictures. The story of Cumbria's part-time soldiers is also told.
Open all year, Mon -Sat, 9.30-6, Sun 10-6, Apr-Oct; daily 10-4 Nov-Mar. (Closed 25-26 Dec & 1 Jan)
✳£2 (ch £1, pen & students £1.50). Price includes entry to Carlisle Castle. Prices under review.
P (400 yds) & (parking for disabled at Castle) shop ✍

Guildhall Museum
CARLISLE
Green Market
☎ (01228) 819925
The Guildhall was once the meeting place of Carlisle's eight trade guilds, and it still has an atmosphere of medieval times. It is an early 15th-century building with exposed timber work and wattle and daub walls. The displays include items relating to the guilds, and other reminders of life in medieval Carlisle.
Open from 31 Mar, Tue-Sun 11-4. Winter by arrangement.
shop ✍
Details not confirmed for 1995

Tullie House Museum & Art Gallery
CARLISLE
Castle St
☎ (01228) 34781
Travel back into the mists of time and let the real stories of historic Carlisle and

Border history unfold before you. Curiosity entices you to begin a journey of discovery as you stroll through LUGUVALIUM (Roman Carlisle), climb part of Hadrian's turf Wall and experience a land inhabited by eagles and peregrines. Peep into Isaac Tullie's study as it might have been when he sat down to record in his diary how the Roundheads laid siege to his Royalist city in 1644, or sit in the 1st-class compartment of a railway carriage and recall the days of steam locomotion.
Open all year, Mon-Fri & Sat 10-5, Thu 10am-10pm, Sun noon-5.
✳*Ground floor (including Art Gallery) - Free. Upper floors - £2.80 (concessions £1.40).*
🍴 ✕ *licensed & (chair lift) toilets for disabled shop* ✍

Wordsworth House
COCKERMOUTH
Main St
☎ (01900) 824805
William Wordsworth was born here on 7th April 1770, and happy memories of the house had a great effect on his work. He played on the garden terrace with his sister Dorothy, and the inside staircase, panelling and other features are original. Portraits and other items connected with the poet are displayed.
Open 3 Apr-Oct, Mon-Fri 11-5. Also Sats 15 & 29 Apr, 27 May and all Sats 1 Jul-2 Sep. (Last admission 4.30pm).
£2.40 (ch £1.20). Family ticket £6.50. Party. Ask for details of discount with Dove Cottage and Rydal Mount.
P 🍴 shop ✍
(NT)

Brantwood
CONISTON
(2.5m SE off B5285, unclass rd)
☎ (015394) 41396
Brantwood, former home of John Ruskin, is one of the most beautifully situated houses in the Lake District with fine views across Coniston Water. Inside there is a large collection of Ruskin paintings and other memorabilia, while outside visitors can enjoy delightful nature walks through the Brantwood Estate. Special events for 1995 include outdoor theatre in fantastic locations.
Open mid Mar-mid Nov, daily 11-5.30. Rest of year, Wed-Sun 11-4.
£3 (ch 18 free). Party.
P 🍴 ✕ *licensed & toilets for disabled shop* ✍

Ruskin Museum
CONISTON
The Institute
☎ (015394) 41164
The Victorian writer John Ruskin lived nearby, and the museum displays photocopies of letters and sketchbooks

and other relics, with portraits of the writer and his circle. There are also minerals and examples of Ruskin Lace, based on a design which he brought back from Italy and which became popular with local lace makers. Other material relates to the Campbells and their Coniston water speed record bids, and to Coniston itself.
Open Etr-Oct, Sun-Fri, 10-1 & 2-4.
✳£1 (school children 50p)
P (50 yds) & ✍

Steam Yacht Gondola
CONISTON
Pier Cottage
☎ (015394) 41288
Launched in 1859, the graceful *Gondola* worked on Coniston Water until 1937, and came back into service in 1980. Now visitors can once again enjoy her silent progress and old-fashioned comfort.
Open 29 Mar-5 Nov to scheduled daily timetable. Trips commence 11 at Coniston; on Sat 12.05. Piers at Coniston, Park-a-Moor at SE end of lake & Brantwood. (Not NT).
Ticket prices on application & published locally.
P ✍
(NT)

Dalemain
DACRE
☎ Pooley Bridge (017684) 86450
The stately home of Dalemain was originally a medieval pele tower, which was added to in Tudor times and later, with the imposing Georgian façade completed in 1745. It has splendid oak panelling, Chinese wallpaper, Tudor plasterwork and fine Queen Anne and Georgian furniture. The rooms include a Victorian nursery and a housekeeper's room. The tower contains the Westmorland and Cumberland Yeomanry Museum, and there is a countryside museum in the 16th-century cobbled courtyard. The grounds include a deerpark and gardens, and there is an adventure playground. The annual Rainbow Craft Fair will be held on 22-23 July.
Open 9 Apr-3 Oct, Sun-Thu 11.15-5. Last entry to house 5pm.
£4 (ch under 5 free, ch 16 £3). Family ticket £11. Wheelchair users free.
P ✕ *licensed & toilets for disabled shop garden centre* ✍

Dove Cottage & The Wordsworth Museum
GRASMERE
(S, off A591)
☎ (015394) 35544 & 35547
Wordsworth called Grasmere 'the loveliest spot that man hath ever found.' He lived at Dove Cottage from 1799 to 1808, and during that time wrote much

of his best-known poetry. The house is kept in its original condition, as described in the journals of his sister Dorothy, and the award-winning museum displays manuscripts, paintings and various items associated with the poet. Near the cottage is the former schoolroom where he taught; and Wordsworth, his wife and sister, and other members of the family, are buried in the churchyard. John Keats: A Bicentenary Exhibition will the the major summer exhibition at the Wordsworth Museum. Please telephone for details of residential courses held by the Wordsworth Trust.
Open daily 9.30-5.30, last admission 5pm. (Closed 9 Jan-5 Feb & 24-26 Dec).
£4 (ch £2). Family ticket available. Party.
P ✕ *licensed & toilets for disabled shop* ✍

Grizedale Forest Park
GRIZEDALE
☎ Satterthwaite (01229) 860010
Grizedale Forest was the first Forestry Commission estate where special efforts were made to provide information and other facilities for visitors. The centre illustrates the story of Grizedale from wild wood to its present role as an area managed for timber, wildlife and recreation. There is a conservation tree nursery, and a number of waymarked walks can be followed, ranging from the one-mile Millwood Habitat Trail to the nine-mile Silurian Way. Routes for cyclists are also provided, and there are woodland sculptures, observation hides, orienteering, children's play area and many picnic sites. The area gives wonderful views, with the possibility of seeing some of the woodland red and roe deer.
Open Apr-Oct, daily 10-5. Rest of year (except Jan) 11-4.
✳*Craft/Sculpture Gallery 50p*
P *(charged)* 🍴 & *(woodland trails suitable for wheelchairs) toilets for disabled shop*

Theatre in the Forest
GRIZEDALE
☎ Satterthwaite (01229) 860291
Dance and drama, classical and jazz music, variety and folk concerts have all been featured at this unique theatre. It was founded in 1969, with an emphasis on quality, and is open during the day for exhibitions. Also of interest is a long-distance Sculpture Trail with around sixty sculptures, and The Gallery in the Forest which houses art, sculpture and craft exhibitions. Other attractions include a painting studio, and a new Sculpture Trail for the disabled.
Open all year, Tue-Sat 11-4.
Ticket prices vary depending on performance.
P *(charged)* 🍴 & *toilets for disabled* ✍

Hardknott Castle Roman Fort
HARDKNOTT CASTLE ROMAN FORT
The fort is at the western end of the hair-pinned (and hair-raising) Hardknott Pass, which has gradients of 1 in 3. On this astonishing site above Eskdale, the Romans built a walled and ramparted fort covering nearly three acres, with a bath house and parade ground outside. The remains of the building can be seen.
Open any reasonable time.
Free.

(EH)

Beatrix Potter Gallery
HAWKSHEAD
Main St
☎ (015394) 36355
An annually changing exhibition of Beatrix Potter's original illustrations from her children's storybooks. Housed in the former office of her husband, solicitor William Heelis. Also a display of her life as an author, artist, farmer and determined preserver of her beloved Lake District.
Open Apr-Oct, Sun-Thu 10.30-4.30 (last admission 4). Admission is by timed ticket including NT members.

Overlooking Coniston Water and the Fells and once home of artist, social reformer and conservationist, John Ruskin, Brantwood is now one of the most beautifully situated museums in England.

The Lakeland Motor Museum is housed at Holker Hall. There are over 80 vintage cars, motorcycles and bicycles displayed, plus a replica of Sir Malcolm Cambell's record-breaking *Bluebird*.

£2.50 (ch £1.30)
P shop ⊘ 🚂
(NT)

Holker Hall & Gardens
HOLKER

Cark in Cartmel, Grange over Sands
☎ Flookburgh (015395) 58328
Dating from the 16th century, the new wing of the Hall was rebuilt in 1871 after a disastrous fire. It has notable woodcarving and many fine pieces of furniture which mix happily with family photographs from the present day. Magnificent 25-acre gardens, both formal and woodland, are adjacent to the Hall; here you will find a fantastic limestone cascade and other water features. The Lakeland Motor Museum, exhibitions, deer park and adventure playground are further attractions. An MG rally will be held here on 27 August.
Open Apr-Oct, Sun-Fri 10-6. Last entry to grounds, hall & motor museum 4.30pm. Prices under review.
🅿 ♨ ♿ *toilets for disabled shop* ⊘ *(ex in park)*

Abbot Hall Art Gallery
KENDAL

Kirkland
☎ (01539) 722464
The ground floor rooms of this splendid house, reputedly designed in 1759 by John Carr of York, have been restored to their period decor, including the original carvings and fine panelling. The rooms make a perfect setting for the Gillow furniture and *objets d'art* displayed here, while the walls are hung with paintings by Romney, Gardner, Turner and Ruskin. The gallery has a fine collection of 18th- and 19th-century watercolours of the Lake District and exceptionally good 20th-century British art, including works by Barbara Hepworth, Frink, Ben Nicholson, Sutherland, Piper and Hitchens. An exhibition of paintings and drawings by L S Lowry is planned for 20 June-4 September.
Open 11 Feb-22 Dec, Mon-Sun 10.30-5 (reduced hours in winter, Feb, Mar, Nov & Dec) please telephone for details.
£2.50 (ch, students & pen £1.25). Family ticket £5.
🅿 ♨ ♿ *(chair lifts in split level galleries) toilets for disabled shop* ⊘

Abbot Hall Museum of Lakeland Life & Industry
KENDAL

Kirkland
☎ (01539) 722464
The life and history of the Lake District has a uniqueness which is captured by the displays in this museum, housed in Abbot Hall's stable block. The working and social life of the area, its people and places are well illustrated by a variety of exhibits including period rooms, a Victorian Cumbrian street scene and a farming display. One of the rooms is devoted to the memory of Arthur Ransome, another to John Cunliffe's Postman Pat.
Open 11 Feb-22 Dec, daily 10.30-5. Reduced hours Feb, Mar, Nov & Dec, please telephone for details.
£2.50 (ch, students & pen £1.25). Family ticket £5.
🅿 ♨ *shop* ⊘

Kendal Museum
KENDAL

Station Rd
☎ (01539) 721374
The archaeology and natural history of the Lakes is dealt with in this popular museum which also features a world wildlife exhibition and a gallery devoted to Alfred Wainwright - the author who was honorary clerk to the museum.
Open 11 Feb-Dec, daily 10.30-5. Reduced hours Feb, Mar. Nov & Dec, please telephone for details.
£2.50 (ch, students & pen £1.25). Family tickets £5.
🅿 ♿ *(chair lift) toilets for disabled shop* ⊘

Beatrix Potter's Lake District
KESWICK

Packhorse Court
☎ (017687) 75173
Peter Rabbit is only part of the tale! A 16 minute dramatic slide and video presentation brings to life Beatrix Potter's most important achievement - her 'saving' of 6000.acres of the Lake District. The careful and sensitive conservation of this magnificent area, on behalf of the nation, is now continued by the National Trust. Japanese commentary is available.
Open Apr-Jun & Sep-Oct, daily 10-5; Jul & Aug, daily 10-5.30; Nov-Mar, weekends 12-4.
£2.50 (ch £1.30) Family ticket £7. Party.
P *(charge payable)* ♿ *(induction loop for impaired hearing) shop* ⊘
(NT)

Keswick Museum & Art Gallery
KESWICK

Fitz Park, Station Rd
☎ (017687) 73263
A mecca for writers, poets and artists, Keswick's attractions are well illustrated in this museum and gallery. Names such as Coleridge, Shelley, Wordsworth, Southey, Lamb and Walpole can be found among the exhibits which include letters, manuscripts and other relics from the time these literary luminaries spent in the Lake District. One of Ruskin's paintings is among the collections in the art gallery and there is a fine scale model of the Lakes dating from 1834. The comprehensive geology collection is of national importance and contains magnificent mineral examples from the Caldbeck Fells. The natural history displays cover animal and bird life of the region, including a golden eagle, and butterfly and moth cabinets. Fitz Park contains formal gardens and a children's adventure playground. There are monthly exhibitions by local artists and craft workers.
Open Etr-Oct, daily 10-4.
£1 (ch, pen, students, UB40's & disabled 50p). Party 10+.
P *(5 mins)* ♿ *shop* ⊘

Lingholm Gardens
KESWICK

Lingholm (S of A66,signposted from Portincale village)
☎ (017687) 72003
Both formal and woodland gardens are seen at Lingholm, which is at its most spectacular when the rhododendrons and azaleas are in bloom. The gardens include meconopsis, primulas, magnificent trees and shrubs, herbaceous borders and gentians. In spring, they are alive with daffodils, and the colours of autumn are breathtaking.
Open Apr-Oct, daily 10-5.
£2.70 *(accompanied ch free). Party 20 +.*
🅿 ♨ ♿ *(wheelchair route, parking near entrance) toilets for disabled* ⊘

Mirehouse
KESWICK

(3m N on A591)
☎ (017687) 72287
Undoubtedly a great place for children - there are four adventure playgrounds - but Mirehouse has its fair share of cultural interest, and a walk along the beautiful lake shore will take you past the place where Tennyson wrote much of *Morte d'Arthur*. Inside the 17th-century house there is much original furniture adorning the graceful rooms. Portraits and manuscripts of Francis Bacon, Carlyle and, of course, Tennyson are on display. Children are welcome inside as well as ouside, with plenty of things to find and do including riding a large Victorian rocking horse. Outside, the flowers in the walled garden attract the bees and butterflies, and make this sheltered spot perfect for picnics.

Mirehouse is also the venue for two concerts attached to Keswick Jazz Festival at the end of May, and bobbin lace demonstrations are held each Wednesday in June, July and September.
Open Apr-Oct. House: Wed, Sun, (also Fri in Aug) 2-last entry 4.30. Grounds: daily 10.30-5.30. Parties by arrangement.
✳House & grounds £3 (ch £1.50). Grounds only £1 (ch 80p). Family ticket £8 (2 adults & up to 4 children)
🅿 ♨ ♿ & ⊘ *(ex in grounds on lead)*

Levens Hall
LEVENS

(5m S of Kendal, on A6)
☎ Sedgwick (015395) 60321 ·
The most remarkable feature is the topiary garden, laid out in 1694 and little changed. The Elizabethan mansion was built onto a 13th-century pele tower and has fine plasterwork and panelling. A steam engine collection adds further interest.
Open - House & gardens Apr-Sep, Sun-Thu 11-5. Steam collection 2-5.
House & garden £4.20 (ch £2.50 & pen £3.80), garden only £2.90 (ch £1.80 & pen £2.70). Party 20+.
🅿 ♨ ♿ *(ramps within garden) toilets for disabled shop (plants on sale)* ⊘

Flying Buzzard & Vic 96
MARYPORT

Elizabeth Dock, South Quay, Maryport Harbour
☎ (01900) 815954
Full guided tours of the Flying Buzzard, a 1951 Clyde tug, bringing to life the story of the ship and her crew. Also explore the VIC 96, and visit the hold - an exciting 'hands on' display for all the family. A chance to try your hand at tying knots, raising and lowering sails and climbing into a hammock.
Open Etr-Oct, Mon-Fri 11-5.30, Sat-Sun 1.30-5.30 (last tour 4.15); Nov-Etr, please telephone for details. Currently under review.
P *(adjacent to dock) shop*
Details not confirmed for 1995

Maritime Museum
MARYPORT

1 Senhouse St
☎ (01900) 813738
The museum houses a wealth of objects, pictures, models and paintings that illustrate Maryport's maritime tradition. From mutineer Fletcher Christian to the great shipowner, Thomas Henry Ismay of the Great White Star Line, owner of the ill fated Titanic.
Open all year, Etr-Oct Mon-Thu 10-5, Fri-Sat 10-1 & 2-5, Sun 2-5; Nov-Etr Mon-Sat 10-1 & 2-4.30.
P ♿ *shop*
Details not confirmed for 1995

Millom Folk Museum
MILLOM

St Georges Rd
☎ (01229) 772555
All the exhibits in this museum illustrate local life, and they are presented in an informative and captivating way with reconstructed room sets of a miner's cottage; a blacksmith's forge, complete with tools; a corner shop and a full scale model of a drift of the Hodbarrow Iron Ore Mine. There is also a tribute to the late Dr Norman C Nicholson, poet and author of 'A Man of Millom'.
Open Etr wk, May Day wknd & Spring-mid Sep, Mon-Sat 10-5.
✳75p (ch 35p)
P *(40yds)* ♿ *shop*

Muncaster Castle, Gardens & Owl Centre
MUNCASTER

(1m E on A595)
☎ Ravenglass (01229) 717614 & 717393 *(owl centre)*
Diverse attractions are offered at this castle, the seat of the Pennington family since the 13th century. Inside is a fine collection of 16th-and 17th-century furnishings, embroideries and portraits, whilst the grounds have a nature trail, an

➜

adventure playground, and a profusion of rhododendrons, camellias, magnolias and azaleas. There is also an extensive collection of owls, as this is the headquarters of the World Owl Trust. Closed circuit television on some nests allows an intimate look, and there are continuous owl videos throughout the day in the Old Dairy Theatre. 'Meet the Birds' daily from 26 March to 29 October at 2.30pm, a talk is given on the work of the Owl Centre and, weather permitting, the birds fly. Special events for 1995 include: Open Field Archery Championships (26-27 August), Models at Muncaster (2-3 September). Embroidery demonstrations first Sunday of each month April to October and most Bank Holiday Sundays.
Open Castle; 26 Mar-29 Oct, Tue-Sun & BH 1-4 (last entry); Garden & Owl Centre, all year, daily 11-5. Parties by arrangement.
Prices not aviailable at time of going to press.
🅿 💺 ✗ *licensed* ⅃ *(wheelchair loan,induction loop,tape for partially sighted) toilets for disabled shop garden centre*

Muncaster Water Mill
MUNCASTER
(1m NW on A595 by railway bridge)
☎ *Ravenglass (01229) 717232*
There has been a mill on this site since the 15th century, and flour and oatmeal are still ground on the premises. The water is brought three-quarters of a mile from the River Mite to the 13ft overshot water wheel, and all the milling equipment is water driven. This old manorial mill is served by the Ravenglass and Eskdale Railway.
Open Apr-Oct, daily, Jun-Aug 10.30-5.30, Apr-May & Sep-Oct 11-5.
✤*£1.20 (ch 60p). Family ticket £3. Party 12+.*
🅿 ⅃ ❀ *(ex grounds)*

Hill Top
NEAR SAWREY
(2m S of Hawkshead)
☎ *(015394) 36269*
Beatrix Potter wrote many Peter Rabbit books in this little 17th-century house which contains her furniture and china.
Open Apr-Oct, Mon-Wed, Sat & Sun 11-5. Last admission 4.30pm. (Closed Thu & Fri (ex Good Fri).
£3.30 (ch £1.70)
🅿 *shop* ❀
(NT)

PENRITH
See Dacre

Wetheriggs Pottery
PENRITH
Clifton Dykes (4m S, off A6)
☎ *(01768) 892733*
Wetheriggs Country Pottery has been working since 1855 and is steeped in rich traditions and set in a nature conservation site. See top crafts people hand-throwing pots and take an educational tour around the surviving steam-powered pottery. Visitors have the opportunity to hand-throw their own pot. There are events throughout the year. Telephone for details.
Open from May 1995.
£3 (concessions)
🅿 💺 ✗ *licensed* ⅃ *toilets for disabled shop garden centre*

Ravenglass & Eskdale Railway
RAVENGLASS
(close to the A595)
☎ *(01229) 717171*
This narrow gauge (15inch) miniature steam railway was laid in the 19th century to carry iron ore from the mines at Boot. It began to carry passengers and then other freight, including quarried stone, once the mines were closed. The railway was given the nickname 'Owd Ratty' after its contractor, a man called Ratcliffe. It is now a passenger line, where both steam and diesel locomotives are used during the summer months to pull the open and saloon coaches. The railway runs through beautiful countryside for the seven mile journey from Ravenglass, on the coast, up to the terminus at Dalegarth. Purpose-built toilets for wheelchair users at Ravenglass and Eskdale. Special events for 1995 include: Family Day (27 May), Friends of Thomas Days (21-22 Oct).
Open: trains operate all year, daily. Closed 22-25 Dec.
Return fare £5.80 (ch 5-15 £2.90). Family ticket £14.50
🅿 *(charged)* 💺 ✗ *licensed* ⅃ *(special coaches - prior notice advisable) toilets for disabled shop*

Rydal Mount
RYDAL
(1.5m, on A5914 to Grasmere)
☎ *Ambleside (015394) 33002*
The family home of William Wordsworth from 1813 until his death in 1850, Rydal Mount incorporates a pre-1574 farmer's cottage. Now owned by a descendant of Wordsworth, the house contains an important group of family portraits, furniture, and many of the poet's personal possessions, together with first editions of his work. Placed in a lovely setting overlooking Windermere and Rydal Water, the house is surrounded by what have been described as the most interesting small gardens in England.

They were designed by Wordsworth himself. Evening visits for groups can be organised on request, including a tour of the house and gardens, with poetry readings, wine and gingerbread at a small charge.
Open Mar-Oct daily 9.30-5; Nov-Feb daily (ex Tue) 10-4 (Closed 10 Jan-1 Feb).
£2.50 (ch 10 £1, pen & student £2). Party 10+
🅿 ⅃ *shop* ❀

National Park Centre
SEDBERGH
72 Main St
☎ *(015396) 20125*
At the north-western corner of the Yorkshire Dales National Park, Sedbergh is set below the hills of the Howgill Fells. The rich natural history of the area and the beautiful scenery created a need for this Visitor Centre; maps, walks, guides, local information and interpretative displays are all found here. There is a full tourist information service.
Open Apr-Nov, weekdays and limited wknds 10-4.
Free.
🅿 *(charged)* ⅃ *(accessible with help Radar key scheme) toilets for disabled shop* ❀

The Sellafield Visitors Centre
SELLAFIELD
(off A595, signpposted)
☎ *Seascale (019467) 27027*
A fascinating insight into the world of nuclear power using audio-visual displays, working models and computer quizzes. Guides are available to answer questions. A range of activities and local art and craft events are planned.
Open all year, Apr-Oct daily 10-6, Nov-Mar daily 10-4. (Closed 25 Dec).
🅿 💺 ⅃ *toilets for disabled shop garden centre* ❀
Details not confirmed for 1995

Shap Abbey
SHAP
Shap Abbey was founded by the Premonastratensian order in 1199, and dedicated to St Mary Magdalene. The abbey was dissolved in 1540 and most of the ruins date from the 13th century, some of which are standing to first floor height. The most impressive feature is the 16th-century west tower of the church.
Open any reasonable time.
Free.
🅿 ⅃
(EH)

Sizergh Castle
SIZERGH
(3.5m S of Kendal)
☎ *Sedgwick (015395) 60070*
The castle has a 60-foot high pele tower,

built in the 14th century, but most of the castle dates from the 15th to the 18th centuries. There is a Great Hall and some panelled rooms with fine carved overmantles and adze-hewn floors. The gardens were laid out in the 18th century and contain the Trust's largest limestone rock garden.
Open 2 Apr-Oct, Sun-Thu 1.30-5.30; Garden open 12.30. Last admission 5pm. £3.30 (ch £1.70). Family ticket £9. Garden £1.70. Party 15+.
🅿 ⅃ *shop* ❀
(NT)

Hutton-in-the-Forest
SKELTON
(on B5305)
☎ *(017684) 84449*
Hutton-in-the-Forest is a beautiful historic house set in magnificent woods which were once part of the medieval forest of Inglewood. The house consists of a 14th-century pele tower with 17th-, 18th-, and 19th-century additions. Inside is a fine collection of furniture, paintings, tapestries and china, a 17th-century gallery and cupid staircase. The lovely 1730s walled garden is a wonderful setting for the large collection of herbaceous plants.
Open Etr Sun & Mon, 30 Apr-1 Oct Thu, Fri & Sun also Wed in Aug and BH Mons, 1-4. Grounds daily (ex Sat) 11-5. Groups any day booked in advance from Apr-Oct. £3.50 (accompanied ch 7 free, ch £1.50). Grounds £2 (ch free).
🅿 💺 *shop*

Acorn Bank Garden
TEMPLE SOWERBY
(N on A66)
☎ *(017683) 61893*
The small but delightful garden of some two and a half acres has a particularly interesting walled kitchen garden. It has been turned into a herb garden with an extensive collection of over 180 varieties of medicinal and culinary herbs. Scented plants are grown in the small greenhouse. A circular walk runs beside the Crowdundle Beck. The mill is being restored but is not yet open to visitors. Apple Day (21 October) celelbrates the different varieties and uses of the apple.
Open Apr-Oct, daily 10-5.30 (last admission 5).
£1.60 (ch 80p). Party.
🅿 ⅃ *toilets for disabled shop* ❀
(NT)

Townend
TROUTBECK
(on S outskirts)
☎ *(015394) 32628*
The house is one of the finest examples of a 'statesman' (wealthy yeoman) farmer's house in Cumbria. It was built in 1626 for George Browne, and the Browne family lived there until 1943. Inside is the original home-made carved furniture, with domestic utensils, letters and papers of the farm. A special event, Theatre at Townend (9-19 May), is planned for 1995.
Open 2 Apr-Oct, Tue-Fri, Sun & BH Mon 1-5 or dusk if earlier. Last admission 4.30pm.
£2.50 (ch £1.30). Family ticket £7.
🅿 ❀
(NT)

Conishead Priory
ULVERSTON
Priory Rd
☎ *(01229) 584029*
A Victorian Gothic mansion on the site of a medieval Augustinian Priory. Now a major Buddist centre, and under restoration, it has fine plaster ceilings, stained-glass windows, a cantilever staircase, Oak Room, vaulted hall and cloister. There is a private woodland walk to Morecambe Bay.
Open Etr-Sep, wknds & BH 2-5. (Closed 22-30 Jul, 5-6 Aug & 12-13 Aug).
✤*Admission free. House tour £1.50 (ch 75p & pen £1).*
🅿 💺 ⅃ *shop*

A stop on the picturesque 7-mile route of the Ravensglass and Eskdale narrow-guage railway is the restored, working Muncaster Mill – on a site occupied by a mill since 1470.

THE WORLD OF BEATRIX POTTER™

ATTRACTION

In 1995 visitors, to the World of Beatrix Potter, will come face-to-face with the dreaded Mr. McGregor in a brand new, walk-through, recreation of Peter Rabbit's garden. For the first time visitors will see, hear and SMELL the hay meadows, flower gardens and pine woods of Beatrix Potter's Lake District, whilst calling on Peter Rabbit and all his friends.

A video-wall, special film about Beatrix Potter's fascinating life, shop and Tailor of Gloucester Tea Room make this an attraction to remember.

OPEN ALL YEAR
EASTER - 30th Sept 10.00am - 6.30pm
Rest of Year 10.00 - 4.00pm. (Closed Xmas Day & 16-27 Jan)

The Old Laundry, Bowness-on-Windermere
Tel: (015394) 88444

Laurel & Hardy Museum
ULVERSTON
4c Upper Brook St
☎ (01229) 582292 & 861614
Ulverston was the birthplace of Stan Laurel, so perhaps it is not then so surprising that the town should boast the world's only Laurel and Hardy museum, now extended to more than double the original floor area. Exhibits include a display of Oliver Hardy memorabilia obtained from Harlem, Georgia (Ollie's birthplace), and waxwork figures of Laurel and Hardy from the House of Wax at Great Yarmouth. Newsreels and documentary films are shown continuously and hourly talks given on Laurel and Hardy. Special children's show at weekends and during school holidays. Voted the finest museum in the Lake District by The Telegraph.
Open all year, daily 10-4.30. (Closed 25 Dec).
P *(100 yds)* & *toilets for disabled shop*
Details not confirmed for 1995

Lake District National Park Visitor Centre
WINDERMERE
Brockhole (on A591, between Windermere and Ambleside)
☎ (015394) 46601
Brockhole, built in 1899 for a wealthy businessman, is a large house, set in 32 acres of landscaped gardens and grounds, standing on the eastern shore of Lake Windermere. It became England's first National Park Visitor Centre in 1969. Its purpose is to help vistors to enjoy and appreciate England's largest National Park. The Centre offers exhibitions, audio-visual programmes, lake cruises, an exciting adventure playground and an extensive events programme.
Open 6 Apr-5 Nov, daily 10-5pm. Grounds and gardens only open all year. Free.
P *(charged)* ⚑ ✗ *licensed* & *(scented garden) toilets for disabled shop*

Windermere Steamboat Museum
WINDERMERE
Rayrigg Rd (0.25m N Bowness Bay)
☎ (015394) 45565
A unique and historic collection of Victorian and Edwardian steamboats and vintage motorboats which reflects the enormous part boating has played over many years in the history of Lake Windermere - a popular lake for both motorboat and sailboat enthusiasts. Many of the exhibits in this extensive collection are still afloat and in working order, including the oldest steamboat in the world - the S L *Dolly* of 1850. There are special displays telling the social and commercial history of England's largest lake. Steamboat trips daily, weather permitting. Special events planned for 1995 include: monthly art exhibitions, Model Boat Rally (14-15 May), Classic Motor Boat Rally (4-6 August), Steam Boat Association Rally (August).
Open 29 Mar-5 Nov daily, 10-5. Steamboat trips subject to availability & weather.
£2.80 (ch £1.40, pen & students £2.50). Family ticket £7.50. Party 12+.
P ⚑ & *toilets for disabled shop*

Helena Thompson Museum
WORKINGTON
Park End Rd
☎ (01900) 62598
Costumes, glass, ceramics and other decorative arts and objects of local historical interest form the core of exhibits in this small museum. The items are displayed in a pleasant 18th-century house and temporary exhibitions are shown in the former stable block.
Open all year, Apr-Oct Mon-Sat 10.30-4; Nov-Mar 11-3. Parties by prior arrangement.
P & *toilets for disabled shop* ⚑
Details not confirmed for 1995

Magpie Mine
BAKEWELL
Sheldon (3m W off B5055)
☎ *Matlock (01629) 583834*
The surface remains of the mine are the best example in Britain of a 19th-century lead mine. It was last worked (unsuccessfully) in 1958, and then stabilised in the 1970s. For further information contact the Peak District Mining Museum, Matlock Bath, Derbyshire.
Open at all times.
Free.

Bolsover Castle
BOLSOVER
(on A632)
☎ *Chesterfield (01246) 823349*
The castle dates back to Norman times, but was rebuilt as a mock castle by Bess of Hardwick's son, in around 1613. His son and grandson continued work on the building, which is unusual because mock castles did not come into vogue until 200 years later. There are fine fireplaces, pseudo-Gothic vaulted ceilings, and ornate panelling. The 'star chamber' is so called because of the stars painted on the ceiling, while the Elysium room has a group of gods on the ceiling, and the Heaven room shows the Ascension of Christ, all elaborately done. There is also an attractive 170ft-long riding school, now used by Riding for the Disabled.
Open all year, Apr-Sep, daily 10-6; Oct 10-4; Nov-Mar, Wed-Sun 10-4. Closed 24-26 Dec & 1 Jan.
£2.20 (ch £1.10, pen, students & UB40 £1.70).
& *(keep not accessible)* ⚑
(EH)

Buxton Micrarium
BUXTON
The Crescent
☎ (01298) 78662
The Micrarium is a fascinating museum, and the first of its kind. Visitors view the displays through push-button, remote-controlled microscopes, seeing the wonders of nature magnified. Snowflakes, flower buds, minerals, crystals, fossils, feathers, live pond water specimens and butterfly wings can all be examined.
Open 8 Apr-29 Oct, daily 10-5.
£2.50 (ch £1.50 & pen £2)
P *(200yds)* & *shop* ⚑

Poole's Cavern (Buxton Country Park)
BUXTON
Green Ln
☎ (01298) 26978
The natural limestone cavern lies in 100 acres of woodland. The cave is 1,000 feet in length, with only 16 steps, making it suitable for all ages. There is a conducted tour with a guide that takes

about 40 minutes. It is rich in beautiful formations which include thousands of stalactites and stalagmites. An exhibition of artefacts from the cave dig, covering the Stone Age to Roman times, also includes the story of limestone and a display of British minerals and fossils.
Open Good Fri-end Oct, daily 10-5. (Closed Wed in Apr, May & Oct).
P ⚑ & *(wheelchairs available) toilets for disabled shop* ⚑ *(ex in woodland)*
Details not confirmed for 1995

Calke Abbey
CALKE
(9m S of Derby, on A514)
☎ *Melbourne (01332) 863822*
This fine baroque mansion dating from the early 18th century was built for Sir John Harpur and remained the family home until its acquisition by the National Trust who describe it as the 'house that time forgot'. Among its treasures are an extensive natural history collection, a magnificent Chinese silk state bed (its hangings in mint condition), and a spectacular red and white drawing room. The house stands in extensive wooded parkland and also has walled flower gardens. An open-air concert will be held 22 July 1995.
Open Apr-Oct Sat-Wed (incl BH Mon); House & church 1-5.30 Gardens from 11am. Last admission 5pm. Park open all year, Apr-Oct closes 9pm or dusk if earlier, Nov-Mar closes at dusk.
£4.50 (charged) ✗ & *toilets for disabled shop* ⚑
(NT)

Blue-John Cavern & Mine
CASTLETON
Buxton Rd
☎ *Hope Valley (01433) 620638 & 620642*
The cavern is a remarkable example of a water-worn cave, and measures over a third of a mile long, with chambers 200ft high. It contains 8 of the 14 veins of Blue John stone, and has been the major source of this unique form of fluorspar for nearly 300 years.
Open all year daily 9.30-6 (or dusk) (telephone for Jan & Feb opening times). Conducted tours every 10-15 mins, tour takes 40-45 mins. Closed 25-26 Dec & 1 Jan).
❄*£3.50 (ch £1.50, pen £2.50). Party. shop*

Peak Cavern
CASTLETON
(on A625)
☎ *Hope Valley (01433) 620285*
This is one of the most spectacular natural limestone caves in the Peak District, and has an electrically-lit underground walk of about half a mile. Ropes have been made for over 500 years in the 'Grand Entrance Hall', and traces of a row of cottages can be seen.
Open Etr-end Oct, daily 10-5.
£3 (ch & pen £2)
P *shop*

Peveril Castle
CASTLETON
Market Place
☎ Hope Valley (01433) 620613
Henry II built the keep in the 12th century. It stands in an impregnable-looking position high above the town, and gives magnificent views.
Open all year, Apr-Sep, daily 10-6; Oct 10-4; Nov-Mar, daily 10-4. Closed 24-26 Dec & 1 Jan.
£1.30 (ch 70p, concession £1)
⌖
(EH)

Speedwell Cavern
CASTLETON
Winnats Pass (off A625, 0.5m W of Castleton Village)
☎ Hope Valley (01433) 620512
Visitors descend 105 steps to a boat which takes them on a one-mile underground exploration of the floodlit cavern with its 'bottomless pit'.
Open all year, daily 9.30-5. (Closed 25 Dec).
£4 (ch 14 £2.50). £4.50 (ch £2.75) at peak times ie wknds, BH's & school holidays).
🅿 shop

Treak Cliff Cavern
CASTLETON
(.75m W on A625)
☎ Hope Valley (01433) 620571
Discover the rich deposits of the rare and beautiful Blue John Stone and fine stalactites and stalagmites on a guided tour of the Caverns, which are illuminated by electric lighting and have safe, clean footpaths. The Dream Cave, Alladin's Cave, Fairyland Grotto, the Seven Dwarfs, the Fossil Cave, the Dome of St Paul's, the Witches Cave and the 'Pillar' - the largest piece of Blue John ever found are all seen in the quarter of a mile tour which lasts about 40 minutes.
Open all year, Mar-Oct daily 9.30-5.30,
Nov-Feb daily 10-4. (Closed 25 Dec). All tours are guided & last about 40 mins.
£3.95 (ch 5-15 £1.95, students £2.50, pen £3). Group 10+
🅿 ♨ shop

Chatsworth
CHATSWORTH
☎ Baslow (01246) 582204
Chatsworth is the palatial home of the Duke and Duchess of Devonshire, and has one of the richest collections of fine and decorative arts in private hands. Inside there is a splendid painted hall, and a great staircase leads to the even finer chapel, which is decorated with marble, paintings, statues and paintings on walls and ceiling. There are magnificent pictures, furniture and porcelain, and a memorable *trompe l'oeil* painting of a violin on the music room door.
The park is one of the finest in Britain. It was laid out by 'Capability' Brown, but is most famous as the work of Joseph Paxton (later Sir Joseph), who became head gardener in the 19th century. Notable features include the Cascade and the Emperor Fountain, which sends up a jet of water to 290ft. Other attractions are the farming and forestry exhibition and the adventure playground. Guided tours are available at extra cost. Numerous events planned for 1995 include: Chatsworth Angling Fair (13-14 May), Country Fair (2-3 September).
Open - House & Garden open 21 Mar-29 Oct, daily 11-4.30. Farmyard & Adventure Playground, 21 Mar-1 Oct 10.30-4.30.
❋ House & Garden £5.75 (ch £3, students & pen £5). Family ticket £15. Garden only £3 (ch £1.50, students & pen £2.50). Family ticket £8. Farmyard & Adventure Playground £2.20. Car park £1.
🅿 (charged) ♨ ✗ licensed ♿ (2 electric wheelchairs available for garden) toilets for disabled shop garden centre ⌖ (ex park & gardens)

Peacock Information & Heritage Centre
CHESTERFIELD
Low Pavement
☎ (01246) 207777
The centre is housed in a medieval timber-framed building which is thought to have been a guildhall before becoming the Peacock Inn. The first floor is now used as an exhibition room, and a video on the history of Chesterfield is available on request. The Tourist Information Centre is situated on the ground floor.
Open all year, Mon-Sat. Information Centre Etr-Jun 9-5.30; Jul & Aug 9-6; Sep-Oct 9-5.30 & Nov-Etr 9-5. Heritage Centre Mon-Sat 11-4. (Closed 25-27 Dec & 1 Jan).
Free.
P (town centre) ♿ shop

Creswell Crags Visitor Centre
CRESWELL
off Crags Rd (1m E off B6042)
☎ Worksop (01909) 720378
The deep narrow gorge of Creswell Crags is pitted with 24 caves and rock shelters which were used for seasonal camps by Stone Age hunter-gatherers. Unusual finds from within the caves include pieces of decorated animal bone and the remains of animals which have long since become extinct, such as the woolly mammoth and hyena. A visitor centre at one end of the gorge explains the importance of the site, with an exhibition and an audio-visual showing what life was like in prehistoric times. From there, a trail leads through the gorge, where visitors can look into the caves through grills; guided cave tours are organised throughout the year. There is a picnic site at the centre, and various events are held.
Open all year, Feb-Oct, daily, 10.30-4.30; Nov-Jan, Sun only 10.30-4.30.
Free (under review). Cave/site tour £2 (ch £1.50).
🅿 ♿ (wheelchair loan) toilets for disabled shop

National Tramway Museum
CRICH
Matlock Rd (off B5035)
☎ Ambergate (01773) 852565
This unique 'action stop' offers a mile-long scenic journey through a period street to open countryside with panoramic views. Visitors can enjoy unlimited tram rides. The exhibition hall houses the largest national collection of vintage electric trams from home and abroad. Other attractions include a video theatre, shops, cafe, a playground and picnic areas. There is plenty to see and do, both indoors and outdoors. Events planned for 1995 include: VE Day, Tramathon, '999' Day, treasure hunt, transport gathering, starlight special. Please telephone for dates.
Open Sun only Mar, daily Apr-Oct (closed some Fri's in Apr, May, Sep & Oct), 10-5.30 (6.30 Sat, Sun & BH).
❋ £4.50 (ch £2.60, pen £3.80). Family ticket £11.70.
🅿 ♨ ♿ (ex trams) toilets for disabled shop

Cromford Mill
CROMFORD
Mill Ln
☎ Matlock (01629) 824297
Sir Richard Arkwright established the world's first successful water-powered cotton mill at Cromford in 1771. The Arkwright Society are involved in a major restoration to create a lasting monument to an extraordinary genius.
Open all year, daily 9.30-5 (Closed 25 Dec). Guided tours 11-4.
🅿 ✗ ♿ toilets for disabled shop
Details not confirmed for 1995

Denby Pottery Visitors Centre
DENBY
Derby Rd (8m N, on B6179)
☎ Ripley (01773) 743644
Guided factory tours show the intricate skills of the potters craft, including throwing, turning, glazing and decorating.

The museum illustrates the history of Denby Pottery. There is a large factory shop selling Denby products. Within the courtyard area are the self service restaurant, a Dartington Crystal Factory Shop, a florist and children's play area. Please check tour times and availabilty prior to arriving at the visitor centre.
Open all year. Full factory tours, Mon-Thu 10.30 &1, Fri 11am. Craftroom only, daily 9.30-3.30. Craftsman's Pantry, daily 9.30-5. Factory shop, Mon-Sat 9-5, Tue 9.30-5, Sun 11-5.
Factory tours £3.10 (ch & pen £2.10). Craftroom only £2.10 (ch & pen 60p). Party 10+.
🅿 ♨ ♿ (lift) toilets for disabled shop ⌖

Derby Museum & Art Gallery
DERBY
The Strand
☎ (01332) 255586 & 255587
The museum has a wide range of displays, notably of Derby porcelain and of paintings by the local artist Joseph Wright (1734-97). Also antiquities, natural history and militaria, as well as many temporary exhibitions. In 1995 there will be a special exhibition commemorating the 250th anniversary of the 1745 Uprising (23 September-7 January 1996).
Open all year, Mon 11-5, Tue-Sat 10-5, Sun & BHs 2-5. (Closed 25-27 Dec).
Free.
P ♿ (lift to all floors) toilets for disabled shop ⌖

Industrial Museum
DERBY
The Silk Mill, off Full St
☎ (01332) 255308
The museum is set in an early 18th-century silk mill and adjacent flour mill. Displays cover local mining, quarrying and industries, and include a major collection of Rolls Royce aero-engines from 1915 to the present. There is also a new railway section. Temporary exhibitions are held.
Open all year, Mon 11-5, Tue-Sat 10-5, Sun & BHs 2-5. (Closed 25-27 Dec).
Free.
🅿 ♿ (lift to all floors) toilets for disabled shop ⌖

Pickford's House Social History Museum
DERBY
41 Friar Gate
☎ (01332) 255363
The house was built in 1770 by the architect Joseph Pickford as a combined workplace and family home, and stands in Derby's most handsome street. Pickford's house now shows domestic life at different periods, with Georgian reception rooms and service areas and a 1930s bathroom. Other galleries are devoted to temporary exhibitions, especially on social history, textiles and costume themes. There is also a display on the growth of Georgian Derby, and on Pickford's contribution to Midlands architecture. The garden has been reconstructed in the Georgian style.
Open all year, Mon 11-5, Tue-Sat 10-5, Sun & BHs 2-5. Times may vary, telephone for details.
Free.
🅿 ♿ shop ⌖

Elvaston Castle Country Park
ELVASTON
Borrowash Rd (signposted from A6 & A52)
☎ Derby (01332) 571342
The 200-acre park was landscaped in the early 19th century, and became one of Britain's first country parks in 1968. Restored after 30 years of neglect, it includes elaborate topiary gardens from the 19th-century scheme, and a walled kitchen garden now planted out as an Old English Garden with herbaceous borders, roses and scented herbs. The old estate workshops have been restored as an Estate Museum, with exhibitions of blacksmithing, saddlery and other traditional crafts associated with country houses at the turn of the century. There

are also nature trails and numerous walks, exhibitions and displays, and a caravan and campsite. A full list of events is available on request.
Open all year, daily dawn-dusk. Museum, Etr-Oct, Wed-Sat 1-4.30, Sun & BH's 11-4.30.
Museum: £1.20 (ch & pen 60p). Family ticket £3.
🅿 (charged) 🍴 ♿ *toilets for disabled shop*

Eyam Hall
EYAM
(W of church)
☎ *Hope Valley (01433) 631976*
A beautiful 17th-century manor house built and still occupied by the Wright family. It is a cosy and intimate house with a stone-flagged hall, Jacobean staircase and old kitchen. Numerous items of furniture, portraits, tapestries and objects of interest, accumulated over the centuries, are on display. A series of concerts, plays and themed events are

planned for 1995.
Open 2 Apr-29 Oct, Wed, Thu, Sun & BH Mon & Tue 11-4.30 (last tour).
£3.25 (ch £2.25, pen & concessions £2.75). Family ticket £9.50. Party.
🅿 🍴 ♿ *(disabled may enter by special gate, avoiding steps) toilets for disabled shop* ⊗ *(ex in grounds)*

Haddon Hall
HADDON HALL
(1.5 S of Bakewell off A6)
☎ *Bakewell (01629) 812855*
Romantic, battlemented Haddon Hall is like a house trapped in time: it has hardly changed for 400 years. It was started in the 12th century; then in the 18th century it was left to lie fallow by its owners, who were Earls and then Dukes of Rutland. They lived at Belvoir Castle instead, leaving Haddon Hall as perhaps the most perfect example of a medieval manor house in England. The oldest part is the painted chapel; the kitchen and the banqueting hall with its minstrels' gallery are of the 14th century; and there is a later long gallery leading to beautiful terraced rose gardens. Dorothy Vernon, a daughter of the house, is said to have eloped from here with John Manners in 1567. The steps and bridge linked with the elopement were not built until the 17th century - but the marriage of Dorothy and John certainly took place, so perhaps the story is true.
Open Apr-Sep, daily (Mon-Sat in Jul-Aug) 11-5.45. Last entry 5pm.
£4.50 (ch £2.80 & pen £3.50). Family ticket £12.50. Party 20+.
🅿 *(charged)* 🍴 *shop* ⊗

See advertisement on page 35

Hardwick Hall
HARDWICK HALL
(2m S M1 Junc 29)
☎ *Chesterfield (01246) 850430*
The splendid Elizabethan mansion is celebrated as the creation of Bess of Hardwick, a redoubtable character, who was married and widowed four times and became immensely rich in the process. She began the magnificent building at 70 after the death of her fourth husband, the Earl of Shrewsbury. They quarrelled and separated, but he left her even richer than before.
The house is remarkable for its vast area of windows, which become taller from the ground floor up. The six towers are topped by Bess's monogram, ES. Inside, the house and contents, such as Bess's great jewel chest, have escaped change because her descendants lived mainly at Chatsworth instead. The High Great Chamber and the long gallery were probably designed to display the tapestries which line them. The latter room is also hung with Cavendish portraits. There are numerous other tapestries, with some fine needlework by Bess and her ladies, and by Mary, Queen of Scots, who was the Earl of Shrewsbury's prisoner for 15 years. In the kitchen are hundreds of 18th-and 19th-century pots, pans and plates, all marked with a ducal coronet. The gardens are laid out in walled courtyards, and there is a large park.
Open Apr-Oct Wed, Thu, Sat, Sun & BH Mon 12.30-5 or sunset. (Closed Good Fri). Last admission 4.30pm. Garden Apr-end Oct daily 12-5.30. Park all year daily dawn-dusk. Car park gates close 6pm. House & garden £5.50 (ch £2.70). Family ticket £13.70. Garden only £2 (ch £1)
🅿 ✗ *licensed* ♿ *toilets for disabled shop* ⊗ *(ex in park)*
(NT)

American Adventure Theme Park
ILKESTON
Pit Ln
☎ *Langley Mill (01773) 769931 & 531521*
This is one of Britain's few fully themed parks, based on the legend of a whole continent. The experiences of a day out here are widely varied, from the heartpounding action of the Missile Rollercoaster in Spaceport USA, to the wet and wild excitement of the Great Niagara Rapids ride and the Cherokee Falls log flume. Take a gentle excursion across Lake Reflection aboard a Mississippi paddle steamer, watch a shoot-out in Silver City, see the glamorous Lazy Lil's Saloon Show, or experience the carnival atmosphere of Mexicoland.
Open from 26 Mar. Telephone for details.
✳*£10.99 (ch 4 free). Party 12+.*
🅿 🍴 ✗ *licensed* ♿ *(free wheelchair hire) toilets for disabled shop* ⊗

Kedleston Hall
KEDLESTON HALL
(5m NW of Derby)
☎ *Derby (01332) 842191*
Thought by many to be the finest Robert Adam house in the country, Kedleston has been the Derbyshire home of the Curzon family for over eight centuries. The original house was demolished at the end of the 17th century when the rather muddled start to the building of the present mansion began. The architect

Matthew Brettingham gave Kedleston its present day plan of a main block and two wings linked by corridors; James Paine is responsible for the imposing north front. It wasn't until 1760 that Adam appeared on the scene. He built the south front and designed most of the interior including the awe-inspiring marble hall, regarded as one of the most splendid rooms in Europe. There are some notable pictures, furniture and china displayed in the house together with an Indian Museum containing the collection accumulated by Lord Curzon, Viceroy of India from 1898 to 1905. The charming boathouse and bridge in the gardens were also designed by Adam. A flock of Canada Geese complement the scene.
Open - House; Apr-Oct, Sat-Wed 1-5.30, last admission 5pm, (closed Good Fri). Garden; same as house but open 11-6. Park; Apr-Oct daily 11-6, Nov-17 Dec, Sat & Sun 12-4 (entry charge £2 on Thu,Fri & during Nov-Dec).
£4.20 (ch £2.10). Family ticket £10.50.
🅿 ✗ *licensed* ♿ *toilets for disabled shop* ⊗ *(ex in park)*
(NT)

Lea Gardens
LEA
(3m SE Matlock off A6)
☎ *Dethick (01629) 534380*
Three and a half acres of attractive woodland gardens with rhododendrons, azaleas and rock plants are open for public enjoyment. A Music Day is planned for 11 June 1995.
Open 20 Mar-16 Jul, daily 10-7.
✳*£2.50 (ch 50p, disabled free). Season ticket £3.50*
🅿 🍴 ♿ *shop garden centre*

Riber Castle Wildlife Park
MATLOCK
(off A615)
☎ *(01629) 582073*
The wildlife park is set in the grounds of ruined 19th-century Riber Castle on 853ft-high Riber Hill and enjoys magnificent views over the Derwent Valley and towards Crich Stand. The park houses a unique collection of animal and birds - rare and endangered species such as lynx, otters, reindeer, wild boar and owls live happily alongside marmots, Shetland ponies, goats, tortoises, wallabies, rabbits and many more. Ornamental pheasants, peafowl and emus can also be seen. Many breeding programmes are in progress. There are daily 'meet a keeper' events with an animal or bird, times and locations are advertised at the gatehouse.
Open all year, daily from 10am. (Summer last admission 5pm, winter 3-4.30pm). Closed 25 Dec.
✳*£3.80 (ch 5-15 £2, pen £3).*
🅿 🍴 ♿ *toilets for disabled shop* ⊗ *(in animal section)*

Heights of Abraham
MATLOCK BATH
(on A6)
☎ *Matlock (01629) 582365*
High on a hill above the village of Matlock Bath are the Grounds of the Heights of Abraham. Until recently the climb to the summit was only for the very energetic, but now alpine-style cable cars provide a leisurely and spectacular way of reaching the top from their starting point near Matlock Bath Railway Station. Once inside the Grounds there is plenty to do for the whole family. Two famous show caverns provide fascinating tours, one is introduced by a multivision programme and the other tells the story of a 17th-century lead miner. A coffee shop, licensed restaurant and picnic sites take advantage of the superb views. There is also a nature trail, the Victoria Prospect Tower and play area, the Owl Maze, the Explorers Challenge and landscaped water gardens.
Open daily Etr-Oct 10-5 (later in high season) for Autumn & Winter opening telephone for details.
Prices under review.

➤

P ♨ ✗ licensed ♿ toilets for disabled shop

Peak District Mining Museum
MATLOCK BATH
The Pavilion (off A6)
☎ Matlock (01629) 583834
A large and rewarding display, ideal for families, explains the history of the Derbyshire lead industry from Roman times to the present day. The geology of the area, mining and smelting processes, the quarrying and the people who worked in the industry, are all illustrated by a series of static and moving exhibits and an audio-visual display. The museum also features an early 19th-century water pressure pumping engine - the only one of its kind in Britain.
Open all year, daily 11-4 (later in summer season). (Closed 25 Dec).
Museum & Mine :£3 (ch, students, disabled & pen £2.25). Family £7. Party.
Museum only or mine only £2 (ch, students, disabled £1.50). Party.
🅿 (charged) ♿ shop

Temple Mine
MATLOCK BATH
Temple Rd (off A6)
☎ Matlock (01629) 583834
In the process of being restored to how it was in the 1920s and 1930s, this old lead and fluorspar workings makes interesting viewing. A self-guided tour illustrates the geology, mineralisation and mining techniques.
Open all year, Oct-Mar, daily 11-4, visits at 12 & 2 only.
Museum & Mine :£3 (ch, pen, disabled £2.25). Family ticket £7. Museum only or mine only: £2 (ch, pen, disabled £1.50) shop

Melbourne Hall
MELBOURNE
(9m S of Derby on A514)
☎ Derby (01332) 862502
In 1133 Henry I gave his royal manor of Melbourne to the first Bishop of Carlisle; hence the surprisingly large parish church of St Michael and St Mary. The lease was then sold to Sir John Coke (Charles I's Secretary of State) in 1628 and the house is still owned by his descendants. Through the centuries the hall has been converted from manor house to a much grander residence which has been the home of two of Britain's most famous Prime Ministers: Lord Melbourne and Lord Palmerston. It features fine collections of pictures and antique furniture, but its chief appeal is its intimate and 'lived in' atmosphere. The glorious formal gardens are among the finest in Britain, and were laid out in about 1720 by royal gardeners London and Wise, who followed the style of the great French garden designer, Le Nôtre.

Special events are usually held each Sunday afternoon in August.
Open, house daily throughout Aug only (ex first three Mons) 2-5. Prebooked parties by appointment in Aug. Gardens Apr-Sep, Wed, Sat, Sun & BH Mon 2-6.
House Tue-Sat (guided tour) £2.50 (ch £1, pen £2), Sun & BH Mon (no guided tour) £2 (ch 75p, pen £1.50). House & Garden (Aug only) £3.50 (ch £2, pen £3). Garden only £2 (pen £1). Family £5.
🅿 (200 yds) ♨ ♿ shop

Middleton Top Engine House
MIDDLETON BY WIRKSWORTH
Middleton Top Visitor Centre (0.5m S from B5036 Cromford/Wirksworth road)
☎ Wirksworth (01629) 823204
Set above the village of Middleton, site of one of Britain's very few limestone mines, a beam engine built in 1829 for the Cromford and High Peak Railway can be seen in its octagonal engine house. The engine's job was to haul wagons up the Middleton Incline, and its last trip was in 1963 after 134 years' work. The visitor centre tells the story of this historic railway, and there is also a picnic area alongside the High Peak Trail, popular with cyclists, walkers and riders.
Open: High Peak Trail all year; Information Centre, wknds all year, wkdays in summer; Bicycle hire, summer season daily (Etr-Dec wknds only). Engine House Etr-Oct first wknd in month (engine in motion).
Static Engine 35p (ch 15p). Working Engine 60p (ch 30p).
🅿 (charged) ♿ (ex Engine house) toilets for disabled shop

Revolution House
OLD WHITTINGTON
High St (on B6052 off A61, signposted)
☎ Chesterfield (01246) 453554 & 559727
Originally the Cock and Pynot alehouse, this 17th century cottage was the scene of a meeting between local noblemen to plan their part in the Revolution of 1688. The house is now furnished in 17th-century style. A video relates the story of the Revolution and there is a small exhibition room.
Open 14 Apr-29 Oct, daily 10-4. Xmas opening 16 -24 Dec & 27 Dec-2 Jan, daily.
Free.
P (100yds) shop

Midland Railway Centre
RIPLEY
Butterley Station (1m N on B6179)
☎ (01773) 747674 & 749788
This centre not only operates a regular steam-train passenger service, but also provides the focal point for a fascinating industrial museum project. Its aim is to depict every aspect of the golden days of the Midland Railway, and its successors.

The working section of the railway line extends for some three and a half miles between Butterley Station and Riddings. Exhibits range from the steam locomotives of 1866 to an electric locomotive of 1986. There is also a large section of rolling stock spanning the last 100 years. 'Specials' run from the centre include Wine and Dine trains and Santa Specials. Also of interest is the narrow-gauge railway, an award-winning country park and a farm park. Special events throughout 1995 include special events celebrating the 25th anniversary of the Midland Railway Trust, Friends of Thomas the Tank Engine Days, vintage weekends and a miniature railway event.
Open: trains operate all year Sun; Mar-Oct & Dec Sat; 12-23 Apr, 27 May-4 Jun, 18 Jul-3 Sep & 21-29 Oct daily; 6 Jun-Jul Tue-Sun. Train times 11.15-4.15.
✽£5.95 (pen £4.95). Two children free with each adult. Party 15+.
🅿 ♨ ♿ (special accommodation on trains) toilets for disabled shop

Sudbury Hall
SUDBURY
(6m E of Uttoxeter)
☎ Burton-on-Trent (01283) 585305
This fine country house was started in 1664 by Lord George Vernon. It has unusual diapered brickwork, a carved two-storey stone frontispiece, a cupola and a large number of tall chimneys. The interior is particularly interesting, with work by some of the best craftsmen of the day: there are plasterwork ceilings by Bradbury and Pettifer, ceiling paintings by Laguerre, a fine carved staircase by Edward Pierce and an overmantel by Grinling Gibbons. The Museum of Childhood, also run by the National Trust, contains a Victorian schoolroom,

collections of toys since the Victorian era, and displays depicting the working lives of children in the early 19th century.
Open Apr-29 Oct, Wed-Sun & BH Mons, 1-5.30 or sunset, last admission 5pm. (Closed Good Fri & Tue after BH Mons). Gardens 12.30-6.
✽House £3.20 (ch £1.60). Family ticket £8. Museum of Childhood £2. Joint ticket £4.40. Joint Family ticket £11. Party
🅿 ♨ ♿ toilets for disabled shop (ex in grounds)
(NT)

Wirksworth Heritage Centre
WIRKSWORTH
Crown Yard
☎ (01629) 825225
The Centre has been created in an old silk and velvet mill. The three floors of the mill have interpretative displays of the town's past history as the hub of a prosperous lead-mining industry. Each floor offers many features of interest including a computer game called 'Rescue the injured lead-miner' and a mock-up of a natural cavern. The lifestyle of a quarryman in the early 1900's is recreated in the Quarryman's House Place. Some unusual local customs such as tap dressing and 'clypping the church' are explained. There are also workshops showing the skills of cabinetmakers and a silversmiths. If you visit Wirksworth during Spring Bank Holiday, you can also see the famous Well Dressings.
Open 11 Feb-7 Apr & Nov-3 Dec, Wed-Sat 11-4, Sun 1-4; 8 Apr-21 Jul & 12 Sep-29 Oct, Tue-Sat 10.30-4.30, Sun 1-4.30 also bank hol Sun & Mon; 22 Jul-10 Sep, daily 10-5. Last admission 45 mins before closing.
90p (ch & pen 60p) Family ticket £2.40. Party 20+.
P (80 yds) ♨ ✗ licensed shop

DEVON

North Devon Maritime Museum
APPLEDORE
Odun House, Odun Rd
☎ Bideford (01237) 474852
Appledore's traditional activities of boat-building and fishing make the village a suitable home for the museum. Each room shows a different aspect of North Devon's maritime history, including steam and motor coasters. There is also a full-size reconstruction of an Appledore kitchen of around 1900. A Victorian schoolroom, recreating an Appledore schoolroom c1890-1900, is available (with costumes) for school parties.
Open Etr-Oct, daily 2-5, May-Sep, Mon-Fri 11-1pm. Also Thu eves in Aug 7pm-9.15pm.
P (opposite) shop
Details not confirmed for 1995

The family home of Lord Melbourne, Queen Victoria's prime minister, Melbourne Hall sits in formal gardens, with tree-lined vistas, velvet lawns, fountains and an exquisite wrought-iron pergola.

Arlington Court
ARLINGTON
(7m NE of Barnstaple, on A39)
☎Shirwell (01271) 850296
Built in 1822, Arlington Court is filled with a fascinating collection of *objets d'art*: pewter, shells and model ships as well as furniture and costumes from the 19th century. The biggest attraction, however, is the collection of carriages and horsedrawn vehicles, and rides are available. Around the house is a landscaped park grazed by Shetland ponies and sheep. There is a Victorian garden and a conservatory, and nature trails may be followed through the woods and by the lake.
Open Apr-Oct, Sun-Fri 11-5.30; also Sat of BH wknds. Footpaths through Park open all year during daylight hours. House & grounds £4.60. Grounds only £2.40.
P ✗ *licensed* & *(wheelchairs available - ramped steps at house) toilets for disabled shop ⌀ (ex in park)*
(NT)

Marwood Hill Gardens
BARNSTAPLE
(signposted off A361)
☎(01271) 42528
The gardens with their three small lakes cover 18 acres and have many rare trees and shrubs. There is a large bog garden and a walled garden, collections of clematis, camellias and eucalyptus. Alpine plants are also a feature, and there are plants for sale.
Open daily dawn to dusk.
£2 (ch 12 free if accompanied, pen £1.50).
P ⛻ & *garden centre*

Pecorama Pleasure Gardens
BEER
Underleys
☎Seaton (01297) 21542
The gardens are high on a hillside, overlooking the delightful fishing village of Beer. A miniature steam and diesel passenger line offers visitors a stunning view of Lyme Bay as it runs through the Pleasure Gardens. These feature 'Melody Close' and the 'Top Spot' where entertainment is staged during high season. Other attractions include an aviary, putting green, crazy golf and children's activity area. The main building

houses an exhibition of railway modelling in various small gauges, displayed in settings around the house and gardens. There are souvenir and railway model shops, plus full catering facilities. In 1995 a circus skills workshop will be held 13-25 August (except Saturdays).
Open Etr-Oct (including Autumn Half Term) , Mon-Fri 10-5.30, Sat 10-1. Also Sun at Etr, Whitsun & early Sep.
❋*Admission fee payable. Disabled helper free.*
P ⛻ ✗ *licensed* & *toilets for disabled shop* ⌀

Gorse Blossom Miniature Railway and Woodland Park
BICKINGTON
(off A38, W of Newton Abbot)
☎(01626) 821361
Unlimited rides are allowed on the three-quarters of a mile, seven and a quarter inch gauge steam railway line, set amid 35 acres of woodland, about half of which is open to the public. Other attractions include a remarkable outdoor model railway in a mountain setting, based on a line through the Swiss Alps; woodland walks, a nature trail, woodland assault course and giant slide, toytown village and children's play area.
Open 9 Apr-8 Oct, daily 10-last admission 4.
£3.50 (ch 3-15 £2.50 & pen £3)
P ⛻ & *toilets for disabled shop* ⌀

Bickleigh Castle
BICKLEIGH
(off A396 take A3072 from Bickleigh Bridge)
☎(01884) 855363
The 'castle' is really a moated and fortified manor house, and was formerly the romantic home of the heirs of the Earls of Devon and later of the Carew family. The small detached thatched chapel is said to be the oldest complete building in Devon. It dates from the Norman period and, like the medieval Gatehouse, survived the destruction which followed the Civil War. The Carew family acquired the house in the 16th century, and it was Admiral Sir George Carew who commanded the *Mary Rose* on her first and last voyage. He drowned with his men when the ship capsized and sank. There is an exhibition on the ship and on Tudor maritime history, with a

feature on the *Titanic* and model ships of bygone days. Also in the house is a museum of domestic objects and toys from the 18th century onwards, and a display of gadgets used by World War II spies and POWs and one of the most complete collections known. More traditional features of interest include the Great Hall, armoury (including fine Civil War armour), guardroom, Elizabethan bedroom and the 17th-century farmhouse. The garden is moated and the tower can be climbed for views of the Exe Valley and of the castle complex.
Open Etr wk (Good Fri-Fri), then Wed, Sun & BH to late May BH, then daily (ex Sat) to 2 Oct.
£3.50 (ch 5-15 £1.80). Family ticket £9.50. Party 20+
P & *(specially arranged tours with experienced guide) shop* ⌀

Bicton Park Gardens
BICTON
East Budleigh (2m N of Budleigh Salterton on B3178)
☎Colaton Raleigh (01395) 568465
Bicton Park offers many attractions, but the central one is over 50 acres of colourful gardens, shrubs, woodlands, lakes, ponds and fountains, with an Italian garden and a wonderful restored palm house. This has tropical and sub-tropical areas, where bananas and other exotica flourish. There are also fuchsia, geranium and temperate houses.
A modern building houses the James Countryside Museum, which has farm tools, wagons and a cider press among its fascinating displays. Not to be forgotten either are the fun world and adventure playground, the Fabulous Forest indoor children's play area, Bicton Woodland Railway, crazy golf, bird garden and tropical house. There is also an open-air arena for equestrian and other events.
Open all year 10-6.
£3.75 (ch 3-15 & pen £2.75). Family ticket £12. Party.
P ✗ *licensed* & *(adapted carriage on woodland railway, wheelchairs) toilets for disabled shop garden centre*

Exmoor Animal & Bird Gardens
BLACKMOOR GATE
South Stowford (off A399)
☎Parracombe (01598) 763352
These natural and landscaped gardens cover an area of 12 and a half acres with a waterfall, streams and a lake with penguins, swans and other water birds, all roaming at liberty. There are aviaries with tropical and exotic birds, and many animal enclosures containing lemurs, marmosets, capybara, rabbits, pigs, tamarins and many more. Set aside from the gardens is Tarzanland for the children.
Open daily, Apr-Oct 10-6; Nov-Mar 10-4. Closed 25 Dec.
£3.50 (ch 3-16 £2, under 3 free, pen £2.75).
P ⛻ & *toilets for disabled shop* ⌀

Parke Rare Breeds Farm
BOVEY TRACEY
Parke Estate (off B3344)
☎(01626) 833909
Over 200 acres of parkland in the wooded valley of the River Bovey make a beautiful setting for the farm, which was established to preserve pure old breeds of domestic animals. Some of the breeds at Parke were common in the Middle Ages, and can be traced back to prehistoric times. They may not be very commercial, but they are an essential reservoir of genes which have been lost in the development of modern farm breeds. In the walled garden there is a fascinating collection of poultry, peafowl, ducks and geese, while in the fields there are pigs, goats, sheep and cattle, including the rare Belted Welsh Black cattle. There is also a pets' corner and a play area. Another great attraction of Parke is the walks which can be taken through woodland beside the river and along the route of the old railway track.

The headquarters of the Dartmoor National Park is also here, and has an information centre.
Open Apr-Oct, daily 10-5 (last admission 4).
Admission charged.
P ⛻ & *toilets for disabled shop*
(NT)

Brixham Museum
BRIXHAM
Bolton Cross
☎(01803) 856267
A museum of general local interest, including the history of fishing and shipbuilding in Brixham.
Open Etr-Oct, Mon-Sat 10-5.
❋*£1.20 (ch & pen 60p). Family ticket £3. P (200 yds)* & *(ramps) shop*

Buckfast Abbey
BUCKFASTLEIGH
☎(01364) 642519
The story of Buckfast Abbey is a remarkable one. The monastery was originally founded in 1018, but the monks left during the Dissolution in the 16th century. Monks returned to the site in 1882 and considered restoring it; in 1907 four (mostly inexperienced) monks began rebuilding the church; and now Buckfast Abbey is once again a religious community. The church was built on the old foundations, using local blue limestone and Ham Hill stone. One of the most beautiful features is the great modern east window, which was the work of Father Charles, a craftsman in stained glass. Other monks have other skills: in beekeeping, farming, and the making of Buckfast tonic wine. Monthly concerts are held at the abbey.
Open all year daily 5.30am-9.30pm. (Shops, tea room 9-5.30). Etr-Oct (exhibition) 10.30-4.30.
❋*Free. (Exhibition 75p, first 2 ch free then 30p)*
P *(charged)* ⛻ ✗ *licensed* & *(braille plan, wheelchair available) toilets for disabled shop* ⌀

Buckfast Butterfly Farm & Dartmoor Otter Sanctuary
BUCKFASTLEIGH
(off A38, at Dart Bridge junct)
☎(01364) 42916
Visitors can wander around a specially designed, undercover tropical garden, where free-flying butterflies and moths from many parts of the world can be seen. The otter sanctuary has four large enclosures with underwater viewing and there are special observation holts.
Open Good Fri-Oct, daily 10-5.30 or dusk (whichever is earlier).
P ⛻ & *shop* ⌀
Details not confirmed for 1995

Buckland Abbey
BUCKLAND ABBEY
(off A386 0.25m S of Yelverton)
☎Yelverton (01822) 853607
Originally a prosperous Cistercian Abbey, and then home of the Grenville family, Buckland Abbey was sold to Sir Francis Drake in 1581. By then the abbey church had been converted into a handsome house with oak panelling and fine plasterwork, and it was his home until he died at sea in 1596. It belonged to the Drake family until 1946. Several restored buildings house a fascinating exhibition about the abbey's history. Among the exhibits is Drake's drum, which is wreathed in legend and is said to give warning of danger to England. There are also craft workshops, which are open at various times, and some lovely walks.
Open all year Apr-Oct, daily (ex Thu) 10.30-5.30; Nov-Mar Wed (booked parties only), Sat & Sun 2-5.
Abbey & grounds £4. Grounds only £2. Car park charge refundable against purchase of admission ticket.
P *(charged)* ✗ *licensed* & *(wheelchairs & motorised buggy available) toilets for disabled shop* ⌀ *(ex in car park)*
(NT)

This complete thatched Norman chapel stands among the later buildings of Bickleigh Castle, really a moated and fortified manor house.

Cobbaton Combat Collection
CHITTLEHAMPTON

Cobbaton
☎ *Chittlehamholt* (01769) 540740 & 540414
World War II British and Canadian military vehicles, war documents and military equipment can be seen in this private collection. There are over fifty vehicles including tanks and a recent Warsaw Pact section. There is also a section on 'Mum's War' and the home front. The children's play area includes a Sherman tank. Special events for 1995 include: VE weekend (6-8 May), VJ Weekend (12-13 August).
Open Apr-Oct, daily 10-6. Winter Mon-Fri 10-4.
£3.50 (ch £1.50, pen £2.75)
P & shop

CHUDLEIGH
See Lower Ashton

The Milky Way & North Devon Bird of Prey Centre
CLOVELLY

(on the main A39, 2m from Clovelly)
☎ (01237) 431255
A visit to the Milky Way and North Devon Bird of Prey Centre is a real 'hands-on' experience. There are twice-daily bird of prey flying displays, bottle feeding show times and hand milking demonstrations. Other attractions include 'cuddling corner', pottery, face painting, laser clay pigeon shooting, a countryside collection, playground, shop and cafe, sheep dog centre, and 18-hole mini-golf.
Open Apr-Oct, daily 10.30-6.
£4 (ch £2.50, under 3 free, pen £3.50).
P & toilets for disabled shop

Bodstone Barton Farmworld & Playland
COMBE MARTIN

Berrydown (2m S, off A3123)
☎ (01271) 883654
Set in an area of outstanding natural beauty, Bodstone Barton is a 17th-century farm covering 160 acres. The farm is run by both traditional and modern methods, and visitors can see goats being milked by hand. Attractions include an adventure playground, and rides by tractor, trailer and horse-drawn cart. There is a nature trail to follow, with an abundance of wildlife to be seen. A large collection of agricultural and domestic items are on show, with 20,000 square feet under cover. Visitors can watch heavy horses being groomed and harnessed. There are lots of rides.
Open all year, daily 10-5.
❋£1.99 (disabled £1.50).
P ▼ ✗ *licensed* & *toilets for disabled shop* ✿

The Combe Martin Motorcycle Collection
COMBE MARTIN

Cross St
☎ (01271) 882346
The collection was formed in 1979 and contains old and new British motorcycles, displayed against a background of old petrol pumps, signs and garage equipment, exhibiting motoring nostalgia in an old world atmosphere.
Open Etr then 20 May-27 Oct, daily 10-5.
£2 (ch & pen £1, ch 10 accompanied free).
P & shop

Combe Martin Wildlife Park
COMBE MARTIN

(off A399)
☎ (01271) 882486
Twenty acres of woodland complete with streams, cascading waterfalls, ornamental gardens, tropical plants and rare trees make this the most natural wildlife park in Britain. Otters living in the streams have produced 29 young in the last five years and for something completely different, visitors can see Meerkats 'on guard', living in the largest

Among the many motorcycles on display at the Combe Martin Motorcycle Collection is this fine example of a 1929 Brough Superior Type S S100.

enclosure in the Europe - a man-made desert. There is also a large selection of primates, mammals and birds. The Domain of the Dinosaurs has partially animated life-size dinosaurs set in prehistoric woodland.
Open Mar-Nov, daily 10-4.30.
❋£4.50 (ch £3 & pen £4). Party 10+.
P ▼ ✗ *licensed* & *(car service) shop* ✿

Compton Castle
COMPTON

(off A381 near Marldon)
☎ *Kingskerwell* (01803) 872112
A fortified house of the 14th to 16th centuries, Compton has been the home of the Gilbert family (related to Sir Walter Raleigh) for 600 years. Much of the appeal of Compton is due to its completeness. The Great Kitchen still has its bread ovens and knife-sharpening marks, and the withdrawing room has squints through which occupants could watch services in the chapel. The original 14th-century hall was restored in the 20th century, complete with the solar, or living room, above. The towers, portcullis entrances and curtain walls were added in the 16th century, when there were French raids in the area. A look-out squint in the wall allows a watch to be kept from the hall door. There is a rose garden outside.
Open Apr-Oct Mon, Wed & Thu 10-12.15 & 2-5.
Castle & garden £2.60
P ✿
(NT)

Bayard's Cove Fort
DARTMOUTH

The low, circular ruined stronghold was built by the townspeople to protect the harbour. It stands at the southern end of the cove, where the cobbled quay was used as a location for *The Onedin Line*.
Open at all reasonable times.
Free.
P
(EH)

Dartmouth Castle
DARTMOUTH

☎ (01803) 833588
The castle dates from 1481 and was one of the first to be designed for artillery. It faces Kingswear Castle on the other side of the Dart estuary, and a chain could be drawn between the two in times of war. The timber-framed opening for the chain can still be seen.
Open all year, Apr-Sep, daily 10-6; Oct 10-4; Nov-Mar, Wed-Sun 10-4. Closed 24-26 Dec & 1 Jan.
£2 (ch £1, concessions £1.50).
P ✿
(EH)

Dartmouth Museum
DARTMOUTH

6 Butterwalk
☎ (01803) 832923
The timber-framed 17th-century house is part of a restored colonnaded arcade, and is encrusted with carvings. It houses a small maritime museum with over 150 ship models and many pictures and artefacts relating to the history of this ancient town.
Open all year, Nov-Etr, Mon-Sat noon-3; Etr-Oct, Mon-Sat 11-5.
80p (ch 5 free, ch 5-15 30p & pen 50p).
P (75 yds) shop

Newcomen Memorial Engine
DARTMOUTH

The Engine House, Mayors Av
☎ (01803) 834224 & 834959
Thomas Newcomen helped to keep open Devon's mines by inventing a steam-driven pump to clear them of water. This building was erected to commemorate the 300th anniversary of his birth (1663) and houses one of his atmospheric pumping engines of 1725.
Open Apr-Sep, Mon-Sat 9.30-5.30, Sun 10-4. Oct-Mar, Mon-Sat 9.30-4.30.
50p. Party.
P & shop

Woodland Leisure Park
DARTMOUTH

Blackawton (W, off A3122)
☎ (01803) 712598
A beautiful 60-acre park with indoor and outdoor attractions for all the family. There are 12 playzones including a commando course, action tracks, amazing matrix and a special toddlers' play village, also 20,000sq ft of under cover play area. The Circus Playdrome has bouncy castles, dressing up in circus costumes, crazy bikes and a circus ring. The large animal complex and wildlife walkabout has 100s of animals and birds, and there is an international wildfowl collection and Bee Observatory. Live entertainment days all through the school holidays and many special events in 1995 including South Hams Game and Country Fair (7-8 May). Other prices under review.
Open all year, 31 Mar-Oct, daily 9.30-6.30; Nov-30 Mar, daily 10-dusk.
❋Discount ticket £13 (2 adults & 2 children). Other prices under review.
P ▼ & *toilets for disabled shop*

Castle Drogo
DREWSTEIGNTON

(4m S of A30)
☎ *Chagford* (01647) 433306
The granite castle is one of the most remarkable designs of Sir Edwin Lutyens, and was built between 1910 and 1930 for Julius Drew, a poor man's son who retired at 33 after founding the Home and

Colonial Stores. It is a fascinating combination of medieval might and 20th-century luxury, with its own telephone and hydro-electric systems, and craftsmanship of a high order. The castle stands at 900ft, on a rocky crag overlooking the gorge of the River Teign. There are wonderful views from the gardens.
Open Apr-Oct, daily (ex Fri but open Good Fri) 11-5.30. Garden open daily, 10.30-5.30.
Castle & grounds £4.60. Grounds only £2.
P ▼ ✗ *licensed* & *(wheelchairs available) toilets for disabled shop garden centre* ✿
(NT)

EXETER
Exeter's history goes back to before the Romans, when the line of the present High Street was already established as an ancient ridgeway. The city prospered under the Romans, who built the wall and a bath house, and in the Middle Ages when the cathedral was built. This is where most visits begin, and it is well worth seeing for its magnificent nave, where clusters of pillars soar up into the web of fan vaulting in the roof. Other notable features are the intricately decorated bishop's throne, and the misericord carvings under the choir seats, including a crocodile and an elephant. Outside the cathedral is the Close, surrounded by charming buildings, and near by there are a number of interesting small churches. Highlights of the city include Rougemont House and its gardens, the Guildhall and the Maritime Museum. A more unusual attraction is the network of underground passages which brought water to the medieval city and can now be explored: the entrance is in the Princesshay shopping precinct.

Guildhall
EXETER

High St
☎ (01392) 77888
This is one of the oldest municipal buildings still in use. It was built in 1330 and then altered in 1446, and the arches and façade were added in 1592-5. The roof timbers rest on bosses of bears holding staves, and there are portraits of Exeter dignitaries, guild crests, civic silver and regalia.
Open when there are no mayoral functions. Times are posted outside weekly. Special opening by arrangement. Free.
P (200yds) & ✿

Maritime Museum
EXETER
The Haven (0.25m from Exe Bridges)
☎ (01392) 58075
Afloat, ashore and under cover, there are over 170 boats at the museum, which is at the heart of the lively quay and canal area. The boats come from all over the world and are very varied, ranging from the oldest working steam dredger, *Bertha*, believed to have been built by Brunel, to dhows and coracles, a junk and a sampan, and a Venetian gondola. There are African dug-out canoes and frail-looking craft from the Pacific, and there is a large Danish harbour tug. One section is occupied by the fascinating Ellerman collection of Portugese craft, and elsewhere is the Ocean Rowers' collection, featuring boats which have been rowed across the Atlantic. Another display shows the 1993/94 Trans-Pacific solo row of Peter Bird.
The museum started with 23 vessels in 1969. It aims to rescue types of boats which are going out of use, and now has the world's largest collection of different boats. Visitors can look at, touch and also climb aboard some of the exhibits. Pleasant river and canal walks can be taken nearby. The Adventure play ship is a replica of the *Mary Rose* sister ship, *Great Harry*, and is complete with boarding nets and hammocks.
Open Apr-Sep, daily 10-5. Oct-Mar daily 10-4. Closed 25 Dec.
£3.80 (ch & students £2.20, pen £2.90). Family ticket £10.50
P (100yds) ☟ & toilets for disabled shop

Royal Albert Memorial Museum
EXETER
Queen St
☎ (01392) 265858
Founded in 1865, the museum is especially interesting for Exeter silver, regional archaeology and Devon paintings. Other displays include a traditional natural history display, a Victorian collection of shells, and beautiful African wood carvings. There is a temporary exhibition programme and children's activities are held during school holidays. Special events include: The Perfection of England - artist visitors to Devon 1780-1850 (June-September). Most well-known artists of this period visited and painted Devon; their paintings are displayed together for the first time.
Open all year, Mon-Sat 10-5.30.
Free.
P (200yds) ☟ & toilets for disabled shop ✿

St Nicholas' Priory
EXETER
Mint Ln, off Fore St
☎ (01392) 265858
The Benedictine priory was founded in 1070, and its remains include unusual survivals such as the Norman undercroft, a Tudor room and a 15th-century kitchen. Some fine plaster decoration can be seen, and there are displays of furniture and wood carving. There is a programme of temporary exhibitions.
Open Etr-Oct, Mon-Fri 10-1 & 2-5., Sat 2-5.
✿£1 (ch, pen & students 50p).
P (200yds) shop ✿

Underground Passages
EXETER
Boots Arcade, High St
☎ (01392) 265858 & 265887
A unique medieval water system with an introductory exhibition. Not recommended unless fit and healthy - definitely not suitable for those inclined to claustrophobia. Britain's only ancient city passageways open to the public. Flat shoes are essential. All tours are guided, and there is an introductory 10-minute videoplus exhibition.
Open Etr-Oct, Mon-Sat 10-5 tours variable. Nov-Etr Mon-Fri 2-5, Sat 10-5.
✿£2.20 (ch, students & pen £1).
P shop ✿

Farway Countryside Park
FARWAY
(1.5m S on unclass rd AA signed on B3174)
☎ (0140487) 224 & 367
A collection of farm animals can be seen in the park, which covers 108 acres of beautiful countryside with magnificent views over the Coly Valley. Attractions include a tropical indoor garden with butterflies and birds; rare poultry, an undercover play area for children, pony rides and nature trails.
Open Good Fri-Sep, daily 10-5pm.
✿£2 (ch £1, pen £1.50).
P (charged) ☟ & toilets for disabled shop

Hartland Quay Museum
HARTLAND
Hartland Quay
☎ Morwenstow (01288) 331353
The displays cover four centuries of shipwrecks on the coasts of Hartland, Welcombe, Clovelly and Morwenstow. Other exhibits include geology, natural history, trade and smuggling.
Open Etr wk then Whitsun-Sep, daily 11-5.
50p (ch 20p).
P (charged) ✿

Allhallows Museum
HONITON
High St (next to parish church of St Paul)
☎ (01404) 831672
The museum has a wonderful display of Honiton lace, and there are lace demonstrations from June to August. The town's history is also illustrated, and the museum is interesting for its setting in a chapel built in about 1200.
Open Etr-Sep, then mid May-Sep, Mon-Sat 10-5; Oct, Mon-Sat 10-4.
80p (ch 30p)
P (400 yds) & shop ✿

Chambercombe Manor
ILFRACOMBE
(1m E off A399)
☎ (01271) 862624
This is one of England's oldest houses, circa 1066, although there are 16th-and 17th-century additions. It boasts a priest's room, private chapel (dating from about 1086) and inevitably, a ghost. The garden includes an ancient wishing well and waterfowl ponds among its many charms. The bird sanctuary is home to many species of pheasant and peafowl.
Open Good Fri-Sep, Mon-Fri 2-4.30, Sun 2-4.30 (Closed Sat). Afternoon bookings by prior arrangement.
£3 (ch £2, pen £2.50)
P ☟ & shop ✿

Hele Mill
ILFRACOMBE
Hele Bay (1m E, on A399)
☎ (01271) 863185 & 863162
Dating back to 1525, this mill still produces wheatflakes and different grades of wholemeal flour. Inside, many interesting items of mill machinery are on view.
Open Etr Sun-Oct, Mon-Fri 10-5, Sun 2-5.
✿£1.60 (ch 5-14 80p)
P shop ✿

Ilfracombe Museum
ILFRACOMBE
Runnymede Gardens, Wilder Rd
☎ (01271) 863541
Ilfracombe was an important trading port from the 14th to the 16th centuries and during the Napoleonic Wars became a popular resort. The history, archaeology, geology, natural history and maritime of the area are illustrated here, along with Victoriana, costumes, photographs and china. There is a brass-rubbing centre. In 1995 there will be special diplays and a video celebrating VE and VJ Days.
Open all year, Etr-Oct 10-5.30 (Jul-Aug 7.30-10), Nov-Etr Mon-Sat 10-1.
70p (ch & students 30p, under 5 free, pen 50p). Disabled free.
P & shop ✿

Watermouth Castle
ILFRACOMBE
(3m NE off A399)
☎ (01271) 863879
Overlooking a beautiful bay, this 19th-century castle is one of North Devon's finest. It caters enthusiastically for the public, offering such unique experiences as a mechanical musical demonstration and the Watermouth Water Fountains. Other attractions include a tube slide, carousel and Gnomeland.
Open 9-13 Apr, Sun-Thu 1-4; 14-21 Apr, Sun-Fri 11-4; 23 Apr-18 May, Sun-Thu 1-4; 21 May-21 Jul, Sun-Fri 11-4; 23 Jul-1 Sep, Sun-Fri 10-4; 3-22 Sep, Sun-Fri 11-4; 24 Sep-19 Oct, Sun-Thu 2-4; 22-29 Oct, Sun-Thu 1-4.
✿£4.50 (ch £3.50 & pen £4)
P ☟ & (special wheelchair route) toilets for disabled shop ✿

Killerton House & Garden
KILLERTON HOUSE & GARDEN
(off B3181)
☎ Exeter (01392) 881345
Although the 18th-century house is rather plain, it is not unattractive, especially with the sweeping lawns, shrub borders and planted beds that surround it. A majestic avenue of beech trees runs from the formal 18th-and 19th-century gardens, up the hillside past an arboretum of rhododendrons and conifers. The dining

Exeter Maritime Museum is in a canal basin crammed with craft from all over the world. In stone warehouses on the quayside of the River Exe, reached by ferry, are hundreds of sailing exhibits.

room, drawing room and upstairs rooms of the house are used to display the Paulise de Bush collection of period costumes: these are shown in a series of room settings, furnished in different periods and ranging from the 18th century to the present day. The family chapel, built in 1840, lies at the eastern edge of the park. A network of footpaths through the parkland, woods and meadow can be enjoyed throughout the year.
Open: House, 18 Mar-Oct, Wed-Mon 11-5.30. Gardens all year, daily from 10.30. House & grounds £4.60. Grounds only £2.80.
P ☟ ✕ licensed & (wheelchairs & motorised buggy available) toilets for disabled shop garden centre ✿ (ex in park)
(NT)

Cookworthy Museum of Rural Life
KINGSBRIDGE
The Old Grammar School, 108 Fore St
☎ (01548) 853235
The 17th-century schoolrooms of this former grammar school are now the setting for another kind of education. Reconstructed room-sets of a Victorian kitchen, an Edwardian pharmacy, a costume room and extensive collection of local historical items are gathered to illustrate South Devon life. A walled garden and farm gallery are also features of this museum, founded to commemorate William Cookworthy, 'father' of the English china clay industry. In 1995 there will be a special display to mark the 50th anniversary of VE Day.
Open all year, Apr-Sep Mon-Sat 10-5; Oct Mon-Fri 10.30-4. Nov-Mar by arrangement.
£1.60 (ch 80p, pen £1). Family ticket £4. Party
P (100yds) & (Braille labels on selected exhibits) shop

Coleton Fishacre Garden
KINGSWEAR
Coleton (2m E on unclass roads)
☎ (01803) 752466
The exotic figure of Lady Dorothy D'Oyly Carte created this equally exotic garden in a stream-fed valley between 1925 and 1940. A wide variety of uncommon trees and rare shrubs were planted.
Open Mar, Sun only 2-5; Apr-Oct, Wed-Fri & Sun & BH Mon 10.30-5.30.
£2.80.
P ☟ garden centre ✿
(NT)

Knightshayes Court
KNIGHTSHAYES COURT
(2m N of Tiverton off A396)
☎ Tiverton (01884) 254665 & 257381
This ornate 19th-century house was designed by William Burges, the creator of

➤

Morwellham was once a great copper port – now restored as a museum. Displayed in the assayer's office are documents relating to the 700,000 tons of copper moved between 1840 and 1900.

the fantastic Gothic towers of Cardiff Castle. He was also partly responsible for the rich Gothic-style interior decoration, although an artist/designer called Crace installed the painted ceilings and stencilled wall decorations which were so popular at the time. The court is most noted for its gardens: both formal and woodland, and containing unique shrubs, azaleas, rhododendrons and carpets of spring bulbs. A 50-year-old topiary animal can be seen, a survivor from one of the older gardens which have all but disappeared.
Open Apr-Oct, House Sat-Thu & Good Fri 1.30-5.30. Nov-Dec, Sun 2-4 for pre-booked parties only. Garden daily 11-5.30. House & garden £4.80. Garden only £2.80.
🅿 ✗ *licensed* ♿ *(wheelchairs available) toilets for disabled shop garden centre* ♨ *(ex in park)*
(NT)

Canonteign Falls & Country Park
LOWER ASHTON
(3m off A38)
☎ *Christow (01647) 52434*
Lakes, wildfowl, a children's play area and miniature horses can be found in this beautiful country park. Covering 80 acres of ancient woodland, this unspoilt valley is also the setting of the highest waterfall in England.
Open all year, Mar-Oct, daily 10-6; Nov-Apr Sun only 10-5.
🅿 👕 ✗ *licensed shop*
Details not confirmed for 1995

Lydford Castle
LYDFORD
The great square stone keep dates from 1195. It is not built on a mound, as it seems to be, but had earth piled against the walls. The upper floor was a Stannary Court, which administered local tin mines, and the lower floor was used to imprison those who broke the forest and stannary laws.
Open all reasonable times.
Free.
🅿
(EH)

Lydford Gorge
LYDFORD
(off A386)
☎ *(01822) 820441 & 820320*
The spectacular gorge has been formed by the River Lyd, which has cut into the rock and caused swirling boulders to scoop out potholes in the stream bed. This has created some dramatic features, notably the Devil's Cauldron close to Lydford Bridge. At the end of the gorge is the 90ft-high White Lady Waterfall.
Open Apr-Oct, daily 10-5.30. (Nov-Mar, waterfall entrance only, daily 10.30-3).
£2.80
🅿 👕 *shop*
(NT)

Lyn & Exmoor Museum
LYNTON
Market St
☎ *(01598) 52317*
One of the oldest buildings in Lynton, this delightful, 18th-century whitewashed cottage was saved from demolition to be run as a museum. The displays reflect the life and occupations of the local population and include traditional arts, crafts and implements, a reconstruction of an Exmoor kitchen of the 1800s, and a scale model of the old Lynton - Barnstaple narrow-gauge railway, together with exhibits on the Lynmouth Flood and Lynmouth Lifeboats.
Open Etr-Oct, Mon-Fri 10-12.30 & 2-5. Sun 2-5.
✱*70p (ch 30p). Family ticket £1.50.*
P *(100 yds)* ♨

Morwellham Quay
MORWELLHAM
(4m W of Tavistock, off A390)
☎ *Tavistock (01822) 832766 & 833808*
When copper was discovered in the hills near Tavistock the town reached new heights of prosperity. Morwellham was the nearest point to which sea-going ships could navigate and became the greatest copper port in Queen Victoria's Empire. Once the mines were exhausted the port area disintegrated into unsightly wasteland, until 1970 when a charitable trust was set up for its restoration. It is now a thriving and delightful open-air museum. Cottages have been faithfully renovated, and visitors can meet a blacksmith, cooper, assayer, quay workers and coachmen, all dressed in period costume to help recreate history in this picturesque old port. There are also underground rides into a copper mine, heavy horse-drawn wagons, slide shows and other displays. Reduced operation during the winter months. Unspoilt countryside, riverside and woodland trails surround the museum.
Open all year (ex Xmas wk) 10-5.30 (4.30 Nov-Etr). Last admission 3.30 (2.30 Nov-Etr). £7 (ch £4.50, pen & students £6.25). Family ticket £21. Party.
🅿 👕 ✗ *licensed shop*
See advertisement on page 44

Bradley Manor
NEWTON ABBOT
(on A381)
☎ *(01626) 54513*
A National Trust property of 70 acres, the 15th-century house and chapel are surrounded by woodland. The River Lemon and a millstream flow through the estate.
Open Apr-Sep, Wed only 2-5; also Thu, 6 & 13 Apr, 21 & 28 Sep.
£2.60
🅿 ♨
(NT)

Tuckers Maltings
NEWTON ABBOT
Teign Rd
☎ *(01626) 334734*
Tuckers Maltings is England's only working malthouse open to the public, producing malt from barley for over 30 West Country breweries. Vistors and learn all about the process of malting - watch a video programme, see a re-constructed Victorian 'Corn Street', visit the hands-on discovery centre and taste the end product at the new in-house brewery. Guided tours last over an hour. Special events for 1995 include: Maltings Beer Festival (21-23 April).
Open Etr-Oct, daily 10-4 (Jul-Aug 5pm).

£3.25 (ch 5-14 £1.95, student & pen £2.95).
🅿 *(charged)* 👕 ✗ *licensed* ♿ *toilets for disabled shop*

Museum of Dartmoor Life
OKEHAMPTON
The Dartmoor Centre, West St
☎ *(01837) 52295*
An attractive three-storey watermill houses this museum, and the Dartmoor Tourist Information Centre and working craft studios are to be found in an adjoining courtyard. There is a cradle-to-grave display of Victorian life, and descriptive reconstructions of local tin and copper mines are complemented by a geological display of the moor. Local history, prehistory, domestic life, industry and environmental issues are explored, and a 1922 Bullnose Morris farm pickup with a wooden back shares pride of place with an ancient David Brown tractor in the agricultural section. An award-winning display depicts everyday life in Dartmoor. A shop sells crafts and books and an exhibition gallery changes its displays regularly. Exhibition galleries feature a reconstructed blacksmith's forge and wheelwright's shop, a cider press and railway relics. Various changing exhibitions, craft events and demonstrations are held throughout the year.
Open Etr-Oct, Mon-Sat 10-5 (also Sun, Jun-Sep). Nov-Mar weekdays only. (Closed Xmas/New Year).
£1.50 (ch 5-16 & students 75p, pen £1.20). Family ticket £4. Party 10+.
🅿 👕 ♿ *toilets for disabled shop*

Okehampton Castle
OKEHAMPTON
(0.5m S in Castle Lane)
☎ *(01837) 52844*
The chapel, keep and hall date from the 11th to 14th centuries and stand on the northern fringe of Dartmoor National Park.

Open all year, Apr-Sep, daily 10-6; Oct 10-4. (Closed 24-26 Dec & 1 Jan).
£2 (ch £1, concessions £1.50).
🅿
(EH)

Otterton Mill Centre
OTTERTON
(off A376)
☎Colaton Raleigh (01395) 68521
Mentioned in the Domesday Book, this water-powered mill grinds wholemeal flour used in the baking of bread, cakes and pies sold on the premises. A gallery houses a series of exhibitions through the summer and autumn, and there are studio workshops for stained glass, blown glass and stone carving as well as pottery, woodturning and printing. There is a 'Millhands' co-operative craft shop.
Open all year, daily Summer 10.30-5.30; Winter 11-4.30.
🅿 ⬛ ♿ toilets for disabled garden centre
Details not confirmed for 1995

Cadhay
OTTERY ST MARY
(near jct of A30 & B3167)
☎(01404) 812432
A mile north-west of Ottery, over Cadhay Bridge, this beautiful Tudor and Georgian house is well worth a visit. It was begun in 1550 and stands around a courtyard.
Open Jul-Aug Tue, Wed & Thu. Also Sun & Mon of late spring & late summer BH's. 2-5.30.
£3 (ch £1.50). Party 20+ by appointment.
🅿 ♿ ✻ (ex in garden)

Paignton & Dartmouth Steam Railway
PAIGNTON
Queens Park Station, Torbay Rd
☎(01803) 555872
Steam trains run for seven miles from Paignton to Kingswear on the former Great Western line, stopping at Goodrington Sands, a popular beach, and at Churston, connecting with the ferry crossing to Dartmouth. Special events for 1995 include: Children's weekend (Easter), Thomas the Tank Engine (August), Santa Specials (December).
Open Jun-Sep daily 9-5.30 & selected days Oct-Nov & Mar-May.
Prices under review.
P (5mins walk) ⬛ ♿ toilets for disabled shop (at Paignton & Kingswear)

Paignton Zoo
PAIGNTON
Totnes Rd (1m, on A385)
☎(01803) 527936
This is one of England's largest zoos set in 75 acres of botanical gardens. Animals in the collection, which first opened 70 years ago, include lions, elephants, giraffes, rhinoceros, zebras, flamingos, crocodiles and ostrich. The Zoo is very committed to conservation and participates in captive breeding programmes for endangered species. A special feature is the lake with Gibbon islands where five Gibbon families roam freely. Children are well catered for with an adventure playground, 'meet the animals' area and the Ark family activity centre - an indoor area with lots to do and learn about wildlife on our planet. Other features include a nature trail which follows a route past disused lime kilns, a jungle express miniature railway and talks by a keeper in the summer. There are special arrangments for educational groups. Special events for 1995 include: Easter Egg Safari (16-17 April), Animal Magic Day (8 May), Jazoo (23 June), Children's Day (24 August).
Open all year, daily 10-6.30 (5pm in winter). Last admission 5pm (4pm in winter). (Closed 25 Dec).
✻£5.75 (ch 3-14 £3.50, pen £4.60). Family ticket £16.50. Party 15+. Reduction for disabled.
🅿 ⬛ ✗ licensed ♿ (free wheelchair loan-booking advisable) toilets for disabled shop garden centre ✻ (kennels available)

PLYMOUTH
To walk the narrow, cobbled streets of Plymouth's Barbican, to visit its ancient houses and to wander beside the quays of its historic Sutton Harbour is to tread in the wake of England's most intrepid seafarers. From here, in 1577, Drake sailed to circumnavigate the world, and 11 years later to defeat the Spanish Armada. In 1620 the Mayflower carried the Pilgrim Fathers to the New World, and in 1768 James Cook left in search of a southern continent. On Plymouth Hoe stands the Royal Citadel built, it is said, on the site where Drake played his game of bowls.

City Museum & Art Gallery
PLYMOUTH
Drake Circus
☎(01752) 264878
A fine building with varied local and worldwide collections of natural history, archaeology, fine and decorative art. Special collections include the Cottonian library of prints and Old Master drawings, paintings from the Newlyn School, prehistoric finds from Mount Batten and minerals from Cornwall. There is a lively programme of contemporary art exhibitions. A special exhibition 'Plymouth in the Age of Discovery', explores 18th-century ideas and discoveries with a 'hands on' section for children.
Open all year, Tue-Fri 10-5.30, Sat 10-5, BH Mon 10-5. (Closed Good Fri & 25-26 Dec).
P ♿ toilets for disabled shop ✻
Details not confirmed for 1995

Merchant's House Museum
PLYMOUTH
33 St Andrews St
☎(01752) 264878
A fine 16th-century house, modernised in 1601 by William Parker, an Elizabethan sea dog and Mayor of Plymouth. Plymouth's history is told here in lively displays through the rhyme 'Tinker, Tailor, Soldier, Sailor, Apothecary, Thief'. A Victorian Schoolroom, opened in 1992, is available to pre-booked school parties; teacher and costumes are provided for which a charge is made.
Open Apr-Sep, Tue-Fri 10-5.30, Sat 10-5 (Closed 1-2), BH Mon 10-5 (summer)
P (400 yds) ♿ shop ✻
Details not confirmed for 1995

Plymouth Dome
PLYMOUTH
The Hoe
☎(01752) 603300 & 600608 (recorded message)
This high-tech visitor centre takes you on a journey through time, exploring the sounds and smells of an Elizabethan street, walking the gun-deck of a galleon, sailing with the epic voyages from Plymouth Sound, dodging the press gang, strolling with film stars on an ocean liner and witnessing the devastation of the blitz. Use high-resolution cameras to zoom in on ships and shoreline, or access computers to identify naval vessels. Examine satellite weather pictures as they arrive from space, keep up to date with shipping movements and monitor the busy harbour on radar. An excellent introduction to Plymouth and a colourful interpretation of the past.
Open all year, daily, Etr-May 9-6; Jun-16 Sep 9-7.30pm; 16 Sep-Oct 9-6; Nov-Etr 9-5.30. (Closed 25 Dec). Last admission one hour before closing.
£3.40 (ch £2.25 & pen £2.70). Family ticket £9.45. Party. Subject to review.
P (200 yds) ⬛ ♿ (induction loop for hard of hearing, wheelchairs available) toilets for disabled shop ✻

Prysten House
PLYMOUTH
Finewell St
☎(01752) 661414 (Mon-Fri 9-1)
Thought to have been erected as a town house by Plymouth and London merchant Thomas Yogge, who bought the site in two lots in 1487 and 1498. It is also believed to have been used as a 'priest's house' by the Augustinian Order of preaching canons from Plympton Priory. After the dissolution of the monasteries in 1539 it fell into secular use for such purposes as a wine store and a bacon factory. Since 1923, it has been owned by St Andrew's Church and the people who give it life are in the main, ordinary Plymouthians, interested in preserving part of our national heritage. Embroiderers are working on a 253ft-long New World Tapestry - a section of it is now on show.
Open Apr-Oct, Mon-Sat 10-4 (last admission 3.30pm). Other times by appointment.
50p (ch & pen 25p). Party 15+.
P (100 yds) ✻

Royal Citadel
PLYMOUTH
Probably designed by Sir Thomas Fitz, this magnificent gateway was built in 1670 for the stronghold commenced by Charles II in 1666. The remaining buildings of the fort include the Guardhouse, Governor's House and Chapel.
Open any reasonable time.
Free.

(EH)

Smeatons Tower
PLYMOUTH
The Hoe
☎(01752) 603300
This famous lighthouse, a triumph of 18th-century engineering, was built on the treacherous Eddystone rocks fourteen miles out at sea to the south west of Plymouth. It was replaced by a larger lighthouse in 1882, and moved stone by stone to its present site on the Hoe.
Open Good Fri-early Oct, 10.30-4.30. Parties by appointment throughout the year.
70p (ch 35p & pen 50p)
P (500 yds) ✻

Saltram House
PLYMPTON
(2m W between A38 & A379)
☎Plymouth (01752) 336546
Built on the site of a Tudor Mansion, this magnificent George II house still has its original contents. The collection of paintings was begun at the suggestion of Reynolds and includes many of his portraits. The saloon and dining room were designed by Robert Adam and have superb decorative plasterwork and period furniture. Set in beautiful surroundings with a shrub garden and 18th-century summer house, Saltram House has a lovely view of the Plym estuary.
Open Apr-Oct, Sun-Thu; House 12.30-5.30. Garden 10.30-5.30.
£5. Gardens only £2.20.
🅿 (charged) ⬛ ✗ licensed ♿ (wheelchairs available) toilets for disabled shop ✻ (ex designated areas)
(NT)

Powderham Castle
POWDERHAM
(signposted off A379 Exeter/Dawlish road)
☎Starcross (01626) 890243
Built between 1390 and 1420, this ancestral home of the Earls of Devon was damaged in the Civil War. The house was restored and altered in later times and fine furnishings and portraits are displayed throughout. It is set in beautiful rose gardens with views over the deer park to the Exe Estuary. Special events for 1995 include Powderham Horse Trials (1-2 July), open air concert (8 July), English Civil War Society Re-enactment (29-30 July).
Open 31 Mar-2 Oct, 10-5.30 (last admission 5pm). (Closed Sat).
✻£3.95 (ch £2.95, pen £3.75). Family ticket £9.85. Party 10+
🅿 ⬛ ♿ shop

Overbecks Museum & Garden
SALCOMBE
Sharpitor (1.5m SW)
☎(01548) 842893
The garden at Overbecks is particularly stunning when the magnolias are in ➤

The Great Kitchen in Saltram House contains many relics of downstairs life two centuries ago, including over 600 copper utensils.

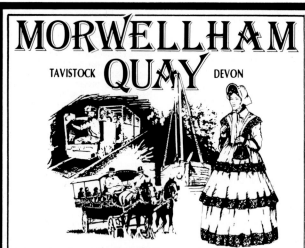

MORWELLHAM QUAY
TAVISTOCK DEVON

A charming riverside village hidden away in 150 acres of Tamar Valley woodland. Founded by monks 1000 years ago, it grew to become by 1868, "The greatest copper port in Queen Victoria's empire". Researched and restored for over 20 years by the Morwellham Trust and vividly brought to life.

* **Ride** the riverside tramway deep underground into an ancient copper mine.
* **Travel** by horse drawn carriage in the beautiful Tamar valley.
* **Explore** the port, boats, shops, cottages and farm and discover the fascinating stories of Victorian life.
* **Try** on a Victorian costume (what a photograph!)
* **Talk** with the people of the past about a bygone age, captured in the craft and costumes of the 1860s.

ALLOW A FULL DAY PLEASE!

Open all year – Winter. Nov–Easter reduced operation.
Summer: 10am – 5.30pm. Last admission 3.30pm.
Winter: 10am – 4.30pm. Last admission 2.30pm.

Off A390 between Tavistock and Gunnislake.
Tavistock (01822) 832766. Information only (01822) 833808

bloom; but its situation, on the most southerly tip of Devon, allows many tender and exotic plants to flourish; one of the most varied collections of trees, shrubs and flowering plants in the country is grown here. The Edwardian house displays toys, dolls and a natural history collection, and there is a 'secret room' for children.
Open Apr-Oct, daily (ex Sat) 11-5.30. Garden all year, daily 10-8 or sunset if earlier.
Museum & gardens £3.40. Gardens only £2.
P *(charged)* ☕ *shop* ✿ 🐕
(NT)

Sidmouth Museum
SIDMOUTH
Church St
☎ (01395) 516139
An elegant Regency house next to the parish church, the museum contains an interesting collection of local prints, many mementoes of Sidmouth's heyday as a Victorian resort, a costume section and an excellent display of old lace. Guided town strolls, lasting approximately one and a half hours, depart from the museum on Tuesdays and Thursdays at 10.15am. Lace-making and other craft demonstrations as announced locally.
Open Etr-Oct, Tue-Sat 10-12.30 & 2-4.30, Sun-Mon 2-4.30. Also open 10-12.30 Sun & Mon in Aug. Other times by appointment.
✱*50p (ch 5-16 20p).*
shop

Vintage Toy & Train Museum
SIDMOUTH
1st Floor, Fields Department Store, Market Place
☎ (01395) 515124 ext 208
A splendid display of toys, games and children's books, covering the 50 years from 1925 to 1975. The exhibits include the first and last Dinky Toy, Hornby 'O' gauge trains and Minic clockwork vehicles, together with a selection of

Britain's military and farm figures and Cadbury's free gift with cocoa - Cococubs. 1995 is the Diamond Jubilee of the Trix Twin train, 1935-1995. A working layout will be on view together with various pre-war sets.
Open 31 Mar-28 Oct, Mon-Sat 10-5. (Closed BH).
£1.30 (ch 3-14 & pen 70p).
P ☕ & *shop* 🐕

Quince Honey Farm
SOUTH MOLTON
(3.5m W of A361)
☎ (01769) 572401
This is the largest bee farm in Britain. Visitors can view the honey-bees, without disturbing them, in a specially designed building with glass booths and tunnels. Observation hives enable visitors to see into the centre of the colony and view larvae and newly-hatched bees in the cells of the comb. Even the queen may be seen at the very heart of the hive. The farm shop sells a wide range of honey, including the local heather honey, as well as pure beeswax candles and polish.
Open daily, mid Apr-Sep 9-6; Oct 9-5; Shop open Nov-Etr 9-5. (Closed 25-26 Dec & 1 Jan).
£2.90 (ch 5-16 £1.45, pen £2.35)
P ☕ *shop* ✿

South Molton Museum
SOUTH MOLTON
Town Hall, The Square
☎ (01769) 572951
The museum is in part of the Guildhall, a Portland stone-fronted building erected in about 1743. The entrance is through an open arcaded frontage. In the museum are objects relating to local history such as old charters, weights and measures, old fire engines and a giant cider press. There are monthly art and craft displays.
Open Mar-Nov, Mon Tue, & Thu 10.30-1 & 2-4; Wed & Sat 10.30-12.30.
Free. Donations accepted.
P *(50 yds)* & *shop* ✿

Finch Foundry
STICKLEPATH
☎ Okehampton (01837) 840046
Finch Foundry was, in the 19th century a water-powered factory (1814-1960) for making sickles, scythes, shovels and other hand tools. Although no longer in production, three waterwheels can still be seen driving huge hammers, shears, grindstone and other machinery, with daily working demonstrations. There is also a display of hand tools and a gallery devoted to water power. Special events for 1995 include: Jazz on the foundry lawn (18 June), craft fair (24 June), folk/square dancing (16 July), demonstrations by blacksmiths using waterdriven machinery (25 November). Access point for Tarka Trail, village trail, cycle route and Two Museums Walk. Information points provided.
Open Apr-Oct, daily ex Tue, 11-5.30. Last entry 5.
£2.20 (ch £1).
P ☕ *shop*

TAVISTOCK
See Morwellham

Tiverton Castle
TIVERTON
☎ (01884) 253200
Dating from 1106, the castle dominates the River Exe. It was originally moated on three sides with the Exe as the fourth defence. One remaining circular Norman tower remains from the original four, and there is also a medieval gatehouse with walls 5ft thick. The castle was a Royalist stronghold during the Civil War but was taken by the Roundheads in 1645. It houses a fascinating clock collection in the tower, and one of the finest collections of Civil War armour and arms in the country. Visitors are encouraged to add their stitches in history to the New World tapestry.
Open Apr-Jun & Sep, Sun & Thu only 2.30-5.30; Jul & Aug, Sun-Thu 2.30-5.30.
£3 (ch 7-16 £3, disabled half price).
P & *toilets for disabled shop* ✿ *(ex on leads in grounds)*

Tiverton Museum
TIVERTON
Saint Andrew St
☎ (01884) 256295
This large and comprehensive museum consists of eight galleries and is housed in a restored 19th-century school. The numerous local exhibits include a Heathcote Lace Gallery featuring items from the local lacemaking industry (started by John Heathcote). There is also an agricultural section with a collection of farm wagons and implements. Other large exhibits include two waterwheels and a railway gallery that houses a GWR 0-4-2T Locomotive No.1442, other railway items, and a display on the Grand Western Canal.
Open Mon-Sat 10.30-4.30. (Closed 21 Dec-Jan).
£1 (ch 16 50p (free on Sat), pen & UB40 75p).
P *(100 yds)* & *shop* ✿

Babbacombe Model Village
TORQUAY
Hampton Av, Babbacombe
☎ (01803) 328669
Set in four acres of beautifully maintained, miniature landscaped garden, the village contains over 400 models and 1200ft of model railway. Authentic sound effects have been added, to create a whole new dimension. In summer, when the village is open until late, it is illuminated. City Lights, a new evening illuminations feature, depicts Piccadilly Circus in miniature.
Open all year, Etr-Sep, daily 9am-10pm; Oct 9-9pm; Nov-Etr 9am-dusk. (Closed 25 Dec).
£3.60 (ch £2.40, pen £3)
P *(charged)* & *(push button audio information) toilets for disabled shop garden centre*

'Bygones'
TORQUAY
Fore St, St Marychurch
☎ (01803) 326108
Step back in time in this life-size Victorian exhibition street of over 20 shops including a forge, pub and period display rooms, housed in a former cinema. Exhibits include a large Hornby railway layout, illuminated fantasyland, railwayana and military exhibits including a walk-through World War I trench. At Christmas the street is turned into a winter wonderland.
Open all year, Jun-Aug 10am-10pm, (Sat 10-6); Sep, Oct, Mar, Apr & May 10-5; Nov-Feb 10-2, Sat & Sun 10-5. (Last admission 1 hour before closing). (Closed 25 Dec). Extended opening during school holidays.
£2.75 (ch 4-13 £1.50, pen £2.50). Family ticket £8.
P *(50 yds)* ☕ *shop* ✿

Kents Cavern Showcaves
TORQUAY
The Caves, Wellswood (1.25m NE off B3199)
☎ (01803) 294059 & 215136
Recognised as one of the most important archaeological sites in Britain, these showcaves provide a set of unique experiences. This is not only a world of spectacular natural beauty, but also a priceless record of past times, where a multitude of secrets of mankind, animals and nature have become trapped and preserved over the last 350,000 years. One hundred and seventy years after the first excavations and with over 70,000 remains already unearthed, modern research is still discovering new clues to our past.
The showcaves are visited along well-lit paths and tours are accompanied by 'storytellers' who bring to life past scenes using props and the natural setting of the caves. Special events during 1995 include The Ghosts of Cavern Past held during selected evenings in July and August. Please telephone 01803 215136 for details.
Open daily (ex 25 Dec). Apr-Jun & Sep 10-6; Jul & Aug 10-9 (6pm Fri & Sat); Oct-Mar 10-5. Last tour 45mins before closing time.
£3.40 (ch 5-15 £2.10 ch under 5 free). Party 20+.
P ☕ & *shop* ✿

Torre Abbey Historic House & Gallery
TORQUAY
The Kings Dr
☎ (01803) 293593
Torbay's most historic building was founded in 1196 as a monastery and later adapted as a country house. It contains historic rooms, the Cary family chapel, mementoes of crime writer Agatha Christie, and mainly 19th-century paintings, sculpture, antiques, and Torquay terracotta pottery. The medieval monastic remains, which include the great barn, guest hall, gatehouse and undercrofts, are the most complete in Devon and Cornwall. Special 'Quest' leaflet available for children. Rooms may be hired. Special exhibitions by local artists throughout the summer.
Open daily Etr-Oct, 9.30-6. (Last admission 5).
✱*£2.50 (ch 15 £1.50, under 8 free; pen & students £2). Family ticket £6 (up to 2 adults & 3 children)*
P *(100 yds)* ☕ & *shop* ✿

Dartington Crystal
TORRINGTON, GREAT
Linden Close (follow brown tourist signs)
☎ Great Torrington (01805) 24233 due to change to 624233
Tours of the factory are conducted from the safety of viewing galleries that overlook the craftsmen. They can be seen carrying out the age-old techniques of glass manufacture and processing, and there are also studio glass-making demonstrations. The factory has a permanent exhibition tracing the history

of glass and crystal over the past 300 years, including items from 1650 and a replica 18th-century glass cone. A video theatre adds a further dimension. A shop sells decanters, goblets and other items of glassware, at attractive prices.
Open all year. Visitor centre: Mon-Fri 9.30-3.30. (Closed 16 Dec-2 Jan) Shop & Restaurant: Mon-Sat 9.30-5. Sun also 10.30-4.30 28 May-17 Dec).
❊*Full tour (inc Glass Centre) £2.20 (ch 6-16 £1, pen £1.90). Party 20+.*
🅿 ⚟ ✕ *licensed & (special tours available, book in advance) toilets for disabled shop* ❦

RHS Garden Rosemoor
TORRINGTON, GREAT ▅▅▅▅
(1m SE of town on B3220)
☎ *Torrington (01805) 624067*
Started in 1959, Lady Anne's garden contains many rare plants. It is sheltered in a wooded valley and covers about eight acres. There are species and hybrid rhododendrons, shrub roses and a wide variety of ornamental trees and shrubs. A new 32-acre garden is nearing completion. It already contains two thousand roses of two hundred varieties, two large colour theme gardens, a herb garden and potager, an extensive herbaceous border, stream and bog gardens, a cottage garden, a foliage and plantsman's garden, and a fruit and vegetable garden. Special events in 1995 include Container Gardening Day (21 May), Rose weekend (15-16 July).
Open: Gardens all year; Visitor Centre Mar & Oct 10-5, Apr-Sep 10-6, Nov-Feb 10-4.
£3 (ch 6-16 £1). Party 20+.
🅿 ✕ *licensed & (Herb garden for disabled) toilets for disabled shop garden centre* ❦

Bowden House Ghostly Tales & The British Photographic Museum
TOTNES ▅▅▅▅
☎ *(01803) 863664*
At Bowden House visitors are welcomed by guides in 1740 Georgian dress. Parts

of the house date back as far as the 12th century, but most of it was built in 1510 by John Giles, supposedly the wealthiest man in Devon. In 1704 the Queen Anne façade was added. The Grand Hall is decorated in neo-Classical Baroque style, and the Great Hall is adorned with 18th- and 19th-century weaponry. The rooms have been beautifully restored.
The museum has a large collection of vintage cameras, a replica Victorian studio, Edwardian darkroom, shops, and the Les Allen movie pioneer display. There are special Ghostly Tales Tours at 2, 3, and 4 o'clock. The house is set in twelve acres of attractive grounds.
Open 3 Apr-26 Oct from noon. Bowden House & Museum Mon-Thu & BH Sun & Mon.
£4.50 (ch 10-13 £2.50, ch 6-9 £1.50, ch under 6 free)
🅿 ⚟ & *(museum only suitable) toilets for disabled shop* ❦

Guildhall
TOTNES ▅▅▅▅
Rampart Walk, off High St
☎ *(01803) 862147*
Originally the refectory, kitchens, brewery and bakery for the Benedictine Priory of Totnes (1088-1536), the building was established as the Guildhall in 1553 during the reign of Henry VIII. A magistrates court and a prison opened in 1624, the same year of the refurbishment of the council chamber which is still used today. There are also relics of the Civil War, and lists of the mayors since 1359. Famous visitors to the Guildhall have included past monarchs such as Charles I and Charles II as well as the present monarch Queen Elizabeth II.
Open Apr-Oct, Mon-Fri 10-1 & 2-5; Other times by appointment.
60p (ch 25p).
P *(50 yds) shop*

Totnes Castle
TOTNES ▅▅▅▅
☎ *(01803) 864406*

A classic example of the Norman motte-and-bailey castle, Totnes dates from the 11th century. The circular shell-keep is protected by a curtain wall erected in the 13th century and reconstructed in the 14th. There are marvellous views from the walls of the keep across the town to the Dart valley.
Open all year, Apr-Sep, daily 10-6; Oct 10-4; Nov-Mar, daily 10-4. Closed 24-26 Dec & 1 Jan.
£1.50 (ch 80p, concessions £1.10)
❦
(EH)

Totnes Motor Museum
TOTNES ▅▅▅▅
Steamer Quay
☎ *(01803) 862777*
This is a private collection of vintage, sports and racing cars and motorcycles, most of which are currently raced. There are also engines and other paraphernalia, and the whole collection covers a 70-year span.
Open Etr-Oct, daily 10-5.30.
£3.50 (ch £2 & pen £2.80). Family ticket £10.
🅿 & *shop*

Totnes Museum
TOTNES ▅▅▅▅
70 Fore St
☎ *(01803) 863821*
This four-storey, partly timbered house, complete with connecting gallery to an additional kitchen/buttery block, dates from about 1575. It has a cobbled courtyard, elaborate plaster ceilings and 16th-century fireplaces. It is now a museum of furniture, domestic objects, toys, dolls, costumes and archaeology. One room is dedicated to Charles Babbage who invented the ancestor of modern computers. There is a Tudor garden and Devon Record Office (study centre).
Open Etr-30 Oct, Mon-Fri & BHs 10.30-5.
£1 (ch 5-16 50p).
P *(440yds) shop* ❦ *(ex small dogs)*

Coldharbour Mill Working Wool Museum
UFFCULME ▅▅▅▅
Coldharbour Mill (off B3181)
☎ *Craddock (01884) 840960*
Originally an important centre for the wool trade, the Culm Valley now has only one working woollen mill. This was built as a grist mill in 1753, but was converted to a wool mill in 1797 by a Somerset woollen manufacturer, Thomas Fox. He added a large red-brick and stone factory in which serge, flannel and worsted yarn was produced for nearly 200 years. The mill closed in 1981 but was reopened as a Working Wool Museum. Visitors can watch every stage in the process of producing woollen cloth and yarn on the two working levels of the mill. There are also displays of interesting machinery and artefacts connected with the wool trade, plus a weaver's cottage, and dye and carpenters' workshops. Visitors can see the 18ft diameter water wheel awaiting restoration, and the 300HP Pollit and Wigzell steam engine which powered the Mill until its closure. Knitting yarn and made-up garments can be bought in the mill shop. Judged Best Museum of Industrial or Social History in 1992.
Open Apr-Oct, daily 11-5. Nov-Mar Mon-Fri (please telephone for times). Last tour 4pm.
🅿 ⚟ ✕ *licensed & shop* ❦
Details not confirmed for 1995

National Shire Horse Centre
YEALMPTON ▅▅▅▅
(On A379, Plymouth to Kingsbridge)
☎ *Plymouth (01752) 880268 & 880806 (recorded info)*
Some fine old farm buildings are at the hub of this 60-acre farm with over 40 Shire horses. With the revival of interest in the gentle giants, the farm has become the National Shire Horse Centre. Visitors are able to see not only the heavy horses and their foals, but a variety of other creatures as well. A butterfly house permits a range of exotic butterflies to be seen in their real habitat. A craft centre, showing the skills of the saddler and the falconer, among others, is in the barns. Daily falconry flying ➤

Once at the heart of a thriving wool region, Cold Harbour Mill at Uffculme is now a working museum. It shows every stage in producing woollen cloth and yarn.

displays (at 1pm and 3.30pm), parades of the Shire horses (at 11.30 and 2.30) and a shire horse musical drive at 4.15pm can be seen from April to the end of October. Children are well catered for with a pets' area, cart rides and an adventure playground with free-fall slide. Special events for 1995 include: a Western Week (15-23 July), a Steam and Vintage Rally (12-13 August), and a Classic Car Show (3 September).
Open all year, daily 10-5. (Closed 24-26 Dec).
P ♥ ✗ *licensed & toilets for disabled shop garden centre*

Paperweight Centre
YELVERTON
4 Buckland Ter, Leg O'Mutton
☎ (01822) 854250
This unusual centre is the home of the Broughton Collection - a glittering display of paperweights of all sizes and designs. The centre also has an extensive range of modern glass paperweights for sale. Prices range from a few pounds to over £500. There is also a series of oil and watercolour paintings by talented local artists, a collection of which are scenes of Dartmoor.
Open all year, 27 Mar-4 Nov, Mon-Sat 10-5. Also Sun 21 May-17 Sep; Nov-Etr, Wed 1-5 & Sat 10-5; 1-23 Dec, Mon-Sat 10-5. Other times by appointment. Free.
P *(100 yds) & (ramp on request) shop*
See advertisement on page 45

DORSET

Abbotsbury Swannery
ABBOTSBURY
New Barn Rd
☎ Weymouth (01305) 871684
The colony was already in existance when, in the 14th century, the monks used the swans as a resource, and Abbotsbury is still a breeding ground for the only managed colonial herd of mute swans. The swans can be seen safely at close quarters, and the site is also home or stopping point for many wild birds. Reeds are harvested for thatching, and there is a 17th-century duck decoy. The highlight of the year is the cygnet season, end of May to the end of June, when there may be over 100 nests on site with an average of six eggs per nest. Hatching can take place before your very eyes. A special event for 1995 is the July round-up '95. Every two years scientists and ornithologists from all over the world gather at the swannery to conduuct an intense two day study of swans, over a weekend in July. Over 600 swans are carefully hearded into an enclosure where they are weighed, tagged, sized and given health checks and necessary treatment before being released. Please telephone 01305 871125 for dates and times.
Open 5 Mar-29 Oct, daily 10-5.

£4 (ch 5-16 £1.25 & pen £3.25). Family ticket £8.50.
P & *(wheelchair loan, herb garden for blind) toilets for disabled shop* ✗

Athelhampton House & Gardens
ATHELHAMPTON
(on A35 1m E of Puddletown)
☎ Puddletown (01305) 848363
The house is built on the legendary site of King Athelstan's palace, and dates from the 15th century. A family home for 500 years, it is one of the finest medieval houses in southern England. The baronial great hall is worth seeing just for its roof structure. Around the house are 10 acres of formal and landscaped gardens, with river gardens and a 15th-century dovecote. Craft fairs will be held here over the Easter and August Bank Holiday weekends, and ther will be a flower show on 28-31 May.
Open 2 Apr-29 Oct, Tue, Wed, Thu, Sun, BH. Also Mon & Fri Jul-Aug. 12-5. House & Garden £4.20 (ch £1.70). Garden only £2.50 (ch free). Family £10. Party.
P ♥ ✗ *licensed & toilets for disabled shop* ✗

Mapperton Gardens
BEAMINSTER
(2m SE off A356 & B3163)
☎ (01308) 862645
Surrounding a manor house dating back to the 16th century are several acres of terraced hillside gardens, with specimen trees and shrubs, and formal borders. There are also fountains, grottoes, stone fishponds and an orangery, and the garden offers good views and walks. The annual Mapperton Courtyard Fair will be held on 26 August 1995 with craft demonstrations, stalls, house tours and local displays.
Open Mar-Oct, daily 2-6.
✳Gardens £2.50 (ch 5-18 £1.50, under 5 free).
P & *shop* ✗

Parnham
BEAMINSTER
(1m S on A3066)
☎ (01308) 862204
The house is a fine Tudor mansion, but it is most famous as the home of John Makepeace and his furniture-making workshop. The workshop is open to visitors, and completed pieces are shown in the house. There are also continuous exhibitions by living designers and craftsmen. Surrounding the house are 14 acres of restored gardens, formal terraces and woodlands.
Open Apr-Oct Sun, Wed & BH's 10-5.
£4 (ch £2, under 10 free).
P ✗ *licensed & toilets for disabled shop* ✗ *(ex in grounds)*

Royal Signals Museum
BLANDFORD FORUM
Blandford Camp
☎ Blandford (01258) 482248
The history of army radio and line

communications is illustrated with paintings, uniforms, medals and badges, vehicles and signalling equipment. Special events for 1995 include a photographic exhibition covering the Royal Signals' contribution to Victory in Europe and the Far East, and another covering the 75 years of the Royal Corps of Signals.
Open all year, Mon-Fri 10-5; Jun-Sep, Sat, Sun & BH 10-4. (Closed 10 days over Xmas).
Free.
P & *(ramps & chair lift) shop* ✗

Bournemouth Bears
BOURNEMOUTH
The ExpoCentre, Old Christchurch Ln
☎ (01202) 293544
Explore the wonderful world of the teddy and meet famous teddy-bear personalities. The Bournemouth Bears are a joy for young and old alike. There are old bears, new bears, gigantic bears, tiny bears, and bears of all kinds, including limited editions and special creations. A nostalgic journey for adults and a delight for the young. Can you bear to miss it!
Open all year, daily 9.30-5-30 (phone for winter hours).
£3.50 (ch £2.25, pen & students £2.75). Family ticket £9.95.
P *(100mtrs) shop*

Dinosaur Safari
BOURNEMOUTH
The Expocentre, Old Christchurch Ln
☎ (01202) 293544
With the aid of modern computer technology you will be able to build your own dinosaur, compare yourself with the largest and the smallest dinosaurs and then actually walk a dinosaur through computerised prehistoric landscapes. See actual-size reconstructions of dinosaurs, fossils and skeletal remains - both real and rare casts. Many 'hands-on' displays.
Open all year, daily 9.30-5.30. (Closed 24-26 Dec).

✳£3.50 (ch £2.25, pen £2.75). Family ticket £9.95
P *(100mtrs) shop*

Russell-Cotes Art Gallery & Museum
BOURNEMOUTH
East Cliff
☎ (01202) 551009 & 551500
The museum was built in 1894 as East Cliff Hall. Together with a new extension called The Display Space, and the recently restored art galleries it houses collections of 17th-to 20th-century paintings, watercolours, sculpture, miniatures, ceramics, furniture and world wide collections. A lively events and educational programme has highlights during the 1995 Bournemouth Festival held in May.
Open all year, Tue-Sun 10-5. (Closed BH's, Good Fri & 25 Dec).
£1 (ch, students, UB40's & pen 50p).
Free wknds.
P *(200 yds)* ♥ & *(2 lifts, induction loop for some events) toilets for disabled shop* ✗

The Shelley Rooms
BOURNEMOUTH
Beechwood Av, Boscombe
☎ (01202) 303571
The Shelley Rooms contain a small museum display commemorating the life and work of Percy Byshe Shelley. Also available is a collection of romantic literature and reference books.
Open all year Tue-Sun 2-5. (Closed BH's, Good Fri, 25 Dec).
Free.
P & ✗

Clouds Hill
BOVINGTON CAMP
(4m SW of Bere Regis)
☎ (01985) 847777
T E Lawrence ('Lawrence of Arabia') bought this cottage in 1925 when he was a private in the Tank Corps at Bovington.

He would escape here to play records and entertain friends to feasts of baked beans and China tea. Lawrence's sleeping bag, marked 'Meum', can be seen, together with his furniture and other memorabilia. Three rooms only are on show.
Open 2 Apr-29 Oct, Wed-Fri, Sun & BH Mon 2-5 or dusk if earlier.
£2.20.
⚲ ♨
(NT)

The Tank Museum
BOVINGTON CAMP
(off A352)
☎ *Bindon Abbey (01929) 463953 (recorded info line)*
At the Tank Museum you can see over 300 vehicles, from over 25 countries, together with displays of weapons, medals, uniforms, memorabilia, engines and supporting artefacts. The museum gives a dramatic insight into the lives and living conditions of tank soldiers since the first tank saw action in 1916. The World War I display includes the finest collection of Great War vehicles in existance. There are things to do and see for all ages, including driving and motion simulators, radio control cars and video theatres. A costume exhibition is dedicated to the army wife and there is a Lawrence of Arabia exhibition. Other facilities include a licensed restaurant, picnic area and junior assault course.
Open all year, daily 10-5. (Closed 10 days over Xmas).
Telephone for details. Party 10+.
Servicemen free.
🅿 ✕ *licensed* ♿ *(wheelchair available, Sound Alive audio tours) toilets for disabled shop* ♨

Bridport Museum
BRIDPORT
South St
☎ *(01308) 422116*
Housed in a Tudor building, this local history museum tells the story of Bridport and its surroundings. The displays cover natural history, agriculture, costume and the history of the town. There is also an extensive local history reference centre, where visitors can research their family history as well as the history of the area.
Open all year, Apr-Oct, Mon-Sat 10-5, Sun 2-5; Nov-Mar, Wed & Sat 10-5, Sun 2-5.
70p (ch 35p).
🅿 *(100yds)* ♿ *shop* ♨

Harbour Museum
BRIDPORT
Salt House, West Bay
☎ *(01308) 420997*
Located in a converted salt house, the museum tells the story of Bridport's rope and net trade and the history of Bridport harbour. Bridport at War exhibition will be held from April to September.
Open Apr-Sep, daily 10-6.
50p (ch 25p)
🅿 *(100yds)* ♿ *shop* ♨

Brownsea Island
BROWNSEA ISLAND
(located in Poole Harbour)
☎ *Canford Cliffs (01202) 707744*
Although it is popular and easy to reach from Poole, Brownsea still offers peace, seclusion and a sense of timelessness. Visitors can wander along woodland paths, lounge on beautiful beaches, admire the fine views of Corfe Castle and the Dorset coast, or join a guided tour of the 250-acre nature reserve managed by the Dorset Naturalists' Trust. The island is perhaps most famous, however, as the site of the first scout camp, held by Lord Baden-Powell in 1907. Scouts and Guides are still the only people allowed to stay here overnight.
The lack of development on the island is due to its last private owner, Mrs Bonham Christie. She kept it as a kind of huge garden for animals, birds and flowers, and let peacocks roam free. Their descendants still thrive here, as do native red squirrels, and sika deer,

introduced in 1896. A less welcome newcomer is the destructive mink. The island is also famous for its dragonflies, moths and butterflies, but most of all for its birds. The brackish lagoon supports a colony of Sandwich and common terns, with numerous waders in autumn and spring, and ducks in winter. There is also a heronry, one of Britain's largest. For details of open air theatre and other summer events please telephone 0891 335235.
Open Apr-1 Oct, daily 10-8 or dusk if earlier.
£2.20 (ch £1.10). Family ticket £5.20 (Apr, May, Jun & Sep). Party 15+.
🍴 ✕ ♿ *toilets for disabled shop* ♨
(NT)

Compton Acres Gardens
CANFORD CLIFFS
Canford Cliffs Rd (on B3065)
☎ *(01202) 700778*
The nine and a half acres of Compton Acres incorporate Japanese, Roman and Italian gardens, rock and water gardens, and heather gardens. There are fine views over Poole Harbour and the Purbeck Hills.
Open Mar-Oct, daily 10.30-6.30 (last entry 5.45)
❋*£3.50 (ch £1, student & pen £2.50).*
Party20+
🅿 🍴 ✕ *licensed* ♿ *(level paths and ramps into shops and cafe) toilets for disabled shop garden centre* ♨
See advertisement on page 48

Chettle House
CHETTLE
(6m NE of Blandford Forum off A354)
☎ *Tarrant Hinton (01258) 830209*
This small country house was designed by Thomas Archer, and is praised as a fine example of the English Baroque. Around the house there are beautifully laid-out gardens. There is an exhibition area and a vineyard.
Open 14 Apr-8 Oct, daily 11-5. (Closed Tue & Sat).
£2 (ch free).
🅿 ♿ ♨

Christchurch Castle & Norman House
CHRISTCHURCH
All that remains of the castle buildings is a ruined keep and a Norman house, which was probably where the castle constable lived. The keep is more dilapidated, but parts of the thick walls can be seen.
Open any reasonable time.
Free.
(EH)

Red House Museum & Gardens
CHRISTCHURCH
Quay Rd
☎ *(01202) 482860*
Local history, archaeology, natural history, Victoriana, dolls and costumes are displayed in this Georgian house. New displays tell the story of early human settlement from the Old Stone Age to the Normans, and there is also an exhibition of fashionable dress from 1865-1914. Temporary exhibitions are shown, and there are gardens with a woodland walk and herb garden.
Open all year, Tue-Sat 10-5, Sun 2-5. (Closed Mon ex BH). Apr-Sep Mon 10-5.
£1 (ch & pen 60p). Family ticket £2.60.
🅿 *(400yds)* ♿ *shop* ♨

Corfe Castle
CORFE CASTLE
(on A351)
☎ *(01929) 481294*
The castle was first built in Norman times, and was added to by King John. It was defended during the Civil War by Lady Bankes, who surrendered after a stout resistance. Parliament ordered the demolition of the castle, and today it is one of the most impressive ruins in England. Special events for 1995 include a Medieval Archery weekend 29, 30 April and 1 May; Civil War Garrison 21-22 October. Please telephone 0891 335237 for further details.
Open Apr-29 Oct, daily 10-5.30 (4.30pm 6-25 Mar) or dusk if earlier; 30 Oct-3 Mar wknds only 12-3.30. (Closed 25-26 Dec).
£3 (ch £1.50). Party 15+ by arrangement.
🅿 *(charged)* 🍴 ✕ *licensed shop*
(NT)

Corfe Castle Museum
CORFE CASTLE
West St
☎ *Corfe (01929) 480415*
The tiny, rectangular building was partly rebuilt in brick after a fire in 1780. It has old village relics, and dinosaur footprints 130 million years old. A council chamber on the first floor is reached by a staircase at one end. The Ancient Order of Marblers meets here each Shrove Tuesday.
Open all year, Apr-Oct, daily 9.30-6; Nov-Mar, wknds and Xmas holidays 10-5.
Free.
♿ ♨

Cranborne Manor Private Gardens & Garden Centre
CRANBORNE
(on B3078)
☎ *(01725) 517248*
The 17th-century gardens are privately owned and include a Jacobean Mount garden and herb garden. The river garden

is particularly beautiful in the spring, with flowering cherries, daffodils and tulips. There are fine avenues of beech and lime and magnificent yew hedges.
Garden Centre all year, Tue-Sat 9-5, Sun 10-5. Manor Gardens Mar-Sep, Wed only 9-5.
£2.50 (students & pen £2).
🅿 ♿ *shop garden centre* ♨

Dinosaur Museum
DORCHESTER
Icen Way
☎ *(01305) 269880*
Britain's only museum devoted to dinosaurs has an appealing mixture of fossils, skeletons, life-size reconstructions and interactive displays such as the 'feelies'. There are audio-visual presentations, and the idea is to provide an all-round family attraction with new displays each year. A temporary exhibition on 'T-Rex' is planned for summer 1995.
Open all year, daily 9.30-5.30. (Closed 24-26 Dec).
❋*£3.50 (ch £2.25, pen £2.75). Family ticket £9.95.*
🅿 *(50 yds)* ♿ *shop*

Dorset County Museum
DORCHESTER
High West St
☎ *(01305) 262735*
A visit to the museum is a must for anyone interested in the Dorset area and its fascinating archaeology. Displays cover prehistoric and Roman times, including sites such as Maiden Castle. There are also sections on the Dorset poet William Barnes, and on the poet and novelist Thomas Hardy, with a reconstruction of his study. Geology, natural history and rural crafts are also explored in the museum which has twice won the Museum of the Year Award. Various exhibitions are planned for 1995 including art exhibitions and another on whales.
Open daily 10-5. (Closed Sun Sep-Jun, Good Fri, 24-25 Dec & 1 Jan).
£2.35 (ch & pen £1.20). Family ticket £6.50. Party.
🅿 ♿ *shop* ♨

Hardy's Cottage
DORCHESTER
Higher Bockhampton (3m E off A35)
☎ *(01305) 262366*
Thomas Hardy was born in this thatched house in 1840. It was built by his great-grandfather and has not changed much in appearance since. The inside can only be seen by appointment with the tenant.
Open Apr-31 Oct, daily (ex Thu) 11-6 or dusk if earlier. Open Good Fri. ➤

The splendid Italianate water gardens at Compton Acres are only one of a number of different styles of garden here. There are Japanese, Roman and rock gardens as well as woodland to explore.

£2.50. Interior by appointment.
🅿 ♿ 🚫
(NT)

Maiden Castle
DORCHESTER
(1m SW)
The Iron Age fort of Maiden Castle ranks among the finest in Britain. It covers 47 acres, and has daunting earthworks which must once have been even bigger, with a complicated defensive system around the entrances. One of the main purposes of such castles may have been to protect grain from marauding bands, and the need for such protection seems to have grown during the Iron Age. The first fort was built in around 700BC on the site of an earlier Neolithic camp, and had just a single rampart. By the time it was completed, probably around 100BC, it embraced the whole plateau and had outer earthworks as well. It was excavated in the 1930s by Sir Mortimer Wheeler, who found a cemetery of defenders killed when the castle was attacked and then taken by Roman troops in AD43. There are good views.
Open any reasonable time.
Free.
🅿
(EH)

The Military Museum of Devon & Dorset
DORCHESTER
The Keep, Bridport Rd
☎*(01305) 264066*
Three hundred years of military history are covered, with displays on the Devon Regiment, Dorset Regiment, Dorset Militia and Volunteers, the Queen's Own Dorset Yeomanry, and Devonshire and Dorset Regiment (from 1958). A VE Day and VJ Day exhibition will run from May to September 1995.
Open Etr-Dec, Mon-Sat 9-5 (Closed Sat 1-2)
✳*£1.50 (ch & pen 75p).*
🅿 ♿ *(purpose built toilets being built) shop* 🚫

Tutankhamun Exhibition
DORCHESTER
High West St
☎*(01305) 269571*
The exhibition recreates the excitement of one of the world's greatest discoveries of ancient treasure using sight, sound and smell. A reconstruction of the tomb and facsimiles of its contents are displayed. The superbly preserved mummified body of the boy king can be seen, wonderfully recreated in every detail. A temporary exhibition The Science of Mummies will run until May 1995 when it will be replaced by the Jewels of Tutankhamun, showing recreations of some of the most famous jewellery found in the king's tomb. This exhibition will close at the end of the summer holidays.
Open all year, daily 9.30-5.30. (Closed 24-26 Dec).

✳*£3.50 (ch £2.25, pen £2.75). Family ticket £9.95.*
P *(200 yds)* ♿ *shop* 🚫
See advertisement on page 47

Minterne Gardens
MINTERNE MAGNA
(2m N of Cerne Abbas on A352)
☎*Cerne Abbas (01300) 341370*
Lakes, cascades, streams and many fine and rare trees will be found in these lovely landscaped gardens. The 18th-century design is a superb setting for the spring shows of rhododendrons, azaleas and spring bulbs, and the autumn colour.
Open Apr-Oct, daily 10-7.
£2 (accompanied ch free).
🅿

Poole Pottery
POOLE
The Quay
☎*(01202) 666200*
Founded in 1873, this well-known establishment has been producing its distinctive Poole Pottery since 1921. There is a display of past and present pottery manufacture. Self-guided factory tour. Other attractions include a factory shop, 'Have a Go' area, and a craft village.
Open all year, daily. (Closed Xmas).
✳*Factory tours £1.95 (ch £1.50, pen & students £1.75)*
P *(500 yds)* 🍴 ✗ *licensed* ♿ *(wheelchairs available) toilets for disabled shop* 🚫

Scaplen's Court
POOLE
High St
☎*(01202) 683138*
Scaplen's Court is a beautifully restored domestic building dating from the medieval period. With its own walled garden and central courtyard the building now houses a museum devoted to domestic life. There is a Victorian school room, a kitchen and scullery in which cooking demonstrations take place from timne to time, a children's room and other displays recalling domestic life in the past. The restored upper hall is the venue for a changing programme of contemporary art and craft exhibitions.
Open all year, Mon-Sat 10-1 & 2-5, Sun 2-5. (Closed Good Fri, 25-26 Dec & 1 Jan).
✳*£1-£1.45 (ch 75p-£1.10). Combined ticket to include Waterfront Museum £1.95-£3.25 (ch 90p-£1.75, pen & students £1.75-£3). Family ticket £7-£10.*
P *shop* 🚫

Waterfront Museum
POOLE
4 High St, The Quay
☎*(01202) 683138*
Set in buildings dating from the medieval period, the Waterfront Museum tells the story of Poole's seafaring past. The visitor can learn of the Roman occupation, hear the smuggler tell his tale, see material raised from the Studland Bay wreck and visualise the first Scout Camp on Brownsea Island. The story is told using

modern and audio visual techniques, hands-on and traditional museum displays.
Open all year, Mon-Sat 10-5, Sun 2-5. (Closed Good Fri, 25-26 Dec & 1 Jan).
✳*£1.95-£3.25 (ch 90p-£1.75, pen & student £1.75-£3.25). Family ticket £7-£10. Includes admission to Scaplen's Court.*
P 🍴 ♿ *(ex Town Cellars) toilets for disabled shop* 🚫

Portland Castle
PORTLAND
Castle Town
☎*(01305) 820539*
Erected by Henry VIII and added to in the 17th and 18th centuries, Portland Castle defended the southernmost coast of Wessex.
Open Apr-Sep, daily 10-6; Oct 10-4.
£2 (ch £1, concessions £1.50).
🅿 ♿ 🚫
(EH)

Portland Museum
PORTLAND
217 Wakeham
☎*(01305) 821804*
Avice's cottage in Thomas Hardy's book 'The Well-Beloved', this building is now a museum of local and historical interest, with varied displays such as domestic bygones and maritime relics. Regular temporary exhibitions are held, including a shipwreck and smuggling exhibition and an exhibition of the work of the late Sir Barnes Wallis and his bouncing bombs. The adjoining Marie Stopes cottage houses domestic bygones and a display of maritime history. A new gallery displays Portland history from the Stone Age to the 19th century. Garden with picnic area. Special events during 1995 include a 50th anniversary exhibition Return to Peace - 1945.
Open all year, Etr-Sep, daily 10.30-1 & 1.30-5. Oct-Etr, Fri-Tue 10.30-1 & 1.30-5. £1.10 (ch, students & UB40's free, pen 60p).

🅿 ♿ *(talking tapes for blind & partially sighted) shop*

Abbey Ruins & Museum
SHAFTESBURY
Park Walk
☎*(01747) 852910*
The abbey at Shaftesbury was part of a nunnery founded by King Alfred in 888. It became one of the wealthiest in the country but was destroyed during the Dissolution in 1539. The excavated ruins show the foundations of the abbey. A museum on the site displays carved stones, decorated floor tiles and other artefacts found during the excavations. A guided trail around the ruins can be followed using a numbered leaflet. An attractive recent addition is the Anglo/Saxon herb garden. A consecration ceremony is planned for the summer of 1995.
Open Apr-Sep daily, 10-5.30; Oct, Sat & Sun only.
✳*90p (ch 30p, pen & student 60p). Parties* ♿ *shop*

Local History Museum
SHAFTESBURY
Gold Hill
☎*(01747) 852157*
The museum is situated at the top of a steep, quaint hill with a cobbled roadway and 18th-century cottages. Inside are exhibits of needlework, toys, agricultural and domestic items, fans, pottery and finds from local markets. There is also an interesting fire engine of 1744.
Open Etr-Sep, daily 11-5, Sun 2.30-5 (other times by appointment).
80p (ch 20p).
♿ *garden centre* 🚫

Conservation Worldwide & Lullingstone Silk Farm
SHERBORNE
Compton House, Over Compton (entrance on A30, 2.5m W)
☎*Yeovil (01935) 74608*

Conservation Worldwide has evolved from Worldwide Butterflies. Visitors see what is being done, and what can be done, for wildlife and the environment. Set in the grounds of lovely Compton House is the superb collection of butterflies from all over the world, flying free in reconstructions of their natural habitats, including natural jungle and a tropical palmhouse. The collection has been built up over 30 years and there are active breeding and hatching areas on view as well as an extensive specialist library for research. Compton is also the home of the Lullingstone Silk Farm which produced unique English-reared silk for the last two coronations and the Queen's and the Princess of Wales' wedding dresses. At the farm the complete process of silk production is shown by exhibits and film.
Open Apr-Oct, daily 10-5.
Admission fee payable.
🅿 🍽 & *shop* ✍

Sherborne Castle
SHERBORNE
☎ *(01935) 813182*
This 16th-century house, built by Sir Walter Raleigh, is the 'new' castle and has been the home of the Digby family since 1617. The house was built beside the ruins of the old castle (see entry below), and in 1625 four wings were added to the original 1594 building. The house contains some fine furniture, painting, porcelain and many items of historical interest. The grounds, with an artificial lake, were designed by 'Capability' Brown in the 18th century. Tea and refreshments are served in a Gothic dairy which is by the lake. Special events for 1995 include a craft fair (29-30 July), open-air production of The Merry Wives of Windsor (3-4 August).
Open Etr Sat-Sep, Thu, Sat, Sun & BH Mons 1.30-5 (grounds 12.30-5).
£3.60 (ch £1.80, pen £3). Grounds only £1.50 (ch 80p). Party 25+.
🅿 🍽 *shop* ✍ *(ex in grounds)*

Sherborne Museum
SHERBORNE
Abbey Gate House, Church Ln
☎ *(01935) 812252*
On show in this museum is a model of Sherborne's original Norman castle, as well as a fine Victorian doll's house and other domestic and agricultural bygones. There are also items of local geological, natural history and archeological interest, including Roman material. Photographs of the Sherborne Missal of 1400 are on display. The latest addition is a 15th-century wall painting originally from a house near the museum.
Open Apr-Oct, Tue-Sat 10.30-4.30, Sun 2.30-4.30.
50p (ch 15p).
🅿 *(400 yds)* & *shop* ✍

Sherborne Old Castle
SHERBORNE
☎ *(01935) 812730*
The castle was built between 1107 and 1135 by Roger, Bishop of Salisbury but was captured and destroyed by Cromwell's forces in the Civil War. The ruins of the main buildings, the curtain wall and the towers and gates date from Norman times. The castle came into Sir Walter Raleigh's possession in 1592.
Open Apr-Sep, daily 10-6; Oct 10-4; Nov-Mar, Wed-Sun 10-4.
£1.30 (ch 70p, concessions £1).
🅿 & ✍
(EH)

Swanage Railway
SWANAGE
Station House
☎ *(01929) 425800 & 424276 (timetable)*
When the branch railway line from Wareham was closed in 1972, Swanage railway station was fortunately saved from destruction, and a band of enthusiasts started work on rebuilding the line. As part of the reconstruction of the railway serving the Isle of Purbeck, steam train rides of about six miles are available.

Built during the Restoration, the interior of Kingston Lacey House was later transformed into an Italian palazzo filled with countless works of art.

Open all year, wknds & BH; Jun-Sep, daily 10.30-5.30; Santa Specials every wknd in Dec.
❃*£4 (ch 5-15 £2,) return. Family ticket £10.*
P *(10 mins)* 🍽 ✗ & *(special disabled persons coach) toilets for disabled shop*

Tolpuddle Museum
TOLPUDDLE
(on A35)
☎ *Puddletown (01305) 848237*
Tolpuddle is celebrated for the agricultural workers from the village who united to improve their wages and conditions of employment. They were arrested and transported in 1834 and became known as the Tolpuddle Martyrs. In the 1930s the TUC built a museum of six cottages named after them. Also in the village is the 'Martyrs Tree', an old sycamore under which it is thought the Martyrs met. The museum within the cottages depicts the story of the martyrs. The Tolpuddle Martyrs Rally is held on the third Sunday of July each year, 12.30-4pm.
Open all year, Apr-Oct, Tue-Sat 10-5.30, Sun 11-5.30; Nov-Mar, Tue-Sat 10-4, Sun 11-4. Open BH Mon. (Closed 24 Dec-1 Jan).
Free.
P & *toilets for disabled shop* ✍

Dorset Heavy Horse Centre
VERWOOD
Edmondsham Rd (1.25m NW, signposted from Verwood).
☎ *(01202) 824040*
Visitors can see the different breeds of heavy horses and miniature and Shetland ponies. There is an information area and a display of farm implements and horse harness. Wagon rides (weather permitting) are an additional attraction. There are two 'live' commentaries daily at 12 noon and 3pm in the summer season, and visitors are welcome to ask staff about the horses and ponies, to sponsor a horse or pony, and enquire about any othr aspect of the Centre.
Open Good Fri-Oct, daily 10-5.
Commentaries at noon & 3pm. Nov-Etr, Tues-Sun 11-4. (Closed Xmas).
£3.50 (ch 14 £2, pen £3). Family ticket £10. Reduced price entry Nov-Etr, but no live commentaries.
🅿 🍽 & *toilets for disabled shop*

Lulworth Castle
WEST LULWORTH
East Lulworth (off A352, 4m S of Wool)
☎ *(01929) 400510*
The ancestral home of the Weld family and set in beautiful Lulworth Park, the castle is a short drive from Lulworth Cove. There are superb views from the

South East tower over the surrounding countryside. Special route-marked paths lead from Castle ranging from 2.5 miles to 5 miles in length and passing through ancient woodland, open heath with historic buildings and sites of wildlife interest.
Open daily, Nov-Mar 10-4; Apr-Oct 10-6 (closed 25-26 Dec).
£1.50 (ch 75p, pen/student/UB40 £1.20).
🅿 *shop*

Lulworth Cove Heritage Centre
WEST LULWORTH
Lulworth Cove
☎ *(01929) 400587*
The centre traces the history of Lulworth from prehistoric through to modern times. There is a comprehensive video display with breathtaking helicopter filming of the coastline and surrounding countryside. Displays include coastal and other local wildlife, flora, geology and fossils of the area. The shop has local crafts as well as books and gifts. The centre is at Lulworth Cove with access to spectacular coastal walks including one to Lulworth Castle, 3 miles away.
Open daily, Nov-Mar 10-4; Apr-Oct 10-6 (closed 25-26 Dec).
£1 (ch 50p).
🅿 *(charged) shop* ✍

Deep Sea Adventure & Titanic Story
WEYMOUTH
9 Custom House Quay, Old Harbour
☎ *(01305) 760690*
This exciting exhibition is an adventure story detailing the struggle to recover wealth from the sea. The exhibition

brings the subject to life by the use of animation, lighting and sound effects. One of the latest additions to the exhibition is 'The Titanic Story: Signals of Disaster', a major collection of actual Titanic signals.
Open all year, daily 10-5.30; winter 10-4.30. Jul & Aug also open 10am-10pm. (Closed 24-26 Dec).
❃*£2.95 (ch 14 £1.95, ch 15-16 , pen & students £2.50). Party 10+.*
& *(lift) toilets for disabled shop* ✍

Sea Life Park
WEYMOUTH
Lodmoor Country Park (on A353)
☎ *(01305) 788255*
The Sea Life Park is situated at the beautiful Lodmoor Country Park. Here you can marvel at the mysteries of the deep and discover amazing sea creatures from around our own shores in spectacular marine displays. Also includes the Tropical Jungle where exotic birds fly freely, the Blue Whale Splashpool, and Captain Kid's World of adventure play area for children.
Open all year, daily from 10am. (Closed 25 Dec).
Admission under review.
🅿 *(charged)* 🍽 & *toilets for disabled shop* ✍

Kingston Lacy House, Garden & Park
WIMBORNE
(1.5m W on B3082)
☎ *(01202) 883402*
One of the finest houses of its period in Dorset, Kingston Lacy House and 1500 of its 9000 acres were bequeathed to the ➤

National Trust in 1981 and opened to the public only in 1986. Until then, the house had been the home of the Bankes family for over 300 years. The original house was built between 1663 and 1665, but in the 1830s it was altered and given a stone façade by Sir Charles Barry for W J Bankes.

W J Bankes was a traveller and a collector and, not only did he add the grand Italian marble staircase and a superb Venetian ceiling, but treasures from Spain and an Egyptian obelisk. There is also a quite outstanding picture collection with works by Titian, Rubens, Velasquez, Reynolds and family portraits by Van Dyck and Lely. Special events in 1995 include a Jazz concert (16 June), Classical Concert with fireworks (14 July).
Open Apr-31 Oct, daily ex Thu & Fri 12-5.30. Last admission 4.30pm; Park & Garden 11.30-6. Last admission 5pm or dusk if earlier.
£5.50 (ch £2.70). Park & Gardens only: £2.20 (ch £1.10). Party 20+. No photography inside house.
🅿 ✕ *licensed* ♿ *(parking by arrangement) toilets for disabled shop* ⊗ *(ex in north park)*
(NT)

Knoll Gardens
WIMBORNE
Stapehill Rd, Hampreston (3m E between Wimbourne and Ferndown off A31)
☎ *(01202) 873931*
Over 4000 plant species from all over the world thrive here, all within a compact, mostly level six-acre site which is continually being expanded. There are water gardens with waterfalls, pools and a stream, a woodland walk, herbaceous borders, and many other features. It it also the home of the NCPG collections of Phygelius and Ceanothus. Plants can be bought here, and there is a tearoom and spacious visitor centre with gift and book shops.
Open from Mar-Oct, daily 10-5.30; Dec, Wed-Sat.
£3.45 (ch £1.70, student £2.40, pen £2.90). Party 20+.
🅿 ✕ *licensed* ♿ *toilets for disabled shop garden centre* ⊗

Priest's House Museum of East Dorset Life
WIMBORNE
23-27 High St
☎ *(01202) 882533*
Explore Wimborne's past through this award-winning local history museum set in an historic house with a working Victorian kitchen where regular cooking demonstrations are held. There are nine other rooms to see, along with regular special exhibitions covering aspects of the collections not normally on view, and a beautiful 300ft-long walled garden. The 'hands-on' archaeology gallery, an ironmonger's shop, Victorian stationer's shop, and toys and dolls are other attractions. Parties are welcome by arrangement.
Open Apr-28 Oct, Mon-Sat, 10.30-5. Also every Sun 4 Jun-24 Sep. Special Christmas season. Closed 12 July.
£1.50 (ch 50p, pen & students (with NUS card) £1). Family ticket £3.50.
P *(200 yds)* ♿ *shop* ⊗

Stapehill Abbey
WIMBORNE
Wimborne Rd West (2.5m E, off A31)
☎ *Bournemouth (01202) 861686*
This early 19th-century abbey, home for nearly 200 years to Cistercian nuns, is now a busy working crafts centre with many attractions under cover. There are award-winning landscaped gardens, parkland and picnic spots, and the Power to the Land exhibition which features the biggest tractor ever produced. Special events for 1995 include: Annual May Festival (14 May), Jazz at Stapehill (10 June), Country World Weekend (12-13 August).
Open Etr-Sep, daily 10-5; Oct-Etr Wed-Sun 10-4. Closed 24 Dec-1 Feb.

£4.50 (ch 4-16 £3, students & pen £4). Family ticket £12. Party 20+.
🅿 ♥ ♿ *toilets for disabled shop garden centre* ⊗

CO DURHAM

The Bowes Museum
BARNARD CASTLE
☎ *Teesdale (01833) 690606*
This splendid French château-style mansion was built in 1869 by John Bowes, who made his fortune in Durham coal and married a French actress. They amassed an outstanding collection of works of art, and built the flamboyant château to house them. The museum is now run by Durham County Council, and its collections include paintings by El Greco, Goya and Canaletto among others; porcelain and silver, furniture, ceramics and tapestries. There is a local history section, and a formal garden. Temporary exhibitions are held.
Open May-Sep, Mon-Sat 10-5.30, Sun 2-5; Nov-Feb closes 4pm; Mar, Apr & Oct closes 5pm. (Closed 20-25 Dec & 1 Jan).
🅿 ♥ ♿ *(lift induction loop) toilets for disabled shop* ⊗
Details not confirmed for 1995

The Castle
BARNARD CASTLE
☎ *(01833) 38212*
The town's name comes from Bernard Baliol, who built the castle in 1125. The castle clings to the steep banks of the Tees and is now a ruin, but it still has a 12th-century keep, and the remains of a 14th-century hall.
Open all year, Apr-Sep, daily 10-6; Oct, daily 10-4 Nov-Mar, daily 10-4 or dusk if earlier. Closed 24-26 Dec & 1 Jan.
£1.80 (ch 90p, students, pen & UB40 £1.40)
P ♿ *shop*
(EH)

Egglestone Abbey
BARNARD CASTLE
(1m SE)
The remains of this Premonstratensian abbey make a picturesque sight on the right bank of the River Tees. A large part of the church can be seen, as can remnants of monastic buildings.
Open any reasonable time.
Free.
🅿 ♿
(EH)

North of England Open-Air Museum
BEAMISH
(off A693 & A6076)
☎ *Stanley (01207) 231811*
Beamish, an open air museum, set in 200 acres of beautiful countryside, vividly recreates life in the north of England early this century. Visitors stroll down the cobbled streets of the town to see fully stocked Co-operative shops, dentist's surgery, working pub and newly opened garage, sweet shop and sweet factory. Guided tours are given underground at a real 'drift' mine in the colliery village and a row of miner's cottages show how pitmen and their families lived. There is a Methodist chapel and a village school here too. Traditional breeds of animals and poultry fill the farmyard at home farm, and in the large farmhouse kitchen the farmer's wife goes about her daily chores. At the railway station, complete with goods yard, signal box and weighbridge house, locomotives and rolling stock are on display. Opening in spring 1995 is Pockerley Manor and horse yard, a fortified medieval manor house illustrating the life of a yeoman farming family almost 200 years ago. Special events for 1995 include: quilting weekends - demonstrations of the traditional craft of North Country quilting and a small exhibition of quilts from the Beamish collection (10-11 June and 13-14 August).

Open all year: Apr-29 Oct, daily 10-5 (last admission 3pm); extended opening until 6pm on 14-23 Apr, 6-8 May, 27 May-4 Jun & 8 Jul-3 Sep; 30 Oct-23 Mar, Tue-Thu & wknds, 10-4 (last admission 3pm). Admission charges under review.
🅿 ♥ ♿ *toilets for disabled shop*

Auckland Castle
BISHOP AUCKLAND
Market Place
☎ *(01388) 601627*
The historic home of the Bishops of Durham with parts dating from the 12th century. The very fine private chapel was remodelled by Bishop Cosin in 1660 from the medieval banquet hall. Portraits of past Bishops line the throne room. There is a large public park and an unusual 18th-century deerhouse.
Open May-18 Sep, Sun, Wed & Thu 2-5, Tue 10-12.30,Sat (Aug) & BH 2-5.
£2 (ch & over 60's £1)
🅿 *shop* ⊗

Bowes Castle
BOWES
(on A66)
Built inside the earthworks of the Roman fort of 'Lavatrae', the castle is a ruin now, but the great Norman keep still stands three storeys high. It was built between 1171 and 1187.
Open any reasonable time.
Free.
♿
(EH)

Killhope Lead Mining Centre
COWSHILL
(3m W off A689)
☎ *Weardale (01388) 537505*
The lead mine and 19th-century crushing mill have been restored to look as they would have done in the 1870s. Visitors are invited to get involved in activities such as separating lead ore from waste by working primitive machinery. A path leads to displays of lead mining through the ages. The 34ft water wheel is now restored and turning. There is a visitor centre and exhibition based on the life of miners and their families. In 1995 there will be a Grand Mineralogical exhibition on the first weekend in September.
Open Apr-Oct, daily 10.30-5. Last entry 4.30. Nov Sun 10.30-5.
✳*£2 (ch & pen £1). Party 10+.*
🅿 ♥ ♿ *toilets for disabled shop*

Art Gallery
DARLINGTON
Crown St
☎ *(01325) 462034*
The gallery has a programme of temporary exhibitions throughout the year. It features the annual Silver Longboat Art Competition which is open to artists throughout the Northern region. A Painter of the Month exhibition, held on a monthly basis and featuring the work of local artists, is held in the Art Gallery Foyer.
Open all year, (during exhibitions) Mon-Fri 10-8, Sat 10-5.30 (Closed Sun & all

weekend BH)
Free.
P *(200 yds)* ⊗

Darlington Museum
DARLINGTON
Tubwell Row
☎ *(01325) 463795*
Displays on local history, agriculture, wildlife and archaeology are shown, with various bygones. There is also an observation beehive, which can be seen from about May to September, and beekeeping exhibits.
Open all year, Mon-Wed & Fri 10-1 & 2-6; Thu 10-1; Sat 10-1 & 2-5.30 (Closed Good Fri, May Day, 25-26 Dec & 1 Jan).
Free.
P *(50 yds)* ♿ *shop* ⊗

Darlington Railway Centre & Museum
DARLINGTON
North Rd Station (0.75m N off A167)
☎ *(01325) 460532*
The museum is housed in North Road Station, built 14 years after the world's first passenger train ran along the Stockton and Darlington line. The building has been carefully restored and part is still in use for train services. The prize exhibit is *Locomotion*, which pulled the first passenger train and was built by Robert Stephenson & Co in 1825. Several other steam locomotives are also shown, together with an early railway coach of about 1845 and a chaldron (coal) wagon. There are also models and other exhibits relating to the Stockton and Darlington and the North Eastern Railway companies. Locomotive restoration work takes place in the former goods shed nearby. A Railway Carnival is planned for mid-September 1995 (please telephone for details).
Open daily 9.30-5 (Closed Xmas & New Year); Last admission 4.30pm. May be subject to amendment.
✳*£1.70 (ch 5-15 85p & pen £1.25). Party.*
🅿 ♿ *(guide tape for visually handicapped) toilets for disabled shop* ⊗

DURHAM
One of the most splendidly sited cities in Britain, Durham's rocky outcrop, washed on three sides by the River Wear, was from the earliest times a secure fortress against invading Scots and Danes. Towering majestically above a loop in the river, Durham Cathedral, with the castle close by makes an unforgettable picture of Norman splendour.
During the Middle Ages the Prince-Bishops of Durham ruled the north of England and, such was their power, they ran Durham as a city state. The castle, now part of the university, was their palace from 1072 until 1836. The steep wooded banks of the river provide lovely walks and among Durham's other attractions are a celebrated Oriental Museum.

Life in north-east England during the early 1900s is recreated at Beamish Open-Air Museum. This authentic tram takes visitors to the museum's centrepiece – the Town.

Durham Light Infantry Museum & Durham Art Gallery
DURHAM

Aykley Heads (0.50m NW, turn right off A691)

☎0191-384 2214

The history of the Regiment is told in displays of artefacts, medals, uniforms and vehicles. The Art Gallery has a continuous programme of temporary exhibitions, and it holds regular lectures and concerts. Events for 1995 include: military vehicle rally August Bank Holiday weekend, and outdoor band concerts throughout the summer.

Open all year, Tue-Sat 10-4.30 & Sun 2-4.30 (Closed Mon, ex BHs).
80p (concessions 40p)
🅿 ▣ ⅙ *(wheelchair available, lift,ramp) toilets for disabled shop* ⌀

Finchale Priory
DURHAM

(3m NE)

The lovely setting of the priory was chosen by St Godric in 1110 as a place for years of solitary meditation. The priory was begun in 1180, and was used by monks from Durham Cathedral. There are considerable remains of the 13th-century church.

Open all year, Apr-Sep, daily 10-6. (Closed 24-26 Dec & 1 Jan).
£1 (ch 50p, concessions 80p)
🅿 ⅙ ⌀
(EH)

Oriental Museum
DURHAM

University of Durham, Elvet Hill

☎0191-374 2911

The museum has a remarkable collection of Oriental artefacts, ranging from Ancient Egypt to Japan. Special exhibitions are held throughout the year.

Open Mon-Fri 9.30-1 & 2-5, Sat & Sun 2-5. (Closed Xmas-New Year).
✳*£1 (ch, pen & students 50p)*
🅿 ⅙ *shop* ⌀

Raby Castle
STAINDROP

(1m N, off A688)

☎(01833) 660202

The stronghold of the powerful Nevill family until 1569, and the home of the Vane family since 1626. The fortress is built around a courtyard and surrounded by a moat (now dry). The castle was erected during Saxon times but is substantially 14th century, with parts added in nearly every century. It has an impressive gateway; nine towers of which the tallest is 80ft; a vast medieval hall; and a Victorian octagonal drawing-room. The 14th-century kitchen, with its collection of Victorian copper cooking utensils, was in use daily until 1954. The castle contains fine pictures from English, Dutch and Italian schools, interesting furniture and ceramics, and a good carriage collection. There are about five acres of gardens and an additional 200-acre park with both red and fallow deer.

Open 15-19 Apr; May-Jun, Wed & Sun; Jul-Sep, Sun-Fri; BHs May, Spring & Aug, Sat-Wed 1-5. Park & gardens 11-5.30, (last admission 4.30pm).
Castle, Gardens & Carriage Collection £3.50 (ch £1.50, pen £3.20). Park, Gardens & Carriage Collection £1 (ch & pen 75p). Party.
🅿 ▣ ⅙ *toilets for disabled shop* ⌀ *(ex in Park)*

Tanfield Railway
TANFIELD

Old Marley Hill (on A6076)

☎0191-274 2002

A 3-mile working steam railway and the oldest existing railway in the world. The Causey Arch, the first large railway bridge and the largest single span arch in Britain of its era, is the centrepiece of a woodland full of picturesque walks around a deep valley. The story of the early railway and collieries is told on a series of display boards, giving an interesting break in a return journey from Tanfield. You can ride in carriages that first saw use in Victorian times, and visit Marley Hill shed, which is the home of 35 engines; inside the shed you can see the stationary steam engine at work driving some of the vintage machine tools. The blacksmith is also often at work forging new parts for the restoration work. ➤

Special events planned for 1995 include: Small Engines Weekend (28-29 May), Enthusiast's Weekend (1-2 July), Children's Weekend (5-6 August), Big Engines Weekend (27-28 August), Santa Steamings in December.
Open all year, summer daily 10-5; winter daily 10-4. Trains: Sun & Summer BH's Sat & Mon; also Thu & Sat 15 Jul-2 Sep. Santa's North Pole Express Sat & Sun in Dec.
Admission free. Train travel £3 (ch & pen £1.50)
P 🍴 & *(some trains can carry disabled visitors) toilets for disabled shop*

EAST SUSSEX

Alfriston Clergy House
ALFRISTON
☎ (01323) 870001
The thatched and timber-framed parish priests' house was built in about 1350 and had not changed very much by 1896, when it was acquired by the National Trust. (It was the first building to be taken over by the Trust.) Now carefully and sensitively restored, it gives a vivid idea of medieval living conditions. Outside the house is a pretty cottage garden. Family Day is on 1 July 1995.
Open Apr-Oct daily 10.30-5 (or sunset if earlier). Last admission 30 mins before closing.
£2 (ch £1)
P shop ⊘
(NT)

Drusillas Park
ALFRISTON
(off A27)
☎ Eastbourne (01323) 870234 & 870656
This famous small zoo features many special areas including 'Out of Africa' with its meerkat mound, otter valley, world of owls, flamingo lagoon and beaver country. There are also beautiful gardens, an adventure playground, a railway, and a farm area. Special events for 1995 include: half-term activities and live music daily throughout the summer holidays. Drusillas Steam-up (10-11 June).
Open all year, daily 10-5 or dusk if earlier, (ex 24-26 Dec).
£5.20 (ch 3-12 £4.50, concessions £3.50). Incl zoo & railway ride & children 3-12 playland. Grounds free.
P 🍴 ✗ *licensed & (sensory trail throughout park) toilets for disabled shop garden centre ⊘ (ex gardens)*

Battle Abbey
BATTLE
☎ (01424) 773792
Built by William to commemorate his victory over Harold at the Battle of Hastings, today one can visit the excavated foundations of the abbey, and the monks' dormitory and common room which survived the Dissolution. An exhibition in the Great Gatehouse tells the day-to-day story of a monk's life at the abbey.
Open all year, Apr-Sep, daily 10-6. Oct-Mar, daily 10-4. Closed 24-26 Dec & 1 Jan.
£3.20 (ch £1.60, concessions £2.40)
P &
(EH)

Battle & District Historical Society Museum
BATTLE
Memorial Hall
☎ (01424) 775955
The focal point is a diorama of the Battle of Hastings and a reproduction of the Bayeux Tapestry. There are also local history exhibits. A Summer Arts Festival is held, and the Battle Festival takes place in June/July. Special displays of old photographs, toys etc are arranged throughout the season.
Open Etr-Sep, daily 10.30-4.30.
80p (ch 20p, ch accompanied free).
P (20yds) shop ⊘

Buckleys Yesterday's World
BATTLE
High St
☎ (01424) 775378
The whole family can experience 'a day in a bygone age' at the largest attraction of its kind in south east England. There are over 30 authentic Victorian and Edwardian shop and room settings, such as a chemists, general store and sweet shop, as well as a 1930's Southern Region railway station, displaying 100,000 nostalgic exhibits. Come face to face with Queen Victoria, an animated, speaking, life-size figure in the Royalty Room, where her nightdress and silk stockings are on display along with other items. Other attractions include an English country garden, children's play village, working model fairground, miniature golf, picnic site and refreshment terrace. Live folk and jazz bands play throughout the summer, usually on Sundays and Wednesdays. The first stage of a new attraction - The Medieval Cellar with a ghost story - is due to open in 1995.
Open all year, daily 10-6 (last admission 5pm) (Oct to Mar times subject to change)
£3.65 (ch £2.50, pen £2.95). Party 20+. Reduced admission Oct-Mar.
P *(100yds)* 🍴 *shop*

Bodiam Castle
BODIAM
(2m E of A21 Hurst Green)
☎ Staplecross (01580) 830436
Small and picturesque, Bodiam is like the castles that children draw. Its tall curtain walls form a rectangular court with round drum towers at each corner, all reflected in the water of the moat. It was built in 1386-8 by Sir Edward Dalrymple, for comfort and defence. The walls measure some 6ft 6in thick, and the great gatehouse was defended by gun loops and three portcullises, of which one has survived. The castle walls have remained remarkably intact, and although the castle was gutted in the Civil War it still has over 30 fireplaces and 28 garderobes (latrines), each with a drain shaft to the moat. The remains of the chapel, halls, chambers and kitchens (with fireplaces) can be seen and the circular stairs to the battlements give access to some lovely views. Special events for 1995 include: Dragon Egg Hunt (14 April), Medieval Spring Fair (29-30 April), Jazz Concert (24 June), Family Fun Day (23 July).
Open 18 Feb-Oct, daily 10-6 or dusk if earlier; Nov-2 Jan, Tue-Sun 10-dusk. (Closed 24-26 Dec & 1 Jan).
£2.50 (ch £1.30).
P *(charged)* 🍴 ✗ *licensed & (Braille guide, special parking on request) toilets for disabled shop ⊘ (ex in grounds)*
(NT)

BRIGHTON
Belief in the benefits of bathing in and drinking seawater had already transformed a south coast fishing village called Brighthelmstone into a seaside resort when the Prince Regent visited the town in 1783, liked it and decided to make a home there. Fashionable society followed, transforming Brighton into 'London by the sea', and the town still retains a singular blend of charm and raffishness in its Regency architecture, outrageous Royal Pavilion, antique shops, yacht marina, idiosyncratic museums and busy promenades.

Booth Museum of Natural History
BRIGHTON
194 Dyke Rd
☎ (01273) 552586 & 713299
The museum was built in 1874 to house the bird collection of Edward Thomas Booth (1840-1890). His collection is still on display, but the museum has expanded considerably since Booth's day and now includes thousands of butterfly and insect specimens, geology

Although now well inland, Bodiam Castle was built as a coastal defence in 1385 – for the River Rother was then navigable by sea-going vessels.

galleries with fossils, rocks and local dinosaur bones and a magnificent collection of animal skeletons, largely collected by F W Lucas (1842-1932), a Brighton solicitor. Conservation is also covered, with displays on the major habitats of Sussex showing how, over the ages, humans have managed and altered them. There is also a programme of exciting temporary exhibitions.
Open all year, Mon-Sat (ex Thu) 10-5, Sun 2-5. (Closed Good Fri, Xmas & 1 Jan). Free.
P & *shop ⊘*

Museum & Art Gallery
BRIGHTON
Church St
☎ (01273) 603005
The museum was built as the Prince Regent's stables and riding school. It now houses paintings and displays of musical instruments, Sussex archaeology, folklife and history, with the Willett collection of ceramics. A section of 20th-century fine and applied art has Art Nouveau, Art Deco and costume. The art gallery has an exciting programme of temporary exhibitions.
Open all year, Mon, Tue, Thu, Fri, & Sat 10-5. Sun 2-5. (Closed Wed, Good Fri, 25 & 26 Dec & 1 Jan). Free.
P *(NCP)* 🍴 & *shop ⊘*

Preston Manor
BRIGHTON
Preston Dr (off A23)
☎ (01273) 603005 ext 3239
This charming Edwardian manor house is beautifully furnished with notable collections of silver, furniture and paintings and presents a unique opportunity to see an Edwardian home both 'upstairs' and 'downstairs'. The servants' quarters can also be seen. The house is set in beautiful gardens.
Open all year, Tue-Sat 10-5, Sun 2-5. (Closed Mon (ex BH Mon), Good Fri & 25-26 Dec).
✱£2.60 *(ch £1.50, pen, students & UB40 £2.10). Family ticket £4.10-£6.50. Party 20+.*
P ⊘

Royal Pavilion
BRIGHTON
Old Steine
☎ (01273) 603005
The most extraordinary palace in Europe. This former seaside residence of King George IV with its myriad of domes and minarets and its brilliant and opulent interiors is a building no visitor to Brighton should miss. The £10 million structural restoration programme is now complete. Group tours by arrangement. Pavilion shop and tea room.
Open all year, Jun-Sep, daily 10-6; Oct-May, daily 10-5. (Closed 25-26 Dec).
✱£3.75 *(ch £2.10, concessions £2.75). Family tickets £5.85-£9.60. Joint ticket with Preston Manor £5.75. Party 20+.*
🍴 & *(facilities for the blind by arrangement) toilets for disabled shop ⊘*

Sea Life Centre
BRIGHTON
Marine Pde
☎ (01273) 604234 & 604233 info line
The sea life centre specialises in British marine creatures from all around the coast of Britain. On show is everything from worms to octopus, from sharks to stingrays as well as special pools where you can actually touch the sea creatures. One section is devoted to the recreation of the Victorian aquarium as it was 130 years ago. This includes many weird and wonderful fish including piranhas, catfish and hawksbill turtle. Visitors can also journey to the bottom of the sea on a walk through Europe's biggest underwater tunnel display. Diving displays during the Easter and summer holidays.
Open all year, daily (ex 25 Dec), 10-6. Last admission 5. (Open later in summer & school holidays)
✱£4.50 *(ch 4-14 £3.25, pen £3.75, students & UB40 £3.25, under 3 free). Party 10+.*
P *(200 yds)* 🍴 & *toilets for disabled shop ⊘*

Bateman's
BURWASH
(0.5m S)
☎ (01435) 882302
Rudyard Kipling lived at this lovely 17th-century ironmaster's house from 1902 to

1936. Kipling's study is kept much as it was then and among his many possessions to be seen around the property is his 1928 Rolls Royce. There are attractive gardens, with a restored watermill which grinds flour (Saturday afternoon only) for sale.
Open Apr-Oct, Sat-Wed 11-5.30, also open Good Fri , (last admission 4.30pm). Sat & Mon-Wed £4 (ch £2); Sun & BH's £4 (ch £2).
P ♥ ✗ *licensed* ♿ *toilets for disabled shop* ✿
(NT)

Moorlands
CROWBOROUGH
Friars Gate (2m N)
Three acres set in a lush valley adjoining Ashdown Forest. There are water gardens with ponds and streams, primulas, rhododendrons, azaleas and many unusual trees and shrubs.
Open Apr-Sep, Wed 11-5. Also Sun 7 & 28 May, 4 Jun & 23 Jul.
✿*£2 (ch free, pen £1.50).*
P

Eastbourne Redoubt Fortress
EASTBOURNE
Royal Pde
☎*(01323) 410300*
This huge fortification was built in 1804 in case of invasion by Napoleon, and has places for 11 guns. It is now the home of the Sussex Combined Services Museum (The Royal Sussex Regiment and the Queen's Royal Irish Hussars).
Open Etr-Oct, 9.30-5.30.
P *(200 yds)* ♥ *shop*
Details not confirmed for 1995

"How We Lived Then" Museum of Shops & Social History
EASTBOURNE
20 Cornfield Ter
☎*(01323) 737143*
Over the last 35 years, Jan and Graham Upton have collected over 75,000 items which are now displayed on three floors of authentic old shops and room-settings, transporting visitors back to the age of their grandparents. Grocers, chemists, sweet shops, iron-mongers, tailors, cobblers, photographers, jewellers, music and toy shops are all represented in fascinating detail, as well as a Post Office, complete with dour postmistress. Other displays, such as seaside souvenirs, wartime rationing and Royal mementoes, help to capture 100 years of social history. The gift shop includes old fashioned sweets, reproduction tins, advertisements and tin-plate and Victorian-style greetings cards.
Open daily Feb-Dec, 10-5.30 (last entry 5pm).
£2.25 (ch £1.25, pen £1.75). Party 10+.
♿ *shop*

Lifeboat Museum
EASTBOURNE
King Edward's Pde
☎*(01323) 730717*
The work of lifeboats which have been stationed at Eastbourne is illustrated here, as is the work of the Royal National Lifeboat Institution in general. Lifeboat models are shown, with the sails and oars from the last sailing lifeboat at the station, and gear worn by lifeboat men. There are also descriptions and photographs of notable rescues.
Open 7-10 days prior to Etr-Dec, 9.30-5. Free.
P *(adjacent)* ♿ *shop* ✿ 🚂

Tower 73 The Wish Tower
EASTBOURNE
King Edward's Pde
☎*(01323) 410440*
The Wish Tower exhibition is housed in Martello Tower 73, completed in 1806 and intended as a defence fortification against Napoleon. Today, an audio-visual show tells the story of Martello towers in south east England and an animatronic figure of the soldier responsible for their building tells his tale.
Open Etr-Sep, daily 9.30-5.30. Contact (0424) 422964 for details of winter opening.
P *shop* ✿
Details not confirmed for 1995

Towner Art Gallery & Local Museum
EASTBOURNE
High St, Old Town (on A259)
☎*(01323) 411688 & 417961*
The Towner is housed in an elegant 18th-century building set in delightful gardens in Eastbourne's Old Town and is home to a splendid collection of 19th-and 20th-century British art. This includes the South East Arts Collection of Contemporary Art and a gallery devoted to Eric Ravilious, Eastbourne's most acclaimed 20th-century artist. A lively programme of changing exhibitions is complemented by talks, workshops and other events. Eastbourne past and present is explored in the fascinating local history collection.
Open all year, Wed-Sat 10-5, Sun & BH Mon 2-5. (Closed Mon, Tue, Good Fri, 24-26 Dec & 1 Jan).
✿*£2 (concessions £1.40).*
P ♿ *shop* ✿

The Living World
EXCEAT
Seven Sisters Country Park (on A259, 2m E of Seaford)
☎*Alfriston (01323) 870100*
This is a living exhibition of small creatures: butterflies, bees, spiders, snails, moths, scorpions, marine life and others, in settings that are as near to nature as possible. The displays of this unique mini zoo are based in two old Sussex barns, situated in a 700-acre Country Park within the Heritage Coastline. A recent display includes the Bearded Dragon Lizards. Every Wednesday during school holidays, children can enjoy the 'mini beast' handling experience - visitors will be allowed to handle certain exhibits.
Open all year, mid Mar-1 Nov, daily;

The exotic, onion-domed pavilion at Brighton was created about 1820 for the Prince Regent, by John Nash, in the newly-fashionable 'Indian-style'.

Nov-mid Mar, wknds & school holidays 10-5.
£2.40 (ch & pen £1.60, ch 5 free). Family ticket £7. Wheelchair users free.
P ♥ ✗ *licensed* ♿ *toilets for disabled shop*

Firle Place
FIRLE
(off A27)
☎*Glynde (01273) 858335*
Home of the Gage family for over 500 years, the house has a Tudor core but was remodelled in the 18th century. Its treasures include important European and English Old Master paintings, fine English and French furniture, and porcelain, including notable examples from Sèvres and English factories. There are family monuments and brasses in the church at West Firle.
Open May-Sep, Sun, Wed & Thu; also Etr, Spring, May & Aug BH Sun & Mon 2-5.
£3.50 (ch £2). Groups 25+. Connoisseurs Day £4.50. Private viewing 25+ by appointment only.
P ✗ *licensed* ♿ *shop* ✿ *(ex in garden)*
See advertisement on page 54

Bedgebury National Pinetum
FLIMWELL
(1.5m N off A21 onto B2079)
☎*Goudhurst (01580) 211044*
Bedgebury Pinetum is the national collection of conifers hardy in Britain. Some 900 species are currently on show, landscaped around three lakes and two streams. Rhododendron species and hybrids add to the collection's beauty and wildflowers are also plentiful. Visitors can walk in most areas, although two waymarked walks with information are included. There are areas of steep ground so it is advisable to wear stout shoes. Special events for 1995 include open-air theatre one night a week in July and August, and a craft fair on 18 June.
Open all year, daily 10-7 or dusk. Visitor centre Etr-Sep, daily 10-5.
£1.80 (ch £1, pen £1.30).
P ♿ *toilets for disabled shop*

Glynde Place
GLYNDE
Lewes (off A27 between Lewes & Eastbourne)
☎*(01273) 858224*
A lovely Elizabethan manor with 18th-century additions, in a beautiful downland setting. It is still a family home, lived in by descendants of the original owner.
Open May-Sep, Wed, Thu & Sun 2-5. Also BH's.
£3 (ch free iaccompanied by an adult). Party 20+
P ♥ ✿

Groombridge Place Gardens & Enchanted Forest
GROOMBRIDGE
(On B2100)
☎*Tunbridge Wells (01892) 863999*
Set against the backdrop of the classical moated mansion are the famous 17th-century walled gardens and the Enchanted Forest which have inspired artists, writers, and connoiseurs of beauty for hundreds of years. Among the attractions are the magnificent Barons Hall, and the walks through the mystical Enchanted Forest with its spring-fed pools and dramatic views of the Weald.
Open Apr-May, wknds & BH 2-6; Jun-Sep, Sun-Wed & Sat 2-6; Oct, 1st & 2nd wknds only, 2-6. Last admission 5.30pm,
P ♥ ♿ *shop* ✿
Details not confirmed for 1995

Michelham Priory
HAILSHAM
Upper Dicker (2.5m W off A22)
☎*Eastbourne (01323) 844224*
Set on a tranquil moated island surrouded by spacious gardens, Michelham Priory is one of the most beautiful historic houses in Sussex. Founded in 1229 for Augustinian canons, the Priory is approached through a 14th-century gatehouse spanning the longest medieval moat in the country. Most of the original buildings were demolished during the Dissolution, but the remains were incorporated into a Tudor farm that became a splendid country house, now containing a fascinating array of exhibits. Outside, the picturesque gardens are ➤

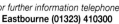

Firle Place

Nr. Lewes on A27 Eastbourne Road Glynde (01273) 858335.

In parkland setting under South Downs, beautiful home of the Viscount Gage. Connoisseurs collection of European and English Old Masters, notable Sèvres and English porcelain and fine French and English furniture. Historic American connections.

OPEN: SUNDAYS, WEDNESDAYS & THURSDAYS (2.00pm till last ticket 5.00pm). May - end Sept also B.H. Suns/Mons during season.

ADMISSION:

Adults	£3.50
Child	£2.00
Pre-Booked Groups of 25+	£3.00
Connoisseurs (NO Group reduction)	£4.50
Private Weekday Exclusive Viewing	£5.50 (£137.50 min.)

(Children = 5-15 inclusive, under 5 no charge)

enhanced by a working watermill, physic garden, smithy, rope museum and the dramatic Elizabethan Great Barn. Facilities include licensed restaurant and tearooms, picnic and play area and a Sussex crafts shop.
Open 25 Mar-Oct, daily; Mar & Nov, Sun only; Mar, Oct-Nov 11-4; Apr-Jul & Sep 11-5; Aug 10.30-5.30.
£3.60 (ch 5-16 £2, pen £2.90, disabled £1.60). Family ticket £9.50 Party 20+.
P ⓧ *licensed & (wheelchairs & braille guide available) toilets for disabled shop* ⌀ *(ex in car park)*

Bentley Wildfowl & Motor Museum
HALLAND
(7m NE of Lewes, signposted on A22/A26/B2192)
☎ *(01825) 840573*
Hundreds of swans, geese and ducks from all over the world can be seen on lakes and ponds along with flamingoes and peacocks. There is a fine array of veteran, Edwardian and vintage vehicles, and the house has splendid antiques and wildfowl paintings. The gardens specialise in old fashioned roses. Other attractions include woodland walks, a nature trail, audio-visual aids in the Education Centre, adventure playground, small animal section, and a miniature train which runs on summer Sundays, and Wednesdays in August. Quiz sheet available. Special events are planned for the summer.
Open 20 Mar-Oct, daily 10.30-4.30 (5pm Jul & Aug), House open from 12. Nov, Feb & part of Mar, wknds only. Estate closed Dec & Jan. House closed all winter.
❄*Summer £3.60 (ch 4-15 £2, pen £2.80). Family ticket £9.95. Winter £2.80. Special rates for disabled.Prices under review.*
P ⓧ & *(wheelchairs available) toilets for disabled shop* ⌀

Fishermen's Museum
HASTINGS
Rock a Nore Rd
☎ *(01424) 461446*
This was once the fishermen's church, and now houses such exhibits as paintings, photographs, model craft, and the last of Hastings' luggers built for sail.
Open end May-Sep, Mon-Fri 10.30-5, Sat & Sun 2.30-5.
Free.
P *(50yds)* &

Hastings Embroidery
HASTINGS
Town Hall, Queen's Rd
☎ *(01424) 718888*
The 80yd embroidery illustrates great events in British history from 1066 to modern times. It was sewn by the Royal School of Needlework, using threads, cords, metals, lace, jewels and appropriate cloths.
Open May-Sep, Mon-Fri 10-5; Oct-Apr, Mon-Fri 11.30-3.30. (Closed BH). Last admission 30 mins before close.
❄*£1.25 (ch & pen 75p). Party 10 +.*
P & *toilets for disabled shop* ⌀

Hastings Museum & Art Gallery
HASTINGS
Cambridge Rd
☎ *(01424) 781155*
A wide variety of displays, including new dinosaur and local wildlife galleries, also local industry and ironwork as well as painting and ceramics. Exhibitions and events are held throughout the year. A new North American Indian gallery is due to open in early 1995.
Open daily Mon-Fri 10-5, Sat 10-1, 2-5, Sun 3-5.
Free.
P & ⌀

Old Town Hall Museum of Local History
HASTINGS
Old Town Hall, High St
☎ *(01424) 781166*
Situated in the heart of Hastings Old Town, the museum was originally a Georgian Town Hall built in 1823. Displays include the History of Hastings, the Battle of Hastings, the Cinque Ports and maritime history - smuggling, shipwrecks and fishing. Famous local personalities, including Logie Baird, inventor of television, are also featured.
Open Etr-Sep, Tue-Sun 10-1 & 2-5; Oct-Dec & Mar 2-4 (ex Wed).
Free.
& *shop* ⌀

Smugglers Adventure
HASTINGS
St Clements Caves, West Hill
☎ *(01424) 422964*
A Smuggler's Adventure is a themed experience housed in a labyrinth of caverns and passages deep below the West Hill. Visitors first tour a comprehensive exhibition and museum, followed by a video theatre, before embarking on the Adventure Walk - a trip through several acres of caves with life-size tableaux, push-button automated models and dramatic scenic effects depicting life in the days of 18th-century smuggling.
Open all year daily, Etr-Sep 10-5.30; Oct-Etr 11-4.30. (Closed 25-26 Dec).
£3.80 (ch £2.50, pen & students £3.20). Family ticket £10.95.
P *(500yds) shop* ⌀

1066 Story in Hastings Castle
HASTINGS
Castle Hill Rd, West Hill
☎ *(01424) 781111*
The ruins of the Norman castle stand on the cliffs, close to the site of William the Conqueror's first motte-and-bailey castle in England. It was excavated in 1825 and 1968, and old dungeons were discovered in 1894. 'The Story of 1066', within the Castle grounds, is an exciting audio-visual experience covering the history of Hastings Castle and the famous battle of 1066. An unusual approach to the castle can be made via the West Hill Cliff Railway which is located in George Street precinct.
Open Apr-Sep 10-5 (5.30 school holidays). Oct onwards 11-3.30 (Closed Jan). £2.50 (ch £1.75, pen & students £2). Family ticket £7.50.
P & *shop* ⌀

British Engineerium-Museum of Steam & Mechanical Antiquities
HOVE
off Nevill Rd
☎ *Brighton (01273) 559583*
This restored Victorian water pumping station has an original working beam engine of 1876, and a French Corliss horizontal engine which won first prize at the Paris International Exhibition of 1889. There are also traction engines, fire engines, and many other fun-size and model engines. Boilers are fired up and 'in steam' the first Sunday of each month and Bank Holidays.
Open all year, daily 10-4 (Closed wk prior to Xmas). In Steam first Sun in month & BH's. £3 (ch, students & pen £2).
P & *shop* ⌀

Anne of Cleves House Museum
LEWES
52 Southover High St
☎ *(01273) 474610*
This 16th-century town house was given to Anne of Cleves by her ex-husband, Henry VIII as part of her divorce settlement, though she never lived in the house. It is now devoted to Sussex arts and crafts, agricultural, industrial and domestic life, with a notable collection of Sussex ironwork including early gun-founding material. There is a medieval herb garden outside.
Open Etr or Apr-Oct, Mon-Sat 10-5.30. Sun 2-5.30. (last admission 5pm). Nov-

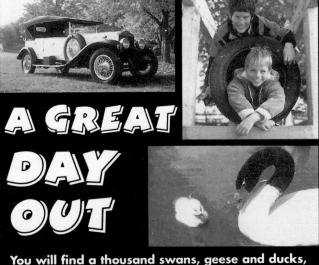

Perfect for steam enthusiasts, trains run regularly along the 10 miles of track revived by the Bluebell Railway. The largest collection of carriages and locomotives in the region is housed here.

Mar, Tue & Thu 10-5.
£1.80 (ch 90p). Party.
P & shop 🐾

Castle & Museum of Sussex Archaeology
LEWES
169 High St
☎(01273) 486290
The imposing ruins of Lewes Castle dominate the town. Originally Norman, it shows signs of rebuilding in the 13th and 14th centuries, and again under Thomas Read Kemp MP and others. The 16th-to 18th-century Barbican House has a museum with displays on prehistoric, Roman, Saxon and medieval Sussex. Lewes Living History Model is a 25 minute tape/slide presentation exploring the town's 1,000 year history, using an accurate model of Lewes in the 1880s as a background. The range of events for 1995 includes Shakespeare in the Spring, Lewes Visual Arts Festival in August, and the Sealed Knot Garrison in October.
Open all year, Castle & Museum Mon-Sat 10-5.30; Sun 11-5.30.
£2.90 (ch £1.50). (Includes Lewes Living History Model).
P & shop 🐾 (ex in Castle grounds)

Garden Paradise
NEWHAVEN
Avis Rd (signposted off A26 & A259)
☎(01273) 513985
Here visitors can wander through two acres of leisure gardens with lakes, fountains and waterfalls. Visit Plantasia, the amazing desert and tropical gardens, and Planet Earth, a world of natural history, where visitors can see how plants and animals live 2000 million years ago. The World of Dinosaurs, the miniature railway and play areas are other features. These attractions are part of a gardening and horticultural centre.
Open all year, daily. (Closed 25-26 Dec).
Admission fee payable.
P 🍽 ✕ & (all areas level or ramped) toilets for disabled shop garden centre 🐾

Great Dixter
NORTHIAM
(off A28)
☎(01797) 252878
Dating back to the 15th century, this half-timbered house has a notable great hall and fine gardens.
Open Apr-15 Oct, Tue-Sun & BH Mon 2-5; Gardens open as house and also from 11am on 28-30 May, Sun in Jul & Aug & 29 Aug.
House & Gardens £3.50 (ch 50p).
Gardens only £2.50 (ch 25p).
Concessions NT members & pen on Fri £3
P shop garden centre 🐾

Pevensey Castle
PEVENSEY
☎(01323) 762604
Built on the site of a 3rd-century Roman fort, Pevensey Castle has Norman and 13th century additions. It has never been taken by force. Ancient fireplaces, dungeons and an oubliette can be seen.
Open all year, Apr-Sep, daily 10-6; Oct, daily 10-4; Nov-Mar, Wed-Sun 10-4. Closed 24-26 Dec & 1 Jan.
✱£2 (ch £1, concessions £1.50).
P 🍽 & 🐾
(EH)

Lamb House
RYE
West St
☎(01892) 890651
This 18th-century house was the home of novelist Henry James from 1898 until his death in 1916, and was later occupied by E F Benson writer of the *Lucia* books, who was at one time Mayor of Rye. The house is surrounded by an attractive garden.
Open three rooms only Apr-Oct, Wed & Sat 2-6 (last admission 5.30pm).
£2. No reductions.
P 🐾 🚃
(NT)

Rye Museum
RYE
Rye Castle, Gun Garden
☎(01797) 226728
The museum is housed in a stone tower built as a fortification in 1249. It was later used for 300 years as the town prison, and the cells remain. The display is of the Cinque Ports and local history, with sections on Rye's maritime interests, Rye pottery and life in Rye over the centuries. A topographical map of Romney Marsh with cliffline and changes in sea levels is part of the display.
Open Etr-Oct, daily 10.30-5.30. (last admission 30 mins before close). Nov-Mar most wknds 11.30-3.30)
£1.50 (ch 16 50p, ch 7 free, students & pen £1). Party 10 +.
P (30yds) shop 🐾

Sheffield Park Garden
SHEFFIELD PARK
(5m E of Haywards Heath off A275)
☎Danehill (01825) 790231
Originally landscaped by 'Capability' Brown, in about 1775, to create a beautiful park with five lakes and a cascade, further extensive planting was done at the beginning of the 20th century. This has given Sheffield Park a superb collection of trees, with particular emphasis on those that give good autumn colour. In May and June masses of azaleas and rhododendrons give colour and later there are magnificent waterlilies on the lakes. The gardens and woodland cover nearly 200 acres.
Open Mar: Sat & Sun 11-4. Apr-5 Nov, Tue-Sun & BH Mon 11-6 or sunset if earlier; 8 Nov-16 Dec: Wed-Sat 11-4. Last admission 1hr before closing.
✱£4 (ch £2) May & Oct. £3.70 (ch £1.80) rest of year.
P 🍽 & (powered self drive car & wheelchairs available) toilets for disabled shop 🐾
(NT)

Bluebell Railway Museum
SHEFFIELD PARK STATION
(4.5m E of Haywards Heath, off A275)
☎Newick (01825) 723777 & 722370 (Train Information)
As its name suggests this ten-mile long, revived steam-railway line runs through woodland that is a mass of bluebells in the springtime. There is a regular service throughout the year, along with Pullman Dining Trains on Saturday evenings, and Luncheon Trains on Sundays which operate daily from June to September. Overnight en suite accommodation is available in luxury 'Queen of Scots' sleeping cars. It is also possible to charter trains with catering for private functions. Part of the station is a museum which has the largest collection of locomotives and carriages in the region. There are many special events organised for 1995, 35th anniversary year.
Open all year, Sat & Sun. Daily May-Sep. Santa Specials run Dec. For timetable

and information regarding trains contact above.
3rd class return fare £7 (ch 3-15 £3.50). Family ticket £19. Museum & locomotive sheds only, £2 (ch £1). Supplementary available for 1st class travel.
P 🍽 ✕ licensed & toilets for disabled shop

Winchelsea Museum
WINCHELSEA
Court Hall
☎Rye (01797) 224395
The Court Hall, one of the oldest buildings in Winchelsea, now houses the museum with the old prison cells underneath. Dating back to the 13th century, it was restored in the 16th and later centuries. There is a model of the town as it was in 1292, collections of clay pipes, bottles and other exhibits of local interest.
Open mid May-Sep, Tue-Sat 10.30-12.30 & 2-5; Sun 2-5.
shop 🐾

ESSEX

Audley End House
AUDLEY END
☎Saffron Walden (01799) 522399
A 17th-century house built by Thomas Howard, Earl of Suffolk, with some work by Robert Adam. Pictures and furnishings in state room. Miniature railway in grounds.
Open Apr-Sep, Wed-Sun & BH's noon-6 (last admission 5).
£5.50 (ch £2.80, concessions £4.10). Grounds £3 (ch £1.50, concessions £2.30)
P (charged) 🍽 & 🐾
(EH)

Colne Valley Railway & Museum
CASTLE HEDINGHAM
Castle Hedingham Station (4m NW of Halstead on A604)
☎Hedingham (01787) 461174
The old Colne Valley and Halstead railway buildings have been rebuilt here. Stock includes seven steam locomotives plus forty other engines, carriages and wagons, in steam from Easter to December. There is also a five-acre riverside nature and picnic area. Visitors may also dine in style in restored Pullman carriages while travelling along the line. Please telephone for a free timetable and details of the many special events which include gala days, summer specials, Great Eastern Victorian Specials, photographic specials and Santa Specials.
Open all year, daily 10-dusk. Steam days, rides from 12-4. (Closed 23 Dec-1 Feb). Steam days £4 (ch £2, pen £3); Family ticket £10. Non-steam days (to view static exhibits only) £2 (ch £1 & pen £1); Family ticket £5.
P 🍽 ✕ licensed & shop 🐾

Hedingham Castle
CASTLE HEDINGHAM
(on B1058, 1m off A604)
☎Hedingham (01787) 460261
This majestic Norman castle was built in 1140. It was besieged by King John, and visited by King Henry VII, King Henry VIII and Queen Elizabeth I and was the home of the de Veres, Earls of Oxford, for over 500 years. The Keep is one of the finest and best preserved in England and stands 100ft high. Children love to explore the castle with its splendid banqueting hall and minstrels' gallery. Visitors can enjoy the peaceful woodland walks and perhaps have a picnic by the beautiful lake.
Open 8 Apr-10 Sep, daily ex Fri, 11-5; 10 Sep-29 Oct, Sat & Sun only. Open 10am bank hol wknds & Good Fri.
£2.75 (ch £1.75). Family ticket £7.50.
🅿 🍴 ♿ *shop*

Chelmsford & Essex Museum, Essex Regiment Museum
CHELMSFORD
Oaklands Park, Moulsham St
☎(01245) 353066 & 260614
On the ground floor of this museum there are displays of fossils, the Story of Chelmsford Galleries, pictures, a Victorian living room, a shop and the Essex Regiment Museum. Other exhibits, on the first floor, include natural history, a bee room with an observation hide, social history and costume, decorative arts, early 18th-century drinking glasses and coins.
Open all year, Mon-Sat 10-5, Sun 2-5. (Closed Good Fri, 25-26 Dec.
Free.
🅿 ♿ *toilets for disabled shop* ⌘

Paycocke's
COGGESHALL
West St
☎(01376) 561305
This timber-framed house is a fine example of a medieval merchant's home. It was completed in about 1505 and has interesting carvings on the outside timbers, including the Paycocke trade sign. Inside there are further elaborate carvings and linenfold panelling. Behind the house is a pretty garden.
Open 26 Mar-29 Oct Tue, Thu, Sun & BH Mon 2-5.30. (Closed Good Fri). Last admission 5.
£1.40 (ch 70p).
♿ ⌘ ⌗
(NT)

Beth Chatto Gardens
COLCHESTER
Elmstead Market (7m E on A133)
☎Wivenhoe (01206) 822007
The gardens were begun only 30 years ago, when Beth Chatto and her husband began working on four acres of wasteland. Today the wasteland has become a garden of three areas, each with their own distinctive character and plants. First is the south-west facing dry garden, which is on gravel and has plants which can cope with drought, such as yucca and pineapple broom. It faces a group of oaks which shade the second area, with woodland and other shade-loving plants, including some chosen for their fine foliage. Lastly, there is the wetland garden, with five large pools filled with fish and surrounded by swathes of exotic and native bog plants. The former grass car park has been transformed into a new gravel garden for plants adapted to drought. A new larger car park is nearby. The nursery has over 2000 different plants.
Open all year, Mar-Oct, Mon-Sat 9-5; Nov-Feb, Mon-Fri 9-4. (Closed BHs).
£2. Prices under review
🅿 ⌘

Colchester Castle Museum
COLCHESTER
Castle Park, High St
☎(01206) 712931 & 712932
This is the largest Norman Castle Keep in Europe. It was built over the remains of the magnificent Roman Temple of Claudius which was destroyed by Boudica in AD60.
Colchester was the first capital of Roman Britain, and the archaeological collections are among the finest in the country. Displays include exciting 'hands-on' learning for all the family, and an exhibition on medieval Colchester. Please telephone for details of the exciting range of associated holiday events.
Open all year, Mon-Sat 10-5, Sun (Mar-Nov) 2-5. Last admission 4.30pm. (Closed 24-26 Dec).
£2.50 (ch & concessions £1.50).
🅿 ♿ *toilets for disabled shop* ⌘

Colchester Zoo
COLCHESTER
Stanway, Maldon Rd (3m W of town B1022)
☎(01206) 331292
One of England's finest zoos, Colchester zoo has over one hundred and seventy five types of animals. Visitors can meet the elephants, handle a snake, and see parrots, seals, penguins and birds of prey all appearing in fun, informative daily displays. New enclosures include Penguin Shores, the Wilds of Asia for orangutans, and Chimps World. 1995 is the Year of the Cat at Colchester Zoo, with informative interactive displays all about cats. There is also an amusement complex, two adventure play areas, several eating places and gift shops, all set in forty acres of beautiful gardens. Special events include Make a Wish Weekend (10-11 June), Teddy Bears' Picnic (30 July), Family Fun Day (20 August).
Open all year, daily from 9.30. Last admission 5.30pm (1hr before dusk out of season). (Closed 25 Dec).
£5 (ch 3-13 £3, pen £4, disabled £2.50).
🅿 🍴 ✗ *licensed* ♿ *toilets for disabled shop* ⌘

Hollytrees Museum
COLCHESTER
High St
☎(01206) 712931
Two centuries of fascinating toys, costume and decorative arts are displayed in this attractive Georgian town house built in 1718.
Open all year, Tue-Sat 10-5. (Closed Good Fri & 23-27 Dec).
Free.
🅿 *town centre* ♿ *shop* ⌘

Natural History Museum
COLCHESTER
All Saints Church, High St
☎(01206) 712931
Displays on the natural environment of north-east Essex from the Ice Age to today's town wildlife, including impressive dioramas and a range of popular 'hands-on' exhibits for children.
Open all year, Tue-Sat 10-5. (Closed Sun, Good Fri & pm 23-27 Dec).
Free.
♿ *shop* ⌘

Social History Museum
COLCHESTER
Holy Trinity Church, Trinity Sq
☎(01206) 712931
Town and country life in the Colchester area over the last two hundred years are displayed in this medieval former Church of Holy Trinity complete with Saxon tower.
Open Apr-Sep, Tue-Sat 10-12 & 1-5 (summer only).
Free.
♿ *shop* ⌘

Tymperleys Clock Museum
COLCHESTER
Trinity St
☎(01206) 712931 & 712932
A fine collection of Colchester-made clocks on display in this restored, late 15th-century house.
Open Apr-Oct, Mon-Sat 10-1 & 2-5.
Free.
♿ *shop* ⌘

Thurrock Museum
GRAYS
Thameside Complex, Orsett Rd
☎Grays Thurrock (01375) 382555
Local history, agriculture, trades and industries are illustrated, with a display on archaeology from the Stone Age to the Medieval period.
Open all year, Mon-Sat 9-8. (Closed BH).
Free.
🅿 *(charged)* ♿ *toilets for disabled shop* ⌘

Hadleigh Castle
HADLEIGH
A familiar sight from Constable's paintings, the castle was first built by Hubert de Burgh and has fine views of the Thames estuary. It is defended by ditches on three sides, and the north-east and south-east towers are still impressive. The latter has a fireplace and three garderobe (latrine) shafts.
Open any reasonable time.
Free.
(EH)

Harlow Museum
HARLOW
Passmores House, Third Av
☎(01279) 454959
Harlow is best known as a new town, but the museum tells its story from Prehistoric and Roman to modern times, with a section on the Harlow Potters and the New Town. It is housed in an early Georgian building set in gardens. Part of the medieval moat from an earlier house can be seen.
Open all year, Tue-Sat 10-12.30 & 1.30-5. £2 (concessions £1). Local residents £1 (concessions 50p).
🅿 ♿ *shop* ⌘

Mark Hall Cycle Museum & Gardens
HARLOW
Muskham Rd off First Av
☎(01279) 439680
The history of the bicycle is illustrated with over 80 examples, from an 1818 hobby horse to a plastic machine of 1982, and a wide range of accessories and memorabilia. There are also three walled gardens, a 17th-century herb garden and a cottage garden.
Open all year, Sun-Fri 10-5 (Closed Xmas & BH)
£1 (ch & pen 50p)
🅿 ♿ *toilets for disabled shop* ⌘

The Redoubt
HARWICH
☎(01255) 503429
The 180ft-diameter circular fort was built in 1808 in case of invasion by Napoleon. It has a dry moat and 8ft-thick walls, with 18 rooms for stores, ammunition and quarters for 300 men. The Redoubt is being restored by the Harwich Society, and contains three small museums. Ten guns can be seen on the battlements. Annual fete 29 May.
Open all year, Sun 10-12 & 2-5. Also 30 May, Sat in Jul & daily in Aug, 2-5. (Closed 25 Dec-29 May).
£1 (accompanied ch free).
P *(200yds) shop*

HEDINGHAM
See Castle Hedingham

Layer Marney Tower
LAYER MARNEY
(off B1022)
☎Colchester (01206) 330784
The only parts of the grand mansion planned by Sir Henry Marney to be completed were the remarkable gatehouse and west wing. However, the red-brick and terracotta-patterned gatehouse is grander than those of some royal palaces, and remains one of the great buildings of the 16th century. Also of interest is a rare breeds farm, the formal gardens, a medieval barn, a church, a farm shop and the deer park. Special events are planned for 1995.
Open Apr-Sep, Mon-Fri 2-6, Sun 12-6 & BHs 11-6.
£3 (ch £1.50). Family ticket £8. Guided tour £4. Party 20+.
🅿 🍴 ♿ *(ramps in garden) toilets for disabled shop* ⌘

The Beth Chatto Gardens have over 1000 species of herbaceous plants in varied terrain – offering water, woodland and Mediterranean gardens.

Mistley Towers
MISTLEY

All that remains of the grand hall and church, commissioned by Richard Rigby and designed by Robert Adam, are the lodges built in 1782 for the hall, and two square, classic towers topped with drums and domes which Adam had added to an earlier church.
Open all reasonable times.
Free.
& *(exterior only)*
(EH)

Mole Hall Wildlife Park
NEWPORT

Widdington
☎ *Saffron Walden (01799) 540400*
Set within the grounds of a part-Elizabethan hall, which is not open to the public, this wildlife park has a large collection of birds and animals in pools and enclosures. It offers a rare opportunity to see otters feeding and at play, and other creatures are housed in attractive pens within a garden setting where many waterfowl roam free. A signposted walk takes visitors through a deer paddock. The butterfly house and insect pavillion allow visitors to wander through a tropical environment with exotic plants and beautiful free-flying butterflies. There is a large pool for Koi and other fish (open to adults only). A small tea shop provides a welcome break, and a gift shop sells interesting items pertaining to natural history, displays of butterflies and mementoes.
Open all year, daily 10.30-6 (or dusk).
(Closed 25 Dec). Butterfly House open mid Mar-mid Nov.
£4 (ch £2.60, pen £3.20). Party.
🅿 🍴 *shop* ⊗

Saffron Walden Museum
SAFFRON WALDEN

Museum St
☎ *(01799) 510333*

In the Middle Ages, the buildings of the prosperous town of Saffron Walden were often decorated with elaborate plasterwork known as pargetting.

Built in 1834, this friendly museum lies near the castle ruins in the centre of town. Its collections include local archaeology, natural history, ceramics, glass, costume, furniture, toys, an ancient Egyptian room and a new geology gallery. Special exhibitions planned for 1995 include: Violet Dix's Trunk childhood in the early 20th century, prints and printmaking, wildlife photography, Chinese embroidery and textiles.
Open all year, Mar-Oct, Mon-Sat 10-5, Sun & BHs 2.30-5; Nov-Feb, Mon-Sat, 11-4, Sun & BHs 2.30-4.30. (Closed 24 & 25 Dec).
£1 (concessions 50p & ch under 18 free).
🅿 & *(lift, ramp to entrance, stairlift) toilets for disabled shop* ⊗

Central Museum & Planetarium
SOUTHEND-ON-SEA

Victoria Av
☎ *(01702) 330214*
A fine Edwardian building housing displays of archaeology, natural history and local history, telling the story of man in the south-east Essex area. Also the only planetarium in the South East outside London. A major exhibition The Stars at our Service is planned forr summer 1995.
Open - Central Museum Mon 1-5, Tue-Sat 10-5 (Closed Sun & BH); Planetarium Wed-Sat, shows at 10, 11, noon, 2, 3 & 4.
❋*Central Museum free. Planetarium £2 (ch & pen £1.50). Family tickets. Party. P (behind library)* & *(planetarium not accessible) shop* ⊗

House on the Hill Toy Museum
STANSTED

☎ *(01279) 813237*
One of the largest toy museums in Europe, housed on two floors covering 7,000 sq. ft. A huge variety of toys, books and games from the late Victorian period up to the 1970s. There is a train room, space display, Teddy Bears' picnic, Action Men, Sindy, Barbie, military displays and much more. A puppet theatre provides lots of animation. Plus a Collector's Shop that buys and sells old toys.
Open daily, 12 Mar-12 Nov 10-5; 13 Nov-11 Mar wknds & school hols.
£2.80 (ch £1.80, pen & student £2.30). Party.
🅿 *shop* ⊗

Mountfitchet Castle & Norman Village
STANSTED

(off B1383, in centre of village)
☎ *(01279) 813237*

Norman motte and bailey castle and village reconstructed as it was in Norman England of 1066, on its historic site. A vivid illustration of village life in Domesday England, complete with houses, church, seige tower, seige weapons, and many types of animals roaming freely. Animated wax figures in all the buildings give historical information to visitors. There are many special events planned throughout the year. Telephone for details and dates.
Open daily, 12 Mar-12 Nov 10-5.
£3.75 (ch £2.75, pen & student £3). Party.
🅿 🍴 & *(laser commentaries) toilets for disabled shop* ⊗

Tilbury Fort
TILBURY

☎ *(01375) 858489*
The fort dates from the reign of Henry VIII, but is most famous for Queen Elizabeth I's review of the fleet and army gathered to fight the Spanish Armada. In about 1670 the fort was extensively altered for defence against the Dutch and the French - ironically, it was designed by a Dutchman in the French style.
Open all year, Apr-Sep, daily 10-6; Oct, daily 10-4; Nov-Mar, Wed-Sun 10-4. Closed 24-26 Dec & 1 Jan.
£1.80 (ch 90p, pen, students & UB40 £1.40).
🅿 & ⊗
(EH)

Hayes Hill Farm
WALTHAM ABBEY

Stubbings Hall Ln, Crooked Mile
☎ *(01992) 892291*
A traditional-style farmyard which has been opened to the public. Visitors can see a range of farm animals, kept in the ➜

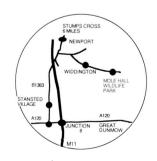

traditional way, plus tools and machinery from earlier times. The centrepiece of the farm is a restored 16th-century barn. On Sundays and Bank Holidays there are demonstrations of traditional crafts. Your visit also includes a look around Holyfield Hall Farm, a working commercial dairy and arable farm of some 435 acres. There are 150 Fresian cows, and milking takes place at 2.45pm every day. Booked guided tours are available.
Open all year, Mon-Fri 10-4.30, wknds & BH 10-6.
🅿 & *toilets for disabled shop*
Details not confirmed for 1995

Waltham Abbey Gatehouse, Bridge & Entrance to Cloisters
WALTHAM ABBEY
Beside the great Norman church at Waltham are the ruins of the abbey buildings. Little remains but a 14th-century bridge and gatehouse, with both pedestrian and vehicle entrances, and part of the 12th-century north cloister. The bridge is named after King Harold, founder of the abbey. The church has an undercroft museum.
Open any reasonable time.
Free.
🅿
(EH)

GLOUCESTERSHIRE

Barnsley House Garden
BARNSLEY
(3m NE of Cirencester on B4425)
☎ Cirencester (01285) 740281
This lovely garden is the creation of Rosemary Verey, who since 1960 has transformed the older garden that was here. There are herbs and a knot garden, and best of all a vegetable garden planted as a French 'potager orné', with small paths forming a chequerboard around fruit trees trained as pyramids, ornamental brassicas and other decorative kitchen plants. They are planted for effect in groups rather than allotment-style rows, but not simply for show, being constantly cut, picked and used by the family. The garden is also interesting for its use of ground cover in the borders. Other features include a laburnum walk (good in early June) and a lime walk. Two 18th-century summerhouses, one Gothic, the other classical, complete the picture. The garden is open in aid of the National Garden Scheme 6 May and 3 June, and for the village festival which will be held in May.
Open all year Mon, Wed, Thu & Sat 10-6; Parties & guided tours by appointment. House not open.
£2 (ch free, pen £1).
🅿 & *shop garden centre* ✣

Birdland
BOURTON-ON-THE-WATER
Rissington Rd (on A429)
☎ Cotswold (01451) 820480
The gardens contain a fine collection of penguins, new aviaries, a tropical house and birds at liberty, including macaws, parrots, cockatoos, lorikeets and flamingoes. Children's play area.
Open all year, Apr-Oct, daily 10-6; Nov-Mar, daily 10-4. (Closed 25 Dec).
✣*£3 (ch £1.50, pen £2.50). Party 10+.*
🅿 *(adjacent)* 🍴 & *toilets for disabled shop*

Cotswolds Motor Museum & Toy Collection
BOURTON-ON-THE-WATER
☎ Cotswold (01451) 821255
Housed in a water mill on the River

Windrush, the museum has cars and motorcycles from the vintage years up to the 1950s, with a collection of 800 advertising signs and some 8000 pieces of automobilia. Also here is the Childhood Toy Collection. Brum, the character from the children's BBC programme, lives at the museum.
Open Feb-Nov, daily 10-6.
£1.40 (ch 14 70p, ch 2 free). Family ticket £3.95. Party. Joint ticket available with Village Life Exhibition.
🅿 *(200 yds) parking for disabled available* & *shop*

Folly Farm Waterfowl
BOURTON-ON-THE-WATER
(2.5 W on A436)
☎ (01451) 820285
Two miles from Bourton, this conservation centre in the Cotswolds has a series of pools and lakes with over 160 types of waterfowl, ducks, geese and poultry, including many rare and endangered species. Undercover pets' area where handreared animals and birds may be stroked.
Open all year, Apr-Sep daily 10-6; Oct-Mar 10-4.
✣*£3 (ch £1.60, pen £2.50).*
🅿 🍴 & *(special car parking) toilets for disabled shop garden centre*

Model Village
BOURTON-ON-THE-WATER
Old New Inn
☎ Cotswold (01451) 20467
The model is built of Cotswold stone to a scale of one-ninth, and is a perfect replica of the village. It includes a miniature River Windrush, a working model waterwheel, churches and shops, with tiny trees, shrubs and alpine plants.
Open all year 9-6.30 (summer), 10-dusk (winter). (Closed 25 Dec).
✣*£1.20 (ch 90p, pen £1). Party 20+.*
🅿 🍴 ✕ *licensed shop*

Village Life Exhibition
BOURTON-ON-THE-WATER
The Old Mill
☎ Cotswold (01451) 821255
A complete Edwardian village shop is displayed with bathroom, kitchen and bedroom above. There is also a blacksmith's forge, a model of the old mill, photographs, toys and period advertising signs.
Open Feb-Nov, daily 10-6.
£1 (ch 50p, under 4 free). Joint ticket available with Costwolds Motor Museum.
🅿 *(200 yds) parking for disabled available shop*

Chedworth Roman Villa
CHEDWORTH
Yanworth (off A429)
☎ Cheltenham (01242) 890256
The remains of a Romano-British villa,

---

excavated 1864-66. Mosaics and two bath houses are well preserved. The museum houses the smaller finds and there is a 10-minute video programme.
Open Mar-Oct, Tue-Sun & BH Mon 10-5.30. (Closed Good Fri). Last admission 5pm; Nov-3 Dec, Wed-Sun 11-4 also 9 & 10 Dec.
£2.70. Family £7.40.
🅿 & *(wheelchair available) toilets for disabled shop* ✣
(NT)

Art Gallery & Museum
CHELTENHAM
Clarence St
☎ (01242) 237431
The museum has an outstanding collection relating to the Arts and Crafts Movement, made famous by William Morris, including fine furniture and exquisite metalwork. The Art Gallery contains Dutch and British paintings from the 17th-century to the present day. Of particular note is the Oriental Gallery which features pottery, costumes and treasures from the Ming Dynasty to the reign of the last Chinese Emperor. An interesting addition to the section devoted to social history and archaeology is a true-to-life depiction of the exploits of Edward Wilson, one of Cheltenham's famous sons, who journeyed with Captain Scott on the ill-fated Antarctic Expedition of 1910. There is a continuous programme of special exhbitions throughout the year. Special exhibitions for 1995 include: Pete Hoida, abstract paintings (22 April-3 June); Robert Welch, designer and silversmith (10 June-5 August), True to Type (12 August-23 September), It's only Rock n' Roll (30 September-18 November).
Open all year, Mon-Sat 10-5.20. (Closed BHs).
Free.
🅿 *(2 mins)* 🍴 & *(handling tables for blind people with Braille labels) toilets for disabled shop* ✣

Holst Birthplace Museum
CHELTENHAM
4 Clarence Rd, Pittville
☎ (01242) 524846 & 237431
The home and birthplace of Gustav Holst composer of *The Planets* who was born at this Regency house in 1874. The museum contains unique displays on the life of the distinguished musician, including his original piano. The rooms of the house have been carefully restored in the tradition of 'upstairs, downstairs' from the nursery at the top of the house to the working Victorian kitchen in the basement, each area evoking a slightly different period in the history of the house from Regency to Edwardian times.
Open all year, Tue-Sat 10-4.20 (Closed Mon & BHs).
£1.50 (concessions 50p)
🅿 *(100 yds) shop* ✣

Pittville Pump Room & Museum
CHELTENHAM
Pittville Park
☎ (01242) 523852
The pump room is generally considered Cheltenham's finest building. It was built in Greek Revival style in the 19th century, and has a colonnaded façade and a pillared and balconied hall. The first pump room was more humble, just a thatched shelter over a spring where pigeons had been noticed pecking at salt crystals. The Pittville Pump Room was bought by the borough in 1890 and has since been restored and the spa fountain was repositioned in 1960. Various functions are held and there is a museum showing the story of the town from the 18th century. Imaginative use of original costumes brings to life the history of Cheltenham from its Regency heyday to the Swinging Sixties. Special exhibitions are held throughout the year.
Open all year, May-Sep, daily 11-4.30; Oct-Apr, daily 11.4 (closed Tue) .
£1.50 (concessions 50p). Pump room free. Party.
🅿 & *toilets for disabled shop* ✣

Berkeley Castle
BERKELEY
(on B4509 1.5m W of A38)
☎ Dursley (01453) 810332
Home of the Berkeleys for almost 850 years, the castle is all one might expect - a great rambling place surrounded by 14ft thick walls, with a Norman keep, a great hall, medieval kitchens and some splendid apartments. It is most famous for the dungeon where Edward II was gruesomely murdered in 1327, at the instigation of his wife and the Earl of Mortimer. Outside there are Elizabethan terraced gardens and an extensive park. There is also a particularly good butterfly farm, with hundreds of exotic butterflies in free flight. Special events for 1995 include a Spring Flower Show in the great hall (14-30 April), with 2500 tulips and amaryllis on display, visitors can purchase or order bulbs.
Open Apr, daily 2-5; May-Sep weekdays 11-5, Sun 2-5. Oct Sun only 2-4.30; BH Mon 11-5. (Closed Mon ex BH).
✣*£3.70 (ch £1.80 & pen £3).*
🅿 🍴 *shop* ✣

Jenner Museum
BERKELEY
Church Ln, High St
☎ Dursley (01453) 810631
This beautiful Georgian house was the home of Edward Jenner, the discoverer of vaccination against smallpox. The house and the garden, with its Temple of Vaccinia, are much as they were in Jenner's day. The displays record Jenner's life as an 18th-century country doctor, his work on vaccination and his interest in natural history. He is buried in the nearby church, which also has some fine monuments to the Berkeley family.
Open Apr-Sep, Tue-Sat 12.30-5.30, Sun 1-5.30. Oct, Sun 1-5.30. (Closed Mon, ex BH Mon 12.30-5.30).
£1.20 (ch 7 40p, students 50p, pen £1). Family ticket £3.
🅿 & *toilets for disabled shop* ✣

The medieval Great Hall of Berkeley Castle still has its minstrels' gallery. The ceiling, supported by splendidly arched timbers, rises to more than 30ft.

Corinium Museum
CIRENCESTER
Park St
☎ *(01285) 655611*
Cirencester was the second largest town in Roman Britain and the Corinium Museum displays use full-scale reconstructions to bring alive the way of life during this period in history. Special exhibitions are held throughout the year. There is a Cotswold Prehistory gallery. 'Building for the Disabled' award winner.
Open all year, Apr-Oct, Mon-Sat 10-5, Sun 2-5; Nov-Mar, Tue-Sat 10-5, Sun 2-5. Also open BHs. (Closed Xmas).
& *(Braille guide for exhibits) toilets for disabled shop*
Details not confirmed for 1995

Clearwell Caves Ancient Iron Mines
CLEARWELL
☎ *Dean (01594) 832535*
The mines were worked in Iron Age times, 2,500 years ago, and the industry grew under the Romans. Over half a million tons of ore were extracted in the 19th century, and the last commercial mining was in 1945. Today nine large caverns can be explores, with deeper trips for the more adventurous. There are engine rooms and exhibits of local mining and geology from the Forest of Dean. Educational visits are a speciality. Special events for 1995 include: Gloucester Museums Week in July - Children in the Mines, a visit to include sections not normally open to the public. Helmet and lamps supplied, suitable for children (and adults) of all ages; Hallowe'en Party (29 October).
Open Mar-Oct daily 10-5. Other times by arrangement. Santa's secret workshop 25 Nov-24 Dec - Mon-Fri 2-6, Sat-Sun 10-5. £2.80 (ch £1.70, concessions £2.50)
🅿 🖢 & *("Hands-on" exhibits, contact in advance) shop* ✵

The ruins of Chedworth Roman Villa date back to AD120 when the villa was built for a rich landowner. The remains show bath suites, underfloor heating, some good mosaics and a water shrine.

Prinknash Abbey Pottery
CRANHAM
(on A46)
☎ *(01452) 812239*
The abbey has become famous for its pottery in the 20th century, but its origins lie in the Middle Ages. Set in a large park, the old abbey building is a 12th-to 16th-century house which was used by Benedictine monks and guests of Gloucester Abbey until 1539. It became a priory and later an abbey for Benedictine monks from Caldey in 1928. Rich beds of clay were discovered when foundations were being dug for a new building, and so the pottery was established. It has a distinctive style, and is sold in many parts of the world. The monks are skilled in other crafts as well, and make many articles for the abbey church. In 1995 St Peter's Grange (Old Abbey) will open to the public on the afternoons of 27-29 May and 4-28 August.
Open all year. Abbey Church: daily 5am-8pm. Pottery: Mon-Sat 11-4.30 (Sun pm). Pottery shop & tearoom 9-5.30. (Closed Good Fri, 25 & 26 Dec). Viewing gallery fee 75p (ch 40p).
🅿 🖢 & *toilets for disabled shop*

Prinknash Bird Park
CRANHAM
Prinknash Abbey
☎ *Gloucester (01452) 812727*
Nine acres of parkland and lakes make a beautiful home for black swans, geese and other water birds. There are also exotic birds such as white and Indian blue peacocks and crown cranes, and the park supports fallow deer and pygmy goats, many of which are tame and can be hand fed. The Golden Wood is stocked with ornamental pheasants, and leads to the restored (and reputedly haunted) monks' fishpond, which contains trout.
Open all year, daily 10-5 (4pm in winter). Park closes at 6pm (5pm in winter).
✳️ *£2.80 (ch £1.60, pen £1.80). Party.*
🅿 🖢 *shop* ✵

Odda's Chapel
DEERHURST
(off B4213 near River Severn)
The rare Saxon chapel was built by Earl Odda and dedicated in 1056. It was discovered as part of a farmhouse and has been restored.
Open any reasonable time.
Free.
(EH)

City East Gate
GLOUCESTER
Eastgate St
☎ *(01452) 524131*
Gloucester was Roman 'Glevum', and the Normans built their walls on Roman foundations. At City East Gate, there are Roman and medieval gate towers and a moat in an underground exhibition chamber.
Open May-Sep, Sat 10.15-11.15 & 2.15-4.15.
40p (ch & pen free).
P (adjacent) shop ✵

City Museum & Art Gallery
GLOUCESTER
Brunswick Rd
☎ *(01452) 524131*
The museum houses the Marling bequest of 18th-century walnut furniture, barometers and domestic silver. The archaeology displays include Roman mosaics and sculptures, and the natural history section has a freshwater aquarium. There are paintings by Richard ➜

Cotswold Farm Park is the home of rare breeds conservation and is home to nearly 50 flocks and herds of ancient British breeds of farm animals.

Wilson, Gainsborough, Turner and others, and art exhibitions are held throughout the year. In the archaeology section is the Gloucester Tables Set - a complete Norman backgammon set believed the oldest in the world, and the Birdlip Mirror - a rare engraved bronze mirror - the natural history section has an extensive collection of dinosaur material.
Open all year, Mon-Sat 10-5. (Also Jul-Sep, Sun 10-4).
Free.
P *(adjacent)* & *(lift) shop* ✸

Folk Museum
GLOUCESTER ▨▨▨▨▨
99-103 Westgate St
☎*(01452) 526467*
A group of Tudor and Jacobean half-timbered houses illustrate the local history, domestic life and rural crafts of the city and county. Displays include Civil War armour, Victorian toys and games, farming, Severn fishing, kitchen equipment, model steam engines, shoemaker's workshop, and a school room c1900. There is a pin factory on the top floor with an 18th-century forge in situ. The new extensions house a reconstructed Double Gloucester Dairy, wheelwright and carpenter's workshops and ironmonger's corner shop. Regular special exhibitions are held. Special events and demonstrations held in 1995 as part of the celebration of the Festival of Arts and Culture include lacemaking, Gloucester Folk Museum 1935-1995 and bee-keeping in Gloucestershire.
Open all year, Mon-Sat 10-5. (Also Jul-Sep, Sun 10-4). Open BH Mon.
Free.
P *(200yds)* & *(parking on request, ramps) shop* ✸

National Waterways Museum
GLOUCESTER ▨▨▨▨▨
Llanthony Warehouse, The Docks
☎*(01452) 318054*
In October 1990, this museum was judged to be one of the top seven museums in Europe in the European Museum of the Year Awards. The

judge's report said 'It has used a strong poetic sense to unlock the images always latent in technology, and has revealed canal and river travel not only as a means of transport, but as a way of life with a character of its own'.
For centuries goods were transferred at Gloucester Docks between inland craft bound for Wales and the Midlands, and larger vessels which could negotiate the Severn Estuary. The heyday of the docks came after the opening of the Gloucester and Berkeley Canal in 1827, and many of the warehouses built in the 19th century still stand. The museum is housed in the Llanthony warehouse, a seven-storey brick building with cast-iron columns, which now shows the role of inland waterways in Britain's fortunes. A traditional canal maintenance yard has been re-created alongside, there are boats to visit, and demonstrations are given of the crafts and skills needed to run the canals. Special events for 1995 include: stationary engine rally (7 May), horses and tugs weekend (20-21 May), Women of the Waterways exhibition (July-August), activities for children (July-August), exhibition The Wheel (21 October-2 December).
Open all year, daily 10-6; (winter 10-5). (Closed 25 Dec).
£4.25 (ch & pen £3.25). Family ticket £9.95.
P *(charged)* 👝 & *(touch exhibits, wheelchair available) toilets for disabled shop* ✸

Robert Opie Collection-Museum of Packaging & Advertising
GLOUCESTER ▨▨▨▨▨
Albert Warehouse, Gloucester Docks
☎*(01452) 302309*
This museum is not only a feast of nostalgia; it is an exploration of the changes in advertising and packaging from 1870 to the present day, covering developments in retailing and marketing in Britain over the last 120 years·as well as changes in taste, style and fashion. The museum is based on the Robert Opie Collection, the largest of its kind in the world. Quiz sheets for children and packs for teachers are available.

Open all year, daily, 10-6; winter Tue-Fri 10-5, Sat & Sun 10-6. (Closed 25-26 Dec). £2.95 (ch 95p, pen & students £1.95). Family tickets £6.95. Party 10+.
P *(charged)* 👝 & *shop* ✸

Cotswold Farm Park
GUITING POWER ▨▨▨▨▨
(off B4077)
☎*Cotswold (01451) 850307*
At the Cotswold Farm Park, the home of rare breeds conservation, there are nearly 50 breeding flocks and herds of the rarest and most fascinating British breeds of sheep, cattle, pigs, goats, horses, poultry and waterfowl. Set on the very top of the Cotswold Hills with magnificent views in all directions, this is the perfect opportunity to get to know a Bagot goat, cuddle a Cotswold lamb, stroke a mighty Longhorn ox, and admire generations of our living agricultural heritage. New born lambs and goat kids can be seen in April, spring calves in May, foals in June and piglets throughout the year. 1995 is the 25th anniversary with special events and exhibitions.
Open Apr-1 Oct, daily 10.30-5. (10.30-6, Sun, BH & daily in Jul & Aug).
£3.50 (ch £1.50, pen £2). Party.
P 👝 & *toilets for disabled shop* ✸

Hailes Abbey
HAILES ▨▨▨▨▨
☎*(01242) 602398*
In the Middle Ages the Cistercian abbey attracted numerous pilgrims because it owned a phial said to contain the blood of Christ. Today the abbey is a beautiful ruin, and the museum has roof bosses, ornate tiles and other evidence of past magnificence.
Open all year, Apr-Sep, daily 10-6; Oct, 10-4; Nov-Mar, Wed-Sun 10-4. Closed 24-26 Dec & 1 Jan.
£2 (ch £1, concessions £1.50).
P & ✸
(EH & NT)

Littledean Hall
LITTLEDEAN ▨▨▨▨▨
☎*(01594) 824213*
The largest known Roman temple in rural Britain was unearthed here in 1984 and the manor itself was built in Norman times; its north front is on the site of a Saxon hall of the 11th century. The house has always been lived in, and remains relatively untouched since the 19th century. Inside there are interpretive displays illustrating the history of the English manor house, the Civil War, and the ghosts and legends of Littledean Hall. The grounds offer beautiful walks, some of the oldest trees in Dean, fish pools in the walled garden and, of course, the Roman excavations. The house features an unusual supernatural history.
Open - House, Grounds & Archaeological site, Apr-Oct, daily 10.30-5.30. Grounds & Archaeological site only, Nov-Mar daily all reasonable times.
✳*£2.50 (ch £1.25).*
P & *shop* ✸ *(ex in grounds)*

Dean Forest Railway
LYDNEY ▨▨▨▨▨
Norchard Centre, New Mills (1m N at New Mills on B4234)
☎*Dean (01594) 843423*
Just north of Lydney lies the headquarters of the Dean Forest Railway where a number of locomotives, coaches, wagons and railway equipment are on show and guided tours are available by arrangement. There is also a gift shop, museum, riverside walk and forest trail. Events for 1995 will include a Vintage Rally (15 October), Thomas the Tank Engine (17-18 June and 16-17 September), and 'Santa Specials' in December.
Open all year, daily for static displays. Steam days: Sun, Apr-Sep; Wed, Jun-Aug; Thu Aug & all BH's (ex Xmas & New Year).
£3.50 (ch £2 & pen £3). Prices include train ride (operating days only).
P 👝 & *(boarded walkways, specially adapted coach for wheelchairs) toilets for disabled shop*

Hidcote Manor Garden
MICKLETON ▨▨▨▨▨
(1m E of B4632)
☎*(01386) 438333*
One of the most delightful gardens in England, created this century by the great horticulturist Major Laurence Johnston and comprising a series of small gardens within the whole, separated by walls and hedges of different species. The gardens are famous for rare shrubs, trees, herbaceous borders, 'old' roses and interesting plant species.
Open, Gardens only Apr-Oct, daily (ex Tue & Fri) 11-7, no entry after 6pm or 1hr before sunset. Closed Good Fri.
£5. Family ticket £13.75. Parties by prior written arrangement.
P 👝 ✗ *licensed* & *toilets for disabled shop* ✸
(NT)

Kiftsgate Court Garden
MICKLETON ▨▨▨▨▨
Mickleton (0.5 m S off A46, adjacent Hidcote NT garden)
☎*(01386) 438777*
Standing adjacent to Hidcote is a magnificently situated house with a garden that is also open to the public. Its chief attraction lies in its collection of old-fashioned roses, including the largest rose in England, the R Filipes Kiftsgate. A wide variety of unusual plants and shrubs and fine trees can be seen.
Open Apr-Sep, Wed, Thu, Sun & BH Mon 2-6. Also Sat, Jun-Jul.
£3 (ch £1).
P 👝 ✸

Batsford Arboretum
MORETON-IN-MARSH ▨▨▨▨▨
(1.5m W, off A44)
☎*(01608) 650722 & (01386)700409(wknds)*
This arboretum of some 50 acres overlooking the Evenlode valley boasts one of the largest private collections of woody plants in Great Britain. Of particular note are the oaks, maples, magnolias and cherries, with many conifers and other rare and unusual trees, shrubs and bamboos. Spring is a procession of colour with masses of naturalised bulbs, particularly daffodils and narcissi, followed by magnolias and cherries. Autumn is equally as attractive with the fiery oranges and reds of the Japanese maples.
Open Mar-early Nov 10-5.
P 👝 *shop garden centre*
Details not confirmed for 1995

Cotswold Falconry Centre
MORETON-IN-MARSH ▨▨▨▨▨
Batsford Park (1m E on A44)
☎*Blockley (01386) 701043*
Conveniently located by the Batsford Park Arboretum, the Cotswold Falconry gives daily demonstrations in the art of falconry. The emphasis here is on breeding and conservation, and eagles, hawks, owls and falcons may be seen flying.
Open Mar-Oct, 10.30-5.30. (Last admission 5pm).
£2.50 (ch 4-14 £1 & pen £2)
P & *shop garden centre* ✸

Sezincote
MORETON-IN-MARSH ▨▨▨▨▨
(1.5m on A44 Evesham rd)
The Indian-style house at Sezincote was the inspiration for Brighton Pavilion; its charming water garden adds to its exotic aura and features trees of unusual size.
Open: House, May-Jul & Sep, Thu & Fri 2.30-5.30. Garden only, all year (ex Dec) Thu, Fri & BH Mon 2-6 or dusk if earlier. House & garden £4. Garden only £2.50 (ch £1 under 5 free). Children not allowed in the House. Groups by appointment only.
P ✸

The National Birds of Prey Centre
NEWENT

(1m SW on unclass Clifford's Mesne Road)
☎ (01531) 820286
Jemima Parry-Jones is becoming increasingly famous for her displays of falconry at shows and fairs all over the country. This is the 'home-base' for her exceptional collection of birds of prey. Trained birds can be seen at close quarters in the Hawk Walk and the Owl Courtyard and there are also breeding aviaries, a gift shop, bookshop, picnic areas, coffee shop and children's play area. Weather permitting, birds are flown four times daily, giving an exciting and educational display.
Open Feb-Nov, daily 10.30-5.30 or dusk if earlier.
£4 (ch £2.25). Family ticket £11.50.
🅿 ☕ & *toilets for disabled shop* ✖

The Shambles
NEWENT

Church St
☎ (01531) 822144
A museum of cobbled streets, alleyways, cottages and houses. Shops, trades, cart sheds and even a tin Chapel and cottage garden all help to recreate the feel and atmosphere of Victorian life.
Open 20 Mar-Xmas, Tue-Sun & BH's 10-6 (or dusk).
✿£2.65 (ch £1.65, pen £2.25).
P (100 yds) ☕ ✖ *licensed* & *toilets for disabled shop*

Cotswold Countryside Collection
NORTHLEACH

Fosseway
☎ Cotswold (01451) 860715
The story of everyday rural life in the Cotswolds is told in this museum, housed in the remaining buildings of the Northleach House of Correction. It was one of a group of Gloucestershire's 'country prisons' built around 1789 by Sir

Onesiphorus Paul. The Lloyd-Baker agricultural collection, one of the best in the country, exhibits a unique collection of Gloucestershire harvest-wagons. There is a 'below stairs' gallery showing a dairy, kitchen and laundry. There are also special exhibitions. Workshops on rag rug making, felt making, patchwork, natural dyeing and basket making are held.
Open Apr-Oct, Mon-Sat 10-5, Sun 2-5 & BHs.
✿£1.25 (ch 75p, students & pen £1). Family ticket £3.25. Party.
🅿 ☕ & *(wheelchair available, parking at entrance) toilets for disabled shop*

Keith Harding's World of Mechanical Music
NORTHLEACH

Oak House, High St
☎ Cotswold (01451) 860181
A fascinating collection of antique clocks, musical boxes, automata and mechanical musical instruments, restored and maintained in the world-famous workshops, displayed in a period setting, and played during regular tours. Winner of 'Come to Britain' award 1988.
Open all year, daily 10-6.
✿£3.50 (ch 16 £1.50, under 3 free, pen & students £2.75). Family ticket £8.50. Disabled-helpers Free.
🅿 & *toilets for disabled shop* ✖

Owlpen Manor
OWLPEN

(3m E of Dursley off B4066)
☎ Dursley (01453) 860261
This romantic Tudor manor house, dating from 1450 to 1616, contains unique 17th-century painted cloth wallhangings, furniture, pictures and textiles. The house is set in formal terraced gardens, and is part of a picturesque Cotswold manorial group including a Jacobean Court House, a watermill dating from 1728 (now holiday cottages), a Victorian church and medieval tithe barn.

This magnificent goshawk is part of the superb collection of hunting birds to be seen at the National Birds of Prey Centre.

Open Etr-Sep, Tues, Thu, Sun & BH Mon 2-5; also Wed in Jul & Aug 2-5.
£3.25 (ch £1.50). Party 20+
🅿 ☕ ✖ *licensed shop* ✖

Painswick Rococo Garden
PAINSWICK

The Stables, Painswick House (on B4073)
☎ (01452) 813204
This beautiful Rococo garden (a compromise between formality and informality) - the only one of its period to survive completely - is currently in the process of being restored. There are fascinating contemporary garden buildings with vistas, ponds and woodland walks, famous for snowdrops in the early spring.
Open 2nd Wed in Jan-Nov, Wed-Sun, 11-5.
£2.60 (ch £1.30, pen £2.20).
🅿 ☕ ✖ *licensed* & *toilets for disabled shop*

Wildfowl & Wetlands Trust
SLIMBRIDGE

(off A38, signed from M5 junc 13 & 14)
☎ Cambridge (Glos) (01453) 890333
Founded in 1946 by the late Sir Peter Scott, Slimbridge is now the home of the world's largest collection of exotic wildfowl and the only place in the UK to hold all six types of flamingo. Up to 8,000 wild birds winter on the 800-acre reserve of flat fields, marsh and mudflats on the River Severn. First class viewing facilities are available and in winter, the towers and hides provide remarkable views of the migratory birds. Other features include a permanent indoor interactive exhibit, with videos, a computer game and large tanks depicting coral reefs, peat bogs and ponds; and a Tropical House. There is a packed programme of events and activities throughout the year including Time Travel Wetland Style throughout the summer holidays in 1995, evening talks and guided walks. Facilities for the disabled include purpose-built toilets for wheelchair users and a braille trail with taped commentaries.
Open all year, daily from 9.30-5 (winter 4pm). (Closed 24-25 Dec).
£4.70 (ch 4-16 £2.35 & pen £3.55). Family ticket £11.75. Party 20+.

🅿 ☕ ✖ *licensed* & *(wheelchairs, tapes for blind) toilets for disabled shop* ✖

Snowshill Manor
SNOWSHILL

(3m SW of Broadway)
☎ Broadway (01386) 852410
Snowshill Manor is a Tudor house with a 17th-century façade. It has 21 rooms containing Charles Paget Wade's collection of craftsmanship, including musical instruments, clocks, toys, bicycles, weavers' and spinners' tools, and Japanese armour. There is a small formal garden and Charles Wade's cottage.
Open Apr & Oct; Sat, Sun & Etr Mon 1-6. (Closed Good Fri). May-Sep; daily ex Tues, 1-6. Last admission to house half hour before closing.
🅿 *shop* ✖
(NT)
Details not confirmed for 1995

Dean Heritage Centre
SOUDLEY

Camp Mill (on B4227)
☎ Dean (01594) 822170
Located in the heart of the Forest of Dean, the Centre is set around a restored corn mill and its mill pond. It tells the fascinating story of this unique area with museum displays which include a reconstucted cottage, coal mine and waterwheel. There are also nature trails (one of which is level), picnic areas and barbecue hearths. Added attractions are an adventure playground, fowl and ducks, gift and craft shops and a cafe. Special events take place throughout the year.
Open all year, daily, Feb-Mar 10-5, Apr-Oct 10-6, Nov-Jan weekends only 10.30-4. (Closed 24-26 Dec). Booked parties at other times by arrangement.
✿£2.60 (ch £1.60, students, pen & UB40 £2.10). Party 20+. Season tickets available.
🅿 ☕ & *toilets for disabled shop* ✖ *(ex in grounds)*

Stanway House
STANWAY

(0.5m E of B4632 or B4077)
☎ Stanton (01386) 584469
A thoroughly lived-in Jacobean manor →

Sudeley Castle was once the home of Katharine Parr, the only wife of Henry VIII who survived him. The house features an impressive art collection and delightful gardens.

house with unusual furniture, set in formal landscaped parkland. There is also a tithe barn and gatehouse. Special events include a daffodil show 23 April.
Open Jun-Sep, Tue & Thu 2-5.
❋*£3 (ch £1, pen £2.50). Party.*
🅿 &

Chavenage
TETBURY
(2m NW signposted off B4014)
☎ *(01666) 502329*
Built in 1576, this unspoilt Elizabethan house contains some stained glass from the 17th-century and earlier, and some good furniture and tapestries. The owner during the Civil War was a Parliamentarian, and the house also contains Cromwellian relics. In more recent years, the house has been the location for 'Grace and Favour' the sequel to the television series 'Are You Being Served?', 'Poirot', 'The House of Elliot' and 'The Noel Edmunds Party'. There is a Shakespeare Week in July. Tours of the house, conducted by the owner or members of his family, are enlivened by many stories of ghosts etc.
Open May-Sep, Thu, Sun & BHs 2-5. Also Etr Sun & Mon. Other days by appointment only.
£2.50 (ch £1.25).
🅿 & ❧

Nature in Art
TWIGWORTH
Wallsworth Hall, Tewkesbury Rd (on A38, from village follow tourist signs)
☎ *Gloucester (01452) 731422*
An ever changing and ever growing collection portraying wildlife in any art medium, from any period and from all over the world, makes this the first museum of its kind. Dedicated to wildlife art of the highest international standards, there are myriads of outstanding exhibits including sculpture (both indoor and outdoor), tapestries and ceramics. There is a comprehensive 'artist in residence' programme for ten months of the year (in 1993 45 artists from 9 countries). Awarded a

Special Commendation in the National Heritage Museum of the Year Awards. Events include regular monthly talks, film showings and a full programme of temporary exhibitions and art courses. A current collection includes the work by over 400 artists from nearly 50 countries, spanning 1500 years. More information about the events being held can be obtained by telephoning or sending for a programme. A purpose-built education/activity centre is used by schools and special interest groups and as a base for the museum's art courses.
Open all year, Tue-Sun & BH's 10-5. Mon by arrangement. (Closed 24-26 Dec).
❋*£2.80 (ch, pen & students £1.95, ch under 8 free). Family ticket £8.50.*
🅿 ☕ & *(lift & ramps at entrance) toilets for disabled shop* ❧ *(ex grounds)*

Uley Tumulus
ULEY
(1m N)
This 180ft long barrow is known as Hetty Pegler's Tump. The Neolithic burial mound is about 85ft wide and is surrounded by a dry-built wall. It contains a central passage, built of stone, and three burial chambers.
Open any reasonable time.
Free.
(EH)

Westbury Court Garden
WESTBURY-ON-SEVERN
☎ *Gloucester (01452) 760461*
This formal water garden with canals and yew hedges was laid out between 1696 and 1705. It is the earliest of its kind remaining in England and was restored in 1971 and planted with species dated from pre 1700, including apple, pear and plum trees.
Open Apr-Oct, Wed-Sun & BH Mon 11-6. (Closed Good Fri). Other months by appointment only.
£2.30. Party.
🅿 & *toilets for disabled* ❧
(NT)

Westonbirt Arboretum
WESTONBIRT
(3m S Tetbury on A433)
☎ *(01666) 880220*
This large arboretum was started in 1829 and contains one of the finest and most important collection of trees and shrubs in the world. There are 18,000 of them, planted from 1829 to the present day, covering 600 acres of landscaped Cotswold countryside. The visitor can follow 17 miles of waymarked trails or simply sit in a leafy glade and admire some of the great varieties of trees and shrubs which provide interest and colour throughout the year, even in winter, when the distinctive barks of the birches and maple are visible. Magnificent displays of Rhododendrons, Azaleas, Magnolias and the wild flowers of Silkwood can be seen in the Spring (March-June). There is a Visitor Centre with an exhibition, shop, and interesting video programme. The arboretum is managed by the Forestry Commission. Special events for 1995 include hanging basket demonstrations (13 May), craft day (30 April), Bonsai day (26 August), Maple day (3 September).
Open all year, daily 10-8 or sunset. Visitor centre & shop Mar-20 Dec.
£2.60 (ch £1, pen £1.70).
🅿 ☕ & *(electric & manual wheelchair for loan) toilets for disabled shop garden centre*

Sudeley Castle & Gardens
WINCHCOMBE
☎ *(01242) 602308*
Set against the rolling Cotswold hills, Sudeley Castle, one of England's most delightful historic houses, has many royal connections. It was once the palace of Katherine Parr, who is buried in the Chapel; Henry VIII, Anne Boleyn, Lady Jane Grey and Elizabeth I stayed here; it was the residence of Charles I; and the headquarters of Prince Rupert during the Civil War. Today the Castle is the home of

Lord and Lady Ashcombe. The impressive art collection includes notable paintings by Turner, Van Dyck and Rubens. The Castle has eight delightful gardens, where visitors can wander through avenues of majestic trees, shrubs, yew hedges and old fashioned roses. A wildfowl sanctuary, exhibition centre, plant centre, picnic area, children's adventure playground. shop and restaurant are other features of Sudeley. Special events are held throughout 1995.
Open Mar, wknds only 11-4; Apr-Oct, daily 10.30-5.30 (Castle apartments 11-5). £4.95 (ch £2.75 & pen £4.55). Gardens only £3.35 (ch £1.60 & pen £2.95). Family ticket £13.
🅿 ✕ *licensed shop garden centre* ❧

Witcombe Roman Villa
WITCOMBE, GREAT
The remains of a large Roman Villa, built around three sides of a courtyard. Several mosaic pavements have been preserved and there is also evidence of underfloor heating from a hypocaust.
Open any reasonable time.
Free.
🅿 &
(EH)

GREATER MANCHESTER

Dunham Massey Hall
ALTRINCHAM
(3m SW off A56, junc 19 off M6 or 7 off M56)
☎ *0161-941 1025*
A fine 18th-century house and park, home of the Earls of Stamford until 1976. It was remodelled in the early 1730s by the 2nd Earl of Warrington and altered again in the early 1900s. It contains fine 18th-century furniture and magnificent

The 500 acres of Westonbirt Arboretum, with some 15,000 specimens of trees and shrubs from all over the temperate world, is beautiful during every season.

silverware made by Huguenot smiths. There are some thirty rooms to be seen including the library and the billiard room. Portraits of the Booth and Grey families (Earls of Warrington and Stamford) include one of Lady Jane Grey. A fully-equipped kitchen, butler's pantry and laundry are not to be missed. Fallow deer roam the park, which also has a working Elizabethan saw mill. The 30-acre garden is on an ancient site with moat, mount and orangery. There are mature trees and fine lawns with an extensive range of shrubs and water-loving plants. Special events for 1995 include: Plantsmans' Day (7 May), open air opera (16-17 June), monthly concerts held in the Great Gallery in the winter.
Open - House Apr-29 Oct, Sat-Wed 12-5. Garden Apr-29 Oct daily 11-5.30. Last admission to house 4.30. Park always open. House & Garden £4.50 (ch £2). House only £3 (ch £1.50). Garden only £2 (ch £1). Family ticket £11. Park only, £2 per car (NT members free), coaches free.
🅿 (charged) 🍽 ✕ licensed 🖐 (large print/braille guide, batricar & wheelchairs for loan) toilets for disabled shop ⌾ (ex on lead in Park)
(NT)

Museum of the Manchesters
ASHTON-UNDER-LYNE
Market Place
☎0161-342 3078
This is an interesting museum illustrating the history of the Manchester Regiment and its relationship with the local community, from the early 19th century to National Service. A new extension follows the story Women at War during World War I and World War II, and features an audio-visual presentation. There is also an exhibition on the history of medals, with medals of the Manchester Regiment on display.
Open all year, Mon-Sat & BHs, 10-4. (Closed Sun).
Free.
P (50yds) 🖐 toilets for disabled shop ⌾

Portland Basin Industrial Heritage Centre
ASHTON-UNDER-LYNE
1 Portland Place, Portland St South (off A635)
☎0161-308 3374
The story of the area over the last 200 years is unfolded here. The harsh times of the Industrial Revolution are highlighted, and there are special sections on political and religious movements. A new exhibition The Canal Age traces the history of the canals and what it was like to live and work on them. Outside is a restored water wheel.
Open all year, Apr-Sep, Tue-Sat 10-6, Sun 10-6; Oct-Mar, Tue-Sat 10-4, Sun 10-4.

Closed Mon (ex BH's).
Free.
🅿 🖐 toilets for disabled shop ⌾

Bramall Hall,Bramhall Park
BRAMHALL
☎0161-485 3708
The large timber-framed hall dates from the 14th century, and is one of the finest black-and-white houses in Cheshire. It has rare 16th-century wall paintings and period furniture, and was the home of the Davenport family for 500 years before coming into the care of the Metropolitan Borough of Stockport.
Open all year, Apr-Sep daily 1-5, Oct-Dec Tue-Sun 1-4. (Closed 25-26 Dec).
✳*£2.75 (concessions £2). Family ticket £8.*
🅿 🍽 🖐 toilets for disabled shop ⌾

East Lancashire Railway & The Bury Transport Museum
BURY
Bolton St Station
☎0161-764 7790(wknds) & 0161-705 5111(day)
The East Lancashire Railway operates a steam hauled train service from Bury to Ramsbotton and on to Rawtenstall. The line runs along the scenic Irwell Valley on the edge of the West Pennine Moors, it crosses and recrosses the River Irwell passing over viaducts, through tunnels and over level crossings. Diesel enthusiasts' weekends (10-18 June and 14-15 October), daily steam trains (5-28 August), teddy bears' picnic (28 August), steam gala (28-29 October), santa specials December weekends, mince pie specials (27-29 December).
Weekend service & BHs, Santa specials Dec; (Closed Xmas & New Year).
✳*Bury-Rawtenstall £5 (ch £2.50). Bury-Ramsbottom £3 (ch £1.50).*
🅿 🍽 🖐 (station area only suitable) toilets for disabled shop

MANCHESTER
Although the Romans established a fort near what is now Manchester's city centre, it was really cotton that created Manchester. In the 14th century Flemish weavers came to Britain and set up their trade. Four centuries later, in the Manchester area, their craft was revolutionised by men such as Samuel Crompton, who invented the spinning mule, Richard Arkwright inventor of the spinning frame and James Hargreaves creator of the spinning jenny who made the mass production of cloth possible. The 18th and 19th century progress brought prosperity to Manchester and there are a number of great houses nearby built from the wealth of cotton. Industrialisation also brought

the need for transport, soon provided by a network of canals and railways which carried cotton and coal for the steam engines from the nearby pits. Manchester's history is celebrated in a heritage park of which Castlefield railway station forms a part and close by Salford Mining Museum gives a taste of life in the coal pits. Although the cotton trade died out and Manchester's canals are now used just for leisure, the city has remained a thriving commercial, cultural and business centre.

City Art Galleries
MANCHESTER
Mosley St/Princess St
☎0161-236 5244
The Mosley Street Galleries have permanent displays of European art, ceramics and silver which are displayed with furniture in an elaborate decorative scheme. The strength of this Gallery lies in the superb collection of Victorian art, especially the group of major Pre-Raphaelite paintings. Decorative and applied arts, including porcelain from early times to the 19th century, furniture and sculpture are also included in this magnificent collection. The Princess Street Galleries house major temporary exhibitions.
Open Mon-Sat 10-5.45, Sun 2-5.45 (Closed May Day BH, 25-26 Dec & 1 Jan).
P 🍽 ✕ licensed 🖐 (notify gallery prior to a visit) toilets for disabled shop ⌾
Details not confirmed for 1995

Gallery of English Costume
MANCHESTER
Platt Hall, Rusholme
☎0161-224 5217
With one of the most comprehensive costume collections in Great Britain, this gallery makes captivating viewing. Housed in a fine Georgian mansion, the displays focus on the changing styles of everyday fashion and accessories, looking back over 400 years. Contemporary fashion is also illustrated and because of the vast amount of material in the collection, exhibitions are constantly changing and no one period is permanently illustrated. The costume library is available for research purposes, by appointment only. New displays include: The New Woman - the change in women's fashions and women's roles, 1890-1939; Home and Dry - an exhibition on protective clothing; Fashin Yesterday and Today 1970-1995 - a new exhibition of recent fasion including brand new outfits by Paul Smith and Vivienne Westwood.
Open all year, daily (ex Tue) 10-5.45, Sun 2-5.45, Nov-Feb closes at 4pm.

Occasional closures at weekends at short notice, telephone to confirm opening.
Free.
🅿 🖐 shop ⌾

Granada Studios Tour
MANCHESTER
Water St
☎0161-832 9090 & 0161-833 0880
Enter the world of television at Granada Studios Tour in the heart of the City Centre. Only here can you walk down Coronation Street, Downing Street and Baker Street in just one day. Visit the Giant Room, from the popular children's programme Return of the Antelope, where chairs loom overhead. See the spectacular Magic Show, then take part in a comedy debate in the House of Commons. Explore the history of cinema at Projections, experience Motion Master where the seats move with the action, see a spectacular 3-D and laser show, gasp as arms are severed in the squeamish make up show, and enjoy the All New Sooty Show. You should allow a possible five hours for your visit.
Open all year, daily summer 9.45-7 (last entry 4); winter 9.45-5.30 weekdays (last entry 3), 9.45-6.30 weekends & BH's (last entry 4). Closed Mon & Tue first half of Feb, Mar, Apr(except Etr), first half of Oct, Nov & Dec(except 28 & 29 Dec). Closed Mon May-Sep (except BH's). Closed 19-25 Dec. Open 1 & 2 Jan and weekends only.
£11.99 (ch £8.99).
🅿 (charged) 🍽 ✕ licensed 🖐 (ramps & lift throughout) toilets for disabled shop ⌾

John Rylands University Library of Manchester of Manchester
MANCHESTER
150 Deansgate
☎0161-834 5343
Founded as a memorial to Manchester cotton-magnate and millionaire John Rylands (1801-88) this former private library now comprises the Special Collections Division of the John Rylands University Library of Manchester. It is a library of international renown, both for its manuscript and printed-book resources as well as its medieval-jewelled bindings. In total its holdings extend to five million books, manuscripts and archival items representing some fifty cultures and ranging in date from the third millenium BC to the present day. It is perhaps best known for its 2nd-century St John Fragment, the earliest known piece of New Testament writing in existence; its St Christopher Woodcut (1423), the earliest piece of western printing with an undisputed date; and its Gutenberg Bible (1455/6), the first book printed using moveable type. The Library's treasures are more than matched by the magnificent neo-Gothic surroundings designed by architect Basil Champneys at the instigation of Enriqueta Augustina Rylands, third wife and widow of John Rylands. Notable items from stock are always displayed as part of the Library's varied exhibitions programme. A wide programme of exhibitions and other events is planned to mark the re-opening of the Library to visitors in Spring 1995.
Open all year, Mon-Fri 10-5.30, Sat 10-1 (Closed BH & Xmas-New Year). Pre-booked groups only at other times. The Library will be closed to visitors, except by proir arrangement until Spring 1995.
Free.
P (400yds) shop ⌾

Manchester Museum of Transport
MANCHESTER
Boyle St, Cheetham (1.5m N of Victoria Station)
☎0161-205 2122 & 0161-205 1082
The City's travel through the ages is illustrated here; among the many interesting exhibits include over 70 buses and other vehicles from the area together with old photographs, tickets and other memorabilia. Special events for 1995 will be the X60 Manchester-Blackpool celebration (3-4 June), weekend for ➤

Manchester's elaborate Town Hall was built during the Victorian era to display the city's wealth and importance.

people with disabilities (17-18 June), Trans-Lancs Historic Vehicle Rally (3 September), Vehicles with Gardner Engines weekend (14-15 October).
Open all year, Wed, Sat, Sun & BH 10-5. Parties at other times by arrangement.
£2 (ch accompanied £1.25). Family ticket £5.
🅿 💺 ⚐ *toilets for disabled shop*

Manchester United Museum & Tour Centre
MANCHESTER ▮▮▮▮
Old Trafford (2m from city centre, off A56)
☎ *0161-877 4002*
This Museum was opened in 1986 and is the first purpose-built British football museum. It covers the history of Manchester United in words, pictures, sound and vision, from its inception in 1878 to the present day. More than 400 exhibits are regularly on display.
Subject to availability, a tour includes a visit to the Museum, then into the stadium, players' lounge, dressing rooms and down the players' tunnel to view the pitch and stadium.
Open all year Tue-Sun & most BH Mons 9.30-4. (Closed 25 Dec).
❋*Ground Tour, Museum & Trophy Room £4.95 (ch & pen £2.95). Museum & Trophy Room only £2.95 (ch & pen £1.95). Family ticket £11.95 & £6.95.*
🅿 💺 ⚐ *toilets for disabled shop* ❊

Museum of Science and Industry in Manchester
MANCHESTER ▮▮▮▮
Liverpool Rd, Castlefield
☎ *0161-832 2244*
The Museum of Science and Industry in Manchester offers endless fascination for adults and children. Located in the buildings of the world's oldest passenger railway station the fun-filled galleries amaze, amuse and entertain. You can take off to the Air and Space Gallery. Try the Super X Simulator and experience the thrills of flying without having to leave your seat. Visit Xperiment! the hands-on science centre where you can shake hands with yourself and walk away from your own shadow. Pit your wits at the puzzle desk and see if you've got what it takes to be a genius. Visit a reconstructed Victorian sewer - complete with sounds and smells. See the wheels of industry turning in the Power Hall which houses the largest collection of working steam mill engines in the world.
Open all year, daily 10-5. Last admission 4.30. (Closed 24-26 Dec).
£3.50-£4 (ch, students, pen, UB40 & disabled £1.50-£2 ch under 5 free). Party 10+.
🅿 *(charged)* 💺 ⚐ *ramps, dropped kerbs & lifts toilets for disabled shop* ❊

Whitworth Art Gallery
MANCHESTER ▮▮▮▮
University of Manchester, Oxford Rd
☎ *0161-273 4865*
The Whitworth Art Gallery runs an exciting programme of temporary exhibitions and displays, many of which highlight our rich and varied permanent collections. Whether you like modern art or gentle English landscapes, there is something for everyone. Surprisingly, we also have important collections of textiles and wallpapers which are frequently on show. Artists represented include Albrecht Durer, William Blake, JMW Turner, William Morris, Barbara Hepworth and Gilbert and George. Items not on public display can be viewed by appointment. To mark the 30th anniversary of Whitworth Young Contemporaries there will be a celebratory exhibtion of the biennial competition of works by students from art colleges from England, Scotland and Wales.
Open Mon-Sat 10-5, Thu until 9pm. (Closed Good Fri & Xmas-New Year).
Free.
🅿 ✗ *licensed* ⚐ *(one wheelchair available, induction loop in lecture theatre) toilets for disabled shop* ❊ ⌗

Heaton Hall
PRESTWICH ▮▮▮▮
Heaton Park (on A665)
☎ *0161-773 1231 or 0161-236 5244 ext 123*
Designed by James Wyatt for Sir Thomas Egerton in 1772, the house has magnificent period interiors decorated with fine plasterwork, paintings and furniture. Other attractions include a unique circular room with Pompeian-style paintings, and the original Samuel Green organ still in working order. Lively exhibitions and events programme in both the Hall and surrounding parkland. *Telephone for details on 0161-236 5244. Free.*
🅿 *(charged)* 💺 ✗ ⚐ *toilets for disabled shop* ❊

Lancashire Mining Museum
SALFORD ▮▮▮▮
Buile Hill Park, Eccles Old Rd
☎ *0161-736 1832*
Two reproduction coal mines, a gallery to illustrate the history and development of coal mining and exhibitions of mining art are housed in this listed Georgian building, designed by Sir Charles Barry, the architect of the Houses of Parliament. The reference library and archives are available for research purposes, by appointment only.
Open all year, Mon-Fri 10-12.30 & 1.30-5, Sun 2-5. (Closed Sat, Good Fri, 24-26 Dec & 1 Jan).
Free.
🅿 *shop* ❊ *(guide dogs)*

Salford Museum & Art Gallery
SALFORD ▮▮▮▮
Peel Park, Crescent
☎ *0161-736 2649*
The pride of this provincial gallery has to be its collection of L S Lowry's works which are displayed in the art gallery together with Victorian paintings and decorative arts. The small museum is equally revealing with its street scene reconstructed in the typical style of a northern industrial town at the turn of the century.
Open all year, Mon-Fri 10-4.45, Sun 2-5. (Closed Good Fri, 25 & 26 Dec, 1 Jan).
Free.
🅿 💺 ⚐ *toilets for disabled shop* ❊

STOCKPORT ▮▮▮▮
See Bramhall

Saddleworth Museum & Art Gallery
UPPERMILL ▮▮▮▮
High St (on A670)
☎ *Saddleworth (01457) 874093 & 870336*
An independent museum displaying the history of Saddleworth in an old mill building next to the Huddersfield Canal. The reconstruction of an 18th-century Weaver's Cottage and the Victoria Mill gallery contain working woollen textile machinery which is run regularly throughout the year. There are also Victorian rooms, a local history gallery, transport and vintage vehicles, and an art gallery with exhibitions of paintings for sale by well-known local artists. Regular craft demonstrations. Groups and school parties welcome. Tourist Information Centre. Special events are planned throughout the year. For 1995 these include Music in Saddleworth (27 May-end August), Saddleworth Festival of the Arts (27 May-4 June), Vintage Vehicle Gala (11 June), Natural History Museum Travelling Discovery Centre (13 July-3 September),
Open all year, Nov-Feb, daily 1-4; Mar-Oct, Mon-Sat 10-5, Sun 12-5.
Small admission fee payable.
🅿 ⚐ *toilets for disabled shop* ❊

Wigan Pier
WIGAN ▮▮▮▮
Wallgate
☎ *(01942) 323666*
Part museum, part theatre, Wigan Pier is a mixture of entertainment and education. Visit the Way We Were

Located on the site of the oldest passenger railway in the world. Manchester's Museum of Science and Industry has exhibits on all forms of power including Energy for the Future.

Heritage Centre with its seaside promenade, coalmine, workshops, market square and pub. Join in with the professional actors of the Wigan Pier Theatre Company as they bring the past to life with a packed programme of themed plays, Victorian music hall shows and the infamous schoolroom. Step aboard a canal boat to experience life in the Lancashire cotton mills across the canal at Trencherfield Mill. Here you will marvel at the world's largest working steam engine, still in steam daily. Special events for 1995 include Wigan International Jazz Festival (8-15 July), Annual Boat Rally and Steam Fair (5-6 August).
Open all year Sat-Thu 10-5 summer; Sat-Thu 11-4 winter. (Closed 25-26 Dec).

✱£4.10 (concessions £3.10). Party 12+.
🅿 ⬛ ✗ ⚬ *toilets for disabled shop* ⌀

HAMPSHIRE

Airborne Forces Museum
ALDERSHOT
Browning Barracks, Queens Av
☎(01252) 349619
Aldershot is the home of the 5th Airborne Brigade, and paratroopers can often be seen practising their drops above the town, so it is an appropriate home for the Airborne Forces Museum. It is easily identified by the World War II Dakota outside, and tells the story of the creation and operation of the parachute forces from 1940 onwards. There are aircraft models and briefing models for World War II operations, and a post-war display includes captured enemy arms, vehicles, dioramas of actions, parachutes, equipment and many scale models. There are Victoria and George Crosses among the medals on show. The Airborne Forces Day Parade and Display is held on the first Saturday in July, and an exhibition commemorating the Rhine Crossing of 1945 is to be held this year.
Open all year, daily 10-4.30. (Closed 22-29 Dec).
✱£2 (ch, students, pen and ex-servicemen £1)
🅿 ⚬ *shop* ⌀

Aldershot Military Museum
ALDERSHOT
Evelyn Woods Rd, Queens Av
☎(01252) 314598
A look behind the scenes at the daily life of both soldiers and civilians as Aldershot and Farnborough grew up around the military camps to become the home of the British Army. Displays include a Victorian barrack room and military tailor's shop, the birth of British aviation, the Canadian Army in Aldershot during World War II, and the Rushmoor Local History Gallery.
Open Mar-Oct, daily 10-5; Nov-Feb, daily 10-4.30. (Closed 13-26 Dec & 1 Jan)
🅿 ⚬ *shop*
Details not confirmed for 1995

Watercress Line
ALRESFORD
The Railway Station
☎(01962) 733810 & 734200
The Watercress Line, a preserved steam railway, runs through ten miles of rolling scenic countryside between Alton and Alresford. All four stations are authentically 'dressed' in period style, with attractive gardens and there are a locomotive yard and picnic area at Ropley. Special events for 1995 include: Friends of Thomas the Tank Engine (14-23 April and two weeks in August), Alton Anniversary Event (27-29 May), War on the Line (9-10 September) and Enthusiast Events (4-5 February, 4-5 March).
Open main operating periods: Sun, Feb. Wknds & BH's Mar-Oct. Mid wk running begins Jun-mid Jul. Daily mid Jul-1st wk Sep (check timetable). "Santa Special" Dec, booking essential. Thomas the Tank Engine events Etr week & 2 weeks in Aug. Unlimited travel for the day, £7.50 (ch £4.50, pen £5.50). Family ticket £22.
🅿 (charged) ⬛ ✗ licensed ⚬ (ramps for trains) toilets for disabled shop

Sir Harold Hillier Gardens & Arboretum
AMPFIELD
Jermyn's Ln (signposted off A31 & B3057)
☎Braishfield (01794) 368787
This is the largest collection of trees and shrubs of its kind in the British Isles. The plants come from different parts of the world, and include many rarities. The setting is 160 acres of attractive landscape, with something of interest at all times of the year. Superb colour is provided in particular during the spring and autumn seasons. Special events for 1995 include: 29 April and 6 May - early opening (6.30am, with breakfast from 7am); June - display of North American plants in conjunction with the National Council for the Conservation of Plants and Gardens; 16-18 July - Flower Arranging Festival/Exhibition in Jermyns House; 2-31 August - Art Exhibition in Jermyns House.
Open all year, Apr-Oct daily 10.30-6, Nov-Mar daily 10.30-5 or dusk. (Closed Xmas, New Year)
Mar-Nov: £4 (ch £1, pen £3.50). Dec & Feb: £3 (ch £1, pen £2.50) Party 30+.
🅿 ✗ licensed ⚬ toilets for disabled garden centre ⌀

Andover Museum & Museum of The Iron Age
ANDOVER
6 Church Close
☎(01264) 366283
The museum is housed in a fine Georgian building. Displays include an aquarium of local fish found in the Test Valley, local history, a natural history gallery and a programme of temporary exhibitions. The Museum of the Iron Age, which interprets Danebury Hill Fort, is housed in an adjacent building.
Open all year Tue-Sat 10-5. Also Apr-Sep, Sun 2-5.
Admission fee payable for "Museum of the Iron Age" £1.20 (ch & pen 60p).
🅿 ⚬ (stair lift to 1st floor) shop ⌀

Finkley Down Farm Park
ANDOVER
(signposted from A303 & A343)
☎(01264) 352195
A wide range of farm animals and poultry can be seen here, including some rare breeds. The pets corner has tame, hand-reared baby animals that can be stroked and petted. There are also a Countryside Museum, housed in a barn, Romany caravans and rural bygones to see, an adventure playground and a large picnic area. A Shetland pony show is planned for July 1995. Tractor and pony rides are available.
Open 26 March-Oct, daily 10.30-6. Last admission 5pm.
Prices under review.
🅿 ⬛ ⚬ toilets for disabled shop ⌀

New Forest Butterfly Farm
ASHURST
Longdown (off A35)
☎Southampton (01703) 292166
The butterfly reserve is set in a glasshouse planted as a tropical garden, with lemon and banana trees, passion flowers and a mass of other plants and shrubs needed by the different types of butterfly. The species come from all over the world, with a separate area devoted to butterflies of Britain. There are also dragonfly ponds, and other creatures to be seen include tarantulas, scorpions, lizards, ants and locusts.
Open 26 Mar-30 Oct, daily 10-5.
🅿 ⬛ ⚬ (ex woodland walk) toilets for disabled shop garden centre ⌀
Details not confirmed for 1995

Willis Museum
BASINGSTOKE
Market Place
☎(01256) 465902
The museum is housed in the handsome Old Town Hall. Displays include a New Town history gallery, exhibits of clocks and watches, embroidery, local interest and a natural history gallery. There are

➤

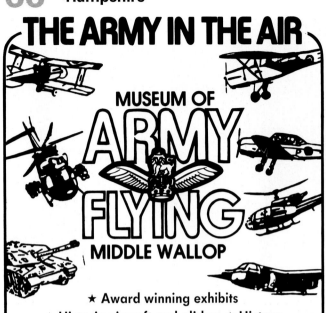

also a gallery for temporary exhibitions and a local Tourist Information Centre.
Open all year, Tue-Fri 10-5, Sat 10-4. Free.
P *(800 yds)* shop

Beaulieu : National Motor Museum
BEAULIEU
(on B3054)
☎*(01590) 612345*
The venerable 16th-century house of Beaulieu is worth seeing just for its lovely setting by the Beaulieu River, but it has become most famous as the home of the National Motor Museum. This is one of the world's largest collections of vehicles and motoring memorabilia, with the extra attraction of 'Wheels', a feature which takes visitors on an automated trip through a spectacular display of 100 years of motoring. Other attractions are a high-level monorail through the grounds, veteran bus rides and a model railway. The main house itself has a collection of fine paintings and furnishings. The house is only the gatehouse of the great abbey which once stood here, and ruins of other monastic buildings can be seen in the grounds. There is also an exhibition of monastic life.
Open all year - Palace House & Gardens, National Motor Museum, Beaulieu Abbey & Exhibition of Monastic Life, Etr-Sep 10-6; Oct-Etr 10-5. (Closed 25 Dec).
P ☕ ♿ *toilets for disabled shop*
Details not confirmed for 1995

Bishop's Waltham Palace
BISHOP'S WALTHAM
(on A333)
☎*(01489) 892460*
The town may have been laid out by the bishops of Winchester, and the remains of their palace are still impressive. It dates from the 12th century, and consists of state apartments round a cloister court, with a great hall and a four-storey tower. It was surrendered to Parliamentary forces in the Civil War.
Open Apr-Sep, daily 10-6. For winter opening telephone 01705 527667
£2 (ch £1, concessions £1.50).
P ♿
(EH)

Spinners
BOLDRE
School Ln (off A337)
☎*Lymington (01590) 673347*
The garden has been entirely created by the owners since 1960. It has azaleas, rhododendrons, camellias and magnolias, interspersed with primulas, blue poppies and other woodland and ground cover plants. The nursery (open all year) is famed for its rare and less common trees, shrubs and plants and attracts visitors from all over the world.
Open 14 Apr-14 Sep daily 10-5. Other times on application. Nursery open all year, but garden and nursery both closed on Sun & Mon.
£1.50 (accompanied ch under 6 free).
P *garden centre*

Breamore House, Countryside & Carriage Museums
BREAMORE
(on A338)
☎*Downton (01725) 512468*
The handsome manor house was built in around 1583 and has a fine collection of paintings, china and tapestries. The museum has good examples of coaches and steam engines, and uses reconstructed workshops and other displays to show how people lived, worked and travelled a century or so ago. A children's playground opened in 1994. On the weekend of 6-7 May the Breamore Museum Special (11am - 6pm) is a mini rally almost all under cover; on Sunday 25 June the Breamore Horse Show is in aid of the Wessex Medical School Trust. Other special events include: the Breamore Craft Shows 27-29 May, live steam model show 5-6 August, and Celebrations of VE Day 12-13 August.
Open Apr Tue, Wed & Sun & Etr, May-Jul & Sep, Tue-Thu & Sat, Sun & all BH, Aug, daily 2-5.30 (Countryside Museum 1pm). Combined tickets £4.50 (ch £3); Party & pen rate available.
P ☕ ♿ *toilets for disabled shop*

Buckler's Hard Village & Maritime Museum
BUCKLER'S HARD
(off B3054)
☎*Bucklers Hard (01590) 616203*
This is a historic shipbuilding village, where wooden warships, including some of Nelson's fleet, were built from New Forest oak. In its busy days the wide main street would have been used for rolling great logs to the 'hard' where the ships were built, and the village would have been stacked high with timber. The 18th-century homes of a shipwright and labourer, and a master shipbuilder's office can be seen.
A typical inn scene has been reconstructed, complete with costumed figures, smells and conversation. The Maritime Museum tells the story of the local shipbuilding industry, and also has items from the voyages of Sir Francis Chichester, who moored his boats here. On the last Sunday in July The Bucklers Hard Village Festival is held with people in period costume to recapture all the atmosphere of the village fête.
Open all year, Etr-Spring BH 10-6; Spring BH-Sep 10-9; Oct-Etr 10-4.30. (Closed 25 Dec).
P ☕ ✕ *licensed* ♿ *shop*
Details not confirmed for 1995

Sandham Memorial Chapel
BURGHCLERE
(4m S Newbury off A34)
☎*(01635) 278394*
The chapel was built in 1926-7 in memory of H W Sandham, who was killed in World War I, and its walls are filled with 19 frescoes by Stanley Spencer. He based the work on his own wartime experiences, which included a period in Salonica and a spell as a hospital orderly. This had helped to make Spencer acutely aware of the humdrum life of the ordinary men. His pictures include soldiers coping with laundry and rubbish, moving baggage and dressing wounds, and laying out kit for inspection. These unsung aspects of war create a haunting and poignant series. Its climax is a resurrection scene that fills one wall. In the foreground is a tangled mass of crosses, each one handed in by a soldier.
Open 25 Mar-Oct, Wed-Sun 11.30-6. Nov & Mar, Sat & Sun 11.30-4. Also open BH Mons. Dec-Feb by appointment only.
**£1.50 (ch 75p).*
P ♿
(NT)

Jane Austen's House
CHAWTON
☎*Alton (01420) 83262*
The house stands in the village street, and is where Jane Austen lived and wrote from 1809 to 1817. It has been restored to look as it would have done in the early 1800s, and items such as the author's donkey cart and writing table can be seen. Visitors are welcome to picnic in the garden in daylight hours. Refreshments are available in the village.
Open daily Apr-Oct, 11-4.30 also Nov, Dec & Mar, Wed-Sun. Jan & Feb, Sat & Sun. (Closed 25 & 26 Dec).
£2 (ch 8-18 50p). Party 15+.
P *(300yds)* ♿ *toilets for disabled shop*

Exbury Gardens
EXBURY
Exbury Estate (3m from Beaulieu, off B3054)
☎*Fawley (01703) 891203*
Exbury Gardens is a 200-acre landscaped woodland garden on the East bank of the Beaulieu River and contains one of the finest collections of rhododendrons, azaleas, camellias and magnolias in the world - as well as many rare and beautiful shrubs and trees. A labyrinth of tracks and paths enable the visitor to explore and enjoy the countless intricate

plantings, the cascades and ponds, a rose garden, rock garden, heather garden and iris garden, daffodil meadow and river walk. In July and August the 53 acres which is kept open is worth a visit and there is an ideal spot for a peaceful picnic by Jubilee Pond. The Autumn colours are spectacular.
Open 12 Feb-23 Oct, daily 10-5.30 (or dusk if earlier). Summer Garden (while part of garden rested) open mid-Jul-mid-Sep.
Spring 200 acres, 12 Feb-10 Jul: £3-£4.50 (ch 10-15 £2-£3.50, pen £2.50-£3.50). Autumn 200 acres, 17 Sep-23 Oct: £2.50 (ch £1.50, pen £2). Summer 53 acres, 11 Jul-16 Sep: £2 (ch & pen £1.50). Party 15+
🅿 ⚐ ♿ *toilets for disabled shop garden centre*

Royal Navy Submarine Museum & HMS Alliance GOSPORT
Haslar Jetty Rd
☎*(Portsmouth) (01705) 529217 & 510354*
The great attraction of this museum is the chance to see inside a submarine, and there are guided tours of *HMS Alliance*. The more conventional part of the museum covers the development of submarines from their earliest days. There is an emphasis on British boats, but an international view is also given, and there are models of practically every kind. Two periscopes from *HMS Conqueror* have now been installed in the museum, giving panoramic views of Portsmouth Harbour. Outside, the dominant presence of the modern Royal Navy gives an exciting, topical flavour to a visit.
Open all year, Apr-Oct 10-5.30; Nov-Mar 10-4.30. (Closed 24 Dec-1 Jan). Allow 2 hrs for visit.
£3.50 (ch & pen £2.50). Party 12+. Combined ticket with Royal Marines Museum & The Royal Navel Museum now available.
🅿 ⚐ ♿ *(information in Braille) shop ❀*
See advertisement on page 69

Havant Museum
HAVANT
East St
☎*(01705) 451155*
The museum shares this late 19th-century building with a flourishing arts centre. There are brand new displays of local history exhibits and a firearms collection made by the engineer Cecil G Vokes (he also developed the automatic windscreen wiper). There is also a regular programme of temporary exhibitions.
Open all year, Tue-Sat 10-5.
Free.
🅿 ♿ *shop ❀*

Highclere Castle
HIGHCLERE
☎*(01635) 253210*
This splendid early Victorian mansion stands in beautiful parkland. It has sumptuous interiors and numerous Old Master pictures. Also shown are early finds by the 5th Earl of Carnarvon, one of the discoverers of Tutankhamun's tomb.
Open Jul-Sep, Wed-Sun 2-6; Aug BH Mon 11-6. Last admission to Castle 5pm.
🅿 ⚐ ♿ *(wheelchair available) toilets for disabled shop garden centre ❀*
Details not confirmed for 1995

Hinton Ampner
HINTON AMPNER
(off A272, 1m W of Bramdean)
☎*(01962) 771305*
It is the site and surroundings which provide the principal charm of Hinton Ampner. The house which now stands with wide views over the placid Hampshire landscape has suffered a chequered history. It was remodelled in the Georgian style in 1936 by Ralph Dutton, the 8th and last Lord Sherborne, and is a tribute to the energy and devotion of this man. Having lovingly restored and refurnished his home, he relinquished it to a school during the war and then saw it largely destroyed by fire in 1960. Undaunted, he rebuilt and refurnished the house with fine Regency furniture, pictures and porcelain.
The gardens juxtapose formality of design and informality of planting, and there are delightful walks with many prospects and unexpected vistas.
Open Apr-Sep. Garden: Sat, Sun, Tue, Wed, 1.30-5.30. House: Tue & Wed only plus Sat & Sun in Aug 1.30-5.30. Last admission 5pm. Closed Good Fri & Etr Mon).
House & Garden £3.70; Garden only £2.40.
🅿 ⚐ ♿ *(Braille guides, special parking) toilets for disabled ❀*
(NT)

Hurst Castle
HURST CASTLE
☎*(01590) 642344*
The castle is one of the many coastal forts built by Henry VIII in case of invasion, and was occupied in the Civil War and then fortified again in the 19th century. It can be reached on foot or by boat from Keyhaven (weather permitting).
Open all year, Apr-22 Jul & Sep 10-5.30 (last admission 4.30) 23 Jul-Aug, daily 10-6 (last admission 5.15. Closed 24-26 Dec & 1 Jan.
£2 (ch £1, concessions £1.50).
⚐
(EH)

Bohunt Manor
LIPHOOK
(on A3)
☎*(01428) 722208*
Bohunt includes woodland gardens with a lakeside walk, a water garden, roses and herbaceous borders, and a collection of ornamental ducks and geese. Several unusual trees and shrubs include a handkerchief tree and a Judas tree. The property has been given to the Worldwide Fund for Nature.
Open all year, daily.
❀*£1.50 (ch free, pen £1).*
🅿 ♿ *flat access around lake ❀*

Hollycombe Steam Collection
LIPHOOK
(1.5m SE on unclass rd)
☎*(01428) 724900*
This all-encompassing collection of steam-driven equipment includes a Bioscope showing old films, fairground organs, steam-driven roundabouts, big wheel, steam yacht, razzle dazzle, a steam farm and paddle steamer engine. There are demonstrations of threshing and steam rolling, and traction engine rides. Three steam-hauled trains run through a woodland setting with spectacular views of the South Downs. Many special events are planned for 1995 to celebrate the twenty-fifth anniversary of the collection.
Open Good Friday, BH & Sun until 8 Oct. £5 (ch & pen £4). Family ticket £15. Party 15+.
🅿 ⚐ ♿ *shop ❀*

New Forest Museum & Visitor Centre
LYNDHURST
Main Car Park, High St
☎*(01703) 283914*
The story of the New Forest, including its history, traditions, character and wildlife, told through an audio-visual show and exhibition displays. The show features life-size models of Forest characters, and the famous New Forest embroidery.
Open all year, daily from 10am (Closed 25 Dec)

Admission charged
🅿 ♿ *toilets for disabled shop ❀*

Marwell Zoological Park
MARWELL
Colden Common (on B2177)
☎*Owslebury (01962) 777406 & 777407*
Devoted to the conservation and breeding of rare wild animals, Marwell has a worldwide reputation. The animals are housed in spacious enclosures or can be seen grazing in paddocks, and there is an enclosure where animals can be approached and stroked by children. Covering 100 acres of parkland, the collection includes over 1000 animals, and some of the species here no longer exist in the wild. New animals are being added constantly. There is also a gift shop and many attractions for younger children, including a children's farmyard, Wallaby Wood and road trains. Numerous events are held throughout the year, including a Christmas 'Winter Wonderland'.
Open all year, daily (ex 25 Dec), 10-6 (or dusk). Last admission 4.30pm or 1 hour before dusk (whichever is earliest). £6.50 (ch 3-14 £5, pen £6). Cars entering zoo circuit £7. Free to orange badge holders. Party 20+.
🅿 ⚐ ✗ *licensed ♿ (special tours for visually impaired by arrangement) toilets for disabled shop ❀*

Museum of Army Flying
MIDDLE WALLOP
(on A343)
☎*Andover (01980) 674421*
This award-winning museum's exhibits include Cody's Kite, World War I aircraft, military Austers of World War II and the largest collection of gliders in Europe. Photographs and diaromas tell the story of army aviation from the 19th century to the present day. Rotary and fixed wing aircraft operate during the week. There is a restaurant with a viewing gallery over the airfield. Special events planned for 1995 include: May 8 - flying display (VE Day); June 17-18 - SAM military glider championship; June 25 - British Electric Flying Association championships; July 8-9 - model aircraft international competition; July 22-23 - British Model Flying Association UK championships; August 5-6 - kite rally; August 19-20 - Wakefield Cup international model competition; September 23-24 - SAM aeromodels meet; October 1 - Bournemouth Model Flying Aircraft Society aeromodels meet.
Open all year, daily 10-4.30. (Closed Xmas-New Year). Evening visits by special arrangement.
❀*£3.75 (ch 5-15 & students £2.25, pen £2.75). Family ticket £10. Party.*
🅿 ✗ *licensed ♿ (lifts to upper levels) toilets for disabled shop ❀ (ex in grounds)*
➤

Highclere Castle is really a sumptuous Victorian mansion. Within the house are many Egyptian relics brought back by the Earl of Carnarvon, who discovered the tomb of the pharaoh Tutankhamun.

The site of Porchester Castle was first fortified by the Romans. The Great Tower, built by Robert Assheton in 1367, is still an impressive sight.

Furzey Gardens
MINSTEAD
☎ Southampton (01703) 812464
The cottage which stands in Furzey Gardens dates from 1560 and with the gallery provides a charming venue for displays of local arts and crafts. The eight acres of peaceful glades which surround the cottage include winter and summer heathers, rare flowering trees and shrubs and a mass of spring bulbs which produce a wonderful display after the winter months.
Open daily 10-5 (earlier in winter). (Closed Xmas).
Gardens, cottage & gallery £3 (ch & disabled £1.50, student & pen £2.50). Nov-Feb reduced admission charge. Party 20+.
🅿 & shop ⊗

Mottisfont Abbey Garden
MOTTISFONT
(4m NW Romsey)
☎ Lockerly (01794) 341220 & 340757
Set picturesquely by the River Test, Mottisfont Abbey is an 18th-century house adapted from a 12th-century priory. The north front shows its medieval church origins quite clearly, and the monks' 'cellarium' is virtually complete. The garden has splendid old trees and a walled garden planted with the national collection of old-fashioned roses. Details for open air events in summer can be obtained by ringing the Rose Garden tel 01794 40757, and Abbey Plays (not NT) tel 01794 40846.
Open: Garden 19-26 Mar, Apr-Oct, Sat-Wed 12-6 (or dusk if earlier); Jun, Sat-Thu 12-8.30pm. Due to major restoration project the Abbey will be closed during 1995.
Gardens £2.50, £3.50 during rose season which varies according to weather.
🅿 & (Braille guide, wheelchair available) toilets for disabled shop ⊗
(NT)

Netley Abbey
NETLEY
☎ (01703) 453076
A romantic ruin, set among green lawns and trees, this was a 13th-century Cistercian abbey founded by Peter des Roches, tutor to Henry III. During the Dissolution part of the early English-style abbey was converted into a house; all that remains is an impressive shell. Nearby is the 19th-century Gothic-style Netley Castle.
Open any reasonable time.
🅿 & ⊗
(EH)

Sammy Miller Museum
NEW MILTON
Gore Rd
☎ (01425) 619696
This museum has machines dating back to 1900 and is accepted as the world's most interesting Motor Cycle Museum with many machines that are the only surviving ones in the world. The Racing collection is of exceptional interest with the opportunity to see these wonderful World Record Breaking Bikes and their history, including the first bike to lap a Grand Prix Course at over 100 miles per hour, the 4 cylinder supercharged 500cc AJS. There are also DKW, NSU, Motoguzzi MV, Norton, Rudge, Velocette, Sunbeam etc, and of course the three-wheel Morgan.
Open all year, daily 10-4.30.
❄£3 (ch & pen £1.50)
🅿 ⬛ & shop ⊗

Basing House
OLD BASING
Redbridge Ln
☎ Basingstoke (01256) 467294
A two-year siege in 1645 culminated in the destruction of the largest house of Tudor England. Built on the site of a Norman castle in 1530, the ruins of Basing House, including a 300ft long tunnel, are a fascinating study. There is a re-creation of a garden of 1600 and exhibitions showing the history of the house. A fine 16th-century tithe barn stands nearby. Special events for 1995 will commemorate the 3rd Siege of Basing House in 1645.
Open Apr-1 Oct, Wed-Sun & BH 2-6.
❄£1.50 (ch & pen 70p). Registered disabled free. Prices under review
🅿 & (disabled parking by prior arrangement) toilets for disabled shop

Paultons Park
OWER
(exit junc 2 M27, near junc A31 & A36)
☎ Southampton (01703) 814455
Paultons Park offers a great day out for all the family with over forty different attractions included in the admission price. Many fun activities include Rio Grande Railway, bumper boats, go-karts, 6-lane astroglide, and exciting Runaway Train. Attractions for younger children include Kid's Kingdom, Spidernet, pet's corner, rabbit ride, pirate ship, flying saucer and the Magic Forest where nursery rhymes come to life. Glimpse the past in the Romany and Village Life Museums. In a beautiful parkland setting with extensive 'Capability' Brown gardens landscaped with ponds and aviaries for exotic birds; lake and hedge maze.
Open mid Mar-Oct, daily 10-6.30. Last admission 4.30pm. Rides close 5.30pm. Earlier closing spring & autumn. Admission fee payable.
🅿 ⬛ ✕ & (some rides unsuitable) toilets for disabled shop ⊗

Bear Museum
PETERSFIELD
38 Dragon St
☎ (01730) 265108
Teddy Bears are the theme of this museum, which children will love because they are allowed to cuddle and play with some of the exhibits. A variety of dolls and bears is displayed in the Victorian-style nursery while downstairs is the 'Teddy Bear's Picnic' where children are encouraged to sing along to the famous song and join in the fun of the large picnic scene. There is a shop selling high-quality limited editions.
Open Mon-Sat 10-5.
Free.
🅿 shop ⊗

Portchester Castle
PORTCHESTER
(off A27)
☎ (01705) 378291
Evidence of the 3rd-century Roman fort can still be seen on this nine-acre site. A church built in 1133 still stands, showing its fine west front and carved font. Robert Assheton built the great tower in 1367, and buildings within the inner courtyard were converted to a palace by Richard II, and the remains of the kitchen, hall and great chamber are still apparent. This was the palace from which Henry V embarked for Agincourt, and Henry VIII stayed here with Anne Boleyn. In later times, although falling into disrepair, the castle was home to prisoners from the Napoleonic Wars.
Open all year, Apr-Sep, daily 10-6; Oct-Mar, daily 10-4. Closed 24-26 Dec & 1 Jan.
£2.50 (ch £1.30, concessions £1.90).
🅿 & ⊗
(EH)

PORTSMOUTH & SOUTHSEA
The history of Portsmouth is the history of England's naval heritage. It was Henry VII who, in the late 15th century, first fortified Portsmouth's sea walls. Behind them he built England's first permanent dry dock, and about 50 years later Henry VIII expanded it into the country's first royal dockyard. Near this dockyard was the birthplace of Charles Dickens - now a museum. Relics of Portsmouth's history include three of the great ships that once sailed from the port - HMS Victory, Mary Rose and HMS Warrior. Portsmouth played a leading role in the World War II D-Day landings which are commemorated in the D-Day Museum at Southsea. Southsea and Portsmouth run into one, Portsmouth being home to the Navy and Southsea being a more traditional seaside town with a promenade, a fair, a leisure centre and a popular aquarium. Southsea also has a castle which formed part of Henry VIII's coastal defences.

Charles Dickens' Birthplace Museum
PORTSMOUTH & SOUTHSEA
393 Old Commercial Rd
☎ (01705) 827261
Built in 1805, this is the birthplace and early home of the famous novelist. Now restored and furnished to illustrate the middle-class taste of the early 19th century, the museum displays items pertaining to Dickens' work and the couch on which he died.
Open Mar-Oct, daily 10-5.30 (last admission 5pm).
£1 (ch & student 60p, accompanied ch 13 free & pen 75p). Family ticket £2.60.
🅿 shop ⊗

City Museum
PORTSMOUTH & SOUTHSEA
Museum Rd, Old Portsmouth
☎ (01705) 827261
The museum features a 'Story of Portsmouth' exhibition. This includes an introduction to the history of Portsmouth, local archaelogy, the early history of the town, room settings showing life in the home from the 17th century to the 1950s, and a gallery of local pictures. Extensive use is made of audio-visuals. Other displays include furniture and decorative arts from the 17th-20th centuries, a specialist contemporary crafts gallery and a regular programme of temporary exhibitions. In 1995 a special display: Destruction and Reconstruction of Portsmouth (during and after the Second World War) is planned.
Open all year, daily 10.30-5.30 (5pm Nov-Mar). (Closed 24-26 Dec).
Admission charged, but will become free from Apr'95.
🅿 & (induction loops) toilets for disabled shop ⊗

Cumberland House Natural Science Museum & Butterfly House
PORTSMOUTH & SOUTHSEA
Eastern Pde
☎ (01705) 827261
The geology and natural history of the area are explained, with a full-size reconstruction of a dinosaur, an aquarium and free-flying butterflies. There are seasonal displays of woodland, downland and marshland ecology.
Open all year, daily 10.30-5.30. Last admission 5pm. (Closed 24-26 Dec).
❄£1 (ch 60p, accompanied ch 13 free & pen 75p). Family ticket £2.60.
🅿 shop ⊗

D-Day Museum & Overlord Embroidery
PORTSMOUTH & SOUTHSEA
Clarence Esplanade (adjacent to Southsea Castle)
☎ (01705) 827261
The story of D-Day is told from the viewpoint of those involved in both sides of history's biggest seaborne invasion, through audio-visual shows, displays, military vehicles and the 272ft-long Overlord Embroidery.
Open all year, daily 10-5.30 (4.30 Nov-Mar). Last admission 1 hr before closing. (Closed 24-26 Dec).
£3.60 (ch £2.20, pen £2.70).
🅿 (charged) ⬛ ✕ & (induction loops available for the hard of hearing). toilets for disabled shop ⊗

HMS Victory
PORTSMOUTH & SOUTHSEA
HM Naval Base
☎ (01705) 839766
Still in commission and manned by regular serving officers and men, Lord Nelson's famous flagship at the Battle of Trafalgar is, because of her age and historic significance, the world's most outstanding example of maritime restoration. A tour around her decks gives some idea of the sailors' way of life in Nelson's day, and visitors can see the spot where the Admiral received his fatal wound, and the surgery below decks where he eventually died.
Open Mar-Oct, daily 10-4.50; Nov-Feb,

daily 10.30-4.30. (Closed 25 Dec).
£4.75 (ch £ 3.50, pen £4.25).
Prices include Royal Naval Museum.
P (charged) & (lower gun deck) toilets for
disabled shop ※

HMS Warrior 1860
PORTSMOUTH & SOUTHSEA
Victory Gate, HM Naval Base
☎(01705) 291379
Originally launched in 1860, HMS
Warrior was the world's first iron-hulled
armoured warship. Restored, with
painstaking accuracy over a period of
eight years in Hartlepool, she is now a
permanent feature beside The Hard in
Portsmouth. Visitors can wander at
leisure throughout the four vast decks,
showing the rich furnishings and
excellent craftmanship. Everything
except the sheer number of crew has
been recreated. HMS Warrior is the only
ship which spans the eras of wood, iron,
sail and steam. Special Victorian Navy
Days are planned for August.
Open all year, Mar-Oct 10-5.30; Nov-Feb
10-5. (Last admission 1 hr before
closing).
P (200 yds) ⚍ & (upper deck only) toilets
for disabled shop ※
Details not confirmed for 1995

The Mary Rose Museum
PORTSMOUTH & SOUTHSEA
HM Naval Base
☎(01705) 839766 & 750521
The spectacular raising of the Mary Rose
in 1982 is remembered by millions.
Remarkably preserved in the Solent silts
for 437 years, Henry VIII's warship was a
Tudor time-capsule, complete with the
everyday possessions, clothing, food,
tools and weapons of her 700 men. One
of Britain's major tourist attractions, the
Mary Rose provides a fascinating family
day out. In her special dry-dock workshop
in Portsmouth's historic dockyard, the
great oak hull is being conserved.
In the Mary Rose Exhibition a twelve
minute audio-visual presentation on the
discovery, raising and conservation of the
ship highlights the enormous endeavour
which has gone into the world's most
ambitious underwater archaeological

project. The visitor will then enjoy all the
more the fascinating exhibition of the
treasures from the Mary Rose: a themed
display of many of the 20,000 artefacts
recovered, including longbows, cannon,
gaming boards, clothing, combs,
pewterware, lanterns, a shaving bowl -
even the contents of the barber-
surgeon's chest, with syringes and jars of
ointment. Several events are to be held
during 1995, including a Festival of Arts
and Culture, the 450th anniversary of the
sinking of the Mary Rose in July, and the
500th anniversary of Portshmouth's
historic dockyard: please write or
telephone for more details. Special
evening openings can be arranged for
pre-booked groups.
Open all year, daily from 10am. (Closed
25 Dec).
£4.75 (ch & students £3.50, pen £4.25).
Family ticket £15.
P (charged) ✗ licensed & toilets for
disabled shop ※

The Royal Marines Museum
PORTSMOUTH & SOUTHSEA
☎(01705) 819385
The Royal Marines Museum offers a
series of exhibitions depicting the
eventful history of the corps from the
17th century to the present day in all
parts of the world, including its service
with the UN. Audio visual shows and a
multi-media cinema vivdly bring to life
campaigns like the Falklands War, the
freezing conditions of the Norway
invasion in the Second World War and
show you just how Commandos survive
in arctic terrain. A 16th-century gallery
shows life at sea, with graphic
descriptions of punishments and food.
Recent attractions include the D-Day film
and exhibition, a Jungle Room and the
Commando Story, and there may be
other events for 1995 - ring for details.
Outside there is a junior commando
assault course, and the chance to climb
aboard a Falklands landing craft.
Open all year, Whit-Aug daily 9.30-5; Sep-
May daily 10-4.30. (Closed 3 days Xmas)
✱£3 (ch £1.50, pen £2) Family ticket
£7.50.
P ✗ licensed shop ※

Now at Portsmouth's Naval Base, the flagship of Nelson's fleet at the Battle of
Trafalgar, HMS Victory is an outstanding example of naval restoration.

Royal Naval Museum
PORTSMOUTH & SOUTHSEA
HM Naval Base (M275 into Portsmouth
then follow signs)
☎(01705) 733060
This is the only museum exclusively
devoted to the overall history of the
Navy. A panorama of Trafalgar, with
sound-effects, is complemented by relics
of Lord Nelson, his officers and men.
Uniforms, medals, figureheads and
model ships are on show, and there is a
wide range of displays, such as 'The Rise
of the Royal Navy', 'Sailing Navy', 'The
Victorian Navy', 'The Navy in the 20th
Century', and to bring the picture right up
to date, 'The Modern Navy'. Starting in
May 1995, the Pacific Fleet Exhibition
commemorates the end of the Second
World War in the Pacific and in July there
will be a Festival of the Sea.
Open all year, daily 10-5. (Closed 25-26
Dec).
£2.65 (ch £1.85 & pen £2.10). Family
ticket £7.50. Combined ticket available
with HMS Victory.
P ⚍ & (exhibit for sight impaired groups
by prior arrangement) toilets for disabled
shop ※ (ex small dogs if carried)

Southsea Castle & Museum
PORTSMOUTH & SOUTHSEA
Clarence Esp
☎(01705) 827261
Part of Henry VIII's national coastal
defences, this fort was built in 1545 and
contains displays illustrating
Portsmouth's development as a military
fortress, aspects of naval history and the
archaeology of the area. Please
telephone for details of the special
events programme for 1995 which
includes a Civil War weekend, a Tudor
weekend and a hawks and owls
weekend.
Open all year, Apr-Oct, daily 10-5.30.
Nov-Mar, Sat & Sun 10-4.30. (Closed 24-
26 Dec).
✱£1.50 (ch & students 90p, ch
accompanied 13 free, pen £1.20).
P (charged) ⚍ & (wheelchair available)
shop ※

Spitbank Fort
PORTSMOUTH & SOUTHSEA
☎Fareham (01329) 664286 & (0831)
608383
This massive granite and iron fortress
was built in the 1860s as part of the
coastal defences against the French.
Standing one mile out to sea, it provides
magnificent views across the Solent. The
interior is a maze of passages connecting
over 50 rooms on two levels. A Victorian
cooking range is still in working order, as
are the forge and a 402ft-deep well from
which fresh water is obtained.
Open May-Sep, Tue-Sun. (Weather
permitting).
£5.75 (ch £4) includes ferry charge. Boat
ride takes approx 20 mins, visitors should
allow 2hr to view. Ferries depart HM
Navel Base Portsmouth.
P ⚍

Roman Villa
ROCKBOURNE
☎(01725) 518541
Discovered in 1942, about a mile outside
the village, these remains of a 40-room
Roman Villa are the largest in the area
and represent a fine display of mosaics
and hypocaust. The site museum reveals
discoveries excavated over many years
and displayed in context. These range
from a coin hoard, jewellery and leather
shoes to pottery vessels, architectural
fragments and human skeletons.
Open Apr-Oct, Mon-Fri 2-6, Sat, Sun &
BH 10.30-6; Jul & Aug daily 10.30-6.
£1.30 (concessions 75p), under review.
P & shop ※

Broadlands
ROMSEY
(main entrance on A31 Romsey by-pass)
☎(01794) 517888
Famous as the home of the late Lord
Mountbatten, Broadlands is now lived in
by his grandson Lord Romsey. An
elegant Palladian mansion in a beautiful
landscaped setting on the banks of the
River Test, Broadlands was also the
country residence of Lord Palmerston,
the great Victorian statesman. Visitors
may view the house with its fine
furniture and pictures and mementoes of
the famous, enjoy the superb views from
the riverside lawns or relive Lord
Mountbatten's life and times in the
Mountbatten Exhibition and spectacular
Mountbatten audio-visual presentation.
Special events for 1995 include: Classic
Car Roadshow (28-29 May), Summer
Garden Show (21-23 Jul),Hampshire Craft
Fair (4-6 Aug), A performance of
Shakespeare's Merry Wives of Windsor
(13 Aug), Romsey Show, (9 Sep), Charity
Firework Display (3 Nov), and Christmas
Craft Fair (18 & 19 Nov).
Open 31 Mar-25 Sep, 12-4; Jul-Aug 12-
last admission 4pm. (Closed Fri ex Good
Fri & Aug).
£4.25 (ch 12-16 £3.25, (ch under 12 free),
pen, students & disabled £4). Party 15+
P ⚍ & toilets for disabled shop ※

Gilbert White's House & The Oates
Museum
SELBORNE
The Wakes, High St (On B3006)
☎(01420) 511275
This historic house, home of the famous
18th-century naturalist, the Rev. Gilbert
White, author of The Natural History
and Antiquities of Selborne. Visitors
can see furnished rooms, the original
manuscript and wander round the
glorious garden. There are also
exhibitions on two famous members of
the Oates family, who were connected
with Selborne: Captain Lawrence Oates,
who accompanied Scott to the South
Pole and Frank Oates, a Victorian
explorer amd naturalist in South America
and Africa.
Special events for 1995 include
Snowdrop Day in Jan/Feb; Unusual
Plants Fair (24 & 25 Jun); Jazz in June (24
Jun); Mulled Wine Day(Nov). Please ➤

GILBERT WHITE'S HOUSE & GARDEN AND THE OATES MUSEUM

The Wakes, High Street, Selborne, Nr. Alton, Hampshire
Tel: 01420 511275

Charming historic home and garden of Rev Gilbert White, 18thC naturalist & author of 'The Natural History of Selborne'. Furnished rooms & glorious grounds. Displays on Capt Lawrence Oates who accompanied Scott to the South Pole and Frank Oates, Victorian explorer.

Snowdrop day Jan/Feb: Weekend of events 24/25th June: Mulled Wine Day November.
Open: 11-5 Daily from end March to end October then weekends during Winter. Evenings also for groups by arrangement.

---

telephone for details.
Open end Mar-Oct, daily 11-5.30 (last admission 5pm). Also open evenings and weekends in winter by appointment.
£2.50 (ch £1, pen & students £2) Party 10+.
P & shop ✍

The Vyne
SHERBORNE ST JOHN ▬▬▬
(4m N of Basingstoke)
☎ *Basingstoke (01256) 881337*
The Vyne was built at the beginning of the 16th century by William Sandys and later came into the Chute family, who owned the property until 1956 when it was bequeathed to the National Trust. Much of the exterior of the house is still 16th century but over the centuries there have been several major alterations, including the classical portico which was the earliest to be added to an English country house. Inside, the chapel with its original 16th-century stained glass, and the Oak Gallery, are both of note. The Gallery has superb linenfold panelling. There is also an 18th-century tomb chamber and a Palladian staircase. The house is set in a pleasant garden with a small lake. Special events are held in the grounds; please telephone for details.
Open 25 Mar-Sep, Tue-Thu, Sat & Sun (open Good Fri & BH Mon, but closed Tue following) House: 1.30-5.30, BH Mon 11-5.30. Grounds 12.30-5.30. Grounds only in Oct 12.30-5.30). Last admission half hour before closing. (Closed Tue following BH).
✻*House & Grounds £4. Grounds only £2. Family ticket £10.*
P (100 yds) ☕ ✗ *licensed* & *(Braille guide) toilets for disabled shop* ✍
(NT)

Calleva Museum
SILCHESTER ▬▬▬
Bramley Rd
The museum deals with the Roman town of Calleva Atrebatum, the remains of which can be visited. Most of the 1.5 mile long city wall still stands, and is an impressive sight, and nearby are the remains of a large amphitheatre. Little else remains. Objects from the site, photos, maps and other material give a brief account of Calleva. Guides to the site are on sale at the Calleva Arms in the village. (See also Reading Museum).
Open daily 9am-sunset.
Free.
P ✍

God's House Tower
SOUTHAMPTON ▬▬▬
Winkle St
☎ *(01703) 635904 & 832768*
An early fortified building, dating from the 1400s and taking its name from the nearby medieval hospital, it now houses the city's Museum of Archaeology with exhibits on the Roman, Saxon and medieval towns of Southampton.
Open Tue-Fri 10-12 & 1-5; Sat 10-12 & 1-4; Sun 2-5(closed BH's)
P (400 yds) shop ✍
Details not confirmed for 1995

Southampton City Art Gallery
SOUTHAMPTON ▬▬▬
North Guild, Civic Centre, Commercial Rd
☎ *(01703) 632601*
This is the largest gallery in the south of England, with the finest collection of contemporary art in the country outside London. Housed in the beautifully refurbished 1930s NorthGuild complex, varied displays of landscapes, portrait paintings or recent British art are always available, as well as a special display, selected and hung by members of the public. Activities, quizzes and taped tours are available for children.
Open all year, Tue, Wed & Fri 10-5, Thu 10-8, Sat 10-4, Sun 2-5. (Closed 25-27 & 31 Dec).
Free.
P (250yds) ☕ & *toilets for disabled shop* ✍

Southampton Hall of Aviation
SOUTHAMPTON ▬▬▬
Albert Rd South
☎ *(01703) 635830*
The Hall of Aviation was inspired by the development of the famous Spitfire aeroplane at the nearby Supermarine Aviation Works at Woolston. The Spitfire evolved from aircraft built for the Schneider Trophy air races, which the company won in 1931 with the Supermarine 6B. There is a Supermarine S6A on display as well as one of the last Spitfires produced, the Mark 24, and other aircraft of local interest.
The museum is built around a huge Sandringham flying-boat which visitors can board. It was operated out of Southampton Airport by Imperial Airways (BOAC) to all parts of the British Empire. There are also exhibits on aviation production and engineering in the south of England, 14 aircraft are on display here.
Open all year, Tue-Sat 10-5, Sun 12-5. Also BH Mon & School Holidays. (Closed Xmas).
P (150 yds) & *(lift to all levels) toilets for disabled shop* ✍
Details not confirmed for 1995

Southampton Maritime Museum
SOUTHAMPTON ▬▬▬
The Wool House, Town Quay
☎ *(01703) 223941 & 635904*
The Wool House was built in the 14th century. It was a warehouse for wool and has buttressed stone walls and chestnut roof timbering. It currently houses an interesting maritime museum with models and displays telling the history of the Victorian and modern port of Southampton.
Open all year, Tue-Fri 10-12 & 1-5, Sat 10-12 & 1-4, Sun 2-5. (Closed BHs).
P (400 yds) & *shop* ✍
Details not confirmed for 1995

Tudor House Museum
SOUTHAMPTON ▬▬▬
St Michael's Square
☎ *(01703) 332513 & 635904*
This fine half-timbered house, built at the end of the 15th century and therefore older than its name suggests, is now a museum. Exhibitions include a Tudor Hall and displays on Georgian and Victorian social and domestic life in Southampton as well as temporary exhibitions. The unique Tudor garden with knot garden, fountain and 16th-century herbs and flowers is not to be missed.
Open all year, Tue-Fri 10-5, Sat 10-4, Sun 2-5. (Closed Mon & BHs). Lunchtime closing 12-1.
P (400 yds) & *(tape guide to garden) toilets for disabled shop* ✍
Details not confirmed for 1995

Stratfield Saye House
STRATFIELD SAYE ▬▬▬
(off A33)
☎ *Basingstoke (01256) 882882*
The house was built in 1630 and given by the nation to the first Duke of Wellington in 1817, after his victory over Napoleon at the Battle of Waterloo. Stratfield Saye remains the home of the Duke of Wellington and contains a unique collection of paintings, prints, and furniture as well as many mementoes of the lst Duke, including his magnificent funeral carriage which weighs 18 tons and stands 17ft high. The Wellington Exhibition shows the life and times of the great statesman soldier, and in the grounds is the grave of Copenhagen, the Iron Duke's horse, who died in 1836. Special events for 1995 include a Craft Show (27-29 May) and the Wellington Prom, an open-air concert (26 Aug).
Open May-last Sun in Sep, daily ex Fri, 11.30-4.
£4.50 (ch £2.25). Party 20+.
P ☕ ✗ *licensed* & *toilets for disabled shop* ✍ *(ex in grounds)*

Wellington Country Park & National Dairy Museum
STRATFIELD SAYE ▬▬▬
☎ *Reading (01734) 326444*
(For full entry see Riseley, Berkshire)

Titchfield Abbey
TITCHFIELD ▬▬▬
Also known as 'Palace House', this used to be the seat of the Earl of Southampton. The abbey was founded in 1232 and closed during the Dissolution, allowing the Earl to build a fine Tudor mansion on the site in 1538. He incorporated the nave of the 13th-century church and the gatehouse into his new home.
Telephone Regional Office 01732 778000 for details of opening.
P & ✍
(EH)

Eling Tide Mill
TOTTON ▬▬▬
Eling Toll Bridge (2m W, signposted from A35)
☎ *Southampton (01703) 869575*
Eling is the only remaining mill still using tidal energy to grind wheat into flour. There has been a mill on this site for at least 900 years - a predecessor appeared in the Domesday Book. The present mill was extensively restored and reopened in 1980.
It has two sets of millstones, each separately driven, but only one set has been restored to working condition. The waterwheels were cast in iron and installed by Armfields of Ringwood at the beginning of the century. Flour ground at the mill is on sale.
Open all year, Wed-Sun, 10-4.
£1.15 (ch 65p, pen 85p).
P & *shop* ✍

The Hawk Conservancy
WEYHILL ▬▬▬
(3m W of Andover, signposted from A303)
☎ *Andover (01264) 772252*
This is the largest centre in the south for birds of prey from all over the world including eagles, hawks, falcons, owls, vultures and kites. Exciting birds of prey demonstrations are held daily at noon, 2pm, 3pm and 4pm. Different birds - from kestrels to condors - are flown at these times and visitors may have the

Once the capital of Norman England, Winchester is still overshadowed by its magnificent Norman Cathedral, the resting place of both St Swithun and King Canute.

opportunity to hold a bird and perhaps fly a Harris hawk.
Open Mar-last Sun in Oct, daily from 10.30 (last admission spring & winter 4pm, summer 5pm).
✼£4 (ch £2, pen £3.50).
🅿 ✗ ♿ *toilets for disabled shop* ✖

WINCHESTER
Winchester was the royal capital of Saxon Wessex and of England until the late 12th century. To medieval and Tudor monarchs Winchester was traditionally the Camelot of King Arthur from whom they claimed descent. As soon as he arrived in England William the Conqueror built a great castle at Winchester but all that remains is the Great Hall. The castle was destroyed during the Civil War but in the 1680s Charles II commissioned Christopher Wren to build a new palace. Sadly it was never completed and became an army barracks. Winchester is dominated by its massive cathedral (one of the longest in Europe) which was also begun just after the Norman conquest. Around the cathedral there are ancient streets with buildings from many ages and an attractive walk along the banks of the crystal clear River Itchen. Winchester was also the home of Jane Austen.

Great Hall of Winchester Castle
WINCHESTER
The Castle
☎ (01962) 846476
The only remaining portion of William the Conqueror's first castle, it was completed in 1235 and is a fine example of 13th-century architecture. Purbeck marble columns support the roof and on the west wall hangs the Round Table purported to belong to King Arthur. A small medieval garden known as Queen Eleanor's Garden, leads off the Hall.
Open all year, Mar-Oct daily 10-5; Nov-Feb, daily 10-4. (Closed Good Fri & 25-26 Dec).
♿ *shop* ✖
Details not confirmed for 1995

Guildhall Gallery
WINCHESTER
The Broadway
☎ (01962) 848296 & 848289
Situated in the refurbished 19th-century Guildhall, the Gallery has a programme of changing contemporary exhibitions including fine art, paintings, prints, drawings, sculpture, ceramics, craft, and occasional displays of topographical works from the Winchester City Collection.
Open during exhibitions, Tue-Sat 10-5, Sun & Mon 2-5. (Closed Mon, Oct-Mar). Subject to alteration.
🅿 ♥ ✗ *licensed* ♿ *toilets for disabled shop* ✖
Details not confirmed for 1995

Gurkha Museum
WINCHESTER
Peninsula Barracks, Romsey Rd
☎ (01962) 842832
This museum tells the fascinating story of the Gurkha's involvement with the British Army. Travel from Nepal to the North-West Frontier and beyond, with the help of life-sized dioramas, interactive exhibits and sound displays. Experience life in the Malayan jungle and the Falklands campaign. Special attractions are held at half term, Easter, summer and before Christmas.
Open all year, BH Mon, Tue-Sat 10-5. (Closed 25-26 Dec, 1 Jan and Tue following BH Mon)
✼£1.50 (ch & pen 75p). Armed forces free. Party 15+.
🅿 ♿ (lift & stair lift) *toilets for disabled shop* ✖

Hospital of St Cross
WINCHESTER
(1.5m S of city, on A333)
☎ (01962) 851375
The hospital was founded in 1136 for the

benefit of 13 poor men and it is still functioning. Throughout the Middle Ages the hospital handed out the Dole - bread and beer - to travellers, and this is still done. The Chapel of St Cross (12th century); the Brethrens Hall and medieval kitchen, and the walled Master's Garden are all worthy of close inspection. It can be reached by footpath across the fields from Winchester.
Open all year, Apr-Oct, Mon-Sat 9.30-12.30 & 2-5; Nov-Mar 10.30-12.30 & 2-3.30. (Closed Sun, Good Fri & 25 Dec). £1.50 (ch 50p, students & pen £1).
P *(200 yds)* ♿ *toilets for disabled shop* ✖

Royal Hampshire Regiment Museum & Memorial Gardens
WINCHESTER
Serle's House, Southgate St
☎ (01962) 863658
This fine, 18th-century, early Georgian house contains an excellent collection of militaria from the history of the Royal Hampshire Regiment. The gardens are a memorial to the Regimental dead.
Open all year, Mon-Fri 10-12.30 & 2-4; Etr-Oct wknds & BH noon-4. Free.
P ♿ *shop* ✖

Royal Hussars (PWO) Regimental Museum
WINCHESTER
Peninsula Barracks, Romsey Rd
☎ (01962) 863751
The Royal Hussars (Prince of Wales Own) were formed by the amalgamation of the 10th Royal Hussars (Prince of Wales Own) and the 11th Hussars (Prince Alberts Own) in 1969, both regiments having been raised at the time of the Jacobite Rebellion in 1715. Visitors to this museum will learn the story of the Royal Hussars (Prince of Wales Own) from its founding to the present day. The displays are laid out in chronological order and the various themes are lavishly illustrated with paintings, prints, photographs and many artefacts, including, weapons, medals, uniforms and a collection of gold and silver. Another interesting exhibit is the cupboard in which a Private Fowler of the 11th Hussars spent three years and nine months whilst hiding from the Germans in World War II. The Royal Hussars (Prince of Wales Own) were amalgamated with the 14th/20th King's Hussars on 1 December 1992. The Regiment is now known as 'The King's Royal Hussars'.
Open 5 Jan-18 Dec, Tue-Fri 10-4, Sat, Sun & BH's 12-4.
✼£1.50 (ch & pen 50p). Groups by arrangement.
🅿 ♿ *toilets for disabled shop* ✖

Westgate Museum
WINCHESTER
High St
☎ (01962) 848269
This small museum of arms, armour and historical objects including the city's standard weights and measures, is housed in the rooms over the medieval Westgate of the city. A Tudor painted wooden ceiling was moved here from Winchester College.
Open Feb-Oct, Mon-Fri 10-5, Sat 10-1 & 2-5, Sun 2-5 (Closed Mon in Feb, Mar & Oct).
shop ✖
Details not confirmed for 1995

Winchester City Museum
WINCHESTER
The Square
☎ (01962) 848269
Located on the edge of the cathedral precinct, the museum has a well-laid-out display relating to the archaeology and history of the city and central Hampshire. An interesting exhibit is the interior of a 19th-century chemist's shop, which used to be in the High Street.
Open all year, Mon-Sat 10-5, Sun 2-5 (4pm Oct-Mar). (Closed Mon Oct-Mar, Good Fri, Xmas & 1 Jan).
♿ *shop* ✖
Details not confirmed for 1995

Built at the end of the 15th-century, Southampton's Tudor House Museum has a fine Hall and a unique restored Tudor garden.

Winchester College
WINCHESTER
College St
☎ (01962) 868778
Founded and built by Bishop William of Wykeham in 1382, Winchester College is one of the oldest public schools in England. The college has greatly expanded over the years but the original buildings remain intact. The chapel and, during school term, the cloisters and Fromond's Chantry are open to the public. Also open is the War Cloister, which is reached by South Africa Gate. Dedicated in 1924, it contains memorials to Wykhamists who died in World War I and all battles since then. There will be a festival in the War Cloister from 10.30am to 6pm from 16-18 June 1995.
Guided tours Mar-Sep daily (ex Sun am) 11, 1 & 3.15. £2.50 (ch £2).
P ♿ *toilets for disabled shop* ✖

HEREFORD & WORCESTER

Berrington Hall
ASHTON
Berrington (3m N off A49)
☎ Leominster (01568) 615721
An elegant neo-classical house of the late 18th century, designed by Henry Holland and set in a park landscape by 'Capability' Brown. The formal exterior belies the delicate interior with beautifully decorated ceilings and fine furniture, including the Digby collection and a recently restored bedroom suite, nursery, Victorian laundry and pretty tiled Georgian dairy. The attractive garden has interesting plants and a recently planted apple orchard in the walled garden.
Open Apr-Oct daily Wed, Sun & BH's (closed Good Fri) 1.30-5.30. Oct, closed 4.30pm. Last admission 30 mins before closing. Grounds open from 12.30. Park Walk open Jul-Oct same days as house.

£3.60. Family ticket £9.90. Grounds only £1.65.
🅿 ✗ *licensed* ♿ *toilets for disabled shop* ✖
(NT)

Bewdley Museum
BEWDLEY
The Shambles, Load St
☎ (01299) 403573
The Shambles is an 18th-century row of butcher's shops, and makes an interesting setting for the attractive museum devoted to the crafts and industries of the Bewdley area, with displays of Bewdley pewter, agricultural implements and charcoal burning. There are also craft workshops within the museum. For those interested in the industrial side, there is a restored brass foundry and the sawyard area gives occasional demonstrations of a 19th-century horizontal reciprocal saw. A working water wheel and hydraulic ram pump can also be seen and there are daily demonstrations of rope-making and clay-pipe making. A range of events, demonstrations and exhibitions take place throughout the year.
Open Etr-early Sep, Wed-Fri 10.30-4.30, Sat & Sun noon-5, BH Mon noon-5. Telephone for details.
P (200yds) ♿ *shop*

Severn Valley Railway
BEWDLEY
☎ (01299) 403816 & (01746) 764361
(For full entry see Bridgnorth, Shropshire)

West Midland Safari & Leisure Park
BEWDLEY
Spring Grove (on A456)
☎ (01299) 402114
A drive-around wild animal safari park with over 40 species of exotic animals to see. Pets' corner, Sealion show, Reptile House, Parrot Show, Goat Walk and Deer Park. Other attractions include a variety of rides in the leisure area.
Open Apr-Oct, daily 10-5.
✼£3.99 (ch 4 free). Book of ride tickets

➤

In the very heart of cider-making country, the Cider Museum has exhibits from the cider-making process going back to the 17th century.

5-£2.50, 10-£4 or 20-£8. Unlimited ride wristband £4.
P ▣ & toilets for disabled shop garden centre

Broadway Tower Country Park
BROADWAY
(off A44)
☎(01386) 852390
This 65ft tower was designed by James Wyatt for the 6th Earl of Coventry, and was built in 1799. There are exhibitions on three floors, and an observation room with telescope, giving wonderful views over 12 counties. Around the tower is a country park with farm animals, an adventure playground, nature walks, a barbeque, ball game areas and giant chess and draughts boards.
Open Apr-Oct, daily 10-6.
P ▣ ✗ licensed & toilets for disabled shop
Details not confirmed for 1995

Lower Brockhampton
BROCKHAMPTON
(2m E of Bromyard)
☎Bringsty (01885) 488099
A late 14th century moated manor house, with an attractive detached half-timbered 15th century gatehouse, a rare example of this type of structure, and the ruins of a 12th century chapel. It lies north of the A44 and is part of a larger National Trust property covering over 1600 acres of Herefordshire countryside.
Open: Medieval Hall & Parlour open Apr-Sep, Wed-Sun & BH Mon 10-5. (Closed Good Fri). Oct: Wed-Sun 10-4.
£1.60. Family ticket £4.40.
P & ✲
(NT)

Avoncroft Museum of Historic Buildings
BROMSGROVE
Redditch Rd, Stoke Heath (2m S, off A38)
☎(01527) 831886 & 831363
The aim of the museum is to save interesting buildings by re-erecting and restoring them here. A working post mill and a blacksmith's shop, a cockpit and a merchant's house are neighbours on the 15-acre site with an 18th-century dovecote, an earth closet and a 1946 prefab. One of the more unusual exhibits is a Georgian icehouse from Tong Castle in Shropshire. It consists of a deep, brick-built pit, where ice could be stored in winter for use in summer. A major acquisition is the great 14th-century roof from Gueston Hall, once a monastic establishment adjoining Worcester Cathedral. An interesting feature of the museum is that the people who work on the buildings have had to relearn traditional skills such as building in wattle and daub. Visitors can sometimes see the skills being used as buildings are added to the museum.

There are wheelchair ramps to the shop and tearoom, and a wheelchair is available on loan. New exhibits include a three cell lock-up dating from the 19th century, an 18th-century perry mill and the National Telephone Kiosk Collection, with models dating back to 1922.
Special events for 1995 include: an Easter Steam Rally (15-17 April), Children's Activity Weekend (5-6 August), Triumph Sports Six Car Club Rally (10 September).
Open Jun-Aug daily 11-5.30; Apr, May, Sep & Oct 11-5; wknds 5.30. (Closed Mon). Mar & Nov 10.30-4 (Closed Mon & Fri). Open BHs.
£3.50 (ch £1.75, pen £2.80). Family ticket £9.40.
P ▣ & (ramps, wheelchair available) toilets for disabled shop

Croft Castle
CROFT
(off B4362)
☎Yarpole (01568) 780246
Home of the Croft family since Domesday (with a break of 170 years from 1750); walls and towers date from the 14th and 15th centuries; the interior is mainly 18th century, when the fine Georgian-Gothic staircase and plasterwork ceilings were added. There is a splendid avenue of 350-year-old Spanish chestnuts, and an Iron Age Fort (Croft Ambrey) may be reached by footpath.
Open Apr & Oct, Sat & Sun 2-5; Etr, Sat-Mon 2-4; May-Sep, Wed-Sun & BH Mon 2-6. Last admission to house half hour before closing. Parkland open all year. Closed Good Fri.
P & (parking available) ✲ (ex in parkland)
(NT)

Dinmore Manor
DINMORE
(off A49)
☎Canon Pyon (01432) 830322
From its spectacular hillside location, the manor enjoys outstanding views of the surrounding countryside. The cloisters, South Room, Roof Walk, Chapel, Music Room (Great Hall), and Grotto are all open to the public. The chapel, dating back to the 12th century, is in a unique setting next to the rock garden, pools, the collection of old acers, and the 1200-year-old yew tree. Among the many attractions here are the remarkable collection of 1930s stained glass, an 18th-century chamber organ, a Victorian aeolian pipe organ, and two medieval sundials.
Open all year, daily 10-5.30
£2.50 (accompanied ch 14 free).
P & shop (plant centre) ✲

The Almonry Museum
EVESHAM
Abbey Gate (on A4184, opposite Merstow Green)
☎(01386) 446944
The 14th-century stone and timber building was the home of the Almoner of the Benedictine Abbey in Evesham. It now houses exhibitions relating to the history of Evesham Abbey, the battle of Evesham, and the culture and trade of Evesham. Evesham Tourist Information Centre is also located here.
Open all year, Mon-Sat & BHs (ex Xmas) 10-5, Sun 2-5 (Aug 10-5).
P (110 yds) & shop ✲
Details not confirmed for 1995

Goodrich Castle
GOODRICH
☎Symonds Yat (01600) 890538
The castle stands above the River Wye, and gives wonderful views in all directions. It was built in around 1150 and then expanded in the 13th and 14th centuries, using the red sandstone rock on which it stands, so that rock and castle seem to merge together. The castle was not severely tested until the Civil War, when it was held by Royalists and was battered by 'Roaring Meg' - a cannon said to have fired 200-pound balls. The siege ended after four and a half months, by which time the castle had lost its water supply. Parliament ordered the slighting of the castle, but the remains are still extensive and impressive.
Open all year, Apr-Sep, daily 10-6; Nov-Mar 10-4. Closed 24-26 Dec & 1 Jan.
£2 (ch £1, concessions £1.50)
P
(EH)

Hanbury Hall
HANBURY
☎Droitwich (01527) 821214
This William and Mary style red-brick house, completed in 1701, is a typical example of an English country house built by a prosperous local family. The house contains outstanding painted ceilings and staircase by Thornhill and the Watney collection of porcelain, while outside there are both a contemporary orangery and an ice house.
Open Apr-Oct, Sat-Mon 2-6. Aug also Tue & Wed 2-6. Closed Good Fri.
£3.70. Family ticket £10. Party.
P ▣ & (Braille guide) toilets for disabled shop ✲ (ex in park)
(NT)

Churchill Gardens Museum & Brian Hatton Art Gallery
HEREFORD
3 Venn's Ln
☎(01432) 268121 or 267409

The museum is laid out in a Regency house with fine grounds, and has 18th- and early 19th-century rooms, displays of costume, and a gallery devoted to works by the local artist Brian Hatton.
Open all year, 2-5, Apr-Sep, Tue-Sun; Oct-Mar, Tue-Sat, inc BH Mons.
£1 (ch & over 60's 40p) Joint ticket with Old House £1.60 (ch & over 60's 75p)
🅿 ⓑ *(access guide & tape,braille guides & plans) shop* ⊗

Cider Museum & King Offa Distillery
HEREFORD
Pomona Place, Whitecross Rd (off A438 to Brecon)
☎(01432) 354207
Housed in a former cider works, the museum tells the fascinating story of cidermaking through the ages. Displays include advertising material, prints, huge English and French beam presses, farm cider house, travelling cidermakers' tack, champagne cider cellars, press house and early bottling equipment. In the distillery cider brandy is produced in Britain for the first time (legally) for over 200 years. A varied programme of temporary exhibitions and events is held throughout the year. Among the special events for 1995 are Object Handling Weekend (15-16 April), Biennial Cidermaking Contest (May), VE Day Display (1-21 May), Apple Day Celebrations (21 October-4 November).
Open all year, Apr-Oct, daily 10-5.30; Nov-Mar, Mon-Sat 1-5. Pre-booked groups at other times.
£1.95 (ch, pen & students £1.40). Party 15+.
🅿 ⓑ *shop* ⊗

Hereford Museum & Art Gallery
HEREFORD
Broad St
☎(01432) 268121 ext 207
Displays range from Roman mosaic pavements to folklife and beekeeping, including an observation hive. English watercolours, local geology and archaeology are also featured. The art gallery has monthly exhibitions.
Open all year, Tue, Wed & Fri 10-6, Thu 10-5, Sat 10-5 (Apr-Sep); Sat 10-4 (Oct-Mar). Also Sun May-Sep 10-4. (Closed Mon ex BH'S).
Free.
ⓑ *(wheelchair available) toilets for disabled shop* ⊗

Old House
HEREFORD
High Town
☎(01432) 268121 ext 225 or 207
This good example of a Jacobean house was built in around 1621, and was once in a row of similar houses. The hall, kitchens, and a bedroom with a four-poster bed can be seen along with a number of wall paintings.
Due to re-open in May 1995. Tue-Fri 10-1 & 2-5.30. (Sat, Apr-Sep 10-1 & 2-5.30; Oct-Mar 10-1). Mon 10-1. Also open BH Mons 10-1 & 2-5.15. (Sun, May-Sep 10-4).

£1 (ch & pen 40p). Joint ticket with Churchill Gardens Museum £1.60 (ch & pen 75p).
ⓑ *shop*

Hartlebury Castle State Rooms
KIDDERMINSTER
Hartlebury (5m S)
☎Hartlebury (01299) 250410
The elegant interior of this castle, the seat of the Bishops of Worcester since 850, reveals little of its long and sometimes troubled history. Its present Gothic appearance dates from the 18th century.
Open Etr Mon-3 Sep, 1st Sun in month plus BH Mon & Tue 2-5. Also Wed (Etr-Aug) 2-4.
75p (ch 25p, pen 50p).
🅿 ⓑ *shop* ⊗

Hereford & Worcester County Museum
KIDDERMINSTER
Hartlebury Castle, Hartlebury (5m S, off A449)
☎Hartlebury (01299) 250416
Housed in the north wing of Hartlebury Castle, the County Museum contains a delightful display of crafts and industries. There are unique collections of toys, costume, domestic life, room settings and horse-drawn vehicles as well as a reconstructed forge, schoolroom, wheelwright's and tailor's shop. Special events for 1995 include: a May Fair (21 May), Transport Event (4 June), Country Fair (6 August), Christmas Festivities (3, 10, 17 December).
Open Mar-Nov, Mon-Thu & BH's 10-5, Fri & Sun 2-5. (Closed Sat & Good Fri).
£1.50 (ch & pen 75p).
🅿 ⬛ ⓑ *shop* ⊗ *(ex in grounds)*

Severn Valley Railway
KIDDERMINSTER
☎Bewdley (01299) 403816 & (01746) 764361
(For full entry see Bridgnorth, Shropshire)

Hergest Croft Gardens
KINGTON
(0.25m W off A44)
☎(01544) 230160
From spring bulbs to autumn colour, this is a garden for all seasons. One of the finest collections of trees and shrubs surround the Edwardian house; an old fashioned kitchen garden has spring and summer borders; and Park Wood, a hidden valley, has rhododendrons up to 30ft tall.
Open 14 Apr-29 Oct daily, 1.30-6.30.
£2.50 (ch 15 free). Party 20+
🅿 ⬛ ⓑ *shop garden centre*

Eastnor Castle
LEDBURY
Eastnor
☎(01531) 633160 & 632302
A magnificent Georgian castle in a fairytale setting with a deer park, arboretum and lake. Inside tapestries, fine art and armour. The Italianate and

Gothic interiors have been restored to a superb standard. There is a children's adventure playground and delightful nature trails and lakeside walks. Homemade teas are available.
Open Etr-Jun & Sep, Sun & BH's 12-5; Jul-Aug, Sun-Fri 12-5.
Castle & grounds £3.50 (ch £1.75). Grounds £1.75 (ch £1).
🅿 ⬛ ✕ *shop*

Malvern Museum
MALVERN
Abbey Gateway, Abbey Rd
☎(01684) 567811
The local history exhibits range from the story of the Malvern Hills to the Water Cure and the lives of Sir Edward Elgar and Bernard Shaw, and from the first British motor car to radar and the silicone chip. The museum is housed in one of the two buildings that survive from the Benedictine monastery.
Open Etr-Oct, daily 10.30-5 (ex closed Wed in term time).
50p (ch 7 10p).
P *shop*

Forge Mill Needle Museum & Bordesley Abbey Visitor Centre
REDDITCH
Forge Mill, Needle Mill Ln, Riverside (off A441)
☎(01527) 62509
The museum is housed in the only remaining water-driven, needle-scouring mill, with machinery from the 18th century which is demonstrated regularly. Displays of finds from the nearby 12th-century Cistercian Abbey are shown in the Visitor Centre. Both the museum and the visitor centre are set in attractive surroundings within the Arrow Valley Park. Regular needlework exhibitions and workshops are held.
Open Apr-Sep, Mon-Thu 11-4.30, Sat & Sun 2-5; mid Feb-Mar & Oct-Nov, Mon-Thu & Sun. Parties by arrangement.
£1.75 (ch 50p, pen £1.25). Family ticket £4.
🅿 ⓑ *(wheelchairs on request) toilets for disabled shop* ⊗

Lost Street Museum
ROSS-ON-WYE
Palma Court, 27 Brookend St
☎(01989) 562752
Discover this unique Edwardian Street, lost in time, with its fully stocked, life-size shops. This is probably the largest privately owned collection of music boxes, toys, dolls, wireless, gramophones, motor cycles, costumes and advertising in the country. There are demonstrations of musical boxes and automata, quizzes with cash prizes and the pub boasts a fine collection of old amusement machines.
Open Feb-Nov, Mon-Sat 10-5; Sun 11-5. Dec-Jan, telephone for opening times.
£2 (ch £1.50, pen £1.75). Family ticket £5.
P *(opposite)* ⬛ ⓑ

Spetchley Park Gardens
SPETCHLEY
(3m E of Worcester, off A422)
☎(01905) 345213 or 345224
The 110-acre deer park and the 30-acre gardens surround an early 19th-century mansion (not open), with sweeping lawns and herbaceous borders, a rose lawn and enclosed gardens with low box and yew hedges. There is a large collection of trees (including 17th-century Cedars of Lebanon), shrubs and plants, many of which are rare or unusual.
Open Apr-Sep, Mon-Fri 11-5, Sun 2-5; BH Mons 11-5. Other days by appointment.
£2.20 (ch £1.10). Party 25+.
🅿 ⬛ ⓑ ⓑ *shop*

Stone House Cottage Gardens
STONE
(2m SE on A448)
☎Kidderminster (01562) 69902
A beautiful walled garden with towers provides a sheltered area of about one acre for rare shrubs, climbers and interesting herbaceous plants. Adjacent

to the garden is a nursery with a large selection of unusual plants.
Open Gardens & nursery Mar-Oct, Wed-Sat 10-6.
£1.50 free for children.
🅿 ⓑ *garden centre* ⊗

The Weir Gardens
SWAINSHILL
☎(01684) 850051
The gardens are at their best in spring when there are lovely displays of naturalised bulbs with woodland and grassland walks. Cliff garden walks can be taken here, with fine views of the River Wye and the Welsh hills.
Open 14 Feb-Oct, Wed-Sun 11-6. Also open Good Friday and Bank Holiday Mon.
🅿 ⊗ 🚼
(NT)
Details not confirmed for 1995

The Jubilee Park
SYMONDS YAT (WEST)
(200mtrs from A40 at Whitchurch jct)
☎(01600) 890360
Visitors can see the world-famous Jubilee Maze, built to celebrate the Queen's Jubilee in 1977, and the Museum of Mazes showing paths of mazes and labyrinths through the ages. In the World of Butterflies, hundreds of colourful butterflies from all over the world fly free in their large tropical indoor garden. There is a craft centre.
Open Good Fri-Sep, daily 11-5.30 (last admission); winter: open at wknds & daily at half term 12-4pm. Closed Dec, Jan and in bad weather.
Admission fee payable.
🅿 ⬛ ✕ ⓑ *toilets for disabled shop garden centre* ⊗

Dovecote
WICHENFORD
☎Tewkesbury (01684) 850051
This large 17th-century dovecote has nearly 600 nesting boxes and is unusual in its timber-framed, wattle and daub construction, which was rarely used for dovecotes. The gabled roof appears to have a chimney, but it is actually an entrance for the birds.
Open Apr-Oct, daily 9-6 or sunset. (Closed Good Fri). Other times by prior appointment with Severn Regional Office, tel (01684) 850051.
60p.
⊗
(NT)

City Museum & Art Gallery
WORCESTER
Foregate St
☎(01905) 25371
The gallery has temporary art exhibitions from both local and national sources; while the museum exhibits cover geology, local and natural history, including River Severn displays and activities. Of particular interest is a complete 19th-century chemists shop. There are collections relating to the Worcestershire Regiment and the Worcestershire Yeoman Cavalry. Exhibitions planned for 1995 include: Abstract Painting (6 May-10 June), New Views on Collection (5 August-16 September), Print Focus (20-30 September).
Open all year, Mon, Tue Wed & Fri 9.30-6, Sat 9.30-5.
Free.
P ⬛ ⓑ *(Lift to all floors from Taylor's Lane entrance). toilets for disabled shop* ⊗

The Commandery
WORCESTER
Sidbury
☎(01905) 355071
This fine 15th-century, timber-framed building was the headquarters of Charles II's army during the Battle of Worcester in 1651. It has an impressive Great Hall with some good 15th-century stained glass, and the building is now England's only Civil War centre. There are spectacular audio-visual displays, including the trial of King Charles I - join

➤

the jury and decide the King's fate, and see the Scots' camp on the eve of the Battle of Worcester. The Commandery is the base of the Worcester Militia who stage regular 17th-century live action weekends.
Open all year, Mon-Sat 10-5, Sun 1.30-5.30. (Closed 25 & 26 Dec).
✱£3 (concessions £2). Family ticket. P *(400 yds)* 💺 *shop* ✆

Dyson Perrins Museum
WORCESTER ▰
Severn St (off A44)
☎(01905) 23221
This museum holds the world's largest and finest collection of Worcester's famous porcelain. Some of the pieces date from 1751 when the porcelain factory was opened in the city. There are also examples on show from services made for the Royal family and European aristocracy. The museum is adjacent to the Royal Worcester Porcelain Factory which is open to the public by guided tour only. A four day event in 1995 - The Festival of Porcelain, Fruit and Flowers (21-24 June), will include china painting, engraving and flower making demonstrations, a flower arranging display and paiting exhibition, children's activities and competitions, lectures, film shows and live theatre. Please telephone for a detailed timetable.
Open all year, Mon-Fri 9.30-5 & Sat 10-5. Royal Worcester factory tours Mon-Fri by prior arrangement.
✱*Royal Worcester factory tours £3.25 (ch 11-16 £2.25). Museum £1.50 (ch & student £1).*
🅿 *(charged)* ✗ *licensed* 💺 *(ex factory, toilets due to open in Jan'95) shop* ✆

Elgar's Birthplace Museum
WORCESTER ▰
Crown East Ln, Lower Broadheath (3m W, off A44 to Leominster).
☎*Cotheridge (01905) 333224*
The cottage where Sir Edward Elgar, the composer, was born in 1857 is now a museum. There is a comprehensive display of musical scores, photographs, letters and personal effects.
Open daily ex Wed, May-Sep 10.30-6. Oct-15 Jan & 16 Feb-Apr 1.30-4.30.
£3 (ch 50p, students £1 & pen £2). Party. P *(50 yds)* 💺 *shop* ✆ *(ex in gardens)*

Hawford Dovecote
WORCESTER ▰
(3m N on A449)
☎*Tewkesbury (01684) 850051*
An unusual square, half-timbered 16th-century dovecote. Access on foot only via the entrance drive to the adjoining house.
Open Apr-Oct, daily 9-6 or sunset. (Closed Good Fri). Other times by prior appointment only with regional office, tel (01684) 850051.
60p.
✆
(NT)

Tudor House Museum
WORCESTER ▰
Friar St
☎(01905) 25371
This interesting 500-year-old timber-framed house has a squint and an ornate plaster ceiling. It is now a museum of local life featuring a children's room, an Edwardian bathroom and displays of the Home Front of World War II. In the yard at the back there are large agricultural exhibits.
Open all year, Mon-Wed & Fri-Sat 10.30-5. Also Sun, Apr-Sep 1.30-5
✱£1.50 (concesssions 75p, school's 60p)
P *(200 yds)* 💺 *shop* ✆

Worcester Cathedral
WORCESTER ▰
Chapter Office, 10A College Green
☎(01905) 28854 & 21004
Worcester Cathedral with its 200 foot tower stands majestically beside the River Severn. The Crypt, built by St Wulstan in 1084, is a classic example of Norman architecture. The 12th century Chapter House and Cloisters are a reminder of the cathedral's monastic past. King John (who signed the Magna Carta) and Prince Arthur (elder brother of Henry VIII) are buried near the High Altar. There are exhibitions and guided tours. The cathedral choir sings during the school term at 5.30 evensong (not Thurs) and 11.00am and 4.00pm Sundays.
Open all year, daily.
Donations.
P *(500yds)* 💺 💺 *(limited access due to nature of building) toilets for disabled shop* ✆

HERTFORDSHIRE

Shaw's Corner
AYOT ST LAWRENCE ▰
(at SW end of village)
☎*Stevenage (01438) 820307*
George Bernard Shaw lived here from 1906 until his death in 1950. He gave the house to the National Trust in 1946, and the contents are much as they were in his time. Among other items to be seen are his hats, including a soft homburg he wore for 60 years, his exercise machine, fountain pen, spectacles and several pictures. Special events for 1995 include: summer play You Never Can Tell (17 June), Candida (22-23 July).
Open Apr-Oct Wed-Sun 2-6. Last admission 5.30pm. (Closed Good Fri)
£3. Family ticket £7.50.
🅿 💺 ✆
(NT)

Berkhamsted Castle
BERKHAMSTED ▰
Roads and a railway have cut into the castle site, but its huge banks and ditches remain impressive. The original motte-and-bailey was probably built by William the Conqueror's half brother, and

there is a later stone keep. The castle was owned by the Black Prince, and King John of France was imprisoned here.
Open any reasonable time.
Free.
🅿 💺
(EH)

Hatfield House
HATFIELD ▰
(2m from junc 4 A1(M) on A1000)
☎(01707) 262823
Robert Cecil built the great Jacobean mansion in 1607-11. It replaced an older palace where Elizabeth I had spent much of her childhood, and is full of Elizabethan associations, important portraits of the queen, and historic possessions such as her silk stockings, perhaps the first pair worn in England. There are also other celebrated pictures, tapestries and armour, including some from the Spanish Armada. Newer attractions include a William IV kitchen (1833) and the National Collection of Model Soldiers.
Around the house are the great park and gardens, including a parterre planted with yews and roses, a scented garden and knot garden with typical plants of the 15th to 17th centuries. Hatfield is still the home of the Cecils, who at one point had a private waiting room at the nearby railway station.
There are nature trails, and an adventure play area for small children. Special events for 1995 are: Living Crafts (11-14 May), Festival of Gardening (24-25 June), Great British Pottery and Ceramics Festival (11-13 August), Transport Spectacular (6 August).
Open 25 Mar-8 Oct. House: weekdays 12-4, Sun 1.30-5. (Closed Mon ex BH 11-5 & Good Fri. Gardens: daily 11-6, except Good Fri.
House Park & Gardens £5 (ch £3.20, pen £4.10). Park, Gardens & Exhibitions £2.80 (ch £2.10, pen £2.50). Party 20+.
🅿 💺 ✗ *licensed* 💺 *toilets for disabled shop garden centre* ✆ *(ex in park)*

Hitchin Museum & Art Gallery
HITCHIN ▰
Paynes Park
☎(01462) 434476
The gallery houses displays on local, domestic and working life. The costume gallery covers two centuries of fashion, and the regimental collection of the Hertfordshire yeomanry is housed here. There is a fascinating reconstructed Victorian chemist's shop, complemented by a physic garden outside. Temporary art exhibitions change monthly.
Open all year, Mon-Sat 10-5, Sun 2-4.30. (Closed BHs).
Free.
🅿 💺 *shop* ✆

Knebworth House, Gardens & Country Park
KNEBWORTH ▰
(direct access from junc7 A1(M) at Stevenage)
☎*Stevenage (01438) 812661*
Home of the Lytton family since 1490, the original Tudor manor was transformed in 1843 by the spectacular high Gothic decoration of Victorian novelist Sir Edward Bulwer Lytton. The interior includes a superb Jacobean Great Hall with a splendid plaster ceiling and magnificent panelling (the reredos, which stretches across the width of the room, is 17th century). Bulwer Lytton was a well known statesman and author and counted among his friends many famous people, including Dickens and Disraeli, who were all guests at Knebworth. There is a fascinating exhibition on the British Raj and some fine furniture and portraits. Outside, the formal-style gardens were simplified by Lutyens (who built several buildings in the town). The 250-acre park now includes many attractions for visitors. There is a maze, a miniature railway, an extensive adventure playground, and a deer park. Knebworth is a popular venue for special events and

activities, including, in 1995, Americal Civil War Battle Re-enactments (16-17 April), Knebworth Country Show (7-8 May), Fireworks and Laser Symphony Concert (30 July), Hertfordshire Craft Fair (19-20 August).
Open - Park & Playground: 1 & 2 Apr, 8 Apr-23 May & 27 May-4 Sep daily. Weekends & BH's 29 Apr-21 May. Weekends only 9 Sep-1 Oct. 11-5.30. House & Gardens as Park (ex closed Mon). 12-5 (last admission 4.30). Closed 30 Jun-3 Jul.
✳£4.50 (ch & pen £4); Park & Playground only: £3. Party 20+.
🅿 💺 ✗ *licensed* ⅍ *(with prior notice visitors can be driven to front door) shop* ⌖ *(ex in park)*

First Garden City Heritage Museum
LETCHWORTH
296 Norton Way South
☎(01462) 482424
Designed by Barry Parker and Raymond Unwin, Letchworth was the first of the garden cities. The museum, housed in the original, thatched offices of the architects, explains the development of this innovative architectural and social concept.
Open all year, Mon-Fri 2-4.30, Sat 10-1 & 2-4. Other times by appointment. (Closed 25-26 Dec).
Free.
P (150 yds) ⅍ *shop* ⌖

Museum & Art Gallery
LETCHWORTH
Broadway
☎(01462) 685647
The museum is housed in an attractive building in the town centre. The main galleries feature local archaeology and natural history, with a regular programme of changing exhibitions being held in the Art Gallery. The Natural History Gallery includes examples of local wildlife in realistic settings representing habitats, such as hedgerows, woodland and farmland. Geology is also covered with a good selection of local fossils on display. The Archaeology Gallery covers the history of man in North Hertfordshire from about 200,000BC to the 17th century. Important finds are included such as a collection of metalwork from a late Iron Age Chieftain's burial, and Roman material from local sites, including the Roman town of Baldock. Exhibitions in the Art Gallery are changed monthly and often feature work by local artists and craftspeople. A programme of events and exhibitions is held throughout the year, including for summer 1995, Dawn on the Farm - an exhibition and related events on the theme of local agriculture from prehistoric times to the present day.
Open all year Mon-Sat 10-5. (Open some BHs).
Free.
P (100 yd) ⅍ *(special provisions on request) shop* ⌖

Mosquito Aircraft Museum
LONDON COLNEY
Salisbury Hall
☎Bowmansgreen (01727) 822051
This museum is the oldest aircraft museum in Great Britain, it was opened on 15 May 1959 to preserve the De Havilland Mosquito prototype on the site of its conception. The De Havilland heritage collection which includes photographs, memorabilia and aero-engine displays is one of the attractions of this museum which exhibits 18 De Havilland aircraft, including three Mosquitoes, a Vampire, Venom, Tiger Moth, DH125 and Horsa. Visitors may walk through the workshops.
Open Mar-Oct, Sat, Sun & BH Mons 10.30-5.30, Thu 2-5.30.
🅿 ⅍ *(wheelchairs available) toilets for disabled shop*
Details not confirmed for 1995

Royston and District Museum
ROYSTON
Lower King St
☎(01763) 242587

Housed in the former congregational chapel schoolroom, the museum contains exhibits which trace the history and development of the town and includes a very fine loan collection of 19th-and 20th-century ceramics and glass. The museum also holds regular temporary exhibitions. The Royston Tapestry has commenced and can be viewed.
Open all year, Wed, Thu & Sat 10-5; Etr-Sep, Sun 2.15-5. Other times by appointment with the Curator.
P (on street) ⅍ *shop* ⌖
Details not confirmed for 1995

Clock Tower
ST ALBANS
Market Pl
☎(01727) 853301
This early 15th-century curfew tower, which faces the High Street, provides fine views over the city (especially of the abbey) and the surrounding countryside. This is one of the only two medieval clock towers in the country. It has a bell which strikes on the hour and is older than the tower itself.
Open Good Fri-mid Sep, Sat, Sun & BH 10.30-5.
shop ⌖
Details not confirmed for 1995

Gardens of The Rose (Royal National Rose Society)
ST ALBANS
Chiswell Green (2m S off Watford Rd in Chiswell Green Ln)
☎(01727) 850461
These are the gardens of the Royal National Rose Society, and include the International Trial Ground for new roses. The gardens contain over 30,000 plants in 1,650 different varieties. These include old-fashioned roses, modern roses and the roses of the future. The National Miniature Rose Show takes place on 29-30 July - entry free to visitors to the gardens. Special events for 1994 include: Craft Fair (3-4 June), Pruning Demonstrations (4-5 March). A special season of musical concerts will be held from June to August.
Open 10 Jun-15 Oct, Mon-Sat 9-5, Sun & BH 10-6.
✳£4 (accompanied ch free, pen & UB40 £3.50, registered disabled £3). Party 20+.
🅿 💺 ⅍ *(ramps where necessary) toilets for disabled shop*

Gorhambury
ST ALBANS
(entry via lodge gates on A414)
☎(01727) 54051
Pleasant house built by Sir Robert Taylor

(1774-1784) to house an extensive picture collection of 17th-century portraits of the Grimston and Bacon families and their contempories. Also of note is the 16th-century enamelled glass collection and an early English pile carpet.
Open May-Sep, Thu 2-5.
✳£2.50 (ch & pen £1.50). Party.
🅿 *shop* ⌖

Kingsbury Water Mill Museum
ST ALBANS
Saint Michael's St
☎(01727) 853502
This 16th-century corn mill, which still has a working waterwheel, is now a museum. Exhibits include a collection of old farm implements, and there is also an art gallery. The mill is on the River Ver half a mile from the city.
Open all year, Tue-Sat 11-6, Sun 12-6. (Closes 5 in winter, closed Mon & 25 Dec-2 Jan).
85p (ch 45p, pen & students 50p).
🅿 💺 ✗ *shop* ⌖ ♿

Museum of St Albans
ST ALBANS
Hatfield Rd
☎(01727) 819340
Exhibits include the Salaman collection of craft tools, and reconstructed workshops. The history of St Albans is traced from the departure of the Romans up to the present day. Temporary exhibitions in the gallery include: Chinese Textiles (January to March), The Home Front - Britain 1945 (from April).
Open all year, daily 10-5, Sun 2-5. Closed 25 Dec.
Free.
🅿 ⅍ *toilets for disabled shop* ⌖

Roman Theatre of Verulamium
ST ALBANS
St Michaels (off A4147)
☎(01727) 835035
The theatre was first discovered on the Gorhambury Estate in 1847 and was fully excavated by Dr Kathleen Kenyon in 1935. It is unique in England. First constructed around AD160, it is semi-circular in shape, 180ft across and could hold 1,600 spectators. Following modification over two centuries, the theatre was used for religious processions, ceremonies and plays.
Open all year, daily 10-5 (4 in winter).
✳£1 (ch 50p, students 80p).
🅿 ⅍ *shop*

St Albans Organ Museum
ST ALBANS
320 Camp Rd
☎(01727) 869693
This unusual museum contains a unique collection of automatically operated organs and other musical instruments. It also has Wurlitzer and Rutt theatre organs. There are recitals every Sunday, 2.15 to 4.30, but they can also be arranged at other times for party bookings.
Open Sun, Recitals 2.15-4.30 (ex 25 Dec). Parties at other times by appointment.
🅿 ⅍ *shop* ⌖
Details not confirmed for 1995 ➤

Hatfield House has been the home of the Cecil family for 400 years. The present house has many memorabilia of Queen Elizabeth I who spent much of her childhood there.

Verulamium Museum
ST ALBANS
St Michaels
☎(01727) 819339
Verulamium was one of the largest and most important Roman towns in Britain. By the lst century it was declared a 'municipium', which gave its inhabitants the rights of Roman citizenship. No other British city was granted this honour. The town was attacked by Boudicca in AD61, but rebuilt after her defeat.
The site is set within a 100-acre park. A mosaic and underfloor heating system can be seen in situ, and the museum shows finds, including mosaics, wall paintings, jewellery, pottery and other domestic items.
There are recreated Roman rooms, excavation videos, 'hands-on' discovery areas and computer data bases which are accessible to visitors. Regular talks and demonstrations at weekends. On the second weekend of every month legionaries occupy the galleries and describe the tactics and equipment of the Roman Imperial Army and the life of a legionary.
Open all year weekdays 10-5.30, Sun 2-5.30.
£2.40 (ch, pen & students £1.40). Family ticket £6.60.
🅿 (charged) & toilets for disabled shop ⌀

Stevenage Museum
STEVENAGE
St George's Way
☎(01438) 354292
The museum, in the undercroft of the parish church of St George, tells the story of Stevenage from earliest times to the present day. There are several exhibitions planned for 1995 including Stevenage 100 years ago (April-November).
Open all year, Mon-Sat 10-5. (Closed Sun & BH's).
Free.
P & toilets for disabled shop ⌀

The Walter Rothschild Zoological Museum
TRING
Akeman St
☎(01442) 824181
This most unusual museum was founded in the 1890s by Lionel Walter, 2nd Baron Rothschild, scientist, eccentric and natural history enthusiast. It is famous for its magnificent collection of thousands of mammals and birds, and there are also displays of reptiles, fishes, insects and domestic dogs. There is even a well known exhibition of dressed fleas. Extinct, rare, exotic and bizarre specimens in a unique Victorian setting. Exhibitions are organised throughout the year (details on request).
Open all year, Mon-Sat 10-5, Sun 2-5. (Closed 24-26 Dec).
£2 (concessions £1).
🅿 & toilets for disabled shop ⌀

Scott's Grotto
WARE
Scott's Rd (off A119)
☎(01920) 464131
Scott's Grotto, built in the 1760s by the Quaker poet John Scott, has been described by English Heritage as 'one of the finest in England'. Recently restored by the Ware Society, it consists of underground passages and chambers decorated with flints, shells, minerals and stones, and extends 67ft into the side of the hill. Please wear flat shoes and bring a torch.
Open beginning Apr-end Sep, Sat & BH only 2-4.30. Other times by appointment only.
Donations
P

Watford Museum
WATFORD
194 High St
☎(01923) 232297
A good art gallery and a museum specialising in the history of Watford from the earliest times to the present day. There are special features on the local industries of printing and brewing, together with a display on wartime Watford, based on the *Dad's Army* TV series, written by Jimmy Perry from his experiences in Watford. Temporary exhibitions take place throughout the year. There are school holiday activities for five to eleven year olds.
Open all year, Mon-Fri 10-5, Sat 10-1 & 2-5. (Closed BH's, 25 & 26 Dec).
Free.
🅿 & (limited parking, lift, wheelchair) toilets for disabled shop ⌀

HUMBERSIDE

Art Gallery
BEVERLEY
Champney Rd
☎Hull (01482) 882255
Local antiquities, Victorian bygones and china are displayed, along with pictures of Beverley and other works of art. Notable among these is the bust of Sir Winston Churchill by Bryant Baker of New York. Solo art exhibitions are held.
Open all year, Mon-Wed & Fri 10-12.30 & 2-5, Thu 10-12, Sat 10-noon & 1-4.
Free.
⌀

Guildhall
BEVERLEY
Register Sq
☎Hull (0182) 867430
The Guildhall was established in 1500 and then rebuilt in handsome classical style in 1762. It is now used as a county court and Mayor's Parlour, but can be visited for its notable ceiling painting in the courtroom, its display of civic regalia, ancient charters and other treasures. A guide service is available.
Open Etr-Sep, Mon-Sat 9.30-5.30, Sun 10-2; Oct-Etr, Mon-Fri 9.30-5.30, Sat 10-4. For opening times of Mayor's Parlour please telephone for details.
Free.
P & ⌀

The Hall, Lairgate
BEVERLEY
☎Hull (01482) 882255
Now used as council offices, the Hall is an 18th-century building with an interesting late 18th-century stucco ceiling, and a Chinese room with rare hand-painted wallpaper.
Open all year, Mon-Thu 8.45-5.30 & Fri 9-4 (subject to availability). Groups at other times by arrangement.
Free.
& ⌀

Museum of Army Transport
BEVERLEY
Flemingate
☎Hull (01482) 860445
The museum tells the story of army transport from horse drawn waggons to the recent Gulf conflict: everything from prototype vehicles to Montgomery's Rolls Royce and the last Blackburn Beverley aircraft. There are also other exhibits to be explored including 'Women at the Wheel' (their role in the war) and an area for children.
Open all year, daily 10-5. (Closed 24-26 Dec).
£2.99 (ch 5-16, £1.50 & pen £1.99). Children under 16 must be accompanied. Party 10+.
🅿 ⛾ & toilets for disabled shop ⌀

Sewerby Hall & Gardens
BRIDLINGTON
☎(01262) 673769 (Park) & 677874 (Hall)
The house was built around 1714-20, and is now an art gallery and museum of history and archaeology. It contains the Amy Johnson Trophy Room, and the gardens are full of interest, especially the walled gardens. There is also a miniature zoo and aviary.
Gardens & zoo open daily all year. Hall open Mar-Apr & Oct-Dec, Sat-Tue 11-4; May-Sep, daily 10-6.

No longer a private gentleman's home, 18th-century Lairgate Hall provides Beverley with some of the most elegant council offices in Britain.

£2.50 (ch £1, pen £2).
🅿 ⛾ ✕ & toilets for disabled shop

Burton Agnes Hall
BURTON AGNES
Estate Office (on A166)
☎(01262) 490324
Built in 1598, this is a magnificent Elizabethan house, with furniture, pictures and china amassed by the family owners over four centuries. There is an old gatehouse, walled garden with maze, potager, herbaceous borders, clematis, campanula and geranium collections, jungle garden and giant board games in coloured gardens as well as walks in woodland gardens. The ghost of a young girl is said to haunt the property. Special events for 1995 include: Easter egg hunt (16-17 April), Gala Day (30 April), gardeners' fair (10-11 June), flower festival (29-30 July). Admission charges will vary on these days.
Open Apr-Oct, daily 11-5.
Hall & grounds £3.50 (ch £2, pen £3). Grounds only £1.80 (ch 80p, pen £1.50). Party 30+.
🅿 ⛾ & (scented garden for the blind) toilets for disabled shop garden centre ⌀

Norman Manor House
BURTON AGNES
This is the house that Burton Agnes Hall replaced. It is a rare survivor from Norman times, and though later encased in brick it still has its Norman piers and the groined roof of a lower chamber. An upper room and an old donkey wheel can also be seen.
Open all year.
Free.
(EH)

Pleasure Island Theme Park
CLEETHORPES
Kings Rd
☎(01472) 211511
The east coast's great new theme park. Re-live traditional pirate adventures in the Old English village, visit Spain and Morocco and explore an African village. Shows and attractions from all over the world including the Boomerang, Mini Mine Train, Giant Wheel, and Tinkaboo Sweet Factory Water Ride. Pleasure Island offers undercover attractions for inclement weather.
Open from 9th Apr, please telephone for further opening times.
Admission fee payable.
🅿 ⛾ ✕ & toilets for disabled shop

Elsham Hall Country & Wildlife Park
ELSHAM
(on M180/A15 Humber Bridge junc5)
☎Barnetby (01652) 688698
Attractions include a children's animal farmyard, clocktower shop and art gallery, carp-feeding jetty, an arboretum and an adventure playground. There are nature trails and quizzes, a garden centre, craft centre with working craftsfolk, a tea room and restaurant and a theatre noted for its medieval banquets and jazz concerts. The Falconry Centre has an excellent selection of birds of prey, and there are flying displays most days, weather and birds permitting. There are special events planned throughout the year, especially during the school holidays. For 1995 these include: lambing and hatching weekend (15-17 April), Magical May Day (30 April-1 May), children's festival (28-29 May), folk dance festival (26-28 August).
Open all year, mid Sep-Maundy Thu, Sun & BH 11-4; Etr Sat-mid Sep, daily 11-5. (Closed Good Fri & 25-26 Dec). May be closed occasionally in winter, phone for details.
£3.95 (ch £2.50, pen £3.50 & ch under 3 free). Party 20+.
🅿 ⛾ ✕ licensed & (fishing facilities for disabled) toilets for disabled shop garden centre ⌀

Old Rectory
EPWORTH
1 Rectory St (on A161)
☎(01427) 872268
John and Charles Wesley were brought up in the handsome rectory, which was built in 1709 and restored in 1957. This

Grade I listed Queen Anne building is maintained by the World Methodist Council as 'The Home of the Wesleys' rather than as a museum. It displays items which belonged to John and Charles Wesley and their parents Samuel and Susanna. Some of the rooms are set out with period furniture much as the family would have known. Also in the house are paintings and prints concerning the lives and times of the Wesley family and commemorative china etc. An exhibition Charles Wesley: Sweet Singer of Methodism, will run from the end June to September 1995.
Open Mar-Oct, Mon-Sat 10-12 & 2-4, Sun 2-4. Other times by prior arrangement.
£2 (ch £1).
🅿️ & *shop* ⊘

National Fishing Heritage Centre
GRIMSBY
Alexandra Dock
☎(01472) 344868
The National Fishing Heritage Centre tells the story of the British Fishing Industry, arguably the nation's most gruelling and demanding occupation, as seen through the eyes of one of the world's greatest fishing ports - Grimsby. Visitors are given a rare opportunity to experience life at sea on a Grimsby trawler in the mid 1950's; they can see, hear, smell and touch a series of recreated environments which take them from the back streets of Grimsby to the distant fishing grounds of the Arctic Circle - and back again. The museum was voted Best Visitor Attraction in 1992, Blue Peter Children's Museum of the Year 1993, and Industrial History Museum of the Year 1994. Guided tours of the fishing boats are available on site. A special event for which will run until 14 January 1996 is The Poseidon Experiment - a science fiction quest. An ingenious mix of high technology and imagination which culminates in a dramatic motion picture experience.

Open all year, daily 10-6. (Closed 25-26 Dec & 1 Jan).
£3.10 (ch £2.30, pen £2.50). Family ticket £8.95.
🅿️ ☕ & *toilets for disabled shop* ⊘

Hornsea Freeport
HORNSEA
☎(01964) 534211
A unique park offering both leisure and retail facilities. Leisure attractions include the Yorkshire Car Collection, Birds of Prey, Model Village, Butterfly World, Neptune's Kingdom, outdoor adventure playground, and guided tours of the pottery. Over 18 famous high street names sell merchandise at reduced prices.
Open all year, daily from 10-6.
Freedom Pass £3.99 (ch £3.50 & pen £2.99).
🅿️ ☕ ✗ *licensed* & *toilets for disabled shop* ⊘ *(ex in park)*

Hornsea Museum
HORNSEA
11 Newbegin
☎(01964) 533443 & 533430
A former farmhouse and its outbuildings now illustrate local life and history, with 19th-century period rooms and a dairy, craft tools and farming implements. Photographs, industries and local personalities are also featured.
Open Etr-Sep, Mon-Sat 11-5, Sun 2-5. Oct-Etr by appointment.
£1.50 (ch & pen £1). Family ticket £4.50.
P (100 yds) & *toilets for disabled shop* ⊘ *(ex garden)*

Maister House
HULL
160 High St
☎(01482) 24114
The house is a mid-18th-century rebuilding, notable for its splendid stone and wrought-iron staircase, ornate stucco work and finely carved doors. Only the staircase and entrance hall are open.
Open all year, Mon-Fri 10-4 (Closed BH).
80p (incl guide book).
P ⊘ 🚗
(NT)

'Streetlife' - Hull Museum of Transport
HULL
High St
☎(01482) 593902
Streetlife is Hull's newest and noisiest museum with a fascinating collection covering over 150 years of road transport. The displays include a recreation of a Georgian inn courtyard, Britain's oldest tram, and several veteran motorcars. A second phase, Bicycle City, explores Hull's strong cycling tradition.
Open all year, Mon-Sat 10-5, Sun 1.30-4.30. (Closed 24-25 Dec & Good Fri).
Free.
P ☕ & *toilets for disabled shop* ⊘

Town Docks Museum
HULL
Queen Victoria Square
☎(01482) 593902
Hull's maritime history is illustrated here, with displays on whales and whaling, ships and shipping, and other aspects of this Humber port. There is also a Victorian court room which is used for temporary exhibitions. The restored dock area, with its fine Victorian and Georgian buildings, is well worth exploring too.
Open all year, Mon-Sat 10-5 & Sun 1.30-4.30. (Closed 25-26 Dec, 1 Jan & Good Fri).
Free.
P (100 yds) & *shop* ⊘

Wilberforce House
HULL
23-25 High St
☎(01482) 593902
The early 17th-century Merchants house was the birthplace of William ➤

Closed in the Reformation, the 13th-century Aylesford Priory is once again a place of prayer. Some shrines have been decorated with ceramic panels.

Wilberforce, who went on to become a leading campaigner against slavery. There are Jacobean and Georgian rooms and displays on Wilberforce, the anti-slavery campaign, silver, costume, historic rooms settings, decorative art and dolls. The house also has secluded gardens. There is a special exhibition The A-Z of Costume, with displays of Hull Museum's extensive costume collection.
Open all year, Mon-Sat 10-5 & Sun 1.30-4.30. (Closed 25-26 Dec, 1 Jan & Good Fri). Free.
P & shop ✗

Burnby Hall Garden & Stewart Collection
POCKLINGTON
The Balk (off A1079 at turning for Pocklington)
☎(01759) 302068
The two lakes in this garden have an outstanding collection of 80 varieties of hardy water lilies, designated a National Collection. The lakes stand within seven acres of beautiful gardens including a lovely walled rose garden, heather beds, a rock garden and a spring and summer bedding area. The museum contains sporting trophies and ethnic material gathered on world-wide travels. Special events for 1995 include: band concerts on the last Sunday of May, June, July and August; craft fair and garden exhibition (1-2 July); Women's Institute craft fair (6 August).
Open 8 Apr-mid Oct, daily 10-6. £2 (ch 5-16 75p, pen £1.50). Party 20+.
P ♥ & free wheelchair hire toilets for disabled shop ✗

Penny Arcadia
POCKLINGTON
Ritz Cinema, Market Place
☎(01759) 303420
This museum houses the world's most comprehensive collection of antique and veteran coin-operated amusement machines. An audio-visual screen show, stage presentation, guided tours and demonstrations introduce you to the

world of the slot-machine.
Open daily, 10-5 Jun-Aug, 12.30-5 May & Sep. Other times groups by arrangement.
P &
Details not confirmed for 1995

Borough Museum & Art Gallery
SCUNTHORPE
Oswald Rd
☎(01724) 843533
The local history gallery in this regional museum includes a reconstruction of a 19th-century ironworker's cottage, a Victorian parlour and a visual display on the iron and steel industries. Other exhibits embrace the natural history, natural science and archaeology of the area together with temporary exhibitions of contemporary arts, crafts and photography.
Open all year, Tue-Sat 10-4, Sun 2-5. (Closed Xmas).
✱*Admission free, but a charge is made for group visits in the evenings.*
P & toilets for disabled shop ✗

Normanby Hall Country Park
SCUNTHORPE
Normanby (5m N off B1430)
☎(01724) 720588
A whole host of activities and attractions are offered in the 350 acres of grounds that surround Normanby Hall including golf, riding, nature trails, gift shop and a farming museum. Deer herds can be spotted grazing in the parkland and many species of wildfowl have their home here. Inside the Regency mansion there are fine rooms decorated and furnished in period style. There are special events including car rallies, craft fairs, demonstrations and guided walks every Sunday during the season.
Open, Park all year, daily. Hall: 27 Mar-1 Oct,daily 1-5; Oct-Mar by appointment only. Farming Museum: 27 Mar-1 Oct, daily 1-5; Oct-Mar by appointment only. Free.
P (charged) ♥ ✗ licensed & toilets for disabled shop

Burton Constable Hall
SPROATLEY
Burton Constable (1.5m N)
☎Hornsea (01964) 562400
This superb Elizabethan house was built in 1570, but much of the interior was remodelled in the 18th century. There are magnificent reception rooms and a Tudor long gallery with a pendant roof: the contents range from pictures and furniture (much of it by Thomas Chippendale) to a unique collection of 18th-century scientific instruments. Outside are 200 acres of parkland landscaped by 'Capability' Brown, with oaks and chestnuts, and a lake with an island. Camping and caravanning sites are available in the park and there is also seasonal fishing.
Open, Hall & grounds Etr-Sep, Sun-Thu, also Sat Jul-Aug. Grounds noon, Hall 1pm. Last admission 4.15pm. House £3.50 (ch £1.50, pen £2.50).
P ♥ & toilets for disabled shop

Thornton Abbey
THORNTON
☎(01469) 40357
A magnificent 14th-century gatehouse and the ruins of the church and other buildings survive from the Augustinian abbey, founded in 1139. The gate is approached across a dry moat, spanned by a long bridge with arcaded walls and circular towers.
Open all year, Apr-Sep, daily 10-6; Oct-Mar 10-4 or dusk if earlier.
& ✗
(EH)

KENT

Aylesford Priory
AYLESFORD
The Friars
☎Maidstone (01622) 717272
Built in the 13th and 14th centuries and then closed down in the Reformation, the priory has been restored and is now a house of prayer, guesthouse, conference centre and a place of pilgrimage and retreat. It has fine cloisters, and displays sculpture and ceramics by modern artists and potters. A potter and an upholsterer are now at the Friars and visitors are welcome to watch them at work. Special events for 1995 are a Fun Run and Family Fun Day on 23 April and a Spring Fayre on 29 May which will include a falcon display, steel band, folk dance groups, children's rides, craft fair and food stalls.
Open all year, daily 9-dusk. Gift & book shop May-Sep, 10-5; Oct-Apr, 10-4. Guided tours of the priory by arrangement. Donations. £1 for special events held on 29th May, 23 Apr & 25 Sep
P ♥ & (wheelchairs available, ramps) toilets for disabled shop ✗

Howletts Wild Animal Park
BEKESBOURNE
(off A257)
☎Canterbury (01227) 721286
Howletts is one of John Aspinall's wild animal parks and has the world's largest breeding gorilla colony in captivity. It also has tigers, small cats, free-running deer and antelope, snow leopards, bison, ratel, the UK's only herd of breeding elephants, and many endangered species of monkeys. All are housed in natural enclosures with the aim of breeding offspring to be returned to safe wild areas. John Aspinall's other wild animal

park is Port Lympne, at Lympne near Hythe.
Open all year, daily 10-5 or dusk. (Closed 25 Dec).
✿£6.50 (ch 4-14 & pen £4.50). Family ticket £19.
P ▆ ✗ licensed Ġ toilets for disabled shop ⊗

Whitbread Hop Farm
BELTRING ▬▬▬▬
(on A228)
☎ Maidstone (01622) 872068
The largest group of Victorian oast houses and galleried barns in the world stands at the centre of this stunning complex. Attractions include the Hop Story Exhibition, designed using modern audio-visual technology, Whitbread Shire Horse Centre, birds of prey including daily owl-flying displays, Rural Museum, Animal Village, Pottery Workshop, restaurant, play area, nature trail and gift shop. Special events are usually held. Please telephone for details.
Open all year, daily 10-6. (Last admission 5pm). (Closed 25-26 Dec & 31 Dec). Admission fee payable.
P ▆ ✗ licensed Ġ toilets for disabled shop

Biddenden Vineyards
BIDDENDEN ▬▬▬▬
Little Whatmans (0.5m S off A262)
☎ (01580) 291726
The present vineyard was established in 1969 and now covers 22 acres. Visitors are welcome to stroll around the vineyard and to taste wines, ciders and apple juice available at the shop. Special events include: Easter Bunny Hunton Easter Sunday, Biddenden Vineyard charity wine run to France on the first Thursday in July (6 Jul, 1995), and at weekends in December, free tasting of hot mulled cider and mince pies.
Open all year, Shop: Mon-Fri 10-5, Sat 11-5 (3pm Nov-Feb), Sun 12-5 (3pm Nov-Dec), BH 11-5 (Mar-Oct). (Closed midday 24 Dec-2 Jan).
Free.
P ▆ Ġ shop

Great Comp Garden
BOROUGH GREEN ▬▬▬▬
(2m E off B2016)
☎ (01732) 882669 & 886154
A beautiful seven-acre garden created since 1957 by Mr and Mrs R Cameron for low maintenance and year-round interest. There is a plantsmans' collection of trees, shrubs, heathers and herbaceous plants in a setting of fine lawns and grass paths. Planting styles vary from woodland and informal walks to terraces and formal paths, with ruins, loved by children, and ornaments for additional interest. Unusual plants for sale. The 17th-century house is not open. Chamber music, classical concerts and other events are organised by the Great Comp Society, details from the Secretary, Great Comp Society at the above address.
Open Apr-Oct, daily 11-6.
✿£2.50 (ch 5 £1). Annual ticket £7.50 (pen £5)
P ▆ Ġ toilets for disabled garden centre ⊗

Emmetts Garden
BRASTED ▬▬▬▬
Ide Hill (1m S of A25)
☎ Ide Hill (01732) 750367 & 750429
Emmetts is a charming hillside shrub garden, with bluebells in spring and fine autumn colours. It has magnificent views over Bough Beech Reservoir and the Weald. Emmetts Country Fair takes place on 19 and 20 Aug 1995, and Emmetts Jazz Concert on 26 Aug 1995.
Open Mar, wknds; Apr-Oct, Wed-Sun & BH Mon 1-6 (last admission 5pm). Special opening for pre-booked parties Thu 11-1.
£2.50 (ch £1.30).
P ▆ Ġ (buggy service from car park to garden) toilets for disabled shop (NT)

Bleak House Dickens Maritime & Smuggling Museum
BROADSTAIRS ▬▬▬▬
Fort Rd
☎ Thanet (01843) 862224
The house was a favourite seaside residence of the novelist Charles Dickens. He wrote the greater part of David Copperfield and other works here, and drafted the idea for Bleak House. There are special exhibitions of relics salvaged from the Goodwin Sands, and of 'The Golden Age of Smuggling'.
Open Etr-Jun & Oct-Nov 10-6, Jul-mid Sep 10-9.
£2 (ch 12 £1.25, pen & students £1.65). Party 10+
P (50 yds) Ġ shop

Dickens House Museum
BROADSTAIRS ▬▬▬▬
Victoria Pde
☎ Thanet (01843) 862853
The house was immortalised by Charles Dickens in David Copperfield as the home of the hero's aunt, Betsy Trotwood. Dickens' letters and possessions are shown, with local and Dickensian prints, costumes and general Victoriana. The parlour is furnished as described in the novel.
Open Apr-mid Oct, daily 2.30-5.30.
£1 (ch 50p).
P (400yds) shop ⊗

CANTERBURY ▬▬▬▬
A visit to Canterbury must naturally start at the cathedral. This is where Chaucer's pilgrims and countless others came to visit the shrine of Thomas à Becket, who was murdered near the steps to the north transept in the 12th century. The treasures of the shrine were carried off during the Dissolution, but its site is still marked, with the tomb of the Black Prince close by. The cathedral has an awe-inspiring high, narrow nave, and the cathedral's medieval stained glass is well worth studying for the stories it tells. Next to the cathedral are the ruins of the former monastery, and the medieval and later buildings of the King's School. An interesting walk can be taken from Christ Church Gate around streets with picturesque old buildings like Queen Elizabeth's Guest Chamber and the weavers' cottages beside the Stour. A short walk leads up the hill to St Martin's church, which was old in the time of the Venerable Bede and is probably the oldest church in England still in use. Older still is the prehistoric tumulus topped by a 19th-century obelisk in Dane John garden.

Blean Bird Park
CANTERBURY ▬▬▬▬
Honey Hill, Blean (3m NW on A290)
☎ (01227) 471666
Exotic tropical birds can be seen flying in a natural setting among the trees. The garden has the largest breeding collection of macaws, cockatoos and parakeets in England. There are also owls, peacocks, pheasants and other birds, with a pets' corner, a small collection of mammals, reptiles and a woodland walk. Children's farm and adventure playground. Falconry displays are held on some weekends, telephone for details.
Open all year, Mar-Oct 10-6; Nov-Feb 10-5.
P ▆ Ġ toilets for disabled shop ⊗
Details not confirmed for 1995

Canterbury Heritage Museum
CANTERBURY ▬▬▬▬
Poor Priests' Hospital, Stour St
☎ (01227) 452747
An award-winning museum in a breath-taking medieval building on the river bank close to the Cathedral, shops and other attractions. The tour starts in Roman times and continues up to the present day. Some of the most exciting of the

city's treasures are shown: the Canterbury Cross, Anglo-Saxon gold, and Viking finds. The displays include (among many others) a reconstruction of Becket's tomb; a medieval street with a pilgrim badge shop; Christopher Marlowe (he was born in Canterbury); the city in the Civil War; and Stephenson's locomotive 'Invicta'. The latest feature is the Rupert Bear Gallery and a collection of Joseph Conrad memorabilia.
Open all year, Mon-Sat 10.30-5 & Sun (Jun-Oct) 1.30-5 (last admission 4pm). (Closed Good Fri & Xmas period).
£1.50 (ch 75p, pen & students £1). Family ticket £3.50. Party 10+
P Ġ shop ⊗

The Canterbury Tales
CANTERBURY ▬▬▬▬
Saint Margaret's St
☎ (01227) 454888
Here you can step back in time to the 14th century and experience the sights, sounds and even the smells of the period. Meet the people, see their animals and visit their homes, inns and workshops and become one of Chaucer's pilgrims walking from Southwark to Canterbury to pray at the miracle-working tomb of St Thomas Becket. The latest electronic presentation techniques bring the experience vividly to life. Commentary is available in English, French, Dutch, German, Italian, Spanish and Japanese and there is also a special children's tape. A recent and successful innovation is an evening programme of medieval entertainment. Students and local actors perform Chaucerian scenes in medieval costume at different locations in the old streets around the cathedral. The entertainment begins at 7pm with a viewing of the Canterbury Tales Visitor Attraction and a glass of mead before the performance, and can finish (optional) with a special traditional meal at a city-centre restaurant. Telephone for details.
Open all year, Mar-Oct, daily 9.30-5.30;

Nov-Feb, Sun-Fri 10-4.30, Sat 9.30-5.30. (Closed 25 Dec).
✿£4.50 (ch 5-16 £3.25, under 5 free, students & pen £3.75). Family ticket £14. Prices under review.
P (5 mins walk) ▆ Ġ (notice required for wheelchairs) toilets for disabled shop ⊗

Roman Museum
CANTERBURY ▬▬▬▬
Butchery Ln, Longmarket
☎ (01227) 785575
Underground, at the level of the Roman town, you will find this famous Roman house with its mosaic floors. Following the discoveries of archaeologists, you walk through a fascinating reconstruction of Roman buildings, including a market place with stallholders' wares of the period. Displays reveal a wealth of objects rescued by the excavation, including 2000-year-old swords and a silver spoon hoard. A computer-generated reconstruction video guides you on the tour, and there is a 'touch the past' area where you can handle artefacts.
Open all year, Mon- Sat 10-5; Sun (Jun-Oct) 1.30-5. Last admission 4pm. (Closed Good Fri & Xmas period).
£1.50 (ch 75p pen & students £1). Family ticket £3.50. Party.
P (500 mtrs) Ġ toilets for disabled shop ⊗

Royal Museum, Art Gallery & Buffs Regimental Museum
CANTERBURY ▬▬▬▬
High St
☎ (01227) 452747
The city's picture collection including the T S Cooper Gallery - England's leading Victorian animal painter; and the Canterbury and Europe Gallery which displays the fine archaeological objects and decorative arts resulting from close links over the centuries. Regular art events are held in the Special Exhibitions Gallery. Also housed here is the Buffs Regimental Museum, telling the story of one of England's oldest infantry ➤

Sir Winston Churchill was a keen bricklayer. At Chartwell, his home, he built the garden walls. The rose garden was planted for his golden wedding.

regiments.
Open all year, Mon-Sat 10-5. (Closed Good Fri and Xmas period).
Free.
P *shop* ⊗

St Augustine's Abbey
CANTERBURY
Longport (off A28)
☎(01227) 767345
The abbey was founded by St Augustine on land given by King Ethelbert in AD598, and the foundations of a 7th-century church can be seen. The remains of the later Norman church and its well-preserved crypt, and the ruins of the medieval monastery can be seen.
Open all year, Apr-Sep, daily 10-6; Oct-Mar, daily 10-4. Closed 24-26 Dec & 1 Jan.
£1.50 (ch 80p, concessions £1.10).
P & *shop*
(EH)

West Gate Museum
CANTERBURY
Saint Peter's St
☎(01227) 452747
The last of the city's fortified gatehouses sits astride the London road with the river as a moat. Rebuilt in around 1380 by Archbishop Sudbury, it was used as a prison for many years. The battlements give a splendid panoramic view of the city and are a good vantage point for photographs. Arms and armour can be seen in the guardroom, and there are cells in the towers.
Open all year (ex Good Fri & Xmas period), Mon-Sat; 11-12.30 & 1.30-3.30.
60p (ch & disabled 30p, pen, students & UB40 40p). Family ticket £1.50. Party 10+.
P (100 yds) *shop* ⊗

Chartwell
CHARTWELL
(2m S of Westerham, off B2026)
☎Edenbridge (01732) 866368
The former home of Sir Winston Churchill is filled with reminders of the great statesman, from his hats and uniforms to gifts presented by Stalin and Roosevelt. There are paintings of Churchill and other

works by notable artists, and also many paintings by Churchill himself. An exhibition gives visitors an insight into his life during his years at Chertwell, and his studio is arranged with easel and paintbox at the ready. The garden has walls and ponds that he laid out, and gives fine views. On 10 June 1995 there is an open-air 1940s dance.
Open Apr-Oct Tue-Sun & BH Mon 11-5.30, last admission 4.30pm. Mar & Nov House only, Sat, Sun & Wed 11-4.30. Last admission 4pm. (Closed Good Fri and Tue following BH Mon).
House & Garden £4.50 (ch £2.25). Studio 50p. Gardens only £2 (ch £1). Entrance by numbered ticket at times in summer to avoid congestion, waiting time can be spent in garden.
P ✕ *licensed* & *toilets for disabled shop* ⊗ *(ex garden)*
(NT)

Fort Amherst
CHATHAM
Dock Rd
☎Medway (01634) 847747
Fort Amherst is the finest Georgian Fortress in the country, comprising a large gatehouse, tunnel complex, ditches, magazines, barracks and Civil Defence exhibition. The parklike setting within the fortifications, together with an 1815 re-enactment most summer Sundays, provides a fascinating visit for all the family.
Open Mar-Oct, daily 10.30-5; Nov-Feb, Thu-Mon 10.30-4.
£3.50 (ch, pen & students £2).
P ⊒ *shop* ⊗

Historic Dockyard
CHATHAM
☎Medway (01634) 812551
A Royal dockyard until 1984, now an 80-acre working museum with 47 Scheduled Ancient Monuments which form the most complete Georgian/early Victorian dockyard in the world. Eight museum galleries cover 400 years of shipbuilding history, and include the award-winning 'Wooden Walls' which shows through sights, sounds and smells, how 18th-century warships such as *HMS Victory*

were built here. Visitors can see a working ropery, sail and flag-making, crafts workshops in action, and witness the restoration of the Victorian sloop *Gannet* in dry dock. Impressive buildings include huge covered slips, a Georgian Officers' Terrace, and the Commissioner's House (1704), Britain's oldest intact naval building whose pleasant garden is open to visitors. Horse-drawn wagon rides are available in the summer. Special events for 1995 include: 16-17 April - Mad Hatter's Tea Party (children's event of the year); 8 May - V E Day Celebrations (historic vehicle rally, march past, open air concert and grand firework finale); 10-11 June - Model Railway Exhibition; 23 July - Heavy Horse Day; 12-13 August - Victorian Fair (steam engines, barrel organs etc).
Open Apr-Oct, daily 10-5; Feb, Mar & Nov, Wed, Sat & Sun 10-4.
£5.60 (ch 5-16 £3.60, student & pen £4.60). Family ticket £15. Party.
P ⊒ ✕ *licensed* & *(wheelchair available, Braille guides) toilets for disabled shop*

Chiddingstone Castle
CHIDDINGSTONE
(off B2027, at Bough Beech)
☎Penshurst (01892) 870347
The 'castle' is a 17th-century house, almost completely rebuilt in the castle style c1800 by William Atkinson. It contains Stewart and Jacobite paintings and other relics, Egyptian and Oriental antiquities, and a fine collection of Japanese lacquer and swords. The interior has recently been refurbished with extra rooms open to visitors. The grounds are now undergoing restoration. Fishing in the lake at £8 a day. Special events for 1995 will include a Spring festival, July open-air event, '45 exhibition and Christmas fair - telephone for details.
Open Apr-Oct. Apr-May & Oct, Wed & Sun; Jun-Sep, Tue-Sun. All BH's. Weekdays 2-5.30; Sun and BH 11.30-5.30. Other times for parties by arrangement.
£3.50 (ch 5-15 £1.50). Party 20+.
P ⊒ & ⊗ *(no exceptions)*

Deal Castle
DEAL
Victoria Rd
☎(01304) 372762
Deal Castle was one of many forts built by Henry VIII in case of invasion by Catholic Europe. It is shaped like a many-leafed clover, with every wall rounded to deflect shot. At the centre is a massive keep. Iron Age weapons and relics of Deal's history are displayed.
Open all year, Apr-Sep, daily 10-6; Oct, 10-4; Nov-Mar, Wed-Sun 10-4. Closed 24-26 Dec & 1 Jan.
£2.50 (ch £1.30, concessions £1.90).
& *shop*
(EH)

The Time-Ball Tower
DEAL
Victoria Pde
☎(01304) 360897 & 201200 (low season)
The tower is a unique four-storey museum of time and maritime communication, built in 1821, with a working time-ball which drops daily on the hour every hour.
Open 31 May-early Sep, Tue-Sun & BH's 10-5.
shop ⊗
Details not confirmed for 1995

Walmer Castle
DEAL
Walmer, Kingsdown Rd (1m S on coast)
☎(01304) 364288
Like Deal Castle, Walmer was built by Henry VIII and has a similar design. It is the official residence of the Lord Warden of the Cinque Ports, a post once held by the Duke of Wellington. His sparsely furnished bedroom can be seen, and there is a delightful garden.
Open all year, Apr-Sep, daily 10-6; Oct, 10-4; Nov-Mar, Wed-Sun 10-4. Closed 24-26 Dec & 1 Jan.
£3.50 (ch £1.80, concessions £2.60)
P &
(EH)

Crabble Corn Mill
DOVER
Lower Rd (off A2)
☎(01304) 823292
Visit this beautifully restored working Kentish water mill, enter the Victorian era and discover when traditional country life changed forever and today's technological world was born. Stoneground wholemeal flour always for sale. Exhibition space now houses the work of local artists and art/craft short courses.
Open all year, Etr-Oct Mon, Wed-Sat 10-5 (& Tue 10-5 in Aug) & Sun noon-5. Nov-Etr, Sat 10-5 & Sun noon-5.
✳*£1.50 (ch 16 80p, students & pen £1). Family ticket £3.50.*
P ⊒ & *shop* ⊗

Dover Castle and Hellfire Corner
DOVER
☎(01304) 201628
The Norman castle has a massive keep built by Henry II in the 1180s, with chapels, a 242ft-deep well, and massive walls and towers. The castle was strengthened and adapted in later centuries. It stands on cliffs which have been fortified since Iron Age times, but the oldest building there now is the Roman lighthouse, the Pharos. The Saxon church of St Mary de Castros is also near the castle. It has been restored but still shows Saxon and Norman work. Secret tunnels underneath the castle were built in Napoleonic times and were more recently used during the Second World War to plan the evacuation of

Dunkirk. A new exhibition is based here called Hellfire Corner.
Open all year, Apr-Sep, daily 10-6; Oct-Mar, daily 10-4. Closed 24-26 Dec & 1 Jan. £5.50 (ch £2.80, concessions £4.10).
P ☕ & shop ✗
(EH)

Old Town Gaol
DOVER
Dover Town Hall, Biggin St
☎ (01304) 201200
High-tech animation, audio-visual techniques and 'talking heads' take visitors back to Victorian England to experience the horrors of life behind bars, listening, as they walk through the reconstructed courtroom, exercise yard, washroom and cells, to the stories of the felons and their jailers. You can even, if you so wish, try the prisoners' beds or find out what it is like to be locked in a 6ft x 4ft cell!
Open all year, Mon-Sat 10-4.30, Sun 2-4.30. (Closed Mon & Tue, 26 Sep-May). Telephone (01304) 202723 for further information.
✳£3.20 (ch & pen £1.90).
P (charged) & toilets for disabled shop ✗

Roman Painted House
DOVER
New St
☎ (01304) 203279
Visit five rooms of a Roman hotel built 1,800 years ago, now famous for its unique, well-preserved Bacchic frescos. The Roman underfloor heating system and part of a late-Roman defensive wall are also on view. There are extensive displays on Roman Dover with video and commentary. Foreign language commentaries are available in French, German, Dutch and Italian. Parties are welcome; tours by arrangement. Special events are held throughout the year.
Open Apr-Oct, Tue-Sun 10-6 (5pm in Apr, Sep & Oct), also BH Mon & Mon Jul & Aug. Last admission half hour before closing.
P & (touch table, glass panels on gallery for wheelchairs) shop ✗
Details not confirmed for 1995

The White Cliffs Experience
DOVER
Market Sq
☎ (01304) 214566
This award-winning attraction uses stunning stage effects and the latest in audio-visual techniques to tell the story of Britain through the eyes of Dover from Roman times through to World War II. Visitors will witness a Roman invasion, step aboard an old ferry deck, see the fantastic Time and Tide show and pick their way through the rubble of a 1940's Dover street. There is an indoor adventure playground and an outdoor picnic area.
Open all year (ex 25 Dec), 8 Apr-Oct, daily 10-5; Nov-7 Apr, daily 10-3. Centre closes one and a half hours after last admissions.
£4.99 (ch 4-14 £3.50, pen & students £3.99).
P (50 yds) ☕ & (Lifts) toilets for disabled shop ✗

Dungeness Visitor Centre
DUNGENESS
☎ Lydd (01797) 321815
The 'A' and 'B' power stations at Dungeness make an extraordinary sight in a landscape of shingle, fishing boats and owner-built houses. There is a high-tech information centre, with 'hands-on' interactive videos and many other displays and models including an environmental exhibition which depicts Dungeness from the Ice Age through to today. The nature trail clearly shows the rare shingle ridges, flora and fauna and completes an interesting day out. Prior bookings for tours is advisable.
Open: Information centre Etr-Oct, daily; Oct-Etr, Sun-Fri. (Closed 23 Dec-4 Jan). Regular Tours of A & B power stations available. No children under 5.
Free.
P & (information centre only) shop ✗

Dungeness Power Station looms large over the shingle beach and flat landscape of the spit on which it is built. There is a 'hi-tech' visitor centre and marked nature trails on the surrounding marshes.

Martello Tower
DYMCHURCH
The tower is one of the series of circular towers built to defend the coast against the expected invasion by Napoleon in the early 19th century. It has a rooftop mounting for a heavy gun.
Open Etr wknd; 23 Apr-16 Jul, wknds only; 22 Jul-2 Sep, daily noon-4.
£1 (ch 50p, concessions 80p)
(EH)

EDENBRIDGE
See Hever

Eynsford Castle
EYNSFORD
☎ (01322) 862536
The walls of this castle, still 30ft high, come as a surprise in the pretty little village. The castle was begun in the 11th century by William de Eynsford, who later retired to become a monk. Also to be seen are the remains of the castle hall and ditch.
Open all year, Apr-Sep, daily 10-6; Oct-Mar, Tue-Sun 10-4. (Closed 24-26 Dec & 1 Jan).
Free.
P &
(EH)

Lullingstone Castle
EYNSFORD
(1m SW of A225)
☎ Farningham (01322) 862114
The house was altered extensively in Queen Anne's time, and has fine state rooms and beautiful grounds. The 15th-century gate tower was one of the first gatehouses in England to be made entirely of bricks, and there is a church with family monuments. There are provisional arrangements to open under the National Gardens Scheme on June 11 and to hold an open-air concert on July 29; the open-air theatre will present *The Beggar's Opera* on July 29.
Open, House Apr-Sep, Sat, Sun & BH 2-6; Wed, Thu & Fri by arrangement.
✳*House & Gardens £3.50 (ch £1.50 & pen £3).*
P ☕ & shop ✗

Lullingstone Roman Villa
EYNSFORD
(1.5m W off A225)
☎ (01322) 863467
The villa dates from the first and second centuries, and its rooms included an extensive bath complex. The mosaic floors are exceptionally well preserved, and fragments of painted wall plaster can also be seen. The site is roofed for protection, with additional exhibits in a lighted gallery.
Open all year, Apr-Sep, daily 10-6; Oct-Mar, Tue-Sun 10-4. Closed 24-26 Dec & 1 Jan.
P & ✗
(EH)
Details not confirmed for 1995

Fleur de Lis Heritage Centre
FAVERSHAM
13 Preston St
☎ (01795) 534542
A thousand years of history and architecture in Faversham are shown in award-winning displays, an audio-visual programme, and a working vintage telephone exchange in this 16th-century building (a former coaching inn). There is a Tourist Information Centre and a bookshop. A special event held every year is the Faversham Open House Scheme (1, 8, 15 July) - over 20 historic properties in Faversham, usually not open to the public, can be visited on these dates. Admission to the properties is by programme only; for more details contact the Fleur de Lis Heritage Centre.
Open all year, Etr-Oct, daily 10-4; Nov-Etr, Mon-Sat 10-4.
£1 (ch, students, UB40's & pen 50p).
Party 10+
P (200 yds) & shop

Eurotunnel Exhibition Centre
FOLKESTONE
St Martin's Plain, Cheriton High St (junc 12 off M20)
☎ (01303) 270111 ➜

Although the romantic manor house of Ightham Mote is actually encircled by a moat, it is more likely that the name was derived from the Saxon word *moot* meaning 'place of assembly'.

The exhibition shows what it will be like to travel with Le Shuttle through the Channel Tunnel. Imaginative displays, interactive videos, a full-size shuttle and a model railway bring the project to life. Follow the 'talking head' family on their journey to France and discover the ease of using the system as a car driver.
Open all year, daily, summer 10-6; winter 10-5.
🅿 ♨ & *(ex observation tower) toilets for disabled shop* ⚅
Details not confirmed for 1995

Museum & Art Gallery
FOLKESTONE
2 Grace Hill
☎ *(01303) 850123*
In the 18th century Folkestone was noted for its fishing fleet; today it is best known as a Channel port. The museum has displays on its history up to World War II and also has fossils, natural history and archaeology exhibits. The Gallery houses changing exhibitions of work by local and national artists and major exhibitions on local themes - programme of events to be published. Music and drama events are occasionally held in the evenings.
Open all year Mon, Tue, Thu & Fri 9-5, Wed 9-1 & Sat 9-5. (Closed BH). Free.
P *(2 mins walk) shop* ⚅

Town Hall
FORDWICH
The Square (off A28)
☎ *Canterbury (01227) 710610*
The timber-framed Tudor town hall and courtroom is thought to be the oldest and smallest in England. It overlooks the River Stour, peaceful now but hectic in the Middle Ages, because Fordwich was the port for Canterbury. The old town jail can also be visited.
Open Etr, Jun-Sep, Mon-Fri 1-4, Sat & Sun 2-4.
50p (ch 10p, students in group 25p).
🅿

Royal Engineers Museum
GILLINGHAM
Prince Arthur Rd, Brompton (off B2004)
☎ *Medway (01634) 406397*
The museum is a treasure trove of the unexpected, covering the world-wide work of the Royal Engineers from 1066. Learn about the first military divers, photographers, aviators and surveyors; see exhibits as diverse as 24 Victoria Crosses, the regalia of 4 Field Marshals, memorabilia relating to General Gordon and Field Marshal Lord Kitchener, Wellington's battle map from Waterloo and a Harrier jump-jet. Conference and corporate facilities are also available. Special events for 1995 include: 18 March - event marking the British

Association for the Advancement of Science week; from 15 April - *The Sapper as Artist* exhibition; 8 MAY - event to mark 50th anniversary of V E Day; 15 August-15 December - *The Forgotten Army*, an exhibition covering the 14th Army and the war against Japan 1941-45.
Open all year, Mon-Thu 10-5, Sat-Sun 11.30-5 Bank Hol Mon 10-5. (Closed Good Fri, 25-26 Dec & 1 Jan). Friday by appointment only.
£2 (ch, pen & UB40s £1). Family ticket £4.50. Guided tour £3.50. Party 15+.
🅿 & *(help available if required) toilets for disabled shop* ⚅
See advertisement on page 80

Finchcocks
GOUDHURST
(off A262)
☎ *(01580) 211702*
This fine early Georgian house stands in a spacious park with a beautiful garden, and contains an outstanding collection of keyboard instruments from the 17th century onwards. They have been restored to playing condition, and there are musical tours on all open days and private visits. Visually handicapped visitors may touch the instruments as well as hear them. Events for 19954 include an exhibition - *The Lost Pleasure Seekers* (prints, costumes etc) - as well as fairs on May 28-29 and October 13-15 and festival weekends throughout September which offer concerts and opera featuring period instruments.
Open Etr-Sep, Sun & BH Mon 2-6; Aug, Wed-Sun 2-6. Private groups on other days by appointment Apr-Oct.
❋*£4.80 (ch £3.20). Party. Private visits £5 (evening £5.50-£6.50).*
🅿 ♨ ✕ *licensed* & *shop* ⚅

Kent Battle of Britain Museum
HAWKINGE
Aerodrome Rd (on A260)
☎ *(01303) 893140*
Once a Battle of Britain Station, today it houses the largest collection of authentic relics and related memorabilia of British and German aircraft involved in the fighting. Also shown are British and German uniforms and equipment, and full-size replicas of the Hurricane, Spitfire and Me 109 used in Battle of Britain films.
Open Etr-Sep, daily 10-5; Oct, daily 11-4.
❋*£2.50 (ch £1.50, pen £2). Party.*
🅿 & *shop* ⚅

"Brambles" Wildlife Park
HERNE COMMON
Wealdon Forest Pk
☎ *Canterbury (01227) 712379*
The 20-acre park has a nature trail leading through woodland where many birds and animals including fallow and sika deer, mara, guanaco, wallaby, owls, Scottish

wildcats and red foxes may be seen. Small rare breed farm animals, ponies and a miniature donkey may be fed with the food sold at the gate. There are also a walk-in rabbit enclosure and an indoor garden, an adventure playground and under-fives' playground.
Open Etr-Oct, daily 10-5. Last entry 4.15. £2.20 (ch £1.40, pen £1.80).
🅿 ♨ & *toilets for disabled shop* ⚅

Hever Castle & Gardens
HEVER
(3m SE of Edenbridge, off B2026)
☎ *Edenbridge (01732) 865224*
This enchanting, double-moated, 13th-century castle was the childhood home of Anne Boleyn. The estate was visited many times by Henry VIII during their long courtship. In 1903 it was bought and restored by the American millionaire William Waldorf Astor, and now shows superb Edwardian craftsmanship and an exhibition on scenes from the life and times of Anne Boleyn. Astor also transformed the grounds, creating a Tudor village (available for conferences and corporate hospitality), a lake, a spectacular Italian garden filled with antique sculptures; maze and a fine topiary. The miniature model houses exhibition contained in a purpose-built centre (no additional charge) illustrates life in English country houses from medieval to Victorian times. Special events for 1995 include Musical Memories on 7-8 May, the official opening of the new Tudor herb garden in mid June, traditional jousting tournaments on 27 May, 29 July, 5, 12, 19 and 26 August and 2 September and a patchwork and quilting exhibition from 15 to 17 September.
Open 14 Mar-5 Nov, daily. Castle 12-6, Gardens 11-6. Last admission 5pm. Private guided tours for pre-booked groups available all year. Castle & Gardens £5.70 (ch 5-16 £2.90, pen £5.20). Family ticket £14.30. Gardens only £4.30 (ch 5-16 £2.50, pen £3.80). Family ticket £11.10. Party 15+.
🅿 ✕ *licensed* & *(wheelchairs available) toilets for disabled shop garden centre* ⚅ *(ex in grounds)*

HYTHE
Romney Hythe & Dymchurch Railway – For details see gazetteer entry under New Romney.

Ightham Mote
IGHTHAM
(2.5m S off A227)
☎ *Plaxtol (01732) 810378*
This medieval manor house, complete

The 14th-century stone tower was built to protect the manor house of the now abandoned Scotney Castle. The ruins have been landscaped to provide one of England's most romantic gardens.

with moat and attractive garden, was given to the National Trust in 1985. It has been extensively remodelled through the centuries but is still a splendid example of medieval architecture: particularly the Great Hall, Old Chapel and crypt c1340. The house also features many important additions from great periods and notable features include the drawing room with its Jacobean fireplace and frieze, its Palladian window and the hand-painted Chinese wallpaper. Once phase six of the major repair programme begins (mid '95) access to the first floor will be limited; the Robinson Library (not normally open) will be shown. Events will include a Conservation Exhibition, the chance to see craftsmen at work, and open-air concerts 14-16 July (that on 16 July being a family concert).
Open 2 Apr-Oct, daily ex Tue & Sat, 12-5.30 wkdays, 11-5.30 Sun & BH Mon. Pre-booked parties wkday am only. Open Good Fri. Last admission 5pm. The house is very busy on Sun & BH between 2 and 4, a timed ticket system may be in operation. Closes 4pm on 16 Jul for family concert.
£4 (ch £2)
🅿 ▣ ♿ *(wheelchairs available,special parking ask at ticket office) toilets for disabled shop* ⌗
(NT)

Bayham Abbey
LAMBERHURST
(2m W in East Sussex)
☎ *(01892) 890381*

Set in the wooded Teise valley, these ruins date back to the 13th century and include parts of the old church, cloisters and gatehouse. Excavation and preservation work is still in progress.
Open Apr-Sep, daily 10-6; Oct 10-4.
£2 (ch £1, concessions £1.50).
🅿 ♿ ⌗
(EH)

Owl House Gardens
LAMBERHURST
(1m NE off A21)
☎ *Tunbridge Wells (01892) 890230*
The Owl House is a small, timber-framed 16th-century house, a former haunt of wool smugglers. Surrounding it are 13 acres of gardens offering the visitor romantic walks with spring flowers, azaleas, rhododendrons, roses, shrubs and ornamental fruit trees. The sweeping lawns lead to lovely woodlands of oak and birch, and informal sunken water gardens.
Open all year, daily 11-6. (Closed 25-26 Dec & 1 Jan).
£3 (ch £1).
🅿 ♿

Scotney Castle Garden
LAMBERHURST
(1m S, on A21)
☎ *(01892) 890651*
The beautiful gardens at Scotney were carefully planned in the 19th century around the remains of the old, moated Scotney Castle. There is something to see at every time of year, with spring flowers followed by gorgeous rhododendrons, azaleas and a mass of roses, and then superb autumn colours. Open-air opera performances will be given 20-23 July and 27-29 July.
Open Garden - Apr-Oct. Old Castle open May-11 Sep Wed-Fri 11-6, Sat & Sun 2-6 or sunset if earlier. BH Sun & Mon 12-6 (Closed Good Fri) last admission 1hr before closing.
£3.20 (ch £1.60)
🅿 ♿ *(wheelchair available) shop* ⌗
(NT)

LEEDS
For Leeds Castle see Maidstone

Lympne Castle
LYMPNE
☎ *Hythe (01303) 267571*
A small medieval castle built between the 12th and 15th century. Although it was largely remodelled and restored in 1905, it retains much of its former character. The view from the castle includes the military canal, dug as part of the coastal defences during the Napoleonic Wars, Romney Marsh and, in fine weather, the French coast across ➤

the Channel. There are exhibitions of toys and dolls, reproduction medieval memorial brasses and scale models of English cathedrals.
Open Etr-early Oct & all BH's, daily 10.30-6. Other times by arrangement. (Closed occasional Sat).
✳£2 (ch 50p).
🅿 *shop*

Port Lympne Wild Animal Park, Mansion & Garden
LYMPNE ▬▬▬
☎ *Hythe (01303) 264647*
The only pair of Sumatran rhinos in Europe have their home in John Aspinall's 300-acre wild animal park along with hundreds of other rare animals: Indian elephants, wolves, bison, black and snow leopards, Siberian and Indian tigers, gorillas and monkeys. The mansion designed by Sir Herbert Baker is surrounded by 15 acres of spectacular gardens. Inside, the most notable features include the recently restored Rex Whistler Tent Room, Moroccan Patio and hexagonal library where the Treaty of Paris was signed after World War I. The Spencer Roberts mural room depicts over 300 animals and birds from South East Asia. Safari trailers journey through some of the animal paddocks during peak times; please telephone to check availability.
Open all year, daily 10-5, 3.30pm in winter (Closed 25 Dec).
£6.50 (ch 4-14 & pen £4.50). Family £19.
🅿 ☕ ✗ *licensed &. (very limited access for disabled) toilets for disabled shop* ♿
See advertisement on page 83

The Archbishops' Palace
MAIDSTONE ▬▬▬
Palace Gardens, Mill St
☎ *(01622) 663006*
Located in the oldest quarter of Maidstone overlooking the River Medway, the 14th-century Palace has recently been restored to its former glory.
Open all year daily 10.30-5.30. (Closed 25 & 26 Dec).
P *(200yds)* ☕ ✗ *licensed &. toilets for disabled shop* ♿

Leeds Castle
MAIDSTONE ▬▬▬
(4m E, at junct 8 of M20/A20)
☎ *(01622) 765400*
The site of a manor of the Saxon royal family in the 9th century, Leeds was described by Lord Conway as 'the loveliest castle in the world'. Visitors may well agree with the sentiment. Built on two islands in the middle of a lake and set in 500 acres of landscaped parkland, it was converted into a royal palace by Henry VIII, and remained a royal residence for over three centuries. Today it has been beautifully restored and furnished; it has some beautiful pictures and other treasures, and, more unusual, a museum of medieval dog collars. Outside there are the Culpeper Flower Garden, the greenhouses, aviaries and vineyard, the 14th-century barbican and mill, the maze and grotto, and water and woodland gardens. Children especially love meeting the free-roaming waterfowl, which include peacocks as well as white and black swans. The Fairfax Hall, a 17th-century tithe barn, is the venue for 'Kentish Evenings' each Saturday night (except during August) and is a fully licenced self-service restaurant during normal opening hours. There are also many special events throughout the year, including a New Year's Day Treasure Trail, Spring Gardens Week (25 March-2 April), a Balloon and Vintage Car Fiesta (3-4 June) and open-air concerts by the Royal Philharmonic Orchestra (24 June and 1 July).
Open all year daily, Mar-Oct 10-5 (Castle 11-5.30). Nov-Feb 10-3 (Castle from 10.15pm).
Castle, Park & Gardens £7.30 (ch 5-15 £4.80, students & pen £6.20); Park & gardens £5.50 (ch 5-15 £3.30, students & pen £4.50). Family ticket £20, Park & gardens only £15. Party 20+.*
🅿 ✗ *licensed &. (Braille information, induction loops & wheelchair lift) toilets for disabled shop garden centre* ♿

Maidstone Museum & Art Gallery
MAIDSTONE ▬▬▬
Saint Faith's St (close to County Hall)
☎ *(01622) 754497*
Set in an Elizabethan manor house which has been much extended over the years, this museum houses a surprising and outstanding collection of fine and applied arts, including oil paintings and watercolours, furniture, Roman, Anglo-Saxon and Medieval archeology, ceramics, costumes and a collection of Japanese art and artefacts. Natural history collections and displays relating to local industry are also featured, together with the museum of the Queen's Own Royal West Kent Regiment. Please apply for details of temporary exhibitions, workshops etc.
Open all year, Mon-Sat 10-5.30, Sun 2-5 & BH Mon 11-5. (Closed 25-26 Dec). Free.
P *(100 yds)* ☕ *shop* ♿

Museum of Kent Life
MAIDSTONE ▬▬▬
Lock Ln, Sandling (From A229, follow signs for Aylesford)
☎ *(01622) 763936*
The story of the Kent countryside unfolds on this 27-acre site close to the River Medway. Exhibitions relating to farming history include displays of agricultural tools and machinery in farm buildings and livestock important to the county, as well as displays of local crafts. The museum also features a 'Darling Buds of May' exhibition.
Open daily, Etr-Oct, wknds to Xmas.
🅿 ☕ ✗ *licensed &. toilets for disabled shop*
Details not confirmed for 1995

Tyrwhitt Drake Museum of Carriages
MAIDSTONE
The Archbishop's Stables, Mill St (close to River Medway & Archbishops Palace)
☎(01622) 754497
A wide array of horse-drawn carriages and vehicles is displayed in these late-medieval stables, which are interesting in themselves. The exhibits include state, official and private carriages, and some are on loan from royal collections.
Open all year, Apr-Oct daily 10.30-5.30; Nov-Mar noon-4.30. Last admission 4pm. (Closed 25-26 Dec).
✸£1.50 (ch & pen £1).
P (100 yds) & shop ⌖

Badsell Park Farm
MATFIELD
Crittenden Rd
☎Paddock Wood (01892) 832549 & 833436
A pleasant day in the country for all the family is offered at this attractive 180-acre fruit and arable farm. Children are able to handle young farm animals and pets in the Animal Park and Pet Area. There are nature trails to follow in beautiful countryside, a butterfly house with live tropical species and a new tropical ant house, picnic facilities and a play barn for toddlers and children up to eleven; outdoor play areas include wendy houses, a fort, fire engine and tractor. An Information Room gives details of farming and wildlife, including live insect displays. Strawberries, apples and other fruit and vegetables can be picked in season. Children's birthday and evening parties are a speciality and pony and tractor rides are available by arrangement. Special events during the year will include a gymkhana, dog shows, classic cars, South American and craft fairs, barn dances and children's parties at Easter, Hallowe'en, Bonfire Night and Christmas.

Open all year, daily 10-5.30.
✸£4 (ch £2.50, pen £3)
P ☕ & toilets for disabled shop ⌖ (ex on nature trail)

Minster Abbey
MINSTER-IN-THANET
☎Ramsgate (01843) 821254
One of the first nunneries in England was built on this site in the 7th century. The house was rebuilt in later centuries, but is still a religious community and is run by Benedictine nuns. The ruins of the old abbey and the cloisters are open to the public and much of the Early English and Norman architecture can still be seen; there is one wing dating back to 1027.
Open all year, May-Sep, Mon-Fri 11-12 & 2-4.30, Sat 11-12; Oct-Apr, Mon-Sat 11-12.
✸Donations
P & shop

Romney, Hythe & Dymchurch Railway
NEW ROMNEY
☎(01797) 362353 & 363256
The world's smallest public railway has its headquarters here. The concept of two enthusiasts coincided with Southern Railway's plans for expansion, and so the thirteen-and-a-half mile stretch of 15 inch gauge railway came into being, running from Hythe through New Romney and Dymchurch to Dungeness Lighthouse. Events planned for 1995 include a Steam and Diesel Gala (14 May), New Romney Bus Rally (18 June) and Friends of Thomas the Tank Engine (10 September) - all dates being provisional at the time of going to press.
Open daily Etr-Sep, also wknds in Mar & Oct. For times apply to: The Manager, RH & DR., New Romney, Kent.
Charged according to journey.
P (charged) ☕ & shop

Penshurst Place & Gardens
PENSHURST
(on B2176)
☎(01892) 870307
The original manor house was built by Sir John de Pulteney between 1340 and 1345 and is perfectly preserved. Successive owners enlarged it during the 15th, 16th and 17th centuries, and the great variety of architectural styles creates an elaborate and dramatic backdrop for the extensive collections of English, French and Italian furniture, tapestries and paintings. The world-famous, chestnut-beamed Baron's Hall is the oldest and finest in the country, and the collection in the Toy Museum is much loved by children.
The house is set in magnificent formal gardens first laid out in the 14th-century, and recently restored to their former glory. The leisure area includes an adventure playground and nature trail. The Weald of Kent Craft Show is held here on 6-8 May and 8-10 September and there are special activities on all Bank Holidays - telephone for details. Events planned for 1995 include a classic car rally (28-29 May), four Weekends of Revelry in July and a Stately Homes music festival (28-29 September).
Open: House Apr-2 Oct, daily 12-5.30; Gardens, Grounds & venture playground open 11-6 and also wknds in Mar & Oct. House & Grounds £4.95 (ch £2.75, pen, students & UB40 £4.50). Grounds, Toy Museum & Venture playground £3.50 (ch £2.25, pen, students & UB40 £3). Party 20+. Family ticket £13.
P ✗ licensed & shop ⌖

Old Soar Manor
PLAXTOL
☎(01892) 890651
Built by the famous Kentish family, the Culpeppers, in 1290, and amazingly intact, the solar, chapel, lavatorium and barrel-vaulted undercroft of Old Soar is

joined to a lovely Georgian red-brick farmhouse. An ancient oak door displays 'graffiti' through the ages.
Open Apr-Sep, daily 10-6.
Free.
(EH & NT)

Maritime Museum
RAMSGATE
Clock House, Pier Yard, Royal Harbour
☎Thanet (01843) 587765
The Maritime Museum Ramsgate is housed in the early 19th-century Clock House, a Grade II listed building, and contains four galleries depicting various aspects of the maritime heritage of the East Kent area. The adjacent restored dry dock and floating exhibits from the museum's historic ship collection include the steam tug *Cervia* and the Dunkirk little ship motor yacht *Sundowner*. Special events for 1995 include: Battles of the Narrow Seas Exhibition (all year), Ships Open Day (2 July) and Children's Open Day (27 July).
Open all year, Apr-Sep Mon-Fri 9.30-4.30, Sat 2-5, Sun 1-6; Oct-Mar Mon-Fri 9.30-4.30.
Combined ticket for museum & steam tug £1 (ch & pen 50p, students 75p)
P (charged) & shop ⌖

Ramsgate Museum
RAMSGATE
Ramsgate Library, Guildford Lawn
☎Thanet (01843) 593532
The museum tells the story of Ramsgate in days gone by with paintings and photographs of Royal Harbour, churches, breweries, pubs, shops, Ramsgate personalities and holiday souvenirs.
Open all year, Mon-Thu 9.30-6, Sat 9.30-5, Fri 9.30-7. (Closed BH).
Free.
P (200 yds) & shop ⌖

Reculver Towers & Roman Fort
RECULVER
The Roman Regulbium was one of the ➤

THE GARDENS · THE HOUSE · THE PLACE

PENSHURST

forts built during the 3rd century to defend the Saxon Shore. The fort was in good condition until the 18th century, when erosion of the cliffs on which it stands caused part of the walls to collapse into the sea below.

During the 7th century an Anglo-Saxon church was built on the site, and its floor plan can still be traced. The church was extended and, during the 12th century, the Normans built on a west front and two huge towers. These are still almost intact, providing a mariners' landmark.
Open any reasonable time.
Free.
 よ ⊗
(EH)

Richborough Castle
RICHBOROUGH ▨
☎*(01304) 612013*
Close to Sandwich, these are the ruins of a Roman castle built to defend the Roman base of *Rutupiae*, the key fort in the defence of the Saxon Shore. The fort covered an area of about six acres and was mostly rebuilt in the 3rd century. Much remains of the Roman walls, parts of which were 12ft thick and up to 24ft high. Excavation has revealed the system of defensive ditches, and the remains of several buildings. There is a museum on the site.
Open Apr-Sep, daily 10-6; Oct 10-4.
£2 (ch £1, concessions £1.50).
🅿よ⊗
(EH)

Charles Dickens Centre
ROCHESTER ▨
Eastgate House, High St
☎*Medway (01634) 844176*
Eastgate House is a fine late Tudor building which contains an audio visual presentation of Charles Dickens' life and works. Two new features have been added - an imaginative and dramatic tableau with state-of-the-art special effects based upon a famous painting

Dickens' Dream, in which many of the great author's most famous characters appear to him whilst he sleeps in his study; and an audio visual theatre showing presentations of Dickens, his life and works and his connections with the Medway Towns (available for groups booked in advance only). Eastgate House appeared as Westgate House in *Pickwick Papers* and The Nun's House in *Edwin Drood*. The garden houses Dickens' chalet from Gad's Hill Place, Higham, which he used as a study in fine weather.
Open all year, daily 10-5.30. (Closed Xmas). Last admission 4.45pm.
£2.70 (ch, pen & students £1.70). Family ticket £7.10. Party 20+. Prices under review.
P (250 yds) shop ⊗

Guildhall Museum
ROCHESTER ▨
High St
☎*Medway (01634) 848717*
Built in 1687, the Guildhall has magnificent decorated plaster ceilings. Recent refurbishment of the adjoining later wing has resulted in new displays of local history from prehistoric times to the beginning of the nineteenth century. There is a feature gallery on the subject of the Medway Prison Hulks. The fine adjacent building, constructed in 1909 as offices for the Conservators of the River Medway, houses the Museum's 19th-century collections. A special exhibition by the Fan Circle International will be held in Spring.
Open all year, daily 10-5.30. (Closed Good Fri, Xmas).
Donations box.
P (250 yds) よ ⊗

Rochester Castle
ROCHESTER ▨
☎*Medway (01634) 402276*
The castle was started in 1087, soon after the Norman Conquest, and the remarkable storeyed keep dates from

1126-39. On the way up are the site of a banqueting hall, a Norman chapel and mural galleries. Parts of the castle walls are still intact.
Open all year, Apr-Sep, daily 10-6; Oct-Mar, daily 10-4. Closed 24-26 Dec & 1 Jan.
£2.50 (ch £1.30, concessions £1.90).
shop
(EH)

C M Booth Collection of Historic Vehicles
ROLVENDEN ▨
Falstaff Antiques, 63 High St (on A28)
☎*Cranbrook (01580) 241234*
The collection is made up of historic vehicles and other items of interest connected with transport. The main feature is the unique collection of three-wheel Morgan cars, dating from 1913. Also here is the only known Humber tri-car of 1904; and items include a 1929 Morris van, a 1936 Bampton caravan, motorcycles and bicycles. There is also a toy and model car display.
Open all year, Mon, Tue, Thu-Sat 10-6 & some Wed pm. Also some Sun & BHs. (Closed 25 Dec).
£1.20 (ch 60p)
shop

Knole
SEVENOAKS ▨
(S end of Sevenoaks, E of A225)
☎*(01732) 450608*
Thomas Bourchier, Archbishop of Canterbury, bought Knole in 1456 and set about transforming it from a simple medieval manor house into his palace; a century later the house was given to Henry VIII who extended it to even grander proportions. In the middle of the 16th century Knole was given to Thomas Sackville by Queen Elizabeth I; the Sackvilles kept the house for ten generations. Thomas lavished a fortune on the refurbishment and decoration of the house. Today, thanks to him, it is the

largest house in England. He employed an army of builders, plasterers, upholsterers and glaziers including 300 specially imported Italians; where most Elizabethan houses had one Long Gallery, Knole has three. The State rooms are rich in architectural detail from the 17th and 18th centuries with fine portraits and outstanding furniture adding to their beauty. Outside, 26 acres of gardens contain formal walks among flower beds and fruit trees while beyond the encircling walls are further acres of undulating pasture and parkland open by courtesy of Lord Sackville.
Open Apr-Oct, Wed, Fri-Sun & BHs 11-5, Thu 2-5. Last admission 4pm. Garden 1st Wed in month May-Sep.
£4 (ch £2). Garden 50p. Deer Park free to pedestrians.
🅿 (charged) ⊕ よ shop ⊗ (ex in grounds)
(NT)

Sissinghurst Garden
SISSINGHURST ▨
(1m E of village)
☎*Cranbrook (01580) 712850*
The Tudor mansion of Sissinghurst Castle was bought in a neglected state in 1930 by Sir Harold Nicholson and his wife, the writer Vita Sackville-West. They set about restoring house and gardens and the gardens now rank among the most attractive and popular in England. Basing the design around the existing high Tudor walls and two stretches of water, axial walks, usually ending with a statue or archway, have been combined with small geometrical gardens.

Each area is planted with a theme: either seasonal, such as the spring or summer garden; or colour, such as the White Garden or the Cottage Garden, planted mainly in orange or yellow. There are a rose garden with many old-fashioned varieties, a nuttery, a herb garden, a moat walk with a small lawn of thyme, woodland walks, an orchard and the beautiful Tower Lawn bordered with

WITH 2,000 YEARS TO DISCOVER IT'S MUCH MORE THAN A DAY OUT!

A fascinating history has produced a City to delight the visitor of today.

If you are looking for true heritage and the perfect day out (or longer!) then why not visit the dramatic Norman Castle? Where King John used the fat of 40 pigs to save his bacon! Or Rochester Cathedral, the second oldest in the Country. Then there is the superbly restored Victorian High Street which is home to the 17th century Guildhall Museum and award winning Charles Dickens Centre where you can enter the grim reality

and curious world of the great Victorian novelist whose links with the City can be found everywhere.

Take a boat trip along the River Medway by paddlesteamer or river bus to the Historic Dockyard at Chatham where Britain's 'Hearts of Oak' were built. Or to the Country's finest Napoleonic Fortress, Fort Amherst, with its

2,000 yards of tunnels and military re-enactments.

Along with the colourful and lively festivals, superb tea rooms and shops, 2,000 years of history is just waiting to be discovered. All this and much more is only 30 miles from London and in a world of its own.

For further information contact the Rochester Tourist Information Centre at the address below, code 2000.

City of Rochester Upon Medway

Rochester Tourist Information, Eastgate Cottage, High Street, Rochester, Kent ME1 1EW. Tel: (01634) 843666

magnolias; there is also an oast house exhibition.
Open: Gardens Apr-15 Oct, Tue-Fri 1-6.30; Sat, Sun & Good Fri 10-5.30 (last admission 30mins before close. Closed Mon incl BH Mon). Due to limited capacity timed tickets are in operation so visitors may have to wait for admission, also the garden may be closed when its capacity has been reached.
£5 (ch £2.50).
P ✗ *licensed* & *(Admission restricted to 2 wheelchairs at any one time) toilets for disabled shop* ✤
(NT)

Dolphin Sailing Barge Museum
SITTINGBOURNE
Crown Quay Ln (N on A2)
☎ *(01795) 423215*
The museum is dedicated to presenting the history of the Thames sailing barge, many of which were built along the banks of Milton Creek. Tools of the trade, photographs of many barges and associated artefacts can be seen at the barge yard along with the sailing barge *Cambria*. Privately owned barges are repaired - there are a forge, shipwright's shop and sail loft.
Open Etr-Oct, Sun & BHs 11-5. Other times by arrangement.
£1 (ch, pen & UB40 50p).
P & *toilets for disabled shop*

Smallhythe Place
SMALLHYTHE
(3m S of Tenterden on B2082)
☎ *Tenterden (01580) 762334*
Once a Tudor harbour master's house, this half-timbered, 16th-century building became Dame Ellen Terry's last home. It is now a museum of Ellen Terry memorabilia. The barn has been made into a theatre and is open most days courtesy of the Barn Theatre Company. Charming cottage garden, including Ellen Terry's rose garden.
Open Apr-Oct, Sat-Wed 2-6. or dusk if earlier. Last admission 30 mins before closing. The Barn Theatre may be closed some days at short notice.
£2.50 (ch £1.30).
P &
(NT)

The Butterfly Centre
SWINGFIELD MINNIS
McFarlanes Garden Centre (on A260 by junction with Elham-Lydden road)
☎ *Selsted (01303) 844244*
A tropical greenhouse garden with scores of colourful free-flying butterflies from all over the world among exotic plants such as bougainvillea, oleander and banana. The temperate section houses British butterflies, with many favourite species and some rarer varieties.
Open 26 Mar-9 Oct, daily 10-5.
P & *shop garden centre* ✤
Details not confirmed for 1995

Tenterden & District Museum
TENTERDEN
Station Rd (off A28)
☎ *(01580) 764310*
The buildings and history of Tenterden, the Cinque Ports and the Weald of Kent are featured at this local history museum. There are corporation records and insignia as well as exhibits on local trades, agriculture and hop growing, and also on display are the Tenterden Tapestry and Colonel Stephens light railway collection. A special exhibition, **Peace 1945** will be held this year.
Open Apr-Oct, Sat-Thu, 2-4.45. (11-4.45 Aug). Mar, Sat & Sun only 2-4.30.
75p (ch 25p, under 5 free, pen 50p).
P *(charged)* & *shop* ✤

Tunbridge Wells Museum & Art Gallery
TUNBRIDGE WELLS
Civic Centre, Mount Pleasant
☎ *Royal Tunbridge Wells (01892) 526121 & 547221*
The museum displays local and natural history, archaeology, toys and dolls, and domestic and agricultural bygones. There

is a fine display of Tunbridge ware. The art gallery has regularly changing exhibitions which include showings of the Ashton Bequest of Victorian oil paintings.
Open all year, daily 9.30-5. (Closed Sun, BH's & Etr Sat).
Free.
P *(200 yds)* & *shop* ✤

Upnor Castle
UPNOR
☎ *(01634) 718742*
Built during Queen Elizabeth I's reign as a River Medway fort, Upnor Castle only saw real action in 1667 when its defences failed to deter the Dutch fleet sailing up the Medway. It is an attractive castle in ragstone brick, with turrets, a square gatehouse, mullioned windows and timber palisades around a neat lawn.
Open Apr-Sep, daily 10-6.
£2.50 (ch £1.30, concessions £1.90).
&
(EH)

Quebec House
WESTERHAM
(off A25)
☎ *(01959) 562206*
Westerham was the birthplace of General Wolfe who spent his childhood in the multi-gabled, square brick house now renamed Quebec House. The house probably dates from the 16th century but was extended and altered in the 17th century. It contains a Wolfe museum and an exhibition on Wolfe and the Quebec campaign.
Open 2 Apr-Oct, daily (ex Thu & Sat) 2-6 (last admission 5.30pm).
£2 (ch £1).
P ✤
(NT)

Squerryes Court
WESTERHAM
☎ *(01959) 562345 & 563118*
This beautiful manor house, built in 1681, was acquired by the Wardes in 1731 and is still their family home. It contains important pictures (including many Italian, 17th-century Dutch and 18th-century English), furniture, porcelain and tapestries, all collected by the family in the 18th century. Also on display are items relating to General James Wolfe of Quebec, a family friend, who received his first commission at Squerryes. The lovely garden was landscaped in the 18th century and has a lake, dovecote, and a restored formal garden.
Open Apr-Sep, Wed, Sat & Sun, also BH Mon 2-6. Mar, Sun only. Last entry to house 5.30pm.
House & grounds £3.50 (ch 14 £1.60 & pen £3.20). Grounds £2 (ch 14 £1 & pen £1.80). Party 20+.
P ☟ & *toilets for disabled shop* ✤ *(ex in grounds)*

St Leonard's Tower
WEST MALLING
The fine early Norman tower is all that remains of a castle or fortified manor house built in about 1080 by Gundulf, Bishop of Rochester.
Open any reasonable time.
Free.
&
(EH)

LANCASHIRE

Lewis Museum of Textile Machinery
BLACKBURN
Exchange St
☎ *(01254) 667130*
A series of period rooms shows the development of the textile industry from the 18th century onwards. The gallery on the first floor has changing exhibitions.
Open all year, Tue-Sat 10-5. (Closed Good Fri, Xmas, 1 Jan & some BHs).
P *(200m)* & *toilets for disabled shop* ✤
Details not confirmed for 1995

Museum & Art Gallery
BLACKBURN
Museum St
☎ *(01254) 667130*
Watercolours, oil paintings, Japanese prints and icons are among the works of art on display. The museum has fine books and manuscripts, militaria, coins and ceramics. The South Asian Gallery shows the heritage of the Indian sub-continent.
Open all year, Tue-Sat 10-5. (Closed Good Fri, Xmas, 1 Jan & some BHs).
P *(200 yds)* & *toilets for disabled shop* ✤
Details not confirmed for 1995

BLACKPOOL
Blackpool is the British seaside town. Within easy access of the large industrial conurbations of Lancashire, its long sandy beaches became a major holiday destination in the 19th century. To add to its attractions the famous 518ft high Blackpool Tower was built, a smaller copy of the Eiffel Tower. At its base is the Circus and the Tower Ballroom, with its mighty Wurlitzer organ, which has been host to thousands of dancers. Today Blackpool has over 6.5 million visitors a year and the small pleasure beach has now become a vast complex of ferris wheels, roller coasters and other thrilling rides. In the evening from dusk till late, the Tower and the mile long Promenade are brightly lit with spectacular illuminations providing a focal point for the many tourists.

Blackpool Zoo Park
BLACKPOOL
East Park Dr
☎ *(01253) 765027*
This modern zoo, built in 1972, houses over four hundred animals within the 32 acres of landscaped gardens. There is a miniature railway and a children's play area, and also a mother and baby room..

Open all year daily, summer 10-6; winter 10-5 or dusk. (Closed 25 Dec).
✱*£3.80 (ch & pen £1.90). Family £9.*
P ☟ ✗ *licensed* & *(limited number of wheelchairs available) toilets for disabled shop* ✤

Grundy Art Gallery
BLACKPOOL
Queen St
☎ *(01253) 751701*
Established in 1911, the gallery has a permanent collection of work by 19th-and 20th-century artists. There are also touring exhibitions.
Open Mon-Sat 10-5 (Closed BH).
P *(adjacent)* &
Details not confirmed for 1995

Sea Life Centre
BLACKPOOL
Golden Mile Centre, Promenade
☎ *(01253) 22445*
Here at the Sea Life Centre you can take a journey underwater without actually getting wet. Marine life can be viewed at close quarters, and visitors can walk through the largest shark display in Europe. Talks and feeding demonstrations throughout the day. Restaurant and gift shop.
Open all year, daily 10-6 (peak season 9.30am-10pm). (Closed 25 Dec).
P *(100yds)* ☟ ✗ *licensed* & *toilets for disabled shop* ✤
Details not confirmed for 1995

Towneley Hall Art Gallery & Museums
BURNLEY
☎ *(01282) 24213*
This 14th-century house contains the museum, which has oil paintings, English watercolours, furniture, ceramics, 18th-century glassware and natural history exhibits. The Museum of Local Crafts and Industries includes displays on Burnley's recent social and industrial history. Special exhibitions and events are held throughout the year including ➤

Noted for its Gothic Revival design, Lancaster's Shire Hall contains the coats of arms of all sovereigns from Richard I.

Founded on the site of three Roman forts, Lancaster Castle dominates Castle Hill, above the River Lune. Its first fortifications date back to the 11th century. The Norman keep was built in about 1170 and King John added a curtain wall and Hadrian's Tower, restored in the 18th and 19th centuries. A turret named after John of Gaunt was used as a beacon to warn of the approach of the Armada. The Shire Hall, chiefly noted for its Gothic revival design, was built within the castle boundaries and contains a splendid display of heraldry, with the coats of arms of all the sovereigns from Richard I. The Crown Court (still sited here) was notorious as having handed out the greatest number of death sentences of any court in the land, while another exhibition displays the grim relics of early prison life.
Open Etr-Oct, daily 10.30 (1st tour)-4 (last tour). Court requirements always take priority - it is advisable to telephone before visiting except in August.
£2.50 (ch & pen 1.75p). Part tour when Court in session £2 (ch & pen £1).
& shop ✪

Wildlife Photographer of the Year 1994 (28 May-28Jul), portraits of Burnley people by David Wild (Apr-May), children's photography (May-Jun), 20th-century prints (20 Aug-1Oct); telephone for details. There are nature trails and a Natural History Centre in the grounds which contains a new aquarium. Educational facilities are available for schools.
Open all year. Hall: Mon-Fri 10-5, Sun 12-5. Natural History Centre: Mon-Sat 10-5, Sun 12-5. (Closed Xmas & New Year). Free.
P ■ ✗ licensed & (toilet for use of card holders) toilets for disabled shop ✪

Camelot Theme Park
CHARNOCK RICHARD
☎*Eccleston (01257) 453044*
This 130-acre theme park brings the legend and pageantry of the medieval world of Camelot to life every day with jousting tournaments, falconry displays, Merlin's Magic Show and Puppet Show. There are over 100 rides and attractions here, including the Tower of Terror and the Beast. There is also the three-star Park Hall Hotel, Leisure and Conference Centre in the grounds with 144 rooms in total, where family weekends and parties are a speciality.
Open Apr-Oct. Telephone for further details.
P ■ ✗ & toilets for disabled shop ✪ Details not confirmed for 1995

Astley Hall
CHORLEY
☎*(01257) 262166*
A charming Tudor/Stuart building set in beautiful parkland, this lovely Hall retains a comfortable 'lived-in' atmosphere.

There are pictures and pottery to see, as well as fine furniture and rare plasterwork ceilings.
Open Apr-Oct, daily. Nov-Mar, Fri-Sun. (Closed 25 Dec-2 Jan). Times not confirmed for 1995.
£2 (concessions £1). Family ticket £4. Party.
P (200 yds) & shop ✪

Clitheroe Castle Museum
CLITHEROE
☎*(01200) 24635*
The museum in Castle House has a good collection of carboniferous fossils, and items of local interest. It is close to Clitheroe Castle, which ranks among Lancashire's oldest buildings and has one of the smallest Norman keeps in England. Displays include local history and the industrial archaeology of the Ribble Valley, while special features include the restored Hacking ferry boat, Victorian kitchen with taped commentary, printer's and clogger's shops. The grounds command magnificent views of the Ribble Valley.
Open Etr-May & Oct 12-4; Jun-Sep & BH wknds 11-4.30.
P & shop ✪ (ex guide dogs) Details not confirmed for 1995

City Museum (also 15 Castle Hill)
LANCASTER
Market Sq
☎*(01524) 64637*
The fine Georgian proportions of the old town hall are the setting for the City Museum, with its new gallery illustrating the history and archaeology of the city from prehistoric and Roman times onwards. Also housed here is the museum of the King's Own Royal

Lancaster Regiment, which has a wealth of paintings, medals and documents relating to three centuries of this famous regiment's history. Changing exhibitions occupy the ground floor. The Cottage Museum, furnished in the style of an artisan's house of around 1820, faces Lancaster Castle.
Open all year, Mon-Sat 10-5, (Closed Xmas-New Year). 15 Castle Hill, Etr-end Sep, daily 2-5.
City Museum free. 15 Castle Hill 50p (concessions 25p)
P & shop ✪

Maritime Museum
LANCASTER
St George's Quay
☎*(01524) 64637*
Graceful Ionic columns adorn the front of the Custom House, built in 1764 and home of the city's Maritime Museum since 1985. Inside, the histories of the maritime trade of Lancaster, the Lancaster Canal and the fishing industry of Morecambe Bay are well illustrated. An extension to the building houses preserved boats, audio-visual shows and reconstructions. Events for 1995 include an Easter Maritime Festival (Good Friday - Easter Monday) which will feature sea shanties, drama, talks and walks on maritime themes.
Open all year, daily, Etr-Oct 11-5; Nov-Etr 2-5.
£1.50 (concessions 75p). Local residents free.
P ■ & toilets for disabled shop ✪

Shire Hall
LANCASTER
Castle Pde
☎*(01524) 64998*

Leighton Hall
LEIGHTON HALL
☎*Carnforth (01524) 734474*
Early Gillow furniture is displayed among other treasures in the fine interior of this neo-Gothic mansion, which has a gallery with resident artist. Outside a large collection of birds of prey can be seen, and flying displays are given at 3.30pm each afternoon (weather permitting). Special events for 1995 include: Music & Fireworks (1 & 2 Jul); Rainbow Craft Fair (9 & 10 Sep); Antiques Fair (6-8 Oct); Doll Fair (15 Oct).
Open May-Sep, Sun, Tue-Fri & BH Mon from 2pm. For Aug only open from 11.10. (Last admission 4.30pm). School parties pre-booked from 10am. Other times by arrangement.
✱£3.30 (ch 5-16 £2.10, pen £2.80). Party 25+.
P ■ & toilets for disabled shop ✪ (ex in park)

British Commercial Vehicle Museum
LEYLAND
King St (0.75m from junct 28 M6)
☎*(01772) 451011*
The largest commercial vehicle museum in Europe is located in a town long associated with the British motor industry. Over forty restored British commercial vehicles are on display, ranging from horse-drawn examples to modern.
Open Apr-Sep, Tue-Sun 10-5; Oct & Nov, wknds 10-5; also BH.
✱£3 (ch & pen £1.50).
P ■ & toilets for disabled shop ✪

Toy & Teddy Bear Museum
LYTHAM ST ANNES

373 Clifton Dr North (on A584, towards Blackpool)
☎*(01253) 713705*
The Tourism Award-Winning Toy and Teddy Bear Museum, set in one of St Annes famous period buildings, has a collection of old toys arranged in five large rooms and the new Toytown Arcade. Charming displays include: Teddy's Wedding, Bears' Picnic and Bears at the Seaside. Other attractions include a Mini Motor Museum, a collection of more than 200 dolls, 35 dolls' houses, toy trains, working layouts, Dinky cars, aeroplanes, meccano, books and games.
Open Whitsun—Oct, daily 11-5 (closed Tue). Winter, Sun & school hols only 11-5.
£1.75 (ch & pen £1.35)
🅿 & shop

Wildfowl & Wetlands Trust
MARTIN MERE

☎*Burscough (01704) 895181*
The Wildfowl and Wetlands Trust Centre at Martin Mere (just off the A59 in Burscough, near Ormskirk) is a 376-acre site of environmental discovery, making a fascinating day out for all the family. Visitors can test their powers of observation on a collection of waterfowl from all over the world, including ducks, geese, swans and flamingos.
The latest development is a new Wetland Adventure designed for children, with a pond maze at the heart of the expedition. To get there, children first have to cross an Indiana-Jones-style swaying bridge which spans a simulated wetland habitat. In the winter, the mere is home to thousands of roosting Pink-footed Geese - up to one tenth of the world's population - plus Whooper and Bewick's Swans who migrate from Arctic climes to winter in safety. They can be seen at close quarters in the many hides or in the heated Raines Observatory overlooking the mere. Special events for 1995 start with an Easter Egg Hunt and other activities (8-23 Apr); Downy Duckling Days when the young birds are hatching

(27 May-4 Jun); Mermaids, Monsters, Myths and Magic, a celebration of wetlands and their wildlife (mid Jul-early Sep); finally, in September, Sweet September Days gives senior citizens a chance to enjoy the mere in peace and quiet.
Open all year, daily 9.30-5.30 (4pm in winter). (Closed 24-25 Dec).
✳£4.20 (ch £2.10, pen £3.15). Family ticket £10.50. Party.
🅿 ⬛ & *(wheelchair loan, Braille trail, heated hide) toilets for disabled shop* ⊗

Frontierland - Western Theme Park
MORECAMBE

The Promenade
☎*(01524) 410024*
Themed on the American Wild West, there are over 30 rides and attractions for all the family with wood and steel roller coasters, dark rides, American carousel, and an all-weather fun house with live country and western music and magic shows in the main season. The Sky Ride offers great views across Morecambe Bay.
Open 12-26 Apr & 24 May-27 Sep, daily; 21 Mar-11 Apr & May Day-23 May, wknds only; Also school hol wk in Oct.
🅿 *(charged)* ⬛ & *toilets for disabled shop*
Details not confirmed for 1995

Gawthorpe Hall
PADIHAM

(0.75m E off A671)
☎*(01282) 778511*
An early 17th-century manor house, Gawthorpe Hall was built around Britain's most southerly pele Tower, restored in 1850. The house contains fine panelling and moulded ceilings, a minstrels' gallery and Jacobean long gallery. A collection of portraits from the National Portrait Gallery and the Kay Shuttleworth Collections of costume, embroidery and lace are on show in the expanded exhibition areas. National Trust members please note: Gawthorpe Hall is financed and administered by Lancashire County Council.
Open all year, Garden: daily 10-6. Hall: Apr-29 Oct, Tue-Thu, Sat & Sun 1-5. Also

The log flume at Morecambe's Frontierland theme park provides a watery experience of the Wild West.

open BH Mon. (Last admission 4.15pm). House: £2.30 (ch £1). Family ticket £6. Garden free. Party 15+.
🅿 ⬛ & *toilets for disabled shop* ⊗ *(NT)*

Harris Museum & Art Gallery
PRESTON

Market Square
☎*(01772) 58248*
The Harris Museum and Art Gallery is an impressive Greek Revival building containing extensive collections of fine and decorative art including a Watercolour, Drawing and Prints gallery and gallery of Clothes and Fashion. The Story of Preston gallery covers the town's history and the lively exhibition programmes of contemporary art and social history are accompanied by events and activities throughout the year.
Open all year, Mon-Sat 10-5. (Closed Sun & PHs).
P *(5 mins walk)* ⬛ & *(Audio and tactile assistance. Wheelchair available) toilets for disabled shop* ⊗
Details not confirmed for 1995

Museum of Childhood
RIBCHESTER

Church St
☎*(01254) 878520*
Three times winner of the Best of England's North-West Tourist Attractions Award, this nostalgic collection of toys, games, models, dolls, dolls' houses, miniatures and curios is housed in an atmospheric museum. There are over 250,000 objects on display and over fifty dolls' houses. There is a working model fairground and special exhibitions including Victorian Punch and Judy Theatre with original puppets, a collection of marionettes, the General Tom Thumb cabinet, the Titanic Bear and the famous Professor Tomlin's Flea Circus. There are normally at least four special events planned each year - details on application.
Open all year, Tue-Sun, also BH Mon, 10.30-5. Last admission 4.30.
✳£2.45 (ch £1.75, pen £2.25).
🅿 *shop*

Rufford Old Hall
RUFFORD

(off A59)
☎*(01704) 821254*
One of the finest 16th-century buildings in Lancashire, the Tudor Hall, timber-framed in late medieval style, is remarkable for its ornate hammer-beam roof and screen. The Carolean wing, altered in 1821, contains fine collections of 17th-century oak furniture and 16th-century arms, armour and tapestries. In 1995, in the week of 9 October theatrical performances by children will take place under the auspices of The Young National Trust Theatre and on Sunday 17 December Father Christmas will visit the Hall, making Christmas at Rufford a family event.
Open Apr-1 Nov, Sat-Wed, Hall 1-5 (Last admission 4.30pm); Garden & shop 12-

5.30, Sun 1-5.30.
£3 (ch £1.50). Family ticket £8. Garden only £1.60.
🅿 ⬛ & *shop* ⊗ *(ex in grounds) (NT)*

Samlesbury Hall
SAMLESBURY

Preston New Rd
☎*Mellor (01254) 812010 & 812229*
Samlesbury Hall is situated in 5 acres of beautiful grounds. A feature of this well restored half-timbered manor house, built during the 15th and 16th centuries, are the windows from nearby Whalley Abbey. Sales of antiques and collector's items, craft shows and temporary exhibitions are frequently held here.
Open all year, Tue-Sun 11-4.30.
£2 (ch 4-16 80p).
🅿 ✗ *licensed* & *toilets for disabled* ⊗

Turton Tower
TURTON BOTTOMS

(1.5m N off B6391)
☎*Turton (01204) 852203*
This historic house incorporates a 15th-century tower house and Elizabethan half-timbered buildings. Restored in the 19th century, the house displays a major collection of carved wood furniture, mostly English, and period rooms depicting the Tudor, Stuart and Victorian eras. A product of the Renaissance, the house became associated with the Gothic revival and later typified the idealism of the Arts and Crafts movement. The gardens are being restored in late-Victorian style and include a tennis court constructed for the All England mixed doubles winner J C Kay. A varied programme of events in 1995 includes: Crafts Display (Feb & Mar); Prints and Print-making Exhibition (Mar-Apr); Country House Landscapes and Follies Exhibition (May onwards). Please telephone for details and dates of other events.
Open May-Sep, Mon-Fri 10-12 & 1-5. Wknds 1-5; Mar, Apr & Oct Sat-Wed, 2-5; Nov & Feb, Sun 2-5. Other times by prior arrangement.
✳£1 (ch & student 50p). Family ticket £2.50. Guided tour £2.
🅿 ⬛ & *shop* ⊗ *(ex in grounds)*

Whalley Abbey
WHALLEY

☎*(01254) 822268*
These ruins of a 13th-century Cistercian abbey are set in the delightful gardens of the Blackburn Diocesan Retreat and Conference House, a 16th-century manor house with gardens reaching down to the River Calder. The remains include two gateways, a chapter house and the abbot's lodgings and kitchen.
Grounds open all year; craft centre, shop & exhibition area, Apr-Oct daily 11-5.
🅿 ⬛ ✗ *licensed* & *(chair lift) shop*
Details not confirmed for 1995

LEICESTERSHIRE

Ashby-de-la-Zouch Castle
ASHBY-DE-LA-ZOUCH
☎(01530) 413343
The impressive ruins of a 14th century castle include a splendid 15th-century extension, the Warwick Tower. Mary Queen of Scots was imprisoned here; later, in the Civil War, the castle was held for over a year by royalists before being demolished. The remains include the tower, walls, solar and large kitchen.
Open Apr-Sep, daily 10-6; Oct 10-4; Nov-Mar, Wed-Sun 10-4.
£1.30 (ch 70p, concessions £1).
🅿 ⑤ ⑱
(EH)

Belvoir Castle
BELVOIR
(between A52 & A607)
☎Grantham (01476) 870262
Although Belvoir Castle has been the home of the Dukes of Rutland for many centuries, the turrets, battlements, towers and pinnacles of the house are a 19th-century fantasy. Amongst the many treasures to be seen inside are paintings by Van Dyck, Murillo, Holbein and other famous artists.
Also here is the museum of the Queens Royal Lancers. The castle's lovely terraced gardens are adorned with sculptures. Jousting tournaments will be held in 1995 on 14 May, 25 Jun, 30 Jul, and 27 & 28 Aug. The 'Siege of the Castle' takes place on 28 & 29 May.
Open Apr-Sep, Tue-Thu, Sat-Sun & BH Mon 11-5.
£4.25 (ch £2.65, pen £3). Jousting days 50p extra per person.
🅿 ⑲ ✗ *licensed* ⑤ *toilets for disabled shop* ⑱

Snibston Discovery Park
COALVILLE
Ashby Rd
☎(01530) 510851 & 813256
This major science and industry museum is set on the 100-acre site of a former colliery. There are themed galleries: Science Alive, Light Fantastic, Virtual Reality, Textiles and Fashion, Engineering, Extractive Industries and Transport.
An outdoor science play area, a fascinating guided tour of the colliery buildings by ex-miners, a country park with a nature trail, picnic areas, a golf course, fishing lakes and a special events arena are further attractions.
Open all year, Apr-Oct daily 10-6; Nov-Mar daily 10-5. (Closed 25-26 Dec).
✴*£4 (ch & pen £2.75). Family ticket £10.*

🅿 ⑲ ⑤ *(Braille labels, touch tables, parking available) toilets for disabled shop* ⑱

Rutland Railway Museum
COTTESMORE
Cottesmore Iron Ore Mines, Sidings, Ashwell Rd (off B668)
☎Oakham (01572) 813203
Run by volunteers, the museum has an extensive collection of industrial locomotives and rolling stock, many of which were used in local ironstone quarries which operated around Cottesmore until the 1960s and 70s. A number are demonstrated in use over three-quarters of a mile of the mineral branch line built for the quarries in the 1880s. This line is also used to give passenger rides.
The 1995 Rutland Steam Gala takes place on 26-28 August. There is also a lakeside walkway which leads to the remains of the Oakham Canal.
Open wknds 11-5 for viewing, with free diesel-hauled rides on request, site conditions permitting.
Steam operating days: 16-17 & 30 Apr; 1 & 28-29 May; 6 & 26-28 Aug; 24 Sep & 3, 10 & 17 Dec.
✴*£2.50 (ch 5-16 £1.50, pen £1). Family ticket £6.50. Includes free train rides (ex Rutland Steam Gala).*
🅿 ⑲ ⑤ *shop*

Donington-le-Heath Manor House
DONINGTON-LE-HEATH
(S of Coalville)
☎Coalville (01530) 831259
This is a rare example of a medieval manor house, tracing its history back to about 1280. It has now been restored as a period house, with fine oak furnishings. The surrounding grounds include rose and herb gardens, and the adjoing stone barn houses a well stocked tea shop.
Open 7 Mar-Sep, Wed-Sun, also BH Mon & Tue (ex May Day Mon only) 1-6. (Closed Good Fri).
Free.
🅿 ⑲ ⑤ *shop* ⑱

Kirby Muxloe Castle
KIRBY MUXLOE
(off B5380)
☎(01533) 386886
When Lord Hastings drew up designs for his castle in the late 15th century, he first had to obtain 'licence to crenellate'. The moated, fortified, brick-built manor house was never completed: Hastings was executed a few years later and building work ceased. Kirby Muxloe Castle now stands as a ruin in his memory.
Open Apr-Sep, daily 10-6.
£1.30 (ch 70p, concessions £1)
🅿 ⑤
(EH)

Belgrave Hall
LEICESTER
Church Rd, off Thurcaston Rd,, Belgrave
☎(0116) 2666590
A delightful three-storey Queen Anne house dating from 1709 with beautiful period and botanic gardens. Authentic room settings contrast Edwardian elegance with Victorian cosiness and include the kitchen, drawing room, music room and nursery.
Open all year, Mon-Sat 10-5.30, Sun 2-5.30. (Closed 25 & 26 Dec & Good Fri).
Free.
🅿 ⑤ *toilets for disabled shop* ⑱

Jewry Wall Museum & Site
LEICESTER
St Nicholas Circle
☎(0116) 2544766
Behind the massive fragment of the Roman Jewry wall and a Roman Baths site of the 2nd century AD is the Museum of Leicestershire Archaeology, which covers finds from the earliest times to the Middle Ages.
Open all year, Mon-Sat 10-5.30, Sun 2-5.30. (Closed Good Fri, 25 & 26 Dec).
Free.
🅿 ⑤ *toilets for disabled shop* ⑱

Leicestershire Museum & Art Gallery
LEICESTER
New Walk
☎(0116) 2554100
This major regional venue houses local and national collections. New galleries include 'Variety of Life' (natural history), 'Leicestershire's Rocks' (geology), Ancient Egyptians and Discovering Art. Decorative arts cover ceramics, silver and glass, and an internationally famous collection of German Expressionism and other displays range from the Rutland Dinosaur, mummies, stunning collections of minerals, and thousands of butterflies.
There are lots of 'hands on' exhibits and a changing programme of temporary exhibitions throughout the year. There are also lunchtime concerts and special events.
Open all year, Mon-Sat 10-5.30, Sun 2-5.30. (Closed Good Fri, 25 & 26 Dec).
Free.
🅿 ⑤ *toilets for disabled shop* ⑱

Leicestershire Museum of Technology
LEICESTER
Abbey Pumping Station, Corporation Rd, Abbey Ln (3m N)
☎(0116) 2661330
Built as a Pumping Station in 1891, this historic building and site have been undergoing refurbishment and restoration; they are due to reopen in April 1995. The Manager's House has been restored to the Second World War period, and sound guides interpret the unique Victorian beam engines.
The Exhibition Hall hosts a public health exhibition dedicated to 'Water - Clean and Foul'.
Open Apr-Dec, Mon-Sat 10-5.30, Sun 2-5.30. (Closed Good Fri, 25 & 26 Dec).
Free.
🅿 ⑤ *shop* ⑱

Leicestershire Record Office
LEICESTER
Long St, Wigston Magna
☎(0116) 2571080
Housed in a converted 19th-century school in Wigston, the Record Office is the centre for the history of Leicestershire. It holds photographs, electoral registers and archive film, files of local newspapers, history tapes and sound recordings, all of which can be studied.
Records of the county's landed estates and families, borough archives dating back to 1103 and census returns for Leicestershire and Rutland going back to 1841.
Open all year, Mon, Tue & Thu 9.15-5, Wed 9.15-7.30, Fri 9.15-4.45, Sat 9.15-12.15. (Closed Sun & BH wknds Sat-Tue).
Free.
🅿 ⑤ *toilets for disabled* ⑱ 🚌

Museum of Royal Leicestershire Regiment
LEICESTER
Oxford St
☎(0116) 2555889
The history of the regiment (17th Foot) is displayed in Newarke Gateway, a building dating back to the early 15th century.
Open all year, Mon-Sat 10-5.30, Sun 2-5.30. (Closed Good Fri, 25 & 26 Dec).
Free.
🅿 *(150 yds) shop* ⑱ 🚌

Newarke Houses
LEICESTER
The Newarke
☎(0116) 2473222
This museum follows the story of Leicestershire's social history from the 16th century to the present day, showing everyday life and social change throughout the county.
Clocks, toys, Victorian toilets, instruments and furniture are among the many collections. A reconstructed street scene gives glimpses of Victorian life and the fascinating tale of Daniel Lambert, the famous 52-stone gaoler of the 18th century, is also told.
Open all year, Mon-Sat 10-5.30, Sun 2-5.30. (Closed Good Fri, 25 & 26 Dec).
Free.
🅿 *(200 yds) shop* ⑱

University of Leicester Botanic Gardens
LEICESTER
Beaumont Hall, Stoughton Dr South, Oadby (3m SE A6)
☎(0116) 2717725
The grounds of four houses, now used as student residences and not open to the public, make up this 16-acre garden. A great variety of plants in different settings provide a delightful place to walk, including rock, water and sunken gardens, trees, borders, heathers and glasshouses.
Open all year, Mon-Thu 10-4, Fri 10-3.30. (Closed BHs).
Free.
🅿 ⑤ ⑱ *(ex guide dogs)*

Wygston's House Museum of Costume
LEICESTER
12 Applegate
☎(0116) 2473056
Behind a Georgian street front hides a beautiful late medieval building which houses selections from the county's extensive collections of costumes and textiles.
Re-displayed in 1993, the exhibits include a recreation of a 1920s draper's shop; fashionable outfits from 1805 to the present day; Victorian menswear, and a children's gallery. Themed temporary exhibitions take place throughout the year.

The private Great Central Railway at Loughborough was established just after the end of the steam era. The steam railway runs over eight miles of track between Loughborough and Leicester.

Battlefield Steam Railway also has a museum containing an extensive collection of fascinating railway artefacts.

Open all year, Mon-Sat 10-5.30, Sun 2-5.30. (Closed Good Fri & Xmas).
Free.
P (150 yds) & shop ≉

Bell Foundry Museum
LOUGHBOROUGH
Freehold St
☎(01509) 233414
Located in the former fettling shop of the John Taylor Bell Foundry, the museum is part of the largest working bell foundry in the world. Exhibits follow the evolution of the bell founder's craft, showing techniques of moulding, casting, turning and fitting, including modern craft practices.
Open all year, Tue-Sat 9.30-12.30 & 1.30-4.30. Evening tours by prior arrangement. Special tours of Bell Foundry on BH Mon 11-2.15.
Museum only 75p (ch under 16 50p). Works tours by appointment for parties of 15+.
P & toilets for disabled shop ≉

Great Central Railway
LOUGHBOROUGH
Great Central Rd (signposted from A6)
☎(01509) 230726
This private steam railway runs over eight miles from Loughborough Central to Leicester, with all trains calling at Quorn, Woodhouse and Rothley. The locomotive depot and museum are at Loughborough Central. A buffet car is run on most trains. Events planned for 1995 include a variety of steam galas (Feb and Sep), Thomas the Tank Engine days and weekends (Jun and Oct) and Christmas Santa Steam Trains.
Open Sat, Sun & BH Mon & midweek May-Sep.
Round trip £6. Family ticket £15.
P ✆ ✗ licensed & (Disabled coach added to train by prior request) shop

Bede House
LYDDINGTON
☎(01572) 822438
The vast diocese of the Bishops of Lincoln, which stretched from the Humber to the Thames, necessitated an episcopal residence in Lyddington. Bede House was built for the purpose in the late 15th century and it remains a good example of the period. It passed out of religious hands at the time of Henry VIII, and was later converted into an almshouse by the Earl of Exeter.

Open Apr-Sep, daily 10-6.
£1.30 (ch 70p, concessions £1).
& ≉
(EH)

Battlefield Steam Railway Line
MARKET BOSWORTH
(3m NW on unclass rd at Shackerstone station)
☎Tamworth (01827) 880754
Together with a regular railway service (mainly steam) from Shackerstone to Shenton, there is an extensive railway museum featuring a collection of rolling stock and a multitude of other relics from the age of steam rail travel. With the opening of the extension in April 1992 of the line to Shenton (site of the Battle of Bosworth Field), the return passenger trip is nine miles. A number of special events are planned for 1995, starting at Easter and running through to the Christmas Santa Specials. There is a dining train, the Tudor Rose, which offers Sunday lunches.
Open all year, Station & Museum, Sat & Sun, 11.30-5.30. Passenger steam train service operates Apr-Oct, Sun & BH Mon. Diesel trains operate Jun-Aug, Wed only.
✳Shackerstone station: 50p (ch 5-15 free). Return train fare £4.50 (ch £2.25). Family ticket £12.
P ✆ & shop

Bosworth Battlefield Visitor Centre & Country Park
MARKET BOSWORTH
Sutton Cheney (2.5m S)
☎(01455) 290429
The Battle of Bosworth Field was fought in 1485 between the armies of Richard III and the future Henry VII. The visitor centre gives the viewer a comprehensive interpretation of the battle by means of exhibitions, models and a film theatre. There are also illustrated trails around the battlefield, and special medieval attractions are held in the summer months. Full details of admission fees for special events and free leaflets are available on application. Special events for 1995 include the re-enactment of battles such as the Battle of Bosworth Field, and a Medieval Jousting Tournament.
Open all year - Country Park & Battle trails all year during daylight hours. Visitor Centre Apr-Oct, Mon-Fri 1-5, (from 11am

Jul & Aug), wknds, BH Mon & Good Fri 11-6. Parties all year by arrangement.
✳Visitor Centre £2 (ch, pen & UB40 £1.30). Party 20+. Special charges apply on event days.
P (charged) ✆ & (parts of footpath network not suitable) toilets for disabled shop ≉ (ex country park)

Harborough Museum
MARKET HARBOROUGH
Council Offices, Adam & Eve St
☎(01858) 432468
The Museum illustrates the history of the town and its surrounding area, from the days of the medieval planned town to its role as a market, social, and hunting area and also as a stagecoach post. Displays incude the Symington Collection of Corsetry and a reconstruction of a local bootmaker's workshop.
Open all year. Mon-Sat 10-4.30, Sun 2-5. (Closed Good Fri & 25-26 Dec).
Free.
P (adjacent) & (ex Sat, Sun & BH) toilets for disabled shop ≉

Melton Carnegie Museum
MELTON MOWBRAY
Thorpe End
☎(01664) 69946
The local museum of the history and environment of the Borough of Melton, including the famous Vale of Belvoir. The area is explored through a wonderful mixture of exhibits such as the fine collection of sporting paintings, local crafts and industries, archaeology, geology and a two-headed calf!
Open all year, Mon-Fri 10-5, Sat 10-4, also Sun 2-5, Etr-Sep only. (Closed Good Fri, 25 & 26 Dec).
Free.
P & toilets for disabled shop ≉

Farmworld
OADBY
Stoughton Farm Park, Gartree Rd (signposted from A6 & A7)
☎Leicester (0116) 2710355
Farmworld is a working farm that offers a feast of fun and surprises for all the family. Children will enjoy the Children's Farmyard and the playground, while their parents might appreciate the Edwardian Ale-house and the craft workshops and demonstrations. There are also Shire horses and cart rides, lakeside and

woodland walks, nature trails and an interesting collection of rare farm animals.
Open all year, daily 10-5.30 (5 in winter). (Closed 25-26 Dec & 1 Jan).
£4 (ch 2-4 £1.75, ch 5-16 £2.75, pen £3.25). Family ticket £11. Party.
P ✆ & (specifically designed viewing gallery) toilets for disabled shop ≉

Oakham Castle
OAKHAM
off Market Place
☎(01572) 723654
An exceptionally fine Norman Great Hall of a 12th-century fortified manor house. Earthworks, walls and remains of an earlier motte can be seen along with medieval sculptures and unique presentation horseshoes forfeited by peers of the realm and royalty to the Lord of the Manor. Please enquire for details of any events in connection with Oakham Festival in June.
Open all year. Grounds daily 10-5.30 (4pm Nov-Mar). Great Hall Tue-Sat & BH Mon 10-1 & 2-5.30, Sun 2-5.30 (4pm Nov-Mar).Closed Mon, Good Fri & Xmas) (Magistrates in session on Mon).
Free.
P (400 yds) & shop ≉

Rutland County Museum
OAKHAM
Catmos St (on A6003)
☎(01572) 723654
The Museum of Rutland Life has displays of farming equipment, machinery and wagons, rural tradesmen's tools, domestic collections and local archaeology, all housed in a splendid late 18th-century cavalry riding school. There is a special gallery on the Volunteer Soldier in Leicestershire and Rutland. A programme of temporary exhibitions takes place - please enquire for details.
Open all year, Mon-Sat 10-5. Sun 2-5 (Apr-Oct, 2-4 Nov-Mar). (Closed Good Fri & Xmas)
Free.
P (adjacent) & toilets for disabled shop ≉

Stanford Hall
SWINFORD
(1m E)
☎Rugby (01788) 860250
This beautiful William and Mary house on the River Avon, was built in 1697 by Sir Roger Cave, ancestor of the present owner Lady Braye. The Ballroom is notable for its decoration and the chimney-piece and the house contains antique furniture, paintings (including the Stuart Collection) and family costumes. There is a replica of Percy Pilcher's flying machine of 1898. In the grounds are a walled rose garden, an old forge, and a motorcycle museum. A craft centre based in the old stables can be seen on most Sundays. Outdoor pursuits include fishing and a nature trail, and the large number of events arranged for 1995 includes car and motorcycle owners club rallies, National Hovercraft Racing Championships on 27-29 May and 26-28 August, the 13th Rugby Raft Races on 25 June and craft fairs on 16-17 April and 30 September-1 October.
Open Etr Sat-24 Sep, Sat, Sun, BH Mon & Tue following 2.30-6; noon on BH & Event Days (House 2.30). Last admission 5.30pm.
House & Grounds £3.20 (ch £1.50); Grounds only £1.80 (ch 70p); Motorcycle Museum £1 (ch 30p). Party 20+.
P ✆ & (museum also accessible) toilets for disabled shop ≉ (ex park)

Twycross Zoo Park
TWYCROSS
(1.5m NW off A444)
☎Tamworth (01827) 880250
Set up during the 1960s, Twycross Zoo Park specialises in primates, and also includes gibbons, gorillas, orang-utangs and chimpanzees. There is a huge range of monkeys from the tiny tamarins and spider monkeys to the large howler monkeys. There are also various other animals such as lions, tigers, elephants and giraffes, and a pets' corner for younger children.

➤

Dating from 1068 and modified through the ages, Lincoln Castle stands in fine grounds beside Lincoln Cathedral. The grounds are a focal point for events in the city.

Other attractions include a Sealion Pool with spectacular waterfall, Penguin Pool with underwater viewing and a Children's Adventure Playground.
Open all year, daily 10-6 (4 in winter). (Closed 25 Dec).
£4.50 (ch £2.50, pen £3). Party25+.
P 🏪 & *toilets for disabled shop* ⌘

LINCOLNSHIRE

Manor House Museum
ALFORD
West St
☎ (01507) 463073
This thatched 17th-century manor house is now a folk museum with local history displays: a chemist's shop, shoemaker's shop, school room, wash house and garden, photographic display, veterinary display and a nursery and maid's bedroom. There are also displays of agricultural and craft tools, sweet making equipment, a kitchen and even a police cell.
Open Etr-first Fri in Oct daily, Mon-Sat 10-5, Sun 1-4.30.
£1 (ch 50p).
P 🏪 *shop* ⌘

Belton House Park & Gardens
BELTON
(3m NE Grantham on A607)
☎ Grantham (01476) 66116
For many people Belton is the perfect country house, a handsome but not overwhelming grand mansion. It was the home of the Brownlow family for nearly three centuries before being given to the National Trust, and the family still has a flat in the house. The ground floor has a succession of state rooms, with the Marble Hall as its centrepiece. The name comes from the black and white marble floor, which is original. The walls are decorated with intricate wood carvings of birds, fruit, flowers and foliage, which have been attributed to Grinling Gibbons but are probably by Edmund Carpenter. There are more remarkable carvings in the formal saloon, which also has ornate plasterwork on the ceiling. Splendid furnishings and decorations throughout the house include tapestries and hangings, both old and modern, lovely garden scenes by Melchior d'Hondecoeter, family portraits, porcelain and fine furniture. Not to be forgotten are the rolling grounds and gardens, including an orangery and formal Italian garden, laid out in the 19th century. There are some attractive sculptures, and an adventure playground for children. In 1995 an open-air concert will be held on 24 June and Belton Horse Trials on 8-9 April.
Open Apr-Oct, Wed-Sun & BH Mon (Closed Good Fri). House open 1-5.30 (last admission 5pm). Grounds open 11-5.30.
£4.30 (ch £2.10). Family ticket £10.70.
P ✗ *licensed* & *toilets for disabled shop* ⌘ *(ex in grounds)*
(NT)

Battle of Britain Memorial Flight Visitor Centre
CONINGSBY
(on A153)
☎ (01526) 344041
View the aircraft of the Battle of Britain Memorial Flight, comprising the only flying Lancaster in Europe, five Spitfires, one Hurricane, DH Devon and a Chipmunk. Because of operational commitments, specific aircraft may not be available. Ring the telephone number given for information before planning a visit.
Open all year, Mon-Fri, conducted tours 10-3.30. (Closed BH's & 2 wks Xmas).
P & *toilets for disabled shop* ⌘
Details not confirmed for 1995

Old Hall
GAINSBOROUGH
Parnell St
☎ (01427) 612669
A complete medieval manor house dating back to 1460-80 and containing a remarkable Great Hall and original kitchen with room settings. Richard III, Henry VIII, the Mayflower Pilgrims and John Wesley all in their day visited the Old Hall. Special events during 1995 include craft fairs on 26 March and 25-26 November, a V E Day concert on 8 May, a medieval fair (27-28 August) and *Yesterday's Shopping*, an exhibition running from 7 October until 6 January.
Open all year, Mon-Sat 10-5; Etr-Oct, Sun 2-5.30.
£1.75 (ch & pen 95p)
P *(100 yds)* 🏪 & *(audio tour, induction loop) shop* ⌘

GRANTHAM
See Belvoir

Grimsthorpe Castle
GRIMSTHORPE
(8m E of A1 at Colsterworth on A151)
☎ Edenham (01778) 591205
An historic home occupied by the Willoughby de Eresby family since 1516. The architecture comprises a medieval tower and a Tudor quadrangular house with a Baroque north front by Vanbrugh. There are eight state rooms and two picture galleries with an important collection of furniture, pictures and tapestries. Formal gardens, parkland and lake. The Castle is now administered by the Grimsthorpe and Drummond Castle Trust.
Open 16 Apr-24 Sep, Sun, Thu & BH's. (24 Jul-7 Sep open Sun-Thu). Park 11-6, Castle & Gardens 2-5.30. (last admission 5pm). Dates and times to be confirmed. Free.
P 🏪 & *toilets for disabled shop*

The Pearoom
HECKINGTON
Station Yard (4m E of Sleaford, off A15)
☎ Sleaford (01529) 60765
The Pearoom has a craft shop, galleries and workshops for ten resident craft workers. Their products include pottery, leather work, toys, and prints; and also there is a musical instrument restorer, a weaver-feltmaker, and a textile designer-printer. An active programme of craft exhibitions runs throughout the year accompanied by a programme of weekend course activities. (For details telephone the Exhibition Officer). A commissioning centre was opened in 1993 showing the work of many local makers willing to work to commission. Members of the public are welcome to consult this register.
Open all year, Mon-Sat & BHs 10-5, Sun 12-5.
Free.
P 🏪 & *toilets for disabled shop* ⌘

City & County Museum
LINCOLN
Broadgate
☎ (01522) 530401
The county's main archaeology museum, housed in a magnificent medieval building, forms part of Greyfriars.
Open all year, Mon-Sat 10-5.30, Sun 2.30-5.30 (Oct-Mar last entry 5). (Closed Good Fri & Xmas).
& *shop* ⌘
Details not confirmed for 1995

Lincoln Castle
LINCOLN
Castle Hill
☎ (01522) 511068
Situated in the centre of Lincoln, the Castle, built in 1068 by William the Conqueror, dominates the Bailgate area alongside the great Cathedral. In addition to its many medieval features, Lincoln Castle has strong 19th-century connections and the unique Victorian prison chapel is perhaps the most awe-inspiring. The beautiful surroundings are ideal for historical adventures, picnics and special events which take place throughout the year. The Castle is now the home of the Magna Carta and there is a new exhibition interpreting and displaying this important document.
Open all year, British Summer Time Mon-Sat 9.30-5.30, Sun 11-5.30. Winter time Mon-Sat 9.30- 4, Sun 11-4. Last admission 30 mins before closing. (Closed 25-26 Dec & 1 Jan).
£2 (ch, concessions & pen £1.20).
P & *(video theatre also accessible) toilets for disabled shop* ⌘

Museum of Lincolnshire Life
LINCOLN
Burton Rd
☎ (01522) 528448
The region's largest and most varied social history museum where the past two centuries of Lincolnshire life are illustrated by displays of domestic implements, industrial machinery, agricultural tools and a collection of horse-drawn vehicles. The Royal Lincolnshire Regiment museum is also housed here. A full list of events and temporary exhibitions is available on request.
Open all year, May-Sep, daily 10-5.30; Oct-Apr, Mon-Sat 10-5.30, Sun 2-5.30.
£1 (ch 50p). From Apr £1.20 (ch 60p).
P 🏪 & *(wheelchair available, parking space) toilets for disabled shop* ⌘

National Cycle Museum
LINCOLN
The Lawn, Union Rd
☎ (01522) 545091
The National Cycle Museum houses the premier collection of cycles and cycling artefacts in the country, with over 100 cycles on display and related artefacts, including photographs, medals, trophies and more.
Open all year, daily 10-5 (Closed Xmas wk).
£1 (ch under 5, ch 5-16, pen & students 50p)
P *(charged)* & *(lift to all floors) toilets for disabled shop* ⌘

Usher Gallery
LINCOLN
Lindum Rd
☎ (01522) 527980
Built as the result of a bequest by Lincoln jeweller, James Ward Usher, the Gallery houses his magnificent collection of

watches, porcelain and miniatures, as well as topographical works, watercolours by Peter de Wint, Tennyson memorabilia and coins. As the country's main visual arts venue, the Gallery also has an active exhibitions and 'outreach' programme; events to take place during 1995 include a major retrospective celebrating forty years of work by the Lincolnshire-based artist Barbara Balmer (from mid-April until mid-June) and an exhibition of the county costume collection (from July until mid-October).
Open all year, Mon-Sat 10-5.30, Sun 2.30-5. (Closed Good Fri, Xmas & 1 Jan).
£1 (ch & students 50p). Free on Fri.
P ⚑ ♿ *toilets for disabled shop* ⚘

LONG SUTTON
see **Spalding**

Church Farm Museum
SKEGNESS
Church Rd South
☎ *(01754) 766658*
A farmhouse and outbuildings that have been restored to show the way of life on a Lincolnshire farm at the end of the 19th century, with farm implements and machinery plus household equipment on display. A timber-framed cottage and a barn have been re-erected. In the barn there is a temporary exhibition and, at weekends during the summer, craftsmen give demonstrations. Special events for 1995 include a V E Day Cook Up (8 May) and Steam Threshing (1 October), and there are also school activity days.
Open Apr-Oct, daily 10.30-5.30
£1 (ch 50p).
P ⚑ ♿ *(wheelchair available) toilets for disabled shop* ⚘

Skegness Natureland Seal Sanctuary
SKEGNESS
North Pde
☎ *(01754) 764345*
Natureland houses a specialised collection of animals including seals, penguins, tropical birds, aquarium, reptiles, pets' corner etc. Also free-flight tropical butterflies (May-Oct). Natureland is well known for its rescue of abandoned seal pups, and has successfully reared and returned to the wild a large number of these beautiful creatures. The new seal hospital unit incorporates a public viewing area, and a large new seascape seal pool (with underwater viewing) should be ready for Easter. Additional attractions include the Sea Life Exhibition, floral displays and an animal brass rubbing house.
Open all year, daily at 10am. Closing times vary according to season. (Closed 25-26 Dec & 1 Jan).
✳*£2.95 (ch £1.95, pen £2.45). Party.*
P *(100 yds)* ⚑ ♿ *shop*

Butterfly & Falconry Park
SPALDING
Long Sutton (off A17)
☎*Holbeach (01406) 363833 & 363209*
The Park contains one of Britain's largest walk-through tropical houses, in which hundreds of butterflies from all over the world fly freely. Outside are 15 acres of butterfly and bee gardens, wildflower meadows, wildfowl and conservation ponds, nature trail, farm animals, a pets' corner and a large adventure playground. At the Falconry Centre, falcons, hawks and owls can be seen, and there are daily falconry displays at 12 noon and 3pm. A farm museum opened in 1994, and 1995 will see the addition of an iguana den and an ant room where visitors can observe leaf-cutting ants in their natural working habitat. 'The Animal Magic Dog Display Team' can be seen every weekend and on Bank Holiday Mondays, and there will be a medieval weekend 22-23 July..
Open 25 Mar-29 Oct, daily 10-6, Oct 10-5.
£3.60 (ch 3-16 £2.40, pen £3.20). Family ticket £10-£12. Party.
P ✘ ♿ *(wheelchairs available) toilets for*

disabled shop garden centre ⚘

Springfields Gardens
SPALDING
Camelgate (1m E on A151, signposted)
☎*(01775) 724843*
The 25-acre gardens provide an amazing spectacle in the spring when thousands of bulbs are blooming among the lawns and lakes. There is a glasshouse and a bedding display with over 50,000 plants during the summer season. Special events for 1995 include: Springfields Horticultural Exhibition (2-5 February), Easter Craft Festival (16-17 April), Spalding Flower Festival and Country Fair (6-8 May). Please telephone for details of these and other events.
Open 24 Mar-1 Oct, daily 10-6.
£2.50 (accompanied ch free, pen £2.30). Prices vary for special events.
P ⚑ ✘ *licensed* ♿ *(free wheelchair hire) toilets for disabled shop garden centre* ⚘

Burghley House
STAMFORD
(1m SE off A1)
☎*(01780) 52451*
This great Elizabethan palace was built by William Cecil, Queen Elizabeth I's first minister, and has all the hallmarks of that ostentatiously wealthy period. The vast house is three storeys high and on the roof is a riot of pinnacles, cupolas and paired chimneys in classic Tudor style. However, inside there is very little of the Tudor period in evidence, as (apart from the kitchen) the house was restyled between 1680 and 1700. The state rooms are now Baroque, with silver fireplaces, elaborate plasterwork and painted ceilings. These were painted by Antonio Verrio, whose finest achievement here is the Heaven Room. The walls of the rooms are hung with superb tapestries and with pictures from the largest private collection of Italian Old Masters.
The grounds were landscaped during the 18th century by 'Capability' Brown and each year, in September, international horse trials are held.
Special events for 1995 include a fireworks and laser concert in the park on 29 July (booking office 01625 573477) and the Burghley Horse Trials (31 August-3 September).
Open Apr-8 Oct, daily 11-5. (Closed 2 Sep).
£5.10 (ch free with one paying adult, pen £4.80). Party 20+.
P ✘ *licensed* ♿ *(chairlift access to restaurant) toilets for disabled shop* ⚘

Stamford Museum
STAMFORD
Broad St
☎*(01780) 66317*
The museum illustrates the history and archaeology of Stamford. Perhaps the most unusual exhibits are the clothes of Daniel Lambert (1770-1809), one of only three men in Britain recorded as weighing over 50 stone (317kg). These are displayed with the clothes of American midget, General Tom Thumb, who was 3ft 4in (102cm) when he died.
Open all year, Apr-Sep, Mon-Sat 10-5, Sun 2-5; Oct-Mar Mon-Sat 10-5.
50p (ch 25p).
P ♿ *shop*

Stamford Steam Brewery Museum
STAMFORD
All Saints St
☎*(01780) 52186*
An authentic steam brewery, with mash tuns, coppers, fermenting vessels and a steam engine. With the aid of an automatic sound system and illustrations of Victorian working life, visitors are given an insight into the activities of a 19th-century brewery employee.
Open Mar-Oct, Wed-Fri 10-4, Sat & Sun 10-6. Also BH Mar-Oct. (Closed Wed during BH weeks).
P ♿ *shop*
Details not confirmed for 1995

Tattershall Castle
TATTERSHALL
☎*Coningsby (01526) 342543*

This large fortified house was built in 1440 by Ralph Cromwell, Treasurer of England, and has a keep 100ft high. On each of the four storeys is a fine heraldic chimneypiece: these were sold at one point, but were rescued from export in 1911. There is also a museum in the guardhouse. A Gilbert and Sullivan concert will take place on 15 July this year.
Open Apr-Oct, Sat-Wed & BH Mons (closed Good Fri) 10.30-5.30. Nov-17 Dec, Sat & Sun only 10.30-4.
£2.20 (ch £1.10). Family ticket £5.50.
P ♿ *toilets for disabled shop* ⚘
(NT)

Woolsthorpe Manor
WOOLSTHORPE
(7m S of Grantham, 1m W of A1)
☎*Grantham (01476) 860338*
A fine stone-built, 17th-century farmhouse which was the birthplace of the scientist and philosopher Sir Isaac Newton, in 1642. He also lived at the house from 1665-66 during the Plague, after his time as an undergraduate at Cambridge. An early edition of his *Principia Mathematica* (1687) is in the house.
Open Apr-Oct, Wed-Sun & BH Mon 1-5.30. (closed Good Fri).
✳*£2.30 (ch £1.10). Family ticket £5.70.*
P ⚘
(NT)

LONDON CENTRAL

LONDON
London is very much a city for exploring. It is rich in history, full of pageantry and culture to suit all tastes, with beautiful shops and parks, characterful pubs and cosmopolitan population. London is served by the largest underground network in the world, but to really see London, there are tours by double-decker bus, or by boat along the canals or the River Thames or, for the truly adventurous, by helicopter. The River Thames is at the heart of London's history from Henry VIII's magnificent Hampton Court Palace in the west, passing the centre of British Government, the Houses of Parliament, then past the City, St Paul's, the Tower and under Tower Bridge. On through London's famous docklands to the great palace at Greenwich in the east. Londoners love pageantry and there is some parade or spectacle almost daily, such as the Lord Mayor's Show, the State Opening of Parliament or the Changing of the Guard at Buckingham Palace. There are magnificent churches such as St Paul's Cathedral, the Byzantine-style Westminster Cathedral and Westminster Abbey, on a site occupied by a church for over 1300 years. In a city with 40 museums and nearly as many art gallleries, over 20 theatres and 30 street markets, a welcome break from the bustle can be found in the hundreds of acres of city parks that make London possibly the greenest capital city in the world.

Agnew's
W1
43 Old Bond St (Underground - Green Park)
☎*0171-629 6176*
If you happen to be shopping for Old Masters, then Thomas Agnew & Son's Ltd is the place to visit. They have a worldwide reputation for exhibiting some of the finest Old Master paintings and drawings, and many works pass through their hands on their way to famous art galleries and museums. Some contemporary English works are also displayed.
➤

The Banqueting House was designed in 1618 for court masques. The spectacular ceiling was painted by Peter Paul Rubens.

Open Mon-Fri, 9.30-5.30, 6.30 on Thu. (Closed BH).
Free ex for some loan exhibitions
P (Arlington St & Saville Row) & ⟡

Bank of England Museum
EC2 ▉
Threadneedle St
☎0171-601 5545
The Museum is housed within the Bank of England itself, right at the heart of the City of London. It traces the history of the Bank from its foundation by Royal Charter in 1694 to its role today as the nation's central bank. There are gold bars from ancient times to the modern market bar, coins and a unique collection of banknotes, as well as pikes and muskets once used to defend the Bank. Documents relating to famous customers such as the Duchess of Marlborough, George Washington and Horatio Nelson, are displayed. The 18th-century Bank Stock Office, designed by Sir John Soane, has been reconstructed and two award-winning interactive systems allow visitors to look behind the doors of The Bank or observe the intricacies of banknote design.
Open Mon-Fri 10-5. (Closed wknds & BH's).
Free.
P & (advance notice helpful) toilets for disabled shop

Banqueting House
SW1 ▉
Whitehall (Underground - Westminster)
☎0171-839 8918
A building which has seen many historic events including the execution of Charles I, the restoration of Charles II and the offer of the throne to William of Orange and Princess Mary. It was the centre of 17th-century London court life and has a sumptuous interior, enriched by Rubens' painted ceiling. The only surviving part of the original Palace of Whitehall, it was designed by Inigo Jones and built in 1619. In 1992 the undercroft was opened to the public for the first time. This houses a video presentation (lasting 17 1/2 minutes) and a small exhibition of 'curiosities' connected with the building.

Open all year, Mon-Sat 10-5. (Closed Good Fri, 23 Dec-2 Jan & BH's). Liable to close at short notice for Government functions.
£2.90 (ch £1.90, students, pen & disabled £2.20).
& toilets for disabled shop

Bramah Tea & Coffee Museum
SE1 ▉
The Clove Building, Butler's Wharf (Underground - London Bridge & Tower Hill)
☎0171-378 0222
The museum tells the fascinating and informative story of the history of the tea and coffee trade carried on in this area for 350 years. A collection of over 1,000 teapots and coffee makers illustrate the many ways that tea and coffee have been made and served. Other displays include expresso machines from the 1950s, advertisements for instant coffee and information on the development of the filter machine. Also on display are 'tetsubin' tea kettles and a 'Raku' tea master bowl, used in the elaborate Japanese Tea Ceremony. Visitors can buy tea and coffee from the museum to take home as a souvenir of their visit.
Open all year, daily 10-6. (Closed 25 & 26 Dec).
✳£3 (ch 14, students, pen, UB40 & disabled £1.50). Group 10+
🅿 (charged) ⛴ & toilets for disabled shop

British Museum
WC1 ▉
Great Russell St (Underground - Russell Sq,Tottenham Court Rd)
☎0171-580 1788 (recorded information)
& 0171-323 8599
The stern façade of the British Museum belies the rich and varied treasures within which make it one of the great museums of the world, showing the works of man from many civilisations, from prehistoric to comparatively recent times. Founded in 1753, the nucleus of the museum was the collections of Sir Hans Sloane and Sir Robert Cotton. The galleries are the responsibility of the following departments: Egyptian, Greek and Roman, Western Asiatic, Japanese, Prehistoric and Romano-British, Medieval and later, Coins and Medals, Oriental, Prints and Drawings, and Ethnography (based at the Museum of Mankind). The museum also displays famous books and manuscripts from the British Library collections. The original building, Montagu House was demolished, and Sir Robert Smirke commissioned to build a more suitable replacement on the site, which was completed in 1852; the famous domed Reading Room was added in 1857. Among the treasures not to be missed are the Egyptian mummies, the notorious and superb Elgin marbles, two of the four existing copies of the Magna Carta, Shakespeare's signature, Nelson's plan of the Battle of Trafalgar and the Sutton Hoo treasure. There is a regular programme of gallery talks, lectures and films, and young visitors can enjoy special children's trails.
Open all year, Mon-Sat 10-5, Sun 2.30-6. (Closed Good Fri, May Day, Xmas & 1 Jan).
Free.
⛴ ✕ licensed & (parking by arrangement; touch tour for visually impaired) toilets for disabled shop

BT Museum Story of Telecommunications
EC4 ▉
145 Queen Victoria St (Underground - Blackfriars)
☎0171-248 7444
A fascinating exhibition featuring the past, present and future of Britain's telecommunications. The many working exhibits chart 200 years of progress from the earliest telegraphs to satellites and optical fibres. Examples of the different styles of domestic telephones through the decades are displayed among the collection of interesting exhibits.
Open all year, Mon-Fri 10-5. (Closed BH). Also open Lord Mayors Show day.
Free.
P (100yds) & (inductive loops) shop

Buckingham Palace
SW1 ▉
Buckingham Palace Rd (Underground - Victoria, Green Park)
☎0171-839 1377
Buckingham Palace is the official London residence of Her Majesty The Queen, whose persoanl standard flies when Her Majesty is in residence. Each August and September the State Rooms are open to visitors. These principle rooms, which form the backdrop to the pageantry of court ceremonial and official entertaining, occupy the main west front overlooking the garden and are all opulently decorated with the finest pictures and works of art from the Royal Collection.
Aug & Sep, specific dates & times under review.
Admission prices under review at present.
P (200yds) & (except gardens) toilets for disabled shop

Cabaret Mechanical Theatre
WC2 ▉
33/34 The Market, Covent Garden (Underground - Covent Garden)
☎0171-379 7961
The museum offers entertainment for the whole family here with an impressive collection of Automata. Buy a ticket in the foyer area, get it stamped by the mechanical stamping man and enter the magical world of Cabaret, where at the touch of a button or the insertion of a coin, machines are set in motion. The collection includes work by Paul Spooner, Ron Fuller and Tim Hunkin.
Open all year, Tue-Sat 10-6.30, Sun 11-6.30, Mon 12-6.30; school holidays daily 10-7. (Closed 25 & 26 Dec & 1 Jan).
£1.95 (ch, students, pen & UB40's £1.20). Family ticket £4.95.
P & toilets for disabled

Cabinet War Rooms
SW1

Clive Steps, King Charles St (Underground - Westminster)
☎0171-930 6961
The underground emergency accommodation provided to protect the Prime Minister, Winston Churchill, his War Cabinet and the Chiefs of Staff during the Second World War provide a fascinating insight into those tense days and nights. Among the 21 rooms are the Cabinet Room, the Map Room (where information about operations on all fronts was collected) and the Prime Minister's room, which have been carefully preserved since the end of the war. Other rooms have been restored to their original appearance.
Open all year, daily 10-6. Last admission 5.15 (Closed 24-26 Dec).
✽*£3.90 (ch £1.90, students £2.80). Party 10+.*
& *toilets for disabled shop* ⊗

Carlyle's House
SW3

24 Cheyne Row (Underground - Sloane Square)
☎0171-352 7087
'The Sage of Chelsea' - distinguished essayist and writer of historical works, Thomas Carlyle - lived in this 18th-century town house from 1834 until his death in 1881. His soundproofed study and the kitchen, where such literary notables as Tennyson, Thackeray and Browning were entertained have been preserved exactly as the Carlyles knew them. Special events planned for 1995 include the centenary of the house bing opened to the public in July and the bi-centenary of Thomas Carlyle's birth in December.
Open Apr-Oct, Wed-Sun & BH Mons 11-5. Last admission 4.30. (Closed Good Fri)
£2.90. No parties over 20 persons.
P *(street metered)* ⊗ ⊞
(NT)

Chelsea Physic Garden
SW3

66 Royal Hospital Rd, (entrance in Swan Walk) (Underground - Sloane Square)
☎0171-352 5646
The second oldest botanic garden in England was begun in 1673 for the study of plants used in medicine by the Society of Apothecaries. By the late 18th century it was famous throughout Europe for its rare and unusual plants, and it is still used for botanical and medicinal research. For the visitor it offers displays of many fascinating plants, and is an oasis of peace and quiet amidst.the hubbub of Chelsea. There will be an exhibition of the history of botanical illustration from the 3rd week in July to the 3rd week in September.
Open Apr-Oct, Wed 2-5, Sun 2-6. Additional opening during Chelsea Flower Show week, 22-26 May & Chelsea Festival week 5-9 Jun, 12-5. Groups at other times by appointment.
£3.50 (ch 16, students & unemployed £1.80).

P *(west end of Battersea Park)* ⅃ &
(disabled parking) toilets for disabled shop garden centre ⊗

Commonwealth Institute
W8

Kensington High St (Underground - High Street Kensington)
☎0171-603 4535
Discover the history, landscapes, wildlife, crafts and economies of the 51 countries of the Commonwealth on three floors of spectacular galleries, where you can visit the Caribbean, see Canada from a skidoo, climb up Mount Kenya or take a rickshaw across Bangladesh. There are also cultural events and exhibitions as well as educational programmes and special activity sheets for children, and holiday workshops. The Commonwealth Shop sells gifts and crafts from around the world.
Open all year, Mon-Sat 10-5, Sun 2-5. (Closed Good Fri, May Day, 24-26 Dec & 1 Jan).
✽*£1 (concessions 50p).*
P *(500yds)* ⅃ ✗ *licensed* & *(lift from car park, advance notice required) toilets for disabled shop* ⊗

Contemporary Applied Arts
WC2

43 Earlham St, Covent Garden (Underground - Covent Garden, Leicester Sq)
☎0171-836 6993
Contemporary Applied Arts is a professional association of craftspeople whose aims include making available the best contemporary craftwork to the public and collectors. The gallery holds several exhibitions a year, from solo and small group shows to larged mixed exhibitions. The basement shop has a constantly changing display including ceramics, glass, furniture, jewellery, textiles, wood and metal. The commissioning service arranges commissions for corporate and private clients. Special events planned for 1995 include: Green Wood (April-May), Enchanted Garden (July-August), Clothes to Collect (October).
Open all year, Mon-Sat 10-6 (7 on Thu). (Closed Sun, BHs & 25 Dec-9 Jan). Free.
& ⊗

Courtauld Institute Galleries
WC2

Somerset House, Strand (Underground - Temple, Embankment)
☎0171-873 2526
The Galleries moved from the Woburn Square premises in March 1990 and opened at Somerset House on 15th June 1990. They contain the superb collection of paintings begun by Samuel Courtauld in the 1920s and 1930s and presented to the University of London in memory of his wife. This is the most important collection of Impressionist and post-Impressionist works in Britain and includes paintings by Monet, Renoir, Degas, Cézanne, Van Gogh and Gauguin.

There are also works by Michelangelo, Rubens, Goya, and other notable Masters, as well as early Italian paintings. British and French 20th-century works given to the University by Roger Fry are also displayed here. Exhibitions are changed regularly.
Open all year, Mon-Sat 10-6, Sun 2-6. (Closed 24-26 Dec & 1 Jan). £3 (ch, pen & students £1.50).
⅃ & *(parking arranged, lift) toilets for disabled shop* ⊗

Cuming Museum
SE17

155-157 Walworth Rd (Underground - Elephant & Castle)
☎0171-701 1342
The museum of Southwark's history. The worldwide collections of the Cuming family joined with the local history of Southwark, from Roman times through the days of Chaucer, Shakespeare and Dickens to the present day. Special exhibitions on local themes.
Open all year, Tue-Sat 10-5. School & adult parties daily by appointment. (Closed BH's & Sat of BH wknd).
P *(20yds) shop* ⊗
Details not confirmed for 1995

Design Museum
SE1

Butler's Wharf, Shad Thames (Underground - London Bridge)
☎0171-403 6933
A museum of everyday objects situated in the Butler's Wharf conservation area. It is the first of its kind to show design in mass production and in the context of our lives. Special events for 1995 include Frank Lloyd Wright in Chicago (4 May-October) and Chief Cook and Bottle Washer: Paul Smith (October 1995-April 1996).
Open all year, Mon-Fri 11.30-6, Sat & Sun 12-6.
✽*£4.50 (concessions £3.50)*
🅿 *(charged)* ⅃ ✗ *licensed* & *toilets for disabled shop* ⊗

Dickens House
WC1

48 Doughty St (Underground - Russell Square)
☎0171-405 2127
Charles Dickens lived in Doughty Street in his twenties and it was here he worked on his first full-length novel, *The Pickwick Papers* and later *Oliver Twist* and *Nicholas Nickelby*, celebrated for their acute observation of society on all levels, and their sympathy for the often unfortunate characters. Pages of the original manuscripts of Dickens's books are on view together with valuable first editions, his special marriage licence and many other personal mementoes. Dickens' drawing room has been reconstructed.
Open all year, Mon-Sat 10-5, last admission 4.30pm. (Closed Sun & Xmas).
✽*£3 (ch under 16 £1, pen & students £2). Family ticket £6.*
& *shop* ⊗

Dr Johnson's House
EC4

17 Gough Square (Underground - Temple, Blackfriars)
☎0171-353 3745
The celebrated literary figure, Dr Samuel Johnson, lived at 17 Gough Square between 1749 and 1759. It was here that he wrote his English Dictionary, and a first edition is on display at the house. The dictionary took eight and a half years to complete and contained 40,000 words. (He then undertook the formidable task of editing the complete works of Shakespeare.).
The house in Gough Square, tucked away behind Fleet Street, is a handsome example of early 18th-century architecture. It was opened as a museum in 1912 and exhibits include a fine collection of prints, letters and other memorabilia from the life of a man who was to become the most quoted Englishman after Shakespeare.
Open all year, May-Sep, daily 11-5.30; Oct-Apr 11-5. (Closed Sun, BH's, Good Fri & 24 Dec).
✽*£3 (ch £1, under 10 free, students & pen £2).*
shop ⊗

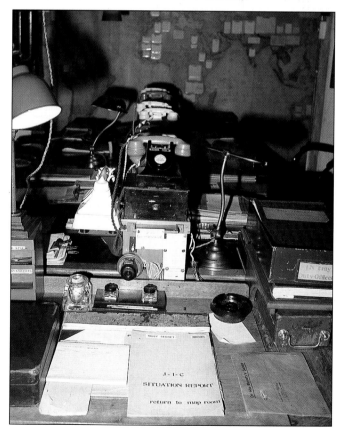

An underground complex in the heart of London forms the Cabinet War Rooms where the Government controlled Britain's defence in WWII.

Florence Nightingale Museum
SE1

2 Lambeth Palace Rd (Underground - Westminster, Waterloo)
☎0171-620 0374
Florence Nightingale needs no introduction, but this museum shows clearly that she was more than 'The Lady with the Lamp'. Beautifully designed, the museum creates a personal setting in which are displayed Florence's prized possessions, a lamp from the Crimean War and nursing artefacts. The centrepiece is a recreated ward scene from the Crimea and audio-visual technology takes the museum beyond its four walls. Set on the site of the first School of Nursing, this museum is an interesting experience, showing the continued relevance of this remarkable woman.
Open all year, Tue-Sun 10-4 (last admission). (Closed Xmas, 1 Jan, Good Fri & Etr Sun).
🅿 *(charged)* 🍴 ♿ *toilets for disabled shop*
Details not confirmed for 1995

Green Park
SW1

(Underground - Green Park)
The smallest of the central London parks, Green Park is aptly named, for the Tyburn stream runs just below the surface, maintaining its lush verdancy. It is situated in the triangle formed by Piccadilly, The Mall and Constitution Hill (where Charles II used to take his constitutional stroll) and was formerly meadowland. This informal character is still maintained today, for there are no flower borders here - just the springtime crocuses and daffodils which grow among the grass.

The Guildhall
EC2

Gresham St (Underground - Bank, St Paul's)
☎0171-606 3030
The Court of Common Council (presided over by the Lord Mayor) administers the City of London and meets in the Guildhall. Dating from 1411, when the Livery Companies raised money for its construction, the building was badly damaged in the Great Fire and again in the Blitz. The great hall, traditionally used for the Lord Mayor's Banquet and other important civic functions, is impressively decorated with the banners and shields of the livery companies, of which there are more than 90. Beneath it lies a 15th-century crypt, the largest of its kind in London. The Clock Museum, which has a collection of 700 exhibits, charts the history of 500 years of time-keeping. The Guildhall Library has an unrivalled collection of manuscripts, books and illustrations on all aspects of the capital city.
Open all year, May-Sep, daily 10-5; Oct-Apr, Mon-Sat 10-5. (Closed Xmas, New Year, Good Fri, Etr Mon & infrequently for Civic occasions).
♿ *shop*
Details not confirmed for 1995

Guinness World of Records Exhibition
W1

The Trocadero, Coventry St, Piccadilly Circus (Underground - Piccadilly Circus)
☎0171-439 7331
Through the use of life-sized models, videos and the latest audio-technology, thousands of world records come alive at the touch of a button. Six themed areas depict: the Human World, the Animal World, Our Planet Earth, Structures and Machines, the Sports World and the World of Entertainment.
Visitors can watch original newsreel footage whilst measuring up to the world's tallest man; select their choice of sporting records from the Sports Recall Data Bank; watch an exciting chronicle of man's exploration of space; listen to the songs that sold millions on a 50's style juke box, and much more.
Open all year, daily 10am-10pm (last admission). (Closed 25 Dec).
✳£5.75 (ch 4-16 £3.75, under 5 free, pen & students £4.50). Group 10+. Prices under review.
P ♿ *toilets for disabled shop*

HMS Belfast
SE1

Morgans Ln, Tooley St (Underground - London Bridge)
☎0171-407 6434
Europe's last surviving big gun, armoured warship from World War II, *HMS Belfast* was launched in 1938 and served in the North Atlantic with the Home Fleet. She led the Allied naval bombardment of naval positions on D-Day, and was saved for the nation in 1971. There are special events for children at Easter, over the summer holidays and the October half term.
Open all year, daily. Mar-Oct 10-6, last admission 5.15; Nov-28 Feb 10-5, last admission 4.15. (Closed 24-26 Dec).
£4 (ch £2, students & pen £3). Prices under review. Party.
P (150yds) 🍴 ♿ (wheelchair lift for access on board) toilets for disabled shop ♿

Houses of Parliament
SW1

Westminster (Underground - Westminster)
☎0171-219 4272
From the time of Edward the Confessor to Henry VIII, the site of the present-day Houses of Parliament was the main residence of the monarch. Hence the often-used term the 'Palace of Westminster'. It was not until Henry VIII moved to Whitehall Palace in 1529 that the building was turned over to state institutions. A disastrous fire in 1834 destroyed most of the medieval palace and a competition was held for the design of a new Parliament building; Charles Barry was awarded the commission with his Gothic-style design (although Pugin was responsible for much of the decorative detail). Today the building stands at 940ft long, covers eight acres and includes 1100 apartments. There are over two miles of passages. To the south stands the lofty Victoria Tower where the Union Jack flies when Parliament is in session. At the north end of the building is the clock tower which contains Big Ben, the 13½-ton hour bell.
Telephone well in advance for information on how to go about arranging permits for a tour of the building, or to listen to debates from the Strangers Gallery.
Free but guides require payment if used.
♿ *(by arrangement) toilets for disabled shop (bookstall)* ♿ 🚻

Hyde Park
W2

(Underground - Hyde Park Corner, Marble Arch)
Situated to the west of Park Lane, between Knightsbridge and Bayswater, and formerly a Royal hunting park, Hyde Park now consists of 340 acres of grass and trees, intersected by paths. The Serpentine, at its centre, provides a habitat for wild creatures which cannot find sanctuary elsewhere in the city centre. It was the venue for the Great Exhibition in 1851, but is probably best known for Speakers' Corner, near Marble Arch, where, every Sunday, anyone can stand up and say just what they please.

Imperial War Museum
SE1

Lambeth Rd (Underground - Lambeth North)
☎0171-416 5000
Founded in 1917 and established in 1920 by an Act of Parliament, this museum illustrates and records all aspects of the two World Wars and other military operations involving Britain and the Commonwealth since 1914. It has recently undergone major renovations and although the vast collections are still housed within the imposing walls of the original building in Lambeth Road, it is now a thoroughly modern museum employing all the latest technology to make its exhibitions more vital and atmospheric for the visitor.
Improvements include a new, large exhibition hall, art galleries and a shop and licensed restaurant. There are always special exhibitions and the programme of events includes film shows and lectures. The Imperial War Museum has a wealth of military reference material, although some reference departments are open to the public by appointment only. Special exhibitions during 1995 include: Fashion on the Ration (4-6 May), Victory Film Season (March-28 August), Victory in the Far East (opening August).
Open all year, daily 10-6. (Closed 24-26 Dec).
£3.90 (ch 5-16 £1.95, students, UB40 & pen £2.90).

Kensington Gardens were once the garden to Kensington Palace and are noted for their tranquillity. An arch by sculptor Henry Moore provides a modern note.

IMPERIAL WAR MUSEUM
The Museum of twentieth century conflict.
Lambeth Road, London SE1 6HZ

IMPERIAL WAR MUSEUM

OPEN DAILY
10.00AM-6.00PM
For information telephone
0171 416 5321

HMS BELFAST
The last of the Royal Navy's big gun armoured warships.
Morgan's Lane,
Tooley Street,
London SE1 2JH

DUXFORD AIRFIELD
A preserved wartime fighter base, now Europe's top aviation museum.
Duxford,
Nr Cambridge,
CB2 4QR

CABINET WAR ROOMS
Churchill's underground HQ in central London.
Clive Steps, King Charles Street, London SW1A 2AQ

P *(metered)* 🍴 ♿ *(disabled parking sometimes available at museum) toilets for disabled shop* ✂

Kensington Gardens
W8
(Underground - Queensway, Lancaster Gate)
This was part of Hyde Park until William III enclosed his palace gardens and today, again, the two areas are not physically divided. A change of character is apparent, though, once you cross the invisible boundary which runs from north to south across the Serpentine Bridge. Kensington Gardens are noted for their tranquility and formality and include the Round Pond, Queen Anne's Orangery, the Sunken Garden and Flower Walk.

Kensington Palace State Apartments & Royal Ceremonial Dress Collection
W8
Kensington Gardens (Underground - High Street Kensington)
☎0171-937 9561
The birthplace of Queen Victoria and today the London residence of the Prince and Princess of Wales, Princess Margaret and Prince and Princess Michael of Kent, Kensington Palace looks out over lovely gardens and an expanse of green parkland. When the house was bought by William III in 1689, it was a more modest town house. He commissioned Sir Christopher Wren to remodel the building and it was enlarged again and decorated by William Kent for George I. It was the principal private royal residence until George II died. The State Apartments display pictures and furniture from the Royal Collection and there is a section on the Great Exhibition. The colourful Royal Ceremonial Robe Collection exhibits some of the magnificent costumes worn at court from 1750 onwards.
Open all year daily; Mar-Oct 9-5, Sun 11-5; (Closed Good Fri, 24-26 Dec & 1 Jan). The Palace will close for major refurbishment in Sep 1995 for approx 18 mths.
£4.50 (ch 16 £3, students, pen & disabled £3.40). Family ticket £12.50.
P 🍴 ♿ *toilets for disabled shop* ✂

Leighton House Museum & Art Gallery
W14
12 Holland Park Rd (Underground - High Street Kensington)
☎0171-602 3316
A uniquely opulent and exotic example of High Victorian taste, Leighton House was built for the President of the Royal Academy, Frederic Lord Leighton, by George Aitchison. The main body of the house was built in 1866 but the fabulous Arab Hall, an arresting 'Arabian Nights' creation, was not completed until 13 years later. The hall is decorated with gilt, ancient tiles from the Middle East and a fountain. Leighton was one of the great Victorian artists, and much of his work is displayed here, along with that of his contemporaries.
Open all year, daily 11-5.30. Garden open Apr-Sep 11-5. (Closed Sun & BH).
Donations
✂

Linley Sambourne House
W8
18 Stafford Ter (Underground - High Street Kensington)
☎0181-994 1019
The home of Linley Sambourne (1844-1910), chief political cartoonist at *Punch*, has had its magnificent artistic interior preserved, almost unchanged, since the late 19th century. Also displayed are many of Sambourne's own drawings and photographs.
Open Mar-Oct, Wed 10-4, Sun 2-5.
£3. (ch 16 £1.50).
P *shop* ✂

London Dungeon
SE1
28-34 Tooley St (Underground - London Bridge)
☎0171-403 0606
The London Dungeon has won the British Tourist Authority's Award for Outstanding Tourist Enterprise. Its modest entrance off a street near London Bridge station will lead the visitor through to a series of slimy vaults where the seamy side of life in past centuries is convincingly re-created. Methods of torture and death, the tools of witchcraft and black magic and some of the more grisly medicinal practices are well represented. Viewing takes about 2 hours; this museum is not recommended for the faint-hearted.
Entry includes the 'Theatre of the Guillotine' show which uses the latest in interactive technology, and the 'Jack the Ripper' show, which presents a 20 minute tour through Jack's Victorian Whitechapel. Several new themed areas and 'shocks' are planned for 1995.
Open all year, daily, Apr-Sep 10-5.30; Oct-Mar 10-4.30.
£6.95 (ch 14 £4, pen & students £5.50).
P *(NCP 200yds)* 🍴 ♿ *toilets for disabled shop* ✂

London Planetarium
NW1
Marylebone Rd (Underground - Baker Street)
☎0171-486 1121
Star shows are performed every 40 minutes throughout the day and visitors can experience a 3 dimensional journey through space. 'Space Station' levels 1, 2 and 3 provide up-to-date information about the stars and planets through touch-sensitive screens. Children under five are not admitted to the Planetarium. Special events are held throughout the year.
Open Etr 1995 after redevelopment, daily (ex 25 Dec), star shows from 12.20, every 40 mins (earlier during wknds & holidays).
£4.20 (ch 16 £2.60, pen £3.25). Family ticket £11.
P ♿ *toilets for disabled shop* ✂

London Toy & Model Museum
W2
21-23 Craven Hill (Underground - Bayswater)
☎0171-706 8000
Having been extensively redeveloped the London Toy and Model Museum reopened in April 1995. There are 21 themed galleries which include an Edwardian railway station with a full scale model of an engine where children can pretend to drive the train. The themed galleries even have sounds and smells to create the atmosphere. The mock-up of an Edwardian Nursery features replicas of Victorian games and toys which children can play with. The oldest toy is a Roman gladiator doll made 2000 years ago. A fascinating display of over 7000 exhibits including detailed working models, villages, railways and funfairs. There are vintage roundabout and train rides for the children in the delightful garden. Special events are planned for 1995 including a 'Whatever Next' gallery featuring the very latest toys before they are even on sale in the UK. There are hands-on workshops for schools.
Open all year, daily 10-5.30.(Closed 25 Dec & 1 Jan).
Prices under review.
P 🍴 ♿ *shop* ✂

London Transport Museum
WC2
The Piazza, Covent Garden (Underground - Covent Garden, Leicester Sq)
☎0171-379 6344 & 0171-836 8557
Set in the heart of Covent Garden, the new London Transport Museum tells the story of London's famous transport system and its effect on the growth of the capital and on people's lives for nearly 200 years. Visitors will discover fascinating collections of buses, trams, trains, posters and photographs. Hands-

on exhibits, videos and touch screen interactive displays bring the story to life - visitors can even put themselves in the driving seat of a London bus or tube train. A full programme of events, activities and temporary exhibitions includes, for 1995, Designed for London (May-December). There is a large shop, cafe and information centre.
Open all year, daily 10-6. Last admission 5.15pm. (Closed 24-26 Dec).
£3.95 (concessions £2.50). Family ticket £10. Party.
P *(5 mins walk)* 🍴 ♿ *toilets for disabled shop* ✂ *guide dogs*

Madame Tussaud's
NW1
Marylebone Rd (Underground - Baker Street)
☎0171-935 6861
Madame Tussaud's world-famous waxwork collection was founded in Paris in 1770. It moved to England in 1802 and found a permanent home in London's Marylebone Road in 1884. The wax models are extremely life-like and the collection is being changed constantly: historical figures, film stars, kings, queens, sportsmen and other popular figures are represented. There are themed areas within the exhibition, and these include the Garden Party, 200 Years of Madame Tussauds, and Hollywood Legends. Another attraction is 'The Spirit of London', a journey in a time taxi through the sights, sounds and smells of London, from the Great Fire of 1666 to the 1960s and 'Swinging London'.
Open all year 10-5.30 (9.30am wknds, 9am summer). (Closed 25 Dec).
£8.25 (ch 16 £5.25, pen £6.25). Family ticket £19.95.
P 🍴 ✖ *licensed* ♿ *(Lift access to all exhibition areas with guide escort) toilets for disabled shop* ✂

Mall Galleries
SW1
The Mall (Underground - Charing Cross)
☎0171-930 6844
These galleries are the exhibition venue for the Federation of British Artists. Eight art societies administered by the federation hold their exhibitions here.
Open all year, daily 10-5.
£2 Depending on exhibition (ch & pen half price) Gallery Friends & Westminster Resident's card holders free.
P *(50 yds)* ♿ *(chairlft to galleries)* ✂

Middle Temple Hall
EC4
The Temple (Underground - Temple, Blackfriars)
☎0171-353 4355
Between Fleet Street and the Thames are the Middle and Inner Temples, separate Inns of Court, so named because of the Knights Templar who occupied the site from about 1160. Middle Temple Hall is a fine example of Tudor architecture and was built during the reign of Elizabeth I (completed in about 1570). The hall has a double

hammerbeam roof and beautiful stained glass showing the shields of past readers. The 29ft-long high table was made from a single oak tree from Windsor Forest; and portraits of George I, Elizabeth I, Anne, Charles I and Charles II, James, Duke of York and William III line the walls behind it. Sir Francis Drake was a visitor to and friend of the Middle Temple, and a table made from timbers from the *Golden Hind* - the ship in which he sailed around the world - is shown.
Open all year, Mon-Fri 10-12 & 3-4 (Closed BH & some legal vacations). Free.
✂ 🚆

The Monument
EC3
Monument St. (Underground - Monument)
☎0171-626 2717
Designed by Wren and Hooke and erected in 1671-7, the Monument commemorates the Great Fire of 1666 which is reputed to have started in nearby Pudding Lane. The fire destroyed nearly 90 churches and about 13,000 houses. This fluted Doric column stands 202ft high (Pudding Lane is exactly 202ft from its base) and visitors can climb the 311 steps to a platform at its summit. The views over the City and beyond are splendid. Because of the steps, access is almost impossible for persons with severe disabilities: there is no lift or escalator.
The Monument will be closed for refurbishment until Spring 1995. Visitors are advised to check the opening date before making a special visit.
Closed from 30 Oct 1994 until late spring 1995 for refurbishment. Visitors are requested to telephone The Corporation of London 0171-606 3030 ext 1174 to confirm re-opening dates.
Prices not confirmed.
✂

Museum of Garden History
SE1
Lambeth Palace Rd (Underground - Waterloo)
☎0171-261 1891 *(between 11am-3pm)*
Adjacent to the south gateway of Lambeth Palace is the former church of St Mary-at-Lambeth, now the Museum of Garden History. There is a permanent exhibition on the history of gardens and a collection of ancient tools. Knowledgeable staff can advise visitors. The shop sells souvenirs, gifts and seeds from the plant collection. In a fine tomb in the replica 17th-century knot garden in the churchyard lie the two John Tradescants, pre-eminent 17th-century plantsmen and gardeners to Charles I and Charles II. Admiral Bligh of the *Bounty* is buried nearby. Special events for 1995 include an exhibition of paintings and photographs (10-30 May).
Open 5 Mar-10 Dec, Mon-Fri 10.30-4, Sun 10.30-5.
Donations
🍴 ♿ *(ramps) shop*

Welcome to the Museum of Garden History. Not just an exhibition of all aspects of garden history, but a flourishing, fully re-created 17c garden packed full of period shrubs and flowers. There's as much to see inside as out! Many fascinating new exhibits are now on display at our beautifully restored premises. We also have an exciting programme of events scheduled for 1995 including lectures, concerts, exhibitions and fairs. These will be taking place both in the Museum and at our newly acquired period building close by – The Ark. Full details on application, with sae, to the address below.

Dept AA, The Museum of Garden History, Lambeth Palace Road, London SE1 7LB
Enquiry telephone line: 0171 401 8865

This gruesome character is one of many artefacts in the Museum of the Moving Image which leads the visitor through cinematic history.

Museum of London
EC2

London Wall (Underground - St Paul's, Barbican)
☎0171-600 3699 ext 24 or 280

Early December 1976 saw the official opening of the Museum of London. The collections of the former London and Guildhall museums were brought together in one specially designed building, located near the Barbican development. The site adjoins a stretch of the original Roman wall which surrounded the city.

Devoted to and detailing all aspects of London life from pre-history to contemporary times, the museum offers a fascinating display presented in chronological order. The exhibits and tableaux are arranged to give the visitor a realistic view of life in the capital through the ages; archaeological levels are illustrated by a relief model of the Thames Valley which provides an apt starting point for the story. Features of special interest include the superb models of William the Conqueror's White Tower and old St Pauls; the audio-visual reconstruction of the Great Fire of London in 1666 (superbly atmospheric) and the exhibition of ceremonial London with the Lord Mayor's State Coach as its centrepiece. It is also worth looking out for the medieval hen's egg, a lift from Selfridges department store, and a 1930s Ford motor car. There is also a programme of temporary exhibitions, lunchtime lectures and evening films throughout the year. A full programme of events is planned.

Open all year, Tue-Sat 10-6, Sun 12-6 (Closed 24-26 Dec, 1 Jan & every Mon ex BH's). Parties by arrangement.
P (NCP 200yds) ☕ ⅙ (wheelchairs available, lifts & induction loops, parking) toilets for disabled shop ⌀
Details not confirmed for 1995

Museum of Mankind
W1

6 Burlington Gardens (Underground - Piccadilly Circus)
☎0171-323 8043

The ethnographical department of the British Museum was re-housed in 1970 at Burlington Gardens to form the Museum of Mankind. Its vast collections embrace the art and material culture of tribal, village and pre-industrial societies from most areas of the world other than Western Europe. It also houses archaeological collections from the Americas and Africa. The museum's policy is to mount a number of fascinating temporary exhibitions (usually lasting for at least a year) rather than have permanent displays on show, although there are a number of outstanding exhibits on permanent display. The reserve collection is stored in Shoreditch and can be made available for serious study. Film shows and educational services are provided.
Open all year, Mon-Sat 10-5, Sun 2.30-6. (Closed Good Fri, May Day, Xmas & 1 Jan).
Free.
P (NCP 50yds) ☕ ⅙ (parking available tel 0171-323 8047) toilets for disabled shop ⌀

Museum of the Moving Image
SE1

South Bank, Waterloo (Underground - Waterloo)
☎0171-401 2636

The Museum of the Moving Image (MOMI)explores the magical world of film, television and video. Original artefacts such as Charlie Chaplin's hat and cane are displayed alongside hundreds of classic film and TV clips. At MOMI you can 'Fly like Superman', read the news, make your own cartoon, or audition for Hollywood with one of our cast of actor-guides.

Open all year, daily 10-6. Last admission 5pm. (Closed 24-26 Dec).
✳£5.50 (ch, UB40's, disabled & pen £4, students £4.70). Party 10+.
P ▣ ✗ licensed ♿ (for details ring 0171-815 1350) toilets for disabled shop ✺

Museum of The Order of St John
EC1

St John's Gate, St John's Ln (Underground - Farringdon)
☎0171-253 6644
One of the most obscure and fascinating museums in London, St John's Gate displays treasures that once belonged to the Knights Hospitaller. Maltese silver, Italian furniture, paintings, coins and pharmacy jars are among the objects on view in the 16th-century gatehouse. Together with the nearby priory church and 12th-century crypt, the Tudor gatehouse now houses the headquarters of the modern Order of St John and displays exhibits from its two charitable foundations: St John Ambulance and the Ophthalmic Hospital in Jerusalem.
Open all year, Mon-Sat 10-5, Sat 10-4 (Closed Etr, Xmas wk & BH's). Guided tours 11 & 2.30 Tue, Fri & Sat.
Donations requested
P meters & NCP 300yds ♿ toilets for disabled shop ✺

National Army Museum
SW3

Royal Hospital Rd, Chelsea (Underground - Sloane Square)
☎0171-730 0717
At the National Army Museum you can discover some of Britain's finest military treasures. It offers a unique insight into the lives of Britain's soldiers, from Privates to Field Marshals, from Tudor times to the present day. The displays include weapons, paintings, equipment, models, medals, and items from one of the world's largest collections of military uniforms. You can see life on the Western Front in a reconstruction of a World War I trench and also learn how soldiers coped with conditions as varied as the jungles of Burma, the mountains of Afghanistan, the plains of India, the snows of Canada, and the deserts of Kuwait. The fascinating exhibits on display include nine Victoria Crosses, a 400sq ft model of the Battle of Waterloo, Florence Nightingale's jewellery, and even the skeleton of Napoleon's horse. New Galleries look at the soldier in the age of Queen Victoria, Women in the Army, and there are regular special exhibitions.
Open all year, daily 10-5.30. (Closed Good Fri, May Day, 24-26 Dec & 1 Jan). Free.
🅿 ▣ ♿ (wheelchair lift) toilets for disabled shop ✺

National Gallery
WC2

Trafalgar Square (Underground - Charing Cross)
☎0171-839 3321 information 0171-747 2885
In 1824 the government bought the collection of pictures accumulated by John Julius Angerstein, a London underwriter, and exhibited them at his former residence in Pall Mall. These formed the major part of the collections of the National Gallery. Further bequests and purchases were made and by 1831 space had become limited, so plans were made for a special building to house the works of art. The present neo-classical building in Trafalgar Square was opened in 1838. All the great periods of European paintings are represented here although only a limited selection of British works is displayed, as most of the national collection is housed at the Tate. The gallery's particular treasures include Van Eyck's *Arnolfini Marriage,* Velázquez's *Toilet of Venus,* Leonardo da Vinci's cartoon (the Virgin and Child with Saints Anne and John the Baptist), Rembrandt's *Belshazzar's Feast* and Titian's *Bacchus and Ariadne.* The British paintings include Gainsborough's *Mr and Mrs Andrews*

and Constable's *Haywain.* There are many more captivating masterpieces to be seen at the National Gallery which houses one of the finest and most extensive collections in the world. The Sainsbury Wing opened in 1991 and contains the early Renaissance works from 1260-1510. Lectures, guided tours and children's quizzes are available. Exhibitions for 1995 include: In Trust for the Nation - Paintings from National Trust Houses (22 November 1995-10 March 1996).
Open all year, Mon-Sat 10-6, Sun 2-6. (Closed Good Fri, early May BH, 24-26 Dec & 1 Jan). Special major exhibitions open normal gallery times, (some late night opening Wed, ring to confirm). Free. Admission charged for some major exhibitions.
P (100yds) ▣ ✗ licensed ♿ (wheelchairs available, induction loop in theatre, lifts) toilets for disabled shop ✺

National Portrait Gallery
WC2

2 St Martin's Place (Underground - Charing Cross)
☎0171-306 0055
With the aim of illustrating British history by means of a collection of portraits of famous, and infamous, men and women, the gallery's first home was established in George Street, Westminster. After several moves the collection was finally housed in its present accommodation in 1896. Located behind the National Gallery, the building was designed in the style of an Italian palazzo. A further wing was added in 1933. The portraits are arranged in chronological order from the top floor, starting with the medieval period and finishing with the present day. As well as paintings, there are sculptures, miniatures, engravings, photographs and cartoons among the displays. Special exhibitions for 1995 include: BP Portrait Award (30 June-15 October), Robert Whitaker - Underground London. Experimental photographs taken at the heart of London's pop and underground culture in the late 1960s (7 July-24 September).
Open all year 10-6, Sat 10-6 & Sun 12-6. (Closed Good Fri, May Day, 24-26 Dec & 1 Jan).
✳Free (ex special exhibitions)
P ♿ (direct access, stair climber, touch tours) toilets for disabled shop ✺

National Postal Museum
EC1

King Edward Building, King Edward St (Underground - St Paul's)
☎0171-239 5420
This museum is a philatelist's paradise; it contains the most comprehensive collection of postage stamps in the world. Established in 1965, the National Postage Museum has obtained a vast collection of material charting the history of the postal system since its inception. Exhibits include a display of numerous stamps issued worldwide since 1878; the R M Phillips collection of 19th-century British stamps, including the celebrated 'Penny Black', the Frank Staff collections of 'postal history' material, and Great Britain's reference display of stamps from King Edward VII to the present day. The museum also holds, on microfilm, the Thomas de la Rue correspondence archives, and a large amount of unique philatelic material, most of which is available for research by prior arrangement. Temporary displays are held throughout the year.
Open all year, Mon-Thu (ex BH) 9.30-4.30, Fri 9.30-4.30. (Possibly closed for 2 weeks late Apr-early May).
♿ (main gallery accessible by prior arrangement) shop ✺
Details not confirmed for 1995

The Natural History Museum
SW7

Cromwell Rd (Underground - South Kensington)
☎0171-938 9123
The Museum's collections were built up around the specimens collected by Sir

Hans Sloane and formed a part of the nucleus of the British Museum. By 1860 the continued expansion of the collections meant that a separate natural history museum was required; it was not until 1881, though, that the new museum - The Natural History Museum - was opened. The vast and elaborate Romanesque-style building, with its terracotta facing showing relief mouldings of animals, birds and fishes, covers an area of four acres. The exhibits cover most aspects of biology and geology. In the Whale Hall a life-size model of the enormous Blue Whale can be seen, and in the Hall of Human Biology visitors can learn about the way their bodies work (including how it feels to be in the womb). Creepy Crawlies shows you how insects, spiders, crabs, and their relatives are important to humans, as both friends and foes. Ecology stresses our relationship with, and responsibility for, the natural world. A major new permanent exhibition on dinosaurs includes new skeletons, recreated robotic models, and displays on how dinosaurs lived, why they became extinct, and how they were dug up and studied by scientists. The Earth Galleries were formerly the Geological Museum, which contains the largest exhibition on basic earth science in the world, as well as a notable collection of gemstones and a piece of the Moon. The entrance to the Earth Galleries is on Exhibition Road, separate from the Cromwell Road entrance to the main museum, but is covered by the same entrance fee. There is a continuing programme of events workshops, lectures and videos throughout the year, but especially at weekends and school holidays.
Open all year, Mon-Sat 10-6, Sun 11-6. (Closed 23-26 Dec).
✳£5 (ch 5-15, student, UB40s & pen £2.50). Family ticket £13.50. Party.
P (180yds) ▣ ✗ licensed ♿ (ex top floor & earthquake machine, wheelchairs available) toilets for disabled shop ✺

Pollock's Toy Museum
W1

1 Scala St (Underground - Goodge Street)
☎0171-636 3452
Teddy bears, wax and china dolls, dolls' houses, board games, toy theatres, tin toys, mechanical and optical toys, folk toys and nursery furniture, are among the attractions to be seen in this appealing museum. Items from all over the world and from all periods are displayed in two small, interconnecting houses with winding staircases and charming little rooms. Toy theatre performances available for school visits.
Open all year, Mon-Sat 10-5. (Closed Sun & Xmas).
✳£2 (ch 18 75p).
P ♿ shop

Public Record Office Museum
WC2

Chancery Ln (Underground - Temple, Blackfriars)
☎0181-876 3444
The Public Record Office houses one of the finest, most complete archives in Europe, comprising the records of the central government and law courts from the Norman Conquest to the present century. It is a mine of information and some of the most interesting material is exhibited in its museum. Domesday Book is on permanent display. Special displays planned for 1995 include: The History of the Building, Wills, The Titanic, The Early Years of the Royal Air Force, and The Railways.
Open all year, Mon-Fri 9.45-4.45. Parties at other times by arrangement. Free.
♿ shop ✺ ▦

The Queen's Gallery
SW1

Buckingham Palace, Buckingham Palace Rd (Underground - Victoria)
☎0171-839 1377
The Queen's Gallery at Buckingham ➤

Springtime tulips bring a splash of colour to the elegance of Regent's Park. The Park, with its surrounding terraced houses, was designed by John Nash in the early 1800s.

Palace was first opened to the public in 1962 to display paintings, drawings, furniture and other works of art in the Royal Collection, one of the finest in the world. The Gallery is sited in a building originally designed as a conservatory by John Nash in 1831 and later converted into a chapel by Blore. The building suffered severe bomb damage in World War II and was not reconstructed until 1962; part of it still remains as the private chapel of Buckingham Palace. Special events for 1995 include a Fabergé exhibition which opens mid-March.
Open all year Tue-Sat & BH Mon 10-5, Sun 2-5 (ex for short periods between exhibitions). Telephone 0171-799 2331 for detailed information.
Prices under review.
P *(200yds)* & *shop* ✗

Regent's Park
NW1
(Underground - Baker Street)
The elegant charm of this park, north of Marylebone Road, can be attributed to John Nash, who laid it out, along with the imposing surrounding terraces, as part of a plan for a new palace which was never built. It now contains London Zoo (see separate entry), a boating lake, open-air theatre, Regent's Canal and the lovely Queen Mary's Rose Garden. There are a number of Victorian garden ornaments around the park and a group of fossil tree trunks are the only reminders that the Royal Botanic Gardens were once situated here.

Rock Circus
W1
London Pavilion, Piccadilly Circus (Underground - Piccadilly Circus)
☎0171-734 7203
Rock Circus is a unique and fun celebration of rock and pop music spanning forty years from the 1950s to the present day. The exhibition is an amazing combination of stereo through personal headsets, audio animatronic and Madame Tussauds figures of over 50 international rock stars. Figures include: Bono, Jon Bon Jovi, Gloria Estefan and Mick Hucknall.
Open all year, daily 11-9, Tue 12-9, Fri & Sat 11-10pm, holiday periods in summer 10am-10pm, Tue 12-10.
✱*£6.95 (ch £4.95, students & pen £5.95). Family ticket £18.85.*
P *(200yds)* & *(lift to all floors with member of staff) toilets for disabled shop* ✗

Royal Academy Of Arts
W1
Burlington House, Piccadilly (Underground - Piccadilly Circus)
☎0171-439 7438 & 0171-439 4996/7
Known principally for its exhibitions, the Royal Academy of Arts was founded in 1768 and is Britain's oldest Fine Arts institution. Two of its founding priciples were to provide a free school and to mount 'an annual exhibition open to all artists of distinguished merit', now known as the Summer Exhibition. Both continue today. Other highlights of the 1995 calendar include From Manet to Gaugin: Impressionism and Post-Impressionism from Swiss Private Collections (29 June-9 October), Africa: the Art of a Continent (14 September-17 December). The Royal Academy's most prized possession, Michelangelo's tondo, *The Virgin and Child with the Infant St John*, one of only four marble sculptures by the artist outside Italy, is on permanent display outside the Sackler Galleries.
Open all year, daily 10-6. (Closed 24-26 Dec & Good Fri.
£4-£6 (ch, students, pen & group visitors reduced price).
🍽 ✗ *licensed* & *toilets for disabled shop* ✗ 🚼

The Royal Mews
SW1
Buckingham Palace, Buckingham Palace Rd (Underground - Victoria)
☎0171-839 1377
Designed by John Nash and completed in 1825, the Royal Mews houses the State Coaches. These include the Gold State Coach made in 1762, with panels painted by the Florentine artist Cipriani. It has been used for every coronation since that date. The collection also includes the Irish State Coach, private driving carriages and royal sleighs. The Windsor greys and Cleveland Bay carriage horses are stabled here.
Open all year, Wed noon-4 with additional days in the summer. Tel 0171-799 2331 for detailed information.
Prices under review.
P *(200yds)* & *toilets for disabled shop* ✗

St James's Park
SW1
(Underground - St James's Park)
Situated between Buckingham Palace and Whitehall, this is the oldest of the Royal Parks in London, drained and converted into a deer park by Henry VIII in 1532. Charles II had the park redesigned in the style of Versailles, but the park as it exists today, with its lake, plantations and walks, was created by Nash for George IV. It remains one of the most delightful and popular places to relax, both for visitors and for workers, who frequently share their sandwiches with the wide variety of waterfowl on the lake. There are also summer band concerts and refreshment facilities.

Science Museum
SW7
Exhibition Rd, South Kensington (Underground - South Kensington)
☎0171-938 8000
Of all the Exhibition Road museums, the Science Museum is the most attractive to children (and often adults too). Among the displays are many working models with knobs to press, handles to turn and buttons to push to various different effects: exhibits are set in motion, light up, rotate and make noises. The collections cover the application of science to technology and illustrate the development of engineering and industry through the ages; there are galleries dealing with printing, chemistry, nuclear physics, navigation, photography, electricity, communications and medicine. A popular feature of the museum is the 'Launch Pad', an interactive children's gallery where children of all ages can carry out their own fun experiments. 'Food for Thought' is a permanent gallery which explains the impact of science and technology on today's food. The centrepiece of the Exploration of Space exhibition is the Apollo 10 space capsule, whilst the world's oldest steam locomotive and Stephenson's *Rocket* can be seen in the huge gallery devoted to rail and road transport. Britain's first 'jump jet' and an executive jet are just two of the exhibits in 'Flight', a fascinating aeronautics gallery. The Wellcome Museum of the History of Medicine features numerous reconstructions of important events in medical history.
Open all year, Mon-Sat 10-6, Sun 11-6. (Closed 24-26 Dec).
🍽 & *toilets for disabled shop* ✗
Details not confirmed for 1995

Sherlock Holmes Museum
NW1
221b Baker St (Underground - Baker Street)
☎0171-935 8866
221b Baker Street, that famous address of super-sleuth Sherlock Holmes, was opened as a museum in March 1990 to the great delight of admirers of the great detective. The first-floor rooms contain all the features familiar to the Holmes enthusiast, and an authentic Victorian atmosphere has been maintained throughout the house. The museum is of unique interest and visitors are encouraged to take photographs.
Open all year, daily 10-6. (Closed 25 Dec).
£5 (ch 8-16 £3 & pens £3). Party
✗ *licensed shop* ✗

Sir John Soane's Museum
WC2
13 Lincoln's Inn Fields (Underground - Holborn)
☎0171-405 2107 & 0171-430 0175 (Info)
Sir John Soane was responsible for some of the most splendid architecture in London, and his house, built in 1812, contains his collections of antiquities, sculpture, paintings, drawings and books. Included amongst his treasures are the *Rake's Progess* and *Election* series of paintings by William Hogarth, and the Sarcophagus of Seti I dating from 1290BC. The architectural drawing collection can be viewed, but by appointment only. An exhibition gallery is due to open in April 1995.
Open all year, Tue-Sat 10-5. Also first Tue of month 6-9pm. (Closed BH). Lecture tour Sat 2.30.
Free.
P *(parking meters) shop* ✗

Tate Gallery
SW1
Millbank (Underground - Pimlico)
☎0171-887 8000 & 0171-887 8008
In 1892 Sir Henry Tate, the sugar magnate and prominent collector of contemporary British painting and sculpture, offered to finance the building of a new and permanent home for his growing collection of British Art. Sidney J R Smith was commissioned to design the new gallery on the site of the former Millbank Prison and the building was officially opened to the public in 1897. A number of extensions to the building have followed, the most recent being the Clore Gallery in 1987 which houses the Turner Bequest. In the early part of this century the gallery was able to expand its collection to include foreign 20th-century art. Amongst the displays for 1995 will be rooms devoted to Tudor and Stuart paintings; John Constable; William Blake; the pre-Raphaelites; Victorian Painting; the London Avante-Garde 1900-1920; Surrealism; Rothko; Pop and Minimal Art; Painting in Britain 1973-1993. The Duveen Sculpture Galleries will include sculpture by Auguste Rodin and Sir Jacob Epstein. Major exhibitions planned include Willem de Kooning (February-7 May), Rites of Passage (15 June-3 September), Dynasties: Painting in Tudor and Jacobean England (12 October-7 January 1996).
Open Mon-Sat 10-5.50, Sun 2-5.50. (Closed Good Fri, May Day BH, 24-26 Dec & 1 Jan).
✱*Free. Charge for major loan exhibitions.*
P 🍽 ✗ *licensed* & *(wheelchairs on request, parking by prior arrangement). toilets for disabled shop* ✗

Theatre Museum
WC2
Russell St, Covent Garden (Underground - Covent Garden, Leicester Sq)
☎0171-836 7891
Major developments, events and personalities from the performing arts are illustrated in this appealing exhibition. Stage models, costumes, prints, drawings, posters, puppets, props and a variety of other theatre memorabilia are displayed. Special exhibitions include 'Slap - the Art of Stage Make-up', and 'From Page to Stage' with the *Wind in the Willows*, based on the National Theatre production. Theatrical events and celebrity interviews are planned for 1995.
Open all year, Tue-Sun 11-7.
✱*£3 (ch under 5 free, ch, students, disabled, UB40's & pen £1.50). Party. Family ticket £7.*
& *toilets for disabled shop* ✗

Tower Bridge
SE1
(Underground - Tower Hill)
☎0171-403 3761
The fairy-tale outline of Tower Bridge remains one of the capital's most popular landmarks. Its glass-covered walkway stands 142ft above the Thames, affording a panoramic view of the river. Much of the original machinery for working the bridge is still in place and can be seen in the engine rooms. The bridge's new exhibition uses state-of-the-art effects to present the story of the bridge in a dramatic and exciting fashion.

There is a glass-covered walkway across the upper part of Tower Bridge offering a spectacular view up and down the River Thames.

Open all year, Apr-Oct, 10-6.30; Nov-Mar 10-5.15 (last ticket sold 75 mins before closing). (Closed Good Fri, 24-26 Dec & 1 Jan).
£5 (ch 15 & pen £3.50, ch 5 free). Party 20+.
P (100yds) & toilets for disabled shop ✵

Tower Hill Pageant
EC3
1 Tower Hill Ter (Underground - Tower Hill)
☎*0171-709 0081*
Computer controlled cars take visitors on a journey to discover the history of the Port of London from Roman times to the present day. Multi-media presentations give an insight into the sights, smells and sounds of the City with on-board commentary in English, French, German and Japanese. Following this are over 1000 fascinating archaeological discoveries to be seen in the museum.
Open all year daily from 9.30am. (Closed 25 Dec).
£5.95 (ch, pen & students £3.95). Family ticket £14.95.
P & toilets for disabled shop ✵

Tower of London
EC3
Tower Hill (Underground - Tower Hill)
☎*0171-709 0765*
Perhaps the most famous castle in the world, the Tower of London has played a central part in British history throughout the ages. The nucleus of the complex is the original White Tower, built by William

the Conqueror as a show of strength to the people of London; it remains one of the most outstanding examples of Norman military architecture in Europe. Today it houses the Royal Armouries, the national collection of arms and armour based on the great arsenal of Henry VIII. For a great part of its history, the Tower of London was used, among other things, as the State Prison. It was here that King Henry VIII had two of his wives executed, here that Lady Jane Grey died and here that Sir Walter Raleigh was imprisoned for 13 years. From the reign of Charles II its main use was as an arsenal, administrative centre and the headquarters of the Royal Mint (until 1812) but during both World Wars it reverted to a state prison and was used to incarcerate German spies.
The unique Yeoman Warders, or 'Beefeaters' play an important role in the protection of the Tower - home of the Crown Jewels - and are most informative and entertaining. Another feature of the Tower are the ravens whose continued residence is said to ensure that the Kingdom does not fail. The first new raven for 300 years was hatched in May 1989, bringing their numbers up to nine.
Open all year, Mar-Oct, Mon-Sat 9-6, Sun 10-6 (last admission 5); Nov-Feb, Mon-Sat 9-5, Sun10-5 (Closed 24-26 Dec & 1 Jan).
£7.95 (ch 16 £5.25, pen, students & disabled £5.25). Family ticket £21.95.
P (NCP Lower Thames St) 🍴 & toilets for disabled shop ✵

Victoria & Albert Museum
SW7
Cromwell Rd (Underground - South Kensington)
☎*0171-938 8500*
The V&A is the world's finest museum of the decorative arts. Its collections span 2000 years and are housed in a magnificent Victorian and Edwardian complex of buildings, including Sir Aston Webbs Cromwell Road façade. The museum's collections comprise sculpture, furniture, fashion and textiles, paintings, silver, glass, ceramics, jewellery, books, prints, and photographs from Britain and all over the world. Highlights include the world's greatest collection of paintings by Constable and the national collection of watercolours; the famous 15th-century Devonshire Hunting Tapestries; the Dress Court showing fashion from 1500 to the present day; a superb Asian collection, including the much-loved Tippoo's Tiger; medieval treasures; magnificent collections of Renaissance and Victorian sculpture; the Jewellery Gallery including the Russian Crown Jewels; and the 20th Century Gallery, devoted to comtemporary art and design. There are also magnificent new galleries devoted to European art and design, glass and ceramics, ironwork, Chinese, European and Indian art, 20th-century design, and architect Frank Lloyd Wright. Exhibitions planned for 1995 include: The Genius of Wedgwood (8 June-17 September) and Botanical Illustrations: The Walter Florilegium Plates (10 May-24 September).
Open all year, Tue-Sun 10-5.50, Mon 12-5.50. (Closed Good Fri, May Day, 27 Aug, 24-26 Dec & 1 Jan). Tel for BH openings.
Donations-suggested £4.50 (ch 12 free, students, pen £1).
P (500yds) ✗ licensed & (braille guide, tour tape) toilets for disabled shop ✵

Wallace Collection
W1
Hertford House, Manchester Square (Underground - Bond Street)
☎*0171-935 0687*
An elegant 18th-century town house makes an appropriate gallery for this outstanding collection of art. Founded by the 1st Marquis of Hertford and brought to England from Paris in the late 19th century by Richard Wallace (son of the 4th Marquis), it was bequeathed to the nation in 1897 and came on public display three years later. As well as an unrivalled representation of 18th-century French art with paintings by Boucher, Watteau and

Fragonard, Hertford House displays a wealth of furniture, porcelain and beautiful works of art. It is the home of Frans Hals' *Laughing Cavalier* and of paintings by Gainsborough, Rubens, Delacroix and Titian. It also houses the largest collection of arms and armour outside the Tower of London.
Open all year, Mon-Sat 10-5, Sun 2-5. (Closed Good Fri, May Day, 24-26 Dec & 1 Jan).
Free.
& (ramps over steps, lift, prior telephone call appreciated) shop ✵

Wellington Museum
W1
Apsley House, 149 Piccadilly, (Hyde Park Corner) (Underground - Hyde Park Corner)
☎*0171-499 5676*
Re-opening in June 1995 after extensive refurbishment, the Wellington Museum is based at Apsley House, known as Number One London. Apsley House was the property of the first Duke of Wellington, Arthur Wellesley, from 1817 until his death in 1852. During the time that he was Prime Minister the windows of Apsley House were broken so frequently that they had to be covered with iron shutters (despite his distinguished military career he was extemely unpopular as Prime Minister). The mansion was designed by Robert Adam, built in 1771-8 and enlarged, under the Duke's direction, by Benjamin Wyatt in the late 1820s. The 7th Duke of Wellington presented it to the nation in 1947 and it opened to the public a few year later. The museum contains the Duke's famous collection of paintings including works by Velazquez, Murillo, Van Dyck, Rubens, Brueghel, Tenier and Wilkie. Canova's colossal marble figure of Napoleon dominates the exhibits which also include his great services of porcelain and silver and personal relics of the Iron Duke.
Re-opening June 1995. Admission times not confirmed.
Admission price details not confirmed.
P & (lift all parts accessible with help) shop ✵

Wesley's House, Museum & Chapel
EC1
49 City Rd (Underground - Old Street)
☎*0171-253 2262*
Wesley's Chapel has been the Mother Church of World Methodism since its construction in 1778. The crypt houses a museum which traces the development of Methodism from the 18th century to the present day. John Wesley's personal possessions, including clothes, books and furniture, are on display in the adjacent house, in which the founder of Methodism lived and died. The House is due to be refurbished over the winter and is scheduled to reopen May 1995.
Open all year, Mon-Sat 10-4 (Closed 25 & 26 Dec). Main service 11am Sun followed by an opportunity to tour the museum and house. House closed Autumn 1994-Spring 1995 for refurbishment.
✹House & museum £3 (ch, students, UB40's & pen £1.50)
& toilets for disabled shop ✵

Westminster Hall
SW1
Westminster (Underground - Westminster Hall)
☎*0171-219 4272*
The great Westminster Hall, where Charles I was tried in 1649, has survived virtually intact since it was remodelled at the end of the 14th century. It even escaped the fire in 1834 which destroyed much of the medieval Palace of Westminster. The magnificent hammerbeam roof is the earliest surviving example of its kind.
Westminster Hall can only be viewed by those on a tour of the Houses of Parliament, which must be arranged by an MP or Peer.
➤

& *toilets for disabled* ✻
Details not confirmed for 1995

Winston Churchill's Britain at War Experience
SE1 ▬▬▬
64 Tooley St
☎ 0171-403 3171
How did it feel to be a British citizen during World War II? Journey back in time for a stunning adventure that's exciting and educational. Take the lift to the London Underground and shelter from the air raids. Crouch in an Anderson Shelter and hear enemy aircraft overhead. The special effects recreate the sights, sounds and even the dust, smoke and smell of the London Blitz to enable you to feel and breathe the War years.
Open all year, Apr-Sep 10-5.30pm; Oct-Mar 10-4.30. (Closed 24-26 Dec)
£4.95 (ch 16 £2.75, student, pen & UB40 £3.75). Family ticket £13.
P (500mtrs) & shop ✻

LONDON OUTER

Bethnal Green Museum of Childhood
BETHNAL GREEN (E2) ▬▬▬
Cambridge Heath Rd (Underground - Bethnal Green)
☎ 0181-980 2415 & 0181-981 1711
This Victorian hall, the original Victorian and Albert building, houses a multitude of childhood delights. Toys, dolls and dolls' houses, model soldiers, puppets, games, model theatres, children's costume and nursery antiques are all included in its well planned displays. There are Saturday workshops for children.
Open all year, Mon-Thu & Sat 10-5.50, Sun 2.30-5.50. (Closed Fri, May Day, 24-26 Dec & 1 Jan).
🅿 shop ✻
Details not confirmed for 1995

Geffrye Museum
BETHNAL GREEN (E2) ▬▬▬
Kingsland Rd (Underground - Old Street)
☎ 0171-739 9893
The Geffrye is one of London's most friendly and enjoyable museums, set in elegant 18th-century almshouses with delightful gardens, just north of the City. The museum presents the changing style of the domestic interior from 1600 to 1950. The displays lead the visitor on a walk through time, from the 17th century with oak furniture and panelling, past the refined elegance of the Georgian rooms and the ornate style of the Victorian parlour, to the 20th-century art deco and post war utility. The museum and garden are brought to life through drama, music, workshops and seminars, with special holiday activities for families and children. The award-winning herb garden is open from April to October. Special events for 1995 include: Rooms within Rooms (4 April-4 June), Christmas Past (1 December-6 January).
Open all year, Tue-Sat 10-5, Sun & BH Mons 2-5 (Closed other PH).
Free.
P ☕ & (wheelchair available) toilets for disabled shop ✻

Hall Place
BEXLEY ▬▬▬
Bourne Rd (near jct of A2 & A233)
☎ Crayford (01322) 526574
Hall Place is an attractive mansion of chequered flint and brick, but it is most interesting for its garden. This has topiary in the form of the 'Queen's Beasts'; rose, rock, peat and water gardens; and a herb garden with a fascinating range of plants (labelled in braille) for medicine and cooking. There is also a conservatory, a local studies centre and museum. Please telephone for details of the programme of temporary exhibitions, lectures and concerts in the museum and Great Hall.
Open all year, House: Mon-Sat 10-5, Sun & BHs 2-6 (summer); Mon-Sat 10-dusk (winter). Gardens: Mon-Fri 7.30-dusk, Sat & Sun 9-dusk.
🅿 ☕ ✗ *licensed* & *shop* ✻
Details not confirmed for 1995

Rangers House
BLACKHEATH (SE3) ▬▬▬
Chesterfield Walk
☎ 0181-853 0035
This beautiful villa, the former home of Philip Stanhope, the 4th Earl of Chesterfield, houses the important Suffolk collection of Jacobean and Stuart portraits. Also featured is the Dolmetsch collection of musical instruments and some fine furniture. There is a busy programme of chamber concerts, poetry readings, holiday projects and workshops.
Open all year, Apr-Sep, daily 10-6; Oct 10-4; Nov-Mar, Wed-Sun 10-4. (Closed 24-25 Dec).
£2 (ch £1, concessions £1.50)
P (limited) & *toilets for disabled shop* ✻ (EH)

Kew Bridge Steam Museum
BRENTFORD ▬▬▬
The Pumping Station, Green Dragon Ln (Underground - Gunnersbury)
☎ 0181-568 4757
The Victorian pumping station has steam engines and six beam engines, of which five are working and one is the largest in the world. A forge, diesel house, waterwheel and old workshops can also be seen along with London's only steam narrow-gauge railway which operates on the second and last weekend of each month from March to November. Free audio tours are available. Special events for 1995 include: Festival of Model Tramways (22-23 April), Festival of Steam (September), live steam model railway show (November). Please telephone for a full list of events.
Open all year, daily 11-5. In steam wknds & BHs. (Closed Good Fri & Xmas wk).
✻*Weekdays £1.70 (ch, students & pen 90p). Family ticket £4.75; Sat & Sun £2.70 (ch, students & pen £1.50). Family ticket £7.25.*
🅿 & *(tours for partially sighted by arrangement) shop*

Musical Museum
BRENTFORD ▬▬▬
368 High St (Underground - Gunnersbury)
☎ 0181-560 8108
This museum will take you back to a bygone age to hear and see a marvellous working collection of automatic musical instruments from small music boxes to a mighty Wurlitzer theatre organ. Working demonstrations. There will be a series of Saturday evening concerts in 1995.
Open Apr-Oct, Sat & Sun 2-5. Also Jul-Aug, Wed-Fri 2-4. (Tour 1hr 30mins).
£3.20 (ch &pen £2.50). Family ticket £10.
P (200 yds) & shop ✻

Bromley Museum & Priory Gardens
BROMLEY ▬▬▬
The Priory, Church Hill, Orpington
☎ Orpington (01689) 873826
The collections are housed in an impressive medieval/post medieval building which stands in attractive gardens. Displays include archaeology of the London Borough of Bromley, the life and work of Sir John Lubbock, First Lord Avebury, and a new 20th-century gallery. There is also a small, but locally important, geological collection and expanding collections of social history, dress and fine art. A full programme of changing exhibitions is planned for 1995.
Open all year, Mon-Sat (ex Thu) 9-5. (Closed BH's).
Free.
🅿 ☕ & ✻ (ex part of gardens)

South London Art Gallery
CAMBERWELL (SE5)
65 Peckham Rd
☎0171-703 6120
The gallery presents six exhibitions a year of contemporary art, some touring, some self-generated. The gallery also houses the Southward art collection, but this is rarely shown.
Open only when exhibitions are in progress, Tue-Fri 10-5, Thu 10-7, Sun 2-5 (Closed Mon & Sat).
shop ✍
Details not confirmed for 1995

Chessington World of Adventures
CHESSINGTON
(on A243, M25 off junc 9)
☎Epsom (01372) 727227
One of Britain's most exciting theme parks, Chessington World of Adventures offers an exciting day out full of fun, thrills and entertainment with spine-tingling rides, amazing attractions, crazy entertainers and rare wild animals all set in magnificent themed lands. There's Transylvania with the Vampire Ride, Professor Burps Bubbleworks, the Runaway Mine Train in Calamity Canyon, Dragon River Water Ride in the Oriental Mystic East and Terrortomb - a spectacular adventure ride in the Ancient Forbidden Kingdom.
Open Apr-Oct, daily. Late opening until 9pm Jul & Aug.
✳*Admission fee payable. Phone for details.*
🅿 ♨ ✗ *licensed & (some rides not accessible) toilets for disabled shop* ✍

Chislehurst Caves
CHISLEHURST
Old Hill (off A222)
☎0181-467 3264
This labyrinth of caves has been called the enigma of Kent. Miles of mysterious caverns and passages hewn out of the chalk over some 8,000 years can be explored with experienced guides to tell the history and legends of the caves.

Open all year, daily during school hols (incl half terms). All other times Wed-Sun, 11-4.30.
£3 (ch & pen £1.50); longer tours: Sun & BH's only £5 (ch & pen £2.50).
🅿 ♨ & *(ramps) toilets for disabled shop*

Chiswick House
CHISWICK (W4)
Burlington Ln, Chiswick (Underground - Gunnersbury)
☎0181-995 0508
Considered to be one of the finest Palladian buildings in Britain, this domed mansion was built between 1725 and 1730 with magnificent interior detailing by William Kent. It has been restored to all its former glory.
Open all year, Apr-Sep, daily 10-6; Oct, 10-4; Nov-Mar, Wed-Sun 10-4. Closed 24-26 Dec & 1 Jan.
£2.50 (ch £1.30, concessions £1.90).
& *shop* ✍
(EH)

Hogarth House
CHISWICK (W4)
Hogarth Ln, Great West Rd
☎0181-994 6757
A small Georgian house once the home of William Hogarth, it is now a picture gallery and has on view many of his famous engravings. It is near the Thames and other 18th-century houses along Chiswick Mall and also Chiswick House. It has a secluded garden and Hogarth's Mulberry Tree.
Open Apr-Sep Mon-Sat (ex Tue) 11-6, Sun 2-6; Oct-Mar Mon-Sat (ex Tue) 11-4, Sun 2-4. (Closed first two weeks in Sep, last 3 weeks in Dec, 1 Jan and Good Fri. Free.
P *(25 & 50yds)* & *shop* ✍

Royal Air Force Museum
COLINDALE (NW9)
Grahame Park Way, Hendon (Underground - Colindale)
☎0181-205 2266 & 0181-205 9191

Seventy full-size original aeroplanes and other exhibits, all under cover, tell the fascinating story of flight through the ages. Extensive galleries show the political and historical impact of this means of transport and communication - including the incredible 'Battle of Britain Experience', the story of history's most famous air battle. Visitor facilities include a daily free cinema programme, a Tornado flight simulator, the Eurofighter 2000 three screen cinema, guided tours and the new 'touch and try' Jet Provost - climb in the cockpit and try out the controls for yourself. Special events for 1995 include: Anne Frank in the World exhibition (4 May-4 June), annual flight activities week from 12 August, and children's workshops during the school holidays.
Open daily 10-6. (Closed 24-26 Dec & 1 Jan).
✳*£5.20 (ch & concessions £2.10). Family ticket £12.60. Party 10+.*
🅿 ♨ ✗ *licensed & (lifts, ramps & wheelchairs available) toilets for disabled shop* ✍

Craft Centre of Silk
CRAYFORD
Bourne Rd
☎(01322) 559401
A guided tour will take visitors along a kind of 'silk road' through the working mill and craft centre which shows the history of silk, associated craft tools and sericulture. As well as the audio-visual presentation, craftsmen can be seen at work hand printing silk. The Mill Shop offers a wide range of silk gifts at mill prices - and it has a sale and other special events. Please telephone for details.
Open all year, Mon-Sat 9.30-5 (4.30 Sat). (Closed Sun & BH).
Museum only £1 (pen & student 75p). Family ticket £3. Guided Tour of Craft Centre & Mill by appointment £2 (pen & student £1.50). Family ticket £6.
🅿 ♨ & *toilets for disabled shop* ✍

Darwin Museum, Down House
DOWNE
Luxted Rd (Off A233, signposted)
☎Farnborough (Kent) (01689) 859119
Down House was the home of Charles Darwin from 1842 until his death in 1882. The drawing room and Old Study are restored and furnished as they were when Darwin was working on his famous, and still controversial book *On the Origin of Species by means of Natural Selection*, first published in 1859. The Museum also includes collections and memorabilia from Darwin's voyage on HMS *Beagle*. There is one room dedicated to his illustrious grandfather Dr Erasmus Darwin. The garden is maintained as laid out by the Darwins, retaining the original landscaping, flint and brick walls and glass house, beyond which lies the famous Sand Walk or thinking path, along which Darwin took his daily walk. There are special displays at various times throughout the year; please telephone for

recorded message.
Open all year, Wed-Sun 1-6 (last admission 5.30). Also BH Mon. (Closed 14 Dec-1 Jan & Feb).
✳*£2.50 (ch 5-15 £1, pen & student £1.50).*
🅿 & *shop* ✍

Dulwich Picture Gallery
DULWICH (SE21)
College Rd (N of South Circular A205)
☎0181-693 5254
The oldest public picture gallery in England is also one of the most beautiful. Housed in a building designed by Sir John Soane in the early part of the 19th century, it displays a fine cross-section of European art, including many Old Masters. Temporary exhibitions are held throughout the year.
Open all year, Tue-Fri 10-1 & 2-5, Sat 11-5, Sun 2-5. (Closed Mon & BHs). Guided tours Sat & Sun 3pm.
🅿 & *shop* ✍

East Ham Nature Reserve
EAST HAM (E6)
Visitor Centre, Norman Rd
☎0181-470 4525
This 10-acre nature reserve with grassland and woodland, has two nature trails with printed guides (braille version in preparation). One trail is suitable for all disabled visitors. There is a visitor centre with displays relating to natural history and the history of the churchyard nature reserve. Expert staff are available to answer wildlife queries or identify natural history objects brought in.
Open Visitor Centre: wknds 2-5. Nature Reserve: summer, Mon-Fri 9-5, wknds 2-5; winter, Mon-Fri 9-4, wknds 2-4.
P *(includes disabled bay)* & *(trails for wheelchairs & blind) toilets for disabled shop* ✍
Details not confirmed for 1995

Forty Hall Museum
ENFIELD
Forty Hill
☎0181-363 8196
The mansion of Forty Hall was built in 1629 for Sir Nicholas Raynton, Lord Mayor of London, and then altered in the 18th century. It has fine plaster ceilings and collections of 17th-and 18th-century furniture, paintings, ceramics and glass. There are also local history displays and temporary exhibitions.
Open all year, Tue-Sun 10-5.
🅿 ♨ & *toilets for disabled shop* ✍
Details not confirmed for 1995

Claremont Landscape Garden
ESHER
Portsmouth Rd (E of A307)
☎(01372) 469421
Laid out by Vanbrugh and Bridgeman before 1720, extended and naturalised by Kent, this is the earliest surviving example of an English landscaped garden. Its 50 acres include a lake with an island pavilion, a grotto and a turf amphitheatre. There are also avenues and viewpoints. A Fête Champetre and ➤

Built in 1869, the *Cutty Sark* was the fastest tea clipper in the world. She carried nearly 10 miles of rigging and an acre of sail.

jazz concert will be held on 12-16 July, telephone (01372) 459950 for details after 25 May.
Open all year, Jan-Mar, Tue-Sun 10-5 or sunset if earlier, Apr-Oct Mon-Fri 10-6, Sat-Sun & BH Mon 10-7 (12-16 Jul, closes 4pm); Nov-Mar Tue-Sun 10-5 or sunset if earlier. Closed 25 Dec & 1 Jan. Last admission 30 mins before closing.
✤*Sun & BH Mon £2.60; Mon-Sat £1.80*
🅿️ 🍴 ♿ *(wheelchairs available, Braille guide) toilets for disabled shop* ✺ *(ex on leads Nov-Mar)*
(NT)

Horniman Museum
FOREST HILL (SE23)
London Rd
☎0181-699 2339 & 0181-699 1872
Situated in 16 acres of gardens, the Horniman Museum has displays from different cultures, natural history collections and an extensive exhibition of musical instruments from all over the world. There is also an Aquarium, a Conservation Centre and a large reference library. Visitors can experience different instruments and the music they create in the Music Room. There are regular concerts, special exhibitions and educational workshops.
Open all year, Mon-Sat 10.30-5.30, Sun 2-5.30 (Closed 24-26 Dec). Gardens close at sunset.
Free.
P (opposite museum) 🍴 ♿ *(chair lift) toilets for disabled shop* ✺

Cutty Sark Clipper Ship
GREENWICH (SE10)
Greenwich Pier
☎0181-858 3445 & 0181-858 2698
The fastest tea clipper to be built (in 1869) once sailed 363 miles in a single day. She has been preserved in dry dock since 1957 and her graceful lines dominate the riverside at Greenwich. Exhibitions and a video presentation on board tell the story of the ship and there is a magnificent collection of ships' figureheads. Restoration work can be seen while the ship is open to visitors, ie shipwrights, riggers etc. A re-enactment of sailing days is planned for early May

1995, please telephone for details.
Open all year, daily 10-5, Sun 12-5; 6pm in summer. (Closed 24-26 Dec). Last ticket 30 mins before closing.
£3.25 (concessions £2.25). Family ticket £8 Party 10+.
P (100 yds metered) (between deck & lower hold deck only) shop ✺

Gipsy Moth IV GREENWICH (SE10)
Greenwich Pier, King William Walk
☎0181-858 3445 or 0181 858 2698
Standing near the famous tea clipper is the yacht in which Sir Francis Chichester made the first single-handed sailing trip around the world, 'Racing against Time' in 1966-7.
Open Apr-Oct, daily 10-6. (Sun 12-6). Last ticket 30 mins before closing.
50p (ch 30p).
P (100 yds) ✺

National Maritime Museum
GREENWICH (SE10)
Romney Rd
☎0181-858 4422
The National Maritime Museum tells the story of Britain and the Sea, from ancient boats and Roman trade, through centuries of boatbuilding, battles and exploration to 20th-century trade and pleasurecraft. Features include items from Henry VIII's naval fleet, detailed 17th-century Navy Board models of wooden warships, masterpieces of great naval battles - including Trafalgar. See Nelson's uniform, elegant gilded Royal barges and shallops. Special events for 1995 include: a children's gallery (open from Easter), Wooden Boat Show and Model Boat Show (June), new Nelson Exhibition (opens mid June). Extra events are held during the school holidays and at half term.
Open all year, Mon-Sat 10-5, Sun 12-5. (Closed 24-26 Dec).
✤*Inclusive ticket to National Maritime Museum, Old Royal Observatory & Queen's House £4.95 (ch 5-16 £2.95, students & pen £3.95) Family ticket £14.95.*
P (50 yds) 🍴 ♿ *(wheelchair available, special needs advisory service) toilets for disabled shop* ✺

Old Royal Observatory
GREENWICH (SE10)
Greenwich Park (off A2)
☎0181-858 4422
Charles II founded the Royal Observatory in 1675 'for perfecting navigation and astronomy'. It stands at zero meridian longitude and is the original home of Greenwich Mean Time. Set in the beautiful grounds of Greenwich Park, which were laid out to plans by the French gardener, Le Nôtre, who planned the grounds at Versailles, the Royal Observatory is part of the National Maritime Museum. Completely refurbished in 1993 it houses an extensive collection of historic timekeeping, astronomical and navigational instruments. Planetarium shows throughout the summer. Events are planned for the school holidays.
Open all year, Mon-Sat 10-5, Sun 12-5. (Closed 24-26 Dec).
✤*Inclusive ticket to National Maritime Museum, Old Royal Observatory & The Queen's House £4.95 (ch 5-16 £2.95, students & pen £3.95). Family ticket £14.95.*
🅿️ ♿ *toilets for disabled shop* ✺

The Queens House
GREENWICH (SE10)
Romney Rd
☎0181-858 4422
The first Palladian-style villa in England, designed by Inigo Jones for Anne of Denmark and completed for Queen Henrietta Maria, wife of Charles I. The recent restoration has been carried out to show the house as it appeared when new, with bright silks and furnishings. The Great Hall, the State Rooms and a Loggia overlooking Greenwich Park are notable features. There is a fine collection of Dutch marine paintings, including some of the finest seascapes ever painted. Events reflecting the music and fashions of the Stuart period are held including during the school holidays.
Open all year, Mon-Sat 10-5, Sun 12-5. (Closed 24-26 Dec).
✤*Inclusive ticket to National Maritime Museum, Old Royal Observatory & The Queen's House £4.95 (ch 5-16 £2.95, students & pen £3.95). Family ticket £14.95.*
🍴 ♿ *(induction loop commentary & special needs adviser) toilets for disabled shop* ✺

Royal Naval College
GREENWICH (SE10)
☎0181-858 2154
With the Queen's House as its focal point, the Royal Naval College occupies one of the masterpieces of English architecture; the grand sequence of buildings originally planned by Sir Christopher Wren towards the end of the 17th century as a hospital and refuge for disabled or veteran seamen of the Royal Navy. Additions were subsequently made by such notables as Vanbrugh, Hawksmoor and Ripley. The College was formerly used as a naval hospital (until 1873) and particularly splendid features include the chapel and the Painted Hall.
Open all year (Painted Hall and Chapel only), daily (ex Thu) 2.30-5 (last admission 4.30). Due to security reasons please telephone to check opening.
Free.
shop ✺ 🚻

Ham House
HAM
(W of A307)
☎0181-940 1950
This lovely house was built in 1610 and redecorated by the Duke and Duchess of Lauderdale in the 1670s. The Duke was a member of Charles II's government, and followed the most fashionable style. There is a 17th-century garden which is currently being restored. Summer concerts are held in the garden, please send SAE for details.
Open gardens: all year, Sat-Thu (open Good Friday) 10.30-6 or dusk if earlier. Closed 25-26 Dec & 1 Jan). House: Apr-

Oct, Mon-Wed 1-5, Sat 1-5.30, Sun 11.30-5.30 (open Good Fri, 1-5 closed Tue following), 4 Nov-17 Dec, Sat & Sun 1-4. Last admission 30 mins before closing.
✤*House £4 (ch £2). Family ticket £10. Garden free.*
P (400 yds) 🍴 ✗ *licensed* ♿ *(Braille guide, wheelchairs available, hearing system) toilets for disabled shop* ✺
(NT)

Fenton House
HAMPSTEAD (NW3)
Windmill Hill (Underground - Hampstead)
☎0171-435 3471
A William and Mary mansion built about 1693 and set in a walled garden, Fenton House is now owned by the National Trust. It contains a display of furniture and some notable pieces of Oriental and European porcelain as well as the Benton Fletcher collection of early keyboard instruments, including a harpsichord once played by Handel. Summer concerts are arranged. For details of Children's Day on 4 June and other events please send SAE to the Custodian.
Open Mar, Sat & Sun only 2-5; Apr-Oct, Sat-Sun & BH Mon 2-5.30, Mon, Tue & Wed 2-5.30. Last admission 30mins before closing.
£3.50. Family ticket £9.
♿ ✺
(NT)

Freud Museum
HAMPSTEAD (NW3)
20 Maresfield Gardens (Underground - Finchley Road)
☎0171-435 2002 & 0171-435 5167
In 1938, Sigmund Freud left his home in Vienna as a refugee from the Nazi occupation and chose exile in England, transferring his entire domestic and working environment to the house at 20 Maresfield Gardens. He resumed work until his death here a year later. Freud's extraordinary collection of Egyptian, Greek, Roman and Oriental antiquities, his working library and papers, and his fine furniture including the famous desk and couch are all here. The house was bequeathed by his daughter Anna Freud (1895-1982), whose pioneering development of her father's work is also represented. The museum has exhibitions on display and historic videos for viewing.
Open all year, Wed-Sun 12-5 (Closed BH's, telephone for Xmas Holiday times).
🅿️ ♿ *(personal tours can be arranged if booked in advance) shop* ✺
Details not confirmed for 1995

Keats House
HAMPSTEAD (NW3)
Keats Grove (Underground - Hampstead)
☎0171-435 2062
The two Regency houses were occupied by John Keats and his fiancée and nurse Fanny Brawne. They have now been converted into one building and form a museum devoted to the life of this famous poet. Manuscripts, letters and personal mementoes are displayed. Special events in 1995 include celebrations of the bicentenary of Keats' birth (11-24 June).
Open all year, Apr-Oct Mon-Fri 10-1 & 2-6, Sat 10-1 & 2-5, Sun & BH 2-5; Nov-Mar Mon-Fri 1-5, Sat 10-1 & 2-5, Sun 2-5. (Closed Good Fri, Etr eve, May Day, 24-26 Dec & 1 Jan).
Free.
P (300yds) shop ✺

Kenwood Iveagh Bequest
HAMPSTEAD (NW3)
Hampstead Ln (Underground - Hampstead)
☎0181-348 1286
Forming the most beautiful part of Hampstead Heath, the wooded grounds of Kenwood were laid out in the 18th century by the first Earl of Mansfield. He engaged Robert Adam to enlarge the house and transform it into a mansion, and the orangery and library are Adam's design. The first Earl of Iveagh bought

the estate in 1925 and bequeathed the grounds, house and its contents to the nation two years later. It contains a fine collection of paintings including Old Masters and 18th and 19th-century portraits by Gainsborough and Reynolds among others. An exhibition of 18th-century shoebuckles and jewellery makes interesting viewing. Kenwood is a popular venue for outdoor summer events and musical evenings.
Open all year, Apr-Sep daily 10-6; Oct-Mar daily 10-4. (Closed 24-26 Dec & 1 Jan).
🅿 💺 ✗ *licensed & toilets for disabled shop ⚙ (ex grounds)*
Details not confirmed for 1995

Hampton Court Palace
HAMPTON COURT ▬▬▬
☎ *0181-781 9540*
The palace was started in the early 16th century by Cardinal Wolsey, Lord Chancellor to Henry VIII. When he fell out of favour he presented it to the king as a placatory gesture. Henry VIII expanded the palace by adding the hammerbeamed great hall, the immense kitchens and the Royal Tennis courts. Later monarchs (and Cromwell) left their own mark: Elizabeth I added plants from the New World to the garden, and William and Mary commissioned Wren to remodel part of the building. The result was the handsome Fountain Court, part of which was devastated by fire in recent years, but has now been gloriously restored after a six year programme.
Today, pictures, furniture and tapestries can be seen, and there are handsome gardens and parkland close to the River Thames. Special attractions are the Tudor Kitchens, the great gatehouse, the orangery, the Hampton Court vine, and the maze, laid out in the time of William III.
Open all year, Palace & maze, Mon 10.15-6, Tue-Sun 9.30-6 (4.30pm mid Oct-mid Mar). (Closed 24-26 Dec & 1 Jan).
£7 (ch 5-16 £4.70, pen, students & disabled £5.30). Family ticket £19.30.
🅿 *(charged)* 💺 ✗ *licensed & toilets for disabled shop 4 shops on site ⚙ (ex in gardens)*

Church Farm House Museum
HENDON (NW4) ▬▬▬
Greyhound Hill (Underground - Hendon Central)
☎ *0181-203 0130*
Dating from the 1660s, this gabled house is a museum of local interest. It features a period furnished kitchen and dining room. In 1995 there will be a major exhibition on the impact of World War II on the London Borough of Barnet (May-September).
Open all year, Mon-Thu 10-5, Sat 10-1 & 2-5.30, Sun 2-5.30. (Closed Good Fri, 25-26 Dec & 1 Jan).
Free.
🅿 & *shop ⚙*

Highgate Cemetery
HIGHGATE (N6) ▬▬▬
Swains Ln (Underground - Archway)
☎ *0181-340 1834*
Highgate Cemetery is the most impressive of a series of large, formally arranged and landscaped cemeteries which were established around the perimeter of London during the first decades of Queen Victoria's reign. Visitors will discover a wealth of fine sculpture and architecture amongst the tombstones, monuments and mausoleums as well as the graves of such notables as the Rossetti family, George Eliot, Michael Faraday and Karl Marx.
Open all year. Eastern Cemetery: daily 10 (11 wknds)-5 (4 in winter). Western Cemetery by guided tour only: Sat & Sun 11-4 (3 in winter); midweek tours 12,2 & 4 (12, 2 & 3 in winter). No weekday tours in Dec, Jan & Feb. Special tours by arrangement. (Closed 25-26 Dec & during funerals).
✱*East cemetery £1. Tour of West*

cemetery £3 (ch 12-16 £1, 8-12 free, no ch under 8 on tours, pen & UB40's £2).
🅿 *shop ⚙*

Syon House
ISLEWORTH ▬▬▬
(Approach via Park Rd off Twickenham Rd)
☎ *0181-560 0881*
The house stands on the site of a monastery, founded by Henry V. After the Dissolution it passed into the hands of the Duke of Somerset but he was accused of treason by John Dudley. Dudley was created Earl of Northumberland and Syon House became his property. The earldom was made a dukedom, and in 1750 the 1st Duke of Northumberland engaged Robert Adam to renovate the mansion. Adam not only adapted the architecture but also was responsible for the furnishings and decoration - the result is spectacular, particularly in the superbly coloured ante-room and gallery library. The Tudor brick was refaced with Bath stone in the late 19th century; this gives the exterior a rather harsh appearance but in no way detracts from the splendours inside.
Open Apr-Sep, Wed-Sun & BH 11-5 (last ticket 4.15). Oct, Sun only.
🅿 💺 & *toilets for disabled shop garden centre ⚙*
Details not confirmed for 1995

Syon Park
ISLEWORTH ▬▬▬
(A315 off A310 to Busch Cnr, entry Park Rd)
☎ *0181-560 0881*
Contained within the 55 acres that make up Syon Park is one of the inspirations for the Crystal Palace at the Great Exhibition of 1851: a vast crescent of metal and glass, the first construction of its kind in the world and known as the Great Conservatory. It was designed by Fowler in 1829. The park also has a butterfly house and the largest garden centre in England. Although the horticultural reputation of Syon Park goes back to the 16th century - when the use of trees purely as ornaments was looked upon as unique - its beauty today is thanks to the master of landscape design, 'Capability' Brown. It is hardly believable that the peaceful haven he has created beside the River Thames is just nine miles from the centre of London. A miniature steam railway runs through the gardens (weekends April to October and Bank Holidays). Special events planned for 1995 include: Syon Summer Festival (10-11 June), motor show (24-25 June), craft fair (3-6 August), and monthly antique and book fairs.
Open all year, daily 10-6 or dusk. (Closed 25 & 26 Dec).
✱*£2.50 (concessions £2). Combined ticket for house & gardens £5.50*

Between 1839 and the 1970s many illustrious people were buried at Highgate Cemetary, Karl Marx, who lived in London from 1849 till his death in 1883, is one of its most well-known incumbents.

(concessions £4).
🅿 💺 & *toilets for disabled shop garden centre ⚙*
See advertisement on page 102

The London Canal Museum
ISLINGTON (N1) ▬▬▬
12/13 New Wharf Rd (Underground - Kings Cross)
☎ *0171-713 0836*
The museum covers the development of London's canals (particularly Regent's Canal on which the museum is situated), canal vessels and trade, and the way of life of the canal people. It is housed in a former ice warehouse and stables and also illustrates horse transport and the unusual trade of importing ice from Norway; there are two large ice wells

under the floor, one of which can be seen through a viewing hole. Facilities include an educational room, and temporary moorings for visitors who arrive by boat. There are occasional special exhibitions.
Open all year, Tue-Sun & BH Mon 10-4.30 (last admission 4). (Closed 24-26, 31 Dec, 1 Jan).
£2.50 (ch, students, pen & UB40s £1.25, under 5's free). Groups 10+
P *(250yds) & shop ⚙*

Kew Gardens (Royal Botanic Gardens)
KEW ▬▬▬
(Underground - Kew Bridge)
☎ *0181-940 1171*
The world-famous gardens at Kew ➤

A curious landmark in south-west London is the 10-storey high Chinese Pagoda which is in the world-famous Kew Gardens.

started as a mere nine-acre site, laid out by George III's mother, Princess Augusta in 1759 (she lived in the White House at Kew which has long since been demolished). In 1841 the gardens were given to the State and by 1904, after Queen Victoria had presented more of the surrounding land to the country, the gardens covered 300 acres - their present size. The 19th-century botanist, Sir Joseph Banks, and head gardener, William Aiton (later curator), were largely responsible for laying the foundations of the great collection of plants, shrubs and trees which exist here today; a collection which not only gives great public enjoyment but also forms part of the world's foremost botanical research centre. The west of the gardens is largely woodland and arboretum, while the formal gardens, with their lawns and neatly manicured beds are in the eastern half. The site has inspired some notable architectural features, both old and very modern. The Palm House is perhaps the most elegant: an early example of glass and wrought iron, it was completed in 1848. But the most famous landmark at Kew is the Chinese Pagoda; it stands 163ft high in ten storeys. Plants that would not otherwise be seen in Britain are grown in houses which reproduce special climatic conditions and among many other features are art galleries, one showing the work of Victorian artist Marianne North. Wheelchairs are available (booking advisable) free of charge and there are purpose-built toilets for wheelchair users. Events for 1995 include Summer Jazz at Kew (18-21 July).
Open all year, Gardens daily 9.30-between 4 & 6.30pm on weekdays, between 4-8pm Suns & BH's, depending on the time of sunset.(Closed 25 Dec & 1 Jan) £4 (concessions £2) Family ticket £10.
🅿 *(charged)* 🍽 ✗ *licensed* ♿ *(16 seat bus tour: enquiries ring 0181-332 5623) toilets for disabled shop* 🐕

Kew Palace
KEW
Royal Botanic Gardens (Underground - Kew Bridge)
☎0181-940 3321
A favourite country residence during the reign of the first three Hanoverian Kings, Kew was the site of several royal houses although only three of the buildings now remain. A fairly modest red-brick building, built in the Dutch style with gables, Kew Palace was built in 1631 and used for nearly a century until 1818 when Queen Charlotte died. It was opened to the public in 1899 and remains much as it was in George III's time, reflecting the quiet country life his family enjoyed here.

Family paintings and personal relics, furniture and tapestries are on display, and a charming 17th-century garden has been recreated.
Open Apr-3 Oct, daily 11-5.30. £1.20 (ch 16 80p, pen, students & disabled 90p). Joint ticket to include Queen Charlotte's Cottage £1.50 (ch 16 £1, pen, students & disabled £1.15). shop 🐕

Queen Charlotte's Cottage
KEW
Royal Botanic Gardens (Underground - Kew Bridge)
☎0181-977 3321
The cottage is typical of the rustic-style edifices built by the gentry in the 18th century and was used by the royal family as a summer house and a place to take tea. The interior is designed to give the impression of a tent.
Open Apr-3 Oct, weekends & BH 11-5.30. 70p (ch 45p, pen, students & disabled 50p). Joint ticket with Kew Palace £1.50. shop 🐕

Osterley Park House
OSTERLEY
(Underground - Osterley)
☎0181-560 3918
This Elizabethan mansion has been transformed into an 18th-century villa, its elegant interior decoration designed in neo-classical style by Robert Adam. The State Apartments include a Gobelin tapestry ante-room and a dressing-room decorated in the Etruscan style. Events for 1995 include: a sculpture exhibition all season, art exhibition (May-June), Children's Day (4 June), band concert (5 August), photographic exhibition (July-December).
Open all year: Park & pleasure grounds, daily 9-7.30 or sunset if earlier. House: Apr-Oct, Wed-Sat 1-5, Sun & BH Mon 11-5. (Closed Good Fri & 25-26 Dec). £3.60. Family ticket £9.
🅿 *(charged)* 🍽 ♿ *(many extra facilities for the less able) toilets for disabled shop* 🐕
(NT)

London Docklands Visitor Centre
POPLAR (E14)
3 Limeharbour, Isle of Dogs
☎0171-512 1111
Exhibition and video show tracing the area's fascinating history, illustrating London Docklands today and looking forward to the final fulfilment of the regeneration programme. A team of experienced information assistants is on hand to answer enquiries and guided tours of London Docklands can be arranged with prior notice.

programmes for schools. Exhibits include the African Aviary, offering unrivalled viewing of the birds within, and the Moonlight World where day and night are reversed. Favourites at the Zoo include black rhinos Rosie and Jos, and the very rare Asiatic Lions which are part of an endangered species breeding programme.
Open all year, daily from 10am. (Closed 25 Dec).
🅿 *(charged)* 🍽 ✗ *licensed* ♿ *(wheelchairs & booster scooter available) toilets for disabled shop* 🐕
Details not confirmed for 1995

Richmond Park
RICHMOND
(Underground - Richmond)
With its herds of deer, abundant wild life and centuries-old oaks, Richmond is a favourite haunt for visitors and

aturalists. There is a formal garden at embroke Lodge, and the various lantations show a wealth of exotic hrubs and wild flowers. Model sail boats re allowed on Adam's Pond, where the eer drink, and the 18-acre Pen Ponds ave been specially made for angling permit required).

The M.C.C. Museum
ST JOHNS WOOD (NW8)
Lord's Ground (Underground - St John's Wood)
☎0171-266 3825
Lord's was established in 1787 and it is the home of the MCC and cricket. When you tour this world-famous arena you follow in the footsteps of the 'greats' of the game, from W G Grace to Ian Botham. Daily guided tours take you behind the scenes at this historic venue. Highlights include the Long Room, a shrine for players and fans the world over, and the MCC Museum where the Ashes and a large collection of paintings and memorabilia are displayed. Other places of interest are the Real Tennis Court, the acclaimed Mound Stand with its magnificent views of the ground, and the Indoor School. The MCC Museum is also open on cricket days for spectators.
Open all year, tours normally at noon & 2pm (times vary on certain cricket days). There are no tours on major match days. Telephone for details and booking. Museum open match days Mon-Sat 10.30-5, Sun 1-5 to visitors who have paid ground admission.
♿ *(by arrangement) toilets for disabled shop* 🐕
Details not confirmed for 1995
See advertisement on page 105

Primrose Hill
ST JOHNS WOOD (NW8)
Once part of the same hunting forest as Regent's Park, Primrose Hill retains in its name the rural character and charm that it undoubtedly had in the past. The view

from the summit is panoramic and encompasses virtually the whole of central London. In 1842 its 62 acres gained gaslights, a gymnasium and respectability as a Royal Park.

Bushy Park
TEDDINGTON
Situated close to Hampton Court, this is one of London's ten Royal Parks, formerly hunting preserves, which were opened to the public by Charles I and Charles II. Bushy Park has a famous 3/4-mile Chestnut Avenue which runs from Hampton Court to the Teddington Gate. This superb double row of enormous trees, laid out by Wren, is best seen in springtime.

Marble Hill House
TWICKENHAM
Richmond Rd
☎0181-892 5115
An example of the English Palladian school of architecture, Marble Hill House was built between 1724 and 1729 for Henrietta Howard, mistress of George II and later Countess of Suffolk. The house is furnished with Georgian furniture and paintings. The Great Room has fine Italian paintings by Panini.
Open all year, daily, Good Fri-Sep, 10-6; Oct-Maundy Thu, 10-4. (Closed 24-25 Dec).
🅿 🍽 ✗ *licensed* ⓗ *toilets for disabled shop* ⌀ *(ex in grounds)*
Details not confirmed for 1995

Orleans House Gallery
TWICKENHAM
Riverside (off A305, along Orleans Rd to Riverside)
☎0181-892 0221
The art gallery holds temporary exhibitions throughout the year and is adjacent to James Gibbs's baroque Octagon Room. Built about 1720, it is all that remains of Orleans House, where Louis Philippe, Duc d'Orleans, King of France 1830-48, lived during his exile.

The Octagon Room and Gallery are in a woodland setting beside the river.
Open all year, Tue-Sat 1-5.30 (4.30pm Oct-Mar), Sun & BH 2-5.30 (Oct-Mar 2-4.30). (Closed Good Fri & 24-26 Dec). Woodland Gardens daily, 9-dusk. Free.
🅿 ⓗ *(handling objects & large print labels for some exhibitions) toilets for disabled shop* ⌀

Vestry House Museum
WALTHAMSTOW (E17)
Vestry Road, near Hoe St (Underground - Walthamstow Central)
☎0181-509 1917
Exhibits of local interest are shown in this small museum housed in a former 18th-century workhouse. It boasts an interesting collection of domestic objects but perhaps its most fascinating piece is the Bremer car: Britain's first vehicle driven by an internal combustion engine. The building is located in Walthamstow Village, a conservation area which is worth a visit in itself. Temporary exhibitions will be held throughout the year including one to commemorate the 50th anniversary of the end of World War II.
Open all year, Mon-Fri 10-1 & 2-5.30, Sat 10-1 & 2-5 (Closed BH). Free.
P *(20 yds)* ⓗ *shop* ⌀

William Morris Gallery
WALTHAMSTOW (E17)
Lloyd Park, Forest Rd (Underground - Walthamstow Central)
☎0181-527 3782
William Morris was a great Victorian artist, craftsman, poet and free thinker. This house, his home from 1848 to 1856 and then known as Water House, has been devoted to the life and work of Morris, his followers, contemporaries and the Morris Company. Recently refurbished displays include fabrics, stained glass, wallpaper and furniture, much of which is still fashionable today.

To complete the picture of this innovative period in the history of art and philosophy there are also Pre-Raphaelite paintings, sculpture by Rodin, ceramics and a collection of pictures by Frank Brangwyn, who worked briefly for Morris. A varied programme of events is run by the museum throughout the year and includes an exhibition of Weaving Techniques (22 April-18 June).
Open all year, Tue-Sat and 1st Sun in each month 10-1 & 2-5. (Closed Mon & BH's). Telephone for Xmas/New Year opening times. Free.
🅿 ⓗ *shop* ⌀

Wembley Stadium Tours
WEMBLEY
Empire Way (Underground - Wembley Park)
☎0181-902 8833
Wembley is the world's most famous stadium and is unique in the history of sport and entertainment. From the FA Cup Final in 1923, the 1948 Olympic Games, the 1966 World Cup, Live Aid in 1985, to the 1992 European Cup Final and Freddie Mercury Tribute Concert, many millions of people have experienced the magic of Wembley Stadium. It has also been the venue for rugby league, greyhound racing, American football, baseball, boxing and speedway.
On your stadium tour you will visit many fascinating behind-the-scenes areas the public do not normally see. Tour highlights include the stadium's event control rooms, television studio, cinema, hospital, England changing room and the player's tunnel. Take a trip around the stadium on Wembley's own land train, walk up the famous 39 steps to receive the cup to the roar of the crowd and sit in the Royal Box.'
Open all year, daily summer 10-4, winter 10-3 (Closed on event days, 25 & 26 Dec).
£5.95 (ch & pen £4.50, students £5.25). Party 20+. Prices under review.
🅿 ⓗ *(limited tour by arrangement) toilets for disabled shop* ⌀

Grange Museum of Community History
WILLESDEN (NW10)
Neasden Ln (Underground - Neasden)
☎0181-452 8311
Housed in a building that dates from around 1700, the Grange museum which was opened in 1977 tells the story of the people of the suburbs of Wembley and Willesden. A new gallery 'Brent People' is about the area that now forms the London Borough of Brent, and features audio listening posts and computerised CDs.
Open all year, Sep-May, Mon-Fri 11-5, Sat 10-12 & 1-5. Closed Sun; Jun-Aug, Tue,-Fri 11-5, Sat 10-12 & 1-5, Sun 2-5. Closed Mon.
🅿 ⓗ *shop* ⌀
Details not confirmed for 1995

Wimbledon Lawn Tennis Museum
WIMBLEDON (SW19)
All England Club, Church Rd (Underground - Wimbledon Park)
☎0181-946 6131
Wimbledon is synonymous with lawn tennis and the museum in the grounds of the All England Lawn Tennis Club is the only one of its kind in the world. Trophies, pictures, displays and memorabilia trace the development of the game over the last century. There is a Special Exhibitions Gallery. See also the famous Centre Court.
Open all year, Tue-Sat 10.30-5, Sun 2-5. (Closed Mon, BHs & Fri-Sun before Championships & middle Sun of Championships).'Phone for Xmas/New Year opening times.
✳£2.50 (ch & pen £1.50, student card £1.50). Party 20+.
🅿 🍽 ⓗ *(lift) toilets for disabled shop* ⌀

Museum of Artillery in the Rotunda
WOOLWICH (SE18)
Repository Rd
☎0181-316 5402
The guns, muskets, rifles and edged weapons that form the collections in this museum are contained in the rotunda designed by John Nash that once stood in St James's Park. The collection tells the story of the gun from its beginning in the 13th-century to the present day, in an unrivalled display of ordnance, including ammunition.
Open all year, Mon-Fri 12-5 (4pm Oct-Mar); Sat & Sun 1-5 (4pm Oct-Mar). (Closed Good Fri, 24-26 Dec & 1 Jan). Due to change in Mar, please ring for details.
Admission prices under review.
🅿 ⓗ *shop* ⌀

Thames Barrier Visitors Centre
WOOLWICH (SE18)
Unity Way
☎0181-854 1373
Built to prevent the possibility of disastrous flooding, the Thames Barrier spans a third of a mile and is the world's largest movable flood barrier. It is sometimes described as the eighth wonder of the world. The nearby visitors' centre and exhibition on the South Bank explains the flood threat and the construction of this £480 million project. Each month a test closure, lasting over 2 hours, is carried out and the annual full day closure of all ten gates takes place in the autumn.
Open all year, Mon-Fri 10-5, Sat & Sun 10.30-5.30. (Closed Xmas - telephone for details). Evening openings by special arrangements for groups - telephone for details.
£2.50 (ch & pen £1.55). Car park 50p Coach park Free. Family ticket £6.80. Party.
🅿 *(charged)* 🍽 ✗ *licensed* ⓗ *(lift from river pier approach) toilets for disabled shop* ⌀

MAN, ISLE OF

MAN, ISLE OF
Tailless cats and motorcycle racing make up the popular image of the Isle of Man. Both have their place among the island's attractions: the cats are bred at Noble's Park, and an entire museum is devoted to motorcycles. But above all Manxmen (as the islanders are called) have been seafarers with a Viking past which is recalled in the island's museums. The ancient castles of Rushen and Peel were built to protect the island against frequent invaders. Rushen was home of Man's Viking kings until 1265 and then, after disputes between Scotland and England over who should rule the island, from 1329 all Lords of Man were English. The island's parliament, The House of Keys, was held in Castle Rushen until 1710. Manxmen were quick to adapt to the Industrial Revolution and a railway network, of which parts still survive today - as steam and electric railways - soon covered the island.

Curraghs Wild Life Park
ISLE OF MAN
BALLAUGH
☎ Sulby (01624) 897323
Developed adjacent to the reserve area of the Ballaugh Curraghs is the wildlife park, which exhibits a large variety of animals and birds in natural settings. Large walk through enclosures let visitors explore the world of wildlife, including local habitats along the Curraghs nature trail. The miniature railway runs on Sundays.
Open Etr-Oct, daily 10-6. Last admission 5.15pm. Oct-Etr, Sat & Sun 10-4.
❋£2.70 (ch £1.20). Party 25+.
🅿 🍴 ⅅ *toilets for disabled shop* ✕

Castle Rushen
ISLE OF MAN
CASTLETOWN
☎ Douglas (01624) 675522
On view to the visitor are the state apartments of this 14th-century stronghold. There is also a Norman keep, flanked by towers from its later rebuilding, with a clock given by Elizabeth I in 1597. The castle is available for private hire.
Open Etr-Sep, daily 10-5.
£2.80 (ch & pen £1.40).
P (100 yds) ⅅ *shop* ✕

Nautical Museum
ISLE OF MAN
CASTLETOWN
☎ Douglas (01624) 675522
The island's colourful relationship with the sea is illustrated here. There is an 18th-century Manx yacht and interesting Cabin Room and Quayle Room. Other areas comprise displays of net-making equipment and sailing ships.
Open Etr-late Sep, daily 10-5.
❋£1.80 (ch & pen 90p).
P (50 yds) ⅅ *shop* ✕

Cregneash Village Folk Museum
ISLE OF MAN
CREGNEISH
(2m from Port Erin/Port St Mary)
☎ Douglas (01624) 675522
A group of traditional Manx cottages with their gardens and walled enclosures. Inside the cottages furniture and the everyday equipment used by typical Manx crofting communities are displayed. A crofter-fisherman's home, a farmstead, a turner's shed, smithy and a weaver's shed are all represented in realistic settings. Spinning demonstrations are given on certain days and sometimes a blacksmith can be seen at work. In the field adjoining the turner's shed, Manx Loghtan sheep can often be viewed; this ancient breed survives in very small numbers. The rams have a tendency to produce four, or even six, horns.
Open Etr-Sep, daily 10-5.

❋£1.80 (ch & pen 90p).
🅿 🍴 ✕ ⅅ *shop* ✕ (*ex in grounds*)

Manx Museum
ISLE OF MAN
DOUGLAS
☎ (01624) 675522
The 'Story of Man' begins at Manx Museum, where a specially produced film portrayal of Manx history complements the award-winning gallery displays. This showcase of Manx heritage provides the ideal starting-point to a journey of rich discovery embracing the length and breadth of the island.
Open all year, Mon-Sat 10-5. (Closed Sun, Xmas, New Year, Good Fri & am of Tynwald Day 5 Jul).
Free.
🅿 ✕ *licensed* ⅅ *toilets for disabled shop* ✕

Laxey Wheel
ISLE OF MAN
LAXEY
☎ Douglas (01624) 675522
Constructed to keep the lead mines free from water, this big wheel, known as the 'Lady Isabella', is an impressive sight at 72.5ft in diameter. It is the largest working wheel in the world.
Open Etr-Sep, daily 10-5.
❋£1.80 (ch & pen 90p).
🅿 ⅅ *shop* ✕

Peel Castle
ISLE OF MAN
PEEL
(on Patricks Isle, facing Peel Bay)
☎ Douglas (01624) 675522
The castle was built to protect the cathedral of St German's, perhaps founded by St Patrick. A phantom black dog, the Moddey Dhoo, is said to have haunted the castle. Sir Walter Scott used the story in *Peveril of the Peak.*
Open Etr-Sep, daily 10-5.
❋£1.60 (ch & pen 80p).
🅿 *shop* ✕

'The Grove' Rural Life Museum
ISLE OF MAN
RAMSEY
(on W side of Andreas Road)
☎ Douglas (01624) 675522
For an intimate glimpse into the everyday life of a previous era this Victorian villa is well worth a visit. Inside there are many of the original furnishings and personal belongings of the former owners, the Gibb family, displayed among the minutiae of Victorian life, both upstairs and downstairs. The outbuildings house a collection of early agricultural equipment including a horse-driven threshing mill; one of the few to survive in working order. There is also an exhibition on bees and bee-keeping.
Open Etr-Sep, daily 10-5.
❋£1.80 (ch & pen 90p).
🅿 🍴 ⅅ *shop* ✕

Murray's Museum
ISLE OF MAN
SNAEFELL MOUNTAIN
Bungalow Corner (Junction A14 & A18)
☎ Laxey (01624) 861719
The TT races are perhaps the best-known feature of the Isle of Man, and not surprisingly the island has a motorcycle museum. Situated at the Bungalow corner on the TT course, this is an historic collection of 150 motorcycles and cycles, plus motoring and motorcycling memorabilia and equipment.
Open 25 May-25 Sep daily 10.30-5.
🅿 🍴 ⅅ *shop*
Details not confirmed for 1995

MERSEYSIDE

Birkenhead Priory
BIRKENHEAD
Priory St
☎ 0151-666 1249
Founded in 1150, the Priory provided accommodation for the Prior and 16 Benedictine monks. Most of the

buildings were neglected after the Dissolution, but not all are ruined. An interpretive centre traces the history and development of the site. St Mary's, the first parish church of Birkenhead, was opened in 1821 adjacent to the Priory: only the tower now stands. However, the original clock mechanism and one bell have been re-installed with new displays. The tower offers superb views of the River Mersey and the surrounding area.
Open all year, Tue-Sat 10.30-1.30 & 2-5, Sun 2-5 (Closed Xmas, New Year & some BH's).
🅿 🍴 ⅅ *toilets for disabled shop* ✕
Details not confirmed for 1995

HMS Plymouth &
HMS Onyx BIRKENHEAD
East Float, Dock Rd
☎ 0151-650 1573
Here is a chance to see the Falklands frigate, *Plymouth* battered by the Argentine Air Force but home safely. She conducted a record breaking 117-day patrol during the conflict; see how her men and the SAS lived in this unique attraction. Also here is *HMS Onyx,* the only submarine afloat in the UK that you can explore.
Open all year, daily 10-dusk.
🅿 🍴 *shop* ✕
Details not confirmed for 1995

Williamson Art Gallery & Museum
BIRKENHEAD
Slatey Rd
☎ 0151-652 4177
English watercolours and works by the Liverpool school are an outstanding feature of the gallery, which was specially built for the purpose. There is a large collection of pictures by P Wilson Steer, and also on view are sculpture, ceramics (English, Continental and Oriental), glass, silver and furniture. Exhibitions are held throughout the year. The museum is linked to the gallery, and has displays on the history of the town and its port. Birkenhead was a hamlet before

the 19th century, but grew large and rich through ship-building and the docks, so model ships are an important feature of this collection. Also on view are the Baxter Motor Collection, cars and motorbikes in a period garage setting. There is a full exhibition programme at the Gallery.
Open all year, Mon-Sat 10-5, Sun 2-5. . (Closed BH's Xmas & Good Fri).
🅿 ⅅ *shop* ✕
Details not confirmed for 1995

LIVERPOOL
Liverpool was a small fishing village which grew to become one of the world's largest ports. Today the huge Liver Building, the last sight of home for millions of immigrants sailing for the New World, still dominates the now silent waterfront. The bustle of the shipping which used to enliven seven miles of waterfront is virtually stilled - but Liverpool's dockland has been reborn, with a superb maritime museum and a wide range of other exhibition centres forming a living village around the Albert Dock complex. This is a city with two cathedrals dominating the skyline, one Victorian Gothic on a splendid scale and one, ultra-modern. Many of the other public buildings are grand and stately, a sign of the wealth of earlier times. The imposing Walker Gallery houses the largest collections of paintings in Britain outside London. During the 1960s, after a period of decline, Liverpool again became famous as the home of the Beatles and the new music.

Animation World
LIVERPOOL
Britannia Pavilion, Albert Dock
☎ 0151-707 1828
A permanent exhibition of cartoon and animation, including hands-on displays, workshops and model studios and

fantasy sets. Also original sets, models and drawings from children's favourite TV characters such as Count Duckula, Danger Mouse and Wind in the Willows.
Open all year, daily 10-6 (Nov-Feb 11-5).
P & toilets for disabled shop %
Details not confirmed for 1995

The Beatles Story
LIVERPOOL
Britannia Pavilion, Albert Dock
☎0151-709 1963
Winner of the English Tourist Board's 'Come to Britain' award 1991, the sights and sounds of the sixties can be relived at The Beatles Story. You can take a trip to Hamburg, 'feel' the cavern beat, 'tune in' to flower power, board the yellow submarine and battle with a Beatle brain computer. A magical history tour for all the family. There is an annual Beatles convention.
Open all year, daily 10-6 (last admission 1 hr before closing). (Closed 25 & 26 Dec).
P & toilets for disabled shop %
Details not confirmed for 1995

Croxteth Hall & Country Park
LIVERPOOL
(5m NE of city centre)
☎0151-228 5311
Visitors can step back in time and join an Edwardian house party when they visit the displays in Croxteth Hall - the Edwardian rooms are furnished with period pieces and character figures. The grounds of this former home of the Earls of Sefton contain a Victorian walled garden, a unique collection of rare breed animals, a miniature railway and an adventure playground. Croxteth Hall is a popular venue for special events, it also boasts an award-winning educational service..
Open, all facilities daily 11-5 in season (phone for details): Some facilities remain open through winter, hours on request. Hall £1.10; Farm £1.10; Walled Garden 60p (ch + pen half price). All inclusive ticket £2.50 (ch & pen £1.25).
P 💺 & toilets for disabled shop % (ex in park & grounds)

HM Customs & Excise National Museum
LIVERPOOL
Merseyside Maritime Museum, Albert Dock
☎0151-207 0001
A chance to experience the activities of customs officers today through interactive, hands-on displays. You get a chance to detect concealed goods or spot the smugglers among a group of suspicious characters. There are a wide range of confiscated goods on display as well as sniffer dog demonstrations and a new exhibition on 18th-century smuggling.
Open all year, daily 10.30-5.30. Last admission 4.30pm. (Closed Good Fri, 24-26 Dec & 1 Jan).
❋£3 (concessions £1.50). Family ticket £8.
P (charged) ✗ licensed & (basement not accessible) toilets for disabled shop %

Liverpool Football Club Visitors Centre Museum
LIVERPOOL
Anfield Rd
☎0151-263 2361
Come to Anfield and enjoy the magnificent display of trophies and mememtoes representing the achievement of one of soccers most successful clubs. Experience and share some of the great moments in the club's history, captured on video.
Open all year, Mon-Fri. Tours starting at 2 & 3pm. (Closed Xmas wk). Advance booking advisable.
P & shop %
Details not confirmed for 1995

Liverpool Libraries & Information Services
LIVERPOOL
William Brown St
☎0151-225 5429
The Picton, Hornby and Brown buildings house Liverpool's collection of over two million books, forming one of Britain's largest and oldest public libraries. First

editions, prints and fine bindings are permanently displayed at Hornby while the reference, international, scientific and technical collections are housed in the Picton and Brown buildings. Regular temporary exhibitions.
Open all year, Mon-Thu 9-7.30 (Fri & Sat 9-5). Closed PHs.
P (300 yds) 💺 & (lift) toilets for disabled %
Details not confirmed for 1995

Merseyside Maritime Museum
LIVERPOOL
Albert Dock
☎0151-207 0001
A large award-winning museum in restored 19th-century docklands, which includes a Cooperage, and the Albert Dock Warehouse, containing varied displays about the Port of Liverpool. There are floating craft, outdoor exhibits of maritime crafts and demonstrations. Permanent displays include Emigrants to a New World, Art and the Sea, World of Models and Transatlantic Slavery Against Human Dignity. Anything to Declare? HM Customs and Excise National Museum is located on the ground floor.
Open all year, daily 10.30-5.30 (last admission 4.30pm). (Closed Good Fri, 24-26 Dec & 1 Jan).
£3 (ch, pen, students & UB40's £1.50). Family ticket £8. Party 20+.
P (charged) 💺 ✗ licensed & (Lifts & free wheelchair) toilets for disabled shop %

Museum of Liverpool Life
LIVERPOOL
Albert Dock
☎0151-207 0001
This new museum explores the history of Liverpool, its people and their contribution to National life. Displays focus on three main themes: Mersey Culture, Making a Living and Demanding a Voice.
Open all year, daily 10.30-5.30. Last admission 4.30.
P (charged) 💺 ✗ licensed & toilets for disabled shop %
Details not confirmed for 1995

Tate Gallery Liverpool
LIVERPOOL
Albert Dock
☎0151-709 3223 & 0151-709 0507
A converted Vicorian warehouse with stunning views across the River Mersey, Tate Gallery, Liverpool offers visitors a unique opportunity to see the best of the national collection of 20th-century art. Complementing collection displays, the Gallery has a changing programme of exhibitions drawing upon works by internationally renowned artists across from public and private collections across the world. Special events for 1995 include: Video Positive '95 - a biennial celebration of some of the most innovative work in video art (29 April-4 June); Venus Re-defined: Sculpture by Rodin, Matisse and contemporaries, held until June; Festival Show (29 July-end October).
Open Tue-Sun 10-6. (Closed Mon ex BH Mon).

Free. Admission to special exhibitions £2.50 (concessions £1) Family ticket £5.
P 💺 & (wheelchairs available) toilets for disabled shop %

Walker Art Gallery
LIVERPOOL
William Brown St
☎0151-207 0001
An outstanding collection of European paintings, and sculpture. Especially notable are the Italian, Netherlands, and Pre-Raphaelite and Victorian paintings. There is an award-winning sculpture gallery and temporary exhibitions are held throughout the year.
Open all year, Mon-Sat 10-5, Sun 2-5. (Closed Good Fri, 24-26 Dec & 1 Jan). Donations.
P (charged) 💺 & (prior notice appreciated, wheelchair on request) shop %

Port Sunlight Heritage Centre
PORT SUNLIGHT
95 Greendale Rd (junc 4 of M53 on B5137)
☎0151-644 6466
The picturesque garden village was built by William Hesketh Lever for the workers in his soap factory, the first sod for the development being cut by Mrs Lever in 1888. The Heritage Centre tells the story of the village, the factory and its workers and a village trail incorporates the varied architecture, beautiful open spaces and the Lady Lever Art Gallery with its world-famous collection of pre-Raphaelite paintings and Wedgwood.
Open all year. Apr-Oct, daily 10-4. Nov-Etr, Mon-Fri 10-4. The Lady Lever Art Gallery will be closed from Sep 1994 for approx 9 mths.
❋40p (ch 20p).
P (on road 1hr limit) & shop %

Knowsley Safari Park
PRESCOT
☎0151-430 9009
A five-mile drive through the reserves enables visitors to see lions, tigers, elephants, rhinos, monkeys and many other animals in spacious, natural surroundings. Extra attractions include a children's amusement park, reptile house, pets' corner plus sealion shows and a miniature railway.
Open, Game reserves Mar-Oct. Other attractions Etr-Sep. Daily 10-4.
£8 per car (incl all occupants). No soft-topped cars (safari bus available). Coach passengers £2.50 (ch 2-15 & pen £1.50).
P 💺 & toilets for disabled shop % (kennels provided)

Prescot Museum of Clock & Watch Making
PRESCOT
34 Church St
☎0151-430 7787
An attractive 18th-century town house contains exhibits pertaining to the clock, watch and tool-making industries of the area. The display includes a reconstruction of part of a traditional ➤

watch-maker's workshop and examples of hand tools and machinery used to make the intricate parts of clock and watch movements. There is a programme of exhibitions, telephone for details.
Open all year, Tue-Sat & BH Mon 10-5, Sun 2-5 (Closed 24-26 Dec, 1 Jan & Good Fri).
Free.
P & shop 🐾

Pilkington Glass Museum ST HELENS
Prescot Rd (on A58, 1.5m from town centre)
☎(01744) 692499 & 692014
Since the 18th century, St Helens has gained a world-wide reputation for flat glass production. The glass museum traces the history of glassmaking from the Egyptians to the present day, with some of the finest examples of glass in the world. Visitors can learn of the many applications of glass in buildings, transport, lighting, science and technology. Other attractions are a special mirrors display and the hands-on interactive exhibits such as the working periscope, and the night vision display. A full programme of temporary exhibitions is planned for 1995.
Open all year, Mon-Fri 10-5; Sat, Sun & BH 2-4.30 (Closed Xmas-New Year). Also evenings for groups by appointment.
Free.
P & (stair lift not suitable for wheelchairs) toilets for disabled shop 🐾

Atkinson Art Gallery SOUTHPORT
Lord St
☎(01704) 533133 ext 2110
The gallery specialises in 19th-and 20th-century oil paintings, watercolours, drawings and prints, as well as 20th-century sculpture. There is also a programme of visiting exhibitions.
Open all year, Mon, Tue, Wed & Fri 10-5, Thu & Sat 10-1. (Closed 25-26 Dec & 1 Jan).
Free.
& shop 🐾

Botanic Gardens Museum SOUTHPORT
Botanic Rd, Churchtown (2m N)
☎(01704) 27547
A small museum with interesting displays of natural history, Victoriana, Liverpool porcelain and dolls. The newly refurbished natural history gallery is due to open Easter 1995.
Open all year, Tue-Fri 11-3, Sat & Sun 2-5, BH's 12-4. (Closed 25, 26 Dec & 1 Jan also Fri following BH Mon).
Free.
P & toilets for disabled shop 🐾

Southport Railway Centre SOUTHPORT
The Old Engine Shed, Derby Rd
☎(01704) 530693
A thousand feet of standard gauge rail connects the museum to the British Rail system. Within the Railway Centre,

which is housed in the former Lancashire and Yorkshire Engine Shed, are ex-British Rail locomotives as well as several industrial locomotives, and also on display are local buses, tramcars, traction engines and a variety of other vehicles, making up what is possibly the largest preservation centre of its type in north-west England.
Open all year, Oct-May, Sat & Sun 1-5; Jun-Sep, Sat & Sun 11-5; Jun & first wk Sep wkdays 1-4.30; Jul & Aug wkdays 10.30-4.30. Also BH periods 11-5.
P 🍴 & toilets for disabled shop
Details not confirmed for 1995

Southport Zoo & Conservation Trust SOUTHPORT
Princes Park
☎(01704) 538102
The zoo is situated in five acres of landscaped gardens. Amongst the many animals to be seen are lions, snow leopards, lynx, chimpanzees, parrots, penguins and llamas. An extension houses a pets' corner barn, a giant tortoise house, primate house, porcupines and a baby chimpanzee house. There is also a reptile house with an aquarium. Gift shop. During the summer there are snake handling sessions with talks.
Open all year (ex 25 Dec) 10-6 in summer, 10-4 in winter,
£2.50 (ch £1.50, pen £2). Party 20+
P (100 yds) 🍴 & toilets for disabled shop

Speke Hall SPEKE
The Walk (follow signs for Liverpool Airport)
☎0151-427 7231
This remarkable manor house was built around a square courtyard and originally had a moat. It is mainly Elizabethan, but was started in 1490, and is one of the most richly timbered houses in England. There is a vast Tudor great hall that contrasts with the later Victorian, small panelled rooms. The kitchen and the servants' hall are open and there is some elaborate 16th-and 17th-century plasterwork to be seen in the great parlour. Additional delights are the priest's hole, examples of William Morris wallpaper, and the Mortlake tapestries. Special events for 1995 include: Centenary Summer Serenade (3-4 June), Blue Peter Day Out (27 May), Midsummer Nights' Dream and the Merry Wives of Windsor (30 June-1 July). For details of special events write to the Administrator, Speke Hall, The Walk, Speke, Liverpool, L24 1XD enclosing an s.a.e.
House open; Apr-29 Oct, daily (ex Mon but open BH Mon) 1-5.30, 4 Nov-17 Dec, Sat & Sun 12-4.30. Garden open daily (ex Mon & Closed 24-26 Dec, 31 Dec, 1 Jan & Good Fri).
Hall & Gardens: £3.60 (ch £1.80). Family ticket £9. Party.
P 🍴 & toilets for disabled shop 🐾
(NT)

NORFOLK

Baconsthorpe Castle BACONSTHORPE
The castle was really a moated and semi-fortified house, built by the Heydon family in the 15th century. It is now a ruin, but the gatehouses, curtain walls and towers can still be seen.
Open any reasonable time.
Free.
P
(EH)

Banham Zoo BANHAM
The Grove (on B1113)
☎Quiddenham (01953) 887771
Enjoy a great day out among some of the world's rare and endangered animals including snow leopards, cheetahs, Grevy's Zebra, jackass, penguins, many exotic birds and a large collection of primates. Daily animal feeding sessions and keeper talks are not only fun but educational too. Find out about penguins, fur seals and squirrel monkeys. Wander through the deer park, woodland walk, and monkey jungle island. Other attractions include an adventure playground, road train, all weather activity centre and soft play area. There are activities and competitions throughout the school half term holidays. Many special events are planned throughout the year.
Open all year, daily from 10am. (Closed 25-26 Dec).
✱*Prices under review. Disabled & party rates available.*
P 🍴 ✗ licensed & (wheelchair available) toilets for disabled shop 🐾

Bircham Windmill BIRCHAM, GREAT
(0.5m W off unclassified Snettisham rd).
☎Syderstone (01485) 578393
This windmill is one of the last remaining in Norfolk. Sails turn on windy days, and the adjacent tea room serves home-made cakes, light lunches and cream teas. The working coal-fired oven in the bakehouse bakes bread which visitors can buy.
Open daily 27 Mar-Sep, 10-6. (Closed Sat).
✱*£2 (ch £1.25, pen £1.75)*
P 🍴 shop

Blickling Hall BLICKLING
(on B1354)
☎Aylsham (01263) 733084
Flanked by dark yew hedges and topped by pinnacles, the warm red brick front of Blickling makes a memorable sight. The house was built in the early 17th century, but the hedges may be earlier. They stand some 17ft tall and 10ft wide. The centrepiece of the house is the carved oak staircase which winds up in double flights from the hall. It was moved from another part of the house and adapted to fit a new 18th-century scheme. (There is also a lift.) On the first floor is Blickling's most celebrated room, the Long Gallery, where the 125ft-long ceiling is covered in ornate Jacobean plasterwork. The work was done by Edward Stanyon, who charged £50.80 for the 'freat seeling'. Stanyon also provided the intricate decorations for the south drawing room, another of the original state rooms, at 'fyve shillings and six pence a yard square' An equally remarkable room is the Chinese bedroom, which still has hand-painted Chinese wallpaper from the 18th-century. Amongst the house's fine furnishing tapestries is a set of eight 17th-century Mortlake works, and the many pictures include a Canaletto. The grounds include woodland and a lake, a formal parterre, and a moat filled with roses, camellias and other plants.

Open 25 Mar-5 Nov, Tue, Wed, Fri-Sun & BH Mon 1-5 (Closed Good Fri). Gardens open from noon, same days as House but daily Jul-Aug, 11-5.
£4.90 (ch £2.45). Gardens only £2.50 (ch £1.25). Party 15+
P 🍴 ✗ licensed & (wheelchairs, Braille guide) toilets for disabled shop garden centre 🐾
(NT)

Bressingham Steam Museum & Gardens BRESSINGHAM
(on A1066)
☎(01379) 687386 & 687382
Alan Bloom is an internationally recognised nurseryman and a steam enthusiast, and has combined his interests to great effect at Bressingham. There are three steam-hauled trains: a 9.5in gauge garden railway, a 15in gauge running through two and a half miles of the wooded Waveney Valley, a 2ft gauge running through two and a quarter miles of Europe's largest hardy plant nursery and a standard gauge engine giving demonstrations on certain days. The Dell Garden has 5000 species of perennials and alpines, grouped in island beds; Foggy Bottom has wide vistas, pathways, trees, shrubs, conifers and winter colour (restricted opening). There is a collection of 50 road and rail engines, many restored to working order. A steam roundabout is another attraction, and the Norfolk fire museum is housed here. Various events are held here during the year including the Bressingham Bus Day (16 July), Steam in Miniature Rally (12-13 August), Annual Model Railway Day (24 September). Services operating will vary according to steaming programme.
Open - Steam Museum & Dell Garden - Apr-Sep, Tue-Sun 10-5.30. Also 24-30 Oct & Sun in Oct. Gardeners Day - Dell Garden & Foggy Bottom every Mon 4 Apr-Oct. Telephone to confirm details.
✱*£3.50 (ch £2.50) Party 12+. Admission to one garden £2, both gardens £3.*
P ✗ licensed & (wheelchair can be taken onto Nursery Line Railway) toilets for disabled shop garden centre 🐾

Berney Arms Windmill BURGH CASTLE
☎(01493) 700605
Access is by boat from Great Yarmouth or by rail to Berney Arms station: the road to the mill is unsuitable for cars. This lonely, seven-storey landmark dates back to the 19th century, and helped to drain the marshes. In earlier years it was also used to grind clinker for cement. The machinery for both functions can be seen.
Open Apr-Sep, daily 10-6.
£1 (ch 50p, concessions 80p)
& 🐾
(EH)

The Castle BURGH CASTLE
(off A143)
Burgh Castle was built in the third century AD by the Romans, as one of a chain of forts along the Saxon Shore - the coast where Saxon invaders landed. Sections of the massive walls still stand, (some parts faced with flint), and are protected by bastions where 'ballistae' or giant catapults may have been mounted.
Open any reasonable time.
Free.
(EH)

Roman Town CAISTER-ON-SEA
The name Caister has Roman origins, and this was in fact a Roman naval base. The remains include the south gateway, a town wall built of flint with brick bonding courses, and part of what may have been a seamen's hostel.
Open any reasonable time.
Free.
(EH)

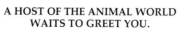
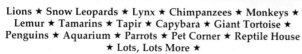

The grounds of Felbrigg Hall have an orangery and a restored walled-garden which is overlooked by a dovecote for 2,000 birds.

Castle Acre Priory
CASTLE ACRE
☎ Swaffham (01760) 755394
The priory was built for the Clunaic order by Earl Warren, son-in-law of William the Conqueror. Twenty-five monks once lived here in great state, but the priory fell into ruin after the Dissolution in 1536. Rising above the extensive remains is the glorious, arcaded west front of the priory church, a reminder of past splendour. The chapel can also be seen, and there is a 15th-century gatehouse.
Earl Warren also built a great castle, which was developed during the Middle Ages. Edward I was entertained there in 1297, at a time when the walls were 7ft thick. Today there are only ruins and earthworks, but even these are on an impressive scale.
Open all year, Apr-Sep, daily 10-6; Oct 10-4; Nov-Mar, Wed-Sun 10-4. Closed 24-26 Dec & 1 Jan.
£2.20 (ch £1.10, concessions £1.70).
🅿 🚻 *shop*
(EH)

Castle Rising Castle
CASTLE RISING
(off A149)
☎ (01553) 631330
The fine Norman keep was probably built by the Earl of Arundel. It stands in massive earthworks and the remains of a bridge and gatehouse can also be seen.
Open all year, Apr-Sep, daily 10-6; Oct, 10-4; Nov-Mar, Wed-Sun 10-4. Closed 24-26 Dec & 1 Jan.
£1.30 (ch 70p, concessions £1).
🅿 🚻 *(exterior only) toilets for disabled shop* ⌘
(EH)

Iceni Village & Museum
COCKLEY CLEY
(off A1065)
☎ Swaffham (01760) 721339 & 24588
A village of the Iceni tribe has been reconstructed here, as it was 2,000 years ago, on the site where it was believed there was an Iceni encampment. There is also a museum, in a 15th-century cottage forge, with models and exhibits of local life from prehistoric times to the present day; and there is a museum of agricultural equipment, vintage engines and carriages. The nearby flint church dates back to around 630. There is also a nature trail and picnic area.
Open Apr-Oct, daily 12-5.30 (Jul-Sep 11-5.30).
✱ £2.80 (ch 5-16 £1.30, pen & students £1.80). Party 10+.
🅿 🚻 *toilets for disabled shop*

Cromer Museum
CROMER
East Cottages, Tucker St
☎ (01263) 513543
The museum is housed in five 19th-century fishermen's cottages, one of which has period furnishings. There are pictures and exhibits from Victorian Cromer, with collections illustrating local natural history, archaeology, social history and geology.
Open all year, Mon-Sat 10-5, Sun 2-5. Closed Mon 1-2. (Closed Good Fri, Xmas period & 1 Jan).
£1 (ch 50p, pen, students & UB40s 60p). shop ⌘

Lifeboat Museum
CROMER
☎ (01263) 512503
The museum in No 2 boat house at the bottom of The Gangway covers local lifeboat history and the RNLI in general. Also of interest is the Lifeboat Station on the pier, where a lifeboat has been stationed since 1804. The history of Cromer from 1804 to the present day is shown together with models of lifeboats. The museum will be housing the recently acquired lifeboat 'The H F Bailey' which served on the station from 1935 to 1945 and which saved 518 lives. Also at the museum are 'The Blogg medals'.
Open May-Oct, daily 10-5. Free.
👤 *shop*

FAKENHAM
See Thursford Green

Felbrigg Hall
FELBRIGG
(off B1436)
☎ West Runton (01263) 837444
The name comes from the de Felbriggs, whose memorials can be seen in the isolated parish church at Felbrigg, but the house was built by the Windham family and was their home for 300 years. It is a splendid house of 1620 with a wing added in 1680, and has not changed on the outside since the 17th-century; inside there are handsome rooms with paintings and furniture which have been in the house since the 18th-century. Felbrigg Hall stands in a large park with fine old trees, and there is also a colourfully-restored walled garden overlooked by a dovecote built for 2000 birds. A Midsummer Open Air Festival will be held on certain evenings in June and July. Further details are available from the Administrator.
Open: House 25 Mar-5 Nov, Mon, Wed, Thu, Sat, Sun 1-5. BH Sun & Mon 11-5. Garden opens 11am. Park walks daily dawn-dusk.
House & garden £4.60 (ch £2.30). Garden £1.80 (ch 90p). Park free. Party.
🅿 🚻 ✗ *licensed* ♿ *(battery operated vehicle for garden, braille guide) toilets for disabled shop* ⌘ *(ex park)*
(NT)

Thrigby Hall Wildlife Gardens
FILBY
(on unclass road off A1064)
☎ Great Yarmouth (01493) 369477
The 250-year-old park of Thrigby Hall is now the home of animals and birds from Asia, and the lake has ornamental wildfowl. There are tropical and bird houses, a unique blue willow pattern garden and tree walk and a summer house as old as the park. The enormous jungled swamp hall, which has special features such as underwater viewing of large crocodiles, won the prestigious 1992 Animal Welfare Award.
Open all year, daily from 10.
£4.50 (ch 4-14 £3, pen £4).
🅿 🚻 ♿ *(wheelchairs available) toilets for disabled shop* ⌘

Bygone Village
FLEGGBURGH
Burgh St. Margaret (on A1064 between Acle and Caister-on-Sea)
☎ (01493) 369770
The Bygone Village is set in over 35 acres of Norfolk countryside. There is a working sawmill, a stone quarry and the Little Lady - a 1929 steam-powered timber wagon, trundling along the lanes. Other attractions include vintage cars, motorcycles, a 2ft narrow gauge railway, two railway engines, peacocks, farmyard animals, fairground, and adventure play area. Special events for 1995 include a Bygone Engine Rally (24-25 June).
Open Mar-Etr, Sun-Thu from 10-dusk; Etr-Oct, daily 10-6.
£4.80 (ch £3.60 pen £4.30).
🅿 🚻 ✗ ♿ *toilets for disabled shop* ⌘

Shell Museum
GLANDFORD
(1.5m off B1156)
☎ Cley (01263) 740081
The appealing little museum with its Dutch gables was built in 1915 to house sea shells and curios collected from all over the world by Sir Alfred Jodrell of nearby Bayfield Hall. Glandford itself is an estate village of the Hall, and its 1906 church is also worth seeing for its decorative carvings.
Open Feb-Nov, Mon-Thu 10-12.30 & 2-4.30, Fri & Sat 2-4.30pm. (Closed Dec-Jan & pm Nov-Feb).
✱ 50p (ch 16 20p). Prices under review.
🅿 ♿ ⌘

Gressenhall Norfolk Rural Life Museum & Union Farm
GRESSENHALL
Beech House (2.5m NW on unclass rd at Gressenhall).
☎ Dereham (01362) 860563
This museum portrays the history of Norfolk over the past 200 years. Housed in what used to be a workhouse, it has displays on all aspects of rural life, with special emphasis on agriculture, rural crafts and village life, with working reconstructions. Union Farm is a typical small mixed farm of the 1920s with heavy horses and rare breeds of sheep, cattle, pigs and poultry. There is a nature trail around the farm.
Open 9 Apr-Oct, Mon-Sat 10-5, Sun 12-5.30. Also BH Mons 10-5.
£3.50 (ch £1.50, concessions £2.50)
🅿 🚻 ♿ *(sound guide & wheelchair loan) toilets for disabled shop* ⌘

Grimes Graves
GRIMES GRAVES
☎ Thetford (01842) 810656
Grimes Graves is a network of hundreds of pits, dug by Neolithic people who were mining for flint between about 3000BC and 1900BC. This is the largest known group of flint mines in Britain, and consisted of vertical shafts leading to galleries through the flint seams. Visitors today can go down a shaft to crouch in the gloom and imagine themselves prising out the flints with antler picks and wooden levers. Each shaft must have provided about eight tons of flint, which went in rough form to other parts of the country to be turned into tools such as axes and knives.
Open all year, Apr-Sep, daily 10-6; Oct, 10-4; Nov-Mar, Wed-Sun 10-4. Closed 24-26 Dec & 1 Jan.
£1.30 (ch 70p, concessions £1). A torch is useful.
🅿 ♿ *(exhibition area, grounds only; access track rough)* ⌘
(EH)

Norfolk Lavender
HEACHAM
Caley Mill (on A149 at junc with B1454)
☎ (01485) 570384
This is the largest lavender-growing and distilling operation in Britain. Different coloured lavenders are grown in strips and harvested in July and August. There are also rose and herb gardens. There are guided tours of the distillery and gardens; and minibus trips visit a large lavender field on Mondays, Wednesdays and Fridays from mid June until mid August. Guardians of the National Collection of Lavenders (Norfolk).
Open all year, daily 10-5. (Closed for 2 wks Xmas).
✱ Admission to grounds Free. Guided tours £1, May, Jun & Sep. £1.50 July & August. Trip to Lavender Field £2.95, 3 times a day Mon, Wed & Fri mid Jun-mid Aug.
🅿 🚻 ♿ *(wheelchairs for loan) toilets for disabled shop garden centre*

Holkham Hall & Bygones Museum
HOLKHAM
(off A149)
☎ Fakenham (01328) 710227
The Palladian mansion was built in 1734 and was later inherited by Thomas William Coke, or 'Coke of Norfolk'. He became famous for pioneering work in the 'Agricultural Revolution' - and he also started a fashion revolution by wearing country clothes at court.
The house has a splendid marble hall and other sumptuous state rooms, with paintings by Rubens, Van Dyck, Claude Poussin, Gainsborough and others. The park is equally fine, with deer, geese on the lake, and an impressive collection of trees, especially ilexes. Also of interest are the Holkham Pottery, and the History of Farming Exhibition with audio-visual guides. The Bygones Museum, housed in the stable block adjoining the Hall, has over 5,000 items on display from gramophones to fire engines, coaches to cars, steam engines to motor cycles, and cameras to kitchens. The Holkham country fair will be held on 22-23 July.
Open 29 May-Sep, Sun-Thu, 1.30-5. Etr, May, Spring & Summer BHs Sun & Mon 11.30-5.
✱ Hall £3 (ch £1.50). Bygones £3 (ch £1.50). All inclusive £5 (ch £2.50). ➤

Elm Hill is a fine example of the narrow, winding, medieval streets, that make Norwich such an attractive city.

🅿 🍴 ⓰ *toilets for disabled shop garden centre* 🐾 *(ex in park & gardens)*

Drainage Windpump
HORSEY

The windpump mill was built 200 years ago to drain the area, and then rebuilt in 1912 by Dan England, a noted Norfolk millwright. It has been restored since being struck by lightning in 1943, and overlooks Horsey Mere and marshes, noted for their wild birds and insects.
Open 25 Mar-Sep, daily 11-5 (Jul & Aug till 6pm). (Closed Good Fri).
£1
🅿 *(charged)* 🍴 *shop*
(NT)

City of Norwich Aviation Museum
HORSHAM ST FAITH

Old Norwich Rd
☎ *Norwich (01603) 625309*
Run entirely by enthusiastic volunteers, this museum offers displays relating to the aeronautical history of the local area, supported by a fine collection of aircraft, engines and equipment featuring the Vulcan bomber. Some of the aircraft cockpits are open to visitors. The location of the museum also offers a good vantage point for viewing aircraft using the airport.
Open all year, Apr-Oct Sun 10-5 (also Wed 2-5pm, Tue & Thu eves 7.30pm-dusk May, Jun, Jul & Aug only); Nov-Mar Sun 10-3.30
£1.50 (ch & pen 75p)
🅿 🍴 ⓰ *shop* 🐾

Lynn Museum
KING'S LYNN

Market St
☎ *(01553) 775001*
Once it was a walled city of considerable importance; its two great churches, two marketplaces and two Guildhalls testify to its size. King's Lynn was also a noted port and a stop on the Pilgrim's Way to Walsingham. The geology, archaeology and natural history of the area are the main collections in the local museum. Specimens include an icthyosaur and a golden eagle. Objects in the archaeology gallery include Bronze Age weapons and the skeleton of a Saxon warrior. Relics from the medieval town of Lynn include an important collection of pilgrim badges. Farm tools, ship models and exhibits from a local fairground machinery firm are also on show.
Open all year, Mon-Sat, 10-5 (Closed BH, Xmas & New Year).
60p (ch 30p, concessions 40p).
⓰ *shop* 🐾

St George's Guildhall
KING'S LYNN

27 Kings St
☎ *(01553) 774725*
Although it has been used for many purposes, the theatrical associations of this 15th-century Guildhall are strongest: Shakespeare himself is said to have performed here. Its present use as the town's theatre was brought about in the 1950s after an 18th-century theatre, incorporated into the hall, was restored and enlarged.
When not in use as a theatre or cinema open Mon-Fri 10-5, Sat 10-12.30 & 2-4. (Closed Good Fri, 25-26 Dec & 1 Jan).
50p
✗ *licensed*
(NT)

Town House Museum of Lynn Life
KING'S LYNN

46 Queen St
☎ *(01553) 773450*
Opened in 1992, this museum shows the life of merchants, tradesmen and families who made Kings Lynn a prosperous place. Historic room displays include: costumes, toys, a working Victorian kitchen and a 1950s living room.
Open all year, Apr-Sep, Tue-Sat, 10-5, Sun 2-5; Oct-Mar Tue-Sat 10-4.
£1 (ch 50p, concessions 60p). Joint ticket with Gaol House £2.50 (concessions £1.80)
⓰ *shop* 🐾

Shirehall Museum
LITTLE WALSINGHAM

Common Place
☎ *Walsingham (01328) 820510*
The museum is in an almost perfect Georgian courtroom with its original fittings, including a prisoner's lock-up. The displays show Walsingham's history, with a special exhibition on the history of pilgrimage. There is also a tourist information centre.
Open Maundy Thu-Sep, Mon 10-1 & 2-5, Tue-Sat 10-5, Sun 2-5; Oct wknds only.
60p (ch 30p, pen, students & UB40s 40p).
shop 🐾

Walsingham Abbey Grounds
LITTLE WALSINGHAM

(take B1105 from Fakenham)
☎ *Walsingham (01328) 820259*
In the grounds of the new abbey are the ruins of the original Augustinian priory built in the 1100s. The priory was built over the shrine of Our Lady of Walsingham which had been established in 1061. The remains include the east wall of the church, the south wall of the refectory and one room, still intact.
Open Apr-Jul Wed, Sat & Sun; Aug Mon, Wed, Fri, Sat & Sun; Sep Wed, Sat & Sun. Also BHs Etr-Sep.
£1 (ch & pen 50p).
🅿 ⓰ *shop*

Creake Abbey
NORTH CREAKE

(1m N off B1355)
Church ruin with crossing and eastern arm belonging to a house of Augustinian canons founded in 1206.
Open any reasonable time.
Free.
(EH)

NORWICH

Norwich Cathedral's lofty spire - the highest Norman tower in Britain - is one among more than 20 towers and spires that thrust above the city's rooftops. The River Wensum winds round the city, enfolding the Norman castle and narrow streets and alleys that display many an old-world shop front. Famous for its mustard, printing and insurance today, in medieval times it was the centre of East Anglia's profitable wool trade and this part of England was among the most populous and prosperous.

Bridewell Museum
NORWICH

Bridewell Alley
☎ *(01603) 667228*
Built in the late 14th century, this flint-faced merchant's house was used as a prison from 1583 to 1828. It now houses displays illustrating the trades and industries of Norwich during the past 200 years, including a large collection of locally made boots and shoes.
Open all year, Mon-Sat, 10-5. (Closed Good Fri, Xmas & New Year)
Joint ticket for Bridewell, Strangers' Hall & Regimental Museum £1.40 (ch 70p, concessions £1.20)
shop 🐾

Guildhall
NORWICH

Guildhall Hill
☎ *(01603) 666071*
Visitors may visit the Council Chamber and view civic plate and insignia dating from 1549. The civic regalia is on view Monday to Friday 2-3.30pm, or at other times for parties by arrangement.
Open all year 6 days a week.
Free.
🅿 *(200 yds)* ⓰ *toilets for disabled* 🐾

Norwich Castle Museum
NORWICH

Castle Meadow
☎ *(01603) 223624*
Norman Castle Keep built in the 12th century, and museum housing displays of art, archaeology, natural history, Lowestoft porcelain, Norwich silver, a large collection of paintings (with special emphasis on the Norwich School of Painters) and British ceramic teapots.

There are also guided tours of the dungeons and battlements. Special events for 1995 include a dinosaur exhibition (17 June-3 September).
Open all year, Mon-Sat 10-5, Sun 2-5. (Closed Good Fri, Xmas period & New Year).
£2.20 (ch £1, concessions £1.50). Party.
🅿 🍴 ⓰ *(lift to first floor, special parking by prior arrangement) toilets for disabled shop* 🐾

Royal Norfolk Regimental Museum
NORWICH

Shirehall
☎ *(01603) 223649*
Museum displays deal with the social as well as military history of the county regiment from 1685, including the daily life of a soldier. It is housed in an old courtroom of the historic Shirehall. It is linked to the Castle Museum by a tunnel through which prisoners were taken to court. This is followed by a reconstruction of a World War I communication trench. Audio-visual displays and graphics complement the collection. There is a programme of temporary exhibitions.
Open all year, Mon-Sat 10-5, Sun 2-5. Closed Good Fri, Xmas period & 1 Jan.
✳ *Joint ticket Strangers' Hall, Bridewell & Regimental Museum £1.40 (ch 70p, concessions £1.20).*
🅿 *(400 yds)* ⓰ *shop* 🐾 🚃

Sainsbury Centre for Visual Arts
NORWICH

University of East Anglia
☎ *(01603) 56060 & 592467*
The collection of Sir Robert and Lady Sainsbury was given to the University in 1973. European art of the 19th and 20th centuries is on display together with ethnographical art. You can see African tribal sculpture and Oceanic works along with North American and Pre-Colombian art. Egyptian, Asian and European antiquities are on show. Various other exhibitions are held during the year.
Open Tue-Sun 12-5. (Closed BH Mon & University closure at Xmas).
Collection & exhibition £1 (concessions 50p)
🅿 🍴 ✗ ⓰ *toilets for disabled shop* 🐾
(guide dogs by arrangement)

St Peter Hungate Church Museum
NORWICH

Princes St (near Elm Hill)
☎ *(01603) 667231*
Built in 1460, this fine church has a hammer-beam roof and good examples of Norwich painted glass. It is now a museum of church art and a brass rubbing centre with a wide selection of brasses to rub from; a charge is made which includes materials and instructions.
Open all year, Mon-Sat 10-5. (Closed Good Fri, Xmas & New Year)
Free. Brass rubbing materials from £1.50.
⓰ *shop* 🐾

Strangers' Hall
NORWICH

Charing Cross
☎ *(01603) 667229*
Strangers' Hall, once a medieval merchant's house, contains a series of rooms furnished in period styles from early Tudor to late Victorian. In addition there are displays of toys and changing exhibitions of costume and textiles.
Open all year, Mon-Sat, 10-5 (Closed Good Fri, Xmas period & New Year)
Joint ticket for Strangers' Hall, Bridewell & Regimental Museums £1.40 (ch 70p, concessions £1.20)
shop 🐾

Oxburgh Hall
OXBOROUGH

☎ *Gooderstone (01366) 328258*
The outstanding feature of this 15th-century moated building is the 80ft high gatehouse which, unlike the rest of the hall, was spared from the alterations made in Victorian times. Two wings are built around a courtyard.

SANDRINGHAM
HOUSE, MUSEUM AND GROUNDS

The private country retreat of HM The Queen and a much-loved family home to four generations of monarchs.

The House, with its fine furniture and porcelain, is set in sixty acres of beautiful grounds amongst woodland paths, rolling lawns, magnificent trees and tranquil lakes.

The Museum, redeveloped for 1995, houses a fascinating collection of Royal motorcars and memorabilia.

Open daily: 13th April – 1st October (except 18th July – 3rd August). Large self-service Restaurant, waitress-service Tea Room, Gift Shop and Country Park. **New for 1995** – a Land Train to transport visitors to the House.

For further information, please contact: Mrs G Pattinson, Estate Office, Sandringham, Norfolk PE35 6EN. Telephone: (01553) 772675.

Henry VII lodged in the King's Room in 1487 and it is now furnished with a 17th-century bed, and wall hangings worked by Mary, Queen of Scots and Elizabeth Countess of Shrewsbury. A spiral staircase links the chambers to the room from which there are fine views across the countryside. A parterre garden of French design stands outside the moat, and there are woodland walks.
Open Gatehouse, principal rooms and garden 25 Mar-5 Nov, Sat-Wed 1-5. (Garden 12-5); BH Mons 11-5. (Closed Good Fri).
£3.80 (ch £1.90). Garden & Estate £2. Party.
🅿 ✕ *licensed & (braille guide) toilets for disabled shop ⌖*
(NT)

Pettitts Animal Adventure Park
REEDHAM
(on B1140)
☎ *Great Yarmouth (01493) 700094*
Farmyard animals - rabbits, goats, ducks many of which have been hand raised, can be seen here along with more exotic creatures like wallabies, falabella horses, peacocks and chipmunks. The art of feather craft and candle carving are among the crafts which are demonstrated. Daily live entertainment is provided by children's entertainers and a country and western singing duo. Other attractions include the play area, train rides, and vintage car ride. Special events are planned throughout the season.
Open Etr Sun-Oct, daily 10-5.30. (Closed Sat).
£4.95 (ch £3.95 & pen £3.50). Disabled & helpers £3.95. Party.
🅿 🍴 ✕ & *toilets for disabled shop*

St Olaves Priory
ST OLAVES
The fine brick undercroft seen in the cloister is one of the most notable features of the ruin of this small Augustinian priory: built in about 1216 it is an exceptionally early use of this material.
Open any reasonable time.
Free.
(EH)

Sandringham House, Grounds, Museum & Country Park
SANDRINGHAM
(off A149)
☎ *Kings Lynn (01553) 772675*
The private country retreat of Her Majesty The Queen, Sandringham House is at the heart of the beautiful estate which has been owned by four generations of Monarchs.
The neo-Jacobean house was built in 1870 for Albert Edward, Prince of Wales and his wife Princess Alexandra, later King Edward VII and Queen Alexandra. The grand and imposing building, where all the main rooms used by the Royal Family when in residence are open to the public, Sandringham House has the warmth and charm of a well-loved family home. Visitors see portraits of the Royal Family, collections of porcelain, jade, quartz, enamelled Russian silver, gold and bronzes set amongst fine furniture.
Sixty acres of glorious grounds surround the House and offer beauty and colour throughout the season with a rich variety of flowers, shrubs and magnificent trees, informally planted around lawns and lakes.
Sandringham Museum, situated within the grounds, contains fascinating displays of Royal memorabilia ranging from family photographs to vintage Daimlers, and an exhibition of the Sandringham Fire Brigade. Special events planned for 1995 include: Rainbow Craft Fair (21-23 April), Street Organ Festival (27 May), Spring Spectacular (28-29 May), Country Weekend (1-2 July), Flower Show (26 July), craft fair (25-28 August).
Open 13 Apr-1 Oct, daily (House closed 18 Jul-3 Aug; Museum & Grounds closed 23 Jul-2 Aug). House 11-4.45. Museum 11-5. Grounds 10.30-5.
House, Museum & Grounds: £4 (ch £2, pen £3). Family ticket £10. Grounds & Museum £3 (ch £1.50, pen £2.50). Family ticket £7.50.
🅿 🍴 ✕ *licensed & (loan of wheelchairs, free transport in grounds) toilets for disabled shop ⌖*

Wolferton Station Museum
SANDRINGHAM
☎ *Dersingham (01485) 540674*
The museum is housed in the former Royal Retiring Rooms at Wolferton Station on the Sandringham Estate. They were built for King Edward VII and Queen Alexandra (when still Prince and Princess of Wales) in 1898, and have been used by all British monarchs from Queen Victoria to the present Royal Family, visiting foreign monarchs and heads of state and Royal guests on their journey to Sandringham. The displays include items and furniture from Royal Trains, Queen Victoria's Travelling Bed, railway relics and curios, Victorian and Edwardian fashions, jewellery, furniture and ephemera, Royal letters and photographs, a representation of a Royal train carriage housed in an 1890's GER coach and much, much more.
Open Apr or Etr if earlier-Sep, Mon-Fri 11-5.30, Sun 1-5, last admission 30 mins before closing.
❋*£1.95 (ch 90p, disabled £1.20, pen £1.50).*
🅿 & *shop ⌖ (ex in grounds)*

Mannington Gardens & Countryside
SAXTHORPE
(2.25m NE)
☎ *(01263) 584175*
The moated manor house, built in 1460 and still a family home forms a centre-piece for the pretty gardens which surround it. Visitors can enjoy the roses - the chief feature of the gardens - and also lovely countryside walks. Special events take place throughout the season, including Nature Discovery Days for children.
Open: Gardens May-Aug, Wed-Fri 11-5; also Sun noon-5 Etr-Oct. Walks open every day from 9am. Hall open by prior appointment only.

🅿 🍴 & *(boardwalk across meadow) toilets for disabled shop garden centre ⌖ Details not confirmed for 1995*

North Norfolk Railway
SHERINGHAM
Sheringham Station
☎ *(01263) 822045*
A steam railway with trains operating on certain days from March to November, with extra days as the season progresses and a daily service in the summer. On Sundays, lunch is served on the train. At the station is a collection of steam locomotives and rolling stock, some of which are undergoing or awaiting restoration. These include several industrial tank engines and ex-Great Eastern mainline engines. The rolling stock includes suburban coaches, the Brighton Belle Pullmans and directors' private saloons and a vintage buffet saloon. There is also a museum of railway memorabilia and a souvenir and book shop. Special events for 1995 include: Thomas the Tank Engine weekends, Diesel Enthusiasts Day, Gala Weekends, Model Railway Exhibition and Christmas Specials.
Open Etr-Oct; daily during summer season; Dec (Santa special). Telephone (01263) 825449 for timetable.
❋*Return £5.50 (ch £3.50, pen £4.50). Family ticket £15. Party 20+.*
P *(adjacent)* 🍴 & *shop*

Park Farm
SNETTISHAM
(signposted on A149)
☎ *Dersingham (01485) 542425*
You can see farming in action here with lambing in the spring, sheep shearing in May and deer calving in June and July. Sheep, goats, lambs, rabbits, turkeys, ducks, chickens, ponies, piglets etc can be seen in the paddocks, and the sheep centre has over 40 different breeds. Take a safari ride around the estate to see the magnificent herd of red deer. Other attractions include a large adventure playground, horse and pony rides, four farm trails, visitor centre and craft workshops. Special events for 1995 include Sheep shearing Spring Bank ➤

The rose-pink of Oxburgh Hall's brickwork creates a romantic image. The house is approached through an iron gate and across the moat.

During winter, the 1,000 acre Wildfowl and Wetlands site at Welney is home to huge numbers of migratory birds. There are numerous hides and a spacious observatory from which to watch the birds.

Holiday weekend.
Open Mar-Nov, daily 10.30-5.
✱*£3.50 (ch £2.50, pen £3.00). Party 10+.*
🅿 ☕ ♿ *toilets for disabled shop ⌀ (ex on farm trails)*

Fairhaven Garden Trust
SOUTH WALSHAM
2 The Woodlands, Wymers Ln (9m NE of Norwich on B1140)
☎*(01603) 270449*
These delightful woodland and water gardens, with a private inner broad, offer peace and tranquility and a combination of cultivated and wild flowers. In spring there are masses of primroses and bluebells, with azaleas and rhododendrons in several areas. Candelabra primulas and some unusual plants grow near the waterways, which are spanned by small bridges. In summer the wild flowers come into their own, providing habitat for butterflies, bees and dragonflies. There is a separate bird sanctuary for bird watchers. Riverboat trips on the *Lady Beatrice* run from the gardens around the two South Walsham Broads. Autumn Colours week will be held 22-29 October.
Open 14 Apr-1 Oct, Tue-Fri & Sun 11-5.30, Sat 2-5.30. Closed Mon ex BH Mon. Autumn colours week, 22-29 Oct, daily.
£3 (ch £1, pen £2). Season tickets £7.
🅿 ☕ ♿

SWAFFHAM
See **Cockley Cley**

Ancient House Museum
THETFORD
White Hart St
☎*(01842) 752599*

An early Tudor timber-framed house with beautifully carved beamed ceilings, it now houses an exhibition on Thetford and Breckland life. This has been traced back to very early times, and there are examples from local Neolithic settlements. Brass rubbing facilities are available and there is a small period garden recreated in the rear courtyard.
Open all year, Mon-Sat, 10-5 (Closed Mon 1-2); Jun-Sep also Sun 2-5. (Closed Good Fri, Xmas period & New Year's Day).
60p (ch 30p, concessions 40p) in Aug. Rest of year free.
shop ⌀

Thetford Priory
THETFORD
The Cluniac monastery was founded in 1103, and its remains are extensive. The 14th-century gatehouse of the priory stands to its full height, and the complete ground plan of the cloisters can be seen.
Open any reasonable time.
Free.
🅿 ♿ ⌀
(EH)

Warren Lodge
THETFORD
(2m NW, on B1107)
The remains of a two-storey hunting lodge, built in 15th-century of flint with stone dressings.
Open any reasonable time.
Free.
(EH)

Thursford Collection
THURSFORD GREEN
(1m off A148)
☎*Fakenham (01328) 878477*
This exciting collection specialises in organs, with a Wurlitzer cinema organ, fairground organs, barrel organs and

street organs among its treasures. There are live musical shows every day, featuring all the material organs and the Wurtlitzer show. The collection also includes showmen's engines, ploughing engines and farm machinery. There is a children's play area and a breathtaking 'Venetian gondola' switchback ride. Special evening musical events, details on request.
Open Apr-Oct, daily 1-5. (Jun-Aug 11-5).
✱*£4.35 (ch 4-14 £1.95, pen £3.95, ch under 4 free). Party 15+.*
🅿 ☕ ♿ *toilets for disabled shop ⌀*

Weeting Castle
WEETING
This ruined 11th-century fortified manor house is situated in a rectangular moated enclosure. It is interesting also for its slight remains of a three-storeyed cross-wing.
Open any reasonable time.
Free.
🅿
(EH)

Wells & Walsingham Light Railway
WELLS-NEXT-THE-SEA
(A149 Cromer rd)
☎*(01328) 856506 (timetable)*
(Wells Station Sheringham Rd (A149). Walsingham Station, Egmere Rd). The railway covers the four miles between Wells and Walsingham. It is unusual in that it uses ten and a quarter inch gauge track and is the longest track of this gauge in the world. The line passes through some very attractive countryside, particularly noted for its wild flowers and butterflies. This is the home of the unique Garratt Steam Locomotive specially built for this line.
Open Good Fri-Sep, daily.
✱*£4 (ch £3.50). Return.*
🅿 ☕ ♿ *shop*

Wildfowl & Wetlands Trust
WELNEY
Pintail House, Hundred Foot Bank (off A1101, N of Ely)
☎*Ely (01353) 860711*
Probably the best time to visit this refuge on the Ouse Washes is during the winter, when the 1000-acre site is home to some 5000 migratory swans and vast numbers of wild ducks and geese. Bewick and whooper swans as well as wigeon and pintail ducks can be seen.
In the spring, the whole refuge is alive with nesting birds including redshank, snipe and blacktailed godwit, and in the summer there is a trail to view the wide variety of Fen vegetation, butterflies, dragonflies and the unique washland habitat. There are numerous hides and also a spacious observatory . On winter evenings the lagoon is floodlit to show

hundreds of wild Bewick's swans. There is a programme of events.
Open all year, daily 10-5. (Closed 24-25 Dec).
✱*£2.95 (ch £1.50, pen £2.20). Party 20+.*
🅿 ☕ ♿ *(wheelchair access to major parts of reserve) toilets for disabled shop ⌀*

Norfolk Shire Horse Centre
WEST RUNTON
West Runton Stables (on A149)
☎*(01263) 837339*
The Shire Horse Centre has a collection of draught horses and nine breeds of mountain and moorland ponies. There are also exhibits of horse-drawn machinery, waggons and carts, and harnessing and working demonstrations are given twice every day. Other attractions include a children's farm, a photographic display of draught horses past and present, talks and a video show. There is a riding school on the premises as well. Many events are planned for 1995 from a programme of working demonstrations, mornings and afternoons, to day events such as sheep dog days, timberloading days, plough days and foal parade days.
Open 2 Apr-last Sun in Oct, Sun-Fri, 10-5. Shire Horse demonstrations 11.15 & 3. School parties by appointment.
£3.50 (ch £2, pen £2.50). Party.
🅿 ☕ ✗ *licensed ♿ toilets for disabled shop*

The Muckleburgh Collection
WEYBOURNE
Weybourne Military Camp (on A149)
☎*(01263) 588210 & 588608*
The Muckleburgh Collection is the largest privately-owned military collection of its kind in the UK and incorporates the Museum of the Suffolk and Norfolk Yeomanry dating from the 18th century. Its 3000 exhibits include restored and working tanks, armoured cars, trucks and artillery of World War II, and equipment including weapons from the Falklands and the Gulf War. Special model displays and diorama include military vehicles, aircraft and ships as well as radios and uniforms. Live tank demonstrations are run daily during summer high season. VE Day anniversary 18 June - Royal British Legion County Rally will be held here, with military bands, static displays etc.
Open mid Mar-Oct, daily 10-5.
✱*£3 (ch £1.80 & pen £2.70). Family ticket £7.90.*
🅿 ☕ ✗ *licensed ♿ toilets for disabled shop ⌀ (ex guide dogs)*

Norfolk Wildlife Centre & Country Park
WITCHINGHAM, GREAT
(on A1067)
☎*Norwich (01603) 872274*
This wildlife park offers a large collection of British and European wildlife. The animals can be viewed in semi-natural surroundings set in 40 acres of beautiful parkland. Britain's only team of trained reindeer pull their wheeled sledge round the park, and there are tame animals to fascinate both young and old. There are also exciting Commando play areas, a narrow gauge Steam Railway and a model farm with numerous rare breeds, most of them tame enough to touch, and with a medieval dovecote as the centrepiece and a carp pool.
Open daily, Apr(or Good Fri if earlier)-Oct, 10.30-6 or sunset if earlier.
🅿 ☕ ♿ *toilets for disabled shop ⌀*
Details not confirmed for 1995

Elizabethan House Museum
YARMOUTH, GREAT
4 South Quay
☎*Great Yarmouth (01493) 855746*
A wealthy merchant built this house in 1596. Although it has a late Georgian front, it contains 16th-century panelled rooms, one with a magnificent plaster ceiling. Other rooms have features from later periods, some containing their contemporary furniture and exhibits illustrating domestic life in the 19th-century. Children's toys, Lowestoft

Although Lyvedyn New Bield appears to be a ruin, it is actually the unfinished shell of a garden lodge dating from 1600.

porcelain and a collection of 18th-and 19th-century drinking glasses.
Open Etr fortnight, Mon-Fri 10-5, Sun 2-5 (closed Good Fri); Sun before Whitsun-end Sep, Sun-Fri 10-5.
£1 (ch 50p, concessions 60p)
shop ⌗

Maritime Museum For East Anglia
YARMOUTH, GREAT
Marine Pde
☎ *Great Yarmouth (01493) 842267*
The sea and the fishing industry have played an enormous part in East Anglia's history and this Maritime Museum has exhibits on each aspect. There are special displays on the herring fishery, the wherry, life-saving and the most recent industry - oil and gas in the North Sea.
Open Etr fortnight, Mon-Fri 10-5, Sun 2-5 (closed Good Fri); Sun before Whitsun-end Sep, Sun-Fri 10-5.
£1 (ch 50p, concessions 60p).
shop

Merrivale Model Village
YARMOUTH, GREAT
Wellington Pier Gardens, Marine Pde
☎ *(01493) 842097*
Set in attractive landscaped gardens, this comprehensive miniature village is built on a scale of 1:12. The layout includes a two and a half inch gauge model railway, radio-controlled boats, and over 200 models set in an acre of landscaped gardens. There are additional amusements, children's rides and remote-controlled cars. During the summer, from June to October, the gardens are illuminated after dusk.
Open Etr 9.30-6, Jun-Oct 9.30-10.
✻*£2.50 (ch 3-14 £1.50).*
P *(opposite)* 🍽 & *shop*

Museum Exhibition Galleries
YARMOUTH, GREAT
Central Library, Tolhouse St
☎ *Great Yarmouth (01493) 858900*
A regularly-changing series of travelling exhibitions are displayed in the library. Also exhibitions of local art, crafts and other activities.
Open (when exhibition showing) Mon-Sat 9.30-5.30. (Closed Sat 12.30-1.30, Etr, late May & Aug BH wknds, Xmas & New Year).
Free.
& ⌗

Old Merchant's House
YARMOUTH, GREAT
Row 117
The 300-year-old house is behind the grand buildings of the waterfront, among narrow parallel lanes, or Rows, of small dwellings. The Rows were so narrow that a specially-built cart had to be used. The restored house shows examples of 17th-and 19th-century local building craft.

Open Apr-Sep, Sun-Fri 10-6.
£1.30 (ch 70p, concessions £1)
⌗
(EH)

Ripley's Believe It or Not!
YARMOUTH, GREAT
The Windmill, 9 Marine Pde
☎ *(01493) 332217*
Collected from the four corners of the world, this fun museum contains the most odd and bizzare things you will ever see. Themed with special effects, you can see, touch and experience an assortment of oddities including videos of amazing human talents. Plenty for the whole family to enjoy - believe it or not!
Open Nov-Apr, wknds & school hols 10-4; Apr-Nov, daily - early season 10-5, main season 10-10.
Free.
P *500yds* & *(free entry) shop* ⌗

Tolhouse Museum
YARMOUTH, GREAT
Tolhouse St
☎ *Great Yarmouth (01493) 858900*
This late 13th-century building was once the town's court house and gaol and has dungeons which can be visited. The rooms above contain exhibits on local history. The museum has become a brass rubbing centre and has a wide range of replica brasses from which rubbings can be made. Prices start at 50p and include materials and instructions.
Open Etr fortnight, Mon-Fri 10-5, Sun 2-5 (closed Good Fri); Sun before Whitsun-end Sep, Sun-Fri 10-5.
£1 (ch 50p, concessions 60p)
& *(lift to ground & 2nd floor) shop* ⌗

NORTHAMPTONSHIRE

Althorp House
ALTHORP
☎ *Northampton (01604) 770107*
Althorp House has been the home of the Spencer family since 1508. The house was built in the 16th century, but has been changed since, most notably by Henry Holland in the 18th century. Restored in 1983, it contains magnificent pictures, furniture and china. Both house and grounds may be closed without notice for security reasons. Special events are planned for 1995 including: falconry fair (28-29 May), classical concert (13 August).
Open: 14-17 Apr incl Easter, 6-8 May incl bank holiday, daily in Aug. For further dates please telephone (01604) 770209.
✻*£4.50 (ch £2.50, pen £3.50). Family ticket £12. Extra charges may be made for special exhibitions.*
P 🍽 & *toilets for disabled shop* ⌗

Canons Ashby House
CANONS ASHBY
☎ *Blakesley (01327) 860044*
Home of the Dryden family since the 16th century, this is an exceptional small manor house, with Elizabethan wall paintings and Jacobean plasterwork. It has restored gardens, a small park and a church - part of the original 13th-century Augustinian priory. Summer fayre 13 August.
Open Apr-Oct, Sat-Wed & BH Mon (closed Good Fri) 1-5.30 or dusk if earlier. Last admission 5pm.
£3.20 (ch £1.60). Family ticket £8.
P 🍽 & *toilets for disabled shop*
(NT)

Deene Park
DEENE
(0.5m off A43, between Kettering & Stamford)
☎ *(01780) 450223 & 450278*
Mainly 16th-century house of great architectural importance and historical interest. Home of the Brudenell family since 1514, including the 7th Earl of Cardigan who led the Charge of the Light Brigade. Large lake and park. Extensive gardens with old-fashioned roses, rare trees and shrubs.
Open BH's (Sun & Mon) Etr, May, Spring & Aug; Jun-Aug, Sun 2-5. Party 20+ by prior arrangement with House Keeper. Admission fee payable.
P 🍽 & *ramps to Old Kitchen and gardens toilets for disabled shop* ⌗

Kirby Hall
DEENE
(1.5m W)
☎ *Corby (01536) 203230*
The hall is a splendid Elizabethan mansion with some later alterations, perhaps by Inigo Jones. The gardens now mainly laid to lawn, were famous in the 17th century.
Open all year, Apr-Sep, daily 10-6; Oct-Mar, Wed-Sun 10-4. Closed 24-26 Dec & 1 Jan.
P &
(EH)
Details not confirmed for 1995

Holdenby House Gardens
HOLDENBY
(off A50 or A428)
☎ *Northampton (01604) 770074*
The gardens have been restored in the style of Elizabethan times (when this was the largest house in England), and have fragrant and silver borders. Other attractions include a museum, rare breeds of farm animals, a falconry centre, a 'cuddle' farm, and craft shop. Please telephone for details of special events.
Open; Gardens, Apr-Sep, weekdays 1-5, Sun 2-6, BH Sun & Mon 1-6. House, BH 1-6 (ex May Day). Parties 25+ by appointment Mon-Fri. Falconry Centre open daily 1-6.

P 🍽 & *(gravel paths with ramps) toilets for disabled shop* ⌗
Details not confirmed for 1995

Alfred East Gallery
KETTERING
Sheep St
☎ *(01536) 410333*
National, regional and local art, craft and photography are all displayed in around 20 exhibitions held each year at this well-run gallery. A collection of paintings by Sir Alfred East RA and Thomas Cooper Gotch on view by appointment, when not on display.
Open all year, Mon-Sat 9.30-5. (Closed BHs).
P *(300 yds)* & *shop* ⌗
Details not confirmed for 1995

Lyveden New Bield
LYVEDEN NEW BIELD
(4m SW Oundle via A427)
☎ *Benefield (01832) 205358*
The 'New Bield', or 'new building', is an unfinished shell of a garden lodge dating from around 1600. It was designed by Sir Thomas Tresham to symbolise the Passion. The shape is a Greek cross, on which a frieze shows the cross, crown of thorns and other 'emblems of the Passion'. Even the building's dimensions are symbolic.
Open daily. Party by arrangement with the custodian.
£1.20 (ch 60p).
🚗
(NT)

Abington Museum
NORTHAMPTON
Abington Park, Park Av South
☎ *(01604) 31454*
A 15th century manor house, once the home of Shakespeare's granddaughter, Elizabeth Barnard, who is buried in the nearby church. It is now a museum showing the social history of the house including a Victorian Cabinet of Curiosities, a 19th-century fashion gallery and exhibits on Northamptonshire's military history and life in the county.
Open all year, BH Mons & Tue-Sun 1-5.
Free.
P *(100 yds)* & *(special parking close to entrance) toilets for disabled shop* ⌗

Central Museum & Art Gallery
NORTHAMPTON
Guildhall Rd
☎ *(01604) 39415*
The Central Museum and Art Gallery reflects Northampton's proud standing as Britain's boot and shoe capital by housing a collection of boots and shoes which is considered one of the finest in the world. Fascinating footwear worn throughout the ages is just one of the attractions in the museum. Other displays include the History of Northampton, Decorative Arts , the Art Gallery, and special temporary exhibitions. Special events for 1995 include: Animal Friends (spring), Northampton, Naseby and the Civil War (early summer), VE Day and the end of Wold War II (early summer).
Open all year, Mon-Sat 10-5, Sun 2-5. (Closed Xmas & 1 Jan). Please telephone to confirm times.
Free.
P & *toilets for disabled shop* ⌗

Rockingham Castle
ROCKINGHAM
(2m N of Corby, on A6003)
☎ *(01536) 770240*
Set on a hill overlooking three counties, Rockingham Castle was built by William the Conqueror. The site of the original keep is now a rose garden, but the outline of the Curtain Wall remains as do the foundations of the Norman Hall, and the twin towers of the gatehouse. The castle was a royal residence for 450 years. Then, in the 16th century Henry VIII granted it to Edward Watson, and the Watson family have lived there ever since.
The current building is basically Elizabethan, but every century since the

➜

The huge mass of Dunstanburgh Castle stands bleakly by the rugged coastline. The castle has been in ruins ever since Tudor times.

Sulgrave Manor was bought in 1539 by Lawrence Washington, wool merchant and twice Mayor of Northampton. It was here that George Washington's ancestors lived until 1656 when his great grandfather, John, emigrated to Virginia. The house that exists today is somewhat different from the one Lawrence Washington bought. His was larger, and much of the present house is a 20th-century restoration. Original parts include the porch, a screens passage, the great hall and the great Chamber. Over the porch is carved the original of the American flag, with three stars and two stripes plus Elizabeth I's arms. Inside there are many relics of George Washington, such as his velvet coat, a lock of hair, documents and portraits. Special events for 1995 include: Indian Rendezvous - an American Indian Living History camp (29 April-1 May), Stars, Stripes and Stitches - an annual needlework event (27 May-4 June), Living History 1580 (1-9 July), Living History 1780 (27-30 August), American Civil War Camp (9-10 September).
Open Apr-Oct, Mon-Fri (ex Wed) 2-5.30, Sat, Sun & BH 10.30-1 & 2-5.30; Mar, Nov & Dec, Sat & Sun only 10.30-1 & 2-4.30; Other times by appointment. Closed 25-26 Dec & Jan.
£3 (ch £1.50). Party 12+. Special event days £3.80 (ch £1.90).
🅿 🍴 ⅄ shop garden centre ✤ (ex in gardens)

Old Dairy Farm Centre
WEEDON BEC ▰
Upper Stowe (2m S of Weedon off A5)
☎ *Weedon (01327) 340525*
Housed in a range of prize-winning converted 19th-century farm buildings and built around a working arable and sheep farm, the centre offers a wide range of shops, craft workshops and demonstration/conference room. There are many animals on view including some rare breed pigs, geese, donkeys, ducks, goats and various breeds of

sheep. The Barn Restaurant serves homemade food. Special events for 1995 include: Living Manger (1-3 December).
Open 10 Jan-28 Feb, daily 10-4.30; Mar-24 Dec, daily 10-5.30.
Free, except for special event wknds.
🅿 🍴 ✗ *licensed* ⅄ *toilets for disabled shop* ✤

NORTHUMBERLAND

Alnwick Castle
ALNWICK ▰
☎ *(01665) 510777 & 603942 wknds*
Described by the Victorians as 'The Windsor of the North', Alnwick Castle is the main seat of the Duke of Northumberland whose family, the Percys, have lived here since 1309. This border stronghold has survived many battles, but now peacefully dominates the picturesque market town of Alnwick, overlooking landscape designed by Capability Brown. The stern, medieval exterior belies the treasure house within, furnished in palatial Renaissance style, with paintings by Titian, Van Dyck and Canaletto, fine furniture and an exquisite collection of Meissen china. The Regiment Museum of Royal Northumberland Fusiliers is housed in the Abbot's Tower of the Castle, while the Postern Tower contains a collection of early British and Roman relics. Other attractions include the Percy State Coach, the dungeon, the gun terrace and the grounds, which offer peaceful walks and superb views over the surrounding countryside. Events this year will include an Easter weekend craft, design and fashion show, a vintage car rally and Alnwick fair at the end of June, and an international music festival at the beginning of August; for a full programme of events and dates please enquire at the Estates Office (tel. 510777).

11th has had an influence somewhere, whether in architecture, furniture or works of art. James I was entertained here in 1603 and Charles Dickens, a frequent visitor, dedicated *David Copperfield* to the owners. Special events planned for 1995 include: craft fair (24-25 June), Civil War re-enactment (1-2 July).
Open Etr Sun-Sep, Thu, Sun, BH Mon & following Tue (also Tue in Aug) 1.30-5.30.
£3.80 (ch £2.30 & pen £3.20). Gardens only £2.30. Family ticket £10. Party.
🅿 🍴 ⅄ *shop*

Triangular Lodge
RUSHTON ▰
☎ *(01536) 710761*
The curious construction of this lodge, built by Sir Thomas Tresham between 1593 and 1596, represents the Holy Trinity and the Mass. There are three walls, with three windows, and three gables to each, on three storeys, topped by a three sided chimney.
Open Apr-Sep, daily 10-6.
£1 (ch 50p, concessions £1).
⅄ ✤
(EH)

Canal Museum
STOKE BRUERNE ▰
(4m S junc 15 M1)
☎ *Northampton (01604) 862229*
The three storeys of a former corn mill have been converted to hold a marvellous collection of bygones from over two centuries of the canals. The museum is near a flight of locks on the Grand Union Canal. Among the hundreds of exhibits is the reconstructed interior of a traditional narrow boat, complete with furniture, crockery, brassware and traditional art. A display on local canals includes a new large working model. There are genuine working narrowboats on show and the opportunity for a boat trip through the mile-long Blisworth Tunnel nearby.
Open Nov-Etr, Tue-Sun 10-4; Etr-Oct daily 10-6. (Closed Xmas).
£2.50 (ch & pen £1.50). Family ticket £6.
🅿 ⅄ *toilets for disabled shop* ✤

Sulgrave Manor
SULGRAVE ▰
Manor Rd
☎ *(01295) 760205*

Open Etr-mid Oct, daily 11-5. Last admission 4.30.
✱£4.50 (ch £2.50, pen & students £4). Family ticket £11. Grounds only £2. Party 12+.
🅿 🍽 ♿ (Castle lift for those able to walk a little) shop 🚫

Bamburgh Castle
BAMBURGH ▬▬▬▬▬
☎(01668) 214208 & 214515
Rising up dramatically on a rocky outcrop, Bamburgh Castle is a huge, square Norman castle. Restored in the 19th century by Lord Armstrong, it has an impressive hall and an armoury with a large collection of armour from HM Tower of London. Guide services are available.
Open daily, Apr-last Sun Oct, from 11am-variable closing times. Other times by prior arrangement.
✱£2.50 (ch £1.20 & pen £2). Party 12+.
🅿 (charged) 🍽 ♿ shop 🚫

Grace Darling Museum
BAMBURGH ▬▬▬▬▬
Radcliffe Rd
☎Seahouses (01665) 720037
Pictures, documents and other reminders of the heroine are on display, including the boat in which Grace Darling and her father, keeper of Longstone Lighthouse, Farne Islands, rescued nine survivors from the wrecked 'SS Forfarshire' in 1838.
Open Etr-Sep, daily 11-6.
Free. Donations to R.N.L.I. welcomed.
P (400yds) ♿ (ramps on request) shop 🚫

Vindolanda (Chesterholm)
BARDON MILL ▬▬▬▬▬
Vindolanda Trust (signposted from A69 or B6318)
☎(01434) 344277
Vindolanda was a Roman fort and frontier town, with remains dating back to the 3rd and 4th centuries. It was started well before Hadrian's Wall, and became a base for 500 soldiers. The headquarters

building is well preserved, and a special feature is a full-scale reconstruction of Hadrian's turf and stone wall, complete with turret and gate tower. The civilian settlement lay just west of the fort and has been excavated. A vivid idea of life for both civilians and soldiers can be gained at the excellent museum in the country house of Chesterholm nearby. It has displays and reconstructions, and its exhibits include such homely finds as sandals, shoes and a soldier's sewing kit. There are also formal gardens. An open-air museum is currently under construction. This year marks the 25th anniversary of the founding of the Vindolanda Trust and special events are currently being discussed.
Open daily from 10 am, all facilities mid Feb-Oct. Wknds only Nov. Site only Jan & Dec.
✱£3 (ch £1.75, student & pen £2.25).
🅿 🍽 ♿ toilets for disabled shop 🚫

Belsay Hall, Castle and Gardens
BELSAY ▬▬▬▬▬
(on A696)
☎(01661) 881636
Belsay Castle, with its splendid turrets and battlements, dates from 1370 and was home for generations of the Middleton family, until they built the Jacobean manor house beside it, and then the magnificent Grecian-style Hall. Aside from the facinating buildings, Belsay has wonderful gardens and an excellent site exhibition.
Open all year, daily Apr-Sep 10-6; Oct-Mar, daily 10-4 or dusk if earlier. Closed 24-26 Dec & 1 Jan.
£2.60 (ch £1.30, concessions £2).
🅿 ♿ toilets for disabled shop
(EH)

Berwick Barracks
BERWICK-UPON-TWEED ▬▬▬▬▬
☎(01289) 304493
These are Britain's oldest purpose-built barracks, constructed in the early 1700s because people objected to soldiers

being billeted in public houses. The design has been attributed to Vanbrugh. The barracks now house the Museum of the King's Own Scottish Borderers, and the Museum and Art Gallery.
Open all year, Apr-Sep, daily 10-6; Oct, 10-4, Nov-Mar, Wed-Sun 10-4 or dusk if earlier. Closed 24-26 Dec & 1 Jan.
£2.20 (ch £1.10, concessions £1.70).
🅿 shop 🚫
(EH)

Museum & Art Gallery
BERWICK-UPON-TWEED ▬▬▬▬▬
Berwick Barracks, Ravensdowne
☎(01289) 330933
The museum is housed in the handsome barracks and has displays of local history, archaeology, fine art and decorative art, including an important collection donated by Sir William Burrell. Temporary exhibitions are held, and in 1995 these will include Magic of Light - Mystery of Shadow - a look at the history of light and shadow across time and in several cultures (June-October) and Light in Northern Lands - interpretations of the landscape by six northern artists (July-October).
Open all year. Winter, Tue-Sat 10-12.30 & 1.30-4, Sun 10-1 & 2-4 (Closed Mon). Summer, Mon-Sat 10-12.30 & 1.30-6, Sun 10-1 & 2-6.
✱£2.20 (ch £1.10, pen & students £1.65). Party 11+. Admission includes entry to Museum of the King's Own Scottish Borderers & English Heritage exhibition 'By Beat of Drum'. Prices under review.
P (50 yds) ♿ toilets for disabled shop 🚫

Museum of The King's Own Scottish Borderers
BERWICK-UPON-TWEED ▬▬▬▬▬
The Barracks
☎(01289) 307426
Designed by Vanbrugh in 1717, these are said to be the oldest barracks in Britain.
Open all year, Mon-Sat 9-4, (Closed BH's).

✱£2.20 (ch & pen £1.10, concessions £1.65). Includes admission to Town Museum and Heritage exhibition.
P (50 yds) shop 🚫

Paxton House
BERWICK-UPON-TWEED ▬▬▬▬▬
(5m from town, signposted from by-pass on A1)
☎(01289) 386291
Paxton House was built in 1758 for the Laird of Wedderburn in anticipation of his marriage to the natural daughter of Frederick the Great of Prussia. Unfortunately the marriage did not take place but the house still stands. It is a fine example of 18th-century neo-Palladian architecture having been designed by John and James Adam. Much of the house is furnished by Chippendale and the picture gallery is the largest private picture gallery in Scotland. The house is in 70 acres of gardens, parklands and woodlands beside the River Tweed.An exciting Adventure Playground was added in 1991.
Open daily from Good Fri-Oct. House & gallery noon-5, grounds 10-sunset. Last tour of house 4.15pm.
🍽 ♿ shop

Wallington House Walled Garden & Grounds
CAMBO ▬▬▬▬▬
(1m S on B6342)
☎Scots Gap (01670) 774283
Dating from the 17th and 18th centuries, the house is set in a great moorland estate of over 12,000 acres. It is famed for its delicate plasterwork, including fine porcelain work and rare British pieces. There are also displays of dolls' houses and model soldiers, and the kitchen is filled with Victorian equipment. In the 19th century Ruskin and other writers and artists came here as guests of Sir William and Lady Trevelyan, who were renowned for their eccentricity and charm. One of the artists, William Bell Scott, painted the ➤

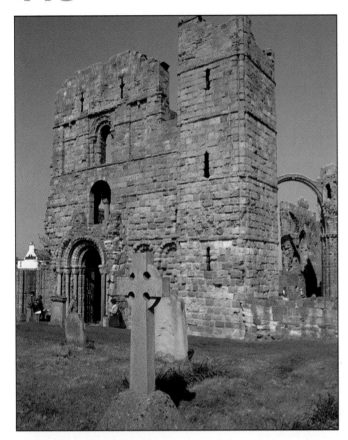

St Aidan first founded the priory on Lindisfarne in AD635. Twice destroyed by Vikings, the final 13th-century priory is also now a ruin.

dramatic murals in the Central Hall. The gardens were partly laid out by Capability Brown, and include formal and woodland areas, and a conservatory with magnificent fuchsias. Special events for 1995 include 'Shakespeare on the west lawn' (28 June-2 July), and free entry day (13 September) as well as centenary events - 'Please, please me' (an open-air concert) on 16 June, classics in the park (12 August), the Jaques Loussier trio (12 November) and a family fun day on 20 August.
*Open: House Apr-Oct, daily (ex Tue) 1-5.30; Last admission 5pm. Walled garden Apr-Sep, daily 10.30-7; Oct, daily 10.30-6 or dusk; Nov-Mar, 10.30-4 or dusk if earlier. Grounds open all year.
House, walled garden & grounds £4.60. Walled gardens & grounds only £2.30. Party.*
🅿 ✕ & *(vessa ventura scooter braille guide scented garden) toilets for disabled shop garden centre ⌾ (ex on lead in grounds)*
(NT)

Roman Wall (Mithraic Temple)
CARRAWBROUGH
(on B6318)
A farmer found the Mithraic Temple in 1949. It was excavated to reveal three altars to Mithras which date from the third century AD. They are now in the Museum of Antiquities in Newcastle, but there are copies on the site. The temple is on the line of the Roman wall near the fort of Brocolitia.
*Open any reasonable time.
Free.*
🅿
(EH)

Chillingham Castle
CHILLINGHAM
☎ Chatton (01668) 215359 & 215390
This remarkable castle fortress with its alarming dungeons and torture chamber, owned by Earl Grey and his descendants continuously since about 1200, is now undergoing restoration - and not only of stone and plasterwork, for state rooms are being brought back to life with tapestries, furniture, arms and armour. Romantic grounds laid out by Sir Jeffry Wyatville - fresh from his triumphs at

Windsor Castle - command views over the Cheviots and include topiary gardens and woodland walks as well as parkland and a lake. Functions and meals can be arranged, and both fishing and claypigeon shooting are available. Special events for 1995 include opera and play performances in June and July.
*Open Etr wknd & May-Sep, daily (ex Tue) 1.30-5. (Last admission 4.30pm). Other times by prior arrangement.
❉£2.50 (ch £1.80, ch under 5 Free, pen £2). Party 20+.*
🅿 ⬛ & *toilets for disabled shop* ⌾

Chillingham Wild Cattle Park
CHILLINGHAM
(off B6348)
☎ Chatton (01668) 215250
The park at Chillingham boasts an extraordinary survival: a herd of wild white cattle descended from animals trapped in the park when the wall was built in the 13th century; they are the sole surviving pure-bred examples of their breed in the world. Binoculars are recommended for a close view. As the cattle can be aggressive and should not be approached, visits are made with a warden.
*Open Apr-Oct, daily 10-12 & 2-5, Sun 2-5. (Closed Tue).
£2.50 (ch 50p & pen £2). Parties 20+*
🅿 ⌾

Corbridge Roman Site
CORBRIDGE
☎ (01434) 632349
The remains of a Roman 'Corstopitum', built around AD210, include granaries, portico columns and the probable site of legionary headquarters. Finds from excavations of the site are displayed in a museum on the site.
*Open all year, Apr-Sep, daily 10-6; Oct, 10-4; Nov-Mar, Tue-Sun 10-4 or dusk if earlier. (Closed 24-26 Dec & 1 Jan).
£2.20 (ch £1.10, concessions £1.70).*
🅿 & ⌾
(EH)

Dunstanburgh Castle
EMBLETON
(1.5m E)
☎ (01665) 576231

The skeletal ruins of the huge castle stand on cliffs 100ft above the North Sea. It was partly built by John of Gaunt, but was in ruins by Tudor times. Its setting has made it a favourite with artists, and Turner painted it three times.
*Open all year, Apr-Sep, daily 10-6; Oct, 10-4; Nov-Mar, Wed-Sun 10-4 or dusk if earlier. Closed 24-26 Dec & 1 Jan.
£1.30 (ch 70p, students, pen & UB40 £1)*
(EH)

Heatherslaw Corn Mill
FORD
(signposted from A697)
☎ Crookham (01890) 820338
This beautifully restored 19th-century water-powered double corn mill is in daily use, and you can see local wheat milled by traditional methods using the original machinery. Everything is visible, from the huge wooden water wheel to the slowly grinding burr stone, and you can taste the full flavour of the flour in delicious biscuits and cakes produced by local bakers. There are also an exhibition area and gift shop.
*Open Apr-29 Oct, daily 10-6. Winter by arrangement.
£2 (ch & pen £1). Family ticket £5.50.*
🅿 ⬛ & *(Braille guide plus tactile facility) toilets for disabled shop* ⌾

Lady Waterford Hall
FORD
(signposted from A697, N of Wooler)
☎ Crookham (01890) 820224
Commissioned as a school in 1862 by Louisa Anne, Marchioness of Waterford, this beautiful Victorian building was decorated with delightful murals of favourite Bible stories. Lady Waterford, a leading light among female artists, spent 21 years painting these outstanding murals, choosing the children of the village and their parents as models; many of her smaller works are also displayed in the gallery.
*Open Apr-29 Oct, daily 10.30-12.30 & 1.30-5.30. Open by appointment in winter.
£1 (ch & pen 50p).*
🅿 ⬛ & *shop garden centre*

Birdoswald Roman Fort
GILSLAND
(signposted off A69)
☎ (016977) 47602
This unique section of Hadrian's Wall enjoys a most picturesque setting overlooking the Irthing Gorge. There is no other point along the Wall where all the components of the Roman frontier system can be found together. But Birdoswald isn't just about the Romans, it's also about border raids in the Middle Ages, about the Victorians, and about recent archaeological discoveries. The Visitor Centre brings its fascinating history to life. A Roman re-enactment is planned - though, at the time of going to press, still unconfirmed - for August Bank Holiday this year.
*Open Etr-Oct, daily 10-5.30. Winter opening by prior arrangement only.
❉£1.75 (ch £1, pen £1.25)*
🅿 ⬛ & *(ramp) toilets for disabled shop*

Lindisfarne Castle
HOLY ISLAND (LINDISFARNE)
☎ Berwick (01289) 89244
The 16th-century castle was restored by Sir Edwin Lutyens in 1903 for the owner of *Country Life* magazine. The austere outside walls belie the Edwardian comfort within, and there is a little garden designed by Gertrude Jekyll.
*Open Apr-Oct, daily (closed Fri ex Good Fri) 1-5.30;. Last admission 5pm. Island not accessible two hours before & four hours after high tide. Other times by arrangement with Administrator.
£3.60.*
P *1m in village* ⌾
(NT)

Lindisfarne Priory
HOLY ISLAND (LINDISFARNE)
☎ Berwick (01289) 89200
St Aidan and monks from Iona founded a monastery here in the 7th century and from it spread Christianity to much of Northern England. They also produced the beautifully illuminated Lindisfarne Gospels (now in the British Museum), but abandoned the monastery because of Viking raids in the 9th century. The beautiful priory ruins on Lindisfarne today date from the 11th century, and the history of life at the Priory is told in the adjacent visitor centre. The island is reached by a causeway at low tide: tide tables are posted at each end of the causeway, or telephone the custodian on the above number.
*Open all year, Apr-Sep, daily 10-6; Oct-Mar, daily 10-4 or dusk if earlier. Subject to tides. Closed 24-26 Dec & 1 Jan.
£2.30 (ch £1.20, concessions £1.70)*
🅿 *shop* ⌾
(EH)

Roman Wall (Housesteads Fort & Museum)
HOUSESTEADS
Nr Bardon Mills
☎ Bardon Mill (01434) 344363
Housesteads was the Roman fort of *Vercovicium*. It has a spectacular site on Hadrian's Wall, and is also one of the best preserved Roman forts. It covers five acres, including the only known Roman hospital in Britain, and a 24-seater latrine with a flushing tank. There is also a museum.
*Open all year, Good Fri-Sep, daily 10-6; Oct-Maundy Thu, daily 10-4. (Closed 24-26 Dec & 1 Jan).
❉£1.60 (ch 16 80p, students, pen & UB40s £1.20). Party reductions in winter. P 0.25m from fort shop* ⌾
(EH & NT)

Brinkburn Priory
LONGFRAMLINGTON
(off B6344)
☎ (01665) 570628
The priory was founded in 1135 for the canons of the Augustinian order, and stands on a bend of the River Coquet. After the Dissolution of the Monasteries it fell into disrepair, but was restored in 1858; remaining medieval fittings include the font, double piscina and some grave slabs.
*Open Apr-Sep, daily 10-6.
£1.30 (ch 70p, concessions £1).*
🅿 ⌾
(EH)

Castle
NORHAM
☎ (01289) 382329
One of the strongest border fortresses, this castle has one of the finest Norman keeps in the country and overlooks the River Tweed.
Open any reasonable time.
🅿 & ⌾
(EH)

Prudhoe Castle
PRUDHOE
☎ (01661) 33459
Standing on the River Tyne, this 12th-to 14th-century castle was the stronghold of the d'Umfravelles and Percys. The keep stands in the inner bailey and a notable gatehouse guards the outer bailey. Access is to the Pele Yard only.
*Open Apr-Sep, daily 10-6; Oct 10-4.
£1.50 (ch 80p, concessions £1.10).*
🅿 *shop* ⌾
(EH)

Cragside House, Garden & Grounds
ROTHBURY
(Entrance for cars 2m N on B6341)
☎ (01669) 620333
This splendid Victorian masterpiece was built for Sir William (later the first Lord) Armstrong in stages, between 1864 and 1895. It was designed for him by the architect Richard Norman Shaw and the interior of the house reflects the taste

and style of both its architect and its owner. The huge drawing room has a curved glass roof and 10-ton marble-lined inglenook. This was the first house in the world to be lit by electricity generated by water-power. The grounds, now 1000 acres of country park, were transformed by Lord Armstrong. He planted seven million trees, diverted streams and created lakes, a waterfall and winding paths. The formal garden includes greenhouses, Italian terraces, a rose loggia and an orchard house. Free entry day is 13 September this year.
Open all year, Grounds: daily, 10.30-7; 4 Nov - 17 Dec, Tue & wknds 10.30-4. House : Apr-Oct, daily (ex Mon, Open BH Mon's) 1-5.30, last admission 4.45pm. Gardens 10.30-5.30. Armstrong Visitor Centre open Apr-Oct daily (ex Mon, Open BH Mon's) 10.30-5.30; Nov & Dec, Tues & wknds, 12-4.
House, Garden & Grounds & Visitor Centre £5.50. Garden, Grounds & Visitor Centre only £3.50. Family ticket for House, Garden & Grounds £14. Party.
🅿 🍴 ✕ *licensed* & *fishing pier braille guide toilets for disabled shop* ⊗ *(ex in grounds on lead)*
(NT)

Chesters Roman Fort & Museum
WALWICK
(.5m E)
☎*Humshaugh (01434) 681379*
One of the Roman forts on Hadrian's Wall is now in the park of Chesters, an 18th-century mansion. The fort named *Cilurnum* housed 500 soldiers and covered nearly 6 acres. The excavations were started in the 19th century by the owner of Chesters, and have revealed a great deal about life in a Roman fort. A large wall and six gatehouses were built to defend the fort, but evidence revealed that it was destroyed and rebuilt three times. The standard of living appears to have been high: water was brought in by aqueduct, the commandant had underfloor heating in his house, and the soldiers' bath house had hot, cold, dry or steam baths, and latrines. The remains of the bath house are very substantial. There is a museum exhibiting artefacts from the site.
Open all year, Apr-Sep, daily 10-6; Oct-Mar, daily 10-4 or dusk if earlier. Closed 24-26 Dec & 1 Jan.
£2.20 (ch £1.10, concessions £1.70).
🅿 & *shop* ⊗
(EH)

Warkworth Castle
WARKWORTH
☎*(01665) 711423*
The castle is situated on a steep bank of the River Coquet, and dominates the town of Warkworth. It is a splendid ruin with its restored 15th-century keep and early 13th-century curtain wall. Near the castle is the 14th-century bridge over the river, with a rare bridge tower. This can now only be used by pedestrians.
Open all year, Apr-Sep, daily 10-6; Oct-Mar, daily 10-4 or dusk if earlier. Closed 24-26 Dec & 1 Jan.
Free.
🅿 & ⊗
(EH)

Warkworth Hermitage
WARKWORTH
Upstream from Warkworth Castle is the Hermitage, a refuge dug into the steep rockface of the riverbank by a 14th-century hermit. It consists of a chapel and two chambers to live in. The hermitage was occupied until the 16th century. Nearby is Coquet island, which was also the home of hermit monks.
Open Apr-Oct, Wed & Sun 11-5.
£1 (ch 50p, concessions 80p)
🅿 & ⊗
(EH)

NORTH YORKSHIRE

Roman Town W
ALDBOROUGH
☎*Harrogate (01423) 322768*
The pretty present-day village occupies the site of the northernmost civilian Roman town in Britain, with houses, courts, a forum and a temple, surrounded by a 9ft thick, 20ft high wall. All that can be seen today are two pavements, the position of the wall and excavated objects in the small museum.
Open Apr-Sep, daily 10-6.
£1.30 (ch 70p, concessions £1)
⊗
(EH)

National Park Centre
AYSGARTH
☎*Wensleydale (01969) 663424*
A visitor centre for the Yorkshire Dales National Park, with maps, guides, walks and local information. Displays explain the history and natural history of the area.
Open Apr-Oct, daily 10-4. Nov-Mar limited wknd opening.
Free.
🅿 *(charged)* 🍴 & *shop* ⊗

Yorkshire Carriage Museum
AYSGARTH
(G W Shaw Carriage Collection), Yore Mill (1.75m E on unclass rd N of A684)
☎*Richmond (01748) 823125*
An old stone mill at Aysgarth Falls now houses over 60 horse-drawn vehicles, including some splendid coaches and carriages.
Open Etr-Oct, daily 11-5.
P *(400 yds)* ⊗
Details not confirmed for 1995

Bedale Hall
BEDALE
(On A684, 1.5m W of A1 at Leeming Bar)
☎*(01677) 424604*
Housed in a building of 17th-century origin, with Palladian and Georgian extensions, the centre of this fascinating little museum is the Bedale fire engine dated 1742. Old documents, photographs, clothing, toys, craft tools and household utensils give an absorbing picture of the life of ordinary people.
Open Etr-Sep, Mon-Sat 10-4. Oct-Etr, Tue only 10-4. Other times by prior arrangement.
Donations.
🅿 & *toilets for disabled shop* ⊗

Beningbrough Hall
BENINGBROUGH
(off A19. Entrance at Newton Lodge)
☎*(01904) 470666*
Beningbrough was built around 1716, and its structure has hardly been altered since then. It houses 100 pictures from the National Portrait Gallery in London. Perhaps the finest feature of the house is the Great Staircase, built of oak with wide parquetried treads and delicate balusters carved to imitate wrought iron. Ornately carved wood panelling is a feature of several of the rooms, notably the drawing room. The other side of country house life can be seen in the restored Victorian laundry, which has its original stoves, drying racks and other equipment.The gardens include formal areas, a conservatory and a wilderness play area.
Open Apr-Oct, Mon-Wed, Sat, Sun, & Good Fri. Also Fri, Jul-Aug.
House, Garden & Exhibition: £4.50 (ch £2.30) Family ticket £9. Garden & Exhibition: £3 (ch £1.50) Family £6.
🅿 ✕ *licensed* & *(access to Victorian laundry, shop & restaurant) toilets for disabled shop* ⊗
(NT)

Brimham Rocks
BRIMHAM
Brimham House, Summerbridge (off B6265)
☎*Harrogate (01423) 780688*
A Victorian guidebook describes the rocks as 'a place wrecked with grim and hideous forms defying all description and definition'. The rocks have remained a great attraction, and stand on National Trust open moorland at a height of 950ft. An old shooting lodge in the area is now an information point and shop.
June-Sept, wknds in Apr, May & Oct, BHs and local school holidays, 11-5.
Cars £1.30. Minibuses £2.50 Coaches £6. Motorcycles 60p.
🅿 & *(specially adapted path) toilets for disabled shop*
(NT)

Bolton Castle
CASTLE BOLTON
(off A684)
☎*Wensleydale (01969) 23981*
The castle is set in the pretty surroundings of Wensleydale, and dates from 1379-97. It was a stronghold of the Scropes family. Mary Queen of Scots was imprisoned here in 1568-9; and the castle was besieged and taken in 1645 by Parliamentary forces. Tapestries, arms and armour, and other artefacts can be seen.
Open Mar-Nov 10-5.
£2.50 (ch & pen £1.50).
🅿 🍴 *shop* ⊗

CASTLE HOWARD
See Malton

Yorkshire Dales National Park Centre
CLAPHAM
☎*(015242) 51419*
A comprehensive information centre with displays on the local countryside and limestone scenery. A wide range of maps, guides, information leaflets, gifts and souvenirs are stocked and knowledgeable staff are on duty to answer questions. Audio-visual

presentation on limestone scenery available.
Open Apr-Oct, daily 10-4.
Free.
🅿 *(charged) (Radar key scheme) shop* ⊗

Byland Abbey
COXWOLD
The abbey was built for the Cistercians and is now a ruin, but enough still stands to show how beautiful it must have been. The ruins date back to the 12th and 13th centuries, and include well-preserved glazed floor tiles. Carved stones and other finds are displayed.
Open all year, Apr-Sep, daily 10-6; Oct, 10-4; Nov-Mar, Wed-Sun 10-4 or dusk if earlier. Closed 24-26 Dec & 1 Jan.
£1.30 (ch 70p, concessions £1).
🅿 &
(EH)

Moors Centre
DANBY
Lodge Ln
☎*Guisborough (01287) 660654*
The former shooting lodge provides information on the North York Moors National Park, with an exhibition, video and bookshop information desk. There are riverside and woodland grounds, with terraced gardens, a children's play area and a brass-rubbing centre. Special events are held in summer - 'phone 0891-664342 to request information.
Open all year, Apr-Oct, daily 10-5; Nov-Mar, Sat & Sun 11-4.
Free.
🅿 🍴 & *(woodland & garden trails) toilets for disabled shop* ⊗

Easby Abbey
EASBY
Set beside the River Swale, the Premonstratensian Abbey was founded in 1155 and dedicated to St Agatha. Extensive remains of the monks' domestic buildings can be seen.
Open all year, Apr-Sep, daily 10-6; Oct-Mar, Tue-Sun 10-4. (Closed 24-26 Dec & 1 Jan).
P *(100yds)* ⊗
(EH)
Details not confirmed for 1995

The granite outcrops of Birmingham Rocks stand over the Yorkshire Moors like sentinels on guard.

Castle Howard, which was the first building designed by Sir John Vanbrugh, has all the grandeur and nobility of a palace. The dome was the first to be built on a private house in England.

Yorkshire Air Museum & Allied Air Forces Memorial
ELVINGTON
☎(01904) 608595
The Yorkshire Air Museum is based on a part of the site of a typical World War II bomber base and its aim is to preserve it as a Memorial to the Allied Air Force air and ground cres who served in World War II, and especially those who served in Yorkshire and Humberside. Visitors can see many examples of interesting aircraft, which include one of the last of the RAF's Victor tankers, one of the last of the Lightnings and one of the early, test, Buccaneers. The Museum is 'the home of the Halifax', and the rebuilding of one - 'Friday the 13th', a unique example in the country - is well advanced. It is also home to a Mosquito rebuild, the Barnes Wallis Collection, a fine display of the Blackburn Heritage, the 609 (WR) Squadron room and displays of aviation artefacts and ephemera. The Museum recreates the sights, and some of the sounds, of an authentic wartime base.
Open all year, Mon-Fri 10.30-4, Sat & Sun 10.30-5, BH's 10.30-5.
£3 (ch 5-16 & pen £2).
🅿 ♿ ✗ *licensed* ♿ *toilets for disabled shop*

Fairburn Ings Nature Reserve
FAIRBURN
Newton Ln
☎Sandy (01767) 680551
One-third of the 618-acre RSPB reserve is open water, and over 200 species of birds have been recorded. A visitor centre provides information, and there is an elevated boardwalk, suitable for disabled visitors.
Access to the reserve from the village at all times. Visitor Centre only open Sat, Sun & BHs 10-5. (Closed 25 & 26 Dec). Car park & walkway at centre open daily 9-6 or dusk.
Free.
🅿 ♿ *(raised boardwalk for wheelchair) toilets for disabled shop*

National Park Centre
GRASSINGTON
Colvend, Hebden Rd
☎(01756) 752774
The centre is a useful introduction to the Yorkshire Dales National Park. It has a video and a display on 'Wharfedale - Gateway to the Park', and maps, guides and local information are available. There is also a 24-hr public access information service through computer screens and a full tourist information service.
Open Apr-Oct daily, 10-4. Also limited wknds Nov-Mar.
Free.
🅿 *(charged)* ♿ *(Radar key scheme) toilets for disabled shop* ♿

Harlow Carr Botanical Gardens
HARROGATE
Crag Lane, Otley Rd (off B6162)
☎(01423) 565418
The gardens were begun in 1950 on a rough site of pasture and woodland. Today there are 68 impressive acres of ornamental and woodland gardens, including the northern trial grounds. Special events for 1995 include: Easter bulb display (1-18 April), *A Midsummer Night's Dream* (4-5 July), Summer Evening Extravaganza (25 July), children's day (22 August), and an art exhibition (4 August-3 September). There are craft weekends throughout the summer. Courses, demonstrations and practical workshops are held in the Study Centre. Prospectus and full programme of events available on application.
Open all year, Mar-Oct, daily 9.30-6. Nov-Feb, daily 9.30-5 or dusk if earlier.
❊£3.20 (ch 16 free, pen £2.50). Party 20+.
🅿 ♿ ✗ *licensed* ♿ *(electric wheelchair available, tape recorded tours) toilets for disabled shop garden centre* ♿

The Royal Pump Room Museum
HARROGATE
Royal Pde
☎(01423) 503340
The octagonal Pump Room building houses changing exhibitions from the museum's own collections. In 1995 these will include 'Togs, Tools and Textiles' - an exhibition of historic needlework - throughout April, 'From Here to Eternity' - cultural approaches to the afterlife - from May to October and 'Get the Message' - the history of script - from October to December. This part of the building still houses the original sulphur wells, now below modern street level. The wells are enclosed by glass to contain their pungent smell, but the water can be tasted, by those brave enough, at the original spa counter, now the ticket counter.
Open all year, Apr-Oct, Mon-Sat 10-5, Sun 2-5, (Nov-Mar close at 4pm). (Closed 25-26 Dec & 1 Jan).
£1 (reductions for ch, pen & families). Prices under review.
P (restricted to 2hrs) ♿ *toilets for disabled* ♿

Dales Countryside Museum Centre
HAWES
Station Yard
☎Wensleydale (01969) 667450
The Dales Countryside Museum contains displays and an extensive collection of bygones and farming implements which explain the changing landscapes and communities of the area. There is a full national park and tourist information service including 24-hr public information terminals, maps, guides, publications and souvenirs.
Open Apr-Oct, daily 10-4. Limited winter opening.
Admission fee payable for museum. National park centre free.
🅿 *(charged)* ♿ *toilets for disabled shop* ♿

Duncombe Park
HELMSLEY
(1m from town centre, off A170)
☎(01439) 770213 & 771115
Duncombe Park stands at the heart of a spectacular 30-acre early 18th-century landscape garden which is set in 300 acres of dramatic parkland around the River Rye. The house, originally built in 1713, was gutted by fire in 1879 and rebuilt in 1895. Its principal rooms are a fine example of the type of grand interior popular at the turn of the century. Home of the Duncombes for 300 years, for much of this century the house was a girls' school. In 1985 the present Lord and Lady Feversham decided to make it a family home again and after major restoration, opened the house to the public in 1990. It is a British Tourist Authority 'Come to Britain' award winner. Part of the garden and parkland were designated a 250-acre National Nature Reserve in 1994.
Open: House & Gardens, Etr, Apr, Wed & Sun, 11-5; May-Jun, Wed-Sun, 11-5; Jul-Sep, daily 11-5; Oct, Wed & Sun, 11-5. Park Apr-Oct, daily.
House & Gardens £4.50 (ch 10-16, £2 & pen £3.75). Gardens & Parkland £2.75 (ch £1). Parkland only £1.
🅿 ♿ ✗ *licensed* ♿ *toilets for disabled shop*

Helmsley Castle
HELMSLEY
☎(01439) 70442
The ruined castle dates from the 12th century and later, and stands within enormous earthworks. It was besieged for three months in the Civil War, and destroyed in 1644.
Open all year, Apr-Sep, daily 10-6; Oct, 10-4; Nov-Mar, Wed-Sun 10-4 or dusk if earlier. Closed 24-26 Dec & 1 Jan.
£2 (ch £1, concessions £1.50).
P (100 yds)
(EH)

Flamingo Land Family Funpark
KIRBY MISPERTON
The Rectory (off the A169)
☎(01653) 668287
With over 100 rides, slides, shows and attractions Flamingoland Zoo and Family Funpark has something for everyone. There are exciting rides such as the Bullet, the Corkscrew and Thunder Mountain, ten shows, and Europe's largest privately-owned zoo with over 1000 different species of animals.
Open from 9th Apr, please telephone for further opening times.
❊Prices on application.
🅿 ♿ ✗ ♿ *(parking) toilets for disabled shop*

Kirkham Priory
KIRKHAM
Set on an entrancing site on the banks of the River Derwent are the ruins of this former house of Augustinian canons. The remains of the finely sculptured 13th-century gatehouse and lavatorium, where the monks washed in leaded troughs, are memorable.
Open Apr-Sep, daily 10-6.
£1.30 (ch 70p, concessions £1)
🅿 ♿ ♿
(EH)

Knaresborough Castle
KNARESBOROUGH
☎Harrogate (01423) 503340
High above the town of Knaresborough, the ruins of this 14th-century castle look down over the gorge of the River Nidd. This imposing fortress was once the hiding place of Thomas Becket's murderers and it also served as a prison for Richard II. Remains include the keep, the sally-port, parts of the curtain wall and the Old Court of Knaresborough, part of which also dates from the 14th century. It now houses a local history museum, and entrance is part of the combined ticket price. A new gallery is devoted to the Civil War in Knaresborough.
Open Etr, May-Sep, daily 10.30-5. Guided tours regulary available.
Combined ticket £1 (ch 60p). Disabled and local residents free. Prices under review.
🅿 ♿ *toilets for disabled* ♿ *(ex grounds)*

Yorkshire Dales National Park Centre
MALHAM
☎Airton (01729) 830363
The national park centre has maps, guides and local information together with displays on the remarkable natural history of the area, local community and work of conservation bodies. Audio-visuals are provided for groups and a 24-hour teletext information service is available..
Open Apr-Oct, daily 10-4. Limited winter opening.
Free.
🅿 *(charged)* ♿ *(Radar key scheme for toilet) toilets for disabled shop* ♿

Castle Howard
MALTON
(NE of York, off A64)
☎Coneysthorpe (01653) 648333
In its dramatic setting of lakes, fountains and extensive gardens, this 18th-century palace was designed by Sir John Vanbrugh. Principal location for the TV series 'Brideshead Revisited', this was the first major achievement of the architect who later created the lavish Blenheim Palace near Oxford. Castle Howard was begun in 1699 for the 3rd Earl of Carlisle, Charles Howard, whose descendants still call the place 'home'. The striking façade is topped by an 80ft painted and gilded dome. The interior has a 192ft Long Gallery, as well as a Chapel with magnificent stained glass windows by the 19th-century artist, Edward Burne-Jones. Besides the collections of antique furniture, porcelain and sculpture, the Castle contains a number of important paintings, including a portrait of Henry VIII by Holbein and works by Rubens, Reynolds and Gainsborough. The grounds include the domed Temple of the Four Winds by Vanbrugh, and the richly designed family Mausoleum by Hawksmoor. The Rose Garden contains both old-fashioned and modern varieties of roses.
Ray Wood is a 30-acre area with unique collections of rare trees, shrubs, rhododendrons and azaleas.
Open 1-16 Mar Grounds only. 17 Mar-29 Oct, Grounds & Plant Centre 10, House 11. Last admissions 4.30pm.
·£6 (ch £3.00, pen £5.00). Party 12+.

P ♥ ✗ licensed ॐ (chairlift, free adapted transport to house) toilets for disabled shop garden centre ⌀

Eden Camp Modern History Theme Museum
MALTON
Eden Camp (junc of A64 & A169)
☎(01653) 697777
The story of the peoples' war - the drama, the hardships, the humour - unfolds in this museum devoted to civilian life in World War II. The displays, covering the blackout, rationing, the Blitz, the Homeguard and others, are housed in a former prisoner-of-war camp built in 1942 for German and Italian soldiers. Voted Yorkshire and Humberside's Visitor Attraction of the Year 1992. Hut 28, opened in 1994, depicts the military and political events of 1944, with a special section covering D-Day. During 1995 there will be V E Day celebrations on 8 May, and later in the summer a new exhibit - Hut 29 - will be opened, covering the events of 1945.
Open 16 Jan-13 Feb wkdays only; 14 Feb-23 Dec, daily 10-5. Last admission 4pm. Allow at least 3hrs for a visit.
£3 (ch & pen £2). Party 10+.
P ♥ ॐ (taped tours, Braille guides) toilets for disabled shop

Malton Museum
MALTON
Old Town Hall, Market Place
☎(01653) 695136
The extensive Roman settlements in the area are represented and illustrated in this museum, including collections from the Roman fort of Derventio. There are also displays of local prehistoric and medieval finds plus changing exhibitions of local interest.
Open Etr Sat-Oct, Mon-Sat 10-4, Sun 2-4. Parties by arrangement.
£1 (ch, pen & students 60p). Family ticket £2.50.
P (adjacent) ॐ shop ⌀

Theakston Brewery Visitor Centre
MASHAM
The Brewery (on A6108)
☎Ripon (01765) 689057
At the Visitor Centre adjacent to the

Brewery visitors can discover how Theakston Traditional ales are brewed and see the ancient skills of the cooper, together with an exclusive video, a museum and a gift shop.
Open Mar, Wed-Sat, 10.30-4; Apr-Oct, Wed-Mon, 10.30-4; Nov-Dec, Wed, Sat & Sun 10.30-1 & 2-4.
Visitor centre & Brewery tour £2.50 (ch 10-18 £2). Visitor centre only £1 (ch 10-18 50p).
P (400yds) ॐ (ex brewery tours) toilets for disabled shop ⌀

Middleham Castle
MIDDLEHAM
☎Wensleydale (01969) 23899
The town of Middleham (much of which is a conservation area) is dominated by the 12th-century keep which saw its great days during the Wars of the Roses. The seat of the Neville family, the Earls of Warwick, it was the home for a time of the young King Richard III, then Duke of Gloucester, who married the Earl's daughter Anne Neville.
Open all year, daily 10-6; Oct, 10-4; Nov-Mar, Wed-Sun 10-4 or dusk if earlier. Closed 24-26 Dec & 1 Jan.
£1.50 (ch 80p, concessions £1.10).
P (30 yds) shop
(EH)

Newby Hall & Gardens
NEWBY HALL & GARDENS
(4m SE of Ripon, 2m W of A1, off B6265)
☎Harrogate (01423) 322583
This late 17th-century house had its interior and additions designed by Robert Adam, and contains an important collection of classical sculpture and Gobelin tapestries. Twenty-five acres of award-winning gardens include a miniature railway, an adventure garden for children, and a woodland discovery walk. Special events take place throughout the year, including craft fairs (10-11 June and 16-17 September), a country fair and horseshow (18 June), a historic vehicle rally (16 July) and the Harrogate MG rally (13 August)..
Open Apr-Sep, Tue-Sun & BH's; Gardens 11-5.30; House 12-5. Last admission 5pm (gardens), 4.30pm (house),

✤House & Garden £5.20, (ch & disabled £3, pen £4). Gardens only £3.30 (ch & disabled £2.20, pen £2.60). Party.
P ✗ licensed ॐ (wheelchairs available, maps of wheelchair routes) toilets for disabled shop garden centre ⌀

Lightwater Valley Theme Park & Village
NORTH STAINLEY
(on the A6108)
☎Ripon (01765) 635321 & 635334
Set in 175 acres of country park and lakeland, Lightwater Valley offers a selection of rides and attractions suitable for all the family. Enjoy the white-knuckle thrills of the world's biggest roller coaster - the Ultimate - as well as the Soopa Loopa, the Rat and the Wave, or, for the less adventurous, there are the Ladybird, the steam train, boating lake, and children's visitor farm. Please telephone for details of special events. This year will see the opening of a new all-year factory shopping village situated next door to the theme park.
Please telephone for details.
P ♥ ✗ licensed ॐ (even pathways) toilets for disabled shop garden centre ⌀

Nunnington Hall
NUNNINGTON
(1.5m N of B1257)
☎(01439) 748283
This large 16th-to 17th-century house has panelled rooms and a magnificent staircase. The Carlisle collection of miniature rooms is on display.
Open Apr-Oct, Tue-Thu, Sat & Sun 2-6, BH Mons 12-6;Also Fri Jul-Aug 2-6, wknds & BH Mon 12-6. Last admission 5pm.
House & garden £3.35 (ch £1.50). Family ticket £7.Gardens only £1 (ch free).
P ♥ ॐ toilets for disabled shop ⌀
(NT)

Mount Grace Priory
OSMOTHERLEY
(1m NW)
☎Northallerton (01609) 883494
A ruined 14th-century Carthusian priory, next to a 17th-century house. One of the monks's cells has been fully restored to show where the monk lived and worked in solitude, and what life was like in this monastery.
Open all year, Apr-Sep, daily 10-6. Oct-Mar, Wed-Sun 10-4. Closed 24-26 Dec & 1 Jan.
P ॐ shop
(EH & NT)
Details not confirmed for 1995

Parcevall Hall Gardens
PARCEVALL HALL GARDENS
☎Burnsall (01756) 720311 (Admin)
720269 (Gardener)
Enjoying a hillside setting east of the main Wharfedale Valley, these beautiful gardens belong to an Elizabethan house which is used as the Bradford Diocesan Retreat House (not open to the public).
Open Good Fri-Oct, daily 10-6. Winter visits by appointment.
✤£2 (ch 5-12 50p).
P ♥

North Yorkshire Moors Railway
PICKERING
Pickering Station
☎(01751) 472508
Operating through the heart of the North York Moors National Park between Pickering and Grosmont, steam trains cover a distance of 18 miles. Beautiful Newtondale Halt gives walkers easy access to forest and moorland. The locomotive sheds at Grosmont are open to the public. Special events for 1995 include an open weekend (1-2 April), a V E wartime weekend (6-8 May), the 150th anniversary gala commemorating the opening of the York to Scarborough line (1-2 July) and a Friends of Thomas the

This miniature room is part of the Carlisle Collection at Nunnington Hall. The model is an example of a classical Palladian entrance hall.

➜

Tank Engine weekend (16-17 September).
Open Apr-Oct, daily; Dec, Santa Specials. Further information available from Pickering Station, North Yorkshire. Prices under review.
P (charged) 🍵 & (ramp for trains) toilets for disabled shop

Pickering Castle
PICKERING
☎(01751) 74989
Standing upon its mound high above the town, the 12th-century keep and baileys are all that is left of this favourite royal hunting lodge.
Open all year, Apr-Sep, daily 10-6; Oct, 10-4; Nov-Mar, Wed-Sun 10-4 or dusk if earlier. Closed 24-26 Dec & 1 Jan. £2. (ch £1 concessions £1.50).
P & shop
(EH)

Georgian Theatre Royal
RICHMOND
Victoria Rd
☎(01748) 823710
Built in 1788, this is the oldest theatre in the United Kingdom still in its original form and still being used for live theatre. Having closed in 1848, it was restored and re-opened in 1962. The audience now watch the actors from the original gallery, boxes and pit. The museum contains old playbills and photographs, and the oldest complete set of painted scenery in the country.
Open Apr-Oct, Mon-Sat 11-4.45, Sun 2.30-4.45. Parties by arrangement. £1 (ch & pen 70p). Party.
P shop

Green Howards Museum
RICHMOND
Trinity Church Square, Market Place
☎(01748) 822133
This award-winning museum traces the military history of the Green Howards from the late 17th century onwards. The exhibits include uniforms, weapons, medals and a special Victoria Cross exhibition. Regimental and civic plate is also displayed.
Open Feb, Mon-Fri 10-4.30; Mar, Mon-Sat 10-4.30; Apr-Oct, Mon-Sat 9.30-4.30 & Sun 2-4.30; Nov, Mon-Sat 10-4.30. £1 (ch 16 50p, pen 75p).
P & shop

Richmond Castle
RICHMOND
☎(01748) 822493
Built high upon sheer rocks overlooking the River Swale, the castle was begun by Alan Rufus in 1071. It is ruined, but has a splendid 100ft high keep. Two of the towers are left on the massive curtain walls, and also well preserved is Scollard's Hall, which was built in 1080 and may be the oldest domestic building in Britain.
Open all year, Apr-Sep, daily 10-6; Oct, 10-4; Nov-Mar, Wed-Sun 10-4 or earlier. Closed 24-26 Dec & 1 Jan. £1.80 (ch 90p, concessions £1.40).
P (800 yds) & shop
(EH)

Rievaulx Abbey
RIEVAULX
☎(01439) 798228
The site for this magnificent abbey was given to a band of 12 Cistercian monks in 1131. Building began in about 1132 and most was completed by the end of the 12th century. The abbey was extremely prosperous, and under its third abbot, Aelred (1147-67), there were 140 monks and over 500 lay brothers. During the 15th century parts of the abbey were taken down as numbers fell, and by the time of the Dissolution there were only 22 monks left.
Surrounded by wooded hills, this site in the Rye Valley is one of the most beautiful in England. The remains of the high church and monastic buildings are extensive, and the choir is a notable example of a 13th-century work. The nave, which dates back to 1135, is the earliest large Cistercian nave in Britain.
Open all year, Apr-Sep, daily 10-6; Oct-Mar, daily 10-4 or dusk if earlier. Closed 24-26 Dec & 1 Jan. £2.40 (ch £1.20, concessions £1.80)
P & shop ⌨
(EH)

Rievaulx Terrace & Temples
RIEVAULX
(on B1257)
☎Bilsdale (01439) 798340
This curved terrace, half a mile long, overlooks the abbey, with views of Ryedale and the Hambleton Hills. It has two mock-Greek temples, one built for hunting parties, the other for quiet contemplation. There are also remarkable frescoes by Borgnis, and an exhibition on English landscape design.
Open Apr-Oct, daily 10.30-6 or dusk if earlier. Last admission 5pm. £2.50 (ch £1). Family £5.
P & (runaround vehicle available) shop
(NT)

Ripley Castle
RIPLEY
(off A61)
☎Harrogate (01423) 770152
This beautiful castle has been the home of the Ingilby family since 1320. The present castle dates mainly from the 16th century but has older and newer areas. The castle has Cromwellian connections and both James I and Cromwell stayed here. It is said that Cromwell was watched throughout the night by Trooper Jane Ingilby, who was armed with a pair of pistols. The castle has, among other things, a priest's hole which was discovered in 1964, and a collection of Royalist armour housed in the 1555 tower. The surrounding gardens and grounds are very fine, and various events are held throughout the year. The gardens now house the National Hyacinth Collection and the Ripley Tropical Plant Collection. Ripley village, one of the last surviving 'model estate villages' in the country, was entirely rebuilt in the 1820s-30s, and is well worth a visit. The Homes and Gardens Grand Summer Fair will be held here (8-11 June) and there will be a Lakeside Viennese Concert with laser and fireworks on 6 August.
Open Apr, May & Oct, Sat & Sun, Good Fri & BH 11.30-4.30; Jun & Sep, Tue, Fri, Sat & Sun 11.30-4.30; Jul-Aug, daily 11.30-4.30. Gardens, Mar, Thu-Sun, 11-4; Apr-Oct, daily 11-5; Nov-23 Dec, daily 11-3.30. Parties any day (ex 25 Dec) by arrangement. Castle & Gardens £3.75 (ch £2, pen £3). Gardens only £2.25 (ch £1, pen £1.75). Party 25+.
P 🍵 & shop garden centre ⌨

Fountains Abbey & Studley Royal
RIPON
(4m W off B6265)
☎Sawley (01765) 608888
Founded by Cistercian monks in 1132, Fountains Abbey is the largest monastic ruin in Britain. It was acquired by William Aislabie in 1768, and became the focal point of his landscaped gardens at Studley. These include formal water gardens, ornamental temples, follies and magnificent views. They are bordered by a lake and 400 acres of deer park. Other interesting features include Fountains Hall, built between 1598 and 1611 using the stone from the abbey ruins.
Open all year. Abbey & garden: Jan-Mar, Nov & Dec, daily (ex 24 & 25 Dec, & Fri Nov-Jan), 10-5 or dusk if earlier; Apr-Sep 10-7 (11 & 12 Jun & 9 & 10 Jul closed 6pm). Fountains Hall & St Mary's Church-restoration work in progress, telephone for opening times. £4 (ch £2). Family ticket £8.
P 🍵 ✕ licensed & toilets for disabled shop
(NT)

Norton Conyers
RIPON
(off A61)
☎*Melmerby (01765) 640333 (house)
640601 (garden)*
This late medieval house with Stuart and
Georgian additions has belonged to the
Grahams since 1624. The pictures and
furniture reflect over 370 years of
occupation by the same family. It was
visited by James I, Charles I and James
II. Another visitor was Charlotte Brontë: a
family legend of a mad woman confined
in the attics is said to have given her the
idea for Mrs Rochester in *Jane Eyre*, and
Norton Conyers is believed to have been
an inspiration for Mr Rochester's
Thornfield Hall. There are displays of
family costumes and wedding dresses.
Please note that ladies are requested not
to wear high-heeled shoes.
*Open - House & Garden: 28 May-10 Sep,
BH Sun & Mon; 24-29 July, daily 2-5.
£2.95 (ch 10-16 £2.50, pen, student,
UB40 & disabled £2).*
🅿 & *toilets for disabled shop* ✹ *(ex
grounds)*

Ripon Prison & Police Museum
RIPON
St Marygate
☎*(01765) 690799 & 603006*
An early 19th-century prison, now a
museum, housing documents, prints and
memorabilia depicting the history of Law
and Order and the Penal system in Ripon
over the last 100 years.
*Open Apr-Oct, Mon-Sun 1-5; Jul & Aug,
Mon-Sat 11-5, Sun 1-5.*
🅿 *(75 yds)* & *shop* ✹
Details not confirmed for 1995

Scarborough Castle
SCARBOROUGH
☎*(01723) 372451*
The ruins of Scarborough Castle stand on
a narrow headland which was once the
site of British and Roman encampments.
The curtain wall was probably built
several decades before the square keep,
which dates from about 1155. The shell
of the keep, the 13th-century Barbican
and remains of medieval chapels and a
house is all that remains of this fine
fortress.
*Open all year, Apr-Sep, daily 10-6; Oct-
Mar, daily 10-4 or dusk if earlier. Closed
24-26 Dec & 1 Jan.
£1.50 (ch 80p, concessionsts £1.10).*
🅿 *(100 yds)* & *(ex in keep)* ✹
(EH)

Craven Museum
SKIPTON
Town Hall, High St
☎*(01756) 794079*
Folk history, archaeology, geology,
costumes, lead mining - this small
museum crammed full of curios is bound
to have something of interest for
everyone. A special exhibition, *Craven at
War*, will be held from May to August
this year.
*Open all year, Apr-Sep, Mon, Wed-Fri 10-
5, Sat 10-noon & 1-5, Sun 2-5; Oct-Mar,
Mon, Wed-Fri 1.30-5, Sat 10-noon &
1.30-4.30. Some BH's & PH's phone to
confirm opening.
Free.*
🅿 *(150 yds)* & *toilets for disabled*

Skipton Castle
SKIPTON
☎*(01756) 792442 (castle) & 792200
(admin)*
Skipton is one of the most complete and
well-preserved medieval castles in
England. Some of the castle dates from
the 1650s when it was rebuilt after being
partially damaged following the Civil War.
However, the original castle was erected
in Norman times, and the gateway with
its Norman Arch still exists. The castle
became the home of the Clifford family in
1310 and remained so until 1676.
Entrance to the castle is through a
massive round-towered gateway with the
family motto 'Desormais' carved above it.
The main buildings inside the walls are
surrounded by well-kept lawns and

cobblestones. Conduit Court is especially
attractive with its ancient yew tree.
Illustrated tour sheets are available in
English, French, German, Dutch, Italian,
Spanish, Japanese or Esperanto.
*Open all year, daily from 10am (Sun
2pm). Last admission 6pm (4pm Oct-
Feb). (Closed 25 Dec).
£3.20 (inc illustrated tour sheet) (ch 18
£1.60, under 5 free, pen £2.70). Party
15+.*
🅿 *(5 mins walk) shop*

Sutton Park
SUTTON-ON-THE-FOREST
(on B1363).
☎*Easingwold (01347) 810249*
The early Georgian house contains fine
furniture, paintings and porcelain. The
grounds have superb, award-winning
terraced gardens, a lily pond and a
Georgian ice house; a new, walled-in
pond garden opens in 1995. There are
also delightful woodland walks and a
nature trail as well as spaces for caravans.
A Flower Festival will be held here on the
weekend of 8-9 July this year.
*Open - Gardens Etr-Oct, daily 11-5.30.
House open Etr Sun & Mon & all BH Sun
& Mon, other times for private parties
only.*
✿*Gardens only £1 (ch 50p). House £3.50
(ch £2, pen £3).*
🅿 🍽 & *shop* ✹ *(ex gardens)*

Whitby Abbey
WHITBY
☎*(01947) 603568*
Dominating the skyline above the fishing
port of Whitby are the ruins of the 13th-
century Benedictine abbey. The stone
abbey was erected on the site of the
wooden abbey of St Hilda, which was
built in 657. It was badly damaged by
shellfire during World War I.
*Open all year, Apr-Sep, daily 10-6; Oct-
Mar, daily 10-4 or dusk if earlier. Closed
24-26 Dec & 1 Jan.
£1.50 (ch 80p, concessions £1.10).*
🅿 *(50 yds)* ✹
(EH)

Whitby Museum
WHITBY
Pannett Park
☎*(01947) 602908*
A charming museum packed full of
fascinating exhibits relating to Whitby's
history. Important collections of fossils,
ship models and Whitby jet jewellery;
Captain Cook material; relics of the
whaling industry and renowned arctic
scientist William Scoresby Jr FRS; fine
ethnographic collection; bygones,
costumes, local archaeology and more.
*Open all year, May-Sep, wkdays 9.30-
5.30, Sun 2-5; Oct-Apr, Mon & Tue 10.30-
1, Wed-Sat 10.30-4, Sun 2-4 (last
admission 30 mins before closing).*

P *(400 yds)* & *(by appointment) shop* ✹
Details not confirmed for 1995

The
ARC YORK
St Saviourgate
☎*(01904) 654324*
The ARC is a 'hands-on' experience of
archaeology, enjoyed by visitors of all
ages. It is housed in the beautifully
restored medieval church of St Saviour.
Be an archaeologist yourself! Sift through
the remains of centuries - bones, shell,
pottery and much more. Piece together
the lives of our ancestors. Solve the
puzzle of how to open a Viking padlock,
decipher Viking-age writing or learn to
make a Roman shoe. Real archaeologists
are on hand to assist you with your
discoveries. A range of special events
and exhibitions of archaeological interest
are held throughout the year.
*Open Mon-Fri 10-5, Sat & Sun 1-5.
Closed Good Fri & 18-31 Dec.*
& *(induction loop) toilets for disabled
shop* ✹
Details not confirmed for 1995

Borthwick Institute of Historical
Research
YORK
St Anthony's Hall, Peasholme Green
☎*(01904) 642315*
Originally built in the second half of the
15th century for the Guild of St Anthony,
the hall, with its fine timber roof, was
later used as an arsenal, a workhouse, a
prison and the Bluecoat School from
1705 to 1946. Now part of York
University, it houses ecclesiastical
archives and exhibitions of documents.
*Open all year, Mon-Fri 9.30-1 & 2-5.
(Closed Etr & Xmas).
Free.*
✹ 🏫

City Art Gallery
YORK
Exhibition Square
☎*(01904) 551861*
This gallery is a treasure-house of
Continental and British paintings
spanning seven centuries and including
the world-famous Lycett Green collection
of Old Masters as well as works by the
remarkable York-born painter of the nude,
William Etty. You can also see the
unrivalled Milner-White collection of
stoneware pottery. In addition, there is a
programme of temporary exhibitions,
lectures and events. The provisional
programme for 1995 includes an
exhibition of work by women artists from
the York area (14 January-5 February), *L
S Lowry: The Man and His Art* (25
March-7 May) and *German Printmaking
in the Age of Goethe* (9 September - 22
October), but dates are unconfirmed at
the time of going to press.

*Open all year, Mon-Sat 10-5, Sun 2.30-5,
last admission 4.30 (Closed Good Fri, 25-
26 Dec & 1 Jan).
Admission under review*
P *(500mtrs)* & *(chairlift) toilets for
disabled shop* ✹

Clifford's Tower
YORK
Clifford St
☎*(01904) 646940*
Known as Clifford's Tower, after Roger
de Clifford who was hung from the castle
by chains, York Castle was built in 1068
by William the Conqueror as part of his
campaign to subdue the Saxons. He built
a large mound, topped with a wooden
castle, on the banks of the River Ouse. In
1190 it was burned down when the Jews
of York hid in it during the pogrom. Under
the reign of King John it was rebuilt in
stone and it was completed in 1313.
However the castle cracked from top to
bottom in 1360, as a result of part of the
mound subsiding into the moat. From the
end of the 15th century the tower was
largely unused. Since 1825 Clifford's
Tower has been part of the prison and is
now looked after by English Heritage.
The wall walk provides one of the best
views of York.
*Open all year, Apr-Sep, daily 10-6; Oct-
Mar, daily 10-4 or dusk if earlier. Closed
24-26 Dec & 1 Jan.
£1.50 (ch 80p, concessions £1.10).*
✹ 🏫
(EH)

Fairfax House
YORK
Castlegate
☎*(01904) 655543*
An outstanding mid-18th-century house
with a richly decorated interior, Fairfax
House was acquired by the York Civic Trust
in 1983 and restored. Prior to this it had
been used as a cinema and a dance hall.
The house contains fine examples of
Georgian furniture, porcelain, paintings
and clocks which form the Terry
Collection. This collection was donated
by Mr Noel Terry who was the great
grandson of Joseph Terry the founder of
the York-based confectionery business.
There is a special display of a recreated
meal dating from 1763 in the dining room
and kitchen. From 1 September until 20
November *Chocolate, Coffee and Tea
Drinking 1600-1850* will explain, through
the use of special set-piece period
displays, the ritual and practice of this
enduring obsession - special loans of
important items from Royal and National
collections helping to chart its
development among members of 18th-
century 'polite society'; the special
annual Christmas exhibition, *The
Keeping of Christmas*, will be held from
3 December to 6 January. ➤

Skipton Castle is one of the best preserved medieval fortresses in England having survived both the Civil War and the
enthusiasm of Victorian 'restorers' without harm.

Open 20 Feb-5 Jan, Mon-Sat 11-5, (Closed Fri). Sun 1.30-5. Last admission 4.30pm.
£3 (ch £1.50, pen & student £2.50).
& (with assistance. Phone before visit) shop ❧

Friargate Museum
YORK
Lower Friargate
☎ (01904) 658775
The award-winning Friargate - the most popular family museum in York, and recently featured on Children's ITV - is celebrated for its role in bringing history to life. Over 70 lifesize waxwork figures are exhibited in carefully reconstructed, realistic sets, showing scenes such as Drake and the Armada, the Dukes of York, and the Crown Jewels. There is even a lifelike Yeti or 'Abominable Snowman' for the very brave - sound effects as well! The 'Chuckles' exhibition of unusual laughter machines forms an additional attraction. Special drawing and photography facilities are available. Events for 1995 include Elsie Wagstaff's V E Day Celebrations and a section on the Jacobean Uprisings.
Open Mar-Oct, daily 10-5; Nov-Feb, 10-dusk. (Closed Jan & 25 Dec).
£2.75 (ch £1.75, pen £2). Party.
P (0.5m) & (touch tours for the blind) shop

Guildhall
YORK
Off Coney St
☎ (01904) 613161
The present Hall dates from 1446 but in 1942 an air raid virtually destroyed the building. The present Guildhall was carefully restored as an exact replica and was re-opened in 1960. There is an interesting arch-braced roof decorated with colourful bosses and supported by 12 solid oak pillars.
Although many of the windows in the Guildhall were unglazed until the 18th century, the west window contains stained-glass from 1682, by a York craftsman, and there is also a superb, modern stained glass window by Henry Harvey. This depicts the story of York through the ages. The Inner Chamber adjoining the Hall has two secret doors and a passageway beneath the Guildhall to the river.
Open all year, May-Oct, Mon-Thu 9-5 (Wed 9-4), Fri 9-4.30, Sat 10-5, Sun 2.30-4.30; Nov-Apr, Mon-Thu 9-5 (Wed 9-4), Fri 9-4.30. (Closed Good Fri, Spring BH, 25-26 Dec & 1 Jan).
Free.
& (electric chair lift) toilets for disabled ❧ ♿

Jorvik Viking Centre
YORK
Coppergate
☎ (01904) 643211
Jorvik was the Viking name for York. Between 1976 and 1981 archaeologists made some remarkable discoveries about Jorvik, during a dig in an area known as Coppergate. In 1984 the Viking Centre was opened over the site of the original excavations. The dig shed a totally new light on the Viking way of life and has revealed many details of tools, clothing, crafts and trade. The Centre displays the archaeological remains - leather, textiles, metal objects and even timber buildings - in a detailed and vivid reconstruction. First there is an audio-visual display to explain exactly who the Vikings were. Then, 'time-cars' carry visitors through a 'time tunnel' from World War II back to Norman times and then to a full-scale reconstruction of 10th-century Coppergate. The busy street scene includes a crowded market, a river wharf with a fully-rigged sailing ship and a family at home. This is all made more authentic by voices speaking in Old Norse and even smells such as cooking, fish, pigsties and rubbish. Finally the tour passes through a reconstruction of Coppergate during the dig of the 1970s. The visit ends in the Skipper Gallery

which has a display of some of the 15,000 small objects found during the dig. This year's Jorvik Festival (11-25 February) is the tenth to feature longship races, combat re-enactment, feasts, crafts, torchlit procession, boat burning ceremony, concerts, lectures - and much more.
Open all year, Apr-Oct daily 9-7; Nov-Mar daily 9-5.30. (Closed 25 Dec).
£4.25 (ch £2.10). (Nov-Mar only pen £3).
P (400 yds) & (time car designed to take a wheelchair) toilets for disabled shop ❧

Merchant Adventurers' Hall
YORK
Fossgate
☎ (01904) 654818
The medieval guild hall of the powerful Merchant Adventurers' Company was built 1357/1361 and is one of the finest in Europe. The Great Hall, where the merchants conducted their business affairs, contains early furniture, one piece dating from the 13th century, paintings, silver, weights and measures, and other objects used by the merchants over the centuries. The building also has an Undercroft where they cared for the poor, a Chapel, and a Jacobean addition for the caretaker.
Open all year, end Mar-early Nov, daily 8.30-5; early Nov-late Mar, Mon-Sat 8.30-3.30. (Closed 10 days Xmas).
£1.80 (ch 7-17 50p, pen £1.50)
P (2 mins walk) & toilets for disabled shop

Museum of Automata
YORK
Tower St
☎ (01904) 655550
The Museum of Automata appeals to adults and children alike, with a unique collection of ingenious machines spanning 2000 years from simple articulated figurines from ancient civilisations to modern day robots. The French Gallery contains a throng of musicians, clowns, artists and eccentrics from Parisian cafe society, brought to life by video, sound and lighting. Visitors can crank exhibits into action in the Contemporary Gallery, and there's a reconstruction of a saucy 1950s seaside pier.
Open all year, daily 9.30-5.30. (Closed 25 Dec)
£3.50 (ch £2, pen & students £3). Family ticket £9.
P (50 yds) & toilets for disabled shop ❧

National Railway Museum
YORK
Leeman Rd
☎ (01904) 621261
At the National Railway Museum visitors can experience nearly two hundred years' history of the technical and social

changes that were brought about by the British invention of railways and their immense contribution to civilisation. In the Great Hall are famous locomotives which illustrate the evolution of motive power; displays explaining the elements of civil engineering, signalling and safety as well completely new exhibitions describing the railway of today and tomorrow, including the Channel Tunnel. The South Hall is all about the social history connected with travelling by train, including the story of Royal Travel. Exhibits range from early third class coaches to Queen Victoria's saloon of 1869 and include the Earl paintings which show the life of a Victorian Railway Station at its busiest. Also in the South Hall, visitors can learn the history of how the railways catered for passengers, whether on trains and ships or at hotels and stations. A restored 1914 third class dining car from the Midland Railway, complete with kitchen facilities, can be visited. Also on show are collections of tableware ranging from refreshment crockery to the fine porcelain and glass used on the Royal coaches.
Open all year, Mon-Sat 10-6, Sun 11-6. (Closed 24-26 Dec). Last admission 5pm.
✻Admission fee payable.
🅿 (charged) 🍴 ✕ licensed & ("Please Touch" evenings) toilets for disabled shop ❧

St Williams College
YORK
College St (adjacent to York Minster at east end)
☎ (01904) 637134
St William's College, a 15th-century timber-framed building, housed chantry priests until 1549. It now contains York Minster's Visitor Centre and the World of the Minster exhibition which offers an insight into the life and times of the people attached to York Minster over 800 years. The entrance fee includes an audio tape to help you around the exhibition of the building and care of the Minster, craftsmen and artisans, intrigues and disasters, amd many priceless treasures including medieval manuscripts and books.
Open all year, Mon-Sat 10-5 (4pm in winter), Sun 11-3. (Closed 24-26 Dec & Good Fri).
🅿 🍴 ✕ licensed shop ❧
Details not confirmed for 1995

Treasurer's House
YORK
Chapter House St
☎ (01904) 624247
There has been a house on this site since Roman times and in the basement of this elegant 17th-century building is an exhibition of its history. The house was

improved during the 18th century with the addition of a fine staircase. Restored between 1897 and 1930, it was left, with its fine furniture, to the National Trust.
Open Apr-Oct, daily 10.30-5. Last admission 4.30pm.
£3 (ch £1.50). Family ticket £6.
P (400 yds) ✕ licensed ❧ (NT)

York Castle Museum
YORK
The Eye of York
☎ (01904) 653611
Four centuries of everyday life are exhibited in the Castle Museum, imaginatively displayed through reconstructions of period rooms and two indoor streets, complete with cobbles, a Hansom cab and a park. The museum is housed in the city's prison and is based on an extensive collection of 'bygones' acquired at the beginning of the century. It was one of the first folk museums to display a huge range of everyday objects in an authentic scene. The Victorian street includes a pawnbroker, a tallow candle factory and a haberdasher's. There is even a reconstruction of the original sweet shop of the York chocolate manufacturer, Joseph Terry. An extensive collection of many other items ranging from musical instruments to costumes and a gallery of domestic gadgets from Victorian times to the 1960s (entitled 'Every home should have one') are further attractions to this remarkable museum. The museum also has one of Britain's finest collections of Militaria; this includes a superb example of an Anglo-Saxon helmet - one of only three known. A special exhibition called 'Seeing it Through' explores the life of York citizens during the Second World War.
Open all year, Apr-Oct Mon-Sat 9.30-5.30 (Wed 10.30-5.30), Sun 10-5.30; Nov-Mar, Mon-Sat 9.30-4 (Wed 10.30-5.30), Sun 10-4. (Closed 25-26 Dec & 1 Jan).
✻£3.95 (ch, pen, students & UB40 £2.85). Family ticket £11. Party 10+.
🍴 & toilets for disabled shop ❧

The York Dungeon
YORK
12 Clifford St
☎ (01904) 632599
Deep in the heart of York, buried beneath Clifford Street, lies the North's most infamous museum of horror. Here, history is brought to life, and execution and torture are everyday events behind its doors. A new feature of the York Dungeon is the Guy Fawkes Experience.
Open all year, daily 10-5.30 (4.30 Oct-Mar).
✻£3.25 (ch & pen £2, students £2.75)
P & shop

Built by the most powerful of the many medieval guilds in York, the Merchant Adventurer's Hall is one of the finest in Europe.

A detail of an embroidery illustrating The York Story. An audio-visual guide and three-dimensional models also help to bring 1000 years of history alive.

York Model Railway
YORK

Tearoom Square, York Station
☎(01904) 630169
One of the biggest and best model railways in Britain, York Model Railway has two very intricate railway layouts. The larger one is set in town and country landscapes. It comprises hundreds of buildings, about 5500 tiny trees, over 2000 lights and around 2500 people and animals. As many as 14 trains can run in this model at the same time, including the Royal Train, the Orient Express, Inter City 125 and the latest freight and passenger trains.
The second model is a much smaller layout and shows a typical German town at night, brightly lit by numerous tiny lights. There are push buttons for children, amid these detailed and accurate scale models, and the Thomas the Tank Engine section will appeal to children of all ages.
Open daily, Mar-Oct 9.30-6, Nov-Feb 10.30-5 (Closed 25-26 Dec).
P *(100 yds)* ё *shop*
Details not confirmed for 1995

Yorkshire Museum & Gardens
YORK

Museum Gardens
☎(01904) 629745
The winner of a European award, Yorkshire Museum - set in 10 acres of botanical gardens in the heart of the historic city of York - displays some of the finest Roman, Anglo-Saxon, Viking and Medieval treasures ever discovered in Britain. The Middleham jewel, a fine example of English Gothic jewellery, is on display in the Medieval Gallery and, in the Roman Gallery, visitors can see a fine marble head of Constantine the Great, household utensils exhibited in a recreated kitchen and many other artefacts. The Anglo-Saxon Gallery houses the magnificent, delicate silver-gilt Ormside bowl and the skilfully wrought Gilling sword. The Museum also has a fine collection of Rockingham porcelain. Part of York's Roman city walls runs through the Museum Gardens where, amongst a variety of flora and fauna, you can visit a working observatory and the ruins of the medieval St Mary's Abbey with its 14th-century guesthouse - the oldest timber-framed structure in Yorkshire. Special exhibitions this year include *Venom - an exhibition with a sting in its tail* (April '95-October '96), *Wildlife Photographer of the Year* (5 March-9 April) and *Travelling Discovery Centre* (25 May-9 July).
Open all year, Apr-Oct, daily 10-5; Nov-Mar, Mon-Sat 10-5, Sun 1-5. Last admission 4.30.
Prices available on application.
ё *(ramps & lift) toilets for disabled shop* ⌘

The York Story
YORK

The Heritage Centre, Castlegate
☎(01904) 628632
The exhibition traces the history of York over the last 1000 years, helped by a large three-dimensional model of York. A model of part of the building of a medieval church, showing the scaffolding and other building techniques, is an unusual feature. There is a comprehensive audio-visual guide to the display of many notable pieces by modern artists and craftsmen and the treasures of the city.
The Heritage Centre is in the predominately 15th-century church of St Mary which has the tallest spire in York, at 152ft.
Open all year, Mon-Sat 10-5 (Wed 10.30-5), Sun 1-5. (Closed 25-26 Dec & 1 Jan).
✳£1.50 (ch, pen, students & UB40's £1).
Joint ticket with Castle Museum £4.95. Family ticket £11.
ё *shop* ⌘

NOTTINGHAMSHIRE

D H Lawrence Birthplace
EASTWOOD

8A Victoria St (follow signs on A610)
☎Langley Mill (01773) 763312
D H Lawrence was born here on 11 September 1885, and the town and its surroundings influenced his writing throughout his life. The carefully restored house offers an insight into the author's early childhood and is also a good example of a Victorian working class home. Audio-visual presentations are held, and two new exhibition rooms show a model of *The Country of My Heart* and Lawrence's travels round the world.
Open all year, Apr-Oct, daily 10-5; Nov-Mar, daily 10-4. (Closed 24 Dec-1 Jan). Evenings by arrangement only.
£1.75 (concessions £1)
P *(100yds) shop* ⌘

White Post Modern Farm Centre
FARNSFIELD

(1m W)
☎Mansfield (01623) 882977 & 882026
This working farm gives an introduction to a variety of modern farming methods. It explains how farms work, with exhibits such as llamas, deer, pigs, cows, snails, quails, snakes and fish, through to 20 arable crop plots. There is also lots to see indoors including the owl houses, incubator room, mousetown and a reptile house. A barn dance is planned for July, and there will be daily Nativity plays before Christmas. The Pet Centre opened in

1994 introduces a brand new concept in pet education.
Open all year, Mon-Fri 10-5. Wknds & BH's 10-6.
£2.95 (ch 4-16 £1.95, under 4 free, pen & people with special needs £1.96). Party 10+.
P 🦽 ё *(sign language, free hire wheelchairs, book if more than 6) toilets for disabled shop* ⌘ *(kennels available)*

Museum & Art Gallery
MANSFIELD

Leeming St
☎(01623) 663088
'Images of Mansfield, Past and Present' uses objects and photographs to illustrate the history of the town, whilst 'Nature of Mansfield' looks at the natural history of the area. The museum has an important display of William Billingsley porcelain and the attractive Buxton watercolours show the town at the turn of the century. The museum also presents a wide range of temporary exhibitions and activities which includes this year 'My Best Friend' - new sculptures by Philip Cox - between 12 August and 17 September.
Open all year, Mon-Sat 10-5. (Closed Sun & BH's).
Free.
P *(120 yds)* ё *shop* ⌘

Millgate Museum of Social & Folk Life
NEWARK-ON-TRENT

48 Millgate
☎Newark (01636) 79403
By reconstructions of shop fronts and street areas from Victorian times to the 1950s, this enterprising museum illustrates the working and home life of local people through the years. A variety

of art and craft exhibitions is planned throughout the year.
Open all year. Opening times under review - phone for details.
Free.
P *(250yds)* ё *toilets for disabled shop* ⌘

Newark Air Museum
NEWARK-ON-TRENT

The Airfield, Winthorpe
☎Newark (01636) 707170
A diverse collection of transport, training and reconnaisance aircraft, jet fighters, bombers and helicopters, now numbering more than forty. A new Undercover Aircraft Display Hall (fifteen exhibits) and an Engine Display have now been opened, making the museum an all-weather attraction. V E Day 50th anniversary celebration days are planned for 1995.
Open all year, Apr-Oct, Mon-Fri 10-5, Sat & Sun 10-6; Nov-Mar, daily 10-4. (Closed 24-26 Dec). Other times by appointment.
£3 (ch & pen £2). Party 10+.
P 🦽 ё *toilets for disabled shop*

Newark Museum
NEWARK-ON-TRENT

Appletongate
☎(01636) 702358
The museum displays the archaelogy and local history of the area. There is some natural history too. Visitors can see an exhibition of 17th-century Civil War items and a collection of militaria of the Sherwood Foresters.
Open all year Mon-Wed & Fri 10-1 & 2-5, Sat 10-1 & 2-5; Apr-Sep also Sun 2-5. BH's 1-4.
Free.
P *(2 mins walk)* ё *shop* ⌘

Vina Cooke Museum of Dolls & Bygone Childhood
NEWARK-ON-TRENT

The Old Rectory, Cromwell (5m N of Newark off A1)
☎(01636) 821364
All kinds of childhood memorabilia are displayed in this 17th-century house: prams, toys, dolls' houses, costumes and a large collection of Victorian and Edwardian dolls including Vina Cooke hand-made character dolls. There will be an Easter Monday extravaganza from 11am to dusk including Morris dancing, puppet shows, craft stalls, displays etc.
Open all year, daily 10.30-noon & 2-5, appointment advisable. Also open evenings for booked parties.
£2 (ch £1, pen £1.50).
P ё *shop* ⌘

Newstead Abbey
NEWSTEAD

(off A60)
☎Mansfield (01623) 793557
This beautiful historic house, set in extensive parklands, is best known as the home of the poet, Lord Byron, who made the house and its ghostly legends famous. Visitors can see Byron's own rooms, mementoes of the poet and other splendidly decorated rooms which date ➤

from medieval to Victorian times. The grounds of over 300 acres include waterfalls, ponds, water gardens and Japanese gardens. Special events planned for 1995 include outdoor theatre and opera.
Open: Grounds all year, daily (ex last Fri in Nov); House Apr-Sep, daily 12-6. Last admission 5pm
✱*House & Grounds £3.50 (ch £1, pen & students £2). Grounds only £1.60 (concessions £1).*
🅿 💺 ✕ *licensed* ♿ *toilets for disabled shop*

NOTTINGHAM
The romance of outlawry still clings to Castle Rock in Nottingham, among the remains of the great medieval fortress that housed the Sheriff of Nottingham and Prince John, opponents of the legendary Robin Hood. His statue stands beneath the castle walls, bow drawn ready for action. However, although the city below the castle still cherishes its legends, it is built on the realities of a textile industry that dates back to the 13th century. The history of Nottingham lace, hosiery and knitwear and the role of canals in trade can be traced in the city museums.

Brewhouse Yard Museum
NOTTINGHAM
Castle Boulevard
☎(0115) 9483504 ext 3602 or 3600
Housed in 17th-century cottages on a two-acre site with unusual local plants, the museum depicts everyday life in Nottingham over the past 300 years. Thousands of locally made or used objects are shown in a mixture of period rooms, re-created shops - including a 'between-the-wars' shopping street - and displays giving an insight into the everyday and special events that make up the lives of the people in Nottingham past and present. Rock Cottage houses a schoolroom and toyshop of the 1930s. Caves behind the houses, used in the

past as air raid shelters as well as for storage and cooking, are now part of the museum.
Open all year 10-5. Last admission 4.45pm. (Closed 25-26 Dec).
Free, but Donations appreciated Mon-Fri. £1 (concessions 50p) weekends & BH. Under review.
🅿 (100 yds) ♿ *toilets for disabled shop* ❧

Canal Museum
NOTTINGHAM
Canal St
☎(0115) 9598835
The history of the River Trent from the Ice Age to the present day is told in the ground and first floors and wharf of this 19th-century warehouse. Life size dioramas, models and an audio-visual presentation add impact to the displays which include local canal and river navigation, boats, bridges and archaeology. There are regular boat trips on Sundays and Bank Holidays during the summer months.
Open all year, Wed-Sun 10-12 & 1-5. Free.
🅿 (400yds) ♿ *(wheelchairs available) toilets for disabled shop* ❧

Castle Museum
NOTTINGHAM
☎(0115) 9483504
This 17th-century building has a much restored 13th-century gateway. Now a museum and art gallery, a guided tour of the underground passages is conducted every afternoon except Sundays. A new, interactive 'Story of Nottingham' exhibition brings the history of the city alive for the visitor. Various special events are held throughout the year, with major temporary exhibitions, both historical and contemporary. There is an automated car in the grounds for disabled people. Various exhibitions are being held during the year.
Open all year, 10-5. Grounds 8-dusk.
✱*weekdays free, weekends & BH's £1 (ch50p). Joint ticket available to Brewhouse Yard Museum.*
🅿 (400 yds) 💺 ♿ *(chair lift) toilets for disabled shop* ❧

Hundreds of samples of Nottingham lace and demonstrations of how it is made, form the main attraction of the Nottingham Lace Centre.

Green's Mill
NOTTINGHAM
Windmill Ln, Sneinton (1m E of city centre, off A612)
☎(0115) 9503635
Restored to working order, this tower mill can be seen in use when conditions allow. The adjacent Science Centre tells the story of George Green, one-time miller here and distinguished mathematician. Flour is on sale.
Open all year Wed-Sun, 10-5, also BH's. (Closed 25 Dec).
Free.
🅿 ♿ *(audio loop, hands-on exhibits) toilets for disabled shop* ❧

The Lace Centre
NOTTINGHAM
Severns Building, Castle Rd
☎(0115) 9413539
Exquisite Nottingham lace fills this small building to capacity; there are even panels hanging from the beamed ceiling. There are demonstrations of lace-making on Thursdays from 2-4pm between Easter and the end of October. Situated below the Castle wall opposite the Robin Hood statue.
Open all year, Jan-Feb, daily 10-4; Mar-Dec, 10-5. (Closed 25-26 Dec).
Free.
🅿 (100 yds) (metered street parking) ♿ *shop*

The Lace Hall
NOTTINGHAM
High Pavement
☎(0115) 9484221
The invention and development of the world-famous Nottingham lace is explained at Lace Hall. Working machines, bobbin lace demonstrations, period settings and talking figures create a lively and educational entertainment, and there are coffee and exhibition shops. Visitors can see the lace being made and buy the product from one of the finest collections in the UK.
Open all year, daily 10-5. (Last admission 1hr before closing). (Closed 25-27 Dec).
✱*£2.75 (ch & pen £1.50). Party.*
🅿 (100 yds) 💺 ✕ *licensed* ♿ *(counters at lower level, lift to upper floor) toilets for disabled shop* ❧

Museum of Costume & Textiles
NOTTINGHAM
43-51 Castle Gate
☎(0115) 9483504
Costume from 1730 to 1960 is displayed in appropriate room settings. Other rooms contain 17th-century costume and embroidery, dress accessories, the Lord Middleton collection and map tapestries. Knitted, woven and printed textiles are also on show, together with embroidery from Europe and Asia.
Open all year, daily 10-5.45. Closed 25-26 Dec.
Free.
♿ *shop* ❧

Natural History Museum
NOTTINGHAM
Wollaton Hall, Wollaton (3m W, off A52 & A6514)
☎(0115) 9281333 & 9281130
Standing in a large deer park, this imposing Elizabethan mansion by Robert Smythson dates back to 1580. A wide variety of displays include birds, mammals, fossils and minerals.
Open all year, Apr-Sep, Mon-Sat 10-5, Sun 1-5; Oct-Mar, Mon-Sat 10-4.30, Sun 1.30-4.30. Park open Mon-Fri 8-dusk, Sat & Sun 9-dusk. Closed 25-26 Dec.
✱*weekdays free, weekends & BH's £1 (ch 50p). Joint ticket available for Wollaton Hall & Industrial Museum.*
🅿 *(charged)* ♿ *(special handling exhibition) toilets for disabled shop* ❧

Nottingham Industrial Museum
NOTTINGHAM
Courtyard Buildings, Wollaton Park (3m W off A609 Ilkeston Rd)
☎(01602) 284602
Housed in the 18th-century stable block, displays illustrate Nottingham's industrial

history, in particular those of lace and hosiery. Exhibits on the pharmaceutical industry, engineering, printing and the tobacco industry are also here. A beam (pumping) engine and heavy agricultural machinery are housed in a new extension. Victorian street furniture is displayed in a yard outside, along with a horse gin from a local coalmine. The beam engine and other engines are in steam the last Sunday in each month and on Bank Holidays.
Open all year, Apr-Sep, Mon-Sat 10-6, Sun 2-6; Oct-Mar, Thu & Sat 10-4.30, Sun 1.30-4.30. 19th-century beam pump engine & other engines in steam last Sun in each month & BH.
🅿 ♿ *(hand & powered wheelchairs available) toilets for disabled shop* ❧
Details not confirmed for 1995

Tales of Robin Hood
NOTTINGHAM
Maid Marian Way
☎(0115) 9483284
A marvel of special effects transporting the visitor to medieval Nottingham and the magical glades of the greenwood in search of Robin Hood. Travelling in the unique adventure cars the experience happens below, around and above you as the commentary (available in seven different languages) is piped into each car by portable compact disc players. Special events are planned for the last full weekend of every month. Please telephone for details.
Open all year, Apr-Oct 10-4.30; Nov-Mar 10-3.30.
£4.25 (concessions £3.25). Family ticket £12.50.
🅿 (NCP) ♿ *(chairlift, specially adapted 'car') toilets for disabled shop* ❧

Sundown Kiddies Adventureland
RAMPTON
(Sundown Pets Garden), Treswell Rd (3m off A57 at Dunham crossroads)
☎(01777) 248274
'The children's story book theme park': every child loves a story, and Sundown Adventureland is every child's favourite - a land where those wonderful fairy tales spring magically to life, a land of nursery rhymes, castles, wizards and dragons, a land as big as any child's imagination. Other attractions include Smugglers' Cove and the Boozey Barrel Boat Ride, the Rocky Mountain Railroad where the bandits hide and Shotgun City with its 'crazy crittur' show as well as an indoor jungle (height restriction), musical pet shop and mini farm with live animals. From this summer the new story book village will also offer an additional indoor ride - 'In Search of Santa'.
Open all year, daily 10-6, earlier in winter. (Closed 25-26 Dec).
✱*£3.50 (ch under 2 free).*
🅿 💺 ♿ *toilets for disabled shop* ❧

Wetlands Waterfowl Reserve & Exotic Bird Park
SUTTON-CUM-LOUND
Off Loundlow Rd
☎Retford (01777) 818099
The collection of waterfowl includes ducks, geese, swans, and flamingos on two lagoons covering some 32 acres, and many wild birds live here. There are also parrots, a variety of trees and plants, and a children's farm.
Open all year, daily 10-5.30 (or dusk whichever is earlier). (Closed 25 Dec).
🅿 💺 ♿ *(wheelchair available) shop* ❧
Details not confirmed for 1995

Clumber Park
WORKSOP
(4.5m SE, signposted from A1)
☎(01909) 476653
An impressive, landscaped park, laid out by Capability Brown. An outstanding feature is the lake running through the park, a haven for wildfowl, covering an area of 80 acres. Although the house itself has been demolished, there is still plenty for the visitor to see and enjoy. Other buildings that have survived include the stables, together with a

restaurant, shop and information point, a classical bridge and Clumber Chapel, built in the Gothic Revival style. The park is a mixture of woodland, open grass and heathland. Events to be held here during 1995 include Clumber Park horse trials (6-7 May), Clumber Park Show (18 June) and open air concerts with fireworks - a centenary jazz weekend on 7-8 July and 'The Swinging Sixties' on 5 August.
Open all year, daily during daylight hours. Walled Garden, Victorian Apiary, Fig House, Vineries & Garden Tools exhibition Apr-Sep Sat, Sun & BH Mon 10-5. last admission 4.30pm. Conservation centre Apr-24 Sep Sat, Sun & BH Mon 1-5. Pedestrians free; cars, motorbikes & caravanettes £2.50.
P ⚑ ✕ *licensed* & *toilets for disabled shop garden centre (NT)*

OXFORDSHIRE

Banbury Museum
BANBURY
8 Horsefair
☎(01295) 259855
This museum, housed in the old boardroom of the Poor Law Guardians, overlooks Banbury Cross. A video introduces visitors to the Cherwell area, and there is an exciting programme of temporary exhibitions. Holiday sessions and special events are regularly organised for children and there is a separate programme of exhibitions and displays by local artists. Events for 1995 include 'Unlaced Grace' - an exhibition on corsetry (28 January-29 April) and 'Seti: Work of a Textile Designer' (6 May-1 July).
Open all year, Oct-Mar, Tue-Sat 10-4.30; Apr-Sep, Mon-Sat 10-5. Free.
P *(behind museum)* ⚑ & *toilets for disabled shop* ⌀

Broughton Castle
BROUGHTON
(2m W on B4035)
☎*Banbury (01295) 262624 & 720041*
Originally owned by William of Wykeham, and later by the first Lord Saye and Sele, the castle is an early 14th- and mid 16th-century house with a moat and gatehouse. Period furniture, paintings and Civil War relics are displayed.
Open Etr & 18 May-14 Sep, Wed & Sun (also Thu in Jul & Aug) & BH Sun & Mon 2-5. £3.50 (ch 5-16 £1.50, pen & students £3). Party 20+.
P ⚑ & *shop* ⌀ *(ex in grounds)*

Cotswold Wildlife Park
BURFORD
(2m S off A40 & A361)
☎(01993) 823006

The 180-acre landscaped zoological park, surrounding a Gothic-style manor house, has a varied collection of animals from all over the world, with tropical birds, a large reptile collection, aquarium and insect house. Other attractions include an adventure playground, animal brass-rubbing centre in the manor house and train rides during the summer months. Also during the summer there are Snake Days and birds of prey demonstrations.
Open all year, daily (ex 25 Dec) 10-6 or dusk if earlier. £4.60 (ch 4 & pen £3). Party 20+
P ⚑ ✕ *licensed* & *toilets for disabled shop*

Buscot Park
BUSCOT
(off A417)
☎(01367) 242094
Much of the character of this 18th-century house is due to two relatively recent owners, the 1st Lord Faringdon, who bought the house in 1889, and his son. They amassed most of the furniture, porcelain and other contents, as well as the many pictures forming the Faringdon Collection. It includes work by Reynolds, Gainsborough, Rembrandt, Murillo, several of the Pre-Raphaelites, and some 20th-century artists. Most memorable is the 'Legend of the Briar Rose', a deeply romantic series by Burne-Jones which fills the walls of the saloon.
The charming formal water gardens were laid out by Harold Peto in the early 20th century. There is also an attractively planted kitchen garden, with unusual concentric walls.
Open Apr-Sep, Wed, Thu & Fri 2-6. Also every 2nd & 4th Sat & immediately following Sun in each month 2-6 (last admission to house 5.30pm). (Closed BH Mon). £4. Grounds only £3.
P ⚑ ⌀ (NT)

Great Coxwell Barn
COXWELL, GREAT
☎(01494) 528051
William Morris said that the barn was 'as noble as a cathedral'. It is a 13th-century stone-built tithe barn, 152ft long and 44ft wide, with a beautifully crafted framework of timbers supporting the lofty stone roof. The barn was built for the Cistercians.
Open all reasonable times. 50p
P (NT)

Deddington Castle
DEDDINGTON
The large earthworks of the outer and inner baileys can be seen; the remains of 12th-century castle buildings have been excavated, but they are not now visible.
Open any reasonable time. Free. (EH)

Didcot Railway Centre
DIDCOT
(on A4130 at Didcot Parkway Station)
☎(01235) 817200
The biggest collection anywhere of Great Western Railway stock is housed in the GWR engine shed, including 20 steam locomotives, a diesel railcar, and a large amount of passenger and freight rolling stock. A typical GWR station has been re-created and original track has been relaid. Special events for 1995 include: Easter Steamings (14-17 April), Teddy Bears' Picnic (16 July), Thomas the Tank Engine (9-10 September), Photographers' Evenings (27-28 October) and Santa Steamings (3, 10, 17, 23, 24 December).
Open all year, 1 Apr-24 Sep, daily 11-5 dusk in winter. Sat & Sun only rest of year. Steam days first & last Sun of each month from Mar, BH's, all Sun's Jun-Aug & Wed 26 Jul-30 Aug. £3-£5 depending on event (ch £2-£5, over 60's £2.50-£4).
P *(100 yds)* ⚑ & *(advance notice recommended) toilets for disabled shop*

Greys Court
HENLEY-ON-THAMES
Rotherfield Greys (3m W)
☎*Rotherfield Greys (01491) 628529*
This appealing house has evolved over hundreds of years. The present gabled building has a pre-medieval kitchen but dates mainly from the 16th century. It stands in the courtyard of its medieval predecessor, facing the mid-14th-century Great Tower. Additions were made in the 18th century and there are some fine 18th-century decorations and furniture. The complex of gardens includes a white garden and a rose garden planted with old-fashioned varieties which leads into the walled area with ancient wisterias. Beyond this is the kitchen garden, and from here a bridge leads to a symbolic brick maze laid out in 1980. Also of great interest is the wheelhouse with its huge wheel, once turned by a donkey to bring water up from the well. Events for 1995 include garden music and fireworks on 12 June.
Open: House Apr-Sep, Mon, Wed & Fri 2-6. Garden Mon-Wed & Fri-Sat 2-6. Last admission 5.30pm. (Closed Good Fri). Garden £3. House & Garden £4. Family ticket £9.50.
P ⚑ ⌀ (NT)

Wellplace Bird Farm
IPSDEN
☎*Checkendon (01491) 680473*
Tropical birds, lambs, goats, monkeys, donkeys, otters, ponies and llamas are just some of the hundred varieties of animals and birds who make their homes at Wellplace Bird Farm; a delightful place for adults and children. Car boot sales will be held here on Bank Holiday Mondays during 1995.
Open all year, Apr-Sep, daily 10-5, Sun 10-6; Oct-Apr. £2 (ch 50p)
P ⚑ & *(use of wheelchair) toilets for disabled shop garden centre* ⌀

Pendon Museum of Miniature Landscape & Transp ort
LONG WITTENHAM
☎*Oxford (01865) 407365*
This charming exhibition shows highly detailed and historically accurate model railway and village scenes transporting the visitor back into 1930s country landscapes. Skilled modellers can often be seen at work on the exhibits.
Open Sat & Sun 2-5, each day of summer BH wknds 11-5 (Closed 13 Dec-7 Jan). £2.50 (ch 16 & pen £1.50, ch 6 free).
P ⚑ & *(phone in advance) toilets for disabled shop* ⌀

Mapledurham House
MAPLEDURHAM
(off A4074)
☎*Kidmore End (01734) 723350*
The small community at Mapledurham includes the house, a watermill and a church, and is reached by travelling down

a 'no through road', or by boat from the Caversham Promenade at Reading. The boat runs only when the house is open to the public but can be chartered by groups. The fine Elizabethan mansion, surrounded by quiet parkland which runs down to the River Thames, was built by the Blount family in the 16th century. Inside are paintings and family portraits collected over five centuries, great oak staircases and moulded Elizabethan ceilings. The estate has literary connections with the poet Alexander Pope, with Galsworthy's *Forsyte Saga* and Kenneth Graham's *Wind in the Willows*, and was the setting for the film *The Eagle has Landed*, as well as featuring in various TV productions.
Open Etr-Sep, Sat, Sun & BH's 2.30-5. Picnic area 12.30-7. Last admission 5pm. Group visits midweek by arrangement.
P ⚑ & *shop* ⌀ *(ex country park area) Details not confirmed for 1995*

Mapledurham Watermill
MAPLEDURHAM
(off A4074)
☎*Kidmore End (01734) 723350*
Close to Mapledurham House (above) stands the last working corn and grist mill on the Thames, still using traditional wooden machinery and producing flour for local bakers and shops. The watermill's products can be purchased in the shops. The mill can also be reached by river launch from Caversham Promenade at 2pm each day the house is open (details from the estate office).
Open Etr-Sep, Sat, Sun & BHs 1-5. Picnic area 12.30-7. Last admission 5. Groups midweek by arrangement.
P ⚑ & *shop* ⌀ *(ex in country park) Details not confirmed for 1995*

Minster Lovell Hall & Dovecot
MINSTER LOVELL
☎*Witney (01993) 775315*
Home of the ill-fated Lovell family, the ruins of the 15th-century house are steeped in history and legend. One of the main features of the estate is the medieval dovecote which has survived intact through the centuries. The village of Minster Lovell is one of the prettiest in this outstanding area.
Open all year, Apr-Sep, daily 10-6; Oct-Mar, daily 10-4. Free.
& *(ex Dovecot)* ⌀ (EH)

North Leigh Roman Villa
NORTH LEIGH
Excavations have found this villa to have been occupied between the second and fourth centuries and reconstructed later in the period. A tessellated pavement and a 2-3 feet high wall span, are on show.
Open any reasonable time. Free. ⌀ (EH)

OXFORD
This ancient and picturesque University city dating back to the 8th century sits comfortably on the rivers Cherwell and Thames. The University, the oldest in Britain, probably dates from the 12th century and consists of a large number of colleges built over a period of several centuries, many of which are among the finest buildings of their age. Access to some colleges is restricted to certain times and details may be obtained from the Oxford Information Centre, St Aldgate's.

Ashmolean Museum of Art & Archaeology
OXFORD
Beaumont St (opposite The Randolph Hotel)
☎(01865) 278000
First opened in 1683 and the oldest museum in the country, the Ashmolean Museum was re-housed in C R ➤

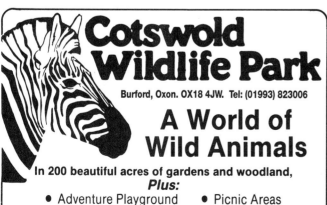

Cockerell's building of 1845. Archaeological exhibits from Britain, Europe, the Mediterranean, Egypt and the Near East are on show and the Herbeden Coin Room contains coins and medals from all countries and periods. Italian, Dutch, Flemish, French and English oil paintings adorn the walls along with Old Masters and modern drawings, watercolours, prints and miniatures. Chinese and Japanese porcelain, paintings and laquer-work are gathered here as well as European ceramics, Tibetan art, Indian sculpture and paintings, metalwork and pottery from Islam and Chinese bronzes. Temporary exhibitions to be held in 1995 include drawings by Edward Lear (21 February-14 May), Ottoman portraits (1 March-30 April) and Dutch and Flemish drawings from the Royal Collection, Windsor Castle (15 August-15 October).
Open all year, Tue-Sat 10-4, Sun 2-4. (Closed Etr & during St.Giles Fair in early Sep, Xmas & 1 Jan).
Free. Guided tours by arrangement.
P & shop ⌖

Carfax Tower
OXFORD ▮▮▮▮▮
☎(01865) 792653
Excellent views of the city are to be seen from the top of this 14th-century tower which is all that remains of St Martin's Church. There is an historic display area on the first floor and an extensive souvenir stall on the ground floor. Bellringings are organised by the Oxford Bell Ringers Society, to celebrate special events.
Open end Mar-Oct, daily 10-6 (last entry 5.30).
P (5 mins walk) shop ⌖

Museum of Oxford
OXFORD ▮▮▮▮▮
St Aldate's
☎(01865) 815559
Permanent displays depict the archaeology and history of the city from earliest times to the present day. There are temporary exhibitions, facilities for school parties and groups, an audio tour, and weekly free lectures and events Thursday lunchtime. Special events for 1995 include: Art Week (23 May-10 June), children's activities every Thursday throughout the summer holiday, an exhibition of international quilting (24 January-12 February), *Changing Images of the Ancient World* - the work of local artist and sculptor Rosamund Chenley (21 March-13 May) and *Paper and Metal* - an exhibition by printmaker Nicola Slattery and silversmith Stella Campion.
Open all year, Tue-Fri 10-4, Sat 10-5. (Closed 25-26 Dec & Good Fri).
Free.
shop ⌖

The Oxford Story
OXFORD ▮▮▮▮▮
6 Broad St
☎(01865) 728822
The 800-year history of Oxford University is brought to life at this innovative exhibition. Sights, sounds - and smells - from the past are described by Magnus Magnusson or Timmey Mallett as visitors take a seat and ride through the exhibition. Foreign language commentaries are available. Special events planned for 1995 include an Easter Egg Hunt and mulled wine - 'the Oxford Nobbler' - during Christmas week.
Open all year, Apr-Jun & Sep-Oct daily 9.30-5, Jul-Aug 9-6.30 & Nov-Mar daily 10-4. (Closed 25 Dec)
£4.50 (ch under 16 £3.25, pen & students £3.95). Family ticket £14.
P (200yds) & toilets for disabled shop ⌖

St Edmund Hall
OXFORD ▮▮▮▮▮
College of Oxford University
☎(01865) 279000
This is the only surviving medieval academic hall and has a Norman crypt, 17th-century dining hall, chapel and quadrangle. Other buildings are of the 18th and 20th centuries.

Open all year. (Closed 23 Dec-3 Jan, 9-17 Apr & 28-31 Aug).
Free.
& toilets for disabled shop ⌖

University Arboretum
OXFORD ▮▮▮▮▮
Nuneham Courtenay (5m SE on A423 just S of the village).
☎(01865) 276920
The gardens consist of 55 acres of mixed woodland, meadow, pond, rhododendron walks and fine specimen trees.
Open May-Oct, daily 10-5; Nov-Apr, Mon-Fri 10-4.30. Closed 22 Dec-4 Jan & Good Fri-Etr Mon.
Free.
& ⌖

University of Oxford Botanic Garden
OXFORD ▮▮▮▮▮
High St (by Magdalen Bridge)
☎(01865) 276920
Founded in 1621, these botanic gardens are the oldest in the country and are of great interest. There is a collection of over 8000 species of plants from all over the world.
Open all year, daily 9-5 (9-4.30 Oct-Mar), Greenhouses, daily 2-4. (Closed Good Fri & 25 Dec).
18 Jun-2 Sep £1, otherwise free.
& (Entry at wknds using Radar key). toilets for disabled ⌖

Rousham House
ROUSHAM ▮▮▮▮▮
(1m E of A4260. 0.5m S of B4030)
☎Steeple Aston (01869) 347110
This attractive mansion was built by Sir Robert Dormer in 1635. During the Civil War it was a Royalist garrison, and had shooting holes cut into its doors. Sir Robert's successors, Masters of Ceremonies at Court during eight reigns, embellished Rousham by employing Court artists and architects. Rooms were also decorated by William Kent and Roberts of Oxford, during the 18th century. The house contains over 150 portraits and other pictures, and also much fine contemporary furniture. The gardens are a masterpiece by William Kent, and are his only work to survive unspoiled. Extending to over 30 acres, with the River Cherwell flowing through, they include classical buildings, cascades, statues, fine walled gardens with herbaceous borders, a small parterre and views over the river. There are longhorn cattle in the park.
Open all year, garden only, daily 10-4.30. House, Apr-Sep, Wed, Sun & BH 2-4.30.
House £2.50; Garden £2.50. Party by arrangement. No children under 15.
P & ⌖

Rycote Chapel
RYCOTE ▮▮▮▮▮
(off B4013)
This small 15th-century private chapel was founded in 1449 by Richard Quatremayne. It has its original font, and a particularly fine 17th-century interior. The chapel was visited by both Elizabeth I and Charles I.
Open all year, Apr-Sep, Sat & Sun 2-6. (Closed 24-26 Dec & 1 Jan).
£1.30 (ch 70p, concessions £1)
P ⌖
(EH)

Stonor House & Park
STONOR ▮▮▮▮▮
(on B480)
☎Turville Heath (01491) 638587
Home of Lord and Lady Camoys and occupied by the Stonor family for 800 years, the house dates back to 1190 but features a Tudor façade. It has a medieval Catholic chapel which is still in use today, and shows some of the earliest domestic architecture in Oxfordshire. Its treasures include rare furniture, paintings, sculptures and tapestries from Britain, Europe and America. The house is set in beautiful gardens with commanding views of the

The dovecote is a feature in the gardens at Rousham House which are one of the finest examples of the work of William Kent. It is one of the first landscaped gardens and remains largely as Kent designed it.

surrounding deer park. The Chiltern craft show will be held here on 26-29 August.
Open Apr-Sep, Sun 2-5.30; May-Sep, Wed 2-5.30; Jul-Aug, Thu 2-5.30; Aug, Sat 2-5.30; BH Mon 12.30-5.30. Parties by appointment Tue, Wed & Thu.
£4 (ch 14 accompanied free). Gardens only £2. Party 12+.
🅿 ⬛ & shop ⌘ *(ex in grounds)*

Castle & White Horse
UFFINGTON
The 'castle' is an Iron Age fort on the ancient Ridgeway Path over the Berkshire Downs. It covers about eight acres and has only one gateway. On the hill below the fort is the White Horse, a 375ft prehistoric figure carved in the chalky hillside. Once thought to have been carved in 871 to celebrate King Alfred's victory over the Danes, now thought to be at least 2000 years old.
Best seen from the B4508.
Open - any reasonable time.
Free.
🅿
(EH)

Vale & Downland Museum Centre
WANTAGE
The Old Surgery, Church St
☎ (01235) 771447
The lively museum centre has displays on the geology, archaeology and local history of the Vale of the White Horse and the town of Wantage, birthplace of King Alfred. There are frequent temporary exhibitions and occasional craft demonstrations. A Tourist Information Centre is now open on the premises.
Open all year, Tue-Sat 10.30-4.30 & Sun 2.30-5.
Free.
P *(100 yds)* ⬛ & *(stairlift installed) toilets for disabled shop*

Waterperry Gardens
WATERPERRY
(2.50m from A40, turn off at Wheatley)
☎ *Long Crendon (01844) 339226 & 339254*
The manor of Waterperry is mentioned in the Domesday Book, and the little church next to the current house incorporates Saxon work, although it dates from early Norman times. It has some very old stained glass, brasses, and woodwork showing the crests of the FitzEly and Curson families who owned Waterperry from about 1250 to 1830.
The present house (not open) was rebuilt by Sir John Curson in 1713 and its elegant proportions reflect the classical tastes of the 18th century. The peaceful gardens and nurseries which surround the house were the home of a celebrated horticultural school between 1932 and 1971, and have fine herbaceous borders, a rock garden, riverside walk, shrub borders, lawns and trees. The horticultural centre now based at Waterperry maintains the earlier traditions with its extensive alpine, fruit, shrub and herbaceous nurseries, and the productive greenhouses. In 1995 there will be a major arts and crafts festival where artists and craftsmen from all over the world will demonstrate their talents (13-16 July). For details please telephone 0171-381 3192.
Open all year, Gardens (ex Xmas & New Year & during "Art in Action" 13-16 Jul).
➜

Mar-Oct 10-5.30, wknds 10-6; Nov-Feb 10-4.30 daily.
Mar-Oct, £2.20 (ch 10-16 £1, ch under 10 free, pen £1.70). Nov-Feb 75p. Party 20+
P ☕ ♿ *shop garden centre*

Cogges Manor Farm Museum
WITNEY
Church Ln, Cogges (0.5m SE off A4022)
☎*(01993) 772602*
Farm museum with breeds of animals typical of the Victorian period, historic site and buildings including Manor House, dairy and walled garden. There are daily cookery demonstrations on the kitchen range, an historic trail and riverside walk. Special events for 1995 include: lambs in April, shearing (28 May), steam threshing (16-17 September), Harvest Home (1 October). In addition, the first floor of the Manor House will be opened, following extensive renovation.
Open Apr-Oct, Tue-Fri & BH Mon 10.30-5.30, Sat & Sun 12-5.30. Early closing Oct.
£3 (ch & student & £1.50, pen & UB40 £1.75). Family ticket £8
P ☕ ♿ *(wheelchair available, staff able to assist) toilets for disabled shop*

Blenheim Palace
WOODSTOCK
☎*(01993) 811091 & 811325 (information line)*
The Royal Manor of Woodstock and the sum of £240,000 to build the Palace were given to the Duke of Marlborough by Queen Anne as a reward for his brilliant military victory over the French at the Battle of Blenheim in 1704. The Palace, begun in 1705, was designed by Sir John Vanbrugh. It was built on a very grand scale, covering seven acres including courtyard, and was completed in 1722. The Palace has splendid State Rooms, a Long Library, magnificent tapestries and paintings as well as fine furniture. Of particular interest are carvings by Grinling Gibbons and the Hall ceiling painted to depict the plan of the Battle of Blenheim by Sir James Thornhill.
The palace is set in a 2100-acre park landscaped by Capability Brown who created a lake spanned by a 390-ft bridge. There are also formal Italian and French gardens.
Sir Winston Churchill was born in the Palace in 1874 and he is buried nearby, at Bladon.
There are a pleasure garden, adventure playground and nature trail through the parkland, and other attractions include a motor launch, train and Butterfly House. Events held in the park during the year include a craft fair (6-8 May), a fireworks concert (29 July), craft fairs (6-8 May and 26-28 August) and the International Horse Trials (14-17 September); two concerts - the Winston Churchill Memorial Concert (4 March) and the Stately Homes Music Festival Concert (14 July) - will be held in the Palace. All events listed are provision; details will be carried in local press.
Open: Palace & Gardens mid Mar-Oct, daily 10.30-5.30 (last admission 4.45pm). Park all year 9-5.
£7 (ch 5-15 £3.50, ch under 5 free, pen, 16-17 yearolds & students £5.10)
P ☕ ✕ *licensed* ♿ *toilets for disabled shop* 🚫🐕 *(ex in park)*
See advertisement on page 129

Oxfordshire County Museum
WOODSTOCK
Fletcher's House
☎*(01993) 811456*
Permanently displayed in Fletcher's House is an exhibition of the story of Oxfordshire and its people, from early times to the present day. The house, which is an elegant townhouse with pleasant gardens, also has temporary exhibitions.
Open all year, Jan-Apr & Oct-Dec, Tue-Fri 10-4, Sat 10-5, Sun 2-5; May-Sep 10-5, Sat 10-6, Sun 2-6. (Closed Good Fri & 25-26 Dec)
Free.
P ☕ ♿ *shop* 🚫🐕

SHROPSHIRE

Acton Burnell Castle
ACTON BURNELL
Now ruined, this fortified manor house was built in the late 13th century by Robert Burnell, the Chancellor of the time. It consisted of a central block with towers at the corners and a great hall and chapel on the upper floor. By 1420 the house was no longer being used, and part of it was converted into a barn in the 18th century.
Open at all reasonable times.
Free.
♿
(EH)

Acton Scott Historic Working Farm
ACTON SCOTT
Wenlock Lodge (off A49)
☎*Marshbrook (01694) 781306 & 781307*
Expertly laid out in an old estate farm, the working museum gives a vivid introduction to traditional rural life. The animals are rare breeds, and the crops are types grown around 1900. They are cultivated on the old crop rotation system, and all the work is done by hand, horse power, or with old machines such as steam-threshers. Butter-making takes place throughout the season, with daily craft demonstrations, and old machinery and equipment are displayed. The farm cottage gives an insight into daily domestic life at the turn of the century with laundry, bread making and cooking at the range. Visitors may take part in some of the work, by becoming resident volunteers. Throughout the season there will be a variety of craft displays, weekend demonstrations of spinning, pottery and more, and seasonal festivals. Special events planned for 1995 include steam threshing, cider making and a harvest festival; a full programme is available on request.
Open Apr-Oct, Tues-Sat 10-5; Sun & BH Mon 10-6.
✻£2.75 (ch £1.50, under 5 free & pen £2)
P ☕ ♿ *(Braille guide, wheelchairs available) toilets for disabled shop* 🚫🐕

Attingham Park
ATCHAM
(4m SE of Shrewsbury on B4380)
☎*Shrewsbury (01743) 709203*
An imposing entrance front with massive portico, colonnades and pavilions greets the visitor to Attingham. The house was constructed around an earlier building, but most of what one sees today dates from the 18th and early 19th centuries. This even applies to the garden, where the planting remains very much as advised by Humphry Repton in 1797-8. The house was designed by George Steuart with the more 'masculine' rooms on the left of the entrance hall and the more 'feminine' rooms on the right. The entrance hall itself is elaborately decorated to imitate marble. Other notable decorations can be seen in the boudoir, which has intricate and delicate designs, the Italian-style drawing room, the oriental Sultana room and the red dining room. The picture gallery was designed by Nash, who made early use of curved cast iron and glass for the ceiling. The River Tern flows through the park, which has a herd of fallow deer. The estate of the house is on the site of the Roman town of Viroconium, and is also crossed by two Roman roads. It is also notable for two fine bridges carrying the A5 over the Tern and Severn rivers. Events planned for 1995 include a balloon and kite fiesta (22-24 September) and Apple Day (15 October).
House open Apr-29 Sep, Sat-Wed 1.30-5, BH Mon 11-5. Oct wknds only. Pre-booked parties allowed daily ex Thu & Fri. Last admission 4.30pm. Grounds open all year, daily (ex 25 Dec), sunrise-sunset.
✻£3.50 (ch £1.75) Family ticket £8.75. Park & Grounds £1.40 (ch 70p).
P ☕ ♿ *(2 electric self drive buggies) toilets for disabled shop* 🚫🐕 *(in Deer park)*
(NT)

Benthall Hall
BENTHALL
(on B4375)
☎*Telford (01952) 882159*
The exact date of the house is not known, but it seems to have been started in the 1530s and then altered in the 1580s. It is an attractive sandstone building with mullioned windows, fine oak panelling and a splendid carved staircase.
Open Apr-Sep, Wed, Sun & BH Mon 1.30-5.30. Last admission 5pm. Other days by appointment only.
✻House £3 (ch £1). Garden only £2.
P ♿ 🚫🐕
(NT)

Boscobel House and The Royal Oak
BOSCOBEL
(off A5)
☎*Brewood (01902) 850244*
The house was built around 1600 by John Giffard, a Catholic, and the structure includes a number of hiding places. One of them was used by King Charles II after his defeat at the Battle of Worcester in 1651. A descendant of the oak tree where he also hid can be seen in the grounds.
Open all year, Apr-Sep, daily 10-6; Oct, 10-4; Nov-Mar, Wed-Sun 10-4. Closed 24-26 Dec & 1 Jan.
£3.30 (ch £1.70, concessions £2.50).
P ☕ ♿ *shop* 🚫🐕
(EH)

Whiteladies Priory (St Leonards Priory)
BOSCOBEL
Only the ruins are left of this Augustinian nunnery, which dates from 1158 and was destroyed in the Civil War. After the Battle of Worcester Charles II hid here and in the nearby woods before going on to Boscobel House.
Open any reasonable time.
Free.
(EH)

Midland Motor Museum
BRIDGNORTH
Stanmore Hall, Stourbridge Rd (2m on A458 Stourbridge Rd)
☎*(01746) 762992*
A notable collection of over 100 well-restored sports and sports racing cars, and racing motor cycles dating from 1920 to 1980 (also a steam traction engine). They are housed in the converted stables of Stanmore Hall and surrounded by beautiful grounds with touring park.
Open 11-5, Oct-Jun wknds only; 11-5 Jul-Sep daily.
£3.50 (ch £1.75, pen £2.80). Family ticket £9.95.
P ♿ *shop* 🚫🐕

Severn Valley Railway
BRIDGNORTH
☎*Bewdley (01299) 403816 & (01746) 764361*
The leading standard gauge steam railway, with one of the largest collections of locomotives and rolling stock in the country. Services operate from Kidderminster and Bewdley to Bridgnorth through 16 miles of picturesque scenery along the River Severn. Special steam galas and Friends of Thomas Weekends take place during the year along with Santa Specials. Saturday evening 'Wine and Dine' and 'Sunday Luncheon' trains are a speciality. There are footplate courses for those wishing to experience the thrill of driving and firing a steam locomotive.
Open wknds early Mar-Oct & daily, 1-8 Apr & mid May-early Oct. Also 24-30 Oct. Santa Steam & Mince Pie Specials wknds, 26 Nov-end Dec, daily 19-24 Dec & 26 Dec-1 Jan.
P ☕ ✕ *licensed* ♿ *toilets for disabled shop*
Details not confirmed for 1995

Buildwas Abbey
BUILDWAS
☎*(01952) 433274*
The beautiful, ruined, Cistercian abbey was founded in 1135, and stands in a picturesque setting. The church with its stout round pillars is roofless but otherwise almost complete.
Open Apr-Sep, daily 10-6.
£1.30 (ch 70p, concessions £1).
♿ 🚫🐕
(EH)

Burford House Gardens
BURFORD
(off A456)
☎*Tenbury Wells (01584) 810777*
Surrounding the Georgian House (1723), the artistically designed gardens contain many rare and unusual plants - including shrubs, herbaceous plants and species roses - and are the home of the national clematis collection. The garden was started by John Treasure in 1954, and next to it is the notable plant centre, Treasures of Tenbury.
Open all year 10-5. dusk if earlier.
✻£1.95 (ch 80p). Party 25+.
P ☕ ✕ *licensed* ♿ *toilets for disabled garden centre* 🚫🐕 *(ex in Plant Centre)*

Aerospace Museum
COSFORD
(off A41)
☎*Albrighton (01902) 374872 & 374112*
This is one of the largest aviation collections in the UK. Exhibits include the Victor and Vulcan bombers, the Hastings, York and British Airways airliners, the Belfast freighter and the last airworthy Britannia. The research and development collection includes the notable TSR2, Fairey Delta 2, Bristol 188 and many more important aircraft. There are a British Airways exhibition hall and a comprehensive missile display. The Large Model Association Aircraft Rally will be held on 15-16 July, and 18 June is Royal Air Force Cosford Open Day.
Open all year daily, 10-4 (last admission). (Closed 24-26 Dec & 1 Jan).
£4.20 (ch £2.40 & pen £3.10). Family ticket £11. Party 20+.
P ☕ ♿ *(limited amount of wheelchairs on request) toilets for disabled shop* 🚫🐕

Haughmond Abbey
HAUGHMOND ABBEY
(off B5062)
☎*Upton Magna (01743) 709661*
The ruined abbey was founded for Augustinian canons in around 1135, and partly converted into a house during the Dissolution. The chapter house has a fine Norman doorway, and the abbot's lodging and the kitchens are well preserved.
Open Apr-Sep, Wed-Sun & BH's 10-6.
£1.30 (ch 70p, concessions £1).
P ♿ 🚫🐕
(EH)

Hodnet Hall Gardens
HODNET
☎*(01630) 685202*
Sixty acres of landscaped gardens offer tranquillity among pools, lush plants and trees. Big game trophies adorn the 17th-century tearooms, and plants are usually for sale in the kitchen gardens. The house, rebuilt in Victorian-Elizabethan style, is not open.
Open daily Apr-Sep, Tue-Sat 2-5, Sun & BH Mon 12 noon-5.30.
✻£2.60 (ch £1, pen £2.10). Party.
P ☕ ♿ *toilets for disabled shop garden centre*

Ironbridge Gorge Museum
IRONBRIDGE
(M54 junc 4, signposted)
☎*(01952) 433522 & 432166 (wknds)*
Ironbridge became famous when the world's first iron bridge was cast and built here in 1779, to span a narrow gorge over the River Severn. Now it is the site of a remarkable series of museums covering some six square miles. Perhaps the most appealing is the Blists Hill Open Air Museum. Set in 42

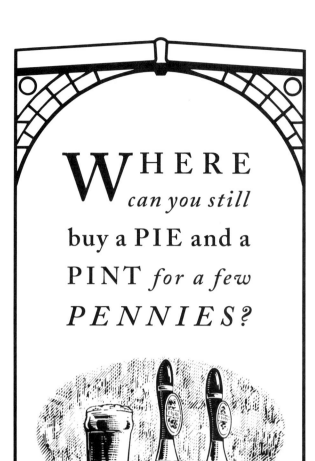
acres of woodland, the recreated Victorian town offers the visitor a chance to step into the past and see how people lived and worked in the 1890s. The Coalbrookdale Furnace Site shows the technique of smelting iron ore, perfected here by Abraham Darby. Associated with the furnace is the Museum of Iron. Another of the museums is housed in the original buildings of the Coalport China Company, based in the area until the mid-1920s. It features workshop and social history displays. There is also the Jackfield Tile Museum where there are tile manufacturing and a mining gallery. An introduction to the Ironbridge Gorge is given at the visitor centre in the Museum of the River, brought to life by an audio-visual display. Special events for 1995 include the opening of Dale House, the re-opening of the new Museum of Iron, *Chinese Whispers: The Willow Pattern Story* at Coalport China Museum and Jackfield, V E Day street party and fireworks at Blists Hill on May 8 and Hallowe'en celebrations.
Open all year, Jul-Aug 10-6, Sep-May 10-5. Some small sites closed Nov-Feb. Telephone or write for exact winter details.
✳*£8 (ch £5, pen £7, family £25). Passport to all sites. A passport will admit visitors to all sites, in any order until all have been visited. It is therefore possible to return to Ironbridge on different days to ensure the whole atmosphere of this unique museum may be captured.*
P 💺 ✕ *licensed & (wheelchairs for loan, potters wheel at Coalport) toilets for disabled shop ⊗ (ex at Blists Hill)*

Lilleshall Abbey
LILLESHALL
(1.5m SW off A518 on unclass road)
Some of the most impressive ruins in Shropshire stand in the beautiful grounds of Lilleshall Hall. Lilleshall Abbey was founded shortly before the middle of the 12th century and from the high west front visitors can look down the entire 228ft length of the abbey church.
Open any reasonable time.
Free.
P ⊗
(EH)

Ludlow Castle
LUDLOW
☎(01584) 873355
Ludlow Castle dates from about 1086 and was greatly extended as ownership passed through the de Lacy and Mortimer families to the Crown. In 1473, Edward IV sent the Prince of Wales and his brother - later to become the Princes in the Tower - to live in Ludlow, and Ludlow Castle became a seat of government with the establishment there of the Council for Wales and the Marches. Another royal resident was Prince Arthur, son of Henry Tudor and elder brother of Henry VIII. John Milton's *Comus* was first performed at Ludlow Castle in 1634; now contemporary performances of Shakespeare's plays, together with concerts, are put on in the castle grounds during the Ludlow Festival (this year to be held between 24 June and 9 July). In 1689 the Royal Welch Fusiliers were formed at Ludlow by Lord Herbert of Chirbury, into whose family, the Earls of Powis, ownership of the castle later passed. The Castle includes buildings ranging from the circular nave of the Norman chapel to an unusually complete range of medieval buildings and the Judges' Lodgings, built in the 16th century. Special events planned for 1995 include a craft fair (27-29 May), and an Autumn Craft Fair and Christmas events in late November; weekly falconry displays take place between July and September.
Open May-Sep daily 10.30-5; Oct-Dec & Feb-Apr 10.30-4. (Closed Jan).
£2.50 (ch £1.50, pen £2). Family ticket £7.50.
P (100 yds) & *toilets for disabled shop ⊗*

Walcot Hall
LYDBURY NORTH
☎0171-581 2782
Built by Sir William Chambers for Lord Clive of India. The Georgian House possesses a free-standing and recently restored Ballroom, stableyard with matching clock towers and extensive walled garden, in addition to its ice house, meat-safe and dovecote. There is an Arboretum, noted for its rhododendrons and azaleas, specimen trees, pools and a lake. In 1995 the Arboretum and Gardens are open for the National Gardens Scheme 28-29 May and the Shropshire Game Fair takes place the second weekend in June; concerts are held in the Ballroom throughout the year.
Open May, Wed, Fri & Sun; Jun Wed & Fri; Jul & Aug Sun; Sep, Wed. 2.15-4.30. Also BH Sun & Mon. (Closed Xmas & New Year).
£2.50 (ch under 15, free)
P & *(lift to 1st floor) toilets for disabled*

Castle
MORETON CORBET
A small 13th-century keep and the ruins of an impressive Elizabethan house are all that remain: the house was destroyed when the Parliamentary forces captured it in 1644.
Open all reasonable times.
Free.
P &
(EH)

Much Wenlock Museum
MUCH WENLOCK
High St
☎(01952) 727773
Much Wenlock has kept its medieval flavour despite encroaching changes from the 20th century. Its museum, in the Old Market Hall, has an admirable collection illustrating the history of the town and its famous priory. There is also a display of memorabilia of the Much Wenlock Olympics, the forerunner of the modern Olympic Games. The town is situated near Wenlock Edge, a limestone escarpment, and there are displays interpreting the geology and natural history of this notable feature.
Open Apr-Sep, Mon-Sat 10.30-1 & 2-5, also Sun Jun-Aug 10.30-1 & 2-5.
50p (ch, pen & UB40 free).
P (100 yds) & *shop ⊗*

Much Wenlock Priory
MUCH WENLOCK
☎(01952) 727466
The original priory was founded here as a convent in the 7th century. It was destroyed by the Danes but was rebuilt and grew over the years. The not inconsiderable remains of the 11th-century priory and subsequent additions are what the visitor will see today.
Open all year, Apr-Sep, daily 10-6; Oct, 10-4; Nov-Mar, Wed-Sun 10-4. Closed 24-26 Dec & 1 Jan.
£2 (ch £1, concessions £1.50).
P ⊗
(EH)

Old Oswestry
OSWESTRY
(0.5m N)
This Iron Age hill-fort covers 68 acres, has five ramparts and an elaborate western portal. It is abutted by part of the prehistoric Wat's Dyke.
Open any reasonable time.
Free.
(EH)

Oswestry Transport Museum
OSWESTRY
Oswald Rd
☎(01691) 671749
This Museum uses over 100 bicycles to display the history of cycling through the ages. Displays include bicycle parts, signs and Dunlop's development of the pneumatic tyre. There is also a large exhibition of the Cambrian Railways where visitors can see 12 railway engines and rolling stock. Short steam rides are planned for late summer along

➡

WESTON PARK

17th Century Ancestral Seat of the Earls of Bradford

This beautiful Palladian House set in 1000 acres of landscaped parkland on Staffordshire/Shropshire border contains a wealth of history, artworks and antiques

★ Formal Gardens ★ Miniature Railway ★ Pets Corner ★
★ Woodland Adventure Playground ★ Museum of Country Bygones ★

Open Easter to the end of September (please enquire for dates and times)

Special events programme throughout the season

Gourmet Dinner Evenings Open to the Public

Licensed Bar and Old Stables Tea Rooms

Facilities also available all year for Residential Conferences, Product Launches, Activity Days, Banquets and Wedding Receptions

At Weston-under-Lizard on the A5. 7 miles west of Junction 12 on M6 or 3 miles north of Junction 3 on M54. Telephone: 01952 850207

---

with a Classic Car Rally/Transport Festival at the end of September.
Open all year, daily 10-4. (Closed 25-26 Dec, 1 Jan & Good Fri).
£1.50 (ch 60p). Party 10+
P ⬛ & shop

Dudmaston
QUATT
(4m SE of Bridgnorth on A442)
☎ *Dudmaston (01746) 780866*
The 17th-century flower paintings which belonged to Francis Darby of Coalbrookdale are exhibited in this house of the same period, with modern works, botanical art and fine furniture. The house stands in an extensive parkland garden and there are dingle and lakeside walks; two estate walks (of 3.5 and 5 miles) start from Hampton Loade car park, six miles southeast of Bridgnorth on the A442. This year there will be an Opera Gala (a finale to the Bridgnorth Hadyn Festival Week) on Sunday 11 June, and 'Illyria' will present *The Merry Wives of Windsor* (July 19) and *A Midsummer Night's Dream* (July 29).
Open 29 Mar-1 Oct, Wed & Sun 2-5.30.
House & Garden £3.50. Garden only £2.50. Family ticket £8.
P ⬛ & (Braille guides, taped tours) toilets for disabled shop ⊘ (ex in grounds)
(NT)

Clive House Museum
SHREWSBURY
College Hill
☎ *(01743) 354811*
Town house with a long history, including a brief association in the 1760s with Robert, Lord Clive (Clive of India). There are outstanding displays of Coalport and Caughley porcelain, and paintings, in contemporary period room settings. Also domestic bygones, a children's room, and local social history 1750-1900. There is an attractive walled garden. Special events for 1995 include new displays, prints and paintings.
Open all year, Tue-Sat 10-4 and Sun end May-end Sep. (Closed Xmas & New Year).
£1 (ch 50p, pen & student 80p). Joint admission to Clive House, Rowley's House, Shrewsbury Castle & Regimental Museum £3 (ch £1, pen & students £2).
P (in town centre) & shop ⊘

Rowley's House Museum
SHREWSBURY
Barker St
☎ *(01743) 361196*
An impressive timber-framed building and attached 17th-century brick mansion. Major displays of the archaeology, geology, prehistory, natural and local history of the region, including much of the material excavated from Roman Wroxeter. There are also a costume gallery, an innovative Medieval Shrewsbury gallery and a varied programme of temporary and touring exhibitions. Day schools, lectures and performance events are held throughout the year. The 160th Anniversary Exhibition of the Collections of Shrewsbury Museums will take place from June until the end of September this year.
Open all year, Tue-Sat 10-5; also Suns from end May-Sep 11-4.
£2 (ch 50p, pen & student £1). Joint admission to Rowley's House, Clive House, Shrewsbury Castle & Regimental Museum £3 (ch £1, pen & students £2)
P (adjacent) & shop ⊘

The Shropshire Regimental Museum at Shrewsbury Castle
SHREWSBURY
The Castle, Castle St
☎ *(01743) 358516*
Re-opened after a two year closure, the museum of The King's Shropshire Light Infantry and The Shropshire Yeomanry is housed within the main surviving building of Shrewsbury Castle. This was a Norman fortification commanding the historic town of Shrewsbury. Thomas Telford was responsible for alterations to the castle in the 18th-century.
Regimental museum re-opening Apr 1995, opening times not confirmed. Castle grounds open Mon-Sat & Sun(end May-end Sep) 10-4.
£2 (ch 50p, student & pen £1). Inclusive ticket toRowley's House, Clive House & Regimental Museum £3 (ch £1, student & pen £2).
P (3 mins NCP) & toilets for disabled shop ⊘

Stokesay Castle
STOKESAY
(1m S of Craven Arms)
☎ *Craven Arms (01588) 672544*
Well-preserved and little altered, this 13th-century manor house has a romantic setting. Special features are the fine gatehouse, the great hall and, reached by an outside staircase, a solar with 17th-century panelling. Special events for 1995 include an historical re-enactment by the English Civil War Society in August.
Open all year, Apr-Oct, daily 10-6; Nov-Mar, Wed-Sun 10-4.
£2.50 (ch £1.25, concessions £1.80)
P & (tape tour for visually handicapped, ramp for wheelchairs) toilets for disabled shop ⊘

Hawkstone Historic Park & Follies
WESTON-UNDER-REDCASTLE
(3m from Hodnet off A53)
☎ *(01939) 200300*
Created in the 18th century by the Hill family, Hawkstone was once one of the greatest historic parklands in history. After almost one hundred years of neglect it has now been restored and designated a Grade I historic park. Visitors can once again experience this magical world of intricate pathways, arches and bridges, towering cliffs and follies, and an awesome grotto. The Grand Valley has wild flowers and tidy lawns, centuries-old oaks, wild rhododendrons and lofty monkey puzzles. The Park covers nearly 100 acres of hilly terrain and visitors are advised to wear sensible shoes and clothing. Allow 3-4 hours for the tour, which is well signposted. There is generally a special event each month, and in 1995 these will include a cryptic clue treasure trail (1 April) and the North Shropshire Tourist Association Country Fair in May.
Open Apr-Oct, daily 10-6; Dec wknds only for Father Christmas visits.
£4 (ch £2, pen & student £3). Family ticket £11.
P ⬛ shop

Roman Town
WROXETER
☎ *(01743) 761330*
These excavated remains of the Roman town of Virconium probably date from 140 - 150AD. There is a colonnade and a municipal bath. The museum has finds from both the Roman town and an earlier legionary fortress on the same site. It also offers educational facilities.
Open all year, Apr-Sep, daily 10-6; Oct, 10-4; Nov-Mar, Wed-Sun 10-4. Closed 24-26 Dec & 1 Jan.
£2 (ch £1, concessions £1.50).
P & shop ⊘
(EH)

SOMERSET

King John's Hunting Lodge
AXBRIDGE
The Square
☎ *(01934) 732012*
Nothing to do with King John or with hunting, this jettied and timber-framed house was built around 1500. It gives a good indication of the wealth of the merchants of that time and is now a museum of local history, with old photographs, paintings and items such as the town stocks and constables' staves.
Open Etr-Sep, daily 2-5. Write for details of tours.
£1 (ch 50p).

(NT)

Barrington Court Garden
BARRINGTON
(off A303)
☎ *South Petherton (01460) 241938*
The house dates from the 17th century, but the gardens were created in the 1920s, with the help (through the post) of Gertrude Jekyll. They are laid out in 'rooms' and there is a large walled kitchen garden supplying fresh fruit and vegetables to the restaurant. Restoration work continues through 1995.
Open: Garden Apr-1 Oct, Sat-Thu, 11-5.30. Court House 26 Mar-1 Oct, Wed only 11-5.30, last admission 5pm.
£3.10 (ch £1.50). 50p. Party. Court house, additional charge £1 (ch 50p).
P ✕ licensed & (batricars available, braille guides) ⊘
(NT)

Glastonbury Abbey is said to have been founded in AD61 by Joseph of Arimathea and is also claimed by some to be the last resting place of King Arthur.

Hadspen Garden & Nursery
CASTLE CARY
Hadspen House (2m SE off A371)
☎ (01963) 50939
Situated within a 17th-century curved wall, this 5-acre garden has borders planted with roses and herbaceous plants, many of which have been developed here. Plants grown in the garden are available in the adjoining nursery.
Open Mar-1 Oct, Thu-Sun & BHs 9-6.
🅿 ⬛ ♿ *toilets for disabled garden centre*
⚑
Details not confirmed for 1995

Forde Abbey
CHARD
(4m S of Chard)
☎ South Chard (01460) 20231
This 12th-century Cistercian monastery was converted into a private dwelling in the mid-17th century by Cromwell's attorney general. In the house there are good pictures and furniture and an outstanding set of Mortlake tapestries. The large gardens are some of the finest in Dorset and include a kitchen garden, rock garden and bog garden as well as herbaceous borders and many outstanding trees. Winner of Christies Garden of the Year Award, 1993.
Gardens, open all year, daily 10-4.30. Abbey & gardens Apr-Oct Sun, Wed & BH 1-4.30 (last admission).
✱*Gardens £3.25 (ch free, pen £2.75). House & Gardens £4.50 (ch free, pen £4). Party.*
🅿 ⬛ ♿ *(electric buggy can be lent for garden tours) toilets for disabled shop garden centre* ⚑ *(ex in grounds)*

Cheddar Showcaves & Gorge
CHEDDAR
☎ (01934) 742343
Britain's two most beautifully illuminated showcaves - spectacular Gough's Cave and the stunning colours of Cox's Cave - plus 'The Crystal Quest', a dark walk fantasy adventure underground. Visit 'Cheddar Man', Britain's oldest complete skeleton, and the world 9,000 years ago. Climb Jacob's Ladder to Pavey's Lookout Tower and clifftop walks. The daring can pre-book an Adventure Caving Expedition (minimum age 12) - so much to do! All set in dramatic Cheddar Gorge.
Open all year, Etr-Sep 10-5.30; rest of year 10.30-4.30. (Closed 24 & 25 Dec). Combined ticket for all attractions £6 (ch 5-15 £4, ch under 5 free). Adventure Caving Expeditions (min 12yrs) £7. Family ticket £19.
🅿 *(charged)* ⬛ ♿ *(free entrance to Gough's cave, access limited) shop*

East Somerset Railway
CRANMORE
Cranmore Railway Station (on A361)
☎ Shepton Mallet (01749) 880417
Nine steam locomotives and rolling stock can be seen at Cranmore station, which has an engine shed and workshops. The new art gallery displays David Shepherd's work. Steam train services (see timetable for Steam Days) include Santa Specials in December, and here also are a museum, wildlife information centre, restaurant and play area. Special events for 1995 include Friends of Thomas Week (27 May-4 June) and Weekend (1-3 September), a jazz night (29 July), the Mendip Steam Dream (7-8 October) and Santa trains each Saturday and Sunday in December.
Open May-Sep, Wed-Sun 10-5.30; Mar, Apr, Oct-Dec, wknds only 10-4. Also open 1 Jan & BH's.
£3.50 (ch £2 & pen £2.80). Non-steam days £1.50 (ch £1).
🅿 ⬛ ✗ *licensed* ♿ *(ramp from road to platform) toilets for disabled shop*

Crinkley Bottom
CRICKET ST THOMAS
(on A30)
☎ Winsham (01460) 30755
Now the home of Crinkley Bottom and Mr Blobby, the old and beautiful park of Cricket House still houses a wide variety

Although originally built by the Normans, much of Dunster Castle is actually Victorian, as is the fine library with its 'leather-look' wallpaper.

of animals and birds, including elephants, camels, sealions, parrots and other exotic creatures. The wildlife enclosures have been designed to blend in with the surroundings as far as possible, and there have been successes with breeding, most notably of black swans. Shire horses can be seen at the Heavy Horse Centre, and there is a woodland railway. The house became well known as 'Grantleigh Manor' in the BBC television series *To The Manor Born*. Please telephone for details of the special events planned for 1995.
Open all year Apr-Oct, daily 10-6; Nov-Mar 10-5 or dusk (whichever is earlier).
✱*£6.80 (ch 3-14 £5 & pen £5.80). Wheelchair users free. Party 20+. Charges for rides extra.*
🅿 ⬛ ✗ *licensed* ♿ *toilets for disabled shop garden centre*

Dunster Castle
DUNSTER
(3m SE of Minehead, approach from A39)
☎ (01643) 821314
The setting of Dunster Castle is dramatic: it lies between Exmoor and the sea. Sub-tropical plants flourish in the 28-acre park and the terraced gardens are noted for exotica such as a giant lemon tree, yuccas, mimosa and palms. The castle's picturesque appearance is largely due to attractive 19th-century work, but handsome older features include intricately decorated ceilings, the superb 17th-century oak staircase and the gallery with its brightly painted wall hangings. The castle was the home of the Luttrell family for 600 years, and there is a dramatic 16th-century portrait of Sir John Luttrell. Other notable features include the elaborate 'thrown chair' and the leather-look wallpaper of the comfortable 19th-century library. Special events for 1995 include: Civil War Garrison (3-4 June), a Victorian weekend (8-9 July) and Christmas week celebrations; for further details ring 0891 335255. Dunster Water Mill will be open to the public on National Mills Day, Sunday 14 May.
Open: Garden & grounds Feb-10 Dec daily 11-4 (5pm in Apr-Sep). Castle Apr-Oct, Sat-Wed 11-5 (4pm in Oct), closed Good Fri. (last admission 30 mins before closing.).
Castle & Garden £4.80 (ch 16 £2.40). Garden & Grounds only £2.70 (ch 16 £1.30). Family ticket to garden & park £6.50, includes exploration trail. Party 15+.
🅿 ♿ *(Braille guide, Batricar for grounds) toilets for disabled shop*
(NT)

Secret World-Badger & Wildlife Reserve Centre
EAST HUNTSPILL
New Rd (Signposted from A38)
☎ Burnham-on-Sea (01278) 783250

Discover the natural world that lives side by side with domestic animals at this Rescue Centre. Foxes, badgers, owls and much, much more can be seen the surroundings of a traditional farm where the listed farmhouse, built in 1675, has been made into tearooms serving meals all through the day. Visit the nocturnal house where night creatures can be seen in their natural surroundings and an observation sett where you can watch badger life or discover the mysteries of the insect house. Feeding routines take place throughout the day, and there is plenty for visitors of any age to do, in any weather, at this all-year-round facility. Dogs are welcome. Badger days this year are May 13-14, July 15-16 and October 14-15; other events include a wildlife weekend (24-25 June) and 'Father Christmas and Sleepy Animals' (9-10 and 16-17 December).
Open Mar-Nov, daily 10-6. Nov-Mar, daily 10-5.
£3.95 (ch £2.75, pen £3.50). Party.
🅿 ⬛ ♿ *toilets for disabled shop garden centre*

East Lambrook Manor Garden
EAST LAMBROOK
(off A303)
☎ South Petherton (01460) 40328
Walter and Margery Fish created the cottage-style garden after buying the 15th-century manor in 1937. Margery Fish's book *We Made a Garden* described the work, and aroused so much interest that she started a nursery to sell the types of plants she used. Plants are still sold. The garden is now Grade I listed and has been fully restored.
Open Mon-Sat 10-5, also 30 May for National Gardens Scheme. (Closed Nov-28 Feb).
🅿 *shop garden centre* ⚑
Details not confirmed for 1995

Farleigh Hungerford Castle
FARLEIGH HUNGERFORD
☎ (01225) 754026
The ruined 14th-century castle has a chapel with monuments to the Hungerfords, a powerful family who owned land from here to Salisbury. Family and castle are linked with various grim tales of hanging and murder.
Open all year, Apr-Sep, daily 10-6; Oct 10-4; Nov_Mar, Wed-Sun 10-4. Closed 24-26 Dec & 1 Jan.
£1.30 (ch 70p, concessions £1).
🅿 ♿ ⚑
(EH)

Glastonbury Abbey
GLASTONBURY
☎ (01458) 832267
Few places in Britain are as rich in myth and legend as Glastonbury and an old tradition maintains that the impressive,

medieval abbey ruins stand at the birth place of Christianity in Britain. This is where Joseph of Arimathea is said to have brought the Holy Grail (the chalice used by Christ at the Last Supper) and to have founded a chapel in AD61, on the site marked by a flowering thorn tree. Later, it is said, King Arthur and Guinevere were buried at Glastonbury; and the abbey was a place of pilgrimage in the Middle Ages. The present abbey ruins date from after a fire in 1184, and are mostly of the 12th and 13th centuries. The Abbey fell into decay after the Dissolution.
The modern display area contains artefacts and a model of the Abbey as it might have been in 1539, which together form a history of the Abbey. Special events for 1995 include: West of England Pilgrimage (24 June), Roman Catholic Pilgrimage (25 June).
Open all year, daily, Jun-Aug 9-6; Sep-May 9.30-dusk or 6 whichever earlier (Closed 25 Dec).
£2 (ch 5-16 £1, pen £1.50).
🅿 *(100yds)* ♿ *toilets for disabled shop*

Lytes Cary Manor
KINGSDON
(off A303)
☎ (01985) 847777
This charming manor, tucked away in the Somerset countryside, takes its name from the family who lived here for 500 years, the Lytes. Much of the present house was built by John Lyte in the 16th century although the oldest part, the chapel, dates from 1343. The Great Hall was a 15th-century addition and still boasts stained glass installed by John Lyte. His son, Henry, was a noted horticulturalist and he transformed the gardens at the manor; unfortunately these have not survived, but the present formal gardens are being restocked with plants that were commonly grown in his day.
Open Apr-28 Oct, Mon, Wed & Sat 2-6 or dusk if earlier. Last admission 5.30.
£3.70 (ch £1.90)
🅿 ♿ ⚑
(NT)

Combe Sydenham Country Park
MONKSILVER
☎ Stogumber (01984) 656284
The 16th-century house was the home of Sir Francis Drake's second wife, Elizabeth, and is currently being restored. The only part of the house that visitors can see is the Court Room, which has been restored using, wherever possible, the materials of the period, and guides are on hand to answer questions from visitors. There are an Elizabethan-style garden, woodland walks, a medieval corn mill, a working bakery and a children's play ➤

area. There is also fly fishing for the beginner, plus day tickets for the more experienced fisherman, and a trout farm for the unsuccessful.
Open 10 Apr-Oct. Country Park: Sun-Fri 10-5. Court Room & Gardens: Mon-Fri. 1.30-4 (Last admission to Court Room & Garden 3pm).
£4 (ch £1.50) Mon-Fri. £3 (ch £1.50) Sun. Family ticket available.
P ⬛ ✗ & *shop* ⊗ *(ex in park)*

Montacute House
MONTACUTE ▰▰▰▰
(off A3088)
☎ *Martock (01935) 823289*
Set amidst formal gardens, Montacute House was built in honey-brown Ham stone by Sir Edward Phelips. He was a successful lawyer, and became Speaker of the House of Commons in 1604. The glittering expanse of windows and Flemish-style rounded gables date from his time, but the heraldic beasts and fluted columns were added in the 18th century. Inside there are decorated ceilings, ornate fireplaces, heraldic glass and fine wood panelling. A collection of tapestries, paintings, furniture and ceramics bequeathed by Sir Malcolm Stewart has enabled the house to be furnished in fitting style. Better still, the Long Gallery displays a permanent collection of Tudor and Jacobean portraits from the National Portrait Gallery in London. Special events in 1995 will include a Medieval Joust and Ox-Roast on 2-3 September (for further details ring 0891 335227) and Horse Trials (ring 01747 840836).
Garden & Park open all year daily (ex Tue) 11.30-5.30 or dusk if earlier. House: Apr-Oct, daily (ex Tue) 12-5.30. Last admission 5pm. (Closed Good Fri). Parties by appointment with the administrator.
House, Garden & Park £4.80 (ch £2.50); Garden & Park only £2.70 (ch £1.20). Party 15+.
P ✗ *licensed* & *(Braille guide) toilets for disabled shop garden centre* ⊗ *(ex park)*
(NT)

Muchelney Abbey
MUCHELNEY ▰▰▰▰
Encircled by marshes, Muchelney seemed a suitably remote spot to found a Benedictine Abbey in the 8th century. All that is left are the 15th and 16th century ruins; the southern range of cloister buildings, containing the Abbot's lodging, is fairly well preserved. Nearby is a 14th-century priest's house, a rare example of domestic architecture from this period.
Open Apr-Sep, daily 10-6.
£1.30 (ch 70p, concessions £1)
P & ⊗
(EH)

Coleridge Cottage
NETHER STOWEY ▰▰▰▰
(off A39)
☎ *(01278) 732662*
It was in this small cottage that Coleridge

was most inspired as a poet and here that he wrote *The Ancient Mariner*. The Coleridge family moved to Nether Stowey in 1796 and became friendly with the Wordsworths who lived nearby, but the group were regarded with suspicion by the local population. The house was smaller and thatched, not tiled, in those days but otherwise little has changed.
Open 2 Apr-3 Oct, Tue-Thu & Sun 2-5 (Parlour & Reading room only). In winter by written application to custodian. £1.50. (ch 80p). Parties by arrangement with caretaker.
P ⊗
(NT)

Nunney Castle
NUNNEY ▰▰▰▰
Built by Sir John de la Mere in 1373, and supposedly modelled on France's Bastille, this crenellated manor house has one of the deepest moats in England. It was ruined by the Parliamentarian forces during the Civil War.
Open any reasonable time.
Free.
&
(EH)

Rode Bird Gardens
RODE ▰▰▰▰
(off A36 between Bath & Warminster)
☎ *Frome (01373) 830326*
Rode Bird Gardens consist of 17 acres of grounds, planted with trees and shrubs, in a pretty and little-visited village. An ornamental lake and a number of ponds surround the aviaries, where more than 200 species are kept. There are also a Pets' Corner, a children's play area, and an information centre. Plants are for sale. Children must be accompanied by an adult. A Woodland steam railway operates daily from Easter until the beginning of October, weather permitting. Events for 1995 include: a Railway Weekend (22-23 April), Parrot Weekend (8-9 July), Clematis Weekend (15-16 July), and a Steam Attractions Weekend (16-17 September).
Open all year daily (ex 25 Dec); Summer 10-6 (last admission 5pm); Winter 10-dusk (last admission 1hr before closing time).
£4.10 (ch3-16 £2.10, pen £3.60).
P ⬛ & *(special route, wheelchairs for hire) toilets for disabled shop* ⊗

Haynes Motor Museum Sparkford
SPARKFORD ▰▰▰▰
(off Castle Cary/Frome Rd).
☎ *North Cadbury (01963) 440804*
The museum contains a unique and extraordinary collection of over 200 veteran, vintage and classic cars, motorcycles, racing cars and bikes. Vehicles range from a 1903 Oldsmobile to sports cars of the 50s and 60s and modern day classics. American cars include a Model T Ford, Haynes V12, Cord, and Supercharged Auburn Speedster. Also at the museum are a 70 seater video cinema, picnic area, and the Pit Stop Cafe. When weather and staff

availability permit, cars are shown on our own vehicle display track. A new extension of 17,500 square feet will be opened in July 1995. (For up-to-date information on any event please contact the museum and ask to speak to Mike Penn).
Open all year, daily 9.30-5.30. Evenings by appointment. (Closed 25,26 Dec & 1 Jan).
✱*£3.85 (ch 5 £2.25, concessions £3.50).*
P ⬛ & *toilets for disabled shop* ⊗

Willow & Wetlands Visitor Centre
STOKE ST GREGORY ▰▰▰▰
Meare Green Court
☎ *North Curry (01823) 490249*
The levels and moors of Somerset are the most important areas of 'wetland' left in England. This centre shows how today's landscape has been created from marsh and swamp. The wetland wild flowers, insects and birds are all illustrated. There are sections on traditional industries based on locally found plants like withies and teasles. Models, drawings and photographs are used to give a fascinating insight into this unique area. There is a guided tour of this working industry, covering all aspects of withy growing and processing and a visit to the basket workshop to see basket making in progress. There is also a Basket Museum.
Open all year, Mon-Fri 9-5 (guided tours 10-4), Sat (no tours) 9-5. Closed Sun.
✱*£1.95 (ch £1, pen £1.50). Party.*
P & *shop*

Stoke-Sub-Hamdon Priory
STOKE-SUB-HAMDON ▰▰▰▰
North St (between A303 & A3088)
☎ *(01985) 847777*
This 15th-century house is built of Ham Hill stone and was once the home of the priests of the chantry belonging to the now vanished Beauchamp Manor. The 14th-and 15th-century farm buildings and the screens passage of the chantry remain, with part of the hall.

Open all year, daily 10-6. Great Hall only open to visitors.
Free.
P
(NT)

The Shoe Museum
STREET ▰▰▰▰
C & J Clark Ltd, High St
☎ *(01458) 43131*
The museum is in the oldest part of the shoe factory set up by Cyrus and James Clark in 1825. It contains shoes from Roman times to the present, buckles, engravings, fashion plates, machinery, hand tools and advertising material. One section illustrates the early history of the shoe firm and its role in the town.
Open all year.
Free.
P *(charged)* ⬛ ✗ & *toilets for disabled shop* ⊗

Hestercombe Gardens
TAUNTON ▰▰▰▰
Fire Brigade Headquarters, Hestercombe House, Cheddon Fitzpaine (3m N, off A361 near Cheddon Fitzpaine).
☎ *(01823) 337222 ext 316*
The late 19th-century house is now the headquarters of the Somerset Fire Brigade. The multi-level gardens and orangery were originally planned in 1905 by Sir Edwin Lutyens and Gertrude Jekyll, with raised walks, sunken lawns and a water garden.
Open all year, Mon-Fri 9-5, also May-Sep Sat & Sun 2-5. Groups by appointment only.
£2 (ch free, pen £1.50). Prices under review.
P

Sheppy's Cider & Rural Life Museum
TAUNTON ▰▰▰▰
Three Bridges, Bradford-on-Tone (on A38)
☎ *(01823) 461233*
Sheppy's is a traditional cider farm which has been producing cider commercially

since 1925. Today the farm has 20 acres of standard and 22 acres of bush orchards. Visitors may walk round the farm and orchard trails, the press room and the excellent museum and can also see a video show of the cidermaking year. Various ciders may be sampled before purchase in the farm shop. The Craft and Cider Country Fayre is held here the last Saturday and Sunday in July (29th and 30th in 1995).
Open all year, Mon-Sat 8.30-6. Sun (Etr-Xmas only) noon-2.
£1.50 (ch 14 £1, pen £1.25).
🅿 💺 & *toilets for disabled shop*

Tintinhull House Garden
TINTINHULL
(.5m S off A303)
☎ (01935) 822545
An attractive, mainly 17th-century farmhouse with a Queen Anne façade, it stands in four acres of beautiful formal gardens and orchard. The gardens were largely created by Mrs Reiss, who gave the property to the National Trust in 1953.
Open Apr-22 Oct (dates not confirmed), Wed-Sun & BH Mons 2-6 (last admission 5.30pm)
£3.50 (ch £1.60)
🅿 ❧
(NT)

Cleeve Abbey
WASHFORD
☎ (01984) 40377
The Cistercian abbey was founded at the end of the 12th century and is now a ruin. There is little left of the church, but the gatehouse, dormitory and refectory are in good condition, with traceried windows, a fine timbered roof and wall paintings to be seen.
Open all year, Apr-Sep, daily 10-6; Oct, 10-4; Nov-Mar, Wed-Sun 10-4. Closed 24-26 Dec & 1 Jan.
£2 (ch £1, concessions £1.50).
🅿 &
(EH)

Tropiquaria
WASHFORD
(on A39)
☎ (01984) 40688
Housed in a 1930s BBC transmitting station, the main hall has been converted into an indoor jungle with a 15-foot waterfall, tropical plants and free-flying birds. (Snakes, lizards, iguanas, spiders, toads and terrapins are caged!) Downstairs is the submarine crypt with local and tropical marine life. Other features include landscaped gardens, outdoor aviaries, a children's playground and the Shadowstring Puppet Theatre.
Open Apr-Sep, daily 10-5; Oct, daily 11-5, Nov & Jan-Mar wknds & school hols 11-5; 27-31 Dec, 11-5. (Closed 1-27 Dec).
🅿 💺 & *shop* ❧
Details not confirmed for 1995

Bishop's Palace
WELLS
☎ (01749) 678691
Close to the cathedral is the moated bishop's palace. The early part of the palace, the bishop's chapel and the ruins of the banqueting hall date from the 13th century; The undercroft remains virtually unchanged from this time. There are several state rooms and a long gallery which houses portraits of former Bishops. The palace is ringed with fortifications as well as the moat and access can only be gained through the 14th-century gatehouse. The name of the city is taken from the wells in the palace grounds.
Open 2 Apr-30 Oct, Tue, Thu & BH Mon; daily in Aug & BHs 11-6. Sun 2-6. Last admission 5.30.
💺 ✕ & *shop* ❧ *(ex in grounds)*
Details not confirmed for 1995

Wookey Hole Caves & Papermill
WOOKEY HOLE
☎ *Wells (01749) 672243*
The Caves are the main feature of Wookey Hole. Visitors enjoy a half mile tour through the Chambers, accompanied by a knowledgeable guide who points out the amazing stalagmites and stalactites, including the famous Witch of Wookey. The guides use remote controlled lighting to highlight geological features and illustrate the history and myths associated with the caves.
Visitors also take in the Victorian Papermill, at one time amongst the largest handmade papermills in Europe, which sold exquisite paper all over the world. Also in the Mill are the Fairground Memories, historically important late 19th-century and early 20th-century fairground rides. The latest attraction is the Magical Mirror Maze, an enclosed passage of multiple image mirrors creating an illusion of endless reflections. After the fun of the maze, visitors move on to a typical Old Penny Arcade where they can purchase old pennies to operate the original machines. In 1995 there will be a Family Funday to raise funds for Arthritis Research on 7 May and a Spirit of the Sixties Classic Motorcycle Run on 14 May.
Open all year, Mar-Oct 9.30-5.30; Nov-Feb 10.30-4.30. (Closed 17-25 Dec).
✱*£5.60 (ch £3.60, pen £4.90). Party 10+.*
Various disabled concessions.
🅿 ✕ *licensed* & *(Papermill only) toilets for disabled shop* ❧

Museum of South Somerset
YEOVIL
Hendford
☎ (01935) 24774
The history of South Somerset can now be experienced in this newly refurbished museum. From prehistoric and Roman occupation, through to agricultural and industrial revolutions, the museum shows, in an imaginative and exciting way, what rural life through the ages was really like. Visitors will discover artefacts set in scenes that recapture the atmosphere of their time.
Open all year, Tue-Sat 10-4. (Closed Sun & BHs).
Free.
🅿 & *shop* ❧

Fleet Air Arm Museum
YEOVILTON
Royal Naval Air Station (on B3151)
☎ *Ilchester (01935) 840565*
Based at the Royal Naval Air Station, the museum portrays the history and achievements of the Royal Naval Air Service, with examples from the early days of kites and airships to the present day. A collection of over 40 historic aircraft, several unique, are on display as well as a vast collection of costume, medals and memorabilia. Special exhibitions using modern audio visual aids and displays put the exhibits in their original context. These include World War I, the Interwar Years, Battle of Taranto, Skua Underwater Experience, Falklands and Gulf Wars and many more. In addition, you can climb aboard and walk through Concorde 002, the British prototype. There are airfield viewing galleries to watch aircraft taking off and landing from the Naval Base. For children there are open cockpits, a flight simulator and a Naval Aviation Adventure playground. In spring 1994 the Ultimate Aircraft Carrier Experience opened, offering all the sights, sounds, smells and action of a real aircraft.
Open all year, daily (ex 24-26 Dec) 10-5.30 (4.30pm Nov-Mar).
✱*£5.50 (ch, disabled & UB40's £3, pen £4.50). Family ticket £14. Price revision due Apr.*
🅿 💺 ✕ *licensed* & *(wheelchairs available) toilets for disabled shop* ❧

SOUTH YORKSHIRE

Monk Bretton Priory
BARNSLEY
(1.5m E)

☎ (01226) 204089

The priory was an important Cluniac house, founded in 1135. The considerable remains of the gatehouse, church and other buildings can be seen, and include some well-preserved drains.
Open all year, Apr-Sep, daily 10-6; Oct, 10-4; Nov-Mar, Wed-Sun 10-4 or dusk if earlier. (Closed 24-26 Dec & 1 Jan).
£1 (ch 50p, concessions 80p).
🅿 & ⌖
(EH)

Conisbrough Castle
CONISBROUGH
☎ *Rotherham (01709) 863329*

The splendid 12th-century keep soars up beside the River Don, and has good views of the surrounding industrial landscape. It is circular with six buttresses - a unique design - and is surrounded by a curtain wall with solid round towers. The castle features in Sir Walter Scott's *Ivanhoe*.
Open all year, Apr-Sep, Mon-Fri 10-5, Sat & Sun 10-6; Oct-Mar, daily 10-4. Closed 24-26 Dec & 1 Jan.
🅿 & ⌖
(EH)

Cusworth Hall Museum
CUSWORTH
☎ *Doncaster (01302) 782342*

The 18th-century house is the home of this museum of South Yorkshire life. There are sections of special interest to children, and the extensive grounds have fishing (in ponds), cricket and football pitches. A children's study base and research facilities are provided.
Open all year, Mon-Fri 10-5, Sat 11-5 & Sun 1-5. (4pm Dec & Jan) (Closed Good Fri, Xmas & 1 Jan).
🅿 & *(wheelchair available) toilets for*

Sheffield City Centre.

disabled shop ⌖ (ex park)
Details not confirmed for 1995

Doncaster Museum & Art Gallery
DONCASTER
Chequer Rd

☎ (01302) 734293

The wide-ranging collections include British and European paintings and sculpture. There are also ceramics, glass, silver, and displays on history, archaeology and natural history. The historical collection of the Kings Own Yorkshire Infantry is housed here, and temporary exhibitions are held. A wide variety of temporary exhibitions are planned for 1995. Please telephone for details.
Open all year, Mon-Sat 10-5, Sun 2-5. (Closed Good Fri, 25-26 Dec & 1 Jan).
Free.
& *(lift) toilets for disabled shop ⌖*

Roche Abbey
MALTBY
(1.5m SE)

☎ (01709) 812739

The walls of the south and north transepts still stand to their full height in this 12th-century Cistercian abbey, providing a dramatic sight for the visitor. There is also a fine gatehouse to the north-west.
Open Apr-Sep, daily 10-6; Oct 10-4.
£1.30 (ch 70p, concessions £1).
🅿 &
(EH)

Art Gallery
ROTHERHAM
Walker Place

☎ (01709) 382121 ext 3624/3635

The Gallery hosts a continuous programme of temporary exhibitions covering a wide range of historic and artistic subjects. The annual programme is drawn together from a variety of sources, some exhibitions being shown at the Art Gallery as part of a national tour, whilst others are drawn from the Museum's own collections or showcase the talents of local people, either in a group show or in one-person exhibitions.
Open all year, Tue-Fri 10-5, Sat 10-5. (Closed Sun, Mon & BH).
Free.
🍴 & *toilets for disabled shop ⌖*

Museum
ROTHERHAM
Clifton Park, Clifton Ln

☎ (0709) 382121 ext 3624/3635

Housed in a mansion designed by John Carr, the museum is noted for its collection of Roman relics from the site of a fort at Templeborough, and also for its Rockingham china. Other attractions include the 18th-century rooms, family portraits, the period kitchen, Victoriana, Natural History displays, local church silver and glassware.
Open all year, Mon-Thu & Sat 10-5, Sun 2.30-5 (4.30pm Oct-Mar).
🅿 & *shop ⌖*
Details not confirmed for 1995

SHEFFIELD

Sheffield was a thriving town, famous for its cutlery, even before Chaucer's time in the 14th century. There is still a Norman castle overlooking the River Don in the city centre and industrial prosperity gave the area several dignified Georgian buildings but, unfortunately not a lot remains from before World War II when the city was severely bombed. It is still a prosperous city and its busy modern heart still finds time and space to recall the history of the steel-making which earned the city a worldwide reputation, and to display with pride some of the finest wares produced in its factories over the years.

Abbeydale Industrial Hamlet
SHEFFIELD
Abbeydale Rd South (4m SW of Sheffield on A621)

☎ (0114) 2367731

A restored water-powered scythe and steel works dating back to the 18th century, the hamlet retains its working water wheels as well as forging hammers, grindstones and the world's only surviving working Huntsman crucible steel furnace. Abbeydale is a magical place where the visitor can wander at will, viewing the Victorian manager's house and workman's cottage, watching local craftsmen at work in the workshops and contrasting today's tranquil atmosphere with Sheffield's rich industrial history. Abbeydale Industrial Hamlet is open all year round, and working days will be held this year on 10-12 March, 26-28 August and 3-5 November (when there will also be a steam rally). Other events planned for 1995 include exhibitions of pewter (March-June) and batik (June-August), a craft fair (27 May-4 June) and a Christmas Fayre (20-21 December).
Open all year, Tue-Sat 10-5 & Sun 11-5. Also open BH Mon. (Closed Xmas & New Year).
£2.50 (ch & pen £1.25). Family ticket £5. On working days £3 (ch & pen £2.25). Family ticket £6. Cfraft Fair £3.50 (ch & pen £1.75). Family ticket £7.
🅿 🍴 & *shop ⌖*

Bishops House
SHEFFIELD
Meersbrook Park, Norton Lees Ln (S of Sheffield, on A61 Chesterfield road)

☎ (0114) 2557701

This 15th-and 16th-century yeoman's house has been restored and opened as a museum of local and social history. Several rooms have been furnished and there are displays of life in Tudor and Stuart times as well as a range of temporary exhibitions. Special educational facilities can be arranged for schools and colleges.
Open all year, Wed-Sat 10-4.30, Sun 11-4.30; also BH Mon 10-4.30. (Closed 24-26 Dec & 1 Jan). Phone to check opening times.
£1 (ch & pen 50p, UB40's free).
& *shop ⌖*

City Museum
SHEFFIELD
Weston Park (on A57)

☎ (0114) 2768588

The museum houses exhibits on regional geology, natural history and archaeology, especially from the Peak District. There is a particularly splendid display of cutlery and Sheffield plate, for which the city is famous, among exhibits on other local industries such as ceramics, clocks, watches and sundials. Educational facilities are available for schools and colleges. A major archaeological, sculptural and visual arts exhibition, *The Bronze Age*, is planned for June-August 1995.
Open all year, Tue-Sat 10-5, Sun 11-5 also BH Mons. (Closed 24-26 Dec & 1 Jan). Please telephone to check opening times.
Free, but charged for special exhibitions & events.
🍴 & *(Inductive loop. Handling sessions for pre-booked groups) toilets for disabled shop ⌖*

Kelham Island Industrial Museum
(.5m NW, take A61 N to West Bar)
SHEFFIELD
Kelham Island, Alma St

☎ (0114) 2722106

Housed in a former generating station, this lively museum tells the story of Sheffield's industrial development over the last 400 years. There are displays of working machinery and traditional cutlery craftsmen can be seen at work, using the time-honoured skills of the industry. These are complemented by exhibitions of a wide variety of goods made in Sheffield, both past and present, film and slide shows and the largest working steam engine in the world 'in steam'. There will be a Christmas market in December.
Open Mon-Thu 10-4, Sun 11-4.30.(Closed last 3 wks of Dec). Please apply for further details.
£2.50 (ch £1.25, pen 1.70). Family ticket £5. Party 12+.
🅿 🍴 & *(wheelchair on request) toilets for disabled shop ⌖*

Shepherd Wheel
SHEFFIELD
Whiteley Woods, off Hangingwater Rd

☎ (0114) 2367731

An early, water-powered, cutlery grinding works that was established in 1584. The works here employed 10 people and used less sophisticated methods than those exhibited in other local industrial museums. The water wheel is operated daily, water levels permitting.
Open all year, Wed-Sat 10-12.30 & 1.30-5, Sun 11-12.30 & 1.30-5 (4pm Nov-Feb).
Free.
&

STAFFORDSHIRE

Alton Towers
ALTON
☎ *Oakamoor (01538) 702200*

Alton Towers, set in 500 acres of stunning Staffordshire countryside, is the UK's most magical experience, with rides and attractions suitable for every member of the family. //Last year saw the introduction of Nemesis, the world's most intense ride experience, and Toyland Tours, a gentle ride for children. //The 1995 season promises to be a somewhat gentler affair with the redevelopment of the farm area and the introduction of two new rides aimed specifically at younger children. //With these, and other recent additions such as the world's spookiest Haunted House dark ride and the rip-roaring Runaway Mine Train, Alton Towers guarantees magic and fun for every member of the family.
Open mid Mar-early Nov 9am until 1 hr after attractions close. Attractions 10-5, 6, 7 or 8 as shown daily at main entrance gate.
£16 (ch £12, under 4's free, pen £5.50). Prices subject to change.
🅿 🍴 ✕ *licensed & toilets for disabled shop ⌖*

Swan boats provide a restful interlude in the hurly burly of Alton Towers theme park which is famous for its exciting rides.

Biddulph Grange Garden
BIDDULPH
Grange Rd (0.5m N)
☎ Stoke-on-Trent (01782) 517999
This exciting and rare survival of a high Victorian garden has undergone extensive restoration which will continue for a number of years. Conceived by James Bateman, the fifteen acres are divided into a number of smaller gardens which were designed to house specimens from his extensive and wide-ranging plant collection. An Egyptian Court, Chinese Pagoda, Willow Pattern Bridge and Pinetum, together with many other settings, all combine to make the garden a miniature tour of the world. An outdoor production of Gilbert and Sullivan's *The Mikado* will take place on June 11 this year - contact the garden office for details.
Open 29 Apr-29 Oct, Wed-Fri 12-6, (Closed Good Fri). Sat-Sun & BH Mon 11-6 (last admission 5.30 or dusk if earlier); 4 Nov-18 Dec, Sat-Sun 12-4.
Apr-Oct; £3.90 (ch £1.95). Family ticket £9.75. Nov-Dec; £2 (ch £1). Family ticket £5.
P 🍴 shop 🚫
(NT)

Bass Museum, Visitor Centre & Shire Horse Stables
BURTON-UPON-TRENT
Horninglow St (on A50)
☎ Burton Upon Trent (01283) 511000
The museum is housed in the Engineers' Department and Company's Joiner's Shop, built in 1866. Three floors of entertaining and interesting exhibits trace the history of the brewing industry from its earliest times to the present day. Outside there are larger exhibits, such as a 1917 steam lorry and a Daimler van in the shape of a bottle of IPA. Other attractions include a model of Burton as it was in 1921, stables with Shire horses, and a steam locomotive. There is a fine collection of drinking glasses - and there is also the beer. Special events take place in the summer and there will be a heavy horse parade on 24 September this year.
Open all year, Mon-Fri 10-5, Sat & Sun 11-5. Last admission 4pm. (Closed 25-26 Dec & 1 Jan).
❋£3.45 (ch £1.85, pen £2.35). Family ticket £9.25. Party. Brewery tours by arrangement only, at extra charge.
P ✕ licensed 🚻 toilets for disabled shop 🚫

Flint Mill
CHEDDLETON
Beside Caldon Canal, Leek Rd
☎ Barlaston (01782) 372561
Two water mills complete with wheels

are preserved here, and both are in running order. The 17th-century south mill was used to grind corn, but the 18th-century north mill was built to grind flint for the pottery industry. The restored buildings have displays on aspects of the pottery industry. Exhibits include examples of motive power, such as a Robey steam engine, and of transport, such as the restored 70ft horse-drawn narrow boat 'Vienna', which is moored on the Caldon Canal. There is also a haystack boiler of around 1770.
Open all year, Sat & Sun 2-5; Apr-Oct, Mon-Fri 10-5.
Donations.
P 🚻

Drayton Manor Theme Park & Zoo
DRAYTON MANOR PARK & ZOO ■
(on A4091)
☎ Tamworth (01827) 287979
A family theme park set in 250 acres of parkland and lakes with an open-plan zoo and zoo farm. There are over 50 rides and attractions for all age groups, including the ultimate white-knuckle ride, 7-Up Shockwave (the UK's first stand roller coaster), Splash Canyon Raft Ride, the amazing Pirate Adventure, Dinosaur Land, Jungle Cruise, Victorian Carousel, Looping Roller Coaster, Paratower, Log Flume, children's corner and many more; a new roller coaster will be introduced in 1995. Wristbands for unlimited rides or ride-as-you-go tickets. Drayton Manor was voted best-value theme park in 1994 by the roller coaster club.
Park & Zoo open Etr-30 Oct, daily 10.30-6. Park (rides) 10.30-5, 6 or 7 (depending on season).
£2.50 (ch 4-15 & pen £1.50). Wristband for unlimited rides £7 (junior-under one metre tall £4.50).
P 🍴 ✕ licensed 🚻 toilets for disabled shop garden centre 🚫 (ex in park)
See advertisement on page 138

Himley Country Park
HIMLEY
(off A449, on B4176)
☎ Wombourne (01902) 324093
The extensive parkland offers a range of attractions, from a model village to a nine-hole golf course and coarse fishing. The hall is *not* open to the public. Permanent orienteering course, a charge is made for the maps. Special events for 1995 include: Dudley Show (5-6 August), firework display (11 November), crafts fairs (April 22-23 and October 21-22) and a family fun day, *It's a Knockout* (9 July).
Open all year, 16 Jun-Sep, daily 6am-30 minutes before dusk; Oct-15 Jun, daily 7.30am-30 minutes before dusk.
Free. Car park 60p
P (charged) 🍴 🚻

Hanch Hall
LICHFIELD
(4m NW on B5014)
☎ Armitage (01543) 490308
A rare Regency four-poster bed said to be used by the poet Shelley; collections of needlework; antique dolls; early parchments; costumes and a postal display are all exhibited in this small country mansion, which has a fine Jacobean staircase and an observation tower. In all there are eighteen rooms open to the public.
Open Apr-Sep, Sun & BH Mon 2-6 (last tour of house 5pm).
P 🍴 🚻 🔘 shop 🚫
Details not confirmed for 1995

Lichfield Heritage Exhibition & Treasury
LICHFIELD ▬▬▬
St Mary's Centre Market Square
☎ (01543) 256611
Fine silver in the Treasury and lively presentations on the Civil War and the siege of Lichfield Cathedral, including a video entitled 'Lichfield - A Walk Through History', are featured here. The displays, housed in the ancient Guild Church of St Mary's, tell the centuries-old story of the city. A viewing platform in the spire gives unique, panoramic views over the city. Changing exhibitions of the City's Charters and Ancient Documents are planned for 1994
Open all year, daily 10-5. Last admission 4.14pm. (Closed Xmas, New Year & Spring BH Mon).
£1.25 (ch, students & pen 75p). Family ticket £3. (Joint ticket with Samuel Johnson Birthplace Museum £1.80, concessions £1). School parties by arrangement. Prices are under review.
P (200yds) 🍴 🔘 (lift) toilets for disabled shop 🚫
See advertisement on page 138

Samuel Johnson Birthplace Museum
LICHFIELD ▬▬▬
Breadmarket St
☎ (01543) 264972
A statue of Dr Johnson sits at one end of Market Square facing his birthplace on the corner of Breadmarket Street. The house, where Samuel's father had a bookshop, is now a museum containing many of Johnson's personal relics. His favourite armchair and walking stick are among the collection. In 1995 Boswell bicentary celebrations are planned around the weekend of 27-27 May.
Open daily 10-5. (Closed, Xmas & New Year).
£1 (ch & pen 60p). Joint ticket with Lichfield Heritage Centre £1.70 (ch & pen 90p). Family ticket £2.70. Party.
P (500 yds) shop 🚫

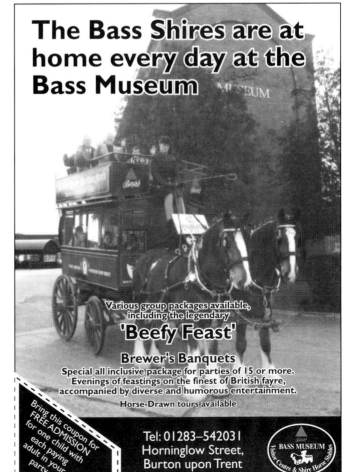

Moseley Old Hall
MOSELEY

☎ Wolverhampton (01902) 782808

Charles II sheltered in Moseley Old Hall after the Battle of Worcester in 1651. He slept in the four-poster bed in the King's Room, and hid in a concealed space below a cupboard in the room. There are numerous pictures and other reminders of the king, and much of the furniture in the panelled room dates from around his time. The house itself is an Elizabethan timber-framed building which was encased in brick in the 19th century. The small garden has a nut walk, period herbs and plants, and a formal knot garden. Special events for 1995 include a 17th-century Royal Garden Party (2 June), an Oak Apple Celebration (24 May), a concert (8 July) and a 17th-century weekend (9-10 September); on 1 April the Charles II Exhibition opens, and from then on there will be lectures on 17th-century topics on the first Tuesday of each month. Full details are available from the Administrator - please send a 9" x 4" envelope.

Open Apr-29 Oct, Wed, Sat, & Sun; Tue, Jul-Aug, 2-5.30. Also BH Mon 11-5. Pre-booked parties at other times.
£3.30 (ch £1.65). Family ticket £8. Party 15+.
🅿 🍽 ✗ *licensed* & *toilets for disabled shop* ❀
(NT)

Wolseley Garden Park
RUGELEY

Wolseley Bridge (at junc of A51 & A513)
☎ (01889) 574888

These beautiful ornamental gardens are the creation of Sir Charles and Lady Wolseley on land that has been in the Wolseley family for over a thousand years. Presently the gardens occupy forty-five acres and comprise excitingly different and beautiful theme gardens. There is the Spring Garden, the Rose Garden and the Scented Garden, whose fragrant herbs and shrubs offer particular enjoyment to the visually handicapped. Other areas of interest are the Water and Bog Garden, the Cathedral Garden and the Lakeside Walks. There is also a garden centre.
Open all year, daily 10-5.30 (or dusk if earlier). Open wknds only in severe winter weather. (Closed 25 Dec).
❊£2 (ch & pen £1.50)
🅿 🍽 & *(scented garden for the blind & audio guides) toilets for disabled garden centre* ❀

Shugborough Estate
SHUGBOROUGH

(6m E of Stafford off A513)
☎ Little Haywood (01889) 881388

Set on the edge of Cannock Chase, Shugborough is the magnificent 900-acre seat of the Earls of Lichfield. The 18th-century mansion house contains fine collections of ceramics, silver, paintings and French furniture. Part of the house is still lived in by the Lichfield family. Visitors can enjoy the Grade I listed historic garden and a unique collection of neo-classical monuments. Other attractions include the museum and the original servants quarters, the laundry, kitchens, brewhouse and coachhouses which have all been restored and are fully operational. Costumed guides show visitors how the servants lived and worked over 100 years ago. Shugborough Park Farm is a Georgian farmstead that has an agricultural museum, working corn mill and rare breeds centre.
Open 26 Mar-28 Oct, daily 11-3. Site open all year to pre-booked parties.
🅿 *(charged)* 🍽 ✗ & *(step climber for wheelchairs, 2 Batricars) toilets for disabled shop garden centre* ❀ *(ex in parkland)*
(NT)
Details not confirmed for 1995

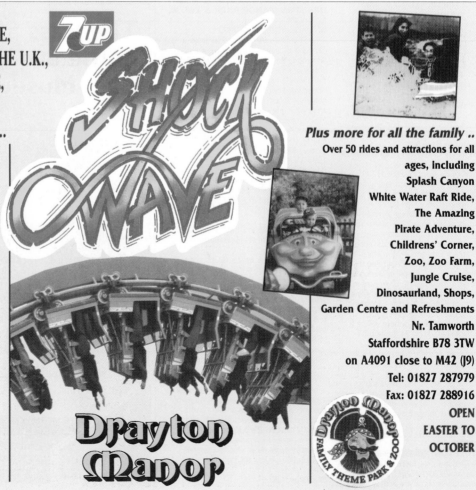

Shire Hall Gallery
STAFFORD
Market Square
☎ (01785) 278345
A fine gallery housed in the 18th-century Shire Hall - one of Staffordshire's most magnificent buildings. Exhibitions of contemporary arts, historic courtrooms and a Crafts Council selected craft shop.
Open all year, Tue-Fri 10-5, Sat 10-5 Free.
P *(200 yds)* & *toilets for disabled shop* ⌘

STOKE-ON-TRENT
Stoke-on-Trent is at the heart of one of Britain's oldest industrial conurbations, known as The Potteries. From the 17th century the towns grew under a thick pall of smoke from the furnaces used to make millions of china articles for home use and export around the world. Perhaps the most famous of these were the exquisite Spode and Wedgwood china. Today the grimy face of the past is disappearing as factories are transformed into living and working museums of nearly 300 years of china production.

Chatterley Whitfield Mining Museum
STOKE-ON-TRENT
Chatterley Whitfield Colliery, Tunstall (on A527)
☎ (01782) 813337
Chatterley Whitfield opened in 1979 as Britain's first underground mining museum on the site of the former million ton per annum Whitfield Colliery Complex. Established to preserve and present the story of coal mining in North Staffordshire, Chatterley Whitfield's purpose has broadened during the site's history as a working museum of the mining industry. With British Coal's decision in 1989 to relocate their national collection of mining artefacts to Whitfield, the museum is now emerging as a major national archive for students of mining history.
The museum can offer tours led by retired miner guides which include pit cage and manrider locomotive rides, together with retired pit ponies in their underground stalls. On the surface visitors can enjoy the sight of restored winding and compressor engines or marvel at the Museum's working steam railway. Visiting school and leisure groups can participate in Whitfield's Sandford award-winning Heritage Education Services. All visitors can take refreshments in the site's 1930s pit canteen.
Open all year, Mar-Oct daily 10-5, last tour 4pm; Nov-Feb, Tue-Sat 11-4, last tour 3pm. Sat 10-5, last tour 4pm.
P ⛴ & *(surface only) toilets for disabled shop*
Details not confirmed for 1995

City Museum & Art Gallery
STOKE-ON-TRENT
Bethesda St, Hanley
☎ (01782) 202173
The history of the Potteries under one roof, including a dazzling display of more than 500 pieces of ceramics, predominantly from Staffordshire - the history of an industry as seen through its products. Other displays introduce the natural, social and archaeological history of the area, and a Mark 16 Spitfire commemorates its locally born designer - Reginald Mitchell. In 1995 there will be a special exhibition for the Year of Arts and Culture entitled *Josiah Wedgwood: The Man and His Mark*.
Open all year, Mon-Sat 10-5, Sun 2-5. (Closed Xmas - New Year).
Free.
P ⛴ & *(lift, induction loop in theatre) toilets for disabled shop* ⌘

Etruria Industrial Museum
STOKE-ON-TRENT
Lower Bedford St, Etruria
☎ (01782) 287557
The Industrial Museum is situated in the Etruscan Bone and Flint Mill which was built in 1857 to grind materials for the agricultural and pottery industries. It is Britain's sole surviving, steam-powered potters' mill and contains an 1820's steam-driven beam engine, 1903 coal fired boiler and original grinding machinery. There is a working blacksmiths forge on site and there are regular demonstration of steam machinery from April to December (phone for details). Also for 1995 there is a Canal boat and folk festival on 3-4 June and a special Christmas on 9-10 December.
Open all year, Wed-Sun 10-4. (Closed Xmas/New Year).
Free.
P ⌘

Ford Green Hall
STOKE-ON-TRENT
Ford Green Rd, Smallthorne (on the B5051)
☎ (01782) 534771
This timber-framed farmhouse was built in 1624 for the Ford family and extended in the early 1700s. It is furnished with items and utensils used by a farming family from the 16th to the 19th centuries. Early music performances will take place on the second Sunday of every month during 1995 and additional events are held throughout the summer - telephone for details.
Open all year, Sun-Thu 1-5. (Closed Xmas & New Year). Tours available at 1.15, 2.15, 3.15 & 4.15.
Free.
P ⛴ & *shop* ⌘

Gladstone Pottery Museum
STOKE-ON-TRENT
Uttoxeter Rd, Longton (on A50, signposted from A500 link with M6)
☎ (01782) 319232

The museum has been created in a restored 'potbank', where day-to-day household chinaware was once produced. This small Victorian pottery is still complete with old warehouses, workshops and four huge bottle ovens. There are daily demonstrations by skilled craftsmen on the making and decorating of pottery. Also to be seen are galleries where colourful examples of tiles and sanitary ware are exhibited, together with colour and decorative techniques. Pottery is sold in the shop. Complete refurbishment and re-interpretation of the complex during 1994 included the recreation of a bottle oven firing where visitors can experience the intense heat, see the glow of flames, smell the soot and hear the noises. Every effort is made to give visitors the opportunity to get their hands on the clay, and hosts are on site to make sure you get the most from your visit. The museum reopens at Easter 1995.
Open all year, daily 10-5 (last admission 4pm). Limited opening Xmas & New Year.
❋ £3 (ch £1.50, students & pen £2.30).
P ✗ & *toilets for disabled shop*

Minton Museum
STOKE-ON-TRENT
London Rd
☎ (01782) 744766
The Minton Museum shows fine examples of the factory's production from 1800 to the present day. The display includes many large exhibits such as the 5ft tall Minton majolica-glazed peacock, fawn, stork and heron. Minton china can be purchased.
Open all year, Mon-Fri 9-1 & 1.45-4.30 (Closed factory holidays). Shop Mon-Sat 9-5.30.
P *shop* ⌘
Details not confirmed for 1995

Sir Henry Doulton Gallery
STOKE-ON-TRENT
Nile St, Burslem
☎ (01782) 292292
A tribute to Sir Henry Doulton, the gallery contains pottery treasures and artistry covering over 175 years. There are nearly 300 figures on display, including some very early and some very rare pieces. There are also displays showing the great variety of Royal Doulton wares, accompanied by archive material, such as catalogues and medals. There are additional displays of ceramic painting by outstanding artists as well as experimental ceramic work. Tours of the factory are also available.
Open all year, Mon-Fri 9.30-4.30. Factory tours by appointment. (Closed factory holidays). Shop Mon-Sat 9-5.30.
Museum Free. Factory tours £2 (students & pen £2.75). Party 30+.
P ⛴ *shop* ⌘

Spode
STOKE-ON-TRENT
Church St
☎ (01782) 744011
This is the oldest manufacturing ceramic factory on its original site (established in 1770) where Josiah Spode first perfected the formula of bone china. Tours commence from the museum and visitors are shown production methods, under-glaze printing and processing to produce the finest tableware. Standard tours are one hour and connoisseur tours are two hours. Prior booking is essential.
Open Tours Mon-Thu 10 & 2, Fri 10 only (Closed during factory holidays). Shop Mon-Sat 9-5 (Closed Etr, 25-26 Dec & 1 Jan). Special tours available for disabled visitors.
Standard tours £2.25; Connoisseur tour £6. By appointment only.
P ⛴ ✗ & *shop* ⌘

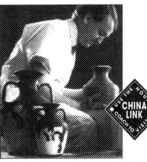

Otters are now a rare sight in the wild, but these delightful creatures are easy to view at the Otter Trust. They are bred here to introduce into the wild.

Wedgwood Visitor Centre
STOKE-ON-TRENT
Barlaston (5m S)
☎(01782) 204141 & 204218
The complex includes an art gallery with works by Reynolds, Stubbs and Romney, and a reconstruction of Wedgwood's original 18th-century Etruria workshops. There are demonstrations of the traditional skills in the production of Wedgwood ware, and a museum containing a comprehensive collection of the works of Josiah Wedgwood from 1750. A video gives the history of Wedgwood wares and demonstrates the craft of Wedgwood production; there is a shop where products may be bought. An exhibition will be held in 1995 to celebrate the bicentenary of Josiah's death.

Open all year, Mon-Fri 9-5, Sat & Sun 10-5; (Closed Xmas & 1 Jan).
£2.95 (ch, students & pen £1.50). Family ticket £6.95. Reductions Nov-Feb.
🅿✗ licensed & toilets for disabled shop
❄

See advertisement on page 139

Tamworth Castle
TAMWORTH
The Holloway
☎(01827) 63563
The castle is a mixture of Norman Gothic, Tudor, Jacobean and early 19th-century architecture, showing the tastes of its inhabitants over 800 years. It started as a Norman motte-and-bailey shell-keep, with the walls of its keep 10ft thick at the base; outer walls and a gatehouse were added in the 13th-century. The Tudor period brought additions of a more domestic sort with a splendid timber-roofed great hall and a warder's lodge.
The Jacobean state apartments have fine woodwork, furniture and heraldic friezes, including 55 oak panels painted with the arms of the Lords of the castle up to 1787. There is a Norman exhibition with 'speaking' knight, a haunted bedroom and Chapel, Annie Cooke's bedroom and a Victorian nursery.
Outside are floral terraces and pleasure grounds with an adventure playground, ten pin bowling alley, Snow Dome and Peaks Leisure Centre. Special events planned for 1995 include Easter at the Castle (16-17 April), Antiques 'Roadshow' (8 May), craft displays and demonstrations (29 May) and Tamworth Flower Club displays (26-28 August).
Open all year, Mon-Sat 10-5.30; Sun 2-5.30. Last admission 4.30.(Closed Xmas).
£3 (concessions £1.50). Family £7.50.
P (100 yds & 400 yds) & shop ❄

Wall Roman Site
WALL
Watling St
☎Shenstone (01543) 480768
Wall was originally the Roman fort of Letocetum. It was situated at the crossroads of Watling Street and Ryknield Street, and was an important military base from about AD50. Excavations started in the 19th century revealed the most complete bath house ever found in Britain. There are three baths: cold, tepid and hot as well as a furnace room and an exercise hall. A small museum at the site exhibits finds from this and other nearby Roman sites.
Open Apr-Sep, daily 10-6; Oct 10-4.
£1.30 (ch 70p, concessions £1).
(EH & NT)

Weston Park
WESTON PARK
(7m W of junc 12 of M6;3m N of junc 3 on M54)
☎Weston-under-Lizard (01952) 850207
Built in 1671, this fine mansion stands in elegant gardens and a vast park designed by 'Capability' Brown. Three lakes, a miniature railway, and a woodland adventure playground are to be found in the grounds, and in the house itself there is a notable collection of pictures, furniture and tapestries. Additional attractions are special events, and in 1995 these will include a Mothering Sunday luncheon in the house (26 March) and a Festival of Transport (16-17 April), Craft Fair (6-8 May) and Caravan, Camping and Leisure Show (14-16 July) in the park.The house is open to the public for special gourmet dinner evenings (please ring for dates), and is

also available for banquets, residential conferences etc.
Open Etr-mid Jun, wknds & BH; mid Jun-Jul daily (ex Mon & Fri); Aug daily; 1-19 Sep wknds only. Park 11-7 (last admission 5pm); House 1pm (last admission 5pm).
❄Park & Gardens £3 (ch £2, pen £2.50). House, Park & Gardens £4.50 (ch £3, pen £3.75).
🅿💺& (disabled route) toilets for disabled shop

Staffordshire Regiment Museum, Whittington Barracks
WHITTINGTON
☎0121-311 3240/3229
Situated adjacent to the barracks, the museum displays a collection of regimental militaria. The exhibits include the regiment's battle honours, captured trophies, a variety of weapons of different ages, medals and uniforms past and present.
Open all year, Mon-Fri 9-4.30. Last admission 4pm. (Closed BH & Xmas-New Year). Parties at other times by arrangement.
Free.
🅿& shop

The Dorothy Clive Garden
WILLOUGHBRIDGE
(on A51 between Nantwich & Stone)
☎Pipegate (01630) 647237
In the small village of Willoughbridge is a 200-year-old gravel quarry converted into a delightful woodland garden. The quarry is at the top of a small hill and the garden, which covers over 8 acres, has fine views of the countryside and adjoining counties. Among the tall oak trees are daffodils, rhododendrons and azaleas in profusion. There is also a variety of rare trees and shrubs, and water and rock gardens have been created among the steep banks. The garden provides colour and interest throughout the seasons from spring to glowing autumn tints.
Open Apr-Oct, daily 10-5.30.
£2.60 (ch £1). Party 20+.
🅿💺& (wheelchairs for use, special route) toilets for disabled

SUFFOLK

Moot Hall Museum
ALDEBURGH
☎(01728) 452730
Standing close to the sea, the Moot Hall is a brick and timber-framed building of the 16th century. An outside staircase leads to the first-floor Council Chamber, where there are old maps and prints and objects of local historical interest with emphasis on maritime history and coastal erosion. Other exhibits include displays on archaeology, geology and natural history. Exhibitions on coastal erosion and the 1953 Floods and a new permanent local flora display.
Open Apr & May, Sat & Sun 2.30-6; Jun, Sep & Oct daily 2.30-5; Jul & Aug 10.30-12.30 & 2.30-5.
45p (accompanied ch free)
P shop ❄

Otter Trust
BUNGAY
Earsham (off A143)
☎(01986) 893470
Otters are a rare sight in the wild nowadays, but at the Otter Trust it is possible to see these beautiful creatures at close quarters. While they are entertaining to watch, one of the Trust's main aims is to breed this endangered species in captivity in sufficient numbers so that it can re-introduce young otters into the wild every year wherever suitable habitat remains to reinforce the vanishing wild population. This re-introduction programme has been running very successfully since 1983 and is carried out in conjunction with English Nature. The Trust has now introduced

captive-bred otters into the wild in Norfolk, Suffolk, Dorset, Hampshire and Hertfordshire and subsequent scientific monitoring has shown that nearly all these animals are breeding successfully. This has resulted in the wild otter population of Norfolk increasing to almost what it was twenty years ago. The Otter Trust covers 23 acres on the banks of the River Waveney. As well as the otter pens there are three lakes with a large collection of European waterfowl, lovely riverside walks and picnic areas.
Open Apr (or Good Fri if earlier)-Oct, daily 10.30-6.
£4 (ch £2.50, pen £3.50). Disabled person & pusher free.
P ▣ ⓥ ♿ *toilets for disabled shop* ✥

Manor House Museum
BURY ST EDMUNDS ▰▰▰▰
Honey Hill
☎*(01284) 757072*
The Georgian mansion specialises in horology and fine and delicate art from the 17th to the 20th centuries. The time-machine gallery introduces the technology of timekeeping in ways that are intriguing and fun. There is a temporary exhibition gallery as well as workshops in textiles and horology. Events for 1995 include a beading exhibition (13 January-5 February), a 1940s Weekend (Easter Sunday and Monday), a lacemaking exhibition (23 June-6 August) and a return to the 18th century in *The Georgian Experience.*
Open all year Mon-Sat 10-5, Sun 2-5. (Closed Good Fri, 25 & 26 Dec).
£2.50 (ch, pen & students £1.50). Party.
▣ ⓥ ✗ *licensed* ♿ *toilets for disabled shop* ✥
(NT)

Moyse's Hall Museum
BURY ST EDMUNDS ▰▰▰▰
Cornhill
☎*(01284) 757488*
This rare 12th-century house of flint and

stone is now a museum of Suffolk history, archaeology and natural history. The clock tower is open by appointment. Temporary exhibitions are held throughout the year, and in 1995 these will include a 60s Exhibition (26 August-10 September) and People's Show (23 September-14 January 1996).
Open all year Mon-Sat 10-5, Sun 2-5. (Closed 25-26 Dec & Good Fri).
Donations welcome
P ♿ *shop* ✥

Cavendish Manor Vineyards & Nether Hall
CAVENDISH ▰▰▰▰
☎*Glemsford (01787) 280221*
The 15th-century manor house stands surrounded by its vineyards in the pretty Stour Valley village. Paintings and rural bygones are shown in the house and museum next to it. Tours of the vineyards and wine tasting are offered.
Open all year, daily 11-4.
£2.50 (ch 16 free)
▣ ♿ *shop* ✥

The Sue Ryder Foundation Museum
CAVENDISH ▰▰▰▰
Sue Ryder Home & Headquarters (on A1092 Long Melford to Clare road)
☎*Glemsford (01787) 280252*
The museum shows the work and history of the small but effective international foundation which cares for the sick and disabled. The Home's garden and chapel are also open.
Open all year, daily 10-5.30. (Closed 25 Dec).
80p (ch 12 & pen 40p). Parties by appointment.
▣ ✗ ♿ *toilets for disabled shop* ✥

Easton Farm Park
EASTON ▰▰▰▰
☎*Wickham Market (01728) 746475*
A Victorian model farm setting situated in the picturesque Deben River Valley.

Framlingham Castle has fine curtain walls, 13 towers and an array of Tudor chimneys.

There are lots of breeds of farm animals, some of which are rare and include Suffolk Punch horses, to be seen here. A purpose built dairy centre enables visitors to watch the cows being milked every afternoon, and, in complete contrast, there is the original Victorian Dairy which houses a collection of dairy bygones. Pets paddocks allow children to feed and touch the smaller animals whilst the Green Trail explores the natural habitats of plants and animals and provides grazing for the larger animals. 150 years of farming and food production are displayed in the 'foodchains' exhibition. Other attractions include: Adventure Playpit, picnic site and working Blacksmiths Forge. Special events are held throughout the season.
Open 19 Mar-1 Oct, daily 10.30-6. Last admission 4.30.
£3.85 (ch 3-16 £2.20, pen £3.15). Party 20+
▣ ⓥ ♿ *toilets for disabled shop*

Euston Hall
EUSTON ▰▰▰▰
(on A1088)
☎*Thetford (01842) 766366*
The 18th-century house is notable for its fine collection of pictures, by Stubbs, Lely, Van Dyck and other Masters. The grounds were laid out by John Evelyn, William Kent and 'Capability' Brown, and include a 17th-century church in the style of Wren.
Open Jun-28 Sep, Thu only & Suns 25 Jun & 3 Sep 2.30-5.
✽*£2.50 (ch 50p, pen £2). Party 12+.*
Wheelchairs free.
▣ ⓥ ♿ *shop* ✥ *(guide dogs by permission)*

Norfolk & Suffolk Aviation Museum
FLIXTON ▰▰▰▰
(off A143, take B1062)
☎*Thurton (01508) 480778*
Situated in the picturesque Waveney Valley, the museum has 23 historic aircraft including a Spitfire replica used in *The Battle of Britain* film; a Sea Vixen that flew in the Fleet Air Arm's aerobatic team 'Freds' Five', and a USAF Super Sabre in the colours of the Skyblazers aerobatic team. There is also a Bloodhound surface-to-air missile, a hangar with smaller buildings housing the museum's smaller exhibits, the 446th Bomb Group Museum, the Royal Observer Corps Museum and souvenir shop. Special events planned for 1995 include *Chocks Away* (8 May-27 May).
Open Apr-Oct Sun & BH 10-5; Also school summer holiday period Tue-Thu

10-5. Parties at other times by arrangement.
Free.
▣ ♿ *(ramp) shop* ✥

Framlingham Castle
FRAMLINGHAM ▰▰▰▰
☎*(01728) 723330*
Built by Roger Bigod between 1177 and 1215, the castle has fine curtain walls, 13 towers and an array of Tudor chimneys. Queen Mary was told here that she was Queen of England. In the 17th century the castle was bequeathed to Pembroke College, which built almshouses inside the walls.
Open all year, Apr-Sep, daily 10-6; Oct-Mar, daily 10-4. Closed 24-26 Dec & 1 Jan.
£2 (ch £1, concessions £1.50).
▣ ♿ *shop*
(EH)

Ickworth
HORRINGER ▰▰▰▰
The Rotunda (2.5m S of Bury St Edmunds).
☎*Bury St Edmunds (01284) 735270*
Ickworth was designed to show off works of art: it is a 100ft-high oval rotunda with two curved corridors, which were meant to be painting and sculpture galleries. The building was commissioned in 1796 by Frederick Hervey (pronounced Harvey), who collected many items for Ickworth, most of which had been confiscated by Napoleon. The house is filled with treasures amassed by the family, however. It has fine furniture and porcelain, one of England's most splendid silver collections, sculptures, and paintings by Velasquez, Lawrence, Kauffmann, Gainsborough and others. The formal gardens are noted for fine trees and there are extensive park walks, a deer enclosure and a children's play area. For details of special events in 1995, please contact the property manager.
Open: House & Garden 25 Mar-5 Nov Tue, Wed, Fri, Sat & BH Mons 1-5; Garden all year daily 25 Mar-5 Nov 10-5. 6 Nov-Mar 10-4; Park daily 7-7pm.
House, Garden & Park £4.30 (ch £2); Garden & park £1.50 (ch 50p). Party 15+
▣ ✗ *licensed* ♿ *(braille guide) toilets for disabled shop* ✥ *(ex in park)*
(NT)

Christchurch Mansion
IPSWICH ▰▰▰▰
Soane St (South side of Christchurch Park)
☎*(01473) 253246 & 213761*
The original house was built in 1548 on the site of an Augustinian priory. At the

end of the 19th century the house and parkland were saved by the Cobbold family from redevelopment; today Christchurch Mansion, set in a beautiful park, shows off its period furnished rooms. There is also an art gallery with a lively temporary exhibition programme, a Suffolk artists' gallery, a good collection of Constables and Gainsboroughs, and furniture and ceramics.
Open all year, Tue-Sat 10-5 (dusk in winter), Sun 2.30-4.30 (dusk in winter). (Closed Good Fri & 24-27 Dec & 1-2 Jan). Open BH mon.
Free.
P *(5 mins walk)* & *(tape guide for partially sighted) shop* ❄

Ipswich Museum
IPSWICH
High St
☎ (01473) 213761 & 263550
The museum has sections on local geology and archaeology from prehistoric to medieval times, and there is a Roman Suffolk gallery and a Victorian natural history gallery. Another section explores the story of mankind all over the world. A temporary exhibition programme is held.
Open all year, Tue-Sat 10-5. (Closed Sun, BH's, 24-27 Dec & 1-2 Jan).
Free.
P *(2 mins walk)* & *shop* ❄

Lavenham Guildhall
LAVENHAM
Market Place
☎ (01787) 247646
Although it has been much restored, there are still many of the original Tudor features left in this picturesque timber-framed building. The hall and its small museum are a testament to the time when East Anglia had a flourishing woollen industry. There is a walled garden with a 19th-century lock-up and mortuary.
Open 25 Mar-5 Nov, daily 11-5. (Closed Good Fri).

£2.50 *(first two ch free then 60p (free Jul-Aug)).Party.*
P 🍴 *shop* ❄
(NT)

The Priory
LAVENHAM
Water St
☎ (01787) 247003
This fine medieval timber-framed building was built for Benedictine monks. It has been well restored, and photographs illustrating the restoration work are on display inside, together with drawings, paintings and stained glass by Erwin Bossanyi. Outside is a uniquely designed herb garden.
Open Apr-Oct daily, 10.30-5.30. Guided tours for groups by appointment.
£2.50 *(ch £1).*
P *(street & 250yds)* 🍴 ✗ *shop* ❄

Leiston Abbey
LEISTON
For hundreds of years this 14th-century abbey was used as a farm and its church became a barn. A Georgian house was built into its fabric and this is now used as a retreat house for the local diocese. The rest of the abbey is in ruins, but remains of the choir and transepts of the church, and the ranges of cloisters still stand.
Open any reasonable time.
Free.
P &
(EH)

Long Shop Museum
LEISTON
Main St
☎ (01728) 832189
The Long Shop Museum, winner of no fewer than seven national awards, features 200 years of Richard Garrett engineering, the town of Leiston and its surroundings. Exhibits include steam engines, steam rollers, traction engines, and a display of USAAF memorabilia from the World War II air base. Projected

events for 1995 include an official opening on 8 April and regular steam days.
Open Apr-Oct, Mon-Sat 10-5, Sun 11-5.
£2 *(ch 75p, pen £1)*
P & *toilets for disabled shop* ❄

St James's Chapel
LINDSEY
Rose Green
Built mainly in the 13th century, this small thatched, flint-and-stone chapel incorporates some earlier work.
Open all year.
Free.
&
(EH)

Kentwell Hall
LONG MELFORD
(signposted off A134)
☎ Sudbury (01787) 310207
A mellow redbrick E-shaped Tudor mansion surrounded by a broad moat. Externally little altered, with many of the 16th-century service areas intact, the house shows internally the changes wrought in a variety of styles by successive owners, including the present family. There is a unique brick-paved mosaic 'Tudor' rose maze, and fine gardens include many clipped yews - some 30ft high - as well as an ancient walled garden with large herb garden and potager. The farm has rare breed animals and a collection of picturesque timber-framed buildings. Kentwell is also the home of living award-winning re-creations of Tudor life when up to 200 participants dress, speak and carry on daily activities as if in the 16th century. This year the Great Annual Re-creation runs from 18 June until 16 July (open to schools only on weekdays and the general public on Saturdays and Sundays, 11am-5pm); re-creations also take place every Bank Holiday weekend and other selected weekends, and there will be an open-air production of *A Midsummer Night's Dream* at 7.45pm on 28 and 29 July.
Open Apr-17 Jun, Sun only; 18 Jun-16 Jul, Sat & Sun for Re-Creation; 18-21 Apr, 30 May-2 Jun & 19 Jul-24 Sep, daily. Noon-5 (11-6 for Re-Creations). For all Re-Creation dates see advertisement. Inclusive ticket £4.50 (ch £2.75, pen £3.75). Garden & Farm only £2.50 (ch £1.75, pen £2.25). Special prices apply for Re-Creations.
P ✗ & *toilets for disabled shop* ❄

Melford Hall
LONG MELFORD
(off A134)
☎ Sudbury (01787) 880286
Queen Elizabeth I was a guest at this turreted, brick-built Tudor house in 1578, and it does not look very different on the outside today. It has its original panelled banquetting hall, and later features include an 18th-century drawing room, a Regency library and a Victorian bedroom. The house was owned for many years by the Parker family, which produced a number of admirals - hence the nautical flavour of the pictures. There is also a large collection of Chinese porcelain, and a display on Beatrix Potter, who was related to the Parkers and often stayed here. The garden has a Tudor pavilion, which may have been built as a guardhouse.
Open Apr, Sat, Sun & BH Mon 2-5.30; May-Sep, Wed, Thu, Sat, Sun & BH Mon 2-5.30; Oct, Sat & Sun 2-5.30. Last admission 5pm
£2.70 *(ch £1.35). Party.*
P & *(stairlift) toilets for disabled* ❄
(NT)

Maritime Museum
LOWESTOFT
Sparrow Nest Gardens, Whapload Rd (on A12)
☎ (01502) 561963
Models of ancient and modern fishing and commercial boats are exhibited, together with fishing gear and shipwrights' tools. There are an art gallery and a lifeboat display as well as a

facsimile of a Drifter's Cabin complete with model fishermen. A ships in bottles demonstration will be given by Tim Pegg on July 21, 22, 23, 24 and August 18, 19, 20, 21.
Open May-Sep, daily 10-5
✳50p *(ch, students & pen 25p)*
P *(100 yds)* & *shop*

Pleasurewood Hills Theme Park
LOWESTOFT
Corton Rd (off A12)
☎ (01502) 508200
After the initial admission fee there is nothing more to pay at this exciting theme park which has over fifty rides, shows and attractions for all the family. After the breathtaking rides such as the Wild Water Falls Log Flume Ride visitors can slow down the pace and enjoy the entertaining shows. Other attractions include the Sealion and Parrot shows, a Fun Factory and Cine 180. Train rides and chairlift make it easier to get around the park.
Open 1-10 Apr, 16-17 & 23-24 Apr, 30 Apr-2 May then daily 14 May-18 Sep, 24-25 Sep & 1-2 Oct. Dates to be revised for 1995.
✳Adult & child £8.95
P 🍴 ✗ & *toilets for disabled shop* ❄

National Horseracing Museum
NEWMARKET
99 High St
☎ (01638) 667333
Newmarket has been the centre of the 'sport of kings' since 1605, and is the headquarters of British racing. The great story of the development of horseracing is told in the museum's five permanent galleries. There is a video of classic races and displays are changed each year. Equine tours give an opportunity to see horses at work on the historic gallops, at home in the yards, on the racecourse and at the National Stud, where some of the world's finest stallions are kept.
The British Sporting Art Trust occupies two additional galleries.
Open 28 Mar-3 Dec, Tue-Sat (also BH Mons & Mon in Jul & Aug) 10-5. Sun 12-4.
£3.30 *(ch £1, pen £2). Party 20+. Equine tour charges on request.*
P *(300yds)* 🍴 ✗ *licensed* & *toilets for disabled shop* ❄

Orford Castle
ORFORD
(on B1084)
☎ (01394) 450472
Built by Henry II circa 1165, this castle has three towers and incorporates an 18-sided keep.
Open all year, Apr-Sep, daily 10-6; Oct-Mar, daily 10-4. Closed 24-26 Dec & 1 Jan.
£2 *(ch £1, concessions £1.50).*
P
(EH)

Bruisyard Winery, Vineyard & Herb Centre
SAXMUNDHAM
Church Rd, Bruisyard (4m W)
☎ Badingham (01728) 638281
This picturesque, 10-acre vineyard produces the award-winning Bruisyard St Peter English wine. There are also a herb garden, water garden, a wooded picnic area, and a children's play area. English wine, herbs, crafts and souvenirs are for sale.
Open Jan-Xmas, daily 10.30-5.
✳£3 *(ch £1.50, pen £2.50)*
P ✗ *licensed* & *shop garden centre* ❄ *(ex in vineyard)*

Saxtead Green Post Mill
SAXTEAD GREEN
(on A1120)
☎ (01728) 685789
One of the finest examples of a traditional Suffolk post-mill can be seen at Saxtead Green. There has been a mill on the site at least since 1796 but the mill has been altered or rebuilt several times. The present structure dates from 1854; for those who climb the steep staircase into the body of the mill there is the reward of

finding the now redundant millstones and other machinery in perfect order.
Open Apr-Sep, daily 10-6; Oct 10-4.
£1.30 (ch 70p, concessions £1).
& *(exterior only)* ⊗
(EH)

Southwold Museum
SOUTHWOLD
Bartholomew Green (A1095 E of A12 nr Blythburgh)
☎(01502) 722375
Housed in a 17th-century Dutch gabled cottage, the museum contains relics of local and natural history and of the Southwold light railway. There are also a display of pictures of the Battle of Sole Bay 1672, fought against the Dutch, and postcards and photographs on the theme 'Southwold and the Sea'.
Open Etr-Sep, 2.30-4.30 daily.
Free.
P *(250 yds)* & ⊗

Museum of East Anglian Life
STOWMARKET
☎(01449) 612229
The extensive, 70-acre, all-weather museum is set in an attractive river-valley site. There are reconstructed buildings, including a water mill, a smithy and also a wind pump, and the Boby Building houses craft workshops. There are videos of a cooper and basket maker at work, as well as a historic film show in a Bioscope cinema. Also here are displays on Victorian domestic life, gypsies, farming and industry. These include working steam traction engines, the only surviving pair of Burrell ploughing engines of 1879, and a working Suffolk Punch horse. Various events are being held throughout the year.
Open Apr-Oct.
Admission charged. Party. Telephone for details.
P ✗ & *(wheelchairs available, special parking facilities) toilets for disabled shop*

Gainsborough's House
SUDBURY
46 Gainsborough St
☎(01787) 372958
Gainsborough's House is the birthplace

of Thomas Gainsborough RA (1727-88). The Georgian-fronted town house, with an attractive walled garden, displays more of the artist's work than any other gallery, together with 18th-century furniture and memorabilia.
Commitment to contemporary art is reflected in a varied programme of exhibitions throughout the year. These include fine art, craft, photography, printmaking and sculpture, highlighting in particular the work of East Anglian artists.
Open all year - House Tue-Sat 10-5, Sun & BH Mons 2-5; (4pm Nov-Maundy Thu).
(Closed Good Fri & Xmas-New Year).
£2.50 (ch, students & disabled £1.25 pen £2). Party.
P *(300 yds)* & *toilets for disabled shop* ⊗

Suffolk Wildlife Park
SUFFOLK WILDLIFE PARK
Kessingland (on A12)
☎Lowestoft (01502) 740291
'Take a walk on the wild side'in 100 acres of Suffolk countryside. During your exploration you will see African lions, cheetahs, chimpanzees, sitatunga, bontebok, Arabian oryx, zebra, giant Poitou donkeys and colonies of lemur monkeys living freely on their islands. Animal feeding times are both informative and fun, and you can find out more about the pets in Farmyard Corner. Other attractions include the safari road train, explorer trails, crazy golf, bouncy castle and children's play area
Open all year, daily from 10am. (Closed 25-26 Dec).
Prices under review.
P ⊞ & *(wheelchairs available) toilets for disabled shop* ⊗

West Stow Anglo Saxon Village
WEST STOW
West Stow Country Park (off A1101)
☎Bury St Edmunds (01284) 728718
The village is a reconstruction of a pagan Anglo-Saxon settlement dated 420-650 AD. Six buildings have been reconstructed on the site of the excavated settlement, using the same techniques, tools and building materials as were used in the original farming village (free audio guides available) and

visitors can also see pigs and crops. The village is situated in the 125-acre West Stow Country Park. There are a Visitors' Centre and children's play area. Facilities for the disabled include purpose-built toilets for wheelchair users and a braille guide to the park. Special events throughout the year include a Saxon Market on Easter Saturday.
Open all year, daily 10-5. Last entry 4.15pm.
£2.50 (ch £1.50). Family ticket £7.
P & *(ramp, audio guides) toilets for disabled shop* ⊗

Woodbridge Tide Mill
WOODBRIDGE
Tide Mill Way
☎Ipswich (01473) 626618
The machinery of this 18th-century mill has been completely restored. There are photographs and working drawings on display. Situated in a busy quayside, this unique building looks over towards the historic site of the Sutton Hoo Ship Burial. Every effort is made to run the machinery for a short time whenever the mill is open and the tides are suitable; details obtainable from tourist information offices or outside the mill.
Open Etr, then daily May-Sep. Oct wknds only. 11-5
✸*80p (ch 40p).*
P *(400 yds)* & *shop* ⊗

SURREY

RAMC Historical Museum
ASH VALE
Keogh Barracks
☎Aldershot (01252) 340212
Some 2,500 items related to the work of the Royal Army Medical Corps are displayed, including a horsedrawn ambulance, a 1942 Austin K2 ambulance, Falklands War items, a mock-up of a patient on an operating table and items from the Gulf War. The RAMC Memorial Chapel is now a wing of the museum. The external displays include a physic garden and an ambulance train coach.
Open all year, Mon-Fri 8.30-4. (Closed Xmas, New Year & BH). Wknds & BH by appointment only. During 1994 the present museum building is being extended to facilitate the co-location of The QARANC Museum. This may have an impact on opening times, It is therefore advisable to phone before visiting.
Free.
P & *toilets for disabled shop* ⊗

Polesden Lacey
BOOKHAM, GREAT
(2m S off A246)
☎Great Bookham (01372) 458203 & 452048
In Edwardian times, this attractive Regency house was owned by a celebrated society hostess, Mrs Ronald Greville. King George VI and Queen Elizabeth (the Queen Mother) spent part of their honeymoon here, and photographs of other notable guests can be seen. The house is handsomely furnished with the Greville collection of tapestries, porcelain, Old Master paintings and other works of art. With its mixed Edwardian and Regency flavour, the house is full of charm, and it is set in spacious grounds. The gardens include a walled rose garden and there are good views and wide lawns. There is also an open-air theatre, where plays are performed in summer; these will run from 16 June-9 July 1995.
Open all year. Grounds: daily 11-6. House: Mar & Nov, Sat & Sun, 1.30-4.30; 30 Mar-Oct, Wed-Sun (inc Good Fri) 1.30-5.30. Also BH Mon & preceeding Sun 11-5.30.
✸*Garden only: £2.50; House: £3.*
P ⊞ ✗ *licensed* & *(braille guide & disabled parking by arrangement) toilets for disabled shop* ⊗
(NT)

Gatwick Zoo
CHARLWOOD
Russ Hill
☎Crawley (01293) 862312
The zoo covers almost 10 acres and has hundreds of birds and mammals. The monkey island has spider and squirrel monkeys, and other animals and birds can be seen in large, naturalised settings. Nearly all species breed each year. A play area for children up to 12 years old has been added.
Open all year, Mar-Oct, daily 10.30-6 (earlier by appointment for schools). Nov-Mar, wknds & school hols 10.30-4 or dusk if earlier. (Closed 25-26 Dec). No butterflies during winter.
£3.75 (ch 3-14 £2.75, pen £3.25 ex Sun & BH). Admission price includes Butterfly House.
P & *toilets for disabled shop* ⊗

Chertsey Museum
CHERTSEY
The Cedars, 33 Windsor St
☎(01932) 565764
The museum is housed in The Cedars, a late Georgian building. Its collections include items illustrating life in the Runnymede Borough from pre-history to the present day; the Matthews collection of 18th-and 19th-century costume and accessories, and furniture, clocks, ceramics and glass. The programme of temporary exhibitions includes an exhibition on World War II, Gerry Cottle's Circus, and In Touch with the Past - an exhibition which allows visitors to touch archaeological exhibits (braille captions).
Open all year, Tue-Fri 12.30-4.30, Sat 11-4. (Closed Xmas).
Free.
P & *shop* ⊗

Thorpe Park
CHERTSEY
Staines Rd (on A320)
☎(01932) 562633 & 569393
The park offers 500 acres of family fun; over 100 attractions are included in the admission price. The attractions include Loggers Leap - one of the highest log theme rides in the UK, Depth Charge water slide, Thunder River, Tea Cup ride, Thorpe Farm, Canada Creek Railway, Carousel Kingdom, the Magic Mill, lots of shows, and much more. There is free transport round the park by land train or water bus. The park is located one-and-three-quarter miles north of Chertsey on the A320.
Open 26 Mar-30 Oct, daily 10-6 (5 early & late season).
P ⊞ ✗ & *toilets for disabled shop* ⊗
Details not confirmed for 1995

CRAWLEY
See Charlwood

Hatchlands
EAST CLANDON
(E off A246)
☎Guildford (01483) 222482
Robert Adam's first commission was to decorate the interior of this 18th-century house, and his work can be admired in the drawing room, library and other rooms. The attractive red brick house itself was probably designed by its first owner Admiral Boscawen, and is on seven different floor levels. It is given a regular appearance from the outside by the use of false windows. In 1988 the Cobbe Collection of keyboard instruments, paintings and furniture was installed here. The garden, by Gertrude Jekyll, has been restored and new walks opened in the Repton park. Concerts are held in the gardens; please send an sae for further information.
Open 2 Apr-Oct, Tue-Thu, Sun & BH Mon 2-5.30. Last admission 5pm. (Closed Good Fri). Also open Fri in Aug. Grounds open as house. Park walks daily Apr-Oct 12.30-6.
✸*£4 (ch £2). Grounds and Park walks £1.50.*
P ✗ *licensed* & *(wheelchair available & special parking) toilets for disabled shop* ⊗
(NT)

This reconstructed windmill is just one of several buildings at the Museum of East Anglian Life showing life as it used to be.

A pair of Macaws at Birdworld bring a sudden flash of colour to the English countryside. They are among a wide range of fish and birds on display.

Birdworld & Underwaterworld
FARNHAM

Holt Pound (3m S on A325)
☎ *Bentley (01420) 22140*
Eighteen acres of garden and parkland are home to a wide variety of birds, from the tiny tanager to the great ostrich, and many rare and unusual species. There are waterfowl as well as land birds; a Sea Shore Walk and Tropical Walk; and an aquarium with tropical, freshwater and marine fish. During the breeding season there are lots of rare baby birds to be seen in the Incubation Research Station. In the Heron Theatre vistiors can meet the keepers along with some of their favourite birds. The Owls Nest bookshop sells books on wildlife. Plant lovers will enjoy the extensive gardens. There is a picnic area with covered seating and a cafeteria for cream teas etc. Children's farm and play area. Facilities for the disabled include purpose-built toilets for wheelchair users. Wheelchairs are available on loan and there are good, solid paths around the grounds. Special Events for 1995 include Aviculture Day - specialist day for people interested in keeping birds (25 June), Mad Hatters Party (24 August).
Open all year, daily from 9.30. (Closed 25 Dec).
❋*Birdworld £3.85 (ch £2.10, pen £2.95); Underwater World £1.10 (ch 55p).*
🅿 ♿ ♿ *(wheelchairs available) toilets for disabled shop* ❦

Farnham Castle Keep
FARNHAM

☎ *(01252) 713393*
The castle was started in the 11th century by Henry of Blois, Bishop of Winchester, at a convenient point on the way to London; his tower stood on the mound of the keep, which was later encased in high walls. Around the keep are a ditch and bank topped by a wall.
Open Apr-Sep, daily 10-6.
£2 (ch £1, concessions £1.50). Admission price includes a free Personal Stereo Guided Tour.
🅿 ❦
(EH)

Museum of Farnham
FARNHAM

38 West St
☎ *(01252) 715094*
Exciting displays tell the story of Farnham and its people, in this newly refurbished Grade I listed Georgian townhouse. William Cobbett memorabilia is also shown, and there is a walled garden.
Open all year, Tue-Sat 10-5. Closed Xmas-New Year.
♿ *toilets for disabled shop* ❦
Details not confirmed for 1995

Godalming Museum
GODALMING

109A High St
☎ *(01483) 426510*
The museum is housed in a 15th-century town house. Displays relate to the local history of Godalming. There is a room dedicated to the architect and gardener team Edwin Lutyens and Gertryde Jekyll; a display about George Phillips, wireless operator on the Titanic and also James Oglethorpe who founded the colony of Georgia in America. In May 1995 there will be an exhibition relating to VE Day in Godalming.
Open all year, Tue-Sat 10-5. From end Oct-Mar 10-4. (Closed 25-26 Dec). Research Library Tues & Sat 10-4. Donations.
🅿 *(behind museum)* ♿ *shop* ❦

Guildford Castle
GUILDFORD

☎ *(01483) 444702*
The three-storey ruined castle keep dates from the 12th century and gives fine views; and the castle ditch has been transformed into a colourful garden which is attractive throughout the spring and summer. Band concerts are held occasionally during the summer months, and an open-air theatre is a feature of the sumemr months.
Open: Grounds daily 8-dusk (Closed 25 Dec); Keep Apr-Sep 10.30-6.
75p (ch 35p).
🅿 *(50yds)* ♿

Guildford House Gallery
GUILDFORD

155 High St (N side of High St, opposite Sainsbury's)
☎ *(01483) 444740*
Guildford House has now reopened after the restoration. Important features of this fascinating building are the finely decorated plaster ceilings, panelled rooms, wrought iron balcony and window catches, together with the richly carved oak and elm staircase. Guildford House dates from 1660 and has been Guildford's art gallery since 1957. A changing selection from the Borough's Art Collection is on display, including pastel portraits by John Russell (1745-1806), topographical paintings and contemporary craftwork, as well as temporary exhibitions. Special events for 1995 include clebrations for the 250th anniversary of the birth of Guildford born artist John Russell RA; Guildford Festival exhibition (July); Guildford Art Society exhibition (November), The Surrey Guild of Craftsmen exhibition (December).
Open Tue-Sat 10-4.45. For details of exhibitions please apply for leaflet. Free.
P *(100 yds)* ☕ *shop* ❦

Guildford Museum
GUILDFORD

Castle Arch
☎ *(01483) 444750*
A local museum with history, archaeology and needlework displays. Various events are planned for 1994 including a Young Archaeologist's Day in July.
Open all year, Mon-Sat 11-5. (Closed 24-26 Dec & Good Fri).
♿ *toilets for disabled shop* ❦
Details not confirmed for 1995

Loseley House
GUILDFORD

(2.5m SW, off A3 onto B3000)
☎ *(01483) 304440*
Familiar to many from yoghurt pots, the Elizabethan house has notable panelling, decorated ceilings, a carved chalk chimneypiece and tapestries. There are trailer rides to the farm to see the famous Jersey herd and many rare breeds of animals. Special events for 1995 include: Craft Fair (2-4 June), Performing Arts Concert (21 July), Classic Car Show and Country Fair (5-6 August).
Open 1 May & 3 May-30 Sep, Wed-Sat 2-5.
❋*House & grounds: £3.50 (ch £2). Grounds: £1.50 (ch 50p). Prices under review.*
🅿 ✕ *licensed* ♿ *(wheelchair available, parking outside house) toilets for disabled shop* ❦

Winkworth Arboretum
HASCOMBE

(1m NW on B2130)
☎ *(01483) 208477*
This lovely woodland covers a hillside of nearly 100 acres, with fine views over the North Downs. The best times to visit are May, for the azaleas, bluebells and other flowers, and October for the autumn colours.
Open all year, daily during daylight hours.
❋*£2.*
🅿 *shop (Apr-14 Nov, Tue-Sun 11-5.30) (NT)*

Old Mill
OUTWOOD

Outwood Common (on A25)
☎ *Smallfield (01342) 843458*
This award-winning example of a post-mill dates from 1665 and is the oldest working windmill in England and one of the best preserved in existence. Standing 400ft above sea level, it is surrounded by common land and National Trust property. Ducks, goats and horses wander freely in the grounds, and there is a small museum and a collection of old coaches. Special events planned for 1995 include Morris dancing, clog dancing and a village show.
Open Etr Sun-last Sun in Oct, Sun & BH Mons only 2-6. Other days & evening tours by arrangement. School parties for educational visits.
Prices under review.
🅿 ♿ *toilets for disabled shop*

Painshill Park
PAINSHILL PARK

(on A245)
☎ *Cobham (01932) 868113*
Painshill Park, a fascinating 18th-century landscape created by the Hon Charles Hamilton, was well-maintained until World War II. In 1981 a charitable trust was formed with the task of restoring this beautiful garden. Visitors can take a circuit walk through a series of delightful scenes. The huge lake, filled by the power of a massive water wheel, meanders through the garden, giving a perfect setting for a Gothic temple, ruined abbey, and a Turkish tent. The magical crystal grotto, hidden among the foliage on one of the islands, is approached across an elegant Chinese bridge. Beyond the lake, through an alpine valley, a castellated, Gothic tower can be seen through the trees. Hamilton was a knowledgeable plantsman and some of his unusual trees and shrubs have survived. Many new shrub beds have been planted with appropriate plant material giving an unusual insight into 18th-century plantings. A series of lectures/workshops on 18-th century architecture and gardens are planned for 1995. Please telephone for details.
Open Sun only, 9 Apr-15 Oct, 11-5. Free optional guided tours. (Tours last one and a half to two hours). Pre-booked parties (10+) & school groups on any other day all year.
£3.50 (ch 5-16 £2.50, pen, students & UB40's £3). Party 10+. Special arrangements for school parties, contact Education Trust (01932) 866743.
🅿 ♿ ♿ *(2 wheelchairs available) toilets for disabled shop* ❦

Priory Museum
REIGATE

Bell St (off A217)
☎(01737) 245065
Originally founded before 1200, this
house was later converted to a Tudor
mansion of which the hall fireplace is a
notable feature. Stucco painting of the
18th century changed the face of the
building, now used as a school. The small
museum has changing exhibitions. There
are 'hands-on' facilities.
Open Wed & Sat 2-4.30.
🅿 ♿ *("Hands On" facilities) shop* ⊘
Details not confirmed for 1995

Rural Life Centre
TILFORD

Reeds Rd (on A287)
☎*Frensham (01252) 792300 & 795571*
The Old Kiln houses a collection of farm
implements and machinery, and
examples of the craft and trades allied to
farming may be seen. The larger exhibits
are displayed in the pleasant garden and
woodland surroundings which cover
some ten acres. In the old farm buildings
are a smithy and a wheelwright's shop,
hand tools and other artefacts. There is
also an arboretum and woodland walk.
Special events for 1995 include VE Day
celebrations (7 May), 'Rustic Sunday'
with craft demonstrations and sideshows
(30 July).
Open Apr-Sep, Wed-Sun & BH 11-6.
£3 (ch £1.50 & pen £2.50).
🅿 ⛽ ♿ *(3 wheelchairs for use) toilets for
disabled shop*

Clandon Park
WEST CLANDON

(on A247)
☎*Guildford (01483) 222482*
An 18th-century house, built by Leoni for
the 2nd Lord Onslow, with stunning
plasterwork and a fine collection of
furniture and pictures. Also on display is a
collection of Meissen Italian comedy
figures and the Gubbay collection of
porcelain, furniture and needlework. This
is also home to The Queens Royal Surrey
regimental museum. There is a garden
with parterre, grotto and Maori House.
Concerts are held in the Marble Hall,
please write for details.
*Open Apr-29 Oct, daily except Thu & Fri
(but open Good Fri) 1.30-5.30, also BH
Mon 11-5.30. Last admission 5pm.
Garden also open weekends in Mar.*
✻*House, Garden & Museum £4 (ch £2).
Family ticket £10.*
🅿 ✗ *licensed ♿ (braille guide & disabled
parking) toilets for disabled shop* ⊘
(NT)

Wisley Garden
WISLEY

(on A3)
☎*Guildford (01483) 224234*
These experimental gardens of the Royal
Horticultural Society were established in
1904 in Wisley village. The property now
covers over 240 acres, of which half is
devoted to garden, and some to
vegetables. The gardens have a wide
variety of trees, shrubs and plants, many
of which are unusual in Britain, and
planted in their correct setting. There are
also greenhouses and specialist gardens.
The Royal Horticultural Society offer an
advisory service at Wisley.
*Open all year, Mon-Sat 10-7 or dusk
(4.30pm Jan, Nov & Dec). Sun members
only. (Closed 25 Dec). Glasshouses close
at 4.15 or sunset Mon-Fri.
£4.70 (ch 6-16 £1.75).*
🅿 ⛽ ✗ *licensed ♿ (free wheelchairs)
toilets for disabled shop garden
centre* ⊘

TYNE & WEAR

Bedes World & St Paul's Church
Museum
JARROW

Church Bank
☎0191-489 2106

The 37 books, many of several volumes,
which the Venerable Bede wrote for his
students represented the collected
knowledge of his time in science,
literature, philosophy and the arts. His
most famous book is the 'Ecclesiastical
History of the English People', and he
also made the first translation of St
John's Gospel into English. St Paul's
Church was part of the monastery where
this impressive man lived from the age of
about fifteen until his death in 735; with
St Peter's, Monkwearmouth, the other
half of the monastery, it is now regarded
as the 'cradle of English learning' and an
important Christian centre.
The chancel incorporates one of the
churches where Bede worshipped and
features some Saxon stained glass. Very
little remains of the original monastery but
archaeological finds from excavations of
the site are housed in Bedes World, where
the story of this important monastery, and
its revered inhabitant, is told. The Museum,
which dates to about 1800, also has an
exhibition on its own occupants; an audio-
visual programme, temporary exhibitions,
tea room, craft shop, herb garden and
Tourist Information Centre. Special events
including concerts, day courses, workshops
and Anglo-Saxon feasts take place
throughout the year. A new museum and
Anglo-Saxon landscape are being
developed on land adjacent to the present
museum to show what life was like in 7th
and 8th century Northumbria.
*Open all year, Apr-Oct, Tue-Sat & BH
Mons 10-5.30, Sun 2.30-5.30; Nov-Mar,
Tue-Sat 11-4.30, Sun 2.30-5.30. (Closed
25 Dec-1 Jan). Church open Apr-Oct 10-
4.30; Nov-Mar 11-4.30 Mon-Sat & Sun
2.30-4.30.*
🅿 ⛽ ♿ *toilets for disabled shop* ⊘
Details not confirmed for 1995

Hancock Museum
NEWCASTLE UPON TYNE

Barras Bridge
☎0191-222 7418
One of the finest museums of natural
history in the country, the Hancock
Museum houses geological exhibits and
John Hancock's magnificent collection of
birds. There is a new Gallery of Ancient
Egypt - Land of the Pharaohs.
Open all year, Mon-Sat, 10-5, Sun 2-5.
✻*£1.80 (concession's £1). Prices vary
with special exhibitions.*
🅿 ⛽ ♿ *toilets for disabled shop* ⊘

Laing Art Gallery
NEWCASTLE UPON TYNE

Higham Pl
☎0191-232 7734 & 0191-232 6989
British paintings and watercolours from
the 18th-century to the present day are on
display here, with works by Burne-Jones,
Reynolds, Turner and others, including the
Northumberland artist John Martin. A
pioneering interactive display called Art on
Tyneside shows paintings, costume, silver
etc in period settings. There is also a
programme of temporary exhibitions.
*Open all year, Mon-Sat 10-5, Sun 2-5.
(Closed 25 Dec).*
⛽ ♿ *toilets for disabled shop* ⊘
Details not confirmed for 1995

Museum of Antiquities
NEWCASTLE UPON TYNE

The University
☎0191-222 7844
Artefacts from north east England from
prehistoric times to AD 1600 are on
display here. The principal museum for
Hadrian's Wall, this collection includes
models of the wall, life-size Roman
soldiers and a recently refurbished
reconstruction of the Temple of Mithras.
There is also a museum book shop.
*Open all year, daily (ex Sun), 10-5 (Closed
Good Fri, 24-26 Dec & 1 Jan).
Free.*
🅿 *(400 yds)* ♿ *shop* ⊘

Newcastle Discovery
NEWCASTLE UPON TYNE

Blandford Square (off A6115/A6125)
☎0191-232 6789
Newcastle Discovery offers something

The magnificent plant specimens are at the experimental gardens of the Royal
Horticultural Society at Wisley which covers over 240 acres.

for everyone. There are displays covering
fashion, military history, maritime
splendours and scientific curiosities.
Local history is covered in the fascinating
Great City story. In summer 1995 a new
gallery will open housing *Turbinia*, once
the world's fastest ship.
*Open all year, Mon-Sat 10-5.30. (Closed
25-26 Dec & 1 Jan & Good Fri).
Free.*
🅿 *(charged)* ⛽ ♿ *toilets for disabled
shop* ⊘

Gibside
ROWLANDS GILL

(6m SW of Gateshead, on B6314)
☎(01207) 542255
The important early 18th-century
landscaped park contains a chapel, an
outstanding example of Palladian
architecture, built to a design by James
Paine as the mausoleum for members of
the Bowes family. It stands at one end of
the Great Walk of Turkey oaks, looking
towards the column of British Liberty.
Walks have views to the ruined hall,
orangery and other estate buildings.
National Trust centenary events for 1995
include Young Musician's Festival (17
June), Midsummer Music (24 June),
Flower Festival (7-9 July). Free entry day
13 September.
*Open Apr-Oct, daily (ex Mon, open BH
Mon's) 11-5. Last admission 4.30pm.
£2.80. Party.*
🅿 ⛽ ♿ *(Stairclimber at chapel braille
guide) shop* ⊘ *(ex on leads)*
(NT)

Arbeia Roman Fort & Museum
SOUTH SHIELDS

Baring St
☎0191-456 1369
In South Shields town are the extensive
remains of Arbeia, a 2nd-century Roman
fort. It was the supply base for the
Roman army's campaign against
Scotland and was occupied for most of
300 years. The remains include fort
defences, stone granaries, gateways, the
headquarters, tile kilns and latrines. On
the site of the west gate is a full-scale
simulation of a Roman gateway with
interior scenes of life at the fort. The

museum exhibits site finds and gives
background information. Archaeological
excavations are in progress throughout
the year.
*Open all year, Tue-Fri 10-5.30, Sat 10-
4.30. Sun (Etr-Sep only 2-5), also BH
Mon.
Free.*
🅿 ♿ *shop*

South Shields Museum & Art
Gallery
SOUTH SHIELDS

Ocean Rd
☎0191-456 8740
The museum shows the history and
natural history of South Shields, and the
Catherine Cookson Gallery reflects the
life and environment of the hugely
popular, local-born author. There is a
programme of temporary exhibitions.
*Open all year, Tue-Fri 10-5.30, Sat 10-
4.30, Sun 2-5 & BH Mon.
Free.*
P *(500 yds)* ♿ *toilets for disabled shop* ⊘

Grindon Museum
SUNDERLAND

Grindon Ln
☎0191-514 1235
The museum specialises in Victorian and
Edwardian period interiors. There are
several rooms, a chemist's shop and a
dentist's surgery.
*Open all year, Mon-Wed & Fri 9.30-12.30,
Sat 9.30-12 & 1.15-4; (Closed Thu, BH &
Sat prior to BH). Opening hours under
review.
Free.*
🅿 ⊘

Monkwearmouth Station Museum
SUNDERLAND

North Bridge St
☎0191-567 7075
The transport museum is housed in a
former station - one of the handsomest
anywhere. It was built in 1848 when the
railway baron George Hudson was the
local MP. The booking office, platforms
and footbridge have all been restored and
there is an outdoor display of rolling
stock. Inside, the 'Going Places' display
shows how transport has affected the

➤

The ruins of Tynemouth Priory stands on a headland at the mouth of the River Tyne. It was a Benedictine priory founded in 1090.

everyday lives of Sunderland people. Thomas the Tank Engine's Great Railway Show will be on display until 8 May 1995.
Open all year, Tue-Fri 10-5.30, Sat 10-4.30, Sun 2-5. (Closed Mon ex BHs). Opening hours under review.
Free.
P & toilets for disabled shop ⊗

Museum & Art Gallery
SUNDERLAND
Borough Rd
☎0191-514 1235
The museum has a wide range of displays, ranging from the wildlife and geology of the north-east to paintings. The 'Sunderland Story' displays the city's history from prehistoric times and there are galleries showing the products of the well-known local glass and pottery industries. There is also a varied programme of temporary exhibitions. A new display 'And Ships Were Born' celebrates Sunderland's once prominent position as the largest shipbuilding town in the world. It takes the visitor deep into the heart of a shipbuilder's yard to look at the history of shipbuilding, design, craftsmanship and working conditions, to bring the experience of shipbuilding to life.
Open all year, Tue-Fri 10-5.30, Sat 10-4, Sun 2-5. (Closed Mon ex BHs). Opening hours under review.
Free.
P (150 yds) ⬤ & toilets for disabled shop ⊗

Tynemouth Castle & Priory
TYNEMOUTH
☎0191-257 1090
The Benedictine priory was built on the site of a Saxon monastery in 1090. The substantial ruins of the priory are enclosed within the castle walls, built during the 11th and 14th centuries. Entrance is through the gatehouse, and there are parts of the curtain wall, the church nave and the chancel to be seen.
Open all year, Apr-Sep, daily 10-6; Oct, 10-4; Nov-Mar, Wed-Sun 10-4 or dusk if earlier. Closed 24-26 Dec & 1 Jan.
£1.30 (ch 70p, concessions £1).
& shop ⊗
(EH)

Washington Old Hall
WASHINGTON
☎0191-416 6879
The home of George Washington's ancestors from 1183 to 1613, the Old Hall was originally an early medieval manor, but was rebuilt in the 17th century. The house has been restored and filled with period furniture. The property was given to the National Trust in 1956. There will be celebrations to mark American Independence Day on 2 July. Free entry day 13 September 1995.

Open Apr-Oct, daily (closed Fri & Sat) 11-5. Last admission 4.30pm.
£2.30. Party.
P ⬤ shop ⊗
(NT)

Wildfowl & Wetlands Trust
WASHINGTON
(signposted off A195 & A1231)
☎0191-416 5454
This Wildfowl Trust park is a welcome refuge on the north bank of the River Wear, between Newcastle and Sunderland. The 100-acre park has over 100 species of wildfowl, which form one of the largest collections in the world. The attractive landscaped park includes 70 acres for wild birds, which can be viewed from several public hides. The Visitor Centre, housed in an attractive log cabin, also has a viewing gallery and large picture windows giving excellent views over the main collection area. The centre provides information on the birds, talks and guided walks as well as a souvenir shop and bookshop.
Open all year, daily 9.30-5 or dusk if earlier. (Closed 24-25 Dec).
❋£3.50 (ch £1.75, pen £2.65). Party.
P ⬤ & (lowered windows in certain hides) toilets for disabled shop ⊗

Souter Lighthouse
WHITBURN
☎0191-529 3161
This 150ft-high lighthouse was opened by Trinity House in 1871 and contains a bi-optic light, still in its original condition, which was the first reliable electrically powered lighthouse light. The Engine and Battery Rooms are all in working order and are included in the guided tour, along with the light tower, museum cottage and video. There is an education room and a restaurant. Free entry day 13 September 1995.
Open Apr, wknds & Wed, Good Friday & Easter Mon 11-5. May-Sep, weekdays (ex Fri) 10.30-4.30, wknds 11-5. Last admission 30 mins before closing time.
£2.30. Party.
P ✕ & toilets for disabled shop ⊗
(NT)

WARWICKSHIRE

Ragley Hall
ALCESTER
(1.5m SW, on A435)
☎(01789) 762090
Ragley Hall is set in four hundred acres of parkland and gardens. The Great Hall contains some of England's finest Baroque plasterwork designed by James Gibbs. Graham Rust's mural *The Temptation* can be seen on the south

staircase. Ample picnic areas beside the lake, as well as an adventure playground, maze and woodland walks. Events planned for 1995 include horse trials (7-8 May), gardens and craft fair (3-4 June), open-air Othello (24 June), symphony concert with fireworks and lasers (5 August), art exhibition (16-24 September).
Open Apr-1 Oct, Tue-Thu, Sat, Sun & BH Mon; Jul-Aug park & garden open everyday. House 11-5, park & gardens 10-6.
House (including garden & park) £4.50 (ch £2.50, pen £4).
P ⬤ & (lift to first floor) toilets for disabled shop ⊗ (ex in park & gardens)

Baddesley Clinton House
BADDESLEY CLINTON
(0.75m W off A4141)
☎(01564) 783294
A romantically-sited medieval moated house, dating from the 14th century, that has changed very little since 1634. With family portraits, priest holes, chapel, garden, ponds and lake walk.
Open 4 Mar-Sep, Wed-Sun & BH Mon 2-6, Grounds from 12.30; Oct Wed-Sun 12.30-4.30 (Closed Good Fri). Last admissions to house 30 mins before closing.
£4.20. Family ticket £11.60. Grounds only £2.10.
P ✕ licensed & (wheelchairs available) toilets for disabled shop ⊗
(NT)

Charlecote Park
CHARLECOTE
(on B4086)
☎Stratford-upon-Avon (01789) 470277
The home of the Ivay family since 1247, the present house was built in the 1550s and later visited by Queen Elizabeth I. The park was landscaped by 'Capability' Brown and has a herd of red and fallow deer, reputedly poached by Shakespeare and a flock of Jacob sheep first introduced in 1756. The principal rooms are decorated in Elizabethan Revival style.
Open Apr-Oct, Fri-Tue 11-6, (last admission 5).(Closed Good Fri, house closed 1-2). Evening guided tours for pre-booked parties Mon May-Sep 7.30-9.30.
£4 Family ticket £11.
P ✕ licensed & (Braille guides available) toilets for disabled shop ⊗
(NT)

Coughton Court
COUGHTON
(2m N,on E side of A435)
☎Alcester (01789) 762435
An impressive central gatehouse dating from 1530. During the Civil War this formerly moated and mainly Elizabethan house was attacked by both Parliamentary and Royalist forces, it suffered damage again in James II's reign. The contents of the Gatehouse

south wing include some notable furniture, porcelain, portraits and relics of the Throckmorton family who have lived here since 1409. Two churches, tranquil lake, riverside walk and newly created formal gardens.
Open Apr & Oct, Sat & Sun 12-5 (all BH Mon incl Etr Mon 12-5). 17-19 Apr 12-5 (Closed Good Fri); May-Sep, Sat-Wed 12-5. Grounds open 11-5.30 (5pm Oct). Last admssion 30 mins before closing.
£4.50. Family ticket £12. Grounds £2.50.
P ✕ & shop ⊗
(NT)

Farnborough Hall
FARNBOROUGH
(.5m W off A423)
☎(01295) 690202
A classical mid 18th-century stone house, home of the Holbech family for 300 years; notable plasterwork, the entrance hall, staircase and two principal rooms are shown. The grounds contain charming 18th-century temples, a 1/4-mile terrace walk and an obelisk.
House, grounds & terrace walk open Apr-Sep, Wed & Sat, 7/8 May 2-6pm. Terrace walk Thu & Fri only, 2-6. Last admission 5.30pm.
House, Grounds & Terrace walk £2.70. Garden & Terrace walk £1.50. Terrace walk only (Thu & Fri) £1.
P & ⊗
(NT)

Heritage Motor Centre
GAYDON
(Exit M40 at junc 12 and take B4100)
☎(01926) 641188
The largest purpose-designed road transport museum in the UK housing the biggest collection of historic British cars anywhere in the world. Far more than a traditional car museum, the Centre has been specifically designed with family visitors in mind. Displays include Corgi and Lucas Museum collections, 1930s reconstruction garage, Engineering Gallery, Art and the Automobile, and Fashion and Motoring. Other attractions on the 65-acre site include a children's adventure playground, compact nature reserve, unique Land Rover shuttle ride and spectacular four-wheel-drive demonstration circuit. There are special activities for families and children at weekends and during school holidays. Special exhibitions and events are held throughout the year.
Open all year, Apr-Oct, daily 10-6; Nov-Mar. daily 10-4.30. (Closed 25 & 26 Dec).
❋£5.50 (ch 5-16 £3.50, under 5 free, & pen £4.50). Family ticket £15.
P ⬤ ✕ & toilets for disabled shop ⊗
See advertisement on page 148

Kenilworth Castle
KENILWORTH
☎(01926) 52078
The castle began life as a 12th-century wooden fortress but rapidly gained importance as first Norman, then Plantagenet and finally Tudor monarchs played a part in its development. John of Gaunt transformed it into a grand castle and in the 16th century it became the property of the newly created Earl of Leicester, John Dudley. Dudley made many further additions including the long barn and gatehouse; it was after his death that the castle went into decline, until finally Cromwell ordered Kenilworth to be demolished. Today it stands as a noble ruin, although the 12th-century keep is still impressive and the outline of John of Gaunt's great hall is recognisable.
Open all year, Apr-Sep, daily 10-6; Oct-Mar, daily 10-4. Closed 24-26 Dec & 1 Jan.
£2 (ch £1, concessions £1.50).
P
(EH)

Warwick District Council Art Gallery & Museum
LEAMINGTON SPA
Av Rd
☎(01926) 426559
Ceramics including Delft, Wedgwood, Whieldon, Worcester and Derby can be

seen, with 18th-century glass. The art gallery specialises in British, Dutch and Flemish paintings of the 16th to 20th centuries and a separate gallery is devoted to local history. A programme if workshops by artists and craft workers, and temporary exhibitions are planned for 1995.
Open all year, Mon, Tue & Thu-Sat 10-1 & 2-5. Also Thu evenings 6-8. (Closed Wed & Sun, Good Fri, 25-26 Dec & 1 Jan).
Free.
& shop

Ash End House Farm "The Childrens Farm"
MIDDLETON
Middleton Ln, Middleton (signposted from A4091)
☎0121-329 3240
Ash End House is a children's farm, specifically set up with children in mind. They love to learn and experience new things, and what better way than when having fun. Children's guided tours give them a unique opportunity to get close to friendly farm animals. A host of animals from the gigantic shire horse, through to hatching tiny chicks and fluffy ducklings can be seen daily. There are also rare breeds such as Bagot goats, Saddleback pigs and Soay sheep. Special events are held during the year.
Open daily 10-5.30 or dusk in winter. (Closed 25 & 26 Dec).
P ☂ & toilets for disabled shop
Details not confirmed for 1995

Middleton Hall
MIDDLETON
(on A4091)
☎(01827) 283095
Once the home of two great 17th-century naturalists, Francis Willoughby and John Ray, the Hall shows several architectural styles, from c.1300 to an 11-bay Georgian west wing. The grounds include a nature reserve, lake, meadow, orchard and woodland - all Sites of Special Scientific Interest - plus two walled gardens. This is also the home of

the Middleton Hall Craft Centre, with craft studios and workshops in the former stable block. Events take place throughout the year including drama and vintage cars; a programme is available on application to the Hon Secretary.
Open Apr-Oct, Sun & BH's 2-5.30.
✱£1.20 (ch 14 & pen 60p)
P ☂ & (lightweight wheelchair available) toilets for disabled shop ⊞

Arbury Hall
NUNEATON
(2m SW)
☎(01203) 382804
The 16th-century Elizabethan house, Gothicised in the 18th century, has been the home of the Newdegate family for over 450 years. It is the finest complete example of Gothic revival architecture in existance, and contains pictures, furniture, and beautiful plasterwork ceilings. The 17th-century stable block, with a central doorway by Wren, houses the tearooms and a large collection of veteran bicycles. There are landscaped gardens with woodland paths and lakes. Special events for 1995 include a motor transport spectacular and spring and summer craft fairs (dates to be announced).
Open Etr-Sep 2-5.30 (last admission 5.10pm). Hall Sun & BH Mon. Garden Sun & Mon. For other opening days & times, contact the Administrator.
£3.50 (ch £2). Gardens only £2 (ch £1).
P ☂ & shop (ex in grounds)

Packwood House
PACKWOOD HOUSE
(on unclass road off A34)
☎Lapworth (01564) 782024
Built as a modest 16th-century farmhouse, Packwood House was extended during the following century and outbuildings were added to make the carefully restored building we see today. Tapestry, needlework and furniture are displayed and Jacobean panelling may be seen. The most notable feature of the gardens is the layout of 17th-century yews clipped to represent Christ's

Sermon on the Mount. Special events for 1995 include open air concert (27 May), open air picnic entertainment (17 June), open air Midsummer Nights' Dream (25 August).
Open Apr-Sep, Wed-Sun & BH Mon 2-6; Oct Wed-Sun 12.30-4.30 (Closed Good Fri). Last admission 30 mins before closing.
✱£3.50 (ch £1.75). Family ticket £9.60. Garden only £2 (ch £1).
P & (wheelchairs available) toilets for disabled shop
(NT)

The James Gilbert Rugby Football Museum
RUGBY
5 Saint Matthew's St
☎(01788) 542426
An intriguing collection of Rugby football memorabilia is housed in the shop in which Gilbert's have made their world famous Rugby balls since 1842. From Monday-Friday 10am-5pm and Saturday 10am-2pm, watch a craftsman at work, hand-stitching the footballs. Situated near to Rugby School and its famous playing field.
Open all year, Mon-Fri 10-5, Sat 10-4. Phone for holiday opening times.
Free.
P (500 yds) & shop

Ryton Organic Gardens
RYTON-ON-DUNSMORE
(on B4029)
☎Coventry (01203) 303517
The gardens are the home of the Henry Doubleday Research Association, which researches organic gardening. The whole site is landscaped with thousands of young trees, and every plant is grown organically. Visitors can stroll around the herb garden, the bee garden, fruit beds, vegetable gardens, shrub borders and many other attractions, all showing how the organic gardener can use plants and planting schemes effectively. Displays on composting and safe pest control. There is a garden centre selling organically grown products, seeds and equipment, and also an Education Centre with exhibitions, courses and special events. For children there is a Swiss Chalet and play area and rare breeds of livestock during summer months.
Open all year 10-5.30. (Closed Xmas).
£2.50 (ch £1.25, students, pen, disabled & UB40 £1.75). Family ticket £6.50. Party 14+
P ✗ licensed & toilets for disabled shop garden centre

Anne Hathaway's Cottage
SHOTTERY
☎Stratford-upon-Avon (01789) 292100
Before her marriage to William Shakespeare, Anne Hathaway lived in this substantial 12-roomed thatched Tudor farmhouse with her prosperous yeoman family. The house now shows many aspects of domestic life in 16th-century England, and has a lovely garden and Shakespeare tree garden.
Open all year, 20 Mar-19 Oct Mon-Sat 9-5.30, Sun 9.30-5.30; Jan-19 Mar & 20 Oct-Dec Mon-Sat 9.30-4, Sun 10-4. (Closed 24-26 Dec, Good Fri am & 1 Jan am).
£2.30 (ch £1.10). Inclusive ticket to all 5 Shakespearian properties £8 (ch £3.60, pen & students £7 Family £21). School and student party rates for groups visiting all five properties.
P (charged) ☂ ✗ licensed shop garden centre

STRATFORD-UPON-AVON
At the very heart of England lies Stratford-upon-Avon, the birthplace of our most celebrated playwright, William Shakespeare. Once a charming market town, it is now bustling with visitors, not only attracted by the lovely timbered houses, Shakespeare's home and the old-world gardens along the banks of the River Avon, but also to the famous

Royal Shakespeare Theatre where his plays are regularly performed by some of the world's greatest actors.

Hall's Croft
STRATFORD-UPON-AVON
Old Town
☎(01789) 292107
A Tudor house with outstanding furniture and paintings where Shakespeare's daughter Susanna, and her husband, Dr John Hall, probably lived before moving to New Place on the dramatist's death. There is an exhibition on Tudor medicine, and fine walled gardens can also be seen.
Open all year, 20 Mar-19 Oct Mon-Sat 9.30-5, Sun 10-5; Jan-19 Mar & 20 Oct-Dec Mon-Sat 10-4, Sun 10.30-4. (Closed Good Fri am, 24-26 Dec & 1 Jan am).
£1.90 (ch 90p). Shakespeare's Town Heritage Trail (inc 3 town properties) £5.50 (ch £2.50, pen & students £5). Inlcusive ticket to all 5 Shakespearian properties: £8 (ch £3.60, pen & students £7 Family £21). School & student party rates for groups visiting all 5 properties.
P ☂ ✗ & toilets for disabled shop

New Place / Nash's House
STRATFORD-UPON-AVON
Chapel St
☎(01789) 292325
Only the foundations remain of the house where Shakespeare spent the last five years of his life and died in 1616. The house was destroyed in 1759, but the picturesque garden has been planted as an Elizabethan knot garden. There is a small museum of furniture and local history in the adjacent Nash's House.
Open all year, 20 Mar-19 Oct Mon-Sat 9.30-5, Sun 10-5; Jan-19 Mar & 20 Oct-Dec Mon-Sat 10-4, Sun 10.30-4. (Closed Good Fri am, 24-26 Dec & 1 Jan am).
✱£1.90 (ch 90p) Shakespeare Town Heritage Trail (inc 3 town properties) £5.50 (ch £2.50, pen & students £5, Family £14). Inclusive tickets for all 5 Shakesperian properties £8 (ch £3.60, pen & students £7, Family £21). School & student party rates for groups visiting all 5 properties.
P & toilets for disabled shop

Royal Shakespeare Company Collection
STRATFORD-UPON-AVON
Royal Shakespeare Theatre, Waterside
☎(01789) 296655
The RSC collection is housed in the original Victorian building which was part of Charles Flower's Shakespeare Memorial, opened in 1879, comprising Theatre, Paintings and Sculpture Gallery, Library and Reading Room, the latter were not destroyed when the Theatre was burnt down in 1926. The permanent exhibition in the RSC Collection contains over 500 items including costumes, props, pictures, sculptures, photographs and sound recordings illustrating the changes in staging from Shakespeare's time to the work of the RSC today. Temporary exhibitions include the work of the current artist(s) in residence, and in 1995 a new temporary exhibition will include costumes from past productions relating to the RSC Stratford 1995 season of plays.
Open all year, Mon-Sat 9.15-end evening interval, Sun 12-4.30 (Nov-Mar Sun 11-3.30).(Closed 25 Dec).Theatre tours usually Mon-Fri (ex matinee days), 1.30 & 5.30, Sun 12.30, 1.45, 2.45 & 3.45 (Nov-Mar, 11.30, 12.30, 1.45 & 2.45).
✱Exhibition £2 (ch, pen & students £1.50). Family ticket £4. Theatre Tours £4 (ch, pen & students £3) - advisable to book in advance.
P (charged) ☂ ✗ licensed & toilets for disabled shop

Shakespeare's Birthplace
STRATFORD-UPON-AVON
Henley St
☎(01789) 204016
Shakespeare was born in the timber-framed house in 1564. It contains

→

Coughton Court has been home for the Throckmorton family since 1409. The house contains notable furniture, porcelain and paintings.

numerous exhibits of the Elizabethan period and Shakespeare memorabilia. The annual Shakespeare Birthday Celebrations will be held on 22 April 1995 and will include a procession, flag unfurling ceremony and street entertainment.
Open all year, 20 Mar-19 Oct Mon-Sat 9-5.30, Sun 9.30-5.30; Jan-19 Mar & 20 Oct-Dec Mon-Sat 9.30-4, Sun 10-4. (Closed Good Fri am, 24-26 Dec & 1 Jan am).
£2.75 (ch £1.30). Shakespeare's Town Heritage Trail (inc 3 town properties) £5.50 (ch £2.50, pen & students £5, Family £14). Inclusive tickets to all 5 Shakespearian properties £8 (ch £3.60, pen & students £7, Family £21). School & student party rates for groups visiting all 5 properties.
P *(100 yds)* & *toilets for disabled shop* ✍

The Teddy Bear Museum
STRATFORD-UPON-AVON
19 Greenhill St
☎ *(01789) 293160*
Ten settings in a house which dates from Shakespeare's time, are devoted to bears of all shapes and sizes. Many very old bears are displayed and there are also mechanical and musical bears. Some of the bears belong to famous people, for example, Jeffrey Archer and Barbara Cartland, or are famous in their own right, such as the original Sooty and Fozzie bear.
Open all year, daily 9.30-6. Closed 25 & 26 Dec.
£1.95 (ch 95p). Family ticket £5.50 Party 20+.
P *(30yds & 200 yds)* & *shop* ✍

World of Shakespeare
STRATFORD-UPON-AVON
13 Waterside
☎ *(01789) 269190*
Travel back in time to 1576 when William Shakespeare was a boy of 11. From the centre of a darkened auditorium

experience the drama, splendour and spectacle of life in Elizabethan times brought to life by dramatic lighting and sound techniques, original music and audio-visual effects.
Open all year, daily 9.05-5. Shows every hour & half hour. (Closed 25 Dec).
£4 (ch, students & pen £3). Family ticket £10. Party 10+.
P *(300 yds)* & *toilets for disabled shop* ✍

Upton House
UPTON HOUSE
(on A422)
☎ *Edge Hill (01295) 87266*
The house, built of mellow local stone, dates from 1695, but the chief attractions are the outstanding collections in the house itself. They include paintings by English and Continental Old Masters, Brussels tapestries, Sèvres porcelain, Chelsea figures and 18th-century furniture. The gardens have terraces, herbaceous borders, fruit, vegetable and water gardens and lakes.
Open Apr-Oct, Sat-Wed & BH Mon. 2-6. (last admission 5.30).
£4.60. Family ticket £12.60. Garden only £2.30. Party.
P 🍴 & *toilets for disabled shop* ✍
(NT)

Lord Leycester Hospital
WARWICK
High St
☎ *(01926) 492797*
These lovely half-timbered buildings were built in the late 14th century and adapted into almshouses by the Earl of Leycester in 1571. The Hospital is still a home for ex-servicemen and their wives. Originally it was built as a Guildhouse and the old Guildhall, Great Hall, Chapel and courtyard remain. The buildings also house the Regimental Museum of the Queen's Own Hussars. The historic Master's Garden will open on Saturday afternoons from April to December.
Open all year, Tue-Sun & BH's 10-5 (4pm

in winter). (Closed Good Fri & 25 Dec).
£2.25 (ch 14 £1, pen £1.50). Party 20+.
P ✗ & *shop*

Warwick Castle
WARWICK
☎ *(01926) 408000*
For centuries Warwick Castle was home to the mighty Earls of Warwick. Richard III once owned the Castle and started new fortifications before meeting his death at the Battle of Bosworth in 1485. Later, the Castle was a Parliamentarian stronghold during the English Civil War. The Castle's medieval history comes alive in 'Kingmaker - A preparation for battle', where you'll experience the dramatic sights, smells and sounds of the household making ready. Set in 1471, these scenes recreate a time during the Wars of the Roses when Richard Neville, Earl of Warwick, known as 'Kingmaker', prepared his army within the safe walls of Warwick Castle.
As history progressed, the military importance of the Castle declined and the main living quarters were converted into a residence of the grandest style. The State Rooms, including the magnificent Great Hall, contain an outstanding collection of arms, armour, furniture and paintings. 'A Royal Weekend Party' recreates an actual Victorian house party in the summer of 1898 with a young Winston Churchill and the future King Edward VII in attendance. Peacocks roam the 60 acres of beautiful grounds and gardens, landscaped by 'Capability' Brown during the 1750s. Special events for 1995 include Medieval Weekend (24-25 June), Jousting Weekends (19-20 August and 2-3 September) Arms and Armour Week (21-29 October).
Open daily 10-6 (5pm 29 Oct-Mar, 7pm Aug wknds & BH). Closed 25 Dec.
❋*£7.75 (ch 4-16 £4.75 & pen £5.50). Family ticket £19.95. Party 20+*
P 🍴 ✗ *licensed* & *(free admission to*

wheelchair bound visitors) toilets for disabled shop garden centre ✍

Warwickshire Yeomanry Museum
WARWICK
The Court House Vaults, Jury St
☎ *(01926) 492212*
After a great fire in 1694, the court house was rebuilt between 1725 and 1728 in a style that befitted the wealthy merchants of the town. In the vaults there is now a museum displaying militaria from the county Yeomanry, dating from 1794 to 1945. It includes regimental silver, some very fine paintings, uniforms and weapons. A small room in the cellars is devoted to Warwick Town Museum.
Open Good Fri-end Sep, Fri, Sat & Sun & BHs 10-1 & 2-4. Other times by prior arrangement.
Donations
P *shop* ✍ 🚼

Mary Arden's House and the Shakespeare Countryside Museum
WILMCOTE
(3m NW off A34)
☎ *Stratford-upon-Avon (01789) 293455*
Mary Arden was William Shakespeare's mother, and this picturesque, half-timbered Tudor house was her childhood home. The house is the main historic feature of an extensive complex of farm buildings which house displays of farming and country life, including a remarkable dovecote, a smithy and cooper's workshop. Daily demonstrations by The Heart of England Falconry. Rare breeds, duck pond and field walk.
Open all year, 20 Mar-19 Oct Mon-Sat 9.30-5, Sun 10-5; Jan-19 Mar & 20 Oct-Dec, Mon-Sat 10-4, Sun 1.30-4. (Closed Good Fri am, 24-26 Dec & 1 Jan am).
£3.20 (ch £1.40). Family ticket £8. Inclusive ticket to all 5 Shakesperian properties £8 (ch £3.60, pen & students £7, Family £21). School & student party rates for groups visiting all 5 properties.
P 🍴 & *toilets for disabled shop* ✍

WEST MIDLANDS

BIRMINGHAM

Birmingham is traditionally associated with the bustling energy of the Industrial Revolution, and its museums today commemorate the city's 19th-century role as one of the great workshops of the world. Most of the scars of industry have now healed, enabling today's visitors to appreciate Birmingham's many noble buildings and beautiful parks. The city has cherished its past, including a canal network which exceeds that of Venice. Today Birmingham's motorway links, modern airport and National Exhibition Centre assure that England's second city has a bright future.

Aston Hall
BIRMINGHAM

Trinity Rd, Aston
☎0121-327 0062
Built by Sir Thomas Holt, Aston Hall is a fine Jacobean mansion complete with a panelled long gallery, balustraded staircase and magnificent plaster friezes and ceilings. It is also said to have the ghost of Sir Thomas's daughter, who by tradition was locked up in a tiny room, went mad and died.
Open Mar-Nov, daily 2-5. Guided tours available at other times if pre-booked. Free.
🅿 shop ✤

Birmingham Botanical Gardens & Glasshouses
BIRMINGHAM

Westbourne Rd, Edgbaston
☎0121-454 1860
The gardens are a 15-acre 'oasis of delight' just 2 miles from the centre of Birmingham. Originally opened in 1832, they continue to be run by an independent educational charity. The Tropical House has a 24ft-wide lily pool and its lush tropical vegetation includes bromeliads, bananas, cocoa and other economic plants. Palm trees, ferns, orchids and insectivorous plants are displayed in the Palm House. The Orangery features a wide variety of citrus fruits and the Cactus House gives a desert scene with its giant agaves and opuntias. Outside there is colourful bedding on the Terrace and a tour of the gardens includes rhododendrons and azalea borders, Rose Garden, Rock Garden and a collection of over 200 trees. There are Domestic Theme Gardens, Herb and Cottage Gardens, the National Collection of Bonsai, a children's adventure playground and aviaries. Plant centre, gift shop, gallery, museum and refreshment pavilion. Bands play every Sunday afternoon throughout the summer. Please telephone for the diary

Birmingham's Museum of Science and Industry has displays of engineering from the beginning of the Industrial Revolution to the present day. Exhibits include the earliest functioning steam engine.

of events and flower shows.
Open daily all year, wkdays 9-8 or dusk, Sun 10-8 or dusk whichever is earlier. (Closed 25 Dec).
£3 (£3.30 summer Sun, concessions £1.70). Party10+.
🅿 💺 ✗ licensed ♿ (3 wheelchairs + 2 electric scooters available free) toilets for disabled shop garden centre ✤

Birmingham Nature Centre
BIRMINGHAM

Pershore Rd, Edgbaston (off A441, in Cannon Hill Pk)
☎0121-472 7775
Animals of the British Isles and Europe can be seen in indoor and outdoor enclosures which are designed to resemble natural habitats. The grounds also have various ponds and a stream, to attract wild birds, butterflies and other creatures.
Open Mar-Oct, daily 10-5. (Winter Sat & Sun 10-dusk).
Free.
🅿 💺 ♿ toilets for disabled shop ✤

Birmingham Railway Museum
BIRMINGHAM

670 Warwick Rd, Tyseley (3m S, A41 Warwick Rd)
☎0121-707 4696
This is a working railway museum with a fully equipped workshop. There are numerous steam locomotives and historic carriages, wagons and other vehicles. Steam-hauled train rides can be taken when available. Driving courses on either an Express Passenger Steam or Tank Loco are also available.

Open daily 10-5 or dusk if earlier. (Closed 25 & 26 Dec & 1 Jan).
✲£2.50 (ch, pen & UB40s £1.25). Family Ticket £6.25
🅿 💺 ✗ ♿ (ramps to platforms) shop

Blakesley Hall
BIRMINGHAM

Blakesley Rd, Yardley
☎0121-783 2193
Built around 1575, the Hall is a timber-framed yeoman's house, which has been furnished according to an inventory of 1684. There are displays on timber

building, pottery and rural crafts, and on the parish of Yardley, as well as the history of the house.
Open Mar-Oct, daily 2-5.
Free.
shop ✤

City Museum & Art Gallery
BIRMINGHAM

Chamberlain Sq
☎0121-235 2834
One of the world's best collections of Pre-Raphaelite paintings can be seen here, including important works by Burne-
➤

Jones, a native of Birmingham. Older schools of art are represented by French, Dutch, Italian and other works from the 14th century to the present day, and also on display are costumes and fine silver, ceramics and textiles. The wide-ranging archaeology section has prehistoric, Greek and Roman antiquities, and also objects from the Near East, Mexico and Peru. This section includes the Pinto Collection of wooden artefacts. Another popular display is the excellent collection of coins. There is a natural history section in the museum, and objects related to local history are also shown. The Gas Hall, Birmingham's state-of-the-art exhibition gallery, has an excellent programme of touring exhibitions.
Open all year Mon-Sat 10-5, Sun 12.30-5. (Closed Xmas & 1 Jan). Free Guided tours Tue 1pm, Sat & Sun 2.30pm or by prior arrangement.
Museum & Art Gallery free, admission charged for Gas Hall Exhibitions tel: 0121-235 1966 for details.
🍴 ✗ *licensed* & *(lift) toilets for disabled shop* ⌖

Museum of Science & Industry
BIRMINGHAM
Newhall St (close to Post Office Tower)
☎0121-236 1022
The displays range from the Industrial Revolution to the present day, with an emphasis on Birmingham's contribution to science and engineering. The Engineering Hall is a former Victorian plating works, and contains machine tools, electrical equipment, and working steam, gas and hot air engines. The Locomotive Hall was built to house the Stanier Pacific loco 'City of Birmingham'; and the aircraft section has a World War II Spitfire and a Hurricane, as well as aircraft engines. The James Watt building houses the earliest still-functioning steam engine in the world, dated 1799. Other sections cover science, transport and arms.
Open all year, Mon-Sat 10-5, Sun 12.30-5 (Closed Xmas & 1 Jan). Free.
🍴 & *toilets for disabled shop* ⌖

Sarehole Mill
BIRMINGHAM
Cole Bank Rd, Hall Green
☎0121-783 2193
An 18th-century water mill, restored to working order and containing displays illustrating various aspects of milling, blade-grinding and English rural pursuits. The writer J R R Tolkein lived nearby and found inspiration for his book 'The Hobbit' here.
Open Mar-Nov, daily 2-5.
Free.
shop ⌖

Selly Manor Museum
BIRMINGHAM
Maple Rd, Bournville (off A38)
☎0121-472 0199
These two timber-framed manor houses date from the 13th and early 14th centuries, and have been re-erected in the 'garden suburb' of Bournville. There is a herb garden and regular exhibitions are held, with an annual craft fair on the first Saturday in November.
Open mid Jan-mid Dec, Tue-Fri & BH 10-5. Open some Saturdays, phone for details.
£1 (ch 50p).
🅿 & *toilets for disabled shop* ⌖

Weoley Castle Ruins
BIRMINGHAM
Alwold Rd
☎0121-427 4270
Only some impressive remains can now be seen of the 13th-century fortified house, but there is a small site museum. It shows objects revealed during excavations, such as coins, keys, a 13th-century shoe, and evidence of a 600-year-old chess game.
Open Mar-Nov, Tue-Fri 2-5.
Free.
⌖

Cadbury World
BOURNVILLE
Linden Rd (1m S of A28 Bristol Rd, on A4040 Ring Rd)
☎0121-451 4159 & 0121-451 4180

Visitors to Cadbury World are first of all transported to see the Aztecs of the 16th century growing and trading cocoa beans, and even sample Emperor Montezuma's favourite drink - a mixture of cocoa, honey and spices. The introduction of chocolate to Europe follows, with a reconstruction of a cobbled square in Georgian England complete with White's Chocolate House. Here the story of the Cadbury family and their chocolate enterprise, including the creation of the Bournville factory and village, is related. There are further displays on packaging and marketing, early machinery, health and safety etc. Although there are no tours of the modern factory, the hand-processing units show all stages in the production of hand-made chocolates. The final part of the exhibition takes visitors through a children's fantasy factory where the production process for chocolate is illustrated in a lighthearted way. An exhibition will record the 90th birthday of Cadbury's Dairy Milk Chocolate, with several events during the year.
Please phone for opening details.
✱*£4.90 (ch £3.40, pen £4.25). Family ticket £14.50.*
🅿 🍴 ✗ *licensed* & *(ex packaging plant) toilets for disabled shop* ⌖

Coventry Cathedral & Visitor Centre
COVENTRY
7 Priory Row
☎(01203) 227597
Coventry's old cathedral was bombed during an air raid of November 1940 which devastated the city. The remains have been carefully preserved. The new cathedral was designed by Sir Basil Spence and consecrated in May 1962. It contains outstanding modern works of art, including a huge tapestry designed by Graham Sutherland, the west screen (a wall of glass engraved by John Hutton with saints and angels), bronzes by Epstein, and the great tapestry window by John Piper. There is also an opportunity to enjoy an audio-visual display in the visitors' centre.
Open all year, daily, Etr-Sep 9.30-7; Oct-Etr 9.30-5.30. Visitor centre closed Oct-Apr. (Closed 13-15 July & 16-18 Nov). Visitor centre £1.25 (ch 6 free, ch 6-16, students & pen 75p).Party 10+. Cathedral £2 donation. Camera charge £1. Video charge £3.
P *(250 yds)* ✗ *licensed* & *(lift, touch and hearing centre, paved wheelchair access) toilets for disabled shop* ⌖

Coventry Toy Museum
COVENTRY
Much Park St
☎(01203) 227560
A collection of toys dating from 1740 to 1980, including trains, dolls, dolls' houses and games, housed in a 14th-century monastery gatehouse.
Open all year, daily 12-6
P *(200yds) shop* ⌖
Details not confirmed for 1995

Herbert Art Gallery & Museum
COVENTRY
Jordan Well
☎(01203) 832381
'Godiva City', an innovative exhibition telling the story of the city's development over 1,000 years, opened in June 1994. Many thousands of visitors have already enjoyed the displays, interactive exhibits and fascinating story. The new tearoom, shop and improved toilet facilities complete the ground floor, while on the first floor are the Sutherland drawings for the Cathedral tapestry, the Phillip Allen collection of Oriental ceramics and a variety of exhibitions of the visual arts.
Open all year, Mon-Sat 10-5.30, Sun 2-5. (Closed part Xmas).
Free.
P *(250 yds)* 🍴 & *toilets for disabled shop* ⌖

Lunt Roman Fort
COVENTRY
Coventry Rd, Baginton (S side of city,off Stonebridge highway,A45)
☎(01203) 832381
The turf and timber Roman fort from around the end of the 1st century has been faithfully reconstructed over many years. An Interpretation Centre is housed in the reconstructed granary. Other features include the main gateway, gyrus and ramparts. The audiotour brings the fort to life with a description of the experience of a soldier stationed at the Lunt, complete with sound effects!
Open Apr-7 Jul & Sep, wknds only 10-5; 14 Jul-Aug, daily 10-5.
£2.50 (ch £1.25), including audiotape guided tour. Party.
🅿 & *toilets for disabled shop* ⌖

Museum of British Road Transport
COVENTRY
St Agnes Ln, Hales St
☎(01203) 832425
The museum illustrates the role of Coventry and the West Midlands in the development of transport throughout the world. There are over 400 exhibits, in displays of motor cars, commercial vehicles, motor cycles and associated items including die-cast models.
Open all year, daily 10-5. Closed 24-26 Dec.
✱*£2.95 (ch & pen £1.95). Family ticket £7.50.*
P 🍴 & *toilets for disabled shop* ⌖

Black Country Museum
DUDLEY
Tipton Rd (on A4037, opposite Dudley Guest Hospital)
☎0121-557 9643 & 0121-520 8054
The museum is really a recreation of a Black Country village, complete with cottages, a chapel, chemist, baker and a pub serving real ale. One of the buildings is a chainmaker's house with a brewhouse, and demonstrations of chainmaking and glass cutting are given in traditional workshops. There is also a canal boat dock with a range of narrowboats, and boats set off daily for canal trips into the Dudley Tunnel, an eerie underground ride.
Transport around the village is provided by an electric tramway. You can go underground in an 1850s mine, and see a replica of the world's first steam engineering venture into a pit-pulled cottage (affected by subsidence due to mining). Costumed guides and demonstrations bring the buildings to life and regular 'Theme' weekends are held throughout the summer.
Open all year, Mar-Oct daily 10-5; Nov-Feb, Wed-Sun 10-4. (Closed 20-25 Dec).
£5.50 (ch 5-17 £4, pen £4.75). Family ticket £15.50. Party 20+
🅿 🍴 ✗ *licensed* & *toilets for disabled shop* ⌖

Dudley Zoo & Castle
DUDLEY
2 The Broadway
☎(01384) 252401
The wooded grounds of Dudley Castle make a wonderful setting for the long-established, traditional zoo, which has animals from every continent. The castle ruins are impressive, and a chairlift and land train take you to the top of Castle Hill. An audio visual show of the castle's history and an interpretation of castle life in the medieval period are shown free of charge.
Open all year, Etr-mid Sep, daily 10-4.30; mid Sep-Etr, daily 10-3.30. (Closed 25 Dec).
£4.95 (ch & pen £2.95). Family ticket £15.50. Party 15+.
🅿 *(charged)* ✗ *licensed* & *(land train from gates to castle) toilets for disabled shop* ⌖

Museum & Art Gallery
DUDLEY
St James's Rd
☎(01384) 456000 ext 5570
The museum houses the Brooke

The late Victorian interior of a chairmaker's cottage has been carefully recreated as part of a whole village at the Black Country Museum.

Robinson collection of 17th, 18th and 19th century European painting, furniture, ceramics and enamels, also Japanese netsuke and inro, and Greek, Roman and Oriental ceramics. A fine geological gallery has spectacular displays of fossils from the local 'Wenlock' limestone and coal measures, and a wide variety of temporary exhibitions are staged throughout the year.
Open all year, Mon-Sat 10-5. (Closed BHs).
& *shop* ✤
Details not confirmed for 1995

Broadfield House Glass Museum
KINGSWINFORD
Barnett Ln
☎(01384) 273011
This magnificent collection of 19th-and 20th-century glass focuses on the cut, etched, engraved and coloured glass made in nearby Stourbridge during the last century. Highlights include cameo glass by Alphonse Lechevrel and George Woodall, and rock crystal engraving by William Fritsche. Also on display are the Michael Parkington collection of 18th-, 19th-and 20th-century British glass, the Hulbert of Dudley collection, and the Notley/Lerpiniere collection of Carnival Glass.
Open all year, Tue-Fri & Sun 2-5, Sat 10-1 & 2-5. BH's 2-5.
P & *shop* ✤
Details not confirmed for 1995

National Motorcycle Museum
SOLIHULL
Coventry Rd, Bickenhill (nr junc 6, of M42, off A45 nr NEC)
☎(01675) 443311
Five exhibition halls showing British motorcycles built during the Golden Age of motorcycling. Spanning 90 years, the immaculately restored machines are the products of around 150 different factories. Over 650 machines are on show, most are owned by the museum,

others are from collections or private owners. Restoration work is carried out by enthusiasts, and new motorcycles are acquired from all over the world. All the machines are made in Britain from the 1898 20mph Beeston 'Trike' to the 1992 TT winning 191mph Nortons, the museum is the legacy of almost a century of world-beating motorcycling and a glorious celebration of speed.
Open all year, daily 10-6. (Closed 24-26 Dec).
✳£4.50 (ch 12 & pen £3.50). Party 20+.
P ✗ *licensed* & *toilets for disabled shop*
✤

The Falconry Centre
STOURBRIDGE
Hurrans Garden Centre, Kidderminster Rd South, Hagley (off A456)
☎Kidderminster (01562) 700014
The centre houses some 80 birds of prey including owls, hawks, falcons and eagles, and is also a rehabilitation centre for sick and injured birds of prey. Spectacular flying displays are put on daily from midday. There are special falconry weekends throughout the year. An animal sanctuary and children's farmyard are due to open early in 1995.
Open all year, daily 10-5.30. (Closed 25 & 26 Dec).
✳£2.50 (ch & pen £1.50, disabled £1)
P ♥ & *shop garden centre* ✤

Walsall Leather Museum
WALSALL
56-57 Wisemore
☎(01922) 721153
Winner of the 'Museum of the Year' award (Social and Industrial History) this museum is housed in a former leather goods factory dating from 1891. In the atmospheric workshops, rich with the aroma of leather, visitors can see how traditional leather goods have been made, and (on most days of the week) talk to leatherworkers about their craft. Historical displays show beautiful

Amberley Museum reflects the industrial history of south-east England. Among exhibits are working traction engines, a wheelwright's and blacksmith's forge.

products from the past, but this museum is not just about the past. Walsall firms of today supply such prestigious customers as Harrods. Regular exhibitions, events and activities are planned throughout the year for all ages. The annual Leather Festival is held in the summer, a Christmas craft fair will be held in November 1995.
Open all year, Tue-Sat 10-5 (Nov-Mar 4pm), Sun noon-5. Open BH Mon.
Free.
P *(opposite)* ♥ & *toilets for disabled shop* ✤ *(ex garden)*

Wightwick Manor
WOLVERHAMPTON
☎(01902) 761108
This house is unusual in that, although barely 100 years old, it is a gem of design and architectural interest. It was begun in 1887 and in its style of decoration it is one of the finest examples of the late 19th-century. The house was designed by Edward Ould, a follower of William Morris. All aspects of William Morris's talents are shown in this house - wallpapers, textiles, carpets, tiles, embroidery and even books. There are also paintings and drawings by Burne-Jones, D G Rosetti, Holman Hunt and others, glass by Kempe and tiles by de Morgan.
The garden was laid out by Alfred Parsons and Thomas Manson, and reflects late Victorian and Edwardian design.
Open Mar-Dec, Thu, Sat & BH Sun & Mon 2.30-5.30.
✳£4.50 (accompanied ch & students £2.25). Gardens only £2.
P &
(NT)

Stuart Crystal
WORDSLEY
Red House Glassworks
☎Brierley Hill (01384) 71161
Fine glass has been made in the area since the beginning of the 17th century when French glass makers arrived in the area. The 200 year old Redhouse Glass Cone and associated building have recently been restored in the first stage

of creating a museum. On the site there is also a factory shop, a chip repair service and glass sculpture. At the Red House factory the focal point is the Redhouse Cone. The tour of the factory shows the complete glassmaking process from glass-blowing to cutting and decorating.
Open all year, daily. (Closed 25-26 Dec & 1 Jan).
Free.
P ♥ *shop* ✤ ⌘

WEST SUSSEX

Amberley Museum
AMBERLEY
Houghton Bridge (off B2139)
☎Bury (01798) 831370
This exciting working museum reflects the industrial history of the south east of England. Here you can visit the craftsmen - the blacksmith, potter, printer or boat-builder, and experience the sights, sounds and smells of their workshops. Take a ride on the workmen's train or on the narrow gauge railway, or enjoy the delights of the vintage motor buses. There are many other exhibits and displays to capture your interest and imagination within the magnificent 36-acre site including the Rural Telephone Exchange, Wheelwright's Shop and the Seeboard Electricty Hall. Allow at least three hours for a visit.
Open 23 Mar-Oct, Wed-Sun 10-5. Also open daily 30 Mar-17 Apr, 25 May-5 Jun, 20 Jul-4 Sep & 19 Oct-30 Oct.
P ♥ & *toilets for disabled shop*
Details not confirmed for 1995

Wakehurst Place Garden
ARDINGLY
(1.5m NW, on B2028)
☎(01444) 892701
Woodland and lakes linked by a pretty watercourse make this large garden a beautiful place to walk, and it also has an amazing variety of interesting trees and shrubs, a Winter Garden, and a ➤

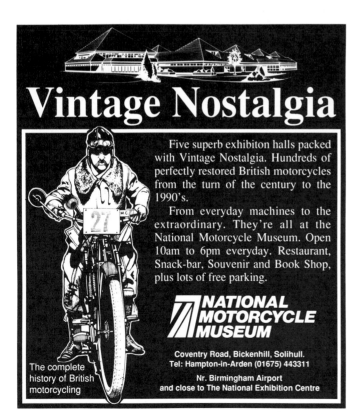

The little town of Arundel nestling beside the River Arun, was protected by Arundel Castle, the ancient home of the Dukes of Norfolk.

Rock Walk. It is administered and maintained by the Royal Botanic Gardens at Kew.
Open all year, Nov-Jan 10-4; Feb & Oct 10-5; Mar 10-6; Apr-Sep 10-7. (Closed 25 Dec & 1 Jan). Last admission 30 mins before closing. Mansion closes one hour before garden.
£4 (ch £1.50, students, UB40 & pen £2).
🅿 ✗ ♿ *(wheelchair available) toilets for disabled shop* ⌖
(NT)

Arundel Castle
ARUNDEL
☎ *(01903) 883136*
This great castle, home of the Dukes of Norfolk, dates from the Norman Conquest. Containing a very fine collection of furniture and paintings, it is still a family home reflecting the changes of nearly a thousand years.
Open Apr-last Fri in Oct, Sun-Fri 12-5. Last admission 4pm (Closed Good Fri).
£5 (ch 5-15 £3.50, pen £4). Party 20+
🅿 *(charged)* ✗ *licensed shop* ⌖

Arundel Toy & Military Museum
ARUNDEL
23 High St
☎ *(01903) 882908 & 507446*
A Georgian cottage in the heart of town displaying a vast and unique collection of interesting old toys, games, dolls, dolls' houses, teddy bears and model toy soldiers. There are also Royal commemoratives, boats, 'Goss' china models, 'Britains' farmyards, puppets, pocillovy (egg-cups), small militaria and curiosities collected from all over the world, and fascinating for all the family.
Open every weekend 12-5, school & BH; Jun-Sep daily 10.30-5. Most days in Spring & Oct.
£1.25 (ch 15, students & pen £1). Family ticket £4. Party 20+.
🅿 *(100 yds)* ♿ *shop*

Wildfowl & Wetlands Trust
ARUNDEL
Mill Rd (signposted from A27 & A29)
☎ *(01903) 883355*
More than a thousand ducks, geese and swans from all over the world live here

in 55 acres of well-landscaped pens, lakes and paddocks; the site is also a sanctuary for many wild birds. Wild diving duck are attracted by the clear, spring-fed pools, while waders come to feed in the damp meadows and 'wader scrape'. Rarities include the shy water rail, whose grunting, squealing call may be heard from the reed beds where it makes its nest. There are hides overlooking the different habitats, and the site also has a large viewing gallery and education complex. Facilities for the disabled include a purpose-built toilet for wheelchair users, free wheelchair loan, access throughout the centre (including hides), and waitress service at the restaurant. Special events for 1995 include: 'half-term in Hawaii' (20-24 Feb), Downy Duckling Days (27 May-4 Jun), mid-summer family evening (7 Jul), Father Christmas grotto (16-23 Dec). Four new activity stations to help visitors explore the wetlands habitats and the wildfowl are due to be opened in April 1995 and will be staffed in the Easter and Summer holidays, West Sussex half-term holiday and all weekends in summer.
Open all year, daily. Summer 9.30-5.30; Winter 9.30-4.30. Last admission Summer 5pm; Winter 4pm. (Closed 25 Dec).
✱*£3.95 (ch £2, pen £2.95). Party.*
🅿 ✗ *licensed* ♿ *(level paths, free wheelchair loan) toilets for disabled shop* ⌖

Holly Gate Cactus Garden
ASHINGTON
Billingshurst Rd (B2133)
☎ *Worthing (01903) 892930*
A mecca for the cactus enthusiast, with more than 30,000 succulent and cactus plants, including many rare types. They come from both arid and tropical parts of the world, and are housed in over 10,000 sq ft of greenhouses.
Open daily, 9-5. (Closed 25-26 Dec).
£1.50 (ch & pen £1). Party 20+.
🅿 🖻 ♿ *shop garden centre*

Bignor Roman Villa & Museum
BIGNOR
(between A29 & A285)
☎ *Sutton (01798) 869259*
Rediscovered in 1811, this Roman house was built on a grand scale. It is one of the largest known, and has spectacular mosaics. The heating system can also be seen, and various finds from excavations are on show. The longest mosaic in Britain (82ft) is on display here in its original position.
Open Mar-May & Oct 10-5 (Closed Mon ex BHs). Jun-Sep daily 10-6.
£2.75 (ch 16 £1.25, pen £1.75). Party 10+. Guided tours by arrangement.
🅿 🖻 ♿ *shop* ⌖

Bramber Castle
BRAMBER
(just N of A283)
A former home of the Dukes of Norfolk, this ruined Norman stronghold lies on a ridge of the South Downs and gives wonderful views.
Open all year, daily.

(NT)
Details not confirmed for 1995

Chichester District Museum
CHICHESTER
29 Little London
☎ *(01243) 784683*
Clues about the people who lived around Chichester in the past are displayed in this welcoming setting, with a new gallery covering 'Chichester since 1900'. Discover the local history in the only museum about Chichester district. There is a programme of changing exhibitions.
Open all year, Tue-Sat 10-5.30. (Closed BH).
🅿 *(100yds)* ♿ *(access leaflet available) shop* ⌖
Details not confirmed for 1995

Mechanical Music & Doll Collection
CHICHESTER
Church Rd, Portfield (1m E off A27)
☎ *(01243) 785421 & 372646*
A unique opportunity to see and hear barrel organs, polyphons, musical boxes, fair organs etc - all fully restored and playing for your pleasure. A magical musical tour to fascinate and entertain all ages. The doll collection contains fine examples of Victorian china and wax dolls, also felt and velvet dolls of the 1920s. A superb array of Victorian artefacts housed in a well-preserved Victorian church.
Open Etr-Sep, Sun-Fri 1-5; Oct-Etr Sun only 1-5; Evening bookings by arrangement. Closed Dec.
£2 (ch 75p).
🅿 ♿ *shop* ⌖

Pallant House
CHICHESTER
9 North Pallant
☎ *(01243) 774557*
The gallery is housed in a restored Queen Anne town house. The rooms contain fine furniture, and there is an Edwardian kitchen. Permanent collections on display include the Modern British Art of the Hussey and Kearley bequests; the Geoffrey Freeman collection of Bow porcelain and enamels. There is a programme of temporary exhibitions, and the small garden is planted in 18th-century style.
Open all year, Tue-Sat 10-5.15. (Closed Sun, Mon & BHs). (Last admission 4.45pm).
£2.50 (ch £1, students & pen £1.70).
🅿 *(3 mins walk)* ♿ *shop* ⌖

Standen
EAST GRINSTEAD
(2m S, signposted from B2110)
☎ *(01342) 323029*
Standen is a showpiece of the 19th-century Arts and Crafts movement. It was designed by Philip Webb for the Beale family, and was meant from the start to be decorated with William Morris wallpapers and fabrics. The interior has

been carefully preserved, and the Morris designs to be seen here include Sunflower, Peacock, Trellis, and Larkspur, among others. The furniture is also in keeping, and includes contemporary brass beds from Heal's, furniture from the Morris firm, and ceramics by William de Morgan. Webb also designed some of the furniture and details such as the fire grates, finger plates for the doors, and the electric light fittings. There is a beautiful hillside garden.
Open Apr-Oct, Wed-Sun (inc Good Fri) House: 1.30-5.30, Garden: 12.30-6. Open BH Mon. Last admission 5pm. Wknds 18-19 & 25-26 Mar 1.30-4.30, last admission 5pm. Entry may be delayed at peak times.
✱*House & garden £4 (£4.80 wknds, Good Fri & BH Mons). Garden only £2.50 (£3 wknds, Good Fri & BH Mons). Children half price. Family ticket £10-£12.*
🅿 ✗ ♿ *shop* ⌖ *(ex woodland walk & lower car)*
(NT)

Roman Palace
FISHBOURNE
Salthill Rd (N of A259 in Fishbourne)
☎ *Chichester (01243) 785859*
This is the largest known Roman residence in Britain, but the reason for building such a magnificent house here is not known. It was occupied from the 1st to the 3rd centuries AD, when its 100 or so rooms must have been a wonderful sight with their mosaic floors and painted walls; 25 of these mosaic floors can still be seen in varying states of completeness, including others rescued from elsewhere in the area. Outside, the northern part of the palace garden has been replanted to its original 1st-century plan. The museum gives an account of the history of the palace, and shows a full-size reconstruction of a Roman dining room. There are also an audio-visual theatre and mosaic-making area for children. Various activity days are planned in 1995. Please telephone for details.
Open all year, daily 14 Feb-16 Dec. Feb, Nov-Dec 10-4; Mar-Jul & Sep-Oct 10-5; Aug 10-6.
£3.50 (ch £1.60, pen & students £2.80). Family ticket £8.70.
🅿 🖻 ♿ *(self guiding tapes & tactile objects for the blind) toilets for disabled shop garden centre* ⌖

Denmans Garden
FONTWELL
(5m E of Chichester on A27)
☎ *Eastergate (01243) 542808*
This garden has been created from land which was part of an estate owned by Lord Denman in the 19th century. The present three-and-a-half-acre garden was begun in the 1940s and has gradually developed over the last 50 years. There is a Walled Garden, bursting with masses of perennials, herbs and old-fashioned roses, and a Gravel Stream with grasses, bamboo and a pond. The South Garden has fine maples and cherry trees, and many mature, rare trees. A school of Garden Design is housed in the Clock House.
Open all year daily 9-5. (Closed 25-26 Dec).
£2.50 (ch £1.50, ch under 5 free, pen £2.25). Party 15+.
🅿 🖻 ♿ *shop garden centre* ⌖

Goodwood House
GOODWOOD
☎ *Chichester (01243) 774107*
The home of the Dukes of Richmond was acquired by the 1st Duke in 1697 so that he could ride with the local hunt. Horses and hunting remained a high priority, and the stable block added during 18th-century alterations outshines the house. The work was started by William Chambers, and taken over after his death by James Wyatt, who also designed an impressive classical building for the hounds. The 'Glorious Goodwood' horse races began in the 19th century. The glories of the house itself, however,

are its beautiful downland setting and its collection of paintings, including numerous Old Masters. There is also some fine furniture, porcelain, tapestries and mementoes of the family. The Festival of Speed will take place in Goodwood Park 24-25 June 1995. This is a time-trial course for classic cars through the park and up Birdless Grove Hill. There is a grandstand in front of the House and there will be trade stands and displays to see.
Open Etr Sun & Mon, then Sun & Mon until 25 Sep, also Tue-Thu in Aug. 2-5. (Closed 23 & 24 Apr, 14 & 15 May, 18, 19 & 25-26 Jun and all event days).
❋£3.40 *(ch & disabled £1.70). Party 15+.*
🅿 💺 ⛄ *toilets for disabled shop* 🚫

Nymans Garden
HANDCROSS
(on B2114)
☎(01444) 400321 & 400002
Set in the Sussex Weald, Nymans has flowering shrubs and roses, a flower garden in the old walled orchard, and a secret sunken garden. There are some fine and rare trees. A musical evening is held in the garden in summer. Telephone or send sae for details.
Open Mar-Oct, daily (ex Mon & Tue) but open BH Mon 11-7 or sunset if earlier. Last admission 1 hour before closing.
❋£3.80 *(ch £1.90).*
🅿 💺 ⛄ *(wheelchair route, wheelchair available, braille guide) toilets for disabled shop* 🚫
(NT)

Borde Hill Garden
HAYWARDS HEATH
(1.5m N)
☎(01444) 450326
The 40-acre gardens have a huge collection of rhododendrons, and the azaleas, camellias and magnolias are also noteworthy. Close to the house are interesting herbaceous beds, and further out there are woodland walks. Recent additions include two lakes and a children's playground. Special events planned for 1995 include: Festival of Gardening (22-23 April), Steam Rally (13-15 May), open-air theatre (28-30 Jul and 4-6 Aug), Christmas Bazaar (3 Dec) and various horse-trial events. Please telephone to confirm dates.
Open Sun in Mar in good weather, daily 18 Mar-1 Oct.
Garden & Parkland £3.50 (ch £1.50 & pen £3). Parkland only £1.
🅿 💺 ✗ *licensed* ⛄ *(wheelchairs available) toilets for disabled shop*

Woods Mill Countryside Centre
HENFIELD
Shoreham Rd (1.5m S Henfield on A2037)
☎(01273) 492630
The centre consists of a wildlife and countryside exhibition in an 18th-century watermill, and a trail through varied habitats. Nets are provided for a pond where children can identify specimens. Inside the Centre is an aquarium, a 25ft-

high replica oak tree, audio-visual theatre and a gift shop.
Open Good Fri- last wknd in Sep, Sat 1-5, Sun & BH 11-5. Also school hols Tue-Thu 1-52-6.
£1 *(ch 50p).*
🅿 💺 ⛄ *shop* 🚫

Highdown
HIGHDOWN
(N off A259 between Worthing & Littlehampton)
☎Worthing (01903) 501054
These gardens were laid out in a chalk pit on Highdown Hill. There are rock plants, flowering shrubs and daffodils, as well as excellent views.
Open all year, Apr-Sep, Mon-Fri 10-6, Sat, Sun & BH Mon 10-8pm; Winter Mon-Fri only, Oct-Nov, 10-4.30; Dec-Jan, 10-4; Feb-Mar, 10-4.30.
Free.
🅿 ⛄ *toilets for disabled* 🚫

Horsham Museum
HORSHAM
9 The Causeway
☎(01403) 254959
The museum is in a timber-framed Tudor house with diverse collections. On show in the recently opened Prehistory room are locally found dinosaur bones; in the new Transport gallery a fascinating collection of early bicycles. The Georgian room has an interesting ceramic collection. There is a display on shops and shopping, a wheelwright's shop, a blacksmith's forge, and a gaol setting. The museum's walled garden has many unusual plants. The latest attractions are the centenary garden, opened in 1993, and a new gallery on the life of the Wealden farmer in 1994. In 1995, as part of Horsham's Arts and Literature Festival, there will be an exhibition on Medwin, biographer and friend of the poet Shelley.
Open all year, Tue-Sat 10-5.
Free.
⛄ *toilets for disabled shop* 🚫 *(ex guide dogs)*

Littlehampton Museum
LITTLEHAMPTON
Manor House, Church St
☎(01903) 715149
A small, friendly museum close to the High Street of this port and seaside resort. This is one of the few maritime museums in West Sussex, and there are also displays of local history, art, archaeology and a lively programme of temporary exhibitions. In 1995 these include: Littlehampton Life 1945-1970 (Apr-Jul), a hands-on geology/natural history and archaeology display of life on earth in the first 3,400 million years (Jul-Sep), and a medieval exhibition (Sep-Dec). Please telephone to check dates and details.
Open all year Tue-Sat (incl Summer BH); 10.30-4.30. Contact for details of possible Mon-Sun opening.
Free.
🅿 *(charged)* ⛄ *(object handling sessions can be arranged for groups) shop* 🚫

Leonardslee Gardens
LOWER BEEDING
(3m SW from Handcross,at junct of A279/A281)
☎Horsham (01403) 891212
Set on the edge of the ancient St Leonard's Forest, this wonderful landscaped garden was created by Sir Edmund Loder at the end of the 19th century. Listed Grade I in importance, there are over 200 acres open to the public. It is best seen in the spring when azaleas and rhododendrons clothe the banks of a series of six ancient hammer ponds. The autumn tints are impressive, and there are wallaby and deer parks. There is also a delightful Rock Garden, a Temperate Greenhouse, Wildflower walk, Bonsai exhibition and Alpine house. Recent improvements and new plantings have now made this a garden for all seasons. Special events for 1995 include: Bonsai Weekend with demonstrations and advice from experts (6-8 May), Country Craft Fair (24-25 June).
Open Apr-Oct, daily 10-6 (May 10-8). Apr & Jun-Oct £3, May £4, (ch £2).
🅿 💺 ✗ *licensed shop garden centre* 🚫

Petworth House & Park
PETWORTH
☎(01798) 342207 & 343929
A 13-mile wall surrounds Petworth's acres. Rebuilt by the Duke of Somerset in the 17th century, all that remains of the 13th-century building is the chapel. The imposing 320ft west front faces the lake and great park, and was re-designed by Anthony Salvin between 1869 and 1872. The state rooms and galleries contain one of the finest art collections in England, including works by Gainsborough, Rembrandt and Van Dyck. Turner was a frequent visitor to Petworth, and a notable collection of his works is kept here. The carved room is said to be the most impressive in the house, with its lovely decoration by Grinling Gibbons. On 23-25 June open air

concerts will be held, (telephone 01798 343748 for information).
Open Apr-Oct, daily (ex Mon & Fri); Open Good Fri & BH Mons, (closed Tue following) 1-5.30. Extra rooms shown Tue-Thu. Last admission to House 5pm. Gardens daily. Park 8-sunset. Park closed 23-25 Jun from noon.
£4 *(ch £2). Family ticket £10.*
🅿 💺 ⛄ *licensed* ⛄ *(wheelchairs available, braille guide) toilets for disabled shop* 🚫 *(ex in park)*
(NT)

Parham House & Gardens
PULBOROUGH
Parham Park (3m SE off A283)
☎Storrington (01903) 744888
Surrounded by a deer park, fine gardens and 18th-century pleasure grounds in a beautiful downland setting, this Elizabethan family home contains a good collection of paintings, furniture, carpets and rare needlework. A brick and turf maze has been created in the grounds - designed with children in mind, it is called 'Veronica's Maze'. The garden at Parham won the prestigious Christie's Garden of the Year Award in 1990. A special Garden Weekend is held on 15 & 16 July 1995. Garden shop.
Open Etr Sun-1st Sun in Oct, Wed, Thu, Sun & BH. Gardens 1-6; House 2-6 (last entry 5). Guided tours on Wed & Thu mornings by special arrangement.
❋*House & Gardens £4 (ch 5-15 £2 & pen £3.50). Gardens £2 (ch £1). Party 20+.*
🅿 💺 ⛄ *(wheelchairs available) shop garden centre* 🚫 *(ex in grounds)*

Marlipins Museum
SHOREHAM-BY-SEA
High St (town centre on A259)
☎Brighton (01273) 462994
The Marlipins Museum has a wide range of exhibits relating to local history and archaeology. There is also a maritime gallery displaying a fine collection of ship portraits, ship models, and other items of local maritime interest. The building in ➤

Leonardslee Gardens
Lower Beeding, Nr Horsham, Sussex

One of several ornately panelled rooms in Bolling Hall, this room is reputedly haunted and is known as the Ghost Room.

which the museum is housed may have been built as a customs house. It dates from Norman times and has a superb knapped flint and stone chequerwork façade. A topographical gallery displays drawings, watercolours, oil paintings and maps of the Shoreham area.
Open May-Sep, Tue-Sat 10-1 & 2-4.30, Sun 2-4.30.
£1 (ch 5-14 50p, students & pen 75p)
P *(200 yds) shop* ⌀

Weald & Downland Open Air Museum
SINGLETON
(6m N of Chichester on A286)
☎(01243) 811348
Situated in a beautiful downland setting, this museum displays more than 35 rescued historic buildings from south-east England. The buildings, ranging from early medieval houses to a 19th-century schoolhouse, have been re-erected to form a village and outlying farms and agricultural buildings. Among the exhibits there is a medieval farmstead working watermill, where corn is ground and flour is sold, a Tudor market hall, a blacksmith's forge, tollhouse and hands-on gallery. Longport House, a farmhouse from the Channel Tunnel site, forms a new reception centre (opening in 1995). There are displays of rural industries, including a charcoal burner's camp, and traditional building crafts. Special events for 1995 include: Traditional Food Fair (16-17 Apr), Midsummer Marvels (19-25 Jun), Show for Rare and Traditional Breeds (23 Jul), Steam Threshing and Ploughing with heavy horses and vintage tractors (21-22 Oct).
Open all year, Mar-Oct, daily 11-5; Nov-Feb, Wed, Sat & Sun 11-5. also 26 Dec-2 Jan, 11-5.
£4.20 (ch & students £2.10, pen £3.70). Family ticket £11. Party.
P 🍴 ⌖ *toilets for disabled shop*

Uppark
SOUTH HARTING
(1.5m S on B2146)
☎(01730) 825317
On 30th August 1989 this late 17th-century house was partially destroyed by fire. The attic and the first floor were completely gutted, but many of the 18th-century contents were saved. In June 1995, following the most ambitious restoration project ever undertaken by the National Trust, Uppark will re-open to the public. The garden, landscaped by Repton, and its magnificent views, can also be enjoyed.
Open Jun-Oct, Sun-Thu. House 1-5.30. Car park, garden, exhibition & woodland walk 12-5.30. Last admission to house 5pm. Timed tickets will be in operation, so delays may occur or tickets may sell out, pre-booking is recommended. Telephone (01730) 825317.
❋*House, garden & exhibition £5. Family ticket £12.50.*
P 🍴 ⌖ *toilets for disabled shop* ⌀ *(ex woodland walk & car park)*
(NT)

Tangmere Military Aviation Museum Trust
TANGMERE
Tangmere Airfield (off A27)
☎*Chichester (01243) 775223*
Based at an airfield which played an important role during the World Wars, this museum spans 70 years of military aviation and has a wide-ranging collection of relics relating to Tangmere and air warfare in the south-east of England. There are photographs, documents, models, uniforms, aircraft and aircraft parts on display along with a Spitfire cockpit simulator. A hangar houses the record-breaking aircraft Meteor and Hunter. The latest acquisition is a Supermarine Swift and there are also full-size replicas of a Spitfire and a Hurricane. Aeromarts will be held in March and September, but please telephone for dates and details.
Open Mar-Oct, daily 10-5.30; Feb & Nov, daily 10-4.30.
£3 (ch £1 & pen £2.50).
P 🍴 ⌖ *(wheelchairs available) toilets for disabled shop*

West Dean Gardens
WEST DEAN
(on A286 between Chichester & Midhurst)
☎*Singleton (01243) 811303*
An historic garden of 35 acres in a tranquil downland setting. Noted for its 300-ft long Harold Peto pergola, mixed and herbaceous borders, rustic summerhouses, water garden and specimen trees. The newly restored walled garden contains a fruit collection, Victorian glasshouses, an apple store, large working kitchen garden and a tool and mower collection. The Circuit Walk (two-and-a-quarter miles) climbs through parkland to the 45-acre St Roches Arboretum with its varied collection of trees and shrubs.
Open Apr-Oct, daily 11-5. Last ticket 4pm.
£3 (ch £1.50, pen £2.50). Party 20+.
P 🍴 ⌖ *toilets for disabled shop* ⌀

Priest House
WEST HOATHLY
(off B2028)
☎*Sharpthorne (01342) 810479*
The 15th-century house has been converted into a small folk museum with a variety of interesting exhibits including samplers, needlework, furniture, kitchen and agricultural implements. The house is set in a traditional English cottage garden, at its best during the summer months, and a formal herb garden is now well established on the site.
Open Mar-Oct, weekdays 11-5.30, Sun 2-5.30.
£1.80 (ch 5-16 90p). Party.
P *(10 yds) shop* ⌀

Worthing Museum & Art Gallery
WORTHING
Chapel Rd (on A24)
☎*(01903) 239999 ext 2528*
A particularly rich collection of archaeological finds is displayed in this museum. There are artefacts from prehistoric, Roman, Anglo-Saxon and medieval times, a downland display, toys, pottery, pictures and a large costume collection from the 18th to 20th centuries. A wheelchair is available for disabled visitors and there are entrance ramps and a lift. A programme of changing exhibitions includes paintings, sculpture, textiles, ceramics and social history.
Open all year, Mon-Sat 10-6 (summer), 10-5 (winter).
Free.
P ⌖ *(wheelchair available) toilets for disabled shop* ⌀

WEST YORKSHIRE

Bagshaw Museum
BATLEY
Wilton Park (best approached from Upper Batley Lane).
☎*Wakefield (01924) 472514*
The museum is housed in a 19th-century building, with displays of local history, Oriental arts, natural history, and a gallery of Egyptology. A new gallery recreates the sights and sounds of a tropical rainforest. There is a full programme of exhibitions and events throughout the year, including a 'Touch and See' exhibition for the visually impaired in summer 1995 - contact the museum officer for details.
Open all year, Mon-Fri 11-5, Sat & Sun 12-5. (Closed Xmas).
Free.
P ⌖ *shop* ⌀

Batley Art Gallery
BATLEY
Market Place
☎*(01924) 435521*
A series of changing exhibitions feature contemporary art in a variety of media by local and regional artists. In the permanent collection are mainly 20th-century paintings and sculpture in the possession of the Local Authority. Workshops and special events run throughout the year and include: Michael Moor prints in May, an exhibition by the Northern Potters Association and a Photographic Exhibition. Please telephone to check dates.
Open all year. Mon, Wed & Fri 10-6, Tue 10-1 , Thu 10-5, Sat 10-4. (Closed Sun & BHs).
Free.
P ⌀

BRADFORD
Bradford, with Leeds and Calderdale, has been associated with wool since medieval times, and the developing techniques of its industry are graphically recreated in the 'living museums'. The city, which became the wool-cloth (worsted) capital of the world in the 19th century, boasts a small cathedral famed for the woolpacks that were hung over the tower to protect it from cannonballs during the Civil War and a magnificent 19th-century Town Hall. Bradford also made railway equipment, cars, trams and motorcycles. The same dynamic spirit that built up the textile industry inspired the establishment in Bradford of the National Museum of Photography, Film and Television and built up Bradford to be a major centre for tourism.

Bolling Hall
BRADFORD
Bowling Hall Rd (1m from city centre off A650)
☎*(01274) 723057*
A classic West Yorkshire manor house, complete with galleried 'housebody' (hall), Bolling Hall dates mainly from the 17th century but has medieval and 18th-century sections. It has panelled rooms, plasterwork in original colours, heraldic glass and a rare Chippendale bed. There is also a 'ghost room'.
Open all year, Apr-Sep, Tue-Sun & BH Mon 10-6; Oct-Mar, Tue-Sun 10-5.

(Closed Mon ex BH, Good Fri, 25 & 26 Dec).
Free.
🅿 & *shop* ⊗

Cartwright Hall Art Gallery
BRADFORD
Lister Park (1m from city centre on A650)
☎(01274) 493313
Built in dramatic Baroque style in 1904, this art gallery has permanent collections of 19th-and 20th-century British art, contemporary prints, and older works by British and European masters, including the 'Brown Boy' by Reynolds. There is an imaginative exhibition programme, featuring in 1995: BT New Contemporaries (18 Mar-14 May); Druie Bowett (20 May-9 Jul); works by the British Guild of Toymakers (20 May-24 Sep); Pamela Melliar ceramic sculptures (27 May-24 Sep) and Sound and Fury, the art and imagery of Heavy Metal music (8 Oct-7 Jan 1996).
Open all year Apr-Sep, Tue-Sun & BH Mon 10-6; Oct-Mar, Tue-Sun 10-5 (Closed Mon ex BH, Good Fri, 25 & 26 Dec).
Free.
🖳 & *toilets for disabled shop* ⊗

Colour Museum
BRADFORD
82 Grattan Rd
☎(01274) 390955
A unique, award-winning museum, run by the Society of Dyers and Colourists, comprising two galleries packed with visitor-operated exhibits demonstrating the effects of light and colour, including optical illusions, and the story of dyeing and textile printing. It even offers the chance to take charge of a modern dye-making factory and to try computer-aided exterior and interior design.
Open all year, Tue-Fri 2-5, Sat 10-4. Booked parties Tue- Fri mornings. (Closed Sun, Mon & BH's).
✳£1.10 (concessions 65p). Family ticket £2.75.
P (300 yds) & (lift from street level) shop ⊗

Industrial and Horses at Work Museum
BRADFORD
Moorside Rd, Eccleshill
☎(01274) 631756
Moorside Mills is an original spinning mill, now part of a museum that brings vividly to life the story of the woollen industry in Bradford. The magnificent machinery that once converted raw wool into finest cloth is on display and the mill yard rings with sound of iron on stone as shire horses pull trams, haul buses, or give rides. The mill owner's house beside the mill is also open and gives an idea of domestic life around 1900 and the back-to-back cottages of Gaythorne Row, just across the street, show how the textile workers would have lived from the late 19th century until the 1950s. There are changing exhibitions and daily demonstrations, plus three special

events for 1995: VE Day Horse Parade (Sun 7 May); Fleece to Fabric (Sun 27 Aug); Christmas Event (Sun 17 Dec).
Open all year, Tue-Sun & BH Mon 10-5. (Closed Mon ex BH)
✳*Free. Charges made for rides.*
🅿 🖳 & *(induction loop in lecture theatre) toilets for disabled shop* ⊗

National Museum of Photography,Film & Television
BRADFORD
Pictureville
☎(01274) 727488
The National Museum of Photography, Film and Television portrays the past, present and future of the media using interactive displays and dramatic reconstructions - ride on a magic carpet, become a newsreader for the day or try your hand at vision mixing. Action Replay, the Museum's own theatre company, regularly performs highlights from the galleries. At the heart of the Museum is IMAX, the UK's largest cinema screen, which is over five storeys high. Vast, brilliant images sweep you into another world, exploring the realms of space to the depths of the ocean or indeed any subject big enough to be turned into this extraordinary experience. Pictureville Cinema houses the only public, wide-screen cinerama in the world. Following the First Bradford Film Festival, which took place in March, there will be events in conjunction with celebrations relating to the centenary of cinema (1995-1996). Telephone for details.
Open all year, Tue-Sun & BH's 10.30-6. (Closed Mon).
Museum free, IMAX Cinema £3.80 (concessions £2.60).
P (NCP) 🖳 & *toilets for disabled shop* ⊗

Bramham Park
BRAMHAM
(on A1 4m S of Wetherby)
☎*Boston Spa (01937) 844265*
This fine Queen Anne house was built by Robert Benson and is the home of his descendants. The garden has ornamental ponds, cascades, temples and avenues. International horse trials are held here 8-11 June.
Gardens open Etr, May Day & Spring BH wknds 1.15-5.30: House & gardens 18 Jun-3 Sep, Sun, Tue, Wed & Thu also Aug BH Mon, 1.15-5.30. (Last admission 5pm).
£3.50 (ch 5 £1.50, pen £2.50). Grounds only £2 (ch 5 £1, pen £1.50). Party 20+.
🅿 & *toilets for disabled* ⊗ *(ex in grounds)*

Smith Art Gallery
BRIGHOUSE
Halifax Rd
☎(01484) 719222
The gallery shows temporary exhibitions of local artists' work and modern works throughout the year.
Open all year, Mon-Sat (ex Wed) 10-5; also Apr-Sep, Sun 2-5. (Closed Xmas & 1 Jan).
Free.
🅿 & ⊗

Red House
GOMERSAL
Oxford Rd (on A651)
☎(01274) 872165
A period house decorated and displayed to reflect the 1830s home of a Yorkshire wool clothier and merchant. The house and family was visited by Charlotte Brontë in the 1830s and featured in her novel *Shirley*.
Open all year, Mon-Fri 11-5, Sat-Sun 12-5. Telephone for Xmas opening.
Free.
🅿 & *(Braille & tape guide available) toilets for disabled shop* ⊗

Bankfield Museum
HALIFAX
Boothtown Rd, Akroyd Park
☎(01422) 354823
Built by Edward Akroyd in the 1860s, this Renaissance-style building is set in parkland on a hill overlooking the town. It has an outstanding collection of costumes and textiles from many periods and parts of the world. There is also a section on toys, and the museum of the Duke of Wellington's Regiment is housed here. Temporary exhibitions are held and there is a lively programme of events, workshops and activities. Please apply for details..
Open all year, Tue-Sat 10-5, Sun 2-5. (Closed Xmas & 1 Jan).
Free.
🅿 & *shop* ⊗

Calderdale Industrial Museum
HALIFAX
Square Rd
☎(01422) 358087
Working machines representing 100 years of local industry from textiles to toffee wrapping; steam engines to washing machines. . . with all the sounds and smells to match! There is an under-6's activity area called the Workplays and also a lively programme of events, activities and workshops. Please apply for details.
Open all year, Tue-Sat 10-5, Sun 2-5 (Closed Mon ex BH's, 25-26 Dec & 1 Jan).
£1.50 (ch, pen & UB40 75p).
🅿 & *(lift) toilets for disabled shop* ⊗

Eureka! The Museum for Children
HALIFAX
Discovery Rd (next to the Railway Station)
☎(01426) 983191 & (01422) 330275
Eureka! is the first 'hands on' museum in Britain designed especially for children up to the age of 12. Wherever you go in Eureka! you can touch, listen and smell, as well as look. There are three main exhibition areas - Me and My Body, Living and Working Together, and Invent, Create, Communicate - where you can find out how your body and senses work, role-play in the buildings around the town square and explore the world of communications from basic forms through to the hi-tech inventions of today.
Outside in the Eureka! Park you can exercise on the Health Trail and experience the Hazard Dome, an audio-visual presentation with special 3-D effects about home safety. A programme of exhibitions, activities, workshops and performances runs throughout the year. Telephone for full details.
Open all year, Mon 10-2 (10-5 during Eureka! school holidays), Tue 10-5, Wed 10-7, Thu-Sun, 10-5. Telephone for details of Eureka! term time and school holiday dates.
£4.50 (ch 3-12 £3.50, under 3 free). Saver ticket £14.50.
🅿 *(charged)* 🖳 & *(lift, staff trained in sign language) toilets for disabled shop* ⊗

Piece Hall
HALIFAX
☎(01422) 358087
The merchants of Halifax built the elegant and unique hall in 1775, as a trading place for pieces of cloth. It has over 300 merchant's rooms around a courtyard, and now houses an industrial museum, art galleries and shops selling antiques, books and other specialities. There is an open market on Friday and Saturday, and a flea market on Thursday. Tourist information point. Free ➔

Bramham Park is a fine Queen Anne house built in the Italianate style by Robert Benson. The house stands in a park inspired by Versailles.

entertainment most weekends and there is a lively programe of exhibitions, workshops, activities and events throughout the year. Please apply for details.
Open all year daily 10-5 (Closed 25-26 Dec). Industrial Museum Tue-Sat 10-5, Sun 2-5. Art Gallery Tue-Sun 10-5.
✲Free (ex small admission charge for the Industrial Museum & when special events are held).
P (50 yds) ⬛ ✗ licensed & (lift to all floors) shop

Shibden Hall & Folk Museum
HALIFAX
Godley Ln
☎(01422) 352246
The house dates back to the early 15th century, and its rooms have been laid out to illustrate life in different periods of its history. The vast 17th-century barn has a fine collection of horse-drawn vehicles and craft workshops such as blacksmiths and saddlers. There is a lively programme of craft events, workshops and family activities. Please apply for details..
Open Mar-Nov, Mon-Sat 10-5, Sun 12-5; Feb, Sun 2-5. (Closed Dec-Jan).
£1.50 (concessions 75p).
P ⬛ & shop ✲

Harewood House & Bird Garden
HAREWOOD
(junc A61/A659 Leeds/Harrogate Rd)
☎(0113) 2886225
The 18th-century home of the Earl and Countess of Harewood contains fine furniture, porcelain and paintings, and its 'Capability' Brown grounds offer lakeside and woodland walks. The Bird Garden has aviaries for over 150 species, and a tropical house. Adventure playground. Numerous special events take place throughout the year including:a Fun Run (1 May); the Harewood Festival of Craft, Fashion and Design (27-30 May) and Harewood Steam Rally (26-28 August). Telephone 0113 2886331 for further details of these and other events.
Open 13 Mar-Oct, daily Bird Garden from 10am, House from 11am.
£5.75 (ch & student £3, pen £5). Party.
P ⬛ ✗ licensed & (electric ramp to front door of house) toilets for disabled shop garden centre ✲ (in House or bird garden)

Keighley & Worth Valley Railway & Museum
HAWORTH
Keighley, Haworth, Oxenhope & Ingrow West
☎Keighley (01535) 645214 & 677777
The line was built mainly to serve the valley's mills, and goes through the heart of Brontë country. It begins at Keighley (also a BR station), and then climbs up to Haworth, the railway headquarters. The terminus is at Oxenhope, which has a museum and restoration building. There are 36 steam engines and eight diesels. Special events are planned throughout 1995.
All year weekend service, but daily all BH wks & Jul-1st wk Sep.
✲Full line ticket £4.50 reduced fares for ch & pen. Family ticket £10. Other fares on request.
P (charged) ⬛ & (wheelchairs can be accommodated in brake car). toilets for disabled shop

Automobilia Transport Museum
HEBDEN BRIDGE
Billy Ln, Old Town, Wadsworth (Take A6033)
☎(01422) 844775
The restored three-storey textile warehouse contains a collection of Austin and Morris cars, motorcycles and bicycles, together with other items of motoring nostalgia. There will be a Vintage Weekend (5-6 August) with vehicles from 1956-1975 on Saturday and vehicles up to 1955 on Sunday.
Open all year, Etr week daily; May-Sep, Tue, Thu, Fri & Sun; Oct-Apr Sun only. BH Mon. 12-5. Groups at other times by arrangement.
£2.20 (ch 5-15 £1.10, pen, students & UB40's £1.50). Family ticket £5.50
P & shop ✲

Holmfirth Postcard Museum
HOLMFIRTH
47 Huddersfield Rd
☎(01484) 682231
Britain's first postcard museum, exhibiting a selection of Bamforth & Co sentimental and comic postcards and lantern slides. There are also video presentations of Bamforth's pioneering silent films and the dramatic story of the Holmfirth flood of 1852.
Open all year, Mon-Sat 10-4, Sun 12-4
£1 (ch 50p). Prices under review.
P (charged) & (lift to all floors) toilets for disabled shop ✲

Art Gallery
HUDDERSFIELD
Princess Alexandra Walk
☎(01484) 513808 ext 216
The permanent collections include British oil paintings, watercolours, drawings and sculpture from the mid-19th century onwards. Temporary loan exhibitions are also held throughout the year. From 2 September - 21 October, Tender Senses - Tampered Surface, contemporary art from Pakistan.
Open all year, Mon-Fri 10-5, Sat 10-4. Closed Sun & Xmas.
Free.
& toilets for disabled shop ✲

Tolson Memorial Museum
HUDDERSFIELD
Ravensknowle Park (on A629)
☎(01484) 530591
Displays on the development of the cloth industry and a collection of horse-drawn vehicles are shown, together with natural history, archaeology, toys and folk exhibits. There is a full programme of events and temporary exhibitions.
Open all year. Mon-Fri 11-5, Sat & Sun noon-5. (Closed Xmas).
Free.
P & toilets for disabled shop ✲

Manor House Gallery & Museum
ILKLEY
Castle Yard, Church St (behind Ilkley Parish Church, on A65)
☎(01943) 600066
The Elizabethan manor house is one of Ilkley's few buildings to pre-date the 19th century. The house was built on the site of a Roman fort and part of the Roman wall can be seen, together with Roman relics and displays on archaeology. Inside there is also a collection of 17th-and 18th-century farmhouse parlour and kitchen furniture, while the art gallery exhibits works by contemporary artists and craftsmen. Exhibitions for 1995 include: 4 Feb-5 Mar & 11 Mar-9 Apr Art Clubs Annual Exhibition; 15 Apr-11 Jun Ruth Fetis & Maggie Melechi; 17 June-10 Sep Robert Lee & Andrew Coates; 4 Nov-3 Dec Hands on History.
Open all year, Apr-Sep, Tue-Sun 10-6; Oct-Mar, Tue-Sun 10-5. Also BH Mon. (Closed Good Fri, 25-28 Dec).
Free.
& shop ✲

Cliffe Castle Museum & Gallery
KEIGHLEY
Spring Gardens Ln (NW of town off A629)
☎Bradford (01274) 758230
French furniture from the Victoria and Albert Museum is displayed, together with collections of local and natural history, ceramics, dolls, geological items and minerals. The grounds of this 19th-century mansion contain a play area and an aviary. Exhibitions for 1995 include: until May, Predators: The Hunters & The Hunted; 4 Mar-2 Apr Art Clubs Annual Exhibition; 8 Apr-11 Jun Yorkshire Pastel Society; 24 Jun-3 Sep Photographs by Lisa Dracup; 9 Sep-19 Nov Ken Graveling & David Greenwood.
Open all year, Apr-Sep Tue-Sun 10-6; Oct-Mar Tue-Sun 10-5. Also open BH Mon. (Closed Good Fri, 25-28 Dec).
Free.
P ⬛ & toilets for disabled shop ✲

East Riddlesden Hall
KEIGHLEY
Bradford Rd (1m NE of town)
☎(01535) 607075
This charming 17th-century Yorkshire manor house is typical of its kind, although the plasterwork and oak panelling are contemporary. A small secluded garden is found in the grounds, which also feature one of the largest medieval tithe barns in the north of England.
Open Apr-Oct, Mon-Wed 12.30-5, wknds 12-5. Also Fri in Jul & Aug 12.30-5. Last admission 4.30pm.
£3 (ch £1.50). Family ticket £6.
P ⬛ & shop ✲
(NT)

Yorkshire Car Collection
KEIGHLEY
Grange St
☎(01535) 690499
Almost 100 cars on display including Star Cars - once owned by celebrities such as Mick Jagger; TV & Screen Cars - which have appeared in *Heartbeat, Taggart* and many more. There are displays of Automotive Memorabilia throughout the museum as well as a collection of arcade machines - penny slot machines of yesteryear, an old time garage, fairground organ, motorcycles and cycles of bygone days.
Open Etr-Oct daily 10-5; Nov-Etr wknds. Closed Dec.
£3.50 (ch, pen, students & UB40 £2.50). Groups 20+
P & toilets for disabled shop ✲

Armley Mills Industrial Museum
LEEDS
Canal Rd, Armley (2m W of city centre, off A65)
☎(01532) 637861
Once the world's largest woollen mill. When the shuttles fly and the bobbins spin, Armley Mills evokes memories of the 18th-century woollen industry, showing the progress of wool from the sheep to knitted clothing. The museum has its own 1920s cinema and illustrates the history of cinema projection, including the first moving pictures taken in Leeds, as well as 1920s silent movies. There are demonstrations of static engines and steam locomotives, and a unique exhibition of underground haulage. Special events for 1995 include machine knitting workshops in March, Lace Guild workshops in April and classic car rallies in May and September; for further details ring Samantha Flavin - Keeper of Events and Exhibitions at the mill.
Open all year, Tue-Sat 10-5, Sun 2-5. Last entry 1 hr before closing. (Closed Mon ex BHs).
✲£2 (ch 50p pen, students & UB40's £1)
P & (chair-lifts between floors) toilets for disabled shop ✲

Kirkstall Abbey & Abbey House Museum
LEEDS
Abbey Rd, Kirkstall (off A65, W of city centre).
☎(0113) 2755821
The most complete 12th-century Cistercian Abbey in the country stands on the banks of the River Aire. The abbey is also the venue for a major folk museum with full-size Victorian shops, workshops and cottages shown in minute detail. An exhibition 'How we Used to Live' is being held 3 September-31 December 1994.
Open all year, Mon-Sat 9.30-5, Sun 1-5. Abbey site open dawn-dusk.
£2 (accompanied ch 50p, pen & concessions £1). Abbey free.
P & toilets for disabled shop ✲

Middleton Colliery Railway
LEEDS
Moor Rd, Hunslet (junc 45/M1 or follow signs from A61)
☎(0113) 2710320 (ansaphone)
This was the first railway authorised by an Act of Parliament (in 1758) and the first to succeed with steam locomotives (in 1812). Steam trains run each weekend in

Most of Harewood House dates from the 1770s and the interior is exquisitely designed by Robert Adam, who produced a particularly fine Gallery with a 76ft long ceiling.

season from Tunstall Road roundabout to Middleton Park. Facilities include a picnic area, nature trail, playgrounds and fishing. There is a programme of special events.
Moor Road Station open for viewing every wknd. Trains run Apr-Dec wknds.
P ♿ (with prior arrangement) shop
Details not confirmed for 1995

Temple Newsam House & Park
LEEDS
(off A63)
☎(0113) 2647321 (House) & 2645535 (Park)
Described as 'the Hampton Court of the North' this Tudor and Jacobean mansion boasts extensive collections of decorative arts in their original room settings, including the incomparable Chippendale collection. An extensive programme of renovation is restoring each room to its former glory, using original wall coverings and furniture. Set in 1,200 acres of parkland (landscaped by 'Capability' Brown), the Rare Breeds Centre in the Home Farm delights visitors. The gardens have a magnificent display of rhododendrons, whilst a riot of roses bloom amid vibrant borders in the old walled garden.
Open all year - House, Tue-Sat & BH Mon, 10.30-5.30 or dusk, Sun, 2-5.30 or dusk; Home Farm, daily 10-4 (3pm in winter); Gardens, 10-dusk; Estate, daily dawn-dusk.
P ☕ ♿ (ramps giving full access to parkland) toilets for disabled shop 🚫🐕
Details not confirmed for 1995

Tetley's Brewery Wharf
LEEDS
The Waterfront
☎(0113) 2420666
Situated in the heart of Leeds, Tetley's Brewery Wharf introduces visitors to the fascinating history of the English pub. With the aid of actors, visitors wiil see life in a 14th-century ale-house, through to Elizabethan, Jacobean, Georgian and Victorian hostelries, a 1940s blitzed pub and finally a futuristic pub at the end of the universe. Crafts associated with the history of pubs are demonstrated - from inn sign painting to a cooper making traditional wood barrels. Other attractions include an adventure playground, picnic area, restaurant, and an amphitheatre where a range of events is planned for the holiday season.
Open all year, Apr-Sep, daily 10-6; Oct-Mar, Wed-Sun 10-6. Last admission 4.30.
£4.50 (ch 14 £2.50, concesssions £3.60). Brewery tour which is optional £2.
P (charged) ✕ licensed ♿ (lift & ramps) toilets for disabled shop

Thwaite Mills
LEEDS
Thwaite Ln, Stourton (2m S of city centre)
☎(0113) 2496453
A knowledgeable guide will take you on a fascinating tour of this water-powered mill which sits marooned between the River Aire, which drives the wheels, and the Aire and Calder Navigation. Two great swishing wheels continually drive a mass of cogs and grinding wheels which crushed stone for putty and paint throughout the 19th century. This was the hub of a tiny island community, and the Georgian mill-owner's house has been restored, and houses displays exploring the mill's history. Visitors can watch the story on video before or after the guided tour. Tours start on the hour and last approximately 45 minutes. There is a fun day on Easter Monday.
Open all year, Tue-Sun 10-5 & BH Mon. Last tour 4pm. (Closed 25-26 Dec & 1 Jan).
P ♿ (wheelchair lifts) toilets for disabled shop
Details not confirmed for 1995

Lotherton Hall
LOTHERTON HALL
(10m E of Leeds, off B1217, near Aberford).
☎Leeds (0113) 2813259
Built in Edwardian times, the former home of the Gascoigne family is now a country house museum. It contains furniture, pictures, silver and ceramics from the Gascoigne collection, and works of art on loan from Leeds galleries. Other attractions include a gallery of Oriental art, a display of British fashion, contemporary crafts and frequent special exhibitions. Outside, the Edwardian garden, bird garden and deer park are delightful places in which to stroll.
Open all year, Tue-Sat 10.30-5.30 or dusk, Sun 2-5.30 or dusk. (Closed Xmas).
P ☕ ✕ licensed ♿ shop 🚫🐕 (ex in park)
Details not confirmed for 1995

The Yorkshire Mining Museum
MIDDLESTOWN
Caphouse Colliery, New Rd (on A642 between Wakefield & Huddersfield)
☎Wakefield (01924) 848806
A unique opportunity to go 450ft underground down one of Britain's oldest working mine shafts, where models and machinery depict methods and conditions of mining from the early 1800s to the present day. Visitors are strongly advised to wear sensible footwear and warm clothing. Surface displays (both indoor and outdoor), pit ponies, 'paddy' train rides, steam winder, nature trail and adventure playground. Special events planned for 1995 include a free familiarisation visit for teachers during the February half term, an Easter egg hunt on 16 April, a horse day on 20 August and Father Christmas underground on 2, 3, 9, 10, 16 and 17 December.
Open all year, daily 10-5. (Closed 24-26 Dec & 1 Jan).
£5.50 (ch £4, concessions £4.55).
P ☕ ♿ (induction loops, braille guide, audio tour, minicom) toilets for disabled shop

Nostell Priory
NOSTELL PRIORY
(6m SE of Wakefield, off A638)
☎Wakefield (01924) 863892
Built by Paine in the middle of the 18th century, the priory has an additional wing built by Adam in 1766. It contains a notable saloon and tapestry room and displays pictures and Chippendale furniture. There is a lake in the grounds. Events being held include the Royal British Legion Rally and a Country Fair.
Open Apr-Jun & Sep-Oct, Sat 12-5, Sun 11-5; Jul-10 Sep daily ex Fri 12-5, Sun 11-5; BH Mon 11-5.
House & Grounds £3.50 (ch £1.80). Family ticket £7. Grounds only £2.20 (ch £1.10). Party.
P ☕ ♿ (lift) toilets for disabled shop 🚫🐕
(NT)

Oakwell Hall
OAKWELL HALL
Nutter Ln, Birstall (6m SE of Bradford)
☎(01924) 474926
A moated Elizabethan manor house, furnished as it might have looked in the 1690s. Extensive Country Park with countryside centre. There are period gardens, an equestrian arena and an adventure playground. Special events for 1995 include a Country Fair (27 August) and Christmas Craft Fair (3 December); in addition, history comes to life in a recreation of 17th-century domestic life in the hall from 27 till 29 May..
Open all year, daily (ex Good Fri, Xmas & New Year).
Admission fee payable.
P ☕ ♿ (herb garden for the blind) toilets for disabled shop 🚫🐕

Pontefract Museum
PONTEFRACT
Salter Row
☎(01977) 797289
Displays on the history of Pontefract from prehistoric times to the present day and a wide range of exhibitions. In 1995 these will include *Dolls and Dolls' Houses* (4 February-26 March), *Snickets and Ginnels* (8 April-11 June), *Woodhall Excavations* (15 July-3 September) and a clothes show (16 September-24 October).
Open all year, Mon-Sat 10.30-5, Sun 2.30-5 & all BH during summer & spring. (Closed Xmas, New Year & Bhs).
Free.
♿ shop 🚫🐕

Commonwealth Institute Northern Regional Centre
SHIPLEY
Salts Mill, Victoria Rd, Saltaire
☎(01274) 530251
The Commonwealth Institute Northern Regional Centre is attractively situated in Salts Mill in the heart of historic Saltaire. A programme of visual arts and crafts exhibitions, educational workshops and cultural events are organised to promote the 50 countries of the Commonwealth.
Open all year, Mon-Fri 10-5, Sun 11-4. (Closed Good Fri, May Day, 24-26 Dec & 1 Jan).
P (200 yds) ♿ toilets for disabled 🚫🐕
Details not confirmed for 1995

Reed Organ & Harmonium Museum
SHIPLEY
Victoria Hall, Victoria Rd, Saltaire
☎Bradford (01274) 585601 after 6pm
Europe's first reed organ museum contains a collection of 70 models. The smallest is no bigger than a family bible and the largest, which belonged to Dr Marmaduke P Conway when he was organist at Ely Cathedral, has three manuals and pedals. If you are a player, you may have the chance to try some of the instruments. There are also harmoniums on display, which have featured on television and radio.
Open Sun-Thu, 11-4. (Closed 2 wks Xmas).
**£1.50 (ch & pen £1). Family £3.50. Party 10+.*
♿ toilets for disabled 🚫🐕

Wakefield Art Gallery
WAKEFIELD
Wentworth Ter
☎(01924) 375402
Wakefield was home to two of Britain's greatest modern sculptors - Barbara Hepworth and Henry Moore. The art gallery, which has an important collection of 20th-century paintings and sculptures, has a special room devoted to these two local artists. There are frequent temporary exhibitions of both modern and earlier works covering all aspects of art and crafts. Special events for 1995 include summer quizzes for children as well as the following exhibitions (some of which may be accompanied by workshops): Rembrandt Etchings (21 January-5 March), Wakefield Art Club (18 March-30 April), Rugs (13 May-25 June), Gyorgy Gordon (8 July-3 September), Stephen Court (9 September-22 October) and Cathy Kollwitz (28 October-26 November).
Open all year, Mon-Sat 10.30-5, Sun 2.30-5. Also BH during spring & summer. (Closed Xmas & New Year).
Free.
P shop 🚫🐕

Wakefield Museum
WAKEFIELD
Wood St
☎(01924) 295351
Wakefield Museum is full of objects and images which depict Wakefield's long and complex history. From flint axes and Roman pottery to steam trains and plastic tea cups. The museum also houses the exotic and eccentric natural history collections of the Victorian explorer Charles Waterton. There are also temporary exhibitions covering a wide range, from wildlife photography to platform shoes. Special events for 1995 include summer quizzes for children as well as exhibitions of fine china (4 February-12 March), Giles' cartoons (29 March-4 June) and quilts and samplers (15 June-30 July) and *Investigating the Past* (12 August-20 October).
Open all year, Mon-Sat 10.30-5, Sun 2.30-5. Also BH in spring & summer. (Closed Xmas, New Year & BH).
Free.
P shop 🚫🐕

Yorkshire Sculpture Park
WEST BRETTON
Bretton Hall
☎Wakefield (01924) 830302
One of Europe's leading sculpture parks, Yorkshire Sculpture Park has pioneered the siting of sculpture in the open air, organising temporary exhibitions of modern and contemporaty sculpture by national and international artists in over 100 acres of beautiful parkland. There are also changing displays from the loan collection by artists including Henry Moore, Barbara Hepworth, Elisabeth Frink, Bourdelle, Igor Mitoraj and Lynn Chadwick. There is a highly active educational programme for children and adults.
Open all year 10-6 (summer) 10-4 (winter). (Closed 25-26 Dec & 1 Jan)
P ☕ ♿ (scooters available for disabled) toilets for disabled shop
Details not confirmed for 1995

WIGHT, ISLE OF

The Needles Old Battery
ALUM BAY
West High Down (.75m SW)
☎Isle of Wight (01983) 754772
This former Palmerston fort, built in 1862, has recently been restored. It sits 77m above sea level. A 60m tunnel leads to a look-out position with spectacular views of the Needles chalk stacks and lighthouse, and across the bay to Dorset. In the fort are two of the original 12-ton gun barrels: they were hauled up from the sea and now lie in the parade ground. The powder house has an exhibition of the history of the Needles headland, from the establishment of the battery to the present day.
Open 30 Mar-2 Nov, Sun-Thu; also open Etr wknd & daily in Jul & Aug. (last admission 4.30).
£2.40 (ch £1.20).
☕ shop
(NT)

The Needles Pleasure Park
ALUM BAY
(signposted, on B3322)
☎Isle of Wight (01983) 752401
Overlooking the Needles on the heritage coastline at the western edge of the Island, the park has attractions for all the family. Super X provides thrills, whilst the Carousel conjures up memories of a bygone age. The chairlift to the beach enables visitors to enjoy the most famous view on the Island and the unique coloured sands. Entertainment is a regular feature of the pedestrianised Festival Street. Vision 180 Thrill Cinema is a new attraction, and events for 1995 include a Spring motor fair (30 April) and the annual firework extravaganza (24 August).
Open Apr-Oct, daily 10-5 (Aug Sun-Thu 10-6).
**No admission charged for entrance to Pleasure Park. Supersaver ticket £5 (ch £3.50). Chargeable attractions individually priced, details not given.*
P (charged) ✕ licensed ♿ toilets for disabled shop

Haseley Manor
ARRETON
☎Isle of Wight (01983) 865420
This is the oldest and largest manor open to the public on the Island. Parts of the south wing have some of the original building, c1350, but the rest of the house is a mixture of styles including Georgian and Victorian. The manor fell into disuse and was derelict by the 1970s but has since been carefully restored and now 20 rooms can be viewed, furnished in period style. Tableaux of figures in costume appear in many of the rooms. ➔

Outside, there is a re-constructed 18th-century farm complete with animals, and a well-stocked herb garden. There is also a children's play area with a tree house, and a small lake with an island castle. Visitors can also see pottery and sweet-making demonstrations, and craftsmen are at work in restored agricultural buildings.
Open Etr-Oct, daily 10-5.30.
£3.95 (ch £2.95, pen £3.15). Party.
🅿 🍽 ✗ & toilets for disabled shop

Bembridge Windmill
BEMBRIDGE
(.5m S on B3395)
☎ Isle of Wight (01983) 873945
The only windmill on the island to survive, Bembridge mill was built about 1700 and was in use until 1913. The stone-built tower with its wooden cap and machinery have been restored since it was given to the National Trust in 1961.
Open 2 Apr-Oct, daily (ex Sat) & Etr Sat & Jul-Aug, daily 10-5. Last admission 4.45.
£1.20 (ch 60p)
🅿 shop ⌀
(NT)

Isle of Wight Shipwreck Centre & Maritime Museum
BEMBRIDGE
Providence House, Sherborne St
☎ Isle of Wight (01983) 872223 & 873125
Situated at the centre of Bembridge village, this fine museum brings alive the maritime history of the Isle of Wight. There are six galleries displaying a unique collection of salvage and shipwreck items, early diving equipment, ship models, HMS *Swordfish,* and a model of the harbour.
Open late Mar-Oct, daily 10-5. (Other times by appointment)
£2.10 (ch £1.35, pen & students £1.50).
🅿 & shop ⌀

Blackgang Chine Fantasy Park
BLACKGANG
(off A3055)
☎ Isle of Wight (01983) 730330
Opened as scenic gardens in 1843 covering some 40 acres, the park has imaginative play areas, water gardens, maze and coastal gardens. Set on the steep wooded slopes of the chine are the themed areas Smugglerland (complete with pirate ship), Nurseryland, Dinosaurland, Fantasyland and Frontierland. Various special events are held throughout the year.
St Catherine's Quay has a maritime exhibition showing the history of local and maritime affairs, including engines in steam. It is in an attractive park that has been 'themed' into different areas, with a complete replica of a Victorian water-powered saw mill and a display of woodland skills and traditional crafts. There is a static engine display from

November to March, and events for 1995 also include *Blackgang Plays the Fool* - a day of zany fun and frolics - on April Fools Day, the Most Amazing Island Tea Party (8 May), Superhero Championships and Pirate Fiesta (28 May) and Wild West Hoe-downs every Friday.
Open 28 Mar-30 Oct daily, 10-6, 28 May-28 Sep, daily 10-10 (floodlit).
Combined ticket to chine, sawmill & quay £4.99 (ch 3-13 £3.99).
🅿 (charged) 🍽 ✗ licensed & toilets for disabled shop

Isle of Wight Wax Museum
BRADING
High St (on A3055)
☎ Isle of Wight (01983) 407286
Rub shoulders with famous and infamous characters through 2000 years of the island's colourful fantsies, legends and facts - brought to life in dramatic scenes with sound, light and animation. Visitors can also see the Ancient Rectory mansion (c1066 AD), the Chamber of Horrors, set in the castle dungeons, and adjacent Aniomal World of Natural History.
Open all year, May-Sep 10-10pm; Oct-Apr 10-5. (Open 25 Dec).
❋£3.99 (ch 14 £2.99, under 3 free). Party 20+. Includes free entry into "Chamber of Horrors" & Animal World of Natural History.
🅿 & shop

Lilliput Antique Doll & Toy Museum
BRADING
High St
☎ Isle of Wight (01983) 407231
This private museum contains one of the finest collections of dolls (and some toys) in Britain. There are over 2000 exhibits, ranging in age from 2000BC to 1945 with examples of almost every seriously collectable doll.
Open daily (ex 15 Jan-15 Mar), 10-5 (winter), 9.30-9.30pm (summer).
£1.35 (ch & pen 95p, ch under 5 free). Party.
P (200 yds) & shop

Morton Manor
BRADING
(off A3055 in Brading)
☎ Isle of Wight (01983) 406168
The manor dates back to 1249, but was rebuilt in 1680 with further changes during the Georgian period. The house contains furniture of both the 18th and 19th centuries, but its main attraction lies in the beautiful gardens and the vineyard. The garden is landscaped into terraces, with ornamental ponds, a sunken garden and a traditional Elizabethan turf maze. In recent years vine-growing for wine has become popular on the island, and Morton Manor is one of the places to have an established vineyard and winery.

A museum of winemaking relics has been set up, and has some unusual exhibits, including a modern working winery and video.
Open Apr-Oct, daily 10-5.30 (Closed Sat).
❋£2.90 (ch £1 & pen £2.50). Party 15+.
🅿 ✗ licensed & shop garden centre

Nunwell House & Gardens
BRADING
(Off Ryde-Sandown Rd, A3055)
☎ (01983) 407240
Set in beautiful gardens, Nunwell is an impressive, lived-in and much loved house where King Charles I spent his last night of freedom. It has fine furniture, interesting collections of family militaria and a Home Guard museum. In summer, concerts are occasionally held in the music room. Phone for details.
Open, House & Gardens, 2 Jul-27 Sep, Sun 1-5. Mon-Wed 10-5. Groups welcome when house open & at other times by appointment.
£2.80 (ch 12 accompanied 60p, pen £2.30).
🅿 shop ⌀

Calbourne Watermill & Rural Museum
CALBOURNE
(on B3401)
☎ (01983) 531227
There has been a mill here since at least 1299, and the present 17th-century machinery still works when turned by the 20ft water wheel. The millpond and stream have been converted into an attractive water garden.
Open Etr-Oct, daily 10-6.
❋£2 (ch £1 & pen £1.50).
🅿 🍽 shop

Carisbrooke Castle
CARISBROOKE
(on B3401)
☎ (01983) 522107
A Norman castle adapted from a Saxon fort, Carisbrooke is the only medieval castle on the island. It is set on a hill 150ft high, and the 12th-century keep is built on an artificial mound of about 60ft. The keep overlooks the later Elizabethan and Jacobean additions and the strong castle walls.
There are two medieval wells in the castle. The keep has a 160ft-deep well, reached by climbing 71 steps, and the other is housed in a 16th-century wellhouse in the courtyard. The winding gear was traditionally driven by a donkey, and a team of donkeys now gives displays of the machinery working. Charles I was a prisoner in the castle from 1647-48, and the castle was the home of the Governor of the island. His lodge is now the Isle of Wight Museum.
Open all year, Apr-Sep, daily 10-6; Oct, 10-4; Nov-Mar, Wed-Sun 10-4. Closed 24-26 Dec & 1 Jan.

£3.50 (ch £1.80, concessions £2.60).
🅿 🍽 &
(EH)

Cowes Maritime Museum
COWES
Beckford Rd
☎ (01983) 293341
The exhibition is a permanent display in the public library, and includes ship models, photographs, paintings, books and other objects showing the island's maritime past.
Open all year, Mon-Wed & Fri 9.30-5.30, Sat 9.30-4.30. (Closed BH's).
Free.
P & ⌀

Barton Manor Vineyard & Gardens
EAST COWES
(on A3021)
☎ Isle of Wight (01983) 292835
Winners of Medina in Bloom and previous winners of Southern England in Bloom, Barton Manor Gardens and Vineyards also boasts the Island's largest hedge maze.
Open Apr-2nd Sun Oct, daily (also Etr) 10.30-5.30.
£3.50 (ch 15 1 per adult free) Prices include guide leaflet, souvenir tasting glass & two tastings.
🅿 ✗ licensed & (wheelchair route around gardens) toilets for disabled shop garden centre ⌀

Old Smithy Tourist Centre
GODSHILL
☎ Isle of Wight (01983) 840364
The former blacksmith's forge has a landscaped flower garden shaped like the Island, aviaries of exotic birds, and a herb garden. There are shops with gifts, clothes, herbs and crafts on sale.
Open Etr-Nov, daily including evenings in mid summer.
80p (ch 40p)
🅿 🍽 & shop

Isle of Wight Steam Railway
HAVENSTREET
The Railway Station
☎ Isle of Wight (01983) 882204
When the Newport to Ryde railway was closed, Haven Street Station was taken over by a private company, the Isle of Wight Steam Railway. A number of volunteers restored the station, locomotives and rolling stock, and steam trains now run the five miles from Wootton, via Haven Street to Smallbrook Junction where there is a direct interchange with the BR Ryde-Shanklin line. Locomotives in operation include former LSWR tank engine *Calbourne*, built in 1891, and LSBCR/Freshwater, Yarmouth & Newport Railway locomotive *Freshwater*, built in 1875. The rolling stock includes 70/80-year-old LBSCR/SECR carriages, plus vintage goods wagons.
At Haven Street, the old gas works houses a display of Island railway memorabilia.
Open 23 Mar-30 Apr, Thu, Sun & BH's; May, Wed, Thu & Sun also BH Mon; Jun-20 Jul, Tue-Thu & Sun; 23 Jul-3 Sep, daily; 5-28 Sep, Tue-Thu & Sun; Oct, Thu & Sun. Nov; Sun.
Return Fares £5.50 (ch 5-15 £3.50).
Family ticket £17.
🅿 🍽 & (with assistance) toilets for disabled shop

Roman Villa
NEWPORT
Cypress Rd
☎ (01983) 529720
Archaeologists have uncovered this 3rd-century Roman villa where visitors can now see the well-preserved baths and re-constructed rooms in which the family once lived. The site museum houses some of the finds from the excavation. Recent refurbishment has provided new displays in reconstructed rooms, a renewed artefact gallery and a Roman garden.
Open Etr-Oct, daily 10-5.30. Other times by appointment.

A sturdy Pirate Ship is one of many attractions at the Fantasy Park on the cliffs of Blackgang Chine.

Admission fee payable.
P *(100 yds)* & *shop* ⍉

Old Town Hall
NEWTOWN
(1m N of A3054)
☎ *Isle of Wight (01983) 741052*
The town hall is unusual in that it stands
alone, surrounded by grass and a few
houses, not in a crowded high street.
Although Newtown was once the
island's capital, it was badly burned in
1377 and never fully recovered. In 1699
the town hall was rebuilt and has been
further restored recently.
*Open 27 Mar-30 Oct, Mon, Wed & Sun
2-5 (also open Good Fri, Etr Sat & Jul-
Aug, Tue & Thu). Last admission 4.45pm.*
£1.10 (ch 55p)
P *(100yds)* ⍉
(NT)

Osborne House
OSBORNE HOUSE
(1m SE of East Cowes)
☎ *Isle of Wight (01983) 200022*
Designed by Prince Albert and Thomas
Cubitt and built between 1845 and 1848,
Osborne was the Royal Family's private
residence and Queen Victoria's favourite
home. She lived at Osborne most of the
time and died there in 1901. The house
was designed to resemble an Italian villa,
with terraced gardens overlooking
Osborne Bay. The state and private
apartments, which have been largely
untouched since Victoria's death, are
open to the public. The private
apartments upstairs are cosy and
comfortable and filled with all the
paraphernalia of daily life. The large
grounds are filled with every kind of
English tree, a miniature fort and a Swiss
cottage, where the Royal children learnt
cooking and gardening. A horse-drawn
carriage takes visitors to the Swiss
cottage gardens and museum.
*Open House - Apr-Oct, daily 10-5;
Grounds - 10-6; Oct 10-5.*
£5.80 (ch £2.90, concessions £4.40).
*Grounds only £3 (ch £1.50, concessions
£2.30)*
P 🖳 & *shop* ⍉
(EH)

Tropical Bird Park
ST LAWRENCE
Old Park
☎ *Isle of Wight (01983) 852583 & 853752*
A bird park situated in the heart of the
almost sub-tropical undercliff, in the
grounds of Old Park. Enclosed by high
stone walls are over 400 birds such as
toucans, macaws and cockatoos.
Woodland Trail is the home of eagles,
storks, vultures and owls. On an
ornamental lake are spoonbills,
flamingoes and ducks. An extra attraction
is a showroom where Isle of Wight glass
is blown and displayed.
*Open Etr-Oct, 10-5; Oct-Etr, 10-4. (Closed
25 Dec).*
*£2.75 (ch over 7 £1.90, pen £2.20), family
ticket £6.25.*
P *(charged)* 🖳 & *shop* ⍉

Museum of Isle of Wight Geology
SANDOWN
Sandown Library, High St
☎ *Isle of Wight (01983) 404344*
The museum houses extensive
collections of fossils and rocks. A special
feature has been made of recently
excavated dinosaur fossils. Modern
displays interpret millions of years of pre-
history on the Isle of Wight.
*Open all year, Mon-Fri 9.30-5.30, Sat
9.30-4.30. (Closed Sun).*
Free.
P *(100 yds) shop* ⍉

Shanklin Chine
SHANKLIN
☎ *Isle of Wight (01983) 866432*
Shanklin Chine is a natural gorge of great
scenic beauty with a spectacular 45ft
waterfall. A path winds down through the
boulders, overhanging trees, ferns and
other flora that cover its steep sides. The

Newtown, once the Isle of Wight's capital, suffered a bad fire in 1377 and never recovered. The Town Hall, although rebuilt in
1699, stands in unusual isolation.

Heritage Centre features details of nature
trails, rare flora and life in Victorian
Shanklin. Features of historic interest
include sections of PLUTO (pipeline
under the ocean), which carried petrol to
the Allied troops in Normandy. There is a
memorial to 40 Commando, Royal
Marines and during 1995, the Island's
Victory '45 Exhibition to celebrate and
commemorate the end of World War II
(Easter to mid October).
*Open 13 Apr-25 May 10-5; 26 May-24
Sep 10am-10pm (illuminated at night); 25
Sep-15 Oct 10-4.*
*£1.80 (ch 50p, pen & students £1.50).
Party.*
P *(400 yds)* 🖳 *shop*

Yafford Water Mill Farm Park
SHORWELL
☎ *Isle of Wight (01983) 740610 & 741125*
The mill is situated in attractive
surroundings with a large mill pond. The
great overshot wheel still turns and all
the milling machinery is in working order.
An unusual attraction is the millpond,
which is home to a seal. The millstream
has pools and falls with flowers and trees
along its banks. There is a nature trail
along the stream to the lakes - home to
ducks, coots and moorhen. Old farm
wagons, agricultural machinery and a
narrow gauge railway can also be seen
along with rare breeds of sheep, pigs and
cattle. Across the lane is a picnic area
and an adventure playground. Special
events for 1995 include: Children's
Treasure Hunt (16-17 April), Traction
Engines & Military Vehicles (VE Day) (6-8
May), Art at the Mill (28-29 May),
Summer Steam Rally (29-30 July),
Transport thro the Ages (12-13 August),
Military Vehicle Rally (2-3 September).
*Open all year, daily 10-6 or dusk in
winter. (Last admission 5pm).*
£2.90 (ch & pen £1.80). Party 10+.
P 🖳 & *toilets for disabled shop* ⍉

Museum of the History of
Smuggling
VENTNOR
Botanic Gardens (on A3055, 1m W of
Ventnor)
☎ *Isle of Wight (01983) 853677*
Situated underground in extensive vaults,
this unique museum shows methods of
smuggling used over a 700-year period
right up to the present day. Each year
there is in Ventnor an 'Isle of Wight
Smuggling Pageant' in the middle of
June. An adventure playground is near
the entrance in the Botanic Gardens.

Open Etr-Sep, daily 10-5.30.
*£1.80 (ch & pen 90p). Parties by
arrangement.*
P *(charged) shop garden centre*

Ventnor Botanic Garden
VENTNOR
Underdiff Dr
☎ *(01983) 855397*
Many rare and tender plants from all over
the world can be found in the 22 acres of
the Ventnor Botanic Garden, one of the
Island's largest gardens. The temperate
house features special displays which
may be seen for a small charge. Facilities
for the disabled include a garden of
raised beds with highly scented plants.
Guided tours by prior arrangement with
the curator. There are two gift shops, a
picnic area, and a children's playground
which is suitable for children of all
abilities, including those in wheelchairs,
pushchairs, and the visually impaired.
*Open all year - Garden; Temperate House
27 Mar-Oct daily 10-5; 7 Nov-27 Feb Sun
only 11-4; 1-26 Mar Tue-Thu 11-3 & Sun
1-4.*
❈*Garden - free; Temperate House - 50p
(ch 20p).*
P *(charged)* ✗ *licensed* & *toilets for
disabled shop* ⍉ *(ex in garden)*

Appuldurcombe House
WROXALL
☎ *Isle of Wight (01983) 852484*
The manor house at Wroxall began as a
priory in 1100. It later came into the
hands of the Worsley family, who pulled
down the original building and built
Appuldurcombe in the Palladian style.
Appuldurcombe has been a ruin since
World War II, but the grounds,
landscaped by Capability Brown, are still
beautiful.
Open Apr-Sep, daily 10-6.
£1.30 (ch £1, concession 70p).
P & ⍉
(EH)

Fort Victoria Country Park
YARMOUTH
Sconce Point (1m W, off A3054)
☎ *Isle of Wight (01983) 760860*
Based around the remains of a fort built
in 1855 to protect the western approach
to Portsmouth, the wide grassy areas,
coastal slopes, beach and sea wall have
been made into a country park. Affording
superb views of the Solent, there are
picnic and barbeque facilities, also guided
walks, exhibitions, a marine aquarium
and planetarium.
Open park daily. Aquarium open Etr-Oct

*10-6. Planetarium daily in season (ring
761555 for out of season opening times).
Maritime Heritage Exhibition open Etr-
Sep.*
P 🖳 & *toilets for disabled shop*
Details not confirmed for 1995

Yarmouth Castle
YARMOUTH
Quay St
☎ *(01983) 760678*
Now tucked away among newer
buildings, this rather homely castle is in
excellent repair. Visitors can see the
Master Gunner's parlour and kitchen,
plus an unusually small great hall. Built
during the reign of Henry VIII as a coastal
defence, the open gun platform provides
an excellent view of the harbour.
Open Apr-Sep, daily 10-6; Oct 10-4
£2 (ch £1, concessions £1.50)
& ⍉
(EH)

WILTSHIRE

Avebury Manor
AVEBURY
☎ *(01672) 539388*
Avebury Manor has a monastic origin,
and has been much altered since then.
The present buildings date from the early
16th century, with notable Queen Anne
alterations and Edwardian renovation.
The flower gardens contain medieval
walls, and there are examples of topiary.
*Open Garden & Keiller Museum Apr-Oct,
daily 10-6. Nov-Mar, daily 10-4. (Closed
24-26 Dec).*
*Garden £2.20 (ch £1.40). Museum £1.50
(ch 80p).*
P & *shop* ⍉
(NT)

Avebury Museum
AVEBURY
(Alexander Keiller Museum)
☎ *(01672) 539250*
This is one of the most important
prehistoric sites in Europe, and was built
before Stonehenge. In the midst of it is
the pretty village of Avebury, which is
surrounded by circles of massive sarsen
stones and an impressive circular
embankment and ditch. An avenue of
great stones leads to the site, which
must have been a place of great religious
significance. The small museum has
recently been refurbished and contains
many new exhibits. It is named after

➤

Bowood House is in a particularly fine setting with over 100 acres of garden laid out by Capability Brown and enhanced by clipped yews and stsuary.

Alexander Keiller, the first archaeologist to analyse the site in a modern way. It shows finds from Avebury and from Windmill Hill, a Neolithic causewayed enclosure about 1.5 miles away, which is also part of the National Trust property. Educational facilities are provided.
Open all year, Apr-Sep, daily 10-6; Oct-Mar, Wed-Sun 10-4. Closed 24-26 Dec & 1 Jan.
🅿 ♿ 🐾
(EH & NT)
Details not confirmed for 1995

Great Barn Museum of Wiltshire Life
AVEBURY
☎ *(01672) 539555*
Close to the prehistoric stones, the museum is housed in a fine 17th-century thatched barn with a splendid roof structure. There are displays on cheesemaking, thatching, saddlery, sheep and shepherds, and the work of blacksmiths, wheelwrights, and other rural crafts. Regular craft sessions take place on Sundays between April and September. During 1995 there is an exhibition on Wiltshire Past & Present.
Open all year, mid Mar-mid Nov, daily 10-6. mid Nov-mid Mar, Sat 11-5, Sun 11-5. 95p (ch & pen 50p). Family ticket £2.30.
P *(100yds)* ✕ *licensed* ♿ *toilets for disabled shop* 🐾

Bedwyn Stone Museum
BEDWYN, GREAT
☎ *Marlborough (01672) 870043*
This small but special open-air museum explains the ancient secrets of the stonemason, showing how carvings have a language of their own. A fine sequence of carvings can be seen in the nearby church.
Open all year.
🅿 ♿ *toilets for disabled*
Details not confirmed for 1995

Great Chalfield Manor
BRADFORD-ON-AVON
(3m SW of Melksham)
☎ *(01985) 847777*

Built during the Wars of the Roses, the manor is a beautiful, mellow, moated house which still has its great hall. It was restored in the 1920s. There is a small 13th-century church next to the house.
Open 4 Apr-31 Oct, Tue-Thu. Tours starting at 12.15, 2.15, 3, 3.45, 4.30. (Closed on PH).
£3.50.
🅿 🐾
(NT)

Tithe Barn
BRADFORD-ON-AVON
Over 160ft long by 30ft wide, the barn stands on Barton Farm, which belonged to Shaftesbury Abbey. It was probably used to store general farm produce as well as tithes of hay and corn. The roof is of stone slates, supported outside by buttresses and inside by an impressive network of great beams and rafters.
Open any reasonable time.
Free.
♿
(EH)

Atwell-Wilson Motor Museum
CALNE
"Downside", Stockley Ln (off A4 at Quemerford)
☎ *(01249) 813119*
The museum contains over 60 exhibits, which include cars from 1924-1983, classic motorbikes, lawn mowers and memorabilia. There will be a classic car, motorbike and tractor rally on 7 May 1995.
Open all year; Apr-Oct, Mon-Thu 10-5, Sun 11-5; Nov-Mar, Mon-Thu 10-4, Sun 11-4.
£2 (ch 75p & pen £1.50)
🅿 ♿ *toilets for disabled* 🐾 *guide dogs*

Bowood House & Gardens
CALNE
(off A4 in Derry Hill village)
☎ *(01249) 812102*
Originally built in 1624, the house was unfinished when it was bought by the first Earl of Shelburne in 1754. He employed celebrated architects, notably Robert

Adam, to complete the work, and what the visitor sees now is a handsome Georgian house. Adam's library is particularly admired, and also in the house is the laboratory where Dr Joseph Priestley discovered oxygen in 1774. There are fine paintings, sculptures, costumes and other displays. The chief glory of Bowood, however, is its 2000-acre expanse, 100 acres of which are pleasure gardens. They were laid out by 'Capability' Brown in the 1760s and are carpeted with daffodils, narcissi and bluebells in spring. The centrepiece is a lake, while terraces, roses, clipped yews and sculptures are a perfect complement to the house. There is also a hermit's cave, a temple and cascade; and for children there is a huge adventure playground.
Open 4 Apr-29 Oct, daily 11-6, including BH. Rhododendron Gardens (separate entrance off A342) open 6 weeks during May & Jun 11-6.
✳*House & Grounds £4.50 (ch £2.30 & pen £4). Party. Rhododendrons only £2.*
🅿 🍴 ✕ *licensed* ♿ *(parking by arrangement) toilets for disabled shop garden centre* 🐾

Sheldon Manor
CHIPPENHAM
☎ *(01249) 653120*
The Plantagenet manor house has a 13th-century porch and a 15th-century chapel. There are beautiful informal terraced gardens, with a water garden, ancient yews, a connoisseur collection of old-fashioned roses and a maze of edible plants. In 1994 Sheldon Manor was awarded the Gold Award for the AA/NPI Historic Houses Award as 'the house which best preserves its character, its authenticity and integrity in terms of architecture, furniture and contents but which, most importantly, remains a lived-in family home'.

Open Etr Sun & Mon, then every Sun, Thu & BH until 1 Oct, 12.30-6. House opens 2pm.
✳*House & gardens £3 (pen £2.75). Garden only £1.75 (pen £1.50).*
🅿 🍴 ✕ *licensed* ♿ *(wheelchair available) shop*

Corsham Court
CORSHAM
(4m W of Chippenham off the A4)
☎ *(01249) 701610*
The Elizabethan manor was built in 1582, and then bought by the Methuen family in the 18th century to house their collections of paintings and statues. 'Capability' Brown made additions to the house and laid out the park, and later John Nash made further changes. There is furniture by Chippendale, Adam, Cobb and Johnson inside, as well as the Methuen collection of Old Master paintings. The garden has flowering shrubs, herbaceous borders, a Georgian bath house, peacocks and a 15th-century gazebo.
Open Jan-Nov; Tue-Thu, Sat & Sun 2-4.30. (6pm Good Fri-Sep & also open Fri & BH) other times by appointment. Last admission half hour before closure.
🅿 ♿ *shop* 🐾
Details not confirmed for 1995

Devizes Museum
DEVIZES
41 Long St
☎ *(01380) 727369*
World-famous collections from the Neolithic, Bronze and Iron Age are on display. There is a Bronze Age gallery, an art gallery with a John Piper window, displays of natural history, and a Wiltshire research library.
Open all year, Mon-Sat 10-5. (Closed PH's).
✳*£1.75 (ch 40p, students & pen £1.25).*
♿ *shop* 🐾

The Courts
HOLT
(3m N of Trowbridge, on B3107)
☎ *Trowbridge (01225) 782340*
Weavers came to The Courts to have their disputes settled until the end of the 18th century. The house is not open, but it makes an attractive backdrop to the gardens - a network of stone paths, yew hedges, pools and borders with a strange, almost magical atmosphere.
Open 2 Apr-31 Oct, daily (ex Sat) 2-5. Out of season by appointment.
£2.80 (ch £1.40). Parties by arrangement.
& ✿
(NT)

Lackham Gardens, Museum and Woodland
LACOCK
(3m S of Chippenham, on A350)
☎ *Chippenham (01249) 443111*
Various visitor attractions are situated within the 210-hectare estate of the Lackham College of Agriculture. Thatched and refurbished farm buildings accommodate the farm museum and the grounds feature a walled garden, glasshouses, rhododendron glades, riverside and woodland walks, a children's adventure playground and two hectares of grassland devoted to rare breeds. There is a major collection of historical roses in the Italian Garden. Also grown in this garden was the largest citron (large lemon) which earned a place in the Guinness Book of Records.There are gardening demonstrations during the year and a vintage tractor rally and an Apple Day have been arranged. Telephone for details. Lackham Country Day will be held on 21 May 1995.
Open Apr-29 Oct, 11-5.
£3 (ch £1, concessions £1-£1.60). Family ticket £7.
🅿 ▬ ✕ & *(wheelchair available) toilets for disabled shop*

Lacock Abbey
LACOCK
(3m S of Chippenham, E of A350)
☎ *(01249) 730227*
Lacock Abbey is not only historic and beautiful, it was also the venue for a series of innovative photographic experiments by William Henry Fox Talbot, which led to the world's first photographic negative being made here in 1835. The abbey, set in a carefully preserved village of 14th-to 18th-century houses, was founded by Ela, Countess of Salisbury in the 13th century. At the Dissolution it was sold to William Sherrington, who destroyed the church and turned the nuns' quarters into a grand home. The cloisters from the original convent remain and other ancient features include an octagonal Tudor tower and half-timbered gables in the courtyard. In 1754 Sanderson Miller was commissioned to design a new entrance hall; this stands today as a superb example of the Gothic Revival style. A museum devoted to Fox Talbot (one of Sherrington's descendants) is housed in an old barn.
Open Apr-30 Oct; House, daily (ex Tue) 1-5.30; grounds & cloisters daily 12-5.30. Last admission 5pm. (Closed Good Fri).
£4.20 (ch £2.20). Grounds & cloisters £2.10 (ch £1). Parties. No pushchairs in Abbey.
🅿 & *(taped guides) toilets for disabled shop* ✿
(NT)

Longleat
LONGLEAT
The Estate Office (Entrance on Warminster-Frome Rd A362).
☎ *Warminster (01985) 844400*
The late lord Marquess of Bath was the first peer to open his house to the public on a regular basis, a trend which many would follow. The Longleat estate has now grown to offer the visitor a safari park (home to hundreds of wild animals, including Britain's only white tiger); an exciting Adventure Castle; a maze; safari boats; narrow-gauge railway and a multitude of exhibitions and other attractions. The centrepiece of all this tourist activity is the majestic Elizabethan house, built by Sir John Thynne in 1580 and decorated in the Italian Renaissance style in the late-19th century. It contains a mixture of furnishings and artefacts reflecting the tastes and interests of the Thynne family through the centuries, and the fully restored Victorian kitchens offer an interesting glimpse of life 'below stairs'. The magnificent grounds, laid out by 'Capability' Brown, offer many lovely walks. Heaven's Gate is particularly spectacular when the rhododendrons are flowering. Rallies and other special events are planned throughout 1995: Easter Balloon Fiesta & Egg Hunt(15-16 April); Prom Concert (8 July); The Wiltshire Balloon Festival (28-30 July); Jazz on a Summer Evening (19 August); Live Crafts (18-19 Nov). Telephone for information.
Open all year. House daily, 10-6 (Nov-Etr 10-4). Safari park, 11 Mar-29 Oct 10-6, last car admitted 5.30pm or sunset if earlier.
House: £4 (ch £2, pen £3). Safari Park: £5.50 (ch £3.50, pen £4.50). Passport ticket for all attractions: £11 (ch & pen £8).
🅿 ▬ ✕ *licensed & toilets for disabled shop* ✿ *(in Safari park-free kennels)*

Ludgershall Castle
LUDGERSHALL
(7m NW of Andover on A342)
Although a ruin since the 16th century, this was once a royal castle and hunting palace. The visitor can see large earthworks of the Norman motte-and-bailey castle and the flint walling of the later hunting palace. The medieval cross stands in the main street of the village.
Open all reasonable times.
Free.
🅿 &
(EH)

Lydiard Park
LYDIARD PARK
Lydiard Tregoze
☎ *Swindon (01793) 770401*
Set in beautiful country parkland, this fine Georgian house belonged to the St John family for 500 years up until 1943 when the house and parkland were purchased by the Swindon Corporation. Since then the sadly dilapidated house has been gradually restored and refurbished with period furniture (in many cases original to the house) and a large St John family portrait collection (also original to the house). Exceptional plasterwork, early wallpaper, a rare painted glass window, and a room devoted to the talented 18th-century amateur artist, Lady Diana Spencer, can also be seen. Adjacent, the church of St Marys has many fine and unusual memorials to the St John family. The Park, now operating as a Country Park, offers a variety of pleasant woodland walks, spacious lawns, lakes and children's adventure playground. A summer exhibition, The Lost Estate, depicting life on the old military camp at Lydiard Park in the 1950's, is just one of a series of events and exhibitions planned to run during 1995. The Wiltshire Festival is held here on August Bank Holiday weekend.
Open all year, House: Mon-Sat 10-1 & 2-5.30, Sun 2-5.30. (Closed Good Fri & Xmas). Winter closing 4pm (Nov-Feb). Park: all year, daily closing at dusk each day.
60p (ch 25p). Car parking 60p for 2 hours, £1 for day.
🅿 *(charged)* ▬ & *(Easiriders may be booked at visitors centre) toilets for disabled shop* ✿ *(ex in park)*

Crofton Beam Engines
MARLBOROUGH
Crofton Pumping Station, Crofton (6m SE of Marlborough, signposted from A338)
☎ *(01672) 870300 & 851639 (Hon.Sec)*
The oldest working beam engine in the world still in its original building and still doing its original job, the Boulton and Watt 1812, is to be found in this rural spot. Its companion is a Harvey's of ➤

The Red Library at Longleat House contains 6,000 books and is decorated in Italian Renaissance style with tooled leather wall coverings.

Hayle of 1845. Both are steam driven, from a coal-fired boiler, and pump water into the summit level of the Kennet and Avon Canal with a lift of 40ft. During steam weekends telephone Marlborough (01672) 870300 for information, or Hon Secretary Ray Knowles (01672) 851639 at other times. The surrounding countryside is pleasant, and walks can be taken along the canal towpath and to a working windmill nearby.
Open Steaming wknds, 10.30-5pm (12.30-5 on Sat): 15-17 Apr; 6-8 May; 27-29 May; 29-30 Jul; 26-28 Aug; 30 Sep-1 Oct. Open all non-steaming wknds Etr-Sep 10.30-5pm (12.30-5 Sat).
Steaming weekend: £3 (ch £1, under 5 free & pen £2). Family ticket £7. Non-steaming weekends £1.50 (ch 50p).
🅿 💺 ♿ *(phone in advance for maximum access) shop ⌗ (ex in grounds)*

Heale Gardens, Plant Centre & Shop
MIDDLE WOODFORD ▰▰▰▰
(4m N of Salisbury, between A360 & A345)
☎ *(01722) 782504*
Heale House and its eight acres of beautiful garden lie beside the River Avon at Middle Woodford. Much of the house is unchanged since King Charles II sheltered here after the Battle of Worcester in 1651. The garden provides a wonderfully varied collection of plants, shrubs, and musk and other roses, growing in the formal setting of clipped hedges and mellow stonework, which are at their best in June and July. Particularly lovely in spring and autumn is the water garden, planted with magnificent magnolia and acers, surrounding the authentic Japenese Tea House and Nikko Bridge which makes an exciting focus in this part of the garden. National Gardens Day 1st Sunday in August.
Open all year, daily 10-5.
£2.50 (ch under 14 accompanied, free). Party 20+.
🅿 ♿ *shop garden centre*

Mompesson House
SALISBURY ▰▰▰▰
Chorister's Green, Cathedral Close
☎ *(01722) 335659*
With its high wrought-iron railings and perfect proportions this Queen Anne house makes an impressive addition to the elegant Cathedral Close in Salisbury. Inside there are no disappointments: the stucco ceilings, carved oak staircase and period furniture are more than matched by the important collection of 18th-century glasses, china and some outstanding paintings. In 1995 there will be an exhibition of watercolours by Barbara Townsend.
Open Apr-31 Oct, daily (ex Thu & Fri) 12-5.30. Last admission 5pm.
£3 (ch £1.50). Party.
🅿 💺 ♿ *shop ⌗*
(NT)

Old Sarum
SALISBURY ▰▰▰▰
(2m N on A345)
☎ *(01722) 335398*
The story of Old Sarum began in pre-history: it was once the location for an Iron Age camp. What the visitor sees today, however, are the remains of a thriving community that grew up around a Norman cathedral and castle. When a new cathedral was built in nearby New Sarum, or Salisbury, the community was gradually abandoned, although until the Reform Bill of 1832 ten voters remained to return two members to parliament; at one time Pitt the Elder represented Old Sarum.
Open all year, Apr-Sep, daily 10-6; Oct-Mar, daily 10-4. Closed 24-26 Dec & 1 Jan.
£1.50 (ch 80p, concessions £1.10).
🅿 *(charged)* ♿
(EH)

Royal Gloucestershire, Berkshire & Wiltshire Regiment Museum
SALISBURY ▰▰▰▰
The Wardrobe, 58 The Close
☎ *(01722) 414536*
An interesting and historic building in Cathedral Close displaying mementoes, relics, uniforms and weapons.
Open Apr-Oct, daily 10-4.30; Feb, Mar & Nov, Mon-Fri 10-4.30. (Closed Dec & Jan).
£1.80 (ch £1, accompanied free, students & pen £1.50).
🅿 💺 ♿ *(restaurant not accessible) shop ⌗*

Salisbury & South Wiltshire Museum
SALISBURY ▰▰▰▰
The King's House, 65 The Close
☎ *(01722) 332151*
One of the most outstanding of the many beautiful buildings in Cathedral Close also houses the local museum, winner of six awards. Covering an area that is so steeped in history - Stonehenge is not far away - there are many fascinating displays. Galleries include Stonehenge, Early Man, History of Salisbury, the Pitt-Rivers collection, ceramics and pictures and the Wedgwood room, and there is a reconstruction of a pre-NHS surgery. A costume, lace and embroidery gallery has recently been added to the museum. A full programme of exhibitions is being held for the Festival of Arts and Culture '95: A Common Thread (15 July-21 October), Photographs of life in an English cathedral city for VE Day (8 May-8 July) plus The Dinosaur Road show and 50th Anniverary of Branksome Pottery (until 3 May), painting of houses in The Close by Gerald Rickards (1 April-1 July), Pilkington Lancastrian Pottery (4 November-January 1996). The event of the year is Medieval Day on 2 September with a re-enactment group. crafts demonstrations and displays.
Open all year Mon-Sat 10-5; also Suns Jul & Aug and Salisbury Festival, 2-5. (Closed Xmas).
£2.50 (ch 50p, pen, students & UB40s £1.75). Party. Tickets give unlimited visits throughout year.
🅿 ✗ *(parking by prior arrangement) toilets for disabled shop ⌗*

Stonehenge
STONEHENGE ▰▰▰▰
(off A344)
Stonehenge is one of the most famous prehistoric monuments in Europe and has been the source of endless speculation by archaeologists and others. The henge was started about 5,000 years ago, but was redesigned several times during the following 1,500 years. The earliest parts are an encircling ditch and bank which were made about 2,800BC. About 700 years later, huge Blue Stones, 80 in all and each weighing 2 tons, were brought from south-west Wales. However, before the work on these was finished, enormous sarsen stones weighing over 50 tons each were dragged from the Marlborough Downs and the whole thing was reorganised into the design we see today. This is made up of an outer ring with mortis-and-tenon-fitted lintels and an inner horseshoe of five pairs of uprights with lintels. Later on, the Blue Stones were re-erected. The axis of the horseshoe points towards the midsummer sunrise.
The whole area was obviously a centre of great ceremonial activity and there are a number of monuments, massive earthworks, and over 300 burial mounds within a relatively small area. Little is known about the Bronze Age society that organised such a vast undertaking, but there was no connection with the Druids.
Open all year, Apr-May & Sep-8 Oct, daily 9.30-6; Jun, 9.30-7, Jul-Aug, 9-7; 9-15 Oct, 9.30-5; 16 Oct-Mar 9.30-4. Closed 24-26 Dec & 1 Jan.
£3 (ch £1.50, concessions £2.30).
🅿 💺 ♿ *shop ⌗*
(EH)

Stourhead House & Garden
STOURHEAD ▰▰▰▰
(off B3092)
☎ *Bourton (Dorset) (01747) 840348*
The Palladian house was built in 1720 by Henry Hoare, a banker. It is not particularly outstanding, although it does contain some fine furniture. However, what makes Stourhead especially memorable are the superb gardens laid out by Henry Hoare in 1741. He returned from his Grand Tour inspired by the gardens and landscapes he had seen in Italy, and was determined to create something similar in England. The result is one of the finest 18th-century landscape gardens in Europe. He built a grotto and a temple to Flora around two springs and then dammed the River Stour to create a large triangular lake. He also erected a Pantheon in 1754 and over the next few years built other temples. Much of the comprehensive tree-planting was done by his grandson who, in 1791, began a planting programme around the lake. There are many varieties of oak, elm, willow and exotic trees, and the rhododendrons, which, with the azaleas, make spring so spectacular at Stourhead, were first planted in 1791. Conifers were introduced in the 19th century, with further planting in the early 20th century. On the edge of the estate is King Alfred's Tower, a 160ft high, red-brick folly built in 1772 by Flitcroft. There are magnificent views across Somerset, Dorset and Wiltshire from the top. Events for 1995: Viennese Symphony Concert with fireworks and lasers (17 June), The Stourhead Fête Champêtre in the gardens will be held on the evenings of 19-22 July (Tickets 0891-335200(24-hours) only ticket holders admitted after 5.00pm), A Midsummer Night's Dream (4-5 August).
Open - House Apr-Oct, Sat-Wed 12-5.30 or dusk if earlier. Last admission 5pm. Garden daily all year 9-7 or dusk if earlier (ex 19-22 Jul when garden closes at 5pm). King Alfreds Tower, Apr-Oct, Good Fri & BH's Tue-Thu 2-5.30, wknds 10-5.30 or dusk if earlier.
House £4.20 (ch £2.20). Garden £4.10 (ch £2.10), Nov-Feb £3.10 (ch 1.50). Family ticket £10. Combined House & Garden ticket £7.50 (ch £3.50) Family ticket £20. Parties 15+ (ex Nov-Feb). No pushchairs or bulky bags in house. King Alfred's Tower £1.50 (ch 5-16 70p).
🅿 💺 ✗ *licensed ♿ toilets for disabled shop ⌗ (ex in gardens Nov-Feb only)*
(NT)

Stourton House Flower Garden
STOURTON ▰▰▰▰
(3m NW of Mere, on A303)
☎ *Bourton (Dorset) (01747) 840417*
Set in the attractive village of Stourton, the house has more than four acres of beautifully maintained flower gardens. Many grass paths lead through varied and colourful shrubs, trees and plants; and Stourton House also specialises in unusual plants, many of which are for sale. It is also well-known for its dried flowers and collection of over 250 different hydrangeas. Events for 1995 include Daffodil Day (16 April), Azalea Day (21 May), Delphinium Day (25 June), Hydrangea Days 20 August-10 September).
Open Apr-30 Nov, Wed, Thu, Sun & BH Mon 11-6 (or dusk if earlier).
£2 (ch 50p).
🅿 💺 ♿ *(wheelchairs available) shop plants for sale ⌗*

The 56-acre site of Old Sarum was once a bustling town with a cathedral, a castle and a bishop's palace. When the Bishop built a new cathedral at Salisbury, the old town fell into disusue.

Great Western Railway Museum
SWINDON
Faringdon Rd
☎(01793) 493189
The museum is in the Great Western Railway Village in Swindon, once one of the busiest railway towns in Britain, and now has a fascinating collection of locomotives and other exhibits relating to the GWR. Among the locomotives are the historic *Dean Goods* and *King George V* and a replica of the broad gauge locomotive *North Star*. There is a comprehensive display of nameplates, models, posters and tickets and other railway paraphernalia, and a new exhibition 'Return to Swindon' celebrates Swindon's Railway Works and Village, complete with recreated Railway Workshop displays.
Open all year, Mon-Sat 10-5, Sun 2-5. (Closed Good Fri, 25-26 Dec & 1 Jan).
❋*£2 (ch & pen £1). Party. (Charge includes admission to the Railway Village museum).*
P *(100 yds)* ᕝ *shop* ⊗

Museum & Art Gallery
SWINDON
Bath Rd
☎(01793) 493188
The museum contains a small collection of items of local interest, and the art gallery has pictures by important British 20th-century artists, including Moore, Sutherland, Wadsworth etc.
Open all year, Mon-Sat 10-5.30, Sun 2-5.30 (Closed Good Fri, 25 & 26 Dec).
Free.
P *(5 mins walk)* ᕝ *(handling table for blind) shop* ⊗

Railway Village House
SWINDON
34 Faringdon Rd (adjacent to GWR Museum)
☎(01793) 526161 ext 4527
This restored foreman's house is furnished as a typical working-class home at the turn of the century. It was originally part of the model village built in Bath stone by the GWR for its workers.
Open all year, Mon-Fri 10-1 & 2-5, Sun 2-5. (Closed Good Fri & Xmas).

Farmer Giles Farmstead
TEFFONT MAGNA
(off A303 at Telfont)
☎(01722) 716338
Set in 175 acres of rolling Wiltshire downland this working dairy farm offers visitors the opportunity to watch the cows being milked, to bottle-feed lambs, and get to know a host of other farm animals and pets. There is an adventure playground and a relaxing walk along the picturesque Beech belt with Highland cattle and Shire horses along the way. Two large exhibition areas and a restaurant. Special events for 1995 include: Sheep shearing - Sheep to the Jumper (2 July and 27 August), Classic Car show (15-16 July), Farmer Giles Country Craft Festival (9-10 September).
Open 25 Mar-5 Nov, daily 10.30-6, wknds until Xmas. Party bookings all year.
£3.50 (ch £2.50, pen £3)
P ✗ *licensed* ᕝ *toilets for disabled shop*

Old Wardour Castle
TISBURY
(2m SW)
☎(01747) 870487
The old castle was a hexagonal building, and there are substantial remains. The walls still stand to their original 60ft and it is possible to climb nearly to the top. It was built in 1392 by John Lord Lovel with later additions after 1570. It was twice besieged and badly damaged during the Civil War.
Open all year, Apr-Sep, daily 10-6; Oct, 10-4; Nov-Mar 10-4. Closed 24-26 Dec & 1 Jan.
£1.50 (ch 80p, concessions £1.10).
P ᕝ
(EH)

Woodland Heritage Museum & Woodland Park
WESTBURY
Brokerswood
☎(01373) 822238 & 823880
Woodland Heritage Museum & Woodland Park nature walks lead through 80 acres of woodlands, with a lake and

❋*80p (ch & pen 50p). Free to those paying for GWR Museum.*
ᕝ *shop* ⊗

wildfowl. Facilities include a woodland visitor centre (covering wildlife and forestry), a children's adventure playground and guided walks and the Smokey Oak railway, over a third of a mile long. (Special catering facilities for parties of 10 or more.) Barbeque sites and fishing permits available. Special events for 1995 include: Easter Bunny Trail (16-17 April), dawn chorus bird walks (23 April, 7 and 21 May), May Bank Holiday Family Fun Day (29 May).
Open all year; Park open daily 10-sunset. Museum open Mon-Fri 10-5 (summer), 12-4 (winter); Sat 2-6, Sun 10-6 (summer); Sun 2-4.30 (winter). Free admission for wheelchair users.
£2 (unaccompanied ch £1, accompanied ch free, pen £1.75).
P ⊑ ᕝ *shop*

Westwood Manor
WESTWOOD
(1.50m SW of Bradford on Avon, off B3109)
☎Bradford on Avon (01225) 863374
The property of the National Trust, this late 15th-century stone manor house has some particularly fine Jacobean plasterwork. The house, which is situated by the parish church, was altered in 1610 but still retains its late Gothic and Jacobean windows. Outside there is a superb modern topiary garden.
Open 2 Apr-1 Oct, Sun, Tue & Wed 2-5
£3.30 no reductions, house not suitable for children under 10.
P ⊗
(NT)

Wilton House
WILTON (near Salisbury)
(3m W of Salisbury, on the A30)
☎Salisbury (01722) 743115
The Black Death, a homicidal drunken Earl and Southern Headquarters for the D-Day landings - these are just some of the fascinating historical links introduced to visitors in the 17-minute film which provides a background to the Earls of Pembroke and the 450-year history of the Estate.
Built on the site of an abbey founded by King Alfred the Tudor, origins of the house can still be seen in the tower

which survived the 1647 fire and is now incorporated within the splendid 17th-century house, based on designs by Inigo Jones. Perhaps the most famous of the six State Rooms are the Double and Single Cube rooms with their fabulous painted ceilings. Gothic Cloisters were added in the early 19th century by James Wyatt. Wilton House boasts a world famous art collection with over 200 paintings on show.
Visitors can step back in time in the reconstructed Tudor Kitchen and the Estates Victorian Laundry, relax in 21 acres of landscaped parkland, rose and water gardens, woodland and riverside walks. There is a massive children's adventure playground. For 1995 there are a number of events organised. Telephone for details.
Open 11 Apr-29 Oct, daily 11-6. Last admission 5pm.
£5.75 (ch 5-15 £3.75, under 5 free, students & pen £4.75). Family ticket £15.25.
P ⊑ ✗ *licensed* ᕝ *toilets for disabled shop garden centre* ⊗

Woodhenge
WOODHENGE
(1m N of Amesbury)
Consisted formerly of six concentric rings of timber posts within a ditch. Positions of the posts are marked by concrete pillars. Discovered accidentally by aerial reconnaissance in 1925.
Open all reasonable times.
Free.
P ᕝ
(EH)

CHANNEL ISLANDS

Le Friquet Butterfly Centre
GUERNSEY
CÂTEL (CASTEL)
☎Guernsey (01481) 54378
European and tropical butterflies fly freely in the lush setting of the Butterfly Farm greenhouse, and may be seen hatching from their chrysalids. Other attractions include putting and croquet.
Open Etr-Oct, daily 10-5.
£2 (ch £1.25 & pen £1.50).
P ⊑ ✗ *licensed* ᕝ *shop*

German Occupation Museum
GUERNSEY
FOREST
☎Guernsey (01481) 38205
The museum has the Channel Islands' largest collection of authentic Occupation items, with tableaux of a kitchen, bunker rooms and a street during the Occupation. Tours of the underground fortifications are arranged, and the 50th anniversary of Liberation Day 9th May will be celebrated with specail events and exhibitions.
Open Apr-Oct 10.30-5; Nov-Mar, Sun 2-4.30. (Closed Jan & Dec).
❋*£2.50 (ch £1, ch under 5 free).*
P ⊑ ᕝ *(ramps)* ⊗

Fort Grey Shipwreck Museum
GUERNSEY
ROQUAINE BAY
☎Guernsey (01481) 726518
The fort is a Martello tower, built as part of the Channel Islands' extensive defences against Napoleon. It is nicknamed the 'cup and saucer' because of its appearance, and houses a museum devoted to wrecks on the treacherous Hanois reefs nearby.
Open Apr-Oct, 10.30-12.30 & 1.30-5.30.
❋*£1.75 (ch 50p, students & pen £1). Joint ticket with Castle Cornet & Guernsey Museum £6.50 (ch £2, students & pen £3).*
P *shop* ⊗

The tower of the original Tudor building can clearly be seen in the 17th-century design of Wilton House by Inigo Jones.

a splendid medieval stronghold dating back to the 13th century. It has high walls and round towers, with machicolations added in the 15th century.
Open all year, Apr-Sep, Mon-Sat 9.30-6.30, Sun 2-6.30; Oct-Mar 9.30-4.30, Sun 2-4.30. (Closed 25-26 Dec & 1-3 Jan).
£2 (ch 16 75p, pen £1.25)
🅿 ⅏ *shop*
(AM)

Wildfowl & Wetlands Trust
CAERLAVEROCK ▰▰▰▰▰
Eastpark Farm
(8m S of Dumfries)
☎ Glencaple (01387) 770200
This is an exciting wildlife refuge of over 1,500 acres on the north Solway shore. There are outstanding hide facilities, observation towers and an observatory giving impressive views of the huge numbers of wildfowl that spend most of the autumn, winter and spring here. The barnacle geese are the most impressive sight. Thousands of them fly in from their Spitsbergen breeding grounds to rest and feed in the waters and marshes. Pink-footed and greylag geese can also be seen, as can waders, whooper swans and ducks such as pintails and wigeons. These in turn may attract interesting predators such as peregrines and merlins. The 'merse', or salt marsh, is also the home of the rare natterjack toad.
Open daily 10-5 (Closed 24-25 Dec).
✱*£2.95 (ch £1.50, pen £2.20). Family ticket £7.40. Party 20+.*
🅿 ⅏ *shop* ⅏

Cardoness Castle
CARDONESS CASTLE ▰▰▰▰▰
(1m SW of Gatehouse of Fleet off A75)
☎ 0131-668 8800
A 15th-century stronghold overlooking the Water of Fleet. It was once the home of the McCullochs of Galloway.
Open all year, Apr-Sep, Mon-Sat 9.30-6.30, Sun 2-6.30; Oct-Mar, wknds only. Sat 9.30-4.30, Sun 2-4.30 (Closed 25-26 Dec & 1-3 Jan).
£1.20 (concessions 70p).
🅿 *shop*
(AM)

Threave Castle
CASTLE DOUGLAS ▰▰▰▰▰
(3m W on A75)
☎ 0131-668 8800
Archibald the Grim built this lonely castle in the late 14th century. It stands on an islet in the River Dee, and is four storeys high with round towers guarding the outer wall. Access to the island is by boat.
Open Apr-Sep, Mon-Sat 9.30-6.30, Sun 2-6.30.
£1.50 (ch 16 75p, pen £1).
🅿 *shop* ⅏
(AM)

Threave Garden
CASTLE DOUGLAS ▰▰▰▰▰
(1m W of Castle Douglas off A75)
☎ (01556) 502575
The best time to visit is in spring when there is a dazzling display of some 200 varieties of daffodil. The garden has something to see all year round, however, and includes a walled garden and glasshouses. The house is the National Trust for Scotland's School of Horticulture.
Open all year. Garden, daily 9.30-sunset. Walled garden and glasshouses daily 9.30-5. Visitor centre, Shop & Exhibition Apr-22 Oct daily 9.30-5.30. (Last entry 30 minutes before closing).
✱*£3.50 (ch & pen £1.80). Party.*
🅿 ✗ *licensed* ⅍ *(wheelchairs available incl. electric wheelchair) toilets for disabled shop garden centre* ⅏
(NTS)

Comlongon Castle
CLARENCEFIELD ▰▰▰▰▰
☎ (01387) 870283
An exceptionally well-preserved 15th-century Border castle currently being restored. It contains many original

features including dungeons, kitchen, great hall, Heraldic devices, and bed chambers with 'privies'. It's set in gardens and woodland with secluded walks, and is haunted by a 16th-century suicide.
Open Mar-Oct, telephone for opening times.
🅿 ⅍
Details not confirmed for 1995

Creetown Gem Rock Museum
CREETOWN ▰▰▰▰▰
Chain Rd (follow signs from A75)
☎ (01671) 820357 & 820554
The museum, completely refurbished in 1993, displays gemstones and minerals collected by the owners from around the world. The beautiful collection also includes gemstone *objets d'art.* There are three large exhibition halls and a gemstone workshop. The Crystal Cave is a major display, built to commemorate the museum's tenth anniversary. There is also a display of replicas of the world's largest diamonds, all 'facet cut'. An audio-visual programme, The Fire in the Stones, explains how minerals are formed. Gemstone polishing demonstrations are held in the workshop. There is an activity bench and fun quiz.
Open Mar-Oct, daily 9.30-6; Nov-23 Dec, Sat-Wed 10-4; 8 Jan-Feb, Sat & Sun only 10-4 or by appointment during the week. Phone for Christmas opening dates.
£2.25 (ch 5-15 £1.25, students & pen £1.75). Family ticket £5.75 Party 20+.
🅿 ⚑ ⅍ *toilets for disabled shop*

Drumcoltran Tower
DRUMCOLTRAN TOWER ▰▰▰▰▰
(7m NE of Dalbeattie)
☎ 0131-668 8800
The 16th-century tower house stands three storeys high and has a simple, functional design.
Open at any reasonable time.
Free.
⅏
(AM)

Burns House
DUMFRIES ▰▰▰▰▰
Burns St
☎ (01387) 255297
It was in this ordinary sandstone house in a backstreet of Dumfries that Robert Burns spent the last three years of his short life; he died here in 1796. It is now a place of pilgrimage for Burns enthusiasts from around the globe. The

house retains much of its 18th-century character and contains many fascinating items connected with the poet.
Open all year, Mon-Sat 10-1 & 2-5, Sun 2-5. (Closed Sun & Mon, Oct-Mar).
✱*80p (concessions 40p). Prices under review.*
🅿 *(100 yds) shop*

Burns Mausoleum
DUMFRIES ▰▰▰▰▰
St Michael's Churchyard
☎ (01387) 255297
The mausoleum is in the form of a Greek temple, and contains the tombs of Robert Burns, his wife Jean Armour, and their five sons. A sculptured group shows the Muse of Poetry flinging her cloak over Burns at the plough.
Unrestricted access.
Free.
🅿 *(100 yds)*

Dumfries Museum & Camera Obscura
DUMFRIES ▰▰▰▰▰
The Observatory, Church St
☎ (01387) 253374
Situated in and around the 18th-century windmill tower, Dumfries Museum is the largest museum in south west Scotland. Its collections were started over 150 years ago and have developed into a vast source of information on the area. Exhibitions trace the history of the people and landscape of Dumfries and Galloway. The Camera Obscura is to be found on the top floor of the windmill tower. It was installed in 1836 when the building was converted into an observatory. On the table-top screen you see a panoramic view of Dumfries and the surrounding countryside. Special events are planned throughout the year.
Open all year, Mon-Sat 10-1 & 2-5, Sun 2-5. (Closed Sun & Mon, Oct-Mar; Camera Obscura closed Oct-Mar).
✱*Free except Camera Obscura 80p (concessions 40p). Prices under review.*
🅿 ⅍ *(ex camera obscura) toilets for disabled shop*

Old Bridge House Museum
DUMFRIES ▰▰▰▰▰
Mill Rd
☎ (01387) 256904
The Old Bridge House was built in 1660, into the fabric of the 15th-century Devorgilla's Bridge; it is the oldest house in Dumfries. A museum of everyday life in the town, it has an early 20th-century dentist's surgery, a Victorian nursery and

kitchens of the 1850s and 1900s.
Open Apr-Sep, Mon-Sat 10-1 & 2-5, Sun 2-5.
Free.
🅿 ⅍ *shop*

Robert Burns Centre
DUMFRIES ▰▰▰▰▰
Mill Rd
☎ (01387) 264808
This award-winning centre concentrates on the connections between Scotland's national poet, Robert Burns, and the town of Dumfries. The centre is situated in the town's 18th-century watermill on the west bank of the River Nith and tells the story of Robert Burns' last years spent in the busy streets and lively atmosphere of Dumfries in the 1790s. In the evening the centre offers top quality feature films in the Film Theatre.
Open all year, Apr-Sep, Mon-Sat 10-8, Sun 2-5; Oct-Mar, Tue-Sat 10-1 & 2-5.
✱*Free except audio-visual theatre 80p (concessions 40p). Prices under review for 1995.*
🅿 ⚑ ⅍ *(Induction loop hearing system in auditorium) toilets for disabled shop*

Dundrennan Abbey
DUNDRENNAN ▰▰▰▰▰
(6.5m SE of Kirkcudbright)
☎ 0131-668 8800
The ruined abbey was founded for the Cistercians. Mary Queen of Scots is thought to have spent her last night in Scotland here on 15 May 1568, before seeking shelter in England, where she was imprisoned and eventually executed.
Open all year, Apr-Sep, Mon-Sat 9.30-6.30, Sun 2-6.30.
£1.20 (concessions 75p).
🅿 *shop* ⅏
(AM)

Glenluce Abbey
GLENLUCE ▰▰▰▰▰
(2m N of village)
☎ 0131-668 8800
The abbey was founded for the Cistercians in 1192 by Roland, Earl of Galloway. The ruins include a vaulted chapter house, and stand in a beautiful setting.
Open all year, Apr-Sep, Mon-Sat 9.30-6.30, Sun 2-6.30; Oct-Mar, Sat 9.30-4.30, Sun 2-4.30. (Closed 25-26 Dec & 1-3 Jan).
£1.20 (concessions 75p).
🅿 ⅍ *shop* ⅏
(AM)

The Robert Burns' Centre in Dumfries is set in the 18th-century watermill, built when Burns was living in the lively town. The centre overlooks the River Nith.

Great Western Railway Museum
SWINDON
Faringdon Rd
☎(01793) 493189
The museum is in the Great Western Railway Village in Swindon, once one of the busiest railway towns in Britain, and now has a fascinating collection of locomotives and other exhibits relating to the GWR. Among the locomotives are the historic *Dean Goods* and *King George V* and a replica of the broad gauge locomotive *North Star*. There is a comprehensive display of nameplates, models, posters and tickets and other railway paraphernalia, and a new exhibition 'Return to Swindon' celebrates Swindon's Railway Works and Village, complete with recreated Railway Workshop displays.
Open all year, Mon-Sat 10-5, Sun 2-5. (Closed Good Fri, 25-26 Dec & 1 Jan).
✳£2 (ch & pen £1). Party. (Charge includes admission to the Railway Village museum).
P (100 yds) & shop ✾

Museum & Art Gallery
SWINDON
Bath Rd
☎(01793) 493188
The museum contains a small collection of items of local interest, and the art gallery has pictures by important British 20th-century artists, including Moore, Sutherland, Wadsworth etc.
Open all year, Mon-Sat 10-5.30, Sun 2-5.30 (Closed Good Fri, 25 & 26 Dec).
Free.
P (5 mins walk) & (handling table for blind) shop ✾

Railway Village House
SWINDON
34 Faringdon Rd (adjacent to GWR Museum)
☎(01793) 526161 ext 4527
This restored foreman's house is furnished as a typical working-class home at the turn of the century. It was originally part of the model village built in Bath stone by the GWR for its workers.
Open all year, Mon-Fri 10-1 & 2-5, Sun 2-5. (Closed Good Fri & Xmas).

✳80p (ch & pen 50p). Free to those paying for GWR Museum.
& shop ✾

Farmer Giles Farmstead
TEFFONT MAGNA
(off A303 at Telfont)
☎(01722) 716338
Set in 175 acres of rolling Wiltshire downland this working dairy farm offers visitors the opportunity to watch the cows being milked, to bottle-feed lambs, and get to know a host of other farm animals and pets. There is an adventure playground and a relaxing walk along the picturesque Beech belt with Highland cattle and Shire horses along the way. Two large exhibition areas and a restaurant. Special events for 1995 include: Sheep shearing - Sheep to the Jumper (2 July and 27 August), Classic Car show (15-16 July), Farmer Giles Country Craft Festival (9-10 September).
Open 25 Mar-5 Nov, daily 10.30-6, wknds until Xmas. Party bookings all year.
£3.50 (ch £2.50, pen £3)
P ✗ licensed & toilets for disabled shop

Old Wardour Castle
TISBURY
(2m SW)
☎(01747) 870487
The old castle was a hexagonal building, and there are substantial remains. The walls still stand to their original 60ft and it is possible to climb nearly to the top. It was built in 1392 by John Lord Lovel with later additions after 1570. It was twice besieged and badly damaged during the Civil War.
Open all year, Apr-Sep, daily 10-6; Oct, 10-4; Nov-Mar 10-4. Closed 24-26 Dec & 1 Jan.
£1.50 (ch 80p, concessions £1.10).
P &
(EH)

Woodland Heritage Museum & Woodland Park
WESTBURY
Brokerswood
☎(01373) 822238 & 823880
Woodland Heritage Museum & Woodland Park nature walks lead through 80 acres of woodlands, with a lake and

wildfowl. Facilities include a woodland visitor centre (covering wildlife and forestry), a children's adventure playground and guided walks and the Smokey Oak railway, over a third of a mile long. (Special catering facilities for parties of 10 or more.) Barbeque sites and fishing permits available. Special events for 1995 include: Easter Bunny Trail (16-17 April), dawn chorus bird walks (23 April, 7 and 21 May), May Bank Holiday Family Fun Day (29 May).
Open all year; Park open daily 10-sunset. Museum open Mon-Fri 10-5 (summer), 12-4 (winter); Sat 2-6, Sun 10-6 (summer); Sun 2-4.30 (winter). Free admission for wheelchair users.
£2 (unaccompanied ch £1, accompanied ch free, pen £1.75).
P & shop

Westwood Manor
WESTWOOD
(1.50m SW of Bradford on Avon, off B3109)
☎Bradford on Avon (01225) 863374
The property of the National Trust, this late 15th-century stone manor house has some particularly fine Jacobean plasterwork. The house, which is situated by the parish church, was altered in 1610 but still retains its late Gothic and Jacobean windows. Outside there is a superb modern topiary garden.
Open 2 Apr-1 Oct, Sun, Tue & Wed 2-5
£3.30 no reductions, house not suitable for children under 10.
P ✾
(NT)

Wilton House
WILTON (near Salisbury)
(3m W of Salisbury, on the A30)
☎Salisbury (01722) 743115
The Black Death, a homicidal drunken Earl and Southern Headquarters for the D-Day landings - these are just some of the fascinating historical links introduced to visitors in the 17-minute film which provides a background to the Earls of Pembroke and the 450-year history of the Estate.
Built on the site of an abbey founded by King Alfred the Tudor, origins of the house can still be seen in the tower

which survived the 1647 fire and is now incorporated within the splendid 17th-century house, based on designs by Inigo Jones. Perhaps the most famous of the six State Rooms are the Double and Single Cube rooms with their fabulous painted ceilings. Gothic Cloisters were added in the early 19th century by James Wyatt. Wilton House boasts a world famous art collection with over 200 paintings on show.
Visitors can step back in time in the reconstructed Tudor Kitchen and the Estates Victorian Laundry, relax in 21 acres of landscaped parkland, rose and water gardens, woodland and riverside walks. There is a massive children's adventure playground. For 1995 there are a number of events organised. Telephone for details.
Open 11 Apr-29 Oct, daily 11-6. Last admission 5pm.
£5.75 (ch 5-15 £3.75, under 5 free, students & pen £4.75). Family ticket £15.25.
P ✗ licensed & toilets for disabled shop garden centre ✾

Woodhenge
WOODHENGE
(1m N of Amesbury)
Consisted formerly of six concentric rings of timber posts within a ditch. Positions of the posts are marked by concrete pillars. Discovered accidentally by aerial reconnaissance in 1925.
Open all reasonable times.
Free.
P &
(EH)

CHANNEL ISLANDS

Le Friquet Butterfly Centre
GUERNSEY
CÂTEL (CASTEL)
☎Guernsey (01481) 54378
European and tropical butterflies fly freely in the lush setting of the Butterfly Farm greenhouse, and may be seen hatching from their chrysalids. Other attractions include putting and croquet.
Open Etr-Oct, daily 10-5.
£2 (ch £1.25 & pen £1.50).
P ✗ licensed & shop

German Occupation Museum
GUERNSEY
FOREST
☎Guernsey (01481) 38205
The museum has the Channel Islands' largest collection of authentic Occupation items, with tableaux of a kitchen, bunker rooms and a street during the Occupation. Tours of the underground fortifications are arranged, and the 50th anniversary of Liberation Day 9th May will be celebrated with specail events and exhibitions.
Open Apr-Oct 10.30-5; Nov-Mar, Sun 2-4.30. (Closed Jan & Dec).
✳£2.50 (ch £1, ch under 5 free).
P & (ramps) ✾

Fort Grey Shipwreck Museum
GUERNSEY
ROQUAINE BAY
☎Guernsey (01481) 726518
The fort is a Martello tower, built as part of the Channel Islands' extensive defences against Napoleon. It is nicknamed the 'cup and saucer' because of its appearance, and houses a museum devoted to wrecks on the treacherous Hanois reefs nearby.
Open Apr-Oct, 10.30-12.30 & 1.30-5.30.
✳£1.75 (ch 50p, students & pen £1). Joint ticket with Castle Cornet & Guernsey Museum £6.50 (ch £2, students & pen £3).
P shop ✾

The tower of the original Tudor building can clearly be seen in the 17th-century design of Wilton House by Inigo Jones.

German Military Underground Hospital & Ammunition Store
GUERNSEY
ST ANDREW
La Vassalerie
☎ *Guernsey (01481) 39100*
This is the largest structure created during the German Occupation of the Channel Islands, a concrete maze of about 75,000sq ft, which took slave workers three-and-a-half years to complete, at the cost of many lives. The hospital was only used for about six weeks, to care for wounded German soldiers brought over from France after D-Day. The ammunition store, however, which was larger than the hospital, was packed with thousands of tons of ammunition during its nine months of use. Most of the equipment has been removed, but the central heating plant, hospital beds and cooking facilities can still be seen.
Open Jul-Aug, daily 10-noon & 2-4.30; May-Jun & Sep, daily 10-noon & 2-4; Apr & Oct, daily 2-4; Mar & Nov, Sun & Thu 2-3.
❋*£2 (ch 60p).*
🅿 ♿ *shop*

Sausmarez Manor
GUERNSEY
ST MARTIN
Sausmarez Rd
☎ *Guernsey (01481) 35571*
The Manor has been owned by the same family for many centuries, a family which has included artists, generals, admirals, privateers, judges, sportsmen, inventors, cartographers, explorers, adventurers and politicians - most of whom have left some mark on the house or its contents. Each room is a happy contrast in style to its neighbour, with collections of Oriental, French and English furniture and an eclectic variety of paintings. The Formal Garden has herbaceous borders in the style of Gertrude Jekyll, while the Woodland Garden, set around two small lakes and a stream, is inter-planted with colourful shrubs, bulbs and wild flowers, many designed to encourage butterflies, birds and other animal life. In a section of the wood, a 7.25-gauge ride-on railway runs for over a quarter of a mile over embankments and through cuttings, while in the 16th-century Tudor Barn there is a 310sq ft model railway layout, with up to eight trains running continuously through meticulously scaled countryside, towns and villages. Another special layout of the Robust Playmobile Train Set is available for visitors to operate. In the Little Barn, is one of the three largest collections in Britain of dolls' houses dating from 1820 to the present day.
House open last BH in May-last Thu in Sep, Tue-Thu & BH Mons. Also Etr-end of May & Oct, Tue-Thu mornings. House £3 (ch 70p). Woodland Garden £1.50(accompanied ch 50p). Dolls House Collection £2. Railway layout 75p (ch & pen 40p). Train rides 60p (ch & pen 30p).
🅿 ♿ ✗ ♿ *shop*

Castle Cornet
GUERNSEY
ST PETER PORT
☎ *Guernsey (01481) 721657*
Castle Cornet has been used in warfare from the 13th to the 20th centuries, and has an impressive array of defences. During the Civil War it was garrisoned by the Royalist governor of the island, and although most islanders sympathised with Cromwell, it was not until 1651 that this last Royalist stronghold surrendered. In 1940 the castle was taken over by German troops and adapted for modern warfare.
Today it houses the new Maritime Museum (opened in 1991), the Spenser collection of uniforms and badges, the Museum of Guernsey's Own 201 Squadron Royal Air Force, the Royal Guernsey Militia Museum, Art Gallery and Armoury. A gun is fired daily at noon on the order of a man who studies the town church clock through a telescope.

Open Apr-Oct, daily 10.30-5.30.
❋*£4.50 (ch £1.50, pen £2.25). Joint ticket with Fort Grey & Guernsey Museum £6.50 (ch £2, students & pen £3)*
🅿 ♿ *shop* ♿

Guernsey Museum & Art Gallery
GUERNSEY
ST PETER PORT
Candie Gardens
☎ *Guernsey (01481) 726518*
The island's first purpose-built museum tells the story of Guernsey and its people. The museum has an audio-visual theatre and an art gallery, and there are special exhibitions throughout the year. It is surrounded by beautiful gardens.
Open all year, daily 10.30-5.30 (winter 4.30).
❋*£2.50 (ch 75p, pen £1.25). Joint ticket with Castle Cornet & Fort Grey £6.50 (ch £2, students & pen £3).*
🅿 ♿ *toilets for disabled shop* ♿

Hauteville House
GUERNSEY
ST PETER PORT
Maison de Victor Hugo, 38 Hauteville
☎ *Guernsey (01481) 721911*
Built around 1800, the house was bought by Victor Hugo, the great French writer, in 1856. He decorated it in a unique way, sometimes carving up and recombining several different pieces of furniture or tapestry. There are fine collections of china, paintings and tapestries.
Open Apr-Sep, Mon-Sat, 10-11.30 (last admission) & 2-4.30.(last admission). (Closed Sun & BH). Due to limited capacity of the house it may be necessary to wait.
♿ *(difficult for wheelchairs)* ♿
Details not confirmed for 1995

Mont Orgueil Castle
JERSEY
GOREY
☎ *(01534) 853292*
The castle stands on a rocky headland, on a site which has been fortified since the Iron Age. It is one of the best-preserved examples in Europe of a medieval concentric castle, and dates from the 12th and 13th centuries. A series of tableaux with a commentary tells the history of the building. Special events for 1995 include Medieval Fayre (28 may), Mont Orgueil under the Yorkists - 1471 (26-31 July).
Open Apr-Oct, daily 9.30-6. Last admission 5.

£2.90 (ch 10-16 & pen £1.90, ch 10 free). Passport to all 5 Jersey Museum Service sites £8.50 (concessions £5.50).
🅿 (200 yds) shop ♿

Greve De Lecq Visitor Centre
JERSEY
GREVE DE LECQ
☎ *(01534) 482238*
The centre focuses on the wildlife, landscape and history of the north coast of Jersey.
Open BH's & Apr & Oct, Thu & Sun only 2-5; May-Sep, daily (ex Mon) 2-5. Free.
🅿 ♿ *shop* ♿ ♿

La Hougue Bie
JERSEY
GROUVILLE
☎ *(01534) 853823*
This Neolithic burial mound stands 40ft high, and covers a stone-built passage and grave which is still intact and may be entered. The passage is 50ft long, and is built of huge stones dragged from quarries; the mound is made from earth, rubble and limpet shells. On top of the mound are two medieval chapels, one of which has a replica of the Holy Sepulchre in Jerusalem below. Also on the site is an underground bunker built by the Germans as a communications centre. It is now an Occupation museum. There are also archaeology and geology displays. A storyteller will interpret the site and relate the 'Legend of La Hogue Bie' on specific dates throughout the summer. Special events for 1995 include Discovery Days (25 June, 23 July, 24 September).
Open Apr-Oct, daily 10-5.
£2.90 (ch 10-16 & pen £1.90, ch 10 free). Passport for all 5 Jersey Museums Service sites £8.50 (concessions £5.50).
🅿 ♿ *shop* ♿

Jersey Lavender Farm
JERSEY
ST BRELADE
Rue du Pont Marquet
☎ *(01534) 42933*
At this lavender farm visitors can see the complete process of production from cultivation through to harvesting and distillation to the bottling, labelling and packaging of the final product. There is also a short video. Visitors can follow walks through the lavender and herb fields and for those interested in plants and gardens there is the National Collection of Lavandula, a fine herb

garden and an extensive collection of dwarf and slow-growing conifers in the Pygmy Pinetum.
Open 22 May- 23 Sep, Mon-Sat 10-5. £1.85 (ch 14 free).
🅿 ♿ *(wheelchair loan) toilets for disabled shop garden centre* ♿

Samarès Manor
JERSEY
ST CLEMENT
☎ *Jersey (01534) 70551*
There are guided tours of the manor, which stands in 14 acres of beautiful gardens. The Japanese Garden occupies an artificial hill, and has a series of waterfalls cascading over Cumberland limestone. One of Britain's largest and most comprehensive herb gardens is here, with a herb and specialist hardy perennial nursery. Other attractions include a craft centre, farm animals and a children's play area.
Open 2 Apr-1 Oct. £3.25 (ch 16 £1.60, pen £2.75).
🅿 ♿ ✗ *licensed* ♿ *toilets for disabled shop garden centre*

Elizabeth Castle
JERSEY
ST HELIER
(access by causeway or amphibious vehicle)
☎ *(01534) 23971*
The original Elizabethan fortress was extended in the 17th and 18th centuries, and then refortified by the Germans during the Occupation. There are many buildings and defences to explore, a museum of the Jersey militia, a Granite and Gunpowder exhibition of cannon and fortifications in war and peace, and an exhibition of life in the castle. Special events for 1995 include 'Muskets and Drums' an 18th-century re-enactment (24-29 August).
Open Apr-Oct, daily 9.30-6. Last admission 5. £2.90 (concessions £1.90, ch 10 free). Passport for all 5 Jersey Museum Service sites £8.50 (concessions £5.50).
♿ ♿ *shop* ♿

Jersey Museum
JERSEY
ST HELIER
The Weighbridge
☎ *(01534) 30511*
The Jersey Museum, winner of the Museum of the Year 1993 Award, is a specially designed purpose-built venue. It

Castle Cornet was originally an island fort built by the French in 1345. It is now joined to St Peter Port by a causeway and forms part of the harbour.

houses 'The Story of Jersey', Jersey's art gallery, an exhibition gallery which features a changing programme, a lecture theatre, and an audio-visual theatre. There is a cafe, shop, and plenty of places to rest and relax. Special events throughout 1995 will be advertised locally and information is available from the museum.
Open all year, Etr-Oct, Mon-Sat 10-5, Sun 1-5. Winter Mon-Sat 10-4, Sun 1-4. (Closed 24, 25 & 26 Dec & 1 Jan). £2.90 (ch 10 free, concessions £1.90). Passport ticket for all 5 Jersey Museums Service sites £8.50 (concessions £5.50).
P *(5 mins walk)* ✗ *licensed* & *(audio loop, audio guide for partially sighted, car park) toilets for disabled shop* ⊗

German Underground Hospital
JERSEY
ST LAWRENCE
Meadowbank
☎(01534) 863442
Close to the entrance is a plaque which records that 'Under these conditions men of many nations laboured to construct this hospital. Those who survived will never forget; those who did not will never be forgotten'. On 1 July 1940 the Channel Islands were occupied by the German forces, and this vast complex dug deep into a hillside is the most evocative reminder of the Occupation. Here in the echoing corridors and chambers visitors can experience the hardships endured by the tunnellers. There is a continuous video presentation which, along with a large collection of memorabilia, brings the experience of the Islanders at war to life.
12 Mar-early Nov, daily 9.30-5.30. Last admission 4.45pm. £4 (ch £2).
P 🍴 ✗ *licensed* & *(ramp to restaurant & lift in Visitor Centre to restaurant) toilets for disabled shop* ⊗

Hamptonne
JERSEY
ST LAWRENCE
☎(01534) 863955
Here at Hamptonne, Jersey's country life museum, you will find a medieval 17th-century home, furnished in authentic style and surrounded by 19th-century farm buildings. Discover the history of rural Jersey and its people in the exhibition gallery, wander through the meadows and apple orchard and see a working cider press and apple crusher. Daily demonstrations include bread-making and spinning etc.
Open Apr-Oct, daily 10-5 £2.90 (ch 10-16 & concessions £1.90). Passport ticket for all five Jersey Museums Services sites £8.50 (concessions £5.50).
P 🍴 & *toilets for disabled shop* ⊗

Jersey Flower Centre
JERSEY
ST LAWRENCE
Retreat Farm
☎(01534) 865585
The Jersey Flower Centre is the largest carnation growing nursery not only in Jersey but in the UK. Take a walk around the giant glasshouses measuring 22,000 sq ft and holding 400,000 plants or view the Flamingo Lake, Wildfowl Sanctuary, Koi Carp Reserve, exotic birds and wildflower meadowland.

Prices under review.
P 🍴 & *toilets for disabled shop* ⊗

Jersey Shire Horse Farm Museum
JERSEY
ST OUEN
Champ Donne, Rue de Trodez
☎Jersey (01534) 82372
There are Shire horses and their foals to meet, and carriage rides can be taken along country lanes. There are also displays of harness, farming implements and a museum.
Open Mar-Oct, daily (ex Sat) 10-5.30. Also all BH's.
P 🍴 *shop* ⊗
Details not confirmed for 1995

Kempt Tower Visitor Centre
JERSEY
ST OUEN
Five Mile Rd
☎Jersey (01534) 483651
The centre has displays on the past, and the wildlife, of St Ouen's Bay, including Les Mielles, which is Jersey's miniature national park. Nature walks are held every Thursday (May to September). Check local press for details.
Open BH's & Apr & Oct, Thu & Sun only 2-5; May-Sep, daily (ex Mon) 2-5. Free.
P *shop* ⊗

Jersey Motor Museum
JERSEY
ST PETER
St Peter's Village (jct off A12 & B41 at St Peters village)
☎Jersey (01534) 482966
The museum has a fine collection of motor vehicles from the early 1900s. There are also Allied and German military vehicles of World War II, a Jersey Steam Railway section, aero-engines and other items. A pre-war Jersey AA box is shown, with a collection of AA badges of all periods.
Open Mar-end Oct, daily 10-5. (Last admission 4.40pm). £1.90 (ch £1). Wheelchair users free.
P & *shop* ⊗

The Living Legend
JERSEY
ST PETER
Rue de Petit Aleval
☎(01534) 485496
Pass through the granite archways into the landscaped gardens and the world of the Living Legend where Jersey's exciting past is recreated in a three dimensional spectacle. Learn of the heroes and villains, the folklore and the story of the Island's links with the UK and her struggles with Europe. Other attractions include an adventure playground, street entertainment, the Jersey Craft and Shopping Village, a range of shops and the Jersey Kitchen Restaurant.
Open Apr-1 Nov daily 9.30-5.30; Mar & Nov-3 Dec, Sat-Wed 10-5.
✱£3.99 (ch £2.50, pen £3.50)
P ✗ *licensed* & *toilets for disabled shop* ⊗

Le Moulin de Quetivel
JERSEY
ST PETER
St Peters Valley (on B58 off A11)
☎Jersey (01534) 483193
There has been a water mill on this site since 1309. The present granite-built mill was worked until the end of the 19th century, when it fell into disrepair; during the German Occupation it was reactivated for grinding locally grown corn, but after 1945 a fire destroyed the remaining machinery, roof and internal woodwork. In 1971 the National Trust for Jersey began restoration, and the mill is now producing stoneground flour again.
Open May-mid Oct, Tue-Thu 10-4. Dates to be confirmed.
P & *shop* ⊗ 🖼
(NT)
Details not confirmed for 1995

St Peter's Bunker Museum
JERSEY
ST PETER
St Peters Village (at junc of A12 & B41)
☎Jersey (01534) 481048
German uniforms, motorcycles, weapons, documents, photographs and other items from the 1940-45 Occupation are displayed in a real wartime bunker. It accommodated 36 men and could be sealed in case of attack. One room has been refitted with authentic bunk beds and figures of soldiers. There will be a photographic exhibition within the museum.
Open end Mar-end Oct, daily 10-5. £1.90 (ch 90p). Groups 10+
P *shop* ⊗

Jersey Zoological Park
JERSEY
TRINITY
Les Augres Manor
☎Jersey (01534) 864666
Gerald Durrell's unique sanctuary and breeding centre for many of the world's rarest and most beautiful animals. In the attractive gardens of the 16th-century manor house, visitors can enjoy the family life of a remarkable collection of exotic creatures, some of them so rare that they are only to be found in Jersey Zoo. Here they have all the benefits of modern, spacious enclosures that encourage natural and entertaining behaviour. Major attractions are the magical Aye-Ayes from Madagascar and the world-famous family of Lowland gorillas.

A comprehensive programme of keeper talks, animal displays and activities enhances the visitor experience and the fascinating story of the work of the Trust around the world is portrayed in a superb film in the Princess Royal Pavilion. The new orang-utang enclosure is opened in 1994 and new developments are planned in 1995.
Open all year, daily 10-6 (dusk in winter). (Closed 25 Dec).
✱£4.60 (ch £2.60, pen £3.10). *Prices under review.*
P ✗ *licensed* & *(trail for the blind, auditory loop in pavilion) toilets for disabled shop* ⊗

Lowland gorillas, an endangered species, are a major attraction at Jersey Zoo which was founded by the naturalist Gerald Durrell to protect endangered animals.

SCOTLAND

BORDERS

Broughton Place
BROUGHTON
(N on A701)
☎(018994) 234
The house was designed by Sir Basil Spence in 1938, in the style of a 17th-century Scottish tower house. The drawing room and main hall are open to the public, and have paintings and crafts by living British artists for sale. The gardens are open and give fine views of the Tweeddale Hills. A full programme of exhibitions is available on request.
Open - Gallery 26 Mar-17 Oct & 19 Nov-17 Dec, daily (ex Wed) 10.30-6. Gallery free; Garden donations.
P & *shop garden centre* ⊗

Hirsel
COLDSTREAM
(0.5m W on A697)
☎(01890) 882834 & 882965
The Hirsel is the seat of the Home family, and its grounds are open all year. The focal point is the Homestead Museum, craft centre and workshops. From there, nature trails lead around the lake, along the Leet Valley and into a wood which is noted for its rhododendrons and azaleas. Tea room, picnic areas. A May Fair (6-8 May), and Christmas Craft Fair (4-5 ➤

Resembling a French château, Floors Castle was transformed from an earlier house into a fairytale castle for the 6th Duke of Roxburgh.

November) are planned.
Garden & Grounds open all year, daylight hours. Museum 10-5. Craft Centre Mon-Fri, 10-5, weekends noon-5.
Free.
P (charged) ⬛ & toilets for disabled shop

Dryburgh Abbey
DRYBURGH
(5m SE of Melrose on B6404)
☎0131-668 8800
The abbey was one of the Border monasteries founded by David I, and stands in a lovely setting on the River Tweed. The ruins are equally beautiful, and the church has the graves of Sir Walter Scott and Earl Haig.
Open all year, Apr-Sep, weekdays 9.30-6.30, Sun 2-6.30 Oct-Mar weekdays 9.30-4.30, Sun 2-4.30. (Closed 25-26 Dec & 1-3 Jan).
P & shop ✗
(AM)

Jim Clark Room
DUNS
44 Newtown St
☎(01361) 83960
Motor racing trophies won by Jim Clark are on display, including two world championship trophies of 1963 and 1965, and other Grand Prix awards. Clark was the first Honorary Burgess of Duns. He was killed in Germany in 1968, and his parents gave the trophies to the town. There is also a growing collection of photographs and other memorabilia.
Open Etr-Oct, Mon-Sat 10-1 & 2-5, Sun 2-5.
P & ✗
Details not confirmed for 1995

Manderston
DUNS
(1.25m E off A6105)
☎(01361) 883450
This grandest of grand houses gives a fascinating picture of Edwardian life both above and below stairs. It was built for the millionaire racehorse owner Sir James Miller. The architect was told to spare no expense, and so the house boasts features such as the world's only silver staircase, a ballroom painted in Sir James's racing colours, and painted ceilings. The state rooms are magnificent, and the domestic quarters are also quite lavish. Outside buildings include the handsome stable block and marble dairy, and there are fine formal

gardens, with a woodland garden and lakeside walks.
Open 11 May-28 Sep, Thu & Sun 2-5.30 (also Spring & Aug BH Mon).
Telephone for details.
P ⬛ & shop

Eyemouth Museum
EYEMOUTH
Auld Kirk, Market Place
☎(018907) 50678
The museum was opened in 1981 as a memorial to the 129 local fishermen lost in the Great Fishing Disaster of 1881. Its main feature is the 15ft Eyemouth tapestry, which was made for the centenary. There are also displays on local history, and temporary exhibitions.
Open Apr-Jun & Sep, Mon-Sat 10-4.30, Sun 2-4; Oct Mon-Sat 10-noon & 1.30-4; Jul-Aug, Mon-Sat 9.30-6, Sun 1-5.30.
£1.50 (concessions £1).
P (250 yds) & shop

Nether Mill (Peter Anderson Ltd)
GALASHIELS
Huddersfield St
☎(01896) 752091
The museum brings the town's past to life with photographs and captions. The focal point is a display on the town's important woollen industry, and there are everyday items of the past on show. Guided tours of the mill take about 40 minutes.
Open all year, Mon-Sat 9-5, Sun (Jun-Sep) 12-5. Mill tours Mon-Thu at 10.30, 11.30, 1.30 & 2.30, Fri am only. Museum free. Mill tour £1.75 (ch 14 free).
P & toilets for disabled shop

Mellerstain House
GORDON
(5m E of Earlston, on unclass road)
☎(01573) 410225
One of Scotland's finest Georgian houses, Mellerstain was begun by William Adam and completed by his son Robert in the 1770s. It has beautiful plasterwork, period furniture and pictures; terraced gardens and a lake. Special events for 1995 include: a vintage car rally (4 June), craft festival (22-24 July).
Open Etr, then May, Jun & Sep Wed, Fri & Sun; Jul & Aug daily ex Sat. 12.30-5 (Last admission 4.30pm).
£3.50 (ch £1.50, pen £3). Party 20+.
P ⬛ & shop ✗

Drumlanrig's Tower
HAWICK
Tower Knowe
☎(01450) 373457
Spring 1995 sees the grand opening of the visitor centre for Drumlanrig's Tower. The Tower has a fascinating history, beginning in its earliest years when the Tower served as a fortified keep in the 12th century - occupied by the Black Douglas of Drumlanrig; through to a more genteel age in the 18th century when Anne, Duchess of Monmouth and Buccleuch transformed it into a glittering residence. Later the Tower served as a gracious hotel. Now transformed into a major visitor attraction with historic room setting, costumed figures, dioramas, sownds, smells and audio visual programmes. Many special events throughout the year.
Open peak season 10-7; other times 10-5.
Adults £2 (concessions £1). Party.
P (300 yds) & toilets for disabled shop ✗

Hawick Museum & Scott Gallery
HAWICK
Wilton Lodge Park (0.75m W from High St, following river)
☎(01450) 373457
Wilton Lodge Park forms a beautiful setting for this museum on the history, trades and wildlife of the Borders. There is an interesting range of exhibitions, including new wildlife displays. The art gallery has exhibitions throughout the year, and the park has riverside walks and gardens. There are displays on the history of Hawick's hosiery and knitwear trade, Hawick Common Riding and the town's sporting associations.
Open all year, Apr-Sep, Mon-Sat 10-noon & 1-5, Sun 2-5; Oct-Mar, Mon-Fri 1-4, Sun 2-4.
£1 (ch, pen, students & UB40's 50p). Party 20+.
P & shop ✗

Hermitage Castle
HERMITAGE
(5.5m NE of Newcastleton off A7)
☎0131-668 8800
An old Douglas stronghold, mainly 14th-century, and well restored.
Open all year, Apr-Sep, Mon-Sat 9.30-6.30, Sun 2-6.30; Oct-Mar wknds only, Sat 9.30-4.30, Sun 2-4.30. (Closed 25-26 Dec & 1-2 Jan).
£1.20 (ch & pen 75p).
P & shop
(AM)

Robert Smail's Printing Works
INNERLEITHEN
7/9 High St
☎(01896) 830206
These buildings contain a Victorian office, a paper store with reconstructed waterwheel, a composing room and a press room. The machinery is in full working order and visitors may view the printer at work and have 'hands-on' experience in typesetting in the composing room.
Open 14 Apr-22 Oct Mon-Sat 10-1 & 2-5, Sun 2-5. (Last tour 45mins before closing morning & afternoon).
✱£2 (concessions £1). Party.
P (300yds) & shop ✗
(NTS)

Jedburgh Abbey
JEDBURGH
4-5 Abbey Bridgend
☎0131-668 8800
Standing as the most complete of the Border monasteries, although it has been sacked and rebuilt many times, Jedburgh Abbey has been described as 'the most perfect and beautiful example of the Saxon and early Gothic in Scotland'. It was founded as a priory in the 12th century by David I and remains of some of the domestic buildings have been uncovered during excavations.
Open all year, Apr-Sep, Mon-Sat 9.30-6.30, Sun 2-6.30; Oct-Mar, Mon-Sat 9.30-4.30, Sun 2-4.30. (Closed 25-26 Dec & 1-3 Jan).
£2.50 (ch £1, pen £1.50).
P (200 yds) & (limited access) toilets for disabled shop ✗
(AM)

Mary Queen of Scots House
JEDBURGH
Queen St
☎(01835) 863331
Mary, Queen of Scots visited Jedburgh in 1566, and had to prolong her stay because of ill-health. This splendid house is now a museum devoted to her memory and tragic history. An unusual feature of this 16th-century fortified dwelling is the left-handed spiral staircase: the Kers, the owners of the house, were left-handed and the special staircase allowed the men to use their sword hands. The museum presents a thought-provoking interpretation of her tragic life with period rooms, stunning murals and personal items connected to Mary, Queen of Scots.
Open Mar-Nov, daily 10-5 (4.30 Sun).
£1.50 (ch, pen, students & UB40's £1). Party 20+.
P (300 yds) & shop ✗

Floors Castle
KELSO
(1m N)
☎(01573) 223333
Sir Walter Scott described this fairy-tale castle as 'altogether a kingdom for Oberon and Titania to dwell in'. Today it is the home of the 10th Duke of Roxburghe and its lived-in atmosphere enhances the superb collection of French furniture, tapestries and paintings contained inside. The house was designed by William Adam in 1721 and extended by W H Playfair over a century later; it enjoys a magnificent setting overlooking the River Tweed and the Cheviot Hills beyond. A holly tree in the grounds is said to mark the spot where James II was killed; and an attractive walled garden, garden centre and play area are among the attractions outside.
Open Etr & late Apr-Jun & Sep (Sun-Thu), Jul-Aug (daily) 10.30-5.30; Oct, Sun & Wed, 10.30-4. Walled Garden & Garden Centre open daily.
£3.80 (ch 5-16 £1.90, pen £3). Family ticket £10.
P ⬛ ✗ licensed & (lift) toilets for disabled shop garden centre ✗ (ex in grounds)

The Ruins of the 14th-century Melrose Abbey are noted for the particularly fine carvings around the cloister and doorways.

Kelso Abbey
KELSO
☎0131-668 8800
Founded by David I in 1128 and probably the greatest of the four famous Border abbeys, Kelso became extremely wealthy and acquired extensive lands. In 1545 it served as a fortress when the town was attacked by the Earl of Hertford, but now only fragments of the once-imposing abbey church give any clue to its long history.
Open at any reasonable time.
Free.
&
(AM)

Kelso Museum
KELSO
Turret House, Abbey Court (off A698)
☎(01573) 225470
Kelso Museum reflects the life and times of this lively market town, going back to prehistoric beginnings and looking at its growth since the establishment of the Abbey in the 12th-century. A Victorian schoolroom, a market scene and the interior of a skinner's workshop are popular features.
Open Etr-Oct, Mon-Sat 10-12 & 1-5, Sun 2-5.
❋80p (ch, pen, students & UB40 40p)
P (50yds) & shop ✖

Thirlestane Castle
LAUDER
(off A68)
☎(01578) 722430
This fairy-tale castle has been the home of the Maitland family, the Earls of Lauderdale, since the 12th century, and part of the family still live in one of the wings. Some of the most splendid plasterwork ceilings in Britain may be seen in the 17th-century state rooms. The former family nurseries now house a sizeable collection of antique toys and dolls, while in the south wing there are several interesting displays illustrating Border country life. The informal grounds, with their riverside setting and views of nearby grouse moors, include a woodland walk and picnic tables. A Kite Festival is planned for 12-13 August 1995 (provisional dates).

Open 12-19 Apr, May-Jun & Sep, Mon & Wed-Thu & Sun; Jul-Aug, daily (ex Sat) 2-5 (last admission 4.30pm). Grounds open on dates listed above noon-6.
£3.50. Family ticket £9. Grounds only £1. Party.
P ✖ shop ✖ (ex in grounds)

Abbotsford House
MELROSE
(2m W off A6091)
☎Galashiels (01896) 752043
Set on the River Tweed, Sir Walter Scott's romantic mansion remains much the same as it was in his day. Inside there are many mementoes and relics of his remarkable life and also his historical collections, armouries and library, with some 9000 volumes. The mansion was built between 1817 and 1822, and Sir Walter Scott lived here until his death ten years after its completion.
Open 20 Mar-Oct, Mon-Sat 10-5, Sun 2-5.
£3 (ch £1.50). Party.
P ✖ & toilets for disabled shop ✖

Melrose Abbey & Abbey Museum
MELROSE
☎0131-668 8800
The ruin of this Cistercian abbey is probably one of Scotland's finest, and has been given added glamour by its connection with Sir Walter Scott. The abbey was repeatedly wrecked during the Scottish wars of independence, but parts of the nave and choir survive from the 14th century, and include some of the best and most elaborate traceried stonework in Scotland. Most of the ruins belong to the 15th-century reconstruction. The abbey has many interesting features: the heart of Robert the Bruce is buried somewhere within the church; note too the figure of a pig playing the bagpipes, set on the roof. The museum, sited at the entrance to the ruins and housed in the 16th-century Commendator's House, is an interesting addition to this historic ruin.
Open all year, Apr-Sep Mon-Sat 9.30-6.30, Sun 2-6.30; Oct-Mar, Mon-Sat 9.30-4.30, Sun 2-4.30.
£2.50 (ch 16 £1, pen £1.50).
P & shop ✖
(AM)

Melrose Motor Museum
MELROSE
Annay Rd
☎(01896) 822624
A short walk from the abbey ruins, this is a fascinating collection of cars, cycles, motorcycles and accessories.
Open Etr-Whitsun, please telephone for opening times. Whitsun-Oct, daily 10.30-5.30. Last admission 5.
❋£2 (ch 50p, pen & students £1.50).
Party 10+ by arrangement.
P shop ✖

Priorwood Garden & Dried Flowers
MELROSE
(off A6091)
☎(01896) 822493
This small garden specialises in flowers which are suitable for drying. It is formally designed with herbaceous and everlasting annual borders, and the attractive orchard has a display of 'apples through the ages' including ancient varieties.
Open Garden & Shop; Apr-24 Dec, Mon-Sat 10-5.30, Sun 1.30-5.30. Shop only; 9 Jan-Mar Mon-Sat 12-4 (Closed 30 Oct-6 Nov).
Honesty box £1.
& shop
(NTS)

Kailzie
PEEBLES
(2.5m SE on B7062)
☎(01721) 720007
These extensive grounds with their fine old trees provide a burnside walk flanked by bulbs, rhododendrons and azaleas. A walled garden contains herbaceous, shrub rose borders, greenhouses and a small formal rose garden. There is a waterfowl pond, a plant centre, an art gallery, and a childrens' play area.
Open 25 Mar-Oct, daily 11-5.30. Grounds close 5.30pm. Garden open all year.

P ✖ ✖ licensed & (ramps in garden & gravel paths) toilets for disabled shop garden centre
Details not confirmed for 1995

Neidpath Castle
PEEBLES
(1m W on A72)
☎(01721) 720333
Successively owned by the families of Fraser, Hay (Earl of Tweeddale), Douglas (Earl of March) and Wemyss (Earl of Wemyss and March), Neidpath Castle occupies a spectacular position on the Tweed. The 14th-century stronghold has been interestingly adapted to 17th-century living; it contains a rock-hewn well, a pit prison, a small museum, and a tartan display, and has picturesque views. There are fine walks and a picnic area. A re-enactment with Highlanders is planned for May.
Open 13 Apr-Sep, Mon-Sat 11-5, Sun 1-5.
£2 (ch £1, pen & students £1.50). Family ticket £5.50. Party 20+.
P shop

Bowhill House and Country Park
SELKIRK
(3m W of Selkirk off A708)
☎(01750) 20732
An outstanding collection of pictures, including works by Van Dyck, Canaletto, Reynolds, Gainsborough and Claude Lorraine, are displayed in this, the Border home of the Duke of Buccleuch and Queensberry KT. In addition to these there is an equally stunning collection of porcelain and furniture, much of it made in the Paris workshop of André Boulle. Memorabilia and relics of people such as Queen Victoria and Sir Walter Scott, and a restored Victorian kitchen add further interest inside the house. Outside, the wooded grounds are perfect for walking, cycling and riding (there is bicycle hire and a riding centre). Children will enjoy the adventure playground and, no doubt, the gift shop. There is also a theatre and ➤

Deep in the beautiful Ochil Hills, Castle Campbell, the lowland stronghold of the Argylls, was known as Castle Gloom.

an audio-visual display. Art courses are held here.
Open, Park: May-Aug 12-5 (ex Fri). House & park: Jul, daily 1-4.30.
House & grounds £4 (ch 5 free, pen £3.50). Grounds only £1. Party 20+.
P ✉ ✗ *licensed ♿ (guided tours for the blind) toilets for disabled shop (Jul)* ⊗ *(ex in grounds)*

Halliwells House Museum
SELKIRK
Halliwells Close, Market Place (off A7)
☎*(01750) 720096*
The former role of Selkirk's oldest surviving dwelling has been recreated in this enterprising museum. The home and ironmonger's shop, lovingly restored, can be seen together with the story of the town's development and frequent temporary exhibitions.
Open Apr-Oct, Mon-Sat 10-5 (Jul & Aug until 6), Sun 2-4; Nov, daily 2-4.
Free.
P ♿ *toilets for disabled shop* ⊗

Sir Walter Scott's Courtroom
SELKIRK
Market Place (on A7)
☎*(01750) 720096*
Built in 1804 as the new sheriff court and town house for Selkirk, it was here that the novelist Sir Walter Scott pursued his work as Sheriff of the County of Selkirk. Now re-opened as a museum with displays and audio-visual presentations about Scott's life, his writing, his contempraries (James Hogg and Mungo Park) and his time as sheriff.
Open Apr-Oct, Mon-Sat 10-4, Sun 2-4.
Free.
P *(100mtrs)* ✗ *shop* ⊗

Smailholm Tower
SMAILHOLM
(1.5m SW on B6937)
☎*0131-668 8800*
An outstanding example of a classic Border tower-house, probably erected in the 15th century. It is 57ft high and well-preserved. The tower houses an exhibition of dolls and a display based on Sir Walter Scott's book 'Minstrels of the Border'. It consists of tapestries and costume figures.
Open Apr-Sep, Mon-Sat 9.30-6.30, Sun 2-6.30. (Closed in winter).
£1.50 (concessions 75p).
P *shop* ⊗
(AM)

Dawyck Botanic Garden
STOBO
(8m SW of Peebles on B712)
☎*(01721) 760254*
An impressive collection of mature specimen trees, some over 40 metres tall, provide an imposing setting for a variety of flowering trees, shrubs and herbaceous plants. Landscaped walks lead visitors through mature woodland which is full of wildlife. Open Day is 7 May.
Open 15 Mar-22 Oct, daily 10-6.
£2 (ch 50p, concessions £1.50). Family ticket £4.50.
P ✉ ♿ *toilets for disabled shop garden centre* ⊗

Traquair House
TRAQUAIR
(1m S of Innerleithen on B709).
☎*Innerleithen (01896) 830323 & 830785*
This is said to be Scotland's oldest inhabited, and most romantic, house. It dates back to the 12th century and 27 English and Scottish kings have stayed here. William the Lion Heart held court at Traquair, and the house has rich associations with Mary, Queen of Scots and the Jacobite risings. The large Bear Gates were closed in 1745, not to be reopened until the Stuarts should once again ascend the throne.
The house contains a fine collection of historical treasures and a unique 18th-century brewhouse which is licensed to make and sell its own beer. Outside there is a maze, croquet, and the opportunity for woodland walks by the River Tweed. There are also craft workshops and an art gallery. Special events for 1995 include: Celebration of Scottish Beer (27-28 May), Sheep and Wool Day (30 July), Traquair Fair (5-6 August).
Open 15 Apr-Sep daily, 12.30-5.30 (ex Jul & Aug 10.30-5.30). Last admission 5pm.
Oct, Fri-Sun, 2-5. Grounds open Apr-Sep,

10.30-5.30.
£3.75 (ch £1.75, pen £3.20). Family ticket £10. Party.
P ✉ ✗ *licensed ♿ shop*
See advertisement on page 167

CENTRAL

Bannockburn Heritage Centre
BANNOCKBURN
Glasgow Rd (2m S off M80/M9 junc 9)
☎*(01786) 812664*
The Heritage Centre stands close to the Borestone site, which by tradition was King Robert the Bruce's command post before the Battle of Bannockburn, June 1314, at which the Scots trounced the English. It was a turning-point in Scottish history, and Bruce is commemorated by a bronze equestrian statue, unveiled in 1964. The site is enclosed by the Rotunda. The centre has an exhibition, 'The Kingdom of the Scots', and an audio-visual display on the battle.
Open - Rotunda & site always open. Heritage Centre & Shop; Feb-Mar & 6 Nov-23 Dec, daily 11-3; Apr-Oct daily 10-5.30. (Last audio-visual showing half hour before closing).
✳*£2 (concessions £1). Party.*
P ♿ *(Induction loop for the hard of hearing) toilets for disabled shop* ⊗ *(ex site only)*
(NTS)

The Birkhill Clay Mine
BIRKHILL
☎*Bo'ness (01506) 825855*
No simulations here, this is a real clay mine deep in the steep wooded Avon Gorge. Experience life underground, and visit the original mill, clay handling buildings and haulage gear. Work is in progress on a car park, picnic area, underground walks and a nature trail.
Open 1 Apr-15 Oct weekends only. 8 Jul-20 Aug daily. Holiday Mon's 17 Apr, 1 & 29 May.
Mine & Train £5.50 (ch £2.80, pen £3.30) Family ticket £13.80. Train only £3.60 (ch £1.80, pen £2.40) Family ticket £9. Mine only £2.40 (ch & pen £1.20) Family ticket £6.
P *shop*

Blair Drummond Safari & Leisure Park
BLAIR DRUMMOND
(M9 exit 10, 4m along A84 towards Callander)
☎*Doune (01786) 841456 & 841396*
Drive through the wild animal reserves and see at close range the monkeys, zebras, North American bison, antelope, lions, tigers and camels. Pets' Farm is home to a wide variety of animals including piglets, llamas, wallabies, rheas, goats and peafowl. Other attractions include the sea lion show, a ride on the boat safari through the waterfowl sanctuary and around Chimpanzee Island, an adventure playground, flying fox cable slide across the lake, giant astraglide, splash cats and pedal boats. Thereis a new den for European brown bears and a new zebra reserve.
Open Apr-2 Oct, daily 10-5.30. Last admission 4.30.
£6 (ch 3-14 & pen £3.50). Party 15+.
P ✉ ♿ *(level foot paths) toilets for disabled* ⊗ *(free kennels at entrance)*

Bo'ness & Kinneil Railway
BO'NESS
Bo'ness Station, Union St
☎*(01506) 822298*
Located in the countryside of Edinburgh, near Linlithgow, the Bo'ness and Kinneil Railway recreates the world of steam with relocated railway buildings, and Scotland's largest collection of locomotives and rolling stock. A visitor trail allows self-guided tours to the engine shed and goods shed. During 1995, the SRPS will open a Scottish Railway Exhibition in a 15,000sq ft

purpose-built building. A seven mile round steam-hauled journey begins on the southern shore of the Firth of Forth and runs to the woodlands of the Avon Gorge at Birkhill, where a Fireclay Mine is open to the public. There, guided tours take the vistiors into the cavernous mine workings, to see for themselves the fossilised trees embedded in the clay some 300 million years ago. Snacks, souvenir shop. Special events for 1995 include Friends of Thomas Spring Weekend (13-14 May), vintage vehicle rally (18 June), diesel enthusiasts weekend (23-24 September).
Open Apr-15 Oct, Sat & Sun; Mon 17 Apr, 1 & 29 May; 8 Jul-20 Aug, daily.
✳*Return fare £3.60 (ch 5-15 £1.80, pen £2.40). Family ticket £9. Inclusive ticket for return train fare and tour of Birkhill Fireclay Mine £5.50 (ch £2.80, pen £3.30), family ticket £13.80.*
P ✉ ♿ *(ramps) shop*

Kinneil Museum & Roman Fortlet
BO'NESS
Duchess Anne Cottages, Kinniel Estate
☎*(01506) 824318*
The museum is in a converted stable block of Kinneil House. The ground floor has displays on the industrial history of Bo'ness, while the upper floor looks at the history and environment of the Kinneil estate. The remains of the Roman fortlet can be seen nearby. An audio visual theatre shows 2000 years of history.
Open all year, Apr-Sep, Mon-Fri 10-12.30 & 1.30-5, Sat 10-5 & May-Aug, Sun 10-5; Oct-Mar, Sat only 10-5.
Free.
P ♿ *shop* ⊗

Rob Roy and Trossachs Visitor Centre
CALLANDER
Ancaster Square (on A84)
☎*(01877) 330342*
The fascinating story of Scotland's most famous outlaw, Rob Roy MacGregor is vividly portrayed through an exciting multi-media theatre and explained in the carefully researched 'Life and Times' exhibition. Also full tourist information centre covering the beautiful Trossachs area, Scottish bookshops and specially themed souvenirs. Evening entertainment, including traditional Scottish music evenings, celidhs and illustrated talks, is arranged 6 nights a week from June to October; telephone for details. School pack available.
Open Feb, Sat & Sun only; Mar-May & Oct-Nov 10-5; Jun & Sep 10-7; Jul-Aug 9-11pm, Dec 10-4.
£2 (ch & pen £1.50).
P ♿ *toilets for disabled shop* ⊗

Wallace Monument
CAUSEWAYHEAD
☎*Stirling (01786) 472140*
The 220ft tower was built in 1869, and Sir William Wallace's two-handed sword is preserved inside. Seven battlefields and a fine view towards the Highlands can be seen. Displays include a Hall of Heroes, an audio-visual show on the life of Wallace, the Forth Panorama, and a sound-and-light show on famous Scots.
Open Feb, Mar & Oct 10-5; Apr & Sep 10-6; May-Aug 10-7.
P ✉ *shop* ⊗
Details not confirmed for 1995

Castle Campbell
DOLLAR
(10m W of Stirling on A91)
☎*0131-668 8800*
The 15th-to 17th-century tower stands in the picturesque Ochil Hills and gives wonderful views. It can be reached by a walk through the magnificent Dollar Glen. Care must be taken in or after rain when the path may be dangerous.
Open Apr-Sep, Mon-Sat 9.30-6.30, Sun 2-6.30; Oct-Mar, Mon-Sat 9.30-4.30, Sun 2-4.30. (Closed Thu pm & Fri in winter, 25-26 Dec & 1-3 Jan).
Castle £2 (ch 16 75p, pen £1.25).
P (440yds) shop
(AM & NTS)

CALLENDAR HOUSE
(Falkirk District Council)
Callendar Park, Falkirk FK1 1YR 🚸 Y
Telephone: (01324) 612134

CALLENDAR HOUSE

Imposing mansion within attractive parkland with a 900 year history. Facilities include a working kitchen of 1825 where costumed interpreters carry out the daily chores including cooking based on 1820s recipes. Exhibition area, "Story of Callendar House" plus two temporary galleries, with regularly changing exhibitions. There is also a history research centre, gift shop and Georgian teashop at the stables.

Location: From Edinburgh exit M9 Junction 5. From Stirling exit M9 Junction 6. To the east of Falkirk Town Centre on Callendar Road (A803)

Open: Jan-Dec Mon-Sat 10-5 Apr-Sept Sun 2-5. Open all Public Holidays
Admission: Adults £1.60. Children and OAPs 80p

Doune Castle
DOUNE
(8m S of Callander on A84)
☎0131-668 8800
The 14th-century stronghold with its two fine towers has been restored. It stands on the banks of the River Teith, and is associated with Bonnie Prince Charlie and Sir Walter Scott.
Open all year, Apr-Sep, Mon-Sat 9.30-6.30, Sun 2-6.30; Oct-Mar 9.30-4.30, Sun 2-4.30. (Closed Thu pm & Fri in winter; 25-26 Dec & 1-3 Jan).
£2 (ch 75p, £1.25).
🅿 🚸 *shop*
(AM)

Doune Motor Museum
DOUNE
(8m NW of Stirling on A84)
☎(01786) 841203
Around 50 cars are displayed, and motoring events are held throughout the season.

Open Etr-Oct, daily 10-5.
Admission fee payable.
🅿 💷 🚸 *toilets for disabled shop* 🐾

Callendar House
FALKIRK
Callendar Park
☎(01324) 612134
Mary, Queen of Scots, Oliver Cromwell, Bonny Prince Charlie, noble earls and wealthy merchants all feature in the the history of Callander House. Today, costumed interpreters describe the early 19th-century life in the well-preserved kitchens and the 900 year history of the house is illustrated in the 'Story of Callendar House' exhibition. The house is set in Callandar Park which offers many leisure attractions including boating, pitch and putt, a play area, and woodland walks.
Open all year, Mon-Sat 10-5. Apr-Sep Sun 2-5.
✽*£1.50 (ch & pen 75p). Family ticket £3.60.*

🅿 💷 ✗ 🚸 *(ramps & lift) toilets for disabled shop* 🐾

Rough Castle
FALKIRK
(1m E of Bonnybridge)
☎0131-668 8800
The impressive earthworks of a large Roman fort on the Antonine Wall can be seen here. The buildings have disappeared, but the mounds and terraces are the sites of barracks, granary and bath buildings. Running between them is the military road which once linked all the forts on the wall and is still well defined.
Open any reasonable time.
Free.
🅿 🐾
(AM)

Inchmahome Priory
PORT OF MENTEITH
(4m E of Aberfoyle, off A81)
☎0131-668 8800
Walter Comyn founded this Augustinian house in 1238, and it became famous as the retreat of the infant Mary Queen of Scots in 1543. The ruins of the church and cloisters are situated on an island in the Lake of Menteith.
Open Apr-Sep, weekdays 9.30-6.30, Sun 2-6.30. (Closed in winter). Ferry subject to cancellation in adverse weather conditions.
£2 (ch 16 75p, pen £1.25).
🅿 *shop*
(AM)

Mar's Wark
STIRLING
Broad St
☎0131-668 8800
Now partly ruined, this Renaissance-style mansion was built in 1570 by the Ist Earl of Mar, Regent of Scotland. With its gatehouse enriched with sculptures, it is one of several fine buildings on the road to Stirling Castle. The Earls of Mar lived

---

there until the 6th Earl fled the country after leading the 1715 Jacobite Rebellion.
Open at all times.
Free.
(AM)

Museum of Argyll & Sutherland Highlanders
STIRLING
☎(01786) 75165
Situated in the King's Old Building in Stirling Castle, the museum tells the history of the Regiment from 1794 to the present day. Displays include uniforms, silver, paintings, colours, pipe banners, and commentaries. There is a fine medal collection covering the period from the Battle of Waterloo to the present day. Five new permanent exhibits mark the bi-centenary of the Regiment.
Open Etr-Sep, Mon-Sat 10-5.30, Sun 11-5; Oct-Etr, Mon-Sat 10-4.
Entry to museum free but entry fee to castle.
P *(castle esplanade) shop* 🐾

Smith Art Gallery & Museum
STIRLING
Dumbarton Rd (junc 10 off M9 follow town centre signs)
☎(01786) 471917
This lively, award-winning museum and gallery presents a variety of exhibitions drawing on its own rich collections and works from elsewhere. A range of programmes and events offers the opportunity to see, find out about and join in art, history, craft and design. There is a small shop.
Open all year, Apr-Oct, Tue-Sat 10.30-5, Sun 2-5; Nov-Mar Tue-Fri 12-5, Sat 10.30-5 & Sun 2-5.
🅿 💷 🚸 *(wheelchair lift) toilets for disabled shop* 🐾
Details not confirmed for 1995

Stirling Castle
STIRLING
Upper Castle Hill
☎0131-668 8800
Sitting on top of a 250ft rock, Stirling Castle has a strategic position on the Firth of Forth. As a result it has been the scene of many events in Scotland's history. Much of the castle that remains today is from the 15th and 16th centuries, when it became a favourite royal residence. James II was born at the castle in 1430. Mary Queen of Scots spent some years there, and it was James IV's childhood home. The old towers were built by James IV, as was the fine great hall. Among its finest features are the splendid Renaissance palace built by James V, and the Chapel Royal, rebuilt by James VI.
Open all year, Apr-Sep, daily 9.30-6; Oct-Mar, daily 9.30-5. Last ticket sold 45 mins prior to closing time.
£3.50 (ch 16 £1, pen & UB40 £2)
🅿 *(charged)* ✗ *licensed* 🚸 *toilets for disabled shop* 🐾
(AM)

DUMFRIES & GALLOWAY

Ardwell House Gardens
ARDWELL
(10m S of Stranraer, on A716)
☎(01776) 860227
Country house gardens and grounds with flowering shrubs and woodland walks. Plants for sale. House not open to the public.
Open Mar-Oct, 10-6. Walled garden & greenhouses close at 5pm, Mar, 'Apr & Oct.
🅿 *garden centre*
Details not confirmed for 1995

Caerlaverock Castle
CAERLAVEROCK
Glencaple (8m SE of Dumfries)
☎0131-668 8800
This ancient seat of the Maxwell family is

For 200 years Stirling Castle was a residence of the Stuart Kings. James V built a splendid Renaissance palace which was further enhanced by the last Stuart King to live there – James VI.

➤

a splendid medieval stronghold dating back to the 13th century. It has high walls and round towers, with machicolations added in the 15th century.
Open all year, Apr-Sep, Mon-Sat 9.30-6.30, Sun 2-6.30; Oct-Mar 9.30-4.30, Sun 2-4.30. (Closed 25-26 Dec & 1-3 Jan).
£2 (ch 16 75p, pen £1.25)
P & *shop*
(AM)

Wildfowl & Wetlands Trust
CAERLAVEROCK
Eastpark Farm
(8m S of Dumfries)
☎ *Glencaple (01387) 770200*
This is an exciting wildlife refuge of over 1,500 acres on the north Solway shore. There are outstanding hide facilities, observation towers and an observatory giving impressive views of the huge numbers of wildfowl that spend most of the autumn, winter and spring here. The barnacle geese are the most impressive sight. Thousands of them fly in from their Spitsbergen breeding grounds to rest and feed in the waters and marshes. Pink-footed and greylag geese can also be seen, as can waders, whooper swans and ducks such as pintails and wigeons. These in turn may attract interesting predators such as peregrines and merlins. The 'merse', or salt marsh, is also the home of the rare natterjack toad.
Open daily 10-5 (Closed 24-25 Dec).
✲*£2.95 (ch £1.50, pen £2.20). Family ticket £7.40. Party 20+.*
P & *shop* ✲

Cardoness Castle
CARDONESS CASTLE
(1m SW of Gatehouse of Fleet off A75)
☎*0131-668 8800*
A 15th-century stronghold overlooking the Water of Fleet. It was once the home of the McCullochs of Galloway.
Open all year, Apr-Sep, Mon-Sat 9.30-6.30, Sun 2-6.30; Oct-Mar, wknds only. Sat 9.30-4.30, Sun 2-4.30 (Closed 25-26 Dec & 1-3 Jan).
£1.20 (concessions 70p).
P *shop*
(AM)

Threave Castle
CASTLE DOUGLAS
(3m W on A75)
☎*0131-668 8800*
Archibald the Grim built this lonely castle in the late 14th century. It stands on an islet in the River Dee, and is four storeys high with round towers guarding the outer wall. Access to the island is by boat.
Open Apr-Sep, Mon-Sat 9.30-6.30, Sun 2-6.30.
£1.50 (ch 16 75p, pen £1).
P *shop* ✲
(AM)

Threave Garden
CASTLE DOUGLAS
(1m W of Castle Douglas off A75)
☎*(01556) 502575*
The best time to visit is in spring when there is a dazzling display of some 200 varieties of daffodil. The garden has something to see all year round, however, and includes a walled garden and glasshouses. The house is the National Trust for Scotland's School of Horticulture.
Open all year. Garden, daily 9.30-sunset. Walled garden and glasshouses daily 9.30-5. Visitor centre, Shop & Exhibition Apr-22 Oct daily 9.30-5.30. (Last entry 30 minutes before closing).
✲*£3.50 (ch & pen £1.80). Party.*
P ✗ *licensed* & *(wheelchairs available incl. electric wheelchair) toilets for disabled shop garden centre* ✲
(NTS)

Comlongon Castle
CLARENCEFIELD
☎*(01387) 870283*
An exceptionally well-preserved 15th-century Border castle currently being restored. It contains many original

features including dungeons, kitchen, great hall, Heraldic devices, and bed chambers with 'privies'. It's set in gardens and woodland with secluded walks, and is haunted by a 16th-century suicide.
Open Mar-Oct, telephone for opening times.
P & ✲
Details not confirmed for 1995

Creetown Gem Rock Museum
CREETOWN
Chain Rd (follow signs from A75)
☎*(01671) 820357 & 820554*
The museum, completely refurbished in 1993, displays gemstones and minerals collected by the owners from around the world. The beautiful collection also includes gemstone *objets d'art*. There are three large exhibition halls and a gemstone workshop. The Crystal Cave is a major display, built to commemorate the museum's tenth anniversary. There is also a display of replicas of the world's largest diamonds, all 'facet cut'. An audio-visual programme, The Fire in the Stones, explains how minerals are formed. Gemstone polishing demonstrations are held in the workshop. There is an activity bench and fun quiz.
Open Mar-Oct, daily 9.30-6; Nov-23 Dec, Sat-Wed 10-4; 8 Jan-Feb, Sat & Sun only 10-4 or by appointment during the week. Phone for Christmas opening dates.
£2.25 (ch 5-15 £1.25, students & pen £1.75). Family ticket £5.75 Party 20+.
P ✦ & *toilets for disabled shop*

Drumcoltran Tower
DRUMCOLTRAN TOWER
(7m NE of Dalbeattie)
☎*0131-668 8800*
The 16th-century tower house stands three storeys high and has a simple, functional design.
Open at any reasonable time.
Free.
✲
(AM)

Burns House
DUMFRIES
Burns St
☎*(01387) 255297*
It was in this ordinary sandstone house in a backstreet of Dumfries that Robert Burns spent the last three years of his short life; he died here in 1796. It is now a place of pilgrimage for Burns enthusiasts from around the globe. The

house retains much of its 18th-century character and contains many fascinating items connected with the poet.
Open all year, Mon-Sat 10-1 & 2-5, Sun 2-5. (Closed Sun & Mon, Oct-Mar).
✲*80p (concessions 40p). Prices under review.*
P *(100 yds) shop*

Burns Mausoleum
DUMFRIES
St Michael's Churchyard
☎*(01387) 255297*
The mausoleum is in the form of a Greek temple, and contains the tombs of Robert Burns, his wife Jean Armour, and their five sons. A sculptured group shows the Muse of Poetry flinging her cloak over Burns at the plough.
Unrestricted access.
Free.
P *(100 yds)*

Dumfries Museum & Camera Obscura
DUMFRIES
The Observatory, Church St
☎*(01387) 253374*
Situated in and around the 18th-century windmill tower, Dumfries Museum is the largest museum in south west Scotland. Its collections were started over 150 years ago and have developed into a vast source of information on the area. Exhibitions trace the history of the people and landscape of Dumfries and Galloway. The Camera Obscura is to be found on the top floor of the windmill tower. It was installed in 1836 when the building was converted into an observatory. On the table-top screen you see a panoramic view of Dumfries and the surrounding countryside. Special events are planned throughout the year.
Open all year, Mon-Sat 10-1 & 2-5, Sun 2-5. (Closed Sun & Mon, Oct-Mar; Camera Obscura closed Oct-Mar).
✲*Free except Camera Obscura 80p (concessions 40p). Prices under review.*
P & *(ex camera obscura) toilets for disabled shop*

Old Bridge House Museum
DUMFRIES
Mill Rd
☎*(01387) 256904*
The Old Bridge House was built in 1660, into the fabric of the 15th-century Devorgilla's Bridge; it is the oldest house in Dumfries. A museum of everyday life in the town, it has an early 20th-century dentist's surgery, a Victorian nursery and

kitchens of the 1850s and 1900s.
Open Apr-Sep, Mon-Sat 10 & 2-5, Sun 2-5.
Free.
P & *shop*

Robert Burns Centre
DUMFRIES
Mill Rd
☎*(01387) 264808*
This award-winning centre concentrates on the connections between Scotland's national poet, Robert Burns, and the town of Dumfries. The centre is situated in the town's 18th-century watermill on the west bank of the River Nith and tells the story of Robert Burns' last years spent in the busy streets and lively atmosphere of Dumfries in the 1790s. In the evening the centre offers top quality feature films in the Film Theatre.
Open all year, Apr-Sep, Mon-Sat 10-8, Sun 2-5; Oct-Mar, Tue-Sat 10-1 & 2-5.
✲*Free except audio-visual theatre 80p (concessions 40p). Prices under review for 1995.*
P & *(Induction loop hearing system in auditorium) toilets for disabled shop*

Dundrennan Abbey
DUNDRENNAN
(6.5m SE of Kirkcudbright)
☎*0131-668 8800*
The ruined abbey was founded for the Cistercians. Mary Queen of Scots is thought to have spent her last night in Scotland here on 15 May 1568, before seeking shelter in England, where she was imprisoned and eventually executed.
Open all year, Apr-Sep, Mon-Sat 9.30-6.30, Sun 2-6.30.
£1.20 (concessions 75p).
P & *shop* ✲
(AM)

Glenluce Abbey
GLENLUCE
(2m N of village)
☎*0131-668 8800*
The abbey was founded for the Cistercians in 1192 by Roland, Earl of Galloway. The ruins include a vaulted chapter house, and stand in a beautiful setting.
Open all year, Apr-Sep, Mon-Sat 9.30-6.30, Sun 2-6.30; Oct-Mar, Sat 9.30-4.30, Sun 2-4.30. (Closed 25-26 Dec & 1-3 Jan).
£1.20 (concessions 75p).
P & *shop* ✲
(AM)

The Robert Burns' Centre in Dumfries is set in the 18th-century watermill, built when Burns was living in the lively town. The centre overlooks the River Nith.

Arbigland Gardens
Kirkbean, Dumfries and Galloway
Telephone: (0138788) 283

The gardens and dower house of this mansion have been evolving through three centuries. Paul Jones, the US Admiral worked here with his father who was the gardener in the 1740's. Woodland, water and formal gardens.

For opening times and admission charges see gazetteer entry.

MAXWELTON HOUSE
Moniaive, Thornhill, Dumfriesshire DG3 4DX

Previously Glencairn Castle but in 1611 Stephen Laurie bought and renamed it Maxwelton House. Extensive additions were made to this early Tower House where in 1682 his great granddaughter Anna, made famous by the well loved ballad, was born. The house remained in the Laurie possession until 1966. Now owned by Mr & Mrs Hugh Stenhouse who have restored the house, chapel, museum and garden. Light, freshly home made refreshments are available in the Tea Room. Craft Shop.

Open: Daily Easter to end of Sept. including Bank Holidays 10.30-5.30pm.

Arbigland Gardens
KIRKBEAN
(1m SE, adjacent to Paul Jones cottage).
☎(01387) 880283
Extensive woodland, formal and water gardens are set around a delightful sandy bay which is ideal for children. John Paul Jones, the US Admiral, worked in the gardens as a young boy (his father was the gardener here in the 1740s). His birthplace, which can be seen nearby, is now a museum.
Open Gardens May-Sep, Tue-Sun 2-6. House 20-29 May. Also open BH Mon. £2 (ch 50p, pen £1.50).
🅿 🍽 ♿ *toilets for disabled shop*

Broughton House & Garden
KIRKCUDBRIGHT
High St
☎(01557) 330437
An 18th-century house where Edward A Hornel, on of the 'Glasgow Boys' group of artists, lived and worked from 1901-1933. A collection of his work, extensive library of local history, and Japanese-style garden created by Hornel.
Open daily, Apr-22 Oct 1-5.30. £2 (concessions £1). Party.
P (on street) ⊗
(NTS)

MacLellan's Castle
KIRKCUDBRIGHT
☎0131-668 8800
This handsome structure has been a ruin since the mid-18th-century: it was once an imposing castellated mansion, elaborately planned with fine architectural detail. Something of its 16th-century grandeur still remains.
Open all year, Apr-Sep, Mon-Sat 9.30-6.30, Sun 2-6.30; Oct-Mar, Sat 9.30-4.30, Sun 2-4.30. (Closed 25-26 Dec & 1-3 Jan).
£1.20 (concessions 75p).
🅿 ♿ *shop* ⊗
(AM)

Stewartry Museum
KIRKCUDBRIGHT
Saint Mary St
☎(01557) 331643
A large and varied collection of archaeological, social history and natural history exhibits relating to the Stewartry district.
Open Mar-Oct, Mon-Sat 11-4 (5pm in May, Jun & Sep;6pm in Jul-Aug also Sun 2-5); Nov-Feb, Sat only 11-4.
❋*£1.50 (ch free with adult, concessions 75p).*
P (outside) ♿ *shop* ⊗

Craigcleuch Collection
LANGHOLM
(2m NW Langholm on B709)
☎(013873) 80137
Baronial stone mansion house with collection of ancient artefacts in wood, jade, ivory and coral, and hundreds of rare tribal sculptures and prehistoric stone pipes, carved as animals and birds. Also Oriental paintings and panoramic views overlooking the 'Gates of Eden' woodland walks.
Open Etr wknd, BH & May-15 Sep, Mon-Sat 10-5.30. Other times by appointment.
🅿 ♿ *shop*
Details not confirmed for 1995

Maxwelton House Trust
MONIAIVE
☎(018482) 385
The house dates from the 14th and 15th centuries and was originally the stronghold of the Earls of Glencairn and later, in 1682, the birthplace of Annie Laurie of the famous Scottish ballad. The house was completely restored by the late Hugh C Stenhouse in 1971 and today's attractions include a museum, chapel, gardens, gift shop and craft shop.
Open Etr-Sep daily 10.30-5.30. £3.50 (ch 16 £2 & pen £3)
🅿 🍽 ✕ ♿ *shop*

New Abbey Corn Mill
NEW ABBEY
(8m S of Dumfries on A710)
☎0131-668 8800
Built in the late 18th century, this water-driven corn mill is still in working order, and regular demonstrations are held.
Open all year, Apr-Sep, Mon-Sat 9.30-6.30, Sun 2-6.30; Oct-Mar, weekdays 9.30-4.30, Sun 2-4.30. (Closed Thu pm & Fri in winter; 25-26 Dec & 1-3 Jan).
£1.50 (ch 16 75p, pen £1).
🅿 *shop* ⊗
(AM)

Sweetheart Abbey
NEW ABBEY
☎0131-668 8800
Lady Devorgilla of Galloway founded Balliol College in Oxford in memory of her husband John Balliol; she also founded an abbey in his memory in 1273. When she died in 1289 she was buried in front of the high altar with the heart of her husband resting on her bosom; hence the name 'Sweetheart Abbey'. This monument, inspired by love and loyalty, now stands as one of Scotland's most beautiful ruins. It features an unusual precinct wall of enormous boulders.
Open all year, Apr-Sep Mon-Sat 9.30-6.30, Sun 2-6.30; Oct-Mar, wkdys 9.30-4.30, Sun 2-4.30. (Closed Thu pm & Fri in winter; 25-26 Dec & 1-3 Jan).
£1 (ch 16 & pen 50p)
🅿 ♿ *(with assistance) toilets for disabled shop* ⊗
(AM)

Orchardton Tower
PALNACKIE
(6m SE of Castle Douglas)
☎0131-668 8800
John Cairns built this rare example of a circular tower in the late 15th century.
Open all reasonable times, on application to key keeper. (Closed 25-26 Dec & 1-2 Jan).
Free.
🅿 ⊗
(AM)

Logan Botanic Garden
PORT LOGAN
☎Stranraer (01776) 860231
Located in the extreme south west of Scotland, virtually surrounded by sea, Logan is one of the most exotic gardens in Britain. Basking in a sub-tropical climate, created by the influence of the Gulf Stream, an array of southern hemisphere plants are grown out of doors. Established over 100 years ago as a kitchen garden, the traditional walled design remains, but today it contains tree ferns and cabbage palms which flourish alongside unusual flowering shrubs, climbers and herbaceous plants. The garden Open Day is on 28 May 1995.
Open 15 Mar-Oct, daily 10-6. £2 (ch 50p, concessions £1.50). Family ticket £4.50.

🅿 ✕ *licensed* ♿ *(wheelchairs available for loan) toilets for disabled shop garden centre* ⊗

Ruthwell Cross
RUTHWELL
(off B724)
☎0131-668 8800
Now in a specially built apse in the parish church, the carved cross dates from the 7th or 8th centuries. Two faces show scenes from the Life of Christ; the others show scroll work, and parts of an ancient poem in Runic characters. It was broken up in the 18th century, but pieced together by a 19th-century minister.
Open all reasonable times. Key from Key Keeper, Kirkyett Cottage, Ruthwell. Free.
🅿 ⊗
(AM)

Savings Banks Museum
RUTHWELL
(6m W of Annan)
☎Clarencefield (01387) 870640
Housed in the building where Savings Banks first began, the museum traces their growth and development from 1810 up to the present day. Exhibits include original letters, books and papers. The museum also traces the life of Dr Henry Duncan, father of savings banks, and restorer of the Ruthwell Cross.
Open all year, daily (ex Sun & Mon Oct-Mar), 10-1 & 2-5. Free.
🅿 ♿ *(touch facilities for blind, guide available) shop* ⊗

Sanquhar Tolbooth Museum
SANQUHAR
High St
☎(01659) 250186
This new museum focuses on the history of Upper Nithsdale and is housed in the town's fine 18th-century tolbooth. It tells the story of the mines and miners of the area, its earliest inhabitants, native and Roman, the history and customs of the Royal Burgh of Sanquhar and local traditions. There is an exhibition on the world famous craft of Sanquhar knitting and a life-like reconstruction of Sanquhar jail. An audio-visual show introduces the visitor to the history and natural beauty of the surrounding countryside.
Open Apr-Sep, Tue-Sat 10-1 & 2-5, Sun 2-5. Free.
🅿

Castle Kennedy Gardens
STRANRAER
Stair Estates (5m E on A75)
☎(01776) 702024
Situated on a peninsula between two lochs, the gardens around the Old Castle were first laid out in the early 18th century and, after years of neglect, were restored and developed in the 19th. They are noted for their rhododendrons and azaleas (at their best in May and early June) and walled kitchen garden with fine

➜

herbaceous borders (best in August and September). The gardens contain many avenues and walks amid some beautiful scenery.
Open Apr-Sep, daily 10-5.
✲£2 (ch 15 £1, pen £1.50). Party 20+.
🅿 ♨ ♿ toilets for disabled shop garden centre

Drumlanrig Castle
THORNHILL ▰▰▰▰▰
(4m NW off A76 on west bank of River Nith).
☎(01848) 331682 & 330248
This unusual, pink sandstone castle was built in the late 17th century in Renaissance style. Ringed by rugged hills, the castle was erected on the site of earlier Douglas strongholds. It contains a celebrated collection of paintings by Rembrandt, Da Vinci, Holbein, Murillo and many others. There is also French furniture, mainly Louis XIV, as well as silver and relics of Bonnie Prince Charlie. The old stable block has a craft centre with resident craft workers, a gift shop, tearoom and a visitor's centre. The grounds offer an extensive garden, a birds of prey centre, cycle hire, a cycle museum, an adventure woodland play area and woodland walks.
Open - Castle & Country Park, 29 Apr-30 Aug, daily 11-5; 29 Apr-16 Jun, reduced weekday opening; (Castle closed Thu). Last admission 4pm. Telephone to confirm times.
Admission fee payable.
🅿 ♨ ♿ (lift) toilets for disabled shop ⌦ (ex in park)

Tongland Tour
TONGLAND ▰▰▰▰▰
(on A762)
☎Kirkcudbright (01557) 330114
This tour of part of the ScottishPower Galloway hydro-electricity scheme includes a video presentation and a visit to the dam and the power station. There is a fish ladder at the dam which provides the chance to see salmon returning to their spawning grounds.

Open May-Sep, Mon-Sat.
Admission fee payable.
🅿

Museum of Lead Mining
WANLOCKHEAD ▰▰▰▰▰
(on B797 at N end of Mennock Pass).
☎Leadhills (01659) 74387
Wanlockhead, Scotland's highest village, set in the beautiful Lowther Hills, is the home of the Museum of Lead Mining. A guided tour takes the visitor into the underground world of Lochnell Lead Mine. The Visitor Centre houses a collection of rare minerals all found locally. There are 'hands-on' displays, mineral collecting areas and an open-air visitor trail. A one-and-a-half-mile walkway takes the visitor to an 18th-century lead mine, smelt mill and miners' cottages furnished in the styles of 1740 and 1890. An unusual feature is a Miners' Reading Society library, which was founded in 1756. Gold panning demonstrations are held monthly throughout the season. Special events planned for 1995 include Gold Panning Championships (28-29 May), craft fair and family fun (August 27), Scottish weekend (23-24 September). All dates are provisional.
Open Mar-Nov, daily 11-4.30 (last mine tour 4pm). Nov-Mar telephone for times & appointments.
✲£2.99 (ch £1.25, concessions £2.50). Family ticket £8.
🅿 ✗ licensed ♿ toilets for disabled shop ⌦

Whithorn-Cradle of Christianity
WHITHORN ▰▰▰▰▰
45-47 George St
☎(01988) 500508
The Whithorn Dig, in Galloway, is the site of the first Christian settlement in Scotland - the Candida Casa of St Ninian. Visitors can learn of the discoveries by way of an audio visual show, exhibitions, murals, models and displays of finds. Friendly guides explain the excavation. Archaeologists are seen at work during

the digging season. Museum of Early Christian stones. The Discovery Centre has a 3-D jigsaw to explain the archaeology. Craft and book shop.
Open Etr-Oct.
✲£2.70 (ch, pen & UB40's £1.50).. Family ticket £7.50. Season ticket. Party.
P (70 yds) ♿ toilets for disabled shop

Whithorn Priory
WHITHORN ▰▰▰▰▰
☎0131-668 8800
The first Christian church in Scotland was founded here by St Ninian in 397, but the present ruins date from the 12th century. The ruins are scanty but there is a notable Norman door, the Latinus stone of the 5th century and other early Christian monuments.
Open all year, Apr-Sep, Mon-Sat 9.30-6.30, Sun 2-6.30; Oct-Mar, Sat 9.30-4.30, Sun 2-4.30. (Closed Mon-Fri in winter, 25-26 Dec & 1-3 Jan).
£2.70 (ch 16 £1, pen £1.70).
🅿 ♿ shop ⌦
(AM)

FIFE

Aberdour Castle
ABERDOUR ▰▰▰▰▰
☎0131-668 8800
The earliest surviving part of the castle is the 14th-century keep. There are also later buildings, and the remains of a terraced garden, a bowling green and a fine 16th-century doocot (dovecote).
Open all year, Apr-Sep, Mon-Sat 9.30-6.30, Sun 2-6.30; Oct-Mar, Mon-Sat 9.30-4.30, Sun 2-4.30. (Closed Thu pm, Fri in winter, 25-26 Dec & 1-3 Jan).
£1.50 (ch 16 75p, pen £1).
🅿 ♿ shop
(AM)

Scottish Fisheries Museum
ANSTRUTHER ▰▰▰▰▰
St Ayles, Harbour Head
☎(01333) 310628
A cobbled courtyard at the harbour is the setting for the displays on Scotland's fishing history. Chief attractions are the boats (real and model), and the fisherman's cottage. The museum is housed in a range of 16th-to 19th-century buildings, and has recently extended into an old boatyard alongside.
Open all year, Apr-Oct, Mon-Sat 10-5.30, Sun 11-5; Nov-Mar, Mon-Sat 10-4.30, Sun 2-4.30. (Closed 25-26 Dec & 1-2 Jan).
✲£2.20 (concessions £1.20). Party 12+.
P (20 yds) ♨ ♿ toilets for disabled shop ⌦

Burntisland Edwardian Fair Museum
BURNTISLAND ▰▰▰▰▰
102 High St
☎Kirkcaldy (01592) 260732
All the fun of the fair at this Scottish Museum of the Year Award Winner.

Burntisland Museum has recreated a walk through the sights and sounds of the town's fair in 1910, based on a painting of the scene by local artist Andrew Young. See reconstructed rides, stalls and side shows of the time and view the local history gallery.
Open all year, Mon-Sat 10-1 & 2-5. (Closed Sun & BH Mon's).
Free.
🅿 ⌦

Fife Folk Museum
CERES ▰▰▰▰▰
The Weigh House, High St (on B939)
☎(01334) 828250 (messages only)
This comprehensive regional collection is displayed in a 17th-century Weigh House and other buildings. Local crafts, farming and trades are illustrated with tools and other items of a social and domestic nature in an attractive and informative way.
Open Etr, mid May-Oct, Sat-Thu 2-5.
✲£1.50 (ch 50p, pen £1.20). Party.
P (100yds) ♿ shop ⌦

Culross Abbey
CULROSS ▰▰▰▰▰
☎0131-244 3101
The Cistercian monastery was founded by Malcolm, Earl of Fife, in 1217. The choir is still used as the parish church, and parts of the old nave remain. The fine central tower still stands complete.
Open all year, Mon-Sat 9.30-7, Sun 2-7, Apr-Sep; Mon-Sat 9.30-4, Sun 2-4, Oct-Mar. (Closed 25-26 Dec & 1-2 Jan).
⌦
(AM)

Culross Palace
CULROSS ▰▰▰▰▰
(off A985, 3m W of Kincardine Bridge)
☎Newmills (01383) 880359
Culross Palace, built between 1597 and 1611, contains unique wall panelling and painted ceilings. The restoration programme is now complete and the Palace re-opened in 1994. Audio guides are available for visitors. A pleasant 17th-century garden has been recreated behind the Palace.
Open Good Fri-Sep, daily 11-5, also 1-22 Oct Sat &Sun only 11-5 (last admission 4).
✲£3.50 (concessions £1.80). Ticket includes visit to Town House & Study.
P shop ⌦
(NTS)

Town House & The Study
CULROSS ▰▰▰▰▰
(off A985, 3m E of Kincardine Bridge)
☎New Mills (01383) 880359
Culross is unique - a Royal Burgh that has remained virtually unchanged for 200 years. It dates mostly from the 16th and 17th centuries, when it prospered in the coal and salt trades developed by Sir George Bruce. When business declined in the 1700s, Culross stayed as it was, unable to afford improvements like wider streets. Its present appearance is due to the National Trust for Scotland, which

has been gradually restoring the burgh since the 1930s. The aim has been to provide modern living standards without destroying the burgh's character, and the small houses with their red-pantiled roofs are still lived in by local people.

The Trust has a visitor centre and exhibition in the Town House (1626). The house called The Study (1610) is also open for visitors to view the Norwegian painted ceiling in the drawing room. The first building bought by the Trust in Culross was The Palace, home of Sir George Bruce. It has terraced gardens and painted rooms. Many other buildings can be seen from the outside.

Open - Town House & Study; 14 Apr-Sep daily 11-5. 1-22 Oct Sat & Sun only 11-5. (last admission 4).
✤*£3.50 (concession £1.80). Ticket includes Palace.*
🅿 ⛟ ✽
(NTS)

Hill of Tarvit Mansionhouse & Garden
CUPAR

(2.5m S off A916)
☎ *(01334) 653127*
The present Mansionhouse was virtually rebuilt in 1906 by Sir Robert Lorimer for F B Sharp to provide a suitable setting for his notable collection which includes tapestries, paintings, furniture and Chinese porcelain. The restored Edwardian laundry is also open. There is a hilltop walk and also a short dog walk in the grounds. Concerts are held regularly throughout the year and there are monthly art exhibitions.
Open 14 Apr-22 Oct, daily 1.30-5.30 (Last admission 4.45pm). Garden & grounds all year, daily 9.30-sunset.
✤*House & Garden £3 (ch £1.50). Garden only, honesty box £1. Party.*
🅿 ⛟ ♿ *shop* ✽ *(ex in grounds)*
(NTS)

The Scottish Deer Centre
CUPAR

Bow-of-Fife (3m W on A91)
☎ *Letham (01337) 810391*
Guided tours take about 40 minutes and allow visitors to meet and stroke deer. Children can help with bottle-feeding young fawns, and facilities include farm, nature and heritage trails. A film presentation and exhibition are provided. Aerial walkways and observation platforms are a special feature, allowing

better views of several species of deer and the landscape. There is a large Adventureland and indoor playroom for children.
Open daily, Apr-Oct 10-5. Telephone for details of winter opening. (Closed Jan-Feb).
✤*£4 (ch £2, concessions £3). Family ticket £11. Party 20+.*
🅿 ✗ *licensed* ♿ *(special parking bay, loan of wheelchairs) toilets for disabled shop* ✽

Andrew Carnegie Birthplace Museum
DUNFERMLINE

Moodie St (400yds from Abbey)
☎ *(01383) 724302*
The museum tells the story of the humble handloom weaver's son who was born here in 1835, created the biggest steel works in the USA, and then became a philanthropist on a huge scale. The present-day work of the philanthropic Carnegie Trust is also explained. Weaving days will be held on the first Friday of every month (May-Oct); on these days, the restored Jacquard handloom will be worked by a member of the Angus Handloom Weavers.
Open all year, Apr-Oct, Mon-Sat 11-5, Sun 2-5; Nov-Mar 2-4.
£1.50 (ch 15 free, concessions 75p).
🅿 ⛟ ♿ *toilets for disabled shop* ✽

Dunfermline Abbey
DUNFERMLINE

Pittencrieff Park
☎ *0131-668 8800*
The monastery was a powerful Benedictine house, founded by Queen Margaret in the 11th century. The foundations of her church still lie beneath the nave of a later, more elaborate Norman nave. The site of the choir is occupied by a modern parish church, at the east end of which are the remains of the 13th-century St Margaret's shrine. The grave of King Robert the Bruce is marked by a modern brass in the choir. The monastery guest house became a royal palace, and was the birthplace of Charles I. The ruins of other monastic buildings can be seen.
Open all year, Apr-Sep, Mon-Sat 9.30-6.30, Sun 2-6.30: Oct-Mar, Mon-Sat 9.30-4.30, Sun 2-4.30. (Closed Thu pm & Fri in winter; 25-26 Dec & 1-3 Jan).
£1.50 (ch 16 75p, pen £1).
🅿 ♿ *shop* ✽
(AM)

Dunfermline District Museum
DUNFERMLINE

Viewfield Ter
☎ *(01383) 721814*
Interesting and varied displays on local history are shown, including domestic articles and damask linen - an important local product. The Small Gallery has changing art and craft exhibitions every month.
Open all year, Mon-Sat 11-5. (Closed Sun & PHs).
Free.
🅿 *(charged) shop* ✽

Pittencrieff House Museum
DUNFERMLINE

Pittencrieff Park
☎ *(01383) 722935 & 721814*
The fine 17th-century mansion house stands in a park with lawns, hothouses and gardens. In the house itself there are galleries with displays of costume, local, social and natural history. Temporary art exhibitions are shown in the top gallery. The house and park were given to the town by Andrew Carnegie.
Open May-Oct, Wed-Mon.
Free.
🅿 *(800yds)* ♿ *(ramp) shop* ✽

Falkland Palace & Garden
FALKLAND

(off A912)
☎ *(01337) 857397*
The hunting palace of the Stuart Kings and Queens, situated below the Lomond Hills. The French Renaissance style of the south range is admired as the best of its kind in Britain. The palace is also noted for the beautiful interiors of the Chapel Royal and the King's Bedchamber, and for the royal tennis court of 1539, the oldest in Britain. The garden has a spectacular delphinium border, and is heavily perfumed in summer. There is a gift shop, and in the Town Hall, an exhibition of the history of the palace and the royal burgh.
Open Apr-22 Oct, Mon-Sat 11-5.30, Sun 1.30-5.30. (Last admission 1hr before closing, garden 30 mins before closing). Town Hall Apr-22 Oct, daily 1-5.30, (last admission 5).
✤*Palace & Garden £4 (ch £2). Garden only £2 (ch £1). Party 20+*
🅿 *shop* ✽
(NTS)

Kellie Castle & Gardens
KELLIE CASTLE & GARDENS

(3m NW of Pittenweem on B9171)
☎ *Arncroach (01333) 720271*
The oldest part of this castle dates from about 1360, but it is as a fine example of 16th-and 17th-century domestic architecture that Kellie is renowned. Inside, the most notable features are the plasterwork and the panelling, which is painted with romantic landscapes, and furniture designed by Sir Robert Lorimer. The castle has a Victorian nursery, an old kitchen, and a Victorian walled garden. There are also audio-visual shows. Special events planned for 1995 include concerts, garden events and a children's day.
Open - Castle Good Fri-22 Oct, daily 1.30-5.30 (last admission 4.45). Gardens & grounds open all year 9.30-sunset.
✤*Castle & gardens £3 (ch £1.50); Gardens only £1 (ch 50p). Party 20+ .*
🅿 ⛟ ♿ *(Induction loop for the hard of hearing) shop* ✽
(NTS)

Museum & Art Gallery
KIRKCALDY

War Memorial Gardens (next to Station)
☎ *(01592) 260732*
A unique collection of Scottish paintings, arts, crafts and historical displays with unusual 'please touch' sections, make a visit to this inspiring museum well worthwhile. The Gallery runs a lively programme of temporary exhibitions.
Open all year, Mon-Sat 10.30-5, Sun 2-5. (Closed Local Hols).
Free.
🅿 ⛟ ♿ *toilets for disabled shop* ✽

Deep-Sea World
NORTH QUEENSFERRY

☎ *Dunfermline (01383) 411411*
Here visitors have the opportunity to get a diver's eye view of a spectacular underwater universe. A moving walkway travels along the largest underwater transparent viewing tunnel and enables visitors to walk along the sea bed without getting their feet wet. On this marine safari through crystal-clear sea water you can come face-to-face with large sharks, giant rays, crabs and lobsters, and conger eels. Other fascinating exhibits include a 'touch pool' and coral reef display. There are children's talks and family lectures throughout the day.
Open all year, daily, Apr-Jun 9.30-6; Jul & Aug 9.30-7pm; Sep-Oct 9.30-6. Closed 25 Dec.
£4.50 (ch, pen, students & UB40 £3.50) Family ticket £13.50. Party.
🅿 ⛟ ✗ *licensed* ♿ *(ramps) toilets for disabled shop* ✽

British Golf Museum
ST ANDREWS

Bruce Embankment
☎ *(01334) 478880*
The museum tells the history of golf with highly visual displays, complemented by the use of visitor-activated touch screens throughout the galleries. Exhibits take the visitor from the misty origins of the game, through to the present day. You'll see amazing images, fascinating collections of clubs, balls, fashion and memorabilia, two period workshops and historic documents. An audio-visual theatre shows historic golfing moments.
Open all year, May-Oct daily 10-5.30; Nov-Apr Thu-Mon 11-3.
✤*£3.50 (ch 15 £1.50, pen & students £2.50). Family ticket £9.*
🅿 *(charged)* ♿ *toilets for disabled shop* ✽

Castle & Visitor Centre
ST ANDREWS

☎ *0131-668 8800*
This 13th-century stronghold castle was the setting for the murder of Cardinal Beaton in 1546. The new visitor centre incorporates an exciting multi-media exhibition describing the history of the castle and nearby cathedral.
Open all year, Apr-Sep, Mon-Sat 9.30-6.30, Sun 2-6.30; Oct-Mar, Mon-Sat 9.30-4.30, Sun 2-4.30. (Closed 25-26 Dec & 1-3 Jan).
£2 (ch 16 75p, pen £1.25) Family ticket £5. Joint ticket with St Andrews Cathedral available.
🅿 ♿ *toilets for disabled shop* ✽
(AM)

Cathedral (& Museum)
ST ANDREWS

☎ *0131-668 8800*
The cathedral was the largest in Scotland, and is now an extensive ruin. The remains date mainly from the 12th and 13th centuries, and large parts of the precinct walls have survived intact. Close by is St Rule's church, which the cathedral was built to replace. St Rule's probably dates from before the Norman Conquest, and is considered the most interesting Romanesque church in Scotland.
The museum is housed in a 14th-century building and contains an important collection of Celtic and medieval sculpture and artefacts. There is also a fascinating array of later gravestones on display.
Open all year, Apr-Sep, Mon-Sat 9.30-6.30, Sun 2-6.30; Oct-Mar, Mon-Sat 9.30-4.30, Sun 2-4.30. (Closed 25-26 Dec & 1-3 Jan).
£1.50 (ch 16 75p, pen £1) Family ticket £4. Joint ticket for St Andrews Castle available.
🅿 ♿ *shop* ✽
(AM)

Culross is the most complete example of a Scottish burgh. Culross Palace has been virtually unaltered since its completion in 1611 – an outstanding example of a rich merchant's home.

GRAMPIAN

ABERDEEN

Proudly known as the 'Granite City', Aberdeen gets its nickname from its handsome grey granite buildings - many of them speckled with mica which shines like silver in the sunlight. Here, old and new live comfortably together with some steets and houses dating from the 16th century and still more from the 19th when fishing was the city's principal industry. The port has flourished since the end of the 13th century and the city boasts two imposing cathedrals - those of St Andrew and St Machar - as well as an ancient university founded by James IV of Scotland in 1505. The North Sea oil boom of the 1970s and 1980s created new prosperity in the city which became a boom town.

Aberdeen Art Gallery
ABERDEEN
Schoolhill
☎(01224) 646333
The gallery's 16th to 20th-century Scottish art includes an outstanding collection of modern paintings. Also here are watercolours, sculpture and decorative arts, and a print room and art library. Special exhibitions and events all year.
Open all year, Mon-Sat 10-5 (8pm Thu) Sun 2-5. (Closed 25 & 26 Dec, 1 & 2 Jan).
P (500 yds) 🍴 & toilets for disabled shop ⦸
Details not confirmed for 1995

Aberdeen Maritime Museum
ABERDEEN
Provost Ross's House, Shiprow
☎(01224) 585788
The museum is in Provost Ross's House, Aberdeen's third oldest building (1593). It highlights the city's maritime history, and its oil industry, in dramatic fashion. A National Trust for Scotland visitor centre and shop is open part of the year; at other times the area is used for special maritime exhibitions.
Open all year, Mon-Sat 10-5 (Closed 25-26 Dec & 1,2 Jan).
& toilets for disabled shop ⦸
Details not confirmed for 1995

Cruickshank Botanic Garden
ABERDEEN
University of Aberdeen, St Machar Drive, (enter by gate in Chanonry, in Old Aberdeen)
☎(01224) 272704
Developed at the end of the 19th century, the 11 acres include rock and water gardens, a rose garden, a fine herbaceous border, an arboretum and a patio garden. There are collections of spring bulbs, gentians and alpine plants, and a fine array of trees and shrubs.

A Scottish baronial-style castle set amid wooded hills by the River Dee, Balmoral Castle was much loved by Queen Victoria and is still the Royal family's holiday home.

Open all year, Mon-Fri 9-4.30; also Sat & Sun, May-Sep 2-5.
Free.
P (200yds) & ⦸ 🏫

James Dun's House
ABERDEEN
61 Schoolhill
☎(01224) 646333
This 18th-century house is used as a museum and puts on temporary exhibitions with special appeal for families.
Open all year, Mon-Sat, 10-5. (Closed 25-26 Dec,1 & 2 Jan)
⦸
Details not confirmed for 1995

Provost Skene's House
ABERDEEN
Guestrow, (off Broad St)
☎(01224) 641086
The handsome old town mansion has notable decorated ceilings and panelling, and is now a museum of local history and social life, with rooms furnished in period style. There is also an audio-visual display on the history of the house.
Open all year, Mon-Sat 10-5. (Closed 25 & 26 Dec, 1 & 2 Jan)
🍴 & ⦸
Details not confirmed for 1995

Satrosphere ("Hands-On" Science & Technology) Centre
ABERDEEN
19 Justice Mill Ln
☎(01224) 213232
Satrosphere, the Discovery Place, is different from many museums or

exhibition centres. It is an Interactive Centre where everything is 'hands-on'. Displays aren't locked in glass cases and there are certainly no Do Not Touch signs. The emphasis is on doing and finding out, not just looking and standing back. There is a shop with exciting and unusual gifts. Special events for 1995 include: children's science workshops during the Easter and summer school holidays, and a special theme - Processes of Life in May and June.
Open all year, Mon & Wed-Fri 10-4, Sat 10-5, Sun 1.30-5. School holidays Mon-Sat 10-5, Sun 1.30-5. (Closed 25-26 Dec & 1-2 Jan).
£3 (ch £1.50, students, UB40's & pen £1.50).
P (charged) 🍴 & toilets for disabled shop ⦸

Alford Valley Railway
ALFORD
☎(019755) 62326
Narrow-gauge passenger railway in two sections: Alford-Haughton Park and Haughton Park-Murray Park approx one mile each. Steam on peak weekends. Diesel traction. Exhibitions. Special events include: Railway Fayre (16 April), Alford Cavalcade Vintage Steam and Car Event (19 July).
Open Apr, May & Sep wknds from 1-5, Jun-Aug daily from 11 (30 min service). Party bookings also available at other times.
£1.50 (ch 80p) return fare.
P & toilets for disabled

Grampian Transport Museum
ALFORD
☎(019755) 62292
There is a strong local theme to this road and rail museum. Its large collection of vintage vehicles includes cycles and motorcycles, horse-drawn and steam vehicles, cars and lorries. 1995 events include Historic Commercial Vehicle Show (28 May), Grampian Classic Sprint (2 July), Alford Cavalcade (23 July), Grampian Motorcycle Convention (10 September).
Open Apr-Oct,10-5.
£2.50 (ch 80p & pen £1.80).
P & toilets for disabled shop

The Glenlivet Distillery
BALLINDALLOCH
(Off B9008 10m N of Tomintoul)
☎Glenlivet (01807) 590427 & (01542) 887471-winter
The first licensed distillery in the Highlands. Produces the famous The Glenlivet a 12-year-old single malt whisky. Visitors are shown round in

parties of not more than ten, and are offered a free sample. Exhibition area, audio-visual display, coffee shop and whisky shop which also sells related souvenirs.
Open Etr-Oct, Mon-Sat 10-4. (Jul-Aug 10-7).
P 🍴 & toilets for disabled shop ⦸
Details not confirmed for 1995

Balmoral Castle Grounds & Exhibition
BALMORAL
(on A93 between Ballater & Braemar)
☎Crathie (013397) 42334 & 42335
Balmoral is the focal point of what is now known as Royal Deeside, a landscape of woodlands and plantations sweeping up to grouse moors and distant mountains. Queen Victoria and Prince Albert first rented Balmoral Castle in 1848, and Prince Albert bought the property four years later. He commissioned William Smith to build a new castle, which was completed by 1855 and is still the Royal Family's Highland residence. The wooded grounds and gardens can be visited from May to July. Country walks and pony trekking can be enjoyed, and an exhibition of paintings and other works of art can be seen in the castle ballroom, together with a Travel and Carriage exhibition and a wildlife exhibition in the Carriage Room.
Open May-Jul, Mon-Sat 10-5.
£2.50 (ch free, pen £2).
P (150 yds) 🍴 & (wheelchairs available) toilets for disabled shop ⦸ (ex in grounds)

BANCHORY
See Crathes

Banchory Museum
BANCHORY
Bridge St
☎(01779) 477778
Newly housed in purpose-built premises, Banchory Museum has displays of Scott Skinner (The 'Strathspey King'), natural history including two stags fighting, royal commemorative china, local silver and local militia artefacts among many other exhibits.
Open Etr-May & Oct, wknds & public holidays 11-1, 2-5; Jun-Sep, daily 10-1, 2-5.30.
Free.
P (100yds) (limited) & (toilet in staff area, ask attendant) toilets for disabled shop ⦸

Banff Museum
BANFF
High St
☎ *Peterhead (01779) 477778*
The museum has an exhibition of British birds, set out as an aviary. The bird display won the Glenfiddich Living Scotland Award in 1989. Armour and items of local history are also on display.
Open Jun-Sep, Fri-Wed 2-5.20.
Free.
P *(200yds)* & shop ✿

Duff House
BANFF
(0.5m S, access south of town).
☎ *(01261) 22872*
The house was designed by William Adam for William Duff, later Earl of Fife. The main block was roofed in 1739, but the planned wings were never built. Although it is incomplete, the house is still considered one of Britain's finest Georgian baroque buildings. There is an exhibition on its history.
Under repair, interior not accessible, can be viewed from outside.
P ✿
(AM)
Details not confirmed for 1995

Braemar Castle
BRAEMAR
(0.5m N on A93)
☎ *(013397) 41219 & 41224 (out of season)*
A picturesque castle beside the River Dee, Braemar was built in 1628 by the Earl of Mar, but burned in 1689 by The Black Colonel, and was largely rebuilt as a garrison post after the 1745 rising. It is now a fully furnished residence of great charm, with many items of historic interest to be seen along with barrel-vaulted ceilings, Laird's pit, iron yett and defensive curtain wall.
Open Good Fri-Oct, Sat-Thu 10-6.
£1.90 (ch 90p, pen £1.50).
P & shop ✿ *(ex on lead in grounds)*

Brodie Castle
BRODIE CASTLE
(4.5m W of Forres, off A96)
☎ *Brodie (01309) 641371*
The Brodie family were granted land in this area in 1160, and lived in the castle for hundreds of years. It was passed to the National Trust for Scotland by the 25th Chief of the family in 1980. It is a handsome, gabled Scottish castle, and contains numerous treasures acquired over the centuries: fine furniture, porcelain, and an impressive collection of paintings including 17th-century Dutch works, 19th-century English watercolours and French Impressionists. The extensive grounds have a woodland walk, daffodils and a wildlife hide. There is also an adventure playground. Facilities for the disabled include wheelchair loan, a wheelchair carrier giving access to all public rooms on the first floor, purpose-built toilets for wheelchair users, audio tape and information in braille. Special events will be held in the Drawing Room and in the Castle grounds.
Open Apr-25 Sep, Mon-Sat 11-5.30, Sun 1.30-5.30; 1-22 Oct, Sat 11-5.30, Sun 1.30-5.30. (last admission 4.30). Grounds open all year, 9.30-sunset.
✱*£3.50 (concessions £1.80). Grounds £1.*
Party.
P ♨ & *(audio tape & information sheet in Braille) toilets for disabled shop* ✿
(NTS)

Buckie Drifter
BUCKIE
Freuchny Rd
☎ *(01542) 834646*
The Buckie Drifter is an exciting new maritime heritage centre. Here you can discover what life was like in the fishing communities of Moray District during the herring boom years of the 1890s and 1930s. Sign on as a crew member of a steam drifter and find out how to catch herring. Try your hand at packing fish in a barrel. Discover the undersea life of the herring through 'hands-on' displays and

find out why conservation is a feature of the fishing industry today. A series of changing displays will be a feature of the museum. Conducted harbour tours, from June to September, will start and end at the museum visting the Buckie Lifeboat, Jones of Buckie Shipyard, the fishmarket and Sinclair net factory. A series of temporary exhibitions will be produced, these include a display on the Moray Firth dolphins, beach donkeys, and the Drifters at War.
Open Apr-29 Oct, Mon-Sat 10-6, Sun 11-5.
£2.50 (ch & pen £1.60). Family ticket £7.
Party.
P ✗ & *(car parking, touch display on upper floor & braille guide) toilets for disabled shop* ✿

Corgarff Castle
CORGARFF
(8m W of Strathdon village)
☎ *0131-668 8800*
The 16th-century tower was beseiged in 1571 and is associated with the Jacobite risings of 1715 and 1745. It later became a military barracks.
Open Apr-Sep, Mon-Sat 9.30-6.30, Sun 2-6.30.
✱*£2 (ch 75p, pen £1.25). Family ticket £4.50.*
P *shop*
(AM)

Speyside Cooperage Visitor Centre
CRAIGELLACHIE
Dufftown Rd (1m S, on A941)
☎ *(01340) 871108*
The only working cooperage in Britain where skilled coopers and their apprentices practise their ancient craft of barrelmaking. Each year they repair around 100,000 oak casks which will be used to mature many different whiskies. The 'Acorn to Cask' exhibition traces the history and development of the coopering industry and includes a Victorian cooperage with life-size models that speak in the local dialect. There is a viewing gallery over the bustling workshop and guided tours.
Open all year, Etr-Sep Mon-Sat 9.30-4.30; Oct-Mar Mon-Fri 9.30-4.30. (Closed Xmas/New Year).
£1.70 (ch & pen £1.20). Family ticket £4.90. Party.
P & *toilets for disabled shop* ✿

Crathes Castle & Gardens
CRATHES
(3m E of Banchory on A93)
☎ *(01330) 844525*
This impressive 16th-century castle with magnificent interiors and painted ceilings has royal associations dating from 1323. There is a walled garden of over three acres and a notable collection of unusual plants. Yew hedges date from 1702, and seasonal herbaceous borders are a special feature. Wild gardens, extensive grounds and six nature trails, including one for the disabled, are among the attractions, plus a wayfaring course and children's adventure playground. There is entertainment within the grounds on most Sundays.
Open: Castle & Visitor Centre Apr-22 Oct, daily 11-5.30. Last admission 4.45). Garden & grounds open all year, daily 9.30-sunset.
✱*Castle, Garden & Grounds £4 (ch & pen £2). Grounds £1.50 (ch 80p).*
P ✗ *licensed* & *toilets for disabled shop* ✿ *(ex in grounds)*
(NTS)

Balvenie Castle
DUFFTOWN
☎ *0131-668 8800*
The ruined castle was the ancient stronghold of the Comyns, and became a stylish house in the 16th century.
Open Apr-Sep, Mon-Sat 9.30-6.30, Sun 2-6.30.
£1.20 (ch & pen 75p).
P & *shop*
(AM)

Crathes Castle is crowned by the square turrets and conical pepper-pot towers typical of a 16th-century Scottish castle.

Dufftown Museum
DUFFTOWN
The Tower, The Square
☎ *Forres (01309) 673701*
This small museum has displays on the local area, including the ancient religious site of Mortlach with a history from the 6th century to the present day. Other displays show aspects of social history and Dufftown's most famous product - malt whisky.
Open from 3 Apr, Mon-Sat 10-5.30; 8-31 May & 1-14 Oct, Mon-Sat 10-5.30; Jun & Sep, Mon-Sat 10-6, Sun 2-5.30; Jul-Aug, Mon-Sat 9.30-6.30, Sun 2-6. Times are provisional for 1995.
Free.
P *(adjacent)* & *shop* ✿

Glenfiddich Distillery
DUFFTOWN
(N of town, off A941)
☎ *(01340) 20373*
Set close to Balvenie Castle, the distillery was founded in 1887 by William Grant and has stayed in the hands of the family ever since. Visitors can see the whisky-making process in its various stages, and then sample the finished product. A theatre provides an audio-visual show (in six languages) on the history and manufacture of whisky, and there is a Scotch whisky museum.
Open all year Mon-Fri 9.30-4.30, also Etr-mid Oct Sat 9.30-4.30,Sun 12-4.30. (Closed Xmas & New Year).
P & *toilets for disabled shop* ✿
Details not confirmed for 1995

Duffus Castle
DUFFUS
(off B9012)
☎ *0131-668 8800*
The remains of the mighty motte-and-bailey castle are surrounded by a moat. Within the eight-acre bailey is a 15th-century hall, and the motte is crowned by a 14th-century tower.
Open at all reasonable times.
Free.
P ✿
(AM)

Elgin Cathedral
ELGIN
North College St
☎ *0131-668 8800*
Founded in 1224, the cathedral was known as the Lantern of the North and the Glory of the Kingdom because of its beauty. In 1390 it was burnt, with most of the town, by the Wolf of Badenoch - Alexander Stewart, Earl of Buchan - who had been excommunicated by the bishop. Although it was rebuilt, it fell into ruin after the Reformation. The ruins are quite substantial, however, and there is still a good deal to admire, including the fine west towers and the octagonal chapter house.
Open all year, Apr-Sep, Mon-Sat 9.30-6.30, Sun 2-6.30; Oct-Mar, Mon-Sat 9.30-4.30, Sun 2-4.30. (Closed Thu pm & Fri in winter; 25-26 Dec & 1-3 Jan).
✱*£1.20 (ch & pen 75p).*
P *shop*
(AM)

Elgin Museum
ELGIN
1 High St (opp 'Safeway'. Follow signs for Cathedral)
☎ *(01343) 543675*
The most notable feature of the museum is its world-famous fossil collection, including fossil fish and reptiles. Other items relating to the history and natural history of Elgin and Moray from prehistoric to modern times are also shown. There is a continuous programme of temporary exhibitions and educational 'workshops' for parties. Themes range from a look at the Wolf of Badenoch (he burnt Elgin to the ground in 1390) to Dinosaur Picnics, Dr Who and football.
Open Apr-Oct, Mon-Fri 10-5, Sat 11-4, Sun 2-5. (Closed Wed).
£1 (ch, pen, students & UB40 50p). Family ticket £2.50.
P *(50 yds)* & *(handrails inside & out. All case displays at sitting level) toilets for disabled shop* ✿

Pluscarden Abbey
ELGIN
(6m SW on unclass road)
☎ *Dallas (01343) 890257*

The original monastery was founded by Alexander II in 1230 and then burnt, probably by the Wolf of Badenoch who also destroyed Elgin Cathedral. It was restored in the 14th and 19th centuries, and then reoccupied in 1948 by Benedictines from Prinknash. It is now once more a religious community. Retreat facilities are available for men and women. Guides on duty at weekends and busy periods. Natural beeswax polish and natural apiary remedies now available.
Open all year, daily 4.45am-8.30pm.
Free.
P & *(induction loop, ramps to shop, toilets planned for '95) shop*

Fasque
FETTERCAIRN
(0.5m N on B974)
☎(01561) 340569 & 340202
Fasque has been the home of the Gladstone family since 1829, and W E Gladstone, four times Prime Minister, lived here from 1830 to 1851. There are impressive state rooms and a handsome, sweeping staircase, but more interesting in many ways are the extensive servants' quarters. The life and work of the large household staff is illustrated, and there are also collections of farming machinery and other local items. The spacious park has red deer and Soay sheep.
Open May-Sep, daily 11-5.30. (Last admission 5pm).
£3 (ch £1.50, pen £2). Party.
P & *(wheelchairs available) shop* ☜

Baxters Visitor Centre
FOCHABERS
(on A96)
☎(01343) 820393
The Baxters food firm started here over 125 years ago and now sells its products in over 60 countries. Visitors can see the shop where the story began, take a guided tour of the factory, watch an audio-visual display, and visit three shops.

Open all year, Mon-Fri 9.30-5, Sat & Sun 10-5.
Free.
P ✕ *licensed* & *(parking facilities) toilets for disabled shop* ☜

Fochabers Folk Museum
FOCHABERS
High St
☎(01343) 820362
This converted church exhibits the largest collection of horse-drawn vehicles in the North of Scotland. There are also displays of the many aspects of village life through the ages, including model engines, clocks, costumes, a village shop and Victorian parlour.
Open all year, daily 9.30-1 & 2-6. Winter closing 5pm.
✱*60p (ch & pen 40p). Family ticket £1.50.*
P & *shop* ☜

Dallas Dhu Distillery
FORRES
(1m S of Forres)
☎0131-668 8800
A perfectly preserved time capsule of the distiller's art. It was built in 1898 to supply malt whisky for Wright and Greig's 'Roderick Dhu' blend. Visitors are welcome to wander at will through this fine old Victorian distillery, or to take a guided tour, dram included.
Open all year, Apr-Sep, Mon-Sat 9.30-6.30, Sun 2-6.30. Oct-Mar, Mon-Sat 9.30-4.30, Sun 2-4.30. (Closed Thu pm & Fri in winter, 25 & 26 Dec, 1 & 3 Jan).
£2 (ch 16 75p, pen £1.25).
P & *toilets for disabled shop* ☜
(AM)

Falconer Museum
FORRES
Tolbooth St
☎(01309) 673701
This museum was founded by bequests made by two brothers, Alexander and Hugh Falconer. Hugh was a distinguished scientist, a friend of Darwin, recipient of many honours and

Vice-President of the Royal Society. On display are fossil mammals collected by him, and items relating to his involvement in the antiquity of mankind. Other displays are on local wildlife, geology, archaeology and history. Regular temporary exhibitions are held throughout the year.
Open all year. May, Jun, Sep & Oct, Mon-Sat 10-12.30 & 1.30-5.30; Jul & Aug, Mon-Sat, 9.30-12.30 & 1.30-6.30, Sun 2-5; Nov-Apr, Mon-Fri 10-12.30 & 1.30-4.30. Times are provisional.
Free.
P *(100yds)* & *shop* ☜

Suenos' Stone
FORRES
☎0131-668 8800
The 20ft-high stone was elaborately carved in the 9th or 10th century, with a sculptured cross on one side and groups of warriors on the other. Why it stands here no one knows, but it may commemorate a victory in battle.
Open & accessible at all times.
Free.
P ☜
(AM)

Huntly Castle
HUNTLY
☎0131-668 8800
The original medieval castle was rebuilt a number of times and destroyed, once by Mary, Queen of Scots. It was rebuilt for the last time in 1602, in palatial style, and is now an impressive ruin, noted for its ornate heraldic decorations. It stands in wooded parkland.
Open all year, Apr-Sep, Mon-Sat 9.30-6.30, Sun 2-6.30; Oct-Mar, Mon-Sat 9.30-4.30, Sun 2-4.30. (Closed Thu pm & Fri in winter; 25-26 Dec & 1-3 Jan).
£2 (ch 75p, pen £1.25). Family ticket £4.50.
P *shop*
(AM)

Huntly Museum
HUNTLY
The Square
☎Peterhead (01779) 477778
The museum has local history displays, and also holds changing special exhibitions every year.
Open all year, Tue-Sat 10-noon & 2-4.
Free.
P *(200yds) shop* ☜

Inverurie Museum
INVERURIE
Town House, The Square
☎Peterhead (01779) 477778
This busy shopping and business centre is ringed by many prehistoric sites; and in more recent times the canal to Aberdeen was started from one of its suburbs. Together with enterprising thematic exhibitions (changed about three times a year), Inverurie's fine museum displays canal relics and items on local history and archaeology.
Open all year, Mon-Tue & Thu-Fri 2-5, Sat 10-1 & 2-5.
Free.
P *(50 yds) shop* ☜

Castle Fraser
KEMNAY
(3m S, off B993)
☎Sauchen (01330) 833463
The massive Z-plan castle was begun about 1575 and completed in 1636. Its architectural embellishments were mainly carried out by two notable families of master masons, Bell and Leiper, and their work helped to make it one of the grandest of the Castles of Mar. An earlier fortified tower house is incorporated in the design.
Open - Castle 14 Apr-Jun & Sep, daily 1.30-5.30; Jul-Aug, daily 11-5.30; 1-22 Oct, Sat & Sun 1.30-5.30 (last admission 4.45). Garden all year, daily 9.30-6; Grounds all year daily 9.30-sunset.
✱*Castle £3.50 (ch £1.80). Garden & grounds £1. Party.*

🅿 ♨ ♿ *garden centre* ✕ *(ex restricted areas/grounds)*
(NTS)

Kildrummy Castle
KILDRUMMY
(10m W of Alford)
☎ *0131-668 8800*
An important part of Scottish history, at least until it was dismantled in 1717, this fortress was the seat of the Earls of Mar. Now it is a ruined, but splendid, example of a 13th-century castle, with four round towers, hall and chapel all discernible. Some parts of the building, including the Great Gatehouse, are from the 15th and 16th centuries.
Open all year, Apr-Sep, Mon-Sat 9.30-6.30, Sun 2-6.30; Oct-Mar, Sat 9.30-4.30, Sun 2-4.30. (Closed 25-26 Dec & 1-3 Jan).
£1.50 (ch 16 75p, pen £1).
🅿 ♿ *toilets for disabled shop*
(AM)

Kildrummy Castle Gardens
KILDRUMMY
(on A97)
☎ *(019755) 71277 & 71203*
With the picturesque ruin as a backdrop, these gardens are not only beautiful but also noted for their botanic interest. An alpine garden in an ancient quarry and a water garden are just two of its features, while the surrounding woods give interesting short walks. There is also a small museum, a video room showing a 15-minute film of the changes in the garden through the seasons, a children's play area and a sales area selling unusual plants.
Open Apr-Oct, daily 10-5.
£1.70 (ch 6-16 50p, under 5 free).
🅿 ♨ ♿ *toilets for disabled shop*

Tamdhu Distillery
KNOCKANDO
☎ *Carron (01340) 810221 & 810486*
A guided tour of the distillery offers visitors the chance to see the process of making malt whisky - from barley through to whisky.
Open Jun-Sep, Mon-Sat 10-4; Apr-May & Oct Mon-Fri 10-4.
✲ *£2*
🅿 ♿ *shop* ✕

Storybook Glen
MARYCULTER
(5m W of Aberdeen on B9077)
☎ *Aberdeen (01224) 732941*
This is a children's fantasy land, where favourite nursery rhyme and fairytale characters are brought to life. Grown-ups can enjoy the nostalgia and also the 20 acres of Deeside country, full of flowers, plants, trees and waterfalls.
Open Mar-Oct, daily 10-6; Nov-Feb, Sat & Sun only 11-4.
✲ *£3 (ch £1.50).*
🅿 ♨ ✕ *licensed* ♿ *toilets for disabled shop* ✕

Glenfarclas Distillery
MARYPARK
(On A95 between Grantown-on-Spey & Aberlour)
☎ *Ballindalloch (01807) 500245 & 500257*
Home of one of the finest Highland malt whiskies, this distillery provides an interesting exhibition illustrating the whisky's history and production. There is also a craft shop and visitor centre. A recent addition is a cask-filling store where visitors may watch new whisky being poured into oak casks.
Open all year, Mar-Oct, Mon-Fri 9-4.30 (Jun-Sep also Sat 10-4); Nov-Feb, Mon-Fri 10-4. (Closed Xmas & New Year). Other times by appointment.
✲ *£2.50 per adult.*
🅿 ♿ *toilets for disabled shop* ✕

Haddo House
METHLICK
(4m N of Pitmedden off B999)
☎ *Tarves (01651) 851440*
Haddo House is renowned for its association with the Haddo Choral Society and is the venue for international concerts which attract top performers

The Great Hall of Castle Fraser is on the first floor and reached by a winding staircase. From the round tower there are views over the castle's wooded parkland.

from around the world. It is a splendid Palladian-style mansion built in the 1730s to designs by William Adam. Home to the Earls of Aberdeen, the house was refurbished in the 1880s in the 'Adam Revival' style and still retains much of its original flavour. The adjoining country park, run by Grampian Regional Council, offers a network of enchanting woodland paths and attracts all kinds of wildlife. Hundreds of birds can be seen on the loch and there is an observation hide for visitors. James Giles painting exhibition. The Haddo House Arts Trust runs a charming small theatre in the grounds.
Open - House Good Fri-Jun & Sep, daily 1.30-5.30; Jul-Aug, daily 11-5.30; 1-22 Oct Sat & Sun 1.30-5.30 (last admission 45 mins before closing). Garden & country park open all year, daily 9.30-sunset.
🅿 ✕ ♿ *(lift to first floor of house & wheelchair) toilets for disabled shop* ✕ *(ex in grounds)*
(NTS)

Aden Country Park
MINTLAW
(1m W Mintlaw off A950)
☎ *(01771) 622857*
The grounds of a former estate provide over 200 acres of beautiful woodland and open farmland for the visitor to explore. A network of footpaths winds through a specially developed nature trail, and gives a chance of seeing many varieties of plants and animals. A countryside ranger service is available by appointment. The wildlife centre is open weekends only, May to September 2-5pm.
Open all year. Farm Heritage centre May-Sep, daily 11-5; Apr & Oct wknds only 12-5. Last admission 30 mins before closing. Park free. Farm Heritage Centre £1 (ch free).
🅿 ♨ ♿ *(garden for blind, reserved parking) toilets for disabled shop* ✕ *(ex in park)*

NE Scotland Agricultural Heritage Centre
MINTLAW
Aden Country Park (1m W on A950)
☎ *(01771) 622857 & Banff (01261) 813390*

The award-winning heritage centre is housed in 19th-century farm buildings, once part of the estate which now makes up the Aden Country Park (above). Two centuries of farming history and innovation are illustrated in an exciting exhibition, a pleasant way to take a break from enjoying the surrounding countryside. The story of the Aden estate is also interestingly illustrated. The newly reconstructed farm of Hareshowe shows how a family in the north-east farmed during the 1950s - access by guided tour only. Winner of a BTA Come to Britain award 1992 and Best Scottish Museum Audio-Visual Presentation 1992.
Open May-Sep, daily 11-5; Apr & Oct, wknds only noon-5. Park open all year, daily 7-10. Last admission 30 mins before closing.
£1 (ch 16 free).
🅿 ♨ ♿ *(garden for blind) toilets for disabled shop* ✕

Deer Abbey
OLD DEER
(10m W of Peterhead)
☎ *0131-668 8800*
The remains of the Cistercian Abbey, founded in 1218, include the infirmary, Abbot's House and the southern claustral range. The University Library at Cambridge now houses the famous Book of Deer.
Open at all reasonable times.
Free.
🅿 ✕
(AM)

Drum Castle
PETERCULTER
(3m W of Peterculter off A93)
☎ *Drumoak (01330) 811204*
The great Square Tower was built in the late 13th century and is one of the three oldest tower houses in Scotland. It has associations with King Robert the Bruce. The handsome mansion was added in 1619. There is a collection of family memorabilia in the Irvine Room. The grounds contain the 100-acre Old Wood of Drum and a walled garden with a collection of historic roses spanning four

centuries. Special events are planned for 1995.
Open Good Fri-Jun & Sep, daily 1.30-5.30; Jul-Aug, daily 11-5.30; 1-22 Oct Sat & Sun 1.30-5.30. Last admission 4.45. Grounds open all year 9.30-sunset.
✲ *£3.50 (ch & pen £1.80). Grounds £1.50 (ch & pen 80p). Party.*
🅿 ♨ ♿ *shop* ✕ *(ex in grounds)*
(NTS)

Arbuthnot Museum & Art Gallery
PETERHEAD
Saint Peter St
☎ *(01779) 477778*
Specialising in local exhibits, particularly those relating to the fishing industry, this museum also displays Arctic and whaling specimens and a British coin collection. The regular programme of exhibitions changes approximately every six weeks.
Open all year, Mon, Tue & Thu-Sat 10.30-1.30 & 2.30-5, Wed 10.30-1. (Closed PH). Free.
P (150 yds) shop ✕

Pitmedden Garden
PITMEDDEN
(1m W on A920)
☎ *Udny (01651) 842352*
The fine late 17th-century 5-acre walled garden has been recreated here, and sundials, pavilions and fountains are dotted among the elaborate floral designs. The Museum of Farming Life has been recently refurbished. There is also a visitor centre, a woodland walk, and a special dog walk.
Open - Garden, Museum of Farming Life & Visitor Centre open 28 Apr-1 Oct, daily 10-5.30 last admission 5pm.
✲ *Garden, Museum of Farming Life & Visitor Centre £3 (ch £1.50). Party.*
🅿 ♨ ♿ *(2 wheelchairs available) toilets for disabled shop* ✕
(NTS)

Tolquhon Castle
PITMEDDEN
(2m NE off B999)
☎ *0131-668 8800*
Now roofless, a late 16th-century quadrangular mansion encloses an early
➡

15th-century tower. There is a fine gatehouse and courtyard.
Open all year, Apr-Sep, Mon-Sat 9.30-6, Sun 2-6; Oct-Mar wknds only Sat 9.30-4, Sun 2-4. (Closed 25-26 Dec & 1-2 Jan).
£1.50 (ch & pen 60p).
P & *toilets for disabled shop*
(AM)

Leith Hall & Garden
RHYNIE
Kennethmont (3.5m NE on B9002)
☎Kennethmont (01464) 831216
Home of the Leith family for over 300 years, the house dates back to 1650, and has a number of Jacobite relics, a major exhibition 'For Crown and Country: the Military Lairds of Leith Hall', and fine examples of needlework. It is surrounded by charming gardens and extensive grounds which contain ponds, trails, a bird hide and unusual semicircular 18th-century stables.
Open - House Good Fri-1 Oct, 1.30-5.30. (Last admission 45 mins before closing). Gardens and grounds all year 9.30-sunset.
✴*£3 (ch £1.50). Party.*
P ☕ & *(parking next to hall, scented garden for the blind) toilets for disabled*
(ex in grounds)
(NTS)

Glen Grant Distillery
ROTHES
(On A941, in Rothes)
☎(01340) 831413 (Apr-Sep) & (01542) 887471
Established in 1840, the whisky produced in this distillery is used in many first-class blends as well as being sold as the single Glen Grant malt in the bottle. Traditional malt whisky methods of distillation are used, together with the most up-to-date equipment. There is a shop on the premises, and a free tot of whisky is provided.
Open Etr-Jun & Sep, Mon-Fri 10-4; Jul-Aug, Mon-Sat 10-4.
P & *(reception centre & still house) toilets for disabled shop*
Details not confirmed for 1995

Tugnet Ice House
SPEY BAY
☎Forres (01309) 673701
The largest ice house in Scotland, built in 1830, now contains exhibitions on the history and techniques of commerical salmon fishing on the River Spey, with an audio-visual programme. There are sections on the geography, wildlife and

industries of the Lower Spey area, such as ship-building at nearby Kingston.
Open 6 May-1 Oct 11-5.
Free.
P & *toilets for disabled shop*

Stonehaven Tolbooth
STONEHAVEN
Old Pier
☎Peterhead (01779) 477778
This was once a 16th-century storehouse of the Earls of Marischal. It was later used as a prison but is now a fishing and local history museum.
Open Jun-Sep, Mon & Thu-Sat 10-noon & 2-5; Wed & Sun 2-5.
Free.
P *(100yds)* & *shop*

Tomintoul Museum
TOMINTOUL
The Square
☎Forres (01309) 673701
Situated in one of the highest villages in Britain, the museum features a reconstructed crofter's kitchen and smiddy, with other displays on the local wildlife, the story of Tomintoul, and the local skiing industry.
Open Apr, May & Oct, Mon-Sat 9.30-1 & 2-5.30, Sun 2-5.30; Jun & Sep, Mon-Fri 9.30-6, Sat 9.30-1 & 2-6, Sun 2-6; Jul & Aug, Mon-Fri 9-6.30, Sat 9-1 & 2-6.30, Sun 11-1 & 2-6.30. Dates & times are provisional. Major redevelopment is planned for Oct 1995.
Free.
P & *(handling display for visually impaired) shop*

Fyvie Castle
TURRIFF
Fyvie (8m SE of Turriff on A947)
☎(01651) 891266
This superb castle dating from the 13th century has five towers, each built in a different century by one of the families who lived here. It is now one of the grandest examples of Scottish baronial architecture. The castle contains the finest wheel stair in Scotland, and a 17th-century morning room which, along with other rooms, has been decorated and furnished in lavish Edwardian grandeur. There is an exceptional collection of portraits, with works by Batoni, Raeburn, Romney, Gainsborough, Opie and Hoppner; and arms, armour and 16th-century tapestries can also be seen.
Open Apr-Jun & Sep daily 1.30-5.30. Jul-Aug daily 11-5.30. 1-22 Oct Sat & Sun

1.30-5.30. (last tour 45 mins before closing). Grounds open all year, daily 9.30-sunset.
✴*£3.50. (ch & pen £1.80). Party 20+. Grounds honesty box £1.*
P ☕ & *toilets for disabled shop* *(ex in grounds)*
(NTS)

HIGHLAND

Strathspey Steam Railway
AVIEMORE
Aviemore Speyside Station, Dalfaber Rd (Off B970)
☎(01479) 810725
This steam railway covers the five miles from Boat of Garten to Aviemore, where trains can also be boarded. The journey takes about 20 minutes, but allow around an hour for the round trip. Timetables are available from the station and the tourist information centre. Special events for 1995 include: Friends of Thomas the Tank Engine weekends (29 April-1 May, 22-24 September), Santa trains (23 December).
Open Jul-Aug daily; Jun & Sep daily ex Sat; selected days Apr, May & Oct; Dec 23, 26, 31 & 1-2 Jan.
£4.20 Basic return; £10.50 Family return.
P ☕ & *shop*

Balmacara (Lochalsh Woodland Garden)
BALMACARA
☎(01599) 566325
The Balmacara estate was bequeathed to The National Trust for Scotland in 1946, and comprises some 5600 acres and seven crofting villages, including Plockton, a conservation area. There are excellent views of Skye, Kintail (the Five Sisters), and Applecross. The area is excellent for walking, both on the estate and on forestry land nearby. A ranger/naturalist service is available on some days. The main visitor attraction is the Lochalsh Woodland Garden.
Open all year daily 9-sunset.
✴*£1 (ch & pen 50p)*
P
(NTS)

Strathnaver Museum
BETTYHILL
☎(016412) 421 due to change to (01641) 521418
The village is named after Elizabeth,

Countess of Sutherland, who built it for families evicted in the Highland Clearances. (The 'clearing' of the Sutherland estates was notorious.) The museum has displays on the clearances, with a fine collection of homemade furnishings, domestic and farm implements, and Gaelic books. There is also a Clan Mackay room. The museum's setting is a former church, a handsome stone building with a magnificent canopied pulpit dated 1774. The churchyard contains a carved stone known as the Farr Stone, which dates back to the 10th century and is a fine example of Celtic art.
Open Apr-Oct, Mon-Sat 10-1 & 2-5; Nov-Mar by appointment only.
£1.50 (ch 40p, pen £1, students 75p).
P *(100yds)* &

Landmark Highland Heritage & Adventure Park
CARRBRIDGE
(off A9)
☎(01479) 841613
The innovative centre has an exhibition on the history of the Highlands and a multi-screen, sound-and-vision presentation, 'The Highlander', which tells of the break-up of Europe's last tribal society. The Forestry Heritage Park has a 65ft forest viewing tower, a working steam-powered sawmill and various exhibitions and buildings. There are demonstrations of timber sawing, and log hauling by a Clydesdale horse throughout the day. Attractions include trails, a fun maze, an adventure play area, a craft and book shop, restaurant, and snack bar with picnic area. A programme of special events is planned to mark the 25th anniversary of Landmark.
Open all year, daily, Apr-Jun 9.30-6; Jul-Aug 9.30-8; Sep-Oct 9.30-5.30; Nov-Mar 9.30-5.
✴*Apr £4.15 (ch £2.75); May-Jun £4.50 (ch £2.95); Jul-Oct £4.75 (ch £3.10); Nov-Mar £3.25 (ch £2.05). Family tickets available.*
P ✕ *licensed* & *toilets for disabled shop*

Cawdor Castle
CAWDOR
(on B9090 off A96)
☎(01667) 404615
Home of the Thanes of Cawdor since the 14th century, the castle has a drawbridge, an ancient tower built round a tree, and a freshwater well inside the house. There are nature trails, a 9-hole golf course and a putting green. The restored Paradise garden and maze will not be open to the public in May and June 1995.
Open May-1 Oct, daily 10-5.30. (Last admission 5pm).
£4.50 (ch 5-15 £2.20, pen £3.50). Family ticket £12.50. Party 20+. Gardens, grounds & nature trails only £2.50.
P ☕ & *toilets for disabled shop*

Clava Cairns
CLAVA CAIRNS
(6m E of Inverness)
☎0131-668 8800
On the south bank of the River Nairn, this group of circular burial cairns is surrounded by three concentric rings of great stones. It dates from around 1600BC, and ranks among Scotland's finest prehistoric monuments.
Open all times.
Free.
P
(AM)

Hugh Miller's Cottage
CROMARTY
Church St
☎(01381) 600245
Hugh Miller, a stonemason who became an eminent geologist and writer, was born in the cottage in 1802. It was built by his great-grandfather in the early 18th century, and now has an exhibition and video on Miller and his work. The cottage garden was redeveloped in 1988.
Open 28 Apr-1 Oct, Mon-Sat 10-1 & 2-5.30, Sun 2-5.30.
✴*£1.50 (ch 80p). Party.*
P *(5mins)*
(NTS)

The Tapestry bedroom at Cawdor Castle, home to the Thanes of Cawdor since the 14th century.

Culloden Battlefield
CULLODEN MOOR
(5m E of Inverness)
☎(01463) 790607
A cairn built in 1881 recalls the last battle fought on mainland Britain, on 16 April 1746, when 'Bonnie' Prince Charles Edward Stuart's army was bloodily routed by the Duke of Cumberland's forces. The battlefield has been restored to its state on the day of the battle. Old Leanach Cottage survived the battle. The Graves of the Clans and the Well of the Dead can also be seen. There is a visitor centre with a display, audio-visual show, (also in Gaelic, German, French, Italian and Japanese), bookshop and restaurant.
Open - site always. Visitor Centre open 4 Feb-Mar & Nov-30 Dec, daily 10-6. (Closed 25 & 26 Dec); Apr-Oct, daily 9-6; Audio visual show closed 30 mins before Visitor Centre.
❋*Admission to visitor centre & museum (includes audio-visual programme & Old Leanach Cottage) £2 (ch, pen & students £1). Party.*
🅿 ✖ ♿ *(wheelchair, induction loop for hard of hearing,raised map). toilets for disabled shop* ✾ *(ex in grounds)*
(NTS)

Official Loch Ness Monster Exhibition
DRUMNADROCHIT
Loch Ness Centre (on A82)
☎(01456) 450573 & 450218
A fascinating computer-controlled, multi-media presentation lasting 40 minutes. Ten themed areas cover the story from the pre-history of Scotland, through the cultural roots of the legend of the monster in Highland folklore, and into the fifty-year controversy which surrounds it. The exhibition was totally renewed in July 1989 and the centre encompasses the Nessie Giftshop, the House of Heraldry, a kilt-maker, coffee shop and a hotel.
Open all year, peak season 9am-9.30pm, otherwise times on application.
❋*£4 (ch £2.50, pen & students £3). Family ticket £10.50.*
🅿 🍴 ✖ *licensed* ♿ *toilets for disabled shop* ✾ *(ex in grounds)*

Urquhart Castle
DRUMNADROCHIT
(on A82)
☎0131-668 8800
The castle was once Scotland's biggest and overlooks Loch Ness. It dates mainly from the 14th century, when it was built on the site of an earlier fort, and was destroyed before the 1715 Jacobite rebellion.
Open all year, Apr-Sep, daily 9.30-6.30; Oct-Mar, Mon-Sat 9.30-4.30, Sun 11.30-4.30. (Closed 25-26 Dec & 1-32 Jan).
£3 (ch 16 £1, pen £2).
🅿 *shop* ✾
(AM)

Laidhay Croft Museum
DUNBEATH
(1m N on A9)
☎(01593) 731244
The museum gives visitors a glimpse of a long-vanished way of life. The main building is a thatched Caithness longhouse, with the dwelling quarters, byre and stable all under one roof. It dates back some 200 years, and is furnished as it might have been 100 years ago. A collection of early farm tools and machinery is also shown. Near the house is a thatched winnowing barn with its roof supported on three 'Highland couples', or crucks.
Open Etr-mid Oct, daily 10-6.
❋*50p (ch 20p).*
🅿 🍴 ♿ *toilets for disabled*

Highland & Rare Breeds Farm
ELPHIN
☎Strathkaniard (01854) 666204
There are over thirty six breeds, both ancient and modern, some of which visitors may stroke or feed, also a pets' corner, riverside walk and a theme shop. Guided tours are available by prior

Strategically placed on Loch Ness, the ruins of Urqhart Castle are all that remains of Scotland's largest castle. The castle is an ideal place for Loch Ness Monster spotting.

arrangement. Sheep-shearing demonstrations are planned for July, and handspinning demonstrations throughout the season.
Open mid May-Sep daily 10-5.
❋*£2.50 (ch £1.50, students & pen £2)*
🅿 ♿ *(assistance available) toilets for disabled shop* ✾

Fort George
FORT GEORGE
(11m NE of Inverness)
☎0131-668 8800
Built following the Battle of Culloden as a Highland fortress for the army of George II, it is one of the outstanding artillery fortifications in Europe and still an active army barracks. Reconstructed barracks of the 18th and 19th centuries, Seafield Collection of Arms, chapel and Regimental Museum of the Queen's Own Highlanders.
Open all year, Apr-Sep, Mon-Sat 9.30-6.30, Sun 2-6.30; Oct-Mar, Mon-Sat 9.30-4.30, Sun 2-4.30. (Closed 25-26 Dec & 1-3 Jan).
❋*£2.50 (ch 16 £1, pen £1.50).*
🅿 ♿ *toilets for disabled shop* ✾
(AM)

Queen's Own Highlanders Regimental Museum
FORT GEORGE
☎Inverness (01463) 224380
Fort George (above) has been a military barracks since it was built in 1748-1769, and was the Depot of the Seaforth Highlanders until 1961. The museum of the Queen's Own Highlanders (Seaforth and Camerons) is sited in the former Lieutenant Governor's house, where uniforms, medals and pictures are displayed.
Open Apr-Sep, Mon-Fri 10-6, Sun 2-6; Oct-Mar, Mon-Fri 10-4. (Closed Good Fri-Etr Mon, Xmas, New Year & BH).
Free. Admission charged by Historic Scotland for entry to Fort George.
🅿 ♿ *toilets for disabled shop* ✾

Inverlochy Castle
FORT WILLIAM
(2m NE)
☎0131-668 8800
The castle was begun in the 13th century and added to later. It is noted in Scottish

history for the battle fought nearby in 1645, when Montrose defeated the Campbells.
Open Apr-Sep. Key available from keykeeper.
Free.
✾
(AM)

West Highland Museum
FORT WILLIAM
Cameron Square
☎(01397) 702169
The displays illustrate traditional Highland life and history, with numerous Jacobite relics. One of them is the 'secret portrait' of 'Bonnie' Prince Charlie, which looks like meaningless daubs of paint but reveals a portrait when reflected in a metal cylinder.
Open all year, Mon-Sat, Jul-Aug 9.30-5.30, Sun 2-5; Apr-Jun & Sep 10-5, Oct-Mar 10-1 & 2-5 closed Mon from Nov.
❋*£1 (ch 40p, pen 60p).*
P *(100 yds) shop* ✾

Gairloch Heritage Museum
GAIRLOCH
Achtercairn
☎(01445) 712287
A converted farmstead now houses the award-winning museum, which shows the way of life in this typical West Highland parish from early times to the 20th century. There are reconstructions of a croft house room, a school room, a shop, and the inside of a local lighthouse. Restored fishing boats are also shown.
Open Etr-Sep, Mon-Sat 10-5; Mar-Oct, Mon-Fri by arrangement.
£1.50 (ch 50p & pen £1)
🅿 🍴 ✖ *licensed* ♿ *(toilets for wheelchair visitors 100yds from entrance) shop* ✾

Glencoe & North Lorn Folk Museum
GLENCOE
Two heather-thatched cottages in the main street of Glencoe now house items connected with the Macdonalds and the Jacobite risings. A variety of local domestic and farming exhibits, dairying and slate-working equipment, costumes and embroidery is also shown.

Open mid May-Sep, Mon-Sat 10-5.30.
❋*£1 (ch 50p).*
🅿 ♿ *shop*

Glencoe Visitor Centre
GLENCOE
(on A82)
☎Ballachulish (01855) 811307
Glencoe has stunning scenery and some of the best climbing (not for the unskilled) and walking country in the Highlands. Its wildlife includes red deer and wildcats, golden eagles and ptarmigan. The A82 Glasgow to Fort William road runs through the glen, so it is also more accessible than some. It is best known, however, as the scene of the massacre of February 1692, when a party of troops billeted here tried to murder all their Macdonald hosts - men, women and children. The Visitor Centre is at the north end of the glen, close to the scene of the massacre. It has a display on the history of mountaineering in the glen, provides information on walks, and has a video programme telling the story of the 1692 Massacre of Glencoe. Ranger service.
Open; Site all year. Visitor Centre Apr-19 May & 1 Sep-22 Oct, daily 10-5; 20 May-31 Aug, daily 9.30-6. (last admission 45 mins before closing).
50p (ch & pen 25p). Includes parking.
🅿 🍴 ♿ *(induction loop in video programme room) toilets for disabled shop* ✾
(NTS)

Jacobite Monument
GLENFINNAN
☎Kinlocheil (01397) 722250
The monument commemorates Highlanders who fought and died for Bonnie Prince Charlie in 1745. It was built in 1815, and has an awe-inspiring setting at the head of Loch Shiel. There is a visitor centre with information (commentary in four languages) on the Prince's campaign.
Open - Site all year. Visitor Centre, Apr-19 May & 1 Sep Oct, daily 10-1 & 2-5; 20 May-Aug, daily 9.30-6.
❋*£1 (ch 50p). Includes parking.*
🅿 🍴 ♿ *(information centre only) shop*
(NTS)

Dunrobin Castle
GOLSPIE ▮
(1m NE on A9)
☎ (01408) 633177 & 633268
The ancient seat of the Earls and Dukes of Sutherland takes its name from Earl Robin, who built the original square keep in the 13th century. The castle is now a splendid, gleaming, turreted structure, thanks largely to 19th-century rebuilding, and has a beautiful setting overlooking the sea. Paintings (including Canalettos), furniture and family heirlooms are on display inside, and the gardens are on a grand scale to match the house (they were modelled on those at Versailles). A summer house in the grounds is now a museum with a variety of exhibits. A vintage car rally is planned for 20 August.
Open Etr & May-15 Oct, Mon-Sat 10.30-5.30, Sun 1-5.30. Closes 1 hr earlier Etr, May & Oct. Last admission half hour before closing.
£3.70 (ch £1.90, pen £2.30). Family ticket £9.40. Party.
🅿 ▮ & *(access by arrangement only) shop* ✸

Timespan
HELMSDALE ▮
Dunrobin St
☎ (01431) 821327
The North's most exciting heritage centre features the dramatic story of the Highlands, from Picts and Vikings, to the last burning of a witch and the Highland Clearances through to crofting, fishing and the present day oil fields. Scenes from the past are re-created using life-size sets, sound effects, and an audio-visual programme. There is a riverside garden and gift shop.
Open Etr-mid Oct, Mon-Sat 10-5, Sun 2-5 (6pm Jul-Aug). Last admission one hour before closing.
✲*£2.75 (ch £1.65 pen & student £2.20). Family ticket £7.20.*
🅿 ▮ & *toilets for disabled shop garden centre* ✸

Castle Stuart
INVERNESS ▮
Petty Parish (5m E of Inverness, off A96)
☎ (01463) 790745
Ancient home of the Earls of Moray and the Stuart family, constructed in 1621 when the Royal House of Stuart had ruled the United Kingdoms of England and Wales, Scotland and Ireland for some twenty years. It is located within the sound of the cannon's roar from High Culloden Moor, where the last attempt to restore the Stuart monarchy ended in defeat. The interior has been restored to its former glory with Jacobean furnishings, armour and historic relics.
Open all year, daily 10-5.
✲*£3 (ch £1, pen & students £2).*
🅿 *shop* ✸

Highland Wildlife Park
KINCRAIG ▮
(on B9152)
☎ (01540) 651270

In countryside of heather and peat bog, a beautiful garden has been made at Inverewe where the warm Gulf Stream creates a frost-free zone area on this windswept coast.

In a magnificent natural setting, native animals from Scotland's past and present can be viewed. There are two parts to the park: a drive through the large main enclsoure with red deer, European bison and wild horses among the animals to be seen here. A walkaround area, including woodland and forest habitats, with capercaillie, pine martens, beavers and owls, to name just a few.
Open Apr-Oct, daily 10-4, (5pm Jun-Aug).
🅿 ▮ & *toilets for disabled shop* ✸
Details not confirmed for 1995

Highland Folk Museum
KINGUSSIE ▮
Duke St
☎ (01540) 661307
The Highland way of life is illustrated with an interesting display of crafts and furnishings, a farming museum, a reconstructed Hebridean mill and a primitive 'black house'. Demonstrations of crafts are held every day throughout July and August, including weaving, spinning and baking.
Open all year, Apr-Oct, Mon-Sat 10-6, Sun 2-6; Nov-Mar, Mon-Fri 10-3. (Closed Xmas-New Year).
✲*£2.50 (ch & pen £1.50).*
🅿 & *toilets for disabled shop*

Ruthven Barracks
KINGUSSIE ▮
(0.5m SE of Kingussie)
☎ 0131-668 8800
Despite being blown up by 'Bonnie' Prince Charlie's Highlanders, these infantry barracks are still the best preserved of the four that were built after the Jacobite uprising. The considerable ruins are the remains of a building completed in 1716 on the site of a fortress of the 'Wolf of Badenoch'.
Open at any reasonable time.
Free.
🅿 ✸
(AM)

Moniack Castle (Highland Winery)
KIRKHILL ▮
(7m from Inverness on A862)
☎ Drumchardine (01463) 831283
A unique Scottish enterprise is undertaken in the former fortress of the Loval chiefs: commercial wine-making is not a usual Scottish industry, but nevertheless a wide range of 'country'-style wines is produced, including elderflower and silver birch; and also mead and sloe gin. A wine bar and bistro are added temptations.
Open all year, Mon-Sat 10-5.
Free.
🅿 ▮ ✗ *licensed shop* ✸

Clan Macpherson House & Museum
NEWTONMORE ▮
Main St
☎ (01540) 673332
Containing relics and memorials of the clan chiefs and other Macpherson families as well as those of Prince Edward Stuart, this museum also displays the Prince's letters to the Clan Chief of 1745 and one to the Prince from his father the Old Pretender, along with royal warrants and the green banner of the clan. Other interesting historic exhibits include James Macpherson's fiddle, swords, pictures, decorations and medals. Highland games take place on the first Saturday in August, and the Clan Macpherson Rally on the same day.
Open May-Sep, Mon-Sat 10-5.30, Sun 2.30-5.30. Other times by appointment.
✲*Free. Donations.*
🅿 & *toilets for disabled shop* ✸

Inverewe Garden
POOLEWE ▮
(6m NE of Gairloch, on A832)
☎ (01445) 781200
The presence of the North Atlantic Drift enables this remarkable garden to grow rare and sub-tropical plants. At its best in early June, but full of beauty from March to October, Inverewe has a backdrop of magnificent mountains and stands to the north of Loch Maree.
Open - Garden all year, daily 9.30-5 (until 7pm Apr-22 Oct). Visitor Centre Apr-22 Oct, daily 9.30-5.30. Guided walks Apr-22 Oct Mon-Fri at 1.30.
✲*£3.50 (concessions £1.80). Party.*
🅿 ✗ *licensed & (some paths difficult) toilets for disabled shop* ✸
(NTS)

Highland Museum of Childhood
STRATHPEFFER ▮
The Old Station
☎ (01997) 421031
The museum is situated in a renovated Victorian railway station of 1885, along with various craft shops. In mid-June Victorian days are held. Strathpeffer also has Highland Games in early August.
Open daily.
🅿 ▮ & *shop*
Details not confirmed for 1995

Countryside Centre
TORRIDON ▮
(N of A896).
☎ (01445) 791221
Set amid some of Scotland's finest mountain scenery, the centre offers audio-visual presentations on the local wildlife. At the Mains nearby there are live deer to be seen, and there is also a static display on the life of the red deer.
Open - Countryside Centre 28 Apr-1 Oct, Mon-Sat 10-5, Sun 2-5. Estate and Deer Museum daily all year.
✲*Deer park, museum & audio-visual display £1 (ch 50p).*
🅿
(NTS)

Caithness Glass Factory & Visitor Centre
WICK ▮
Airport Industrial Estate
☎ (01955) 2286
All aspects of glassmaking are on view, from the initial processing of the raw

materials to the finished article. Visitors can see the jewellery and engraving depatments at work and learn about the history of Caithness glass at the exhibition. There is a shop, which also sells factory seconds, and a restaurant.
Open all year, Factory shop & restaurant Mon-Sat 9-5 (Sun, Etr-Oct 11-5).
Glassmaking Mon-Fri 9-4.30.
P ✕ *licensed & toilets for disabled shop* ⊗ *(ex in shop)*
Details not confirmed for 1995

Castle of Old Wick
WICK ▬▬▬
(1m S)
☎ *0131-668 8800*
A ruined four-storey, square tower that is probably of the 12th century. It is also known as Castle Oliphant.
Open except when adjoining rifle range is in use.
Free.
⊗
(AM)

Wick Heritage Centre
WICK ▬▬▬
20 Bank Row
☎ *(01955) 605393*
The heritage centre is near the harbour in a complex of eight houses, yards and outbuildings. The centre illustrates local history from Neolithic times to the herring fishing industry. In addition, there is a complete working 19th-century lighthouse, and the famous Johnston collection of photographs. The centre has won five major awards including 'Best of Better Britain 1992'.
Open Jun-Sep, daily 10-5. (Closed Sun).
£1.50 (ch 50p).
P & *toilets for disabled*

LOTHIAN

Myreton Motor Museum
ABERLADY ▬▬▬
(1.5m from A198, 2m from A1)
☎ *(01875) 870288*
This is a charming and wide-ranging collection, with cars and motorcycles from 1896, cycles from 1863 and commercial vehicles, historic British military vehicles, advertising signs and automobilia.
Open all year, daily 10-6 (summer); 10-5 (winter). (Closed 25 Dec & 1 Jan).
£2 (ch 16 50p).
P & ⊗

Malleny Garden
BALERNO ▬▬▬
(off Bavelaw Rd)
☎ *0131-449 2283*
The delightful gardens are set around a 17th-century house (not open). There is a good selection of shrub roses, a woodland garden, and a group of four clipped yews, the survivors of a group of 12 which were planted in 1603. The National Bonsai Collection for Scotland is also at Malleny.
Open daily 10-sunset. House not open.
❄*£1*
P & ⊗
(NTS)

Crichton Castle
CRICHTON ▬▬▬
(2.5m SW Pathhead)
☎ *0131-668 8800*
The castle dates back to the 14th century, but most of what remains today was built over the following 300 years. A notable feature is the 16th-century wing built by the Earl of Bothwell in Italian style, with an arcade below.
Open Apr-Sep, Mon-Sat 9.30-6.30, Sun 2-6.30.
£1.20 (ch 16 & pen 75p).
P *shop*
(AM)

Edinburgh Butterfly & Insect World
DALKEITH ▬▬▬
(At Dobbies Gdn World 1m N on A7)
☎ *0131-663 4932*
Richly coloured butterflies from all over the world can be seen flying among exotic plants, trees and flowers. The tropical pools are filled with giant waterlilies and colourful fish, and are surrounded by lush vegetation. Also displayed are scorpions, leaf cutting ants, beetles, tarantulas and other remarkable creatures. There is a unique honeybee display. Events planned for 1995 include rainforest, minibeast and bee tours.
Open Mar-7 Jan, daily 10-5.30, (10-4 winter).
❄*£3.25 (ch 5 free, ch £1.90, pen & students £2.55). Family ticket £9.30. Party 10+. Prices under review*
P ♨ & *toilets for disabled shop garden centre* ⊗

Dirleton Castle
DIRLETON ▬▬▬
(on A198)
☎ *0131-668 8800*
The oldest part of this romantic castle dates from the 13th century. It was besieged by Edward I in 1298, rebuilt and expanded, and then destroyed in 1650. Now the sandstone ruins have a beautiful mellow quality. The garden, established in the 16th century, has ancient yews and hedges around a bowling green.
Open all year, Apr-Sep, Mon-Sat 9.30-6.30, Sun 2-6.30; Oct-Mar, Mon-Sat, 9.30-4.30, Sun 2-4.30. (Closed 25-26 Dec & 1-3 Jan).
£2 (ch 16 75p, pen £1.25). Family ticket £4.50.
P & *shop*
(AM)

Museum of Flight
EAST FORTUNE ▬▬▬
East Fortune Airfield (Signposted from A1 near Haddington)
☎ *(01620) 880308 or 0131-225 7534*
Aircraft on display include a Supermarine Spitfire MK 16, De Haviland Sea Venom, Hawker Sea Hawk and Comet (4). The museum is set out in a former airship base, and also has a section on Airship R34 which flew from here to New York and back in 1919. There is also an extensive display of rockets and aero-engines. Special events for 1995: Free Weekend (22-23 April), Enthusiasts' Day (20 May), Gala Days (15-16 July).

Open Etr-Sep, daily 10.30-5.
❄*Admission fee payable.*
P ♨ & *toilets for disabled shop* ⊗

Hailes Castle
EAST LINTON ▬▬▬
(1m SW on unclass rd).
☎ *0131-668 8800*
The castle was a fortified manor house of the Gourlays and Hepburns. Bothwell brought Mary Queen of Scots here when they were fleeing from Borthwick Castle. The substantial ruins include a 16th-century chapel.
Open at all reasonable times.
Free.
⊗
(AM)

Preston Mill
EAST LINTON ▬▬▬
(signposted from A1)
☎ *(01620) 860426*
This is the oldest working water-driven meal mill to survive in Scotland, and was last used commercially in 1957. It has a conical roof and red pantiles. There is an old mill pond with ducks. A short walk leads to Phantassie Doocot (dovecote), built for 500 birds.
Open Good Fri-Sep, Mon-Sat 11-1 & 2-5.30, Sun 1.30-5.30; 1-22 Oct, Sat & Sun 1.30-4. Last entry 20 mins before closing morning and afternoon.
❄*£1.50 (ch 80p). Party.*
P & *toilets for disabled shop* ⊗
(NTS)

EDINBURGH

Edinburgh has a glorious setting, with unexpected views of the sea and hills wherever you happen to be, and a skyline dominated by the great crag on which the castle stands. From here the medieval Old Town runs down to the Palace of Holyrood House, and through the heart of the Old Town runs the Royal Mile, lined with historic buildings like the Outlook Tower with its camera obscura, the tall tenement of Gladstone's Land, Lady Stair's house and a number of museums, all full of interest. It is also well worth spending time exploring the many 'wynds' and alleys that run down steeply from either side of the Royal Mile. Edinburgh's second main area is the New Town, a place of elegant squares and terraces built for the city's merchants and aristocrats in the late-18th century, seen at its grandest in Charlotte Square. There is a third town as well - the districts of grand Victorian houses - and Edinburgh is also a city of villages, each with their own character. Always fascinating to visit, Edinburgh becomes a riot of theatre and music both on and off the streets during the International Festival and Fringe Festival in August. An especially popular event is the military searchlight tattoo held in front of the castle.

Brass Rubbing Centre
EDINBURGH ▬▬▬
Trinity Apse, Chalmers Close, High St
☎ *0131-556 4364*
Housed in the historic, 15th-century remnant of Trinity Apse, the Centre offers the chance to make your own rubbing from a wide range of replica monumental brasses and Pictish stones. Tuition is available.
Open Jun-Sep, Mon Sat 10-6; Oct-May, Mon-Sat 10-5.
Charge made for use of materials.
shop ⊗

Camera Obscura
EDINBURGH ▬▬▬
Castlehill, Royal Mile
☎ *0131-226 3709*
Step inside this magical 1850s 'cinema' for a unique experience of Edinburgh. As the lights go down a brilliant moving image of the surrounding city appears. The scene changes as a guide operates the camera's system of revolving lenses and mirrors. As the panorama unfolds the guide tells the story of the city's historic past. Also of interest is the Rooftop Terrace, and exhibitions on International Holography, Pinhole Photography and Victorian Edinburgh.
Open all year, daily, Apr-Sep 9.30-6; Oct-Mar 10-5. (Closed 25 Dec & 1 Jan). Open later Jul-Aug, phone for details.
❄*£3.20 (ch £1.60, pen £2 & students £2.50). Family ticket £8.70.*
P (300yds) shop

City Art Centre
EDINBURGH ▬▬▬
2 Market St
☎ *0131-529 3541*
The City Art Centre houses the city's permanent fine art collection and stages a constantly changing programme of temporary exhibitions drawn from all ➤

Spectacular butterflies fly free in the artificial rainforest created at Edinburgh Butterfly World in Dalkeith, where tropical insects and plants also flourish.

As night falls over Edinburgh, the Castle on its huge volcanic outcrop is silhouetted against the skyline.

parts of the world. It has six floors of display galleries (linked by an escalator), a shop, cafe and facilities for disabled visitors. The 1995 exhibitions programme includes: Dream City (10 May-24 June), Lions and Unicorns - Heraldry in Scotland (27 May-8 July), A Picture of Edinburgh (15 July-16 September).
Open Jun-Sep, Mon-Sat 10-6 (Sun 2-5 during Edinburgh Festival); Oct-May, Mon-Sat 10-5.
Free. Admission charged for exhibitions.
P (500yds) 🍴 ♿ (induction loop, lifts) toilets for disabled shop ⊗ guide dogs

Craigmillar Castle
EDINBURGH
(2.5m SE)
☎0131-668 8800
Mary Queen of Scots retreated to this 14th-century stronghold after the murder of Rizzio, and the plot to murder Darnley, her second husband, was also hatched here. There are 16th-and 17th-century apartments.
Open all year, Apr-Sep, Mon-Sat 9.30-6.30, Sun 2-6.30. Oct-Mar, Mon-Sat 9.30-4.30. Sun 2-4.30. (Closed Thu & Fri in winter, 25-26 Dec & 1-3 Jan).
£1.50 (ch 75p, pen £1).
P ♿ shop
(AM)

Edinburgh Castle
EDINBURGH
☎0131-668 8800
This historic stronghold stands on the precipitous crag of Castle Rock. One of the oldest parts is the 11th-century chapel of the saintly Queen Margaret, but most of the present castle evolved later, during its stormy history of sieges and wars, and was altered again in Victorian times. The apartments of Mary Queen of Scots can be seen, including the bedroom where James I of England and VI of Scotland was born. Also on the rock is James IV's 16th-century great hall. The vaults underneath have graffiti by 19th-century French prisoners of war. The Scottish crown and other royal regalia are displayed in the Crown Room, and the spectacular Military Tattoo is held on the Esplanade, built in 1753 - shortly after the castle's last siege in 1745. Also notable is the Scottish National War Memorial, opened in 1927 on the site of the castle's church. A new 'Honours of the Kingdom' exhibition tells the fascinating story and history of the Scottish crown jewels. There is still a military presence in the castle, and some areas cannot be visited.

Open Apr-Sep, daily 9.30-6. Oct-Mar, daily 9.30-5. Last ticket sold 45 mins earlier than closing time.
£5.50 (ch £1.50, pen £3.50).
P (charged) 🍴 ✗ licensed ♿ (free transport to top of Castle Hill lift) toilets for disabled shop ⊗
(AM)

Edinburgh Zoo
EDINBURGH
Corstorphine Rd (2m W on A8)
☎0131-334 9171
Set in 80 acres of hillside parkland, Edinburgh Zoo houses Scotland's largest animal collection with over 1500 animals including many endangered species. The zoo has the world's largest penguin enclosure; four different species of penguins and almost 180 penguins altogether can be seen here. There are daily 'penguin parades' at 2pm April-September, and October if weather permits. Other attractions include animal handling classes and brass-rubbing. Panoramic views of Edinburgh and the surrounding countryside can also be enjoyed here.
Open all year, Mon-Sat 9-6, Sun 9.30-6 in summer, but closes 5pm or dusk in winter.
P (charged) 🍴 ♿ (wheelchair loan) toilets for disabled shop ⊗
Details not confirmed for 1995

General Register House
EDINBURGH
(East end of Princes St)
☎0131-556 6585
The headquarters of the Scottish Record Office and repository for the national archives of Scotland, designed by Robert Adam and founded in 1774. The historical and legal search rooms are available to researchers, and changing exhibitions are held. An exhibition 'The Jacobites' is planned for July-September 1995.
Open Mon-Fri 9-4.45. Exhibitions 10-4. (Closed certain PHs & part of Nov).
No charge for historical searches or exhibitions.
♿ toilets for disabled shop ⊗ ⊞

Georgian House
EDINBURGH
7 Charlotte Sq
☎0131-225 2160
The house is part of Robert Adam's splendid north side of Charlotte Square, the epitome of Edinburgh New Town architecture. The lower floors of No 7 have been restored in the style of around

1800, when the house was new. It gives a vivid impression of Georgian life, in both the grand public rooms and the servants' areas. Visitors can watch videos on life in the Georgian house, and the New Town.
Open Apr-22 Oct, Mon-Sat 10-5, Sun 2-5. Last admission 4.30pm.
✱£3.50 (ch & pen £1.80); (includes audio-visual show). Party.
(induction loop for hard of hearing) shop ⊗
(NTS)

Gladstone's Land
EDINBURGH
477b Lawnmarket
☎0131-226 5856
Built in 1620, this six-storey tenement, once the house of a prosperous Edinburgh merchant, still has its arcaded front - a rare feature now. Visitors can also see unusual tempera paintings on the walls and ceilings. It is furnished as a typical home of a 17th-century merchant, complete with ground-floor shop front and goods of the period.
Open Apr-22 Oct, Mon-Sat 10-5, Sun 2-5. Last admission 4.30pm.
£2.50 (ch, pen & students £1.30).
P (440yds meters) ♿ (tours for the blind can be arranged) shop ⊗
(NTS)

Huntly House
EDINBURGH
142 Canongate
☎0131-529 4143
This is one of the best-preserved 16th-century buildings in the Old Town. It was built in 1570 and later became the headquarters of the Incorporation of Hammermen. It is now the main museum of local history, and has collections of silver, glassware, pottery, other items such as street signs, along with a collction relating to Field Marshal Earl Haig, a World War I general.
Open all year, Mon-Sat, Jun-Sep 10-6, Oct-May 10-5. (During Festival period only, Sun 2-5).
Free.
P (100 yds) meters ♿ shop ⊗

John Knox House
EDINBURGH
The Netherbow, 43-45 High St
☎0131-556 9579
John Knox is said to have died in the house, which was built by the goldsmith to Mary, Queen of Scots. Renovation work has revealed the original floor in the

Oak Room, and a magnificent painted ceiling. The house is traditionally associated with John Knox the Reformer and contains an exhibition about his life and times.
Open all year, Mon-Sat 10-5. (Closed Xmas & New Year). Last admission 30 mins before closure.
£1.30 (ch 75p, students & pen £1). Party 20+.
🍴 ♿ toilets for disabled shop ⊗

Lauriston Castle
EDINBURGH
Cramond Rd South, Davidson's Mains (NW outskirts of Edinburgh, 1m E of Cramond)
☎0131-336 2060
The castle is a late 16th-century tower house with 19th-century additions but is most notable as a classic example of the Edwardian age. It has a beautifully preserved Edwardian interior by one of Edinburgh's leading decorators, and still has the feel of an Edwardian country house. There are spacious, pleasant grounds. Special events planned for 1995 include Lauriston Castle Edwardian Extravaganza (20-21 May), Davidsons Mains and Cramond Children's Gala (17 June), Lace at Lauriston (2-3 September). Please telephone to confirm dates.
Open all year by guided tour only; Apr-Oct, 11-1, 2-5; Nov-Mar, wknds 2-4. (Last tour commences 40 minutes before each closing time). Closed Fri.
£2 (ch £1). Grounds only free.
P ♿ shop ⊗

Museum of Antiquities
EDINBURGH
1 Queen St
☎0131-225 7534
The museum illustrates the history and everyday life in Scotland. A gallery displays 'Dynasty: The Royal House of Stewart' - 300 years of Stewart rule in Scotland, illustrated by portraits and objects from the Scottish national collections.
Open all year, Mon-Sat 10-5, Sun 2-5. (Closed 25-26 Dec & 1-2 Jan).
Free.
🍴 ♿ toilets for disabled shop ⊗

Museum of Childhood
EDINBURGH
42 High St (Royal Mile)
☎0131-529 4142
One of the first museums of its kind, it was reopened in 1986 after major expansion and reorganisation. It has a wonderful collection of toys, games and other belongings of children through the ages, to delight visitors both old and young. Special exhibitions are held throughout the year, please telephone for details.
Open all year, Mon-Sat, Jun-Sep 10-6; Oct-May 10-5. (During Festival period only, Sun 2-5).
Free.
P ♿ (3 floors only) toilets for disabled shop ⊗

National Gallery of Scotland
EDINBURGH
The Mound
☎0131-556 8921
Recognised as one of Europe's best smaller galleries, the National Gallery of Scotland occupies a handsome neo-classical building designed by William Playfair. It contains notable collections of works by Old Masters, Impressionists and Scottish artists. Among them are the *Bridgewater Madonna* by Raphael, Constable's *Dedham Vale*, and works by Titian, Velázquez, Van Gogh and Gauguin. Drawings, watercolours and original prints by Turner, Goya, Blake and others are shown on request, Monday to Friday 10-12.30 and 2-4.30. Special exhibitions for 1994 include: an exhibition of the works of Raphael (5 May-10 July), Monet to Matisse - Landscape painting in France 1874-1914 (11 August-23 October).
Open all year, Mon-Sat 10-5, Sun 2-5; (Extended opening hours during the Festival period). Winter (Oct-Mar) some

rooms may be closed. (Closed May Day, Xmas & New Year)
Free. Admission charged to some major exhibitions.
& (ramps & lift) toilets for disabled shop ✥

Nelson Monument
EDINBURGH
Calton Hill
☎0131-556 2716
Designed in 1807 and erected on Calton Hill, the monument dominates the east end of Princes Street. Visitors climbing to the top will enjoy superb views of the city. Every day except Sunday the time ball drops at 1pm as the gun at the castle goes off.
Open all year, Apr-Sep Mon 1-6 Tue-Sat 10-6; Oct-Mar Mon-Sat 10-3.
❋£1
P shop ✥

Newhaven Heritage Museum
EDINBURGH
Fishmarket, Newhaven Harbour
☎0131-551 4165
The museum tells the story of the village and its people. It looks at fishing, other sea trades, customs and superstitions. There are displays on the development of this tightly-knit community, its leisure activities and choirs. The story is told through reconstructed sets of fisherfolk, objects, photographs, first-hand written and spoken accounts of people's lives. Also features hands-on exhibits, music and video.
Open all year, Mon-Sat 12-5.
Free.
& toilets for disabled shop ✥

Palace of Holyroodhouse
EDINBURGH
(at east end of Royal Mile)
☎0131-556 7371 & 0131-556 1096 (info)
The Palace grew from the guesthouse of the Abbey of the Holyrood, said to have been founded by David I after a miraculous apparition. Mary, Queen of Scots, had her court here from 1561 to 1567, and 'Bonnie' Prince Charlie held levees at the Palace during his occupation of Edinburgh. The Palace is still used by the Royal Family, but can be visited when they are not in residence. Little remains of the original abbey except the ruined 13th-century nave of the church. The oldest part of the palace proper is James V's tower, with Mary's rooms on the second floor. A plaque marks the spot where Rizzio was murdered. The audience chamber where she debated with John Knox can also be seen. There are fine 17th-century state rooms, and the picture gallery is notable for its series of Scottish monarchs, starting in 330BC with Fergus I. The work was done by Jacob de Wet in 1684-5, many of the likenesses are based on imagination. The grounds are used for royal garden parties in summer.
Open Winter, Mon-Sat 9.30-4.15 (last ticket sold at 3.45pm), Sun 10-4 (last ticket sold 3.15). Summer, Mon-Sat 9.30-6 (last ticket sold at 5.15pm), Sun, 10-5.15 (last ticket sold at 4.30pm).
❋£3.50 (ch 16 £1.80, pen £3). Family ticket £9.
P & (first floor by lift, wheelchair available) toilets for disabled shop ✥

Parliament House
EDINBURGH
Supreme Courts
☎0131-225 2595
Scotland's independent parliament last sat in 1707, in this 17th-century building hidden behind an 1829 façade. It is now the seat of the Supreme Law Courts of Scotland and has been adapted to its changed use, but the Parliament Hall still has its fine old hammerbeam roof. A large stained glass window depicts the inaugration of the Court of Session in 1540.
Open all year, Mon-Fri 10-4.
P 🍵 ✗ & toilets for disabled ✥
Details not confirmed for 1995

The People's Story
EDINBURGH
Canongate Tolbooth, 163 Canongate
☎0131-225 2424 ext 4057
The museum, housed in the 16th-century tolbooth, tells the story of the ordinary people of Edinburgh from the late 18th century to the present day. Reconstructions include a prison cell, 1930s pub and 1940s kitchen supported by photographs, displays, sounds, smells and a video.
Open Jun-Sep, Mon-Sat 10-6; Oct-May, Mon-Sat 10-5. Also, open Sun during Edinburgh Festival 2-5.
Free.
& (first floor accessible by lift) toilets for disabled shop ✥

Royal Botanic Garden
EDINBURGH
Inverleith Row (1m N)
☎0131-552 7171
The gardens offer 70 acres of peace and greenery close to the city centre. They were founded as a physic garden in 1670 at Holyrood and came to Inverleith in 1823. The largest rhododendron collection in Britain can be seen here, and the different areas include an arboretum, a peat garden, a woodland garden, and rock and heath gardens. There is a splendid herbaceous border, and the plant houses have orchids, cacti and other specialities from a variety of climates. The gardens have colour all year round, even in winter when the plants with coloured bark come into their own. The exhibition hall has informative 'hands-on' displays, and Inverleith House Gallery has art exhibitions. All major routes and areas of interest are accessible to wheelchairs, and there are purpose-built toilets for wheelchair users. Wheelchairs are available at the entrance.
Open all year Garden, Nov-Feb 10-4, Mar-Apr & Sep-Oct 10-6, May-Aug 10-8. (Closed 25 Dec & 1 Jan).
❋Free. Donations.
P 🍵 ✗ licensed & (wheelchairs available at east/west gates) toilets for disabled shop garden centre ✥

Royal Museum of Scotland (Chambers St)
EDINBURGH
Chambers St
☎0131-225 7534
This magnificent museum houses extensive international collections covering the Decorative Arts, Natural History, Science, Technology and Working Life, and Geology. A lively programme of special events including temporary exhibitions, films, lectures and concerts takes place throughout the year.
Open all year, Mon-Sat 10-5, Sun 12-5. (Closed 25-26 Dec & 1-2 Jan).
Free.
🍵 & toilets for disabled shop ✥

Royal Observatory Visitor Centre
EDINBURGH
Blackford Hill
☎0131-668 8405
The Visitor Centre explains the fascinating world of modern astronomy and the work of Scotland's national observatory. The main exhibition, 'The Universe', takes visitors on a tour of space and time from the present day Solar System to the beginning of it all. Models, 'hands-on' exhibits, videos, computer games and stunning deep-sky photographs explain the latest discoveries about the Universe in simple, everyday language. 'Reaching for the Stars' describes 100 years of work athe Royal Observatory; the 'Star Chamber' is an interactive discovery room where the science important to astronomy is explained. The Visitor Centre rooftop gives panoramic views over the city and the Braid Hills. There is a collection of telescopes and during the dark winter evenings two small telescopes on site are used to give guided visual tours of the night sky. To book a session at the telescopes telephone the observatory.
Open all year, Apr-Sep, daily, 12-5.30; Oct-Mar, Mon-Thu 1-5, Fri 1-9pm, wknds 1-5. Closed 25 Dec & 1 Jan
£2 (ch £1.25). Season ticket £5. Family season ticket £10.
P & (lift) toilets for disabled shop ✥

Scottish National Gallery of Modern Art
EDINBURGH
Belford Rd
☎0131-556 8921
This is the home of the national collection of 20th-century painting, sculpture and graphic art. Among the many modern artists represented are Derain, Picasso, Giacometti, Magritte, Henry Moore, Hepworth and Lichtenstein. There is also the national collection of modern Scottish art, with paintings and sculpture by Peploe, Fergusson, Cadell, Bellany, Paolozzi and Conroy. A programme of temporary exhibitions is planned for 1995. The print room and library are open by appointment.
Open all year, Mon-Sat 10-5 & Sun 2-5. (Extended opening hours during the Festival). (Closed May Day, Xmas & New Year).
Free. Admission charged to some major exhibitions.
P 🍵 & (ramps & lift) toilets for disabled shop ✥

Scottish National Portrait Gallery
EDINBURGH
1 Queen St
☎0131-556 8921
The collection housed within this striking red Victorian building brings Scottish history to life with portraits of royals, rebels, soldiers, scientists, writers and many others, in all media including sculpture. The building also houses the National Collection of Photography. Special events planned for 1995 include: Light from the Dark Room - Scottish Photography (20 July-16 September, dates are provisional).
Open all year, daily, Mon-Sat 10-5, Sun 2-5. (Extended opening hours during the Festival. (Closed May Day, Xmas & New Year).
Free. Admission charged to some major exhibitions.
🍵 & (ramps & lift) toilets for disabled shop ✥

Scottish United Services Museum
EDINBURGH
Edinburgh Castle
☎0131-225 7534
The museum is in Edinburgh Castle.

The Palace of Holyrood House and the rugged hills of Arthur's Seat make a superb vista from Carlton Hill in Edinburgh.

Exhibitions include 'The Story of the Scottish Soldier' and 'For Your Freedom and Ours: Poland, Scotland and World War II'.
Open all year, Apr-Oct, Mon-Sat 9.30-6, Sun 11-6; Nov-Mar, Mon-Sat 9.30-5, Sun 12.30-5.
❋*Free admission after paying entrance fee to the Castle.*
& *toilets for disabled shop* ⌘

Scott Monument
EDINBURGH
East Princes St Gardens, Princes St
☎*0131-529 4068*
Opened in 1846, the 200 foot high, Gothic monument dominates Princes Street. Visitors can climb to the top and enjoy stunning views of the city.
Open Apr-Sep, Mon-Sat 9-6; Oct-Mar, Mon-Sat 9-3; Jun-Sep, Sun 12-5
❋*Admission £1.*
P *shop* ⌘

West Register House
EDINBURGH
Charlotte Square
☎*0131-556 6585*
The former church of St George (1811) was designed by Robert Reid in Greco-Roman style and is now the modern record branch of the Scottish Record Office. It houses the exhibition '800 Years of Scottish History', and the Search Room is available to researchers. From April 1995 onwards there will be an exhibition to mark the centenary of the Scottish Poor Law.
Open Mon-Fri 9-4.45. Exhibitions 10-4. (Closed certain PHs & part of Nov). No charge for historical searches or exhibitions.
& *toilets for disabled* ⌘ ⌘⌘

The Writers' Museum
EDINBURGH
Lady Stair's House, Lady Stair's Close, Lawnmarket
☎*0131-529 4901*
The Writers' Museum is situated in the historic Lady Stair's House which dates from 1622. It is now a museum housing various objects associated with Robert Burns, Sir Walter Scott and Robert Louis Stevenson. Temporary exhibitions are

planned throughout the year.
Open all year, Mon-Sat, Jun-Sep 10-6; Oct-May 10-5. (During Festival period only, Sun 2-5).
Free.
shop ⌘

Suntrap Garden Oatridge College Horticultural Centre
GOGAR
43 Gogarbank (between A8 & A71 W of city bypass)
☎*0131-339 7283 & (01506) 854387*
The three-acre garden comprises of many gardens within a single garden, including Italian, Rock, Rose, Peat and Woodland. Details from the Principal, Oatridge Agricultural College, Ecclesmachan, Broxburn, West Lothian, EH52 6NH. Open day 3 June 10am-5pm, plant sales and refreshments.
Open all year; Apr-Sep, daily 9.30-4.30; Oct-Mar, Mon-Fri 9.30-4.30. Closed 2 weeks Xmas & New Year.
£1 (accompanied ch free).
P & *toilets for disabled garden centre*

Scottish Agricultural Museum
INGLISTON
(at East Gate of Royal Highland Showground)
☎*0131-333 2674*
A fascinating collection illustrating rural Scotland through the ages: the tools and equipment, the workers and their families. Visitors can see the oldest threshing mill in the world, models of the first reaping machines, numerous old photogrphs, interesting folk art and a range of excellent audio-visual presentations.
Open Apr-Sep, daily 10-5; Oct-Mar, Mon-Fri. Closed Xmas & New Year.
Charge for admission to Showground in Jun.
P ⬤ & *toilets for disabled shop*

Inveresk Lodge Garden
INVERESK
☎*(01592) 266566*
With a good deal of appeal, this charming terraced garden specialises in plants, shrubs and roses suitable for growing on small plots. The 17th-century house makes an elegant backdrop.

Open all year, Mon-Fri 10-4.30, Sat-Sun 2-5 (Closed Sat Oct-Mar).
❋*£1*
⌘
(NTS)

Blackness Castle
LINLITHGOW
(4m N)
☎*0131-668 8800*
Once this was one of the most important fortresses in Scotland. Used as a state prison during covenanting time and in the late-19th century as a powder magazine, it was one of four castles left fortified by the Articles of Union. Most impressive are the massive 17th-century artillery emplacements.
Open all year, Apr-Sep, Mon-Sat 9.30-6.30, Sun 2-6.30. Oct-Mar, Mon-Sat 9.30-4.30, Sun 2-4.30. (Closed Thu pm & Fri in winter; 25-26 Dec & 1-3 Jan).
£1.50 (ch 75p, pen £1).
P *shop*
(AM)

House of The Binns
LINLITHGOW
(4m E off A904)
☎*Philpstoun (01506) 834255*
An example of changing architectural tastes from 1612 onwards, the House of The Binns now stands as a Regency-style mansion. It was once a tall, grey, three-storeyed building with small windows and twin turrets; and after additions, reshaping and refacing it has evolved into a pretty U-shaped house, with crenellations and embellished windows. The most outstanding features are the beautiful early 17th-century moulded plaster ceilings inside. This is the historic home of the Dalyell family - General Tam Dalyell raised the Royal Scots Greys here in 1681. There are panoramic views from a site in the grounds.
Open: House, 27 Apr-1 Oct, daily ex Fri, 1.30-5.30 (last admission 5). Parkland, all year, daily 10-7 (last admission 6.30).
❋*£3 (ch & pen £1.50). Party. Members of the Royal Scots Dragoon Guards free when in uniform.*
P & *(braille sheets)* ⌘
(NTS)

Linlithgow Palace
LINLITHGOW
☎*0131-668 8800*
The magnificent ruin of a great Royal Palace, set in its own park or 'peel'. All the Stewart kings lived here, and work commissioned by James I, III, IV, and VI can be seen. The great hall and the chapel are particularly fine. Mary, Queen of Scots was born here in 1542.
Open all year, Apr-Sep, Mon-Sat 9.30-6.30, Sun 2-6.30; Oct-Mar, Mon-Sat 9.30-4.30, Sun 2-4.30. (Closed 25-26 Dec & 1-3 Jan).
£2 (ch 75p, pen £1.25).
P & *shop* ⌘
(AM)

Scottish Mining Museum
NEWTONGRANGE
Lady Victoria Colliery (on A7)
☎*0131-663 7519*
Newtongrange is the largest surviving coal company village in Scotland, and after a working life of almost 90 years, Lady Victoria Colliery is being restored and developed as a museum. An exhibition of talking tableaux in the visitor centre portrays characters involved in the creation of the mine and its day-to-day organisation. The steam winding machine and pit-head can also be visited. Guided tours by a former miner are popular.
Open Apr-Sep, daily 11-4. Last tour 3pm.
P ⬤ & *toilets for disabled shop* ⌘
Details not confirmed for 1995

North Berwick Museum
NORTH BERWICK
School Rd
☎*(01620) 895457*
The former Burgh School contains a museum with sections on natural history, local history, golf, archaeology and domestic life. Exhibitions are held

throughout the summer. In 1995 there will be a special exhibition on the history of radio and TV, and displays on natural history, local history and archaeology.
Open Apr-Sep, daily 11-5.
Free admission.
P *shop* ⌘

Tantallon Castle
NORTH BERWICK
(3m E on A198)
☎*0131-668 8800*
A famous 14th-century stronghold of the Douglases facing towards the lonely Bass Rock from the rocky Firth of Forth shore. Nearby 16th-and 17th-century earthworks.
Open all year, Apr-Sep, Mon-Sat 9.30-6.30, Sun 2-6.30; Oct-Mar, Mon-Sat 9.30-4.30, Sun 2-4.30. (Closed Thu pm & Fri in winter; 25-26 Dec & 1-3 Jan).
£2 (ch 75p, pen £1.25).
P & *shop* ⌘
(AM)

Edinburgh Crystal Visitor Centre
PENICUIK
Eastfield Industrial Estate (on A701)
☎*(01968) 675128*
A tour around the factory allows visitors to see the various stages in the art of glassmaking, including glass blowing, the 'lehr', cutting, polishing, engraving and sand etching. An exhibition and video entitled 'The Story of Edinburgh Crystal' exlains the process further.
Open all year. Factory tours Mon-Fri 9-3.30. Also (Closed 25-27 Dec & 1-2 Jan). Visitor Centre Mon-Sat 9-5, Sun 11-5. Tours £2 (ch 50p, pens £1). Party.
P & *toilets for disabled shop* ⌘ *(ex guide dogs)*

Scottish Mining Museum
PRESTONPANS
Prestongrange (on B1348)
☎*0131-663 7519*
The oldest documented coal mining site in Britain with 800 years of history, this museum shows a Cornish Beam Engine and on-site evidence of associated industries such as brickmaking and pottery, plus a 16th-century customs port. The 'Cutting the Coal' exhibition, in the David Spence Gallery, has an underground gallery, a coalface, a reconstruction of a colliery workshop and a wonderful collection of coal-cutting machines and equipment. There is a guided tour of the site by a former miner.
Open Apr-Sep, daily 11-4. Last tour 3pm.
P ⬤ & *toilets for disabled shop* ⌘
Details not confirmed for 1995

Dalmeny House
SOUTH QUEENSFERRY
☎*0131-331 1888*
This is the home of the Earl and the Countess of Rosebery, whose family have lived here for over 300 years. The house, however, only dates from 1815 when it was built in Tudor Gothic style. There are vaulted corridors and a splendid Gothic hammerbeamed hall, but the main rooms are in classical style. Dalmeny House has a magnificent situation on the Firth of Forth and there are delightful walks in the wooded grounds and along the shore. Inside, it has fine French furniture, tapestries and porcelain from the Rothschild Mentmore collection. Early Scottish furniture is also shown, with 18th-century portraits, Rosebery racing mementoes and a display of pictures and items associated with Napoleon.
Open May-26 Sep, Sun 1-5.30, Mon-Tue 12-5.30. Last admission 4.45.
£3.50 (ch 10-16 £1.80, pen £2.80, students £2.80). Party 20+.
P ⬤ & *toilets for disabled* ⌘ *(ex in grounds)*

Hopetoun House
SOUTH QUEENSFERRY
(2m W of Forth Road Bridge, off B904)
☎*0131-331 2451*
Scotland's greatest Adam mansion is the home of the 4th Marquess of Linlithgow. It was built in 1699 to a design by William

Gutted by fire in 1746 Linlithgow Palace is just a shell surrounding an inner courtyard. The castle was the birthplace of Mary Queen of Scots in 1542.

Bruce, but between 1721 and 1754 it was enlarged by William and Robert Adam. The magnificent reception rooms have notable paintings by artists such as Canaletto, Gainsborough and Raeburn, and there are also fine examples of furniture and a collection of china. A museum in the stables features an exhibition entitled 'Horse and Man in Lowland Scotland'.
The grounds are extensive, and include deer parks with red and fallow deer, and a herd of the rare St Kilda sheep. There are formal gardens as well, and it is possible to play croquet or pétanque for a fee. Walks along the coast give views of the Forth bridges, which can also be seen from a special viewing platform. Facilities include a garden centre, a nature trail and a free Ranger Service. If prior notice is given special arrangements can be made for blind and disabled visitors.
Open 1 Apr-2 Oct, daily 10-5.30 (last admission 4.45).
🅿 ♿ ♿ *toilets for disabled shop garden centre*
Details not confirmed for 1995

Inchcolm Abbey
SOUTH QUEENSFERRY
Inchcolm Island (1.5m S of Aberdour Access by ferry Apr-Sep)
☎0131-668 8800
Situated on a green island on the Firth of Forth, the Augustinian abbey was founded in about 1123 by Alexander I. The well-preserved remains include a fine 13th-century octagonal chapter house and a 13th-century wall painting.
Open Apr-Sep, Mon-Sat 9.30-6.30, Sun 2-6.30.
£2 (ch £1, pen £1.25). Additional charge for ferry trip.
shop ♿
(AM)

Queensferry Museum
SOUTH QUEENSFERRY
53 High St
☎0131-331 5545
The museum tells the story of South Queensferry and its people. It looks at the development of the Queensferry Passage, the growth of the former Royal Burgh and the building of the rail and road bridges which span the Forth. There are displays on the life work and pastimes ofQueensferry people and a life-size model of the Burry Man, a centuries-old custom. There are changing exhibitions and a new hands-on display on the natural history of the Forth is being developed.
Open all year, Mon & Thu-Sat 10-1, 2.15-5 (Sun 2-5).
Free.
P *(0.25m) shop* ♿

STRATHCLYDE

Burn's Cottage
ALLOWAY
(2m S of Ayr)
☎(01292) 441215
Thatched cottage built in 1757, now a museum, birthplace of Robert Burns in 1759. The cottage has recently undergone extensive refurbishment and contains an audio-visual presentation.
Open all year, Jun-Aug 9-6 (Sun 10-6); Apr-May & Sep-Oct 10-5 (Sun 1-5); Nov-Mar 10-4 (Closed Sun).
✳*£2.20 (ch & pen £1.10) includes entry to Burns Monument & Gardens. Family ticket £5.25. Prices under review.*
🅿 ♿ ♿ *toilets for disabled shop*

Burn's Monument
ALLOWAY
(2m S of Ayr)
☎(01292) 441321
Robert Burns was born in the thatched cottage in 1759, two years after it was built. It is now a museum. The monument was built in 1823 to a fine design by Thomas Hamilton Junior, with

sculptures of characters in Burns' poems by a self-taught artist, James Thom.
Open as for **Burns' Cottage** *(ex closed Nov-Mar).*
Admission included in entrance to **Burns' Cottage**
🅿 ♿ *shop*

Arduaine Garden
ARDUAINE
(20m S of Oban, on A816)
☎(01852) 200366
An outstanding 18-acre garden on a promontory bounded by Loch Melfort and the Sound of Jura, climatically favoured by the North Atlantic Drift or Gulf Stream. Nationally noted for rhododendrons and azalea species and other rare trees and shrubs.
Open all year, daily 9.30-sunset.
£2 (concessions £1). Party.
🅿 ♿
(NTS)

Auchindrain Township-Open Air Museum
AUCHINDRAIN
(5.5m SW of Inverary)
☎Furnace (01499) 500235
Auchindrain is an original West Highland township, or village, of great antiquity, and the only communal tenancy township to have survived on its centuries-old site. The township buildings, which have been restored and preserved, are furnished and equipped in the style of various periods to give the visitor a taste of what life was really like for the Highlander in past ages.
Open Apr, Sun-Fri 10-5; May-Sep, daily 10-5.
✳*£2.40 (ch £1.60, pen £1.90). Family ticket £7.40.*
🅿 ♿ *shop*

Maclaurin Art Gallery & Rozelle House
AYR
Rozelle Park, Monument Rd (on B7024)
☎Alloway (01292) 445447 & 443708
A modern art collection in the house and Henry Moore sculptures are permanent fixtures, with art, craft, photography and sculpture all featured in temporary shows. The park has a nature trail and there is a small military museum. A programme of International art exhibitions is planned.
Open all year, Mon-Sat 10-5, Sun (Apr-Oct only) 2-5. (Closed Xmas & New Year).
🅿 ♿ ✗ ♿ *shop* ♿
Details not confirmed for 1995

Balloch Castle Country Park
BALLOCH
☎Alexandria (01389) 758216
Set beside Loch Lomond, the country park spreads over sloping ground with woodland trails, a walled garden, and lawns for picnics giving wonderful views. Overlooking the lawns is Balloch Castle, built in 1808. Its visitor centre gives an introduction to local history and wildlife. An events programme is available in March. The park is part of a larger regional park which covers an area of 170 square miles.
Open Visitor Centre, Apr-Sep daily 10-6. Country Park 8-dusk. Garden 10-6 (4.30 winter).
Free.
🅿 ♿ *toilets for disabled shop*

Sea Life Centre
BARCALDINE
(10m N of Oban on A828)
☎Ledaig (01631) 72386
Set in one of Scotland's most picturesque locations, Oban Sea Life Centre provides dramatic views of native undersea life from stingrays and seals to octopus and catfish. There are daily talks and feeding demonstrations and during the summer young seals can be viewed prior to their release back into the wild. There is a restaurant, gift shop, children's play park, and nature trail.
Open all year, Feb-Nov, daily 9-6. (Jul-Aug 7pm); Dec & Jan, Sat & Sun only.

This magnificent memorial is to Robbie Burns and was built at Alloway in 1823 to commemorate Scotland's most famous poet at his birthplace.

✳*£4.25 (ch £2.95, pen £3.25). Party 10+.*
🅿 ✗ *licensed* ♿ *(assistance available for wheelchairs) toilets for disabled shop* ♿

BARGANY
See Old Dailly

Roman Bath-House
BEARSDEN
Roman Rd
☎0131-668 8800
Considered to be the best surviving visible Roman building in Scotland, the bath-house was discovered in 1973 during excavations for a construction site. It was originally built for use by the Roman garrison at Bearsden Fort, which is part of the Antonine Wall defences.
Open all reasonable times.
Free.
♿ ♿
(AM)

Younger Botanic Garden
BENMORE
(7m N of Dunoon on A815)
☎Sandbanks (01369) 706261 & 840599 (shop)
This is a woodland garden on a grand scale, with many species of conifers and rhododendrons. It became a specialist garden of the Royal Botanic Garden in Edinburgh in the 1930s, but the garden's origins go back much further. The colours are especially good in late spring and early summer, and there are fine views. About half the garden is accessible to the disabled. Wheelchairs are available on loan and there are purpose-built toilets for wheelchair users. The garden is famous for its Redwood Avenue, and has some of the largest conifers in the British Isles. A Ranger Service and Discovery Centre are planned for 1995.
Open 15 Mar-Oct, daily 10-6.
✳*£1.50 (ch 50p, concessions £1).*
🅿 ♿ ♿ *toilets for disabled shop garden centre*

Gladstone Court Museum
BIGGAR
(entrance by 113 High St)
☎(01899) 21050
An old-fashioned village street is portrayed in this museum, which is set out in a century-old coach-house. On display are reconstructed shops, complete with old signs and advertisments; a bank; a telephone exchange; a photographer's booth and other interesting glimpses into the recent past.
Open Etr-Oct, daily 10-12.30 & 2-5, Sun 2-5.
£1.20 (ch 50p, pen £1). Family ticket £3. Party.
🅿 ♿ *shop* ♿

Greenhill Covenanters House
BIGGAR
Burn Braes
☎(01899) 21050
This 17th-century farmhouse was brought, stone by stone, ten miles from Wiston and reconstructed at Biggar. It has relics of the turbulent 'Covenanting' period, when men and women defended the right to worship in Presbyterian style. Rare breeds of sheep and poultry are also kept.
Open Etr-early Oct, daily 2-5.
50p (ch 30p, pen 40p). Family ticket £1.20. Party.
🅿 ♿ *shop* ♿

Moat Park Heritage Centre
BIGGAR
☎(01899) 21050
The centre illustrates the history and geology of the Upper Clyde and Tweed valleys with interesting displays.
Open all year, Apr-Oct, daily 10-5, Sun 2-5; Nov-Feb, weekdays during office hours. Other times by prior arrangement.
£1.50 (ch 80p, pen £1.20). Family ticket £4. Party.
🅿 ♿ *(with assistance) toilets for disabled shop* ♿

David Livingstone Centre
BLANTYRE
165 Station Rd
☎(01698) 823140 ➤

David Livingstone was born in a single-roomed house in Shuttle Row, Blantyre, and the whole row is now an unusual museum. It has displays on the town, and on Livingstone's life and his work in Africa. The story continues in the African Pavilion, which looks at the continent today, and also has a cafe and a shop. The Centre is situated in spacious grounds with riverside walks, an adventure playground and picnic sites. Events are planned for each Sunday afternoon throughout the season; contact the Events Officer for details.
Open mid Jan-mid Dec, Mon-Sat 10-6, Sun 1-6. Last admission 5pm. Other times by arrangement.
P 💺 & *toilets for disabled shop* 🐾 *(ex in grounds)*
Details not confirmed for 1995

Bothwell Castle
BOTHWELL
(approach from Uddingston off B7071)
☎ 0131-668 8800
Besieged, captured and 'knocked about' several times in the Scottish-English wars, the castle is a splendid ruin. Archibald the Grim built the curtain wall; later, in 1786, the Duke of Buccleuch carved graffiti - a coronet and initials - beside a basement well.
Open all year, Apr-Sep, Mon-Sat 9.30-6.30, Sun 2-6.30; Oct-Mar, Mon-Sat 9.30-4.30, Sun 2-4.30. (Closed Thu pm & Fri in winter; also 25-26 Dec & 1-3 Jan). £1.50 (ch 75p, pen £1).
P & *shop*
(AM)

Carnassarie Castle
CARNASSARIE CASTLE
(2m N of Kilmartin off A816)
☎ 0131-668 8800
Built in the 16th-century by John Carswell, first Protestant Bishop of the Isles, the castle was taken and partly destroyed in Argyll's rebellion of 1685. It consists of a tower house with a courtyard built on to it.
Open at all reasonable times.
Free.
P 🐾
(AM)

Summerlee Heritage Trust
COATBRIDGE
West Canal St
☎ (01236) 431261
Summerlee is a major 20-acre museum of social and industrial history centring on the remains of the Summerlee Ironworks which were put into blast in the 1830s. The aim of the Trust is to preserve and interpret the history of the local iron, steel and engineering industries of the communities that depended upon them for a living. The exhibition hall features displays of social and industrial history including working machinery and recreated workshop interiors. Outside, Summerlee operates the only working tram in Scotland, and new exhibits include an underground coalmine and reconstructed miners rows with interiors dating from 1840. The gallery shows regularly changing exhibitions. Special events throughout the year include a Spring Fling with children's entertainment, Historic Vehicle Festival, Circus Activity Week, Models and Hobbies Fair and Hallowe'en Activity Week.
Open daily 10-5pm. (Closed 25-26 Dec & 1-2 Jan).
Free.
P 💺 & *(wheelchair available & staff assistance) toilets for disabled shop* 🐾

Culzean Castle & Country Park
CULZEAN CASTLE
(4m W of Maybole, off A77)
☎ Kirkoswald (01655) 760274 & 760269
The castle and country park together make one of the most popular days out in Scotland. The great 18th-century castle stands on a clifftop site in spacious grounds and was designed by Robert Adam for David, 10th Earl of Cassillis. It is noted for its oval staircase, circular drawing room and plasterwork. The Eisenhower Room explores the general's link with Culzean.
Culzean was Scotland's first country park, and covers 563 acres with a wide range of attractions - shoreline, woodland walks, parkland, an adventure playground, and gardens, including a walled garden of 1783. The visitor centre has various facilities and information, and is also the base of the ranger naturalists who provide guided walks and other services. Many events are held each year, both in the castle and park.
Country park open all year, daily 9.30-sunset. Castle & visitor centre open Apr-22 Oct, 10.30-5.30. Last admission 5pm. Other times by appointment.
❄*Country Park £3, concessions £1.50. Castle £3.50 (concessions £1.80). Combined ticket for castle and country park £5.50 (concessions £3) Party20+*
P *(charged)* 💺 ✗ *licensed* & *(wheelchairs available, lift in castle) toilets for disabled shop garden centre (ex castle)*
(NTS)

Dumbarton Castle
DUMBARTON
☎ 0131-668 8800
The castle is set on the 240ft Dumbarton Rock above the River Clyde, and dominates the town (the capital of the Celtic kingdom of Strathclyde). Most of what can be seen today dates from the 18th and 19th centuries, but there are a few earlier remains, and the rock gives spectacular views.
Open all year, Apr-Sep, Mon-Sat 9.30-6.30, Sun 2-6.30; Oct-Mar, Mon-Sat 9.30-4.30, Sun 2-4.30. (Closed Thu & Fri pm in winter also 25-26 Dec & 1-3 Jan). £1.50 (ch 75p, pen £1).
P *shop* 🐾
(AM)

Achamore Gardens
GIGHA ISLAND
☎ Gigha (01583) 505267 or 505254
The wonderful woodland gardens of rhododendrons and azaleas were created by Sir James Horlick Bt, who bought the little island of Gigha in 1944. Many of the plants were brought in laundry baskets from his former home in Berkshire, and others were added over the following 29 years. Sub-tropical plants flourish in the rich soil and virtually frost-free climate, and there is a walled garden for some of the finer specimens.
Open all year, daily.
£2 (ch £1).
P &

GLASGOW
Glasgow was the second city of the British Empire, a 'dear, dirty city' which was a hub of the Industrial Revolution. Now it is clean, and has become a major attraction for visitors, who are discovering its artistic and architectural riches and its inimitable atmosphere. The biggest surprise for newcomers is the amount of open space in the city, which has over 70 richly varied public parks and several public golf courses. Glasgow Green has been open common land for centuries, but the heyday of the park was in the 19th century, when numerous stretches of land were
bought and laid out for the public. In the heart of the city is the medieval cathedral, close to Provand's Lordship, Glasgow's oldest house, and to an array of splendid Victorian buildings. At the end of the Victorian era, Charles Rennie Mackintosh led the way in making Glasgow a centre for Art Nouveau; his style is epitomised by the Willow Tea Rooms, which are serving tea once more. Mackintosh's home has been reconstructed in the Hunterian Art Gallery, one of Glasgow's impressive galleries and museums. The most astonishing is the Burrell Collection, but there are many others in easy reach of the city centre.

Bellahouston Park
GLASGOW
Ibrox
☎ 0141-427 4224
The park was the site of the Empire Exhibition in 1938, and covers 171 acres only three miles from the city centre. There are sweeping lawns, a sunken garden and a walled garden, a multi-purpose sports centre at the west end and an all-weather athletics track next to it. A Charles Rennie Mackintosh-designed house is under construction. The Glasgow Show will be held here 23-24 July, and the world pipe band championships in August 1994.
Open all year, 8am-dusk.
P 💺 & *toilets for disabled* 🐾 *(ex in park)*
Details not confirmed for 1995

Botanic Gardens
GLASGOW
Queen Margaret Dr, off Great Western Rd
☎ 0141-334 2422
The gardens were established in 1817 from an older university physick garden, and moved to this site in 1842. There is an outstanding plant collection, but the most remarkable feature is the 23,000 sq ft Kibble Palace, a spectacular glasshouse with soaring tree ferns inside, set off by a number of Victorian sculptures. There are more conventional glasshouses too, showing orchids and other exotica. The grounds are laid out with lawns and beds, including a chronological border and a herb garden. At the northern edge the ground slopes down to the River Kibble, which is crossed by footbridges.
The Kibble Palace open 10-4.45 (4.15 in winter).The main glasshouse open Mon-Sat 1-4.45 (4.15 in winter), Sun 12-4.45 (4.15 in winter). Gardens open daily 7-dusk.
& *toilets for disabled* 🐾 *(ex in grounds)*
Details not confirmed for 1995

Burrell Collection
GLASGOW
Pollok Country Park (2m S of city centre)
☎ 0141-649 7151
John Julius Norwich has said that 'in all history, no municipality has ever received from one of its native sons a gift of such munificence'. The Burrell Collection was amassed over some 80 years by Sir William Burrell, who presented it to Glasgow in 1944. It is now beautifully housed in a specially designed gallery, opened by Her Majesty The Queen on 21 October 1983.
Among the 8000 items in the collection are Ancient Egyptian alabaster; Chinese ceramics, bronzes and jade; Japanese prints; Near Eastern rugs and carpets; Turkish pottery; and European medieval art, including metalwork, sculpture, illuminated manuscripts, ivories, and two of the world's best collections of stained glass and tapestries. There are also medieval doorways and windows, now set in the walls of mellow sandstone; British silver and needlework; and paintings and sculptures, ranging from the 15th to the early 20th centuries, with work by Cranach, Bellini, Rembrandt, Millet, Degas, Manet, Cezanne and others. Wise visitors come back more than once, partly because there is too much to see at one go, and partly to revisit their favourite treasures.

Built on a clifftop 150 feet above the sea, Culzean Castle is one of Scotland's finest castles with lavishly furnished public rooms and walled and terraced gardens.

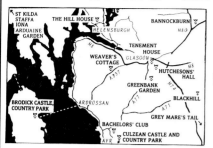
Open all year, Mon-Sat 10-5, Sun 11-5. (Closed 25-26 Dec & 1-2 Jan).
Free.
🅿 *(charged)* ✗ *licensed* & *(wheelchairs available, tape guides for blind) toilets for disabled shop* ⌘

Cathedral
GLASGOW ▮▮▮▮▮▮
Castle St
☎*0131-668 8800*
This is the most complete medieval cathedral surviving on the Scottish mainland. It was founded in the 6th century by St Kentigern, better known as Mungo ('dear one'), Glasgow's patron saint, and dates from the 13th and 14th centuries. The Cathedral was threatened at the time of the Reformation, but the city's trade guilds formed an armed guard to ensure that no damage was done. The choir pews are named after those guilds, and after more modern city organisations which helped with renovation work in the 1950s. The Cathedral is on two levels, and the lower church contains the tomb of St Kentigern, covered by an embroidered cloth. Nearby is the St Kentigern tapestry, presented in the 1970s.
Open all year, Apr-Sep, weekdays 9.30-6.30, Sun 2-6.30; Oct-Mar, weekdays 9.30-4.30, Sun 2-4.30. (Closed 25-26 Dec & 1-3 Jan).
Free.
shop ⌘
(AM)

Glasgow Art Gallery & Museum
GLASGOW ▮▮▮▮▮▮
Kelvingrove (1m W of city centre)
☎*0141-221 9600*
The gallery's extraordinary wealth of pictures includes works by Giorgione and Rembrandt, and is especially strong on the French Impressionists, Post-Impressionists, and Scottish artists from the 17th century to the present day. Other areas show sculpture, porcelain, silver, and a magnificent display of arms

and armour. One section is devoted to the 'Glasgow Style', with furniture by Charles Rennie Mackintosh and others. Archaeology, ethnography and natural history are also featured, and special attention is paid to Scottish wildlife.
Open all year, Mon-Sat 10-5, Sun 11-5. (Closed 25-26 Dec & 1-2 Jan).
Free.
🅿 ✗ *licensed* & *toilets for disabled shop* ⌘

Greenbank Garden
GLASGOW ▮▮▮▮▮▮
Flenders Rd, Clarkston (off B726 on southern outskirts of the city)
☎*0141-639 3281*
The spacious walled and woodland gardens are attractively laid out in the grounds of an elegant Georgian house (not open), and are best seen between April and October. The aim is to help local owners of small gardens, and a very wide range of flowers and shrubs is grown to show what is possible. There is also a garden and greenhouse designed for disabled enthusiasts, with special gardening tools. A programme of the many walks and other events is available on request.
Garden open all year, daily 9.30-sunset. (Closed Xmas & New Year).
✱*£2 (concessions £1). Party.*
🅿 ♨ & *(wheelchairs available) toilets for disabled shop (& plant sales)* ⌘
(NTS)

Haggs Castle
GLASGOW ▮▮▮▮▮▮
100 St Andrews Dr (2m S)
☎*0141-427 2725*
Adults are welcome, but the museum is really meant for children. The house was built in the 1580s, taken over by the Army in World War II, converted into flats and finally transformed into a museum in the 1970s. Children are encouraged to find out its history through worksheets and quizzes, and can explore the house, from the old-style kitchen up to the 17th-

century bedroom and Victorian nursery. The hands-on approach to education extends to weekend and holiday activities, including learning traditional crafts. Regular temporary exhibitions are held.
Open all year, Mon-Sat 10-5, Sun 11-5. (Closed 25 & 26 Dec & 1-2 Jan).
Free.
& *(assistance on request)* ⌘

Hunterian Art Gallery
GLASGOW ▮▮▮▮▮▮
The University of Glasgow
☎*0141-330 5431*
The core of the collection is a group of paintings bequeathed in the 18th century by Dr William Hunter, but it has grown a good deal since his time. There are important works by James McNeill Whistler, an ever-growing collection of 19th-and 20th-century Scottish paintings, contemporary British art and sculpture, and a remarkable re-creation of Charles Rennie Mackintosh's home, including the windows and front door. The print collection has some 15,000 items, from Old Masters to modern, and there is a changing programme of print exhibitions. Special events for 1995 include: Whistler - The Master on Paper (1 July-2 September), Mackintosh Flowers (9 September-4 November), Lutyens Drawings (11 November-13 January).
Open all year. Main gallery Mon-Sat 9.30-5. Mackintosh House Mon-Sat 9.30-12.30 & 1.30-5. Telephone for PH closures.
Free.
🅿 *(500 yds)* & *(lift, wheelchair available) toilets for disabled shop* ⌘

Hunterian Museum
GLASGOW ▮▮▮▮▮▮
The University of Glasgow (2m W of city centre)
☎*0141-330 4221*
The museum is named after the 18th-century physician, Dr William Hunter, who bequeathed his large and important collections of coins, medals, fossils,

geological specimens and archaeological and ethnographic items to the university. Since the museum opened in 1807 there have been many additions, and the emphasis is now on Geology, Archaeology, Coins and Anthropology. The exhibits are shown in the main building of the university, and temporary exhibitions are held. The main exhibtions are Earth....Life - a history of the evolution of our planet and life on it; and Roman Scotland, outpost of an Empire.
Open all year, Mon-Sat 9.30-5. (Closed certain PH's phone for details).
Free.
🅿 *(100yds)* ♨ & *(access by lift, prior arrangement) shop* ⌘

Hutchesons' Hall
GLASGOW ▮▮▮▮▮▮
158 Ingram St
☎*0141-552 8391*
This handsome early 19th-century building was designed by David Hamilton and is now a listed building. There is a visitor centre and a shop. A video about Glasgow's Merchant City is shown daily during July and August.
Open - Visitor centre & Function Hall all year Mon-Fri 9.30-5, Sat 10-4. Shop Mon-Sat, 10-5. (Closed PH's & 24 Dec-9 Jan). Hall on view subject to functions in progress.
Free.
🅿 *(on street)* & *toilets for disabled shop* ⌘
(NTS)

Linn Park
GLASGOW ▮▮▮▮▮▮
Cathcart (southern outskirts of Glasgow).
☎*0141-637 1147*
The park covers 200 acres of hillside by White Cart Water, with riverside and woodland walks, a nature trail, a children's zoo and a collection of British ponies and Highland cattle. The 18-hole golf course is another attraction, and also in the park is a ruined 14th-century castle. Countryside ranger service; ➤

See how we make electricity with a hollow mountain and a fish ladder.

Cruachan

No, this isn't a clever little trick from Blue Peter, but an invitation to visit Cruachan and Tongland, two of our power stations which offer guided tours in the summer months.

Cruachan, set in the rugged grandeur of the Highlands next to Loch Awe, is 15 miles from Oban on the A85. Here you are taken by electric coach deep inside Ben Cruachan, the Hollow Mountain, to the power station turbine hall, where water is drawn down 364 metres from the reservoir above to drive the turbines. Back on the surface there's a Visitor's Centre with a video, display material, shop and a pleasant picnic area.

Tongland

Tongland is near Kirkcudbright in Galloway, Scotland's bonnie south west, and although much smaller than Cruachan, is the largest power station in the Galloway Hydro Scheme. Your tour starts with a video featuring popular radio and TV personality, Jimmie MacGregor, and features a look at Tongland's turbine hall, still producing power 60 years after being commissioned. The impressive dam and fish ladder, set among the tranquil beauty on the Galloway countryside, offer a most enjoyable holiday trip.

For full details call 0186 62 673 for Cruachan and 01557 330114 for Tongland during summer months.

ScottishPower

McLean
MUSEUM & ART GALLERY
Greenock

Displays on local history, James Watt, ship and engine models, maritime collections, big game mounts, ethnography and fine art.

15 Kelly Street, Greenock
Open 10-12, 1-5 MONDAY TO SATURDAY
(closed local and national public holidays)

Admission free

Tel: (01475) 723741
Inverclyde District Council

---

various events. Adventure playground for the disabled adjacent to park (Netherlee Road).
Open all year, daily 7am-dusk.
🅿 & *(some parts of river walkway unsuitable)*
Details not confirmed for 1995

McLellan Galleries
GLASGOW
270 Sauchiehall St
☎0141-331 1854
The McLellan Galleries were officially re-opened on 2nd March 1990 by Her Majesty The Queen, on her visit to inaugurate Glasgow as European Cultural Capital 1990. With over 1,200 sq metres of top gallery space, the McLellan Galleries provide Glasgow Museums with the opportunity to bring to Glasgow major exhibitions and establish Glasgow as Britain's second art city, with a popular and international exhibition programme.
Open Mon-Sat 10-5, Sun 11-5 during exhibitions. For details of 1995 exhibitions please write or telephone. £1-£3 (concessions 50p-£1.50).
P *(500mtrs)* & *(assistance available) toilets for disabled shop* ⚅

Museum of Transport
GLASGOW
Kelvin Hall, 1 Bunhouse Rd (1.5m W)
☎0141-221 9600
The first Museum of Transport was an old tram depot, but in 1988 the collections were handsomely rehoused in Kelvin Hall. The new museum is a feast of nostalgia for older Glaswegians and a fascinating look at the past for younger visitors, with Glasgow buses, a reconstruction of a Glasgow side street in the year 1938, and Glasgow trams (last used in 1962, when they made their way around the city in a grand, final procession). There are Scottish-made cars, fire engines, horse-drawn vehicles, cycles and motorcycles, and a walk-in car showroom with vehicles from the 1930s to the present day. Railways are represented by steam locomotives and a Glasgow subway station; and the already notable collection of ship models has been expanded.
Open all year, Mon-Sat 10-5, Sun 11-5. (Closed 25-26 Dec & 1-2 Jan). Free.
🅿 *(charged)* ✗ *licensed* & *(assistance available) toilets for disabled shop* ⚅

People's Palace
GLASGOW
Glasgow Green (1m SE of city centre)
☎0141-554 0223
This museum looks at the work and leisure of the ordinary people of Glasgow, with exhibits ranging from a 2nd-century Roman bowl to mementoes of the Jacobite risings, football games and boxing matches. Glasgow's trades and industries are illustrated with fine products of the city's potteries, textile mills and foundries; and there is an interesting section on Glasgow's tobacco

---

trade and immensely rich 'Tobacco Lords'. There are also numerous banners, posters and other material from Glasgow's days of campaigning for wider voting rights, votes for women and recognition of trade unions.
Beyond the main museum building is the glass-and-iron expanse of the Winter Gardens, a huge conservatory with tropical plants.
Open all year, Mon-Sat 10-5, Sun 11-5. (Closed 25-26 Dec & 1-2 Jan). Free.
🅿 & *toilets for disabled shop* ⚅

Pollok Country Park
GLASGOW
2060 Pollokshaws Rd
☎0141-632 9299 & 0141-649 0331
The leafy 361-acre park was presented to the city in 1966 by Mrs Anne Maxwell Macdonald, whose family owned the Pollok estates for nearly 700 years. It is home to two major museums, the Burrell Collection and Pollok House, and its many outdoor attractions range from a jogging track to a display rose garden and a demonstration garden. Amateurs are given advice here on a wide range of gardening matters. There are waterside and woodland trails to follow. The Countryside Rangers' Centre gives information on these and on the park's history and wildlife (ranger service available). The park is also home to a championship herd of Highland cattle, which represents the City of Glasgow at agricultural shows around the country.
Open - Park always. Demonstrations & display garden open Mon-Thu 8-4, Fri 8-3, wknds 8-6.30 (winter wknds 8-4pm).
🅿 ✗ & *toilets for disabled shop (at Ranger Centre)*
Details not confirmed for 1995

Pollok House
GLASGOW
(2m S of city centre)
☎0141-632 0274
Given to the city at the same time as the land for Pollok Country Park, the house contains the remarkable Stirling Maxwell collection of Spanish paintings, including works by El Greco, Murillo and Goya. Silver, ceramics and furniture collected by the family over the generations are also on display.
Open all year, Mon-Sat 10-5, Sun 11-5. (Closed 25-26 Dec & 1-2 Jan). Free.
🅿 ⚅ & *shop* ⚅

Provand's Lordship
GLASGOW
3 Castle St (1m E of city centre)
☎0141-552 8819
The Prebend of Provan (see Provan Hall) used this house as his city residence. It was built in 1471 as a manse for the Cathedral and St Nicholas Hospital, and is the city's oldest house. Mary, Queen of Scots is reputed to have stayed here; in Victorian times it was used as an alehouse; in the early 1900s it was a sweet shop; and the city hangman used

---

to live in a lean-to next door (now demolished). The house has been carefully restored and displays furniture, pictures and stained-glass panels from various periods in the city's history. There is a fine collection of 17th-century Scottish furniture, and the machines which made the sweets in the house's sweetshop days can be seen.
Open all year, Mon-Sat 10-5, Sun 11-5. (Closed 25-26 Dec & 1-2 Jan). Free.
P *(50 yds) shop* ⚅

Provan Hall
GLASGOW
Auchinlea Rd
☎0141-771 6372
This 15th-century mansion house has remained virtually unchanged since before the Reformation - a remarkable survivor in a built-up part of Glasgow. Once the country residence of the Prebend of Provan (a canon of Glasgow Cathedral), it stands in Auchinlea Rd, which has formal and informal gardens, including a garden for the blind.
Telephone for opening hours.
🅿 & ⚅ *(ex in grounds)* 🐕
Details not confirmed for 1995

Rouken Glen Park
GLASGOW
Giffnock
☎0141-638 1101
Fine walks can be taken along riverside pathways through the deep, wooded glen, and the waterfall at the head of the glen is a noted beauty spot. The park also offers the pleasures of a large walled garden and spreading lawns, a picturesque loch for boating, a large enclosed children's play area (dog free), an 18-hole pitch and putt course, 'Butterfly Kingdom' and an art gallery.
Open all year, daily. Free.
🅿 ⚅ ✗ *licensed* & *toilets for disabled shop garden centre*

St Mungo Religious Life & Art Museum
GLASGOW
2 Castle St (1m NE)
☎0141-553 2257
This unique museum, opened in 1993, explores the universal themes of life and death and the hereafter through beautiful and evocative art objects associated with different religious faiths. Three galleries focus on art, world religions and religion in Scotland. Britain's only authentic Zen garden contributes its own unique sense of peace.
Open all year, Mon-Sat 10-5, Sun 11-5. Closed 25 & 26 Dec & 1-2 Jan. Free.
🅿 *(charged)* ✗ *licensed* & *(taped information & lift) toilets for disabled shop* ⚅

Tenement House
GLASGOW
145 Buccleuch St, Garnethill (N of Charing Cross)
☎0141-333 0183
This National Trust for Scotland property shows an unsung but once-typical side of Glasgow life: it is a first-floor flat, built in 1892, with a parlour, bedroom, kitchen and bathroom, furnished with the original recess beds, kitchen range, sink, and coal bunker, a rosewood piano and other articles. It was the home of Miss Agnes Toward from 1911 to 1965, and was bought by an actress who carefully preserved its 'time capsule' quality until the Trust acquired and restored it. Today the contents of the flat are interesting for the vivid picture they give of one section of Glasgow society. Two flats on the ground floor provide reception, interpretative and educational facilities.
Open Mar-22 Oct, daily 1.30-5. (Last admission 30 mins before closing).
❄£2 (ch £1). Party (not exceeding 15).
P 100yds ⚅
(NTS)

University of Glasgow Visitor Centre
GLASGOW
University Av
☎0141-330 5511
The University of Glasgow's Visitor Centre is a spacious, pleasant attraction with leaflets, publications and video displays explaining how the university works, what courses are available and which university events are open to the public. It forms the starting point for guided tours of the university's historic attractions, including the Hunterian Museum, Memorial Chapel, Bute and Randolph Halls, Professors' Square, Lion and Unicorn Staircase, and Main Gates.
Open all year, Mon-Sat 9.30-5. Also May-Sep, Sun 2-5. Free.
P *(880yds)* ⚅ & *toilets for disabled shop* ⚅

Victoria Park
GLASGOW
Whiteinch
☎0141-959 2128
Workmen who were digging a path in the park in 1887 came across stone-like tree stumps which turned out to be fossil remains, some 230 million years old. They are the best-known examples, and can be seen in the Fossil Grove building. Elsewhere the park has tree-lined walks, an arboretum and formal beds.
Fossil Grove Building telephone 0141-950 1448 for details.
&
Details not confirmed for 1995

Museum of the Cumbraes
GREAT CUMBRAE ISLAND
MILLPORT
Garrison House
☎(01475) 530741 (Mon-Fri)
The Garrison House was built in 1745 by Captain Crawford as a barracks for his crew of 'The Royal George', a customs ship. It now houses a small museum which displays the history and life of the Cumbraes. Along with artefacts from the collection, the museum displays a major exhibition each summer. There is also a fine collection of local photographs.
Open Jun-Sep, Mon-Sat 11-1 & 1.30-5. Free.
P &

McLean Museum & Art Gallery
GREENOCK
15 Kelly St (close to Greenock West Railway Station)
☎(01475) 723741
James Watt was born in Greenock, and various exhibits connected with him are shown. The museum also has an art collection, and there are displays on shipping (including river paddle steamers and cargo vessels), natural history and ethnography.
Open all year, Mon-Sat 10-noon & 1-5. Closed local & national PH. Free.
P & *(disabled toilet from early 1995) shop* ⚅

Chatelherault
HAMILTON
Ferniegair
☎(01698) 426213
Chatelherault was built by William Adam for the Duke of Hamilton in the 1730's, as a hunting lodge, staff accommodation and kennels. It is set in 500 acres of park containg areas of outstanding natural beauty and nature conservation, as well as physical evidence of land use including mining, quarrying, Cadzow Castle, a possible hillfort, and ancient oak fort and deer park, and a herd of white Cadzow cattle.
Open daily, Visitor Centre 10-5.30 summer, 10.30-4.30 winter; Lodge House 11-4.30 summer, 11-4 winter; Country Park open all year round. Parts may be closed during 1995 for redevelopment. Prices under review.
🅿 ⚅ & *(architect designed for disabled access) toilets for disabled shop garden centre* ⚅ *(ex grounds)*

Hamilton District Museum
HAMILTON
129 Muir St
☎ (01698) 283981
This local history museum is housed in a 17th-century coaching inn complete with its old stables and an 18th-century assembly room. Permanent exhibitions look at the history of the area, the devlopment of the town, industry and agriculture and key local themes, for example the Covenanting period. There is a regular temporary exhibition programme, including exhibition openings, private views etc, along with a programme of musical concerts organised by the local arts guild.
Open - redevelopment under way - Apr, Mon-Sat 10-5 (closed noon-1 on Wed & Sat).
Free.
🅿 ♿ (disabled toilet being built) shop ✍

Hill House
HELENSBURGH
Upper Colquhoun St (off B832, between A82 & A814)
☎ (01436) 673900
The Hill House is a handsome example of Charles Rennie Mackintosh's work, modern but part-inspired by Scottish tower houses. It was commissioned by the publisher Walter Blackie. The gardens are being restored to Blackie's design, with features reflecting the suggestions of Mackintosh. There is also a special display about Mackintosh.
Open Apr-23 Dec, daily 1.30-5.30. Last admission 5pm.
🅿 💷 shop ✍
(NTS)

Hunterston Power Station
HUNTERSTON
☎ West Kilbride (0800) 838557
This is a nuclear power station of the advanced gas-cooled reactor (AGR) type. A purpose-built visitor centre contains exhibits, interactive models, videos, and a lecture theatre. Parties of up to 40 are taken on guided tours of the power station and shown a video presentation on the generation of nuclear power.
Open - Visitors' Centre, daily 9.30-4.30 (Closed Xmas & New Year). Tour times 9.45, 11.15, 1.30 & 3.
❋ *Free. (ch accepted if accompanied by an adult)*
🅿 ♿ (trained guides for visually impaired visitors) toilets for disabled shop ✍

Bell Tower of All Saints' Church
INVERARAY
The Avenue
☎ Inverary (01499) 302259
The tower was built in the 1920s and stands at 126ft. It has the world's second heaviest ring of ten bells, installed as a Campbell War Memorial in 1931. An exhibition on campanology is mounted inside and there are visiting bell ringers who give recitals, usually once a month. A splendid view rewards those who climb to the roof.
Open mid May-Sep, daily 10-1 & 2-5.
❋ £1 (ch & pen 50p).
🅿 ♿ shop ✍

Inveraray Castle
INVERARAY
☎ (01499) 302203
The third Duke of Argyll (the chief of Clan Campbell) engaged Roger Morris to build the present castle in 1743; in the process the old Burgh of Inveraray was demolished and a new town built nearby. The beautiful interior decoration was commissioned by the 5th Duke from Robert Mylne; the great armoury hall and staterooms are of particular note but the furniture, tapestries and paintings throughout are well worth viewing. The gardens are open by appointment.
Open Apr-Jun & Sep-Oct, Sat-Thu, 10-1 & 2-5.30, Sun 1-5.30; Jul-Aug, Mon-Sat 10-5.30, Sun 1-5.30. Last admissions 30 mins before closing.

£3.50 (ch 16 £1.75, pen £2.50). Family ticket £9.
🅿 💷 ♿ shop ✍

Inveraray Jail
INVERARAY
Church Sq
☎ (01499) 302381
Enter Inveraray Jail and step back in time. See furnished cells and experience prison sounds and smells. Ask the 'prisoner' how to pick oakum. Turn the heavy handle of an original crank machine, take 40 winks in a hammock or listen to Matron's tales of day-to-day prison life as she keeps one eye on the nursing mother, barefoot thieves and the lunatic in her care. Visit the magnificent 1820 courtroom, hear trials in progress and imaginative exhibitions including 'Torture, Death and Damnation'.
Open all year, Nov-Mar, daily 10-5 (last admisssion 4); Apr-Oct, daily 9.30-6 (last admission 5pm). (Closed 25 Dec & 1 Jan). Extended hours in summer.
❋ £3.95 (ch £2, pen £2.50). Family ticket £10.90. Party.
🅿 (100 yds) ♿ toilets for disabled shop

Glasgow Vennel Museum & Burns Heckling Shop
IRVINE
10 Glasgow Vennel
☎ (01294) 275059
The Glasgow Vennel Museum has a reputation for exciting and varied exhibitions, ranging from international artists to local school groups. Behind the museum is the Heckling Shop where Robert Burns, Scotland's most famous poet, spent part of his youth learning the trade of flax dressing. In addition to the audio-visual programme on Burns, there is a reconstruction of his lodgings at No.4.
Open all year - Jun-Sep, Mon-Sat 10-5, Sun 2-5 (Closed Wed); Oct-May, Tue, Thu-Sat 10-5. Closed for lunch 1-2.
Free.
🅿 ♿

Scottish Maritime Museum
IRVINE
Harbour St
☎ (01294) 278283
The museum has displays which reflect all aspects of Scottish maritime history. Vessels can be seen afloat in the harbour and undercover. A 1910 tenement house shows a shipyard worker's house. The Irvine Harbour Festival takes place 21-23 July and there will be boat jumbles on the first Sunday in May and October.
Open Apr-Oct, daily 10-5.
£2 (ch & pen £1). Family ticket £4.
🅿 💷 ♿ shop ✍

Weaver's Cottage
KILBARCHAN
Shuttle St, The Cross (off A737)
☎ (01505) 705588
Together with a fascinating display of weaving equipment, occasional demonstrations of the craft are given in this characterful museum. Also displayed in the 18th-century weaver's cottage is a collection of early domestic utensils.
Open Good Fri-30 Sep, daily, 1.30-5.30; 1-22 Oct, Sat & Sun 1.30-5.30 (last admission 5).
❋ £1.50 (ch 80p). Party.
✍
(NTS)

Dean Castle
KILMARNOCK
Dean Rd
☎ (01563) 26401 ext 136 & 22702
This fine castle has a 14th-century fortified keep and 15th-century palace, and is the ancestral home of the Boyd family. The restoration work which has taken place shows the building in almost its original splendour, and inside there is an outstanding collection of medieval arms and armour, musical instruments and tapestries and a display of Burns' manuscripts. The castle is set in a beautiful wooded country park with rivers, gardens, woodlands, adventure

playground, children's corner and aviaries.
Open all year, daily noon-5. (Closed 25-26 Dec & 1-2 Jan).
🅿 💺 ⛶ *(special disabled garden) toilets for disabled shop* ⚘ *(ex in grounds)*
Details not confirmed for 1995

Dick Institute
KILMARNOCK
Elmbank Ave
☎(01563) 26401
Museum exhibiting geology, natural history, engineering, archaeology and local history. Newly modernised art gallery with an important permanent collection of paintings and touring exhibitions of prints, photography and crafts. Works by contemporary artists often for sale.
Open all year, Gallery: Mon, Tue, Thu & Fri 10-8, Wed & Sat 10-5. Museum: May-Sep, Mon, Tue, Thu & Fri 10-8, Wed & Sat 10-5; Oct-Apr Mon-Sat 10-5.
🅿 ⛶ *toilets for disabled shop* ⚘
Details not confirmed for 1995

Dunadd Fort
KILMARTIN
(1m W of Kilmichael Glassary)
☎0131-668 8800
Dunadd was one of the ancient capitals of Dalriada from which the Celtic kingdom of Scotland was formed. Near to this prehistoric hill fort (now little more than an isolated hillock) are carvings of a boar and a footprint; these probably marked the spot where early kings were invested with their royal power.
Open & accessible at all reasonable times.
Free.
⚘
(AM)

Kilmun Hill: Arboretum & Forest Walks
KILMUN
(on A880 1m from junc with A815)
☎(01369) 840666
The Argyll Forest Park extends over a large area of hill ground and forest, noted for its rugged beauty. Numerous forest walks and picnic sites allow the forest to be explored in detail. The Arboretum walks and the route from the Younger Botanic Gardens to Packs Glen are of special scenic quality; a series of guided walks within the forest park is planned; contact the above address for details.
Open all year.
Free.
🅿 Y⛶

Colzium House & Estate
KILSYTH
Colzium-Lennox Estate (on A803)
☎(01236) 823281
The old castle was associated with Montrose's victory over the Covenanters

in 1645; the museum, courtyard, ice-house and walled garden make interesting viewing and the grounds include a children's zoo and forest walks.
Open - House Etr wknd-Sep wknd, Mon-Fri, 9-5 & Sun, 10-6. (Closed when booked for private functions). Grounds open at all times. Museum open Wed 2-8.
Free.
🅿 💺 ⛶

Souter Johnnie's Cottage
KIRKOSWALD
Main St (on A77)
☎(01655) 760603 or 760274
'Souter' means cobbler and the village cobbler who lived in this 18th-century cottage was the inspiration for Burns' character Souter Johnnie, in his ballad *Tam o'Shanter*. The cottage is now a Burns' museum and life-size stone figures of the poet's characters can be seen in the restored ale-house in the cottage garden.
Open Good Fri-Sep daily. Apr-22 Oct, Sat & Sun only. 1.30-5.30. Last admission 5pm.
❄£1.50 (ch & pen 80p). Party.
P (75yds) ⛶ ⚘
(NTS)

Finlaystone Country Estate
LANGBANK
(1m W on A8)
☎(01475) 540285 & 540505
A charming exhibition of Victoriana and an international collection of dolls, are displayed in a homely family house with historical connections to John Knox and Robert Burns. The house, though, is only a foil to the considerable natural beauty; most visitors to Finlaystone are drawn by the formal gardens, walled gardens, woodland walks and adventure playgrounds. Disabled visitors will enjoy the small scented garden. There are purpose-built toilets for wheelchair users in the visitor centre; and a lift to second floor in the Mansion House. A Celtic Craft Fair is planned for 2-3 September 1995.
Open all year. Woodland & Gardens daily, 10-5. House, open wknds Apr-Aug or by appointment.
❄*Garden & Woods £1.50 (ch & pen £1); House, Victorian Kitchen only, 90p (ch 40p). Guided tour of house (Sun only), £1.40 (ch £1).*
🅿 ⛶ *(lift to second floor) toilets for disabled shop*

Kelburn Country Centre
LARGS
(2m S off A78)
☎Fairlie (01475) 568685
Eighteenth-century farm buildings have been neatly converted here to resemble a village square, with craft shops, workshops, display rooms, special exhibitions, cafe and restaurant. The

setting is the historic estate of the Earls of Glasgow, which also provides the visitor with beautiful gardens and magnificent scenery. The most famous part of the estate is Kelburn Glen, areas of which are still in a wild state, with waterfalls and pools. There are also rare trees, nature trails, a pets' corner, pony-trekking centre and adventure playgrounds. For those looking for some real action, there is a Marine Commando assault course and various special events during the year, including a Woodcraft and Forestry Fair (29 April-1 May), Noah's Ark Carnival (21 May), Viking Day (3 September).
Open all year, Etr-Oct, daily 10-6; Nov-Mar, daily 11-5.
£3.50 (concessions £2). Low season £1.75 (concessions £1).
🅿 💺 ✕ *licensed* ⛶ *(Ranger service to assist disabled) shop*

Cruachan Power Station
LOCHAWE
(3m W off A85, near Pass of Brander)
☎Taynuilt (018662) 673 due to change to (01866) 822673
A vast cavern inside Ben Cruachan contains a 400,000-kilowatt hydro-electric power station which is driven by water drawn from a high-level reservoir up the mountain. A guided minibus tour starts from the visitor centre which also provides fascinating displays on the site. The picnic area gives spectacular views.
Open late Mar-late Oct, daily 9-4.30.
❄£1.80 (ch 8-16 50p).
🅿 💺 ⛶ *toilets for disabled shop* ⚘

Lochwinnoch Community Museum
LOCHWINNOCH
High St
☎(01505) 842615
Local agriculture, industry and village life are reflected in the series of changing exhibitions displayed in this enterprising museum. There is an annual art exhibition and occasional special exhibitions based on the district's varied collections.
Open all year, Mon, Wed & Fri 10-1, 2-5 & 6-8; Tue & Sat 10-1 & 2-5. (Closed public holidays).
Free.
🅿 ⛶ ⚘

RSPB Nature Centre
LOCHWINNOCH
Largs Rd (on A760)
☎(01505) 842663
An attractive Norwegian timber building in the Lochwinnoch Nature Reserve, incorporating an observation tower offering fine views of the reserve and the surrounding countryside, an RSPB shop, and an exhibition and lecture room with a video system and displays. A nature trail leads from the centre, through deciduous woodland to two observation hides. An

attractive second trail, featuring a boardwalk across the marsh, leads from the centre to a third birdwatching hide; this one has been designed specifically for the convenience of disabled visitors.
Open all year, daily 10-5. (Closed Xmas, New Year & BH's).
£2 (ch 50p).
🅿 💺 ⛶ *(wheelchairs available, access one hide) toilets for disabled shop* ⚘

Crossraguel Abbey
MAYBOLE
(2m S)
☎0131-668 8800
The extensive remains of this 13th-century Cluniac monastery are impressive and architecturally important. The monastery was founded by Duncan, Earl of Carrick and the church, claustral buildings, abbot's house and an imposing castellated gatehouse can be seen.
Open Apr-Sep, Mon-Sat 9.30-6.30, Sun 2-6.30.
£1.20 (ch & pen 75p).
🅿 ⛶ *shop* ⚘
(AM)

Crarae Gardens
MINARD
☎(01546) 86614 & 86388
Set in a Highland Glen beside Loch Fyne, these gardens are among Scotland's loveliest. They are noted for their rhododendrons, azaleas, conifers and ornamental shrubs, which include a number of rare species.
Open all year, daily, summer 9-6; winter during daylight hours. Visitor centre, Etr-Oct 10-5.
£2.50 (ch £1.50). Family ticket £7.50.
🅿 💺 ⛶ *toilets for disabled shop*

Dunstaffnage Castle
OBAN
(3m N on peninsula)
☎0131-668 8800
Now ruined, this four-sided stronghold has a gatehouse, two round towers and walls 10ft thick. It was once the prison of Flora MacDonald.
Open Apr-Sep, Mon-Sat 9.30-6.30, Sun 2-6.30.
£1.50 (ch 75p, pen £1).
🅿 shop
(AM)

Oban Glass Studio
OBAN
Heritage Wharf, Railway Pier
☎(01631) 63386
Visitors can watch the art of making paperweights here, and also purchase both perfect and slightly imperfect paperweights and glassware in the shop which stocks a wide range to choose from.
Open all year, Factory Shop: Mon-Sat 9-5 (later Jun-Sep), also Etr-Oct, Sun 11-5. Glassmaking Mon-Fri 9-5.
P (100yds) 💺 ⛶ *shop* ⚘
Details not confirmed for 1995

Bargany Gardens
OLD DAILLY
Girvan (4m NE on B734 from Girvan)
☎(01465) 871249
Woodland walks display snowdrops, daffodils and blubells in spring, and a fine show of azaleas and rhododendrons is to be seen around the lilypond in May and June. Ornamental trees give autumn colour, and visitors can buy plants from the gardens.
Open Gardens Mar-Oct, daily 7pm (or dusk).
❄*Contribution Box.*
🅿 ⛶

Coats Observatory
PAISLEY
49 Oakshaw St West
☎0141-889 2013
Astronomy, meteorology and space flight, along with the history of the building, are the subjects of displays on show in this observatory built in 1883. Recent renovations have installed modern technology, and the observatory has resumed an important role in ➤

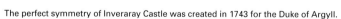
The perfect symmetry of Inveraray Castle was created in 1743 for the Duke of Argyll.

astronomy and meteorology.
Open all year, Mon, Tue & Thu 2-8, Wed, Fri & Sat 10-5. Oct-Mar Thu 7-9 weather permitting. (Closed Xmas & New Year).
Free.
shop ✤

Paisley Museum & Art Galleries
PAISLEY
High St
☎0141-889 3151
Pride of place here is given to a world-famous collection of Paisley shawls. Other collections illustrate local industrial and natural history, while the emphasis of the art gallery is on 19th-century Scottish artists. There is also a study centre for studio ceramics.
Open all year, Mon-Sat 10-5. (Closed PH).
✤*Free.*
🅿 ♿ *toilets for disabled shop* ✤

Newark Castle
PORT GLASGOW
☎0131-668 8800
The one-time house of the Maxwells, dating from the 15th and 17th centuries. The courtyard and hall are preserved. Fine turrets and the remains of painted ceilings can be seen, and the hall carries an inscription of 1597.
Open Apr-Sep, Mon-Sat 9.30-6.30, Sun 2-6.30.
£1.50 (ch 75p, pen £1).
🅿 *shop*
(AM)

North Ayrshire Museum
SALTCOATS
Manse St, Kirkgate
☎(01294) 464174
This museum is housed in a prime example of mid-18th-century Scottish church architecture. On display is a rich variety of artefacts from the North Ayrshire area, including archaeological and social history material. The museum also houses a fine collection of Ayrshire Whitework, a town hall clock and a recreation of a turn-of-the-century kitchen. There is a continuing programme of temporary exhibitions.
Open all year, Mon-Sat (ex Wed) 10-1 & 2-5.
Free.
P (75 yds) ♿ *toilets for disabled* ✤

Bachelors' Club
TARBOLTON
Sandgate St (on B744, 7.5m NE of Ayr)
☎(01292) 541940
In this 17th-century thatched house, Robert Burns and his friends formed a debating club in 1780. Burns attended dancing lessons and was initiated into freemasonry here in 1781. The house is furnished in the period.
Open 14 Apr-Sep, daily 1.30-5.30; 1-22 Oct, wknds 1.30-5.30.
£1.50 (concessions 80p). Party.
P ✤ 🚻
(NTS)

Bonawe Iron Furnace
TAYNUILT
(0.75m NE off B845)
☎0131-668 8800
The furnace is a restored charcoal blast-furnace for iron-smelting and making cast-iron. It was established in 1753 and worked until 1876. The most complete furnace and ancillary buildings in Britain, the works exploited the Forest of Lorne to provide charcoal for fuel.
Open Apr-Sep, Mon-Sat 9.30-6.30, Sun 2-6.30.
£2 (ch 75p, pen £1.25).
🅿 ♿ *toilets for disabled shop*
(AM)

Glasgow Zoopark
UDDINGSTON
Calderpark
☎0141-771 1185
The developing, open-plan zoo has birds, mammals and reptiles housed in spacious new enclosures and buildings. There are many rare animals and the zoo's specialities are cats and reptiles. Other attractions include ample picnic

Blair Atholl was the last castle in Britain to be besieged. The tower named after the first owner, Cummings, was damaged during a Jacobite seige in 1746.

sites, children's farm and seasonal displays.
Open all year, daily 10-5 (or 6pm depending on season).
✤*£3.95 (ch, students, pen & UB40 £2.30). Family ticket £10.30. Party 16+.*
🅿 🍴 ♿ *(wheelchairs available) toilets for disabled shop* ✤

Arbroath Abbey
ARBROATH
☎0131-668 8800
The 'Declaration of Arbroath' - declaring Robert the Bruce as king - was signed at the 12th-century abbey on 6 April 1320. The abbot's house is well preserved, and the church remains are also interesting.
Open all year, Apr-Sep, Mon-Sat 9.30-6.30, Sun 2-6.30; Oct-Mar, Mon-Sat 9.30-4.30, Sun 2-4.30. (Closed 25-26 Dec & 1-3 Jan)
£1.20 (ch & pen 75p).
🅿 ♿ *shop* ✤
(AM)

Arbroath Museum
ARBROATH
Signal Tower, Ladyloan (On A92)
☎(01241) 875598
Fish and Arbroath Smokies, textiles and engineering feature at this local history museum housed in the 1813 shore station of Stevenson's Bell Rock lighthouse. Other displays include maritime wildlife, school days, and a wash house and parlour with a wailing baby and a cat.
Open all year, Mon-Sat 10-5.
Free.
🅿 ♿ *shop* ✤

Barry Mill
BARRY
(2m NW of Carnoustie)
☎(01241) 856761
This restored 18th-century mill works on a demonstration basis. Records show that the site has been used for milling since at least the 16th century. Displays

highlight the important place the mill held in the community, milling and supplying oats for all the local farms. Waymarked

walk and picnic area.
Open Good Fri-Sep, daily 11-5; 1-22 Oct, Sat & Sun only 11-5.

✹£1.50 (ch 80p). Party
🅿 ♿ ramp from car park to mill toilets for disabled (grounds only)
(NTS)

Atholl Country Collection
BLAIR ATHOLL ▰
The Old School
☎(01796) 481232
Artefacts and photographs illustrate local life and trades from 1850 onwards. Displays include a crofter's kitchen, a 'smiddy' (smithy), dress, a byre (with stuffed Highland cow), a gamekeeper's corner, road, rail and postal communications, the church and school. There is a Kiddies' Kist, where everything can be lifted up and examined.
Open end May-mid Oct 1.30-5.30 also from 9.30am Jun-Aug & Sep weekdays.
£1.50 (ch 75p).
🅿 ♿ toilets for disabled shop

Blair Castle
BLAIR ATHOLL ▰
(7m NW of Pitlochry, off A9)
☎(01796) 481207
Home of the Duke of Atholl, chief of the Murrays, and his unique private army, the Atholl Highlanders. The castle dates back to the 13th century but was altered in the 18th century and later given a castellated exterior. The oldest part is Cumming's Tower, built in about 1270. There are 32 rooms open to the public, with paintings, Jacobite relics, lace, tapestries, china, arms and armour, and Masonic regalia to be seen. The extensive grounds include a deer park, and visitors may follow nature trails or go pony trekking. Numerous events are held throughout the year, including the annual parade of the Duke's Private Army (27 May), Highland Games (28 May), a Charity Day (6 July), and the Glenfiddich Piping Championships (28 October).
Open Apr-27 Oct, daily 10-6. Last entry 5pm.
£5 (ch & pen £4). Family ticket £14. Party.
🅿 ♨ ✗ licensed ♿ (toilets, but not suitable for severely disabled) shop (ex in grounds)

Clan Donnachaidh (Robertson) Museum
BRUAR ▰
☎Calvine (01796) 483264
Robes, uniforms, weapons, silver, glass, books and pictures associated with the clan are shown. The Battle of Bannockburn and the Jacobite risings are also featured.
Open Apr-Oct, Mon-Sat 10-1 & 2-5, Sun 2-5. Other times by arrangement. (Closed on Tue.)
£1 (ch 50p)
🅿 ♿ shop

Scottish Tartans Museum
COMRIE ▰
Drummond St (A85 town centre)
☎(01764) 70779
Just about every aspect of tartan is covered here. There are details of nearly 2,200 tartans, with over 450 tartans on display, and the period costume room shows costumes and artefacts from the early 18th century to the present day. At the rear is a reconstructed weaver's cottage and a dye-plant garden, which grows the plants which were traditionally used to dye the wool for tartans. The Scottish Tartans Society can also offer a research service into surnames associated with clans or tartans. Children's corner. There are also spinning demonstrations every weekday afternoon during the summer months.
Open Mar-Oct, Mon-Fri, 10.30-5.30. Nov-Dec week days only. Jan & Feb by appointment only.
P (500yds) ♿ also shop
Details not confirmed for 1995

Glenturret Distillery
CRIEFF ▰
The Hosh (1.5m NW off A85)
☎(10764) 656565
The distillery dates from 1775 and is the

oldest in Scotland. It uses the pure water of the Turret Burn to make award-winning whiskies, sold at twelve, fifteen and twenty-one years of age.
Open Mar-Dec, Mon-Sat 9.30-6 (last tour 4.30), Sun 12-6 (last tour 4.30), Mon-Fri 11.30-4 (last tour 2.30).
🅿 ✗ licensed ♿ toilets for disabled shop
Details not confirmed for 1995

Innerpeffray Library
CRIEFF ▰
(4.5m SE on B8062)
☎(01764) 652819
This is Scotland's oldest free lending library. It was founded in 1691 and is still open every day except Thursdays. It is housed in a late-18th-century building which is interesting in itself, and contains a notable collection of bibles and rare books. Adjacent is St Mary's Chapel, the original site for the library and the Drummond family burial place.
Open all year, Mon-Wed & Fri-Sat 10-12.45 & 2-4.45, Sun 2-4. (Closed Thu.)
✹£1.50 (ch 10p, pen £1)
🅿 ♨ shop

Barrack Street Natural History Museum
DUNDEE ▰
Barrack St
☎(01382) 432020
Displays on Scottish wildlife of the Lowlands and Highlands are shown, including the skeleton of the Great Tay whale. A major gallery for changing art exhibitions explores nature and environmental themes. Head for the Hills, an exhibition on upland areas, habitats and conservation, is on the ground floor.
Open all year, Mon 11-5, Tue-Sat 10-5. (Closed 25-26 Dec & 1-3 Jan).
Free.
P (NCP 500 yds) shop

Broughty Castle Museum
DUNDEE ▰
Broughty Ferry (4m E, off A930)
☎(01382) 776121
The 15th-century castle was rebuilt to defend the estuary in the 19th century. It now houses displays on Dundee's whaling history, a major industry for Dundee, which built most of Britain's whaling ships. Other sections display arms and armour, local history and seashore life. There are superb views across the Tay estuary from the observation room.
Open all year, Mon 11-1 & 2-5, Tue-Thu 10-1 & 2-5. (Sun.2-5 Jul-Sep only). (Closed 25-26 Dec & 1-3 Jan).
Free.
🅿 shop

Camperdown Country Park
DUNDEE ▰
(signposted off A90)
☎(01382) 434296
The 19th-century mansion of Camperdown House was built for the son of Admiral Lord Duncan, who defeated the Dutch at the Battle of Camperdown in 1797. The house is set in nearly 400 acres of fine parkland with a wide variety of trees, some of them rare. Most notable is the Camperdown elm, a weeping form of wych-elm. The park also offers attractions such as a golf course, a wildlife centre with a big collection of native and domestic animals, and an award-winning adventure play area with the Battle of Camperdown as its theme. There is an extensive network of footpaths and forest trails to follow, and the house itself has a restaurant and function area. The Countryside Ranger service is based in the Park. They are available for environmental projects and interpreting the Park. They also organise various events and walks and have a Ranger Centre in Templeton Woods. There is a playground designed for the disabled and able-bodied. Special events for 1995 include: The Dundee Flower Show - including craft and food fairs and trade stands (1-3 September).

Open all year - park. Wildlife Centre - daily, Apr-Sep 10-3.45, Oct-Mar 10-2.45. Park free. Wildlife Centre £1.10 (ch & pen 80p, under 3 free). Party 12+.
🅿 ♨ ✗ ♿ toilets for disabled shop in Wild Life Centre

Discovery Point
DUNDEE ▰
Discovery Quay
☎(01382) 201245
Discovery Point is the new home of *RRS Discovery*, Captain Scott's famous Antartic ship. Within the £6 million complex there are eight exhibition areas. Spectacular lighting, graphics and special effects re-create key moments in the *Discovery* story, including Locked in Ice, a dramatic presentation on three giant screens showing how Scott and his men adapted to their harsh environment, culminating in *Discovery* being blasted free from the crushing pack ice. The ship has been extensively restored below decks.
Open all year, 28 Mar-Oct, Mon-Sat 10-5, Sun 11-5; Nov-27 Mar, last admission 4pm.
✹£4 (concessions £2.90)
🅿 (charged) ♨ ♿ (in-house wheelchairs & lifts) toilets for disabled shop

HM Frigate Unicorn
DUNDEE ▰
Victoria Dock (on north side of Tay Road Bridge)
☎(01382) 200900
The *Unicorn* is the oldest British warship still afloat, and is Scotland's only example of a wooden warship. Today she makes an apt setting for a fascinating museum of life in the Royal Navy during the days of sail, with guns, models and displays.
Open all year, daily 10-5. Closed 25 Dec & 1 Jan.
£3 (concessions £2). Party.
🅿 ♨ ♿ shop (no exceptions)

McManus Galleries Museum
DUNDEE ▰
Albert Square (off A85)
☎(01382) 432020
A resplendent Victorian building in the city centre is the home of Dundee's main

museum. It has collections of silver, ceramics, glass and furniture, and displays on local archaeology, civic and social history, trades and industries. The major art gallery has an important collection of Scottish and Victorian works of art, and touring exhibitions are a regular feature.
Open all year, Mon 11-5, Tue-Sat 10-5. (Closed 25-26 Dec & 1-3 Jan).
Free.
P (100 yds) ♿ (wheelchair available & high arm chairs) toilets for disabled shop

Mills Observatory
DUNDEE ▰
Balgay Park, Glamis Rd
☎(01382) 667138
The observatory was built in 1935, and has a Victorian 10in Cooke refracting telescope among its instruments. The gallery has displays on astronomy and space exploration. There is a small planetarium for booked groups only. Open nights during the winter months, children's activities during the summer holidays.
Open all year, Apr-Sep, Tue-Fri 10-5, Sat 2-5; Oct-Mar, Tue-Fri 3-10, Sat 2-5. (Closed 25-26 Dec & 1-3 Jan).
Free.
🅿 shop

Little Houses
DUNKELD ▰
The Cross (off A9, 15m N of Perth)
☎(01350) 727460 & 728641
The National Trust for Scotland owns two rows of 20 houses in Dunkeld, and has brought them up to modern standards without destroying their character. Most were built after the Battle of Dunkeld in 1689. The houses are let, and therefore not open to the public. There is a Trust display and audio-visual show in the tourist information centre.
Open Ell Shop Apr-Sep, Mon-Sat 10-5.30, also Sun Jun-Aug 1.30-5.30; Oct-23 Dec, Mon-Sat 10-4.30. (Closed 30 Oct-5 Nov). Exterior of houses can be viewed all year.
Free.
P (300yds) shop
(NTS)

Now moored at Victoria Dock in Dundee the *Unicorn* is the oldest British warship.

Edzell Castle
EDZELL

(on B966)

☎0131-668 8800

The 16th-century castle has a remarkable walled garden built in 1604 by Sir David Lindsay. Flower-filled recesses in the walls are alternated with heraldic and symbolic sculptures of a sort not seen elsewhere in Scotland, with niches for birds to nest in above. There are ornamental and border gardens and a garden house.
Open all year, Apr-Sep, Mon-Sat 9.30-6.30, Sun 2-6.30; Oct-Mar, Mon-Sat 9.30-4.30, Sun 2-4.30. (Closed Thu pm & Fri in winter; 25-26 Dec & 1-3 Jan).
£2 (ch 75p, pen £1.25).
🅿 & *toilets for disabled shop garden centre*
(AM)

Angus Folk Museum
GLAMIS

Kirkwynd Cottages (off A94, in Glamis)

☎(01307) 840288

A row of stone-roofed, early 19th-century cottages now houses the splendid Angus Folk Collection of domestic equipment and cottage furniture. Across the wynd, an Angus stone steading houses The Life on the Land Exhibition.
Open Good Fri-2 Oct, daily 11-5. (Last admission 4.30pm). 1-22 Oct, Sat & Sun only 11-5.
❋*£2 (ch £1).*
🅿 & *toilets for disabled shop* ✲
(NTS)

Glamis Castle
GLAMIS

(5m W of Forfar on A94)

☎(01307) 840242 & 840393

The splendid, turreted and battlemented castle was the family home of the Earls of Strathmore, and was the childhood home of HM The Queen Mother. The present castle dates from the 15th century, but there is known to have been a building here for many centuries. One of the oldest parts is known as Duncan's Hall, a reminder of the murder of King Duncan in Shakespeare's *Macbeth* ('All hail, Macbeth! hail to thee, Thane of Glamis!'). Other noteworthy rooms are the chapel with its painted panels, and the drawing room. There are fine collections of china, pictures, tapestries

and furniture, and the grounds can also be explored. Various events during the summer, including Strathmore Vehicle Vintage Club Extravaganza, 16 July, Grand Scottish Promenade Outdoor Concert (22 July).
Open Apr-30 Oct 10.30-5.30. Last admission 4.45pm. Other times by prior appointment.
Castle & grounds £4.50 (ch £2.40, pen & students £3.50). Grounds only £2.20 (ch & pen £1.10).
🅿 ✗ *licensed* & *toilets for disabled shop* ✲ *(ex in grounds)*

Glengoulandie Deer Park
GLENGOULANDIE DEER PARK

(8m NW of Aberfeldy on B846).

☎Kenmore (01887) 830509 & 830261

Various native birds and animals are kept in surroundings as similar to their natural environment as possible, and there are herds of red deer and Highland cattle. Pets must not be allowed out of cars.
Open Apr-Oct, 9am-1hr before sunset.
❋*95p. Cars £3.50*
🅿 *shop* ✲

Killiecrankie Visitor Centre
KILLIECRANKIE

(3m N of Pitlochry on A9)

☎Pitlochry (01796) 473233

The visitors' centre at this historic spot features an exhibition illustrating the battle that took place near here in 1689; there are also displays on the natural history of the area and ranger services. The battle site was where the Jacobite army, led by 'Bonnie Dundee' (who was mortally wounded in the attack) routed King William's troops. The wooded gorge is a notable beauty spot admired by Queen Victoria, and there are some splendid walks.
Open Visitor Centre, Exhibition, shop & snack bar Good Fri-23 Oct, daily 10-5.30. Site all year daily.
❋*£1 (ch free). Includes car park toilets, exhibitions & walks.*
🅿 *(charged)* 🍵 *shop*
(NTS)

Kinross House Gardens
KINROSS

☎(01577) 63467

Yew hedges, roses and herbaceous borders are the elegant attractions of these formal gardens. The 17th-century house was built by Sir William Bruce, but

is not generally open to the public.
Gardens only open May-Sep, daily 10-7.
❋*£2 (ch 50p).*
🅿 & ✲

Loch Leven Castle
KINROSS

Castle Island

☎0131-668 8800

Mary Queen of Scots was imprisoned here in this five-storey castle in 1567 - she escaped 11 months later and gave the 14th-century castle its special place in history.
Open Apr-Sep, Mon-Sat 9.30-6.30, Sun 2-6.30.
£2 (ch 75p, pen £1.25).
🅿 *shop* ✲
(AM)

Barrie's Birthplace
KIRRIEMUIR

9 Brechin Rd (on A926)

☎(01575) 572646

The creator of Peter Pan, Sir James Barrie, was born in Kirriemuir in 1860. The upper floors of No 9 Brechin Road are furnished as they may have been when Barrie lived there, and the adjacent house, No 11, houses a new exhibition about his literary and theatrical works. The wash-house outside was his first 'theatre' and gave him the idea for Wendy's house in 'Peter Pan'.
Open Good Fri-Sep, Mon-Sat 11-5.30 & Sun 1.30-5.30; 1-22 Oct Sat & Sun only. Last admission 5pm.
❋*£1.50 (ch & pen 80p). Party 20+.*
P *(100yds)* 🍵 & *shop* ✲
(NTS)

Burleigh Castle
MILNATHORT

☎0131-668 8800

Dating from 1582, this tower house has an enclosed courtyard and roofed angle tower.
Open all year, daily.
Free.
✲
(AM)

House of Dun
MONTROSE

(4m W, on A935)

☎Bridge of Dun (01674) 810264

A Georgian house, overlooking the Montrose Basin, built in 1730 for David Erskine, Lord Dun, to designs by William

Adam, and particularly noted for its exuberant plasterwork. The house was opened to the public in 1989 after extensive restoration, and displays a fine collection of family portraits, fine furniture and porcelain. The courtyard buildings house a working loom, restaurant and NTS shop. Walled garden and woodland walks. On Sundays during the summer there will be a special steam train service from Brechin station, run by Caledonian Co Ltd.
Open 14 Apr-Jun & Sep, daily 1.30-5.30; Jul-Aug daily 11-5.30; 1-22 Oct, Sat & Sun 1.30-5.30. (last admission to house 5). Garden & Grounds, all year daily 9.30-sunset.
£3 (ch £1.50). Party.
🅿 ✗ & *(braille sheets, house wheelchair & stair lift) toilets for disabled shop* ✲ *(ex in grounds)*
(NTS)

Montrose Museum & Art Gallery
MONTROSE

Panmure Place (opposite Montrose Academy)

☎(01674) 673232

Extensive local collections cover the history of Montrose from prehistoric times to local government reorganisation, the maritime history of the port, the natural history of Angus, and local art. Exhibits include Pictish stones, Montrose silver and pottery, whaling artefacts and Napoleonic items (including a cast of his death mask); also paintings by local artists and sculpture by William Lamb.
Open all year, Mon-Sat 10-5. Closed 25 & 26 Dec.
Free.
P & *shop* ✲

Drummond Castle Gardens
MUTHILL

(1m N)

☎(01764) 681257

The gardens of Drummond Castle were originally laid out in 1630 by John Drummond, 2nd Earl of Perth. In 1830, the parterre was changed to an Italian style. One of the most interesting features in the garden is the multi-faceted sundial designed by John Mylne, Master Mason to Charles I. The Formal garden is said to be one of the finest in Europe and is the largest of its type in Scotland. Open in aid of Scotland's Garden Scheme first Sunday in August.
Open - Gardens May-Oct, daily 2-6 (Last admission 5pm).
£3 (ch £1.50 & pen £2).
🅿 &

Black Watch Regimental Museum
PERTH

Balhousie Castle, Hay St

☎(01738) 621281 ext 8530

The treasures of the 42nd/73rd Highland Regiment from 1739 to the present day are on show in this museum, together with paintings, silver, colours and uniforms.
Open all year, May-Sep, Mon-Sat 10-4.30 (Closed last Sat in Jun); Oct-Apr, Mon-Fri, 10-3.30 (Closed 23 Dec-3 Jan). Other times & Parties 16+ by appointment.
❋*Donations.*
🅿 *shop* ✲

Branklyn Garden
PERTH

Dundee Rd (on Dundee Rd, A85)

☎(01738) 625535

Once described as the finest garden of its size in Britain, Branklyn covers little more than two acres and is noted for its collection of rhododendrons, shrubs and alpines. There are regular conducted tours of the garden, and botanical painting courses are held.
Open Mar-Oct, daily 9.30-sunset.
❋*£2 (ch £1). Party 20+.*
🅿 *shop* ✲
(NTS)

The childhood home of J M Barrie, creator of Peter Pan, has been preserved. His father's woodcarving shop is on the ground floor and the living rooms above.

At Scone Palace is a replica of the Stone of Scone on which Scottish monarchs were traditionally crowned. In 1296 Edward I of England took the original stone to Westminster Abbey.

Caithness Glass Factory & Visitor Centre
PERTH
Inveralmond Industrial Est
☎(01738) 37373
All aspects of paperweight-making can be seen from the viewing gallery at this purpose-built visitors' centre. There is a collectors' museum and a factory seconds shop.
Open all year, Factory shop Mon-Sat 9-5, Sun 11-5 (Oct-Mar, Sun 1-5). Glassmaking Mon-Fri 9-4.30.
🅿 ✗ *licensed* ♿ *toilets for disabled shop* *Details not confirmed for 1995*

Huntingtower Castle
PERTH
(2m W)
☎0131-668 8800
Formerly known as Ruthven Castle and famous as the scene of the so-called 'Raid of Ruthven' in 1582, this structure was built in the 15th and 16th centuries and features a painted ceiling.
Open all year, Apr-Sep, Mon-Sat 9.30-6.30, Sun 2-6.30; Oct-Mar, Mon-Sat 9.30-4.30, Sun 2-4.30. (Closed Thu pm & Fri in winter; 25-26 Dec & 1-3 Jan).
£1.50 (ch 75p, pen £1).
🅿 *shop* ♿
(AM)

Perth Museum & Art Gallery
PERTH
78 George St
☎(01738) 632488
This purpose-built museum houses collections of fine and applied art, social and local history, natural history and archaeology. Temporary exhibitions are held throughout the year.

VISITORS CENTRE AND FISH LADDER
A friendly welcome awaits you at the Hydro-Electric Visitors Centre here at Pitlochry.
Open: April–October
7 days a week 9.40am-5.30pm
For group booking please phone the supervisor
01796 473152

Open all year, Mon-Sat 10-5.
Free.
P *(adjacent)* ♿ *shop* ♿

Edradour Distillery
PITLOCHRY
(2.5m E on the A924)
☎(01796) 472095
It was in 1825 that a group of local farmers founded Edradour, naming it after the bubbling burn that runs through it. It is Scotland's smallest distillery and is virtually unchanged since Victorian times. Visitors can have a dram of whisky while watching an audio-visual in the malt barn and then see the disillers' art practised here as it has been for over 160 years.
Open early Mar-end Oct, Mon-Sat 9.30-5. Winter months, Mon-Sat 10-4, shop only. Free.
🅿 ♿ *toilets for disabled shop* ♿

Faskally
PITLOCHRY
Forestry Commission (1m N on the B8019)
☎Dunkeld (01350) 727284
On the shores of Loch Faskally, the mature, mixed woodland incorporates forest walks, a nature trail, picnic area and toilets.
Open Apr-Oct, dawn to dusk.
Free.
🅿 ♿ *toilets for disabled* ♿

Hydro-Electric Visitor Centre, Dam & Fish Pass
PITLOCHRY
☎(01796) 473152
The hydro-electric visitor centre consists of a souvenir shop; an exhibition showing how electricity is brought from the power station to the customer; access to the

turbine viewing gallery and video shows. The salmon ladder viewing chamber allows visitors to see the fish as they travel upstream to their spawning ground. There is also a walkway across the top of the dam.
Open Apr-Oct, daily 9.40-5.30.
✳*£1.50 (ch 60p, concessions £1). Family ticket £3.*
🅿 ♿ *(monitor viewing of salmon fish pass) toilets for disabled shop* ♿

Queen's View Visitor Centre
QUEEN'S VIEW
(7m W of Pitlochry on B8019)
☎Dunkeld (01350) 727284
Queen Victoria admired the view on a visit here in 1866, and there is a splendid viewpoint which also has access for the disabled. Forest walks take the visitor to viewpoints, an excavated ring fort and a reconstructed 18th-century farm village. The Visitor Centre has an exhibition describing the history of the area and places to visit.
Open Apr-Oct, daily 10.30-6.
Free.
🅿 *(charged)* ♿ ♿ *toilets for disabled shop*

Scone Palace
SCONE
☎(01738) 552300
Scottish kings were crowned at Scone until 1651; it was the seat of government in Pictish times; and it was the site of the famous coronation Stone of Destiny, brought there in the 9th century until it was seized by the English in 1296. The castellated edifice of the present palace dates from 1803 but incorporates the 16th-century and earlier buildings. The displays inside include a magnificent collection of porcelain, furniture, ivories, clocks and 16th-century needlework; one of the bed hangings was worked by Mary, Queen of Scots. The grounds include an outstanding pinetum, woodland garden and brilliant displays of rhododendrons and azaleas (at the right time of the year). Although one of the most historic houses in Scotland, its chief attraction lies in its much-loved and 'lived-in' atmosphere - it still remains a family home. Events for 1995 include horse trials (29-39 April), a Coronation pageant (25 June), a Scottish game fair (1-2 July), and Farming of Yesteryear (10 September).
Open 14 Apr-9 Oct, Mon-Sun 9.30-5, (Jul-Aug 10-5). Special parties outside normal opening hours & during winter by arrangement.
✳*Palace & Grounds £4.50 (ch £2.50). Grounds only £2.25 (ch £1.25) Family £13. Party 20+.*
🅿 ♿ ✗ *licensed* ♿ *toilets for disabled shop* ♿ *(ex in grounds)*

SCOTTISH ISLANDS

Castle Menzies
WEEM
(1.5m from Aberfeldy on B846)
☎Aberfeldy (01887) 820982
Restored seat of the Chiefs of Clan Menzies, and a fine example of a 16th-century Z-plan fortified tower house. Involved in the turbulent history of the Highlands it was occupied by various military forces on occasions up to World War II. Prince Charles Edward Stuart stayed here briefly on his way to Culloden in 1746. Special events for 1995 include the Menzies Clan Gathering (11-13 August).
Open 11 Apr-14 Oct, wkdays 10.30-5, Sun 2-5. Last entry 4.30pm.
£2.50 (ch £1, pen £2).
🅿 ♿ ♿ *toilets for disabled shop* ♿

SCOTTISH ISLANDS

Brodick Castle, Garden & Country Park
ISLE OF ARRAN
BRODICK
(2m from Brodick village)
☎(01770) 302202
The site of Brodick Castle has been fortified since Viking times, but the present castle dates from the 13th century, with extensions added in 1652 and 1844. It was a stronghold of the Dukes of Hamilton and more recently became the home of the late Duchess of Montrose. Splendid silver, fine porcelain and paintings acquired by generations of owners can be seen, including many sporting pictures and trophies.
There is a formal garden, dating from the 18th century and restored in Victorian style, but the most impressive part of the grounds is the woodland garden. It was started by the Duchess in 1923, and is world-famous for its rhododendrons and azaleas. A self-guided walk leads to its heart, and there are weekly guided walks in summer. The grounds also have an ice house, a Bavarian summer-house and an adventure playground, ranger service and display centre.
Open all year, Garden & Country Park, daily 9.30-sunset. Castle open Good Fri-30 Sep daily 11.30-5; 1-22 Oct, Sat & Sun only 11.30-5. Last admission 4.30pm.
✳*House & Gardens £4 (concessions £2). Garden only £2 (ch £1). Party.*
🅿 ✗ ♿ *(Braille sheets, motorised buggy, wheelchairs & stairlift) toilets for disabled shop* ♿ *(ex in park)*
(NTS)

Isle of Arran Heritage Museum
ISLE OF ARRAN
BRODICK
Rosaburn
☎(01770) 302636
The setting is an 18th-century croft farm, including a cottage restored to its pre-1920 state and a 'smiddy' where a blacksmith worked until the late 1960s. There are farming and shipping displays, as well as a heritage project carried out in conjunction with a local high school. A feature on village halls is planned for 1995.There are also occasional demonstrations of horseshoeing, sheepshearing and of the horse-mill working.
Open Apr-Oct, Mon-Sat 10-5.
✳*£1.50 (ch 75p, pen £1).*
🅿 ♿ ♿ *shop*

Ardencraig
ISLE OF BUTE
ROTHESAY
(1m off A844, S of Rothesay)
☎(01700) 504225
Particular attention has been paid to improving the layout of the garden and

➤

introducing rare plants. The greenhouse and walled garden produce plants for floral displays throughout the district. A variety of interesting fish is kept in the ornamental ponds and the aviaries have some interesting birds.
May-Sep.
🅿 ♨ ♿ ⌖
Details not confirmed for 1995

Bute Museum
ISLE OF BUTE
ROTHESAY
Stuart St
☎*(01700) 502248*
The contents are all from the Isle of Bute, and are divided into sections. The natural history room has birds, mammals and seashore items; and the history room has varied collections of recent bygones, such as models of Clyde steamers, photographs of 'old' Rothesay, farming and history items. There is a collection of early Christian crosses, and the prehistoric section has flints and pots from two Neolithic burial cairns. A comprehensive geological survey of the island can be seen, and there is also a children's 'touch table'. Details of nature trails on the island are on sale. A special exhibition of local interest is held during Highland Week, and there will be an exhibition of local common wild flowers from spring to autumn. Guided walks of Rothesay take place on Tuesdays and Thursdays during the summer months. Walkers meet at the museum.
Open all year, Apr-Sep, Mon-Sat 10.30-4.30, Sun 2.30-4.30; Oct-Mar, Tue-Sat 2.30-4.30 (Closed Sun & Mon).
❈*£1 (ch 30p, pen 60p).*
🅿 ♿ *(touch table for blind) shop* ⌖

Rothesay Castle
ISLE OF BUTE
ROTHESAY
☎*0131-668 8800*
The focal point of Rothesay is this 13th-century castle. It has lofty curtain walls defended by drum towers and enclosing a circular courtyard.
Open all year, Apr-Sep, Mon-Sat 9.30-6.30, Sun 2-6.30; Oct-Mar, Mon-Sat 9.30-4.30 Sun 2-4.30. (Closed Thu am & Fri in winter; also 25-26 Dec & 1-3 Jan).
£1.50 (ch 75p, pen £1).
🅿 ♿ *shop*
(AM)

Black House Museum
ISLE OF LEWIS
ARNOL
☎*0131-668 8800*
A traditional Hebridean dwelling is built without mortar and roofed with thatch on a timber framework. It has a central peat fire in the kitchen, no chimney and a byre under the same roof. The Black House museum is an excellent example and it retains many of its original furnishings.
Open Apr-Sep, Mon-Sat 9.30-6.30; Oct-Mar, Mon-Sat 9.30-4.30.
£1.50 (ch & pen 80p).
🅿 ♿ *shop* ⌖
(AM)

Callanish Standing Stones
ISLE OF LEWIS
CALLANISH
(12m W of Stornoway)
☎*0131-668 8800*
An avenue of 19 monoliths leads north from a circle of 13 stones with rows of more stones fanning out to south, east and west. Probably constructed between 3000 and 1500BC, this is a unique cruciform of megaliths.

Open & accessible at all times.
Free.
🅿
(AM)

Dun Carloway Broch
ISLE OF LEWIS
CARLOWAY
(1.5m S of Carloway)
☎*0131-668 8800*
Brochs are late-prehistoric circular stone towers, and their origins are mysterious. One of the best examples can be seen at Dun Carloway, where the tower still stands about 30ft high.
Open at all reasonable times.
Free.
🅿
(AM)

Mull & West Highland Narrow Gauge Railway
ISLE OF MULL
CRAIGNURE
Craignure (old pier) Station
☎*(01680) 812494 (in season) or (01680) 300389*
The first passenger railway on a Scottish island opened in 1984. Both steam and diesel trains operate on the ten-and-a-quarter inch gauge line, which runs from Craignure to Torosay Castle. The line is one-and-a-quarter miles long, and there are extensive and dramatic woodland and mountain views. The latest acquistion - a steam locomotive built in Sheffield in 1993 - has been named Victoria because of the help received from the Puffing Billy Railway in Australia, based near Melbourne, Victoria. The engine is based on their 2' 6" gauge engines.
Open Etr-mid Oct.
Return £2.50 (ch £1.70); Single £1.70 (ch £1.10). Family ticket return £6.50, single £4.50.

🅿 ♿ *(provision to carry person seated in wheelchair on trains) shop*

Torosay Castle & Gardens
ISLE OF MULL
CRAIGNURE
(1m S of Ferry Terminal at Craignure)
☎*(01680) 812421*
Much of this Victorian castle is open to the public together with its delightful Italian terraced gardens, designed by Lorimer. The Scottish baronial architecture is complemented by the magnificent setting and inside the house there are displays of portraits and wildlife pictures, family scrapbooks and a study of the Antarctic. The Edwardian library and archive rooms particularly capture the flavour of their era. Allures of the garden include a statue walk and water garden, an avenue of Australian gum trees, a Japanese garden, many rare shrubs, a narrow gauge steam and diesel railway and a weaver's workshop.
Open Etr then late Apr-mid Oct, daily 10.30-5.30. Gardens all year.
❈*Castle & garden £3.50 (ch £1.50, pen & students £2.25). Garden only £1.50 (ch, pen, & students £1). Party.*
🅿 ♨ ♿ *toilets for disabled shop* ⌖ *(ex in gardens)*

Earl's Palace
ORKNEY
BIRSAY
☎*0131-668 8800*
This ruined palace dates from the 12th century. The round tower was built by Bishop Reid and other additions were made in the 1600s by Patrick Stewart, Earl of Orkney.
Open Apr-Sep, Mon-Sat 9.30-6.30, Sun 2-6.30.
£1.20 (ch & pen 75p).
🅿 ⌖
(AM)

Brough of Birsay
ORKNEY
DOUNBY
(6m NW)
☎*0131-668 8800*
This ruined Romanesque church stands next to the remains of a Norse village. The nave, chancel and semicircular apse can be seen along with claustral buildings. Crossings must be made on foot at low-water - there is no boat.
Open at all reasonable times.
Free.
(AM)

Click Mill
ORKNEY
DOUNBY
(NE of village,off B9057)
☎*0131-668 8800*
This is an example of the rare Orcadian horizontal watermill, and is in working condition.
Open at all reasonable time.
Free.
(AM)

Skara Brae
ORKNEY
DOUNBY
(4m SW)
☎*0131-668 8800*
Engulfed in drift sand, this remarkable group of well-preserved Stone Age dwellings is the most outstanding survivor of its kind in Britain. Stone furniture and a fireplace can be seen.
Open all year, Apr-Sep, Mon-Sat 9.30-6.30, Sun 2-6.30; Oct-Mar, Mon-Sat 9.30-4.30, Sun 2-4.30. (Closed 25-26 Dec & 1-3 Jan).
£2.50 (ch £1, pen £1.50).
🅿 *shop* ⌖
(AM)

Maes Howe Chambered Cairn
ORKNEY
FINSTOWN
(9m W of Kirkwall, on A965)
☎*0131-668 8800*
The masonry of Britain's finest megalithic tomb is in a remarkable state of preservation. Dating from neolithic times,

The 12ft high Standing Stones at Callanish on the Isle of Lewis were put in place about 4,000 years ago. In the centre are the remains of a burial chamber.

it contains Viking carvings and runes.
*Open all year, Apr-Sep, Mon-Sat 9.30-
6.30, Sun 2-6.30; Oct-Mar, Mon-Sat 9.30-
4.30, Sun 2-4.30. (Closed 25-26 Dec &
1-3 Jan).*
❄£2 (ch 16 75p, pen £1.25). Family ticket
£4.50
🅿 ✕ licensed ⅃ shop ⌕
(AM)

Stenness Standing Stones
ORKNEY
FINSTOWN
(3m SW off A965)
☎0131-668 8800
Dating back to the second millenium BC,
the remains of this stone circle are near
the Ring of Brogar - a splendid circle of
upright stones surrounded by a ditch.
Open at any reasonable time.
Free.
🅿
(AM)

Orkney Farm & Folk Museum
ORKNEY
HARRAY
☎(01856) 771411 & 771268
The museum consists of two Orkney
farmhouses with outbuildings. Kirbuster
(Birsay) has the last surviving example of
a 'Firehoose' with its central hearth;
Corrigall (Harray) represents an improved
farmhouse and steading of the late
1800s. Both display period furnishings,
farm implements and native breeds of
sheep among their exhibits.
*Open Mar-Oct, Mon-Sat 10.30-1 & 2-5,
Sun 2-7.*
£1.50 (ch, students, pen & UB40 free) .
🅿 ⅃ shop ⌕

Earl Patrick's Palace
ORKNEY
KIRKWALL
☎0131-668 8800
Although roofless, much still remains of
this palace. Considered one of the finest
Renaissance buildings in Scotland, its
oriel windows are of particular interest.
*Open Apr-Sep, Mon-Sat 9.30-6.30, Sun 2-
6.30.*
£1.20 (ch & pen 75p).
🅿 ⅃ shop
(AM)

Tankerness House Museum
ORKNEY
KIRKWALL
Broad St
☎(01856) 873191
One of the finest vernacular town houses
in Scotland, this 16th-century building
now contains a museum of Orkney
history, including the islands' fascinating
archaeology. From April to September
1995 there is an exhibition on Orkney in
the Second World War.
*Open all year, Mon-Sat 10.30-12.30 &
1.30-5 (May-Sep Sun 2-5).*
£1.50 (ch, students, pen & UB40's free).
P (50yds) ⅃ shop ⌕

Orkney Natural & Maritime
History Museum
ORKNEY
STROMNESS
52 Alfred St
☎(01856) 850025
Founded by the Orkney Natural History
Society in 1837, this museum includes
exhibits on birds, shells, butterflies,
whaling and fishing. There are items
relating to Hudson Bay and the German
Fleet in Scapa Flow.
*Open May-Sep, Mon-Sat 10.30-12.30 &
1.30-5, Sun 10.30-5; Oct-Apr, Mon-Sat
10.30-12.30 & 1.30-5. (Closed Xmas,
New Year & 3 wks Feb-Mar).*
❄80p (ch 30p). Family ticket £2.
P (50yds) ⅃ shop ⌕

Pier Arts Centre
ORKNEY
STROMNESS
☎(01856) 850209
The collection is housed in a warehouse
standing on its own stone pier. A
children's workshop operates during the
school holidays and there is a constantly

In the distance, beyond Sandwick, is Mousa Island on which stands Mousa Broch, the best-preserved Iron-Age stone tower
in Scotland.

changing programme of exhibitions.
*Open all year, Tue-Sat 10.30-12.30 &
1.30-5.*
P (100 yds) ⅃ shop ⌕
Details not confirmed for 1995

Noltland Castle
ORKNEY
WESTRAY
☎0131-668 8800
Started in the 16th century, this ruined
castle was never completed. It has a fine
hall, vaulted kitchen and a notable
winding staircase.
*Open all reasonable times. Application to
key keeper.*
Free.
⌕
(AM)

Clickhimin
SHETLAND
LERWICK
(1m SW)
☎0131-668 8800
The remains of a prehistoric settlement
that was fortified at the beginning of the
Iron Age with a stone-built fort. The site
was occupied for over 1000 years. The
remains include a partially demolished
broch (round tower) which still stands to
a height of 17ft.
Open at all reasonable time.
Free.
(AM)

Fort Charlotte
SHETLAND
LERWICK
(overlooking harbour)
☎0131-668 8800
An artillery fort, begun in 1665 to protect
the Sound of Bressay during the Anglo-
Dutch War. The fort was burned by the
Dutch in 1673, together with the town of
Lerwick. It was repaired in 1781 during
the American War of Independence. The
fort is pentagonal with high walls and
seaward-facing gunports.
Open at all reasonable time.
Free.
(AM)

Shetland Museum
SHETLAND
LERWICK
Lower Hillhead
☎(01595) 5057
The massive brass propeller blade outside
the building is from the 17,000-ton liner
Oceanic, wrecked off Foula in 1914. The

museum itself has a fascinating range of
items recovered from shipwrecks, and
houses a permanent collection of
artefacts, models, displays and
specimens which illustrate the history of
Shetland from prehistoric times to the
present day. Exhibits include replicas of
the St Ninian's Isle Treasure. Regular
exhibitions of photographs and paintings
are held in the Back Gallery.
*Open all year Mon, Wed, Fri 10-7, Tue,
Thu, Sat 10-5.*
Free.
🅿 ⅃ (lift, wheelchair available) toilets for
disabled shop ⌕

Mousa Broch
SHETLAND
MOUSA ISLAND
(Accessible by boat from Sandwick)
☎0131-668 8800
This broch is the best-preserved example
of an Iron Age drystone tower in
Scotland. The tower is nearly complete
and rises to a height of 40ft. The outer
and inner walls both contain staircases
that may be climbed to the parapet.
Open at all reasonable time.
Free.
(AM)

Scalloway Castle
SHETLAND
SCALLOWAY
☎0131-668 8800
The ruins of a castle designed on the
medieval two-step plan. The castle was
actually built in 1600 by Patrick Stewart,
Earl of Orkney. When the Earl, who was
renowned for his cruelty, was executed
in 1615, the castle fell into disuse.
Open at all reasonable time.
Free.
🅿
(AM)

Jarlshof Prehistoric Site
SHETLAND
SUMBURGH
(At Sumburgh Head, approx 22m S of
Lerwick)
☎031-244 3101
One of the most remarkable archaeological
sites in Europe. There are remains of
Bronze Age, Iron Age and Viking
settlements as well as a medieval farm.
There is also a 16th-century Laird's House,
once the home of the Earls Robert and
Patrick Stewart, and the basis of 'Jarlshof'
in Sir Walter Scott's novel *The Pirate*.
Open all year, Apr-Sep, Mon-Sat 9.30-

6.30, Sun 2-6.30.
🅿 ⅃ shop
(AM)

Clan Donald Vistor Centre
ISLE OF SKYE
ARMADALE
(0.5m from Armadale Pier A851)
☎Ardvasar (01471) 844305 & 844227
Skye's award-winning Visitor Centre is
situated at the south end of the island.
Armadale Castle and Gardens were built in
1815 as the home of Lord Macdonald. The
sculptured ruins of the castle now house
the Museum of the Isles, with an exhibition
and slide-show. A library and study centre
offer genealogical research and access to
historical records. Surrounding the castle
are 40 acres of beautiful woodland gardens
and nature trails. The Countryside Ranger
Service provides a full summer programme
of walks, talks and children's afternoons.
The converted stables house a
restaurant/tearoom and gift shop.
*Open 3 Apr-21 Oct daily, 9.30-5.30.
Limited winter opening.*
£3.20 (concessions £2.20). Family ticket
£9. Party.
🅿 🍴 ✕ licensed ⅃ (wheelchairs available,
hearing loop in Audiovisual room) toilets
for disabled shop garden centre

Dunvegan Castle
ISLE OF SKYE
DUNVEGAN
☎(01470) 521206
This fortress stronghold set on the sea
loch of Dunvegan has been the home of
the Chief of Macleod for 790 years. On
view are books, pictures, arms and
treasured relics of the clan. There is a
display that traces the history of the
family and the clan from their days as
Norsemen until the present day. A
pedigree Highland Cattle fold is also a
major attractions as is the boat trip to the
nearby Seal Colony - take your camera as
the boatmen are trained to get close
enough to the seals to enable some
wonderful photographs to be taken.
There is also the opportunity for a cruise
of the loch aboard a turbo diesel boat
MacLeod of MacLeod which seats 35.
*Open 20 Mar-31 Oct, Mon-Sat 10-5.30,
Sun, castle 1-5.30, gardens 10-5.30. Last
admission 5pm. Nov-Mar by appointment
only.*
❄£4 (ch £2.20, pen & students £3.60).
Gardens £2.50 (ch £1.50). Seal boats
£3.50 (ch £2.50)
🅿 🍴 ✕ licensed shop ⌕ (ex in grounds)

WALES

CLWYD

Bodelwyddan Castle
BODELWYDDAN
(adjacent to A55)
☎St Asaph (01745) 584060
Set in rolling parkland against the impressive background of the Clwydian Hills, this imposing Victorian country house has been magnificently restored to its former glory. The lavish interiors reflect various periods and design styles from the 19th century and provide a sumptuous setting for a collection of over 200 portraits on loan from the National Portrait Gallery. It is the finest collection of Victorian portraiture outside London and contains work by William Holman-Hunt, John Singer Sargent and G F Watts. The portraits are complemented by furniture from the Victoria and Albert Museum and sculptures from the Royal Academy of Arts. A 'hands-on' exhibition of Victorian amusements and inventions features parlour games, puzzles and optical illusions - a veritable extravaganza of Victorian fun and games for all ages. A programme of events and temporary exhibitions takes place throughout the year. Events include: VE Day Celebrations - a street party, a Firework and Laser Symphony Concert and an Historic Vehicle Rally. Exhibitions on Four Women Photographers (15 Jan-19 March) and The Art of the Brontës (8 April-2 July).
Open all year; 8 Apr-Jun & 8 Sep-Oct, daily (ex Fri) Jul-7 Sep daily, 10-5; Nov-Mar Sat, Sun & Tue-Thu 11-4.
£4 (ch, students & disabled £2.50, pen & UB40's £3.50). Family ticket £10.
🅿 ♨ ✗ *licensed* ♿ *(lift to first floor) toilets for disabled shop* ⊗

Llyn Brenig Visitor Centre
CERRIGYDRUDION
(on B4501)
☎(01490) 420463
The 1,800-acre estate has a unique archaeological trail and round-the-lake walks of 10 miles (completion certificate available). The Nature Trail can offer glimpses of native trout or crossbills. A hide is available: best viewing is November to March. Disabled anglers are catered for with a specially adapted fishing boat and an annual open day. The centre has a bilingual exhibition on geology, archaeology, history and natural history.
Open all year, mid Mar-Oct daily 10-5; 1 Nov-mid Mar, Mon-Fri 10-4. (Access in winter may be limited by snow; cross-country skiing is then available).
❋*Free. (ex water sports & fishing).*
🅿 *(charged)* ♿ *(boats for disabled & fishing open days) toilets for disabled shop* ⊗

Chirk Castle
CHIRK
(off A5,0.5m W Chirk village, 1.5m driveway)
☎(01691) 777701
Chirk is one of a chain of late-13th-century Marcher castles. Its high walls and drum towers have hardly changed, but the inside shows the varied tastes of 700 years of occupation. One of the least-altered parts is Adam's Tower. Elsewhere, many of the medieval-looking decorations were by Pugin in the 19th century. The elegant stone staircase and delicate plasterwork of the state rooms date from the 18th century when Chirk was transformed in neo-classical style. There is a 17th-century Long Gallery, and the servants' hall has its old list of rules. The equally varied furnishings include fine tapestries. Outside is a formal garden with clipped yew hedges, and a landscaped park with splendid wrought-iron gates by the Davies brothers. To celebrate the 700th anniversary of the castle and 100 years of the National Trust there will be an outdoor concert with fanfare and fireworks on 23 July 1995.
Open 2 Apr-29 Sep, daily (ex Mon & Sat) (open Mon in Jul & Aug also BH Mon); 1-29 Oct, Sat & Sun only; Castle 12-5, Grounds 11-6. Last admission 4.30pm.
£4 (ch £2) Family ticket £10. Party.
🅿 ♨ ♿ *toilets for disabled shop* ⊗
(NT)

Welsh Mountain Zoo
COLWYN BAY
Old Highway (off bypass, A55)
☎(01492) 532938
The zoo and gardens are set in a 37-acre estate overlooking Colwyn Bay, with magnificent panoramic views of the coast and mountains. The animals are housed in natural settings, interspersed with gardens and woodland. The traditional range of zoo animals can be seen, from lions and elephants to penguins and parrots, and the zoo also attracts a variety of local wildlife. There are falconry displays during the summer months, and Californian sealions can be seen performing tricks at feeding time. Visit the Chimpanzee World complex, featuring the unique Chimp Encounter, and a South American small monkey breeding centre. There is also a Jungle Adventureland and Tarzan Trail activity area, and a Children's Farm. The 7th annual Easter Egg Safari will be held on 14-15 April.
Open all year, 9.30-last admission 5pm. (4pm Nov-Feb).
🅿 ♨ ✗ *licensed* ♿ *(free admission for the blind & wheelchair visitors) toilets for disabled shop* ⊗

Denbigh Castle
DENBIGH
(via A525, A543 & B5382)
☎(01745) 813979
The castle was begun by Henry de Lacy in 1282 and has an inspiring and impressive castle gatehouse, with a trio of towers and a superb archway, which is surmounted by a figure believed to be that of Edward I.
Open May-Sep daily 10-5; Oct-Apr open at all times.
❋*£1.50 (reductions £1), Family ticket £4, summer. Free winter.*
🅿 ♿ *shop* ⊗
(AM Cadw)

Town Walls & Leicester's Church
DENBIGH
Noted for their almost complete circuit, the town walls were started in 1282 at the same time as the castle. The remains include one of the gateways and the unfinished Leicester's Church, built by the Earl of Leicester, favourite of Elizabeth I, who meant it to become the cathedral of the diocese.
Open May-Sep daily 10-5.
🅿 ⊗
(AM Cadw)
Details not confirmed for 1995

Ewloe Castle
EWLOE
(NW of village on B5125)
The remains of Ewloe Castle stand in Ewloe Woods. It was a native Welsh castle, and Henry II was defeated nearby in 1157. Part of the Welsh Tower in the upper ward still stands to its original height, and there is a well in the lower ward. Remnants of walls and another tower can also be seen.
Open at all times.
Free.
⊗
(AM Cadw)

Flint Castle
FLINT
☎(01352) 733078
The castle was started by Edward I in 1277 and overlooks the River Dee. It is

---

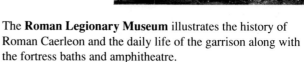

Transformed from a large cottage. Plas Newydd was created between 1780 and 1829 into a fantasy of timber, oriel windows and stained glass by the 'Ladies of Llangollen'.

exceptional for its great tower, or Donjon, which is separated by a moat. It may have been the castle's chief residence. Other buildings would have stood in the inner bailey, of which parts of the walls and corner towers remain.
Open at all times.
Free.
🅿🚫
(AM Cadw)

Chwarel Wynne Mine & Museum
GLYN CEIRIOG
Wynne Quarry (on B4500)
☎(01691) 718343
Chwarel Wynne Mine extends two and a ʼ half miles underground and was continuously worked from 1750 to 1928, during which time it produced more than 2000 tons of slate annually. The methods of mining and processing the slate are explained in a half-hour guided tour of the underground workings. The museum illustrates the history of the slate industry in North Wales. On show are tools, photographs and documents relating to mining along with objects relating to life in a slate-quarrying village almost a century ago. Film show. The mine has a beautiful setting in a 12-acre site, and there is a nature trail.
Open Etr-Oct, daily 10-5. Parties welcome at other times by prior appointment.
🅿🅿♿ *shop*
Details not confirmed for 1995

Horse Drawn Boats and Canal Exhibition Centre
LLANGOLLEN
The Wharf, Wharf Hill
☎(01978) 860702 & (01691) 75322
Visitors can enjoy horsedrawn boat trips along the beautiful Vale of Llangollen, as well as a fascinating museum illustrating the heyday of canals in Britain. The imaginative displays include working and static models, photographs, murals and slides. There is also a narrowboat trip which crosses Pontcysyllte Aqueduct.
Open Etr-Aug, daily; Sep-Oct Tue-Thu, Sat & Sun.
✳*Museum £1 (ch 70p). Horse Drawn Boat Trip £2 (ch £1.30). Narrowboat Trip £4.50 (ch £3.50).*
🅿 *(400 mtrs)* 🍴♿ *(alighting/pick-up point available) toilets for disabled shop*🚫

Llangollen Station
LLANGOLLEN
☎(01978) 860951 & 860979
The restored Great Western Railway Station is situated in the town centre and beside the River Dee. Locomotives and rolling stock are displayed, and passenger trains run on a ten-and-a-half-mile round trip between Llangollen and Glyndyfrdwy. A special coach for the disabled is sometimes available. During 1995 work

should be completed on an additional two miles of track. Events for 1995 will include Transport Extravaganza weekends in the Spring and Autumn, Thomas the Tank Engine weekends, Santa Specials, and special 'Wine and Dine' trains on Saturday evenings (summer only) and Sunday lunchtimes.
Open - Station wknds, Steam hauled trains Apr-Oct Sun & daily in Jul & Aug, diesel trains May-Oct Sat, daily during Jun. Santa specials during Dec.
✳*Station Free, except for special event days when charge of £1 (ch 50p) this is deducted from fare if travelling; Return Fares 1st class £5.60 (ch £2.80) 2nd class £5 (ch £2.50). Single Fare 1st class £3.50 (ch £1.90) 2nd class £3.20 (ch £1.70).*
🅿 *(400 yds)* 🍴♿ *(special coach for disabled parties) toilets for disabled shop (at stations)*

Plas Newydd
LLANGOLLEN
Hill St
☎*Oswestry (01691) 773291*
The 'Ladies of Llangollen', Lady Eleanor Butler and Sarah Ponsonby, lived here from 1780 to 1831. The original stained-glass windows, carved panels, and domestic miscellany of two lives are exhibited along with prints, pictures and letters.
Open Apr-Oct, daily, 10-5. Rest of the year by arrangement.
✳*£1.70 (ch 85p)*
🅿 *(0.5m)*♿ *toilets for disabled*🚫 *(ex in grounds)*

Valle Crucis Abbey
LLANGOLLEN
(on B5103, off A5 W of Llangollen)
☎(01978) 860326
Set in a deep, narrow valley, the abbey was founded for the Cistercians in 1201 by Madog ap Gruffydd. Substantial remains of the church can be seen, and some beautifully carved grave slabs have been found. There is a small exhibition on the Cistercian monks and the abbey.
Open all year, late Oct-late Mar, Mon-Sat 9.30-4, Sun 2-4; Late Mar-late Oct, daily 9.30-6.30. (Closed 24-26 Dec & 1 Jan) £1.50 (reductions £1). Family £4.
🅿♿ *shop*🚫
(AM Cadw)

Minera Lead Mines
MINERA
Wern Rd (through village down hill past City Arms)
☎Wrexham (01978) 751320 & 753400
Minera was one of the largest lead mines of the 19th century. Now much of the site has been transformed into a country park with a restored engine house and a visitor centre with fascinating displays on the mines and the people who worked there.
Open Etr-Sep, Tue-Sat 10-5. Last

admission 4.30pm.Country Park open daily, dawn-dusk.
80p (concessions 40p). Prices under review.
🅿♿ *(Radar key access to toilet) toilets for disabled shop*

Bersham Ironworks & Heritage Centre
WREXHAM
Bersham (2m SW)
☎(01978) 261529
The foundries and furnaces which produced cannon for the American War of Independence, and cylinders for James Watt's steam engines, are brought alive again at this fascinating museum which tells the story of John 'iron mad' Wilkinson and his 18th-century ironworks. Special events for 1995 include: Rebels and Redcoats Weekend (27-29 May) and a Veteran & Vintage Machinery Rally (6 August).
Open Etr-Sep, Mon-Fri 1-5, Sat-Sun & BH noon-5; Heritage Centre open all year, Mon-Fri 10-4, Sat & Sun noon-4.
£1 (ch, pen & student 75p). Family ticket £2.50. Party 20+. Free admission to Bersham Heritage Centre.
🅿♿ *toilets for disabled shop*🚫

Erddig
WREXHAM
(off the A525, 2m S of Wrexham)
☎(01978) 355314
Owned by the National Trust, Erddig is a treasure house of furnishings, utensils and tools of a country house since the 1700s. Built in 1680, the house was enlarged and improved during the next half century by a wealthy London lawyer with a passion for gilt and silver furniture. The house still has its original furnishings including a magnificent state bed in Chinese silk.
The house is especially notable for the view it gives of both 'upstairs' and 'downstairs' life. There is a range of restored outbuildings which show the workings of the laundry, the bakehouse - where bread is still baked - and the estate smithy and sawmill.
The gardens are unusual in that they have been very little changed since the 18th century.
Open 14 Apr-10 Oct, daily (ex Sat, Wed & Good Fri); 11-6 (house 12-5); last entry 4pm. 2-29 Oct, whole house Sat & Sun; below stairs Mon, Tue & Wed; 11-6 (house 12-4); last entry 3pm.
Family rooms (inc below stairs, outbuildings & gardens) £5 (ch £2.50). Below stairs only £3.20 (ch £1.60). Party.
🅿✕ *licensed*♿ *toilets for disabled shop*🚫
(NT)

DYFED

Carmarthen Museum
ABERGWILI
(2m E of Carmarthen, on A40)
☎Carmarthen (01267) 231691
Housed in the old palace of the Bishop of St David's and set in seven acres of grounds, the museum offers a wide range of local subjects to explore, from geology and prehistory to butter making and pottery and Welsh furniture and folk art. There are Roman and medieval displays, and temporary exhibitions are held. During 1995 these will be VE Day and the Impact of the War, Civil War in West Wales 1645-1995 and B A Lewis - a Carmarthen watercolourist.
Open all year, Mon-Sat 10-4.30. (Closed Xmas-New Year).
✳*50p (ch free, pen, students & unemployed 25p). Party 10+.*
🅿♿ *toilets for disabled shop*🚫

National Library of Wales
ABERYSTWYTH
Penglais Hill
☎(01970) 623816
The huge library is one of Britain's six copyright libraries, and specialises in Welsh and Celtic literature. It has maps, manuscripts, prints and drawings, as well as books in all languages. A major permanent exhibition 'A Nation's Treasury' is on view and there is a programme of travelling exhibitions.
Open all year, Library & reading rooms Mon-Fri 9.30-6, Sat until 5. (Closed BH's & first wk Oct).
Free.
🅿🍴♿ *toilets for disabled*🚫

Colby Woodland Garden
AMROTH
☎Saundersfoot (01834) 811885
The tranquillity and seclusion of this sheltered valley combined with the splendour of the woodland garden makes Colby one of the most beautiful National Trust properties in Pembrokeshire. There are many pleasant meadow and woodland walks. From early spring to the end of June the garden is a blaze of colour, from the masses of daffodils to the rich hues of rhododendrons, azaleas and bluebells. Events for 1995 include Blue Peter Competion Day (29 May), Supper and Shakespeare in the Meadow - A Midsummer Night's Dream (end June), Centenary Country Fayre (5-7 July), Outdoor Concert (6 July).
Open Apr-3 Nov, daily 10-5. Walled garden 11-5.
£2.60 (ch £1.10).
🅿🍴♿ *toilets for disabled shop garden centre*
(NT)

Rheidol Hydro Electric Power Station & Visitor Centre
CAPEL BANGOR
Cwm Rheidol (Off A44 at Capel Bangor)
☎(01970) 880667
A guided tour of the power station can be taken. It lies in a secluded valley, and other facilities include a fish farm, forest walks and a lakeside picnic area. There is a visitor centre.
Open Apr-Oct, daily 10-4 for tours of the Power Station & visitor centre.
Free.
🅿🍴♿

Carew Castle & Tidal Mill
CAREW
(on A4075, 5m E of Pembroke)
☎(01646) 651657 & 651782
This magnificent Norman castle - later an Elizabethan residence - has royal links with Henry Tudor and was the setting for the Great Tournament of 1507. Special events for the year include theatre interpretation, a schools programme, holiday activities and concerts - details available spring 1995. Nearby is the Carew Cross (Cadw), an impressive 13ft Celtic cross dating from the 11th century. ➤

Perched on the edge of a 330ft limestone cliff, Carreg Cennan is all that a castle should be – even as a ruin.

Carew Mill is one of only three restored tidal mills in Britain, with records dating back to 1558. The fine four-storey building houses a theatre showing an introductory film, and there are talking points explaining the milling process. A permanent exhibition 'The Story of Milling' - milling through the ages. Events for 1995 include a Civil War battle re-enactment and holiday activities.
Open Etr-Oct, daily 10-5.
❄£2 (ch & pen £1.20). Single ticket (castle or mill) £1.50 (ch 90p).
🅿 & *toilets for disabled shop*

Carreg Cennen Castle
CARREG CENNEN CASTLE
☎Llandeilo (01558) 822291
A steep path leads up to the castle, which is spectacularly sited on a limestone crag. It was first built as a stronghold of the native Welsh and then rebuilt in the late 13th century. Most remarkable among the impressive remains is a mysterious passage, cut into the side of the cliff and lit by loopholes. The farm at the site has a rare breeds centre and a tea room.
Open all year, late Oct-late Mar, daily 9.30-4; Late Mar-late Oct daily 9.30-6.30.(9.30-8 Jun-Aug). (Closed 24-26 Dec & 1 Jan).
❄£2 (reductions £1.50). Family ticket £6.
🅿 & *shop*
(AM Cadw)

Cilgerran Castle
CILGERRAN
(off A484 & A478)
☎Cardigan (01239) 615007
Set picturesquely above a gorge of the River Teifi - famed for its coracle fishermen - Cilgerran Castle dates from the 11th to 13th centuries. It decayed gradually after the Civil War, but its great round towers and high walls give a vivid impression of its former strength.
Open all year, late Oct-late Mar, Mon-Sat 9.30-4, Sun 2-4; Late Mar-late Oct daily 9.30-6.30. (Closed 24-26 Dec & 1 Jan).
❄£1.50 (reductions £1). Family ticket £4.
& *shop*
(AM Cadw)

Castell Henllys Fort
CRYMYCH
Pant-Glas, Meline (Off A487)
☎Crosswell (0123979) 319 due to change to (01239) 891319
This Iron Age hill fort is set in the beautiful Pembrokeshire Coast National Park. Excavations began in 1981 and

three roundhouses have been reconstructed. A forge, smithy, and looms can be seen, with other attractions such as trails and a herb garden. Special events for 1995 include visits by re-enactment groups displaying authentic Celtic costumes, weaponry and day to day life in the Iron Age and Celtic feasts; and exhibitions of spinning, weaving and dyeing, local craft demonstrations and courses. Please telephone for details.
Open Apr-late Oct, daily 10-5
£2 (ch & pen £1). Family ticket £4.80.
🅿 & *toilets for disabled shop*

Museum of the Welsh Woollen Industry
DRE-FACH FELINDRE
(signposted from A484)
☎Velindre (01559) 370929
The museum is housed in the former Cambrian Mills and has a comprehensive display tracing the evolution of the industry from its beginnings among the present day. Demonstrations of the fleece to fabric process are given on 19th-century textile machinery.
Open all year, Apr-Sep, Mon-Sat 10-5; Oct-Mar, Mon-Fri 10-5. (Closed 24-26 Dec & 1 Jan). Evening visits by prior arrangement.
❄£1 (ch 50p, pen 75p). Family ticket £2.50. Party.
🅿 💺 & *toilets for disabled shop garden centre (ex galleries)*

Dryslwyn Castle
DRYSLWYN
☎(01222) 500200
The ruined 13th-century castle was a stronghold of the native Welsh. It stands on a lofty mound, and was important in the struggles between English and Welsh. It is gradually being uncovered by excavation.
Open - entrance by arrangement with Dryslwyn Farm.
Free.
🅿
(AM Cadw)

Felinwynt Butterfly & Rainforest Centre
FELINWYNT
Rhosmaen (From A487, turn onto B4333. Signposted)
☎Cardigan (01239) 810882
A chance to wander amongst free-flying exotic butterflies accompanied by recorded sounds from the cloud forests of Ecuador and wildlife sounds of the Peruvian Amazon. A waterfall, ponds and streams combine to a humid tropical atmosphere and provide a habitat for fish

and native amphibians. There is a display of butterfly life from eggs to adult. Personal attention at all times especial in the Tropical House.
Open daily last Sunday May-last Sunday Sep, 10.30-5.
£2.75 (ch 4-14 £1 pen £2.25)
🅿 💺 & *shop*

Cardigan Island Coastal Farm Park & Waterfowl Centre
GWBERT-ON-SEA
☎(01239) 612196
A beautiful farm park located right on the cliff tops opposite Cardigan Island, which is just 200 yards offshore. The island is a Dyfed Wildlife Trust Nature Reserve, and is home to many species of birds. A colony of Atlantic grey seals breed in the many caves below the park, and can be seen at close quarters for most of the year. Bottle-nosed dolphins can also be seen as they chase the salmon up the nearby Teifi Estuary. Visitors can mix with the rare breeds of sheep and goats, and meet the animals in pets' corner. The waterfowl centre has colourful ducks and geese from all parts of the world, including Mandarins, Carolinas, Whistling Ducks and Egyptian Geese.
Open all year; farm park until dusk, waterfowl centre 10-5.
🅿
Details not confirmed for 1995

Haverfordwest Castle
HAVERFORDWEST
☎(01437) 763707
The ruined 12th-century castle was used as a jail and a police headquarters before it became a museum. The museum has been moved to Scolton House, Spittal but the castle grounds are still open to the publice and the Record Office is on the premises.
Open all year. Record Office Mon-Thu 9-4.45, Fri 9-4.15. Castle ruins daily during daylight, at visitors' own risk. Admission free on Sat, Oct-Mar.
Free.
🅿 & *(ex in grounds)*

Kidwelly Castle
KIDWELLY
(via A484)
☎(01554) 890104
This is an outstanding example of late-13th-century castle design, with its 'walls within walls' defensive system. There were later additions made to the building, the chapel dating from about 1400. Of particular interest are two vast circular ovens.

Open all year, late Oct-late Mar, Mon-Sat 9.30-4, Sun 11-4; Late Mar-late Oct, daily 9.30-6.30. (Closed 25-26 Dec & 1 Jan).
❄£2 (reductions £1.50). Family ticket £6.
🅿 & *toilets for disabled shop*
(AM Cadw)

Kidwelly Industrial Museum
KIDWELLY
Broadford
☎(01554) 891078
Two of the great industries of Wales are represented in this museum: tinplate and coal mining. The original buildings and machinery of the Kidwelly tinplate works, where tinplate was hand made, are now on display to the public. There is also an exhibition of coal mining with pit-head gear and a winding engine, while the more general history of the area is shown in a separate exhibition.
Open Etr, Jun-Aug, PH wknds, Mon-Fri 10-5 (6pm Jul-Aug), Sat-Sun 2-5 (6pm Jul-Aug). Last admission 4pm (5pm Jul-Aug). Other times by arrangement for parties only.
🅿 & *toilets for disabled shop (ex in grounds)*
Details not confirmed for 1995

Lamphey Palace
LAMPHEY
(off A4139)
☎Pembroke (01646) 672224
This ruined 13th-century palace once belonged to the Bishops of St Davids.
Open all year.
❄£1.50 (reductions £1). Family ticket £4. No charge Oct-Mar.
🅿 & *toilets for disabled shop*
(AM Cadw)

Dylan Thomas' Boat House
LAUGHARNE
Dylans Walk (14m W of Carmarthen)
☎(01994) 427420
Under Milk Wood was written here by Wales's most prolific 20th-century poet and writer. The waterside house, set on the 'heron priested' shore of the Taf estuary, contains much original furniture, family photographs, an art gallery and displays on the life and works of Dylan Thomas. There is an audio-visual presentation available. Nearby is the writing shed where Dylan Thomas actually wrote so many of his well-known poems and short stories. Telephone for detail of special events in celebration of the Swansea Year of Literature 1995.
Open all year, Etr-Oct, daily 10-6 (last admission 5pm); Nov-Etr, Sun-Fri 11-4 (last admission 3pm).
£1.75 (ch & pen £1.25). Party 5+.
P (10mins walk) 💺 *shop*

Llanelli Wildfowl & Wetlands Centre
LLANELLI
Penclacwydd
☎(01554) 741087
Penclacwydd salt-marsh is on the northern shore of the Burry Inlet (10 miles west of Swansea). The Inlet is a premier estuary for wildfowl and waders in Wales with up to 50,000 birds including oystercatchers, curlew, widgeon, pintail and knot. At the visitor centre there is a resident population of over 1,000 wildfowl including the endangered White-wing Wood Duck from Asia. Among the facilities offered are a major bird hide, pond dipping facilities and a garden specially designed to attract butterflies. On the last weekend in July, there is a Conservation Fair for all the family.
Open summer 9.30-5.30, winter 9.30-4.30. Closed 24-25 Dec.
❄£3.50 (ch £1.75, pen £2.65). Family ticket £8.75. Party.
🅿 ✕ & *toilets for disabled shop*

Parc Howard Art Gallery & Museum
LLANELLI
☎(01554) 773538
Llanelli pottery, local museum exhibits and a permanent collection of paintings are housed in this gallery, which is set in a pleasant park.

Open all year, daily. Apr-Sep 11-1 & 2-6;
Oct-Mar 11-1 & 2-4.
Free.
P (50 yds) ☕ ⌀

Llansteffan Castle
LLANSTEFFAN
☎(01267) 241756
The ruins of this 11th-to 13th-century
stronghold stand majestically on the west
side of the Towy estuary.
Open - access throughout the year.
Free.
⌀
(AM Cadw)

Penrhos Cottage
LLANYCEFN
☎Clarbeston (01437) 731328
Local tradition has it that cottages built
overnight on common land could be
claimed by the builders, together with the
ground a stone's throw away from the
door. This thatched cottage is an
example, built with help from friends and
family; and it remained in the same family
from the time it was built until the late
1960s, when the county council bought it.
Its character has been maintained, and it
gives the visitor an insight into traditional
Welsh country life. Various outbuildings
complete the picture.
Open Etr Sun & Mon, then mid May-Sep,
Tue-Sat 10-1 & 2-5 & Sun afternoons.
✻20p (ch free, pen & UB40 10p).
⌂ shop ⌀ (ex in grounds)

Llawhaden Castle
LLAWHADEN
☎(01437) 541201
The castle was first built in the 12th
century to protect the possessions of the
bishops of St David's. The 13th-and 14th-
century remains of the bishops' hall,
kitchen, bakehouse and other buildings can
be seen, all surrounded by a deep moat.
Open at all times. Key keeper arrangement.
Free.
⌂ ⌀
(AM Cadw)

Oakwood Park
NARBERTH
Canaston Bridge (signposted off the A40)
☎Martletwy (01834) 891373 891376
The activities offered here are numerous
and include rollercoaster, waterfall and
bobsleigh rides, miniature trains, go-karts
and assault courses and a theatre show.
There is a huge undercover playland as
well as an outdoor children's play area.
Open 26 Mar-Sep, daily from 10am.
Restricted in Oct.
P ✗ licensed ⌂ toilets for disabled shop
⌀
Details not confirmed for 1995

Pentre Ifan Burial Chamber
NEWPORT
(3m SE from B4329 or A487)
☎(01222) 500200
Found to be part of a vanished long
barrow when excavated in 1936-37, the
remains of this chamber include the
capstone, three uprights and a circular
forecourt.
Open - access throughout the year.
Free.
⌀
(AM Cadw)

The Museum of the Home
PEMBROKE
7 Westgate Hill
☎(01646) 681200
A pleasant domestic setting provides an
opportunity to view some of the objects
that have been part of everyday life over
the past three hundred years.
Open May-Sep, Mon-Thu 11-5, other
times by arrangement.
£1.20 (ch & pen 90p). Party.
⌀ ⌂

Pembroke Castle
PEMBROKE
☎(01646) 681510
This 12th-to 13th-century fortress has an
impressive 80ft-high round keep. There is
also a new Interpretative Centre. ➜

Although a ruin, the towering three-storey gatehouse and the curtain walls of
Kidwelly Castle are almost complete.

Open all year, daily, Apr-Sep 9.30-6; Mar
& Oct 10-5; Nov-Feb, 10-4. (Closed 25-26
Dec & 1 Jan).
✱£2 (ch 16 & pen £1.20, ch 5 &
wheelchairs free). Family ticket £6.
P (200 yds) 💺 & toilets for disabled shop

Graham Sutherland Gallery
PICTON CASTLE
(5m E of Haverfordwest, S of A40)
☎(01437) 751296
Graham Sutherland was enchanted with
Wales, and this unique gallery reflects
the artist's fascination. A large collection
of Sutherland paintings hangs here, and
visitors can discover for themselves the
lanes and estuaries that inspired one of
Britain's greatest artists. Videos on
Sutherland can be seen in the lecture
theatre. There is an annual programme of
temporary exhibitions of work by other
artists; lectures and events. Activity
sheets for children.
Open Apr-Oct, Tue-Sun 10.30-12.30 &
1.30-5. Also open BH Mons. Open Nov-
Mar & evenings for groups by prior
arrangement
✱£1 (ch 5-15 50p, pen, UB40 & disabled
75p). Family ticket £2.50. Visitors to the
gallery get a free ticket to the Museum of
the Woollen Industry at Drefach Velindre.
P 💺 ✗ licensed & toilets for disabled
shop

Llywernog Silver-Lead Mine
PONTERWYD
(11m E of Aberystwyth on A44)
☎(01970) 890620
The Llywernog Silver-lead Mine is an
award-winning family attraction located
high up in the beautiful Cambrian
Mountains of Mid Wales. Visitors can
safely explore tunnels and chambers
dating from the 18th century and see
veins of silver-lead ore running through
the rocks. At surface, the old mine
buildings contain exhibitions which tell
the colourful story of the 'boom days',
and heritage collections of old tools,
working water wheels and quaint
machinery. Children (and adults) can pan
for silver and 'fools gold' and operate
simple pumps and equipment. Rocks,
mineral specimens and mining souvenirs
can be purchased at the shop, together
with locally-made silver jewellery.
Open Etr-Oct, daily 10-6 (Oct 5pm). Last
admission 1 hour before closing time.
Winter by appointment.
P 💺 & shop
Details not confirmed for 1995

Dolaucothi Gold Mines
PUMSAINT
☎(01558) 650359
Here is an opportunity to spend a day
exploring the gold mines and to wear a
miner's helmet and lamp while touring
the underground workings. The
information centre and a walk along the
Miners' Way disclose the secrets of 2000
years of gold mining. A unique blend of
history and beauty, this is the only place
in Britain where the Romans mined gold.
Open Apr-3 Nov, daily (incl BH's) 11-5.
Underground tours 20 May-24 Sep, daily
10-5. Other guided tours and activities
available, contact the Visitor Centre
Manager for further information.
✱£1 (ch 50p). Underground tours £3.50
(ch £1.50).
P 💺 shop
(NT)

St Davids Bishop's Palace ST
DAVID'S
(on A487)
☎(01437) 720517
These extensive and impressive ruins are
all that remain of the principal residence
of the Bishops of St Davids. The palace
shares a quiet valley with the cathedral,
which was almost certainly built on the
site of a monastery founded in the 6th
century by St David. The Bishop's Palace
houses an exhibition: 'Life in the Palace
of a Prince of the Church'.
Open all year, late Oct-late Mar Mon-Sat,
9.30-4, Sun 2-4; Late Mar-late Oct, daily
9.30-6.30. (Closed 24-26 Dec & 1 Jan).

✱£1.50 (reductions £1). Family ticket £4.
P & toilets for disabled shop
(AM Cadw)

Manor House Wildlife & Leisure
Park   ST FLORENCE
Ivy Tower (on B4318)
☎Carew (01646) 651201
The park is set in 35 acres of delightful
wooded grounds and award-winning
gardens. The wildlife includes exotic
birds, reptiles and fish. Also here are a
pets' corner, a children's playground,
amusements and radio-controlled
models. Other attractions include a giant
astraglide slide, a go-kart track and model
railway exhibition. There are falconry
displays daily.
Open Etr-Sep, daily 10-6.
£3.50 (pen £2, ch & disabled/helpers
£1.50). Party 20+.
P 💺 & toilets for disabled shop garden
centre

Scolton House & Museum
SCOLTON
(5m N of Haverfordwest, on B4329)
☎Clarbeston (01437) 731328 (Mus) &
731457 (Park)
Scolton House is situated in Scolton
Country Park. The early Victorian mansion
and stables and the large exhibition hall
illustrate the history and natural history of
Pembrokeshire. Within the mansion are
period rooms on three floors. The 60
acres of grounds are rich in fine trees and
ornamental shrubs while three nature
trails provide interesting diversions.
Special events are held in the Country
Park, please telephone the warden at the
Park.
Open; Museum Apr-Oct, Tue-Sun & BH's
10-4.30; Country Park all year,
✱50p (ch free, pen & UB40 25p). Party
10+.
P (charged) 💺 & toilets for disabled
shop (ex in grounds)

Strata Florida Abbey
STRATA FLORIDA ABBEY
☎Pontrhydfendigaid (01974) 831261
Little remains of the Cistercian abbey
founded in 1164, except the ruined
church and cloister. Strata Florida was an
important centre of learning in the Middle
Ages, and it is believed that the 14th-
century poet Dafyd ap Gwilym was
buried here.
Open all year, Oct-Apr at all times; May-
Sep daily 9.30-6.30 (Closed 24-26 Dec &
1 Jan).

✱Summer only :£1.50 (reductions £1).
P & shop
(AM Cadw)

Talley Abbey
TALLEY
☎(01558) 685444
Only beautiful ruins now remain of this
once magnificent abbey, including two
pointed archways set in the remains of
the north and east walls of the church's
central tower. The abbey was founded in
1197 by Rhys ap Gruffudd, and was
virtually destroyed in the uprising led by
Owain Glyndwr.
Open all year, late Oct-late Mar, Mon-Sat
9.30-4, Sun 2-4; Late Mar-late Oct, daily
9.30-6.30. (Closed 24-26 Dec & 1 Jan).
Key keeper arrangement.
✱£1 (reductions 60p).
P
(AM Cadw)

Tenby Museum
TENBY
Castle Hill
☎(01834) 842809
The town museum is situated on Castle
Hill. It covers the local heritage from
prehistory to the present in galleries
devoted to archaeology, geology,
maritime history, natural history, militaria
and bygones. The picture gallery
concentrates on local associations with
an important collection of works by
Augustus and Gwen John. In 1995 there
will be summer exhibitions in the picture
gallery and a special exhibition of local
history.
Open all year, Etr-Oct, daily 10-6; Nov-Etr,
Mon-Fri 10-4.
✱£1 (ch 40p, pen 60p).
P (5 mins walk) & shop

Tudor Merchant's House
TENBY
Quay Hill
☎(0834) 842279
Recalling Tenby's history as a thriving
and prosperous port, the Tudor
Merchant's house is a fine example of
gabled 15th-century architecture. There is
a good Flemish chimney and on three
walls the remains of frescoes can be
seen. The ground floor houses a National
Trust information centre.
Open 2 Apr-Oct, Mon-Fri 10.30-5.30, Sun
1.30-5.30. (Closed Sat).
£1.60 (ch 80p).
P (440yds) shop
(NT)

GWENT

Abergavenny Museum & Castle
ABERGAVENNY
Castle St (off A40/A465 Abergavenny rbt)
☎(01873) 854282
Craft tools, a Welsh kitchen, a saddler's
shop and local exhibits are displayed at
the museum, and the remains of the
castle's walls, towers and gateway can
be seen.
Open all year. Museum open Mar-Oct,
Mon-Sat 11-1 & 2-5; Sun 2-5. Nov-Feb,
Mon-Sat 11-1 & 2-4. Castle open daily 8-
dusk.
£1 (ch, pen & students 50p)
P & (limited) toilets for disabled shop

Big Pit Mining Museum
BLAENAVON
(off B4246, follow brown tourist signs)
☎(01495) 790311
The 'Big Pit' closed as a working mine in
1980, but today visitors can don safety
helmets and cap lamps, and descend the
300ft shaft to find out what life was like
for generations of miners in South Wales.
There is an exhibition in the old pithead
baths and changing rooms, and a
reconstructed miner's cottage can also
be seen. Stout shoes and warm clothes
are recommended for tours of the mine.
Open Mar-Nov, daily 9.30-5. (Last tour
3.30). Dec-Feb telephone for opening
details.
Underground & surface £4.95 (ch £3.50
& pen & students £4.50) surface only
£1.75 (ch £1, pen & students £1.50).
Family ticket £15.
P 💺 & (underground tours by prior
arrangement) toilets for disabled shop

Caerleon Fortress Baths,
Amphitheatre & Barracks
CAERLEON
(on B4236)
☎Newport (01663) 422518
Caerleon was an important Roman
military base, with accommodation for
thousands of men. The foundations of
barrack lines and parts of the ramparts
can be seen, with remains of the
cookhouse, latrines and baths. The
amphitheatre nearby is one of the best
examples in Britain. The Fortress Baths
were excavated in the 1970s and
represent the most complete example of
a Roman legionary bath building in
Britain.

Big Pit Mining Museum offers visitors an exceptional chance to visit a coal mine. Donning helmnets and lamps, they are
taken down the 300ft shaft by lift.

Open all year, late Mar-late Oct daily 9.30-6.30. Late Oct-late Mar, Mon-Sat 9.30-4, Sun 2-4. (Closed 1 Jan & 24-26 Dec).
✱£1.50 (concessions £1). Family ticket £4. Three site ticket (with National Museum of Wales) £2.50 (concessions £1.50).
🅿 & N shop ✍
(AM Cadw)

Roman Legionary Museum
CAERLEON
High St (2m N of M4 junc 25)
☎(01633) 423134
The museum illustrates the history of Roman Caerleon and the daily life of its garrison. On display are arms, armour and equipment, with a collection of engraved gemstones, a labyrinth mosaic and Roman finds from the legionary base at Usk. Please telephone for details of children's holiday activities.
Open all year, 15 Mar-15 Oct, Mon-Sat 10-6, Sun 2-6; 16 Oct-14 Mar, wkdays 10-4.30, Sun 2-4.30. (Closed Xmas period).
✱£1.50 (ch & pen £1). Also joint ticket available with Roman Baths & Amphitheatre.
P (100yds) & toilets for disabled shop ✍

Caerwent Roman Town
CAERWENT
(off A48)
☎(01222) 500200
A complete circuit of the town wall of 'Venta Silurum', together with excavated areas of houses, shops and a temple.
Open - access throughout the year.
Free.
✍
(AM Cadw)

Caldicot Castle, Museum & Countryside Park
CALDICOT
(on B4245)
☎(01291) 420241
Caldicot Castle's well-preserved fortifications were founded by the Normans and fully developed, in royal hands, by the late 14th century. Restored as a family home by a wealthy Victorian, the castle offers the chance to explore medieval walls and towers in a setting of tranquil gardens and wooded Country Park.
Open Mar-Oct, Mon-Fri 10.30-5, Sat & BH 10.30-5, Sun 1.30-5.
✱£1.20 (ch, pen & student 60p). Party 10+.
🅿 ⬛ & (Radar key for toilet) toilets for disabled shop

Chepstow Castle
CHEPSTOW
☎(01291) 624065
Built by William FitzOsbern soon after the Norman Conquest, Chepstow is the first recorded Norman stone castle. It was used as a base for advances into Wales, and stands in a strategic spot above the Wye. Not only could it easily be defended, but it also overlooked a harbour. The castle was strengthened in the following centuries, but was not besieged (as far as is known) until the Civil War, when it was twice lost to the Parliamentarians. The remains of the domestic rooms are evidence of past splendour, and the massive gatehouse with its portcullis grooves and ancient gates is still impressive, as are the walls and towers with their variety of slots for arrows and guns. An extension of the castle was the Port Wall, which ran round the town. An exhibition, 'Chepstow - A Castle at War', provides visitors with an insight into the building of the medieval castle and its role in the Civil War.
Open all year, late Oct-late Mar Mon-Sat 9.30-4, Sun 11-4; late Mar-late Oct daily 9.30-6.30. (Closed 24-26 Dec & 1 Jan).
✱£2.90 (reductions £1.80) Family ticket £8.
🅿 & shop ✍
(AM Cadw)

Chepstow Museum
CHEPSTOW
Gwy House, Bridge St
☎(01291) 625981
Now set out in a fine 18th-century house, the museum has exhibitions of the history of Chepstow, the lower Wye Valley and the surrounding area. Exhibition themes change monthly. Special facilities, activities and information is available to pre-booked groups in the new education resource centre, nearby. Contact the Education Resource Officer at Chepstow Museum for more details. Events for 1995 include Milk (8 April-11 June), Crysése - textile designs (17 June-29 July), The dynamic toys of Rosey Peppé (18 November-Jan 1996).
Open Jan-Jun & Oct-Dec, Mon-Sat 11-1 & 2-5, Sun 2-5; Jul-Sep, Mon-Sat 10.30-1 & 2-5.30, Sun 2-5.30.
✱£1 (ch free if accompanied, pen 50p). Party. Pre booked educational groups free.
P (opposite) & toilets for disabled shop ✍

Cwmcarn Forest Drive
CWMCARN
(8m N of Newport on A467)
☎Newport (01633) 400205
A seven-mile scenic drive with spectacular views over the Bristol Channel and surrounding countryside. Facilities include barbecues, picnic and play areas, and forest and mountain walks. The area is run by the Forest Enterprise. Special events are being held throughout the year, telephone for details.
Open Etr-Oct, daily 11-7pm.
Cars & Motorcycles £2, Minibus fr £6, Coaches £20.
🅿 & shop

Grosmont Castle
GROSMONT
(on B4347)
☎(01981) 240301
Grosmont is one of the 'trilateral' castles of Hubert de Burgh (see also Skenfrith and White Castle). It stands on a mound with a dry moat, and the considerable remains of its 13th-century great hall can be seen. Three towers once guarded the curtain wall, and the western one is well preserved.
Open - access throughout the year.
Free.
& ✍
(AM Cadw)

Llanthony Priory
LLANTHONY
☎(01222) 500200
In the early 12th century William de Lacey discovered the remains of a hermitage dedicated to St David, built six centuries earlier; by 1108 a church had been consecrated on the site and just over a decade later the priory was complete. Forty years after an uprising in 1135, when the priory was brought to a state of seige, Hugh de Lacey provided the funds for a new church, and it is this that makes the picturesque ruin seen today. Its architectural styles range from Norman to Early English, and the visitor can still make out the west towers, north nave arcade and south transept. The former priest's house is part of a hotel. The priory is reached by narrow roads through lovely scenery.
Open - access throughout the year.
Free.
🅿 & toilets for disabled ✍
(AM Cadw)

Hen Gwrt
LLANTILIO CROSSENNY
(off B4233)
☎(01222) 500200
The rectangular enclosure of the former medieval house, still surrounded by a moat.
Open - access throughout the year.
Free.
✍ 🚻
(AM Cadw)

Nelson Museum & Local History Centre
MONMOUTH
New Market Hall, Priory St
☎(01600) 713519
The bulk of the Nelson Museum collection was formed by Lady Llangattock who lived near Monmouth. On show are commemorative glass, china, silver, medals, books, models, prints and the prize exhibit: Admiral Nelson's fighting sword. The local history displays deal with Monmouth's past as a fortress market town in the Wye Valley, and include a section on the co-founder of the Rolls Royce company, Charles Stewart Rolls, who was also a pioneer balloonist, aviator and, of course, motorist.
Open all year, Mon-Sat 10-1 & 2-5; Sun 2-5 (Closed Xmas & New Year).
✱£1 (accompanied ch 18 free, pen 50p). Party 10+.
P (200 yds) & shop ✍

Tredegar House & Park
NEWPORT
Coedkernew (2m W, signposted from A48/M4 junc.28)
☎(01633) 815880
Tredegar was home to one of the greatest of Welsh families, the Morgans, later Lords Tredegar, for over five centuries, but for years their house has remained relatively unknown. Today it stands out as one of the most magnificent 17th-century houses in Britain. A tour of the interior vividly illustrates what life was like for the Morgans and their servants, giving visitors a fascinating insight into life 'above' and 'below' stairs. The house and gardens are set within a 90-acre landscaped park. Carriage rides, formal gardens, self-guided trails, craft workshops, boating, and an exciting adventure playfarm provide a wide variety of things to do and see. There are events each month in 1995 including a folk festival (May) and a vintage car rally (September). Telephone for further details.
Open Good Fri-end Sep, Wed-Sun & BHs 11.30-4.(Tue during school holidays. Wknds only in Oct. Special Xmas opening).
House £3.50 (ch & pen £2.70) Family ticket £9. Garden only £1.
🅿 (charged) ⬛ ✕ licensed & (wheelchairs for loan) toilets for disabled shop

Penhow Castle
PENHOW
(On A48 between Newport & Chepstow)
☎(01633) 400800
This, the oldest inhabited castle in Wales, was originally a small border fortress and was the first British home of the famous Seymour family. The building presents a fascinating picture of life from the 12th to 19th centuries. The ramparts, with views of three counties, are 12th-century, while the great hall, its reconstructed screen and minstrels' gallery, are of the 15th century. The kitchen represents life in the 17th century, and there is a housekeeper's room of the Victorian era. Walkman tours, pioneered here, are included in the admission price. There will be Christmas Candlelit Tours from 15 November to 5 January.
Open Etr-Sep, Wed-Sun & BH 10-5.15; "Candlelit Tours" by arrangement; Aug open daily; Winter Wed only 10-5.
£3.15 (ch £1.85). Family ticket £8.15. Party 20+.
🅿 Refreshment bar & (audio-tours for blind) shop ✍

The Valley Inheritance Museum
PONTYPOOL
Park Buildings (off A4042)
☎(01495) 752036
Housed in the Georgian stable block of Pontypool Park House, exhibitions and films tell the story of a South Wales valley. Temporary exhibitions are also held.
Open Feb-Dec, Mon-Sat 10-5 & Sun 2-5 (Closed 25 Dec).
£1.20 (ch 60p).Family ticket £2.40. Party.
🅿 ⬛ & toilets for disabled shop ✍

Raglan Castle
RAGLAN
☎(01291) 690228
This magnificent 15th-century castle is noted for its 'Yellow Tower of Gwent'. It was built by Sir William Thomas and slighted during the Civil War, after a long siege. The ruins are still impressive, however, and the castle's history is illustrated in an exhibition situated in the closet tower and two rooms of the gate passage.
Open all year, late Oct-late Mar, Mon-Sat 9.30-4, Sun 11-4; late Mar-late Oct, daily 9.30-6.30. (Closed 24-26 Dec & 1 Jan).
✱£2 (reductions £1.50). Family ticket £6.
🅿 & shop ✍
(AM Cadw)

Skenfrith Castle
SKENFRITH
☎(01222) 500200
This 13th-century castle has a round keep set within an imposing towered curtain wall. It was built by Hubert de Burgh as one of three 'trilateral' castles to defend the Welsh Marches.
Open - access throughout the year. Key keeper arrangement.
Free.
🅿 ✍
(AM Cadw & NT)

Tintern Abbey
TINTERN
(via A466)
☎(01291) 689251
Standing serenely beside the banks of the River Wye, the ruins of the Cistercian monastery church are still surprisingly intact. The monastery was established in 1131 and it continued to thrive and become increasingly wealthy well into the 15th century. During the Dissolution, the monastery was closed and most of ➤

the buildings, other than the church, were completely destroyed. During the 18th century the ruins of Tintern were considered to be one of the essential sites to visit. Many poets and artists came to see the majestic arches, fine doorways and elegant windows, and recorded their experiences in poetry and paintings. An exhibition, situated near the new shop, illustrates the lifestyles of the monks.
Open all year, late Oct-late Mar, Mon-Sat 9.30-4, Sun 11-4; late Mar-late Oct, daily 9.30-6.30. (Closed 24-26 Dec & 1 Jan).
✱*£2 (reductions £1.50). Family ticket £6.*
🅿 ✿ *toilets for disabled shop* ✤
(AM Cadw)

Gwent Rural Life Museum
USK
Malt Barn, New Market St
☎(01291) 673777
An award-winning collection of farm tools, machinery, wagons and domestic items.
Open Apr-Oct, daily 10-5 (ex Sat & Sun am). Winter hours contact the Museum.
£1.50 (ch 75p, pen £1). Party.
🅿 ✿ *(special tape recording of tour for deaf) shop*

White Castle
WHITE CASTLE
(7m NE of Abergavenny, unclass rd N of B4233)
☎*Llantilio (0160085) 380*
The impressive 12th-to 13th-century moated stronghold was built by Hubert de Burgh to defend the Welsh Marches. Substantial remains of walls, towers and a gatehouse can be seen. This is the finest of a trio of castles, the others being at Skenfrith and Grosmont.
Open all year.
✱*£1.50 (reductions £1). Family ticket £4. No charge for admission Oct-Mar.*
🅿 ✿ ✤
(AM Cadw)

GWYNEDD

Penrhyn Castle
BANGOR
(3m E at Landegai on A5122)
☎(01248) 353084
The splendid castle with its towers and battlements was commissioned in 1827 as a sumptuous family home. The architect was Thomas Hopper, who was also responsible for the panelling, plasterwork and furniture, still mostly in the 'Norman' style of the mid-19th century. Notable rooms include the great hall, heated by the Roman method of hot air under the floor, the library with its heavily decorated ceiling and great arches, and the dining room, which is covered with neo-Norman decoration. Among the furniture is a slate bed weighing over a ton, and a decorated brass bed made specially for Edward VII at the then huge cost of £600.
The Penrhyn Castle Industrial Railway Museum occupies the stableyard. The 40-acre grounds include a walled garden, wild garden and attractive woodland. There are wonderful views over Anglesey, Puffin Island, the North Wales coast and Snowdonia.
Open 29 Mar-29 Oct, daily (ex Tue) 12-5 (Jul-Aug 11-5). Grounds 11-5. Last admission 4.30pm. Last audio tour 4pm.
£4.40 (ch £2.20). Family ticket £11. Party 20+. Audio tours 50p.
🅿 🍴 ✿ *toilets for disabled shop* ✤
(NT)

Beaumaris Castle
BEAUMARIS
☎(01248) 810361
Beaumaris was the last of the great castles built by Edward I around the coast of North Wales, and there is an exhibition on his castles in the Chapel Tower. The building took from 1295 to 1312 to complete and involved a huge workforce: a record for 1296 mentions 400 masons and 2000 labourers, besides 100 carts and wagons and 30 boats carrying stone and seacoal. In the early 1400s it was captured by Owain Glyndwr and then retaken, and in later centuries it was plundered for its lead, timber and stone. Despite this it remains one of the most impressive and complete castles built by Edward I. It has a perfectly symmetrical, concentric plan, with a square inner bailey and curtain walls, round corner towers and D-shaped towers in between. There are also two great gatehouses, but these were never finished. Around it is an outer curtain wall with small towers, and a moat which has been restored. The original defended dock for shipping has also survived.
Open all year, late Oct-late Mar, Mon-Sat 9.30-4, Sun 11-4; Late Mar-late Oct daily 9.30-6.30. (Closed 24-26 Dec & 1 Jan).
£1.50 (concessions £1). Family ticket £4.
🅿 ✿ *shop* ✤
(AM Cadw)

Beaumaris Gaol & Courthouse
BEAUMARIS
☎(01286) 679098
With its treadmill and grim cells, the gaol is a vivid reminder of the tough penalties exacted by 19th-century law. One particularly gruesome feature is the route that condemned prisoners took to the scaffold. The courthouse, built in 1614 and renovated early in the 19th-century, is a unique survival of a Victorian court room.
Open Etr, end May-Sep, daily 11-5.30. Court 11.30-5.30 (ex when in session), wknds 2-5.30. Other times by arrangement only.
✱*Gaol £2.30 (ch & pen £1.55). Courthouse £1.35 (ch & pen £1.05). Combined ticket £2.80 (ch & pen £2.10). Family ticket £6.75.*
🅿 ✿ *(audio tape tour available) shop* ✤

Museum of Childhood
BEAUMARIS
1 Castle St (on A545)
☎*Bangor (01248) 712498*
Many rare and valuable exhibits are shown in the nine rooms of the museum, which illustrates the life and interests of children and families over 150 years. They include money boxes, dolls, educational toys and games, early clockwork trains, cars and aeroplanes, push toys and cycles. Also shown are things that were used rather than played with by children, such as pottery and glassware, and pieces of furniture. A gallery shows paintings and prints of children. Winner of the BTA and National Heritage Museum of the Year Awards. In 1990, the museum was voted 'Star Choice' out of 35 top museums by the Sunday Express Magazine travel writers.
Open daily 10.30-5.30, Sun 12-5. Last admission 4.30pm, Sun 4pm. (Closed Nov-2nd wk Mar).

✱*£2.50 (ch £1.25, pen £1.50). Family ticket £6.50. Free entry for wheelchairs.*
🅿 2 ✿ *shop* ✤

Sygun Copper Mine
BEDDGELERT
(1m E of Beddgelert on A498)
☎(01766) 890595
With the help of an expert guide, and an audio-visual underground tour, visitors can explore the workings of this 19th-century copper mine set deep within the Gwynant Valley where magnificent stalactite and stalagmite formations can be seen. The less energetic can enjoy a continuous audio-visual presentation and a display of artefacts found during excavations.
Open all year, daily 10-6. (Last tour 5pm).
£3.90 (ch £2.75, pen £3.25). Family ticket £12.
🅿 ✿ *toilets for disabled shop*

Conwy Valley Railway Museum
BETWS-Y-COED
Old Goods Yard
☎(01690) 710568
The two large museum buildings have displays on both the narrow-and standard-gauge railways of North Wales, including railway stock and other memorabilia. There are working model railway layouts, a steam-hauled miniature railway in the grounds, which cover over four acres, and a 15in-gauge tramway to the woods. The latest addition is the quarter-size steam 'Britannia' loco which is now on display. For children there arealso self-drive mini-dodgems, Postman Pat, school bus and Toby Tram. For 1995 there is a weekend meeting of 'Denver & Rio Grande' steam locomotives. Telephone for details.
Open Etr-Oct, daily 10-5.30.
✱*£1 (ch & pen 50p). Family ticket £2.50. Steam train ride 75p. Tram ride 60p.*
🅿 🍴 ✿ *toilets for disabled shop*

Ffestiniog Pumped Storage Scheme
BLAENAU FFESTINIOG
Ffestiniog Information Centre, Tan-Y-Grisiau (off A496)
☎(01766) 830310
The scheme was the first hydro-electric pumped storage scheme, and was opened by Her Majesty the Queen in 1963. Water is released from an upper dam, through turbines, to generate electricity when needed, and then pumped back up when demand is low. Guided tours are available, and the information centre includes a souvenir shop and cafe.
Open Etr-Oct, Sun-Fri, 10-4.30. Other times by prior arrangement.
£2.50 (ch, students & pen £1.25)
🅿 ✿ *shop* ✤ *(ex in grounds)*

Gloddfa Ganol Slate Mine
BLAENAU FFESTINIOG
(1m N on A470)
☎(01766) 830664
Visitors can put on safety helmets and go into the extensive underground workings

of this slate mine, which is the world's largest. There are special conducted tours by Land Rover for the more adventurous, which explore some of the miles of chambers and tunnels hundreds of feet up in the mountain. The massive machinery used in slate mining is displayed in the mill, and the art of slate splitting is demonstrated. Gloddfa Ganol is an active mine. Today's open-cast blasting operations can be seen from the safety of the Mining Museum, and with the help of video films, exhibitions and demonstrations visitors achieve a valuable insight into the complex nature of the slate industry.
Open Etr-Oct, Mon-Fri, also Sun BH wknds & summer school holidays.
❋£4 (ch £2).
🅿 💺 ✗ licensed & shop

Llechwedd Slate Caverns
BLAENAU FFESTINIOG
☎ (01766) 830306
The Miners' Underground Tramway carries visitors into areas where early conditions have been recreated, while the Deep Mine is reached by an incline railway and has an unusual audio-visual presentation. Free surface attractions include several exhibitions and museums, slate mill and the Victorian village which has Victorian shops, bank, Miners Arms pub, lock-up and working smithy.
Open all year, daily from 10am. Last tour 5.15 (Oct-Feb 4.15). (Closed 25-26 Dec & 1 Jan).
❋Single Tour £4.75 (ch £3.25, pen £4.25). Combined Tour £7.25 (ch £5, pen £6).
🅿 💺 ✗ licensed & toilets for disabled shop 🐾 (ex on surface)

Bryn Celli Ddu Burial Chamber
BRYN-CELLI-DDU
(3m W of Menai Bridge off A4080)
☎ (01222) 500200
Excavated in 1865, and then again in 1925-9, this is a prehistoric circular cairn covering a passage grave with a polygonal chamber.
Open at all times.
Free.
🅿 🐾
(AM Cadw)

Anglesey Sea Zoo
BRYNSIENCYN
The Oyster Hatchery (follow Lobster signs along A4080 to zoo)
☎ (01248) 430411
The sea zoo is a unique collection of marine life found around Anglesey and the North Wales coast. The sea creatures are housed in glass-sided and open-topped tanks of all shapes and sizes, which are intended to provide as natural and unrestricted an environment as possible. Another important consideration has been providing cover for visitors. There are also shoaling tanks, a wave tank, tide tank, wreck room and touch pools. A recent addition is an exhibit called 'The Big Fish Forest'. This is a huge kelp forest enclosed by the largest unsupported acrylic panel in Britain.
Open Mar-Oct, daily 10-5; Nov-Feb, daily 11-3. Closed 19-26 Dec, 1 & 3-6 Jan.
❋£4 (ch £3, pen £3.50). Family ticket £12-£14. Party 12+.
🅿 💺 ✗ licensed & (wheelchair available) toilets for disabled shop

---

Caernarfon Castle
CAERNARFON
☎ (01286) 677617
Edward I began building the castle and extensive town walls in 1283 after defeating Llywelyn ap Gruffyd (the last independant ruler of Wales). Completed in 1328, it has unusual polygonal towers, notably the 10-sided Eagle Tower, and the walls have bands of colour. There is a theory that these features were copied from the walls of Constantinople, to reflect a tradition that Constantine the Great was born nearby, at the Roman fort of Segontium. Caernarfon was the largest of Edward I's castles in Wales, and the Chamberlain Tower has an

Viewed from across the river and with a backdrop of Snowdonia, Conwy Castle is a most impressive sight. It still retains its eight round towers and two barbicans.

exhibition on the castles of Edward I. His son and heir was born and presented to the Welsh people here, setting a precedent that was followed in 1969, when Prince Charles was invested as Princes of Wales - there is a 'Prince of Wales' exhibition in the North-East Tower and a display of investiture robes. A wall walkway links the Eagle Tower to the Queen's Tower, which houses the museum of the Royal Welch Fusiliers. The regiment dates back to 1689 and eight Victoria Crosses are on display. There is also a 'Prospect of Caernarfon' exhibition on the ground floor of the Eagle Tower.
Open all year, late Oct-late Mar, Mon-Sat 9.30-4, Sun 11-4; Late Mar-late Oct daily 9.30-6.30. (Closed 24-26 Dec & 1 Jan)
❋£3.50 (reductions £2.50). Family ticket £10
🅿 shop 🐾
(AM Cadw)

Segontium Roman Fort & Museum
CAERNARFON
Llanbeblig Rd (on A4085)
☎ (01286) 675625
The Roman fort dates from AD78 and was an important base for 300 years. It was rebuilt a number of times, and remains of the various phases can be seen, including four gateways and an underground storeroom. Sir Mortimer Wheeler directed excavations in the 1920s, and the museum shows finds from the site.
Open all year, daily; Mon-Sat 9.30-6 (closes 5.30 Mar, Apr & Oct; 4 Nov-Feb). Sun all year 2-5.
❋£1 (concessions 60p).
🅿 & shop 🐾
(AM Cadw)

Coed-y-Brenin Forest Park & Visitor Centre
COED-Y-BRENIN
☎ Dolgellau (01341) 422289
Located in the heart of Coed-y-Brenin, the visitor centre provides an excellent introduction to the area with its range of displays and audio-visual programmes. Coed-y-Brenin means King's Forest, and it was named to commemorate the Silver Jubilee of King George V in 1935. There are over 50 miles of waymarked walks, delightful picnic spots and a wildlife conservation hide. Guide leaflets on the surrounding trails are provided by the centre, where visitors can also see a fascinating display on the gold mines

which were once worked in this area. Mountain bikes are available for hire at the visitor centre. There is a children's play area, and a new orienteering course. A Forest Festival is planned for late spring 1995.
Open Apr-Oct 10-5. Other dates by prior bookings.
Free.
🅿 (charged) 💺 & toilets for disabled shop

Aberconwy House
CONWY
☎ (01492) 592246
This house dates from the 14th century; it is the only medieval merchant's house in Conwy to have survived the turbulence, the fire and pillage of this frontier town for nearly six centuries. Furnished rooms and an audio-visual presentation show daily life in the house at different periods in its history.
Open 31 Mar-30 Oct, daily (ex Tue) 10-5. Last admission 4.30pm.
£1.80 (ch 90p). Family ticket £4.50. Party 20+.
shop 🐾
(NT)

Conwy Castle
CONWY
(by A55 or B5106)
☎ (01492) 592358
The castle is a magnificent fortress, built from 1283-9 by Edward I. There is an exhibition on Edward I and his castles in Wales within the shop area. The castle forms part of the same defensive system as the extensive town walls, 1400yds long and some 30ft high, which are among the most complete in Europe. They have 21 (originally 22) towers, and sweep up and down hills as they encircle the town. The best view of the castle and walls is from the other side of the river, which is spanned by three bridges designed to complement the scene. The graceful suspension bridge was built by Telford in 1826, the tubular bridge by Stephenson in 1848, and the road bridge was completed in 1958.
Open all year, late Oct-late Mar, Mon-Sat 9.30-4, Sun 11-4; Late Mar-late Oct daily 9.30-6.30. (Closed 24-26 Dec & 1 Jan)
❋£2.90 (reductions £1.80). Family ticket £8.
🅿 & toilets for disabled shop 🐾
(AM Cadw)

Smallest House
CONWY
The Quay
☎ (01492) 593484
The 'Guinness Book of Records' lists this as the smallest house in Britain. Just 6ft wide by 10ft high, it is furnished in the style of a mid-Victorian Welsh cottage.
Open Apr-mid Oct daily 10-6 (10-9.30/10pm in Jul & Aug). In winter by arrangement.
50p (ch 5 free).
P (100 yds) & shop

Criccieth Castle
CRICCIETH
(off A497)
☎ (01766) 522227
The castle dates from the 13th century and was taken and destroyed by Owain Glyndwr in 1404. Evidence of a fierce fire can still be seen. The gatehouse leading to the inner ward remains impressive, and parts of the walls are well preserved. There are two exhibitions - one on the castles of native Welsh Princes and another on Gerald of Wales and the Welsh Princes. Perched on its rocky peninsula, the castle commands superb views over the resort and Tremadog Bay.
Open all year, late Oct-late Mar, Mon-Sat 9.30-4, Sun 2-4; Late Mar-late Oct, daily 9.30-6.30. (Closed 24-26 Dec & 1 Jan)
❋£2 (reductions £1.50). Family ticket £6.
P shop 🐾
(AM Cadw)

Cymer Abbey
CYMER ABBEY
(2m NW of Dolgellau on A494)
☎ Dolgellau (01341) 422854
The abbey was built for the Cistercians in the 13th century. It was never very large, and does not seem to have been finished. The church is the best-preserved building, with ranges of windows and arcades still to be seen. The other buildings have been plundered for stone, but low outlines remain.
Open all year, late Oct-late Mar, Mon-Sat 9.30-4, Sun 2-4; Late Mar-late Oct, daily 9.30-6.30. (Closed 24-26 Dec & 1 Jan)
❋£1 (reductions 60p)
🅿 & 🐾
(AM Cadw)

Dolwyddelan Castle
DOLWYDDELAN
☎ (016906) 366

➤

Steam trains have struggled up Snowdon for almost 100 years on a track that climbed 3140ft in just over 4½ miles. It operates on a rack and pinion system.

The castle is reputed to be the birthplace of Llywelyn the Great. It was captured in 1283 by Edward I, who immediately began strengthening it for his own purposes. A restored keep of around 1200, and a 13th-century curtain wall can be seen. An exhibition on the castles of the Welsh Princes is located in the keep.
Open all year, late Oct-late Mar, Mon-Sat 9.30-4 & Sun 2-4; Late Mar-late Oct daily 9.30-6.30. (Closed 24-26 Dec & 1 Jan).
❋*£1.50 (reductions £1). Family ticket £4.*
🅿 ♿
(AM Cadw)

Fairbourne Railway
FAIRBOURNE
Beach Rd
☎ (01341) 250362
One of the most unusual of Wales's 'little trains' - it was built in 1890 as a horse-drawn railway to carry building materials for the seaside resort of Fairbourne. It was later converted to steam, and now runs two-and-a-half miles from Fairbourne to the end of the peninsula and the ferry for Barmouth. Its route passes one of the loveliest beaches in Wales, with views of the beautiful Mawddach Estuary. An enjoyable round trip can be made from Barmouth in summer, crossing the Mawddach by ferry, catching the narrow gauge steam train to Fairbourne and then taking the British Rail train - or walking - across the Mawddach Viaduct. At Gorsaf Newydd terminus visitors can see locomotive sheds and engineering works.
Open Etr-Oct 2, times vary according to season and events.
🅿 ✗ *licensed* ♿ *shop*

Felin Isaf Watermill
GLAN CONWY
(on A470, 1m S from junc A55 & A470).
☎ Aberconwy (01492) 580646
This award-winning 17th-century mill with a working water wheel has recently been restored, and stands in its own secluded gardens. Nine rooms can be seen, including the Ghost Room! There is a mini golf course, craft, souvenir and bric-a-brac shops. There is a picturesque woodland walk and mill pond. School groups are a speciality. Children can take part in a Discovery Project.
Open Apr-Oct, Sun-Thu from 10.30am; daily Jul & Aug. Last tour 5.30pm.
£2.50 (ch £1.50, pen £2).
🅿 ☕ ♿ *shop* ♿

Harlech Castle
HARLECH
(from A496)
☎ (01766) 780552
Harlech Castle was built in 1283-81 by Edward I, with a sheer drop to the sea on one side. Owain Glyndwr starved the castle into submission in 1404 and made it his court and campaigning base. Later, the defence of the castle in the Wars of the Roses inspired the song *Men of Harlech*. Today the sea has slipped away, and the castle's great walls and round towers stand above the dunes. The gatehouse is especially impressive, and there are magnificent views of Snowdonia and across Tremadog Bay.
Open all year, late Oct-late Mar, Mon-Sat 9.30-4, Sun 11-4; Late Mar-late Oct, daily 9.30-6.30. (Closed 24-26 Dec & 1 Jan)
🅿 *(disabled spaces in car park) shop* ♿
(AM Cadw)

Din Llugwy Ancient Village
LLANALLGO
(1m NW off A5025)
The remains of a 4th-century village can be seen here. There are two circular and seven rectangular buildings, still standing up to head height and encircled by a pentagonal stone wall some 4 to 5ft thick.
Open at all times.
♿
(AM Cadw)
Details not confirmed for 1995

Maes Artro Centre
LLANBEDR
(on A496)
☎ (01341) 23467 due to change to 241467
An old wartime RAF camp has been imaginatively converted to display a varied range of exhibitions and activities. An original air raid shelter has been restored with light and sound effects; the history of RAF Llanbedr is illustrated; and a Spitfire, used in the TV series *A Piece of Cake*, is on show. Rural Heritage Exhibition, a 'Village of Yesteryear', military tanks, RAF Rescue helicopter, a log fort playground and nature trails are all set among the lovely wooded grounds. Large Marine Life Aquarium. Musicians play live in the village most days.
Open Etr-Sep, daily 10-5.30.
❋*£2.75 (ch & pen £2).*
🅿 ☕ ♿ *toilets for disabled shop*

Dinorwig Power Station
LLANBERIS
(on A4086)
☎ Caernarfon (01286) 870636
The tours of the Power Station begin at the 'Power of Wales' Centre. A new introductory, interactive audio-visual show and electricity gallery are features of the centre. New displays are being produced for 1995.
Mar-Oct, daily. Feb & Nov, Sun, Tue, Wed & Thu. 10-5 peak season, 10.30-3.30 mid-season & 11-3 low season.
❋*£5 (ch £2.50, concessions £3.75) includes show, museum & underground.*
🅿 ☕ ♿ *toilets for disabled shop* ♿

Dolbadarn Castle
LLANBERIS
☎ (01222) 500200
Built by Llywelyn the Great in the early 13th century, this Welsh castle overlooks Llyn Padarn in the Llanberis pass.
Open all year, late Oct-late Mar, Mon-Sat 9.30-4, Sun 2-4; Late Mar-late Oct, daily 9.30-6.30.
❋*£1 (reductions 60p).*
🅿 ♿
(AM Cadw)

Llanberis Lake Railway
LLANBERIS
Padarn Country Park (off A4086)
☎ (01286) 870549
Steam locomotives dating from 1889 to 1948 carry passengers on a four-mile return journey along the shore of Padarn Lake. The terminal station is adjacent to the Welsh Slate Museum, within the Padarn Country Park. The railway was formerly used to carry slate.
Open Etr-late Oct. Trains run frequently every day (ex Sat), 11-4.30 in peak season.
❋*£3.60 (ch £2). Family ticket available.*
🅿 *(charged)* ☕ ♿ *toilets for disabled shop* ♿ *(train & shop)*

Museum of the North/Power of Wales
LLANBERIS
☎ Caernarfon (01286) 870636
Amgueddfa'r Gogledd/Museum of the North, the National Museum of Wales's main centre in North Wales is located at the foot of Snowdon, overlooking Lake Padarn. In order to complete your understanding of the fascination of Snowdonia, wander through the museum's splendid exhibition galleries. Various aspects of the culture and history of the area are featured and you can also discover the National Grid Company's story of electricity generation in Snowdonia.
Open all year; Jun-15 Sep daily, 9.30-6; 16 Sep-Oct & Mar-May daily, 10-5; Nov & Feb, Tue-Thu & Sun, 10.30-4 (prebooked only Mon & Fri). Dec & Jan prebooked parties only Mon-Fri.
❋*£3.50 (ch £1.75, pen £2.60. Power Station; £1.50 (ch 75p, pen £1.15).*
🅿 ♿ *(lift to first floor) toilets for disabled shop* ♿

Snowdon Mountain Railway
LLANBERIS
(on A4086, towards Capel Curig)
☎ (01286) 870223
Britain's only public rack-and-pinion railway is operated by seven vintage steam and four modern diesel locomotives. The journey of just over four-and-a-half miles takes passengers more than 3000ft up to the summit of Snowdon; breathtaking views include, on a clear day, the Isle of Man and the Wicklow Mountains in Ireland. The railway was opened in 1896.
Open 15 Mar-1 Nov, daily from 9am (weather permitting).
❋*Return £13.20 (ch £9.50). Single £9.50 (ch £7). Party 15+ by prior arrangement (out of season only).*
🅿 *(charged)* ☕ ♿ *(2 carriages suitable for disabled) toilets for disabled shop*

Welsh Slate Museum
LLANBERIS
Gilfach Ddu (0.25m off A4086)
☎ (01286) 870630
Until its closure in 1969 the Dinorwic Quarry was one of the largest in Britain, employing over three thousand men in its heyday. The workshops, most of the machinery and plant have been preserved, including the foundry and the Dinorwic water wheel. The museum which was subsequently founded on the site includes displays and audio-visual presentations depicting the life here, and

much of the original atmosphere still prevails. Nearby is a group of craft workshops and a woodcraft centre where visitors can watch craftsmen at work.
Open daily, Apr-Sep 9.30-5.30; Oct-Mar prebooked parties only.
✿£1.50 (ch 80p, pen £1.20) Family ticket £3.80.
🅿 (charged) ᵰ shop
(AM Cadw)

St Cybi's Well
LLANGYBI
☎(01758) 612179
Cybi was a sixth-century Cornish saint, known as a healer of the sick, and St Cybi's Well (or Ffynnon Gybi) has been famous for its curative properties through the centuries. The corbelled beehive vaulting inside the roofless stone structure is Irish in style and unique in Wales.
Open at all times.
ᵰ ✍
(AM Cadw)
Details not confirmed for 1995

Bryn Bras Castle & Gardens
LLANRUG
(0.5m SE of A4086)
☎Llanberis (01286) 870210
Against a backdrop of high mountains, this extravagant neo-Norman style mansion, thought to be the work of Thomas Hopper, was built in 1830. The charm of the interior lies in its 'lived-in' atmosphere, and the richly carved furniture and panelling, stained glass, interesting ceilings and galleried staircase are special features. The grounds are splendid with herbaceous borders, rhododendrons, roses and hydrangeas, waterfalls, pools and streams. Perhaps the chief attraction is the walled knot garden, but the woodland and mountain walks with their panoramic views are strong contenders.
Open Spring BH-mid Sep, Tue-Fri 1-5; mid Jul-Aug 11-5. Also bank hol Sun & Mon.
✿£3.50 (ch £1.75).
🅿 ⬛ shop ✍

Gwydir Uchaf Chapel
LLANRWST
(.5m SW off B5106)
☎(01492) 640978
Built in the 17th century by Sir John Wynn of Gwydir Castle, the chapel is noted for its painted ceiling and wonderfully varied woodwork.
Open all year, Mon-Fri 8.30-4.
✿£1 (reductions 60p).
🅿ᵰ✍
(AM Cadw)

Bala Lake Railway
LLANUWCHLLYN
The Station (off A494)
☎(016784) 666 due to change to (01678) 540666
Steam locomotives which once worked in the slate quarries of North Wales now haul passenger coaches for four-and-a-half miles from Llanuwchllyn Station along the lake to Bala. The railway has one of the four remaining double-twist lever-locking framed GWR signal boxes, installed in 1896. Some of the coaches are open and some closed, so passengers can enjoy the beautiful views of the lake and mountains in all weathers; the latest corridor coach has facilities for the disabled. Special events for 1995 include: Teddy Bear Weekend (22-23 July).
Open 14 Apr-1 Oct, daily (ex certain Fri in Apr-Jun & Sep).
£5 return. Family ticket £11.
🅿 ⬛ ᵰ shop

Lloyd George Memorial Museum & Highgate Victorian Cottage
LLANYSTUMDWY
(on A497)
☎(01766) 522071
Visitors can explore the life and times of David Lloyd George. His boyhood home is recreated as it would have been when he lived there between 1864 and 1880, along with his Uncle Lloyd's shoemaking workshop. Also

Highgate Cottage's Victorian garden. 1995 is the 50th anniversary of the death of Lloyd George. Many events are being organised for all ages. Telephone for details.
Open Etr-Sep, Mon-Fri 1-5, wknds 2-5; Oct, Mon-Fri, 11-4. Other times by appointment, telephone (01286) 679098 or (01766) 522071 for details.
✿£2.10 (ch & pen £1.35). Family ticket £5.20.
🅿ᵰ (limited access to Highgate) toilets for disabled shop ✍

Penarth Fawr
PENARTH FAWR
(3.5m NE of Pwllheli off A497)
☎Pwllheli (01766) 810880
The hall, buttery and screen are preserved in this house which was probably built in the 15th century.
Open at all times.
Free.
ᵰ ✍
(AM Cadw)

Penmachno Woollen Mill
PENMACHNO
(2m off A5, between Llangollen/Betws-Y-Coed)
☎Betwys-y-Coed (01690) 710545
The 17th-century quarrymen and farmers wore flannel shirts made from cloth woven by local cottage weavers. The cloth was washed and finished in the Pandy (fulling mill). Power looms introduced in the 19th century now weave lightweight tweed and rug cloth. The Story of Wool exhibition explains the process and its history, and there is a mill shop and cafe. In June there is a sheep shearing competition and sheepdog trial sponsored by Penmachno Wollen Mill.
Open daily 10-6.
Free.
🅿 ⬛ shop ✍

Plas Newydd
PLAS NEWYDD
(1m S of Llanfairpwll, on A4080)
☎Llanfairpwll (01248) 714795
Built by James Wyatt in the 18th century, this house stands on the Menai Strait in unspoilt surroundings, and enjoys uninterrupted views of the Snowdonia mountain range. Beautiful lawns and parkland surround the house and there is a fine spring garden. An exhibition of Rex Whistler's work is on show with his largest wall painting. Relics of the first Marquess of Anglesey and the Battle of

Waterloo are kept here, along with the Ryan collection of military uniforms and headdresses.
Open 31 Mar-29 Sep, daily (ex Sat). 1-29 Oct, Fri & Sun only. House 12-5, Garden 12-4. Last admission 4.30pm.
£3.80 (ch £1.90). Family ticket £9.50. Party 20+.
🅿 ⬛ ᵰ toilets for disabled shop ✍
(NT)

Plas-yn-Rhiw
PLAS-YN-RHIW
(on unclass road 4.5m NE of Aberdaron)
☎Rhiw (01758) 780219
House with gardens and woodlands down to the sea on west shore of Porth Neigwl (Hell's Mouth Bay). This is a small manor house, part medieval, with Tudor and Georgian additions and ornamental gardens with flowering trees and shrubs including sub-tropical specimens, divided by box hedges and grass paths. There is a stream and waterfall, rising behind to the snowdrop wood.
Open 2 Apr-29 Sep, daily (ex Sat) 12-5. Last admission 30 mins prior to closing.
£2.30 (ch £1.15). Family ticket £6.
🅿ᵰ toilets for disabled ✍ 🚲
(NT)

Ffestiniog Railway
PORTHMADOG
Harbour Station
☎(01766) 512340 & 831654
Narrow gauge steam railway running for 13.5 miles through Snowdonia National Park, between Porthmadog and Blaenau Ffestiniog. Breathtaking views, superb scenery. Buffet service on all trains including licensed bar (in corridor carriages). Comfortable seating, some trains heated, toilet facilities on corridor carriages. To coincide with VE Day 50th Anniversary a massive Steam Gala '95 has been organised (6-8 May). Telephone for details.
Open late Mar-early Nov, daily service and also 26 Dec-2Jan. Weekend service Nov-Dec (most days). Limited service Feb & Mar. Talking timetable (01766) 514114.
Full distance return £11.60 (1 child free with each adult).
🅿 ⬛ ᵰ shop

Ffestiniog Railway Museum
PORTHMADOG
Harbour Station
☎(01766) 512340
The harbour station is home to exhibits

including an old four-wheeled hearse converted from a quarryman's coach, one of the original steam locos from 1863, a slate wagon and model steam engine. Maps and diagrams illustrate the history of the famous narrow-gauge railway.
Open Mar-Nov when train services operating (see Ffestiniog Railway).
🅿 ⬛ ᵰ shop
Details not confirmed for 1995

Portmeirion
PORTMEIRION
☎Porthmadog (01766) 770228
Welsh architect Sir Clough Williams Ellis built his fairy-tale, Italianate village on a rocky, tree-clad peninsula on the shores of Cardigan Bay. The nucleus of the estate is a sumptuous waterfront hotel, rebuilt from the original house and containing a fine 18th-century fireplace and a library moved here from the Great Exhibition of 1851. A bell-tower, castle and lighthouse mingle with a watch-tower, grottoes and cobbled squares among pastel-shaded picturesque cottages let as holiday accommodation. A number of shops sell a variety of goods and the whole village is set in 175 acres of sub-tropical coastal cliff and wooded gardens.
One of the finest wild gardens in Wales is here - the 60-acre Gwyllt Gardens. They include miles of dense woodland paths and are famous for their fine displays of rhododendrons, azaleas, hydrangeas and sub-tropical flora. There is a mile of sandy beach and a playground for children. Toll-paying visitors can see the place where Noel Coward wrote 'Blithe Spirit', and the location for the cult TV series 'The Prisoner'.
Open all year, daily 9.30-5.30.
✿£3 (ch £1.30, pen £2.40). Party 20+. Winter rates (Nov-Mar) £1.50 (ch 75p, pen £1.50).
🅿 ⬛ ✗ licensed ᵰ toilets for disabled shop ✍

Museum of Old Welsh Country Life
TAI'N LON
Felin Faesog
☎Clynnogfawr (01286) 660311
Set in a 17th-century watermill in the hills by the River Desach, the museum has a wide range of exhibits from Wales of the past, including displays on the old farming year, the women's week, children's work and play, a miller's room, and clog making.
➤

Portmeirion is a fantasy Italianate village of colour-washed houses created among the grey-slate villages of Gwynedd by Clough Williams-Ellis in the 1920s.

Open Good Fri-Sep, daily (ex Sat) 10-5.
❋*£1.20 (ch 16 60p). Party 15+.*
🅿 ♿ *(special entrance) shop ⊗ (ex in
grounds)*

Bodnant Garden
TAL-Y-CAFN ▓▓▓▓▓▓
(8m S of Llandudno & Colwyn Bay on
A470)
☎ *Tyngroes (01492) 650460*
Situated above the River Conwy with
beautiful views over Snowdonia, these
gardens are a delight. They were first laid
out in 1875 but in 1900 the 2nd Lord
Aberconway started to improve them
dramatically. Five terraces in the Italian
style were constructed below the house,
and between two large, existing cedars
he placed a lily pool. On the lowest
terrace is a canal pool with an open-air
stage at one end and a reconstructed Pin
Mill at the other.
Part of the grounds have been made into
a beautiful woodland garden in a
sheltered valley. This is notable for its
rhododendrons and other delicate shrubs.
There are also many azaleas, a rock
garden, and a laburnum walk. To
celebrate the National Trust's centenary a
gala evening in the garden is scheduled
for 30 June 1995.
*Open 18 Mar-30 Oct, daily 10-5 (last
admission 4.30pm).*
£3.90 (ch £1.95). Party 20+.
🅿 ♨ ✗ ♿ *(steep in places with many
steps not easy for wheelchairs) shop
garden centre ⊗*
(NT)

Trefriw Woollen Mill
TREFRIW ▓▓▓▓▓▓
Trefriw Woollen Mills Ltd (on B5106)
☎ *Llanrwst (01492) 640462*
Established in 1859, the mill is situated
beside the fast-flowing Afon Crafnant,
which is used to drive two hydro-electric
turbines to power the looms. All the
machinery of woollen manufacture can
be seen here: blending, carding, spinning,
dyeing, warping and weaving. The mill
produces Welsh tapestries and tweeds,
and there is a large shop selling its
products. In the Weaver's Garden, there
are plants traditionally used in the textile
industry, mainly for dyeing.
*Mill open Etr-Oct, Mon-Fri 9-5.30. (Closed
BHs & 3rd Mon Oct). Weaving
demonstrations & turbine house: open all
year, Mon-Fri 9-5. Also Spring BH-Aug,
Sat & BH's 10-5 & Sun 2-5.*
*Free (ex school parties which must be
pre-booked).*
🅿 *(35 yds)* ♨ ♿ *shop ⊗*

Narrow-Gauge Railway Museum
TYWYN ▓▓▓▓▓▓
Wharf Station
☎ *(01654) 710472*
An interesting small museum displaying a
number of locomotives, wagons and
signalling equipment used on the non-
standard narrow-gauge railways. There
are also displays of other relics, from
tools to signs.

*Open Apr-4 Nov, daily 10-5. Winter by
arrangement.*
❋*50p (ch 10p).*
P *200yds* ♿ *toilets for disabled shop
⊗*

Talyllyn Railway
TYWYN ▓▓▓▓▓▓
Wharf Station
☎ *(01654) 710472*
This is the oldest 27in-gauge railway in
the world. It was built in 1865 to run from
Tywyn on Cardigan Bay to Abergynolwyn
slate mine some seven miles inland. The
railway was also the first to be saved by
a voluntary preservation society, after the
slate quarry closed in 1947. The railway
climbs the steep sides of the Fathew
Valley and on the way there are stops to
admire the Dolgoch Falls or to allow
passengers to visit the Nant Gwernol
forest. The train takes 2 hours and 30
minutes to cover the round trip. Each
year in August there is a 'Race the Train'
charity competition. This will be held on
19 August in 1995. Nearly 1,000 runners
follow the track and usually as many as
100 will beat the train. Other events for
1995 include: Colt Vehicle Rally and
1940's weekend (27-28 May), Victorian
Week (30 July-5 August), Landrover Rally
(27 August).
*Open 12 Feb-26 Mar, Sun only; Apr-4
Nov, daily. Xmas holiday sevice 26 Dec-2
Jan. Timetable available.*
*£7 return ticket (ch accompanied £2).
Intermediate fares available.*
🅿 *(charged)* ♨ ♿ *(by prior arrangement
on trains) toilets for disabled shop*

MID GLAMORGAN

Newcastle
BRIDGEND ▓▓▓▓▓▓
☎ *(01656) 659515*
The small castle dates back to the 12th
century. It is ruined, but a rectangular
tower, a richly carved Norman gateway
and massive curtain walls enclosing a
polygonal courtyard can still be seen.
*Open - accessible throughout the year.
Key keeper arrangement.*
Free.
🅿 *⊗*
(AM Cadw)

Caerphilly Castle
CAERPHILLY ▓▓▓▓▓▓
(on A469)
☎ *(01222) 883143*
The concentrically planned castle was
begun in 1268 by Gilbert de Clare and
completed in 1326. It is the largest in
Wales, and has extensive land and water
defences. A unique feature is the ruined
tower - the victim of subsidence - which
manages to out-lean even Pisa!
*Open all year, late Oct-late Mar, Mon-Sat
9.30-4, Sun 11-4; late Mar-late Oct, daily
9.30-6.30. (Closed 24-26 Dec & 1 Jan).*

❋*£2 (reduced £1.50). Family ticket £6*
🅿 ♿ *shop ⊗*
(AM Cadw)

Coity Castle
COITY ▓▓▓▓▓▓
☎ *Bridgend (01656) 652021*
A 12th-to 16th-century stronghold, with a
hall, chapel and the remains of a square
keep.
*Open all year, at all times. Key keeper
arrangement.*
Free.
P *⊗*
(AM Cadw)

Brecon Mountain Railway
MERTHYR TYDFIL ▓▓▓▓▓▓
Pant Station Dowlais (2.5m NE to the N
of A465)
☎ *(01685) 722988*
After eight years of planning and
construction, this narrow-gauge railway
was opened in 1980. It follows part of an
old British Rail route which was closed in
1964 when the iron industry in South
Wales fell into decline. The present route
starts at Pant Station, three miles north
of Merthyr Tydfil, and continues for 3.5
miles through the beautiful scenery of
the Brecon Beacons National Park, as far
as the two-and-a-half-mile long Taf
Fechan reservoir. The train is pulled by a
vintage steam locomotive, a delight in
itself, and for lovers of vintage
locomotives the workshops at Pant
Station are well worth a visit. The display
includes engines built in Germany and
the USA as well as Great Britain, and
some have spent their days on railways
in far-flung corners of the earth.
*Opening times on application to The
Brecon Mountain Railway, Pant Station,
Merthyr Tydfil, Mid Glamorgan.
Fares are under review, please ring for
details.*
🅿 ♨ ✗ *licensed* ♿ *toilets for disabled
shop*

Cyfarthfa Castle Museum & Art Gallery
MERTHYR TYDFIL ▓▓▓▓▓▓
Cyfarthfa Park
☎ *(01685) 723112*
The home of the Crawshay family, who
took over the Cyfarthfa Ironworks which
employed 1,500 men by the turn of the
century, is an imposing Gothic mansion.
It was built in 1825 and the magnificent
gardens, designed at around the same
time, still survive today. The state rooms
are given over to a museum which not
only covers the social and industrial life of
the area, but also houses collections of
fine and decorative art, natural history
items, archaeology and Egyptology.
Temporary exhibitions are held.
*Open all year, Apr-Oct, Mon-Fri 10-6, Sat
& Sun 12-6. Oct-Mar, Mon-Fri, 10-5, Sat
& Sun 12-5. (Last admission 30 mins
before closing).*
80p (ch, pen & UB40's 40p).
🅿 ♨ ♿ *(stair lift & wheelchair available)
toilets for disabled shop ⊗*

Joseph Parry's Cottage
MERTHYR TYDFIL ▓▓▓▓▓▓
4 Chapel Row, Georgetown (off A470)
☎ *(01685) 383704*
The cottage was the birthplace of the
musician and composer, Dr Joseph Parry,
and contains an exhibition devoted to his
life and works. Also shown here are
displays of the industrial and social
history of 19th-century Merthyr Tydfil
during its heyday as an industrial centre.
The ground floor of the cottage has been
restored and furnished in the style of the
1840s. An excavated section of the
Glamorganshire Canal provides an open-
air exhibition. The Merthyr Heritage Day -
a heritage based day with activities and
entertainment for the family will be held
in June/July 1995.
*Open Etr-Oct, Mon-Fri 2-5, Sat, Sun & BH
2-5. Other times by appointment.*
*60p (ch 6-16, pen, students & UB40's
50p).*
🅿 ♨ *shop ⊗*

Ynysfach Iron Heritage Centre
MERTHYR TYDFIL ▓▓▓▓▓▓
Ynysfach Rd (off A470)
☎ *(01685) 721858*
Opened in July 1989, this heritage centre
once housed the beam-blowing engine of
the Ynysfach Iron Works. Exhibitions in
the superbly restored building introduce
the history of Merthyr Tydfil's once-
famed iron industry with an 18-minute
audio-visual programme narrated by actor
Philip Madoc, full-size models of
ironworkers, maps and photographs.
Winner of the Prince of Wales Award in
1989 and two others in 1990. The
Merthyr Heritage Day - a heritage based
event with activities for all - will be held
in June/July 1995.
*Open Mar-Oct, Mon-Fri 10-5, wknds &
BH 2-5. Nov-Feb, Mon-Fri 10-5. (Closed
wknds & Xmas).*
*£1.15 (ch 6-16, students, pen & UB40's
70p). Party.*
🅿 ♨ *shop ⊗*

Llancaiach Fawr Manor
NELSON ▓▓▓▓▓▓
Gelligaer Rd
☎ *Treharris (01443) 412248*
Step back in time to the exciting Civil
War period at this fascinating living
history museum. The year is 1645 and
you are invited into the Manor to meet
the servants of 'Colonel' Edward Prichard
- the gossipy housekeeper Anne Thomas
or the gregarious cook Sioni Mawr.
Special events for 1995 include the visit
of King Charles I on 5 August, monthly
Murder Mystery evenings, winter Ghost
Tours, May Eve and Celtic New Year
Celebrations. Please telephone for
further details.
*Open all year, Mon-Fri 10-3.30 (last
admission), Sat-Sun 10-4.30 (last
admission). (Closed 25-26 Dec & 1 Jan).*
❋*£3.50 (ch £2, concession £2.20). Family
ticket £9.50.*
🅿 ♨ ♿ *(lift in visitor centre to audio
visual show) toilets for disabled shop ⊗
(ex in grounds)*

Ogmore Castle
OGMORE

☎*Ogmore-by-Sea (01656) 653435*
Standing on the River Ogmore, the west wall of this castle is 40ft high. A hooded fireplace is preserved in the 12th-century, three-storey keep and a dry moat surrounds the inner ward.
Open - access throughout the year. Key keeper arrangement.
Free.
🅿️ ♿ ✆
(AM Cadw)

Rhondda Heritage Park
TREHAFOD

Lewis Merthyr, Coed Cae Rd (off A470)
☎*Porth (01443) 682036*
The Rhondda Heritage Park, based at the Lewis Merthyr Colliery, is a living testament to the coal mining communities of the Rhondda. Visitors can journey back in time on the underground tour 'A Shift in Time' and experience for themselves the sights, sounds and smells of the Lewis Merthyr in the 1950s. Accompanied by guides visitors ride in the cage to Pit Bottom and discover the secrets of the Lewis Merthyr at work. A lively multi-media exhibition illustrates the unique character and culture of the Rhondda as seen through the eyes of one local mining family. Other attractions include children's play area, restaurant and gift shop.
Open all year, daily 10-6. Closed Mon from Oct-Etr. Last admission 4.30pm. Closed 25 & 26 Dec.
£4.95 (concessions £4.25). Family ticket £16.
🅿️ 🍴 ♿ *toilets for disabled shop* ✆

POWYS

Dan-Yr-Ogof Showcaves
ABERCRAF

(midway between Swansea & Brecon on A4067)
☎*(01639) 730284*
Winner of twelve major tourism awards, Dan-Yr-Ogof Showcave is the longest in Britain. Cathedral Showcave is the largest single chamber in any British showcave and Bone Cave was home to man 3,000 years ago. There is also a Dinosaur Park, an Iron Age village, museum, craft shop and new Shire Horse Heritage Centre. Special events for 1995 include: Music in the Mountains (27-28 August).
Open Apr-Oct, daily from 10am. Please telephone for Oct.
❄£5.50 (ch £3.75).
🅿️ ♿ *toilets for disabled shop*

Brecknock Museum
BRECON

Captain's Walk
☎*(01874) 624121*
A wealth of local history is explored at the museum, which has archaeological and historical exhibits, with sections on folk life, decorative arts and natural history. There is a 19th-century Assize Court and one of the finest collections of Welsh Lovespoons. A full exhibition programme is planned for 1995.
Open all year, Mon-Fri 10-5, Sat 10-1 & 2-5 (also Sun Apr-Sep) . Closed Good Fri & Xmas-New Year.
Free.
🅿️ ♿ *(limited parking, must be accompanied by able-bodied) shop* ✆

South Wales Borderers (24th Regiment) Museum Museum
BRECON

The Barracks, The Watton
☎*(01874) 613310*

This is the museum of the South Wales Borderers and Monmouthshire Regiment, which was raised in 1689 and has been awarded 23 Victoria Crosses. Amongst the collections is the Zulu War Room, devoted to the war and in particular to the events at Rorke's Drift, 1879, when 121 men fought 4500 Zulus.
Open all year, Apr-Sep daily; Oct-Mar, Mon-Fri 9-1 & 2-5. (Closed Xmas & New Year).
£1
🅿️ ♿ *shop* ✆

Welshpool & Llanfair Light (Steam) Railway
LLANFAIR CAEREINION

(on A458)
☎*(01938) 810441*
The Llanfair Railway is one of the Great Little Trains of Wales - the nearest to England. It offers an 8-mile trip through glorious scenery by narrrow-gauge steam train. The line is home to a collection of engines and coaches from all round the world. Special events for 1995 include: Friends of Thomas the Tank Engine Weekend (8-9 July), Narrow Guage Steam Gala (2-3 September).
Open Etr-1 Oct, wknds; Etr, May Day BH, Spring BH wk; 20 Jun-13 Jul, Tue-Thu; 17 Jul-10 Sep, daily. Trains from Llanfair at 10.30, 1.30 & 4.15pm; from Welshpool 11.45, 2.45 & 5.15. Extra trains at BHs. £6.50 return (ch 5-15 £3). Family ticket £15.
🅿️ 🍴 ♿ *(two coachs adapted for wheelchairs) toilets for disabled shop*

Centre for Alternative Technology
MACHYNLLETH

(2.5m N on A487)
☎*(01654) 702400*
The Centre for Alternative Technology is an internationally renowned display centre, promoting practical ideas and information on sustainable technologies. The exhibition includes displays of wind, water and solar power, organic gardens, low-energy dwellings, and a unique water-powered railway which ascends a 200ft cliff from the car park. There is a restaurant and bookshop on site. Educational services and residential courses are available.
Open all year, daily 10-5. Phone for winter opening details.
❄£4.50 (ch £2.50, pen & UB40 £3.50). Family ticket £12.50
🅿️ 🍴 ✕ *licensed ♿ (wheelchair available) toilets for disabled shop garden centre* ✆

Tretower Court & Castle
TRETOWER

☎*Crickhowell (01874) 730279*
The castle is a substantial ruin of an 11th-century motte and bailey, with a three-storey tower and 9ft-thick walls. Nearby is the Court, a 14th-century fortified manor house which has been altered and extended over the years. The two buildings show the shift from medieval castle to more domestic accommodation over the centuries, and an audio-cassette tour is available.

Open all year, late Oct-late Mar, Mon-Sat 9.30-4, Sun 2-4; late Mar-late Oct, daily 9.30-6.30. (Closed 24-26 Dec & 1 Jan).
❄£2 (reductions £1.50). Family ticket £6.
🅿️ ♿ *toilets for disabled shop* ✆
(AM Cadw)

Powis Castle
WELSHPOOL

(1m S on A483)
☎*(01938) 554336*
This medieval castle was built in about 1200 for a Welsh prince and has been continuously inhabited ever since. Later improvements to the castle have added 16th-century plasterwork and panelling and a fine 17th-century staircase. There are also murals by Lanscroon. Over the centuries many articles and treasures have been collected by both the Herbert family and the Clive family, who lived here and formed one of the finest country-house collections in Wales, including paintings, tapestries and early Georgian furniture. The most celebrated of the Clive family was Clive of India, and there are relics of his life and career in the house. The gardens at Powis, with their magnificent early 18th-century terraces, are of great horticultural and historical importance.
Open Apr-Jun & Sep-29 Oct, Wed-Sun; Jul-Aug, Tue-Sun & BH Mon. Castle Museum: 12-5; Garden: 11-6. Last admission 30 mins prior to closing. Castle, Museum & Gardens £5.80 (ch 2.90). Family £14.50. Garden only £3.80 (ch £1.90). Family £9.50. Party 20+.
🅿️ 🍴 ♿ *toilets for disabled shop* ✆
(NT)

SOUTH GLAMORGAN

Welsh Hawking Centre
BARRY

Weycock Rd (on A4226)
☎*(01446) 734687*
There are over 200 birds of prey here, including eagles, owls and buzzards as well as hawks and falcons. They can be seen and photographed in the mews and some of the breeding aviaries, and there are flying demonstrations at regular intervals during the day. A variety of tame, friendly animals, such as donkeys, goats, pigs, lambs, cows and rabbits will delight younger visitors.
Open all year, daily 10.30-5, 1hr before dusk in winter. (Closed 25 Dec).
❄£3 (ch & pen £2).
🅿️ 🍴 ♿ *shop* ✆

CARDIFF
Cardiff - the capital city of Wales - has been a prominent town since Roman times and Cardiff Castle dates back 1,900 years. The castle, having been magnificently refurbished in the 19th century, reflects Cardiff's history as a ➤

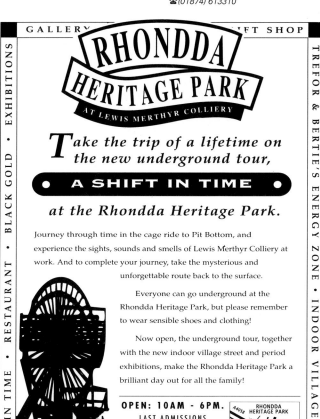

flourishing industrial city and port. The city's wealth depended on coal mining, iron and steel works and tinplate mills. Today it is a flourishing commerical city with an exciting cultural base. The castle is a stone's throw from one of the finest civic centres in Britain and from a fine shopping centre with a colourful covered market reputed to have the finest wrought-iron structure since the Crystal Palace. At its heart is a magnificent 2,000-seat concert hall with a worldwide reputation. There are thousands of acres of beautiful parks in the city offering a lovely riverside walk to Llandaff Cathedral as well as several excellent museums illustrating life in Wales.

Cardiff Castle
CARDIFF
Castle St
☎ (01222) 822083
The Norman castle was built on the site of a Roman fort, and Roman walls some 10ft thick can still be seen. There is also a Norman keep and a 13th-century tower. Apartments were started in the 15th century, but the present-day character of the castle comes from its transformation in the 19th century, when the immensely rich 3rd Marquess of Bute employed William Burges to restore and rebuild it. Together they created a romantic fantasy of a medieval castle, decorated with wall paintings, tapestries and colourful carvings of birds, animals, knights and ladies. Also here are the military museums of the Royal Regiment of Wales and Queen's Dragoon Guards.
*Open all year, daily (ex Xmas & New Year BH's). Royal Regiment of Wales Museum, Wed pm, Thu-Sat. Queen's Dragoon Guards Museum, Mon-Tue, Wed am, Sat-Sun. Conducted tours Mar, Apr & Oct, daily 10-12.30 & 2-4 (Castle closes 5pm). May-Sep, daily 10-12.40 & 2-5 (Castle closes 6pm); Nov-Feb daily 10.30-3.15 (Castle closes 4.30pm). Only short tours when functions in progess. Conducted tours all year.
Conducted tour, military museums, green, Roman Wall & Norman Keep £3.50 (ch & pen £1.70). Short tour, military museum, green, Roman Wall & Norman Keep £2.90 (ch & pen £1.50) Green, Roman Wall, Norman Keep, & military museum £2.20 (ch & pen £1.10). P (200 yds) ♨ & toilets for disabled shop ⊘ (ex in grounds)*

Dyffryn Gardens
CARDIFF
St Nicholas (6m W of city centre off A48)
☎ (01222) 593328
'A Garden for all Seasons', describes Dyffryn, one of Wales' finest landscaped gardens. The beautiful grounds offer an endless variety of colour and form with many small theme gardens, a heather bank, arboretum and glass houses. The 55 acres also include a butterfly house. Various events are held throughout the year including craft fairs and music and arts festivals.
*Open all year, Apr-Oct 10-5.30; Mar wknds 10.30-4.30; Winter please check for details as facilities are limited. ✲£2 (ch & pen £1.50). Family ticket £6. Party 20+.
P ♨ ✕ licensed & (wheelchairs, parking) toilets for disabled shop*

National Museum Of Wales (Main Building)
CARDIFF
Cathays Park
☎ (01222) 397951
Treasurehouse of the principality, the National Museum of Wales' main building at the heart of Cardiff's elegant Civic Centre boasts excellent collections including paintings, silver and ceramics, coins and medals, fossils, minerals, shells, archaeological artefacts and even dinosaur skeletons. The recent refurbishment of the East Wing has provided a splendid new setting for the museum's impressive art collections and, for the first time, shows them in their European context.
The new galleries enable the museum to focus more attention on contemporary art. The highlights include the renowned Davies Collection of French Impressionists, and the Evolution of Wales Exhibition. Children's activities are planned for the school holidays, and there is a continous programme of temporary exhibitions.
*Open all year, Tue-Sat 10-5, Sun 2.30-5. (Closed Mon (ex BHs), Good Fri, 24-26 Dec & 1 Jan). ✲£2.50 (ch £1.25, pen £1.85). Family ticket £6.25.
P (charged) ✕ licensed & (wheelchair available) toilets for disabled shop ⊘*

Techniquest
CARDIFF
72 Bute St, Pier Head
☎ (01222) 460211
Science and technology made accessible - and fun - at Britain's largest hands-on science centre, where visitors of all ages can participate in the activities and experiment with the exhibits. See yourself as others see you, instead of the mirror-image you are used to.
Understand how aircraft fly . . . Techniquest makes it easy. Special events take place throughout the year.
*Open all year, Tue-Fri 9.30-4.30; Sat-Sun & BH's 10.30-5. Also Mon during school hols. ✲£3 (ch & concessions £1.60). Family ticket £7.60
P ♨ & toilets for disabled shop ⊘*

Welsh Industrial & Maritime Museum
CARDIFF
Bute St (on A4232)
☎ (01222) 481919
In Cardiff's docklands, one of the world's most famous maritime districts, the Welsh Industrial and Maritime Museum stands alongside the waterfront. Thematic presentations, with hands-on activities and events, provide a meaningful experience for visitors of all ages. There is a regular programme of activities and events. The museum is located at the heart of the Inner Harbour of the Cardiff Bay development, one of the largest and most exciting of its kind in Europe. Special events are planned during the school holidays.
*Open all year, Tue-Sat 10-5, Sun 2.30-5. (Closed Mon (ex BHs), 24-26 Dec, 1 Jan, Good Fri).
£1.50 (ch 75p, pen £1.15). Family ticket £4.15.
P & (wheelchair available) toilets for disabled shop ⊘*

Cosmeston Medieval Village
PENARTH
Cosmeston Lakes Country Park, Lavernock Rd
☎ Cardiff (01222) 708686
Deserted during the plagues and famines of the 14th century, the original village was rediscovered through archaeological excavations. Now the buildings have been faithfully reconstructed on the excavated remains, within the Cosmeston Lakes Country Park, creating a living museum of medieval village life. Special events throughout the year.
*Open all year, daily 10-6 (10-5 Oct-Mar). Closed 25 Dec.
✲Country Park free. Tours £1 (ch 75p).
P ♨ ✕ & toilets for disabled shop*

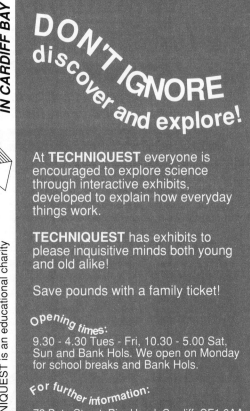

Historic buildings from all over Wales have been carefully reconstructed at St Fagans to form a living monument to the past.

Turner House
PENARTH
Plymouth Rd
☎Cardiff (01222) 708870
This small gallery holds temporary exhibitions of pictures and *objets d'art* from the National Museum of Wales and other sources.
Open all year, Tue-Sat 11-12.45 & 2-5, Sun 2-5. (Closed Good Fri, May Day & Xmas).
✼*50p (ch 25p, pen 30p).*
shop ✿

Wales Aircraft Museum
RHOOSE
Cardiff (Wales) Airport
☎(01446) 711141 & 710135
The museum displays military and civil aircraft of post World War II interest, including the magnificent Vulcan B2 bomber - XM569 as well as undercover exhibitions, models etc.
Open May-Aug, daily 10-5; Sep-Apr, wknds.
🅿 ➽ & *toilets for disabled shop*
Details not confirmed for 1995

Welsh Folk Museum
ST FAGANS
☎Cardiff (01222) 569441
Once the home of the Earls of Plymouth, St Fagans is a 16th-century house built within the curtain walls of the original 13th-century castle. Donated to the National Museum in 1947, it is now the home of the extensive Welsh Folk Museum. The museum is designed to represent the life and culture of Wales, and there is a huge amount to see. Old farmhouses, cottages, a tannery, a school and a chapel have been reconstructed, and are just a part of the range of the building styles and living conditions to be seen. Numerous skills are also demonstated throughout the year, and traditional Welsh cooking is part of the facilities. Special events for 1995 include: May Fair (29 April-1 May), Midsummer Festival (24-25 June), Harvest Festival (23-24 September), Christmas Celebrations (6-8 December).
Open all year, Apr-Oct, daily 10-5; Nov-Mar, Mon-Sat 10-5. (Closed Good Fri, 24-26 Dec & 1 Jan).
✼*£4 (ch £2, pen £3).*
🅿 ➽ ✗ *licensed* & *(wheelchairs available) toilets for disabled shop* ✿ *(ex in grounds)*

Old Beaupre Castle
ST HILARY
(1m SW, off A48)
☎(01446) 773034
This ruined manor house was rebuilt during the 16th century. Its most notable features include an Italianate gatehouse and porch. The porch is an unusual three-storeyed structure and displays the Basset arms.
Open - access throughout the year. Key keeper arrangement.
Free.
🅿
(AM Cadw)

Castell Coch
TONGWYNLAIS
☎Taffs Wells (01222) 810101
Castell Coch is Welsh for red castle, a good name for this fairy-tale building with its red sandstone walls and conical towers rising out of the wooded hillside. The castle was originally built in the 13th century but fell into ruins, and the present castle is the late-19th-century creation of William Burges and the 3rd Marquis of Bute, who commissioned him to restore it. An exhibition provides an illustrated history of Bute, of Burges and of the building they created. It has three round towers with conical roofs, a drawbridge and portcullis. Inside, the castle is decorated in fantasy style with many murals, giltwork, statues and carvings. The most spectacular room is probably Lady Bute's bedroom, which has a domed ceiling painted on the theme of the Sleeping Beauty.
Open all year, late Oct-late Mar, Mon-Sat 9.30-4, Sun 11-4; Late Mar-late Oct, daily 9.30-6.30. (Closed 24-26 Dec & 1 Jan).
✼*£2 (reductions £1.50). Family ticket £6.*
🅿 *shop* ✿
(AM Cadw)

WEST GLAMORGAN

Aberdulais Falls
ABERDULAIS
(on A465)
☎Neath (01639) 636674
For over 300 years this famous waterfall has provided the energy to drive the wheels of industry. Nestling amongst the site's historic remains, a unique hydro-electric scheme has been developed to harness this great natural resource. The Turbine House provides visitor access to the top of the falls, with views of the power equipment, fish pass and displays. A special lift has been installed to allow disabled visitors access to roof level with excellent views of the Falls and the new water wheel. Special events will be held during 1995 to celebrate the centenary of the National Trust.
Open Apr-3 Nov, Mon-Fri 10-5, Sat-Sun & PH 11-6.
£2.80 (ch £1.20). Party.
🅿 & *(lift for disabled to view falls) toilets for disabled shop*
(NT)

Penscynor Wildlife Park
CILFREW
(off A465)
☎Neath (01639) 642189
Tropical birds, penguins, meerkats, and parrots are seen here in an attractive setting among trees, streams and ponds, where visitors can also feed rainbow trout or see their tropical relatives, touch or hold the animals in the Zoo Centre and feed llamas and donkeys. A chair lift goes to the cliff top for the alpine ride (summer only), and there is a children's playground.
Open all year, daily 10-6, dusk in winter. (Closed 25 Dec).
✼*£4 (ch 3 free, ch & pen £3). Family Ticket £12. Party 20+.*
🅿 *(charged)* ➽ & *toilets for disabled shop* ✿

Cefn Coed Colliery Museum
CRYNANT
(1m S on A4109)
☎Neath (01639) 750556
The museum is on the site of a former working colliery, and tells the story of mining in the Dulais Valley. A steam-winding engine has been kept and is now operated by electricity, and there is also a simulated underground mining gallery, boilerhouse, compressor house, and exhibition area. Outdoor exhibits include a stationary colliery locomotive. Forest walks and picnic sites nearby. Exhibitions relating to the coal mining industry are held on a regular basis.
Open daily, Jan-Mar 10.30-4; Apr-Sep 10.30-6; Oct-Dec 10.30-4. (Closed 25 Dec-1 Jan).
✼*£1.25 (ch & pen 80p) ch under 5 & registered disabled free. Party 10+.*
🅿 ➽ & *toilets for disabled shop*

South Wales Miners Museum & Afan Argoed Count Country Park
CYNONVILLE
(on A4107)
☎Cymmer (01639) 850564 & 850875
The picturesquely placed museum gives a vivid picture of mining life, with coal faces, pit gear and miners' equipment. Guided tours of the museum on request. The country park has forest walks and picnic areas, and a visitor centre.
Open all year daily, Mar-Sep 10.30-6, (5pm rest of year).
✼*50p (pen & ch, 5 and over 25p). Disabled free of charge.*
🅿 ➽ ✗ & *toilets for disabled shop* ✿

Weobley Castle
LLANRHIDIAN
(from B4271 or B4295)
☎Swansea (01792) 390012
A 12th-to 14th-century fortified manor house with an exhibition on the history of Weobley and other historic sites on the Gower peninsula.
Open all year, late Oct-late Mar, Mon-Sat 9.30-4, Sun 2-4; Late Mar-late Oct, daily 9.30-6.30. (Closed 24-26 Dec & 1 Jan).
✼*£1.50 (reductions £1). Family ticket £4.*
🅿 & *shop* ✿
(AM Cadw)

Margam Park
MARGAM
(off A48)
☎Port Talbot (01639) 881635
Margam Park's 850 acres of open parkland and forest are full of natural and historic treasures. The castle and abbey ruins, the waymarked walks, gardens and adventure playground, all go toward a memorable day out for the visitor. Fairytale Land, road train and farm train, a large hedge maze, a fallow deer herd and the Margam Orangery, the largest of its kind in Britain, add to the appeal of this notable beauty spot.
Open all year, Apr-Sep daily 10-6 (last admission 5pm). Oct-Mar, Wed-Sun 10-5 (last admission 3pm).
🅿 ➽ ✗ *licensed* & *(free wheelchair loan, garden for disabled) toilets for disabled shop*
Details not confirmed for 1995

Oystermouth Castle
MUMBLES
☎Swansea (01792) 368732 & 368517
The former stronghold of the Breose family is now an impressive ruin. The gatehouse, chapel and great hall date from the 13th or 14th centuries and there is also a small park to explore.
Open Apr-Sep, daily 11-5.
✼*75p (ch 35p).*

Neath Abbey
NEATH
☎Swansea (01792) 812387
These ruins were originally a Cistercian abbey founded in 1130 by Richard de Grainville.
Open at all times. Key keeper arrangement. Free.
🅿 & ✿
(AM Cadw)

Glynn Vivian Art Gallery
SWANSEA
Alexandra Rd
☎(01792) 655006 & 651738
The gallery has an outstanding collection of Swansea porcelain and pottery, European and Oriental pottery, and glass including paperweights. There are paintings, drawings and sculptures by British and foreign artists, with the emphasis on Welsh artists. Major exhibition programme all year round (Swansea Festival, September-November); progressive education and community arts services.
Open all year, Tue-Sun & BH Mon 10.30-5.30. (Closed 25, 26 Dec & 1 Jan).
✼*Donations*
& *also sculpture court toilets for disabled shop* ✿

Swansea Maritime & Industrial Museum Service
SWANSEA
Museum Square, Maritime Quarter
☎(01792) 650351
This musuem complex in the Swansea docks contains a complete, working woollen mill as well as a selection of floating boats to explore from April to October. These include a trawler, a tug and a lifeboat. There are also displays relating to the Port of Swansea, its industries and its environment, transport exhibits, and maritime and agricultural sections.
Open all year, Tue-Sun 10.30-5.30.(last admission 5.10pm). Closed Mon except BH Mon, 25, 26 Dec & 1 Jan).
& *shop* ✿
Details not confirmed for 1995

Swansea Museum
SWANSEA
Victoria Rd, Maritime Quarter
☎(01792) 653763
Archaeological finds, and natural and local history exhibits are shown, including a reproduction of a 19th-century Welsh kitchen and an exhibition on the history and future of the Lower Swansea Valley. There is a special section on Swansea and Nantgarw china and pottery. There will be a series of changing temporary exhibitions throughout the year.
Open all year, Tue-Sun 10.30-5.15. (Closed 25-26 Dec & 1 Jan). Free.
🅿 *shop* ✿

BELFAST

BELFAST
The bustling city of Belfast is enviably situated within easy access of the coast and the peaceful countryside. Within the city, there are some beautiful parks, including the famous Botanical Gardens, where there is plenty of interest throughout the year; winter is an especially good time to visit the Tropical Ravine and the Palm House, the earliest surviving structure of curvilinear glass and cast iron in the world. Shoppers are served by all leading High Street stores, as well as by more specialist shops which market the famous Waterford crystal, Belleek china, linen, damask, and Donegal tweed. Eating out can be quite an adventure, especially in the area between the City Hall and Shaftesbury Square, which has been known as the Golden Mile. In its length one can dine on Italian, French, Indian, Mongolian and Chinese specialities, but do not forget the traditional Irish dishes - Ardglass herring, or Guinness with Strangford oysters, which you can sample in the congenial surroundings of The Crown Liquor Saloon. This Victorian pub dates from 1849 and is a notable Belfast landmark, now owned by the National Trust.

Belfast Castle
BELFAST
Antrim Rd
☎ (01232) 776925
This great Scottish baronial-style castle with its great square six-storey tower and baroque staircase, was built in 1870 by the 3rd Marquis of Donegal. It was presented to the city by the Earl of Shaftesbury in 1934 and was restored in 1980 at a cost of £2.2 million, re-opening to the public in October 1988. It is used for all types of functions and is open daily for morning coffee, lunch, afternoon tea and dinner. The castle stands on the lower wooded slopes of Cave Hill, an area popular for walks and picnics. The climb to the top of the hill will reward you with far-reaching views.
Open all year, daily. Internal tours of Castle by prior arrangement.
🅿 💺 ✕ *licensed & (lift to all floors) toilets for disabled shop* ⊗
Details not confirmed for 1995

Belfast Zoological Gardens
BELFAST
Antrim Rd (6m N)
☎ (01232) 776277
The 50-acre zoo has a dramatic setting on the face of Cave Hill and enjoys spectacular views. Attractions include the award-winning primate house (gorillas and chimpanzees), penguin enclosure, free-flight aviary, African enclosure, and underwater viewing of sealions and penguins. There is a group of very rare spectacled bears, also red pandas. Free-ranging lemurs and other animals can also be seen.
Open all year (ex 25 Dec), daily Apr-Sep 10-5; Oct-Mar 10-3.30 (Fri 10-2.30)
✼*Admission charged (ch 4, pen & disabled free). Party.*
🅿 💺 & *toilets for disabled shop* ⊗

Botanic Gardens Park
BELFAST
Stranmillis Rd
☎ (01232) 324902
Thirty-eight acres to the south of the city make up these lovely botanic gardens. One highlight of the park is the beautiful

glass-domed Victorian Palm House, built by Richard Turner, the Dublin iron founder, between 1839-52. This palm house predates the one in Kew Gardens and is one of the earliest curved-glass and iron structures in the world. It has recently been re-stocked with exotic plants. Another feature is the Tropical Ravine - visitors stand on a balcony to get a wonderful view through a steamy ravine full of exotic plants.
Open all year, Park daily 8.30-dusk. Tropical ravine and palmhouse Mon-Fri 10-12.30 & 1-5 (summer), closes 4.30 (winter); wknds open 2-5 (summer), 2-4 (winter).
&
Details not confirmed for 1995

Giant's Ring
BELFAST
(0.75m S of Shaws Bridge)
☎ (01232) 235000
A huge, circular, Bronze-age enclosure nearly 200ft in diameter similar in style to Stonehenge, with a stone chambered grave in the centre and bordered by banks 20ft wide and 12ft high. Very little is known for sure about this site, except that it was used for ritual burial. The circular enclosure was used as a horse-racing circuit in the 18th century, while the punters stood on the banks.
Open all times.
Free.
🅿
(AM)

Grovelands
BELFAST
Stockmans Ln
☎ (01232) 381996
Horticultural Training Centre open to the public. Visitors may also look round the enclosed garden.
Open all year, daily 8am to dusk.
Free.
🅿 & 🕀

Malone House-Barnett Demesne
BELFAST
Upper Malone Rd
☎ (01232) 681246
An early 19th-century Georgian mansion overlooking the River Lagan, beautifully restored in 1983 after fire gutted the interior. Owned by Belfast City Council, the house is now used for trade shows and functions. There is a restaurant. The Higgin Art Gallery is also open to visitors.
Open all year, Mon-Sat 10-4.30 (Closed BHs).
🅿 ✕ *licensed & toilets for disabled* ⊗
Details not confirmed for 1995

Ulster Museum
BELFAST
Botanic Gardens
☎ (01232) 381251

The Ulster Museum is both a national museum and an art gallery. The collections are Irish and International in origin and cover antiquities, art, botany and zoology, geology and local history (including industrial archaeology). Some of the permanent displays on show include The Dinosaur Show; Made in Belfast; Armada Treasures; The Irish Flora and Fauna and many more. A programme of temporary exhibitions, films and Sunday afternoon events is also available. Educational activities for adult groups, families and schools. Access to research collections by appointment. Telephone for information, ext 207.
Open all year, Mon-Fri 10-5, Sat 1-5, Sun 2-5. (Closed 12 Jul, 23-27 Dec & 1 Jan). Free. Admission charged for some temporary exhibitions.
P (100 yds) 💺 & *(all galleries except one. Loop system for hearing impaired) toilets for disabled shop* ⊗

CO ANTRIM

Antrim Round Tower
ANTRIM
(N of town)
☎ (01232) 235000
Antrim round tower stands among lawns and trees but it once was surrounded by monastic buildings. Antrim was an important early monastery, probably a 6th-century foundation, closely linked with Bangor.
Open all year.
Free.
🅿 &
(AM)

Shane's Castle
ANTRIM
(on A6)
☎ (01849) 463380 & 428216
The entrance to Shane's Castle is on the A6 Randalstown Road. Home of the O'Neills, the first castle was built in the 17th century. Nash redesigned the castle in the early 19th century, but it was destroyed by fire before his designs could be fully realised. Only the fine conservatory (where camellias are grown) and the terraces remain of his work. A second castle was built in the mid-19th century, but this too was gutted by fire in the troubles of 1922. Part of the estate, which stretches from the outskirts of Antrim along the shores of Lough Neagh to the village of Randalstown, is open to the public. Visitors can take a trip on the narrow-gauge steam railway through a lovely wooded nature reserve to the castle ruins, where ancient cannons point out over the lake.
Open Apr-May, Sun & BH's; Jun, Wed,

Sun & BH's; Jul-Aug, Tue-Thu, Sat-Sun & BH's; Sep, Sun only noon-6.30. Diesel service only Jun, Wed; Jul-Aug, Tue-Thu. Please telephone to confirm details.
🅿 💺 ✕ & *toilets for disabled shop*
Details not confirmed for 1995

Bonamargy Friary
BALLYCASTLE
(E of town, at golf course)
☎ (01232) 235000
Founded by Rory MacQuillan around 1500 and later passed on to the MacDonnells, Earls of Antrim, there are still remains of the friary gatehouse, church and cloister for visitors to see.
Open all year.
Free.
🅿 🕀
(AM)

Ballylumford Dolmen
BALLYLUMFORD
(on B90 on NW tip of Island Magee)
☎ (01232) 235000
Incorporated in the front garden of a house in Ballylumford Road are the remains of this huge 4-5,000-year-old single-chamber Neolithic tomb, also known as the Druid's Altar.
Open all year.
Free.
&
(AM)

Harryville Motte
BALLYMENA
(N bank of river Braid)
☎ (01232) 235000
On a ridge to the south of the town, this Norman fort, with its 40ft-high motte and rectangular bailey, is one of the finest examples of Norman earthworks left in Northern Ireland.
Open all year.
Free.
🅿 🕀
(AM)

Heritage Farm Park
BALLYMONEY
Leslie Hill (1m NW)
☎ (012656) 66803
An 18th-century estate with a Georgian house, magnificent period farm buildings, and fine grounds with paths, lakes and trees. Among the attractions are an extensive collection of rare breeds, poultry, horsedrawn machinery and carriages, exhibition rooms, a museum, working forge, walled garden and an adventure playground. There are horse and trap rides and donkey rides for children. Special events throughout the year.
Open Jul-Aug Mon-Sat 11-6, Sun 2-6; Jun Sat-Sun & BH's 2-6; Etr-May & Sep Sun & BH's 2-6.
£2.10 (ch & pen £1.40).Family ticket £6.50.
🅿 💺 & *(ramps) shop garden centre* ⊗

The splendid palm house, designed by Charles Lanyon and constructed in 1840, is a prominent feature of Belfast's lovely Botanical Gardens.

Strong nerves are all that are needed to make the crossing of the Carrick-a-Rede Rope Bridge and the views are wonderful – if you can bear to look!

Old Bushmills Distillery
BUSHMILLS
☎(012657) 31521
Old Bushmills was granted its licence in 1608 and is the oldest licenced whiskey distillery in the world. There is a good visitor centre from which guided tours of the distillery start. Hospitality and shops are available at the end of the tour.
Open all year, Mon-Thu 9-noon & 1.30-3.30, Fri 9-11.45. Extended hours during summer. No tour May Day, 12-13 Jul, first wk Oct & Xmas. Please telephone to confirm details.
£2 (pen £1.50, accompanied ch free). Party 15+.
P (shops only accessible) shop

Carrick-a-rede Rope Bridge and Larrybane Visitors Centre
CARRICKARDE ISLAND
☎*Ballycastle (012657) 62178 & 31159*
This shaky rope bridge, made of planks of wood and wire and suspended 80ft above the sea, bridges the 60ft gap between cliffs and a small rocky island. The bridge owes its existence to the salmon who regularly make the dash through the chasm and get netted for their efforts, and to the fishermen who need access to the commercial fishery on the south-east side of the island. The bridge has been put across the gap each spring and dismantled every autumn for about the last 300 years. From the Larrybane car park, where there is a National Trust Information Centre, the Trust have made a clifftop path to the bridge and the views are lovely.
Open - Visitor centre Etr, daily 11-6; May-June wknds & BH, 11-6; Jul-Aug, daily 11-6.
Parking, cars £1.50, coaches £6.
P (charged) ♿ (information centre) toilets for disabled
(NT)

Carrickfergus Castle
CARRICKFERGUS
(on N shore of Belfast Lough)
☎*(01960) 351273*
Imposingly placed on a rocky headland overlooking Belfast Lough, this is the best preserved and probably the most fought-over Norman castle in Ireland. Built by John de Courcy, Earl of Ulster, after 1180, it served a military purpose for more than eight centuries. Exhibits include a giant model of the castle, a short film, and a banqueting suite. The castle is often used as a venue for medieval banquets and fairs. There is a new visitors' centre, shop and refreshment point.
Open all year, Apr-Sep, weekday 10-6, Sun 2-6; Oct-Mar closes at 4.
£2.70 (ch £1.35).
P ☕ ♿ toilets for disabled shop
(AM)

Town Walls
CARRICKFERGUS
☎*(01232) 235000*
Lord Deputy Sir Arthur Chichester enclosed Carrickfergus with stone walls from 1611 onwards and more than half the circuit is still visible, often to its full height of 4 metres to the wall walk.
Visible at all times.
Free.
P ♿
(AM)

Cranfield Church
CHURCHTOWN
(3.75m SW of Randalstown)
☎*(01232) 235000*
This small medieval church is situated on the shores of Lough Neagh. Beside it is a famous holy well.
Open all year.
Free.
P ♿
(AM)

Giant's Causeway Centre
GIANT'S CAUSEWAY
44 Causeway Rd (2m N of Bushmills on B146)
☎*(012657) 31855*
Only discovered in 1692 and now designated a World Heritage Site, this dramatic rock formation is undoubtedly one of the wonders of the natural world. The Centre provides an exhibition and audio-visual show, and tourist information.
Open all year, daily 10-4 (6pm Jun & Sep-Oct; 7pm Jul-Aug).
Audio-visual show (25 min) £1 (ch 50p). Family ticket £2.50. Admission to causeway free.
P (charged) ☕ ✕ ♿ (mini bus transport with wheelchair hoist) toilets for disabled shop

Olderfleet Castle
LARNE
☎*(01232) 235000*
A 16th-century tower house, the last surviving of three which defended Larne.
Open at all times.
Free.
(AM)

Duneight Motte and Bailey
LISBURN
(2.3m S beside Ravernet River)
☎*Belfast (01232) 235000*
Impressive Anglo-Norman earthwork castle with high mound-embanked enclosure, making use of the defences of an earlier pre-Norman fort.
Open all year.
Free.
(AM)

Irish Linen Centre & Lisburn Museum
LISBURN
Market Sq
☎*(01846) 663377*
The new Irish Linen Centre adjacent to Lisburn Museum tells the story of the Irish linen industry both past and present. The recreation of individual factory scenes brings the past very much to life and a series of imaginative hands-on activities describe the linen manufacturing processes. A highlight of the exhibition is the handloom weaving workshop. A speciality linen shop on the ground floor provides the opportunity to purchase a piece of linen.
Open all year, Apr-Sep, Mon-Sat 11-5.30, Sun 2-5.30; Oct-Mar, closing time 5pm. Thu all year, late night closing 9pm.
Adult £2.50 (concessions £1.50). Family ticket £4-6. Party.
P 250yds ☕ ♿ (special lift) toilets for disabled shop

Dunluce Castle
PORTBALLINTRAE
(off A2)
☎*Bushmills (012657) 31938*
Extensive and picturesque ruins of a 16th-century castle perched on a rocky crag high above the sea. Stronghold of the MacQuillans and MacDonnells, who significantly altered the original stonebuilt fortress. Randal MacDonnell built a house in the centre of the castle, of which parts of the Great Hall remain, as do the towers and early 17th-century gatehouse. The castle has new displays and there is an audio-visual show. The cave below the ruins provided a secret way into and out of the castle from the sea.
Open all year, Apr-Sep, weekdays 10-7, Sun 2-7; Oct-Mar, Tue-Sat 10-4, Sun 2-4.
£1.50 (ch & pen 75p)
P ♿ toilets for disabled shop
(AM)

Pattersons Spade Mill
TEMPLEPATRICK
☎*(01238) 510721*
This is the last surviving water-driven spade mill in Ireland. It has been completely restored by the National Trust and is now back in production. For details of events in 1995 please telephone (01849) 433619.
Open Etr, Apr-May & Sep, wknds 2-6; Jun-Aug, daily (ex Tue) 2-6.
£2.50 (ch £1.25). Party.
P ♿ (ramps wheelchair available) toilets for disabled
(NT)

Templetown Mausoleum
TEMPLEPATRICK
Situated in the graveyard of Castle Upton, this family mausoleum is in the shape of a triumphal arch and was designed by Robert Adam.
Open daily during daylight hours.
Free.
(NT)

CO ARMAGH

Armagh County Museum
ARMAGH
The Mall
☎*(01861) 523070*
Housed in an interesting 19th-century schoolhouse, this museum contains an art gallery and library, as well as an interesting collection of local folkcrafts and natural history that excellently illustrate the life and history of the city and county of Armagh. Special events are planned thoughout the year, including 'Consequences' one-woman show by Biddy Healy, Barbara Allen watercolourist (April), Irish Vernacular Furniture Exhibition (May-June), Art Club Exhibition (November).
Open all year, Mon-Fri 10-5, Sat 10-1 & 2-5.
Free.
P shop

Armagh Friary
ARMAGH
(SE edge of town)
☎*(01232) 235000*
Situated just inside the gates of the former Archbishop's Palace are the remains of the longest friary church in Ireland (163ft). The friary was established in 1263 by Archbishop O'Scanail and destroyed by Shane O'Neill in the middle of the 16th century to prevent it being garrisoned by Elizabethan soldiers.
Open all year.
Free.
P ♿
(AM)

Armagh Planetarium & Science Centre
ARMAGH
College Hill
☎*(01861) 523689 & 524725*
A trip to Armagh Planetarium is just the start of a journey that takes visitors to the outer limits of the universe. Attractions include: The Star Theatre, a multi-media environment equipped with the latest technology and featuring a virtual reality digital system; The Hall of Astronomy, devoted to 'hands on' explanations of astronomical concepts: The new Eartharium Building, containing exhibits on the environment scale, the seasons and the sturcture of the earth. Surrounding the Planetarium is the Astropark, a 25-acre 'hands on' park devoted to explaining scale in the universe. Special events for 1995 feature a meteor watch in August.
Open all year, Hall of Astronomy Mon-Fri 11.30-4.45, shows daily at 3pm. Also open Sat & Sun 1.30-4.45, shows every Sat 2 & 3. Additional shows during Etr, Xmas & BH's.
£3.50 (ch & pens £2.50). Family ticket £11. Exhibition area £1.
P ☕ ♿ toilets for disabled shop

Navan Centre
ARMAGH
Killylea Rd (2m W on A28)
☎(01861) 525550
Navan Fort is one of Europe's most important Celtic sites; the seat of the ancient Kings of Ultster ans setting for the legends of the mythical Cuchulainn. When the Navan Centre was opened in mid-summer 1993 it was voted the Best Tourism Project. The Centre unveils the history and archaeology of the fort and its landscape in a stunning visual interactive display.
Open all year, Apr-Jun & Sep, Mon-Sat 10-6, Sun 11-6; Jul-Aug, Mon-Sat 10-7, Sun 11-7; Oct-Mar, Mon-Fri 10-5, Sat 11-5, Sun noon-5.
£3.75 (ch 16 £2.10, pen, students & UB40's £2.50). Family ticket £7 (1 adult) & £10 (2 adults). Party.
🅿 🎫 ⅃ toilets for disabled shop ⌗

Palace Stables Heritage Centre
ARMAGH
The Palace Demesne
☎(01861) 522722
This picturesque Georgian building, set around a cobbled courtyard, has been lovingly restored and now houses a heritage centre where visitors can experience stable life in the 18th century. An exhibition A Day in the Life uses audio-commentary, life-like models and spectacular, colourful murals. Visitors can browse around the Tack Room and the Coachman's House and glimpse the working and living conditions of a coachman. Other attractions include the hayloft, children's play area, Ice House & servants tunnel, education room, audio-visual theatre, craft shop and restaurant.
Open all year, Apr-Sep, Mon-Sat 10-7, Sun 1-7; Oct-Mar, Mon-Sat 10-5, Sun 2-5. Last tour 1hr before closing.
✳£2.50 (ch 4-16 £1.50, pen £2). Family ticket £7. Party.
🅿 ✗ ⅃ toilets for disabled shop (courtyard only)

St Patrick's Trian
ARMAGH
English St
☎(01861) 527808
This exciting complex situated in the centre of Armagh City illustrates the development of Armagh from prehistoric times to the present day, and also reveals Armagh's importance as a world ecclesiastical centre. The development also houses The Land of Lilliput, which is based on Gulliver's Travels; craft shops, a restaurant and educational facilities. Special events are planned for 1995.
Open all year, Apr-Sep, Mon-Sat 10-7, Sun 1-7; Oct-Mar, Mon-Sat 10-5, Sun 2-5. Last tour 1hr before closing.
🅿 (charged) ✗ ⅃ (specially designed for disabled) toilets for disabled shop ⌗

Killevy Churches
CAMLOUGH
(3m S lower eastern slopes of Slieve Gullion)
☎(01232) 235000
The ruins of the two churches (10th- and 13th-century) stand back to back, at the foot of Slieve Gullion sharing a common wall, but with no way through from one to the other. The churches stand on the site of an important nunnery founded by St Monenna in the 5th century. A huge granite slab in the graveyard supposedly marks the founder's grave. A holy well can be reached by climbing the path north of the graveyard. The nunnery was in use until the Dissolution in 1542.
Open all year.
Free.
⅃
(AM)

Kilnasaggart Inscribed Stone
JONESBOROUGH
(1.25m S)
☎(01232) 235000
A granite pillar stone dating back to 8th century, with numerous crosses and a long Irish inscription carved on it.
Open all year.
Free.
🅿
(AM)

Argory
MOY
Derrycaw Rd (3m NE)
☎(018687) 84753
Originally the home of the McGeough family, this Regency house is situated on a hillside overlooking the Blackwater River. The Argory is full of period furniture and bric-a-brac. Of particular interest is the house's very unusual acetylene lighting, installed by the family in 1906, the cast-iron stove in the hall and the cabinet barrel organ. Lovely rose garden and walled pleasure gardens. For details of special events telephone (018687) 84753.
Open Etr, daily; Apr-Jun & Sep, wknds & BH; Jul-Aug, daily (ex Thu) 2-6. Open from 1pm on BHs. Last tour 5.15.
House & grounds £2.20 (ch £1.10). Car park £1. Party.
🅿 (charged) ▣ ⅃ (special parking facilities, wheelchair available) toilets for disabled shop

Moyry Castle
NEWRY
(7.5m S)
☎(01232) 235000
This tall, three-storey keep was built by Lord Mountjoy, Queen Elizabeth's deputy, in 1601, its purpose to secure the Gap of the North which was the main route into Ulster.
Open all year
Free.
(AM)

Ardress House
PORTADOWN
Annaghmore (7m W on B28)
☎Annaghmore (01762) 851236
Plain 17th-century house transformed around 1770 by its visionary, architect owner George Ensor, who added elegant wings and superb Adamesque plasterwork carried out by the Dublin expert, Michael Stapleton. The house has a fine picture gallery on loan from the Earl of Castlestewart. The grounds are beautifully unspoilt and there is a farmyard with livestock and a display of farm implements.
Open Etr, daily; Apr-Jun & Sep, wknds & BH's; Jul-Aug, daily (ex Tue) 2-6. Farmyard also open May-Jun & Sep, wkdys (ex Tue) noon-4.
House, grounds & farmyard £2 (ch £1). Party.
🅿 ⅃ toilets for disabled
(NT)

Village Cross
TYNAN
☎(01232) 235000
A carved High Cross, 11ft tall, which lay broken in two pieces for many years, but was skilfully mended in 1844. The carvings depict Adam, Eve and the serpent entwined around an apple tree.
Open all year
Free.
🅿 ⅃
(AM)

CO DOWN

Jordan's Castle
ARDGLASS
☎(01232) 235000
Although Ardglass is an important fishing port today, it was once the busiest seaport in Northern Ireland. Between the 14th and 15th centuries a ring of tower houses and fortified warehouses was built to protect the port. Jordan's Castle, a late-15th-century, four-storey tower house situated in the centre of town, is one of these. Besieged in the early 1600s and held for three years, the castle was bought, repaired and filled with bygones by a Belfast solicitor in the early part of this century.
Open Jul-Aug; Tue-Sat 10-7, Sun 2-7. Other times on request telephone (01232) 235000.
75p (ch 40p)
⌗
(AM)

Grey Abbey
BALLYWALTER
(on east edge of village)
☎(01232) 235000
Founded in 1193 by Affreca, daughter of the King of the Isle of Man, these extensive ruins of a Cistercian abbey, sitting in lovely sheltered parkland, are among the best preserved in Northern Ireland. The chancel, with its tall lancet windows, magnificent west doorway and an effigy tomb - believed to be Affreca's - in the north wall, are particularly interesting.
The abbey was burned down in 1572, and then re-used as a parish church. There are many 17th- and 18th-century memorials to be seen in the church ruins, which occupy a pleasant garden setting. The abbey now has a beautiful medieval herb garden, with over 50 varieties of plants, and a new visitors' centre.
Open Apr-Sep; Tue-Sat 10-7, Sun 2-7.
✳£1 (ch accompanied 50p)
🅿 ⅃ toilets for disabled
(AM)

Drumena Cashel
CASTLEWELLAN
(2.25m SW)
☎(01232) 235000
There are many stone ring forts in Northern Ireland, but few so well preserved as Drumena. Dating back to early Christian times, the fort is 30m in diameter and has an 11m accessible underground stone-built passage, probably used as a refuge and for storage.
Open all times
Free.
🅿
(AM)

Castle Espie Wildfowl & Wetlands Centre
COMBER
Ballydrain Rd (3m SE)
☎(01247) 874146
Located on the shores of Strangford Lough, Castle Espie is home to the largest collection of wildfowl in Ireland. New hides enable visitors to watch the splendour of migratory waders and wildfowl. Beautiful landscaped gardens, a taxidermy collection and fine paintings by wildlife artists can also be seen. Visitors, especially children, are encouraged to feed the birds, many of which are rare and endangered.The Centre is of interest all year round - woodland walks are especially enjoyable in the summer, as are the Downy Duckling Days during July. Thousands of birds migrate to the reserve in winter and Bird Walks are held on the last Thurday of every month. The Centre's effluent is treated in a reed bed filtration system which can be seen on one walk.
Open all year, Mon-Sat 10.30-5, Sun 11.30-5. (Closed 25 Dec).
✳£2.50 (ch 4 free, ch £1.25, pen & students £1.85); family ticket £6.25.
🅿 ▣ ⅃ (hides have wheelchair platforms) toilets for disabled shop ⌗

Ballycopeland Windmill
DONAGHADEE
(1m W, on B172)
☎Millisle (01247) 861413
The only complete working windmill in Northern Ireland, this tower cornmill was built in the late-18th century. Fully operational until 1914 for the milling of wheat, oats and the making of animal foodstuffs, the mill has intricate wooden machinery. There are additional displays in the Miller's House and drying kiln.
Open all year Apr-Sep, Tue-Sat 10-7, Sun 2-7; Oct-Mar, Sat 10-4, Sun 2-4.
£1 (ch 50p)
🅿 shop ⌗
(AM)

Down County Museum & St Patrick Heritage Centre
DOWNPATRICK
The Mall
☎(01396) 615218
The museum occupies the old county gaol built between 1789 and 1796. The

Ardress House provides a fascinating insight into the life-style of the gentleman-farmer during the 17th, 18th and 19th centuries.

Saint Patrick Heritage Centre in the former gatehouse tells the story of Ireland's patron saint. In the recently restored governor's residence are galleries relating to the human and natural history of County Down. The story of man's settlement from 7000BC to recent times, is told with texts and artefacts ranging from flint arrowheads to Dinky toys. The three-storey cell block has been renovated and some of the 18th-century cells on the ground floor can be seen, together with additional exhibition areas. Special events for 1995 include: Down in the War - Life in Co Down during the second world war (11 Apr), Ulster rambles - paintings by Barbara Allen (27 June).
Open all year, Jul-mid Sep, Mon-Fri 11-5, wknds 2-5; rest of year, Tue-Fri 11-5 & Sat 2-5.
Free.
P *(100yds)* ☙ & *(wheelchair available) toilets for disabled shop* ☙

Inch Abbey
DOWNPATRICK
(0.75m NW off A7)
☎(01232) 235000
Beautiful riverside ruins of a Cistercian abbey founded by John de Courcy around 1180. Of particular note is the tall, pointed, triple east window.
Open Apr-Sep 10-7. Sun 2-7. Oct-Mar free access.
Apr-Sep 75p (ch 40p)
P &
(AM)

Loughinisland Churches
DOWNPATRICK
(4m W)
☎(01232) 235000
This remarkable group of three ancient churches stands on an island in the lough, accessible by a causeway. The middle church is the oldest, probably dating back to the 13th century, with a draw-bar hole to secure the door. The large North church was built in the 15th century, possibly to replace the middle church and continued in use until 1720. The smallest and most recent church is the South (MacCartan's) church.
Open all times
Free.
P & ☙
(AM)

Mound of Down
DOWNPATRICK
(on the Quoile Marshes, from Mount Crescent)
☎(01232) 235000
A hill fort from the Early Christian period, conquered by Anglo-Norman troops in 1177, who then built an earthwork castle on top. This mound in the marshes, beside the River Quoile, was the first town before the present Downpatrick.
Open all times
Free.
P
(AM)

Struell Wells
DOWNPATRICK
(1.5m E)
☎(01232) 235000
Pilgrims come to collect the healing waters from these holy drinking and eye wells which are fed by a swift underground stream. Nearby are the ruins of an 18th-century church, and, even more interesting, single-sex bath-houses. The men's bath-house is roofed, has an anteroom and a sunken bath, while the ladies' is smaller and roofless.
Open all times
Free.
P ☙
(AM)

Legananny Dolmen
DROMARA
(4m S)
☎(01232) 235000
Theatrically situated on the slopes of Slieve Croob, this tripod dolmen with its three tall uprights and huge capstone is

the most graceful of Northern Ireland's Stone Age monuments. There are views to the Mourne Mountains.
Open at all times
Free.
& ☙
(AM)

Hillsborough Fort
HILLSBOROUGH
☎(01846) 683285
On a site that dates back to early Christian times, the existing fort was built in 1650 by Colonel Arthur Hill to command a view of the road from Dublin to Carrickfergus. The building was ornamented in the 18th century. It is set in a forest park with a lake and pleasant walks.
Open all year; Apr-Sep, Tue-Sat 10-7, Sun 2-7; Oct-Mar, Tue-Fri 10-4, Sat 10-4, Sun 2-4.,
Free.
P &
(AM)

Ulster Folk and Transport Museum
HOLYWOOD
Cultra (on A2)
☎Belfast (01232) 428428
Opened in 1964, in the grounds of Cultra Manor, this museum is in two parts. The Folk Museum, which covers a 137-acre site, has a wonderful collection of rural and urban buildings that have been taken from original settings all over Ulster, and reconstructed at the Museum. They include: farmhouses, cottages, watermills, a small town with shops, a school, churches, printer's workshops, bank and terraced houses, which recreate the Ulster landscape of the 1900's. In the rural area there are farm animals native to Ireland and the fields are cultivated using traditional farming methods. The Transport Museum exhibits all forms of transport, including the popular Titanic exhibition and the spectacular Irish Railway Collection. Events for 1995 include Easter Monday & Tuesday activities; a Storytelling Festival and a Wool Day (June); a Linen Day and the Rare Breeds Show & Sale (August); Classic Road Show (September); Halloween Celebrations (October);

opening of new Road Transport Gallery (December). Telephone for details on 24hr-information line (01232) 421444
Open all year Apr-Jun & Sep, Mon-Fri 9.30-5, Sat 10.30-6, Sun noon-6; Jul-Aug, Mon-Sat 10.30-6, Sun noon-6; Oct-Mar, Mon-Fri 9.30-4, Sat-Sun 12.30-4.30.
✽£3 (ch £2). Family ticket £8. Prices to be reviewed Apr.
P ☙ & toilets for disabled shop

Greencastle
KILKEEL
(4m SW)
☎(01232) 235000
Looking very much like an English Norman castle with its massive keep, gatehouse and curtain wall, this 13th-century royal fortress stands on the shores of Carlingford Lough, with fine views of the Mourne Mountains. Greencastle has an eventful military history, it was beseiged and taken by Edward Bruce in 1316, attacked and spoiled by the Irish at least twice later in the 14th century, and maintained as a garrison for Elizabeth in the 1590s.
Open Jul-Aug, Tue-Sat 10-7, Sun 2-7. 75p (ch 40p).
P &
(AM)

Sketrick Castle
KILLINCHY
(3m E on W tip of Sketrick Islands)
☎(01232) 235000
A badly ruined tall tower house, probably 15th-century. The ground floor rooms include a boat bay and prison. An underground passage leads from the north-east of the bawn to a freshwater spring.
Open at all times.
Free.
P &
(AM)

Dundrum Castle
NEWCASTLE
(4m N)
☎Belfast (01232) 235000
This medieval castle, one of the finest in Ireland, was built in 1777 by John De Courcy in a strategic position overlooking

Dundrum Bay, a position which offers visitors fine views over the sea and to the Mourne Mountains. The castle was captured by King John in 1210 and was badly damaged by Cromwellian troops in 1652. Still an impressive ruin, it shows a massive round keep with walls 16m high and 2m thick, surrounded by a curtain wall, and a gatehouse which dates from the 13th century.
Open Apr-Sep, Tue-Sat 10-7, Sun 2-7. 75p (ch & pen 40p).
P & toilets for disabled
(AM)

Maghera Church
NEWCASTLE
(2m NNW)
☎Belfast (01232) 235000
The stump of a round tower, blown down in a storm in the early 18th century, survives from the early monastery, with a ruined 13th-century church nearby.
Open all year.
Free.
P &
(AM)

Mount Stewart House, Garden & Temple of the Winds
NEWTOWNARDS
Greyabbey (5m SE)
☎Greyabbey (012477) 88387 & 88487
On the east shore of Strangford Lough, this 18th-century house was the home of the Stewart family (who later became Marquesses of Londonderry) and the place where Lord Castlereagh, Foreign Secretary from 1812 to 1823, grew up. The house is the work of three architects - James Wyatt in the 1780s and George Dance and probably Vitruvius Morrison in the early 19th century. Much of the house's contents have associations with Castlereagh, and there are interesting paintings, including one by Stubbs, as well as silver and porcelain. Outside, in the lovely, inspired gardens (among the very best of the National Trust's), many rare and subtropical trees thrive, while by the shore of Strangford Lough is the Temple of the Winds, built by James Stewart in 1782 for the first Marquess. ➤

The interior of Lismacloskey House – one of the many fascintaing buildings reconstructed at the award-winning Ulster Folk and Transport Museum.

The lustrous cream colour and the delicate, skilfully woven basketwork of Belleek pottery is prized by collectors from all over the world.

Open House Etr, daily; May-Sep daily (ex Tue); Apr, Sep & Oct wknds, 1-6. Temple of The Winds (open dates as house) 2-5. Garden Apr-Sep, daily; Oct, wknds 10.30-6.
House Garden & Temple £3.30 (ch £1.65); Garden & Temple £2.70 (ch £1.35). Temple only 90p. Party
🅿 🐶 🍴 ♿ *(electric wheelchair available) toilets for disabled shop*
(NT)

Scrabo Tower
NEWTOWNARDS
Scrabo Country Park, 203A Scrabo Rd
(1m W)
☎ *(01247) 811491*
The 135ft high Scrabo Tower, one of Northern Ireland's best-known landmarks, dominates the landscape of North Down and is also the centre of a country park around the slopes of Scrabo Hill. The Tower provides a fascinating series of interpretative diplays about the surrounding countryside and the viewing platform boasts spectacualr views over Strangford Lough and Co. Down. The park provides walk through fine beech and hazel woodlands and the unique sandstone quarries display evidence of volcanic activity as well as breeding sites for peregrine falcons.
Open Etr, May-Sep, Sat-Thu 11-6.30. Country park open all year, daily, 11-6.30. Free.
🅿 *shop* 🐶
(AM)

Rowallane Garden
SAINTFIELD
(1m S on A7)
☎ *(01238) 510131*
Beautiful, exotic, 50-acre gardens started by the Rev John Moore in 1860 and continued by his nephew Hugh Armytage-Moore. The gardens contain exquisite plants from all over the world. Particularly noted for its rhododendrons and azaleas and for the wonderful floral displays in spring and summer displayed in a natural setting. The gardens have the national collection of Large-flowered Hybrid Penstemons. There are monthly demonstrations on The Art of the

Gardener. Events for 1995 include Jazz at the Bandstand (17 June), Horse Drive (18 June) The French Connection concerts (23-24 June), Annual plant Sale (28-29 October), Yuletide Market (9-10 December).
Open Apr-Oct, Mon-Fri 10.30-6, Sat & Sun 2-6; Nov-Mar, Mon-Fri 10.30-5 Apr-Oct £2.50 (ch £1.25); Nov-Mar £1.50 (ch 75p). Party.
🅿 🐶 ♿ *(parking facilities) toilets for disabled shop*
(NT)

Audley's Castle
STRANGFORD
(1.5m W by shore of Strangford Lough)
☎ *Belfast (01232) 230560*
Fifteenth-century tower house on Strangford Lough which offers lovely views from its top floor. The internal fittings are complete.
Open Apr-Sep, daily 10-7. Free.
🅿 🐶
(AM)

Castle Ward
STRANGFORD
(0.5m W on A25)
☎ *(01396) 881204*
The curious diversity of styles in this house is due to the fact that its owner, Bernard Ward, later First Viscount Bangor, and his wife could never agree; so the classical style preferred by the Viscount and the more elaborate Gothic look favoured by his wife were both incorporated in the house. Not altogether surprisingly, the couple separated shortly after the house was completed! The servants' living quarters are separate from the house and are reached by an underground passage. Fully equipped laundry in the courtyard. Small theatre in part of the large barn. Castle Ward is beautifully placed overlooking Strangford Lough. The gardens, complete with a small lake, home to a collection of waterfowl, and a classical summerhouse, are richly planted and especially beautiful in spring.
House open Etr, daily; Apr & Sep-Oct, wknds; May-Aug, daily (ex Thu) 1-6. Estate grounds all year, daily dawn-dusk.

House £2.60 (ch £1.30). Estate £3.50 per car (Nov-Mar £1.75). Party.
🅿 *(charged)* 🐶 🍴 ♿ *(wheelchair available, may be driven to house) toilets for disabled shop*

Strangford Castle
STRANGFORD
☎ *(01232) 235000*
A three-storey tower house built in the 16th century, overlooking the small double harbour of Strangford.
Visable from outside. Free.
🐶
(AM)

Narrow Water Castle
WARRENPOINT
(1m NW)
☎ *Belfast (01232) 235000*
Both picturesque and complete in detail, this 16th-century battlemented tower house is surrounded by a wall and juts out into the river estuary which it was originally built to defend.
Open Jul-Aug, Tue-Sat 10-7, Sun 2-7. 75p (accompanied ch 40p).
🅿
(AM)

CO FERMANAGH

Belleek Pottery
BELLEEK
☎ *(013656) 58501*
Known worldwide for its fine Parian china, Ireland's oldest and most historic pottery was started in 1857 by the Caldwell family. Although the Caldwells originally used felspar from the Castle Caldwell estate, today it is imported, mainly from Norway. Visitors watch this delicate porcelain being handcrafted and visit the museum which exhibits pieces dating back over 100 years. There is a shop and display area.
Open all year, Mar-Jun, Mon-Fri 9-6, Sat 10-6, Sun 2-6; Jul-Aug, Mon-Fri 9-8, Sat 10-6, Sun 11-6; Sep, Mon-Fri 9-6, Sat 10-6, Sun 2-6; Oct, Mon-Fri 9-5.30, Sat 10-5.30, Sun 2-6; Nov-Feb, Mon-Fri 9-5.30. Guided tours £1.
🅿 🍴 ♿ *toilets for disabled shop* 🐶 *(small dogs allowed)*

White Island Church
CASTLE ARCHDALE BAY
(in Castle Archdale Bay; ferry from marina)
☎ *Belfast (01232) 235000*
Lined up on the far wall of a small, roofless 12th-century church are eight uncanny carved-stone figures. Part Christian and part pagan in appearance, their significance has been the subject of great debate. The church ruins sit on an early monastic site.
Open Jul-Aug, Tue-Sat 10-7, Sun 2-7. £2.25 (ch & pen £1.20).
🅿 🐶 🚣
(AM)

Tully Castle
DERRYGONNELLY
(3m N, on W shore of Lower Lough Erne)
☎ *Belfast (01232) 235000*
Extensive ruins of a Scottish-style stronghouse with enclosing bawn overlooking Lough Erne. Built by Sir John Hume in the early 1600s, the castle was destroyed, and most of the occupants slaughtered, by the Maguires in the 1641 Rising. There is a replica of a 17th-century garden in the bawn.
Open Apr-Sep Tue-Sat 10-7, Sun 2-7; Oct-Mar 10-4.(2-4 Sun).
£1 (ch & pen 50p).
🅿 ♿ 🐶
(AM)

Castle Coole
ENNISKILLEN
(1.5m SE on A4)
☎ *(01365) 322690*

One of the finest classical mansions in Northern Ireland, if not in the British Isles. No expense was spared in the building of this mansion for the First Earl of Belmore between 1789 and 1795. James Wyatt was the architect, the lovely plasterwork ceilings were by Joseph Rose, and the chimneypieces the work of Richard Westmacott. Vast amounts of Portland stone were specially imported, together with an Italian expert in stonework, and joiners from England were brought in to make the shutters and doors. The house is filled with beautiful Regency furniture. Don't miss the sumptuous state bed in scarlet silk. Outside the lawns slope gently towards Lough Coole which is home to a flock of greylag geese.
Open Etr, daily; Apr-May & Sep, wknds & BH's; Jun-Aug, daily (ex Thu) 2-6. Last tour 5.15.
£2.50 (ch £1.25). Estate £1.50 per car. Party.
🅿 🐶 ♿ *(may be driven to house) toilets for disabled shop*
(NT)

Devenish Island
ENNISKILLEN
(2m N)
☎ *Belfast (01232) 235000*
In an attractive setting, two miles downstream from the city centre, this island (once the site of a monastery founded in the 6th century by St Molaise - regarded as one of the 12 apostles of Ireland) has a considerable number of interesting ecclesiastical remains. The ruins of Teampull Mor, with its fine south window, date back to the 13th century, while St Molaise's house - the remains of a tiny but sturdy church (roofless now) - to the 12th century. Facing this little church is a perfect 80ft-tall round tower. Also dating back to the 12th century, this tower is built on five floors accessible by ladders. The ruins of the Augustinian priory of St Marys' has an elaborately carved north chancel door and a pretty 15th-century cross in the graveyard.
Open Apr-Sep, Tue-Sat 10-7, Sun 2-7. £2.25 (incl ferry access to museum & tower) (ch & pen £1.20) ; 50p (tower & museum only)
🅿 🐶
(AM)

Enniskillen Castle
ENNISKILLEN
☎ *(01365) 322711*
Overlooking Lough Erne, this castle, a three-storey keep surrounded by massive stone-built barracks and with a turreted fairytale 17th-century water gate, now houses two museums and a heritage centre. In the castle keep is a small museum displaying Royal Enniskillen Fusiliers regimental exhibits, while the other rooms contain the Fermanagh County Museum's collection of local antiquities.
Open all year Mon 2-5, Tue-Fri 10-5 (closed 1-2, Oct-Apr), Sat 2-5 May-Aug, Sun 2-5 Jul-Aug, all day BH's.
£1 (ch 50p, pen 75p)
🅿 ♿ *shop* 🐶
(AM)

Florence Court
ENNISKILLEN
(8m SW via A4 & A32)
☎ *(01365) 348249*
Named after the wife of John Cole, the father of the First Earl of Enniskillen, this 18th-century mansion overlooks wild and beautiful scenery towards the Mountains of Cuilcagh. The interior of the house, particularly noted for its flambuoyant rococo plasterwork, was gutted by fire in 1955, but has been miraculously restored. The mansion is situated in beautiful parkland full of fine old trees, including the Florence Court Yew - mother of all Irish yews. There are pleasure grounds with an Ice House, Summer House and Water Powered Sawmill, also a walled garden and fine views. Special events include Victorian Tea Party (25 June), Craft Fair (13

August).
Open Etr, daily 1-6; Apr, May & Sep wknds & BH's 1-6; Jun-Aug, daily (ex Tue) 1-6.
£2.50 (ch £1.25). Estate only £1.50 per car.
🅿 💺 ♿ *(electric wheelchair available) toilets for disabled shop*
(NT)

Marble Arch Caves
ENNISKILLEN
Marlbank Scenic Loop (off A4 Enniskillen-Sligo road)
☎ *(01365) 348855*
Magical cave system - one of Europe's finest - under the Mountains of Cuilcagh. Here visitors are given a tour round a wonderland of stalagmites, stalactites, underground rivers and lakes, which starts with a boat trip on the lower lake. The streams which flow down and then disappear into the mountain feed the caves and then emerge at Marble Arch, a huge 30ft detached limestone bridge. Special events to mark the centenary of the original exploration (10-16 July).
Open Apr-Oct, daily (weather permitting). Tours Mon-Sun 11-4.30 (11-5 in Jul & Aug). Admission prices under review.
🅿 💺 *shop* ✂

Monea Castle
ENNISKILLEN
(6m NW)
☎ *Belfast (01232) 235000*
A fine example of a plantation castle still with much of its enclosing bawn wall intact, built around 1618. Of particular interest is the castle's stone corbelling - the Scottish method of giving additional support to turrets.
Open at any reasonable time.
Free.
🅿 ♿
(AM)

Castle Balfour
LISNASKEA
☎ *Belfast (01232) 235000*
Dating from 1618 and refortified in 1652, this is a T-plan house with vaulted rooms. Badly burnt in the early 1800s, this house has remained in ruins.
Open at all times.
Free.
🅿 ♿
(AM)

Crom Estate
NEWTOWNBUTLER
(3m W)
☎ *(013657) 38174*
About 1,350 acres of woodland, parkland and wetland on the shores of Upper Lough Erne. This is one of Northern Ireland's most important native conservation areas of international significance. There is a visitor information centre on Lough Shore. For details of events for 1995 telephone (01365) 322633.
Open 29 Mar-Sep, daily 2-6.
Free.
🅿 *(charged)*
(NT)

CO LONDONDERRY

Hezlett House
COLERAINE
Castlerock (5m W on Coleraine/Downhill coast rd)
☎ *Castlerock (01265) 848567*
A low, thatched cottage built around 1690 with an interesting cruck truss roof, constructed by using pairs of curved timbers to form arches and infilling around this frame with clay, rubble and other locally available materials.
Open Etr, daily; Apr-Jun & Sep wknds & BH's; Jul-Aug, daily (ex Tue) 1-6.
£1.50 (ch 75p). Party.
🅿 ✂ *(ex in gardens)*
(NT)

Mount Sandel
COLERAINE
(1.25m SSE)
☎ *Belfast (01232) 230560*
This 200ft oval mound overlooking the River Bann is believed to have been fortified in the Iron Age. Nearby is the earliest known inhabited place in Ireland, where post holes and hearths of wooden dwellings, and flint implements dating back to 6,650BC have been found. The fort was a stronghold of de Courcy in the late 12th century and was refortified for artillery in the 17th century.
Open at all times.
Free.

(AM)

Tullaghoge Fort
COOKSTOWN
(2m S)
☎ *Belfast (01232) 235000*
This large hilltop earthwork, planted with trees, was once the headquarters of the O'Hagans, Chief Justices of the old kingdom of Tyrone. Between the 12th and 16th centuries the O'Neill Chiefs of Ulster were also crowned here - the King Elect was seated on a stone inauguration chair, new sandals were placed on his feet and he was then anointed and crowned. The last such ceremony was held here in the 1590s; in 1600 the stone throne was destroyed by order of Lord Mountjoy.
Open at all times.
Free.
🅿
(AM)

Wellbrook Beetling Mill
COOKSTOWN
Corkhill (4m W in Co Tyrone, 0.5m off A505)
☎ *Tulnacross (016487) 51735*
This 18th-century water-powered linen mill was used for bleaching and, until 1961, for finishing Irish linen. Beetling was the name given to the final process in linen making, when the material was beaten by 30 or so hammers (beetles) to achieve a smooth and slightly shiny finish. The National Trust acquired the mill and restored it to working order.
Open Etr, daily; Apr-Jun & Sep, wknds & BH's; Jul-Aug, daily (ex Tue) 2-6.
£1.40 (ch 70p). Party.
🅿 ♿ *shop*
(NT)

Mussenden Temple Bishop's Gate and Black Glen
DOWNHILL
Mussenden Rd (1m W of Castlerock)
☎ *(012658) 48728*
Spectacularly placed on a cliff edge overlooking the Atlantic, this perfect 18th-century rotunda was modelled on the Temple of Vesta at Tivoli. Frederick Hervey, Bishop of Derry and 4th Earl of Bristol, had the temple built as a summer library for his cousin, but sadly she died before its completion, so he studied there himself. The temple, with its magnificent views of the Antrim and Donegal coasts, is only a part of the Earl Bishop's Downhill demesne; visitors entering by the Bishop's Gate can enjoy a beautiful glen walk up to the headland where the temple stands.
Open 1-12 Apr, booked parties only; Temple: Etr, daily, noon-6; Apr-Jun & Sep, weekends & BH's noon-6; Jul-Aug, daily noon-6.
Free.
🅿 ♿
(NT)

Banagher Church
DUNGIVEN
(2m SW)
☎ *Belfast (01232) 235000*
This church was founded by St Muiredach O'Heney in 1100 and altered in later centuries. Today impressive ruins remain. The nave is the oldest part and the square-headed lintelled west door is particularly impressive. Just outside, the perfect miniature stone house, complete with pitched roof and the sculpted figures of a saint at the doorway, is believed to be the tomb of St Muiredach. The saint was said to have endowed his large family with the power of bringing good luck. All they had to do was to sprinkle whoever or whatever needed luck with sand taken from the base of the saint's tomb.
Open at all times.
Free.
🅿
(AM)

Dungiven Priory
DUNGIVEN
(SE of town overlooking River Roe)
☎ *Belfast (01232) 235000*
Up until the 17th century Dungiven was the stronghold of the O'Cahan chiefs, and the Augustinian priory, of which extensive ruins remain, was founded by the O'Cahans around 1150. The church, which was altered many times in later centuries, contains one of Northern Ireland's finest medieval tombs. It is the tomb of Cooey na Gall O'Cahan who died in 1385. His sculpted effigy, dressed in Irish armour, lies under a stonework canopy. Below are six kilted warriors.
Open - Church at all times, chancel only when caretaker available. Check at house at end of lane.
Free.
✂ 🚌
(AM)

Rough Fort
LIMAVADY
(1m W)
Early Christian rath.
Open at all times.
🚌
(NT)

City Walls
LONDONDERRY
☎ *Belfast (01232) 235000*
The finest and most complete city walls to be found in Ireland. The walls, 20-25ft high, are mounted with ancient canon, and date back to the 17th century. The walled city is a conservation area with many fine buildings. Visitors can walk round the city ramparts - a circuit of one mile.
Open all times.
Admission free from various points.
🅿 *(charged)* ♿
(AM)

Foyle Valley Railway Heritage Centre
LONDONDERRY
Foyle Rd
☎ *(01504) 265234*
A fascinating collection of relics from the four railway companies which served Londonderry are on display here at the Foyle Valley Railway Heritage Centre. Majestic steam locomotives, diesel railcars and all the paraphernalia of a station can be seen, along with the Railway Gallery which tells the story of the people who ran the railways and those who used the trains.
Open all year, Apr-Sep Tue-Sat & PH's 10-5, Sun 2-6; Oct-Mar Tue-Sat 10-5.
Free.
🅿 ♿ *toilets for disabled shop garden centre* ✂

This traditional homestead and farmyard, ancestral home of President Ulysses Grant of the United States of America, is furnished in period style.

Tower Museum
LONDONDERRY
Union Hall Place
☎*(01504) 372411*
The exhibition recounts the history of Londonderry from pre-historic times to the present day using real artifacts, theatrical displays and eleven audio-visual programmes showing the spread of Irish monasticism, the famous Siege of Derry and the road to the partition of Ireland.
Open all year, Tue-Sat 10-5.
✱£2.50 (concessions, pre-school ch & pen free).
P *(300 yds)* ♿ *toilets for disabled shop* 🐕

Maghera Church
MAGHERA
(E approach to the town)
☎*Belfast (01232) 235000*
Important 6th-century monastery founded by St Lurach, later a bishop's see and finally a parish church. This much-altered church has a magnificently decorated 12th-century west door. A cross-carved stone to the west of the church is supposed to be the grave of the founder.
Key from Leisure Centre.
Free.
P ♿
(AM)

Springhill
MONEYMORE
(1m from Moneymore on B18)
☎*(016487) 48210*
Dating back to the 17th century, this attractive, pleasingly symmetrical manor house was originally the home of the Scottish Conyngham family. Today much of the family furniture, books and bric-a-brac have been retained. Outside, the laundry, stables, brewhouse, and old dovecote make interesting viewing, as do the old Irish cottage kitchen and the excellent costume museum.
Open Etr, daily 2-6; Apr-Jun & Sep, wknds & BH's 2-6; Jul-Aug, daily (ex Thu) 2-6.
£2.20 (ch £1.10). Party.
P ☕ ♿ *toilets for disabled shop*

CO TYRONE

Ardboe Cross
ARDBOE
(off B73)
☎*Belfast (01232) 235000*
Situated at Ardboe Point, on the western shore of Lough Neagh, is the best example of a high cross to be found in Northern Ireland. Marking the site of an ancient monastery, the cross has 22 sculpted panels, many recognisably biblical, including Adam and Eve and the Last Judgment. It stands over 18ft high and dates back to the 10th century. It is still the rallying place of the annual Lammas, but praying at the cross and washing in the lake has been replaced by traditional music-making, singing and selling of local produce. The tradition of 'cross reading' or interpreting the pictures on the cross, is an honour passed from generation to generation among the men of the village.
Open at all times.
Free.
P ♿
(AM)

U S Grant Ancestral Homestead & Visitor Centre
BALLYGAWLEY
Dergenagh, Ballygawley Rd (off A4, 3m on Dergenagh road)
☎*Aughnacloy (016625) 57133*
Ancestral homestead of Ulysses S Grant, 18th President of the United States of America. The homestead and farmyard have been restored to the style and appearance of a mid-19th-century Irish smallholding. The small thatched cottage consists of two rooms, furnished with replica period pieces, and the farmyard contains examples of agricultural implements used by the 19th-century

The west coast of Clare has some of Ireland's most spectacular scenery, and the cliffs of Moher are undoubtedly the most impressive of all.

farmer. The Visitor Centre houses a shop and a display area with exhibitions on the Ulster Scots Plantation and the U S Grant story. There is also a small audio-visual theatre, and a small cafeteria in which each of the five tables represents a different period in local history.
Open Etr-Sep, Mon-Sat 12-5, Sun 2-6. Other times by arrangement. (Closed 25-26 Dec & 1 Jan).
✱60p (ch & pen 30p). Party 10+
P ☕ ♿ *shop*

Beaghmore Stone Circles and Alignments
BEAGHMORE
☎*Belfast (01232) 235000*
Discovered in the 1930s, these impressive, ritualistic stones have been dated back to the early Bronze, and maybe even Neolithic Ages. There are three pairs of stone circles, one single circle, stone rows or alignments and cairns, which range in height from one to four feet. This is an area littered with historic monuments, many discovered by people cutting turf.
Open at all times.
Free.
P ♿
(AM)

Benburb Castle
BENBURB
☎*Belfast (01232) 235000*
The castle ruins - three towers and massive walls - are dramatically placed on a cliff-edge 120ft above the River Blackwater. The northwest tower is newly restored and has dizzy cliff-edge views. The castle, built by Sir Richard Wingfield around 1615, is actually situated in the grounds of the Servite Priory. There are attractive walks down to the river.
Castle grounds open at all times. Special arrangements, made in advance, necessary for access to flanker tower.
Free.
P ♿ 🐕
(AM)

Castle Caulfield
CASTLECAULFIELD
☎*Belfast (01232) 235000*
Sir Toby Caulfield, an Oxfordshire knight and ancestor of the Earls of Charlemont, built this manor house in 1619 on the site of an ancient fort. It was badly burnt in 1641, repaired and lived in by the Caulfield/Charlemont family until 1670. It boasts the rare distinction of having had Saint Oliver Plunkett and John Wesley preach in its grounds. Some fragments of the castle are re-used in the fine, large 17th-century parish church.
Open at all times.
Free.
P ♿
(AM)

Harry Avery's Castle
NEWTOWNSTEWART
(0.75m SW)
☎*Belfast (01232) 235000*
The hilltop ruins of a Gaelic stone castle, built around the 14th century by one of the O'Neill chiefs, are the remains of the oldest surviving Irish-built castle in the north. Only the great twin towers of the gatehouse are left. A new stairway enables the public to gain access to one of these.
Open at all times.
Free.
🐕
(AM)

Ulster American Folk Park
OMAGH
(5m NW Omagh)
☎*(01662) 243292*
An outdoor museum, established in 1976, that traces the history of Ulster's links with America and the emigration of Ulster residents to North America during the 18th and 19th centuries. The 15-acre site is divided into two parts - Old World and New World. The Old World is centred around the restored farmhouse of Thomas Mellon, who emigrated to Pennsylvania in 1818, and later founded the Mellon Bank of Pittsburgh. In the New World are log houses and outbuildings - all are suitably furnished. There is also the cottage of John Joseph Hughes, who emigrated from Augher in 1817, became first Catholic Archbishop of New York and initiated the building of St Patrick's Cathedral there in 1858. There are also demonstrations of Old and New World crafts, such as horseshoeing and thatching. A modern visitor centre, with exhibitions and audio-visual presentations, provides further information. A special feature is the Emigration Gallery area complete with dockside buildings and emigrant ship. A full programme of special events is planned for 1995 and includes: Easter Weekend - Easter Bonnet Parade, Egg Painting Competition; American Independence Day (to be held in July), and the fourth annual Appalachian and Bluegrass Music Festival (to be held on the 1st weekend in September).
Open Etr-Sep, daily 11-6.30, Sun & BH 11.30-7; Sep-Etr Mon-Fri 10.30-5. Last admission 1hr 30mins before closing.
£3 (ch & pen £1.50)
P ☕ ♿ *toilets for disabled shop* 🐕

Ulster History Park
OMAGH
Cullion (7m on B48)
☎*(016626) 48188*
The Ulster History Park tells the story of settlement in Ireland with the aid of the full-scale models of the houses and monuments built through the ages. These range from a mesolithic encampment (c8000-4000BC); the houses and megalithic tombs of the first farmers (c4000-2200BC); a ring fort, crannog, round tower and Norman motte-and-bailey, and a 17th-century Plantation settlement. Exhibitions and audio-visual presentations expand the theme. There is a cafeteria, shop and picnic facilities.
Open all year, Apr-Sep Mon-Sat 10.30-6.30, Sun 11.30-7, BH's 10.30-7; Oct-Mar Mon-Fri 10.30-5. Last admission 1hr 30mins before closing time.
✱£3 (ch, students & pen £1.50). Family ticket £8. Group 15+
P ☕ ♿ *toilets for disabled shop* 🐕

Mountjoy Castle
STEWARTSTOWN
Magheralamfield (3m SE, off B161)
☎*Belfast (01232) 235000*
Ruins of an early 17th-century brick and stone fort, with four rectangular towers, overlooking Lough Neagh. The fort was built for Lord Deputy Mountjoy during his campaign against Hugh O'Neill, Earl of Tyrone. It was captured and re-captured by the Irish and English during the 17th century and was also used by the armies of James II and William III.
Open at all times.
Free.
P
(AM)

Gray's Printing Press
STRABANE
49 Main St
☎*(01504) 884094*
Strabane was once an important printing and book-publishing centre, the only relic of which is a small shop in Main Street - Gray's Printing Shop. The shop now houses a Printing Museum containing three 19th-century presses, while upstairs the development of printing techniques over sixty years is illustrated. Two young men who served their apprenticeships in Strabane during the 18th century went on to great things: John Dunlap emigrated to Philadelphia, where he founded 'The Pennsylvania Packet' - America's first 'daily'; James Wilson who also emigrated to Philadelphia becoming a printer, newspaper editor and judge whose grandson was President Woodrow Wilson.
Open Apr-Sep, daily (ex Thu, Sun & BH's) 2-5.30. Other times by prior arrangement.
£1.40 (ch 70p). Party.
P *(100yds) shop* 🐕
(NT)

REPUBLIC OF IRELAND

CO CLARE

Aillwee Cave
BALLYVAUGHAN
☎ (065) 77036 & 77067
An underground network of caves beneath the world famous Burren. Guided tours take you through large caverns, over bridged chasms and alongside thunderous waterfalls. There are craftshops where cheese is made and charcoal burning, coppicing and woodcraft exhibitions.
Open mid-Mar-Nov, 10-5.30 (Jul-Aug 6.30pm).
IRE3.95 (ch IRE2.20). Family ticket IRE12.
P ☕ shop ✻ (in cave)

Bunratty Castle & Folk Park
BUNRATTY
☎ Limerick (061) 361511
Restored in 1960, this is Ireland's most complete medieval castle. It houses the Lord Gort collection of furniture, objet d'art, and paintings and tapestries dating from before 1650. One-day tours operate in season from Limerick and include a medieval banquet at the castle. Irish village life at the turn of the century is tellingly re-created in the folk park in the grounds, with its typical 19th-century rural and urban dwellings. There are eight farmhouses, a watermill, a blacksmith's forge, and a village street complete with shops and pub.
Open all year, daily 9.30-5.30.
IRE4.50 (ch IRE2.20, pen IRE4.25). Family ticket IRE11.
P ☕ ✗ licensed & (castle not accessible) toilets for disabled shop

O'Brien's Tower & Cliffs of Moher
LISCANNOR
(4m N)
☎ (065) 81565
Just north of Liscannor on the coast of West Clare, are the famous Cliffs of Moher, defiantly standing as giant natural ramparts against the aggressive might of the Atlantic Ocean. They rise in places to 700ft, and stretch for almost 5 miles. O'Brien's Tower was built in the early 19th century as a viewing point for Victorian tourists on the highest point. From here you can view the Clare coastline, the Aran Islands and mountains as far apart as Kerry and Connemara. There is a visitor centre with tourist information.
Open - Cliffs of Moher accessible all year. O'Briens Tower, daily 10-5.30.
IRE1 (ch IR60p).
P (charged) ☕ & toilets for disabled shop

The Craggaunowen Bronze Age Project
QUIN
☎ Limerick (061) 367178
Contains a full-scale reconstruction of a crannog, a Bronze Age lake dwelling. The project includes a reconstructed ring fort and replicas of furniture, tools and utensils. Also on display is the *Brendan*, a replica of the leather boat used by St Brendan the Navigator in the 6th century. The boat was sailed across the Atlantic Ocean in 1976 and 1977. Special events: The Living Past (April-October daily), Traveling exhibition on the Bronze Age (mid Jul-mid Apr).
Open Mar-Oct, daily 10-6. Groups by appointment during the winter.
IRE3.50 (ch & pen IRE2.75). Family ticket IRE9.50
P ☕ & shop

CO CORK

The Royal Gunpowder Mills
BALLINCOLLIG
The Long Range
☎ (021) 874430
The Royal Gunpowder Mills is an amazing industrial complex on the banks of the River Lee. The mills supplied vast quantities of explosives for the British military forces, throughout the world from 1794 to 1903. Today visitors can experience the sights and sounds of this enormous factory. Personalised tours are provided from 10am to 6pm daily. The highlight of the tour includes a visit to the restored incorporating mill. An audio visual display is also provided.
Open daily, Apr-Sep 10-6. Last tour at 5.15pm.
IRE2.50 (ch IRE1.50, pen & students IRE2). Family ticket IRE7.
P ☕ & toilets for disabled shop

Bantry House
BANTRY
☎ (027) 50047
A Georgian mansion, surrounded by gardens, with a collection of furniture, tapestries etc by the Second Earl of Bantry. A tea room and craft shop are housed in the wings and there is an exhibition in the stables.
Open all year. (Closed 25 Dec)
IRE3 (ch free if accompanied, pen & students IRE1.75)
P ☕ & shop ✻ (ex in grounds)

Blarney Castle & Rock Close
BLARNEY
(5m from Cork on main road towards Limerick)
☎ Cork (021) 385252 & 385669
The site of the famous Blarney Stone, known the world over for the eloquence it is said to impart to those who kiss it. The stone is in the upper tower of the castle, and the visitor, held by his feet, must lean backwards down the inside of the battlements in order to receive the gift of the gab.
Open - Blarney Castle & Rock Close, Jun-Jul Mon-Sat 9-7.30; Aug Mon-Sat 9-7.30; May Mon-Sat 9-7; Sep Mon-Sat 9-6.30; Apr & Oct Mon-Sat 9-sunset; summer Sun 9.30-5.30; winter Sun 9.30-sunset. Blarney House & Gardens Jun-mid Sep Mon-Sat noon-6.
Blarney Castle & Rock Close IRE3 (ch IRE1, pen & students IRE2.50). Blarney House & Gardens IRE2.50 (ch IRE1, pen & students IRE2.50)
P & shop ✻

Fota Wildlife Park
CARRIGTWOHILL
Fota Estate
☎ (021) 812678
Situated 10 miles from Cork, on the Cobh road. Established in 1983 with the primary aim of conservation, Fota has more than 70 species of exotic wildlife in open, natural surroundings with no obvious barriers. Giraffes, zebras, ostrich, antelope and other animals enjoy 40 acres of grassland through which visitors can walk on an unfenced road in complete safety. Monkeys swing through mature trees on lake islands, while kangaroos, macaws and lemurs have complete freedom of the park. Only the cheetahs have a conventional fence. Facilities include children's corner, tour train, lakeside coffee shop and picnic benches. Also here is an internationally renowned arboretum, with a particularly good selection of trees from China, Japan, New Zealand, Australia, South America and the Himalayas.
Open 13 Mar-3 Oct, Mon-Sat 10-6, Sun 11-6 (last admission 5); Reduced rates and facilities in Oct.
✻IRE3.50 (ch & pen IRE2, students IRE3). Family day ticket IRE13.50.
P (charged) ☕ & toilets for disabled shop ✻

Best known these days for the 'gift of the Blarney', this 15th-century castle was the strongest in Munster. There are fine views from the top of its walls.

West Cork Model Village Railway
CLONAKILTY
Inchydoney Rd
☎ (023) 33224
The Model Railway village depicts the prominent buildings landmarks and way of life in the six major towns and villages of West Cork, namely Clonakilty, Bandon, Skibbereen, Dunmanway, Kinsale and Bantry. The towns are modelled at the height of activity. Fair days and the hectic day-to-day life of the mills and breweies are depicted. Phase one is currently open and shows a detailed model of Clonakilty. Visitors enter through a lifesize replica of Clonakilty Station as it was in the 1940s. In the centre a series of models, artefacts and diplays prepare the visitor for their model village experience. Phase two opens in July 1995 with the addition of an audio-visual display and access to the control room.
Open Mon-Sun 11-5. Last admission 4.30pm.
✻IRE2 (concessions IRE1). Family ticket IRE5.
P ☕ & toilets for disabled ✻

Cork City Gaol
CORK
Convent Av, Sundays Well
☎ (021) 305022
A superbly restored prison building which housed prisoners in the 19th century, often in very wretched conditions. Furnished cells, lifelike characters, sound effects and amazing exhibits combine to allow visitors to experience day-to-day life for prisoners and gaoler. Inter-active multimedia are incorporated into an audio-visual presentation of the social history of Cork City, which mirrors national history. Suitable for all ages, individual sound tours are available in English, French and German.
Open Apr-Oct, daily ; Nov-Mar wknds. Opening times Mar-Oct from 9.30am, Nov-Feb from 10am. Last tour May-Sep 6pm, Oct 5pm, other times 4pm.
IRE3 (ch 12 IRE1.50, pen & student IR£2.50). Family ticket IRE7.50.
P ☕ & toilets for disabled shop ✻

Cork Heritage Park
CORK
Bessboro, Skehard Rd, Blackrock
☎ (021) 358854
Located approximately four kilometres from the centre of Cork, this heritage theme park covers about six acres of the former Bessboro estate. There is an Environmental Centre with information about wildlife on the Douglas Estuary; a scale model and photographic exhibits of Cork Harbour and the Port of Cork; an exhibition on the Pike family who formerly owned the estate; exhibits on Cork's boat building, maritime and archeological heritage, plus many other interesting exhibits. A restored 19th century farmyard is a new attraction for 1995.
Open Etr-Sep, 10-5 (Etr-1 May wknds only).
✻IRE2 (concessions IRE1.50). Family ticket IRE5. Party.
P ✗ & toilets for disabled shop ✻

Cork Public Museum
CORK
Fitzgerald Park, Mardyke (N of University College)
☎ (021) 270679
Displays illustrating the history of the city are housed in this museum. The collections cover the economic, social and municipal history from the Mesolithic period, with emphasis on civic regalia, and the trades and crafts of the 19th and 20th centuries. There are fine collections of Cork Silver and Glass and Youghal Needlepoint Lace.
Open all year, Jun-Aug Mon-Fri 11-1 & 2.15-5, Sun 3-5; Sep-May Mon-Fri 11-1 & 2.15-5, Sun 3-5. (Closed Sat, BH wknds & PH)
✻Mon-Fri free; Sun, Family IRE1 individual IR50p. Students, pen & unwaged free
P (100 yds) shop ✻

Garinish Island
GLENGARRIFF
☎ (027) 63040
An Italianate garden, designed by Harold Peto, bathed in the warm waters of the Gulf Stream provides an ideal setting for the collection of tender plants which

➤

thrive here. A Martello Tower, Clock Tower, a Grecian Temple overlooking the sea and magnificent pedimented gateways are some of the architectural features of the garden.
Open Jul-Aug, Mon-Sat 9.30-6.30, Sun 11-7; Apr-Jun & Sep, Mon-Sat 10-6.30, Sun 1-7; Mar & Oct, Mon-Sat 10-4.30, Sun 1-5. Last landing 1 hour before closing. IR£2.50 (ch IR£1 & pen IR£1.75) Family ticket IR£6
&. *toilets for disabled shop*

Jameson Heritage Centre
MIDLETON
☎ (021) 613594 & 613596
A tour of the Jameson Heritage Centre consists of a 20 minute audio/visual presentation, then a 35 minute guided tour of the Old Distillery and then back to the Jameson Bar for a whiskey tasting - minerals are available for children. The guided tour and audio-visual aids are available in five languages.
Open daily, Mar-20 Nov 10-6. Last tour commencing 4.15pm.
✱*IR£3.50 (ch £1.50). Family ticket IR£9.50*
🅿 🍽 &. *toilets for disabled shop*

CO DONEGAL

Ardara Heritage Centre
ARDARA
☎ (075) 41704
The Heritage Centre offers information about this fabulous region mountain passes, forests, lakes and historical landmarks. It is an area rich in folklore and archeology, as well as a cultural centre for traditional music. Ardara is the heart of Ireland's manufacture of handwoven tweed, hand knitwear and hand loomed woollens and there are many craft and factory shops as well as exhibitions within the Heritage Centre. In 1995 the Old Fair Day is held from 30 June to 2 July and and the Agricultural show on the second weekend in August.
Open Apr-Sep, 9.30-6.
IR£2 (ch14 IR50p, pen & student IR£1). Party.
🅿 🍽 ✕ &. *toilets for disabled shop* ⊗

The Water Wheels
BALLYSHANNON
Abbey Assaro (cross Abbey River on Rossnowlagh Rd)
☎ (072) 51580
Abbey Assaroe was founded by Cistercian Monks from Boyle Abbey in the late 12th century. The Cistercians excelled in water engineering and canalised the river to turn water wheels for mechanical power. The mills were restored in 1989 and there is a coffee shop and auditorium. One waterwheel now powers a generator which supplies light and heat. The site occupies an unusual position overlooking the Erne Estuary and the Atlantic.
Open Etr wk & May-Aug, 10.30-6.30.

Other times, Sun 1.30-dusk.
Charge for audio-visual display IR£1
🅿 ✕ &. *toilets for disabled shop garden centre*

Guns of Dunree Military Museum
BUNCRANA
Fort Dunree, Dunree (6m N, on eastern shore of Lough Swilly)
☎ (077) 61817
Fort Dunree Military Museum is the first and only permanent and professionally-designed military museum in Ireland. It is located a few miles north-west of Buncrana along the Inis Eoghain 100, the motoring circuit of the beautiful Inishowen Peninsula in North Donegal. The museum houses a collection of artefacts and an audio-visual display which vividly illustrates the working of a coastal defence battery extending back of 180 years.
Open daily Jun-Sep 10.30-6, Sun 1-6.
✱*IR£1.50 (ch IR75p)*
🅿 🍽 &. *shop* ⊗

Glebe House & Gallery
LETTERKENNY
Church Hill
☎ (074) 37071
The Regency house set in beautiful woodland gardens along the shore of Lough Gartan, was given to the nation, along with his art collection, by the artist Derek Hill. The interior of the house is decorated with original wallpapers and textiles by William Morris. The art collection is extensive with paintings by many leading 20th century artists, Japanese prints including works by Hokusai and Hiroshige and a fabulous collection of Victoriana.
Open 15-23 Apr & 20 May-1 Oct. Closed Fri.
IR£2 (ch & student IR£1, pen IR£1.50). Party.
🅿 🍽 &. *shop* ⊗

Letterkenny Pottery
LETTERKENNY
Pinehill Industrial Estate, Mountaintop
☎ (074) 22738
Letterkenny Pottery was founded by Brian McGee. The pottery produced at Letterkenny is extremely popular in Ireland. It is notable for its very colourful wax resistant decoration. Brian McGee is well-known for his Raku pots and demonstrations of Raku pottery-making are planned throughout 1995. Telephone or contact the local tourist office for details.
Open all year, Mon-Sat 10-6 (Dec-Apr Mon-Fri).
🅿 &. *(accessible with assistance) shop* ⊗
Details not confirmed for 1995

Cavanacor Historic House & Craft Centre
LIFFORD
Ballindrait (1.5m from town off Strabane/Letterkenny rd)
☎ (074) 41143
Built in the early 1600s and commanding a view of the Clonleigh valley and the

River Deele, Cavanacor House is the ancestral home of James Knox Polk, 11th President of the USA (1845-1849). King James II dined under the sycamore tree which still stands in front of the house in 1689. There is a display of the history of the house and the surrounding area and over 10 acres of landscaped gardens and an old-fashioned walled garden. 1995 is the 200th anniversary of the birth of President James Knox Polk and a series of events are planned.
Open Etr- Sep, Tue-Sat 12-6, Sun 2-6. Closed Mon ex BH's.
IR£2 (ch & pen IR£1). Family ticket IR£6. Party
🅿 🍽 ✕ &. *shop garden centre*

CO DUBLIN

Ardgillan Castle
BALBRIGGAN
(on R127)*
☎ (01) 8492212
A large and elegant country manor house built in 1738, set amid 194 acres of parkland overlooking the sea and coast as far as the Mourne Mountains. There are exhibitions throughout 1995: Mar/Apr - 17th Century maps of Ireland; May - Craft Potter Society of Ireland; June - Art Group; July - Malmö (Sweden) Photo-Club Exhibition;Sep/Oct - Famine in Fingal.
Open 20 Dec-Jan, Sun & BH's 2-4.30 (closed 25 Dec); Apr-Sep, Tue-Sun & BH's 11-6; Oct-Mar, Wed-Sun & BH's 11-4.30.
✱*IR£2 (pen IR£1). Family ticket IR£4.50. Party.*
🅿 🍽 &. *toilets for disabled* ⊗

Newbridge House and Traditional Farm
DONABATE
☎ *Dublin (01) 8436534 & 8462184*
Newbridge House was designed by George Semple and built in 1737 for Charles Cobbe, Archbishop of Dublin. The house contains many splendidly refurbished rooms featuring plasterwork, furniture and paintings. The finest room in the house is the Red Drawing Room, which has a beautiful white marble chimney piece and a rococo plaster ceiling attributed to Richard Williams. Other rooms open on the ground floor include the library, dining room, sculpture gallery and Museum of Curiosities. The latter features many artefacts collected by the Cobbe family on their travels throughout the world. Downstairs you will find the kitchen and the laundry. Special events throughout the year include demonstrations of sheep shearing, weaving, dying, pottery and harness making.
Open Apr-Sep Tue-Fri 10-1 & 2-5, Sat 11-6, Sun & PH 2-6; Oct-Mar Sat-Sun & PH 2-5. Parties at other times by arrangement.
✱*House IR£2.50 (ch IR£1.35, concessions IR£2.15). Family ticket IR£6.95; Farm IR£1 (concessions IR80p).*
🅿 🍽 &. *shop* ⊗

DUBLIN
Dublin is a delightful city with many outstanding examples of 18th-century architecture. Birthplace and inspiration of many great authors, its contrasts are apparent everywhere: sweeping avenues and intimate sidestreets, chic shops and smokey pubs, stately museums and colleges, and terraces with faded exteriors emanating distinctive character. A good place to begin a tour of this compact city is O'Connell Bridge, leading to the city's main shopping area, O'Connell Street, where the best buys are local products, such as linen and lace, homespun tweeds and knitwear. City attractions include Parnell Square, one of Dublin's earliest and most attractive squares of handsome brick-faced

Georgian houses; Charlemont House, containing the Hugh Lane Municipal Gallery of Modern Art; Nassau Street, with its bookstores; the National Gallery, housing more than 2000 works of art; the National Museum's fascinating collection of Irish treasures; the Civic Museum, and Trinity College Library. Dublin Castle's state apartments have guided tours every half-hour, and the Guinness brewery offers visitors a 30-minute film show, followed by a tasting.

Ashtown Castle Visitor Centre
DUBLIN
Phoenix Park
☎ (01) 6770095
Situated in Phoenix Park the Visitor Centre provides an historical interpretation of the park from 3500BC through a series of attractive displays. Part of the building is devoted to nature and there is a colourful film of Phoenix Park. The castle, probably dating from the early 17th century has been restored to its former glory.
Open daily all year; Mar & Oct-Nov 9.30-5, Apr-May 9.30-5.30; Jun-Sep 9.30-6.30; Dec-Feb 9.30-4.30. (last admission 45 mins before closing).
IR£2 (ch & students IR£1, pen IR£1.50). Family ticket IR£5.
🅿 🍽 &. *toilets for disabled shop* ⊗

Drimnagh Castle
DUBLIN
Long Mile Rd, Drimnagh
☎ (01) 4502530
The last surviving medieval castle in Ireland with a flooded moat, Drimnagh dates originally to the 13th century. The Great Hall and Undercroft have been restored to their medieval grandeur, set off by the 17th-century style formal gardens, all of which are open to the public. Continuously inhabited until 1954, it is now populated by a team of crafts men, apprentices and young trainees, restoring the later tower, stables and coach-house with the same meticulous attention to detail as was used for the older parts. In June 1995 it is hoped there will be a training workshop in building conservation skills which is open to all.
Open Apr-Sep, Wed, wknds & BH's 12-5; Oct-Mar, Sun & BH's 2-5.
IR£1.50 (ch IR50p, pen & students IR£1). Party.
🅿 🍽 &. ⊗

Dublin Writers Museum
DUBLIN
18/19 Parnell Square North
☎ (01) 8722077
The Dublin Writers Museum and Irish Writers Centre is housed in two restored 18th-century buildings which retain many of their Georgian characteristics, and a modern annexe with lecture rooms and exhibition spaces. Dublin's rich literary heritage can be followed through displays tracing the written tradition in Ireland from the Book of Kells in the 8th century to the present day. Paintings, letters, photographs and artefacts are also on show. An audio tour, in French, Spanish, German, Italian and Japanese is included in the admission price.
Open all year, Mon-Sat 10-5 & Sun & BH 11.30-5.30. Jun-Aug, Mon-Fri 10-7pm.
IR£2.60 (ch IR£1, concessions IR£3). Family ticket IR£7
P (200 yds) 🍽 ✕ *licensed shop* ⊗

Guinness Hop Store
DUBLIN
Crane St
☎ (01) 536700
Established in 1876, the Hop Store remained crammed with hopsacks until 1957, when a new hop store came into use. It has now been converted to 'The World of Guinness' which shows the history of the famous brewery through museum exhibits and audio-visual presentations. In 'The Cooperage', there is a comprehensive collection of cooper's

---

The superb glasshouses at the National Botanic Gardens in Dublin were erected between 1843 and 1869.

tools and oak casks displayed in an authentic brewery setting. There is also a Transport Gallery and a Sample Bar, where you can taste the famous drink.
Open all year, Mon-Fri 10-4 (last complete tour 3.30). (Closed Sat-Sun & PH/BH)
P & *toilets for disabled shop* ⚘
Details not confirmed for 1995

Howth Castle Rhododendron Gardens
DUBLIN
Howth (9m NE)
☎(01) 322624 & 322256
On the northern boundary of Dublin Bay, the castle is justly famous for its attractive gardens and it is especially lauded for its rhododendron walk. The walk is open all year, but is at its floral best in May and June. There are views north to the Mourne Mountains and to the west of Dublin Bay.
Open all year, daily 8am-dusk. (Closed 25 Dec).
P ⚑ ✖ *licensed*
Details not confirmed for 1995

Hugh Lane Municipal Gallery of Modern Art
DUBLIN
Charlemont House, Parnell Square
☎(01) 8741903
The gallery occupies Charlemont House, a lovely Georgian mansion. Included here are collections of Irish works and art from the modern French and British schools.
Open all year, Tue-Fri 9.30-6, Sat 9.30-5, Sun 11-5. (Closed Mon). (Closed Good Fri & 24-25 Dec).
Free.
P *100 metres (meter parking)* ✖ *licensed* & *toilets for disabled shop* ⚘

Irish Museum of Modern Art
DUBLIN
Royal Hospital Kilmainham, Kilmainham
☎(01) 6718666
The museum is housed in the Royal Hospital Kilmainham, a large impressive 17th-century building laid out around an elegant courtyard. It presents a wide-ranging programme of Irish and International 20th-century art from its own collections and through temporary exhibitions, along with talks, seminars and musical events.
Open all year Tue-Sat 10-5.30, Sun & BH's 12-5.30. (Closed 24-26 Dec).
P ⚑ & *toilets for disabled shop* ⚘
Details not confirmed for 1995

National Botanic Gardens
DUBLIN
Glasnevin
☎(01) 8374388 & 8377596
The National Botanic Gardens, established in 1795 and covering an area of 48 acres, contains fine collections of trees and shrubs, as well as renowned herbaceous borders. Separate areas are devoted to annuals and vegetables, and to native Irish plants, arranged according to habitats. A self-guiding trail, highlighting some interesting hardy Chinese species, has been laid out for the visitor to follow. The glasshouses contain collections of palms, rare cycads, tropical ferns, cacti and alpines. Restoration of the famous iron-and-glass Curvilinear Range (1843-1869), principally designed and built by Richard Turner, will be completed in 1995.
Open all year, summer Mon-Sat 9-6, Sun 11-6; winter Mon-Sat 10-4.30, Sun 11-4.30. (Closed 25 Dec).
Free.
P & *toilets for disabled* ⚘

Natural History Museum
DUBLIN
Merrion St
☎(01) 6618811
The Natural History Museum was recently described by Professor Stephen Jay Gould as one of the world's finest and fullest exhibits in the old and still-stunning cabinet style. Founded by the Royal Dublin Soceiety in 1792, it has occupied its present premises since 1857. It was taken over by the state in 1877. There are extensive zoological exhibitions and geological specimens are also on display. The ground floor is devoted to Irish fauna while the first floor contains examples of all the major animal groups including many rare specimens. The Blaschka glass models of marine animals are world-famous. The museum is also an important research institute.
Open Tue-Sat 10-5, Sun 2-5.
Free.
P *(parking meters wkdays)* & ⚘

Newman House
DUBLIN
University College Dublin, 86 St Stephens Green
☎(01) 7067422 & 4757255
Newman House consists of two superb Georgian townhouses which contain some of Ireland's finest 18th-century plasterwork and decoration. As the founding home of University College Dublin in 1854, the house has been associated with many famous literary and historical figures, including James Joyce, Gerard Manley Hopkins, and Cardinal Newman. A major restoration programme, begun in 1989, has restored the rooms to their early Georgian splendour.
Open Jun-Sep, Tue-Fri 10-4.30, Sat 2-4.30, Sun 11-2. Parties by appointment all year.
✳*IR£1 (concessions IR75p).*
P ✖ *licensed shop* ⚘

Number Twenty Nine
DUBLIN
Lower Fitzwilliam St
☎(01) 7026165
Number Twenty-Nine is an exhibition of the homelife of a middle-class merchant family in late 18th and early 19th century Dublin. It is presented by the Electricity Supply Board and the National Museum of Ireland and one visit will only whet the appetite for more! There are occasional evening talks. Ring for details.
Open all year, Tue-Sat 10-5, Sun 2-5. (Closed Mon & 2 wks prior to Xmas). Free.
P *(on street meters)* ⚏ *shop* ⚘

Royal Zoological Society of Ireland
DUBLIN
Phoenix Park
☎(01) 771425
The gardens were founded in 1830 and today exhibit many species of birds and animals, notably lions and other large cats. Inhabitants occupy spacious buildings and outdoor enclosures on beautifully landscaped grounds. Two large lakes are the home of pelicans and flamingos; and the largest collection of waterfowl in Ireland.
Open all year, Mon-Sat 9.30-6, Sun 11-6. Gardens close sunset in winter. (Closed 25 & 26 Dec)
P ⚏ ✖ *licensed* & *toilets for disabled shop* ⚘
Details not confirmed for 1995

George Bernard Shaw House
DUBLIN
33 Synge St
☎(01) 4750854 & 8722077
The modest 1840s terrace house where the playwright and Nobel prizewinner George Bernard Shaw was born and spent the first eleven years of his life. It was here he began to gather a store of characters whom he would later recreate in his plays. The house has been fully restored and refurbished in such a way as to recreate the atmosphere and character it must have had when the Shaw family lived there.
Open May Oct, Mon-Sat 10-1 & 2-5, Sun & BH's 11.30-1, 2-6.
IR£2 (ch 3-11 IR£1.10, other concessions and under 18 IR£1.60). Family ticket IR£5.80.
P *(charged)* ⚘

James Joyce Tower
DUN LAOGHAIRE
Sandycove
☎(01) 2809265 & 8722077
Built by the British as a defence against a possible invasion by Napoleon, the tower has walls approximately 8ft thick and an original entrance door 13ft above the ground. The tower was once the temporary home of James Joyce, who depicted this setting in the opening scene of *Ulysses*. The structure is now a museum devoted to the author. The annual Bloomsday celebrations will be celebrated on 16 June, and will include readings and performances.
Open Apr-Oct Mon-Sat 10-1 & 2-5, Sun & PHs 2-6; Nov-Mar by arrangement (phone (01) 8722077).
IR£2 (ch 3-11 IR£1.10, pen & ch 12-17 IR£1.60). Family ticket IR£5.80. Parties 20+.
P *(100 yds)* & *shop* ⚘

Fry Model Railway
MALAHIDE
Malahide Castle
☎*Dublin (01) 8463779 & 8462184*
The Fry Model Railway is a rare collection of '0' gauge trains and trams, depicting the history of Irish rail transport from the first train that ran in 1834. Cyril Fry began to build his model collection in the late 1920s, in the attic of his home. All the models are built to scale, and they are now housed in a purpose-built setting adjacent to Malahide Castle.
Open all year, Apr-Oct, Mon-Thu 10-1 & 2-5, Sat 11-1 & 2-6, Sun & PH 2-6 (also Jun-Aug Fri 10-1 & 2-5, Jul-Aug Sun & PH's 11.30-1 & 2-6); Oct-Mar Sat-Sun & PH 2-5. Parties at other times by arrangement.
✳*IR£2.35 (ch 3-11 IR£1.30, concessions IR£1.75). Family ticket IR£6.75.*
P & *shop* ⚘

Malahide Castle
MALAHIDE
☎*Dublin (01) 8462184 & 8462516*
One of Ireland's oldest castles, with a late medieval core as the nucleus to the romantic and beautiful structure, in 250 acres of grounds; the contours of the castle have changed very little in 800 years. Tours offer views of Irish period furniture and historical Irish portrait collections. Additional paintings from the National Gallery depict Irish life from the last few centuries.
Open all year, Apr-Oct, Mon-Fri 10-5, Sat 11-6, Sun & PH 11.30-6; Nov-Mar, Mon-Fri 10-5, Sat-Sun & PH 2-5. Closed for tours 12.45-2pm.
IR£2.75 (ch 3-11 IR£1.40, pen & students IR£2.15). Family ticket IR£7.50.
P ⚏ ✖ *licensed shop* ⚘

CO GALWAY

Royal Tara China Visitor Centre
GALWAY
Tara Hall, Mervue
☎(091) 751301
Royal Tara China is the country's leading manufacturer of fine bone china. The china is made at Tara Hall, a beautiful Queen Anne-Georgian style mansion which was formerly the home of the Joyces - one of the ancient tribes who founded Galway City. The last family occupant Colonel Pierce Joyce was an associate and intimate friend of the legendary Lawrence of Arabia and took part with him in the famous desert campaigns. The visitor centre has five factory showrooms showing the extensive range of hand-crafted giftware, tableware and collectable miniatures from Galway Art Creations. There are guided factory tour at 11.00am and 3.00pm.
Open all year, Mon-Sun 9-6 (9pm Jul-Sep & Dec).
Free.
P ⚏ ✖ & *shop* ⚘

Spanish Arch Civic Museum
GALWAY
City Hall, College Rd
☎(091) 67641
In the south-west quarter, the arches date from the days when Spain and Ireland had trading ties. Galway City Museum at the arch is devoted to the city's history. A large map of the city in 1651 can be seen in the museum.
Open Whitsun-mid Oct, daily 10-5 (Jun-Sep 8pm).
P *(parking discs required)* ⚘
Details not confirmed for 1995

Thoor Ballylee
GORT
☎(091) 31436
This tower house is the former home of the poet William Butler Yeats and where he completed most of his literary works. The tower has been restored to appear exactly as it was when he lived there, and houses an Interpretative Centre with audio-visual presentations and displays of his work.
Open Ětr-Sep, daily 10-6.
IR£2.50 (ch IR75p, pen & students IR£2). Family ticket IR£5. Party.
P ⚏ ✖ *(audio-visual presentation) toilets for disabled shop* ⚘

Dunguaire Castle
KINVARRA
☎(091) 37108
Dunguaire Castle has stood for hundreds of years on the site of the 7th-century stronghold of Guaire, the King of Connaught. The castle bridges 13 centuries of Irish history from the skirmishes, battles and sieges that characterise its colourful past to the

literary revival of the early 20th century. Today the restored castle gives an insight into the lifestyle of the people who lived there from 1520 to modern times.
Open May-Sep, daily 9.30-5.30 (last admission 4.30).
IRE2.25 (ch IRE1.25, pen IRE1.75). Family ticket IRE6.
🅿 shop

Roundstone Musical Instruments
ROUNDSTONE
Craft Centre
☎ (095) 35875
Situated in an old Franciscan monastry at Roundstone is the craft workshop of Malachy Kearns who makes Ireland's oldest product - the Bodhrán (Bow-rawn). It is an 18inch one-side drum made from goatskin treated by a traditional process. The drum is played with a tipper or beater while the tone is varied by pressing the back of the skin with the other hand. Visitors can see the drums being made and also decorated with handpainted designs by Anne Kearns. Bodhráns can be purchased and special designs commissioned.
Open daily Mar-Oct, 9-7. Closed some days in winter.
Free.
🅿 💺 ⠿ shop

CO KERRY

Crag Cave
CASTLEISLAND
(1m N, signposted off N21)
☎ (066) 41244,
Crag Cave is one of the longest surveyed cave systems in Ireland with a total length of 3.81km (12,510ft). The existance of the cave was known locally for many years but the present show cave was only discovered in 1983 by a Welsh diver Martyn Farr. It is a

spectacular world where pale forests of stalagmites and stalagtites, thousands of years old, throw eerie shadows around vast echoing caverns complemented by dramatic sound and lighting effects.
Open daily, Mar-Nov 10-6 (Jul-Aug until 7pm).
🅿 💺 ✗ *licensed & (ramp to visitor centre) toilets for disabled shop* ⠿
Details not confirmed for 1995

The Blasket Centre
DUNQUIN
☎ (066) 56444 & 56371
In the early part of this century a small group of writers from the remote Blasket Island, just of the coast of County Kerry, achieved world renown. They told their own story in their own language - Irish. The centre describes the lives of the hardy Blasket Islanders before the sad abandonment of the island in 1953. The literary works produced in the 1920s and 30s included masterpieces such as "The Islandman" and "Twenty Years A-Growing" which have been translated from the Gaelic to English, French, German and many other languages. Facilities include a state-of-the-art exhibition and an audio-visual documentary on the Blasket Heritage.
Open daily, Etr-early Oct 10-6 (7pm Jul-Aug)
IRE2.50 (ch & student IRE1, pen IRE1.75). Family tcket IRE6.
🅿 ✗ *licensed & toilets for disabled shop* ⠿

Kenmare Heritage Centre
KENMARE
The Square
☎ (064) 31633
Kenmare has been designated a Bord Failte Heritage Town under the theme of "A Planned Estate Town". The town grew around the mineworks founded in 1670, planned by Sir William Petty, ancestor of the Lansdownes, local landlords. The Heritage Centre covers the

history of Kenmare including famous visitors. The effects of the Famine; the landlords; historical sites; the Nun of Kenmare and a Kenmare lace exhibition.
Open Apr-Sep, Mon-Sat 9.30-5.30 (also Sun Jul-Aug)
IRE2 (ch 12 IRE1, pen & student IRE1.50). Family ticket IRE5.
P *(400mtrs) & toilets for disabled shop* ⠿

Killarney Transport Museum
KILLARNEY
Scotts Hotel Gardens
☎ (064) 32638
The glorious years of motoring can be re-lived in this unique collection of fascinating Irish veteran, vintage and classic cars, motorcycles, bicycles, carriages and fire engines. Exhibits include the 1907 Silver Stream (reputed to be the rarest car in the world, it was designed and built by an Irishman and he only made one!); a 1904 Germain, and a 1910 Wolseley Siddeley driven by WB Yeats. The museum also has a 1930s garage with the tools, spare parts, oil cans and even a mechanic working on a car.
Open 17 Mar-Oct, daily 10-6 (Jul-Aug 7pm).
IRE2.50 (ch IRE1, students & pen IRE1.50). Family ticket IRE6. Wheelchair visitors free.
🅿 & shop

Blennerville Steam Railway
TRALEE
Ballyard Station, Dingle Rd (follow signs for Dingle on N86/R559)
☎ (066) 28888
The Tralee-Blennerville Steam Railway is part of the famous Tralee & Dingle Light Railway (1891-1953) restored in 1993 from Tralee to Blennerville (3km). Steam trains, powered by T & D Loco No. 5 (1892), operate from Tralee (Ballyard Station) to Blennerville. The carriages, though not original, are fitted out in the traditional style. An on-board commentary is provided. The line was featured in the Great Railway Journeys of the World TV series. For 1995 the Steam Traction and Vintage Machinery Display is on Sun, 1 Oct at Blennerville Station. Telephone for other events.
Open daily. Apr-Sep (ex 2nd Mon each month). Trains depart Tralee 11am and then hourly until 5pm & depart Blennerville 11.30am and then hourly until 5.30pm. Open wknds only in Oct.
IRE2.50 (ch15 IRE1.50, pen & student IRE2). Family ticket IRE6.50.
🅿 & shop ⠿

Blennerville Windmill Visitor & Craft Centre
TRALEE
Blennerville (1m W, on N86/R559)
☎ (066) 21064
The largest working windmill in Britain and Ireland is the focal point of a major visitor and craft complex. Blennerville was a major port of emigration during the mid-19th century. Visitor facilities include an audio-visual theatre, exhibitions on flour milling and 19th-century emigration, craftworkshops, craft shop and restaurant. Admission includes the guided tour. On a site adjoining the windmill a reconstruction of the 19th-century Tralee emigrant vessel, the "Jeanie Johnston" (1847-58), is being built in preparation for the 150th anniversary of the Great Irish Famine (1845-48) in 1997/8 when it will sail to North America. For 1995, the Harvest Festival and Steam Traction Rally will be on Sun 1 Oct.
Open daily, Apr-Oct 10-6.
✳☆✳£2.75 (ch15 IRE1.50, pen & student IRE2.25). Family ticket IRE7.50.
🅿 💺 ✗ *licensed shop* ⠿

Kerry The Kingdom Museum
TRALEE
Ashe Memorial Hall, Denny St
☎ (066) 27777
This is one of Ireland's most visited attractions. The museum tells the story of Kerry (and Ireland) from earliest times.

The centre comprises three attractions within the splendidly restored Thomas Ashe Memorial Hall (1923-28): an audio-visual presentation on Kerry's spectacular scenery and historic monuments; the priceless treasures of Kerry origin in the Kerry Museum, which was listed among Europe's top twenty museums in 1994; Geraldine Tralee - a reconstruction of Tralee during the Middle Ages when Tralee was the principal seat of the Anglo-Norman FitzGeralds (Geraldines). Visitors travel by time car through the reconstructed streets and houses of the medieval town. Synchronised sound, lighting and odour effects help to make this an almost life-like experience!
Open daily, Mar-Oct 10-6; Aug 10-7; Nov-Dec 12-5. (Closed 24-26 Dec).
IRE3.95 (ch15 IRE2.50, pen & student IRE3.50). Family ticket IRE12.
P *(100mtrs) (disc parking area)* 💺 & *(enter through tourist office entrance) toilets for disabled shop garden centre* ⠿

The Skellig Experience
VALENTIA ISLAND
☎ (064) 31633
The Skellig Rocks are renowned for their scenery, sea bird colonies, lighthouses, Early Christian monastic architecture and rich underwater life. The two Skellig island - Skellig Michael and Small Skellig - stand like fairytale castles in the Atlantic Ocean, rising to 218 metres and their steep cliffs plunging 50 metres below the sea. The Heritage Centre has an audio visual show running at regular intervals to tell the story of the Skellig Michael monastery. Other information is provided on the seabirds and their habitat, the 161 years of lighthouse service to mariners and the the colour and magic of underwater Skellig using graphics models and sound.
Open May-Jun & Sep 10-7, Jul-Aug 9.30-7.
IRE3 (ch IRE1.50, pen & student IR £2.70). Family ticket IR £7.
🅿 💺 & *toilets for disabled shop* ⠿

CO KILDARE

Castletown House
CELBRIDGE
☎ Dublin (01) 6288252
Ireland's largest and finest Palladian country house, begaun c1722 for William Conolly, speaker of the Irish House of Commons. Designed by Italian architect, Alessandro Galilei, and also in part by Irish architect Sir Edward Lovett Pearce. The state rooms include the 'Pompeian' Long Gallery with its Venetian chandeliers, the only surviving 18th-century print room in Ireland, the recently restored green silk drawing room and magnificent staircase hall with Lanfranchini plasterwork. There is a fine collection of 18th-century Irish furniture and paintings. Summer concerts include two in the series of Music in Great Irish Houses.
Open all year, Apr-Sep Mon-Fri 10-6, Sat 11-6, Sun & BH 2-6; Oct Mon-Fri 10-5, Sun & BH 2-5; Nov-Mar Sun & BH 2-5 & Mon-Fri for pre-booked groups. Last admission 45 mins before closing.
IRE2.50 (ch IRE1, pen & students IRE1.75). Family ticket IRE6. Party.
🅿 💺 shop ⠿

Japanese Gardens
KILDARE
Irish National Stud, Tully
☎ (045) 21617
Situated in the grounds of the Irish National Stud, the gardens were established by Lord Wavertree between 1906 and 1910, and symbolise 'The Life of Man' in Japanese-style landscape. Visitors can explore the gardens using self-guide leaflets; guided tours are available for groups booked in advance. Facilities include a picnic area, souvenir centre, bonsai store and tearoom.
Open 17 Mar-Oct, daily 9.30-6.

IR£4 (ch IR£2, students & pen IR £3). Family ticket IR£10.
🅿 ✗ licensed & toilets for disabled shop garden centre

CO KILKENNY

Kilkenny Castle
KILKENNY
☎ (056) 21450
Situated in a beautiful 50-acre park, the castle dates from 1172 and was the key stronghold of the Butler family, Earls and Dukes of Ormonde from 1391 to the present day. The castle has recently been restored to its former 1830s splendour and houses the National Furniture Collection. It illustrates the life of the most powerful family in Ireland over the centuries. The Butler Art Gallery, situated in the former servants' rooms, mounts frequently changing exhibitions of contemporary art.
Open all year - Jun-Sep daily 10-7; Apr-May daily 10.30-5; Oct-Mar Tue-Sat 10.30-12.45 & 2-5, Sun 11-12.45 & 2-5. Last tour 45mins before closing. Closed Xmas & Good Fri.
✱IR£3 (ch, students IR£1.25 & pen IR£2). Family ticket IR£7.50.
💺 & ✿ ❀

CO LIMERICK

Flying Boat Museum (on N69)
FOYNES
☎ (069) 65416
The museum recalls the era of the flying boats during the 1930s and early 1940s when Foynes was an important for air traffic between the United States and Europe. The flying boats brought in a diverse range of people from celebrities to refugees. Located in the original terminal building, it is the only museum of its kind in the world. There is a comprehensive range of exhibits, graphic illustrations and a 1940s style cinema featuring a 17 minute film - all original footage from the 30s and 40s. It was here that Irish coffee was first invented in 1943 by Chef Joe Sheriden. In 1995, the Powers Irish Coffee Festival is to be held here 17-20 August.
Open daily, 31 Mar-Oct 10-6.
IR£3 (ch IR£1, student IR£2). Family ticket IR£8.
🅿 💺 & toilets for disabled shop ❀

Lough Gur Stone Age Centre
HOLYCROSS
Bruff Rd
☎ (061) 385186
Lough Gur introduces visitors to the habitat of Neolithic Man on one of Ireland's most important archaeological sites. Near the lake is an interpretative centre which tells the story of 5000 years of man's presence at Lough Gur. The centre features an audio-visual presentation, models of stone circles, burial chambers and facsimiles of weapons, tools and pottery found in the area. Walking tours covering the archaeological features of the area are conducted at regular intervals.
Open mid May-Sep, daily 10-6 (last admission 5.30)
✱IR£1.90 (ch IR£1, pen IR£1.60). Family ticket IR£5.50.
🅿 💺 & shop

Celtic Park & Gardens
KILCORNAN
(N69 coast road)
☎ (061) 394243
The Celtic Park and Gardens are located on an original Celtic settlement within one of the most important Cromwellian plantations in the south-west of Ireland. The park, its two loughs and its environment are completely unspoilt by modern man. Visitors walking through the park are able to see a church built in 1250, a Mass rock, dolmens, a 6/7th

century wooden church, a stone circle, lake dwellings, cooking site and other fascinating sights including one of the finest examples of an early surviving historic ring fort. The surrounding landscape offers meadow, scrubland, cragland and bog with many species of wild flower. The classic-style gardens afford a panoramic view.
Open daily, Mar-Oct 9-7. Last entry 6pm.
IR£3 (pen & students IR£2)
🅿 💺 shop

Hunt Museum
LIMERICK
University of Limerick
☎ (061) 333644
The Hunt Museum at the University of Limerick holds Ireland's finest collection of Celtic to Medieval treasures outside Dublin's National Museum. On display is a treasury of antiquities and art objects from Europe and Ireland, including some excellent examples of ancient Irish metal work, with European objects crafted in medieval bronzes, ivories and Limoges enamels.
Open daily 10-5 (ex Sun). Guided tours at 11 & 3.
IR£2 (pen & student IR£1). Family ticket IR£5.
🅿 💺 ✗ licensed & toilets for disabled shop ❀

King John's Castle
LIMERICK
Castle St, King's Island
☎ (061) 411201
A national monument marked by an imposing twin-towered gatehouse and battle-scarred walls. The 13th-century King John's Castle is an impressive Anglo-Norman fortress where imaginative models and three-dimensional displays demonstrate 800 years of Limerick's and Ireland's history. An audio-visual show depicts the wars, sieges and treaties of its past, and in the courtyard there are copies of ancient war machines.
Open all year, Apr-Oct daily 9.30-5.30 (last admission 4.30); Nov-Apr, Sun 11-4. Groups by arrangement in off season.
IR£3.50 (ch IR£1.90, pen IR£3.20). Family ticket IR£9.
🅿 💺 & (lifts and ramps) toilets for disabled shop ❀

CO MONAGHAN

Patrick Kavanagh Rural & Literary Resource Centre
INNISKEEN
☎ (042) 78560
Inniskeen, birthplace of Patrick Kavanagh, one of Ireland's foremost 20th-century poets, is a village at the heart of Irish legend and heritage. Examples of early rock art and stone circles testify to the ancient history of Inniskeen. The town grew around the ancient monastry of St Daig MacCairill which was founded by 562, and its strong, 10th-century round tower still stands. The rolling hills have inspired poets and scholars, bards and heroes. The Patrick Kavanagh Rural and Literary Resource Centre, housed in St Mary's Church, chronicles the ancient history of the region and its role in developing Kavanagh's genius. There are exhibitions and an audio-visual on Kavanagh as well as a research library and Kavanagh country tours. There is a weekly performance of Kavanagh's works - Sundays 3.30pm - and evenings of traditional storytelling.
Open all year, Mon Fri 11-5, wknds & BH's 2-7.
IR£1.50 (ch 12 free, concessions IR£1).
🅿 💺 & toilets for disabled shop garden centre

Monaghan County Museum
MONAGHAN
1-2 Hill St
☎ (047) 82928

This is a modern European and national prize-winning museum of local archaeology, history, arts and crafts. Throughout the year various special exhibitions with take place, notably for 1995, the Monaghan Open Exhibition in May featuring Irish artists in a competitive show held every second year for artists North and South.
Open all year, Tue- Sat 11-1 & 2-5. Free.
🅿 & ❀

CO OFFALY

Birr Castle Demesne
BIRR
☎ (0509) 20056
A large landscaped park with a lake, rivers and waterfalls, containing important plant collections particularly of magnolias, maples, limes and oaks. A catalogue is available of the 2650 listed plants in the collection, some of which are labelled. The demesne is particularly colourful in the spring and autumn, and is possibly best noted for its formal gardens, containing cloisters or alleys, of hornbeam and the tallest box hedges in the world. The demesne also contains the remains of the world's largest 19th-century telescope, which projects from Gothic supporting walls in the centre of the park like a giant cannon. Work will commence on its restoration in the spring of 1995. Special events for 1995 include the All-Ireland Carriage Driving Championships (9-10 November), classical or chamber music concerts (11 June and 13 August), Georgian cricket match (12 August).
Open all year - May-Sep daily 9-6; Jan-Apr & Oct-Dec daily 9-1 & 2-5 (or dusk if earlier). Exhibition open May-Sep daily 2.30-5.30.
Apr-Oct IR£3.20 (ch IR£1.60); Jan-Mar & Nov-Dec IR£2.60 (ch IR£1.30).
🅿 💺 & toilets for disabled garden centre

CO ROSCOMMON

Strokestown Park House & Famine Museum
STROKESTOWN
Strokestown Park
☎ (078) 33013
Strokestown Park is a good example of an early 18th-century gentleman farmer's country estate. Built in Palladian style in the 1730's for Thomas Mahon MP, the house reflects perfectly the confidence of the newly emergent ruling class. The Famine Museum, located in the stable yards commemorates the Great Irish Famine of the 1840's when blight devastated the Irish potato crop, the staple food of Ireland, and one-quarter of the Irish population - in excess of 2 million people - either died or emigrated. Strokestown was particularly significant in that the landlord, Major Denis Mahon, was assassinated as a result of his attempts to clear two-thirds of his destitute tenants through eviction and assisted-emigration to North America.
Open May-Sep
Prices under review.
🅿 ✗ licensed & toilets for disabled shop ❀ (ex grounds)

CO TIPPERARY

Swiss Cottage
CAHIR
Kilcommon (1m from town on Ardfinnan road)
☎ (052) 41144
A delightful thatched "cottage orné" built in the early 1800's on the estate of the

Co Kildare – Co Waterford 223

Earls of Glengall to a design by the famous Regency architect John Nash.
Open mid Mar-Apr & Oct-Nov 10-1 & 2-4.30; May-Sep 10-6. Last admission 30mins before closing.
IR£2 (ch & student IR£1, pen IR£1.50). Family ticket IR£5. Party.
🅿 shop ❀

Brú Ború Heritage Centre
CASHEL
☎ (062) 61122
Brú Ború - the palace of Ború - is a national heritage centre at the foot of the Rock of Cashel, a 4th century stone fort. It is a cultural and interpretative village designed around a village green and is home to the study and celebration of native Irish music, song, dance, story telling, theatre and Celtic studies. There is a Folk Theatre where three performances are held daily in the summer and in the evening, banquets evoke the Court of Brian Bor£ the 11th-century High King of Ireland with songs, poems and sagas. The Teach Ceoil - music house - has a more informal atmosphere for the celebration of Irish music, song and dance. The Heritage School offers and opportunity to explore and study the history of Ireland. In addition there is a Genealogy Centre and a display and exhibition hall.
Open Jan-May & Oct-Dec, Mon-Fri 9.30-5.30; June-Sep Tue-Sat 9.30-11pm, Sun-Mon 9.30-5.30.
Free.
🅿 (charged) ✗ licensed & toilets for disabled shop ❀

Cashel Folk Village
CASHEL
Dominic St
☎ (062) 62525
A thatched 18th, 19th and 20th century "village" consisting of Pub, Kitchen, Butcher's shop, Forge, Penal chapel, tool and trades exhibition and museum. From June 19-Sep 15 1995 the Cashel Heritage Society is producing a colourful pageant of music, song, dance and drama in the village depicting the Great Famine of 1845 to commemorate the 150th anniversary of this horrendous period in history. Proceeds to charity.
Open Mar-May 10-6; Jun-Oct 10-7.30. IR£2 (ch IR50p).
🅿 & shop

CO WATERFORD

Touraneena Heritage Centre
BALLINAMULT
Tourannena, (off R672, signposted)
☎ (058) 47353
A 300 year old traditional Irish thatched farm, authentically furnished, home of the O'Keefe family for eight generations, featuring a working dairy, blacksmith's forge, vintage farm machinery, gypsy wagon, stable loft and hatchery, depicting Irish rural life in 1890s. The authentic atmosphere is enhanced by staff dressed in costume, live butter-making demonstrations on Sunday afternoons and daily bread and scone baking on a traditional open turf fire.
Open May-Oct, daily 10-7; Oct-Apr, Sun 11-4.
🅿 💺 & shop

Lismore Castle Gardens
LISMORE
☎ (058) 54424
Lismore castle is the Irish home of the Duke of Devonshire. It has been in the Cavendish family since 1748 when the 4th Duke of Devonshire married Lady Charlotte Boyle, the only daughter and heiress of the 4th Earl of Cork. The beautifully situated walled and woodland gardens contain a fine collection of camellias, magnolias and other shrubs and a remarkable Yew Walk. It is said that Spenser wrote part of his *Faerie* ➤

Queene in these gardens. The walls and towers at the western boundary of the garden were built in 1626-7 by the first Earl of Cork, they played an important part in the siege of the castle in 1642.
Open 29 Apr-10 Sep, Sun-Fri 1.45-4.45. IRE2.50 (ch 16 IRE1.50). Party 20+.
🅿

Celtworld
TRAMORE ▬▬▬▬▬
Railway Square
☎(051) 386166
Here the myths and legends that are so much a part of Ireland's past are re-told in an informative and entertaining way. Audio-visual technology, combines with the stunning visual imagery of renowned Irish Celtic artist, Jim Fitzpatrick to create a dramatic presentation of Ireland in this magical era. A fascinating journey back in time to where legend lives.
Open Apr-May, daily 10-5; Jun, daily 10-8; Jul-Aug, daily 10-10; Sep, daily 10-6. Last admission 1 hr before closing. Rest of the year by arrangement.
❊*IRE3.95 (ch IRE2.95, students & pen IRE3.25). Family ticket IRE12. Party 10+.*
🅿 ⅏ *toilets for disabled shop* 🐾

Waterford Crystal Visitor Centre
(on N25, 1m from city centre)
WATERFORD ▬▬▬▬▬
☎(051) 73311
These are the largest manufacturers of mouth-blown and hand-cut crystal. There are factory tours everyday to see mastercraftsmen mouth-blow and hand-cut this famous crystal. Visitors can talk to the master engravers and see the crystal being sculptured. In the gallery there is the finest display of Waterford crystal on display and and audio-visual presentation every 20 minutes.
Tours of factory: Mar-Oct, daily 8.30-5; Nov-Feb, Mon-Fri 9-5.
🅿 ☕ ✕⅏ *(special tours on request) toilets for disabled shop* 🐾

CO WEXFORD

Irish National Heritage Park
FERRYCARRIG ▬▬▬▬▬
(2m from Wexford, on N11)
Fourteen historical sites set in a magnificent 35-acre mature forest explaining Ireland's history from the Stone and Bronze Ages, through the mighty Celtic period and concluding with the Vikings and Normans. Among the exhibits are a reconstructed Mesolithic camp, a Viking boatyard with 2 full size ships and a Norman motte and bailey. There are audio-visual aids and guided tours.
Open 17 Mar-mid Nov.
IRE3 (pen & students £2.50). Family ticket £8.
🅿 ☕ ⅏ *toilets for disabled shop* 🐾

Dunbrody Abbey Visitors Centre
NEW ROSS ▬▬▬▬▬
Dunbrody Abbey, Campile
☎(051) 88603
The visitor centre is based around the Abbey itself and Dunbrody Castle. There is an intriguing yew hedge maze with 1550 yew trees and a museum. In addition there is a golf pitch and putt course with competions organised twice a month. In July there is an open day of Irish Music and Dance and on 25/26/27 Sep 1995 is the Mussel Festival.
Open Apr-Sep 10-6 (7pm Jul-Aug). IRE1 (ch IR50p). Family ticket IRE2.
🅿 ☕ ⅏ *shop garden centre*

Dunmain House
NEW ROSS ▬▬▬▬▬
☎(051) 62122
An imposing slate-covered, 17th-century house with a history of intriguing stories. The house and its history has been the subject of many novels namely *Guy Mannering* by Sir Walter Scott, Smolletts *Peregrine Pickle* and Charles Reade's *The Wandering Heir*. Learn about the these

and see the olde world kitchen, private oratory, jail cell, old forge and old farm machinery. Groups can arrange for a traditional bread baking on an open fire.
Open May-Sep, daily 10-12.30, 2-5.30.
IRE2 (ch free). Party.
🅿 ☕ ⅏ *toilets for disabled*

John F Kennedy Arboretum
NEW ROSS ▬▬▬▬▬
(12km S, off R733)
☎(051) 388171
The John F Kennedy Arboretum, formally opend in 1968, covers 622 acres across the hill of Slievecoiltia which overlooks the Kennedy ancestral home at Dunganstown. Six counties can be seen from the viewing point. there are 4,500 types of trees and shrubs representing the temperate regions of the world. There is a lake and 200 forest plots, planted according to their geographic origin. There is a visitor centre and during the season there are pony and trap transport and a miniature railway.
Open daily, May-Aug 10-8; Apr & Sep 10-6.30; Oct-Mar 10-5. Last admission 45 mins before closing. (Closed Good Friday & 25 Dec).
IRE2 (ch & student IRE1, pen IR1.50). Family ticket IRE5. Party.
🅿 ☕ ⅏ *toilets for disabled shop garden centre*

The Irish Agricultural Museum
WEXFORD ▬▬▬▬▬
Johnstown Castle Old Farmyard (4m SW, signposted off N25)
☎(053) 42888
This interesting museum has extensive displays on rural transport, farming and the activities of the farmyard and the farmhouse. Large scale replicas of different workshops, including a blacksmith, cooper and basket worker can be seen here. Other attractions include displays on dairying, cycling, and sugar-beet harvesting and a collection of Irish country furniture. The museum is situated in the estate farm buildings which were erected in 1810 and are themselves now of historic interest.
Open all year, Jun-Aug Mon-Fri 9-5 & Sat-Sun 2-5; Apr-May & Sep-14 Nov Mon-Fri 9-12.30 & 1.30-5, Sat-Sun 2-5; 15 Nov-Mar Mon-Fri 9-12.30 & 1.30-5. (Closed 25 Dec-2 Jan).
IRE1.75 (ch & students IRE1). Parking charge May-Sep.
🅿 *(charged)* ☕ ⅏ *toilets for disabled shop* 🐾 *(ex.small dogs)*

Johnstown Castle Gardens
WEXFORD ▬▬▬▬▬
(4m SW)
☎(053) 42888
The 19th-century mansion is closed to the public but visitors can explore the 50 acres of grounds containing over 200 different varieties of trees and shrubs, ornamental lakes with wildfowl, and walled gardens and hothouses. The ruins of Rathlannon Castle, a medieval tower house can also be seen.
Open all year, daily 9-5.30. (Closed 25 Dec).
Car (plus passengers) IRE2.50. Pedestrians IRE1.50 (ch & students IR50p).
🅿 ☕ ⅏ *toilets for disabled shop*

Wexford Wildfowl Reserve
WEXFORD ▬▬▬▬▬
North Slob (take Gory road over bridge for 1.50m)
☎(053) 23129
The reserve is of international importance for Greenland Whitefronted Geese as it has one-third of the world's population, Brent Geese, Bewick's Swans and Widgeon. The reserve is a superb place for birdwatching and there are hides and tower hides available as well as a visitor centre with an audio-visual display. Special items will be arranged during the Wexford Festival (last 2 weeks October).
Open all year, 15 Apr-Sep 9-6; Oct-14 Apr 10-5.
Free.
🅿 ⅏ 🐾

CO WICKLOW

Powerscourt Gardens
ENNISKERRY ▬▬▬▬▬
Powerscourt Estate (just off N11 S of Bray)
☎Dublin (01) 2867676
Includes beautiful Italian and Japanese gardens and walled gardens, herbaceous borders and a famous collection of trees. It is one of the last formal gardens to have been created in Europe. The waterfall is the highest in Ireland (400ft) and is 5km from the formal gardens. Special events for 1995 include musical afternoons each Sunday in June as part of the Wicklow Gardens Festival, Morris Dancers Easter Sunday and Monday, Village and Veteran Car Rally 13 August.

Open - Gardens Mar-Oct daily 9.30-5.30; Waterfall Mar-Oct daily 9.30-7; winter daily 10.30-dusk.
❊*Gardens: IRE2.80 (ch IRE1.70 & students IRE2.30). Waterfall: IRE1.50 (ch IR80p & students IRE1). Under 5's free. Party 20+*
🅿 ☕ ⅏ *toilets for disabled shop garden centre*

National Gardens Exhibitions Centre
KILQUADE ▬▬▬▬▬
Calumet Nurseries
☎(01) 2819890
The centre offers plenty of ideas of the gardener or new home-owner. There are 15 different gardens designed by some of Ireland's leading landscapers and designers, in which there are several water features and a man-made mountain stream. There is a garden centre adjacent to the exhibition. There are lectures during the year, ring for details.
Open Feb-22 Dec.
IRE2.50 (ch free Mon-Sat, pen IRE2). Party.
🅿 ☕ ⅏ *garden centre* 🐾

Avondale House & Forest Park
(1.6km S of town)
RATHDRUM ▬▬▬▬▬
☎(0404) 46111
It was at Avondale House in 1846 that one of the greatest political leaders of modern Irish history, Charles Stewart Parnell, was born. The house is now a musem to his memory and a major refurbishment programme has restored much of the house to its decor of 1850. Parnell spent much of his time at Avondale until his death in October 1891. Visitors are introduced to Avondale by way of a specially commissioned video which describes the life of Parnell. Events for 1995 are Parnell Spring Day - early April; Synge Summer School - end of June; Parnell Summer School - end of Aug. Telephone for details.
House & Park open daily. House 11-6, last entry May-Sep 5pm, other times 4pm. (House closed Good Friday & Xmas).
House IRE2.50 (pen IRE1.50). Family ticket IRE6. Party. Park car IRE1, coach IRE3. Prices under review.
🅿 *(charged)* ☕ ⅏ *shop* 🐾 *(ex on lead in park)*

At the foot of the ancient Rock of Cashel is the Brú Ború Heritage Centre, which is for the study and celebration of native Irish music, dance and storytelling.

Shakespeare's mother, Mary Arden, lived in this Tudor farm with its extensive and well-preserved outbuildings.

PEOPLE AND PLACES

Hundreds of places throughout the British Isles can claim a link with the famous. Birthplaces, or other buildings associated with the famous, are often top tourist attractions.

Many places claim that 'Queen Elizabeth I slept here'. In fact, according to one historian, there are 241, giving her a head start in the commemorative plaque stakes! Charles Dickens also laid his weary head on a pillow or two although, unlike Elizabeth, he tended to stay longer than one night.

LITERARY LIVES

Dickens was born in Portsmouth(Hants), home now to his Birthplace Museum, but he spent his childhood in Chatham (Kent). His favourite town, however, was neighbouring Rochester, despite calling it Mudfog or Dullborough in his books. The Charles Dickens Centre is in one of several old houses still recognisable from his descriptions. Further east, in Broadstairs – 'our little watering place' to his family – are the Bleak House Maritime and Smuggling and Dickens House museums. He lived in several London properties too, but another Dickens House, in Bloomsbury, is the only surviving example.

Even more intimately, you can see the actual bed in which the Ploughman Poet, Rabbie Burns, was born, still in his cottage at Alloway (Strathclyde), and in Dumfries

Many places claim that 'Queen Elizabeth I slept here'. In fact, according to one historian, there are 241 giving her a head start in the commemorative plaque stakes!

The Dickens House at Broadstairs is full of momentoes of his life, including this stained glass panel of David Copperfield set in his bedroom window.

(Dumfries & Galloway) are his house, mausoleum and the Robert Burns Centre.

William Shakespeare's birthplace in Stratford-upon-Avon (Warks), restored in typical 16th-century, middle-class style, is visited by more than half a million people annually. A few miles away, at Wilmcote, is the large Tudor farm where the Shakespeare's mother Mary Arden was born and raised and young William, no doubt, visited his grandparents.

FROM RAKES TO PURITANS

Three decades after Shakespeare died the Byron family was raised to the peerage for their support of Charles l during the Civil War. When poet George Gordon, the 6th Lord Byron, inherited Newstead Abbey (Notts) in 1798, it was in poor condition and he declined to move in for 10 years. A decade later he had to sell it to pay off his debts but today the house has a fine display of Byron treasures.

At Jordans, near Chalfont St Giles (Bucks), you will find the poet John Milton's Cottage, the interior apparently little disturbed since his day, and in the house at Chawton (Hants) in which Jane Austen spent her final years, there is a collection of her furniture, documents and letters. Nearby, lived the naturalist Gilbert White, whose fame rests on *The Natural History and Antiquities of Selborne*, a book based on 40 years of observing local flora and fauna. His house, 'The Wakes', is today shared by one museum dedicated to him, and another to both Francis Oates, the explorer, and his nephew, Captain Lawrence Oates, who accompanied Scott on his ill-fated Antarctic expedition.

ALL-EMBRACING TALENT

In Ireland there are strong literary connections too. James Joyce is remembered in the old Martello tower at Dun Laoghaire, near Dublin, in which he lived, and in the city itself George Bernard Shaw's house has been restored to 19th century condition with furniture, arte-

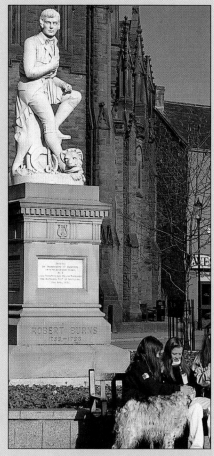

In the heart of Dumfries is a statue of Scotland's most famous poet, Robert Burns, who lived there for the last few years of his life.

facts and works of art. The poet and novelist Patrick Kavanagh, renowned for his masterly poem 'The Great Hunger', was born, and is now buried, at Innisheen (Co. Monaghan), where the Rural and Literary Resource Centre spotlights his work.

The homes of artists and musicians are pretty numerous, too. For example, the house in Sudbury (Suffolk) belonging to Thomas Gainsborough, the 18th-century landscape and portrait painter, is now his museum while William Morris, founder of the Arts and Crafts Movement, lived for a time in an 18th-century Walthamstow (London) house where all aspects of his work are now on view.

Gustav Holst, the British composer of Swedish descent, was born in Cheltenham (Glos), home today of his Birthplace Museum, and Sir Edward Elgar is similarly remembered in Worcester (Hereford & Worcester). After the sculptor Barbara Hepworth died in a fire, her St Ives (Cornwall) studio became a museum, and its grounds a sculpture garden, as a permanent showcase of her work.

The Scott Polar Reasearch Institute at Cambridge is named after the intrepid Antarctic explorer Captain Robert Scott. Exhibits from his expeditions are on display.

THE BRITISH ARCTIC EXPEDITION 1875-76

Chartwell is the former home of Sir Winston Churchill. He lived there for many years until his death in 1965.

HEROES AND HEROINES

Island living encouraged our ancestors to be adventurous. Captain Cook, discoverer of Australia and New Zealand, came from Middlesbrough (Cleveland), now home to his Birthplace Museum, and in Monmouth (Gwent) the Nelson Collection features items from the admiral's life. Lifeboat heroine Grace Darling is remembered in a museum at Bamburgh (Northumberland), while at the David Livingstone Centre in Blantyre (Strathclyde) you can find out all about the Scottish explorer. Born in the town in 1813, he died in Africa in 1873, his long search for the source of the Nile unfulfilled.

Charles Darwin, more of an adventurous naturalist perhaps, made a formative voyage round the world on 'The Beagle', before spending nearly 30 years collecting evidence for his theory of evolution, published as *The Origin of Species* in 1859. Down House near Bromley (Kent), where he lived for 40 years, is now the Darwin Museum.

In the world of medicine, Edward Jenner, whose discovery of vaccination against smallpox helped to lay the foundations of modern immunology, has a museum recording his work at his Georgian home at Berkeley (Glos).

Florence Nightingale's associations with medicine are more readily recalled, and a museum of nursing history named after her can be found near London's Lambeth Palace.

Politicians have not been ignored either, Among many examples of museums in the homes of former statesmen are Benjamin Disraeli's Hughenden Manor (Bucks), the Wellington Museum (London), the Cromwell Museum in Huntingdon (Cambs) and the Lloyd George Memorial Museum in Llanystumdwy (Gwynedd). Chartwell, Sir Winston Churchill's long-time home, near Westerham (Kent), is full of mementoes of his life, ranging from walking sticks to the famous garden wall that he built.

LATTER-DAY HEROES

One does not have to be long dead (or even dead at all) to have achievement commemorated. Motor racing fans will find the Jim Clark Room in the late Grand Prix winner's home town of Duns (Borders), and in Laugharne (Dyfed) is the secluded boathouse where the mercurial Welsh poet Dylan Thomas lived and wrote. And probably everything worth knowing about John, Paul, George and Ringo is told in The Beatles Story in Liverpool's Albert Dock (Merseyside).

But reality is not necessarily the only passport to immortality. At the Granada TV Studios in Manchester you can stroll along the hallowed cobbles of Coronation Street, home for more than 30 years to a never-ending succession of famous screen characters. And in Yorkshire, the gritstone town of Holmfirth is a magnet for fans of the television series 'Last of the Summer Wine', hoping for a glimpse of Norah Batty. Maybe, one day, there'll be a plaque saying 'Compo slept here'!

The poet John Milton wrote his masterpieces Paradise Lost and Paradise Regained in his cottage at Chalfont St Giles.

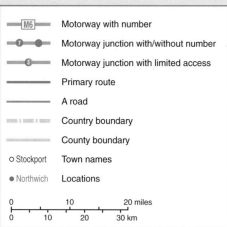

Motorway with number
Motorway junction with/without number
Motorway junction with limited access
Primary route
A road
Country boundary
County boundary
○ Stockport   Town names
● Northwich   Locations

0   10   20 miles
0   10   20   30 km

Any establishment may be located by using the National Grid Reference given beside its Index entry. The grid for Ireland is unique to this map and the Grid References given beside all Irish entries in the Index refer to this map only.

The first number of the Grid Reference refers to the atlas page (eg Map 02). The following two letters (eg ST) refer to the major squares marked by the heavier blue lines on the atlas pages. For a more precise location, each of these grid squares is subdivided by marks along the edge of the map indicating smaller squares (numbered horizontally 0-9 from west to east and 0-9 vertically from south to north). The large square is subdivided by a fainter blue line on grid mark 5 for easier use. The point where two grid 'lines' intersect forms the bottom left-hand corner of the square in which the establishment is located.

For example, if the reference is Map 02 ST97, the place (in this case Chippenham) is to be found on atlas page 2, in major grid square ST, after grid line 9 along from the left, and above grid line 7 up from the bottom.

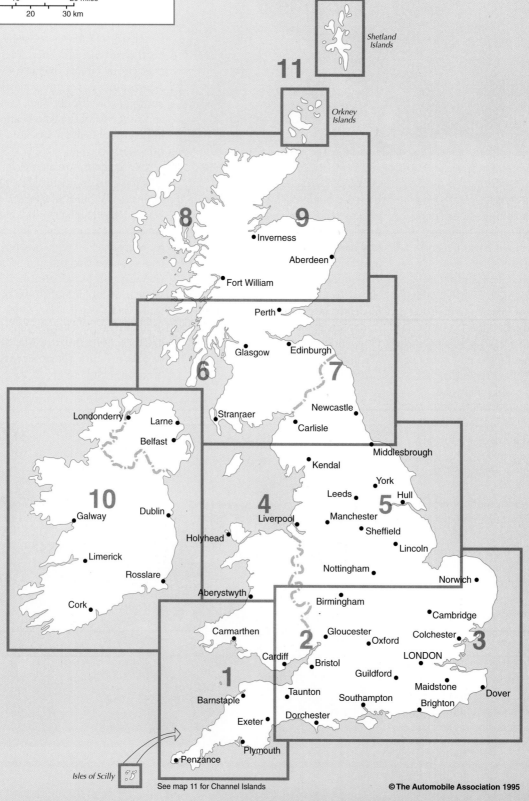

Shetland Islands

11

Orkney Islands

8

9
● Inverness
● Aberdeen
● Fort William
● Perth
● Glasgow   ● Edinburgh

6

7
● Stranraer   ● Newcastle
● Carlisle
● Middlesbrough
● Kendal
● York
● Leeds   ● Hull
● Londonderry   ● Larne
● Belfast

10
● Galway   ● Dublin
● Holyhead
● Limerick
● Rosslare
● Cork

4
● Liverpool
● Manchester
● Sheffield
● Lincoln
● Nottingham
● Norwich

5

2
● Aberystwyth
● Birmingham
● Cambridge
● Carmarthen
● Gloucester   ● Colchester
● Oxford
● Cardiff   ● Bristol   LONDON
● Guildford
● Maidstone
● Dover

3

1
● Barnstaple   ● Taunton   ● Southampton
● Dorchester   ● Brighton
● Exeter
● Plymouth
● Penzance

Isles of Scilly
See map 11 for Channel Islands

© The Automobile Association 1995

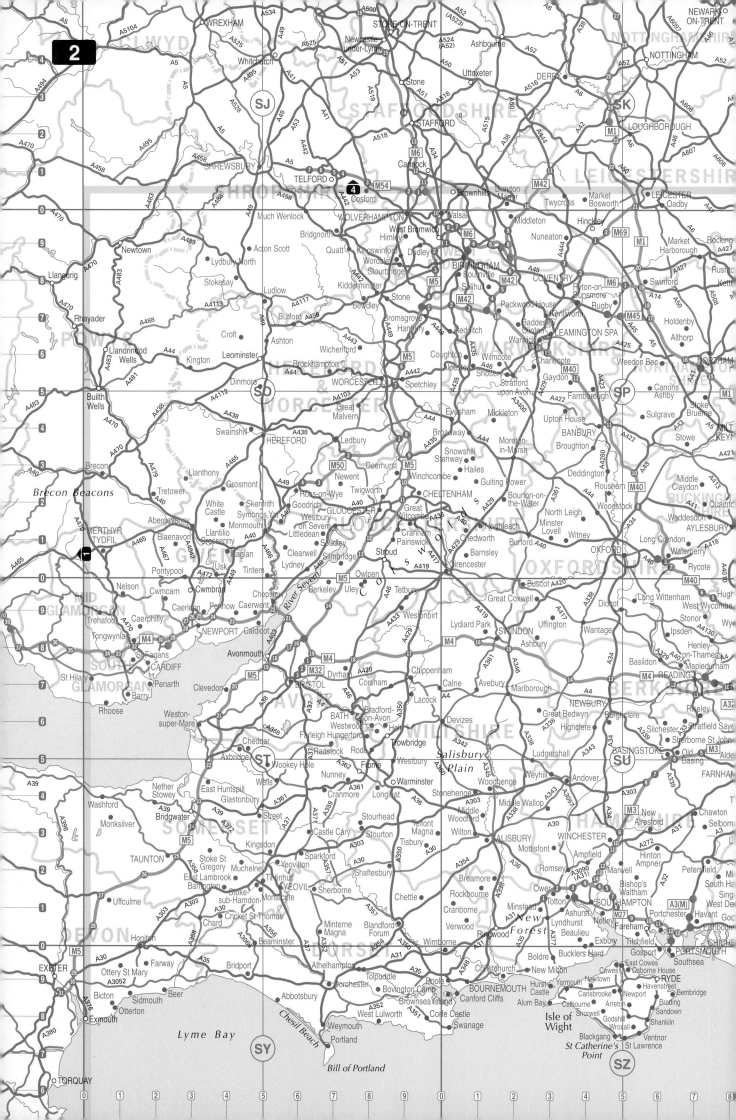

7
6
5
4
3
2
1
0
9
8
7
6
5
4
3
2
1
0
9
8
7
6
5
4
3
2
1

ountains

NO
SN
NU
NZ
NT
NY

A93
A924
A822
A926
Forfar
A935
A90
A92
Dunkeld
A94
Arbroath
A92
A933
Barry
Scone
PERT H
Firth of Tay
DUNDEE
Leuchars
A90
A914
St Andrews
Milnathort
Cupar
A91
Ceres
Kinross
Falkland
A92
Kellie Castle & Gardens
Anstruther
Dunfermline
Culross
A985
Burntisland
Kirkcaldy
Firth of Forth
North Berwick
Aberdour
Dirleton
Bo'ness
North Queensferry
Aberlady
East Fortune
South Queensferry
Prestonpans
Linlithgow
Ingliston
EDINBURGH
Inveresk
East Linton
Gogar
Balerno
Newtongrange
Dalkeith
A1
Penicuik
Crichton
A68
Lammermuir Hills
St Abb's Head
A1107
Eyemouth
Broughton
Peebles
Lauder
A697
Duns
A6105
Berwick-upon-Tweed
Innerleithen
Gordon
A6112
Norham
A698
Holy Island
Stobo
Galashiels
Smailholm
A8089
Coldstream
Lindisfarne
Traquair
Dryburgh
Kelso
A1
Bamburgh
Melrose
Ford
Selkirk
Chillingham
Embleton
The Cheviot Hills
Jedburgh
Hawick
A68
A697
Alnwick
A1068
Warkworth
A6088
A1
Rothbury
Hermitage
NORTHUMBERLAND
Longframlington
Langholm
Ashington
Cambo
Morpeth
Belsay
A1
A696
Carrawbrough
Walwick
Housesteads
A68
Gisland
A69
Corbridge
A69
Prudhoe
NEWCASTLE UPON TYNE
Tynemouth
South Shields
Brampton
Bardon Mill
A695
Gateshead
Jarrow
Whitburn
A689
Rowlands Gill
Sunderland
CARLISLE
Consett
Tanfield
Washington
Alston
Beamish
NORTH SEA
Cowshill
A689
Durham
A691
Skelton
M6
Penrith
Bishop Auckland
A689
HARTLEPOOL
Keswick
A66
Temple Sowerby
Staindrop
Redcar
Dacre
Brougham
A688
Stockton-on-Tees
Saltburn-by-the-Sea
Appleby-in-Westmorland
MIDDLESBROUGH
Skinningrove
CUMBRIA
DARLINGTON
Lake District
Scotch Corner
North York Moors
NORTH YORKSHIRE
Thirsk

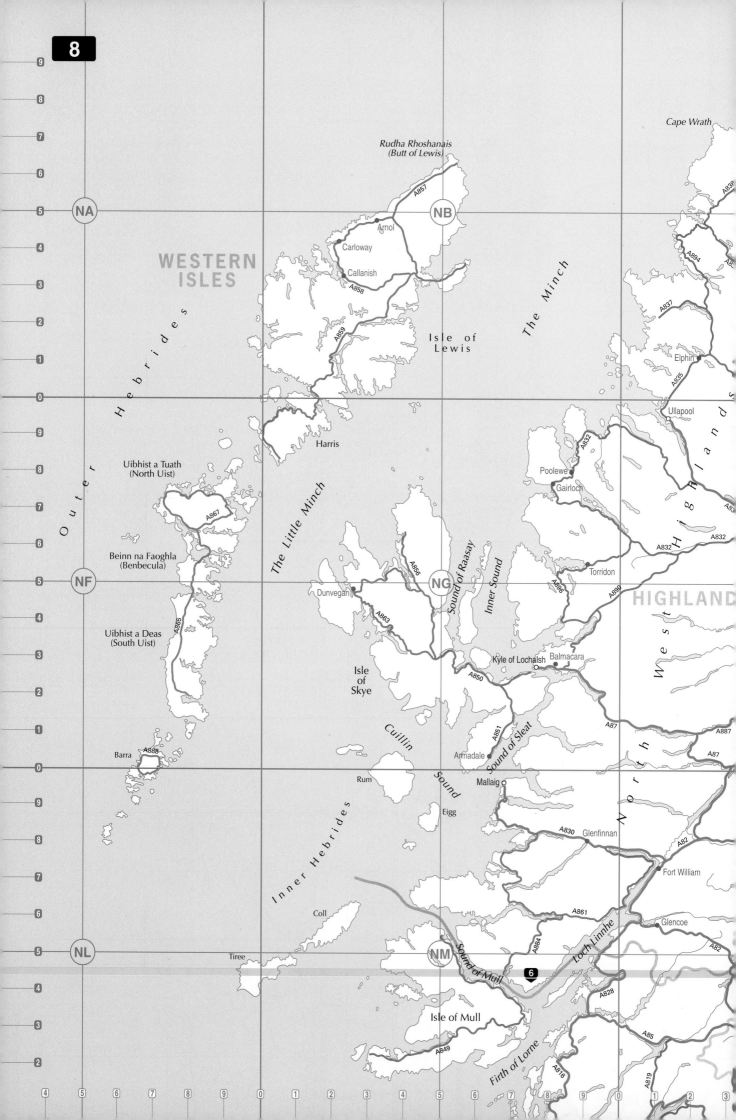

WESTERN ISLES

NA

NB

Rudha Rhoshanais
(Butt of Lewis)

Cape Wrath

A857

A894

Arnol

Carloway

A837

Callanish

A858

The Minch

A859

Isle of
Lewis

Elphin

A835

Ullapool

Harris

A832

Poolewe

Uibhist a Tuath
(North Uist)

Gairloch

Outer Hebrides

A867

A832

A832

Beinn na Faoghla
(Benbecula)

The Little Minch

NF

NG

Sound of Raasay

Inner Sound

Torridon

A896

A890

Dunvegan

A856

HIGHLAND

A863

A865

Uibhist a Deas
(South Uist)

Kyle of Lochalsh Balmacara

Isle
of
Skye

A850

West

A851

A87

A887

Barra

A888

Armadale

Sound of Sleat

A87

Cuillin Sound

Rum

Mallaig

North

Eigg

Inner Hebrides

A830 Glenfinnan

A82

Fort William

A861

Coll

Loch Linnhe

Glencoe

NL

Tiree

NM

Sound of Mull

6

A884

A82

A828

Isle of Mull

A85

A849

Firth of Lorne

A816

A819

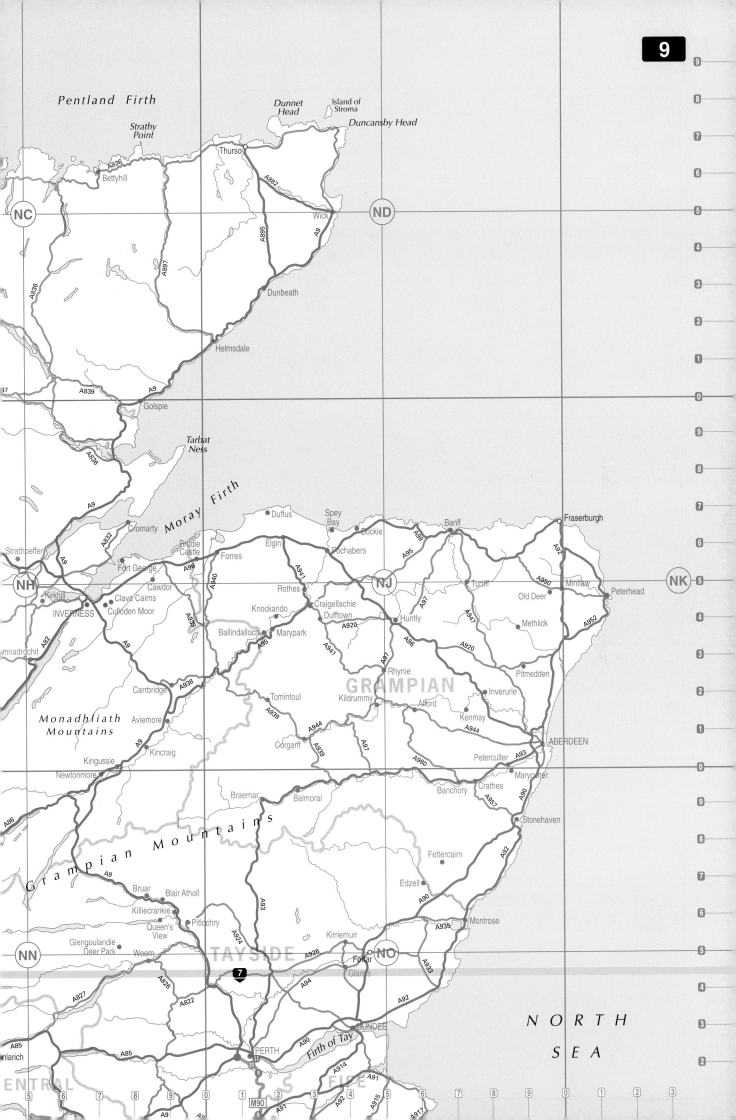

9

Pentland Firth

Strathy
Point

Dunnet
Head

Island of
Stroma

Duncansby Head

Bettyhill

A836

NC

Thurso

A882

A895

A9

Wick

Dunbeath

A897

A839

Helmsdale

A9

Golspie

Tarbat
Ness

Moray Firth

A836

Duffus

Spey
Bay

Buckie

Banff

Fraserburgh

Cromarty

Elgin

Fochabers

A98

A92

Strathpeffer

Brodie
Castle

Forres

A95

NJ

A96

NH

Fort George

A940

Rothes

Turriff

A950

Mintlaw

Peterhead

NK

Kirkhill

Cawdor

A941

Craigellachie

A97

Old Deer

A952

INVERNESS

Clava Cairns

Culloden Moor

A939

Knockando

Dufftown

A920

Huntly

A947

Methlick

A9

Ballindalloch

Marypark

A95

A941

A97

A96

Rhynie

A920

Pitmedden

GRAMPIAN

Carrbridge

A938

Tomintoul

Kildrummy

Alford

Inverurie

Monadhliath
Mountains

Aviemore

A939

Kenmay

A944

ABERDEEN

A9

Kincraig

Corgarff

A944

A97

Peterculter

A93

Kingussie

A939

A980

Maryculter

Newtonmore

Braemar

Balmoral

Banchory

Crathes

A90

Stonehaven

A957

A86

Grampian Mountains

A9

Bruar

Blair Atholl

Fettercairn

A92

Killiecrankie

Edzell

Pitlochry

A93

A90

Queen's
View

Kirriemuir

A935

Montrose

Glengoulandie
Deer Park

Weem

TAYSIDE

A924

A926

NN

7

Forfar

NO

A933

Glamis

A827

A94

A92

A822

A826

NORTH

A85

A85

DUNDEE

A90

Firth of Tay

SEA

nlarich

PERTH

A914

CENTRAL

M90

A91

FIFE

A92

A9

A915

A917

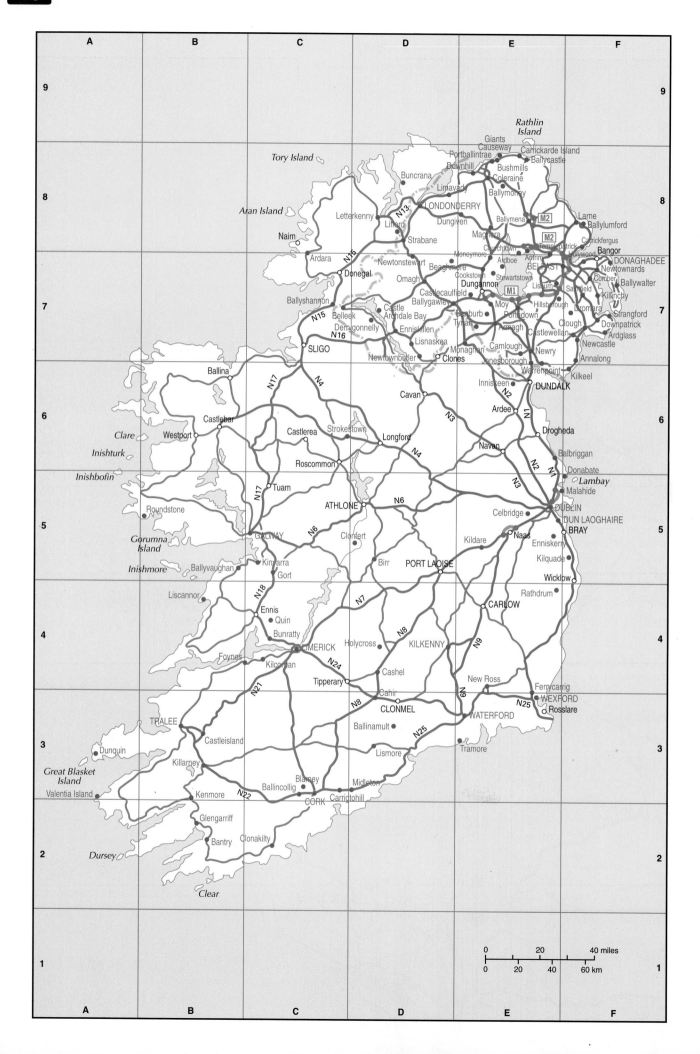

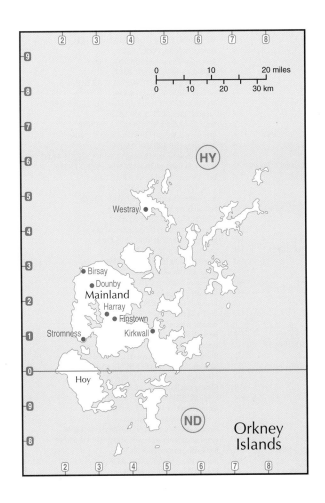

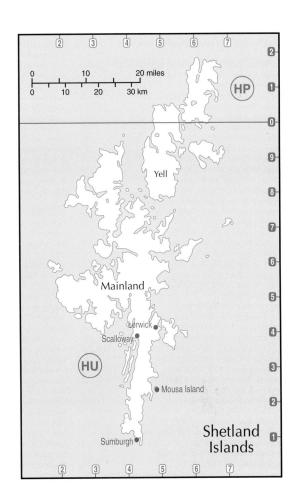

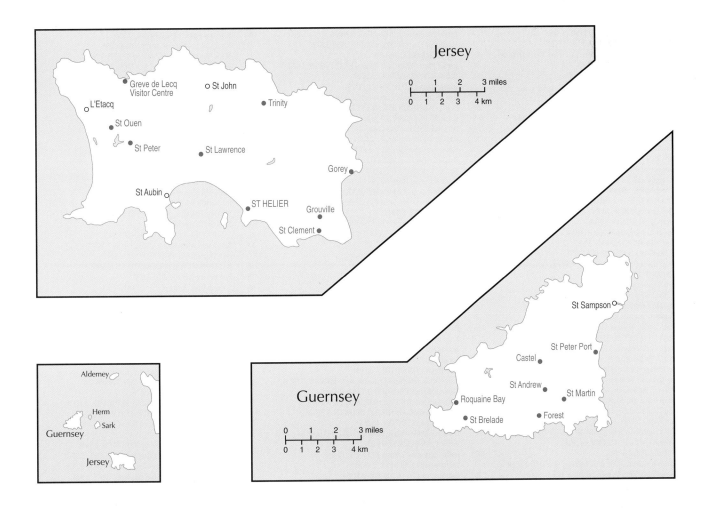

Orkney Islands

9
8
7
6
5
4
3
2
1
0
9
8

2 3 4 5 6 7 8

0   10   20 miles
0   10   20   30 km

HY

Westray ●

Birsay ●
● Dounby
Mainland
Harray ●
● Finstown
Stromness ● ● Kirkwall

Hoy

ND

2 3 4 5 6 7 8

Shetland Islands

0   10   20 miles
0   10   20   30 km

HP
0
9
8
7
6
5
4
3
2
1

2
1

Yell

Mainland

Lerwick ●
Scalloway ●

HU

● Mousa Island

Sumburgh ●

2 3 4 5 6 7

Jersey

0   1   2   3 miles
0 1 2 3   4 km

● Greve de Lecq
Visitor Centre
○ St John
● Trinity

○ L'Etacq

● St Ouen
● St Peter
● St Lawrence

● Gorey

St Aubin ○
● ST HELIER
● Grouville
St Clement ●

Alderney

Herm
○
Sark
Guernsey

Jersey

Guernsey

0   1   2   3 miles
0 1 2 3   4 km

St Sampson ○

St Peter Port ●
Castel ●

St Andrew ●
St Martin ●
Roquaine Bay ●
● Forest
St Brelade ●

Index

Letters in **bold** are map numbers and grid references